* * *

Remembrance

Rock

*

By Carl Sandburg

★ ★ ★

ABRAHAM LINCOLN: THE PRAIRIE YEARS

ABRAHAM LINCOLN: THE WAR YEARS

MARY LINCOLN: WIFE AND WIDOW

THE AMERICAN SONGBAG

STEICHEN THE PHOTOGRAPHER

STORM OVER THE LAND

HOME FRONT MEMO

REMEMBRANCE ROCK

★

Poems

SMOKE AND STEEL

SLABS OF THE SUNBURNT WEST

CHICAGO POEMS

CORNHUSKERS

GOOD MORNING, AMERICA

SELECTED POEMS
Edited by Rebecca West

THE PEOPLE, YES

★

For Young Folks

ROOTABAGA STORIES

ROOTABAGA PIGEONS

ABE LINCOLN GROWS UP

CARL SANDBURG

* * * * *

Remembrance Rock

* * * * * * * * * * * * * * *

New York

HARCOURT, BRACE AND COMPANY

The quotations on page 999 from *Up Front* by Bill Mauldin are reprinted by permission of Henry Holt and Company, Inc.; the poem "The young dead soldiers do not speak," quoted on page 1003, is reprinted by permission of the author, Archibald MacLeish; the selection on pages 1007-1008 from *Not So Wild a Dream* by Eric Sevareid, copyright 1946 by Eric Sevareid, and the selection on page 1061 from *The Last Days of Sevastopol* by Boris Voyetekhov, copyright 1943 by Alfred A. Knopf, Inc., are reprinted by permission of Alfred A. Knopf, Inc.; the selection on page 1046 is reprinted from *Tucker's People* by Ira Wolfert, copyright 1943 by Ira Wolfert, and published by A. A. Wyn, Inc.

*personal Book Shop
3.00*

1-4-49 cb

Notes and Acknowledgments

*   *   *

A few of the characters in this book are from real life, their names of documentary record. The others are fictional creations and if any should prove identical with names of the present time, the circumstance is a coincidence.

Amid various toils and tribulations in the progress of this work I had the friendship and counsel of publisher Donald C. Brace, and the unfailing assistance of his coadjutors Catherine McCarthy and Robert Giroux. (It was no hindrance that the creative editor Giroux had served in World War II on the carrier *Essex* in the Pacific, ending as Lieutenant Commander.) Library and research labors of my wife and daughters should be mentioned, with a rose pinned on Helga for sustained industry and enterprise as a trouble-shooter. For occasional long hours day and night on manuscript, credits should go to Louise Howe Bailey and Sarah Sandifer of Hendersonville, North Carolina, and William P. Schenck of Chicago. Salutations should go to Voldemar Vetluguin, Sidney Franklin, and Olin Clark for their quiet faith and worthy silence. For reading the manuscript as it progressed and for their encouragement and suggestions I am beholden to Oliver R. Barrett and Mary Hastings Bradley of Chicago and to Don and Lyal Shoemaker of Asheville, North Carolina. For scrutiny and aid on the Epilogue I should mention Marjorie Arnette and William Braye, also Hazel and Jane Buchbinder, of Chicago. Nor could I omit Mitchell and Rose Dawson of Winnetka, Illinois. For consultations and materials I am grateful to Keith Wheeler, the war correspondent who out of personal experience wrote *We Are the Wounded,* and to Earle Davis, professor, poet and infantry officer, author of *An American in Sicily.* And we could put in bronze the name of Lieutenant Commander Kenneth MacKenzie Dodson, executive officer of a Navy attack transport, a true mariner and a man of rare faith in the American dream.

C. S.

TO THE KNOWN AND UNKNOWN TOILERS AND FIGHTERS
WHOSE DUST IS BEYOND GATHERING FOR REMEMBRANCE

★ ★ ★ ★ ★ ★ ★ ★ ★
★   ★
★   *Prologue*   ★
★   ★
★ ★ ★ ★ ★ ★ ★ ★ ★

JUSTICE WINDOM'S BOX

Bowbong Walks in Washington Moonlight

THE boy not yet two years old tried to say "Grandpa" and it came out "Bowbong." That, anyhow, was the one they picked from bowbong, buppong, boohbong, bahbong, babbong, pahpong and still other variations. The older ones took to saying and writing it Bowbong and it was really nobody's business except Bowbong the grandfather's and Raymond the grandson's.

More than twenty years ago, that was. And now from the South Pacific letters had come that began with "Dear Bowbong." And from India, Egypt, Italy, England, Pearl Harbor, Los Angeles, had come letters or postal cards that began with "Dear Bowbong," these from Raymond, a pilot, "on a mission" here, "on a mission" there, leading a global life that neither he nor Bowbong had expected in the years just before 1944.

Now Bowbong wore a sack coat, a rather battered panama hat, and spoke a shy greeting to a few who had recognized him and wished him good evening and mentioned his name. Also he nodded in a shy way to others who nodded their heads as though they knew him, though they had not met formally. He had walked, taken a bus, walked again, taken a taxi, and again was walking. He had sat on a bench in Lafayette Square, looked at the bronze Andrew Jackson in the saddle on a bronze horse pawing the air with its forefeet while Jackson holding the reins with his left hand salutes America, the future, the moon, with the cocked hat raised in his right hand. Jackson had come to this city of Washington in a time about halfway between George Washington and Abraham Lincoln. Elected for one term in the Executive Mansion across the street, then again elected for a second term, the nickname had been given him of "King Andrew." Eight Presidents since Jackson had come to the Executive Mansion across the street until Lincoln moved in alive and was carried out of the great front doors with the breath gone from him and since then fourteen Presidents of the United States had moved into the White House, twelve of them no longer in the land of the living.

The white haze of a full moon came down on Lafayette Square, on Pennsylvania Avenue, on the White House framed in stately and quiet trees across the way, and Bowbong on the park bench could remember shaking hands with nine of those fourteen Presidents. Quiet in the shadows and the moonfall looked the White House this night. He

3

knew, however, it was never quiet under that roof over there and whatever of peace and stillness might seem to be there, it was a momentary screen behind which lurked the surging trials, heartaches and turmoils of the American people. His own life went back as far as the year that Abraham Lincoln died. His father, from Peoria, Illinois, had fought three years in what was variously called the Civil War, the War between the States, the War of the Brothers, the War of the Rebellion, the War of the 1860's. And his mother had come down from Boston in January of '65 and they were married that month and he had been born in October of that year and it was in April of that year of '65 that Bowbong's father and mother had shaken hands with President Lincoln and exchanged greetings and good wishes. Many years afterward it was his father and mother were utterly and momentously solemn when they told him of looking into Lincoln's face and feeling his handclasp there in the White House across the way, and his mother's eyes hazy and moist as she gave her thought, "It would not be stretching the truth, my boy, for you to say you were in the same room with President Lincoln, though neither of you saw the other—he would have meant the handclasp he gave me to be shared by the child I was carrying."

He had crossed the street, strolled past the State Department Building, the Treasury Building, and taken a streetcar to the Capitol grounds, holding a little imaginary conversation with the bronze Chief Justice John Marshall, and walking up the wide stone stairs to stand at the West Front where many a crowd had seen and heard a new President take the oath of office and kiss the Bible handed him by a Chief Justice —and far up and near lost in the haze of a moon bath the Capitol Dome surmounted by the bronze full-breasted matron with helmet and sword symbolizing Armed Freedom. A year or two before he was born, it was, the iron-curved beams and sections of the dome lay scattered on the ground where he now stood and had been hoisted and joined and fastened into the unity of form intended by architect and builders. Past the time-washed Library of Congress he had strolled, and its neighbor building air-conditioned to keep inviolate manuscripts and data of the great Englishman William Shakespeare, and then a few steps away the new white glittering sanctuary of the Supreme Court of the United States. His eyes roved its immaculate marble front, his ears caught the dim jumble of juke boxes a block away. The hour was getting late and time to go home.

The taxis sped by, a dozen perhaps, before he could double with passengers going his way, two young couples who had been dancing and taken a few drinks. They asked him gay questions and got short, gruff answers. He was pondering, brooding, questing in thought as he rode the taxicab, carrying on the mood of shy and solemn meditation that had held him through the evening and night as he had rambled and troubled himself with the oldest involved questions threshed out on

4

the floors of Congress under the Capitol Dome, in the White House, on the Supreme Court bench. And he knew his meditations would have to be good, worthy, keen and, if possible, cadenced and singing. This because tomorrow night he was to give his first radio address to the American people. They had urged him that millions who knew his name and took him as a significant American figure would like to have coming into their homes his voice with a message for the time and hour. He had refused and again refused this request and had finally given in to their insistence that others might have a right to keep silence during the fourth year of the Second World War, but not he.

He was aware that the two girls got off at their rooming house and a few blocks farther the two young men got out and before kicking the starter the driver, speaking gently so it could be taken he was talking to himself, "Kinda fresh, huh?" and farther along the driver volunteering that when in college he had studied one of his passenger's essays in *An Anthology of Modern American Prose*. The taxi-driver had recognized his passenger and resented it that such a passenger should get from a youth who couldn't well carry what was under his belt the query as to what they had in the Gay 90's as nice as boogie-woogie.

They drove on. The driver, he learned, had a wife and two children and would be in the Marines but for one kidney missing. As he was getting out of the cab and paying his fare, the driver had started the radio and, making change, very respectfully, "I'll be listening tomorrow night."

(This place he had named Hopecrest. Around the wide front of the two-story stone house with its four-dormer garret he loafed in a slow and easy stroll to the large wooded yard at the rear, a few oaks and elms older than himself, and a score of pines, Lombardy poplars, Chinese elms and a privet hedge that his own hands had planted across twenty years and more. Here among his own trees, bushes, paths, with no interfering street lights, he could be alone with the moon, with the latticed crossplay of shadows, with the timeless patterns of black patch and silver curve flowing to the confluence of branches, leaves, and moonfall to the earth, each pattern silent, certain, yet infinitely transient. He came to a rugged boulder, tall as himself and longer and wider than it was high.)

(Here stood four pointed cedars he had planted for the four cardinal points from which any and all winds of destiny and history blow. So much he had told others. Also he had told others he named the boulder Remembrance Rock, for it could be a place to come and remember.) What he had not told them was the kind of thing a shy man of sensitive imagination would not choose to tell others. Here he had brought a handful of dust from Plymouth, Massachusetts, and here a colonial silver snuffbox filled with earth from Valley Forge,

5

and here a small box of soil from Cemetery Ridge at Gettysburg, Pennsylvania, and here another handful of dust from the Argonne in France. As each man has his personal secrets, often whimsical and beyond explanation though deeply sacred, so it had been his decision many years back to spread around this Remembrance Rock and these four trees a small box of soil from Plymouth, others from Valley Forge and Gettysburg, and a precious handful of loam from the Argonne. The earth smell of early summer came as he leaned and joined his shadow to that of the boulder and saw the full moon pouring a thin white-gold to filter among tree branches and become a silver haze among forks of black and fingers of purple on the ground. Alone he had gone to far places and brought back dust and soil of high meaning to men and women at Plymouth and Valley Forge, his father at Gettysburg, his son with the La Fayette Escadrille in France. The silence of each held the personal secret of each. He had lived shy and rated himself lower than any of his friends or kinfolk might guess. And he would go on shy, with a humility that could border on shame when he measured the little that he had given to his country, to the world and the Family of Man.

In the house he sat in the study corner of his library and wrote for an hour, recasting his address to the American people tomorrow night, to go from coast to coast in America and then rebroadcast to the Armed Forces of the United States over the earth. Bowbong went to bed haunted by what he had written and after an hour of wakeful thought knew he would tomorrow again rewrite the message.

* * * * * * * * * *

Chapter 2

* * * * * * * * * *

One Big Geographical Kiss

ON the morning of June 1, of 1944, shortly after Maria had brought her baby christened Joseph Stilwell to Hopecrest, a day when the sky over Europe had never before been so full of bomber and fighter formations in death grapple—on this day of full green leaves with the bosom of the earth aching to bloom and yield—on this morning Bowbong looked up from his library table where he had started a piece of writing. Someone was quietly opening the door, aiming not to disturb him. He noticed two feet step through the doorway and two persons enter the room. It was Maria, in her left arm twelve-pound Joseph Stilwell. She had been rereading some of Raymond's letters and on the big globe wanted to locate the islands in the Pacific where Raymond and his squadron had "put on a good show."

Bowbong held young Joseph Stilwell while Maria made her findings. She was nearly the same height as the old man, the top arcs of the globe just below the level of her eyes. "Nice you don't have to stand tiptoe," she murmured. While she spoke the baby burped and made a wry mouth at his father's grandfather. She repeated her remark. The old man chuckled, "Yes, I measured it for you, Mimah." Raymond had begun it and Bowbong followed in calling her Mimah ("Mee'mah"), among themselves, while to outsiders she was strictly Maria, her father tracing back to First Comers on the *Mayflower*, her mother stemming from Czech and Lithuanian forebears.

Mimah felt sentimental about reaching a hand out to arm's length and turning the planet Earth around to the various locations where her husband, her brother and other kin and next of kin were last heard of with the Armed Forces. She turned again to where Raymond had been, as he once wrote, "skybusting and hell-bent" before going to base hospital. Then Mimah turned for a long look at the shape of the island of Sicily where her brother Peter Enders, now hospitalized with face wounds, had met a booby-trap blast at an innocent-looking doorway in a quiet village.

Little Joe Stilwell now definitely belched, stuck out a thick underlip, and sent a trickle of milk out over his chin. Bowbong stepped over to his desk for a tissue and returned to Mimah, wiping the milk off the chin and studying the face of Joe Stilwell which he believed now meant to say, "I beg your pardon if I looked ugly at you a moment ago. I feel better now and you might as well forget it."

Her eyes shifting to the baby, Mimah said, "Did I tell you on the night Raymond went away, we agreed if the baby was a girl we would name it Beulah Bathsheba and if a boy Joseph Stilwell? Don't people take notions when they get to picking one name out of thousands for a baby that has nothing to do with picking its parents or the name of its parents? Out of millions of homes our baby Joe had to come to this one." She blew a flick of lint off one baby ear. "A long time before he'll do any worrying about that. Raymond spoke prayers that your great-grandchild should come here. He said you told him there are times one baby means more to you than all your books."

"I told Raymond," said Bowbong, "about the man rebuked for sleeping through a play he was to give his opinion about. The man said, 'Sleep is an opinion.' And a baby is God's opinion that life should go on. A book that does nothing to you is dead. A baby, whether it does anything to you, represents life. If a bad fire should break out in this house and I had my choice of saving the library or the babies, I would save what is alive. Never will a time come when the most marvelous recent invention is as marvelous as a newborn

7

baby. The finest of our precision watches, the most supercolossal of our supercargo planes, don't compare with a newborn baby in the number and ingenuity of coils and springs, in the flow and change of chemical solutions, in timing devices and interrelated parts that are irreplaceable. This baby here is very modern. Strictly. Yet it is also the oldest of the ancients. This Joe Stilwell here doesn't know he is a hoary and venerable antique—but he is. Before man learned how to make an alphabet, how to make a wheel, how to make a fire, he knew how to make a baby—with the great help of woman and his God and Maker."

"Raymond had a way of laughing at modern love," Mimah smiled. "He'd say ancient love was hairy wild, naked, terrible with consequences, and it can't be modernized with any helps, conveniences, devices. When a couple in a fifteen-story apartment house is nice and crazy about each other today it's the same as a one-room log-cabin couple nice and crazy about each other two hundred years ago. And when a jealous man now kills a woman with an automatic, it's the same kind of jealousy as ten thousand years ago when he killed with a large hand-picked pebble. Perhaps Raymond heard that from you, Bowbong."

"Whatever Raymond heard from me about love was amateur after he met you."

"The only jealousy I've had about Raymond is planes. I think he might grow to love some skybuster more than any woman."

"He does stroke and caress the controls, doesn't he? His letters tell us he reads his instrument board like it was a good woman's face."

Bowbong and Mimah had occasionally glanced at Joe Stilwell. Under the lull of their conversational babble he had faded into sleep.

"Before I take away ancient Joseph, perhaps I should give you Raymond's names for the B-26 bomber. You remember I saw him take a new one up, at the Glenn Martin plant near Baltimore, right after the test pilot had put her through its first flight? You can't land going slow with her. You put her down at ninety miles an hour. She is tricky. You have to know her. The English named her the Marauder. Later the Americans nicknamed her Murder, Incorporated. And one squadron that couldn't make her behave nicknamed her the Prostitute—no visible means of support."

"That isn't fair to the prostitute," said Bowbong. "She not only wears but flaunts her visible means of support. I remember as a boy going with my father and mother to Chicago. Late one night walking to our horsecar connection, we met and passed along three or four blocks some five or six women, one by one, alone on the street, 'dressed to kill,' as the slang of the day had it, in gowns bespangled, their necks bejeweled. Mother said, 'I should think those women would be afraid to be out alone on the streets so late at night.' And father very softly, 'It's the men better be afraid.'"

8

"Next we'll be in a tangle about what makes a good woman and a bad woman bad."

"I'm talking too much—as usual. Those are all fit names they the murderous and temperamental B-26. It's their demon. They it. They study its whims and humor it. I favor any name they give it. Did Raymond tell you about one they named Mud Flat?"

"No."

"Three of them took her from Pearl Harbor on a practice flight. She did some twisting and landed in a mud flat on the island of Oahu. Two of them piled out safe. She began sinking. They saw the muddy, black, incoming tidewater rise inch by inch to the elbows, to the shoulders, to the chin of their buddy pinned so he couldn't get loose. They worked like fury and pulled him out just as the black, briny water reached his mouth. Raymond said if they had lost two or three minutes on that operation their buddy would have been a goner. Raymond chuckled telling it, so damned funny, he said, they were so damned lucky."

"What an odd fool thing to happen. And how many odd fool things they'll be telling when they come back. And now," said Mimah as she softly lifted a dangling arm of Joe Stilwell and put his fist up near the chin, "with one more look at this globe I'll relieve you of holding this future squadron commander."

She stepped to the globe, moved a finger in a wide circle of the South Pacific. "Somewhere here in a base hospital Raymond rests between clean white sheets and has the best of care and perhaps in six weeks or three months will come home and tell us about it. It's too complicated and bothersome to write the details, he says. Look, Bowbong," as she slowly revolved the globe twice.

"Yes, Mimah," he murmured to meet her vivid imaginative mood.

"When he went away he said, 'I'm going places, birdie, and when I get back I'll tell you about it—and if there's a little fellow to listen it'll make his ears grow.' They put him on missions, here and there missions."

Her hands smoothed and patted the globe as she went on. "He's been over this ocean, the Atlantic, three times, and once over this the Indian Ocean and here in the Himalayas, he climbed the Hump and waved it Good-by, Hump, nice Hump, and here on the Pacific he's crossed it four times. Here on this island he saw the boy that took on seven enemy planes and in twenty minutes of zigzag skybusting that boy brought down all seven and then scrammed and when Raymond asked him how did he feel afterward the boy grinned, 'I didn't sleep two nights thinking about it.'"

"And these continents, Bowbong, your grandson has been over this and this, every one of them. Do you get it? This fellow you once saw as a helpless bundle like Joseph here, he takes the round globe in his stride asking, What's one ocean more or less? And only yester-

9

day he stood in that door and held my face in his hands and chucked me under the chin and pushed me in the ribs and gave me one long, soft, slow kiss as he said, 'Kiss your husband one last kiss he can take around the world before you give him another.' Who would have thought it? Around the planet Earth, the globe, up, down and criss-cross around the world he's been with that kiss."

Mimah's wild gaiety slowed down, her face solemn. "Now he'll be here again this summer, with stories past any of our imagining." Then just a touch of the bitter in her tone. "What fancy wars we have these days when a wife gives her husband a good-by kiss to take" —and she turned the globe and swept her hand here and there—"over this ocean, that continent, this bloody atoll, this hazy, crazy, crimson man-eating archipelago where my guess is he got whatever sent him to that base hospital."

Bowbong noted her tincture of the bitter, put a hand on her shoulder, drew her toward him, and spoke in her earlier and lighter mood. "Yes, Mimah, kisses go farther these days, they surely do. I expect one of these days to see a keen young sweetheart standing on her toes reaching her lips to a young fellow in pilot togs telling him, 'Now I'm going to give you a big geographical kiss that'll bring you good luck and keep you warm in the Aleutians and keep you cool in the Caribbean.' And he'll tighten his lips on hers in one long kiss, stopping to say, 'That was for the Western Hemisphere,' and before another one, 'This is for the Eastern Hemisphere.'"

"Like as not," beamed Mimah, "they'll go on from there to one kiss for each ocean, each continent, and then itsybitsy kisslets for every little island and atoll they can think of."

"And like as not her last little whimpering words to him will be, 'You mug, you, you mug, why do you do me like you do?'"

"It could be," said Mimah, taking the baby into her arms. "You are a comfort, Bowbong."

She walked to the door as he moved to his worktable. "Come again, Mimah, that globe is yours by natural right."

"I will."

"And bring the little fellow."

"For any particular reason?"

"He's the future, you're the present. I'm the past."

Only her face in sight before closing the door, "I think you are all three, Bowbong. I thank you."

The door closed. Bowbong sat looking at the Box and its papers. They meant much to him.

Chapter 3

Listening Millions

HIS books were part of him. Each year of his life, it seemed, his books became more and more a part of him. This room, thirty by twenty feet, and the walls of shelves filled with books, had for him the murmuring of many voices. In the books of Herodotus, Tacitus, Rabelais, Thomas Browne, John Milton, and scores of others, he had found men of face and voice more real to him than many a man he had met for a smoke and a talk. The ancients and moderns of history and biography were there, sections of science, folklore, fiction with special stress on the supreme short stories, and a collection of English-language Bibles going back to the Coverdale Bible of 1535, and a variety of famous prayer books and hymnals. Three sections or groupings of books had been most used and worn, filled with markers and notes, these dealing with the Pilgrims, the American Revolution, and the War of the 1860's in the United States. His living thought and heaviest anxieties of many years, along with some of his deepest pleasures of life, had centered in this room, these books, and what he had met in them to make his own. He saw it as fitting that in this room where he had tried to keep a fellowship with great minds and rare human spirits of the past and the present and where so often he had put away all the books and tried to get at the best of his own thought and experience and throw it into written form on paper— here he saw it as fitting he should make an address reaching millions of the American people.

Now the hour for speaking that address had come and they were watching the minute hand of a watch on the table, placed between the two disks. A little marvel was this six-inch disk. Inside it waited an infinitely sensitive piece of machinery. At any moment it was either dead or alive. If it was dead you could shout into it at the top of your voice, you could wear your voice ragged, and you wouldn't be heard except by yourself and the people in the room. If it was alive it would pick up your whisper and carry that whisper to millions of people listening in their country and farm homes, in their trucks and cars driving along highways, in planes above clouds in the sky, in ships plowing the sea or at anchor in harbor. To housewives washing dishes, to families eating their evening meal, to lonesome drinkers in taverns and cocktail lounges, to men at rest on their fishing boats, to the club cars of overland limited railway trains, to sick folk pale and hoping in their beds, to crowded city apartment houses and lonely mountain cabins and desert shacks where they prize their ten-dollar mail-order midget sets, to a vast swarming mass of listeners, each with his own face and human personality, would go your whisper, if and when the little disk into which you sent your whisper was alive.

The old man wondered how many there might be like the taxi-driver who had said "I'll be listening" and how many would be tuning in accidentally not knowing what was on the air for this evening. He looked at his "script." That was their name for it, the script, mimeographed and tabbed with signals. They had come to his home in the afternoon and he had gone over it with them. "The script has to be exactly correct, neither too long nor short for the time you're on the air," he was told. He took a pencil and crossed out a long sentence. He wrote in two short sentences that would take less time. He looked at it and doubted whether he had improved what he had to say.

He looked across the room and at once felt more easy. His eyes met the face of a smiling young woman, the mouth large with thin lips over white even teeth, her eyes set wide apart, her hairdress too elaborate to please him and her little hat no hat at all but just a whimsical ornament. A good face, somewhat gaunt, she had, and a rich grave smile he always liked. But more important was the small bundle she held in her lap. Now she raised this bundle and let him have a look at the sleepy, blinking, noncommittal face of his great-grandson, sixty days old, still well satisfied with the breast feeding he had a few minutes ago. This was the clinching reason that had brought Bowbong to this broadcast on a June evening of 1944. The future, the next generation, the young ones who would be carrying on when his generation had vanished—yes, he would do his best at giving them a message—not so easy an assignment for a shy man who had come more and more to value silence, but he would do his best and they could not rebuke him nor he reproach himself with having hidden idle in a background of misgiving and evasion.

A drone and a roar came on the air, an even monotone of a thundering drone that rattled the windows of the house and sent tremors to the table and the disks before them. Three or four low-flying bombers had come and gone overhead. They could only hope there would be no such interference during the broadcast.

The announcer pleasantly suggested that the baby might cry or make sounds interfering with the broadcast and they should perhaps not have the child present. "I want that child here," and Bowbong motioned toward the baby. "There will be no harm." To Mimah he said, "If he cries I shall tell them it is the Future they hear crying."

Mimah's eyes rested on the face of the great-grandfather still reading his script and studying about it and ready to make last-minute changes. A slash of a wide gargoylish mouth, half-solemn, the upper lip thin as against the heavy and mournful lower lip, the jaws having a flow

12

of lines that joined to shape the chin and it reminded her of battleships, anvils and tall crags because though they are so very different there is common likeness in battleships, anvils and tall crags. The skin held a ruddy sun-and-wind tan, the nose ran straight with wide nostrils, his yellowed and uneven teeth showing but little when he laughed. His brown eyes, she knew, could drowse, then bore deep into your own, then drowse again, then dance and flutter at a sudden keen interest, at times the right eye all open and the left a peering narrow slit. His mouth was changeful with a gamut of shades and twists. The sloping, thick-muscled shoulders often had their own way of talking without words and running along with whatever he might be laughing or solemn about. He stood five feet eight inches, weighing one hundred eighty pounds, thickset and powerful of build, his silvered head of hair, once brick-red in the sun and a sunset maroon in shadow, one side of his face at peace in calm and the other side half-snarling and dark with endless combat. At times, in moments and flickering instants when he was deeply moved—and she could see those instants occasionally now—his gargoylish mouth became a crooked slash varying like the progressions of a storm sky. His face had the ranging contrasts of his personality, for though he was most of the time grave, calm, slow-spoken, his moods could run to banter and persiflage, the airy fooling of broomstraws in a high wind. Thus the wife of his grandson, mother of his great-grandson, saw him as his eyes ran over the script and occasionally sent a glance toward her.

That afternoon he had seen her dance for the first time. He didn't know about her dancing till it slipped from her just as a casual report on how she had been spending a little spare time lately. Three dances she had now for Raymond when he should come home. She used to make up dances for him and do them and ask him how she was doing. Once in a while they would say it together that one of her dances had nearly everything. One was the Old Zip Coon, another Moonlight on the White House Lawn. Three now she had ready for Raymond: the American Dream, Bomber Formation, and the Soldier's Letter to His Wife and Baby. She hesitated, made sure Raymond's grandfather was in the mood and wouldn't take it as too irregular or ridiculous, and because he sort of insisted, she did the three new dances that she would not be sure about till later. He saw it was her way of singing. Her feet, her long slim legs and winding torso, along with her ideas and quirks of imagination, could make things come alive. She had no career in mind except as wife and homebody. She did the dances because they came to her and sometimes they were more than just keen fun. She was six feet in height like Raymond and it was in their private sessions after dancing for hours to a swing band that she had got to saying, "I'm going to do some steps and whirls now and we'll see how they come out."

13

Her face a trifle gaunt, the cheekbones high, the skin sea-pale, there was a bright burnish to her sweeps of chestnut hair. Her eyes were blue and Raymond said that in some moods they had sea-green and stormwind in them. She had written Raymond that the baby had his father's deep-blue eyes, a danger-blue as she called it, and the baby had her chestnut hair.

During the eight or ten minutes before the broadcast was to begin, she kept on wondering as she had often in recent weeks what it might be that so preoccupied the old man, giving him a faraway look that didn't stay faraway at all when suddenly his brown eyes were boring straight to her heart with a steady flame-line of care and love and it was almost as though it left a mark there on her bosom, her face, that she and Raymond must not forget. He gave her that look for the both of them. What the look meant he would try to get said to them both. The roots of it could be nothing ordinary and the lights of it could sky-high with spokes, wheels and sprockets of sacred and momentous action. Whether it was something he would speak to them about, whether it was something in writing, some manner of a testament or other document, she couldn't make out for sure, she could merely guess. When it came it would be for her and Raymond, directly to them, and yet beyond them it was to be meant for many other young people, many other young American couples seeking their way out of the present war and what lay beyond the war. And she could tell now beforehand that it would be meant for Joe Stilwell when his time came, for the little one represented the Future. And something told her too that part of what burned in Bowbong when he dropped that faraway look and his drowsy brown eyes took on fateful meaning, part of it would get told tonight in this radio address.

Suddenly she was making the past come alive again. She saw ropes and thongs of tough weave, threads of thick white linen, fine-spun and almost invisible shimmers of scarlet and blood-mist silk, that interwove between her and Raymond and his grandfather. And these bonds that held the three of them, bonds they could feel growing from year to year, even month to month since the war began, these were in part a private family affair and nobody's business beyond their home roof—and then again these interwoven rootholds of their hearts ranged out far and wide touching their country and what the American people, the American flag, the American citizen might stand for in relation to the world scene and the widespread Family of Man over the earth.

In those minutes ticked off by the precision watches on the table between the microphone disks, her mind ran back over the four years since she first met Raymond and his grandfather, her graduation at eighteen from Bryn Mawr and his happening to be there and "so pleased" to meet the daughter of the first violinist of a great symphony orchestra and she "truly delighted" to know the grandson of a jurist of national fame. And they started "going together" and it seemed to work out nicely and they attended Washington University together until he enlisted and was stationed near Washington for training. She was about as good on the violin as he was on the harmonica and it was in weekends at Hopecrest that Justice Windom got them to learn and play for him his old favorites "Kathleen Mavourneen," "Then You'll Remember Me," and "Down in the Valley." They played blues, swing and boogiewoogie for him and he said it was interesting but he couldn't quite get the intentions of it—if he could just get their intentions he would know why they went so "wide and handsome" with it. There had been the time they learned "Old Zip Coon" because the Justice liked it and they could play it straight the way he wanted it and then they had a wild changeable way of playing it for themselves with the variations never the same. They sensed what they were heading into, and nothing said about it until one afternoon they played "Old Zip Coon" crazier and sweeter, as they themselves admitted, than ever before. "Either we're kidding ourselves," Raymond had proposed, "or we're going to take one of those high dives into what for the want of a better word they call matrimony." She met his mood.

And they knew they weren't casual, flip nor offhand, something terribly real about it, as basic as the training that made him so handy a flier that he was put in charge of instruction. It was early 1942 before he went into active service and it was on leave in August of '43 they were married and September he had gone away and weeks until she had letters from him.

The baby had come as a miracle of consolation and there had been solace in meeting Justice Windom's request that she live at Hopecrest. The old man had come to lean on her. She broke his loneliness and eased his shyness, knew when he needed the hush of her hands and long fingers over his forehead. And what he had done for her was not easy to explain. She had learned new ways to go at books and handle them like people she was not afraid of—where she used to be either scared of ideas or else shut them out as sort of useless for her it got so that he would offer her all kinds of ideas as though he was at the same time asking himself and her how about them. She would offer him what came to her mind and after a while he had given her a clear notion that she ought to trust what went on in her mind and to take what lay deep, cherished and insistent in her mind as having value for the guidance of her life. It was perhaps not so easy and plain as that, but what Bowbong had given her seemed priceless to her and in return he knew she adored an inner flame in him and some flicker of that flame would be with her for a long time.

Then there had been those few letters from Raymond. The whole island bristled with guns, under every house one or more pillboxes, with gun magazines and bomb shelters connected by underground tunnels for their last desperate stand. How the landing was made you will probably read about in the newspapers. Somehow it seems hard to talk about it." So often would be that from Ray. "Somehow it seems hard to talk about it." Kwajalein was a pretty island, thick with green leaves and fresh tropical foliage and tall coco palms. "Now it is seared and blasted beyond human comprehension, the stink of death everywhere, the awfullest retching stench imaginable."

Where had this merry harmonica chum of hers been? She would ask knowing he could never tell her when he came back. He was saying so, writing it, "beyond human comprehension" the waste and terror his eyes had lived on, stenches of death that made you retch. "Infantrymen drove on from pillbox to pillbox, using high explosives, hand grenades, and flame-throwers to smoke the Japs out. The Japs would run underground and keep popping up behind again, which is why so many of our men were shot in the seat of their pants. All the time dive bombers and naval gunfire delivered on call. By afternoon the smoke poured out and up high into the sky all over the islands under attack. From gas, oil, and ammunition dumps blown up, the explosions and gunfire shook the ship, the roar never ending. Landing later we saw bodies seared and bloated. I saw one half-buried in a pillbox, the skin burned off his back and his head off a few feet away. Another stood dead in a half-crouch, both hands holding to a coconut log of the pillbox. In bed at night remembering the awful sweetish sickening stench of powder, kerosene, decaying human flesh, I wonder, after all, what war is all about."

And much more. In his letters he piled horror on horror as though no matter how horrible it might seem to one reading about it, the reality was so far worse and beyond any telling that it would be no kindness to omit the horrors. He had hope in two of the earlier letters, writing that hope rather desperately. "We are going to fight and work our heads off to win this war. But we are fighting because we bungled the past peace, and we must never let it happen again. They can't tell me war is a fine and noble thing. I wish they could see the difference between the Saturday morning parades at Alameda and the stench of Kwajalein. General Sherman, how right he was in 'War is hell.' I heard a blinded veteran of the last war say that, low and bitter. It didn't sound like it reads in print."

Farther along in that letter his hope bordered on despair. "One night I watched them transferring 62 wounded men to a hospital ship. Some groaned, some talked out of their head. One fine-looking tall boy extended over both ends of his stretcher. He was shot through the leg and the bone shattered. For some reason I felt compelled to ask him where he was from. He said, 'Southeast Oregon,' and mentioned a small town near Ashland. I told him my brother-in-law had a fox farm at Eagle Point. We were just picking him up to put him in the boat and he smiled in the moonlight and said, 'Eagle Point

16

Fox Farm. I know him. He sure has beautiful foxes.' He gripped my hand hard, and then they picked up his litter and lowered it into the boat to start him on his way back home. Well, I'd got through all the groaning and the screaming and kept a stiff upper lip, but as that smiling kid left, I had to rub away the tears with my fist. I hate war." The tone was desperate though not lost to all hope. "Here we are in the third year of it, and it is just beginning to come home to me. I know we all love our country more than we ever did. But the average soldier and sailor wants to get the war over as soon as possible and come home."

And then there were lines she cried over because of the loveliness of their personal thought as between just her and him. From a small island untouched by gunfire he would try to send her a bag of "beautiful sand" to go in a goldfish bowl for her and Joe Stilwell, "the prettiest sand I have ever seen."

Another man, a changed lover with hungers neither he nor she had ever heard of when he went away, would be coming back to her. "The war leaves a stamp on you. You take a bath and don't feel clean. You want a spiritual purge of the whole stinking business. You feel you'd like to be baptized and have communion. You want to lie on the grass and watch the cumulus swimming by in the blue of the sky. You want to have your arms around one very near and dear to you and snuggle your head deep beside your beloved and feel the tenderness of her lips on yours and the clean warm living scent that is her. And then sleep, and there shall be no more war, no parting, no killing, no smell of death: just peace."

Aware he had gone far in this black mood he confessed, "Well, this has been about the most morbid letter I have ever written. Don't take it too bad. I'm very healthy and eat my three square meals (out of tin cans). I certainly would like to see you. When I can come home for good, it will be for good, you bet your boots it will. I've got a lot of hugs to hug and kisses to kiss. No more going to fight a war, a chance to really live, there will be a way. God has never failed us and He will see us through. . . . The soldiers are laughing and telling stories. Life goes on. Boy, are we looking forward to mail next week. Hope you did your stuff, honey, for I'm ready for a long session reading letters from you."

Then for a time no letters. Then a few short letters. He had been free-spoken. He could and did pour out bitterness that burned inside him. Now no more of that. Some change had come over him. Its reason or cause couldn't be read in those abrupt short notes with a hint that he felt completely useless about what he was doing now or would try to do tomorrow.

This dark turmoil, the poignant and cutting parts and those of moving loveliness, she had shared with Bowbong. And Bowbong had intimated that he had so much to say that for the time it was best

17

for him to say little or nothing. And he implied directly that when he would come to speak his heart, his mind and imagination, for her and Raymond, by way of such light and counsel as he might offer to them, it might be something far out of the ordinary.

She had seen him in morning hours and late at night working on papers, perhaps a long and strange manuscript, and they were kept carefully in the Box that so often stood on his table and that went into a little fireproof vault when he was not working with them. Those papers, she knew, and the radio address he was to give this evening, would be directed at Raymond and her, and if he could rightly keep his faith with them, with his "dearest ones," as he phrased it, then he could not fail of a message worth the time of the listening millions of the American people.

They had motioned him to his place before the microphone disk. He heard on a receiving set a droning butterball voice ending its vehement praise of the merit and quality of all brands manufactured by the Miracle Products Corporation. He heard an announcer, "We are taking you now to our Washington studios."

A silence of a few seconds and he watched the face of an announcer at a microphone opposite him, in a smooth, quiet and perfect gravity, "It is a rare privilege and an honor that does not come often—to present for his first radio address to the American people—an American citizen of world renown—a man whose conception of civic responsibility and whose devotion to duty in public service have endeared him to millions of patriotic Americans—a man whose long years of distinguished service have given him a peculiar niche in the historic annals of our nation—" The announcer had lifted his eyes from the script and was glancing toward him. "It is a unique honor to present to you one of the greatest of living Americans, former Justice of the United States Supreme Court, Orville Brand Windom," and the announcer gave his head a definite down-sweeping nod while saying, "Mr. Justice Windom."

He was surprised at how easy and natural he sent his voice into the disk before him. This was partly because he forgot about how many millions might be listening when his eyes could always find for a swift glance of greeting the lovable face of his grandson's wife and the face bundled in her arms that was the Future. There was the thought too that his grandson in a hospital somewhere in the South Pacific might be hearing him tonight or soon would certainly be hearing him in the rebroadcast.

"When we say a patriot is one who loves his country," ran the voice of Justice Windom, "what kind of love do we mean? A love we can throw on a scale and see how much it weighs? A love we can take apart to see how it ticks? A love where with a yardstick we record how long, high, wide, it is? Or is a patriot's love of country a thing invisible, a quality, a human shade and breath, beyond all reckoning and measurement? These are questions. They are old as the time of man. And the answers to them we know in part. For we know when a nation goes down and never comes back, when a society or a civilization perishes, one condition may always be found. They forgot where they came from. They lost sight of what brought them along. The hard beginnings were forgotten and the struggles farther along. They became satisfied with themselves. Unity and common understanding there had been, enough to overcome rot and dissolution, enough to break through their obstacles. But the mockers came. And the deniers were heard. And vision and hope faded. And the custom of greeting became 'What's the use?' And men whose forefathers would go anywhere, holding nothing impossible in the genius of man, joined the mockers and deniers. They forgot where they came from. They lost sight of what had brought them along.

"When we say a patriot is one who loves his country, what kind of love is it we mean? Those are tremendous questions. I could write a book trying to answer those questions. You have heard that the shroud has no pockets and the dead to whatever place they go carry nothing with them—you have heard that and you know its meaning is plain. Whatever cash or collateral a man may have, whatever bonds, securities, deeds and titles to land, real estate, buildings, leases and patents, whatever of jewels, medals, decorations, keepsakes or costly apparel, he leaves them all behind and goes out of the world naked and bare as he came. You have also heard the dead hold in their clenched hands only that which they have given away. In this we begin to approach the meaning of a patriot though we do not unlock the secret that hides in the bosom of a patriot. The dead hold in their clenched hands only that which they have given away. When men forget what is at the heart of that sentiment—and it is terribly sentimental—they are in danger of power being taken over by swine, or beasts of prey or men hollow with echoes and vanities. It has happened and the records and annals cry and moan with specific instances.

"As I speak to you from the seclusion of my home, I can see many of your faces. They are faces I have seen in our America, faces I have met from coast to coast, from the Great Lakes to the Gulf. They are the faces of today, of now, of this hour and this minute. Yet it is worth considering that many of those same faces have had their shining moments in our America of the past. We can go back fifty or a hundred years, two and three hundred years, and we meet these same faces of men, women and children. They shared in the making of America, in bringing this country on from the colonial wilderness days through one crisis after another. Their faces moved through shattering events and the heartbreak of war and revolution. Their faces gazed from the canvas slits of the covered wagon, from the glass windows of railway coaches, from the shatterproof glass of motorcars on concrete high-

19

ways, from the plexiglas nose of the latest make of airplane curving in the sky. They saw years of startling change and dazzling invention, till America took her place among nations as one of the great world powers. In each time of storm, in each period of development, have been these faces—and I can see them out among you who are listening tonight.

"I get familiar with you tonight to the extent of saying that in this room from which I am speaking, I see faces out of long before our time, long ago playing their parts and taking their roles in the making of America. Across the room I see the face of a baby sixty days old. That high-pitched squealing sound you heard a few moments ago came from him. The sound experts suggested that he might interrupt our talk tonight and he ought to be removed from the room and I told them we must keep the little fellow near by us. What you heard from him was the cry of the Future, the voice of the next generation. Their faces will rise to take the place of our faces which year by year they will see vanishing. And across the room holding this precious bundle of a baby I see his mother, wife of my grandson. He is in a hospital in the South Pacific tonight. I hope of course that he is listening in and that my voice is reaching him. That low-flying bomber you heard as I was beginning my talk—he was piloting one of those before he went to hospital. He and his wife represent young America that is making the present and will shape the future of our country. And among you who listen tonight, I am sure, are thousands of other young couples whose faces hold the dreams and resolves of the present looking toward the future. The same expectant and resolved faces from the hill at Plymouth gazed over the harbor three hundred years ago—I can see their faces at Valley Forge in that bitter winter and the faces of the women that those men there couldn't forget—I can see them saying good-by before their menfolk marched away to the campaign that brought them to Gettysburg.

"I get personal with you tonight. About your faces and dreams I get personal. Like myself nearly every one of you listening has dear ones. And we remember their faces. And we dream about them.

"Now at this moment I wonder about two people. One of them happens to be my granddaughter-in-law. I love her very much. And there is her husband, my grandson, somewhere in the South Pacific, I don't know where. I know you people are troubled. I confess I am troubled, too. I'm selfish enough to admit I'm troubled about my own flesh and blood—my grandson and his wife and the little great-grandson sitting in front of me now.

"It is perfectly natural we should be troubled. Yet we must keep it in mind and press it home in our minds that something like what is happening to our dear ones now has happened before. This is one crisis, the latest one. There have been others in the making of this

20

nation. The call to hardship, toil and combat runs like a blood-scarlet thread over and through the story of our people. It has cost to build this nation. Living men in struggle and risk, in self-denial and pain, in familiarity with sacrifice, wounds and death—those living men of the past paid that cost.

"I have reached the period of life when I am somewhat behind a cloud. Past, present and future become one. I know it is more reality than illusion when I look back and see my grandson and his wife three hundred years ago in the town of Plymouth—and in the next moment I see him in a place named Valley Forge and she is at home with their child wondering when the war will end—and again I see him in that tornado of action called Gettysburg and amid the suffering afterward he finds time to write her a letter.

"I see their faces the same in those days as now. From one spot of time to another the faces repeat. The mother of my great-grandson, seated here holding that child as I speak to you—she could have stood on the New England shore three hundred years ago. And her man who is away could have been there, too, in that time, hewing planks for a shelter, hoeing corn for their food, three hundred years ago. And so through the ups and downs and windings of the whole story of the American people there have been these people, these faces. My children and yours have been given this heritage, this land of ours, by their toil and struggle. And has it been worth the cost they paid? I think it has. To do it took men willing to throw in with all they had. And they did that. And we've got to let those who now are to shape the future know what the present time came from and what it's worth as a heritage.

"In a very real sense there is no such thing as a death of thought and energy. The will and vision that motivated people in Plymouth did not fade but moved on alive and written on faces at Valley Forge. It is still with us. Generations vanish, people disappear, the earth stays and the transmissions of energy. Life goes on.

"Long before this time of ours America saw the faces of her men and women torn and shaken in turmoil, chaos and storm. In each major crisis you could have seen despair written on the faces of the foremost strugglers. Yet there always arose enough of reserves of strength, balances of sanity, portions of wisdom, to carry the nation through to a fresh start with an ever renewing vitality.

"You may bury the bones of men and later dig them up to find they have moldered into a thin white ash that crumbles in your fingers. But their ideas won. Their visions came through. Men and women who gave all they had and wished they had more to give—how can we say they are sunk and buried? They live in the sense that their dream is on the faces of living men and women today. In a rather real sense the pioneers, old settlers, First Comers as some called themselves—they go on, their faces here now, their lessons worth our seeing. They ought not to be forgotten—the dead who held in their clenched hands that which became the heritage of us, the living."

Justice Windom had finished. His face lighted, the right eye full open and the left a narrow slit, his mouth and forehead alive with many shadings of thought and emotion, Bowbong looked at Mimah while the announcer was saying, "You have just heard the first radio address ever given to the American people by the former Justice of the United States Supreme Court, Mr. Orville Brand Windom. This is Station WBXJ, Washington, D. C."

He stepped quickly over to where Mimah stood with the little one in her arms. He reached his long arms around the two of them, and in an eager whisper, "I hope Raymond was listening."

Telegrams came that night and the next morning. For a week the mail was heavy with letters, almost too many, he said, taking his time from what he wanted to do and must be doing. But they were worth while if only for new-found friends and for words from old-timers he had lost track of.

★ ★ ★ ★ ★ ★ ★ ★ ★ ★

Chapter 4

★ ★ ★ ★ ★ ★ ★ ★ ★ ★

The Box

DURING this week it came to the notice of Mimah that Justice Windom was not taking his time nor any ease at what he did among his books and papers. On the long oak table in his work corner always stood the Box, more than a foot long and again as high, of heavy metal meant to be fireproof. Twice before leaving the room, as he filled it with the papers that seemed to belong in it, Mimah had seen him lock it once with one key and again with another key. She couldn't guess what his anxiety might be nor did he offer any explanation of why he had changed from the even pace of his usual working habits and why the smooth tone, the patience and measure that had always been a part of him, now had become something else. His hands moved too fast, his fingers reached too swiftly, his flashing brown eyes had a fever of impatience as he snatched his way among books, documents, keepsakes, possessions.

His foremost anxiety seemed to be the Box. He put things in the Box, took them out, put them back. He could touch and handle the

Box as though perhaps jealous of it, as though it might hold fear, love, consecration, despair, anything good or evil you might like to imagine. She noticed the two sides of his face as never before so vivid in contrast. She had heard of a friend once saying of those two profiles, "One side he's been to heaven, the other side he's been to hell," and it struck her she had never seen the combat profile so doggedly, even viciously, determined in its will and purpose nor the grave calm of the other profile so brightly composed and luminously serene.

She set a pitcher of iced lemonade on his table one mid-afternoon and at the doorway before leaving heard him call her and turned to hear him asking, while quizzical lights played on his face, "You didn't hear someone calling, did you, Mimah, someone in the hallway or down near the front door, calling 'Mr. Windom, Mr. Justice Windom, telegram for Mr. Windom'?"

No, she had heard nothing of the kind. She was sure. Very gently she assured him she had heard nothing of the kind.

She saw him bend his head and move his hands among his papers, a mystifying pleasant look on his face, and she believed he chuckled low to himself as though he could make it all quite clear to her when he'd so choose. He had never been much of a joker, as she knew him directly and through others, and her mind troubled itself about the phantom voice in the hallway or down near the front door that called, "Mr. Windom, Mr. Justice Windom, telegram for Mr. Windom."

In the twilight before dusk that evening came a wild rain and a spit of storm soon over. Two black clouds, rolling as smoke rolls, met and mixed and parted and five stars shone in a dim glimmer through a white mist drift. Mimah going down the hall through the open doorway saw the Justice at a tall window, standing erect and quiet, seeming to enjoy the sky drama. The two black clouds returned and joined again, a light wind coming up with a drizzle of raindrops. The wind came stronger, driving wild, sending rainsheets in skirls around the four cedars and Remembrance Rock, beating down its raindrench on a little flag of Stars and Stripes the Justice had laid on the Rock that morning. Against the walls and windows of Hopecrest house the rainsheets broke amid thunder-drums and split-second forks of lightning rolling and echoing off toward the Atlantic, the Alleghenies, Canada, the Great Lakes, and the Gulf. Some fifty yards from where Justice Windom stood, one fierce crashing prong of fire sent itself straight into an arching majestic oak that had lived too long and clove it in two and shattered the halves and left it a mass of splinters and charred grandeur.

Eating his light dinner with her that evening the Justice spoke little and what he did say seemed to her rather airy and somewhat absent-minded, except for the care-laden and solemn wishes he mentioned for Raymond in that far-off South Pacific hospital and his surmise that a plane might be bringing Raymond home any day now and his deep hope of better days to come for the grandson who had seen hard going. He was actually shy, thought Mimah, when, starting upstairs to his library worktable, he asked her to look in on him sometime in an hour or two. After a little more than an hour she looked in to find he had been working at the long oak table, then feeling tired had turned off all lights except a single one darkly shaded, then laid himself to rest on the leather couch. And she was baffled at his faraway voice and his dreaminess in telling her: "There is a stranger lurking around the house trying to get to see me alone. I think I saw his face at one window and then another window. I'm sure he means me no harm. He has something very personal he wants with me. I thought I recognized him and then it got away from me because he turned his face as though he wasn't ready to show it to me as yet. An old-time face he has and I think I have heard men tell about it yet I can't place it and what I have heard about him is that he means no harm. I am sure I saw him moving around out in the storm as though he was the personal manager of the storm, in some way of speaking, or it might be that he needed to hurry getting here and the storm could bring him quickly for what it is he wants with me. It is something very personal and I must be alone when I see him. I say he is a stranger but of course that can't be so or I would be suspicious of him and I am not suspicious and when we have our talk alone I will recognize him and we will get along and I will find out what it is so personal he wants with me."

Mimah could think of no answer to this except to say that the storm of the early evening had been strange and wild, they would miss the great oak that had gone down, and it could be expected that any kind of a stranger might have come riding in on that whirling wind. She smoothed his forehead softly with her hands, told him he must go to his sleep early this night. Looking in an hour later she saw him in bed well asleep.

The next morning, when the breakfast table had waited longer than usual for the Justice, she went to his room and saw him in bed, lying on his back, his face upturned. And he seemed asleep and her thought was to tiptoe away and leave him to finish his sleep. Then came the second thought that he could not have slept from early last night till this late in the morning. Then came a third and terrifying thought and she stood still and clenched her hands and rested her eyes on the two profiles of his face that seemed almost to speak and to clash in what they would speak. She made her right hand infinitely gentle in its touch at the forehead. Then she slowly put both hands to the sides of the face. And when her two hands held his right hand and there too sensed the same final chill, the same icy and rigid certainty, she knew then that he knew better than she had known the night before that a stranger had lurked around the house and no harm was meant and "He has something very personal he wants with me."

The quiet ceremonials and functions of the burial of Justice Windom were over. And Mimah knew that for many years she would have moments of illusion when his liquid brown eyes framed in that baffling multiple face would be looking straight into her eyes and then slowly and shyly turning away. And after such a moment she would be asking herself, "How am I doing? I've got freedom enough—what am I doing with it?"

Tuesday it was he died and the burial on Thursday and on the Monday following came the telegram that set her heart jumping. At Los Angeles Raymond was taking a plane for Washington; he had tried to phone her but all circuits were busy. Another telegram—at Kansas City he had tried to get her long distance and the circuits all busy. Tuesday morning now he would be arriving at the Washington airport.

And this Tuesday morning she was studying herself before a full-length oval mirror. Perhaps she was a little thinner, somewhat worn, the cares of bearing and watching over the baby, the heavy grief of the death the week before, and the burrowing curiosity and lurking fears over Raymond—yes, she was definitely not as fresh a flower as spoke good-by to him last year—and she would hope to God the change in him could be less than in her.

She wasn't long fixing herself before the antique, gilt-framed, oval mirror. But in that space of time her mind again ran over the four years since they first met, his grandfather he would not see again, his child he would see for the first time, the questions each would be asking.

She smoothed her hair and knew she must not, whatever befell, show him the tumults that ran in her about him. She patted out every possible crimp and crinkle in her gown and stockings, aware she must keep the manner of calm that would have been on the face of Orville Brand Windom if he were going with her today to the Washington airport to meet his grandson Raymond.

They put down the plane he was on. She saw him step out, saw him come on a slow walk to the gate, saw him try to bring to his face the light, elation and merriment she had seen when he was on leave and they were married. But no gaiety came from him. The light was a low flicker that faded to return and fade from his eyes and face. The elation and the old merriment were a mockery of the real thing. Tired, he was so tired. After a long rest, so they had told him, he would be his old self and make for her this and that like he used to. So he was saying, his arms around her, holding her tight, but his old hard strength or will not there. The hospital had been good, they gave him all they had. The trip was nice, you couldn't ask better accommodations. "And let's not talk for a while, honey." He stopped and put

25

his arms around her again. "Be good to me, honey, we'll see what gives. We'll have to wait."

They got in the car and drove to Hopecrest. Inside she was smoldering and burning, letting none of it show as she told him smoothly and slowly, putting a shade of warmth into her tone occasionally, of the storm last week, of the lightning crashing the old oak, of his grandfather mentioning the lurking stranger who must be seeing him alone, of Tuesday morning a week ago and the cold face and cold hands she touched and then the burial on Thursday.

Raymond turned his head toward her, his face showing no sign of feeling, his eyes closing twice, his long eyelashes perhaps slightly tremulous, Mimah thought, and then she heard him, "It sounds like more of where I've been, Mimah, that's all. Life is a fake. Life cheats you even if you play fair. The best men get the worst breaks and the worst men never get what's coming to them." And Mimah had the suspicion that he would have liked to have tears to spend on grief but he had now left only dry tears.

He had vitality and flame in him, Mimah was sure of that. The grip of his hands on her, the fierce press of his ribs against hers once—strength and plenty of it he had left. Something in his mind and will didn't want to connect with his flowing vitality, didn't care about waking any of the old flame or depths of desire. When she tried to look at this as though the Justice were alive and he and she were trying to fathom Raymond's malady, she recoiled at the questions that crossed her mind. Could it be that Raymond had about as fine a bodily physique as ever but something at the center and pivot of it had been squeezed, pushed, pressed, tortured and become haunted, so now he didn't care whether he lived or died?

Time was when he laughed with his grandfather—and a rollicking gay laugh—at the Irish bull of the flamboyant orator, "Life is a phantom and a shadow. We pursue it and the bubble bursts and leaves only ashes in our hands." Now he would say that and say it was nothing to laugh at and was the real goods any way you figure it. He could hold her tight in his arms and let her go, suddenly himself going limp not from being weak but from something that crossed his mind and acted on his will, something not made clear in his muttered "I'm just one of God's mistakes, Mimah—forget it—let's skip it."

On Wednesday evening at dinner he had talked about a captain of Marines who had a bed next to his in hospital. "He could tell about fog so thick you didn't know what was front or rear or where to find the fighting you came for." On Thursday morning at daybreak she heard Ray in the hallway and found him pointing at the windows at the two ends of the hall, then taking her to his own room and there outside his own windows the same fog, a grayish white wall of thick mist, and you couldn't see the nearest trees, and you might have reached your arm out and three feet away you could hardly see your hand. She had

26

heard him mumbling to the men of his command how they should handle themselves. "Low ceiling, fellows," she heard him with a shade of mockery, and, "We'd better not move, fellows, wait till she blows away and we can see a little ahead of us." She coaxed him back into bed, put his head in one of her arms, and began talking smoothly and slowly about how lovable his grandfather had been all the days he was away, talking an hour or more until she saw him sink into sleep.

Early one afternoon Mimah, with hands slow and soft, turned the knob of the door to Ray's room, making sure not to wake him. She eased the door open and put her head in, to see Ray pulling on a shirt. She heard him singing, a touch of both the maudlin and the defiant in his voice. The words he sang struck through her, sharp and merciless. As he buttoned his shirt and ended singing, she drew the door shut, stood a moment with a shivering body, eyes tight-closed, then went to her room and threw herself on the bed. The song words she heard gave her a brief storm flash of a world he knew and one she could never know, a world of dark gay mockery, flaunting strange ironics and travesties. Slowly it came to her, "He's earned the right to sing it and it did him good." The opening line she could remember or rather couldn't forget. The other lines had rolled away from her. The song ran:

> I wanted wings till I got the goddam things,
> Now I don't want them any more.
> They taught me how to fly when they sent me here to die,
> I've had a belly full of war.
>
> I'm too young to die in a damned old PBY,
> That's for the eager, not for me.
> I don't trust to luck to be picked up by a Duck,
> After I've crashed into the sea.
>
> You can save those Mitsubishis for the other sonsabitches,
> For I'd rather lay a woman than be shot down in a Grumman;
> I wanted wings till I got the goddam things,
> Now I don't want them any more.

Not yet could she tell him about his grandfather's will and the Box. He must have a few days, perhaps a week, and then they would do together what the will instructed. Next Monday, perhaps sooner, if Ray improved, they would open the Box.

The pipsqueak—Raymond liked the pipsqueak. He came nearer the rim of his old delights a moment or two when handling Joseph Stilwell Windom. After the baby's bath one morning he held the little one in his hands. "He's as clean as that beautiful coral sand I sent you— Jesus, he's clean—God, how I'd like to be that clean." He handed her the child, the lighting of his face vanished, and back again the cold deadpan look. "Yeah—one time I was clean as him—and how do you know, how do I know? He'll grow up and fight a war and come out of it dirty as I am. He'll take bath after bath and scrub and scrub and he can't scrub off that feeling."

Raymond had read in a book where a woman came to General Robert E. Lee and asked his blessing for her baby. The General spoke the sacred words and put the baby into the mother's arms with "Teach him he must deny himself." Ray liked the picture they made for him. He tried for a paraphrase of General Lee's line. "Teach him he must be a stinker and sleep with himself." That wouldn't quite do. "Teach him to be stinking dirty and like it." That wouldn't quite do either. So he doubted he could improve on General Lee.

Was he light-minded? Mimah asked that and instantly reproached herself for letting such a question occur to her mind. He was groping. In dark winding tunnels he was feeling his way. Or again and more rarely he was dazed and bewildered in labyrinths of memories and phantoms. "Concussion syndrome and a guilt complex, Mimah, that's what the doctors say I've got to crawl out of," he said one morning after a long night of deep sleep alongside of Mimah. "You can ask me how the concussion syndrome is coming and I'll tell you pretty good but don't you dare ever say guilt complex to me."

Five days had passed and he had said nothing of hearing Bowbong's broadcast. After many delays and hesitations Mimah asked him whether he had heard it. Yes, he had heard it. He was going to mention to her that he had heard it. But the way he heard it and what it did to him was not easy to tell her about. "It gave me a lift at first, a rather wonderful lift. But it didn't last. I sagged down lower than before I heard it, then I came back part-way again, then I lost it. I don't know whether I want to talk about it. Just his voice had something to do with the lift I got. When I was a kid he'd reach me like nobody else. When he'd tell me that he had been about all the different kinds of fools there are I'd open up and tell him what particular kinds of a fool I had been which was what he wanted and after that we'd talk it over without my ever being afraid. Maybe I should read his broadcast and see what would happen. But that wouldn't give his voice. And he's gone."

Mimah's face gleamed. She had ordered a recording they could play on their phonograph. It would arrive next Monday. They would hear his voice again giving that speech. Then they would open the Box.

She had held off telling him about the Box. Now it poured from her, slowly, for she was keeping clear of speed and excitement, but pouring it out, how she had long ago guessed that the Box held something the Justice rated as precious or certainly precious as between him and Raymond and her, how the lovable old man had somehow realized in the last month that his end was near and he showed not merely a constant anxiety but a sort of passionate devotion toward having the Box complete and finished in what it held. When his will was read, bestowing

28

his entire estate on Raymond and Maria, there were instructions that the two keys to the Box would be found in the little fireproof vault, that Raymond and his wife, with no others present, should open the Box and see for the first time for their use "certain personal papers, documents, manuscripts, which I have not been sufficiently egregious and self-regarding to share with my family or friends nor have I any basis for definite and final judgment whether they should ever at any future time be made public for the world at large, which are entirely matters for the discretion and decision of my grandson Raymond Windom and his wife Maria." Further instructions ran that for the period of one year the contents of the Box should be considered confidential, should not under any conditions be divulged to other persons beyond Raymond Windom and his wife, toward the end and purpose that their eventual course might be "certain, deliberate, final, and proper to all concerned." In this both Raymond and Mimah saw the shyness of Bowbong with a dim glint of his humor.

Mimah saw Raymond picking up an interest, a flare of zest for living, only a flash, but she would hope. She explained how while Bowbong worked on his radio speech he hinted to her that it belonged with what was in the Box, that she had seen him dig among materials in the Box as though it held vast confirmations of what he would say over the air to the American people along with what he wanted to say to his next of kin, to his own flesh and blood including a great-grandson who embodied the Future.

The recording arrived Monday morning. On the long oak table in his library work corner they had set the Box. Now alongside it they set the phonograph, arranged the turntable, made sure of the needle, and set the record going. Mimah saw Raymond sink deep in a chair with his legs stretched far out, a hand over his eyes. The same voice came again in the same room—for two listeners' and those two only—instead of five or six million listeners as before when the same voice shaped the same words. . . . "When we say a patriot is one who loves his country, what kind of love do we mean? A love we can throw on a scale and see how much it weighs? . . . Or is a patriot's love of country . . . beyond all reckoning and measurement? . . . These are questions . . . the answers to them we know in part . . . when a nation goes down and never comes back, when a society or a civilization perishes, one condition may always be found. They forgot where they came from . . . faces of today, of now, of this hour and this minute . . . many of those same faces have had their . . . shining moments in our America of the past. . . . That high-pitched squealing . . . was the cry of the Future, the voice of the next generation. . . . Like myself nearly every one of you listening has dear ones. And we remember their faces. And we dream about them. . . . This is one crisis, the latest one. There have been others in the making of this nation. . . . It has cost to build this nation. . . . I look back and see my grandson and his wife three hundred years

29

ago in the town of Plymouth—and in the next moment I see him in a place named Valley Forge and she is at home with their child wondering when the war will end—and again I see him in that tornado of action called Gettysburg and amid the suffering afterward he finds time to write her a letter. I see their faces the same in those days as now . . . ."

The recording had closed. "The moment it ended," said Mimah, "he stepped over and reached his arms around the baby and me and whispered, 'I hope Raymond was listening.' "

Mimah turned one key in the Box, Raymond turned the second key. They lifted easy at the lid of the Box and it came up. At the top lay a note they read without a word to each other.

My dear ones—Mimah and Raymond—you whose faces I cherish—you whose faces I have seen far back in other times of the American Republic long and long before you were born—you will please me for the love I bear you—by reading this manuscript in the sequences I have carefully arranged them—book by book— and may it be that as you live with these repeating faces that weave a blood-scarlet thread over and through the story of our country—may it be that you find tokens and values worth your time in living with them and my time in the many years I have given them—so be it—a thousand deep prayers I speak for you— my blessings go with you always—may your intercessions to an all-wise Providence be heard—so be it—and farewell—

Then there was his bold sweeping signature, distinctly bold for all of two or three shy twists of letter shapes.

"So," breathed Mimah, "that was what he was doing those years I thought I saw him at it and many years before I first saw him. His heart's blood is here. We will be slow and careful."

"We'll go into it," breathed Raymond, "with the care we know he'd like to think we were giving it."

A light summer rain had blown up outside. The thunder was a soft rolling recessional. Against the windows came a light steady drumming.

Mimah took the top sequence, its cover marked Book One, turned to the first page and read: "Time eats all things. The brown gold of autumn says so. The falling leaves in the last rainwind before the first spit of snow—they have their way of saying, Listen, be quiet, winter comes: Time eats all things."

* * * * * * * * *
*   *
*   *Book One* *
*   *
* * * * * * * * *

THE FIRST COMERS

Chapter 1

Home to Austerfield and Scrooby

TIME eats all things. The brown gold of autumn says so. The falling leaves in the last rainwind before the first spit of snow—they have their way of saying, Listen, be quiet, winter comes: Time eats all things.

In such a mood on a late October afternoon of 1607 Oliver Ball Windrow sat his old sorrel mare Babs on the horse path winding from London to Edinburgh, the Great Northern Road, only a few feet wide, where coach or wagon wheels would tangle in the going.

There were times Windrow searched his mind by talking to himself or by long conversations with Babs wherein the horse never argued, or he made little speeches, abrupt orations, with pauses, declaimed to Matilda Bracken, the woman who never talked back and kept silent during his pauses. To look at him gave her half she wanted. He stood five feet eight inches, well over a hundred and eighty pounds, thickset of build, a massive head of hair brick-red in the sun and a sunset maroon in shadow, one side of his face smooth in peace, the other side half-snarling and set for combat, his mouth straight, wide, full-lipped. In dark moods and deeply moved the mouth became a crooked slash changing with the progressions of a storm sky. Usually grave, slow-spoken, his moods often ran to banter and persiflage, airy as milkweed floss in a high wind. In rare outbursts he ran to the broadly comic, vulgar and odorous as a barnyard. With regret he had come to the end of the one book of Rabelais.

Four times in ten years he had made the hundred-and-fifty-three-mile journey from Austerfield to London and back, on each visit saying he would seek out William Shakespeare if he could find the time. Early this afternoon he did get to the house where Shakespeare stayed when in London, a grave woman telling him, "Come this evening at candlelight, says Master Shakespeare. This afternoon he goes deep in the fourth act of a tragedy that has occupied him long." But Windrow had overstayed in London, begged pardon for his boldness, presented his compliments, untied Babs and in saddle on the Great Northern Road was saying, "Shakespeare is forty-three, I am thirty-nine—another time I will pay my profound respects and ask him whether he too is baffled about certain of his plays and poems."

In one saddlebag Windrow had a play by Shakespeare, a thin affair dated 1603 titled: *The Tragical Historie of Hamlet, Prince of Denmark, as it has been diverse times acted by his Highness servants in the Cittie of London as also in the two Universities of Cambridge and Oxford, and Elsewhere.* Windrow had read it several times since buying it in York three years ago and on this stay in London had learned it was set up by the printer from "an acting copy" stolen or more likely borrowed from, as he was told, "some actor who might have needed wine for his belly or a new scarlet velvet waistcoat for his vanity or a jeweled comb for a maid he desired."

Time eats all things. He would soon be home again, amid open fields, tangled thickets, forest and moor of the North Country of Yorkshire and Nottinghamshire, for his eyes to see the last brown gold of autumn and the final rainwind before the first flurry of snow. There he would feel, as never in London, that time is as young as it is old and no sorrow time does not touch and change and weave into something else.

Faces—after the street-crowd faces in London would he not be wanting the human procession? A worker in wood, a good fellow carver like himself, an old friend whose work he respected, had asked that. And he had replied that in Austerfield or a mile farther in Bawtry or another mile and a half in Scrooby, "the faces of a thousand years and more come alive for me."

Over the church door in Austerfield the pagan Danish invaders of eight hundred years back had put their signs, had carved in oak the forked-lightning zigzag of Thor, their god of hammer and fire, and the beaks of their pagan luck bird, the raven. Scrooby had its name from the Danes, "by" meaning a town or village. Farther back, a matter of fifteen hundred years, the men with long spears and short swords, dark-eyed men with black hair, swarthy men from far south in Europe, had crossed the Channel and overrun England and swarmed into the North Country. "At York, forty-two miles to the north of my town of Austerfield, they will show you where the Emperor Hadrian lived while directing the building of the Hadrian Wall, to stand as the northern limit of the Roman Empire. They will show you at York where the Roman Emperor Severus died and had his imperial body publicly, ceremonially and honorably, burned to an ordinary mortal crisp. The Celtic invaders came and in part went away and in part stayed. The invading conquerors under William of Normandy, they, we know, stayed and became rulers. Under Queen Elizabeth came ten thousand Dutch for refuge—they named Ranskill, near Scrooby, a 'kill' being to them a creek. And a part of all of them is alive on faces in the North Country, Romans, Danes, Celts, Normans, Dutch, and still others, their blood mingled with Saxons and Angles and other native-born and earlier breeds—faces beyond reading for the tale of whence they came and what seed of time and spawn of love or conflict brought them hither."

Faces within the memory of living men—faces of those who danced on air at a rope's end in "Hangman's Lane" and on "Gibbet Hill," not far from Scrooby. "London not so far away when the long arm of Queen Elizabeth could reach up the horse path of the Great Northern Road and make important, even exemplary, the broken necks of unbelievers and rebels against authority."

Faces—a man could wonder what were the faces of the pagan Danes who defiled and burned the churches of Christ. "They bred hate that more than once brought on revolt and reprisal. There were Danes taken alive, skinned alive, and told to look where their bleeding skins hung nailed fast to a church door. I have seen pieces of skin, centuries old, found under the nailheads of oaken church doors. The Danes came and went. Some of their violence, laughter and fair hair mingled in the English breed."

One face stayed always with him, Mary Windling, her dear face, amid plaits of chestnut hair faintly bronzed, twenty years younger than he—and he was sure her eyes and heart would never bring him to harm or hurt. What would the next year bring her face? Would she marry John Spong? And was he worth any part of her? The next year 1608 would tell much.

The old manor house at Scrooby, you could write the history of the North Country and of England itself and Scotland too, if you could read and know the faces of the Archbishops of York going in and out its doors for hundreds of years. It was a hunting lodge and around and beyond lay the hunting park of the Archbishop of York, forest, thicket, moor and swamp for the chase of game. A variety of Faces, no two alike, smiling, mocking, sober and reverent, had moved in its thirty-nine chambers and apartments, had seen in the great hall three screens, six tables, nine benches, one cupboard—and in the chapel a timber altar and two superaltars of topstone to lay over the wood, a reading desk, a pair of organs, and a clock out of repair lacking weights and cords—and in the dining chamber or refectory the ceiling and walls of carved oak panels and beams, the oak "ceiled and dressed with the 'wainscot,'" the Dutch word for the finest of oak without knot or flaw.

"A market place and a village of no more than one hundred fifty people, Scrooby post is the seat of Scrooby Manor," explained Windrow. "There the Archbishop of York sheltered for a night's sleep Margaret Tudor, the daughter of Henry VIII on her way to marry a Scottish king and by the bonds of wedlock to unite England and Scotland. There her father Henry VIII and his retainers stayed overnight and found room enough in the thirty-nine chambers. There for many days stayed Cardinal Wolsey, a master mind of politics, shorn of power and living on memories. There in many a hunting season of the past the Archbishop of York had invited his fellow heads of the North Country Church of England to ride, shoot, eat, drink—and to discuss the mutterings and rumblings over the kingdom, the revolts put down, the rebels jailed, the heretics hanged, beheaded, their ears cropped, their

35

noses slit—and the muttering had not died down and events rumbled on toward unknown changes.

"Now the old place lacks gaiety and needs repair. King James seeing it four years ago said it showed 'exceeding decay.' " And at that point Windrow hesitated and did not speak his thought: "What goes on there now is done in secret and King James I when he learns of it will move to end it."

Austerfield and Scrooby were intensely alive and human, Oliver Ball Windrow made clear to his wood-carving brother, aware that in London folk from Yorkshire and Nottinghamshire were regarded as peculiar yokels, with speech of their own and odors of the cowhouse. "You may gather from what I say that I am not well pleased to meet so frequently in London and elsewhere those superior persons who cannot tell whether Scrooby is a town, a place, a disease resembling the scurvy, or a game of cards where the loser is a scrooby and has his nose smutted with charcoal as penalty for being scrooby."

As he rode back home from London, gazing at flame runners on the woodlands and the hill slopes, he was not at all at ease. He had heard enough in London at the taverns and among old friends and struggling artist-workmen such as himself, seeing the same unfathomable elements of change at work over England and Europe as in the little human swirls he knew so well at Austerfield and Scrooby.

"Get along, Babs, old quadruped," he spoke to the mare once. "It may be as well you know nothing of the matters disputed by the eminent learned men. For you heaven is plenty of hay and hell any place lacking hay."

"Babsworth," addressing her once by her full name—and it was his whim she flicked her right ear when so spoken to, and the left ear if he called her Babs for short—"Babsworth, this is a riddle: What secret have you that makes you like unto Queen Elizabeth who died four years ago after ruling England forty-five years? The answer? A moment of thought gives the answer. Each of you so conducted your life and speech that no one could say you were at heart either Catholic, Protestant, or Reformed."

* * * * * * * * * *

Chapter 2

* * * * * * * * * *

One Small Candle May Light a Thousand

ON the edge of Austerfield, forty yards back from the Great North Road, stood Oliver Ball Windrow's one-room stone house, built with his own hands. On a November day, an hour before noon, a woman turned off the road, walked to the big front door, gazed a moment at the brass script "Windrow," took the hem of her dress and wiped a blemish from two of the letters, turned the brass knob, and without knocking entered. She saw Windrow at the other end of the room with mallet and chisel and a panel of wood eight feet by ten. They moved toward each other, met and stood holding each other's hands, gazed with utter solemnity into each other's faces. He returned to his panel and wood-carving. She moved about the room, sweeping, cleaning, straightening, then seated herself in a cupboard and pantry corner and prepared mutton, carrots and cabbage, to go into the pot over the fire.

Windrow turned to let his eyes rove over her. She had taken off the black kerchief she wore on arriving. Her flaxen hair flowed down in long ropes of braid to her hips, summer sun over waving grain with the run of windfeet on it, slants of silver—her hair, head and torso Windrow hoped to shape some day if he could find wood of the right bleach. Her large eyes of cornflower-blue looked from a forehead and face of cream-smooth skin with freckles so distinct that people counted them and found seven. Below medium height, she was rather massive of build, curves from head to toe, her powerful frame and torso impressive with ease of movement. Some inner grace of mind and poise of spirit spoke in the way she handled herself. She did her work with the fewest number of easy, knowing motions. Often between pieces of housework and cookery, she glanced toward Windrow. When he at his work suddenly started talking, she caught it at the first word, turned her face toward him, seemed listening to every word, her face in response to his sometimes breaking into a slow smile. Her lighted face could suddenly go as though she had wiped it off, leaving her eyes and mouth in a quiet, grave composure.

"They call themselves a church, meet in secret and in fear of what may happen to them," spoke Windrow as he worked, Matilda Bracken nodding slightly to him to let him know she was aware he was talking. "More than a year now, some forty to sixty of them have met often at the decaying Scrooby Manor in discussions led by Elder William Brewster. They are watched. Some have been questioned by authorities. They change their meeting places, send word to members where they meet in secret the next Sabbath. Our neighbor, young William Bradford, born in Austerfield and at twelve put to the plow in fields near by here, terrible determination and will on his face, his eyes lighted by hunger no man can read, he is saying, 'Out of small beginnings great things have been produced by God's hand that made all things of nothing and gives being to all things that are—and as one small candle may light a thousand, so the light here kindled may shine to many, yea in some sort to a whole nation.'

"They have wearied of form, ceremonial, the Book of Common

Prayer. They say the living heart should confess and petition God. They seek religious liberty. They hate prayer and worship by compulsion. They carry their hate far. I cannot go with them in that hate. Here we have Hugh and Anne Bromhead writing to William Hamerton of London, writing last year from Amsterdam"—and Windrow took manuscript papers from a shelf and read as though not trusting his memory—" 'As the prophet Isaiah spake of the people of the Jews, so may we speak of the Church of England—"from the sole of the foot unto the head there is nothing whole therein, but wounds and swellings, and sores full of corruption,—the whole head is sick, and the whole heart is heavy." '

"They have stiff-necked, sanctimonious fools, yet they are chiefly a sweet and decent people seeking a way of life and worship not yet tried. What do they do and say in these guilty heretical meetings? Here it is told in this letter. Hugh and Anne Bromhead, I can hear them and see their lips"—and he read from a copy of their letter:

"The order of the worship and government of our Church is, 1. We begin with a prayer; after, read some one or two chapters of the Bible, give the sense thereof, and confer upon the same; that done, we lay aside our books, and after a solemn prayer made by the first speaker, he propoundeth some text out of the Scripture, and prophesieth out of the same by the space of one hour or three quarters of an hour. After him standeth up a second speaker, and prophesieth out of the said text, the like time and place, sometimes more, sometimes less. After him the third, the fourth, the fifth, &c., as the time will give leave. Then the first speaker concludeth with prayer as he began with prayer, with an exhortation to contribution to the poor, which collection being made, is also concluded with prayer. This morning exercise begins at eight of the clock and continueth until twelve of the clock. The like course and exercise is observed in the afternoon from two of the clock until five or six of the clock. Last of all, the execution of the government of the Church is handled."

He brandished the telltale paper high overhead in his right hand and spoke high-pitched. "I give this letter ten readings and damn me if I find guilt, heresy or treason in it." He put the letter on a shelf and went on even-voiced. "In their innocent proceedings I shall not join them. Nor shall I betray them. Even it may be I can help these people, so strangely resolved. They may, as young Bradford believes, become one small candle to light a thousand and mayhap kindle a nation. I have seen their eyes unflinching. My bones tell me half of them will die before they find the church they seek."

Then a long silence. Then a light nod and just the flicker of a smile passed between Windrow and the woman whose ropes and braids of hair sang from her head to her hips as a noonday sun streamed through the two big south windows.

She followed him with her eyes as he shifted and handled three sections of a panel, put them together in the order they would be fitted on a hallway wall in the summer home of a London merchant and importer, Sir Humphrey Cavendish: "Ai ai, Sir Humphrey, and it may be your summer guests will both laugh and weep and some knock their heads together over the portent of the ancient Jewish fable of the Tower of Babel in three chapters. You may guide them, Sir Humphrey, and help them with lessons and elucidations: Here, my friends, you see the Tower has been building till it reaches into the clouds and above the clouds. And here they are swarming on a great plain, tens of thousands of people, a vast heaving mass of people pressing toward the Tower on their work and errands—shouting, toiling, sweating, singing toward the Tower—in time it will stretch and pierce far enough so they can journey to heaven on it—and the Tower being finished their children and their children's children will find the going to heaven easy and ever easy—so then they will bow down before their work and worship it as an idol—it will be their one and only God—they will praise it with loud hosannahs—you can see their faces pleased and vain over their labors. And we come to Chapter Two: They had not seen nor thought to look at One who rode on a great black mist of smoke in the clear, clean sky, a jealous God in anger over their folly—they run, fight, cry, in wild grimaces at each other as their feet take them rushing in flight from the Tower of Terror—for now they speak to each other and they hear each other and what they say is babble without meaning sent into the ears of others—an evil has smitten them deeper than if they had been struck deaf and dumb and yet could make signs and trust each other. Then Chapter Three: There is only the Tower of Babel, supreme monument to man the babbler, standing lonely pointing at the sky—no shouting, swarming, singing people—only the stones piled high on stones and some of the masonry so soon falling away and loosening among the foundations—and a scrawl on one of the cornerstones: 'They would have wrought a jest and mocked at God with an easy journey to heaven.'"

Windrow had stepped back from the panels, speaking with clenched fists. He stretched wide both arms, stood with arms akimbo, shot one vehement fist high in the air, slowly let it down, stood hushed and inquiring before his own work. He had not turned to look but he knew the silent woman had dropped her work and was there at his right elbow as he finished. He saw her face with a light near ecstasy in her eyes, a peace of finality in the carved strengths under her cream-fair skin and the seven distinct freckles. His two hands at her shoulders, his lips moved lightly over her right cheek.

She set a table. They ate in silence, a stew of mutton and vegetables, a tankard of beer that each raised to the other in a manner more like reverence than mere respect or affection. Once he wiped his fingers, running them through his thick sunset-maroon hair—his way of saying, "We must be polite but not too polite for convenience."

They rose from the table. He slid into a leather coat, a doublet, put on a cap, walked to the door, opened it, waved a gay salute and good-by to Matilda Bracken, and was gone.

She washed the dishes, put them in the cupboard, arranged the leftover victuals in the pantry. She walked the mile to where she lived with her father, marking a brilliance and health in a late afternoon sunshine of early November.

Her own life, she knew, ran in patterns zigzag as the wild geese flying in dips and detours from their main course that afternoon. She knew Oliver Windrow had started that afternoon on a walk he took two or three times a week, three miles to the home, near Scrooby, of Mary Windling. She knew he would again be asking Mary Windling to marry him, asking her with such foolery and such a comic twist of his crooked mouth, and such a clown tilt of his massive head, that a listening stranger could take him for a jester talking nonsense. But Mary Windling would know, as Matilda Bracken knew, that it was no joke about his wanting to marry her. He had so told Matilda. He was thirty-nine and Mary nineteen but it wasn't the difference in their ages that stood against their marriage. Matilda knew this as well as she knew how deep was his love for Mary. Matilda had put it to Oliver, "If Mary Windling should ever ask me I will tell her that she lives for you always as a sweet ghost and of her you have said the same to me once for every high night star in the sky." And if Mary should ask her, "What does Oliver Windrow mean to you?" her answer to Mary would be short: "I cool his anger." These in many variations were Matilda's thoughts as she walked home to her father's house with silver glints of November sun on her long flowing braids of flaxen hair from her head to her hips.

Oliver Ball Windrow sat before the fireplace of his workroom holding in his hands a wooden box, smooth, round, small—he could have held six of the same size in one hand. He had carved, oiled, sanded, smoothed the wood. A neat cover on the box slid out at a thumb-push.

Carved in the circle of the cover was a girl's head, lean-faced, impudent, long black eyelashes sleepy with passion, a head sweeping with its tumble of curls hiding the ears and framing the face. He slid out the cover, studied a few moments one winding and glossy black curl. Then with thumb and fingers he lifted the curl from the box, laid it on a living wood ember and watched the strand of hair crackle and sputter, a slow dark crimson of the hair blended and lost with the yellowish crimson of the ember. This distinctly over and completely ended, he laid the box on the same place in the fire. The box took longer to burn, to die down, and the dying less clean. There lay at the finish a hard black oily wafer defying the flame to consume it. With a stick he flipped this into the main pile of ashes at the back of the fire.

Ten years back he had promised he would keep the box for ten years—as a reminder. In that year a vagrant drifted into Scrooby, a strolling player who when sober could earn a bare living at speaking scenes from the *Love's Labour's Lost, Romeo and Juliet,* and *Midsummer Night's Dream* of Will Shakespeare. A petty thief this player, who sneaked clothes or food when chance tempted. He and his daughter, in a clump of bushes off the Great Northern Road, when caught were eating the final shreds off a well-smoked ham vanished from a farmhouse pantry two miles away. The thief sat in the stocks two days and nights at Scrooby. His daughter, her light fine paid by Oliver Windrow, stayed at the home of Richard Spong. Dirty, disheveled, lazy—this Ellie Marmon the daughter of Hambleton Marmon —refused to wash and comb herself properly. Yet she was vital, swift, flashing white teeth and darting black eyes. She swept Windrow out of himself. He couldn't stay away from her. After her broken and starved father was let out of the stocks, worn black-and-blue at the wrists and ankles, he and his daughter stayed four days at Windrow's home, and it was Windrow walked four miles with them toward the city of York.

Ellie Marmon at twenty-one didn't care to marry thirty-year-old Oliver Windrow, nor any other man. "Why should a one-woman man yoke with a many-men woman?" she asked him. He had never heard of such a question and couldn't think of an answer, except that she didn't know herself, didn't know her own wild heart, and if they lived together she would find such a life, with its comfort, warmth and assurance, changing her.

He carried these points far enough to make her say mayhap time would change her heart and find her willing to yoke herself to one man for life. She kissed him hard tight kisses and told him to come of an afternoon to York in sixty days, to the Maypole Tavern, "the filthiest, the gayest, the most loose-hearted and loose-minded tavern in the North Country," she promised him.

And Windrow had arrived of an evening two days sooner than the date set, to find her in a corner of a taproom. There, while he slowly drank two tankards of ale, she sat bare-bosomed first in one man's lap, then another's, letting three men make free with her while all four made free with a bottle of rum. Her glance caught Windrow. He would never forget that glance. While a man played with her breasts she tilted back her head and poured down her throat the last of a glass of rum. Bringing her head down after that guzzle, with a casual sweep of her eyes she found the face of this man at the bar, the fellow she had known at Scrooby and Austerfield. In an instant she was on her feet, standing to take one steady look to make sure what she was seeing. Then she ran to him, stopping two paces away, her feet planted wide, her body swaying and tipsy, her arms on her hips, her word to the bartender "Ale." Nothing was said. She glanced where the bartender put a glass of ale, then she blazed, "Of all the damned one-woman fools I ever set eyes on, you . . ." threw the glass of ale into his face, ran to the door and vanished, leaving an echo of one sharp moan that came from her and cut across the air as she ran.

Windrow saddled Babs, then a fast colt, rode halfway home, slept under a hawthorn tree, woke in the morning to laugh, a grand crazy laughter at himself for a fool. How could he hate such a woman? She was wiser than he in knowing herself well enough not to enter his life and make a mockery of it by what she knew she would be doing when they were yoked. Was that it? Should he go back to York, seek her out, and tell her how well he now understood this, and that he still loved her but now he wouldn't marry her if she begged and pleaded for it? No—she might surprise him again—she lived by surprises—the chief pleasure she had from washing herself was to see how clean and changed she looked. No, he would go back to his wood, to the planks, slabs and blocks, inside and outside of his workshop home, waiting for him to cut, trim, shave, carve the forms he wanted to come out from them. He was then well along on a full-figured John the Baptist for a very sober churchman—and a scowling, furtive, malignant Judas for a London goldsmith, a whimsical unbeliever who drank hard. "I return to my work with a more proper humiliation," he laughed to himself. And the laughter over: "What I do with any woman in the days to come must not be sudden. Why, after this lesson, should any woman sweep me off my feet and spin my head round as though it were a top?"

The curled strand of hair in the box with the tender portrait carved on the cover, "I will keep it by me as a reminder and on the eve of my fortieth birthday I will burn it. And by then—by then—in her way of life Ellie Marmon will be a broken decrepit hag, and more likely rotted away in some pauper's field, having her unspoken prayer answered that she would burn soon and fast in that furnace we call life."

Came the only year in his life he drank hard and drank often—Spanish wines, French brandy, Holland rum, all the hard English and Scotch liquors. Then he quit, holding himself to beer and ale at meals. He had been heard to say, "I know why some men drink. They are trying to dust off a memory that keeps coming back."

Passing through Austerfield the next afternoon Oliver Windrow stepped into the front room of the house of Richard Spong, a stone-mason who gave part of his time to clock repair, a small, lean-muscled man who attended the secret meetings of the Scrooby congregation. When he approved of anything said, Richard Spong took the lower flap of his right ear between thumb and finger—when it was hard for him to make up his mind he locked the fingers of his two hands behind his head. "I welcome thee always, Oliver Windrow," ran his greeting. And Windrow took out a small sheet of tough parchment. On this he had written large and plain "The Four Causes of Error"—as set forth by Roger Bacon some three hundred and fifty years earlier. He had recited them to Spong on his previous visit and promised to copy them for Spong to keep by him. Spong ran his eyes over the text:

The Four Stumbling Blocks to Truth

1. The influence of fragile or unworthy authority.
2. Custom.
3. The imperfection of undisciplined senses.
4. Concealment of ignorance by ostentation of seeming wisdom.

"As for the first," he told Windrow, "I accept our Lord Christ Jesus as neither fragile nor unworthy but on the contrary as an absolute authority in whom I can hold complete trust and unquestionable faith. As for the second, I follow not custom but the lights and decrees of my own heart, wherefore I would take my stand against the whole world, as one man alone, prepared for torture and death sooner than join my testimony in acceptance of a creed or a belief sanctioned merely by custom. As for the third, I must take what my own voices and visions report. I must follow their gleam and call even though it lead to earthly shame and degradation. As for the fourth, I hope to be humble and bring wrong to no other man by my folly, vanity or arrogance."

"The world is no loser by thy way of life—so much I know," said Windrow gravely, and in a lowered tone more grave, "Mayhap you should not keep this writing of Roger Bacon in your house. I have been told of your being watched and warned. The family of Roger Bacon had their houses, lands and money taken away, Bacons driven into exile for their way of thought under Henry III."

A quiet luminous glow came in the eyes of the small well-knit Richard Spong. He stood a moment with two hands interlocked at the back of his head. Then with a thumb and forefinger holding the lower flap of his right ear in approval of an irrevocable decision in his mind: "I will keep it and pray no harm come. At worst a man can die but once before going to the great reward that awaits him beyond."

Windrow turned to a clock he liked and asked Spong to make it perform. Spong moved the hands to a minute before the hour, took a key and wound it, and at the hour striking, out on a platform walked the Twelve Apostles and in a procession one by one back into the clock.

"I count and they are ever and always twelve," said Windrow.

"Twelve precisely."

"Why not eleven? Why must they include Judas?"

"He is not here. These are the Twelve Apostles—not Disciples—you cannot confound me."

In this mood they stepped out of the door, stood in a mellow sunshine with a bright chill on it, Spong saying as they shook hands: "Carry my fond esteem and affection to Mary Windling. Like you I have more than a distant interest in her."

"I will do so and gladly."

"And I thank thee for coming today. Roger Bacon and his stumbling blocks to truth I shall not mislay. They will stand on the little platform back of the Twelve Apostles."

* * * * * * * * * *

Chapter 3

* * * * * * * * * *

The First Secret Departure That Failed

MARY WINDLING stood tall, looked bony, often talked dreamy. Four inches taller than Oliver Windrow, twenty years younger, she saw that his eyes gathered her dreaminess and actually prized some of her strange ways and talk not quite accepted by Scrooby congregation members. She saw in his face a rare and deep adoration for her, never telling of it in so many words, though he talked endlessly to her and woke a smooth-flowing tongue in her when for days she had said little. On one of his afternoon visits, no sooner was he out the door than her father and mother wished to know whether either of them had tried keeping a still tongue in quiet pauses of their talk. "I know he talks too much," Mary answered. "He is not sure what his thoughts are till he finds words for them. I am the same. We both talk too much because our thoughts crowd and come rushing when we are together."

While thus answering, the daughter knew she could not straighten the uneasy feeling of her father and mother, the dim misgivings they held, over a difference of fact, not a dispute of opinion. Richard Spong had taught her to read the Bible. They read together proclamations of the King, leaflet prints of ballads, the play of *Hamlet* lent them by Windrow. And Windrow taught her to write. Mary's father and mother could put their eyes on print and the words meant nothing. They could not take a pointed goose quill, dip it in ink and with scratches on paper spell out words to make sense—as their daughter could. This made a difference. The parents were quicker to scold her faults, pick at her imperfections. Nor could they be truly easy with

44

Windrow nor with Richard Spong's son John who also could read and write. Those of the Scrooby neighborhood able to read and write were few and conspicuous. What they did wrong or with fault did not miss notice and mention by various others who took writing for a suspect craft and an evil mystery. "He reads? He writes? Can it be? We must watch him close." This had been heard.

When Mary was learning to read she had come home one day smiling to her mother, "Should God be kind one day we shall have a Bible in our home and mayhap one or two other books. I will read to you and father what chapters and verses you wish. What a day that will be when we have two or three books in our house!" Her mother gave her a glare of mistrust.

A few sheets of paper whereon Mary had practiced writing and a few other sheets of sentences that snared and held random thoughts from her mind—this was the only reading matter in the house. Like neighbors in near-by houses, like most of the people over all of Britain and over all of Europe, the Windlings had not so much as one book in the house. Until Mary learned to read, if by any chance the house had suddenly become flooded with books the father and mother could not have read a page, line or word—nor wrenched a fragment of meaning from the print.

Pompous fools, windy and hollow men there were and had been in religion and politics, in the church and the government—and they could read—wherefore came several versions of a saying, "He had mother wit and a little wisdom till he read a book," or, "He learned to read and now if he knew a mite more he'd be a half-wit."

A house and two acres the Windlings owned, other acres they rented. They lived plain and sober, working the land, Jasper Windling sharing with the owner the crops he raised on land not his own. Their sheep gave them enough wool to card, spin, and weave into clothes—and yarn to knit into stockings and shawls. Their deepest interest was Scrooby congregation, the furtive and secret meetings of their little but living church and their faith in their Lord Jesus Christ.

For two years Oliver Ball Windrow had been making his afternoon calls on Mary two and three times a week, often helping her spin, get meat and vegetables ready to cook, joining the family more than once in sheepshearing, carrot and turnip digging and like helps.

On the afternoon of March 10, 1608, she was expecting him, he and she knowing of trouble in the air. "When I know him for a fool, I seek in myself and find the same fool," she said to herself, washing parsnips she had dug and coaxed out of frozen ground. Washing the table near the fire she said, "I am not as wise as Oliver Windrow, yet I am near to him in wisdom others cannot gather—and with him when he talks idly." Seating herself on the table and dangling her long, lean legs and quick feet, "I would marry him today if no John Spong had come into my life, if John Spong and I had not learned to read together from John's father, if John Spong and I had not so often had our own meeting before and after the Scrooby church meetings, if we had not walked hand in hand in the moonlight among thickets beyond the meadows, in the blowing snow of winter nights when we struck knee-deep in white drifts coming home from the secret meeting. We four—father and mother—John and I—what is written for us to see together?" She leaped off the table, whirled on one foot, and shouted to the ceiling, "Even though he has not yet bespoken himself!" She repeated it with a half-mocking laughter.

A knocking at the door—she ran to it and let in Oliver Windrow, seeing one side of his face smooth and calm, the other twisted in a grimace: "You know you find me bespoken any time you say the word. Earlier than this I would have come." He threw his coat in a corner, whirled his cap after it. "In a ditch out of Austerfield a fellow lay sleeping off his drink. I kicked him, rubbed him, got him up and walked him to his brother's house. It was ten years ago when I had been a fool over a woman who was a worse fool, I fell into a snowdrift and lay as in cozy white feathers and the sky full of white feathers coming down warm on me—and it was a good neighbor kicked me, rubbed me, dragged me, slapped me, made me walk home to live and tell the tale as I am telling it now to a sweet woman with a profound heart, with eyes of starpools and sea-wind anger."

"You brought your tongue again—and no lack of costly words to pour over a helpless woman."

"I brought more than a tongue and words. And you are not helpless."

He took from a pocket a plaque of bronze two inches long, an inch and a half wide, a silver cord through a slit at the top. He reached it over her head, slid it down around her neck, leaned lightly against her while she held it and read:

"The Four Stumbling Blocks to Truth

1. The influence of fragile or unworthy authority.
2. Custom.
3. The imperfection of undisciplined senses.
4. Concealment of ignorance by ostentation of seeming wisdom."

She spoke the words slowly. After learning the alphabet and the look of single words by themselves, the Sermon on the Mount gave the first long reading lesson she had with Windrow. At Scrooby meetings she had heard elders dispute over words, too often enjoying the disputes. She turned to Windrow now saying she could see these words on bronze pressed hard and heavy with meanings, "a book by themselves." What is "authority"? What is "ostentation"? What is "custom"? Other words struck her, Windrow stood silent. Her eyes fell to the parsnips, slanted to a window out over the land. She turned

46

her sea-blue sea-wind eyes on the man, her hushed voice barely reaching his left ear: "It will go far—this keepsake—Oliver Windrow."

They stood in quiet dreaminess a few moments. Then they talked while she scoured pewter and they shared in preparing mutton, carrots, peas, turnips for the large iron pot over the fire.

She mentioned John Spong as being, to her, strong, bashful, solemn, quaint. Not yet had they come clear on betrothal or wedding. About candlelight she expected him and they were to have meat and await her parents' return from the meeting of a select committee of Scrooby congregation. As though a lurking ear could be near she lowered her voice in mention of the meeting. Windrow spoke low. "They plan to go away again, to leave England?"

"Their troubled faces show it. What they do must be in secret. The fewer who know the safer for all. John Spong, weighed down about his father, fears to speak of it. Of last October I know only that the best part of our Scrooby congregation sold what they could, took clothing, keepsakes, bundles, journeyed to the seacoast and came home weary, sore, or failed to reach home at all. Father, mother and I would have been with them, only for a fever that took father in late summer and kept him too weak for the venture. Now he is well and strong. What they plan I will be part of, with John. What do you know of last October and why have you not told me?"

Oliver Windrow spoke. "This winter—dark enough—good men hunted. For what? For beliefs that harm neither man, child nor field mouse. Hardly more than two hundred years now since the Bible translated from Latin to English. Seventy years only since the first Bible printed in English. Seventy years—and what? For reading the Bible to make what they will of it, men taken in the night, pulled from their beds and clapped into jail. A man caught with a Bible, reading it as pleases him, judging it by his own heart, what is he? A Nonconformist, a heretic, a mocker and scorner, a criminal with the law after him, a rat to be trapped and tossed on a dung pile. Not long since the loud-mouthed King Henry VIII instructed Parliament: 'We must have a law to abolish diversity of opinion.' Now King James sounding the threat 'I will make them conform or I will harry them out of the kingdom or else do worse.' "

"Oliver Windrow, I mislike naught you say. You should answer my question. And I know you will in God's good time."

Oliver Windrow spoke on. "So what events befall? Enough to let us know change is in the air beyond any man's foretelling in this hour, Scrooby men confessing ignorance of the shape of the change. What have we? It seemed that Queen Elizabeth wished the head of Mary Stuart, Queen of Scotland, to be cut off, the ax of the headsman to fall straight and exact between chin and collarbone of the woman. She tells this privately, confidentially, to her Secretary of State, Davison. The Secretary sees to it. The thing is done. The ax sinks in the

47

lady's neck and her head duly falls. The private wish of Queen Elizabeth now fully met. Then publicly Queen Elizabeth says it was wrong, 'A horrible accident' and she had no hand in it. Also the world hears of the Queen sending to the Tower of London her Secretary of State Davison and he is fined ten thousand pounds. The Secretary shoulders the blame and curses for Mary Stuart's head fallen away at a cleaving ax. Therefore what? Therefore no other course open to Secretary Davison's clerk and attendant William Brewster than to leave the court. Brewster it was traveled with Ambassador Davison to the Low Countries, to Rotterdam, Delft, The Hague, on high royal matters, and when the States of the Netherlands honored Ambassador Davison with a gold chain for him to remember them by, Davison placed that chain around the shoulders of his loyal clerk, attendant, friend, William Brewster. What is right? Or wrong? Mayhap, as was said at the time, Mary Queen of Scots did seek to buy household servants to send a poisoned bullet into Queen Elizabeth. Mayhap, as was also said at the time, Mary Queen of Scots had a share in letters and arrangements for a Spanish fleet to override the English. And mayhap, as the affairs of state go, Queen Elizabeth had reasons that justified her to herself in making it appear to the English and the Scots that it was not the Queen of England who had the Queen of the Scots' head struck off. Her only course, she said to herself, as a woman of decision, was to name it 'a horrible accident' and lay the infamy of it on her Secretary of State. The pith of the matter for William Brewster was that he must come home to Scrooby. Manor. A kindly man, a gentle man, a man of reverence, a man with a strangely decent respect for the opinions of others.

"The years pass and William Brewster holds quiet Sabbath meetings with friends and neighbors. After a time they became a little congregation. What is it they wish? Free-spoken liberty of conscience, freedom to worship God as they see fit, the right to read their Bible for instruction and faith."

Mary Windling quietly scoured pewter. "I still listen and mislike naught you say. Please say all. I need it. And in due time you come to my question."

Oliver Windrow proceeded. "I am nearly arrived. What the men and women of the Scrooby congregation do flows from a long past. We can see light breaking, something in the air, Mary Windling. England shall see better days with more freedom for all men. William Brewster sees the way hard and long yet the way must be taken. In April of 1594, William Brewster was appointed postmaster of Scrooby to serve Her Majesty at 'twenty pence per diem,' which later became 'two shillings sterling per diem.' The years pass till September of 1607 and William Brewster resigns this post at Scrooby. He sells land, goods, chattels, throwing his fortune in with men of lesser means.

And for what? To hire a ship, to pay a shipmaster well, to take Scrooby congregation to Holland, and all in secret. For the law says church Nonconformists must leave England, yea verily, but the law further says they must stand examination and buy a license before they can leave England.

"In other places straight connected with Scrooby, other bodies of churches of men form their congregations. They arise into living, growing forms out of the earth and air, the breath of these times. And who would have believed or expected that this holy zeal of a new-found congregation should come to life in the very corner of England where Robin Hood and his men hid out from the law? Yet farther away in towns and villages of Nottinghamshire, in Lincolnshire, near the Yorkshire border, they hold their meetings and look toward the future, under the counselings and preaching of Mr. John Smith, of Mr. Richard Clifton, of the very grave and reverend Mr. John Robinson."

Oliver Windrow hesitated, took papers from a pocket. "Here a man tells it in his own words. You know the man. You have heard him set forth his Satan, his Christ, his zeal and gospel. His name for the Lord's free people? Pilgrims. What moves this young Scrooby believer William Bradford? He tells it in a letter, in a language of his own, taking pains to be exact, as his heart bids." Windrow unfolded the paper and read:

"Since the breaking out of the light of the gospel in our Honorable Nation of England, Satan hath raised, maintained, and continued against the Saints, from time to time, in one sort or another. Sometimes by bloody death and cruel torments; other whiles imprisonments, banishments, and other hard usages; as being loath the kingdom of Satan should go down and the truth prevail. And when the old serpent could not prevail by persecution, torture and tragedy, he began another kind of war to ruinate and destroy the kingdom of Christ by more secret and subtle means, by kindling the flames of contention and sowing the seeds of discord and bitter enmity. Against his barbarous and profane force, our side labors to have the right worship of God and discipline of Christ established in the church, according to the simplicity of the gospel, to be ruled by the laws of God's word, according to the scriptures.

"At Scrooby and hard by these parts, are new Pilgrims whose hearts the Lord has touched with heavenly zeal, as the Lord's free people in the following of the gospel. And it shall cost them something, hunted and persecuted, on every side their former afflictions are but as flea-bitings, some taken in their beds at night and clapt in prison, others their houses beset and watched night and day.

"So they resolved to go to Holland where they heard there was freedom of religion for all men, where exiles from London and other parts had gone. Many thought it marvelous, their decision to tear loose from their roots in native soil, their lands and livings. Where they proposed to journey they must learn a new language and get livings they knew not how. The trades and employments to which they were going would be new to men of plain country life and the innocence of husbandry."

Oliver Windrow paused.
"Now you come to it," said Mary Windling.
"Here you have it in William Bradford's own words. He was there. He lay in jail with Brewster and others."
He held the copied letter toward her. She took it and read aloud:

"A large company purposed to get passage at Boston and for that end had hired a ship wholly to themselves, and made agreement with the master to be ready on a certain day, and take them and their goods in, at a convenient place, where they accordingly would all attend in readiness. So after long waiting, and large expenses, though he kept not day. with them, yet he came at length and took them in, in the night. But when he had them and their goods aboard, he betrayed them.

Now I see why father and mother shrank from telling it. They feared it could lessen any craving of mine to go with them in the next trial they face getting to Holland."
"Even now," said Windrow, "they shrink at the full particulars. Secretly their leaders got the money to hire a ship. Secretly they bargained with a shipmaster who made it cost them high. Then the fellow kept them waiting, day after day, each day of waiting at cost. At last came the ship, in the darkness of night, somewhere not far from Boston Harbor, mayhap in a cove or inlet where he sent a shallop ashore for them or they had rowboats or other small craft to take them to the ship. At last all were aboard, some with their little chests of clothing and books, others with a few bundles and belongings.
"Then came the betrayal. The shipmaster had told searchers and officers of the law to be on hand. Whether he divided his gold with them or was paid for delivering them up, we do not know. Whether he issued commands or stood by and mocked at them while he jingled gold coins in his pockets, we do not know. He had taken from them, as Bradford writes it, 'extraordinarie rates for their passages.' They having sold their safety to him, he sold them to the man-hunters who sought them. So much we know. Was it a night of fog or stars or moon? How many were these Pilgrims hoping for Holland? We do not know. We may surmise fifty or sixty, others to follow if this

voyage should win. We do know they were suddenly searched, detained and held in prison.

"By dim lanterns showing the way overboard they were made to climb down into the open boats waiting for them in smooth waters. Their goods, chests of books and knapsacks, bundles of belongings, had all been piled in the boats. Then the men searched, pockets of their cloaks and waistcoats, every inch of their shirts rifled and ransacked. Then the women, their clothes and bodies handled beyond modesty."

Windrow had been standing at first, leaning occasionally on the table where Mary was fixing meat and vegetables. Then he seated himself in a large oak chair at the fireplace. Now he paced back and forth the length of the room, raising his voice, in an ironic mood:

"On smooth waters in the dark of night they were carried back to the town of Boston, amid noise and gabble about the shrewd and swift actions of the man-hunters serving the law. The officers took pride in their night's work. Like hunters of wild game showing trophies they paraded their victims as a spectacle for a crowd to have its gaze at these captured creatures, outlandish men and women trying on a dark night to steal away to another country and cleverly taken in the act of the law.

"Then came trifles of decency and justice. Some had lost money, books, other goods seized. But the magistrates showed them favor, held them guilty of no crime, kept them prisoners for a month till order came from the Council table, when all were released except seven bound over for trial, later released without trial. The gentle William Brewster was one of the seven, with William Bradford.

"So they came straggling back to Scrooby and their other towns for the winter. They had been forty and fifty miles to Boston and back, not to Holland. They were farmers and workers on the land, some taking their first glimpse of the sea. All, and William Brewster most of all, had lost money and belongings. And the winter spent how? They say only in the inner secret circles. They have plans. In the light of their eyes I can read they are, as Bradford has it, resolved —aye, resolved."

The man leaned on his left hand at the table, faced her as she scraped a carrot, put out his right arm, once stroked lightly with his fingers her brow and the partings of her hair above, laid lightly the flat of his hand to the side of her head, joined his two hands behind his back, turned and walked to a corner of the room in silence and returned toward her.

"So now, Mary Windling, you have heard all, of October. To no one else roundabout Scrooby would I tell these many things."

Mary gave the last scrape to a carrot. "I speak thanks to you. Never has my affection for you run deeper than this afternoon. I pray deep for the proud calm of the left side of your face and again for the storm, the anger, the humility pressed so plain on the right side of your face."

And Windrow, "Had your father not gone down with fever in late summer you would have been there, crowded into one of the boats, your clothes ransacked, your body prodded by customs officers as if a lousy common smuggler."

"Yes. And soon I go whither they go. I fear what the year may bring. And again no fear, like them not afraid."

"And John Spong? Does he fear? And will he delay farther this matter of when he speaks for you to be his wife?"

She brought her troubled face close to his, looked him in the eyes. "He comes tonight. He will speak if it is the time. He is heavy in his mind for I know not what. He will clear the air tonight. Afterward more fog."

"I go now," said Windrow. They walked toward the door, his right hand softly on her left shoulder. "Remember me. The stars will be out before my legs get me home. I will look at the stars and make wishes for you. Star after star will hear me wishing you keep your outward comeliness and your inward grace."

He put his arm around her and kissed her on the hair above the left ear.

Then he went out the door.

She closed the door after him.

She leaned against the door, her head sunk in her arms.

She moaned, "Oh, what a weak vessel of the Lord I am!"

★ ★ ★ ★ ★ ★ ★ ★ ★ ★

Chapter 4

★ ★ ★ ★ ★ ★ ★ ★ ★ ★

The Second Secret Departure Looms

PERHAPS two hours later Mary Windling took from a shelf four pewter bowls and set them on a table with a pewter spoon alongside each, as though expecting four persons to eat. Two large candles on the table lit the room. At times she stood still and listened to a wind lashing rain against the sides of the house. At times a sleet rattled and drummed, lapsed and came back to drum and pound.

In the branches of two oaks and five cedars near the house she heard sounds she knew, straightened herself and cried at the top of her voice, "Weep, ye rains, wail, ye winds. Ye make a storm and in our hearts storm as wild."

She talked to herself about Windrow. She hoped he was not caught in the storm. "A mile or two he could stand. More would soak and chill him to the bone. I make a prayer for him."

She wondered about John Spong in the storm. "Only a mile he has to come. Should he be wet and cold he'll soon be dry and warm here." She stirred the fire and threw on an extra log. The fresh blaze lit the room, outshone the two candles. This gladdened her heart a moment. Her feet did a little quickstep. With arms straight out from shoulders, she made five whirls and turns of her body, bowing at each turn to an invisible partner.

A loud knocking at the door. She ran, unbolted it, opened it for a young man blown in on a gust of frozen rain and wind. The two of them pushed the door shut against a furious, pressing wind. She bolted the door. They stood with arms around each other, close-pressed, and he kissed her lips and eyes.

She stood six feet tall, he an inch taller, his black hair trimmed close, his face a pale white and the smooth-shaven skin darkened by stubborn beard the razor couldn't reach. The stoop of his shoulders had come in the later years from heavy work on the land. Mary could feel on his hands the calluses that came from spade, fork, shovel, hoe, rake, ox goad, flail. She liked his small dark-gray eyes best when he was meeting her own moods of whimsy and fun, with a left eye squinting to hide its twinkle. The main fault she had to overlook was his mixing a cruelty with his wit and fun. He could be mean when jealous of her or when belittling someone else for queer and petty reasons. Then his tongue-end might run out from the right corner of his mouth while his bushy black eyebrows rose and quivered. Or his underlip would thrust out under a down-press of the upper lip. He had lived clean of body, spare in his eating and drinking, could work hard and long.

And Mary Windling knew she might not risk marrying him unless for this merit he had of actually enjoying hard work and long hours of it. Work for itself pleased him: he couldn't be idle and enjoy himself for long. Smallpox had taken his mother when he was ten years old and a mild attack of that scourge had given his face a few pit marks noticeable only on second close glance. His father had scraped a living at wood carving, clock repairs in a region with few clocks worth repair, and writing letters for many who had not learned to write. Some could pay when a letter must be written. His father had taught John Spong to read, though he had found little time for books and books were scarce—on his father's urging he had learned to earnestly and slowly scrawl words and sentences. His father Richard Spong was a little man in physical size, and an invisible rampart of a man in point of will and vision. Mary Windling believed the son must have gleams of his father sneaking through him. Some of

Richard Spong's bright gold and wit, tall peaks of moral grandeur, must be in his son John.

Thus Mary Windling read her John. She might be reading what wasn't there. "It is a chance I take, whosoever I marry," she said. "I am not afraid. It is not a trouble eating my heart. I love him for the way we get along together and the way he needs me even more than I need him."

So they stood this March afternoon, meeting again after absence, meeting to hold each other close.

They loosened their holds, walked toward the fire as she felt of his doublet and, "Ye'll soon be dry and warm."

"I waited, hoping the storm to die down. Then I began the walk, stopped under trees and sheds. I asked the wind to blow more easy. And it didn't hear me."

"Wit on your part to speak so to the storm." She brought a wooden basin, set it on stones before the fireplace, unhooked the kettle and took it to the table saying, "You dry and warm while I make ready the table."

He wrung out his stockings, sat barelegged to the knees, holding the stockings before the fire to dry. She hung his doublet to dry near the fire, also his hat. She cut a loaf of bread, did various table errands. He warmed his stockings, pulled them on, turned inside out, saying they would dry sooner and better so.

At the table they bowed their heads and John Spong, "We thank thee, O Lord, for watch and guidance given us through the storm of today and we beseech thee in the storms to come thou will give us watch and guidance. To thy will we bow. We thank thee for this daily bread before us and we ask thy blessing in the name of thy son Jesus Christ. Amen."

They ate, lifting a heavy soup or stew with pewter spoons, breaking pieces of bread to put in the soup, pulling out skewers and carving mutton, cutting off pieces of the meat and taking it from the platter to their mouths with fingers, occasionally dipping the fingers in a bowl and wiping the fingers on a cloth or large napkin. They talked, sometimes swiftly and portentously, then lapsed into silences. They seemed at ease with each other in silences.

The rain kept pounding the roof and sides of the house. The roar and high wailing in the two oaks and five cedars outside went on.

Out of long-time touch and training under her ways and speech, the munching John Spong said, "Fit we should hear a storm. We have further storm to meet."

"Yes, the storm sings of changes." She held a hand, an open palm, toward him. "Now you must tell me what you have held back these many days."

"Doubts and fears have gnawed at me like rats. My father, twelve years ago I saw him at his work in Austerfield, fitting pieces into a

54

clock that had fallen on its face. He was full of goodwill to all men, said a stupid man is sometimes perfect in wisdom 'like a stopped clock which once during the day and once during the night is correct to the minute.' From a hiding place he brought out his Bible, telling me again you and I are the only persons he has ever let see it and hold it. A book for all men, he said, for the solemn who lead holy lives or the light-minded who enjoy wit. He chose one verse as having humor, 'Whoso hath a proud look and high stomach, I will not suffer him' and how completely bitter and unforgiving was the psalmist who put the curse on his enemy 'That thy foot may be dipped in the blood of thine enemies, and that the tongues of thy dogs may be red through the same.' Then he spoke of how often women and children bring their will and desire to pass over their men, and the curse Isaiah put on women of his day. He read this from Isaiah, and I made a copy of it for its glitter and terror." John Spong took out a sheet of rag paper with the inked letters somewhat splotched in his rain-soaked coat and read:

"Because the daughters of Zion are haughty, and walk with stretched forth necks and wanton eyes, walking and mincing as they go, and making a tinkling with their feet: therefore the Lord will smite with a scab the crown of the head of the daughters of Zion, and the Lord will discover their secret parts. In that day the Lord will take away the bravery of their tinkling ornaments about their feet, and their cauls, and their round tires like the moon, the chains, and the bracelets, and the mufflers, the bonnets, and the ornaments of the legs, and the headbands, and the tablets, and the earrings, the rings, and nose jewels, the changeable suits of apparel, and the mantles, and the wimples, and the crisping pins, the glasses and the fine linen, and the hoods, and the vails. And it shall come to pass, that instead of a sweet smell there shall be stink; and instead of a girdle a rent; and instead of well set hair baldness; and instead of a stomacher a girding of sackcloth; and burning instead of beauty.

"Then he said how different is the spirit of the New Testament and the blessed Jesus and turned the pages to the Sermon on the Mount and read the Beatitudes to me. 'Blessed are ye when men persecute you for my sake'—and those other blessings that comfort our people."

Mary Windling reached into her bosom and brought out the small bronze plaque, loosened the silver cord, and moved it across the table to him. "Your coming made me forget. I should have told you sooner."

John Spong read the engraved lines. "This lacks piety, I would say. How came it to you?"

"Oliver Windrow was here, two hours, this afternoon. I shall tell you of him."

"And did he not go too far with you?"

"Not even at the door when he kissed me over the left ear."

"I think he must have faults we know not of, an unbeliever with secret beliefs. He drinks alone, he gets stone-blind drunk alone and goes unwashed and blood-red in his eyes for days. He sits by himself and vents curses on himself and then names one by one everyone he knows and curses them one by one. He is a louse who sits wishing he were a wolf."

"John, you go too far. The print of his chaste mouth over my ear is still there and I cannot forget it."

"We have sorrow to talk, doings of moment or I would question you. This Oliver Windrow must have faults."

They kept a stubborn silence. John Spong softened, told more of his father. "Half the winter he kept in his house a man with wife and two children who had returned saying the October ship would not sail for Holland. They would say little more only they had lost money and belongings. They were sad yet saying they would try another day."

"And then?"

"He talked of the English, the Welsh, of young William Bradford saying we are to light candles that shall glimmer far and shine long. Then of watchers. Day and night six days in September they had stood by his house, else he might have gone with those who were to sail for the Low Countries. Now again for two days they had watched night and day. He had considered giving me his Bible to take away and keep from harm. For if they should search his house and find the Bible he would go to prison for refusing to tell them where he had gotten it. 'Here,' he said, 'here is the name of the man who gave me this Book of Books. There it is written.' Then he showed the same name in a list of eighteen men who went to that prison in London, the Clink, a little straw between their bodies and the damp stone floor, often no food for two days, hunger and cold bringing jail fever. Between the years 1586 and 1592 these eighteen died in the jail where they were thrown for their beliefs."

John Spong gave messages he had been entrusted to deliver in the country near Austerfield. He returned two days later to find his father troubled. "The officers had come in the morning, searched his house, and taken away his Bible, then returned and questioned him. He told them his belief in the Father, the Son and the Holy Ghost, that he was a member of no established church, that his life would be guided by the teachings he found in the Book of Books they had taken away. Had they thundered and raged at him he would have been less troubled. They were quiet with a cold hate and scorn. He had considered taking flight but could not think what would be his course. At the worst, he said, if he should be taken he would be merely one more whose resistance, whose light of the free human spirit, would in God's good time be of help to men. He put his arms around me. He knows my work on the land here and my work with the Scrooby congregation were calling me back, that I had messages to deliver with no delay. And I told him of you and our hopes."

"Me?"

"You."

"And you said our hopes?"

"Yes."

"And you meant our hopes together side by side, each with each and sometimes both the same and again each is both and both each? Thus? Are you speaking what you long held back?"

"Yokefellows—the man yoked to the woman and the woman yoked to the man—for life—for weal or woe. Bedfellows, each warming the bed for the other on nights when the frost bites deep with chill and the firelogs have gone out and the man and wife sleep spoon-fashion."

"God love you, John Spong."

"God keep you, Mary Windling."

"Is it not as though we had so soon now these moments spoken the words and seals of holy matrimony?"

"It is."

"Yet listen. Why should this be? The wind has gone down in the two oaks and the five cedars. The rain drums soft on the roof. The fury is over. Now father and mother will be home. Only the storm could have kept them from coming early this evening. We will both tell them."

She did a little quickstep, waited while he turned his stockings and put his shoes on. Arms straight out from shoulders she made five turns of her body, bowing at each turn to John Spong who bowed low in reply four times and the fifth time clutched her tight in his arms, held her for six heartbeats, then the two of them went through the motions of an old folk dance.

They took two mugs of beer from the table, touched them, and with laughing faces cried Mary's toast, "To the storms to come and the stars coming after the storm."

They drew a bench and sat close together by the fire, after a long kiss.

John Spong with his right arm about her gave her a slow long print with his lips over her left ear, saying, "On the burnish of chestnut hair over your left ear I put one token not knowing why."

"Be so good as to forget and leave me alone in the remembering. You have no better friend than Oliver Windrow and both of us no better friend."

She fastened the silver cord at the back of her neck and put the keepsake in her bosom. The beer, the dancing, the arousals of the night, set John talking. Parts of it Mary had heard before and often.

"When I doubt there is an Evil One," he began, "I have only to look into myself. There he is, the chief of all evil. Men have seen his shadow. though no man ever set eyes on him, except the Master when

57

he said, 'Get thee behind me, Satan.' I have heard of men finding a track of his cloven foot and men hearing his laugh mock at them, 'I will get thee yet. Wait and I will put my clutches on thee.' He was in the storm early this night. In one dread moment when the wind had slackened and then commenced with worse fury than before, I heard a swish of black wings high in the sky and I heard an echo from east to west and from west back to east, a faint howl and a thin cry, 'I will get thee yet, miserable little John Spong, worm of the dust, John Spong. I shall yet snare thee and hear thee cry for pity and then obey commands I give thee.' He was outside this house tonight hoping to snare us, hoping to clamp evil and fear over our hearts so we would quarrel and commit folly and spit in each other's faces instead of pledging ourselves in betrothal. He slipped a spell under the door or through a window crack and had it got all the way through, the spell would have wrought evil on us. The spell came far enough so that I spoke wrong of Oliver Windrow. It failed to reach and strike you. Had any part of the spell touched you, then you would have spoken as mad as I did."

"Yes, John, I would have answered that you too sit alone and drink and blaspheme and vent curses on every name of friend or foe you can call."

"Then instead of sweet words and our little dance we would have flung beer in each other's faces and mocked at each other."

"Who knows," said Mary, "what can come when the Dark One lurks in hearing and tries his spells, till the thing you do is what you never would have believed you could do, like the man in York who knew the Archdemon was following him night and day trying to catch him off guard? Twice he found himself standing over his wife as she slept, him with a knife in his hand and about to drive it into her throat as she slept. He caught himself with upraised hands about to give her a bloody and awful death. He fell to the floor in tears, on his knees giving thanks to the watching angels of the Lord who had broken the Archdemon spell thrown over him. Twice he broke from that spell, the same knife in his hand each time over the same woman he came near slaying. Day and night he said he felt that Shadow near him. The third time he came out of the spell the knife was in the woman's throat. The red blood gushing from her brought him out of the spell. He came to his senses crying and ran to his best friend, a neighbor, crying, 'O God, it was not my doing. It was a God-damned hell-born fiend who crazed my brain.' Then he went and threw himself into the thin ice of the millpond and they found him in the morning with his face up toward the red dawn, the knife still clutched in his right hand. And a strange face he had turned toward the east, half of it twisted in torment, the other half at peace with himself and his God. So my mother heard it when she was a girl."

John Spong, as if the two of them might search and approach the source of such tragedy: "Bedeviled, yes, he was bedeviled. Someone close to the black art could have helped him. Men and women shrewd in black art put spells on each other and throw them off. It is a game for those sold to the high prince Satan. Before he killed his woman that man could have looked at his face in a looking-glass and shifted the glass so it caught the new moon shining on it. Plain to be seen there was his face and the new moon. From then on he could escape the fate set for him in one way, by hurling the glass from his hand and shattering it. To break it with a hammer, a stone, an ax, would not help. He must throw it away from himself. Then if the glass should not stop itself in the air and fall slow and unbroken, the spell would still be on him. By hurling it away from him, he gives the demons of black art a fair chance to stop it before it destroys itself. Some of the black-art men would say it was the woman at fault. A spell came on her the day of her wedding. She was completely dressed and had put the last touch on standing before the looking-glass, then turned and went out of the door to meet the bridegroom and the clergyman. The black-art demons chuckle with their strange glee when a bride does that. She should have been told that she must leave some part of her dressing, some last action, to be done without looking in the glass. If she had combed one tress of hair or put on a glove, or taken off a glove and put it on again, without looking in the glass, the spell would have been off. So they say. So they tell it. I believe half of it. I ask you, Mary, when you dress yourself for our wedding, leave something undone, take off a glove or a shoe and put it on again without looking in the glass before you make your way to the ceremony."

This he said rather lightly, with a drollery she liked in him, what she had told Oliver Windrow was the "quaint" side of him. Then with his utmost solemnity which she also liked: "The prayers and good works of a servant of Christ who is unceasingly anxious to follow the Lord's instructions as given in the Bible, such a Christian cannot be overcome by any black art or witchcraft. He can say as the Lord said, 'Get thee behind me, Satan.' Then if he has been faithful to the Lord, the Lord will be with him and the temptations of the Evil One in vain."

"I follow you, John. We shall do our best with faith and works. I give you the promise when I put on the best clothes I have for our wedding, and they will be plain clothes indeed, I shall nevertheless take off a shoe and put it on again or give my handkerchief some last touch without looking in the glass before I go to meet you for the ceremony."

A pounding at the door. Mary ran to the door, John Spong following. They heard voices "Mary, Mary." She slid the door bolt. A smallish man with an owlish face, a wide slit and thin mouth, entered followed by a woman half a head taller than himself, she more rugged of build than he. He was swift and again deliberate, a puzzle of a man.

"Father, mother," cried Mary. "I said you would come home when

59

I heard the storm go down." He kissed her on the cheek. Mary bolted the door. The elders hung their cloaks on wooden pegs in a corner. Mary put bowls of soup, a mutton stew, on the table. The four pulled chairs to the table and talked.

Mary began. "John Spong and I must tell you of one little matter. And not so little either."

Jasper Windling rasped, "Lose no time. Tell it."

"John Spong has this night bespoken himself and I have given my troth."

"He has been slow. The storm has helped him? The wind blew him into a haste not seen before this?"

"Leave your humor, father, we are bespoken."

"Till death do you part?"

John Spong stood stony-faced, half defiant and resentful of Jasper Windling's tone. "For weal or woe. The icy arms of death will not put us asunder."

"So be it."

The mother Sarah Windling murmured in echo, "So be it."

Jasper Windling, his rasp gone, "So be it. Our prayers go with you. God speed you. On all your pathways God speed you."

Sarah Windling again echoed, "May God speed you on all your pathways."

John Spong gave what he believed was called for. "We shall stand with you in whatever heavy darkness may hang over your heads and be true whenever candles are lighted to the grace of God in the name of Christ and in token of the Holy Ghost."

"You speak fairly," said Jasper Windling.

"He speaks well, father. I speak with him," Mary joined in softly. "Tell us of your meetings yesterday and today."

A meditation of Jasper Windling to himself and a speech to the others—he intoned it slowly as though a voice of fate spoke through his. He broke the intonation with sudden high-keyed pronouncements. "Soon we sail, again for Holland. The plan will be told to you—the time, the place, what you may carry, who your companions. We shall not fail. We go. Make preparations for your needs, with few knapsacks and belongings. Prepare your minds to be calm for whatever events befall. Prepare your souls with fortitude and high resolves. We go. 'We shall be pilgrims,' said young Bradford, 'we may light a candle that shall send its gleam far.' We go. No tyrant constables shall stop us. Only storm or death or the act of God in His great wisdom can stop us. We go. It is in our bones we must go. We cannot do else."

After a pause Sarah Windling spoke shyly. "Tell John Spong of his father."

Jasper Windling waited and after hesitation, "It will not brighten your heart, lad. They have him now in the Clink in London, the vilest prison the land knows. He will not answer who gave him his Bible

60

they took in his house, nor the names of men and women who hold
secret meetings. They tell him he is surely the wretch intended by
King James saying they must conform or he would harry them out of
the land or else do worse. He has pleaded he will leave the land. Yet
they hold him in a narrow cell with a few straws between him and
the stone floor he sleeps on. Jail fever may be his end. Yet his spirit
is not broken, his humor not gone. He sent word by a man released:
'Why should a little man like me who has wronged no other man
have so elaborate attention from the majesty of the law?' "

Mary Windling burst into a high wail, checked herself and spoke
as a storm gone down, with a shrug of shoulders toward John Spong:

"Alone he can do nothing for his father. No army to send against
the King's attorney to knock down the prison, no friends at court who
can win a pardon. Should he make public outcry he would be seized
and put in the Clink with his father. Were the prison of wood and
his father a rat he might consider gnawing a hole for a body to wriggle
out. But the Clink is of stone. And were it of wood he is not a rat.
Wherefore John Spong and all of us stand free to wring hands like a
woman seeing her man drown far at sea while on shore her cries go to
the blue heaven in prayer. The child in John would like to weep now,
the child that still loves the hand and voice of his father."

John's voice was shaken. "The man in me, remembering the light
of my father's face and eyes when last I saw him, with neither hate
nor curses for those doing evil to him, the man in me shall seek and
hope to do likewise. That is what he would have me do: read the
Book of Books and join with others in a fellowship around that Book
of Books. He would say I justify him and his death in jail by going with
Scrooby congregation."

Jasper Windling consoled. "You will have friends who have known
bitterness near your own."

"There will be your wife Mary with her hand in yours, a helpmeet,"
said Sarah Windling. "She can pray and speak of holiness. Then too,
she may dance for you. I have caught her in quickstep dancing near to
sin. Her feet lead her to pleasure too easy. I told her so once. She an-
swered so long as the communions of her heart were proper the Lord
would blame only her feet."

Mary Windling swung her head in a bright silver laughter. "Yes,
my feet may go to hell though my soul will not follow my feet. The
good Lord should not have made my feet so glad. They cannot help
it they dance a thankfulness over the light of morning and the light
of faces I love or the evensong of the coming out of the stars. A great
moment at the end of the day when scarlet runners of the sun beckon
and bow low as if seeing before we do the first evening stars and say-
ing to them, 'Now comes your time to bring your light to the children
of men.' My tongue goes silent and failing to speak my thanks to the
Lord of Creation who made that sun and those stars, that sky where

they move. My tongue fails. Yet my feet can say part of it. My feet can sing praise to God for letting me have eyes to see it. My knees sway and bend in thanking."

"Mary Windling, my own daughter, you speak like a heathen and a pagan. How in such an hour as this can you think of pleasuring yourself?"

"Is it your doing, John Spong," continued the father, "that this maid forsakes the pathway of the Lord and dallies with the dangers of lust and dancing?"

"Jasper," said the mother, "you should know she always had a singing heart and dancing feet. Now she begins to dance with her eyes and her talk."

"The day has been crowded for her," said John Spong. "You yourself saw me too slow in bespeaking myself. I do not know why I waited so long."

Mary Windling leaped from her chair, did a quickstep and two swift turns, bowed low before each of the three. They sat silent and amazed. She paused.

"You have not gone daft," said the father. "By queer ways you act nonetheless. Why so queer, Mary? Are you sure no spell is over you?"

"Only the spell of my love bespoken."

She twirled once, stood at the left shoulder of the seated John Spong, threw a right arm around him, kissed him bold on the mouth, danced away doing two turns, then: "I am crazed, father. Not in the head. In the feet and the knee-bones. Crazed with a dark delight. When you get what you want overflowing and you hadn't been sure you would get it, then you wear the morning stars at your naked ankles and your very toes hold conversations with the moon, the baby moon, the cradle moon."

She did two quaint slow gyrations, ending with two arms slowly outstretched, swung her head, then slowly raised it, showing an utterly solemn face, then: "I could have been singing today that heartbreaking song—

"When cockle shells turn silver bells,
Then will my love return to me,
When roses blow in wintry snow,
Then will my love return to me.

"O waly waly, but love is bonny,
A little while when it is new.
But it grows old and waxeth cold
And fades away like morning dew.

So I could have been singing. Now instead of such emptiness and hunger I bring you good tidings and the bread of life."

"There may be a spell on you," the father warned. "Watch yourself with care. You have heathen feet. You pleasure yourself." The mother added, "I brought you up to be a good woman. Had I not seen you in these mad moments, more than once, I would find no comfort in these antics."

Both Jasper Windling and Sarah Windling spoke words they believed fitting their duties as parents, their loyalty to church teachings. Yet a vitality and gleam of Mary's performance actually deepened the hold of their affection for her. Yet doubts crept in. They could not be fully rid of a feeling that the Evil One had cast a spell on her and sold her to the fleshpots of Babylon. She had her defense. "You should know well I have not been sold to the fleshpots of Babylon. Only when I am alone or with you, my three dear ones, my love, my father, my mother, only then shall I let my feet be glad. You shall have no bad name over my glad feet."

She skipped to a shelf, came away in a slow walk, her body drawn fully erect, the head bowed and the face abstracted, the wide lips parted in a gravity near the awe of a beholder. Her eyebrows lifted, tangled shags of a darker chestnut tint than her hair, not unlike a wild grass rain-and-wind beaten with long play of sun on them, a touch of the outdoor lawless in their twists of disorderly growth.

"Paper," said Mary Windling, holding at arm's length a six-by-six-inch sheet. "Linen rags and old fishing nets and castoff garments boiled and pressed smooth and dried, paper for those who write and print. Paper—not one house in a hundred in England or Europe has a sheet of paper." She seemed to hold back from going so far as to ask her father and mother, "Why should those who scorn reading and writing need paper? What more useless to them than paper?"

Then holding high the sheet of paper, "A token given me by Richard Spong. From his Bible I copied." Her arm brought the sheet down and her eyes scanned words and turned to the others in the room. "Many times I have read these alone. Now I read them for the first time to others." Her voice became songlike with cadence and color, reading the Beatitudes from the Sermon on the Mount, asking at the end, "What is the meaning?" They marveled she could be so certain of herself. She rambled on with a peculiar low-toned elation:

"What is the meaning? We are entitled to rejoice. We pay for this joy by the load of the Cross, by enduring as Richard Spong this night endures, as he waits unafraid in the Clink of London. These words bid our faces shine. They prophesy fellowship. We shall leave England. What we seek shall in due time come to England. I can tell it in the air, change to come. God is sifting and winnowing. God takes His time. Europe, Africa, dim and far-off Asia, the wilderness of America, wherever mankind struggles, is to come change, fellowship over the whole earth. Either so, in the end, or the words of Jesus mean nothing. The truth of Christ is as tangled as those blessed words."

Jasper Windling's eyes had blinked with suspicion, then his head nodded a mild approval. "Sarah, who would have believed you once carried so strange an unborn child?"

"She preached when a child," said Sarah, "and seemly enough in church never rises to say a word. I have heard her preach to the two oaks and five cedars not knowing I listened. Today loosed her tongue."

"The words of Jesus go smooth and rough and wear many faces," said Mary. "We too shall wear many faces ere we arrive in Holland, ere we find our way to free worship. 'For with what measure ye mete, it shall be measured to you again.' Back to your bosom comes the pay for struggle and prayer. I ask you to let my feet be glad when they must rejoice. Let me have that between ourselves. My feet may go to hell. But Jesus knows my bosom prays to hold no wrong. My bosom and my soul will go on high with the saved and the blessed if my feet get acquainted with enough thorns and stones. I have preached nothing to you. I have spoken thoughts crowding on me this day when life has given me good measure, pressed down, shaken together."

Jasper Windling spoke in anger, jealousy, or a mixed mood, sharptoned. "I listen to you pleasure yourself, child. You vaunt yourself about your feet going to hell and brag of your bosom and soul going to heaven. On the great day of doom when all human creatures rise from their graves and receive sentence from the Great Judge, who are you to be set apart and have your feet go to hell and the rest of you to heaven? Will there be some who have a little toe or a big toe go to hell while the rest goes to heaven? And by the same token will others have feet go to heaven and the bosom and soul to hell? This somber night we have burdens of care on us and I try to think whether you are not quite bright or whether you are overbright, which is the same in the end."

Sarah snarled, "Let her alone. You talk as though the Evil One has put a black hand and a claw mark on her."

Jasper Windling snarled back. "I talk no such stuff. I would rebuke my daughter. There is holy work to be done. She talks folly and nonsense. What she does may prepare her for the Evil One. The shadow of Satan lurks in such pleasuring."

John Spong in his first interposition spoke softly. "Judge not and ye shall not be judged."

The father asked Mary to draw him a pot of beer. He took a swig, smacked his lips, swept a finger over his mouth and instructed John. "You were not asked to put in a word, young man. I am the one by law who giveth away this woman to the one she weds."

"She giveth herself away. If any other giveth her away she is not given."

"You would begin scandal and strife in Scrooby church. Is there not enough confusion and secrecy without your muddling?"

"You fathered an excellent child that grew to be a comely and rare young woman."

The father snarled. The others saw it gave him relief and happiness. "She talks too much. She dances. At the Gate of Heaven she is prepared to shed her feet and abide with the angels footless for all eternity. I will be asked, 'Is that your daughter, Jasper Windling, who goes about here with no feet?'"

John Spong when near Mary at times had a way of speech and thought somewhat like hers. He could often guess her answers. What she termed the "quaint" in him came more vivid when he was in the circle of her personal vibrations. He told the father: "The angels with wings will not care if one of them is footless, while flying. And in that blessed abode the angels will be forgiving. Even mayhap some tall angel by grace and appointment from Jesus will lay a hand on her and say, 'Let there be feet on her, let there be glad feet good to look upon.' Surely stranger things have happened in heaven."

Again Jasper Windling took comfort if not happiness in snarling: "You keep a sober face and mock at me. She mocks. You join her in mocking. You make game of me. You would make me a fool in heaven and on earth!"

John Spong rose and took two steps to where Mary Windling had stood white and motionless with folded hands, put his right arm around her waist and looked toward the father. "You chose your woman and your woman chose you. So we have chosen each other. If it be the will of God we have a daughter as rare and pleasant as you and your woman brought into life, we will give prayers of thanks, hosannahs and shouts."

"She had a hard day, Jasper," said the mother. "A day of wild storm over sky and oaks and her heart."

Jasper moderated a little. "She may yet learn she has spoken drivel tonight. It would be unseemly the church hear of it."

Rousing a bit out of dreaminess, Mary went on: "Oliver Windrow this afternoon told me in full of October—of the Scrooby people at last on the boat to take them to Holland when the shipmaster betrayed them. I could have wept and did not weep. Then Oliver Windrow spoke with his brown eyes and his evensong voice of what he and I have between us that death cannot take away. He went out the door and I bolted it and leaned against it and wanted to weep and I had only dry tears. Then the storm came and later John, the chosen John Spong with the story of seeing his father, holding the Bible of his father, the watch on his father night and day. Then sorrow and care swept away in our betrothal. Then much else. Then you came home with this blow of Richard Spong in the foulest prison in London. I could have wept yet I did not weep. I danced. Every step of the dance kept tears away."

She danced slowly, then faster, then slowly again, weaving in count and cadence, the repeated steps of the dance. "I could have wept yet I did not weep," then suddenly reeling into her mother's arms. "And now, and now, at last," and her body trembled and the tears came as in a storm long withheld.

John Spong printed a soft kiss on her hair and forehead, bowed to the mother, bowed and offered his hand to Jasper Windling, who silently held it a moment and went to the door with John Spong, who left saying he would come again tomorrow.

Spong outside paused between two oaks, looked up at the quiet branches and beyond to an arch of serene night stars. "Her feet will never see hell. Not one hair of her will ever go to hell."

* * * * * * * * * *

Chapter 5

* * * * * * * * * *

Out of Oak the Heart of Christ

AN April night of stars saying winter long gone, summer soon to come and a light breeze with earth smells reporting the land ready for seedtime, ready for apple blossoms. Outside the big door of his workroom Oliver Windrow stood barefoot and barekneed in his sleeping shirt, searching with his eyes among the squares and sprockets of the changing dome.

"Three times this night," came his words to the Big Dipper, "three times I say to hell with sleep and come out here to see if the sky has news knowing well there is no news. Yesterday came news enough—of Richard Spong gone with jail fever, racked and rotted with jail scurvy, dying in the dirt and damp of the Clink in London. Somewhere up there beyond the Milky Way floats his shadow and soul. Here among living men his name and shadow will be alive for long. 'I go not alone,' he told me last winter. 'Over Britain, over Europe, other men prepare to pay the great price so that men after them may in the great days to come be free to meet, to pray, to worship, to speak, to think, and to keep that freedom so long as they harm no other man's life, person or goods.' Good-by, my friend," and Windrow kissed his hand toward the morning stars and gleams of daybreak. "Many another night I shall wake out of a dream of you and hear you saying, 'I go not alone.'"

He went inside, lay wakeful awhile as a slow daylight crept into the room. He got up, put on his clothes, warmed a dish of dried apples he had put to soak the evening before, ate it with a thick slice of rye bread and a small cut of cold roast pork. Around a block of oak tall as himself he moved, stood still, moved again, making measurements, wondering what a year of work would bring forth breathing and warm from that dumb, cold, dry shape once of a living, massive tree. For

66

two hours he drew lines and set marks where the preliminary cuts and chiselings were to follow the drawings and designs he consulted every few moments.

He heard the door open. He turned and bowed to Matilda Bracken. He stepped toward her, took her two hands, kissed her mouth lightly, went to his work and she to hers. Now he broke his silence. Now while doing his work he let go free and careless the words telling his mood, occasionally pausing as though to ask himself what was it he had just said:

"I might have been a juggler or a strolling player or a fortuneteller living by my wits, an astrologer, a numerologist, a palmist, three in one.

"You, good sir, I would predict, shall marry a rich widow, though I cannot tell you fat and lousy you shall die.

"And you, most excellent madam, shall fall into money and take to yourself three husbands one by one, though I cannot tell you before your time you will die weary of bought young husbands.

"Or I might have been one of those villainous persons the law terms a vagabond or an incorrigible rogue.

"Certainly I am incorrigible and had I been a rogue I would have been an incorrigible rogue.

"I might have been a heretic and a traitor and King James with his big head, his glut of learning from books, his slobbering mouth, his rickety spindly legs, his gabble and clowning, might have sat down one day and signed my death warrant, signed a piece of paper saying, 'This rat is better out of the world than in it.' So they would have put a rope around my neck, driven a cart from under my feet.

"And I would have dropped the length of my body and the drop might have been ten thousand sea fathoms with my neck broken and my face a twisted look in surprise at how soon a man can forget familiar names and faces. Then would come the special and high honors paid only to those heretics guilty of treason.

"They would let me to the ground, slit my bowels and thrust them over my face as a function and a ritual duly provided in the text of the law.

"Thus my human dignity would be sunk to lower depths, the majesty of the law elevated and redeemed, the stature of the King raised higher, his royal bowels rendered more holy, their content sacrosanct.

"Why should they assume the wrongdoer, gone on a journey they must all take, nevertheless is still on earth to feel the infamy of his personal bowels forming a cover over his hated face?

"Or I might have been a plain heretic, not quite a traitor, wherefore I would be privileged to have first my left ear cut off and then my right ear cut off so I would thereupon walk as a warning to citizens saying, 'Take care not to be a heretic or you lose your ears and wear your hair long to cover your lost heretical ears.'

"Or again I might have had my heretical head neatly severed, cut

67

off with skill and dispatch, the beholders saying of the executioner, 'That man has had practice and deserves praise.'

"And the blood streaking the face and matting the hair would be left quaintly so, a work of art in the realm of the mighty and proficient ax.

"Soon there would be my isolated head, an achievement, stuck on a spike at the end of a tall pole at a street corner near a market place.

"And my head would dry and shrivel and become august and austere with time. The rains would beat on it and the snow fall on it and the wind tell it many an idle fable.

"Tireless elements would be washing the dry blood from the forehead, the nose, the chin, and the jaw.

"And the sun would be kind to the face muscles over the bones and bake them—and heavy fog sheets come and shroud them.

"And the fog moving away the moon would come down with a velvet golden light on the teeth at the lips drawn back and curled in a meditative mockery: 'Here is the tongue of heretic words, here the mouth of speech brings doom to close the mouth and make it shut up forever.'

"Then the years would go by and men would forget—it has happened—they would forget the name of the heretic and what the heretic had said that made the heresy.

"For the heresy of one generation is the heroism of another and some generations are forgetful.

"And here on a sweet April morning I blather, having kept my head and ears, I blather."

His work was going well, off to a good start. His wild talk rose in part from his wrath and scorn of the high authorities who gave mean death to Richard Spong, in part from self-reproach that he measured poorly alongside of Spong, and more definitely over the feeling ever deep-rooted in him that the rulers of Britain and of Europe are, with few exceptions, and have been for generations, coarse, ignorant, superstitious, blind, greedy, rapacious, cruel with a practiced and studied cruelty wherein they take satisfaction, pride and pleasure. "They guise themselves in glittering garments and dazzling jewels of pomp and panoply yet they know less of what they do and truly are than the peasants they mislead by keeping them in fear and ignorance." His talk was incidental, his work the main thing. He would not have been sure what he had been saying if asked to repeat his words.

A head of Christ was to come out of the block of oak tall as himself. He hoped and prayed the work might come off well. His friends and good patrons Sir Reginald Overstreet and Lady Bathsheba Overstreet of Hawksby Manor had talked with him about it, urging him against his feeling that a head of Christ was next to impossible to achieve truly in any of the arts. Six important chairs Windrow across years had made for their great hall, two stairways with singing banisters, special frames for ancestral portraits, a bas-relief of the characters in Jack the Giant Killer for a child's room, a bas-relief of David and Goliath, portrait heads of Alfred the Great and of William of Orange, the Dutch titan. They would now accept his best effort at a head of the Saviour of Man and pay more generously than for any of his previous work. He had delayed years in this commission that was to be his great life effort.

Matilda Bracken saw him move with impetuous fury, then pause in perfect composure, then again in changing low strides and short steps, make his beginnings at taking away the first surplus of wood from that block of oak. She saw passing over the two contrasting sides of his face the questioning, the bewilderment, the simple wonderment, the amazement and awe, of a straightaway seeker dominated completely by the purpose and motive of his quest. Her face held a calm light as she watched him. His eyes caught hers more than once and his head nodded to her briefly, abruptly, with a grim gladness. She was to go soon but she knew he wished her to stay through a meditation he began, speaking as an accompaniment to the broken cadences of his work motions:

"The Christ head, the Christ face, what man will ever paint, chisel or carve it? When finished it would float and gleam, cry and laugh, with every other face born human. And how can you crowd all the tragic and comic faces of mankind into one face?

"Two of them died last year who strove and failed to make that mystic face come alive. One of them painted more than a hundred Christ faces, then died saying a thousand would not be enough of learning in heartbreak. The other prepared himself by painting Matthew, Mark, Luke, John. At fifty years he had made portraits of the Twelve Disciples, saying, 'Of them all only Judas made me weep.' Mary and Martha he put on canvas, Nicodemus, Pontius Pilate, Barabbas, the Roman soldier whose spear sent vinegar into the wound on the left side. Each year he said, 'Next year I will paint the Christ face, I am not ready, next year I begin.' Into the sleep of death he faded with 'Next year I begin my Christ face.'

"Once I woke from a dream of day on day, month after month, seeking faces. I found one at an autumn fair, a tall peasant with flaxen hair. His smooth, waving tresses of oat straw had the gleam of summer sun ripening the grain, a mouth of compassion and resolves, eyes of anger and pity. He seemed beyond all others in a face made of all the good faces swarming at the booths, peddlers, acrobats. 'This,' I said in my dream, 'must be in the Christ face I shall foreshadow from a block of oak.'

"Then in my dreams I sought an evil face and found another tall man, gloss and black in his hair and eyes, a mocking mouth, eyes of cunning, cruelty and sly greed, seeking possessions to pile on his accrued and fat-dripping possessions. Pride, sloth, gluttony were all there in his face. In him were blended all the sinners seeking land, gold, power, hunting women, wine, bargains beyond their needs. Lust, thievery, murder, sat on his face made of many vile sinner faces.

"And I said in my dream I would join these two faces, with the good one having its will over the evil one, the Child of Satan overcome by the Son of God, the sinner subdued by the saint. With fury and prayer I carved those two faces into one. Then I stood back and looked at it. What I had made was a gargoyle of two faces in combat. I needed thousands of other faces. The surge and wail of mankind, the pity of circumstance, were not there, nor the betrayers nor the saviors.

"Then in my dream I saw too that the face of Christ must have in it the essence and mystery of the sea and the sky, the valleys and the mountains overlooked by sun, moon, stars, and the heavy darkness where men grope and stumble. For the face of Christ would hold what every man sees, hears, smells, touches, tastes. And it would be very old and very young, older than bare hilltop boulders burnt and time-washed, younger than the latest fresh-born child seeking its mother's nipples.

"The face of the landless man having no piece of soil he can call his own—and the face of the landlord owning more acres and miles of land than he will ever in his life have time to ride over—their mutual obligations, mistrust and hate—they would be there on the face and head of Christ.

"The look he gave the Magdalene when she washed his feet and wiped them with her hair, the look he gave Judas to let Judas know he knew of the thirty pieces of silver, the look he gave the crowd when he turned water into wine and when he magnified the loaves and fishes for the feeding of the multitude, the private gaze he turned on the Twelve Disciples when they journeyed by themselves from city to city, the peace in his eyes when he turned them on the Galilee storm and commanded the waters to be still, the series of faces at the Stations of the Cross, the majestic anger in his nostrils when he drove the money-changers from the Temple, the awful quiet on his lips when he bade Lazarus rise from the dead, the music and serenity of his mouth as the syllables poured forth in the Sermon on the Mount, the desperate gleam and twisted grimace over the mouth muscles in those blinding instants when the earth trembled and the sky darkened and he cried, 'My God, my God, why hast thou forsaken me?' the baffling and dazzling radiance that issued from his hallowed head when he rose from the tomb in white robes and announced his work done and he would go home to his Father and await them to join him—must not all of these faces be joined, melted and composed into one for setting forth the face of Jesus the Christ? Otherwise is it not less than the Christ face?"

Now he bordered on bewilderment. He dropped his tools. He walked to the door, back to the block of oak, to the door again, and back and forth. Then in pantomime and speech he told himself and Matilda

Bracken that to carve the Christ head he wanted, he would have to be sunk in blacker sorrow than he had ever known and be lifted into flame-white ecstasy he had never yet known. He brought a goose-quill pen and inkpot with paper to the big table and began writing in a large free script:

Before my Christ head comes alive out of oak, my heart must be sunk deeper and get closer interwoven with the hearts of all other men, the good who have some bad in them and the bad who have some good in them, none being utterly good, none being utterly bad. I must be shameless dust of the earth and roots singing underground till they become blossoms of harvest triumphant in the sunlight above. I must know the sorrow of endless tears and the deeper sorrow that has forgotten how to weep. I must come near the miracle of those who can give and go on giving when it is a mystery where they get what it is they give and never fail in the having to give. I must be silent often and break my silence only with prayer. I must believe in many deeds beyond my doing in the hope that one or two such unbelievable deeds may come from my hands.

He knew Matilda Bracken leaned over his shoulder and read as his pen shaped the words. He rose and swept his arms around her. Their eyes met with meaning, their lips in a long deep kiss of both measure and abandon. She threw him a kiss at the door when leaving. He moved in his work at the block of oak with a deepened faith in deeds beyond his doing.

A knocking at the door—he unbolted and swung it open to see two shy women, their faces pale, thin, trouble-worn. They looked slimpsy, nerve-racked. He saw their cloaks thorn-torn, creased and wrinkled as though they had no other cloaks and these had been slept in and stained with leaves, grass, gravel, clay. He saw their eyes unsteady, their shoulders swaying. They seemed to him weak and like to faint before him. At the moment the younger one said his first name, he got her voice and cried, "Mary Windling, in the name of God—and your mother—and where in the name of God have you been?" He stepped between them, taking them by the arms. They leaned on him. They had taken a few steps into the big room. The mother reeled and was about to fall. Oliver and Mary caught her and led her to his couch alongside the wall next the fireplace. He lifted her head and put his pillow under it.

"She needs food and drink," he said with his eyes on Sarah Windling. "She has been through torment." And turned his eyes to Mary. "Likewise you."

He moved swiftly to the fireplace, got the fire going under a kettle. He brought a bottle and two glasses, motioned Mary to a chair, poured

71

them a glass each. "This Madeira wine will warm your insides and set you up. We shall soon have barley broth and mutton roast."

He arranged a bench covered with rushes in a corner, led Mary to it and told her she must lie down and rest till food came. Mary said no word, her face woebegone, a mute look he had never seen before on her. It startled him. He put on his own face the best slow calm look of cheer he could think of. Then he lost that look and before going to the fireplace and pantry to get food and dishes, his lighted face turned dark with melancholy. "I shall serve the mother, then your turn."

He brought Sarah Windling broth, mutton, rye bread, then the like for Mary. "You are hungry and tired. It will go away. Eat now. Then rest. And we will talk. You are the same brave Mary Windling I saw in March. Food and rest will be yours here."

He went about work and errands over the big room. Looking toward her as she finished the food and drank a mug of beer, he saw her beckoning him. He went to her. She asked weakly, "Shall we talk now? So much to say."

"Not yet. You lie quiet. Take a nap. If you can't nap, close your eyes and say, 'Quiet is good.' Say it slow six times and then six times again, 'Quiet is good.'"

He turned her on her side, moved a soft hand over her brow and eyes, kissed ever so softly her pale mouth and again went about his work and errands over the big room. Twice he stepped over to the mother to see she had eaten and now slept well. Later he saw Mary slept deep. He bent over her, saw her coming nicely and walked away, rubbing his hands and chuckling.

An hour or more and he stole a look over Mary as she stirred, turned from one side to lying on her back, stretched a little, opened her eyes. "Good Oliver Windrow, blessed Oliver Windrow."

"I know part of what happened," he said. "It is in this letter from one who was there. I will read it to you. You will tell me more, the risks you took and what came of it." He read to her from a letter written in jails and elsewhere:

"It so fell out, that the light of a Dutchman at Hull, having a ship of his own belonging to Zealand; they made agreement with him, and acquainted him with their condition, hoping to find more faithfulness in him, than in the former of their own nation. He bade them not fear, for he would do well enough. He was by appointment to take them in between Grimsby and Hull, where was a large common a good way from any towne. Now against the prefixed time, the women and children, with the goods, were sent to the place in a small bark, which they had hired for that end; and the men were to meet them by land. But it so fell out, that they were there a day before the ship came, and the sea being rough, and the women very sick, prevailed with the seamen to put into a creek hard by, where they lay on ground at lowwater. The next morning the ship came, but they were fast and could not stir till about noon. In the meantime, the ship master, perceiving how the matter was, sent his boat to be getting the men aboard whom he saw ready, walking about the shore. But after the first boat full was got aboard, and she was ready to go for more, the master espied a great company, both horse and foot, with bills, and guns and other weapons; for the country was raised to take them. The Dutch-man seeing that, swore his country's oath, 'sacremente,' and haveing the wind fair, weighed his anchor, hoist sails and away. The rest of the men that were in greatest danger, made shift to escape away before the troop could surprise them; those only staying that best might, to be assistant unto the women. But pitiful it was to see the heavy case of these poor women in this distress; what weeping and crying on every side, some for their husbands, that were carried away in the ship as is before related; others not knowing what should become of them, and their little ones; others again melted in tears, seeing their poor little ones hanging about them, crying for fear, and quaking with cold. Being thus apprehended, they were hurried from one place to another, till in the end they knew not what to do with them; for to imprison so many women and innocent children for no other cause (many of them) but that they must goe with their husbands, seemed to be unreasonable and all would cry out of them; and to send them home again was difficult, for they aledged, as the truth was, they had no homes to go to, for they had either sold, or otherwise disposed of their houses and livings. To be shorte, after they had been thus turmoiled for a good while, and conveyed from one constable to another, they were glad to be rid of them in the end upon any terms; for all were wearied and tired with them. In the meantime they (poor souls) endured misery enough."

Windrow folded the paper. "You could have fared worse. You are alive, none of you hanged and," as he touched her two ears, "you possess these entire and neat on your gracious head. Also," as he held her nose a flickering instant, "there is no slit of a knife through here."

Mary Windling gave her news. "First you should know father was on the ship—and John Spong. They are safe in Holland. We have a letter from William Bradford. Death came near to some of our best loved. We still hold our breath and give thanks. Here is the letter." She reached into her bundle, unfolded a paper for him and his eyes gathered it.

Oliver Windrow fingered and rustled the letter, shook it at arm's length, rehearsed what he had read. "What a piece of paper with a few scribbles on it can tell! We can see them on that small sailing vessel. Strong men choke, their shoulders shake, they sob at the last view of their loved ones on shore. They wave their hands asking, 'Shall we ever see them again? Oh, that we could be there to help them against the men with guns and swords and catchpoles. Oh, my baby! Oh, my good wife!' Night comes, no clothes but those on their backs. The night wind goes through them. The hours pass and the winds bite deeper in their bones. The squall becomes a gale and the gale a hurricane. Wave after wave taller than the ship itself leaps before them as though to bury the ship. Down between tall waves they see the ship ride. They see it climb up one long wave after another, riding that wave till it falls into a trough between two waves. By some wonder they do not go down. They forget the compass. No use to steer a course for Holland. They ask only to save the ship from sinking. The driving rain pelts them. Day after day for seven days no sun, moon, star. They are lost on the sea, the ship out of its course four hundred miles and near the coast of Norway. Fourteen days of cold, hunger, rain, black thoughts of dear ones left on the shore of England at the Humber River, salt water soaking every timber of the ship, every stitch of their clothes, their ribs under their wet skins salt-soaked like beef pickled in brine. Not only the landsmen scared of their lives and of going to the sea bottom. The mariners, the hardened seamen, they despaired, they gave over all, they shrieked and cried as though the ship had foundered and would go down. I can see a sailorman crying, 'This lousy slobbering sea has gone crazy and wants to tear the ship to pieces.' We can see the Scrooby congregation men, the Lord's free people, Pilgrims seeking a free church of their own, on their knees in the driving rain on the deck, water in their ears, water in their mouths when they open to speak. While the mariners cry, 'We sink, we sink,' the kneeling Pilgrims call, 'Yet Lord thou canst save, yet Lord thou canst save.' Their God was with them, they believed, when the winds began to go down and the sky clearing. Again one morning they saw the sun that had hidden for seven days. Again at night they could witness the ancient stars moving in quiet and dignity over the sky saying, 'Ye may take hope to your hearts again.' The Dark One, the Archdemon, had put a spell on the sea and their God had overcome the spell and bade the sea be quiet as the Son of God did at Galilee. So they believed. So they came safe to the harbor where people came flocking, admiring their deliverance. Meaning to sail two hundred miles they sailed one thousand."

Oliver Windrow spoke partly in low monotone, with pauses and accents that soothed Mary, who closed her eyes and seemed near sleep as his quiet word picture of the storm went on. At the words "We sink" she moved her head, slowly half-opened her eyes, gave him a look he answered with a slow nod. In the comfort of the end, somewhere there, she faded into sleep. He kissed her ever so softly on a

74

strand of hair over an ear and stole gently away. After a while, when he was puttering at a kettle over the fire, Mary sat up for the first time, called him and talked songlike her dreaminess:

"Precious Oliver Windrow, friend of man and kinsman of the angels. I heard you tell the end of the storm. You made the sea quiet and sleepy with your words. I fell into a catnap. Since I saw you I have seen the sea. I must tell you, for the first time, you should know, I saw it. The sea folds away, from you like a mystery. You can look and look at it and mystery never leaves it. It runs away from your eyes and loses itself against the sky. It will flow away from you deep-blue with green shadows. Then with the sun lost in the overcast of the sky it will change its face and you know not where the sea ends and the sky begins. And when you listen to the sea that you heard brawling and roaring an hour ago, it is now as though you listened to nothing and as though the sea might be saying, 'I am nothing and you are nothing and we are all nothings and it is good to look in yourself and find yourself to be nothing, only gray mist and gray air moving from gray empty shores to gray empty horizons.' My first thought then was, 'I am a believer and I shall not let the atheist sea make me an atheist.' Then the gray mist folded away. So slow, so easy, so thin and fine the gray mist went folding away you could not swear what the sea was doing or going to do. A long fork of violet drifted down into a pool of silver light for a moment and then was gone. Then came two bars of gold crying their lights and crossing each other like the letter X and they were gone quite as soon as they came. Then the west began a march of changing banners and chariots. I saw Elijah in red-gold robes with a sweeping beard of fire riding in the last and greatest of the chariots vanishing into horizon shadows, coming to a standstill one moment before the shadows gathered him. And it was as though he bowed and threw a kiss to five evening stars that began glimmering over the marvelous night quiet of the sea. Then my thought came, 'I did wrong by you not knowing you are both friend and stranger, oh shambling and mysterious sea. You are one of God's belongings. He made you and shaped you for his own ends, as He did the sky and the sea's sunset lights.' I saw the sea is a believer having many dark fathoms such as I find when I look deep in myself and loneliness presses deep and hard, the kind of loneliness that whispers, 'I'll be good for you if you know how to use me.'"

Oliver smiled. "Thank you for making me acquainted with the sea. From this time on when I think of you I shall think of the sea and when I think of the sea I shall think of Mary Windling. She is the sea herself."

"I was a victim of the sea and shall tell you about it. First I must wash the sleep from my face."

Oliver Windrow led her to a wooden basin, poured from a bucket: "Fresh from a rain off the eaves yesterday."

She held her wet palms to her face long and cool. "Now, may I have a chair and we will talk?"

"No, you must lie down again. You need rest, my girl. Your bones were too sore when you came in at that door this noon. Where did you sleep last night?"

"Among five cedars like those in the home we sold. Sweet-smelling cedars a few miles out of Bawtry."

"The ground wet from that rain yesterday."

"We scraped pine needles in heaps and slept like good Egyptians, gypsies, fortunetellers. At noon we shared food with gypsies who told our fortunes. May I see your hand?" She took Windrow's hand, studied the palm, and with mock gravity, "You shall live long. Misfortunes I see. One, two, three, heavy misfortunes and you shall come out of them laughing. You shall meet a good woman, very fair, her skin like fresh cream, her hair shining like oat straw. You will have two sons and a daughter. The daughter will be a wastrel and go to France, then Spain, dance her life away, marrying a rich Spanish merchant and when he threatens to kill her she runs away to Peru in South America with an English gold-seeker and they are never heard of again."

"And the two sons?"

"One will be a poet and die in a brawl with another poet over which writes the better. But two of his poems will be famous and you will be pointed out in London as the father of the famous poet."

"And the other son?"

"He will be a preacher. He will make a great name for burning words. Twice he will be tried for heresy and fail of conviction. You and his mother will live with him and he will preach to you and you will say you are as good a believer as he, only your belief is your own and kept secret."

"You are keen this day, Mary. Had Scrooby congregation and its men not gotten you, the fortunetellers and the dancers would have. You are a wild girl."

"You light up the wild in me. Ever it has been you that makes every fool in me brighter and more daring. I was a shut-mouth till I met you."

"Now lay you down here on the pallet and tell me of the hard going, of what happened."

Windrow sat crosslegged on the floor alongside the pallet. She closed her eyes, lay silent a few minutes, then:

"A small bark was hired to carry the women and children and the baggage. We sailed from the Idle River to the Trent, then to the Humber River. Not being room for the men it was better they should walk overland. They walked in couples, spread far apart, not wishing to seem an expedition or a strange company that would invite questions. All must be secret, as though we were lawbreakers, conspirators, criminals, avoiding the town officers and the country constables. Our boat sailed chiefly at night so we would not be seen in the daytime

76

and questioned. Day and night the women wondered would their men be there to meet them at the appointed place by the sea near Grimsby. Or would their men fall into the clutches of justice and lie in a jail and not be there when we came? At last our boat came to where the broad Humber River joins the sea. There we met our men and saw they were safe. On a common in between Grimsby and Hull, we met, no town near by. There, yes, our men on solid land and we being on rough waters that rocked our boat. The farm and village women took seasick, sick of the sight of the endless, meaningless sea, sick with the tossing of the boat. They went to the deck rail and gave up their guts. Sick too with news of the ship to take us to Holland not arrived and again mayhap betrayal. What to do? The seamen obliged us. They ran the bark into a creek and we stood in low water that was quiet and soothed us. The next morning there was the Dutch ship waiting for us. We saw a boat from the ship go to shore and take out, filled with as many of our men as it would hold. It got them aboard the ship. It stood ready to go for the remainder of our men when there was a crying out loud, oh, such a crying. On horse, on foot came riding men and running men. We could see them, man-hunters. The Dutch shipmaster saw he could not reach our remaining men in time, saw our boat helpless because the tide had gone out and left us on a mud flat waiting the tide. So there we stood wringing our hands and crying to high heaven, while the Dutch ship hoisted sail and got away to the open sea for Holland. We raised our hands high and waved them. We put kerchiefs in our hands and waved to our men crying, 'Good-by and God keep you.' Of our men on shore some ran fast as their legs would take them, knowing they could do more good if they were free than if clapped in jail. Some men stayed, knowing we would need their help and comfort. So we were taken and our baggage and belongings examined. And officers spoke of money as though it might help us if we had enough of it.

"From then on it was one misery after another, in mean houses under guard, days with little or no food for women and children, men behind bars in narrow cells with damp straw to sleep on, some coughing with lung sickness, one racked with scurvy. Mothers with little ones hanging about them crying with fear and quaking with cold. They learned crying would do no good and like their mothers took on stony faces, made moan and gave whimpers so low scarce to be heard. From one justice to another, from town to town, we were sent. We perplexed them, uncertain of our crime or evidence against us, having found we were not thieves nor smugglers but children of God seeking to accommodate the King and the authorities by leaving a land where we had to worship in secret from Sabbath to Sabbath. To imprison so many women and innocent children, for no other cause than they sought to go with their husbands and fathers, this seemed unreasonable to the small magistrates who examined us. And what justice

77

would lie in their sending us back to our old homes where we had parted with our houses, lands and livings? Onc constable after another wearied of us and sent us to another constable who on occasion would return us to the constable who had us in the first instance. After there was a sufficiency of this turmoil they said they would be glad to be rid of us on any terms. So we have scattered and wandered, seeking means whereby to make passage to Holland and join our men. Hither and yon have been folk who do not believe as we do, yet they are impressed with the godly carriage and Christian behavior of the men and women of our Scrooby congregation. They have helped with generous hearts so that by now, even now, a few of our women with their children have joined their men in Holland."

Mary paused, then went on. "Some have shrunk and lost their faith in being Pilgrims. Others go on. Mother's heart beats strong as ever. We will go."

"And John Spong? Still the one man enshrined in your heart? He was on the ship in the storm?"

"Yes and yes. On our last day at Scrooby, before taking the boat, we were married before Elder Brewster. And think it not silly—when I put on my one best dress and fixed myself before the looking-glass and combed my hair the prettiest way I knew and tied one satin ribbon the way it should look for a wedding, then I stooped and took off my right shoe. Then without looking in the glass again I ran to where I was to give myself away for life. I will mimic it for you. Like this I tied the satin ribbon, looking in the glass. Like this I took a last look. Like this I took off my right shoe. Like this I ran away and like this put on my shoe again."

"I know that superstition. No spell would get on you."

"John wanted it that way. No harm—and like playing a game with the Devil."

"And now? Now you seek in Scrooby and Austerfield the means for you and your mother to make passage to Holland?"

"You read it."

"I shall find the means for you. You well knew I would, and with a glad heart."

"What you give shall be a loan, a trust in our distress. Our hope is you will be paid back, though your heart tells you that your sort of loving-kindness can never be paid back. It is matter not to be rewritten nor blotted away."

"What I lack for your passage to Holland others I can find here will supply. Write on this sheet the amount. Tomorrow night it shall be in your hands. Now lie back. Forget your miseries like you would blind rats and lousy curs. Let yourself dream of that sea sunset, the fork of violet and two bars of gold and Elijah kissing his hand to the first evening stars."

She sank back toward rest.

Oliver talked to himself, preparing the evening meal. "My child, my daughter she is. It can and does so happen. I read her like her own father can never read her. Her husband will not fathom her deeper than I do. She is mine and knows it because she knows I give her away. Freely and with no questions I give her to whomsoever she wishes to be given. It is my secret that I could have been there when she was taken in marriage, to shout if the words rose, 'Who giveth away this woman?' the reply 'I do! I do!' "

Mary Windling stirred, coughed, shook with a coughing spell. Her mother had risen and she and Oliver leaned over Mary. The long coughing over, she looked from her mother to Oliver. "I am sorry. I should not make trouble for you."

Windrow brought a pot of syrup with a spoon. "A throat balsam—pine and honey."

He handed it to the mother who spooned it to her daughter. Windrow comforted the mother, "Rest and good food she needs. That is all."

The room darkened with twilight and dusk. Oliver lighted candles, brought food to Mary and her mother, insisted they rest and sleep. He blew out four candles one by one. There was darkness and quiet.

The next morning shortly after daybreak Mary Windling woke, stretched and sat up with a lighted face, refreshed and renewed by good food and deep sleep. She had opened her eyes half-dozing, looked at her mother still asleep. Her eyes roved to the corner where Oliver had made his pallet of rushes. There sat a large woman holding her breasts to a nursing child. Mary got up and walked softly over to see three other figures, a man and two boys sleeping. She recognized Miles Goodridge and his family, spoke softly to the nursing mother and returned to her pallet. She had fallen into a doze. The mother and nursing baby had gone to sleep. The room was quiet.

The big front door opened. A woman entered. She took off a black headkerchief. Her head of flaxen hair flowed down in long ropes of braid. Her large blue eyes were serene. Below medium height, rather massive of build, having ease of movement, curves from head to toe, an impressive, powerful torso. She found a broom and swept the room with no disturbing of sleepers. When sweeping near Mary's bed, Mary awakening, whispered, "Good morning" and at no response whispered a loud, "Good morning." And it was as though the woman had not heard.

The woman attended to the fire, carried ashes from the fireplace outdoors, returned and began preparing a porridge, showing a complete familiarity as to where things were and what to do.

Mary went, "Psstt! Psstt!" Mary got up and sidled over to the woman bowing face to face, smiled and whispered, "Good morning."

The woman bowed gravely with quick blinking eyes and a slight

79

trace of a smile. Then as the woman proceeded with mixing meal to go in a pot over the fire Mary spoke softly though pertinently, "Where do you come from, good woman? What is your name? And where has gone Oliver Windrow?"

Again it was as though she was unheard, and Mary, "You refuse to speak? Are you proud? Has not Oliver Windrow told you pride is the first of the seven deadly sins?"

And again no response, and Mary, "You wish to be wooden?"

Mary went to the door, stepped out. The woman finished preparing porridge and had it on the fire. She had begun scrubbing the large table in the middle of the room when Mary entered with "It is a golden morning with the sun shedding brightness from a great dome of blue sky as though the world is very young and all wrongs men have done one to another are forgiven."

The woman finished scrubbing the table and had laid out a pile of knives and spoons she had washed earlier and now was polishing till they shone, this while seated at the table. Mary seated herself opposite. Something dawned on Mary after a long look at the woman's silent, composed and admirable face. Mary went to a cabinet and brought out a goose quill pen, a pot of ink and sheets of paper, seated herself and wrote, "Greetings, and I wish you well."

The woman in turn took pen and paper, writing, "Sweet morning. God love you."

Mary writing, "My name Mary Windling—and yours?"

The woman writing, "Matilda Bracken."

Mary: "What do you do?"

Matilda: "Whatever should be done my hands find to do."

"Why are you so kind?"

"Oliver Windrow said, so be it."

"What are you to Oliver Windrow?"

"I cool his anger."

"And if he is not angry?"

"I wake him to anger."

"Is anger so good?"

"His kind of anger."

"You would be yoked to him?"

"Yes."

"And he would be yoked to you?"

"No. Yes. No. Mayhap. No."

"May I thank you for your loving-kindness to him?"

"If also you thank yourself for being a sweet ghost to him."

"How should you know I am such to him?"

"He has said so once for every high night star in the sky. Now sleep with you once more. There will be food."

Mary returned to her bed. Matilda Bracken shined knives and spoons. Mary tried to sleep. Twice she sat up straight and looked at

Matilda, then sank into another doze. But not till once more she had sat up, caught the eyes of Matilda and thrown her a kiss swift. Matilda put the knuckles of her right hand under chin and moved the fingers right and left, then gestured with her right hand at her drooped head a go-to-sleep sign.

Noon arrived. Matilda Bracken finished trimming and scraping carrots and sat peeling potatoes. The Goodridge family was stirring and saying they would get up. Mary and her mother had completed washing their faces in the wooden basin and drying with a gray linen towel.

There was a sound of horse hoofs outside, voices and feet scrambling. The door opened and there entered Oliver Windrow with an assured and elegant gentleman and lady.

The Goodridges all came to a standing position, the mother holding her baby. Mary and her mother and Matilda likewise stood. One of high rank had entered. It was a summons to show respect by standing. Oliver Windrow pointed to each one. They bowed low one by one, including the mother and baby, as Windrow gave the names, while the gentleman and the lady gave a curt, precise nod of the head at each name. Of course, on entering, Oliver had made the announcement, "Sir Reginald Overstreet and Lady Bathsheba Overstreet of Hawksby Manor."

Sir Reginald Overstreet beckoned to all, "Come close in a circle here that your ears may not miss what I am about to say." They all came closer. He continued:

"About midmorning of this day Master Oliver Windrow arrived at Hawksby Manor," this in a rather high piping voice faintly touched with humor as though a man can't help his voice. "He was dusty and footsore," this with a slight chuckling and a sidelong look at Oliver, who grinned. "He left his place here in the dark before daybreak when a light rain had ended. In a roadside thicket two miles from here he heard a child crying, an infant, so his ears told him. There he found the Goodridge family, somewhat wet and hard put where to go dry themselves and sleep. He brought them back here and set out again for Hawksby Manor, pausing at the house where Matilda Bracken resides with her father and mother, requesting her to proceed here and make herself useful."

He cast a glance at Matilda as did the others. Her blue eyes did several blinks. Her head and shoulders straightened as though she knew whatever was being said of her. She had pride rather than shame. Her glance finally rested on Oliver Windrow, who grinned to her and for the first time that day she definitely smiled.

Sir Reginald continued: "We welcome Oliver Windrow at Hawksby Manor. We have known him long and my father knew his father. He told us of your misfortunes, of how you are sinned against rather than sinning and every last gold piece and copper farthing he has

81

hidden about this house he is prepared to lend to your enterprise. Yet such monies as he has would need doubling to carry Jasper Windling's wife and daughter to Holland and considerably more of the wherewithal is required for the five Goodridges. I gave Oliver Windrow plain words as man to man that I could not join with him in this undertaking to help such Dissenters and Separatists as you. Howsoever, I told him, I would summon Lady Overstreet and she would hear him and we would deliberate. To her ears," and here he cast a half-merry glance at Lady Overstreet, "and to mine he poured out his tale at greater length adding fresh and more harrowing details of what you have undergone. I made plain that I am opposed to your devices and your teachings, that I think you are doing harm to the Established Church and to the kingdom with the unrest you stir. You go too far in your contempt of what is tried, established and true. Bad manners, evil manners, some of your speakers have shown. You wish to pray in your own way without use of the Book of Common Prayer though I have yet to hear one of you make a prayer equal to those found in the established Book. Thus what is in my mind I make clear to you, hoping you will come to more charity in your hearts for those who oppose you in doctrine. Nevertheless the officials, constables and clergy, who approve of the persecution accorded you, those who have harried you from place to place and made you distress and misery, they, in such actions, have put themselves more in the wrong than you. In any case whatever doubts I might have had about helping you were swept away when Lady Overstreet gave her immediate and unreserved decision that Hawksby Manor must do for you what can be done. To be brief and sum up the matter, we gave Master Oliver Windrow our word that if he chooses to strip himself of all available coin of the realm he has at hand, we will join with him and do the best we can. You should all know, naturally, in this matter, that the sooner you act the better. Each day you put off leaving for Holland, each day you stay hereabouts, you may be found by prying manhunters who place undue value on their own importance and who are so completely self-righteous that they cannot understand any part of what you mean when you explain yourselves. And now I shall have a view of the block of oak from which our friend is to carve a head of the Christ for the great hall of Hawksby Manor."

He walked, following Oliver to the oak block, and stood in contemplation of it a few moments. "You have been correct, Oliver Windrow, in saying you will have difficulties in bringing from this inanimate wood the head and face of the Saviour of Mankind. Lady Overstreet and I shall join our prayers with yours that it comes through a noble and exalted work." He went toward the door, taking the arm of Lady Overstreet, his parting words at the door: "I will lose standing if it is known I have helped the likes of you, howsoever deserving you are. Get out of England and lose no time in doing it. Get out as fast as you can. These are troubled days and you may save yourselves further misery by moving fast. I have gone over with Oliver Windrow the practical matters and he will see to you. My final advice is that some of your people talk too much. You enjoy dispute and argument too much. Tell them there are moments when quiet is a help. And may God speed you." He stepped toward the baby, kissed it on the forehead and went out with Lady Overstreet and Oliver Windrow. The sound of a cracking whip was heard, horse hoofs and rolling wheels.

Oliver came in and gave particulars. "A boat has been hired to take you as a party to Grimsby where a ship sails soon for Amsterdam, Holland. Sir Reginald will get word to an officer at Grimsby, an old acquaintance who has none of the customary loathing for you. He will give you every help toward getting away." This Oliver told slowly and deliberately as though the outlook was bright and the plans could not fail. He gave a nod to Matilda, pointed to the fireplace and the food, then to the table: "Matilda Bracken will set a table for us. We shall eat with glad hearts. She will make bundles of food for your journey. On the doorstep are two hams well baked, a large cheese and a bag of rye loaves, all from Hawksby Manor, which should last you to Grimsby and farther. Now get ready to eat. Wash your fingers, you little jackanapes," tousling the hair of the two Goodridge boys. "A cart and horse with a good man for driving will be here midafternoon and take you to the boat."

The Goodridges and Sarah Windling proceeded to washing themselves, and making their bundles.

Mary's face through all of this had been alive and changeful. While others were about their readying she spoke low-voiced to Oliver. "Not an easy going away, greatheart. Your wit and love sink deep in me. They will come back to me in noonday sun and black midnight wherever I am." She took from her bosom the bronze keepsake. "This has the right tumult. Please remember I said that much of this sweet token. It goes where I go so long as breath remains in me." She nodded her head toward the silent Matilda Bracken at her duties. "We talked this morning, writing our talk. You taught her to write as you taught me. And your two pupils talked about their writing teacher. I am glad you have her."

"How do you know I have her?"

"I asked her, 'What are you to Oliver Windrow?' and she wrote, 'I cool his anger.' Deep under she is enough like you to be yours for long."

"What else did you two women write?"

"I asked what if you are not in anger? She wrote, 'I wake him to anger.' To my question, 'Is anger so good?' she wrote, 'His kind of anger.' I did not know anger could be so strange. We wrote like two honest women. I would not have believed it. She said she would be yoked to you but only you could know whether you would be yoked to

83

her. Last of all she thanked me for being a sweet ghost to you. And when I asked how could she be sure I was any sweet ghost to you, she answered you had said so over again once for every high night star in the sky. She will comfort my thinking of you."

"In a world of too many women who talk too much there are merits of salt, bread and wine in a silent woman."

"You will marry Matilda Bracken?"

"No man knows whom he will marry till it happens. Your John Spong, the man you married, would be food for the fishes of the North Sea, his bones now cleaned white, but for the whim and grace of God."

"What you do with one simple gloomy thought!"

"I am neither simple nor gloomy. I read it as written I shall never see you again."

"We shall meet once more before parting for all time. I do not know how nor where it shall be. The bones of my dancing feet say it. And after that one time when we meet again I shall journey far to desperate shores and eat bitter bread and see blood and moaning."

"Now it is you simple and gloomy."

"You stay with the England you love. It is ordered that I leave the England I love. Yet neither of us is simple nor gloomy in saying again, 'There is change in the air. Though freedom comes slow it does come. And there are hidden resolves in the hearts of the people of England. They shall be wrought out on the anvils of time.'"

"Will you pray for my Christ head, Mary?"

"No day, no night I am gone that I will not be saying, 'Let the best priceless heart of Oliver Windrow shine in the Christ head he carves.'"

"I shall drop chisel and mallet at the dusk of many an evening and reach long invisible arms wherever you are."

"The table is almost ready. It is sweet beyond words we could have had this last talk."

"All has been said. It will come back to me many a time in the presence of a silent woman who understands better than ourselves how certain it is that there must be struggle and wise accommodation to cruel circumstance before there can be love."

"And who can say God has not fixed an afterworld or a thousand afterworlds where we poor seekers can go on seeking what we did not find in this hungering and groping world?"

"Thy God shall be mine and mine shall be thine, Mary. That shall stand out over all the miles and wild winds blowing between us. Each shall stand with the other to banish fear. With fear gone we can welcome death or any circumstances worse than death." He kissed her softly on the pale mouth.

"So be it, greatheart."

They ate. They moved food, bundles, belongings out to the horses

84

and saddlebags. The big room was empty. They were saying good-by. There was laughter, outcry, voices diminishing.

Oliver entered, took up chisel and mallet, began on the Christ head, Matilda straightening the room. In one pause of his work he talked briefly with Matilda Bracken in a pantomime and finger-letter speech at which they were improving, telling Matilda, "She asked me naught and I told her naught of her beloved husband's beloved father dying of jail fever and scurvy in the Clink—because of his thoughts that harmed no man. Her cross hangs heavy enough for her now."

The lashes of Matilda's great eyes of cornflower-blue swept downward slowly twice and on the sorrowing red mouth of her nodding face was written fellowship with those who sorrow.

PART TWO

Chapter 6

Store We Up Therefore Patience

THE boy Freeborn, ten years old, had a pale flower face, black hair smooth along the temples, black eyes and the hair of the eyebrows clear black pencilings. The boy Oliver, nine years old, had a like face. They had been taken for twins.

Their big sister Remember, eleven years old, had blue eyes, bright chestnut hair, shaggy brown eyebrows. Her bony face, wide mouth, skin somewhat enamel-like rather than flower-soft, gave her a look of strength the boys were lacking.

Their first home had been in a house in the Stincksteeg, a Dutch name translated into either Stench Lane or Stink Alley, a winding street so narrow "men with arms just a little longer could reach across and shake hands."

This sunny May day of the year 1620, Freeborn, Oliver and Remember walked along the Donckeregracht to their favorite three knotholes at the boards of that covered canal. Standing with eyes at these peepholes they saw ships and barges, boats and sailormen, flags, masts, men at oars, ropes and hawsers coiled on decks, a cook out of the galley for a breath of fresh air and wiping sweat off his forehead, vessels so long from stem to stern that one eye at a knothole caught only parts of a ship as it passed. On one ship they saw bags of wool piled high, later another ship of wool cargo. In church and at home the children had seen wool combers and carders, remembering one in their house with flecks of wool over his clothes, wool dust in his hair and ears.

The ships went gliding by, a sea smell on them, dripping brine. One with ragged masts and a hull green and thick with barnacles seemed to say, "I have been to sea many times—where have you been?" On another ship large tall men with no two sets of mustaches and beards alike, danced, capered, and laughed, as though good news had come, two of them with monkeys on their shoulders. Here a seaman shook his fist at another who stuck out his tongue and put a thumb and wiggling fingers to his nose. There a captain bawled at his crew and Freeborn at his knothole repeated their "Aye aye, sir." On other ships quiet men stood ready to put in at a wharf and unload cargo. Once last year on an outgoing ship they saw a tipsy seaman

86

playing a fiddle for two other tipsy ones who tried to dance a horn-pipe, and the boys heard Remember say, "They please Satan." On another day they saw four men holding playing cards before their faces and Oliver called out, "They read the Devil's Bible."

They saw the outside world go by there in that canal, the Donckere-gracht. They had heard of the English, the French, the Flemish and Walloons, the Swedes, Danes and Russians. Here they saw them go by in ships. This knothole show had wonder for their eyes, from Other countries Other faces with Other tongues. Once on a ship that moved close to them the three children on a summer day had seen two dark-skinned men begin a fight. They couldn't understand the name one of them called the other. But they saw the fists flying and the blood run on one man's face, as the ship moved beyond their knotholes.

Freeborn had asked afterward, "Remember, did you hear the name he called the other man that started the fight?"

"I heard. I couldn't understand. It was jabber I never heard before."

"Then the other man, if he had been like you and didn't know what the bad name meant, he wouldn't have hit at the fellow that called him the name?"

"I wouldn't be sure. The man that called the bad name made a wicked face with it. He wanted to fight. He was mad."

They started home this May day. On the way they stopped to look where two cripples sat on a bench in the sun. Tall blond long-legged men, their hats off, the sunshine falling on their straggly hair and ruddy weatherworn faces. One had a crutch taking the place of his left leg. He didn't interest the three children for they had seen him before and a dozen one-legged men in the city like him. The other one they had heard most about. They could see, as they came along, his right sleeve hung loose and an arm gone. They saw too it must be the other side of his head where they should look. They were shy about it. They couldn't walk up and stare at what they had heard of, at what they were curious to see. They would have had manners enough for that without their mother having taught them a certain reverence for cripples and particularly this one.

They played at chasing each other, back and forth and around the bench where the two men sat in easy and friendly talk. They stole glances as they ran, looked out of eye corners. They saw what they had meant to see. They ran up the street, slowed to a walk, and Freeborn said to Remember, "You don't have to cry about it."

"I'm not crying."

"Your eyes show wet."

"What if they do? Have I ever yet seen where an ear was cut off?"

"It hurt you to look."

"Let's not talk till we get home."

Remember had heard other old men tell about it, how the horse-

87

man's sword had come down as though to cleave the soldier's head in two and the soldier had moved his head so the blade scraped down along the skull-bone and took off hair, skin—and an ear.

The boys had never cared, as Remember did, about the wars those two had seen and the great men who led the Dutch people in those wars. From others, from Dutch children who could speak English, and from her mother mostly, Remember had heard the stories and they haunted her. It was forty-six years ago that the people of this city of Leyden at first hungered, then starved and saw thousands die of starvation, while a powerful Spanish army waited outside to take the city. From May till October no food came into the city. Dogs, cats, rats were killed and eaten. A plague struck six thousand dead. For weeks the wind had blown from the east and when on October 1 it shifted, dikes were cut and waters flooded in, bringing a fleet, and putting the Spanish army on the run.

At the head of the Dutch people in that war and other wars stood William the Silent, William of Orange. Remember had learned to say the name like her mother did, sort of holding her breath. She had asked, "William the Silent, William of Orange, did he look like Moses or Joshua or St. Paul or others in the Bible?" And her mother, "An old man who saw him told me he was tall, well built, with a dark-skinned face and brown hair and eyes, that's all I know." He would fight a war, said her mother, losing one battle after another but in the end winning the war and against heavy odds.

"How did he die?" asked Remember.

"His enemy King Philip of Spain offered twenty-five thousand crowns in gold to any man who would kill William of Orange and 'rid the world of such a pest.' King Philip used those words. To him William of Orange was a pest and he offered gold to pay any slayer of the Dutch leader. Two or three tried and at last one of them did put a pistol bullet through William of Orange."

"Why was he fighting so many wars all the time?"

"He had to. They came to him. They wanted to take over Holland and make it their own. He beat them. Out of it came the Dutch Republic. Freedom of worship, liberty. You could read the Word of God from your own Bible, because the Dutch people kept on fighting alongside of William the Silent, William of Orange who believed in people, books, schools, let everybody read and write and talk things over."

And Remember knew her own heart this May afternoon on the way home. The man with the missing ear had fought five years in armies of William of Orange. The long tangled ugly scar, where the ear had been, William of Orange had touched it with his hand once and said to the man that war costs and freedom costs and a free people pay for their freedom. Later the man paid his right arm for Dutch liberty and had to leave the army. So Remember's mother told it. And Remember was near crying, hardly held the tears back: she felt something sacred in that man with the missing ear. Her mother's words came back to her. "The day they buried William of Orange, the Dutch people, young and old, low and high, came with their tears and wept without shame. They laid him to rest to wait for the Doomsday trumpets knowing he would meet those trumpets not afraid."

Remember said to herself, "I could weep today for that man with his ear gone—like the Dutch everywhere wept when they laid away the great William the Silent, William of Orange."

Twelve years had passed since the little congregation left Scrooby, England, for Leyden, Holland, where in 1620 they numbered some three hundred members. At first they held services in this house and that on the Lord's Day. On weekdays they scrabbled their livings at many kinds of work—in wool, fustian, say, bombazine, silk, felt, at making beer, buttons, gloves, shoes, pumps, pipes, blocks, at carpentry, printing, barbering, at merchandising, at teaching English in private lessons to students at the University of Leyden as did Elder Brewster.

Straight across from the south transept of an immense and old-time cathedral, no longer in Roman Catholic use, named the Pieterskerk or St. Peter's, they bought from Heer van Poelgeest a big old house for church meetings and a parsonage where the minister John Robinson lived. In an open lot alongside they built twenty-three houses, each of two and a half stories, tall, thin, high-gabled houses that stood tight against each other as pointed dominoes in a row. Near the very center of the city was this. Around them swirled the life of the 80,000 people of Leyden, two branches of Der Rhyn, the old Rhine River, entering the city and joining, canals and bridges in any direction you chose to walk, tenement districts where the poor looked out on crooked narrow shadowed streets. And Leyden had come to a great name for its university, for its baize and camlet cloths, for its schools and the number of children who could read and write, and for liberty of religion.

The year 1620 it was, waters of time washing on the shores of Europe, the few clocks here and there telling twelve noon, twelve midnight— or five minutes to midnight—four years since Shakespeare died—ninety years since the first Bible printed in England—not yet two hundred years since the first books fresh with black sticky ink came off the first printing presses—only a century and a little more, less than the life of one grandmother and her child, since a Genoese navigator on Spanish ships put a foot on a new world and Magellan soon after set out on a ship that went round the world and proved the planet Earth to be global—and on the land over the plains and valleys of Europe the peasant, millions of peasants, and a peasant was, to the nobles and their clergy in general, a beast of the fields, a thing and a utensil, a service animal to be driven, deluded, managed, kept ignorant of the alphabet and of the Bible or other print to be read, to be held down in a proper place and made to obey through fear of the lash and hunger in the present and hell in the hereafter.

The year 1620 and the clocks said midnight here and five minutes to midnight there—the Spanish, Dutch, French, and English in a race for lands and colonies in the New World—English at Jamestown, Virginia, buying Negroes brought from the African Gold Coast, buying slave labor from Dutchmen on a warship—America become a place for speculations and bets, a gambler's dream and an investor's fever to kings, nobles, financiers, bishops of England, France, Spain, Holland—the bloodiest war that ever drenched middle Europe bursting to run its thirty-year course—and a bigoted palavering king of England on a satisfied throne besotted and unaware of a fanatic flame heaving and swaying under the upper human crust of Britain or of how soon Cavalier and Puritan would be at each other's throats in civil war— glimmerings of change and of daybreak lights—and beyond the smoke of a chaos never the same from day to day.

Parts of this time and its tumult were in the personal book of Mary Windling Spong, known to her in the twelve years of life and housekeeping in Leyden, bearing to John Spong a daughter they named Remember and sons they named Freeborn and Oliver.

Bright days, sun-washed and affirmative, had come to her brooding mind and romance-lighted heart, to her gaunt face, to her lithe torso and lean swift legs. And dank overcast days had dragged at her feet and had marked her mouth and forehead.

News had come from year to year, now by a letter, now by the report of someone in their church fellowship returning from a visit to Scrooby and Austerfield. Oliver Windrow and his wife Matilda Bracken, their first child, a boy named Geoffrey, eleven years old now, they called him "promising" and said he had the look of his father. Their twin girls would have been nine now. They were fair, flaxen-haired, blue-eyed, deaf-mute like their mother—and they with their father had in one week died of smallpox and the three of them in a wide pine box, their oat-straw curls next to his shoulders, laid in one grave. At Hawksby Manor Matilda and the boy Geoffrey were taken in as near to kinfolk.

In the great hall at Hawksby stood the massive Christ head of oak, impressive, exalted, mute yet vibrant and moving. The look of a torn and worn mankind was there, branches tangled in storm and fiery trial, roots fastened deep in many faiths. On the face were sealed strengths of sea and wind, of wide plains and slow rainfall giving soil and seed the promise of crops and harvest. It whispered rebuke and murmured comfort. Thus ran report.

Sir Reginald had one day asked Lady Bathsheba what meaning came to her most often when looking at it and she answered, "Blessed are ye that weep now: for ye shall laugh." She asked him the same and he spoke, "As ye would that men should do to you, do ye also to them likewise." Matilda Bracken stood by. She hesitated as between the lines she wrote, one "Charity vaunteth not itself and is not puffed up" and the other, "With what measure ye mete, it shall be measured to you again." And the boy Geoffrey spoke to the others words he made with sign language of his fingers to his mother, "It says what my father was always saying, 'Be not afraid.'"

Twelve crowded years they had been for Mary Windling Spong, from 1608 to 1620. Housewife she was, yokefellow, bedfellow, mother, sewing woman, scrubwoman, cook, dishwasher, mender, helpmeet for her husband and their brood of three children. Health permitting they were all there, the family of three, then four, then five, when the church held its Lord's Day meeting of two and three hours singing psalms, hearing Scripture reading, the sermon—and again in the afternoon services, discussion or "prophesying" by the men—no woman venturing ever to rise and speak. The children slept, listened, slept and if they winked or grimaced at other children later heard rebuke.

Their girl Remember, born seven months after they were married, there were friends who said, "She is a good woman and the child was born early" and gossips who chattered, "The baby spilled from her too soon and we do no wrong to ask if it began out of wedlock and the mother guilty of unlawful maternity, the father ungodly and the mother a slattern."

This furtive whispering grew less, though five years after Remember's birth Mary told of a woman persistent in referring to Remember as "the one born too early," and "the child that came too soon." Mary sent back word, "Tell that wench I can write my own name, more than she can do; tell her that foul and evil tongue of hers will bring no good to the innocent children of her household; and if that shakes no wrath in her ugly bosom, tell her I said she is a slut too lazy and dirty to lick herself; tell her I mind my own matters and if she cannot do the work of the Lord to the extent of keeping a decent tongue in her head I will grapple with her after Sabbath meeting and I will scratch her eyes out and tear the clothes off her."

From then on the busybody took it that Mary would make a scene and raise public scandal. From then on the gabmouth contented herself with raising her eyebrows at mention of the Spongs. Also the busybody could purse her lips in a way to her very significant and satisfying.

Mary clutched Remember to herself as having her own childhood English roots and flickers of the storm night of her betrothal. She saw Remember as dark, sober and quaint, not unlike her father, at

91

moments vivid and reckless as her mother. For others Mary never danced in the later years at Leyden, though often for Remember she stepped out and in quick footwork and twirls. Remember more than anyone else woke the high lights in her and brought back the shadow and voice of Oliver Windrow, his whims and blessings. Often with Remember on her knee the mother had given the girl a reading lesson from the lines on the bronze keepsake she still wore for more than memory's sake.

John had worked at hauling clay and preparing it for the potters in a small shop that made earthenware of reputation. Their potters' guild hesitated long at letting an English-born worker learn their craft. But he had proven himself. And now for two years he had been a full-fledged craftsman, either at the turning wheel shaping the clay into a well-formed high or low jug, or in the drying kiln or among the enamelers. With higher wages had come better victuals for the table and more of other comforts.

John had driven a fish cart ten weeks coming home with a fish smell in clothes, hair and skin. He had driven a night-wagon, emptying the accumulations of indoor privy closets, coming home at daybreak with heavy odors, getting his sleep during the day, Mary taking care that the crying of the baby Remember or other sounds, in their small two-room quarters, didn't wake him. She welcomed his change to driving a pottery clay cart when the only smell he brought home was faintly of the horse he curried and drove. She saw her husband step out and battle for wages, for a bare living, for the few coins a week that gave the family food, shelter and clothing, with always a small coin to drop in the collection box as it passed on the Lord's Day.

After her father Jasper Windling had died of a fever in the first year at Leyden, Mary had seen her mother come to live with them, to linger bedridden for a year and pass away. Through that trial John Spong with no complaints gave his help, Mary saying to him once, "as though she could be your own mother."

Mary and John had watched Jasper Windling in his last year with pity. They saw him a landsman who had lost his land, cut off from crops and animal husbandry. His city work as porter and hostler at an inn, then a sweeper, choreman and barrel-hoister and wagon-loader at a brewery, wore him down. He said he would go straight back to his land at Scrooby if he hadn't sold that land and given about all the money to their church. He died of the fever—and of an aching loneliness for his land, crops, animals—so his daughter believed.

The years went by. Mary came to a feeling that John less often had the bright and quaint flashes she had seen in him in their earlier years together. He had grown toward her for a time and then the growing came to an end. The quivers of his small dark-gray eyes, the comic squint of the left eye when lighted over something odd and original that pleased him and that he knew would please her, this as a habit was gone. She hoped he would move into some phase of the grandeur that had been part of his martyred father, and her hope had dwindled. It was a chance she had taken, aware she must not expect too much. She had prayed for him to move into the will, vision and depth of his father and the prayers had failed. She had fallen back on herself never failing to value him and give him full outpouring of her love for what he was and what he did of genuine worth.

Yet when John had sat in their church meeting on the day they voted, he gave his voice with the younger men who favored sailing across the Atlantic to found a colony. Holland would again before long be at war with Spain, reports ran. The children grew up in Leyden with misgivings among elders as to what forces outside their church were doing to the young ones. Young men of the congregation had become soldiers and sailors, lost touch with the church and their upbringing. Others of the youth had taken to drink and bawdyhouses. Girls had married Hollanders, Zeelanders, and drifted away. Always came the appeal of other faiths, Catholic, Calvinist, Presbyterian, Lutheran, Baptist, Anabaptist, Separatist, Arminian, Brownist, many shepherds of other and different flocks gathered for shelter in the Dutch Republic. Their own faith and church must test itself by what it did with its young people. They were to carve the future.

The congregation considered going in Dutch ships with Dutch financing and protection to small Dutch possessions in America, deciding against it. They were English and must hold to the English language, ways and customs. In sessions that ran till midnight and past the church leaders sat in discussions and listened to reports of their agents. Some seventy merchants and others, chiefly in England, had subscribed two funds for ships to take colonists across the Atlantic. After a seven-year settlement, they were to divide the profits and property, half to the investors and half to the colonists. Before signing a contract, the English managers reported that King James at first favored a charter confirming their rights to a local self-government and other privileges, including religious liberty. They reported the King asking wherefrom these highly religious colonists would get their profits and being told "fishing" had replied, "So God have my soul, 'tis an honest trade; 'twas the Apostles' own calling!"

Then at a later interview the King had changed his mind and thrown the whole matter over to the bishops and archbishops. Next the English managers wanted from the church at Leyden a statement that would clear up points around the question of how radical or disturbing their faith might be, how they stood on the matter of loyalty to the King whose domain they had fled in 1608. Signed by their minister John Robinson and their elder William Brewster, this document in reply, headed "The Seven Articles," dated the year 1618, went to the Council of England and to whom it might concern. The

93

document, reverent in tone, held dry, keen implications under its fair and solemn pledges, behind its façade. It read as follows:

1. To the confession of faith published in the name of the Church of England, and to every article thereof, we do, with the Reformed Churches where we live, and also elsewhere, assent wholly.

2. As we do acknowledge the doctrine of faith there taught, so do we the fruits and effects of the same doctrine, to the begetting of saving faith in thousands in the land, Conformists and Reformists as they are called, with whom also as with our brethren we do desire to keep spiritual communion in peace and will practice on our parts all lawful things.

3. The King's Majesty we acknowledge for supreme governor in his dominion, in all causes and over all persons; and that none may declare or appeal from his authority or judgment in any cause whatever, but that in all things obedience is due unto him, either active if the thing commanded be not against God's word, or passive, if it be, except pardon can be obtained.

4. We judge it lawful for His Majesty to appoint bishops, civil overseers, or officers in authority under him in the several provinces, dioceses, congregations, or parishes and govern them civilly according to the laws of the land, unto whom in all things they are to give an account, and by them to be ordered according to godliness.

5. The authority of the present bishops in the land we do acknowledge, so far as the same is indeed derived from His Majesty unto them, and as they proceed in his name, whom we will also therein honour in all things, and him in them.

6. We believe that no synod, classes, convocation, or assembly of ecclesiastical officers hath any power at all, but as the same by the magistrate given unto them.

7. Lastly, we desire to give unto all superiors due honour to preserve the unity of the spirit of all that fear God; to have peace with all men what in us lieth, and wherein we err to be instructed by any.

John Spong two days after hearing the Articles read to the congregation rubbed the stubble of an unshaven chin and said to Mary at the evening meal, "I am not clear in my mind—what do the Seven Articles mean?"

"Yes," chimed in Remember. "I can't make head or tail of them."

"Very gently," said Mary, smiling, her eyebrow shags moving up, "very gently they say we are tired of disputing true religion and would like to try living it. Very gently too they say we have no wish to fight any other church and above all we are not out to damage or destroy the Church of England. We will obey the King—unless he screws us too hard. Most of all we desire to plant and grow the tree of our own little church, whatever it may come to, while any and all others may plant and grow theirs. 'To have peace with all men what in us lieth, and wherein we err to be instructed by any,' that is plain enough gospel."

"Why didn't they say it like you say it?" chirped Remember.

"They were asked to put it in writing and it came out like writing. They were asked for words and poured out words—for the moneybag men and the lawyers in London. Yet even so they spoke fair and with meaning."

Remember was satisfied. So was her father. He was no longer glum and suspicious about the Seven Articles.

Yet more light was wanted by the English investors and authorities, on the points of what kind of people they were, why they planned to go straight on into such hardship, toil and danger as lay ahead. What special training or qualities did they have that might promise success? Considering how often colonies had bogged down in failure and death, what of these matters? So the Seven Articles were followed by Five Reasons shaped by strong men of wieldy strengths:

1. We verily believe and trust the Lord is with us, unto whom and to whose service we have given ourselves in many trials; and that he will graciously prosper our endeavours according to the simplicity of our hearts therein.

2. We are well weaned from the delicate milk of our mother country, and inured to the difficulties of a strange and hard land, which yet we have in a great part by patience overcome.

3. The people are, for the body of them, industrious and frugal, we think we may safely say, as any company of people in the world.

4. We are knit together in a body in a most strict and sacred bond and covenant of the Lord, of the violation whereof we make great conscience, and by virtue whereof we do hold ourselves straightly tied to *all care of each other's good*, and of the whole by every one, and so mutually.

5. Lastly, it is not with us as with other men whom small things can discourage, or small discontentments cause to wish themselves home again. We know our entertainment in England and Holland; we shall much prejudice both our arts and means by removal; if we should be driven to return, we should not hope to recover our present helps and comforts, neither indeed look ever for ourselves to attain unto the like in any other place during our lives, which are now drawing towards their periods.

This pleased John Spong. At breakfast and supper he repeated, "We are well weaned from the delicate milk of our mother country." They were telling those who wished to invest in them that already in degree they had learned patience and endurance in a strange land. They asked comparison with "any company in the world" on the points of "industry and frugality." Knit in sacred bonds of fellowship, they were "tied to all care of each other's good." No small things, no small discontentments, could make them wish themselves back home again. If driven to a return to England, they would claim none of their old helps and comforts. Could the financial investors, the Adventurers, as they were termed, ask more?

The Adventurers were satisfied. But the archbishop, whose consent to the charter was needed, frowned at the idea that a congregation should reserve to itself by vote to choose or dismiss its minister, its clergyman.

Across the years 1618 and 1619 the affair went up and down, hung by an eyelash, so it seemed to the waiting congregation at Leyden. They had reached King James with an appeal, finding him not unfriendly though for reasons of state he couldn't openly endorse them. He would "connive at them and not molest them, provided they carried themselves peaceably." Elder William Brewster, the trusted John Carver, and one Robert Cushman made connections in London that finally brought the charter. Articles of contract with the Adventurers were signed.

On the news reaching Leyden, a fast day was held. The congregation heard John Robinson preach from a text in the twenty-third chapter of I Samuel: "And David's men said unto him, see, we be afraid here in Judah: how much more if we came to Keilah against the hosts of the Philistines? Then David asked counsel of the Lord again." Less than fifty were to go and they made their preparations. Those having property turned it into money as best they could.

John and Mary Spong shared in the news, the excitements, promises and fears. They parted with furniture, larger pots and pans, gave away their surplus of few clothes, racked their brains to pick and choose of garments, blankets, cooking utensils, keepsakes, and so on, to go in two small chests. Then Mary, one day late in July of 1620, hand in hand with Remember, and John between the two boys, walked to their church meeting in the lower story of John Robinson's house. It was near noon. They had eaten no food in the morning. They had none at noon. It was a fast day. They were leaving Leyden, starting on their long winding trip to America, the next day. It was their farewell fast together.

They heard Robinson preach from his text in the eighth chapter of Ezra: "And there at the river by Ahava, I proclaimed a fast, that we might humble ourselves before our God, and seek of him a right way for us, and for all our children, and all our substance." He preached long on this, "spent a good part of the day very profitably" on it, noted William Bradford, "the rest of the time was spent in pouring out prayers to the Lord with great fervency, mixed with abundance of tears."

Remember, Freeborn and Oliver couldn't keep their eyes open through the preaching, the more sleepy for being hungry. They dozed off. The father nudged the boys. They awoke, sat up straight for a while, dozed off again. Mary let Remember sleep through the whole sermon. She and John realized that John Robinson was giving them the ripest fruit of his many years of contemplation. He charged them to follow him no farther than they found him to follow Christ, and to hold themselves as ready to receive new truth from any other messenger.

Edward Winslow wrote of the fast day, "We refreshed ourselves, after tears, with singing of psalms, making joyful melody in our hearts as well as with the voice, there being many of our congregation very expert in music; and indeed it was the sweetest melody that ever mine ears heard."

A peculiar group, with leadership and unity, no man denied his say or vote in church affairs, William Bradford wrote of it: "They grew in knowledge and other gifts and graces of the spirit of God, and lived together in peace and love and holiness. If at any time any differences arose, or offences broke out (as it cannot be, but sometimes there will, even amongst the best of men) they were ever so met with, and nipped in the head betimes, or otherwise so well composed, as still love, peace, and communion was continued; or else the church purged those that were incurable or incorrigible, when, after much patience used, no other means would serve, which seldom came to pass."

Pastor John Robinson, his able ministry and prudent government, it was he, more than any other one, who brought them to "many years in a comfortable condition, enjoying much sweet and delightful society and spiritual comfort together." Bradford wrote for himself and others. "Such was the mutual love and reciprocal respect that this worthy man had to his flock, and his flock to him, that it was hard to judge whether he delighted more in having such a people, or they in having such a pastor. His love was great toward them, and his care was always bent for their best good, both for soul and body. In civil affairs, in dangers and inconveniences, he was very helpful to their outward estate, and so was every way as a common father to them." Hard cases did Pastor Robinson handle? "None did more offend him than those that were close and cleaving to themselves, and retired from the common good; as also such as would be stiff and rigid in matters of outward order, and inveigh against the evils of others, and yet be remiss in themselves, and not so careful to express a virtuous conversation." Later Robinson might join them in America. He was staying to hold together the Leyden church.

Bradford saw the members of this congregation make good names for themselves. "Though many of them were poor, yet there was none so poor, but if they were known to be of that congregation, the Dutch (either bakers or others) would trust them in any reasonable matter when they wanted money. Because they had found by experience how careful they were to keep their word, and saw them so painful and diligent in their callings; yes, they would strive to get their custom, and to employ them above others, in their works, for their honesty and diligence."

High praise Bradford gave the men he worked with, gave freely, as true. Had they been slack, slow to pay debts, irresponsible, drinking up money and forgetting where it came from, or meaning well yet slipshod and lazy, he would have written so. When they slipped and it became a habit for them to slip, Bradford told it. He loved them for keeping sober, working hard, and with no flinching making themselves ready for the misery, monotony, dangers of sickness and death involved in sailing the Atlantic for the sake of a dream. A bare living, those years in Holland, was about all they had for heavy labor and long-hour workdays, noted Bradford. Many that came from England to try the liberty of Holland "could not endure the great labor and hard fare, with other inconveniences, and they left, as it were, weeping; yes, some preferred and chose the prisons in England, rather than this liberty in Holland, with these afflictions." So it was thought "if a better and easier place of living could be had, it would draw many and take away these discouragements. Yes, their pastor would often say, that many of those who both wrote and preached now against them, if they were in a place where they might have liberty and live comfortably, they would then practice as they did." What with "crosses and sorrows" old age was stealing on many of them, hastened by their difficulties.

What was harsh and bitter Bradford could tell without shrinking, as in recording what elders felt about their young. "As necessity was a taskmaster over them, so they were forced to be such, not only to their servants, but in a sort to their dearest children; the which as it did not a little wound the tender hearts of many a loving father and mother, so it produced likewise sundry sad and sorrowful effects. For many of their children, that were of best dispositions and gracious inclinations, having learned to bear the yoke in their youth, and willing to bear part of their parents' burden, were, often times, so oppressed with their heavy labours, that though their minds were free and willing, yet their bodies bowed under the weight of the same, and became decrepit in their early youth; the vigour of nature being consumed in the very bud as it were. But that which was more lamentable, and of all sorrows most heavy to be borne, was that many of their children, by these occasions, and the great licentiousness of youth in that country, and the manifold temptations of the place, were drawn away by evil examples into extravagant and dangerous courses, getting the reins off their necks, and departing from their parents. Some became soldiers, others took upon them far voyages by sea, and some worse courses, tending to dissoluteness and the danger of their souls, to the great grief of their parents and dishonour of God. So that they saw their posterity would be in danger to degenerate and be corrupted."

Of the congregation of three hundred built in Leyden, less than fifty chose to make this danger plunge toward America. They were leaving "that goodly and pleasant city which had been their resting place for twelve years," wrote Bradford. "But they knew they were Pilgrims and looked not much on those things, but lifted up their eyes to heaven, their dearest country, and quieted their spirits." Not last nor least of their purposes lay in "a great hope and inward zeal they had of laying some good foundation, or at least to make some way thereunto, for the propagating and advancing of the gospel of the kingdom of Christ in those remote parts of the world." They were humble. Others after them would carry the dream further. "Yes, though they should be but even as stepping-stones unto others for the performing of so great a work." Their promises of widespread religious liberty might fall short. Yet the unborn to come might thank these pilgrims and pathfinders. For what? For having made themselves "stepping-stones."

Down the canal they went the next day of that last week in July 1620, the fourteen miles from Leyden to Delfthaven, a full channel lifting the boat. They saw the wide level plain, cattle knee-deep in green grass, farms, villages, sober little houses white and clean, proud sprawling mansions with yellow barriers and gilt posts, gardens floating by dreamlike with roses and pansies flaunted alongside marigolds and larkspur. Pastor Robinson and many others had come along for the farewell at Delfthaven. There too at Delfthaven would be fellow members from Amsterdam. They talked of the past and worn-out members left behind, of days to come and shining expectations. They landed at Delfthaven. The old town had stood there more than a thousand years. It had seen much. But never quite the like of this day and these Pilgrims risking an Atlantic voyage and the wilderness of America for a vision of the Heavenly City, for what they termed religious liberty.

At church meetings and among themselves in little huddles the Pilgrims had talked up, down and across what they had heard of the American continent. While the eastern American coast, toward Europe, was fairly well known, the interior of the continent ran immense with forest, plain, mountains, rivers not yet measured or mapped. The impression common then was reported by Bradford. "Fruitful and fit for habitation," such land they could find, yet nearby no "civil inhabitants," rather "only savage and brutish men who range up and down, little otherwise than wild beasts." The miseries they met would be hard, "and likely consume, and ruinate them altogether." They would be liable to "famine, nakedness, the want, in a manner, of all things," while "the change of air, diet, drinking water, would infect their bodies with sore sickness and grievous diseases." Escaping these there would be the treacherous, merciless savages who delighted "to torment men in the most bloody manner, flaying some with the shell of fishes, cutting of the members and joints of others by piecemeal and broiling them on coals, eating the collops of their flesh in their sight whilst they live; with other cruelties horrible to be related." Thus the embarking

Pilgrims had talked, Bradford noting "the very hearing of these things could not but move the very bowels of men to grate with them, and make the weak to quake and tremble."

The sea could be cruel and sudden, Bradford noted. "Many precedents of ill success and lamentable miseries befallen others in like designs, were easy to be found." Their own earlier troubles, first at Boston Harbor and again at Grimsby, in their removal to Holland, could not be forgotten. Nor was it a cheerful incident, as it came in a responsible letter from London, of a ship arrival at Gravesend two years before when the streets there rang with cries and wails. For at that port had landed ragged and grief-smitten people, the last remnants of a group of Separatists. One Francis Blackwell had tried to take them to Virginia. "Packed together like herrings," ran the chronicle of one hundred and eighty persons taken aboard that boat—and of them one hundred thirty dying. Northeast winds had blown them southward out of their course. "And the master of the ship and some six of the mariners dying, it seemed they could not find the bay, till after long seeking and beating about. Mr. Blackwell is dead, and Mr. Maggner, the Captain; yea, there are dead one hundred thirty persons, one and other in the ship. Yes, the streets at Gravesend rung of their quarrelings, crying out one of another, 'Thou hast brought me to this, and, I may thank thee for it.' Heavy news!"

The saying was heard, "The land is for men, the sea for fishes and birds." They might say that with new light, on their last night in hospitable Holland.

Their goods, baggage, bundles put aboard their ship the *Speedwell*, on the wharf they spent the night, most of them, "with little sleep, but with friendly entertainment and Christian discourses and other real expressions of true Christian love." There was feasting too, singing, refreshments provided by devout and anxious ones who were to return to Leyden and Amsterdam. Lanterns burned from the evening dark till daybreak while those to go and those to stay looked at each other's faces they hardly expected ever to see again and tried to find the words perhaps worth each other's remembering so long as they might live.

A fair wind blew that morning of July 31, 1620. The passengers went aboard, their friends with them. "Sighs, sobs and prayers did sound amongst them," noted Bradford. "Tears did gush from every eye, and pithy speeches pierced each heart. Sundry Dutch strangers on the key as spectators could not refrain from tears. Yet comfortable and sweet it was to see such lively and true expressions of dear and unfeigned love. They were loathe to depart. The Reverend pastor falling down on his knees, and they all with him, with watery cheeks commended them to the Lord and his blessing. With mutual embraces and many tears, they took their leaves."

Sailing for Southampton, England, they were, on the *Speedwell*, a sixty-ton vessel they bought through financial backers. They were to meet in Southampton another, the *Mayflower*, a hundred-and-eighty-ton ship hired to carry passengers across the Atlantic to the land they had chartered. The two ships were to keep together, help each other if need be.

Into Southampton they came in four days, their eyes lighting on the *Mayflower*. Now came twelve bad days of waiting. Ninety passengers were to go on the *Mayflower*, thirty on the *Speedwell*. But the days passed and they didn't stir out of the harbor. Disputes came up. In a rewritten new contract the Pilgrims were asked to sign, two clauses in the old contract were dropped; first, that at the end of the seven years each planter should own the house and garden land occupied by him; and second, that he should during the seven years work four days in each week for the colony, and have two days for himself and family. The agent of the Adventurers, one Thomas Weston, on being told the old and original contract must stand, showed temper, left for London, telling them to "look to stand on their own legs," and refused to pay one hundred pounds owing for port charges and equipment. The Pilgrims, run out of money, sold eighty firkins of butter for sixty pounds "to clear the port." They decided to sail lacking oil, leather, swords, lacking muskets for every man and other things needed.

At last they made ready to sail. So the whole company was called together. They elected John Carver to be Governor with two or three assistants for each ship, "to order the people by the way and see to disposing of their provisions, and such like affairs." The two shipmasters agreed they should have such responsible heads for routine or emergency. With serious faces all listened while a letter from Pastor John Robinson, dated July 27, was read. He had said much of it to them personally at Delfthaven and Leyden. Now they had it in writing. He signed himself "an unfeigned wellwiller of your happy success in this hopeful voyage." And they could feel velvet and steel, great compassion and an iron will, weaving and interweaving through his counsels that ran:

"Loving and Christian Friends, I do heartily and in the Lord, salute you all . . . though I be constrained for a while, to be bodily absent from you . . . God knowing how willingly I would have borne my part with you in this first brunt. . . . First, as we are daily to renew our repentence with our God, special, for our sins known, and general, for our unknown tresspasses; so doth the Lord call us, in a singular manner, upon occasions of such difficulty and danger as lieth upon you, to a both more narrow search, and careful reformation, of our ways in his sight. . . . Now next after this heavenly peace with God and our own consciences, we are carefully to provide for peace with all men, what in us lieth, especially with our associates: and for that end, watchfulness must be had, that we neither at all in ourselves do give, no, nor easily take offence being given by others. . . . How unperfect and lame is the work of grace in that person who wants charity to cover a multitude of offences, as the Scriptures speak. . . . Persons ready to take offence, either want charity to cover offences, or wisdom duly to weigh; or lastly, are gross, though close, hypocrites, as Christ our Lord teacheth. As indeed, in mine own experience, few or none have been found, who sooner give offence, than such as easily take it; neither have they ever proved sound and profitable members in societies, who have nourished in themselves that touchy humour. . . . Lastly, your intended course of Civil Community will minister continual occasion of offence, and will be as fuel for that fire, except you diligently quench it with brotherly forbearance. And if taking offence causelessly, or easily at men's doings be so carefully to be avoided, how much more heed is to be taken that we do not take offence at God himself, which yet we certainly do, so often do we murmur at his providence in our crosses, or bear impatiently such afflictions as wherewith he pleases to visit us. Store we up therefore patience against the evil day! . . . Let every man repress himself, and the whole body, in each person (as so many rebels against the common good) all private respects of men's selves not sorting with the general conveniency! And as men are careful not to have a new house shaken with violence before it be well settled, and the parts firmly knit, so be you, I beseech you, brethren, much more careful that the House of God, which you are, and are to be, be not shaken with unnecessary novelties, or other opportunities, at the first settling thereof—Whereas you are to become a Body Politic, and are not furnished with any persons of special eminency above the rest to be chosen by you into Office of Government, let your wisdom and Godliness appear, not only in choosing such persons as do entirely love and will diligently promote the common good; but also in yielding to them all due honour and obedience in their lawful administrations. Not beholding in the ordinariness of their persons, but God's ordinance for your good, nor being like unto the foolish multitude, who more honour the gay coat than either the virtuous mind of the man, or glorious ordinance of the Lord. . . . Sundry other things of importance I could put you in mind of, but I will not so far wrong your godly minds, as to think you heedless of these things. . . . These few things, therefore, I do earnestly commend unto your care and conscience, joining therewith my incessant prayers unto the Lord, that he (who hath made the heavens and earth, the sea and all rivers of water, and whose Providence is over all his works, especially over all his dear children for good) guide and guard you in your ways."

To this the Pilgrims listened, this the counsel of their long-time shepherd. On the ship deck on a summer day they heard it read. Should they live and build their church in the American wilderness, their worst dangers would rise in and among themselves rather than outside. That was the gist of the lesson from their pastor and "wellwiller" John Robinson.

"Store we up therefore patience against the evil day," said Mary as she brushed a hand through Remember's hair and Remember whispered "Store we up therefore patience" to Freeborn who repeated it to Oliver who asked his father, "What is patience?" and heard the short answer, "You will learn."

Out of Southampton they sailed for America August 15, having by delay lost a favoring wind, their way slow. Four days and Captain Reynolds of the *Speedwell* reported his ship leaking and he "durst not put further to the sea until she was mended." The two ships put in at Dartmouth August 23, spent ten days in repairs from bow to stern of the *Speedwell*, and again put to sea for America. Three hundred miles out Captain Reynolds again hoisted distress signals and reported his ship leaking and kept afloat only with endless pumping. Then back and back many of the miles they had sailed for America, they went to the port of Plymouth. There again they overhauled the *Speedwell* and heard from Captain Reynolds and his crew that she was not seaworthy. So the *Speedwell* sailed for London, keeping eighteen of her passengers who had decided they would as soon not go to the American wilderness and found a colony. The other twelve of her passengers were crowded into the already well-filled *Mayflower*. Her companion ship lost, alone the *Mayflower* was to try crossing the Atlantic, alone, and vivid meaning to be fixed in the word "alone," by herself, no companion ship.

The port of Plymouth, England, they saw as an open shallow bay. They heard of southwesterly gales that had rocked and tossed anchored ships and dashed them to pieces. "God give us fair weather," they said at Plymouth. Among the townspeople were those who didn't care what happened to a queer congregation of colonists leaving because the religion in England wasn't good enough for them. And Plymouth held still others of those ready for change who welcomed pilgrims seeking change. At the house of the latter kind of people John and Mary Spong stayed several days with their children and did a fateful thing. Their boys Freeborn and Oliver had both weakened in health since leaving Leyden. They took poorly to the sea, ate little, played little, hated the roll of salt water and shrank from it. John and Mary feared for them on the ship journey to America. And when the offer came from the couple Angus and Joanna Smith that they would care for those two boys as their own till a later time when they could send them across the ocean in better health, John and Mary saw it as the wise thing to do. Angus Smith was a ship carpenter and of three children Joanna had borne, two had been lost in a typhoid-fever epidemic, and they welcomed Freeborn and Oliver to the empty corners where their own boys had lodged, and as playmates for their seven-year-old girl. Others on the *Mayflower* had likewise left children with friends in England. William Bradford and his wife prayed nightly for their son they had put in the care of a family in London.

* * * * * * * * * *

<h2 align="center">Chapter 7</h2>

* * * * * * * * * *

<h1 align="center">A Girl from the Queer People</h1>

ON September 16, 1620, on the day the *Mayflower* sailed from Plymouth for America, twelve-year-old Remember Spong found a corner where she said to herself, "I like it alone here. I can tell myself what I wish and no one will hear my wish and it will be a secret between Me and Myself and when the wish comes true, then Me will say to Myself, 'That was pretty to be wishing.'"

Along the wharf went sailors, passengers, idlers, onlookers, helpers, bustling to and fro with last-minute cargo, belongings, repairs, materials for the *Mayflower* voyage. Visitors, idlers, onlookers, some for mere curiosity, ambled or stood around, some just gaping and daydreaming. A few, saying farewell with anxious faces, favored the ship, its people and their hopes. Others wore scowls of contempt or smiles of amusement at the foolhardiness of these queer people setting out for nowhere to do nothing worth the time and effort of respectable persons.

John and Mary Spong had brought Remember to the wharf after an early morning visit to say farewell and Godspeed to the boys Freeborn and Oliver. Remember put her arms around each of her brothers, kissed them with tears, hugged and kissed Angus Smith and his wife saying she knew they would take good care of her brothers. Then Remember had run out of the house, to wait outside for her father and mother, the parting not easy for her.

John and Mary had gone up the gangplank with things for use on the voyage, telling Remember to go play a while on the wharf. She had asked that. Before the ship sailed they would be back for her, join with her in walking English soil for perhaps the last time in their lives. And Remember with glad feet had strolled, run, skipped. Her feet took her away from the crowd to a wharf shed filled with cargo, ship junk and salvage. With the shed between her and the crowd, she stood look-

104

ing at the sea, then toward the town of Plymouth, then ships at anchor, enjoying her meditations, finding a cozy quiet and loneliness about it. "I can tell myself what I wish and no one will hear my wish and it will be a secret between Me and Myself and when the wish comes true then Me will say to Myself, 'That was pretty to be wishing.'"

She had her mother's dreaminess at times. On the human-packed ships the faces and voices gave her small chance for her kind of dreaminess. To the sea, to the town, to the ships at anchor, her eyes turned. She felt rich. The quiet of the spaces and slants of the morning sun on the town, the ships, the sea, wrapped her in dreaminess. "I clear forgot you, Tamia," she broke her mood, speaking to what she held tucked in her right arm, a bright yellow kitten with black spots on its haunches. "Now you make wishes like I do, Tamia, and after any of them come true you tell me of it."

Of a sudden came voices hailing her, calling at her. From around the corner of the shed came five boys, glee in their voices and mischief on their faces. The four smaller seemed twelve to fourteen years in age, the tall one perhaps sixteen. A small pretty mouth he had, the tall one, the leader, black silk stockings, a short black velvet waistcoat, long blond curls falling to the shoulders. They formed a half-circle around her where she stood between two small empty beer barrels. Remember met the flashing light brown eyes of the leader, met on his face a look of overstressed importance as though he had waited this chance to show his quality, his leadership, to himself and to his four young followers.

"You are sailing on the ship *Mayflower* today?"

"Yes."

"And ye knew not we had been seeking you?"

Remember shrank. Her eyes roved the five for a breach to run through swiftly. They had her hemmed in and cornered.

"Why should you be seeking me?"

"We know all there is need to be known of you." The small pretty mouth spoke loftily, the eyebrows lifting, the light-brown eyes screwing to a slit. "The queer people, we call you. A pack of fanatics, my father calls you, and my mother holds you to be a shameless set of busybodies and troublemakers and she hopes the ship will sink with all of you when you get far enough from land so you can see no land. England not good enough for you. You hate our church. You detest our prayer book. You mislike our faces. So you must flee to be rid of our church, our prayer book, our faces."

He paused, bent toward the right, then the left, as though studying her ears. "What excellent white ears stand forth from your excellent head! Yet they are evil ears accustomed to hearing evil preached. What if we should cut off your ear on this side," as he pinched her right ear, "and then," as he pinched her left ear, "this other one?"

Remember felt herself tremble from head to toe. Her dry lips she moistened with moving them over and under each other. She began to speak and the words stuck on the tongue at the roof of her mouth. With another effort the words came. "Do you know what you do? Let me be. Let me go to my father and mother, who wait for me on the ship. I would give answers if I could think the answers for you. I have heard it many times those who measure out evil to me I should measure out good in return."

"So you have." And the leader's eyes left her for a moment and swept along the faces of his four open-eyed and admiring companions. "So you have. Truly those are pretty ears." He held her two ears with his hands and spoke with sarcasm and plainly with a vehemence of feeling caught from association with elders passionate in their hate of Dissenters from the Established Church order and methodical in their ways of dealing with heresy. "Pretty ears. And they heard no evil. And they listen to good doctrine only, yea, yea." His mock gaiety rose on a tone near laughter. "Have you seen the man now here with two ears missing? They were cut off. By the law they were cut off. When his hands feel for his ears, he finds they are not there and he asks, 'Why did I lose my ears?' Then he remembers his ears heard too much evil and his tongue spouted the evil he heard. He may give thanks they did not slit his nose, seeing the high manner of his proud nose. Now your pretty ears—" His hands let go her ears, he paused. Remember, though fearing she would crush the yellow kitten under her arm, made a dash, trying to break through their line, first at one place, then at two more places. At each place they stopped her, pushed her back between the two small empty beer barrels. She stood scared and mute as he went on: "We leave you soon now, after we give you your lesson according to law. What do you say? Why is your tongue tied? You can talk. Your people talk. Your people talk, talk, talk. Make us a speech."

Remember, her wits coming back in part, stroking Tamia, spoke rather as though to herself than to them. "You hate me. And why do you hate me? For my thoughts? And what do you know of my thoughts? I came to this quiet place to wish, not to think. And how have my little wishes and thoughts ever touched you, ever harmed you?"

"You dispute well. You devote your days to argument and your lives to dispute, I have heard my good father say. We will leave you. We will go." His tone was casual as though each thing done was of the moment, each move of sudden impulse and prompting. "Now before we go, suppose I spit in your face. Your ears you can keep though mayhap"—and he paused with a malicious, steady gaze—"mayhap you will speak and make yourself known if we spit in your face."

He stooped and set one of the empty beer barrels on end and commanded, "Mount and stand there." Two of them lifted her up on the barrel as he mounted the other barrel and faced her. He swung a short piece of thick-tarred rope, swinging it so near her face that she drew back to escape it as he was saying, "Now I will show you we have mercy. I shall not lash you with this rope. Many of your people have tasted this but I shall not touch you with it." Again he swung it swiftly within an inch of her face. Remember, still clutching the kitten Tamia, leaped off the barrel, tried for escape, but they caught her. She wrestled and wriggled to get away but they put her back on the barrel.

The leader went on with his mockery. "I shall not lash you, though your people deserve lashing, all of you." He took out a fisherman's knife, opened a long saw-tooth blade for gutting fish, brandished it toward Remember. "We shall not harm your ears, your nose." He closed the knife, put it away back in a pocket. "And yet how would it be if I should spit in your face and you tried to wipe it off and you should find you could never wipe it off and the shame of it would be there on your face for life and whatever you might forget you could never forget our compliments to you and your people, how would it be?"

His face brightened with what he regarded as a whimsical smile. "At least you will speak enough to tell us what is the name of your kitten."

Her shoulders hunched forward and a little dreamlike, Remember drew her left hand across her mouth and face as though perhaps cleansing it of spittle.

"You scare easy, you queer people."

Two boys echoed, "Queer people, queer people," two others in a timebeat as though marching to drums, "Queer—queer, queer—queer." And the small pretty boy mouth framed in blond curls snapped words like a whiplash: "Speak and give the name of your dirty yellow kitten."

"Mesopotamia."

"You say the name Mesopotamia? That long name for that little dirty scared kitten?"

Weakly and shrinkingly, "Tamia for short."

"Who would have believed it? Tamia for short! And now before we go, how would it be if I spit in your face so you will not forget us when your ship is on the sea or when your ship arrives in America if God does not punish you by sending you to the bottom of the sea?" And the small whiplash boy mouth snarled, "Speak now." He leaned toward her, his teeth shining, his lips twisting.

Remember and her tormentors had been fascinated by the ingenuity, wild words, garrulity and fury that piled one shame on another. None of them had seen a boy of perhaps fourteen years who had come near and stood listening. Now this newcomer could no longer stand still and listen. He leaped forward, threw all the weight of his body he could bring into the shove of his right foot against the barrel the leader was mounted on. The blond curls, black velvet and silk stockings tumbled to the ground sprawling. The pretty boy picked himself up, and somewhat dizzy rubbed sore spots on his buttocks and shoulders.

The newcomer swung an ax handle, circling it in all directions, doing a mad club dance as he whirled and howled, once narrowly missing the blond curls by just the margin he meant to miss. From his wild face showing all its front teeth came the howling, "Get away from her, your dirty dogs, you lousy rats. If you don't get away from this girl I'll break your goddam skulls, I'll kill you, I'll knock your bones loose, I'll mash your noses flat on your bloody goddam faces."

The leader and his four followers wondered what had happened and stood dazed, awaiting they knew not what. The followers would have run if the leader had said the word or had himself run.

The newcomer's war dance with an ax handle had ended. But he stood wide-eyed, every muscle tensed, his body swaying as he held the club over his right shoulder ready to swing, leap and swing again. His eyes ranged the four small ones, then turned straight to the light-brown eyes of the leader and the small pretty mouth, and, now talking cool, loud and slow: "If one of you bastards takes a step this way, you'll go down with your goddam head broken."

Two of the small followers slowly began walking away. The other two nodded their heads toward the leader as though it was time to be going. The leader looked at the piece of tarred rope in his hand. His fingers loosened and it fell to the ground. Not yet out of his daze, dusting off spots that came from his sudden fall off the barrel, he moved away, mumbling to the followers who were leading him away, "We do not have time for this poor fool out of his right mind."

The newcomer walked with Remember along the wharf so alive with all the last errands of a ship leaving for a long voyage. She thanked him and said she could not speak enough thanks. He asked why she had left the wharf for the shed.

"To be alone once after being on ships so long—and to wish."

"And even your wish to be alone—you can't have that little wish."

Remember said, "Was there need for thee to take the name of the Lord in vain as thee did?"

"They would not believe me lest I spoke as though I came from the Head Demon of Hell. And I was not myself. I was out of my head when I ran in swinging this ax handle I found in the shed."

She spoke thanks again to him. Her eyes enjoyed his eyes and ranged over his face and shoulders. She tingled with more than admiration for him.

They came to the gangplank of the *Mayflower*. She must go up on the ship.

"Let me hold the yellow kitten once."

He stroked the fur, touched his fingers to the black spots on its haunches, and called it by name, "Mesopotamia—and Tamia for short."

They shook hands and said Godspeed with their faces very near each other, both of them bashful.

Remember ran up the gangplank, waved to him from the deck and he waved back. Then she held Mesopotamia high as her arms could reach and the boy waved to Mesopotamia, turned, walked farther away and looked back to see Remember with her upstretched arms swaying the yellow kitten to and fro. The boy watched her, suddenly swung his ax handle breaking two imaginary heads, threw a kiss first with one hand and then the other to the girl and the kitten, turned and ran fast as his feet would take him. She saw him climb into a one-horse cart with a man who took the reins and they drove off and faded up a Plymouth street.

At supper in a little farm cottage near Plymouth that evening the boy told his mother what he had seen and done at the wharf. Later that evening she tucked a blanket around him in his pallet of rushes on the floor and kissed him good night, and he told her more, ending, "The name of the yellow kitten was Mesopotamia and for short Tamia."

"And the girl's name?"

"She didn't tell me."

"And the name of the ship?"

"I don't remember."

* * * * * * * * * *

Chapter 8

* * * * * * * * * *

The *Mayflower* Fights the Deep Sea

THEY knew it might cost them that the *Mayflower* was starting on her voyage later by far than expected. Miserable delays they had seen. Negotiations with the investors, the Adventurers, delayed them. The King delayed them. An Archbishop held them back. They had hoped by now, this September sixteenth, to be halfway across the Atlantic. Their agents and managers had been slow, incompetent, faithless, or the *Speedwell* would have been abandoned at Southampton in July instead of weeks later at Plymouth in September. The delays and bickerings had worn out the faith of some who had gone back to London on the *Speedwell*. Now at best they would arrive in America in a cold November or in the dead of winter amid snow and ice. But they were going. Nothing could stop them, unless an act of God. "Store up therefore patience," the pastoral letter had said. They would need all they could store of that invisible quality.

"Pass by my weak manner, for my head is weak, and my body feeble," their agent from Leyden to England, Robert Cushman, had written in a letter at Dartmouth to Bradford. The buying and loading of supplies had not worked well, victuals would be scant, there was disunity, "violence will break all," believed Cushman, writing, "I see not in reason how we shall escape even the gasping of hungry starved persons. I write it as upon my life, and last confession in England." So Cushman had been willing to join those safely sailing in the *Speedwell*, to London. Those on the *Mayflower* were taking their chances against the prediction they would be meat for the fishes or skeletons of famine.

Forward in the ship the crew of some twenty-five men slept, ate, talked, sang, cursed, drank, mended their clothes, took out their decks of cards or penny tracts. Aft, and some of them amidship, were the passengers. Bradford listed the roster of one hundred and two of these who made up the church and who were to found a colony or, as the contract termed it, "a plantation." Among these one hundred and two a few Pilgrims listed as crew members, such as John Alden, the ship cooper, Christopher Martin, an officer known as a factor, and three seamen. Governor Carver, William Bradford, Edward Winslow, Elder Brewster and the small group of original Leydeners kept active in the management or government of the passengers as a body, quietly watching and guiding affairs as best they could, wakeful that no course of events should turn the enterprise into something else than its first purpose.

Eighteen married couples were on board. Two of the mothers carried babes in arms. Seven daughters of Pilgrims could be counted and one female cousin. A half-dozen children, and several quite grown up, were on deck in fair weather. Three men, Richard Warren, Francis Cooke and Degory Priest, had left wives and children behind them in England and hoped to send for them later when "the plantation" was going. Of children and youths were listed thirty-two. Minor employees named as "servants" were some of them, such as John Howland assigned to Governor Carver, important assistants. They numbered eleven. Miscellaneous "other men," some of them Leydeners and others Londoners, numbered twenty-three.

The *Mayflower* this September day lay waiting for a good wind and the right tide. A ship meant for cargo, only last May she had brought more than fifty tons of wine from France, her hold having a wine smell, a telltale "bouquet." A tubby, bark-rigged vessel with three masts, considered high-lifted in her forward works and higher still in the afterworks. The foremast and mainmast rigged with two sails each, with "bonnets" or strips for use in fine weather, at the bow a spritsail, square-cut, and the mizzenmast carrying a lateen-shaped (triangular) sail, all these sails spreading well but heavy to handle. Amidship spray could be expected any time. In a rough sea wave crests would reach over to the decks.

A cargo ship now made into a passenger transport. Guns she carried, a few of 3¼-inch bore, shooting 340 yards, enough to warn off or damage pirates or savages. Perhaps 113 feet long, 26 feet wide at her broadest. Rough partitions had been thrown up, with bunks and cubbyholes using all available space. Not many years later it was found best to have a ship of about twice the size of the *Mayflower* for her number of passengers.

Soon after four o'clock that afternoon the tide was running out, a fair gale blowing, or as Bradford wrote, "a prosperous winde, which continued diverce days togeather, which was some incouragemente." Then sails bellied out. On shore came crying farewells. On the ship were answering cries of "Farewell, dear England, farewell!" Leaving that country they still counted it their country and had faith believers like themselves would make gains in it for their faith.

They saw the land lines fade in wavering silver mist. They stood at the *Mayflower* rails and looked on deep waters. "Only these oak timbers between us and the sea bottom," said Mary to John Spong, as they stood holding the little hands of Remember between them. "This is the sea, Remember. The sea is kind. And the sea can be merciless."

Shaking herself out of this mood, Mary straightened her body and swayed as though she might twirl into a dance, while she pointed at white gulls flirting with white-capped waves, at the changing bosoms of clouds rolling and unrolling their white folds against the cool calm blue of the sky.

"It is deep water—and how deep?" asked Remember.

"Deeper," said the mother, "than any man has ever told. For those who know how deep have never come back to tell us."

Again she shook herself, knowing this no way to talk to her child. "The fish like it," she murmured, squeezing Remember's hand. "The birds like it, and you and father and I are going to like it."

The music of the endless faces of the sea had entered her. Mary Windling knew she might as well try not to be practical. The dreaminess of the deep waters overcame her. The changing shingles of light and color, the heave and slap of the never-ending swells against the few timbers of oak that held them safe, the perfect insignificance of one little two-legged human creature and the arch of sky and the level reaches of water running to the skyline, one flying fish she saw skitter from wave to wave seeming to have her own gaiety in her dancing days —a series of impressions, some of them vague in her blood, some sharp to her ears and dazzling to her eyes, held her to this dreaminess.

She spoke to John and Remember of how what they looked on, vast, unspeakable and immeasurable as it was, nevertheless counted as only a little part of the framework that was the handiwork of the Lord. Beyond their words saying the Lord shaped the heavens and the earth, the sea and all rivers, mankind and all other forms of life, there were no more words to tell it with complete meaning.

The heart could be silent in a sea-blue hush, and try to hold it all as one breath of air gives the whole firmament and one thimble of salt water reports the endless ocean. Many were the times during sermons, during discussions when one member after another paid his respects to

God and the godly life, Mary forgot to listen to them, letting herself into reverie and vague brooding, saying to herself, "What they find by search of tongue and language I may find by my quest into silence."

Then as often before a fact came like the bong of a bell breaking a dream. Her dreaminess vanished as a smoke wreath in a headwind. For John was lifting Remember to where over the deck rail Remember could give the sea what was left in her stomach of her noon meal. Having so helped Remember, John took her to their cubbyhole aft. Then John returned, stood quiet a while, then himself leaned over the rail and did what the seasick do. Mary herself was one of the immune. The heave of the ship did not faze her. She helped Remember for five days and John for the eight days they were down, bringing them water and food where they lay nauseated and disgusted, almost elbow to elbow with other suffering brothers and sisters.

Fair winds, fair skies, and smooth sailing over the blue plain of the sea they had, this company of people who were a church at sea, this group of home-seekers hunting a foothold on the earth to prove their faith and try their hope. Human, frail, mortal, they were not satisfied with themselves. They had the unrest that burns in those prepared to make history or lose their shirts, belongings—their very lives.

Had some fortuneteller in Plymouth, some wandering Egyptian known as a Gypsy, a dark-skinned woman with copper earrings and a scarlet bandanna around her head and knotted under her chin, told them, "Half your passengers aboard the *Mayflower* shall die within a year—it will go hard with all—there shall come days when only six or seven of you will be on your feet, all others dead, stricken or writhing," the answer from any one of the general run of the Pilgrims would have been, "If it is so written, we are ready." As Bradford saw them, they had prayers, hope—and intestinal fortitude.

Some of the children were homeless strays that now on the *Mayflower* for the first time had steady connections. From the London slums they came, from overcrowded quarters. One way the authorities found to take care of children lost or abandoned, who had to be sent somewhere, was to ship them off to the colonies. The records showed one hundred so going overseas in 1618, another one hundred in 1619. Each of these little ones was "bound" to the grownup taking him or her along, the chronicles saying "the child was put to him."

Mostly the passengers were farm and country folk, neither seafaring nor city-wise. Some were middle-class, fairly well-to-do, affording cabins or better quarters than the mass huddled and cramped aft. The Leydeners and a good part of the others were pious and joined in church services. Others were indifferent, held aloof and even mocked. These spoke English only and when they behaved too ungodly or profane, Carver, Bradford, and other Leydeners talked in Dutch of how when they reached land they might try to teach such fellows better manners.

The families, the good and the bad, the young and the old, on the Bradford roster of the *Mayflower* passengers read as follows:

Mr. John Carver; his wife, Katherine; Desire Minter; John Howland; Roger Wilder, and William Latham (employees); a maidservant, and Jasper More ("a child that was put to him").

Mr. William Bradford and his wife, Dorothy May. [Their son John to come later.]

Mr. Edward Winslow; his wife, Elizabeth Barker; George Soule and Elias Story (employees); Ellen More, who was "put to him."

Mr. William Brewster; his wife, Mary; their sons, Love and Wrestling; Richard More and his brother, who were "put to him."

Mr. Isaac Allerton; his wife, Mary Norris; their children, Bartholomew, Remember, and Mary; John Hooke (employee).

John Crackstone and his son, John.

Captain Miles Standish, and his wife, Rose.

Mr. Samuel Fuller. [His wife and child to come later.]

Mr. Christopher Martin; his wife; Solomon Prower and John Langemore (employees).

Mr. William Mullins; his wife; their children, Joseph and Priscilla; Robert Carter (employee).

Mr. William White; his wife, Susanna; their son, Resolved; Wm. Holbeck and Edward Thompson (employees).

Mr. Stephen Hopkins; his wife, Elizabeth; their children, Giles, Constance (by a former wife), Damaris, and Oceanus; Edward Dotey (or Doten) and Edward Lister (employees).

Mr. Richard Warren. [His wife and five daughters to come later, also two sons.]

Francis Cooke and his son John. [His wife to come later.]

John Billington; his wife, Eleanor; their sons, John and Francis.

Edward Tilley and his wife, Ann; their cousins, Henry Sampson and Humility Cooper.

John Tilley; his wife, Bridget Van der Velde; their daughter Elizabeth.

Thomas Rogers and his son Joseph.

Thomas Tinker; his wife, and their son.

John Ridgdale and his wife, Alice.

[John Spong; his wife, Mary, and their daughter, Remember.]

James Chilton; his wife, and their daughter, Mary.

Edward Fuller; his wife, and their son, Samuel.

John Turner and his two sons.

Francis Eaton; his wife, Sarah, and their infant son, Samuel.

Degory Priest. [His wife and children to come in 1623.]

Moses Fletcher; John Goodman; Thomas Williams; Edmund Margeson; Richard Britteridge; John Allerton; Richard Clark; Thomas Clark; Thomas English; Peter Brown; Gilbert Winslow;

Richard Gardner; John Alden (cooper); William Trevor and
—— Ely (hired seamen).

The weeks passed and each of these names took on meaning for the
other *Mayflower* passengers. No chance had they to be strangers. And
each had favorite faces on that ship 113 feet long and 26 feet at its
widest as they sailed amid autumn cross-winds, saw their first iceberg,
heard the mutter of storms coming, the ruthless equinoctials. Crowded
in bunks and passageways, they stumbled into each other, climbed over
and around each other, caught the smells of one another, saw and
touched one another's unwashed clothes, unwashed skins, getting more
soiled from week to week. When they talked their wishes they named
clean clothes and the itching skins of their bodies to be scrubbed with
soap and warm water. Another big wish was for cooked food, fresh,
warm and steaming from a fire. Each morning the Governor and
his assistants rationed out the few cold food staples, monotonous with
sea biscuit or hard tack, salt beef, salt pork, smoked herring, cheese—
and beer, the standard beverage common in Britain and over Europe.
Occasionally came butter, vinegar, mustard, more rarely lemons and
prunes, and still more rarely the luxury of gin, brandy or Madeira wine.
Damp was the ship everywhere, known as a "wet" ship, her upper
works none too tight, and being loaded with extra cargo therefore
lower in the water and easier reached with spray and wave.

Faces they saw. Never before so many of the same faces met their
eyes, day after day the same faces. The grave face of John Carver, their
colony Governor, forty-four years old, a face worth looking at and
thinking about. Up from Nottinghamshire, not so far from Scrooby,
he had gone to London in the last years of Queen Elizabeth, a good
businessman, making what was a comfortable fortune for those days.
Going to Holland in 1609, he joined the Scrooby group of Pilgrims
at Leyden in 1610. His honesty in dealing, his ability, what they saw
as his true piety and love of God, put him among their leaders.
Managing to transfer his fortune from England, he used it to help
that struggling congregation. Freely he threw in his money toward
the Great House where Pastor John Robinson lived and the Pilgrims
worshiped. Pastor Robinson, Elder Brewster, Deacon Carver, William
Bradford, seemed the ranking of the leaders. Carver had brought Eng-
lish merchants in as financial backers of the colony. He had hired this
ship the *Mayflower*, his home since July 15 when he sailed on her
from London to meet the Leydeners on the *Speedwell* at Southampton;
for three years he had spent far more time in England than Holland.
Carver's practical organizing mind had sought and finally found the
plan, the money, the influence, resulting in this ship and its pilgrims
journeying they knew not where of a certainty. Carver had standing
in England, had affection for it as "the mother country." He was
among those who could not say, "Farewell, Babylon" but rather "Fare-

well, dear England." Carver had personally signed up Miles Standish, John Alden, John Howland and others, good and not so good, who came on board at London. Master Carver still had means, with six "servants" all "bound out" to him. His wife Katherine and their desired daughter named Desire had sailed with him and he was staking all money at hand and all lives dear to him on the *Mayflower* coming through and his brethren proving themselves.

The face of William Bradford, in practical leadership ranking next. A shrewd face, at first look, a practical man, yet underneath this mask often slid out a solemn Pilgrim mouth and eyes, a scholar, a seeker on the borderline of becoming dreamer and poet. Only thirty years since he was born at Austerfield near Scrooby, the son of a well-off yeoman, brought up to drive horses and follow a plow, seeing too many of the people roundabout as "ignorant and licentious," a spindling of a boy at twelve beginning to read the Bible, and at Babworth listening to sermons of the Nonconformist preacher, the Reverend Richard Clyfton. While yet a boy Bradford joined, though his elders were wrathy about it, the Scrooby people meeting at Brewster's house and forming their Separatist church in 1606. He had gone in 1607 with those who at Boston were sold out by the treacherous shipmaster and jailed by the authorities. He had walked overland to Grimsby in 1608, saw the women and children left helpless and wailing on shore, Bradford one of the passengers blown to the coast of Norway, praying in the two-week voyage that should have taken four days, when good sailormen cried out they were sunk.

Coming of age in 1611 with "a comfortable inheritance" from his parents, Bradford took care a good part of it went to service for the Leyden church. The house he owned on the Achtergeracht in Leyden he sold in 1619 when the other colonist Pilgrims were selling off what they could and staking it on a new world. The trade of weaver he learned, working first in fustian, a thick-twilled, short-napped cotton cloth, then in say, a fine sergelike cloth. He spoke fair Dutch, could manage a little French, had mastered the reading of Latin and Greek, had read enough of Hebrew to be sure that someday, with more time, he would revel in that language and perhaps read his way through a Hebrew Bible. Bradford followed the terrific John Calvin in ideas about God, sin, hell, redemption, salvation, though in practice he favored each congregation seeking its own way. He was shy of putting labels on good Christians and wished fellowship among all reformed churches. He had scorn of Catholics in general, calling them papists, leaning toward those who termed the Vatican "the Whore of Babylon," though he could sit in fellowship with a Jesuit not too dogmatic and superior, believing, as he wrote, "It is too great arrogance for any man or church to think that he or they have so sounded the word of God to the bottom." He was among the foremost in organizing the minority of the Leyden church that sailed down the canal to Delfthaven and boarded the *Speedwell* and rode her to Southampton, to Dartmouth, to Plymouth. He had stuck foremost among the stubborn ones who would not revise the contract at Southampton.

Bradford wore sober black, "sad-colored" clothes, as they were called. But on a festive or important occasion, he could step out in a red vest with silver buttons, a violet cloak, blue hat with a high crown and broad brim. However, clothes were a secondary matter to one who had heard the clang of iron jail doors in Boston, where he had awaited the trial that didn't come, sleeping with little straw between him and the stone floor, waking through the night chilled to the bone.

A peculiar calm vitality had Bradford—it spilled over into light, color and cadence at times when he wrote. He depended on "the might of Him who walked the wave." Death to him had merely the shadow of "the angel of the backward look." In December of 1613 at Amsterdam he married the daughter of a member of the English church, sixteen-year-old Dorothy May, and took her back to Leyden. Their little son John, left in London, was to join them later. No scandal rose, no evil gossip, but some of the Pilgrims puzzled quietly about William Bradford and two women. Reports had it he asked Alice Carpenter, the daughter of Thomas Carpenter, to marry him. She enjoyed being fickle, had played with him, and Bradford had gone to Holland with news of Thomas Carpenter's daughter married to the well-to-do Edward Southworth. Then and not till then did Bradford marry Dorothy May. Thus ran the undercurrent talk of gossips, busybodies, and even the well-meaning who said they didn't know what was fact or idle rumor. Out of pleasant chatter, part truth, part guess and surmise, a tradition was forming. Some who saw the faces of William Bradford and Dorothy May tried to read whether it might be that his heart was back in England with another woman and whether the melancholy on the face of Dorothy May was that of a woman knowing herself less loved, less cherished—or of a woman finding no real fault in her husband yet sick of the sea and so weary of it that she could leap into it to end the weariness.

The face of Elder William Brewster—on looking at it one might not forget the wet ship timbers, the damp through garments to the skin, the damp mingled with odors of many folk huddled in close living quarters, the food served cold, the gabble of those who had little thought for their own privacy and no respect for the privacy of others —one might not forget but the Brewster face would help. Water suited him for drink, water only. Brewster had no objection to others pouring beer, wine or other liquor, but for him plain water. Austere but graciously human of iron and velvet, they would have elected him Governor but for his place as the elected ruling elder of the church. For him to be also Governor would be joining the authority of Church and State, unthinkable in men opposed to such joint authority in Britain and Europe. No ordained preacher, Brewster's place was to teach, advise, help, lead. Of the well-to-do upper class, of distinguished political service under a right-hand secretary of Queen Elizabeth, he could have gone high in affairs of church, state, or trade. Instead he threw in his life and fortune with these people known to the English authorities as a pack of fanatics, a herd of ne'er-do-well busybodies, and good riddance to England they were out of the kingdom and realm. No forced growth was that germinating Scrooby group. Quietly they met with Brewster at Scrooby Manor, prayed, sang, discussed, heard the Bible read, and made their decision to go it alone and see what would happen.

A quiet modesty glimmered on the face of Elder Brewster. Modesty could have been his middle name. To anyone anxious to walk before him he would bow, "After you, my friend." He didn't want to shake the world to pieces and put it together again by any plan of his. He wanted to be let alone with his Bible and his own thoughts about the Bible and his fellowship with others who saw likewise. He had walked overland to Boston Harbor with the others later put off the ship, searched, taken ashore to be jeered at and shamed in the streets of Boston, then jailed. He had walked to the Grimsby rendezvous, on shore waved farewell to those sailing into storm on the North Sea, stayed with a few other men to comfort and help the women and children, hustled from jail to jail. Brewster at Leyden had helped guide a decision that a majority stay in Leyden with Robinson, a minority to go with him and risk their all on a colony in America, others from Leyden to come later if so it could be. Teaching Latin and English earned him a plain living the first years in Leyden. Then he went in with a printer, Thomas Brewer, in whose house garret in Bell Alley near Robinson's house they set up the type and sent it to Dutch printers for the presswork—books in both Latin and English, those in English of a sort "not allowed to be printed in England." First was a *Commentary*, in Latin, *on the Proverbs of Solomon*, by Thomas Cartwright, a professor of theology, with a preface by John Polyander, also a professor of theology, 1513 pages, published at Leyden, Choralis Street, A.D. 1617, "a practical work much esteemed." Second came *Confutation of the Remists'* (or Romans') *Translations, Glosses, &c., of the New Testament*, by Thomas Cartwright, a book asking whether certain pages of the New Testament stood correct and true as done in translation by Roman Catholics, a book, wrote the old church historian Fuller, having defects, yet "so complete that the Remists durst never return the least answer thereto." Third was a Latin treatise concerning "the True and Genuine Religion of Our Lord and Saviour Jesus Christ." The fourth book was momentous, in both Latin and English, titled *The People's Plea for the Exercise of Prophecying*, by John Robinson, holding "in a moderate and guarded manner" and in effect, that within certain proper limits, any member of the church could go through exercises as though he might be a prophet and find at times that he was one. Fifth, in Latin a theological dispute titled *Ames' Reply to Grevinchovius*, which proved fascinating to those who knew Grevinchovius and wanted him, as to argument, put in a hole. Two books by David Calderwood, published in 1619, *Perth Assembly* and *A Brief Account of Discipline in the Scotch Church*, made Brewster and Brewer hunted men.

Parties interested had informed King James of Englishmen printing books in Holland that they couldn't print in England, and smuggling the books over to England. King James had his ambassador to Holland instructed to take up the matter with the Dutch government and end this nuisance by closing the printshop and taking into custody the men responsible. The ambassador reported as of July 22, 1619, that the suspect William Brewster seemed to have disappeared, "both his family and his goods," reports being that Brewster had gone to London. As of September 12 the ambassador reported to King James that there had been expectation Brewster would be "taken at Leyden" and this had failed because "the schout [scout] employed by the magistrates for his [Brewster's] apprehension, being a dull drunken fellow, took one man for another." The printshop, however, was searched, "the types, books, and papers seized and searched as well as sealed."

Brewster's associate, Thomas Brewer, owner of the printshop, was thrown into jail, later taken to England, held in custody, finding friends at work for him, especially the University of Leyden which had more satisfaction than did the ambassador Sir Dudley Carlton at the eventual honorable discharge of Brewer. Yet later his enemies were to get Brewer, lay heavy fines on him, and the bishops of the King's Bench sentence him to prison till his health was broken and his release by petition to the House of Lords coming only a month before he died.

Thus Elder Brewster had known the right moment to flit, migrate and depart as a free man to the London where they wished to have him in custody. There he had helped as he could toward getting ships, funds, supplies. When his feet stepped on the deck of the *Mayflower* for the first time last July 15 at London, with his wife Mary, their sons Love and Wrestling and the two More brothers, "bound boys," he was sixty-three years of age, a man unafraid, no one on the ship *Mayflower* having more hope than he that it would please God to bring them over safe "to do His gracious work." Sober clothes Elder Brewster wore and neat, impressive at formal meetings, his coat of violet-colored cloth, his black silk stockings, his ruff of starched linen fluted and crimped from breast and up around the neck—and the face composed, serene, fissured with chariots and flights known to his inner and mystic self.

Younger than Brewster by forty years was the face of Edward Winslow, outstanding in activity and leadership. He came from Worcestershire, of upper middle-class people of property and education. At twenty-three, a youngster traveling over Europe, word came to him of the Robinson congregation at Leyden. "He was so struck with the Christian life of the brotherhood that he cast in his lot with them." Supposed to be "peculiar," Winslow found them highly reasonable. He joined them, married Elizabeth Barker there in 1618, earning his way as a printer, staying along, an active church worker, investing sixty pounds in stock of the Virginia Company, sailing on the *Speedwell* and moving over to the *Mayflower*. He had means, could afford his two servants or employees, George Soule and Elias Story, and the "bound" girl Ellen More. A massive, stubborn, round head, a somewhat chubby face he had, not strictly looking the combination he was of a man of affairs and a student, writer, debater, yet to show himself keen and able in defending the Pilgrims against unfair accusations.

Isaac Allerton, thirty-four years old, that face of his, who could read it? He left his tailor shop in London to arrive in Leyden before the Scrooby group, joined them at once, married Mary Norris, became a citizen of Leyden, arranged the buying and overhauling of the *Speedwell*, on which he sailed with wife and three children, taking on the "bound" boy John Hooke at London. Ability he had, this Isaac Allerton. They were to elect him to high office and trust him with big dealings and heavy money affairs and in the end find him a liar and a cheat, his word no good, his fingers greedy for coin and the name and power of material riches. On his face now, of course, they couldn't read it.

The face of Christopher Martin could get ugly as sin. He had temper and could rage and tear the air. Not for this had they elected him to the office variously called "governor," "factor," or "supercargo," to receive and pay out money, to keep accurate accounts of all business transactions as between the colonists and the Adventurers of the Virginia Company. Into the enterprise he had put his own money. The Adventurers favored him. So did the colonists, at first. The gloomy and nerve-shattered Robert Cushman, who had returned to London on the *Speedwell*, was unjust though not all wrong August 17 at Southampton in his written report: "Master Martin if he be called upon for accounts, he crieth out of unthankfulness for his pains and care, that we are suspicious of him, and flings away, and will end nothing. Also he so insulteth over our poor people, with such scorn and contempt, as if they were not good enough to wipe his shoes. It would break your heart to see his dealing, and the mourning of our people. They complain to me, and alas! I can do nothing for them; if I speak to him, he flies in my face, as mutinous, and saith no complaints shall be heard or received but by himself, and saith they are forward, and waspish, discontented people, and I do ill to hear them. There are others that would lose all they have put in, that they might depart; but he will not hear them, nor suffer them to go ashore, lest they should run away. The sailors are so offended at his ignorant boldness, in meddling and controlling in things he knows not what belongs to, as that some threaten to misscheefe him, others say they will leave the ship, and go their way. But at the best this cometh of it, that he makes himself a scorn and laughing stock unto them!" There was more of the same, unjust but not all wrong, for men of better temper and nerves than Cushman rated Christopher Martin as careless in his bookkeeping, far from conciliatory, overbearing, impatient, self-conceited, arrogant. Some read in his face that time, hardship and trial might improve him. Others didn't care what happened to him. They would have liked to change his face.

The face of William Mullins would not tell offhand that he came from Dorking in Surrey near London, a boot and shoe dealer. Among the English merchants who had led in endorsing and joining the Adventurers he had been steadfast and worthy of trust, investing five hundred pounds of his own and further backing his faith by sailing on the *Mayflower* with his wife (his second) and a son Joseph and a daughter Priscilla.

Stephen Hopkins, was his face at home on the *Mayflower?* Yes, as much as anyone's. His face could flush and redden as he roared and blustered. Then with his noise and blow went tough hands for building or fighting and a heart for danger and risk. Eleven years now since he sailed with Governor Gates for Virginia as lay reader to the chaplain and attested as one who had "much knowledge of the Scriptures, and could read well in them." After shipwreck at Bermuda the stubborn Hopkins held that as they had contracted to serve in Virginia, the landing at another place wrecked the contract too, so they no longer had to take orders from their officers. Gates termed this treason. A court-martial sentenced Hopkins to death. His wailing over what would happen to his wife and children won the chaplain, admiral and other officers to plead for him till Gates gave in with a pardon. Six months then they stayed on the island, running out of food and trapping deer to eat.

The sea Hopkins liked, arguments, backtalk, even fist fights Hopkins liked. Queer things that other men would not think of Hopkins liked to do, if the idea took him, tough and hard, opinionated. He would be heard from, and not merely because his wife Elizabeth had given birth to the first child born to the colony on the *Mayflower*, a baby they named Oceanus. The party Hopkins brought to the ship numbered eight. He was well-off. His face said so. He was independent, free-going, worshiping God as he pleased and ready to spit in any man's eye who would dispute his right to say or do anything he wanted to do. The two servants or employees "bound" to him had already caught some of his swagger and readiness to fight. These two, Edward Dotey and Edward Lister, had violence in their eyes and were yet to come to a duel with each other, a sword in the right hand and a dagger in the left. Their faces were worth studying on the *Mayflower*.

Profanity loomed on the face of John Billington and his sons John and Francis, with impudence and ready backtalk on the face of the wife Eleanor. Hard, swaggering, quick to quarrel and go on from insults to blows this bad man Billington. He differed from Stephen Hopkins who could bluster and then fight. For Hopkins was not a killer. Billington was. He could carry hate and violence to where he must see the other man die. For what Bradford termed Billington's "miscarriages" of conduct they were to punish him often. "One of the profanest families amongst us," wrote Bradford. "They came from London and I know not by what friends shuffled into our company." Their stateroom rated one of the best on the *Mayflower*. They had not been invited or welcomed aboard by any of the Pilgrims. It was supposed that some of the Adventurers either had reasons for wishing to get rid of John Billington or expected to use him as a spy and a watcher making reports to them on how their investment was prospering and who was at fault or lacking honesty. While the *Mayflower* was still anchored at a London wharf, the Billingtons were seen as unfit but it seemed too late to put them off the ship. They had paid their passage, the leaders were busy with a thousand more important matters. So the Billingtons stayed on. The *Mayflower* passengers couldn't enjoy it that one of the Billington boys went to the Billington family stateroom when it was empty, found a loaded gun, pressed the trigger and let go a terrific blast of lead and fire. Others came in and found the boy barely missed hitting a small keg half-full of powder—and this only four feet from a fire in the main cabin where passengers had gathered to keep warm on a chilly evening. The faces of the Billingtons were not always easy to look at on the ship.

Tall, blond and blue-eyed, no passenger at all but a member of the *Mayflower* crew, John Alden had a face worth more than one look. The ship's cooper, he was, English maritime law, because of wood scarcity, saying that a ship taking out beer must give bonds to bring back as many beer-cask staves as they sailed away with. The cooper should see to that, as well as other jobs of timber and plank repair best suited to a cooper. Alden at twenty-one shipped from Southampton and began to like these Pilgrims. His eyes enjoyed roving the face of fourteen-year-old Priscilla Mullins particularly and especially. And the solemn men at their services, the psalm-singers, preaching, Bible discussions—it struck him as a way of life. Hard, shrewd men, no soft livers, a kind of bittersweet about them, about Carver, Brewster, Bradford and their loyal hard women. Their dream and doctrine seemed to make sense. "Mayhap I will throw in with them all my strength and whatever skill I have," seemed Alden's thought about these people. "If queer I will be queer with them and see what comes. I belong with them. I would so be saying even if I did not see Priscilla Mullins as the sweetest girl ever to set foot on an English ship." They saw this crewman coming closer to them. His face was welcome. Also his hands; for they could use a good young cooper like him.

Captain Miles Standish and John Alden liked each other's faces at first sight. Both were practical men, Standish fifteen years older, Alden listening to him and finding that mayhap he could work or fight nicely alongside this undersized, short hammer of a man. A man of arms, this Standish, a soldier of fortune, of proven fighting service in the Low Countries. He knew guns, military drill, tents, marching, camping. Well-knit, plump, sturdy, he was to be their leader in bloody warfare, if need be for their cause. Quick of wit and cat-swift with every muscle when a pinch came, it took a second or third look to see what he had, and it took combat to bring out his real temper. "Very little stature" was noted of him, also "hot and angry temper," wherefore he was "a little chimney soon fired." One story ran that he came from a Roman Catholic family in Lancashire. Certainly he made no pretense on the *Mayflower* of being a devout Pilgrim. But they had his respect. And he had theirs. Already he leaned toward their form of worship and way of life here, their hopes beyond. He leaned, too, on his good wife Rose, both their faces good and steady.

Faces enough, young and able John Howland and the face he turned to the daughter of John Tilley, Elizabeth, and her face, each faintly aware as the *Mayflower* plowed her way over the Atlantic that they were to be, in the wording of that time, yokefellows and bedfellows. The face of Master Richard Warren, abstracted and lost in meditation over his wife, his five daughters, his two sons, the eight of them now in England to join him later if God prospered them all. Faces—yes, the faces of five husbands who in five months were to bury five wives, the faces of five children who in that same five months would see their fathers and mothers laid in graves, the faces of nine husbands and their nine wives who were to have burial couple by couple in the five months to come.

The calm fate on the face of Christopher Jones, master of the *Mayflower*, a middle-aged, sedate family man who could ride a rocking ship into the teeth of a winter gale, cold and drenched, keeping his head as commander. He could build a ship and had so once done. From Harwich, known as a good port in the time when the Romans held England, came this Jones, at eighteen years of age owning the ship *Marie Fortune* willed to him by his mariner father. Shipboy, sailor, pilot, navigator, then commander, he had gone up the ladder, learning maps, winds, sails, sea lanes, traders, cargo, harbors, landmarks, cautions against scurvy and fever, ship signals, sea slang, mutiny, aye aye sir, and orders is orders. His first wife, Sarah Twitt, daughter of a shipmaster and whaler, bore him a son, and died ten years after their marriage. His second wife, a widow, Josian Thompson Gray, he christened with her name Josian the one ship he built to show he could build one and sail it as master. Six children Josian gave him, two in

Harwich, four in their home in the Redriffe district of London where he made his headquarters with the ship *Mayflower* of which he was a quarter-owner. To Rochelle, Bordeaux, Gascon towns of France he had sailed the *Mayflower*, the cargo generally wine casks, though the hold was no stranger to taffeta, satins, stockings, perpetuanas, "coney" (rabbit) skins, and once an item of Virginia leaf tobacco.

When Christopher signed up the *Mayflower* and himself and crew for her first crossing of the Atlantic, when he made his decision to go it alone without a sister ship, though the written and signed agreement specified the two ships should go together, when he at fifty years of age and not bad off in worldly goods said Yes to a more dangerous voyage than any hitherto in his life, what moved him? The money gain was minor for he could have done as well or better in safer sea lanes. The English flag waving over colonies in that new world—if he could have a hand in making history toward that end—could he not then rate himself more than a merchant trader? Then as a mariner why not round out his life with trying himself, proving himself, playing his ability, wit and skill against the mighty and treacherous Atlantic and winning? Such questions it is supposed he asked himself.

Perhaps Christopher Jones knew the Pilgrims underrated him. Partly it was their suspicion as landsmen of all seafaring men who are a tribe by themselves with a slang their own. They were sure, the Pilgrims were, that Captain Reynolds of the *Speedwell* was crooked as a dog's hind leg and a liar and rascal, though there were reasonable doubts in evidence that Captain Reynolds was no double-dealer. They couldn't quite fathom the master of the *Mayflower*, and he was a better man than they believed and reported. On his face was some of the decent sagacity of a man grave and calm over his responsibility and his use of the power of life and death over any and all on the ship. The *Mayflower* was a second-rate ship, wet and overloaded, and his only ship and the only one they could hire. The record, too, ran that he was a good family man, with thoughts of home often. Behind his weatherworn features lurked often his passing wish to be safe at a fireside in Redriffe of London with Josian and the four living children left to him, two boys and two girls, one of the boys arriving only last spring and not yet weaned from the mother's breast.

John Clark, first mate, and Robert Coppin, second mate, had seasoned faces. Clark, now around forty years of age, had seen two voyages to the Virginia coast, had piloted one ship in the fleet Sir Thomas Dale took to Jamestown. From a Spanish caravel that sailed up the James River in 1611 the English took prisoners and the Spaniards in retaliation carried off Clark, as he told it, "his feet kicking in the air." After holding him in a lousy cell in Havana for a time, they shipped him to Spain and held him prisoner four years in Madrid, exchanging him in 1616 for a Spaniard let loose from an English jail. Mate Coppin had been to Cape Cod. Four of the crew, William Trevor, John

Allerton, Thomas English, and one Ely, had been hired for a year of service by the Pilgrims. Master's mates Andrew Williamson and John Parker and there were four quartermasters, a carpenter, boatswains, cooks, gunners, as many as thirty-six men before the mast. These faces on their many errands, duties and jobs, became familiar, even fascinating, but not strictly lovable to the landsmen Pilgrims.

For each mess of four men of the crew, the customary rations were two pieces or six pounds of beef on "meat days" (three days a week); four pounds of bread; a pint and a half of peas; and four gallons of beer. Fish, cheese, oatmeal or "water-gruel" also were served. In the fare of the officers, of course, were added delicacies of wheat-flour biscuit, fruit, wine, liquor. The crew, it was understood, fed better than the passengers, or at least the poor passengers, who were the majority of the Pilgrims.

Fair winds and good weather the *Mayflower* enjoyed at first. Then she met storms, the equinoctials, and plunged groaning and soaked through heavy buffers and twists of curving water, coming through as though the brute elements meant to bring her down spent and strangled at the sea bottom—and had failed this time and the next time might not. Cross winds came when no hoist of sail could catch wind so as to bring her on. So all sails were taken in and they drifted and moved out of the course intended as charted. Then she was no ship at all but rather a mere house they lived in amid howl of wind and anger of water, going nowhere with them and nothing to do but look on helpless while they went on nowhere.

"A leak in the upper works," came the word one day. And the storm waves pounded at the weakening oaken wood till the one leak became more and more. Then fear came. Bradford wrote it, "One of the main beams amidship was bowed and cracked, which put them in some fear that the ship could not be able to perform the voyage." Then the head men of the Pilgrim company put their heads together. It was time to do so. For among the seamen, among good men manning the ship, fear set in as to whether the *Mayflower* could take what was to come and sail on with a main beam broken and buckled, whether she would hold together or be shaken to pieces in more rugged weather that lay ahead. Carver, Bradford, Brewster, Winslow, they went to Captain Christopher Jones and the first and second mates. They "entered into serious consultation." The Pilgrim decision was to sail on. The officers reported among the seamen "great distraction and difference of opinion." Having now crossed half the Atlantic course they had marked, many were willing to do "what could be done for their wages sake and on the other hand they were loath to hazard their lives too desperately."

Had the Pilgrims said, "Turn back and sail for England," had they joined in the fear of what lay ahead, the ship *Mayflower* would have shifted and pointed east instead of sailing on west. Joining them was the shipmaster, Christopher Jones, whose word and authority, along with willing seamen, could have dictated a turnabout.

"What do you deem right to be done?" was asked of every man in this momentous session where the head Pilgrims and the heads of the crew made a decision. Jones and other officers "affirmed they knew the ship to be strong and firm under water." The ship carpenter was there, sober, his wits going good. To him had come word of a great iron screw the passengers had brought out of Holland for possible use in their colony in America. This screw would raise that beam buckled amidship into its right place. This done, the carpenter and the shipmaster agreed that with a post put under, set firm in the lower deck, and otherwise bound, the main beam would serve well. The decks and upper works calked new, with the working of the ship they would not long keep her watertight, yet there would be no great danger, if the ship was not overpressed with sails. This was agreed on. "So they committed themselves to the will of God," wrote Bradford, "and resolved to proceed. In sundry storms the winds were so fierce, and the seas so high, they could not bear a knot of sail."

In one of these storms the *Mayflower* had no sail on, drifted and took her beating from headwinds. John Howland, young, lusty, and adventurous, came up above the hatchways, stood on the upper deck and had his look at the roaring sea, a landsman curious to see from the upper deck what it was all about over the ocean. A twist of galloping wind, a treacherous lurch of the ship, and his feet lost their place on the wet and slippery deck. Flung loose into mid-air he found himself thrown overboard. Down under wild and churning water he went. "But," wrote Bradford, "it pleased God he caught hold of the top-sail halyards which hung overboard and ran out at length. Yet he held his hold though he was sundry fathoms under water, till he was hauled up by the same rope to the brim of the water. Then with a boat-hook and other means he was got into the ship again, and his life saved, though he was something ill with it."

From then on, it was believed, a favorite Bible story of John Howland was the one of Jonah. Cast into the sea and sunk out of sight he nevertheless was fished up with a boat hook to live, breathe, speak. Soaked through and half-frozen, he came out of death's door by an eyelash, by the accident of those halyards trailing the sea that his hands got hold of as he went under. When rest, food, warmth and sleep brought him on deck again, all were glad to rest their eyes on him, especially the girl Elizabeth Tilley who found him good to look on and was to know him as near and dear.

The ship sailed on. Using a crutch, but sailing. Some passengers had thought to take along this piece of hardware, a big jackscrew, common on Dutch ships, a *vijzel* to the Dutch. Lacking this *vijzel* they would have turned back. Now they sailed. On west and ever westward to the goal, whatever it might be.

Rains came blowing, snow, hail and sleet wind-driven. The ship timbers strained on into the storms. Water on the upper deck seeped wet and cold down into cabins, dripped into partitions and cubbyholes. The passengers fastened below decks took it mute and uncomplaining or moaning and praying, with shirts and blankets sticky and stinking, with shivering skins and the dumb acceptance of the half-alive.

The crying of Oceanus Hopkins, to those who heard that newborn baby boy wanting milk from the breasts of his mother Elizabeth, that crying came welcome. He was the future. He was tomorrow. He might come through and live to see one or two generations of men after all the elders on the *Mayflower* had vanished. They had to wonder what their children's children would see of shock and change. Were they not to plant their seeds in a vast continent, a giant domain that dwarfed England in land, gold and the means of life?

Hugging Remember to her breast one day Mary Windling Spong said, looking away toward a far indefinable skyline, "We move on a sea beyond fathoming into horizons God made inscrutable." This she was telling herself. To her child she said, "I have found archangels. They came to me. We will need them."

"How did they come?" asked Remember. "What is an archangel?" The mother took long in giving her visions. The little one understood less than half yet was comforted.

* * * * * * * * * *

Chapter 9

* * * * * * * * * *

Drink, Dreams, and Death on the *Mayflower*

THE passenger John Billington sat in his stateroom of the *Mayflower* with a bottle of French brandy on the table before him and his two invited guests, the ship carpenter and a quartermaster. For nearly an hour they had reached for the bottle one by one and taken a pull at it and talked about the sea, the ship, the weather, the voyage, the crew, the "puke-faces," America, women, drink and dreams. It was the last week of October, heavy seas for days. The ship pitched and rolled as they passed the bottle. Billington was lush and agreeable to his guests and they in turn lush and agreeable to him. Between the quartermaster and the ship carpenter, however, occasionally passed lush insults and loose threats. To them the sea was everywhere the sea and the authority of the liquor had given them self-importance and loosened their tongues. Billington had announced he would tell them a dream he had the night before. "Yes, I had a dream—and such a dream!"

The quartermaster could stand to hear it. "Tell us the dream. We want to know all the dreams on this ship. While we listen to the dream we forget the goddam ship."

"For Christ's sake, let him tell his dream, can't ye?" the carpenter exploded. "He brought this bottle," taking a pull at it, "and any man wot brings his bottle can bring his dream. Tell us. Let us have it, Master Billington. And if it's a funny dream we'll laugh, and if it's sad we'll cry." He passed the bottle to the quartermaster who before drinking looked at the carpenter, and: "We talk too much with our goddam mouths. If it's a short dream by now he could have told it. If it's a long dream by now he would be halfway through the beginning. Why don't we shut our mouths? Why don't we clap locks on our lips?" He illustrated with a gesture of his thumb and forefinger holding his lips shut. "Is it we are sick of these puke-faces, these psalm-singers who tell themselves they are going to plant a king's colony in the howling wilderness of America, if the goddam ship ever gets us there?"

"You talk too much," came the carpenter. "You dabble dabble too much with words. The puke-faces have got into you. They know too many words. They dabble dabble with words all the time. They know more words than we do. We have words only from England and the sea. They have words from England and the sea and then thousands of words from heaven and thousands more from hell and they like to spill their words."

"It was I talked too much, now it is you," the quartermaster babbled. "The puke-faces have put a spell on you too." He turned to Billington and handed him the bottle, "You are a passenger and a gentleman and we request you to tell your dream and this carpenter I will kick him in the nuts if he spills another word that stops your telling the dream."

"You pass the time for me," babbled Billington. "Mayhap my dream will pass the time for you." He took a light swig from the bottle. "A hell of a dream it was, come to think on it, the damnedest dream I ever had."

"I'm ready to say it's going to be a good dream, a goddam sweet dream," agreed the lush carpenter.

The quartermaster snarled, "Still your tongue, you lousy fornicatin brute of a ship carpenter."

"I will."

"You will or as I said I'll kick you in the nuts."

"I'm not sayin a word." And this was in a low tone near a whisper.

Billington had enjoyed this byplay and now began: "The damnedest dream I ever had. To my cabin I went early last night and it was more damp and more of a chill in the damp than any time on this goddam journey o'er this slobberin dirty sea they call the Atlantic. Into the damp bedclo'es I got with my wife, a lady I adore for her lower works are good and tight as the *Mayflower* and her upper works better by far than the loose-jointed timbers of this vessel. I slept quick. And I slept deep. Toward daybreak it was the dream came."

The carpenter drowsed and in a tone hardly to be heard, "Aye aye, the dream, the dream." The quartermaster lifted a threatening open palm toward the carpenter.

Billington resumed. "Morning it was the dream came. I became a high lord, in a house of two hundred rooms, a manor house where I stood at my window and looked out on ten thousand acres of forest and plain and five hundred peasants to do my will. But lords are human and must sleep. So to my bed of mahogany with a canopy of rich satin over its four posts, and silk coverlets and quilts of goose down, to my bed I went. Good God, what a bed! May God damn me for a cur with fleas and the mange if it wasn't more soft and warm and grand than any king or queen ever had by way of a bed to lie on your back and see and smell and feel—Jesus, what a bed! So I slept me a fine sleep. I woke up in the dark and there being nothing worth seeing in the dark I said to myself, 'To sleep again, my lord.' When I woke again it was past daybreak and the sun streaming through the windows of the big long room. I paused a few moments enjoying the faces of my ancestors in paintings on the walls and their armor, their swords and spears, that hung on the ancestral walls. Then far at the end of the room I see a door open. 'Who can this be?' I ask myself. Then I take note she is the handsome young wench I have chosen to serve me according to what I wish. She trips smiling and gay and I take note I have done well to choose her for she is neither plump nor lean but correct according to my choice of a fair maid, with fair locks of hair you might say edged toward smooth gold, with a skin milk-white, with breasts suited for a man to fondle, hips and buttocks shaped for the revelry of a true lord who could stand at his window and look out on ten thousand acres with five hundred peasants toiling for him. There at my bedside she stood with smiles over her mouth and sweet mischief in her eyes. I took one of her hands and pressed the fingers. Then I took both of her hands and fondled them and kissed the palms. Then she pulled her hands loose with a quick motion, as she stroked my forehead with her right hand and said, 'Not so soon, my lord most high and gracious. What will thee have by way of food for thy breakfast this sunshiny morning?' 'Come to think of it,' I said, 'a brisket of good meat would go well.' 'Ram, lamb, sheep, or mutton?' she asked brightly in a bantering way. 'Mutton roast,' was my reply, 'with a little of London ale and plenty of home beer, just a whiff of French brandy and to begin perhaps a small herring not wider than your thumb and wheat-flour bread, white and clean of a sort unknown to the peasants, a delicate chunk of goose liver. Vegetables and fruit I will reserve for the midday dinner.' 'It will be a joy and delight to serve you, my noble and gracious lord,' she answered. 'And have you forgotten the oatmeal or should I remind you of that lowly dish?' 'Oatmeal,' I said. 'By all the angels that wing their way through the firmament above us, there should be a small bowl of oatmeal first of all to begin the day.' Then slow, like she had been suddenly dazed and wasn't sure what she was saying, came her words, 'Would you have your oatmeal plain or covered with fresh rich cow's cream?' Then like a goddam fool I told her, 'Covered with fresh rich cow's cream,' and it was then I woke and find myself saying to myself, 'You goddam fool, why didn't you say you wanted your oatmeal plain?' For she was gone, that fine young wench I had chosen for myself was gone and the big bed was gone and the big long room. And instead of the great bed with satin drapes and the coverlets of silk and the quilts of goose down there I was in the damp blankets of a bunk in the *Mayflower* and the air stinking with wet brine. My wife heard me groaning in the dark sometime before daybreak and called, 'You must have had a dream, John.' And I told her about the most wonderful bed I had ever slept in though I let her know nothing of the fair young wench I came so near having for my own. And all my life I'll be saying, 'You goddam fool, why didn't you tell her you wanted just plain oatmeal and to hell with the cover of fresh rich cow's cream?' "

The quartermaster looked at the carpenter. "There's the dream, you fiddle-faddle carpenter. Now you tell a dream up to that one."

The carpenter received the bottle from Billington who had taken a drink and after his own pull at it the carpenter rambled on, "It's a funny dream and I should be a-laughin. Then too it's a sad dream and I should be a-cryin. Somehow it sets me to wishin. I wish I had a ship twice the size of this *Mayflower* and a crew twice as keen as this one and I wish I was the captain, the commander and the one and only passenger, and I would sit at a table and the cabin boys would bring me in the fat of the land, roasts drippin with gravy and garnished with sauces and four kinds of white bread to sop up the gravy, and grapes and apples before and after, and plum puddin and custards, and the best of London old musty ale, and gin all the time and brandy in between. And best of all there would be ten young wenches I had picked for myself in England and France, Spain and Italy, some fair, some dark-skinned, one or two with golden hair twisted fine down their bare necks. There at the table they would be sittin and they would dance for me and sing for me and come up and cuddle me under the chin and call me their darlin. There would be some with dark eyes a man would get lost lookin into and they would have on blue velvet gowns givin me only a little peep at the shinin round breasts they had and—"

The quartermaster had drained the last of the bottle and was tipsy.

"Say, carpenter, you would let me come on your ship and have one of those dark women for myself, wouldn't you?"

The carpenter exploded in a snarl. "Nah, ye goddam greedy fool, why don't ye go and wish yourself a ship and whatever dark women ye want on it? Why would ye want to come over on my ship and take my women? Go do your own wishin."

All three straightened up and took on a sober look as a bos'un stepped in after knocking. "Ye know Amber Shreeve took sick yesterday morning."

The quartermaster, "Yes, we heard."

The bos'un, very gravely as though it was not easy to take, "And last night he got desperate and died."

"We heard." And now the quartermaster had control of his lush tongue. "He should have lived longer. He did his work. Too much blather and bobbery to the passengers and puke-faces. But a good fellow, Amber Shreeve. He could fight. A-land I had to fight with him to get him safe home to his mother. She'll be a-weepin for her boy so pretty to look at with his chest out and his fair curls in the wind. Hot in the head. And a tongue hotter. But he was learnin and might yet have made a master's mate. And now?"

"The burial is soon. Ye go up with me. They're nearly ready."

The four wound their way to where below the half-deck the crew stood bareheaded, Billington moving over to where the sober-faced Pilgrims stood with hats on as they did not recognize the Established Church custom of uncovering the head. The faces of the crew were utterly solemn. To those who knew Amber Shreeve his going was sudden and fearful. One of their own no longer was alive and sailor belief holds that a dead body on a ship can bring any kind of evil.

On the deck amid lashing winds and occasional flying spray, in the gray twilight of early evening and the first dogwatch, on a bier, on a plank lay a body sewn with skill into a canvas shroud, weights at head and feet, where the well-muscled shoulders bulged out and could be seen. The winding sheet tapered toward the feet.

Shipmaster Christopher Jones, whose faith was rigorously that of the Established Church, stood bareheaded with a worn prayer book, stood perfectly balanced as though it might be a fair day and they were on land, stood and read the passage:

"Forasmuch as it hath pleased Almighty God of his great mercy to take unto himself the soul of our dear brother here departed, we therefore commit his body to the deep, to be turned into corruption, looking for the resurrection of the body, when the Sea shall give up her dead, and the life of the world to come, through our Lord Jesus Christ; who at his coming shall change our vile body, that it may be like his glorious body, according to the mighty working whereby he is able to subdue all things to himself."

Six men stooped and lifted the rough bier with the humble shrouded body on it, and at the nod of the captain gently slid it over the rail and gave it to the sea.

Some of both passengers and crew went to the rail and looked over to where the waters had closed and covered and taken the body. It was as though they need not have looked for what was buried and gone from the eyesight of men.

The crew went to their stations and quarters, the passengers to their cabins, bunks, cubbyholes. William Bradford came to write his testimony, his impression of what had gone before, and as follows:

> I may not omit here a special work of God's providence. There was a seaman, a proud and very profane young man, of a lusty, able body, which made him the more haughty. He would always be condemning the poor people in their sickness, and cursing them daily with grievous execrations, telling them that he hoped to cast half of them overboard before they came to their journey's end, and to make merry with what they had. And if he were by any gently reproved, he would curse and swear most bitterly. But it pleased God to smite this young man with a grievous disease, of which he died in a desperate manner, and so was himself the first that was thrown overboard on the *Mayflower*. Thus his curses light on his own head; and it was an astonishment to all his fellows, for they noted it to be the just hand of God upon him.

* * * * * * * * * *

Chapter 10

* * * * * * * * * *

They Sign a Strange Paper

THE *Mayflower* sailed on. Some of the men, women and children passengers had coughing spells and their hacking and spewing became part of them. The cold fish and beef, the cold carrots and turnips, the monotonous fare, became part of the daily dreariness. One and another saw the scurvy come to his arms and legs with itches and scabs, its ravages slower at the gums and teeth in the form known as mouth rot. This was the food lacking acids to tone the body, lack of fruit and vegetables. The man with the rotting gums, not easy to look at, needed the pity Jesus gave to the lepers. Some had strength to come on deck in fair weather but when the ship heaved in storm, they stayed in their quarters, hugged close to the damp boards and their damp blankets and prayed for soon deliverance from the brute, pitiless ocean. They could have loathed the sea and put curses on it but for their faith in a God somewhere who had made that ocean and had His purposes in so doing.

As ships and voyages go they were doing well enough for their time. They were nearly in sight of land. And only one passenger had died. William Button, employee of Samuel Fuller, lay in a canvas shroud on a plank. Elder Brewster read from the Scriptures, spoke a brief burial service, and the body gently slid over the rail.

Hard times, mean conditions, on the *Mayflower*, they had expected. But not so much damp, cold, filth, wearing monotony, storm after storm. Why did they stand it so well with only one passenger lost? Partly it was that the Leydeners had always lived hard, spare, no excesses. Gaunt when in health were many—and now on the *Mayflower* some worn haggard. Fellowship there was adding to their strength, the faces of good companions they had shared hard life with in Holland or in England. Nor did fear wear them down. They were trained in faith and disciplined in a trust of high invisible powers sustaining them and ordering their lives.

On the skyline daybreak of November 9 they could hardly believe their eyes—a thin brown line shadowed on the horizon—a tremulous shadowline first caught by only the keenest eyes on the *Mayflower*— thin as haze or cloud. The ship drew nearer and the line grew black and nearer and the cry was "Land ho!" They had at last sighted America, the continent, Cape Cod, off Massachusetts. The Pilgrim men and Captain Jones huddled in consultation. Wind and weather being fair they would sail southward toward the Hudson River and the land chartered to them. They tacked about and sailed half a day, getting tangled in shoals and breakers, the wind going down. Back to Cape Cod they headed and for the first time since sight of land at Plymouth, England, they sailed from open sea into the safety of a long protecting land hook, Cape Cod.

"Being thus arrived in good harbor and brought safe to land," wrote Bradford, "they fell upon their knees and blessed the God of Heaven, who had brought them over the vast and furious ocean, and delivered them from all the perils and miseries thereof, again to set their feet on the firm and stable earth, their proper elements."

Mutterings had been heard. They were far north of the land named in their charter. And after landing who should have authority? Who to command obedience and bring unity, law and order? Was this a time for anyone to be saying, "Every man for himself and the devil take the hindmost"? To clear the air on this the men of the colony joined their signatures as equals in covenanting themselves. The document became known as the Mayflower Compact and read:

In ye name of God, Amen! We whose names are under-written, the loyall subjects of our dread soveraigne Lord, King James, by yᵉ grace of God, of Great Britaine, Franc, & Ireland King, defender of yᵉ faith, &c., haveing undertaken, for yᵉ glorie of God and advancemente of yᵉ Christian faith, and honour of our king and countrie, a voyage to plant yᵉ first colonie in yᵉ Northerne parts of Virginia, doe by these presents solemnly and mutually in yᵉ presence of God, and one of another, covenant and combine our selves togeather into a civill body politick, for our better ordering and preservation and furtherance of yᵉ ends aforesaid; and by vertue hereof to enacte, constitute, and frame such just and equall lawes, ordinances, acts, constitutions, and offices from time to time, as shall be thought most mete for yᵉ general good of yᵉ Colonie, unto which we promise all due submission and obedience. In witnes whereof we have hereunder subscribed our names at Cap-Codd yr 11 of November, in yᵉ year of yᵉ raigne of our soveraigne lord, King James, of England, France, & Ireland yᵉ eighteenth, and of Scotland yᵉ fiftie-fourth. A. Dom. 1620.

John Carver	Edward Tilley	Degory Priest
William Bradford	John Tilley	Thomas Williams
William Brewster	Thomas Rogers	Edmund Margeson
Edward Winslow	Francis Cook	Gilbert Winslow
Isaac Allerton	Thomas Tinker	Peter Brown
Miles Standish	John Rigdale	Richard Britteridge
John Alden	Edward Fuller	George Soule
Samuel Fuller	John Turner	Richard Clarke
Christopher Martin	Francis Eaton	Richard Gardiner
William Mullins	James Chilton	John Allerton
William White	John Crackston	Thomas English
Richard Warren	John Billington	Edward Dotey
John Howland	Moses Fletcher	Edward Lister
Stephen Hopkins	John Goodman	John Spong

* * * * * * * * * *

Chapter 11

* * * * * * * * * *

A Conclusion by the Most Voices

THREE and a half months since the *Mayflower* passengers set foot on board ship. Fourteen weeks since the *Speedwell* met the *Mayflower* at Southampton. One hundred and eight days since those two ships hailed each other and delayed over contract disputes. One hundred and three days since they put in at Dartmouth and anchored ten days for the *Speedwell* repairs. Ninety-nine days since the *Mayflower*, crowded with more passengers from the *Speedwell*, sailed alone out of Plymouth for the open sea.

And now they were to stay on the *Mayflower* many more days, all of them except a few hard men chosen to explore, freeze, fight and toil on water and ashore—many more days on the same wet ship.

Was it a foretokening one day when word went round that twenty-four-year-old Dorothy May Bradford, the wife of William Bradford, had been drowned and there seemed to be no particulars known or given out on whether she drowned by accident or by choice let herself drop into the sea? It could have been, thought some, that she foresaw a harvest of death, an ordeal of fiery trial, to come that winter and she wished to have no part of it. The chronicle ran, "She fell from the ship and was drowned."

The hoary old Atlantic Ocean had tried for a death grip on the *Mayflower*, and only one of the crew and one passenger had gone to sea bottom. They had come through on the high sea road leading from the ancient continent of Europe, much people and its land much planted, to the new continent of North America, thin with people and endless with virgin soil.

As they traveled that sea highway John and Remember Spong recovered from their first spell of seasickness and kept to their feet through most of the days of the voyage. Mary Windling Spong lay on the damp bedding occasional days, and the final two weeks kept to her bed with sometimes coughing spells and a stiffness of her knees from a mild scurvy. There were days she had no taste for the salt meat and fish brought her. Her face was sea-pale, her eyes fevered with a brightness that startled and troubled Remember, now twelve years old, as she heard her mother talking not to her but to archangels.

"I have seen your gold hair in the sky over the ship, I have heard your wings dip in the waves." The words came as a thin moan and yet a calm, triumphant chant. "One of you I saw guiding our ship through storm and you stayed till the stars came out and then you soared high till I could no longer see you for you were lost among the stars, and I knew you had gone back to the bosom of God. Early one morning when the sunrise flamed with blood and gold, over the east three of you came, a trinity of you in white robes and shining silver wings."

One evening Remember heard the words moaned low with assurance, "Ye will take me through this land of bondage. Ye will bid me rise, walk and be glad again. The stiff knees beyond my helping now ye will oil them and smooth their hinges so mayhap once again I shall dance for my dear ones."

One morning Remember came laughing and shouting to her mother. "They cried 'Land ho!' at daybreak." Her mother roused, smiled, took

Remember's two hands, spoke slow words, "Our good archangels are bringing us through the days of trial. Great days are to come in this new land of ours. 'There must be those who begin,' said Oliver Windrow, 'and after the beginning it is not so hard for those who come after. Banish fear,' said the good Oliver, 'then you have made the great beginning.'"

She sank back, promising that when they dropped anchor in sight of land, she would rise and take her vision of the long-sought land. The day arrived. Leaning on John and Remember, taking short steps with her stiff, pain-shot knees, she willed she must get to the deck, which she did. She stood in silence, sweeping her eyes along a beach, across a bluff, over a tall blue mound, along trees and woodland that sort of sang to her with promises. Then she swayed and fell and they carried her back to the cubbyhole, where she slept and late that day for once ate what was for her a hearty meal of salt beef, sea biscuit and boiled carrots. Soon, in a few days, they would be on land and she would be her old self, she believed. After the hundred and eight days of sea travel she was to be held many days yet on the ship *Mayflower*. She did not know it must be so long a stretch of days till again her feet would feel land under them.

One way they looked from the *Mayflower* whined the ocean they had traveled. The other way lay wilderness, hiding what behind its beaches and blank, secretive forest? They must seek the answers. Here, somewhere, they knew not where as yet, they must find the place to unload cargo, build shelters, find food, worship their God in their own way, and found a colony.

Gulls came with high screeching and winter birds wheeling in silence, "the greatest store of fowle that ever we saw," it was written, "flocks of duck, plover, and furthermore, everie day we saw whales playing hard by us, of which in that place, if we had instruments and meanes to take them, we might have made a verie rich return . . . three or four thousand pounds worth of oyle."

Wednesday November 15 men with musket, sword, breast armor, sixteen of them, jumped into the longboat, rowed to shore, wading knee-deep to land, under command of Miles Standish, with Bradford, Hopkins and Edward Tilley as advisers. A mile along shore they saw six people with a dog who turned, ran and vanished in the woods. They followed, walking through underbrush and thickets that near tore their heavy armor off.

Night coming they built a barricade and windbreak, got a fire going, ate biscuit and Holland cheese, suffering from thirst for all day they had found no water and had drunk only a small bottle of "aqua vitae" they shared. The next day following Indian barefoot prints they met deer paths, fishponds, sassafras, strawberry plants, walnut trees festooned with grapevines, shallow graves they opened to find the bones and relics of white men, springs of fresh water "as pleasant unto them as beer or wine had been to them in fore-time."

A little pile of sand, padded over by human hands—what was this? They dug under to uncover a small, old basket of shelled corn and farther down a new basket of three or four bushels, thirty-six whole ears, yellow ears, red and blue ears. Was this corn the Indian maize? They had never seen any. It might serve for seed. Into a big ship kettle picked up "where a house had been" they poured the corn, filled their empty pockets with more corn, buried what they couldn't carry, marched on with the kettle slung on a staff resting on the shoulders of two men. Were they stealing good corn from someone who had worked to get it? They asked that. It troubled them. "Much consultation" they had on this, concluding "if we could find any of the people and come to parley with them, we would give them the kettle again and satisfy them for their corn."

Again that night they barricaded themselves, put guards on watch, and slept little because of a blinding rain all night. In the morning they sank in a pond their kettle of corn too heavy for carrying miles back to the *Mayflower* where they were expected, having promised they would not stay away more than two nights.

"It's a deer trap, be wary," warned Stephen Hopkins as they marched single file, Bradford at the rear not hearing. A sapling flew up and there was Bradford, a trapped animal with a wild-hemp cord of Indian make holding one good leg of his. They got him loose, laughed, marched on taking with them the cord to study and learn of Indian skill. Three buck deer they saw, partridges, flocks of wild geese and duck—bringing down no game with their muskets—they were English farmers and Leyden weavers—wading creeks—marching on to arrive at the *Mayflower* landing place where Governor Carver and Shipmaster Jones with others were ashore and anxious about them. On shipboard they emptied their pockets of corn and Bradford later wrote, "Thus we came weary and welcome home, and delivered our corn into the store to be kept for seed; for we knew not how to come by any, and therefore were very glad, purposing as soon as we could meet with any of the inhabitants of that place, to make them large satisfaction." Bradford and others had in mind the words: "Thou shalt not steal."

Ten long days went by, colder weather setting in. On a fair Monday a party of women with men helpers, set ashore from the longboat, waded in through icy waters, walked, ran, stood in wet shoes and stockings, washed clothes, the first washing since Leyden four months ago, the first cleansing of garments soiled, worn, stench-laden, some of them not lacking vermin. The men cut wood, fetched fresh water, built fires under the kettles. The women rubbed and pounded the soaked fabrics and hung and laid them to dry and shine in the sun. They returned that night in the gladness they could now have sweet-smelling linen next to the skin, and woolen, hempen or linsey-woolsey clean to feel about their legs, arms, bodies.

Ten days and the ship carpenter a sick man with scurvy. Delay followed delay in the repair and fitting of the shallop taken ashore, a small sailboat meant for exploring quiet waters, "a sloop-rigged craft of twelve or fifteen tons." She was in bad order, "much opened with people lying in her."

Ten days and they set off in the shallop, Captain Jones in command, nine sailors, twenty-four picked men of the Pilgrims. "It blowed and did snow all that day and night, and froze, withal . . . being very cold and hard weather."

Six inches of snow fell. The fury of the winds drove them to the shelter of a harbor with their shallop. In the longboat they rowed to land, wading ashore in pelting snow and freezing air, marching five miles till they found shelter from a cutting wind, some saying afterward it might have been only three miles they marched in wet shoes and stockings that froze to their feet and legs.

They were seeking where they would settle and make their homes and a colony. They had to find such a place. By morning the storm let down. They made wide circuits beyond the limit of their first two days of exploring, "up and down steep hills, and deep valleys, which lay half-a-foot thick with snow," going back to the shallop, sailing up a river, tramping four or five miles up one branch of the river, followed by the shallop, wallowing through snow, tugging through underbrush, making camp at night in a pine clump, having the luck to bring down three fat geese and six ducks for a roast supper after a day of little to eat.

The next day under sand heaps and in pits they chopped and dug out from the frozen ground seed corn, "about ten bushels." Captain Jones read threatening weather to come and went to the shallop taking "the weakest people and some that were sick and all the corn," while eighteen Pilgrims sought "further discovery."

Five or six miles into the woods they went, uncovering mounds to find bowls, trays, dishes and "such like trinkets," abandoned wigwams with earthen pots, woven baskets, vessels holding crab shells, parched acorns, silk grass, tobacco, seeds, sedges and rushes for mat-weaving, taking along some of these things and hoping later to "conciliate" the owners. One mound gave up two finely wrapped bundles, holding a fine dry, pungent red powder, in one bundle the bones of a man, in the other the bones of a child. A glossy yellow hair covered the skull of the man, and by his side a knife, a pack needle, a few articles of iron, bound in a pair of cloth breeches and a sailor's canvas cassock. Around the child bones were bracelets, strings of white beads, a small bow and other playthings. The man plainly had not been an Indian though it was plain he had been buried in Indian style with honors. This mound tomb the Pilgrims covered over smooth again with reverence.

Not yet had they found a place to settle when they set foot on the shallop and cruised back to the *Mayflower*. A few of them favored places they had seen on this trip, the others saying No.

Four days they stayed on the *Mayflower*. Then, as their journal said, "Wednesday, the 6th of December [1620], we set out, being very cold and hard weather." Slow going it was to get clear of a sandy point an eighth of a mile from the *Mayflower*, "in which time two were very sick, and Edward Tilley had liked to have sounded [swooned] with cold. The gunner also was sick unto death . . . and so remained all of that day and the next night."

The shallop reached smoother water and better sailing. "But it was very cold; for the water froze on our clothes, and made them many times like coats of iron." For safety, comfort and health they could have turned back. They went on. "The spray of the sea lighting on their coats, they were as if they had been glazed."

Eighteen they were, ten picked from men "of themselves willing," seven Leydeners, three London passengers, two Pilgrim seamen, four *Mayflower* seamen. Standish, Carver, Bradford, Winslow, John and Edward Tilley, John Howland were the Leydeners, John Allerton and Thomas English the Pilgrim seamen, and Richard Warren, Stephen Hopkins and Edward Dotey the Londoners.

Far down Cape Cod they coasted twenty miles, saw Indians cutting up a grampus, a fish of baby-whale size, saw the Indians run inland, camped for the night with lookouts ready for the Indians. Leaving eight men on the shallop, ten moved north finding a harbor not what they wanted for a settlement, finding three eighteen-foot grampuses, the blubber two inches thick. Turning south they met empty wigwams, burial mounds, acorn hoards, at sunset hailing the shallop, making camp and a barricade in woods, leaping to arms at a midnight alarm over wild-animal noises.

After morning prayer they sat eating breakfast when a piercing yell came and a sentinel crying, "They are men! Indians! Indians!" All but four of the Pilgrim party had piled their muskets on the beach near the shallop. They ran for their guns. Standish, Bradford and two others fired two at a time, while the other two reloaded. Some thirty to forty Indians circled them, shooting arrows from behind trees. They dodged three well-shot arrows of one copperface they could see as he stepped from behind a tree. Three times they sent musket shots near him without scaring him. A fourth shot hit the tree, near his face, showering bark and splinters around his ears. With "an extraordinary cry" he leaped away, the other Indians vanishing after him. Their war cry through the fight, wrote Bradford, sounded like "Woach, woach, ha hach woach."

"We followed them about a quarter of a mile," ran the journal, "but we left six to keep our shallop; for we were very careful of our business. Then we shouted all together two separate times, and shot off a couple of muskets, and so we returned. This we did, that they might see we were not afraid of them, nor discouraged. Thus it pleased God to vanquish our enemies and give us deliverance. By their noise we could not guess they were less than thirty or forty, though some thought that they were many more; yet, in the dark of the morning, we could not so well discern them among the trees as they could see us by our fireside. We took up eighteen of their arrows, some whereof were headed with brass, others with hart's horn, and others with eagles' claws. Many more, no doubt, were shot; yet, by the especial providence of God, none of them either hit or hurt us, though many came close by us, and on every side of us; and some coats which hung up in our barricade were shot through and through. So, after we had given God thanks for our deliverance, we took our shallop, and went on our journey, and called this place 'The First Encounter.' "

They sailed an hour. Rain came, then snow, high wind, rough seas. "The hinges of the rudder broke, so that we could steer no longer; but two men, with much ado, were fain to serve with a couple of oars. The seas were grown so great, that we were much troubled and in great danger; and night drew on. Anon Master Coppin bade us be of good cheer: he saw the harbor. As we drew near, the gale being stiff, and we bearing great sail to get in, split our mast in three pieces, and were like to have cast away our shallop. Yet by God's mercy, recovering ourselves, we had the flood [tide] with us, and struck into harbor."

Near death's door they had been, they well knew, with the rudder broken, steering by two men with oars, their mast in three pieces, the sail fallen overboard. Had the tide been out they would have been sunk. But the tide was in. And that was, to them, "God's mercy."

They passed over surf and entered a sound, got to a rise of land for wind shelter. In the dark of a beating rain they hunted enough dry wood to start a fire. "Yet still the Lord kept us, and we . . . kept our watch all night in the rain upon that island. And in the morning we marched about it and found no inhabitants at all; and here we made our rendezvous all that day, being Saturday, ninth of December. On the sabbath day we rested; and on Monday we sounded the harbor, and found it a very good harbor for our shipping. We marched also into the land, and found divers cornfields, and little running brooks—a place very good for our situation: so we returned to our ship [the *Mayflower*] again with good news to the rest of our people, which did much comfort their hearts."

Thus ran their own account of what became afterward known as the Landing of the Pilgrims. They had found where they would settle and make a colony and a free church.

They had found Plymouth Harbor, so named nearly five years before, by one Captain John Smith, and on his map spelled "Plimmoth." It met their four conditions, a ship harbor, cleared land, good water, natural defenses. There were broad cornfields vacated three years before by Indians dying of a plague, brooks of pure water, to the south a great ravine, to the west a sheer hill one hundred sixty-five feet high, and northward an open field for palisades and cannon. Such news they brought back to the *Mayflower*.

On Friday, December 15, 1620, by the Old Style Calendar used by the Pilgrims, the *Mayflower* lifted anchor and set sail for neat little Plymouth Harbor near by. Headwinds rose and beat the ship back to her old anchorage. The next day again she sailed and this time rode smoothly in to drop anchor in Plymouth Harbor. For three days as many as were able rowed ashore, waded in over bars and spits of sand dragging their boat, then tramping miles here and there looking over the lands and waters proposed for their new home. They were to vote by voice, the "most voices" to decide, one of them writing:

"The nineteenth of December, after our landing and viewing of the places as well as we could, we came to a conclusion, *by most voices*, to set on the main land, on the first place, on a high ground, where there is a great deal of land cleared, and hath been planted with corn three or four years ago. . . . Saturday, the three and twentieth, so many of us as could went on shore, felled and carried timber, to provide ourselves stuff for building. . . . Monday, the five and twentieth, being Christmas day, we began to drink water aboard; but at night the master caused us to have some beer; and so on board we had divers times now and then some beer, but on shore none at all."

They divided themselves into nineteen families, allotting single men, servants, bound children to the smaller families, and marked plots of ground sized for the larger and smaller families. Now they began cutting down trees, hewing them into clapboards, setting the walls and roof of the Common House, twenty feet square.

Peter Browne and John Goodman had not come back on a Friday night with what they cut of wild grasses to finish thatching the roof in their English style. Searching parties went for them Friday night and Saturday morning, finding no sign of them. When on Saturday afternoon Browne and Goodman staggered in, worn and frozen, they told of it. Their pets, a spaniel and a mastiff bitch they had brought over the sea, chased a deer they saw at a pond drinking. They followed the dogs that chased the deer—and got lost. They tramped in a pouring rain, soaked through their thin clothes. The rain turned snow and freezing and they had no food and for weapons only their sickles against two wild animals they heard howling in the dark, the snow and wind. They stood by a tree holding back the mastiff from rushing toward the howling animals. The howling grew less, the animals went away, and the two men spent the night walking back and forth to keep from freezing. At sunrise taking the sun for a guide they walked more than eight miles, came in the afternoon to a hilltop sighting Plymouth and by night reached friends and home. Goodman's shoes had to be cut from his swollen feet and for long he walked slow and lame. "It was a long time after ere he was able to go."

After this Friday and Saturday came the Sunday morning when those on the *Mayflower* saw the Common House on fire, the grass of the roof thatch in flames and a high wind fanning it. In that house those able were to come to worship that Sabbath. In that house twenty men had their beds, their muskets, their store of powder. Governor Carver lay sick there. They had seen Bradford with rheumatic ankles and terrible aches "shot to his hucklebone" or hip, in such pain they believed Bradford would die. Rather swiftly in the blowing wind the thatch grass burned away, the wind swept off the cinders, and the roof, not dry from the late rains, "stood good" and the main loss was thatch.

All who looked on and saw, echoed Edward Winslow in writing of it: "Blessed be God, there was no harm done." Winslow wrote of the fire caused "by a spark that flew up into the thatch" and, "The most loss was Master Carver's and William Bradford's, who then lay sick in bed, and if they had not risen with good speed had been blown up with powder; but through God's mercy, they had no harm. The house was as full of beds as they could lie one by another, and their muskets charged; but blessed be God, there was no harm done."

Until mid-April their offshore home was the *Mayflower* and on land the Common House. They cut down trees and sawed clapboards to begin building first seven houses on Leyden Street, crossed by Main Street.

Across those winter months of late 1620 and early 1621 the new-founded colony paid high for having crossed the Atlantic on a wet, crowded ship with salt food and bad diet. Those on the *Mayflower* saw seamen of that ship die and vanish with sea burial. Of Captain Christopher Jones' crew, the half of them died, or as Bradford wrote: "So allmost halfe of their company dyed before they went away, and many of their officers and lustyest men, as the boatson, gunner, three quartermaisters, the cooks and others . . . they that before had been boone companions in drinking and jollity in the time of their health and wellfare, begane now to deserte one another in this calamitie, saing, they would not hasard their lives for them, they should be infected by coming to help them in their cabins, and so, would do little or nothing for them, but if they dyed to let them dye. But shuch of the passengers as were yet abord shewed them what mercy they could, which made some of their harts relente, as the boatson, who was a prowd yonge man, and would often curse and scofe at the passengers; but when he grew weak, they had compassion on him, and helped him; then he confessed he did not deserve it at their hands, he had abused them in word and deed. O! saith he, you, I now see, shew your love like Christians indeed one to another, but we let one another lye and dye like doggs."

141

The joints of their bones swollen, their skins running with scurvy, or their lungs inflamed with "quick consumption," their behavior was not up to Bradford's desire and standard as he wrote: "Another seaman lay cursing his wife, saing if it had not ben for her had never come this unlucky viage, and anone cursing his fellows, saing he had done this and that, for some of them, he had spente so much, and so much, amongst them, and they were now weary of him, and did not help him, having need. Another gave his companion all he had, if he died, to help in his weakness; he went and got a little spise and made him a mess of meat once or twise, and because he died not so soone as he expected, he went among his fellows, and swore the rogue would cousen him, he would see him chooked before he made him any more meat; and yet the poor fellow dyed before morning."

The tree-cutting, plank-sawing, house-building, went slow. The unloading of cargo, stores and goods from the *Mayflower* went slow. The spread of the scurvy and of lung inflammation, "galloping consumption," went fast, for they caught it from one another. Only two stood up and kept their feet and never went down in this time they named as the days of the Great Sickness. Only Elder William Brewster and Captain Miles Standish kept their feet and health. Everyone else, at one time or another, took to bed.

In December six died, in January eight more, in February seventeen, and in March thirteen. On some days two or three died. And there were times when only six or seven men could stand and move, able to help the stricken, able to do what they did night and day carrying wood, keeping fires going, tending to beds, washing clothes, cooking food, performing needed service. All told in those four months, forty-six died, Bradford writing, "Of 100. & odd persons, scarce 50. remained. And of these in yᵉ time of most distress, ther was but 6. or 7. sound persons, who, to their great comendations be it spoken, spared no pains, night nor day, but with abundance of toyle and hazarde of their owne health, fetched them wood, made them fires, drest them meat, made their beds, washed their lothsome clothes, cloathed and uncloathed them; in a word, did all yᵉ homly & necessarie offices for them wᶜʰ dainty and queasy stomacks cannot endure to hear named; and all this willingly and cheerfully, without any grudging in yᵉ least, shewing herein their true love unto their friends & brethren. A rare example & worthy to be remembered."

To Brewster and Standish, noted Bradford, "my selfe, & many others, were much beholden in our low and sicke condition." Bradford saw "the Lord so upheld these persons [Brewster and Standish] as in this generall calamity they were not at all infected either with sickness, or lamnes." He could name many others, some who had died, others yet living, "that whilst they had health, yea, or any strength continuing, they were not wanting to any that had need of them."

The grownups stood through the Great Sickness better than the young, the little ones. Ten of the eleven girls died, fifteen of the twenty-one boys. The Pilgrims of English hardships and of the toiling and managing at Leyden stood through better than the Londoners.

At the end of year 1621, of the one hundred and two passengers on the *Mayflower* sailing list, fifty-one were alive. In April Governor Carver died and in the summer Katherine Carver was buried next to her husband and their boy Jasper. "Thomas Tinker and his wife and son all dyed in the first sickness," wrote Bradford. "And so did John Rigdale and his wife." Of Christopher Martin, his wife and two servants Solomon Prower and John Langemore, noted Bradford, "Mr. Martin, he and all his, dyed in the first infection not long after the arrivall." Edward Tilley and his wife had burial side by side, "Edward Fuller and his wife dyed soon after they came ashore." The leader Edward Winslow saw his wife Elizabeth pass away and two servants and the little girl Ellen More. Captain Miles Standish buried his lovable Rose. William Mullins, his wife, their son Joseph and their servant Robert Carter, vanished, leaving the daughter Priscilla. "John Turner and his two sones all dyed in the first siknes." And so on and on ran the death toll. Day and night they were asking, "Who is amongst us and who hath passed away?"

Remember Spong saw her father carry her mother ashore from a longboat and then with rests between-times, carry her to the new cottage that served as a hospital. "I wish I could stay and fight with you for this place in the wilderness, this place in America," she had smiled once when John and Remember held her two bony hands. Little would she eat, and she had wasted away, and knew she was haggard and pale, and for them to look at her came hard. Her blue eyes kept a burning loveliness and her chestnut hair a wave of flame sheen. One moment John had paused for her to stand leaning against him, her feet on the ground. She had said, "Whatever betide, you must put me down once so my feet touch this new land."

Early afternoon, several days in January, Remember came to the cottage where on the floor were crowded men, women, and children, in misery. Each time for a few minutes she held her mother's hand in silence. Once the mother did not open her eyes, pressed Remember's hand slowly, and that was their visit for that day.

By an effort of will one day with a cold wind blowing snow outside the rough cottage walls, the mother tightened her hold on Remember's hand and with wide, bright eyes, "Stay with them, Remember, my love, and fight. They will win, Remember, stay with them. Do not forget, my baby." Her hands struggled and fluttered at her bosom and her weak, slow fingers brought out the bronze plaque, the keepsake of long ago, tarnished and spotted. "Keep it. My archangels will be watching. Wear it sometimes for memory's sake. Read it. Keep it. Be good to your father. He is a good man. Speak in the dark to my archangels. I will be near. Go now. God love you."

The sentences each came clear; some in hoarse whispers and between there would be a rest and a wait for strength to say more. She lifted Remember's hand to her lips and kissed it. She would not let the lips of her child meet her own lips that had gushed with blood from sore and inflamed lungs.

Remember turned away, tears blinding her eyes, groping to the door, finding something that pleased her as appropriate in the relentless snow outside and the inexorable wail of the January wind.

The next day she followed her father and five others who carried her mother's body on a board litter to the burying ground, up Burial Hill where axes had chopped and spades dug a grave in the frozen earth. To the service of solemn words Remember listened stony-faced. The grave was shallow. They soon covered it, then leveled snow over it, as with other graves, whereby no curious Indians might read how large a number there were of the dead.

Not until just before daybreak and after troubled sleep did Remember weep. Then her frame shook and the silent sobs came. It was so for weeks. She woke in the dark to shake with grief till past daybreak, clutching the bronze keepsake.

In time the sorrow left her and became an exquisite memory, the hurt gone and in its place an exaltation. They had been part of each other, she and her mother. The words lasted and never failed at coming back: "Stay with them, Remember, my love, and fight. They will win, Remember, stay with them."

* * * * * * * * *

Chapter 12

* * * * * * * * *

The Hard Beginnings

CARING for their sick and burying their dead—unloading stores from the *Mayflower*, while keeping lookouts against the Indians hovering near by at lighted campfires—on Sunday quitting work and holding services in praise of God in their free church—the Pilgrims at the same time in four months built the Common House, seven cottages and shaped a stockade with cannon mounted for defense, a fort.

On April 5 they watched the *Mayflower* lift anchor, set sail, and take to the sea and fade from sight, on her way to England. They had their grudges against the captain and crew. But she had brought them safely over. And the reckoning was about even in mortality—passengers and crew losing half their numbers.

The next November 21 there arrived in Plymouth harbor the ship *Fortune*, from the Merchant Adventurers, bringing thirty-five new settlers, lacking stores, food, clothes, thirty-five more to be fed and sheltered. They stood less sober and reverent than Bradford would have liked, "most of them lusty young men, many of them wild enough, who little considered whither, or about what they went." The colony had to go on half-rations. What each had to eat before was now cut in half. Spring came and what they had laid by to eat was gone. The good Christian captain of a fishing vessel listened to Winslow, let them have provisions, so there was "a quarter of a pound of bread a day to each person" till the corn was ripe that year of 1622. But they found hungry pilferers had gone into the fields and taken unripe ears to eat, Bradford noting, "Now the welcome time of harvest approached, in which all had their hungry bellies filled. But it arose but to a little in comparison of a full year's supply." They were farm and city folk from England and it took time to learn what food they could get from the sea. In those first two years they were always on the near edge of famine and starvation.

Yet they were alive. They had come through. They had a foothold on a vast continent, a new country with a new future. Only half of them had died. It might have been worse. Some twenty able-bodied men had been fit for a hard day's work every day till harvest and the first frosts and the signs of winter. It was time to lay off work, give thanks and rejoice. Governor Bradford sent out four hunters who brought back game and enough good eating for a week. They had made friends with Indians and on invitation Chief Massasoit brought ninety red men as guests, bringing also five deer. So there was a day of great Thanksgiving and two more days, opening with prayer and Bible reading and going on into games, marches, frolics and a good time for all.

A little of sea fish they got, mostly bass, and occasionally they shot a deer. From outright and straightaway starvation they were saved by clams. They learned to dig for shellfish. "God fedd them out of ye sea for ye most parte," wrote Bradford. "Wonderful is his providence over his in all ages; for his mercie endureth forever." In three or four of the worst months of the famine, Winslow noted, he saw men at noonday staggering in their weakness for want of food. Elder Brewster of Scrooby Manor, who had dined off gold plates in palaces with nobility, now ate from a wooden platter of boiled clams, washed it down with cold water, called it a good meal and thanked God for his "suck of the abundance of the sea" and for "treasures hid in the sand."

Across June and July of 1623 for seven weeks they saw no rainfall on their planted corn and beans. Indian-style they had put dried fish as fertilizer and to hold moisture in each hill of corn or beans. They saw the last moisture give out among the beans. They had hoped for their corn. If the corn failed they would fail as a colony and break up into some harder future they couldn't picture.

Late in July they gathered at their hilltop fort and meeting house. For nine hours they spoke to the Lord that ruleth the earth and sky their many sacred promises and psalms, pleading how helpless they were without the divine help that could bring water to the scorched land, to the soil hardened and cracking around the corn hills.

Hobomok and his copper-faced brethren saw the white men trying to "conjure" rain. They wondered what the Great Spirit of the white men would do in answer to the cries for the healing waters to come down and freshen the earth.

The red men were amazed, so were the whites, so was the corn, when on the evening of that day a fine, gentle rain came down, "distilled out of the heavens," as Winslow phrased it, and day after day for fourteen days kept on coming, making sure they would have enough corn to live another year.

Late that same July came the ship *Anne* and ten days later the *Little James* bringing about one hundred more people to be fed and cared for, which meant that each and all must starve or else dig and eat more clams and "treasures hid in the sand." Fear and Patience, a son and daughter of Elder Brewster, with others of the Leyden congregation, were among the newcomers. Governor Bradford's eyes lighted on a face beloved to him, the thirty-three-year-old widowed Alice Carpenter Southworth bringing her two children, and the Governor and she were married that year, the bonds to last long.

On looking over some of the newcomers Bradford saw them as too slack for what they had come to and sent them back to England at the colony's expense. At the dinner in honor of their arrival the newcomers saw spread before them a lobster, a piece of fish, and "a cupp of fair spring water." Bradford noted, "Some wished themselves in England again. Others fell a weeping . . . all were full of sadness . . . for they were in a very low condition, many were ragged in apparell, and some little better than half-naked." And a noble remnant of them Bradford saw whose hearts were wrung at "pitying the distress they saw their friends had long been in." It came hard at first yet all but three or four stayed on at Plymouth, a colony of some hundred and eighty souls at the end of 1623, its men, women, children to be known in the later years as the Pilgrims, the First Comers, or the Forefathers.

Their leaders, chosen at elections, acted as statesmen, politicians, military organizers, police administrators, court judges, labor directors, and in still other offices. They kept sober and asked moderation in all things and self-control, self-discipline, in the personal behavior of those registered as Citizens, those not yet admitted to citizenship and known as Inhabitants, and those whose stay would not be permanent, known as Sojourners. From each and all the Governor and his assistants would

146

like to see these rules followed: "Profane no Divine ordinance. Touch no State matters. Urge no healths [drinking toasts]. Pick no quarrels. Encourage no vice. Repeat no grievances. Reveal no secrets. Maintain no ill opinions. Make no comparisons. Keep no bad company. Make no long meals. Lay no wagers."

Late in that fall of 1623 one Governor Robert Gorges on his way from Virginia to England put in at Plymouth and his sailors came ashore. They were drinking and roistering, piling the wood on a big fire, in a house next to the main storehouse where the Pilgrims kept their corn harvest and goods for trading with the Indians. Outside it was cold. The more the seamen drank and the gayer they felt the more logs they threw on the fire. The chimney couldn't carry the heat. Flames swept out of the chimney and lighted the thatch roof. The house burned to the ground. So did three other houses. Worst of all the main storehouse soon had flame flickers over it. Enough sober citizens came rushing to smother the fire and to put out the falling sparks. Again they were thankful and called it, not good luck, but Divine Providence, that had saved their food and goods against the folly of godless seamen.

They announced a public day of 1623 thanksgiving for rain, for crops and harvest, for being alive, for their foothold on the new continent being a little more sure, for their God having heard them. England was still dear to them. It was the mother country that had borne them into life. They called themselves Englishmen. Yet it might be they were coming to know they could live without England. Such thought, such feeling, was hazy. Yet deep in their bones and blood ran their hope that what they might shape of the future, in the new land of this virgin continent, would hold some shine of honor to their many dead who had carried a dream through storm and across a wide sea.

They were on their own. The land was theirs to do with. Early 1623 "they begane to thinke how they might raise as much corne as they could, and obtaine a better crope than they had done, that they might not still thus languish in misery." All concerned threshed it out in long talks, deciding in the end "that they should set corne every man for his own perticular." Each family should plant for itself. To each person was given in fee an acre of land, his own. "It made all hands very industrious," noted the Governor, with much more corn planted and "farr better contents." Women who had held back went willingly into the fields, "tooke their little-ones with them to set corne, which before would aledg weakness, and inabilitie; whom to have compelled would have been thought great tiranie and oppression." Young men worked harder who before had complained they worked without pay for other men's wives and children. Strong men threw in their effort now who before had felt it wrong for the product of their labor to be shared out to weaker men, noted Bradford. "The aged and graver men . . .

thought it some indignities and disrespect unto them." Yet there were men's wives pleased to be rid of serving other men, "as dressing their meate, washing their cloaths, etc.," which "they deemed a kind of slaverie, neither could many husbands brooke it." Under the new plan many people worked harder and longer and produced more. To those objecting that "this is men's corruption," Bradford would answer, "Seeing all men have this corruption in them, God in his wisdome saw another course fiter for them." And he translated Seneca: "A greate part of liberty is a well-governned belly and to be patiente in all wants."

So they had carried into planting and harvesting the same theory of private ownership as in their housing two years earlier, Bradford writing in his Register January 9, 1621: "We labor in building our town, in two rows of houses, for greater safety: divided by lot the ground we build on: agree that every man shall build his own house, that they may make more haste than when they work in common."

To reports reaching England that "many of the particular members of the plantation will not work for the general," Bradford sent reply: "This is not wholly true, for though some do it willingly, and others not honestly, yet all do it; and he that doth worst gets his own food, and something besides. But we will not excuse them, but labor to reform the best we can, or else quit the plantation of them." To the objection reported from England of "children not catechised nor taught to read" he would say neither was true, for divers families "took pains with their own" as best they could, and "indeed, we have no common school for want of a fit person [to teach], or hitherto means to maintain one; though we desire now to begin." He disputed further objections from England, making clear Plymouth had water "good as any in the world" and in England "they shall not find such grass" as in Plymouth fields and meadows. Further rumor in England had it of the colony that "many are thievish and steal from one another." True enough, admitted Bradford, and refuted: "Would London had been free from that crime, then we should not have been troubled with these here; it is well known sundry [thieves in Plymouth] have smarted well for it, and so are the rest like to do, if they be taken." The London element, not the Leydeners, did the stealing and some had been caught and punished. There was annoyance from foxes and wolves, they had heard in England. "So are many other good countries too," urged Bradford, "but poison, traps and other such means will help to destroy them." And with sharp humor the Governor met the objection, "The people are much annoyed with mosquitoes." His answer: "They are too delicate and unfit to begin new plantations and colonies, that cannot endure the biting of a mosquito; We would such to keep at home till at least they be mosquito proof. Yet this place is as free [from mosquitoes] as any."

The years came and went with summer rainfall and winter snowdrift, seven years going by before the first of nineteen more signers of the Mayflower Compact died, Richard Warren. They carried him up Burial Hill and one commentary came: "He was a useful instrument, and during his life bore a deep share in the difficulties and troubles of this first settlement." Two sons and five daughters were to go on and see their children spread far, the widow to live long and have it entered on the colony record that she, "having lived a Godly life, came to her grave as a shock of corn fully ripe."

Two years later died another signer of the compact, the profane and turbulent John Billington. John Newcomen it was that Billington hated, claiming the young man "interfered" with his hunting. He waited with his gun, meaning to kill, his finger on the trigger as Newcomen came nearer. Newcomen saw Billington and saw a killer's face. He ran for a tree. Billington circled and shot and sent a bullet into the youth's body. Newcomen died of the wound. They arrested Billington, tried and convicted him of murder. Then came a hard decision for the colony. With all his faults the man nevertheless had voyaged on the *Mayflower* and had come through the hard years with them. Punishment he must have. But must they go to the extreme of hanging him? They discussed and argued the death penalty, they consulted long and agreed that the murderer "ought to die, and the land be purged of blood." Many echoed Bradford that it was "a matter of great sadness."

Four years after landing from the *Mayflower* the Plymouth settlement had thirty-two dwelling houses, one hundred and eighty-four inhabitants, stores of goods, and rated as an investment of seven thousand pounds. With little more than bare hands they had put up their shelters against cold and storm, planted and reaped their crops against hunger. Drought, fire, disease, famine, anxiety, fear, drink, uncertain and skulking Indians, these threats of circumstance they had overcome.

The pious, faithful in keeping the Sabbath and building the church, stood foremost in making the laws and teaching respect for law and order—they were chiefly of Scrooby congregation and the John Robinson flock at Leyden. These loyal and active church members numbered perhaps one out of four in the colony. To the objection from England that there was "diversity about religion" Bradford replied, "We know no such matter, for here was never any controversy or opposition, either public or private (to our knowledge), since we came." To the further objection from English investors and churchmen that there was "neglect of family duties on the Lord's day," Bradford answered, "They that thus report it, should have shown their Christian love more if they had in love told the offenders of it. . . . To say no more, we wish themselves had given better example." And finally in this regard was the objection from England of the "want of both the sacraments" on which point Bradford gave light: "The more is our grief that our pastor is kept from us, by whom we might enjoy them; for we used to have the Lord's Supper every Sabbath, and baptism as often as there was occasion of children to baptise."

So a pastor had been sent to them from England. John Lyford stepped from a ship with his wife Sarah and four children. And he proved baffling. They swarmed to meet him as he came ashore. He saluted them "as is seldom to be seen." He bowed low, "would have kissed their hands" had they let him, "yea, he wept and shed many tears, blessing God that had brought him to see their faces; and admiring the things they had done etc. as if he had been made all of love, and the humblest person in the world." He was given a house, the largest food allowance in the colony, and a man to run his errands and attend his business. He made public confession of his "former disorderly walking, and being entangled with many corruptions," which had burdened his conscience. Now he blessed God for this opportunity and freedom to live in purity. As the weeks passed however he seemed to spend considerable time with Billington, with another new-come troublemaker named John Oldham, and still other disturbers and malcontents. What was he planning—or plotting?

Many letters wrote Lyford, giving them to a ship captain sailing one day for England. To Bradford came word that Lyford had shared with some of his new-found friends the "juicy" spots in his letters and they had laughed in their sleeves. Bradford took a shallop two leagues out to sea and aboard the ship with the captain they went through more than twenty of Lyford's letters, copying some, keeping originals of others. On reaching Plymouth Bradford for weeks said nothing, did nothing, as to the letters. It came out that Lyford and his group aimed at a sweeping change, an overthrow of the church and the colony government. A Lord's Day came when Lyford and those with him, "without ever speaking one word either to the Governor, Church, or Elder, withdrew themselves and set up a public meeting apart, with sundry such insolent carriages."

Governor Bradford called a court and summoned Lyford, Oldham and others before him. They were charged with trying to ruin the church and wreck the colony. They denied the charges. Lyford asked for proof. It came when some of his letters were read, "at which he was struck mute." Oldham however held his tongue, then raged and threatened, when his writings were read. Oldham's rage was nothing new to Captain Miles Standish close by, for only a short time before, when ordered to take his turn at a watch kept on the fort palisades, Oldham called Standish a rascal, drew a knife and found himself jailed with time to think it over.

The trial went on. The letters made out a case Lyford couldn't answer. He had written that John Robinson and the Leyden members must be watched and kept from coming over to Plymouth, with the further suggestion that the Merchant Adventurers could ship to Plymouth enough people to outvote the Pilgrims in the General Court. He told in his letters what procedure of finance and indenture would make each bond servant shipped over a free man and citizen with a right to vote, suggesting further that a true military man be sent over, "for this Captain Standish looks like a silly boy and is in utter contempt."

Lyford now found his tongue and made the claim that what he had written he had from the mouths of good Pilgrims. Being asked who these Pilgrims were, he gave the names. And one by one these Pilgrims took the stand and called Lyford a barefaced liar. Both Lyford and Oldham had expected others to come forward and join their revolt. Nobody came.

Oldham was ordered to leave the colony at once. He so did. Lyford was told he could stay six months, perhaps longer if he showed signs of reforming himself.

Before long Oldham came back, bawling, loud-mouthed, calling the Pilgrims names they were "ashamed to repeat." They locked him up to cool off and tame down. Then they opened their jail door and let him out—out into a row of musketeers, and as he passed, "everyone ordered to give him a blow on his hinder parts." Then to the harbor and as a boat carried him away he heard their farewell, "Go mend your manners."

Now an arriving ship brought Edward Winslow back from England on colony business, with word that they didn't know the worst about Lyford. The Merchant Adventurers' Council had called Winslow before them to answer accusations brought by friends of Lyford. And Winslow had witnesses. They tore to shreds the pretenses and claims of Lyford. A liar he was, plain to see, a hypocrite beyond doubt, and a moral pervert whose curious sins could not be told in full. It came out Lyford while a Puritan minister of a congregation in Ireland had "ruined" a girl. But the course of her ruin was extraordinary. A young man came to Lyford asking his advice about marrying a certain maid. Lyford said that before he could advise he must first "take better knowledge of her, and have private conference with her." So at "sundry times" Lyford had conferences with her "and in conclusion commended her highly to the young man as a very fit wife for him."

So they were married. "But sometime after marrying the woman was much troubled in mind, and afflicted in conscience, and did nothing but weep and mourn, and long it was before her husband could get from her what was the cause." Soon was to come a child. "And she prayed her husband to forgive her, for Lyford had overcome her, and defiled her body before marriage, after he had commended him unto her for a husband, and she resolved to have him when he came to her in that way. The circumstances I forbear [so wrote Bradford] for they would offend chaste ears to hear them related, for though he satisfied his lust on her, yet he endeavored to hinder conception."

The husband took "some godly friends with him" to deal with Lyford for this evil. "At length he confessed it, with a great deal of seeming sorrow and repentance, but was forced to leave Ireland upon

151

it, partly for shame, and partly for fear of further punishment, for the godly withdrew themselves from him; and so coming into England unhappily he was light upon and sent hither [to Plymouth]."

What few friends Lyford had in Plymouth could no longer stand for him. He had to go. With his wife Sarah and four children he had to go. To Salem he went, then to Virginia, where he died. And it may be guessed where Bradford believed he went after death, Bradford writing, "I leave him to the Lord." In Plymouth it was agreed that they never had among them a liar so barefaced, a double-dealer so smooth yet clumsy, a hypocrite who could act so many different parts. He it was, and those like him in thirst for personal power, enjoyment of plot and conspiracy, who had spread false reports in England of Plymouth Colony and its management.

The Lyford affair was thick and tangled. Not so ran Bradford's account of another who came to preach. "Mr. Allerton brought over a young man for a minister to the people," without the church's sending for him. "They had been so bitten by Mr. Lyford, as they desired to know the person well whom they should invite amongst them. His name was Mr. Rogers; but they perceived, upon some trial, that he was crazed in his brain." So they sent him back to England. "And Mr. Allerton was much blamed that he would bring such a man over."

A different creature was Thomas Morton at Wollaston, some forty miles away. Merry Mount he named his settlement. He favored songs, poetry, learning, scholarship, and wrote verses and essays. He favored dancing, sport, hunting, games, wine and plenty of it, women and plenty of them including Indian squaws and maids. The gay Cavalier of the Established Church of England, a society of natural aristocrats by hunting and by trading with the red men to make fortunes and spread their culture over the new America, so in brief ran the model and the vision of Morton of Merry Mount. He despised the Pilgrims at Plymouth and failed to reckon on what they might do to him if they truly came to likewise despise him. He spoke and wrote of them as a low sort with a low religion and treacherous to the church and crown of England. This was not his undoing. That came because of what he sold and traded to the Indians, regularly, persistently, as a business and a habit. Drink, strong drink, wines, rums and brandies, "strong water" new to the Indians who learned how to pour it down their throats till they staggered and fell and might come up sullen and dangerous. The Pilgrims found the red men difficult enough to deal with when sober and they might have overlooked Thomas Morton's liquor trade if not for still another business he had started. Muskets he gave the Indians in exchange for corn and furs. Powder and shot to load the muskets he traded them for piles of fur to ship back to England for good cash. Lessons he and his men gave the Indians in how to load and fire and kill with the white man's firearms. They would thus kill more animals and bring him more furs.

Adventurers, pirates, drifters, desperadoes, rascal Indians, runaway indentured servants from other colonies, gamblers and drink victims, an odd assortment of humanity Morton collected. He heard from Plymouth and other settlements that he must quit arming the Indians but Morton wasn't interested. He wrote bacchanalian verse and told his people to go on with dancing and drinking around an eighty-foot Maypole. It was a festival day when the Pilgrims arrived, well armed, headed by Captain Standish. Morton seems to have hid out at first and then come back, somewhat drunk and not in condition to lead his drunken armed men who were fuddled in handling their muskets, and fuddled about whether to fight while there was still drink to be poured and women waiting to dance. Morton pointed his loaded gun at Standish who pushed it one side and arrested Morton. The expected bloodshed was limited, wrote Bradford, to "one so drunk that he ran his nose up the point of a sword held before him, but he lost but a little of his hot blood."

They took Morton to Plymouth, shipped him to England with letters reporting why. Nothing by way of justice then happened to Morton in England. He lived on to write a book *New English Canaan* with implications that the Pilgrims had church practices and teachings aimed to undermine the Church of England, Bradford terming it "an infamous and scurrilous book against many godly and chief men of the country; full of lies and slanders, and freighted with profane calumnies against their names and persons, and the ways of God." When again Morton came to Massachusetts he took a hand in shady schemes so that he was again "sent prisoner to England, where he lay a good while in Exeter Jail." Besides, wrote Bradford, "he was vehemently suspected for the murder of a man that had adventured moneys with him, when he first came into New England." Now being rid of him, "they demolished his house, that it might be no longer a roost for such unclean birds to nestle in."

How did slanders and misleading reports arise in England for the worry of investors and churchmen? Part of it came from religious prejudice and the jealousy of factions that welcomed any bad news from Plymouth and would like to see the colony fail. And there were important men, trusted by the Pilgrims, who could have done better. They found Edward Winslow able and honest in the business trips he made to London and back. But Isaac Allerton, a First Comer and one of their active church members, mishandled some affairs, made a bad record for himself in several deals, and proved in the end to be a mere money-getter rather than a true Pilgrim. Thomas Weston, the agent of the Merchant Adventurers, showed finally as a poor manager, a bungler, and a sad case.

Sixty of the "lusty young men" who arrived on the ship *Fortune* stayed a while in Plymouth and then told the colonists they saw too much want, poverty and mismanagement at Plymouth. So they were

153

going to Weymouth and make a colony worth looking at. Part of this scheme was Weston for he had put them on ship at London and they were known as "Weston's men." While their provisions from Weston lasted at Weymouth they rode high and gay, nothing to do till to-morrow which would take care of itself. The kindness, fellowship and equity that the Pilgrims tried to practice with the Indians wouldn't do for them. Indians, to this Weymouth settlement, were inferiors and so to be met and kept. They dug into ground where the Indians had stored corn and carried it away. They stole skins the Indians meant to trade. They used Indian women as they chose. They did the amazing thing of putting Indians in stocks and whipping them, having no slightest notion of what a whipped Indian can remember. This was in the high days.

The high days of plenty passed. The Indians learned to outwit them. Winter came. And they must eat. But how? Then in their want of food many sold away their clothes and blankets to get corn and meat from the Indians. "Others, so base were they, became servants to the Indians," wrote Bradford, "and would cut them wood and fetch them water, for a cap full of corn; others fell to plain stealing, both night and day. In the end they came to that misery, that some starved and died with cold and hunger. One in gathering shell-fish was so weak he stuck fast in the mud, and was found dead in the place." At last most of them, in fives and tens, "left their dwellings and scattered up and down in the woods and by the water-sides, where they could find ground nuts and clams."

Now it was the Indians who put on scorn and rode high. Many times the white men as they sat around their fire with a pot of acorns or shellfish cooking, "the Indians would come and eat it up." At night it happened more than once an Indian came and snatched off and walked away with the ragged blanket that covered a cold and shivering Englishman. So low had they sunk that when the Indians insisted they must hang one of their white men, a thief, they did so, to accommodate the red men, to meet the wishes of copper-faced men they had put in the stocks and whipped. Bradford related it, "Yea, in the end they were faine to hange one of their men, whom they could not reclaime from stealing, to give the Indian contente."

Their food gone, living lean from day to day past midwinter of 1623, their powder and shot gone, what was to come of them? They asked that. Not many months before Weston's men were going to make a colony and settlement of comfort where Plymouth had want. Now they wondered how long they would live. One of them, named Phineas Pratt, took a chance on escaping to the woods, "running south-ward till three o'clock in the afternoon, snow lying on the ground." In his winding route toward Plymouth he got lost and through Chief Massasoit learned of a plot laid by one Chief Wituwamat for all the petty Indian chiefs between Boston and Narragansett Bay to join their strengths and kill off every last white person in that district—nothing less.

Hard going in the snow it was for the weak Phineas Pratt but arriving in Plymouth he told them the terrible news. "He durst stay no longer" at Weymouth. "They would bee all knocked in the head shortly." This tallied with other word from Chief Massasoit. Only a short time before the Plymouth men had visited Massasoit when he was sick and given him medicine and helped him through the sickness. Massasoit had sent them word he was not joining Chief Wituwamat's scheme to blot out the white man, his women and his children, from Boston to Narragansett Bay.

Captain Standish and eight picked men with muskets, powder and shot toward the end of March arrived in Weymouth, finding Weston's settlers unarmed, careless, slack. The Indians, hearing that a delegation from Plymouth had arrived, flocked in from the woods, to mock at the newcomers. Several enjoyed sharpening their knives and going through the motions of stabbing and slitting. One chief brandished his knife, saying he had a better one at home and he had killed both Frenchmen and Englishmen with it, saying too that by and by his knife would eat and not speak. One tall strapping red man, the ringleader, Chief Peksuot, spoke his pity of Standish being so little and who would expect that one so little could make fight? Standish burned at this, held himself and waited.

The next day Standish managed to get four Indians into a room, two of them chiefs, one of them none other than Wituwamat, the head one himself. With the door fastened, Standish gave the word to his three men to attack and kill. Then the fierce little javelin Standish leaped at Big Chief Peksuot, who the day before had mocked at his small size. He snatched the chief's knife from his neck and sunk it in him. Peksuot still struggled and Standish was amazed at how many times he had to stab and slash before he had killed his man. When Standish got his breath and looked around he saw the head one, Wituwamat, twisted and blood-spattered on the floor and a third Indian likewise done for. The fourth one, eighteen years old, a brother of Wituwamat, they took out and hanged. Three men were killed in skirmishes. The Pilgrims were on a rampage. They wanted now to spread terror of what the white man could do against a conspiracy to kill all whites between Boston and Narragansett Bay.

When they went back to Plymouth they carried with them the bloody head of Chief Wituwamat. On a spike up over the meeting house of their fort in Plymouth they stuck the head of Wituwamat. There it stayed long as a sign and a warning. "By the good providence of God they were taken in their own snare," wrote Bradford, "and their wickedness came upon their own pate; we killed seven of the chief of them, and the head of one of them stands still on our fort for a terror unto others."

On a small ship they had, Weston's men sailed away from Plymouth and scattered. Of the first settlers three had been killed by Indians, one died on their ship, and Phineas Pratt numbered ten as dying of starvation and not a few others from cold and sickness.

And Thomas Weston? The man who had led them to believe they were born colonizers and children of fortune, the man who at Southampton had tried to force a changed contract on the Pilgrims and failing had told them "to look to stand on their own legs" and left them to pay a port fee of one hundred pounds with the selling of eighty firkins of butter—what of him now? He came over from England with some fishermen, under another name, disguised as a blacksmith. Hearing his colony was vanished, he got a shallop and one or two men, and sailed to have a look at the ruins of Weymouth colony of "Weston's men." By bungling the management of the big ship, it went to bottom between Meremek River and Pascataquack. Weston made shore, fell into the hands of Indians who took from him everything but his shirt. Getting to Pascataquack he borrowed a suit of clothes and means to reach Plymouth. "A strange alteration there was in him to such as had seen and known him in his former flourishing condition; so uncertain are the mutable things of this unstable world." He lied, cheated, and swindled further, had continuous patience, benefits and help from the Pilgrims. "But he requited them ill, never repaid them anything for it, but reproaches and evil words."

Such affairs and people were among Plymouth beginnings. The colony had expected to export fish, fur, lumber to England and little came of it. Their small cargo to England sold at a loss. Supplies sent them had been lost at sea, one ship captured by pirates. Sixty young men scorning the Plymouth short rations and moving to Weymouth had brought on the one great Indian threat, which like so many other threats had failed to wreck them. They were hewing toward the purpose Elder Brewster wrote in 1619, "That they might make way for and unite with others what in them lieth, whose consciences are grieved with the state of the Church in England." So many other colonies had sought fortunes or profits or a way of life the same as they had left in England. At Plymouth the aim was to see what they could do on their own, what would come when they were free from the pressures on them in England and Europe. Besides a free church they were to be "a body politic," Pastor John Robinson had told them, or in Bradford's phrase "to live as a distinct body by themselves." As many as thirteen of the Merchant Adventurers in 1624 had signed a letter saying they were persuaded "You are the people that must make a plantation in those remote places when all others fail and return." A year earlier the Adventurers had written, "You have been instruments to break the ice for others who come after with less difficulty; the honor shall be yours till the world's end."

Fear of starvation, so real at first, was gone. A handful of corn for a day's subsistence, that was past. With meal and meat for the body assured, now what?

"When I seriously consider of things," wrote Winslow from England, "I cannot but think that God hath a purpose to give that land, as an inheritance to our nation." Winslow was speaking as an Englishman, as a son of England who believed the Plymouth experiment would become a good inheritance to his mother country. He and his Pilgrim brethren liked to quote from Isaiah, "A little one becomes a thousand, and a small one a great nation."

＊ ＊ ＊ ＊ ＊ ＊ ＊ ＊ ＊ ＊

Chapter 13

＊ ＊ ＊ ＊ ＊ ＊ ＊ ＊ ＊ ＊

Remember Spong Gropes Toward Light

A QUIET snow with no wind gives a hushed look to what it touches. After such a snow the cedars wear cloaks of fresh stainless authority while the hemlocks bowed in white hoods listen to a low music heard by each one alone. Such a snow had crept on through a March afternoon and night of 1627 in Plymouth and the grass-thatched roofs of Leyden Street had the added thatch of snow and seemed twice as important as the day before.

A single line of foot tracks—or rather the shoe prints of a man—led from Leyden Street through the gate of the fort stockade. Where this path in the snow ended, a man stood looking up at the head of Chief Wituwamat fastened to a rusty spike over the storehouse and arsenal. The snow had made something else of Wituwamat's head. And the man stood looking, a short massive man whose reddish hair ran out from under his hat and over his ears.

A girl of eighteen, tall and bony, with a chestnut burnish on her hair, with sea-blue eyes having sea wind in their look, stepped from Leyden Street and walked in his shoe prints in the six-inch snow till she stood near him. She too had noticed that Wituwamat's head took on quite a change during the night and afternoon of snow.

Neither spoke to the other. They had gazed several minutes at the six-inch hat of snow, a new hat, a pretty hat, that sat on the head of Wituwamat. The ugly and straggling black hair of Wituwamat now had a spotless cover as though he might be asking, "How do you like the fresh dignity given me by a tall hat of snow dropped on me in the night from a tall sky?" Over the stuck-out lower lip of Wituwamat had come a fringe of white snow, giving him a new mouth. On the

157

right and left eyebrows had fallen two lines of snow. In the middle of the forehead a crinkle of dried skin had caught another line of snow. So Wituwamat this morning gave the illusion, at first glance, of looking out over Plymouth, the harbor and the sea with three eyes.

The girl's eyes dropped two or three times for a glance at the massive hunched shoulders of the man, and the locks of rust-color hair between his hat rim and the collar of his cloak. She knew he had turned toward her and was looking at her. She went on, cool and composed, still gazing at Chief Wituwamat's new hat and changed face. She was aware too that he had turned and begun to study again the snow hat and that he and she both knew that when the sun came, the hat would vanish and melt down over the face and ears of Chief Wituwamat.

Quietly, before she knew, he had turned again and was saying, "God be witness and it is strange what a little snow can do to an old and familiar face." His voice came velvet and low-spoken. "Is he speaking to me?" she asked. "Or to himself?" She saw his eyes, brown and neither bold nor shrinking, his mouth a wide slash, and she felt him at once sad, comic, sensitive. "And he is older than I, a matter of twenty years."

"Aye, sir." She paused. "And the hat is well worth looking at before the sun comes to melt it."

"All things must vanish." This man could be very solemn. "And of all things a snow hat must not be proud for long." The light of an odd smile crisscrossed his face as though he could be happy alone and had no fear of any tricks of his mind.

"You are the man Orton Wingate. They tell of you this winter."

"Yes, I am Wingate. Not a citizen of Plymouth. A sojourner and an inhabitant. And I have twice heard mention of you, I believe, the brightest head of chestnut hair in the colony, Remember Spong."

"You speak well. I am she. And you live alone a mile or more from Plymouth?"

"In a hut I blame myself only if it is not weatherproof. I plant enough corn and beans. I trap, fish and hunt enough for my needs."

"They say you read books."

"Yes."

"They say you read any book whether good doctrine or bad."

"Yes."

"They say your mind is full of many conceits and you incline toward all faiths, even the Indians', having no steadfast faith of your own."

"If so then so be it. Whatever faith I have I pray it will be ever a living and growing thing."

"I have heard one woman say it is like as not you hold converse with the Evil One."

"What she heard was that I have said if the Evil One should come to me desiring that I hold converse with him, I should have no fear of such converse and I should have no fear of any spell he could cast on me and until I meet a good and true man who can tell me honestly he has seen the Antichrist in person and held converse with him and seen the horns and tail and heard the mocking laugh and smelled the smoke of brimstone on the scarlet cloak of the Archdemon—until then I wish to hear less speech regarding the Head of Hell being among us and I would hear more of the Nazarene who can make us shed our fears and stand calm before any judgment."

"The same woman spoke evil of my mother till my mother gave warning she would tear the clothes off her at public meeting unless she left off her evil speech."

They walked together to the Spong house. Her father was mending a wolf trap and went on short-spoken while Remember worked at her spinning wheel and carried on talk with Orton Wingate. He was the first ever to tell her of the Greeks in ancient times believing that an immense giant named Atlas stood under the world, holding it up, and if Atlas should become tired or angry and drop it the world would crash to its doom. John Spong looked from his work in disgust at this idea, new to him and of course a fantasy. After Wingate said, "God be with you" and was out the door, the father, "You may well beware of this man and of speech with him. He is an unbeliever and comes to our meetings to listen and say nothing and to go away with no light from our Master and Saviour. To hold counsel with the like of him can bring you no good."

Wingate came again to the Spong house but not often and always bringing fish or a cut of deer meat or a brace of partridges. When there was need, they heard, Wingate had gone to more than one house where there was sickness near death. When others were worn and spent he had fetched wood and water, washed sores, moved silently, spoken little, his calm and his complete faith being a help. He stayed no longer than wanted, knew the moment to go, and was baffling in his quiet strength and humility, being a favorite in one house where his twisted mouth spoke an understood greeting to an idiot boy, "How is my little brother?" and being the only man on the streets of Plymouth to stress one point of justice, "Wituwamat and his red men would not have plotted to kill all the whites between Boston and Narragansett Bay if white men had not publicly lashed with bloody whips the backs of helpless red men. Wrong breeds wrong."

Remember had grown as Plymouth grew, at first somewhat groping and desperate, then smoother and stronger. She had walked faint from want of food in days of the first two years. She had many a week joined her father in digging clams to piece out the quarter-pound of bread given them daily when the colony went on half-rations. She saw the Indians standing amazed when the Great Spirit sent rain for answer to the white men's beseechings. In that first year she saw her Mesopotamia walk stunted, lean and dizzy, learning to get strength from dead fish washed up and dried on the beach, learning as she became cat size how to take field mice in the meadows and small rabbits in the woods. On such fare, as the cat grew keener in stalking it, her fur took on a sheen while Remember waxed pale in her weakness. The time had passed that Remember stroked her fur and said, "Tamia, you grow slow from a kitten to a cat. Till better days we live hard and you too." And she would speak her curiosity and memory to Tamia, saying, "Where is our strong boy with the quick wit now, the boy who swung the ax handle on our enemies and stood ready to smite them?"

Tamia was in Remember's arms to see the new faces arriving from England when the ship *Fortune* rode into the harbor late November of 1621, and again the new faces of the ships *Anne* and the *Little James* in late July of 1623—and again that memorable day in 1624 when Edward Winslow returning from England marched down the gangplank to the wharf leading three young heifers and a young bull, the colony's promise that they were going to have milk and butter when they pleased.

Of kittens Remember kept one she named Little Mesopotamia who had the bright yellow fur of Big Mesopotamia and black spots on the haunches. On the rare occasions when the mother and daughter cat disappeared in the woods two or three days they came back sleek and stout. Yet Remember came to fear the woods, especially in winter. She scolded her father and stopped him from going into the winter woods alone. She had seen John Goodman many months walking lame and in pain from his swollen and frostbitten feet. She had seen the men set out on a shallop in the winter of 1621 to bring home John Billington who one bright day in the woods turned to go home and lost his direction and wandered for five days living on berries and what he could find till he came on Indians, and Massasoit arranged for him to be delivered to the shallop from Plymouth. She had seen young John Crackston on the *Mayflower* and had seen him six years later in Plymouth and the winter he went hunting alone in the woods and came back with his feet frozen and from a fever that followed he died.

She kept a sweetness and brightness like that of her mother. But she could be harder than ever her mother had been. And she could be stony-faced from some warping inner bitterness that grew on her from year to year. The same course of growth but not so definite went on in her father who from year to year had less of the quaint and whimsical that Mary Windling had loved in him. Together each Sabbath when there was no preacher they came early to the meeting house, heard the opening prayer and Scripture reading, joined in the psalm-singing, and occasionally her father stood up and joined in the "discussion." Together Remember and her father had heard the Reverend John Lyford preach his first sermons and seen the later unfolding of his involved hypocrisy. Together they had seen and heard the pathetic efforts of the preacher named Rogers whose wandering mind and incoherent remarks from the pulpit showed him to be "crazed in the brain." They had seen the Reverend Ralph Smith installed as minister, a good and well-behaved man who served well, though at speaking and prophesying he had no such inner light as either Elder Brewster or Edward Winslow had revealed at many a meeting.

In America as in Europe were the beginnings of movements to take from the Church and give to the State added authority to regulate man's behavior and conscience. From Europe came trickles of news about the long bloody conflict later named the Thirty Years' War. In the colonies of America could be seen in miniature the same bitter contentions, the same prejudice and intolerance, that before long were to drench the British Isles with civil war. And those settled in America, men of rather humane and tolerant spirit such as Bradford, Brewster and others of the Pilgrims, nevertheless kept and used somewhat the standards of judgment and methods of punishment customary in England and Europe.

Remember Spong had joined the crowd in March of 1621 who gathered to see John Billington punished. The man had been tried by "the whole company" and found guilty of cursing Captain Miles Standish and refusing to obey an order. "For his contempt of the Captain's lawful command, with opprobrious speeches," he was "adjudged to have his neck and heels tied together." That month thirteen of the colony had died. There was work to be done. So the record read: "Upon humbling himself and craving pardon, and it being his first offence, he is forgiven."

Four months later "the whole company" again "adjudged." Before them came Edward Dotey and Edward Lister, found guilty of fighting a duel. Each with a sword in the right hand and a dagger in the left, had hacked, thrust and stabbed at each other, meaning to kill. One gashed in the hand, the other slashed in the face, these two servants of Stephen Hopkins were arrested and adjudged "to have their head and feet tied together, and so to lie for twenty-four hours, without meat or drink; which is begun to be inflicted, but within an hour, because of their great pains, at their and their master's humble request, upon promise of better carriages they are released."

Remember, holding Tamia in her right arm, had looked on, had seen the chains cutting the men's wrists, had stood limp on seeing their eyeballs bulge as a pull of their feet pressed the chains deeper to their throats. She had slipped a hand out of her father's hand and walked swiftly to where her eyes swept the cool blue harbor of Plymouth and white wisps of clouds drifting in changes on the blue sky.

Later she heard of punishment never known in Plymouth, the news of one Philip Ratcliffe at Salem found guilty of "uttering malicious and scandalous speeches against the government and church of Salem," fined forty pounds, publicly whipped and banished with his ears cut off. From England, where Ratcliffe returned, came complaints that there was scandalous severity in New England government "cutting off the Lunatick man's ears, and other grievances."

Remember grew and came to know the ways of gossips and idle talkers. A few enjoyed the cunning wag of their malicious tongues, as did the woman who could not check herself from an occasional reference to Remember as "a child that came early," as also did the widow of John Billington. Deacon John Doane sued Mrs. Billington for slander and one hundred pounds damages. The Court gave Doane nothing but found Mrs. Billington's slander to be flagrant, fined her five pounds and ordered her to sit in the stocks and be publicly whipped. Then there were those men and women too goodhearted for malice and slander, who picked up this and that and by repeating it first one way and then another after a time had made what came to be known as "a tradition." Thus arose the entertaining story, passed along from year to year, giving it out that Captain Miles Standish had sent his friend and comrade John Alden to Priscilla Mullins to ask her hand in marriage for Captain Standish, Priscilla asking the bashful Alden, "Why not speak for yourself, John?" In truth and fact John was bashful and Priscilla would have been bright enough to ask precisely such a question. And it made a pleasant story to pass the time. Less pleasant the story gained headway and became a tradition of the colony that Governor William Bradford had wooed Alice Carpenter in England before he went to Holland and after the drowning of his first wife Dorothy May had at once sent to England for the widowed Alice Carpenter Southworth. It was unfair to Bradford because he left England at eighteen years of age and could never have traveled the two-week journey from Austerfield to Wrington, near Bath, where Alice lived, at a time when he was among the foremost men active in forming the Scrooby church and transplanting it to Holland. But those who speculated, guessed and surmised on the strange drowning of Dorothy May and the voyage so soon thereafter of Alice Carpenter Southworth from England to Plymouth, they enjoyed rounding out the story, giving it added and mysterious motives not true in cold fact. They would have it a rather loveless match when Bradford married the sixteen-year-old Dorothy May in Amsterdam, that his heart was really lost to Alice and that he had not married Dorothy till word came of Alice marrying a Southworth. They took pleasure in weaving dark complications not there in the plain facts.

Remember could have married Orton Wingate. She knew so by the light on his face, and aware too that he knew it would make scandal and vast difficulty for her to marry one twice her age, not of the church membership, and "misliked" by her father. They would see what time

162

might bring. Neither could she be knowing she was stony-faced more often though she suspected some inner bitterness she could not put a finger on was beginning to warp surfaces she would rather have smooth. Those little dances learned from her mother and done only for her father and mother—was she beginning to mistrust them as having an edge of sin and shame? When such a suspicion came to her and her mind and conscience took trouble about it, she could put it away by making her thoughts blank and empty about it. There were the moments, long or short, when she was stony-faced.

So often she wished her mother had lived on. Her mother had a wisdom and insight that could have put a finger on what was empty in her that should be filled. Then would come the doubt that even her mother might have grown deeper in misgivings as to her sins and in fears related to her personal shames. She tried to get at what her mother would have done the winter afternoon when Orton Wingate recited for her and her father "some very old verses known among the Irish." Wingate gave the lines as though he might be whiling away shuttling monotones of time in his hut in the woods:

"Thanks be to God for the light and the darkness,
    Thanks be to God for the hail and the snow,
Thanks be to God for shower and sunshine,
    Thanks be to God for all things that grow;

"Thanks be to God for lightning and tempest,
    Thanks be to God for weal and for woe,
Thanks be to God for His own great goodness,
    Thanks be to God that what is, is so;

"Thanks be to God when the harvest is plenty,
    Thanks be to God when the barn is low,
Thanks be to God when our pockets are empty,
    Thanks be to God when they again o'erflow."

Wingate now paused long in his reciting and Remember spoke: "It is like some fresh and sacred music gushing out, is it not so, father?"

"It is good to hear, mayhap too good, too smooth and pleasant for true reverence to the Lord God and Creator."

After the long pause Orton Wingate's voice went on to give the two closing stanzas:

"Thanks be to God that the Mass bell and steeple
    Are heard and are seen throughout Erin's Green Isle,
Thanks be to God that the priest and the people
    Are ever united in danger and trial.

"Thanks be to God that the brave sons of Erin
    Have the faith of their fathers as lively as aye,
Thanks be to God that Erin's fair daughters
    Press close after Mary on heaven's highway."

All three sat silent a short while, Wingate in a bronze and perfect calm of face and feet, Remember chilled and frozen in certainty of condemnation to come, and John Spong with his thoughts in a fury and his tongue stuck fast. The moment came however when his wrath let loose:

"What we have heard, my child, is a service of praise for the Whore of Babylon, for the Romish papacy, for the Roman Catholic Mass, for the pagans who blaspheme at the very throne of God."

And Spong went on in a harangue, the words tumbling off his tongue, practiced and familiar words of denunciation. When he came to an end of words all three sat silent again. It was the only time that Orton Wingate in his few and rare visits quietly went out the door without his customary "God be with you" to John and Remember Spong.

The little incident lingered with Remember and haunted her. She tried to make her mind pierce through the complicated implications of it and pluck so much as one clear and simple meaning from it. Meantime the colony struck roots and grew.

Of a total of one hundred and ninety-nine persons come to Plymouth, in 1627 there were living one hundred and fifty-six. Fifty-two died the first year, only six in the next six years. Of sixty-eight born at Plymouth in those years fifty-three had moved away. In all shifts and changes the same group of Leydeners formed the center of the church and community. Bradford and his council of five re-elected, kept hewing to their purpose, Bradford writing, "With their miseries they opened a way to these new lands, and after these storms, with what ease other men came."

Now in 1627 they arranged to break from the Merchant Adventurers. Payments not easy to make they pledged for a term of years, after which they would be the owners of their plantation. In this ownership by the "Purchasers" were fifty-seven men, twenty-nine women, thirty-four boys and thirty-six girls, of whom forty-two had come in the *Mayflower*. Besides the single acre each already had, they now divided so there were twenty acres for each person or Purchaser's share, the meadows being owned in common and each entitled to cut hay in proportion to his shares. Their livestock by now numbered four cows, seven young heifers, four young bulls, eighteen goats, besides hogs and poultry.

Chapter 14

A Girl Sees a Ghost, a Watch, and Books

THOSE first years of living bare and gaunt had become part of Remember, part of her bones, shape and face. That time, those days gone, pressed their imprint on her. She wondered what other kind of a girl she might have been without work that put calluses on her hands. Chores had toughened her leg muscles, arms and torso. Many an afternoon she longed for twilight and sunset for then came supper, bedtime, sleep to shut out the monotony of things done over and over the same way. It was in one of those early years of the hard beginnings that Remember had a strange visitant.

On a windy night of gripping cold and blowing snow, the leather-hinged door shaken and its wooden latches rattling, Remember came out of a dream. She lay awake repeating for herself the pictures that followed one after the other in the dream. A pine smell came from twigs under her. Over pine twigs next the floor she had laid thatch, rushes, a blanket folded three times. Her head lay on a pillow of rough linen filled with pine needles. Over her spread two blankets; one had covered her on the *Mayflower*, one her mother had used on the *Mayflower*. Over these blankets she had piled her own cloak and one from her mother.

Her feet stretched a little farther could touch her father's floor bed, pallet, five or six feet from the fireplace. Farther away from the fire would be too cold, nearer would be too close to loose flying sparks and embers from the crackling firelogs. A small burnt hole in her pillow and two large ones in a blanket were ugly to look at, ominous. Once or twice during the night she or her father awoke shivering and threw on fresh firewood.

Drafts of cold air circled the room, coming in through chinks between the hewn planks: she had helped her father put clay over the large cracks. They hoped next summer to line with clay every space between the planks on the outside of the house. They hoped, too, for the day they could plaster the inside walls.

The bucket of drinking water on a shelf next to the chimney she knew in the morning would be topped with a thin layer of ice. The wind kept up a high howling outside. The walls shook. The house swayed. Once she wondered how it would be if the house should turn over and lie on one side with the roof thatch on fire.

The fireplace of stones chinked with clay sent most of its heat up that chimney of planks coated with clay. When the fire was low you were cold. When it blazed high you worried about the clay breaking apart, the wooden planks catching fire.

On this January night of bitter cold Remember heard the wooden latch of the front door rattle. She turned her head on the pillow toward the door. She saw someone come in and stand in the middle of the room. The door had not opened, she knew, or there would have been a terrific sweep of wind and snow through the room. Now who or what was it her eyes saw? Or what was it her mind reported her eyes as seeing? A tall, lithe woman with a sea-pale, bony face—thin shoulders narrowed with sharp corners, the hips curved hardly at all. Her gown seemed to flow with a soft light from shoulder to ankle. Then a returning flow of light ripples moved slow from ankle to shoulder and out along the two thin outstretched arms. Remember stared, trying to feel the lighted fabric of the gown. "A white-gold silk woven of moonmist," she told herself. Then Remember's eyes played straight on the now more distinct face and the chestnut hair of rare bright burnish. And she knew it was her mother, a thin band of gold shimmering across the forehead and around above the ears to hold coils of hair perfectly in place.

Remember lifted her head from the pillow, sat up. Tears filled her eyes, ran down her face. And she heard, "Stay under the covers, child. Do not take cold for that I have come this once."

The words came slow, clear, cozy and warming. Remember whispered slow, "Mother! Mama! you—this bitter winter night—how came you?"

Then she saw the forearms and hands raised as in blessings over her and the words, "Follow your deep inner lights, Remember, my love, follow them."

Then her mother's shape, a thin and shimmering white-gold, slowly turned on its ankles, to glide and slide rather than walk to the door. Again Remember heard the wooden door latch rattle and saw her mother go through the door without opening it.

This was the instant Remember awoke to find herself sitting amid bedclothes tangled about her, her face wet with tears, her body from waist to neck shivering with cold. She got up, threw on fresh firewood, crept into her blankets and cloaks. For an hour she lay quietly awake, turning her eyes occasionally to the door and the middle of the room. Thinking it over she believed she could be sure she had had a dream of her mother's ghost moving into that room. Yet she could not shake off a feeling that it might have been no dream of a ghost at all but a true and real shape of her mother. Why out of some other world shouldn't her mother be permitted to come to her for a few brief moments to bring unforgettable, shining loveliness into this rough-hewn, earthbound, smoke-smelling, one-room house?

And neither her dream nor her make-believe reality of her mother's ghost would she report to her father. He was practical, year by year more practical. Her dreams interested him only when practical, when they made sense, when they were like everyday life.

In his earlier years John Spong had let himself be freely whimsical and Mary Windling had lighted that element in him and brought it into rich speech at times. Then with her passing these streaks in him dwindled. Remember noticed this. During the first three years at Plymouth she hesitated more and more about telling him a fancy or folly that came to her mind.

A bluebird or a redwing might please her as she sat in the doorway to shell corn, darn stockings, sew patches on clothes. Wildflowers in May gave her delight: she spoke greetings and told them how well they kept hid through the long winter. Her bare feet ran glad on the first days in late May. Her feet sang eagerness for life as she drove cows and goats to the common pasture. And such keen and singing pleasures she would either not mention to her father or she would take care and not babble and gush gay and carefree. She saw him grow more suspicious of joy or fun. Not that he would tell her it was wrong or forbid her joy or fun. Rather she felt him more and more apart from her in things that lighted her and made her want to sing and dance. So often he somberly nodded or mildly grumbled at her fun. He would deny her nothing the church would not deny her. So it seemed. She must expect he would overlook her childish ways. So it further seemed. And the time must soon come when she would leave off childish ways and be an older person like him going through life practical, sober, grave and reverent. So indeed he said he hoped. This process had done something to her. She felt her father shaping her toward his own patterns of life. More often now she checked herself, held back from him little affairs that made her feet glad and her eyes merry.

She questioned herself about God in a blue sky, God in a blinding snow of a great white storm from the northwest, about a regard for things her mother called sacred. Bread was sacred, her mother taught her: to throw away a scrap of bread was a sin against the God who gave the seed to the earth that brought the grain for the bread. Sea and land were sacred, so was the soup for dinner and the spoons that lifted it to the mouth. A tall tree and its branches were sacred, so was a knucklebone of her little finger, so was each of the five small faint freckles on her face. She could tell this to herself. But not to her father. He could be like to say, "You speak well one moment. Then you lapse into peril of becoming a trifler, a flippant and irreverent child." She prayed to grow like her mother. She too would like personal archangels to call by name and send them on errands for her.

Such matters ran through her mind that bitterly cold January night. She was fifteen, groping for meanings. Her father on his pallet by the fire stirred in his sleep, turned from one side to the other, half-awak-

167

ened but unaware of his shivering daughter in tears on her pillow. Her tears came more from joy than from pain. She had seen her mother in a startling white-gold loveliness rattle the wooden door latch and enter the room without opening the door, speaking a few sweet words to her and then vanishing. Though it was a dream she was going to make believe it happened true and real, and the roughhewn, earthbound house would evermore hold hope and holiness for her because this had happened.

She was slow getting warmed and going to sleep again but it was a deep sleep.

When later her eyes opened she saw gray streaks of light straggle through a window of heavy white paper soaked with linseed oil, breaking the long night's darkness of the room. She welcomed another winter morning. Her father awoke. They sat up facing each other. The fire had gone low, a few ruddy embers glowing through the cover of ashes. Remember chirped another day had come. Her father warned they must take care no hour of it be wasted.

She could have sung out to him, "I saw mother last night—there in the middle of the room I saw her. She came rattling the door latch and moved through the door without opening it. She spoke to me. I heard her." She could have sung out that to her father. And it would have spoiled the beginning of the day for him. Late that afternoon or the next day he would have spoken fear over the fantasies possessing her mind or mumbled something like, "You dream of your mother in too gaudy a garb."

Having slept in their undergarments and wool stockings, they were soon dressed, wearing their heavy cloaks. The father soon had a rousing fire going. The girl skipped to warm a pot of corn meal. Out of pewter bowls they had brought from Leyden they ate their breakfast of cornmeal mush, seated on stools they brought close to the fire. They could feel the cold come in and take its hold on the hand or ear away from the fire. They bowed their heads before eating. John Spong spoke grace and thanks for the food. They were in health, with sharp appetites, taking each spoon of mush slowly and with relish. They could have eaten a second bowl as they did before the colony's corn supply ran low. But they could see near by the sack of corn meal that must last them till the next issue weeks away. In the other houses over Plymouth they knew it was the same: those who had eaten one bowl of mush would have liked a second bowl for warmth and strength.

"The taste is so good I can feel it in my bones," said Remember as the last spoonful of warm corn meal slid down her throat. She smacked her lips, clucked her tongue at her father with mischief and glee in her eyes. She threw back her head, shut her eyes tight and sat still murmuring, "Now I'm going to keep my eyes shut and I will see my self eating a second bowl of that good yum-yum corn, that sweet yummy-yummy corn, warming my belly and then my warm belly making me warm all over me."

"Contain thyself, child," she now heard. "Such nonsense does not well begin the day. The little food we have for these mortal bodies of ours should be held sacred."

His voice was kind. He was gently admonishing her. But he wouldn't join her in a little fun to start the day as they sat where a hand or an ear turned away from the fire could feel the grip and chill of winter air. He might have said to her, "I will shut my eyes and join you in having that second yummy-yummy bowl warming my belly and making me warm all over me." Then he would have brought her into telling her sweet dream to him. Instead of which, as she sat with head thrown back and eyes shut, she changed from seeing herself eat a second bowl of corn meal, changed the picture in her mind to where she saw her mother poised in the middle of the room and herself saying of what her mother wore, "A white-gold silk woven of moonmist."

Remember at nineteen had not at all broken away from those first years of the hard beginnings. They were part of her. Now she and her father had each their beds a foot above the floor. And they had mattresses filled with cornhusks. They had that added human dignity, along with many others.

She had held blazing pine knots to light her father on winter nights. He smoothed with a plane the rough boards to go lengthwise for their beds. He sawed and planed the foot and head boards. He whittled with a knife the wooden pegs to go here and there in auger-bored holes. She learned by the nods of his head and the motions of his hand where he wanted the light of the pine knot brought closer. They had then two candles half burned down and they had to save on candles. When cattle should be doing better in Plymouth they would have tallow, they said then. And that time had come and Remember had taken her turn with the women at candle-dipping. Sometime too they would have a watch or a clock. They were not sure when that day would come. But every year now they were a little better off so John Spong talked occasionally about how it would be to rise any time of the night and open a watch and look at the numbers on its face and read the time—or how it would be morning or midday to turn to a watch and know the exact hour and minute. On a day of sun in winter or summer he could read shadows near the exact hour. On their little wooden sundial, that he had carved and fitted in four winter nights by the fire, he could read time to the half-hour. But a watch in their house would be a kind of testimony to man and his ingenious calculating mind that could so measure out time in days, half-days, hours, and then go farther and measure out the little minutes of which sixty make an hour.

They would not soon forget the day Goodman Spong made changes and repairs on the floor, bookshelves, and fireplace of Elder Brewster's house. On the Elder's study table lay his silver-cased watch, nearly as wide across as Remember's hand. Elder Brewster noticed her curiosity. Open-eyed, her eyebrows raised, her lips pursed in a smile she listened to the ticking of the watch. She had been told that same ticking goes on night and day, never faster and never slower, that tick-tick-tick-tick and never any stop to the tick-tick-tick-tick—what was it doing? Keeping watch on time, ready to tell the time whenever you should look at its face.

Elder Brewster explained this as he held the watch against her left ear so she could hear how clear and how regular was tick-tick-tick-tick. Slowly and softly he moved it from her and laid it back on the table. It wasn't perfect, he would have her know. There had been times when the shadow lines of the sun pointed straight north and the watch was a half-hour and once more than an hour behind noon, the strictly correct time of the sundial.

Then five or six of the Plymouth men best skilled in mechanics sat around the table and studied the inside of the watch and made little changes here and there, so it told correct time again. Elder Brewster smiled telling this, for it seemed the cleverest mechanics respected the watch as a work of master mechanics and they took it as a holiday when they could sit around it, touch and handle it, ask questions and talk to it, "What is wrong with you? Tell us. We want to make you right again."

Remember slowly reached her fingers toward the watch and felt of the scrolls engraved on the silver case. "The dial they call this," said Elder Brewster, pointing with a finger. And Remember, "I can read the numbers. They are the same numbers that stand at the beginning of chapters in the Bible." Elder Brewster, pleased at this, went on telling of more than twenty different kinds of watches he had seen, some egg-shaped, some formed like a skull to remind those looking at it that each second ticked off brought them nearer to death; other watches oval, eight-sided, or square or shell-shaped. And he blinked with a shine to his eyes mentioning two watches he would have liked for his own; one of Swiss make and oblong opened like a book and inside the cover engraved on the gold was the Saviour on the Cross. The other was French made in the form of a Cross with the dial at the center.

Now Elder Brewster had to raise his voice above the noise made by Goodman Spong and a hammer driving wooden pegs into the new-made bookshelf ends. What few iron nails Spong had went into the floor work, and no more iron nails to be had till weeks or months ahead when the blacksmith could get to it. So Spong whittled his own nails of wood, fitted them, drove them in with his hammer. Spong hoped sometime for plenty of iron nails so he could work faster and be more sure of what he nailed holding together, for even the hardest hickory-wood pegs would in time warp and come loose. He wiped the wood dust off his hands on his leather breeches. He came over to join Remember in marveling at the watch on the table.

"The day shall come and it must in God's good time," said Elder Brewster, "when every house and family in Plymouth will have its own watch. It is not an easy matter to foresee that far in the future. Yet I believe it will come. A watch is a help, not a necessity, but rather a convenience. The dark of the night tells us when to go to bed. Daybreak tells us when to get up. The healthy and temperate man knows when to eat or drink, when to work hard or slacken and rest.

"The man of sloth would not go to work earlier or later by reason of a watch telling him the time. Nor can a watch tell a glutton when to quit stuffing himself. Nor would any drunkard stop guzzling of drink because a watch told him it was time to stop. Yet decent folk and punctual men can use a watch to advantage. They would rather say, 'I will come to your house at thirty minutes after six by our watches' than as they say now, 'I will come soon after candlelight.' The exact watch enables us on each Lord's Day to begin our meeting at the proper and correct time. The watch tells the drummer when to beat the drum roll for the members to leave their homes for worship."

John Spong bent his head down, laid an ear close to the watch, raised his head, on his face a peculiar shrewd look, too shrewd. Remember had seen this look before. She knew her father had been struck with an idea on which he set value. Brewster had seen this look when Spong in meetings stood up to "prophesy," to speak some personal interpretation of the Bible, usually with a touch of vanity as though to imply, "You may not expect it from me. Nevertheless I have testimony to give worth your hearing and in favor to compare with that of others who have spoken."

Now Spong was saying of the watch, "It is a wonderful contrivance of man. We may see it as a work of man which reflects the powerful craft of his mind. We may go farther and see it as a work of man in which he endeavors to measure those moments of his life which constitute a part of eternity, that part of eternity in which God has permitted him to have life. As an offering of man's humility and a constant reminder of the short shrift of his life, it may contain no portion of sin. Nevertheless should man have too high a degree of pride and praise himself too highly for his playfulness with time, which belongs to God, one might conceive that a jealous God, seeing and knowing this, would regard this undue pride and praise as a false assumption on the part of man. Thereupon the Lord would enact a decree as forthright and severe as when He stopped the false and vain assumptions of those who gave themselves praise and pride while building the Tower of Babel. The Lord then decreed that all tongues should be confounded and tangled. So likewise the Almighty could decree that all the watches of men should be entangled and struck with confoundment, so their reports of time should be false and not worthy of trust."

Remember saw her father's underlip stuck out, his eyes shining with a gleam of sly triumph. In the short silence that followed she felt sorry for him, then less so. She saw he was sorry for himself that he had spoken too soon. Her father knew he could just as well have waited and lived with his fresh idea before giving it so freely in the very house and among the very books of Plymouth's foremost authority on the Bible, Plymouth's chief interpreter of the plan, intention and character of God.

A quiet remark came from Elder Brewster. Remember could read that her father's venture into theological interpretation and his needless vehemence about it were not quite called for. With a kindly imperturbable gravity Elder Brewster was saying, "Should the watch become common and receive devotion as a heathen idol, the beneficent All-Wise Creator may direct it be destroyed through confoundment as at the Tower of Babel or He may in His wisdom permit the watch to continue to exist for His own divine purposes as He has permitted other idols to go unharmed."

"His ways and works are mysterious," mumbled Spong, going back to his boards and pegs.

Remember knew her father would be miserable for days over this little affair. The spoken conceit of his mind was nice enough. But he had been vehement, proud, vain in the speaking of it. He should have offered it as an odd fancy; it had crossed his mind and he wasn't sure what to make of it. Instead he presented it as original, not yet heard in any sermon in Plymouth and probably not found in the four hundred books on Elder Brewster's shelves. His tone had been, "I may not be a learned man but I can report grave matters not yet found in the books."

For two whole days Remember noticed him short-spoken about the house. Twice when Remember tried to make talk his response was, "I have reason to be a say-nothing."

Days later Remember ventured, "When I awoke this morning I had thoughts about a long time from now, two or three hundred years from now. Many things will be different, comforts and helps we dream not of now, the streets full of horses and gaudy wagons, houses with many more rooms than now and so many candles that every room will have two candles, a wide glass window. Think of it, a glass window for every room, thick walls with every chink plastered and the walls whitewashed. Chimneys of stone, with enough cows on the common pasture for milk, butter, cheese, every day for all. And in every house a watch, some with two watches, one on the ground floor, another on the upper, and—"

She had bubbled with enthusiasm about this Plymouth of the future. She saw her father listening with interest till she mentioned watches. Then his underlip went out. She heard him, "Let us say no more about it."

The future, the long time ahead, changes to come in that long time, how certain were those changes, this crept as a wonder in Remember's thinking. Especially when she was allowed visits and talks with Elder Brewster among his books. Nothing else like that book corner in all of Plymouth. More than four hundred books stood on those shelves. She would take them from the shelves one by one. She would feel the heavy boards and leather bindings, feel the thick and tough rag-paper pages, run her fingers along pages where the printed words stood black and clear. And you couldn't make a letter come loose out of a word by rubbing it with your thumb or scraping it with a fingernail.

Elder Brewster told her that two hundred and eighty-one of the books had come over on the *Mayflower*. Since then more than a hundred other books had come on ships from England. He saw her hushed and awed before the array of volumes that marched along the bookshelves. The books stood still and seemed to say, "We can speak to you—open the covers and put your eyes on our letters and you will find we speak—we only seem to be silent."

The books awed her by size, thickness, the staggering mass of lines and words to read before she could read all of them. Then having read all of the books must she carry in her head all that knowledge from the books? This too staggered her.

"Wouldn't my head feel queer?" she asked Elder Brewster. "Wouldn't my head feel heavy carrying so much knowledge? Could any of it spill out if there was too much?"

"No, my child, I have read all of them. Each writer of a book repeats himself. And they all repeat each other more or less."

He pointed to a long row of "Commentaries." First a Commentary on the whole Bible, then a Commentary on the New Testament, followed by a Commentary on the Four Gospels, another on the Pentateuch, more and more, one by one, on the Prophets, on the Psalms, on the Proverbs of Solomon, on Ecclesiastes, on the Song of Solomon, on Genesis, Joshua, Samuel, Jeremiah, Isaiah, Lamentations, Ezekiel, Daniel, Hosea, Matthew, Luke, John, the Epistles to the Romans, Corinthians, Thessalonians, Ephesians, Colossians, Timothy, Titus, Hebrews, James, Peter, Jude, and the Apocalypse.

In each commentary, the Elder explained, the writer told what some part of the Bible meant to him. Another man searching the Bible for meanings might find such a book a help. As time passed there would be more commentaries written, till there were thousands. Then would come danger. A man might spend too much time reading the inquiries and discussions of others: he would then lose his own time for reading the Bible and searching his own heart many times over for the meanings.

Remember was surprised. The humility and frankness of Elder Brewster pleased her. Near seventy years old, he had read all those books, besides the Bible, several times. And he was saying he didn't know it all. He read books hoping they would help him to know. And he was saying furthermore that all the commentaries, a long row of books, wouldn't help you unless you read the Book of Books for yourself and searched your own heart many times over.

She held in her hands a Hebrew grammar, then Morelius's *Latin, Greek and English Dictionary*, then Buxtorf's *Hebrew and Chaldee Lexicon*. For a moment the shadowy, ancient mystery of the languages of mankind swept her. It was as though she had dropped into a deep well. Dutch was the only language besides English she had seen in printed letters. Now she saw Greek and Hebrew for the first time.

Not often was Remember open-mouthed. Now with an open mouth and staring eyes she said to Elder Brewster, "For thousands of years millions of people, one generation after another of Hebrews and Greeks, have been using these letters and talking the tongues that go with them."

"Yes, Remember. The earliest manuscripts of the Bible are in those languages. Some manuscripts written in Hebrew are lost. We have them only in translations into Greek."

Slowly Remember's mouth closed. Her awe edged into bewilderment. She tried to think how old is time, what long spaces of years mankind has been on the earth. She heard swarming of life behind those books. They whispered of toil, struggle, death, love, war and clashing faiths, long ago—oh, so long ago—in Rome, Athens, Jerusalem, Damascus, Bethlehem.

She took the Hebrew grammar in her hands again. She asked Elder Brewster to find the words "love," "death," and "mother." He did so, pronouncing the words in Hebrew for her. The look of the words on the printed page, the way those Hebrew syllables were shaped by the mouth—gave her wonder. She asked him to repeat them with her. She said the strange words after him as best she could.

She handled two volumes on civil government, *The Six Bookes of a Commonweale* by Knowles translated from *Les sez livres de la ré-publique* by the French jurist Jean Bodin—and *Commonwealth of England & maner of Government thereof* by Sir Thomas Smith. A government in Plymouth she knew they had, and each year they elected a governor and a council. Now the thought struck her: there is government everywhere, either good or bad. And men who know about government write big bulging books about it.

She held the volume *Two Bookes, of the proficience and advancement of Learning, divine and humane* by Lord Francis Bacon. Remember had heard him mentioned a few times: the man who had read and written more books than any other man in England. This crossed her mind. Elder Brewster smiled gravely. "Should you read it, you would find he desires men of learning should rehearse and revise their learning with more care. Their learning often is less deep and certain than they believe."

Once more this afternoon Remember was puzzled. "Should I get time to read many books I would find the men of learning in dispute

174

and argument among themselves? They challenge each other how much they know and do not know—would that be so, Elder Brewster?"

His slow grave smile came. "Yes, my child."

She handled De Serre's *Perfect use of Silkwormes and their benefit,* two works on surveying, one on herbs, John Smith's *Description of New England,* Abbot's *Briefe Description of the whole world,* a volume on how to grow more firewood and timber on the same ground, Bedford's *Sufficiencie of English Medicines for the cure of all diseases cured with Medicine,* two volumes of verse, Henoch Clapham's *A briefe of the Bible,* Braithwait's *Description of a Good Wife,* many pages of Latin verse by Reverend Dr. Francis Herring in praise and celebration of King James I, and Henry Ainsworth's book giving the tunes he wrote for his rearrangements of the Psalms of David.

Holding in her hands Hornsby's *Scourge of Drunkenness* in verse Remember turned her eyes toward Elder Brewster. Tall, well-formed and erect, clear-eyed and well-kept, a man good to look at—all his life he had spared himself from wines and liquors, not so much as touching beer—one of the six men who had not taken to his bed during the Great Sickness. He pointed at one little row of books very personal to him. His dearest old friend and teacher, John Robinson, wrote four of these. Eleven he had written himself, helped print them in Leyden. When copics reached England they roused the anger of bishops and archbishops who got orders sent to Holland for officers to arrest and deport Elder Brewster, so when later Elder Brewster went to England he kept in hiding: he could not be found by those who would put him in jail. Jail for him then would not have been the first time, thought Remember. She had heard from her father and mother of his lying in Boston jail many days after the first attempt of the Scrooby Pilgrims to leave England.

She went away with a kindly handshake and a smile of blessing from Elder Brewster. She walked home a little dazed. She seethed with pictures, questions, imaginings about the world of books and thought.

* * * * * * * * * ★

Chapter 15

* * * * * * * * * ★

Remember's Birthday

THE year 1628 came and with it the October day which was Remember's birthday. She always kept it as a solemn day—and a gay one. Her mother had seen to it that no matter how mean or pinched their living

175

in Leyden, there were always cakes and gifts. Little and trifling the gifts might be, but her mother brought them with festival gaiety. And she and her mother did a birthday dance together—holding hands and swinging in a circle one way as many years as Remember was old, again swinging the other way the number of years with the right knee raised high with the left hand slapping the face of the other, then the left knee raised high and the right hand slapping the face of the other, then they bowed profoundly smiling in each other's eyes, "We bow to the year to come."

Remember didn't forget she was "an early child" by two months, reckoning by the marriage date. "When you are grown older I shall tell you all you need and wish to know," said her mother more than once. "You are lawful a child as ever born. And should it hap you were lawless conceived and baseborn I would hug you all the harder."

Even on the *Mayflower* when Remember's birthday came and a wide sea of breakers tossed the *Mayflower* like an eggshell and the winds howled, Mary Windling Spong brought from somewhere a little inch-wide foot-long ribbon of blue satin. This Remember had kept, always wearing it around her neck on this October day, never failing to picture the one supreme anger of her mother's life. She was sure her mother would have kept that threat sent to the woman who went on, in spite of mild warnings, in scandalizing, mouthing, insinuating with malicious mischief, as to Remember being "an early child." Remember was sure her mother would have waited till after meeting in the house of worship on the Lord's Day and leaped on her enemy and torn the clothes off her.

"She might have killed that evil gossip, I am not sure," Remember said to herself many a time. She wondered whether she had from the blood of her mother any such marvelous anger. "I hope so," ran her thought. "I believe so. The time has not come, yet it may when I will need that scorn and proud anger from the blood of my mother."

"Twenty, twenty, twenty," she babbled like a song when she woke this October morning. "Who says twenty? I say twenty. The sky says twenty. The Atlantic Ocean says twenty. God says twenty." Here she paused. She had babbled this so glad, so loud, so emphatic that her father might have heard it. And if her father heard it he would be sure to admonish her. And she would like him to enjoy himself with some admonishing on her birthday. She would see him revel in the pleasure of indulging himself in a long admonition on profanity, blasphemy, the perils of taking the name of God in vain.

She listened. She heard a stirring below and knew that her father had got out of bed into his clothes and gone to the trapdoor, climbed down the ladder. The crackling she heard was fresh firewood he had put on. He was making ready their breakfast. The one waking first in the morning would do these chores. Sometimes she woke first and got into her clothes and tiptoed through the door of the thin partition between their rooms and went down the ladder without waking him. In the winter, unless it was so cold that they both slept next to the fire below, she would take her clothes, on jumping out of bed, and scurry with all speed to the trapdoor and down the ladder to dress by a warm fire.

"Somewhat gladsome, somewhat nice, neat, pretty," said Remember, "when I look back to my other birthdays in Plymouth." Clean white sheets she had slept in this night. The first year, this was, she and her father had clean white sheets over and under them. The year before they had a white sheet under and a wool blanket over. The years before that it had been a blanket under and a blanket over. White pillowcases they had had for four years. And before this year the pillows had been stuffed with straw, pine needles, cornhusks. Now this gladsome year they had goose down in the pillows. "We are coming up in the world," Remember had told her father on their first night with their heads on goose-down pillows. "We are rising. We may become soft."

Her father's face was enigmatic. "You may speak more truth than you know. We are in the keeping of the Most High. My father told me of his grandfather and their forebears for generations sleeping on straw laid on a clay floor and for pillow a log of wood. Those peasants of England had no chimneys. The firesmoke went through a hole in the center of the roof. A hundred and two hundred years ago and in generations farther back much of the common folk lived bare and gaunt like the beasts of the fields that huddle uncomplaining under sheds not sheltering them but merely breaking the severity of the storm."

Remember could see what her father had when he rose into one of his rare fine moments. It moved her that her father should have gathered to his mind and kept this picture of a hardened humanity in former times living so meager that what they now had in Plymouth was luxury.

She burrowed her face in her goose-down pillow. Personal, quite personal was this pillow to her. Habakkuk and Hannaniah, Beulah and Bathsheba, had helped make the pillow soft. Then Peter and Paul, Dainty and Deborah, had helped. Then Hezekiah and Zachariah, Sheba and Shallott had added their goose down. Remember had been a goosegirl, a gooseherd, feeding and tending her geese year after year, giving them goose names that pleased her. One she had named after Breakheart Hill, ten miles from Plymouth, its Indian name Paukopunnakuck. To a plump, fat, important-looking gosling she gave this name of Paukopunnakuck, or Pauko for short. But the months went by and Paukopunnakuck proved the scrawniest and most wretched goose she had ever raised. On the other hand the unpromising and peaked Dainty became a flock leader and eventually provided much good meat and plenty of worthy goose grease for a variety of purposes around the household. Her burrowed face came out of the pillow with a little laugh, "Dainty, 'twas you gave more down than any other," and with a mock sobriety, "and you, Paukopunnakuck, you gave what down you had to give and no other goose did more, so on my birthday, I do not forget you, Paukopunnakuck."

Her bed stood ten inches from the floor, made of pit-sawn oak boards. It was seven feet long, and, as Remember once noted to herself, "Twice as wide as I am at the hips wherefore I could not ask more."

Out near Breakheart Hill, which also had the name of Heartbreak Hill, ran a stream named Labor-in-Vain Creek. Remember had seen enough on the *Mayflower* and in her eight years in Plymouth to understand why any stream or hill got the name of Breakheart, Heartbreak, or Labor-in-Vain. This day, however, it was her resolution to shut out dark thoughts. The clean white sheets, for instance, where her long, lean, lithe, snow-white body snuggled, it was a pleasant thought that she washed the sheets herself, that last year they got a new washtub, deep as her arm-lengths. And had she helped to make the soft soap for washing clothes and scrubbing floors? She had. Ashes from oak and maple wood she had saved, drippings from venison and other roasts, however little it might be. She had helped carry her personal ashes and her personal grease to where she joined with neighbors around a big washtub where with fire and the right use of lye, lime, and boiling water, the neighborhood soapmaking went on to its finish and Remember helped carry home a year's supply to be stored in a barrel in their house cellar. The smooth soft rain water she now had for washing—that was an improvement of this year of 1628. Before this year she had carried water in buckets from springs and creeks and later had helped in the hauling from springs or creeks of casks of water on an oxcart.

Now in this year it was, early spring, her father with five other men had torn off the heavy grass thatch roof and put on a roof of heavy clapboards with shingles. Then they had made wooden troughs to hang under the eaves and catch the rain water that ran into barrels and was nice and handy for washing. Well it was the grass thatch roof was gone, for the houses burned to the ground in Plymouth had nearly all started from sparks falling into dry grass thatch, wherefore the law now forbade thatch roofs.

A day for looking back it was. Till this year of 1628 she and her father had lived, cooked, slept and gone through necessary routines of the day, all in that one room below. With removal of the thatch roof had come this addition of a second story of two rooms. Four years back the six-foot cellar was dug under their house, John Spong himself laying the flat stones of a curve of stairway like his folks had in Scrooby, England. The crowded clutter of the main living room below her was easier to look at and take care of now in 1628.

By sitting up straight and holding her hand high as she could, Remember's finger tips could touch the ceiling of her room, five feet from the floor. Above was a garret reached by a ladder and through a trapdoor. Here were discards, castaways, clothes and utensils, rags, pieces of leather and all sorts of oddities not now of use. And often the exact little thing needed to fix or repair something could be found here. Wooden pegs on the walls of her room held the few dresses, gowns, and cloaks of Remember. A leather-covered oak chest brought from Leyden, and used for herself and her mother on the *Mayflower*, stood against a wall. Roasting the last of Paukopunnakuck Remember took spoons of grease to rub well through the leather of this chest. With soap and grease for years she had rubbed this trunk leather, her intention it should last her lifetime. The chest held her two bodices, her few lace trimmings, two lawn kerchiefs a yard square each, one black and one white, two hoods, two white nightgowns, a white night jacket her mother had used, gloves, mittens, woolen hose, cloth hose. Alongside the chest stood her two pairs of shoes. Until a week ago this October she had since the middle of May worn shoes only on the Lord's Day at worship. Now would come frosty mornings and until next May she would be wearing shoes every day. All of her shoes had patches. Next summer she hoped to go to a shoemaker to measure her feet and cut and sew for her a shape of leather into which she could shove her feet. Buckles to pull the shoe more snug around the ankles—or a heavy ribbon of black silk or taffeta tightened and tied in a bow at the ankles —these she would afford when better-off.

Her birthday—a day for looking back. A long time back it seemed to that winter seven years ago when pressed and hurried with other things that must be done, they had no outhouse built when winter came— and the people of six houses utilized the one outhouse. The two earthenware chamber pots they had brought from Leyden, turned at the potter's wheel by John Spong himself, had proved convenient. Now they had their own little edifice, four by four and seven feet high, weatherproof, private, truly a privy. On bitter-cold winter nights when a northeast wind blew in from the Atlantic with a driving, whirling snow to the Plymouth hilltop houses, there were the occasional moments when a chamber pot was saluted with depths of gratitude for being what it was and where it was, having almost a sacramental quality.

A day to look back—and there came the mental picture of the eight days she lay on the floor of the Common House with more than forty others of men, women and children, some writhing with scurvy and running sores, a stench over the room, many like herself feverish and worn near to skeletons with scant food, coughing and spewing from sore throats and lungs, others far gone, their white lips speaking faint final testimonies. Remember's eyes caught each day one or two carried out for burial and one day no less than four bodies borne out. That was nearly eight years ago and she twelve years old in the Great Sickness that struck hard among children, she had come through alive. And for all of scant food, the cold, bad shelter, hard work and long hours of it, she nevertheless got back and held her strength and had never a sick day. That is, never a sick day in her body. Her mind and heart, however, had often been sick. She could get along with God. The goodness of God she never questioned. It was God's great antagonist troubled her, Satan, the Dark One, the Evil Shadow. Many an hour came when she believed the Evil Shadow to be near. It took possession of her thoughts to an extent that could and did frighten her. She asked herself whether a Dark Power that could so completely hold her thought and occupy her mind so often—was it not already a very real danger?

While her mother was alive the Dark One had no hold on her. Her mother so often lighthearted, even gay, could banish the Evil Shadow. In Leyden she and her mother did a dance they called Sweeping Out the Devil. Remember would stand still and her mother skipstep in a circle around her, laughing, "We will sweep out the Devil." Three times around and her mother would stop stock-still and throw her the broom saying, "Sweep out the Devil, child." Then Remember would hold the broom high as she could with her two hands and skipstep three times around her mother, laughing, "Sweep out the Devil." Stopping stock-still, Remember would sling the broom to her mother's hands, crying, "Sweep out the Devil, mother." They went through more variations and ended with opening a window and sweeping the Devil out of the window and then opening the kitchen door and each one with long fast, curving sweepstrokes saying and laughing, "We have swept the Devil out—if the Devil was here, he's gone—we swept him out."

Until her mother died Remember had believed in the Devil only slightly. Since her mother's guardian face and voice had gone she had heard of the powerful mysterious Dark One, heard it from grave elders, heard it from men and women with whom she had gone through hardship and trials. Talked and preached and taught it was, that Satan, sly, conniving, subtle beyond fathoming, lurked about every house, in every room, seeking ever to seduce and betray even the best of men and women.

Also with the passing of her mother, she saw her father from year to year more fascinated and occupied with the reality of the Devil.

"A woman can become a witch active in the service of the Evil One without her knowing what it is haps to her while it goes on," Remember heard her father say not once but a hundred times. "It is little by little in the brightness of midday or the dark of the moon, though more often by the dark of the moon it is, little by little the Devil can take a good enough woman and make her into a vile witch sold to him."

A woman visited with sick spells, somewhat out of her mind the last two years of her life, died suddenly, with much lively talk in some quarters about her way of dying. "They say," Remember heard her father one night at supper in the tone of a man who believed what "they" were saying as if "they" could tell still more and far worse if they told all. "They say she had vomiting spells the long afternoon of the evening before she died. They say she gave up nails, pins, and needles from her innards. Then came a vomit of jewels which were mostly rubies. She vomited rubbish and ashes. The last she gave up from her ghastly and wicked guts were five live coals. They burned red and sent up a black smoke spelling strange letters no one could read. Her dying eyes read them nevertheless and on reading them she breathed her last words, 'I go to my Master.' "

Neither Remember nor John Spong said anything for a while, then the father, as more he should have included, "Some of the needles were knitting needles, long sharp bloody knitting needles." The father cut a morsel of the pork before him, put his fingers round it, raised it to his mouth and chewed it and smacked over it.

Remember found her food tasted flat. An afterthought came from her father and plainly he had discussed it with others and they had agreed. "No doubt the Antichrist works by his dark and subtle ways in Plymouth. Had we known of her condition or suspected it any day in the last year we could have challenged her to the one test infallible, to several tests infallible. Tell her she must say the Lord's Prayer and she will shrivel in fear, well aware she dare not say the opening words, 'Our Father, who art in heaven,' in betrayal of her master, the Evil One to whom she is sold. Or make the woman to weep, and if she is a witch, you will see she can weep only three small tears and those from the left eye. The supreme test for a witch is to strip the woman naked. Then you cross-bind her, the right thumb to the left toe, the left thumb to the right toe. Then you throw her into a pond or a river. If she is guilty she cannot sink. In her bargain with the Devil, she renounced the benefit of the water of baptism wherefore the element of water renounces her, refuses to receive her to its bosom, and she floats, she swims without moving arms or legs, and we know her to be a witch."

And with this additional information from her zealous father, Remember lost interest in the food before her.

Her father believed what he had been telling her. Or else he wanted to believe it and it pleased him in some dark winding fashion to believe it. Of so much Remember was sure. And how much of it was she herself believing? She recoiled from believing all of it. It was too nasty for her to believe all of it, yet part of it stayed with her. Months went by and she could not rid herself of a certain definite little shiver of terror over what happened at the death of that woman.

She spoke of this affair to Orton Wingate. He edged on anger, then laughed. "In the first vomit something glistened like a needle. In the retelling of the story it became pins, needles, nails, and finally knitting needles. A small blotch of blood in another vomit became a ruby and with further telling became all kinds of jewels although mostly rubies. And who that has puked has not seen the like of rubbish and ashes in it? The five little coals burning red, sending up black smoke, spelling strange letters no one could read but her. That was a figment of a pigment originated by goddam liars who know not what they do. I have my surmise, as good as any other. She died in a simple honest Christian faith and her last words, 'I go to my Master,' meant she was glad to leave blab-mouthed Plymouth and go to the arms of Jesus, her Lord and Master."

Remember agreed with half of this, perhaps nearly all. Yet her small shiver of terror about it would not be gone. There was a Satan, a Dark One, the Evil Shadow working in Plymouth. He might be working through her father on her. How did she know? It haunted her. A shade of terror, a cruel fear, came and went in her mind and heart. She would be rid of it, clean gone from her. Then it came again, with the creep of a poison mist.

She yawned on this birthday morning—and stretched. "A slugabed am I. I know what I be—a slugabed. The sluggard's guise—loath to bed and loath to rise." She yawned again, threw her arms far back and stretched from finger tips to toes. "Twenty, twenty, twenty," she babbled again this October morning. "Who says twenty? I say twenty. The sky says twenty. The Atlantic Ocean says twenty." And in a whisper, "God says twenty."

She held her hands before her eyes, looked at them, turned them around palm and back, looked. They were hard hands, near gnarled. The handles of broom, bucket, hatchet, hoe, fork, sickle, had worn calluses. She had gripped work in this house of her father, in the cornfields and in the grassy meadows allotted for cutting. She had helped at planting the corn, hoeing, cutting, stacking the shocks, husking with her bare hands the ripe corn. Still later at home in the winter her bare hands shelled corn and put the blue, brown and white kernels in bags her father carried to mill. She had let no corncob go to waste; they fed the fire and had other uses. She had washed and prepared corn for parching, corn meal for bread, for cakes, for gruel she ate with her father. Food she ate she had seen as the seed her hands put in the ground and tended and harvested. "I am earthy and of the earth," she had said, "and in my blood and bones and hair flows the strength of the kindly earth—I must live hard—and kindly—it may be so—yes hard and kindly shall be my life."

She exulted in her strength, in being swift, in the skill of her measured motions at cooking, cleaning, at house and farm work. She had learned to work slow enough to last through a task and not be worn-out. At service one summer Lord's Day she fought against sleep that overcame her. The congregation saw her bright head of burnished chestnut had slimpsed down, her chin at her collarbone, her underlip in a helpless pout. And the congregation saw the tithingman reach a rod of authority toward her. A rabbit foot on its end tickled her nose. She awoke, straightened herself, and saw smiles in the eyes of some who would not let their mouths smile. Was it not this summer that a woman was publicly reproached for letting her face, eyes and lips smile during Lord's Day service? And it was this Lord's Day that Elder Brewster patted her cheek and, "I have seen thee. In the corn you go too fast with the hoe. Take more time, child. The Lord will allow of thee taking more time. It is many years in old England they have said: Fair and softly goes far in a day." That stayed with her. In the corn rows, at the washtub, bringing buckets of water from a rain barrel or a well she studied how to go fair and softly.

Her hands pleased her. Not so she was vain of her hands. There they were. She turned them around, palm to back to palm again, fingers and thumbs and they had never forsaken her. They pleased her, these hands. They could take hold. They served. Going much by herself and alone, leaning her weight on no others for help, she paid honor to her hands this morning as though they were not part of herself but two independent, warm, close friends. And wherever she went these two friends came along and leaped to do what she wanted the moment her mind thought it. "Thankful I am to thee, my right hand, and to thee, oh, left hand, I give equal thanks. The three of us this morning say twenty, twenty, twenty." Now her clear voice rang loud as a hosannah. "The sky says so. The wide blue sea says so." Then in a clear whisper not to be heard beyond the room, "And the good sweet God high above us says so."

She had guessed that any moment her father might be in hearing, and calling her. Now his voice came up through the trapdoor of the next room, "Slugabed—slugabed!" And her ringing shouted answer, "Twenty, twenty, twenty years I have had."

She was out of bed and into her day clothes. Out of the chest she picked the satin ribbon of blue. Down the ladder she slid rather than stepped, ran out the back door, took a wooden basin off a bench next the house, stepped to a rain barrel at the house corner and scooped it full of water, sprang with it to the bench, washed her hands, face, ears, neck, reached her hand into a small wooden bowl of soft soap under the bench, again washed her hands, face, ears, neck, took the basin in her two hands and threw the water out of it as far as she could, stepped over to the rain barrel, reached down and picked up a bowl and dipped water that she threw into the washbasin to rinse it, then throwing that water to follow the other, she laid the basin one end up on the bench against the house. Soon would come the cold weather lasting till next April or May and no more of this morning facewash outdoors.

Here at a corner rain barrel she had several times made a wish. She wished the rain barrel to be in the house and two spigots on it. "One spigot I would turn and out would come cold water. The other spigot I would turn and out would come hot water. And the barrel would always give me the water I wanted, hot or cold, and no filling of the barrel with buckets and buckets day after day. What a handy and pleasant barrel that would be! Hot water on my saying come hot, cold water on my saying cold—what a wishing barrel!"

She stood on the first stones that formed the doorstep. She waved her hand to her favorite wind-worn cedar tree twenty feet off and again waved her hand and gave a long sweeping salute to the Atlantic Ocean and the lean white sandbar of Clark's Island with the mournful sunfall on them and a lingering roll of mist off where Cape Cod made its curving arm.

Inside the house she closed the door, turned and bowed low, "Good morning, father." The even-toned stern reply came, "A slugabed speaks. Are you up for all day?"

"My birthday comes but once a year and if it came twice or thrice a year, on the morning of each one of them I would wish to be a slugabed, looking back and wondering how I came to live so long."

He sat near the fire, whittlings and leather at his feet from pieces he was shaping for beaver, fox, and wolf traps. And again his even-toned, stern voice, "Slugabed nonetheless."

Her feet whisked around the kitchen and pantry corner. On a table near the middle of the room and toward the fire she set bowls, spoons, knives, a pitcher of milk. The corn-meal mush that had been long coming to a boil she brought to the table in a large pewter bowl with its large pewter serving spoon. Between two pewter mugs she stood a pitcher of cider fresh-made that week. They took their stools facing each other at this table. They bowed their heads and John Spong said grace, spoke pious meditations and phrases habitual to him at home, at week-night prayer meetings and at Lord's Day service when lay members arose and prophesied. Occasionally at these morning prayers Remember noticed her father speaking in the simplest of plain words about weather, about food and garments, even feet, shoes and stockings, about the mystery of daybreak light and how it came—and on such mornings and at such prayers the girl had a reverence for her father. Most often however she felt his prayers a sort of mummery. Along with others of the church he scorned prayers to be read out of a book. Prayers must rise from a fresh and living heart and not be read from a cut-and-dried book such as the Church of England's Book of Common Prayer. To be caught in Plymouth with that Book of Common Prayer, to own a copy of it or to be seen reading it, set a man under suspicion and he might be charged and put on trial and given penalties for it. Remember tried to clear her mind on how when her father prayed long he prayed cut-and-dried, his phrases having become a habit with him and a habit with others. Once when he had pain in his sore throat his almost inaudible and husky voice, driven by necessity to brevity, spoke grace and the prayer, "Help us poor mortals and bless this food to divine uses, O Lord, we ask thee in Christ's name." And this was one of the very few out of the many prayers she heard her father speak that Remember was pleased to keep and repeat on the rare mornings he called on her to say grace. She had bowed her head and slowly spoken, "Help us poor mortals and bless this food to divine uses, O Lord, we ask thee in Christ's name."

A thousand times and more at this table near the fireplace in this room they had eaten breakfast together. A few weeks in late spring and early summer they could open wide the back and front doors and throw open the windows on the two other sides of the house. Only on those weeks of the year did a full daylight flood into the room. Cheese-cloth over the two windows, three feet by two, kept flies and mosquitoes out through summer and early autumn. The window frames holding oiled paper swung in on their leather hinges, in summer cheesecloth fastened outside with wooden pegs. A drab gray daylight came through in these warmer months. With the first icy grips of winter a solid clap-board fastened outside the windows kept the cold out, in degree. Until late March they lived in this room of darkness, lighted by the burning wood of the fireplace and for further need pine knots or candles. Here was the fireplace they had shared more than six years, for warmth to their bodies, for the cooking of food, for the heating of water to wash bodies or clothes or dishes, bowls, pots, pans. Into the fireplace they coughed their phlegm, relieved their nostrils and saved the soiling of cloth and handkerchief. Thousands of times Remember had carried one or two buckets of water to pour into the big iron kettle over the fire. Thousands of odd jobs with wood, leather, cloth, John Spong had done at this fireplace. The few times they had spoken of glass windows to give this room full daylight, summer and winter, it was to laugh. In their lifetimes they expected to see glass windows in only one building in the town of Plymouth. In ten years, it might be, the church would have a new meeting house and, it could be, the glass to make four windows brought from England on a ship.

Their one piece of glass was a jagged chip from the bottom of a bottle. "I found it between two street stones in Leyden and digged it out," John Spong explained when showing it. "It is glass. You can see through it. We hope to have a house of worship with windows made of this, windows brought over from England."

The Spong mirror, though small, looked important and was kept with care. Four inches long by three wide, they could drop their mirror and pick it up. They might nick it or dent it, but they weren't afraid of its breaking, made as it was of steel, highly polished.

By this mirror John Spong shaved each Wednesday morning and on each Saturday afternoon before sunset and the Lord's Day which began on the instant the last rim of the sun went down Saturday evening. By this looking-glass Remember saw her mouth wide with thin lips over white even teeth. She could see her smile widen to be luminous as a little sunslant from an open door. By this mirror she fixed her hair in braids, coils, plaits—or on special occasions she let the masses of hair fall over her ears and downward to make a frame for her face. On occasion, and this birthday was that kind of an occasion, she tied the blue satin ribbon from her mother in a bowknot where it pleased her in her hair. Of course she often wished the looking-glass larger—three times larger then she could see her whole head all at once. She saw in the mirror her face bony, a little gaunt. She saw her cheeks with an apple blush, hardy winter apples. Her eyebrows rough, the hairs twisting and curling, neither her fingers nor her small tortoise-shell comb nor her large hickory-wood comb could lay them smooth. Her thick tangled eyebrows reminded her of gnarled underbrush she had seen. But the lashes of her eyes curved smooth and long. Often when she spoke her long eyelashes seemed to sweep up, down, sidewise in punctuations and stresses of what she was saying. And most definitely from her mother had come her eyes—smooth sea-blue that could change to greenish storm-blue—the darkest kind of sea-blue always alurk with sea wind.

Thousands of times her father had sat at this table facing her in his leather jerkin, leather breeches, a dark-gray wool shirt with a wide collar. The jerkin was really a tight-fitting coat without sleeves, laced with a cord. The leather breeches, held at the waist with a belt, hung loose, baggy, roomy, running below the knees and held in place there by a tightened cord. The breeches went over the homemade stockings Remember had knitted; they were woolen and fitted to above the knees. With years of wear and occasional scrubbings with soap and cold water the breeches were a drab brown in color. Over these clothes, John Spong at work often wore a smock. For weekday wear a black cloth cap, for the cold of winter a wool cap rabbit-furred on the flap for pulling over his ears. For Lord's Day wear the year round he had a hat of wide brim and high crown, a doublet and breeches of a brown known as "sad-colored." The plain cloth of part wool on the doublet shone with small finely braided scrolls of say, a sort of silk. These braided scrolls running out two inches from the buttons and buttonholes seemed the only betokenings of personal vanity in John Spong's garb. The steeple crown of his hat was an excess, its height making it cumbersome, but such a hat was the custom. Also he followed a handsome custom in a white linen collar that ran out wide over his shoulders. Starched and snow-white, stiff, proper, affirmative, this collar betokened purity, or, of a certainty, the desire for purity. In the main corner of the living room stood Spong's musket. With this he drilled and marched under command of Captain Miles Standish. On his shoulder, the one or two nights each month he stood watch at the colony fort, on his shoulder this musket.

Her father's black hair, Remember noticed this morning, reached over his ears a little, hung smooth and black nearly to his shirt collar. Allowed to grow much longer it would, of a certainty, be regarded by others as a vanity. One day this week he would be coming home rather close-cropped, with jagged edges of scissor marks here and there over his head. Or it might be a neighbor's turn to come to this room and Spong would sit on a stool near the fire as the neighbor held hair between forefinger and middle finger and snipped away, perhaps grunting occasionally, "It mought be a little jagged, Master Spong, but I'll try to smoothen it the best I can." "Botch it and I'll be wreaking my vengeance on you when it comes my turn," Remember once heard her father grunt in reply. And when they had cut each other's hair and after Remember swept the loose hairs from their shoulders and arms with a clean broom, she then took a less clean broom and swept the hair from the floor into the fireplace.

The former pale white of her father's Leyden face had tanned and roughened with summer sun and winter winds. The lurking hair of a stubborn black beard lingered on his face as though a razor couldn't reach it. "He has secrets, even from himself, like his beard not reached by his razor," Remember once surmised.

She had noticed more of a curve come to the stoop of his shoulders from the many days of heavy work and long hours. On his hands the calluses had thickened. Like her mother she enjoyed his small dark-gray eyes best when he was meeting his own moods of whimsy and fun. A merry squint of his left eye, sort of flirting with a twinkle in his other eye, now came less often, though precisely why Remember was not sure. She could be certain that now more often than formerly he could mix cruel shafts in his wit.

His fun might shade swiftly into fear of fun. More often his underlip would thrust out under a down-press of his upper lip. What few lines of age or care had come on his face were heightened by the little pitmarks of smallpox from that scourge when he was ten years old. He had gone on living clean of body, as neat as time would allow in the care of his person, spare in his eating and drinking, seemingly able to work harder and longer in these days than in any years before. The nearest to dissipation or indulgence that Remember saw in him had to do with his self-righteousness. He had moods more often now when directly or indirectly he seemed to put high value on his attainments in personal holiness.

From time to time Remember kept up her practice in writing. Not many, not half the Plymouth people, could write. Some could read, slow and awkward, who hadn't learned to write even their own names. They couldn't find time to learn—they had work—or they didn't care.

Remember practiced, kept on writing—often just for fun. Her father didn't. She prized the look of letters, enjoyed putting an inkhorn on the table, dipping a goose-quill pen in it and then shaping letters on a square of birch bark, making words come alive on the white bark surface. Her father had suspicions: in this she enjoyed herself with some manner of vanity.

Once he seated himself opposite her at the table as she practiced at writing that pleased her. And she heard him. "You may be wasting golden moments of life at this game that seems a vanity with you." He had watched her face very sober in a line of writing. Then a mischievous mirth came over her face writing a second line. "The sun has gone down and the Lord's Day began an hour ago and you pleasure yourself at this game," came his voice again. She looked at his face with a wish. Her wish was that his left eye could squint and flirt with an elusive twinkle in the other eye as happened years ago in Leyden when he dandled her on his knee. How long a time it was since he threw her toward a ceiling and caught her in his arms as she came down. Her wish was for that squint and twinkle of fun. Instead he was telling her that with sundown an hour ago the Lord's Day began and she must be warned against the sin of pleasuring herself.

She could think of no answer except action. She would be bold with a complete sincerity and accept any consequence. "At least half of this is not sin," she said as she moved the candle toward him and placed before his eyes the square of birch bark with two lines:

A soft answer turneth away wrath.
A soft answer turneth away rats.

Then came the tirade, a spell of scolding. Back and forth the length of the room strode John Spong crying his fear of her being a careless sinner and ending in Gehenna, in a lake of fire, in a hell timeless and everlasting. Part of it hurt him to be telling her. She noticed it hurt him. She was dizzy at one moment when the suspicion struck her that he wanted to hurt himself with his wailings and self-reproaches; that it pleased him, definitely gave him some weird pleasure to lash both himself and her with fierce accusations and alarms. He hurled questions at her. He demanded solemn pledges from her that she turn a more grave face toward the issues of life. "The ladder to heaven is made of crosses," he cried with his face toward the roof, took the text apart and put it together again, spun out lessons and instructions from it and wailed it once as though the louder his lungs and mouth could cry it, the more deeply it would sink in her as a warning to last.

Her moods—Remember could not help her moods as her father's tirade ran on for more than an hour. She pitied him. She pitied herself. And she was carrying the weight on her shoulders and in her mind of the sorrows of all of Plymouth, of all other folk of white, copper, or black skins in America, of swarming multitudes in Britain and Europe. And a little shaft of terror, a now familiar and cruel sliver of fear, came and went in her mind and heart. There was Satan, a Dark One, an Evil Shadow at work in Plymouth. He might be working on her father and he might through her father be working on her. How did she know? It haunted her. It came to her that Lord's Day night when she crept into the new-washed sheets of her bed and in the darkness could not push away with her strong hands nor thrust out of her anxious mind this fear of the Evil One that had its seed in her. The little beginning of it in her—her father and others not lacking authority wanted it to take root and grow and flourish as a controlling fear shaping her life.

That was of the past. Yet part of it was here now, here at the birthday breakfast table. Her father's voice had caught on the walls and the corners of the room and was still there crying, "The ladder to heaven is made of crosses."

Silhouettes of the past moved between her face and her father's face at this birthday breakfast. They moved as fingers of blue light and thumbs of maroon shadows. They made a crisscross pattern of dancing question marks. Once she had thrown a square of birch bark into the fire when her father came in the door. He might then have asked her why her quill pen had shaped a row of straight and crooked question marks and after each one an exclamation point—in rows of ten, perhaps forty running along—?! ?! ?! ?!—arranged in pairs or couples. If he had asked her what is this folderol and what can this nonsense mean she would have said the same she said when shaping them with her pen, one pair, one couple after another. "Each question mark stands for my ignorance and asks if I may learn and know the answer. And each exclamation point stands for my surprise at how little I know, my amazement at my vast ignorance, my utter astonishment at how much there is for me to learn." Some couples she made straight in elegant companionship, others she twisted, and others crept horizontal. This led to her practicing that week on a March of the Dancing Question Marks.

Now this birthday breakfast she felt between her face and her father's face a whole world of dancing, floating, tumbling, cavorting question marks and exclamation points. She would tell him about this. Yes, she would brighten her face and tell him. And he would brighten his face and answer, "Tell me more—I am one of God's fools, too." "No," she hesitated, "it couldn't be. His answer would be more like, 'Are you going out of your head, child?' Or, 'Daft—you have not gone daft, I hope.' Or, 'Eat your victuals, daughter. Question marks and exclamation points would make you a sorry breakfast. Cleanse yourself of this folly.'"

Such answers he had given her when, smaller and younger, she asked, "Does the wind ever blow stars off the sky?" And "What if all the short people should wake up long tomorrow morning and all the long people wake up short, would the world be different?"

No, she would not tell him this birthday morning that a world of dancing question marks and whirling exclamation points floated between his face and hers. She finished her bowl of mush when he did his, spooned out a second bowl for him and for herself a second. Then she prattled brightly, "I like the gloss of your black hair smooth and pretty as it is now. And I mislike it, I do mislike it, that you must have it slashed off this week with marks on your head where the scissors snip too deep." He ate several spoons of mush. He ate more and with the last spoon, "Long hair is a vain show and an abomination. Try and be pleased your father is not a creature of pomp and panoply."

Remember had heard before of pomp and panoply. The Church of England, she was sure, did go too far with pomp and panoply that glorified man rather than God. So, she was also sure, did the Romish Church which her father so frequently termed the Whore of Babylon. Now why couldn't he let her enjoy the smooth black downflow of his hair this one birthday morning without bringing in "pomp and panoply"? His hair would have to grow far longer, far down over his ears, before she could begin to see any possible pomp or panoply in it. With her final spoonful of mush she ventured, "It is so smooth, so black and glossy, where it falls to your ears. You will not think me wicked if I say it is the smoothest handsome head of hair of all the men in Plymouth." She caught now a dim glint of a smile in his eyes, though his upper lip pressed down on the stuck-out underlip as he mumbled, "Babble as you please, little one. Babble me more compliments. This week my locks get shorn and none shall say me nay." By this she knew he had been on the brink of a moment of happiness and then checked it.

The birthday breakfast was over. Mainly their fare had been corn and plenty of it. They could say, as others had said, "Horses and oxen take strength from this fare—why not man?"

John Spong sat at the fireplace repairing and making traps, putting a new sideboard on a wheelbarrow. He would have thrown open the front and back doors and let in a flood of daylight to work by—or he would have gone out into his back yard and sat pleasantly working on his traps. But these were the warm October days of mosquitoes at their worst.

A knock at the door and Remember let in two men. They talked with her father about repairs to be made that day on the colony's storehouse nearly filled with corn to be traded to the Indians for skins to export. They left, understanding Spong would soon join them with traps to be set for rats and field mice that had lately found their way into the colony's storehouse.

Not long after came a knocking at the door. Remember opened it and let in a short, wiry, compactly built young man in his middle twenties, red-haired, his hair and clothes somewhat disheveled, his eyes a trifle bloodshot. She knew him to be Hode Latch. She had seen him in the stocks only last week, under punishment for profanity, disorderly conduct, assault and battery. He had a name for bad temper and could hurl himself at a man much bigger and heavier than himself and bring him down. His reputation credited him, when sober, as an able man on a fishing boat. His pretty young wife, light-haired, blue-eyed, and completely in love with her husband, had come and begged Remember to go to Stephen Hopkins' taproom. "He's drinking again and drinking hard. Unless you can bring him away he will spend the last of the money the baby and I need at home." And why couldn't the woman go herself to the taproom and bring away her husband? Remember had queried. "He would ask me to drink with him, and he's that sweet and lovable I would be drinking with him. Last April it was we sat in the stocks together for being beastly drunk. You go, please go, and bring him away."

Remember went. She found Hode Latch with a mug of rum in his hand telling four other men no one else in Plymouth had a wife like he.

"All women are good," he laughed, taking a drag of the rum, and then, "good for something, or good for nothing."

Remember stood just inside the door, her wits at work on how to get Hode Latch to one side where she could quietly tell him he must go with her to his home. She saw all five of the men rather heavy with liquor. She gathered that the biggest fellow of the five made some leering insinuation about Latch's wife having sat in the stocks alongside her husband with an incidental query as to how many women in Plymouth had that distinction.

Hode Latch had leaped with a blow to the man's mouth, had swiftly got him by one leg, thrown him to the floor, straddled his chest with his hands at the man's throat, crying, "Take that back, you bastard. Take it back, or I'll kill you, you son of a bitch."

And as he pressed harder on the throat, Latch cried, "Say you're sorry." The big fellow's mouth bleeding from the first blow struck him, his dazed brain sent to the bruised lips the words that quivered hoarse, "I'm sorry, I'm sorry."

Hode Latch stood up. The beaten man rose, moved to the door, and as he went out Hode Latch's eye caught Remember, saw her beckoning. He came to her and she told him quietly the message from his wife: he must go home to her and the baby, she didn't dare come here herself for fear she would again get drunk with him.

Hode Latch smiled. "You're a lovely lady to do this. In a minute I'll finish that mug of rum," nodding his head toward the bar, "and then I'll go with you to the best girl in Plymouth."

He had finished his rum and was turning toward Remember when two constables came in. And after a night in jail Hode Latch was on trial next day, sentenced to a day in the stocks. To an inquiry from one of the judges, and with his shoulders thrown back, the look of his eyes straight and no sign of humiliation, Remember among the spectators had to admire him saying, "You ask if I like fighting. It is that I get mad too quick. I would fight any man slurring my wife, however bigger than me he might be. I am one of those men don't take insults easy."

In a cool voice as from another sphere, aloof and distant, the judge's meditation, "Hode Latch, you are a truculent vagabond." And Hode Latch straight into the judge's face blazed, "I don't know what dirty name you mean by truculent. But no vagabond be I. I have fought with a boat against a slobbering sea for many a big catch of fish brought into this Plymouth town. And if I'm a vagabond I don't know how to take it, not from any goddamned court in Plymouth."

For that he was given an extra day in the stocks, one for fighting, the second for profanity.

Remember saw, on this, her birthday morning, that Hode Latch would rather she be alone, would rather her father were not in the house there at the fire working on traps and a wheelbarrow. Sober and out of trouble, Latch kept himself clean and neat. He knew he now looked disorderly and had a plain humiliation, telling John Spong, "I had heavy ale and rum yesterday afternoon, too much of it and my tongue got loose again. The constables are after me. I slept in the woods last night, damp and cold, and nothing to eat have I had this morning."

Then the cold inquiry of John Spong, "Profanity again?"

"Aye, sir."

"What were the unholy words you said?"

"It was cheap, I'll say it was cheap. A foul ale we drank and a worse rum. To sell it should be a sin. We put it under our belts with the toast many times, 'Better belly burst than good drink lost,' but it wasn't good drink, 'twas foul and my head feels split open as I speak to you."

"What will they testify were the unholy words?"

"The ale was foul. It made me vaunt and blow and brag."

"And the unholy words?"

"It got to where my tongue thick with that foul ale was saying, 'What do we care for the goddam governor and council? What do we care for their goddam court?'"

And Hode Latch would like food before traveling away from Plymouth. He might walk. But he was weak and his head felt split open. He would like food, to stay him, to keep him on his feet.

"Do me this help." Hode Latch ended his plea. "Do me this help."

John Spong would lend a hand to no such help. There was the door. "And be thankful I put you out of my house rather than I put you under arrest and led you to the wicked vagabonds of Plymouth jail."

"So be it." Hode Latch was speaking to John Spong who did not raise his head from his work on a beaver trap. Latch bowed his head with understanding of the pity he saw in Remember's eyes, opened the back door, stepped out, closed the door, and was gone from the room.

Not long after, Spong thrust his traps in a canvas bag, put on a smock and went out the front door.

Remember waited a few minutes, stepped out of the front door to the sundial, ran a cloth over and around it, slapped two mosquitoes dead on her left wrist, and went back in the house. She had seen no one about or approaching. She opened the back door, saw Hode Latch seated on the wash bench. In the clear daylight she could see the swellings on his face and hands from mosquito bites. "I covered my head with my coat most of the night, keeping them away," he murmured, "and that left my body damp and shivering."

She asked him into the house, told him if anyone came he must go to the cellar. She seated him at the table, brought him hot cornmeal mush with milk poured over it, and a mug of cider. She handed him dried corncake and a cut of roast pork. "Victuals for your pocket, on the way." He thanked her. He finished his meal, began brightening, and seemed a new man after Remember brought him a basin of water and a towel for his morning wash.

About now it dawned on both of them that it might not be safe for him to walk out in daylight. Nighttime would be safer.

Three knocks sounded on the front door. A little wait and three more knocks. Remember saw Hode Latch vanish down the cellar stairway. She opened the door and saw the sharp, sober faces of two constables. They were asking if Hode Latch were in the house.

"Hode Latch came here a while ago when father was here. He talked with father and then went out the back door."

"We will take a look in your back yard and then go farther. Thanks be to you."

She closed the door, talked down the cellar stairway with Latch, waited an hour, then went out to see if a watch were kept on the house. It seemed so. They managed to pass the house often enough to know who was going in or coming out.

As she entered her home and closed the door, she stood and took a long breath. What a day! What a birthday morning! She had thought all would be easy enough. "Could aught but the Evil One have brought this to pass?"

She was tempted to go tell the limbs of the law to come take their man. In so doing she would confess to at least two false statements to the constables. The penalty laid on such a false witness could be the stocks, the pillory, and twenty or forty lashes with the whip.

Soon would be noon hour and her father home for the midday meal. What if he went to the cellar and a toolbox there? She sent a loud whisper down the cellar stairway. No answer. She called in a low voice, low enough not to be heard outside the house, "Hist, you, come up, come up." No answer. Again she called, and hearing no sound, she lighted a candle at the fire and hurried down the cellar to find in a far corner stretched on a board, Hode Latch in a deep sleep. She pushed him awake, pulled him up and told him to hurry follow her.

A deep sleep had made him over. He looked clean, stood straight, could walk or turn swift as a panther. The bloodshot eyes now shone clear and danced with challenge. "I'll go out now and face any music they want to give me. I can't say what I owe you. You do me these helps beyond price. While I talk here they might be coming. Should I go now this moment without more risk to you?"

What before Remember had done out of pity she did now in admiration. She pointed, "Up that ladder and through my father's room into my room. Father may not come home till early candlelight. Before he comes it may be dark enough to hide your getting away."

John Spong came, ate his noon meal, went to his cellar toolbox, himself answered a doorknock and let in the two constables to join him in a glass of cider, and Remember saw the three of them walking away towards the colony storehouse.

She washed the dishes, straightened all things in the kitchen and pantry corner, swept the room and put every utensil and garment in its accustomed place. She began the shelling of a half a bushel of corn about midafternoon. Her chair was near the window. A fair daylight came in. She liked the shine of it on the corn. A whole day of corn-shelling she found wearing, monotonous, and it hurt her hands. Two or three hours of it were pleasant. Her right hand dropped the red, white, brown, purple kernels into a sack. Her left hand dropped the cob back in the basket. It was a pleasure to run her hand and forearm down among the cobs to hunt for the last three or four ears till finally none was there. Then she would rise from her chair, stoop over the basket, run both hands and forearms down among the cobs and laugh with high glee when she found one that had tried to hide out on her. The cat Mesopotamia left the fireside, came over and sat on its haunches near her and looked up into her face, sleepily blinking its eyes as though to say, "If you will trouble your memory you may recall who I am. Must I remind you that I am supposed to be here to keep you company?"

She talked in low tones to the cat who kept turning its head slowly and scrupulously licking each of the four black spots on its yellow haunches. She talked low, in confidence. "Tamia, it is well I have with me one like you I can trust, and I am telling you, Tamia, it must all come out for the best." She went on shelling in silence. She heard a crow cawing and made her guess the crow sat high in the back-yard cedar. Stillness hung over the room. The hush was broken only by a sound that could be heard only in a deep stillness. It came from the swift patter of the lightest kind of feet. Tamia heard it. A field mouse had gotten into the room, and was dashing toward the cellar stairway. Tamia saw and leaped for it. Remember stood up and shouted at the top of her voice, "Get him, Tamia! Get him and shake him!" She seated herself to go on shelling with little doubt that Tamia would bring the mouse up from the cellar.

A half a minute or more went by. Then a knocking at the door. Remember opened, to see one of the constables. He was asking, "What are the voices here? What is the shouting?"

"I would not say you are a meddler. I would not say you had better be minding your own business. A field mouse got in the house, found a hiding place and suddenly made a dash for our cellar stairway. I shouted to our cat Tamia to get him and shake him." Remember felt very bold. This time she was telling the truth. And her claims were justified and the constable looked a little sheepish as Tamia slowly and gravely walked up to Remember with a mouse in her teeth and dropped the mouse on the floor so each and all concerned could bear witness it was a mouse.

The constable departed with a mumbled apology, Remember took up her shelling, Tamia let out the front door with the mouse. There was no clock in the room and Remember made a wish and dwelt on it, to have in this room now the tall important clock she had seen and heard in the Governor's house. Once on an errand there she had sat sixteen minutes, watching the minute hand move from one minute mark to another minute mark. She liked the tick-tock, tick-tock of the clock. It kept her company. In Leyden she had seen five clocks in five different shops and houses. In Plymouth she had never seen but this one clock in the Governor's house. Someday, a long time from now, and yet a time sure to come, to come somehow, every house in Plymouth would have a clock, the big houses with tall dignified clocks, the little houses with short cozy clocks. If she had a clock now she could tell how many minutes and seconds it took to shell one ear, two ears, four ears of corn.

She knew she was using these clock follies to keep off darker thoughts. Whatever should come of the doings of this day, whether or not there would be public disgrace, condemnation, punishment, for her the worst would be her fear that the Evil Shadow had wrought one of its marvels. When Satan sought to make you captive he might do it by the subtle, roundabout fashion of today's happenings. She had planned nothing. She had held no design of evil. Yet tomorrow might find her facing a community wrath, accusations beyond her answering, public shames never yet in her personal experience, black and crooked shames for her whose name had been kept clean and white.

She threw a cob, just shelled, with all her might across the room into the fire. She followed it with five, six more cobs, flung with all her might.

She saw this came to no use. She must keep cool for what was to come. She would have kept cool but for thoughts of the Dark One, who could make himself unseen hovering about the house. At the root of her trouble was that mystic Evil Presence that had her mind baffled and could pierce her heart with fears.

The half-bushel was shelled. She put the basket of cobs next to the fireplace, the sack of shelled corn into the pantry. She opened the back door and looked out to see daylight growing dim, dusk creeping on. She called up the ladder to Hode Latch. No, he was not asleep. He had kept awake ready for a call at any time all afternoon. The next hour would see the test, she told him. He had eaten his corncake and meat, she was certain. She handed him more for his pockets on the journey they hoped he would be free to make.

She looked out the back door again. It was not yet dark. She closed the door. She lighted a candle, set supper dishes on the table, made ready and warmed food.

The front door opened. John Spong came in, pulled off his smock, hacked with his throat and spewed phlegm into the fire, reported that the well-rotted and sun-dried dead fish used for bait in the traps at the storehouse would probably work as they all expected. "Should this bait not attract them, we shall use cheese, which costs more."

Remember put the food on the table, seated herself facing her father, noticed him searching her face as he said, "What is burning you?"

"I have done a good day's work though I know not why I should be feeling weak. Would you, for this evening, go down cellar and fetch up the cider?"

Without a word he rose and went to the cellar stairway. She saw his head go out of sight. And she glided with all speed to the ladder and sent up her loud whisper, "Now."

Down the ladder smooth and perfect as she could have asked it to be came Hode Latch, reaching the floor in quiet, moving with a smooth speed to the back door she held open. She closed the door, let the latch down with no noise, and sat at the supper table as her father came through the cellar stairway opening, bringing the pitcher of cider. As he put it on the table his eyes again searched her face, "What is burning you? Have you a fever, child? Your eyes—their light is unnatural."

She said nothing. She ate little. The word "unnatural" struck her. Often in sermons, often in everyday talk, that word "unnatural" carried meaning the Dark One was at work.

In her bed early that night she groped with her thoughts. What a twentieth birthday for a girl! Not again would she care to live it. What could such a mingle-mangle of niminy-miminy affairs be unless it had devices of the Evil One? The most restless night of her life was this. How could she know but Hode Latch would be taken by the law, and sloven that he could be with his mouth, tell all? Late into the night, past midnight, hour on hour and sleep would not come. She slipped into a cloak, tiptoed past her sleeping father, went down the ladder and out the back door, stood on the flat stone door-step, stood looking up at moving arches of stars, twisted her head swiftly toward one and another house corner, saying to herself it would ease her if the Dark One would show himself, even if he mocked at her and claimed her.

She pulled a stool before the fire, squatted with her feet wide apart, her elbows on her knees, her chin in her cupped hands. Her wish was that the Archdemon might come sliding down the chimney, as there was testimony he had done when wishing to speak to one of his victims. She was not yet a fully snared victim. If so there would be a wild joy in it, a cunning and riotous joy she had not known this day or night. He had not yet gained sway over her. For her wish was that he should appear and make himself known. She would defy him and give him combat. With what words, with what weapons, she could not think now but she would welcome the chance to tell him her scorn and hate.

Up in her room and bed she turned and tossed, dropped into a light sleep and saw herself brought to court for public trial. The respectable and upright people of Plymouth that she had known were all there. They believed her guilty. She had given false statements and conducted herself perfidiously before authorities of the law who solicited her aid in their search for a hardened lawbreaker and an incorrigible rogue. She had sheltered and aided the most profane drunkard in Plymouth—they so believed. What intercourse had taken place between her and this light-minded vagabond—they would know further. What lust and cohabitation had taken place toward the corruption and defilement of community life—of this, too, they would know further. These faces of the respectable and upright peering at her with a curious pleasure—this could not break her. Here and there were sweet faces, beloved ones she had known in many ways and they had come to know her in many ways. And it was on their faces they could not believe her guilty. Yet they were helpless. These few old and faithful friends sat overwhelmed in the tide of feeling that beat against her and the hot smolder of the scorn poured on her. This nearly broke her. At the sight of these faces and their sorrowing eyes she was faint and giddy and afraid she would fall helpless.

A magistrate pointed a long finger and spoke in the tone desired by the respectable and upright certain of her guilt. "You had knowledge the man you aided and sheltered was a guilty man, a habitual offender, a man foul and evil in his guilt. He had so made confession to you. And yet you did him the helps he asked of you. You provided him the assistance of food and a roof while your false tongue misled and mocked at the majesty of the law and justice seeking him." At this she saw nodding heads and pleased glances among the respectable and upright, faces turning sullen again as their eyes once more dwelt on her face. She cried out her answer, her defense, "In naught of what I did can you say I knew what I was doing. What I did was done by a Dark Power beyond me, the Archdemon."

Soon and with short shrift they put her in the stocks with her father. On a warmish sultry autumn day, from dawn to past noon until the going down of the sun, Remember and John Spong sat with their hands and feet locked in merciless wooden clutches. Taunts and cries came but not many. There was pity in some eyes at the swellings that came on the hands and faces of her and her father from the flies and mosquitoes that could not be shaken off.

One face lightened the burden of the day for Remember. That was a light-haired and blue-eyed woman with a baby in her arms. She came early in the morning, again at noon, again late in the afternoon. Tears coursed freely down her cheeks. She came near with love and trust in her voice, saying, "I know it is hard. And you know I would trade places with you if I could, if they would let me." This was Hode Latch's wife and she took the curse off the day. Mrs. Hode Latch stood forth in contrast to John Spong, dazed and out of his mind, saying, "You are my daughter and you spoke false as hell to me. Why did you send me to the cellar for cider? Can you be my daughter that you should speak false as hell to me?"

Remember came out of this dream in a hot sweat that turned cold as ice. The anguish that cut through her must come to an end. It did spend itself, though no more sleep came to her. Thin wide slants of daybreak filtered in. She held her hands calm before her eyes, turned them around palm and back and palm. "I am of the earth and in my blood and bones flows the strength of the hard and kindly earth. I shall live on and make my life hard and kindly."

She was first down and had breakfast ready when her father came. They ate with few words. His were, "The burning is gone. You slept well."

And Remember wondered where by now was Hode Latch. Her will hewed to a purpose, "If I must sit in the stocks, I will not give them one moan for mercy, not one prayer for pardon. I can take death as did my father's father in the Clink of London."

This seemed new to her. Why should her father be joined so often with others who took what seemed a fierce pleasure in being cruel and relentless toward victims who harmed only themselves and not others? Her father's father had a Bible and by it brought no harm to others. Yet for but little more they gave him death.

A few days went by. Orton Wingate came, for presents bringing four good fowl he had shot. He shared dinner, lighted the room with the comic slash of his mouth and his dancing brown eyes.

Up near Salem, Wingate had heard, two hunters had been out for two days and brought down no game to eat. On the third day they were ravenous with hunger and brought down a crow they roasted over a fire. They picked the bones bare with their teeth, saying not a word till they had finished. One drawled, "How do you like crow?" And the other, "I mought say I can eat it, but I don't hanker after it."

Remember laughed. Her father sniffled and went to his afternoon's work. They talked half the afternoon, Remember and her trusted friend. To him she told the whole story of Hode Latch. She had been to the Latch home, had carried them what they needed of corn meal and fish, besides a little pork.

Three weeks later when Wingate came she gave him the news that Mrs. Latch had a message from her husband, he was doing well on a fishing vessel, and had sent her a little money and before long would send for her and the baby. And yesterday afternoon had come Mrs. Latch with her baby, her light hair combed with brightness and her blue eyes beaming. In the dark of that night on Plymouth wharf she would step onto a fishing vessel. And the Hode Latches, the three of them, would wave farewell in the dark to Plymouth. And Deliverance Latch—for the name of Deliverance had been given to her—brought out a small silver earring. "Hode had it from his mother. He wanted to give you something he believed he would part with only at death."

Remember had not meant to leave it on the chest against the wall in her room. The silver gleam of it caught her father's eye as he glanced through the doorway in the morning. He came in and took it between thumb and finger, turned it round and about, held it toward the light.

"Whence this gaudy little ornament?"

"It is pure silver."

"And you are vain over it! Whence comes it to you and your room?"

Remember hesitated, then again, "It is pure silver."

Then came one of her father's morning tirades. They were not so long as his evening tirades but they were more vehement.

Much pleasant talk, many good times of talk, Remember and her father had in this room. At his work with other men, at meetings of committees of which he was a member, on errands and dealings that the church leaders entrusted to him, he naturally heard much of what was going on in the town, heard early the news and events. Likewise Remember going to the houses of neighbors to borrow salt or to return molasses she had borrowed or merely to exchange interesting gossip, she too gathered news and rumors. When a ship came in to Plymouth Harbor from England or Virginia or the West Indies, there was always a little news, sometimes much news. And Remember and her father would exchange such items of news and either of them could ask questions so as to make sure of having all the details of the reports and rumors.

They had lived in a city where were thousands of faces. They had walked the streets of Southampton, Dartmouth and Plymouth, England, seeing hundreds of houses, thousands of faces. Now these years since 1620 they had made their lives in a village of less than sixty houses. Walk between two rows of houses slowly along a roadway or street and in five minutes you had seen the town's houses and buildings.

Yet the hundred and fifty-odd people of the town, the old familiar faces, the few new faces always arriving, the behavior and the babble of them, made plenty to talk about. Yorkshiremen there were whose dialect was almost another language when heard alongside the speech of the men and women from London. Remember could manage nice little snatches of conversation with her father in Dutch and he could talk with any of the Leydeners enough of Dutch so that a listening Londoner wouldn't know what they were saying about him if they were discussing his good or bad conduct. Colony members there were who had been brought up in the Anglican, Scottish, and Welsh churches, in Walloon, French and Dutch churches. Some had come over from England whose fathers and mothers had fled France, Belgium or Holland for refuge to be had under Queen Elizabeth in England. They termed themselves Englishmen and Englishwomen and it was accepted that they were under the English crown and government. A humanity varied of people and languages, mixed in their village of less than sixty houses. Any of the leaders, Brewster, Bradford, Winslow, Hopkins, Alden, each active in political government and their church, was worth talking about. Likewise the sawed-off, red-faced, fiery little javelin of a man, Captain Miles Standish who had shown perfection as their military organizer and commander, who had risked his life so often and undergone hardships that Plymouth Colony might live—yet the years passed and he had not joined the Plymouth congregation.

The wide wild sea to the east, the treacherous thousand-mile wilderness to the west, their little huddle of houses stood as the first settlement on the coast of New England to stand up and stay put. Northward the French had forts in Canada. Southward the Dutch had trading posts, two hundred and seventy people and more than a hundred cattle, at the mouth of Hudson River and on Manhattan Island. Far down on the curving and jagged Atlantic coastline lay the Jamestown settlement. Who in Plymouth had not heard of death, starvation and ruin tracked across Jamestown and Virginia for twenty years? Shipmasters, seamen, officers of the crown, their vessels anchored in Plymouth Harbor, had their tales and reports of Jamestown. Across twenty years out of the ports of England, ships had carried more than five thousand and six hundred emigrants for Virginia. And hundreds had fled back to the old country, sick of hardship and terror. In a single massacre three hundred and forty-seven men, women and children went down under the hatchets, knives and arrows of the Indians. Nearly one thousand died of sickness or want of food on the way to Virginia or in the colony. Its governor officially termed the year 1610 as the Starving Time. About one in five who had left England for Virginia was now alive and aboveground, the Virginia colony population numbering one thousand and ninety-five people—four out of five had fled or died.

From day to day to month after month in 1627 Remember and her father had news of the passengers and crew of a Virginia-bound ship lost at sea. The first they heard of it was from Indians and two white men who walked into Plymouth one summer day with a letter to the Governor. They wanted help. Six weeks at sea after leaving England with many passengers and considerable goods. They had run out of beer and water. For quenching thirst they had come near the bottoms of two hogsheads of wine one of the passengers had brought. The captain had tried to run the ship with orders from where he lay in the cabin sick and lame with scurvy. Crew and passengers decided to run the ship straight for land. So they had run stumbling in the night over the shoals of Cape Cod and it pleased God not to wreck them. In a small harbor to the southward of Cape Cod with a small gale of wind, high water and a smooth sea, they had laid out an anchor on a sandbar. Toward evening a wind sprang up at sea and blew so rough it broke their cable and beat them over the bar into a harbor, where they saved their lives and goods. A butt end of a ship plank had sprung and they were in luck to run on a dry flat, close to a beach where at low water they got out their goods and were glad they had saved their lives. But where were they? And what of the Indians paddling toward them in canoes? And did they find it pleasant that the naked savages could speak English? And was it further pleasant that the Indians believed them to be men of Plymouth or friends of the Governor? It was. With help from Plymouth the wrecked ship was mended and supplied. But she got into bad mooring, took heavy beatings from wind and breakers, all cargo was unloaded and the ship abandoned.

Passengers and crew stayed in Plymouth the best part of a year, well and courteously entertained, some passengers paying well. Most of them got some kind of passage to Virginia. The shipmaster, a Scotchman named Johnston, got well of his scurvy and could walk again.

A few stayed on in Plymouth, among these one Peter Ladd, an able seaman. Remember noticed him particularly, seeing him exactly her own height of six feet, lean and hard like herself, very light blue eyes and a fair blond face that could suddenly be all a smile, thick wavy light hair that came below his ears, his left shoulder lower than the right, a white scar over his right eye, his hands peculiarly nimble. As he stayed on in Plymouth Peter Ladd took far more notice of Remember than she did of him.

Ships bound to or from Virginia found their way to Plymouth Harbor, on business, or blown out of their course. They told of things seen and heard in the royal colony farther south, its leaders staunch for the Established Church of England, one of their purposes being to get land, trade and riches to lay the groundwork for an aristocracy as in England. When they got going they would have good living, gay apparel, lively parties, manorial houses, ladies and gentlemen of titles and nobility. They favored a way of life rather different from the Plymouth settlers.

"They are saying," John Spong began one evening. And Remember knew he meant by "they" the men of Governor Robert Gorges on a ship from Virginia anchored in Plymouth Harbor. "They are saying one ship from England arriving with cargo in Virginia unloaded sixty young women, sent to Virginia to be wives, and they were bought by various bidders who paid from a hundred and twenty to a hundred and fifty pounds of tobacco for each wife. The tobacco was worth three shillings a pound."

"And what are *men* selling for?" Remember in asking this could not be sure whether she was serious or mocking and gay.

They were saying, her father reported, that men who had signed papers in England, binding themselves for seven years to be indentured servants, sold in Virginia at forty to sixty pounds of tobacco. Of this class, Plymouth was not lacking. Remember and her father could name more than a score of men, women and children in Plymouth "indentured" for service: after their seven years of service they would be free and on their own.

"They are saying," and what her father had next to tell she could not quite grasp and picture at that time. A Dutch warship had landed at Jamestown, Virginia, in August of 1620 twenty Negroes brought from Africa, put on sale and the money paid and taken for them to be slaves and from then on kept, bought, sold, the same as oxen, cattle, sheep or other property. Remember tried to picture it but couldn't. She had never seen a Negro till 1627. A ship from Virginia laid anchor at Plymouth and Remember saw the shipmaster walking to Governor Bradford's house followed by a boy naked except for short ragged breeches, a gleaming black skin from head to toe, the hair on his head like short kinks of tight-woven wool, his nose flat, his mouth wide with thick lips, on one shoulder a chest he lugged for his master. He looked smooth, lithe, quick on his feet, rippling and gay under his black skin.

"I do believe he can dance," Remember murmured. Her mind kept going over this, her first sight of a Negro. She kept asking herself what the Negro might think to himself about being owned by someone else. It was being done and the law said it was right. It seemed right to Remember till suddenly she found herself asking how it would be with her if she was *owned* by someone else. She asked her father about it. "Does the owner and master own the soul of the slave? Or does the slave have a soul?"

She tried to make something of this. John Spong didn't welcome it. He had heard no preaching about it so he had to work it out in his own mind and told his daughter, "It is a condition that has been wrought by the black hands and the dark evil spirit of Satan. They are children of the Dark One. It is of his design and purpose they are born black." He recoiled as though his daughter had struck him an insolent stinging blow across the nose with a flat fist on her blurting, "What if I had been born black? What could I have done about it? Did I choose to be born white—did you?"

He let silence be his answer. The angers twisting in him could not find tongue. The best he could do after a time was, "It is a complication. We must give it our meditation and prayer." And Remember when occasionally her mind dwelt on it asked herself, "Is it wrong for one man to own another? If so is there not a curse of God on it?" And one of the perplexities her mind wrestled with was around the question whether there could be so strange and devious an evil as man selling man, man buying man, man owning man, unless there were a Satan, an active Archdemon, who conceived it.

A lonesome little village Plymouth had seemed to Remember when more than once of a summer morning before daybreak she slid out of bed and out the front door and ran barefoot to where the two streets crossed, on one corner the fort and meeting house with its flat roof and six cannon pointed every direction but the sea. In the daybreak stillness and looking to the red-mist sunrise over the sea she would say, "Plymouth is a promise. It must come true. Mother said so—it must."

Hardship, struggle, barren days and bitter deaths she had seen in this Plymouth of hers. The bonds and thongs holding her to Plymouth were sacred, familiar and of mystic strengths. Only some great price, only causes and reasons more dazzling than any yet come into her life, could take her away from this Plymouth. She would not say she had love for Plymouth any sooner than she had love for her right and left hands. They were part of her. Plymouth was part of her.

She had seen Isaac de Rasière, fat, broad, heavy and waddling, welcomed in Plymouth on the fourth of October, 1627. His bark *Nassau* loading and unloading at Manomet, twenty miles from Plymouth, he had started to walk to Plymouth, having heard of his Dutch friend John Jacobson in six hours walking the twenty miles from Manomet to Plymouth. De Rasière started. Then his feet told him they would give out. He sent word to Governor Bradford asking a boat be sent for him, which was done. Remember saw Isaac de Rasière delivered at a Plymouth wharf, saw guardsmen and attendants in bright scarlet velvet as an escort, and leading his procession—the trumpeters. Remember clapped her hands, held her joined hands in front of her, and her feet would have danced if she dared. She had never seen trumpeters nor heard trumpets. Here they were blaring loud, pompous and gay, followed by as funny a man as she ever looked at, a nice worthy man, broad, fat, waddling. This was the first Ambassador she had seen in Plymouth. Isaac de Rasière—who was he? He was the Secretary, by appointment of the Governor and Council, of New Netherland at Manhattan and Fort Amsterdam at the mouth of the Hudson River.

And the trumpeters blaring their brass salutations, they were repeating the lines that opened his letter in the Dutch language which translated:

"Noble, worshipful, wise, and prudent Lords, the Governor and Councillors residing in New Plymouth, our very dear friends:— The Director and Council of New Netherland wish to your Lordships, worshipful, wise, and prudent, happiness in Christ Jesus our Lord, with prosperity and health, in soul and body."

A pleasant and chubby man, this Isaac de Rasière. Remember liked his pink blond face, his twinkling eyes. Her father told her about Governor Bradford and his assistants sitting at a table with Secretary-Ambassador Isaac de Rasière and talking things over and making arrangements so there should be no disagreement, no fighting, no violence and bad feeling between the peace-loving Englishmen of Plymouth and the peace-loving Dutchmen of New Amsterdam. Were they not, in their own words "very loving friends, and Christian neighbors"? The Dutch were not sure but what their government by right controlled trading in fields occupied by Plymouth men to the south of Plymouth. Bradford had to caution his Dutch neighbors against settling in territory definitely claimed by England. Good feeling came of it all. De Rasière stayed for several days of discussions and entertainment. They carried him back to his bark *Nassau* at Manomet. He brought out for them "cloth of three sorts and colors, and a chest of white sugar, besides small wares." And the Plymouth authorities paid him mainly with Plymouth-raised tobacco.

When, soon after, in that year of 1627, Isaac de Rasière sat at a table and dipped a goose-quill pen in an inkhorn and wrote a letter to authorities in Holland, Remember Spong would have been delighted at reading the exact and detailed portrait he made of her town. One paragraph read:

New Plymouth lies on the slope of a hill, stretching east towards the sea-coast, with a broad street about a cannon shot of eight hundred [yards] long, leading down the hill, with a [street] crossing in the middle, northwards to the rivulet, and southwards to the land. The houses are constructed of hewn planks, with gardens also enclosed behind and at the sides with hewn planks, so that their houses and court-yards are arranged in very good order, with a stockade against a sudden attack; and at the ends of the streets there are three wooden gates. In the center, on the cross-street, stands the Governor's house, before which is a square enclosure, upon which four patereros (steen-stucken) are mounted, so as to flank along the streets. Upon the hill they have a large square house, with a flat roof, made of thick sawn planks, stayed with oak beams, upon the top of which they have six cannon, which shoot iron balls of four and five pounds, and command the surrounding country. The lower part they use for their church, where they preach on Sundays and the usual holidays. They assemble by beat of drum, each with his musket or firelock, in front of the captain's door; they have their cloaks on and place themselves in order, three abreast, and are led by a sergeant without beat of drum. Behind comes the Governor, in a long robe; beside him, on the right hand, comes the preacher with his cloak on, and with a small cane in his hand, and so they march in good order, and each sets his arms down near him. Thus they are constantly on their guard night and day.

A new kind of money that Remember began saving for a necklace came into use at Plymouth after de Rasière left. The Dutch had used it in trading with the Indians and the Plymouth men took de Rasière's word that what he handed them was the equivalent of fifty English pounds for tobacco they sold him. As this new money got into circulation, Remember laid it by for a necklace, each piece a cylinder bead, about a quarter-inch long and an eighth-inch in diameter, ground smooth as glass and strung together by a hole drilled through the center. The dark purple beads came shaped from hard-shell clams which the Indians called *quahaug* or *quahog*, the white beads from the shell of whelks. *Wampum* and *wampunpeage*, meaning white bead, the Indians called this money. To cut, grind, polish and finish these beads took slow and careful workmanship, and the white men learned in this they were less skilled than the Indians. They learned wampum must have the right feel to the finger and eye of an Indian or he wouldn't take it for animal skins the white man wanted—and it was wampum only when the beads were strung or woven together. This money for trading with the Indians became useful, as de Rasière had predicted. Remember told her father they would lay by wampum, four of them worth an English penny, and with three hundred and sixty they would have a "fathom" of wampum. Then they would buy things needed in their house, perhaps even a mirror "high and wide enough to see your face without twisting your head right and left and up and down."

Meantime the wampum would be nice to look at. Remember beamed about that. She quit beaming when her father soberly, "Thee would make an idol of a glittering string of Indian money pieces?" In the little chest from her mother, far down in a bottom corner, Remember kept the string of wampum they hoarded. She would take it out to look at. She put it on once when alone in the living room. She opened front and back door and danced her version of Sweep Out the Devil.

Gambling forbidden by law in Plymouth, many a day had seen incorrigible gamblers in the stocks. On June 1 of the year 1627 however all of the Purchasers, those who had paid in on the plantation as an investment, shared the excitement of a game of chance—or a legal procedure as fascinating as any merry game of chance. On this day came the cattle division. In March of 1624 Edward Winslow had walked down the gangplank of the ship *Charity* leading the colony herd of one bull and three heifers. These four with other heifers arriving on the *Anne* and the *Jacob* had grown to fifteen head. And the hundred and fifty-six Purchasers had formed themselves in twelve groups of thirteen each. To each group would go an animal for their care and use for ten years, when they should restore to the public the animal and its increase, if any. The fifteen cattle, on basis of points and merits, were thrown into twelve divisions. Each division, except the fourth, had a pair of she-goats thrown into it.

For these divisions they drew numbers. They decided by chance, "by lot." Who would get what nobody knew beforehand. Not since they divided the land "by lot" had there been such excitement over who would win what. The animal described as "the least of the four black heifers" that came in the ship *Jacob* went by the number drawn to Francis Cooke, his wife Hester, John Cooke, Jacob Cooke, Jane Cooke, Hester Cooke, Mary Cooke, Moses Simonson, Philip Delaney, Experience Mitchell, John Faunce, Joshua Pratt, Phineas Pratt.

The animal described as "the great black cow" which came in the ship *Anne*, along with "the lesser of the two steers," went by chance, by number, by lot, to "Mr. Isaac Allerton and his company," his wife Fear, Bartholomew Allerton, Remember Allerton, Mary Allerton, and Sarah Allerton, Mariah Priest, Sarah Priest, Edward Bumpas, John Crackstone, and verily in this company were Cuthbert Cuthbertson, Sarah Cuthbertson, Samuel Cuthbertson. This particular transaction interested Remember Spong who when she burnt a finger handling a hot pan or pot at the fire would vent her feelings with crying rapidly, "Cuthbert Cuthbertson! Cuthbert Cuthbertson!" There were houses in Plymouth where they refused to say a child had learned to talk until "Now at last he can say Cuthbert Cuthbertson."

The animal described as "the red cow which belongeth to the poor of the Colony; to which they must keep her calf of this year, being a bull, for the company [Colony]," went by chance, by lot, by number to Captain Miles Standish, his wife Barbara Charles Standish, Alexander Standish, John Standish, Abraham Pierce, Thomas Clarke, Edward Winslow, Susanna Winslow, Edward Winslow, Jr., John Winslow 2d, Resolved White, Peregrine White. There were eyes turned on the six-year-old child born December 10, 1620, the first English child born in New England, now owning a share in a red cow.

Raghorn, another of the four heifers, went by fortuity of number to John Howland, his wife Elizabeth, John Howland, Jr., Desire Howland, William Wright, Thomas Morton, Jr., Edward Doten, John Alden, Priscilla Mullins Alden, Elizabeth Alden, John Alden, Jr., Clement Briggs, Edward Holman.

The blind heifer, another of the ship *Jacob* four, went by unpredictable chance to William Brewster, Love Brewster, Wrestling Brewster 2d, Jonathan Brewster, Lucretia Brewster, William Brewster, Mary Brewster, Richard More, Henry Sampson, Thomas Prence, Rebecca Prence, Humility Cooper.

An animal described as "the lesser of the black cows," from England on the ship *Anne*, along with "the bigger of the two steers," went by the whimsical dictate of a number, by chance, by lot, to John Shaw and joined to him John Adams, Eleanor Adams, Elizabeth Basset, William Basset, Jr., Elizabeth Basset, Jr., Francis Sprague, Anna Sprague, Mercy Sprague, John Spong, Remember Spong.

To the next group, headed by Stephen Hopkins, ran the record, "To this lot fell a black weaning calf; to which was added the calf of this year, to come of the black cow which fell to John Shaw, etc.," which proving a bull, they were to keep it for five years for common use, and after to make the "best of it," with the proviso, "nothing belongeth of these two for the company of the first stock, but only half the increase." Joined to Stephen Hopkins in this were his wife Elizabeth, Giles Hopkins, Caleb Hopkins, Deborah Hopkins, Nicholas Snow, Constance Snow, William Palmer, Frances Palmer, William Palmer, Jr., John Billington, Eleanor Billington, Francis Billington.

The record of this division of cattle in two items made reference to "the poor" of the colony though how many were the poor and what the character and degree of their poverty was not implied though the implication was definite that Plymouth had its class or human stratum whose members passed officially into the designation or category of "the poor." With the eighth division went the notation: "To this lot fell a red heifer, come of the cow which belongeth to the poor of the Colony, and is of that consideration, viz.: these persons nominated to have half the increase; the other half, with the old stock, to remain for the use of the poor." This eighth lot fell to Samuel Fuller, his wife Bridget Fuller, Samuel Fuller, Jr., Peter Browne, Martha Browne, Mary Browne, John Ford, Martha Ford, Anthony Annable, Jane Annable, Sarah Annable, Hannah Annable, Damaris Hopkins.

The smooth-horned heifer, last of the four black ones from the ship *Jacob*, went by the inexplicable upflip of the number 9 to Richard Warren, his wife Elizabeth, Nathaniel Warren, Joseph Warren, Mary Warren, Ann Warren, Sarah Warren, Elizabeth Warren, Jr., Abigail Warren, John Billington, Jr., George Soule, Mary Soule, Zachariah Soule.

The white-bellied heifer, "an heifer of the last year," went to Francis Eaton, his wife Christian, Samuel Eaton, Rachel Eaton, Stephen Tracy, Triphosa Tracy, Sarah Tracy, Rebecca Tracy, Ralph Wallen, Joyce Wallen, Sarah Morton, Robert Bartlett, Thomas Prence, Jr.

Governor William Bradford headed the eleventh lot to whom fell "an heifer of the last year, which was of the great White-back Cow brought over in the *Anne*." Joining the Governor in ten-year ownership of this heifer were his wife Alice, William Bradford, Jr., Mercy Bradford, Joseph Rogers, Thomas Cushman, William Latham, Mannasseh Kempton, Julian(a) Kempton, Nathaniel Morton, John Morton, Ephraim Morton, Patience Morton.

Now the excitement was over. Everybody laughed or smiled except a few of the constantly frozen-faced who stood wary of betraying mirth. There was left only "the great White-back Cow; to which cow the keeping of the bull was joined for these presents to provide for." She fell to John Jenny, his wife Sarah, Samuel Jenny, Abigail Jenny, Sarah Jenny, Jr., Robert Hicks, Margaret Hicks, Samuel Hicks, Ephraim Hicks, Lydia Hicks, Phebe Hicks, Stephen Dean, Edward Bangs.

Not again would famine stalk the streets of Plymouth, so they believed. Not another summer when men wobbled on their feet, weak from the want of food. The sober and industrious men whose management and straight dealing had brought the colony along, they saw themselves moving into comfort and prosperity, even riches, compared to the years of hard beginnings. On January 13, 1628, each of the Purchasers received, in the division of land on that day, twenty acres for himself, besides the single acre allotted him five years before. One hundred and fifty-six fields there were, covering some five square miles, ranging from Jones River to Eel River, about six miles, with the village at the middle. Each field had its personal owner, doing about what he liked with his four-sided plot of ground, four acres by five. The Governor and Council gave mowing rights to livestock owners and according to their needs they cut and hauled grass from meadows on the poorer land. Those whose land lay away off were allowed to share the use of land near the village.

So when Remember's twentieth birthday came in October of 1628, she could look on the village and colony of Plymouth in its hard beginnings. And she could look at her hands and say they were hard and they had helped. And she could look at her father with the added stoop of his shoulders and his hard hands—and she felt deep bonds between him and her. Barriers had come and her affection for him had grown less yet there still were thongs of loyalty and fidelity. Should he by any chance catch her dancing Sweep Out the Devil he would be frightened at her as a sinner. He would not begin to understand, in case she might try to tell him how and why she helped Hode Latch escape the constables. And he had his dark suspicions and was mentioning them to her often enough, his mistrust of the blond Peter Ladd, with his thick wavy light hair coming below his ears. "He sees you more often than need be," the father would mutter. Remember liked Peter Ladd as company. The two had pleasant hours. Time was to tell what they had between them.

Meantime too it was no help that her fear of the Evil One, a cold terror that came and went in her heart and her meditations, did not lessen. When heartsease rested too soft in her, when any pleasure swept her and became too keen a delight, there would come the shadow, the mistrust of it as perhaps a device of the Dark One, the Archdemon. Her elders never left off teaching from day to day how real was this cunning Agent of Evil. Her companions of somewhat her own age likewise had this fear that so often moved Remember though none of these companions probed, questioned, troubled themselves so deeply about it as did Remember.

Hundreds of times now she had begun, with the downgoing of the sun on Saturday, to ready herself for the Lord's Day, having meat, fish, vegetables so prepared—and the sweeping of floors and carrying in of firewood from the woodpile outside—and such other tasks as could be attended to beforehand so that neither she in her own heart nor anyone else could say she was disobedient to the commandment:

Remember the sabbath day, to keep it holy. Six days shalt thou labour, and do all thy work: But the seventh day is the sabbath of the Lord thy God: in it thou shalt not do any work, thou, nor thy son, nor thy daughter, thy manservant, nor thy maidservant, nor thy cattle, nor thy stranger that is within thy gates: For in six days the Lord made heaven and earth, the sea, and all that in them is, and rested the seventh day: wherefore the Lord blessed the sabbath day, and hallowed it.

Hundreds of times on the Lord's Day she had done her best to look neat and clean as she sat in the Lord's Day service—and in the latter years being painstaking that as she walked down the middle aisle of the meeting house and turned into the high-backed bench of her appointed place and personal pew, that her face and head rose out of a broad snow-white collar, that her own arrangement of the bright smooth coils and braids of her chestnut hair evidenced a young woman "comely but not vain."

Hundreds of times she had sat through the morning and afternoon services of the Lord's Day five to six hours, listening to hours of preaching and prayer. A prayer running long would recall to her the deacon invited by her father to their house to share food and discuss church matters. She had put on the table a roast of pork browned and hot, set in nice drippings of brown grease hot and tasty—and the deacon had prayed as to the sins of Europe in general, the kingdom of England more particularly, and especially the savages of North America and still more especially first the inhabitants, then the sojourners and finally the citizens of Plymouth village and plantation—and the prayer eventually did come to an end and all the living sinners in the world had been prayed for; and all the dead sinners preceding them were represented in petitions to the Most High nor were forgotten the unborn whom God was yet to permit to come alive and tread the earth.

Early in the prayer Remember was sure the pork had lost its hot early savor. Midway in the prayer she had her suspicion the pork was no longer warm. As the prayer came to its Amen she knew the pork was cold and the hot tasty brown grease drippings stiffened, coagulated and not worth sopping with fresh corncake. So the roast had to go back on the fire. She could see the face of that deacon among the other deacons seated just below the pulpit and facing the congregation like sentinel guardians. She was mischievous enough at times to read in the deacon's face during a long prayer his pride that he could pray as long as the preacher and bring in a wider variety of sinners not forgotten by the good Lord.

More than twice a hundred times on Sundays of penetrating cold Remember had brought along a shawl for her shoulders and back, a blanket for her legs, knees and ankles, not forgetting a flat stone heated by the fire at home and wrapped in wool, which made a footwarmer and a footrest. In the third hour of the services on such a cold Sunday she could swing her head slowly for a gaze at the congregation and take notice of those not come prepared, or low in health, how they were shivering with the cold and the only person in the room of a certainty having comfortable blood circulation was the earnestly expounding and vociferating preacher.

More than a hundred summer Sundays when the earth baked and blistered under the sun and heat waves curled from the roof and from each iron cannon on the roof, Remember sweated in her pew and wished the ordinances of the church not so strict against a woman's neck being "naked." The starch soon sweated out of the snow-white collar—and she further wished that on such a Lord's Day she could go barefoot and barelegged as she did weekdays.

More than a thousand times in that high-backed bench she had noticed a feeling grow and deepen in her, an admiration and affection for three of the colony and church leaders, Brewster, Bradford, Winslow. When they spoke she listened. They talked as though they wanted to grow in what they termed "inner grace." They prayed for it. She prayed and thirsted with them for this inner grace. Her eyes came away from dwelling on their faces as though she had received a candle-beam of inner grace. The faces of Stephen Hopkins, of Isaac Allerton, of John Billington, from these she gathered impressions that they wanted more from life than could be had—and it was coming about that Stephen Hopkins had an itch for property and dominance, that Isaac Allerton had secret yearnings for money beyond all his needs, that Billington could nurse anger to where it was a sick fool's indulgence. Remember straightened and drew her chin in at hearing Winslow speak of "light and vain persons who stumble," and his affirmation when plots and treacheries threatened the colony, "If any honest mind be discouraged I am sorry. I am far from being discouraged myself, offering you Christian consideration, beseeching you to make a good construction of my simple meaning, beseeching God to crown our Christian and faithful endeavors, with his blessings temporal and eternal. It would be hard and difficult to us that have endured the brunt of the battle and yet small profits return. Only, by God's mercy, we are safely seated, housed, and fortified." She heard a letter by Winslow read: "To all well-willers and furtherers of plantations in New England," and saluting in England, "Right Honorable and Worshipful Gentlemen, or Whatsoever," and begging, "Accept, I pray you, my weak endeavours, pardon my unskillfulness, and bear with my plainness." He named three things as "the overthrow and bane" of New England plantations or colonies.

1. The vain expectation of present profit, which too commonly taketh a principal seat in the heart and affection, though God's glory, etc., is preferred before it in the mouth with protestation.

2. Ambition in their governors and commanders, seeking only to make themselves great, and slaves of all that are under them, to maintain a transitory base honour in themselves, which God oft punisheth with contempt.

3. The carelessness of those that send over supplies of men [from England] unto them, not caring how they be qualified; so that ofttimes they are rather the image of men indued with bestial, yea, diabolical affections, than the image of God, indued with reason, understanding and holiness.

Remember had seen these people of "diabolical affections" come off the ships, and had seen them by scores put back on the ships for return to England. The investors, the Merchant Adventurers in London, sent these unwanted specimens to the colony as part of an English policy to rid their own country of vagrants, foot-loose wanderers and petty criminals. Also they had sent over Lyford, Weston, Oldham, and other men of education whose secret aim was to wrest control of the colony and the church and put it into the hands of the Church of England. These it was that Winslow meant in his letter: "what great offence hath been given by many profane men, who being but seeming Christians, have made Christ and Christianity stink in the knowledge of the poor infidels, and so laid a stumbling block before them. But woe be to them by whom such offences come."

Winslow was trying to tell the English investors to be more careful about what human timber they transported overseas. "I praise God I speak not these things experimentally, but by way of complaint of our own condition, but having great cause on the contrary part to be thankful to God for his mercies towards us; but rather, if there be any too desirous of gain, to entreat them to moderate their affectations, and consider that no man expecteth fruit before the tree be grown; advising all men, that as they tender their own welfare, so to make choice of such to manage and govern their affairs, as are approved not to be seekers of themselves, but the common good of all for whom they are employed."

A round head, broad across the brow, massive from ear to ear, with a jaw and chin in proportion—and always well carried—Remember liked Mr. Winslow's head. His black hair parted on the top of his head with a line about even with the middle of his left eyebrow, and it hung down into a rich mass of wide curls covering the ears and touching the white collar that fitted close around his neck to the chin. His black cloth coat fitted snugly around his muscular compact body. Sixteen silver buttons Remember counted on this coat. Sixteen she counted if she started at the top and went down, again sixteen if she started at the bottom button and counted up. At the top a cord, drawn close, hung with tassels down to the third or fourth button. Remember talked with Damaris Hopkins about this coat and they agreed it must be a doublet —being sure, however, that they could find others who would say it was a jerkin, a jacket, a cassock, a paltock. A doublet, she and Damaris agreed, was always of two thicknesses and wadded. A wadding of wool between double thicknesses of leather made a very warm garment for the coldest time of the year. A jerkin would be of a single thickness so what Master Winslow wore was not a jerkin. A jacket would be tighter-fitting. A cassock would be more like what a preacher would wear. A paltock—both Remember and Damaris had heard but forgotten what was a paltock. At the sleeve ends of the Winslow doublet, and from under the sleeve, came ruffled linen cuffs folded back perhaps six inches.

What if Plymouth leaders had been lesser men than they were in honesty and sagacity? Remember and her father along with others of the church asked that question. The colony had been saved several times by such narrow margins that they knew with lesser men they had been sunk. Between the conniving London money-makers allied to the King and the Church of England, on the one hand, and on the other hand the primitive savages who in one massacre in Virginia had slaughtered twice the population of Plymouth, they would have been erased, rubbed out, unless for extraordinary leadership and the ever dependable loyalty of about one-third of the colony to that leadership.

Among the dependables ever loyal Remember counted herself and her father. They had poured toil, hardship, the lifeblood of their best years, into the making of a church, the rooting of a colony. In the planting of Plymouth and its growth, Remember felt herself among the deeper roots. She knew its beginnings and kept wondering over its future, how Plymouth and New England would look after five or ten generations. Often came her twist of curiosity, her personal query as to when Plymouth, now having watches and books in only five houses, would have them in every house. Often, too, she wished for rows of standing books either read or waiting for her to read them.

And what with watches and books, would Plymouth people be so very different? Would they value and use time more wisely? Would the books correct their ignorance and lessen their fear? Or would the

Evil Shadow, the Archdemon, the Subtle One, employ the watches and the books of the future for his own ends and the corruption of men and women and the winning of them for his own purposes? With unfailing regularity her questing mind came back to the existence of a Supreme Mocker, God's Archantagonist who was hurled out of heaven for his ambition to dethrone God and rule heaven himself, the furtive and oily Satan who had sought to tempt Jesus on a mountain, the King of Masks who could change his form as he chose and took the shape of a Snake for the betrayal and fall of Adam and Eve—back he came to her waking mind, over and again returning to her dreams and sleep.

The Antichrist, the Head of Hell with its swarming fiends, the conniving and execrable Evil One beyond description because he took many shapes and could make himself invisible in the twinkling of an eye—grave and kindly elders had taught her to beware of this Terror. Her father never forgot that always near by lurked this Dark Shadow.

Sweet women she knew, clean women who kept their houses and children trim and neat, they had their eyes out for the Devil and they believed those who had seen his Satanic hoofprints in dust and snow. And who was it that had raised up flames of contention and sowed seeds of discord and enmity among the supposed authorities and teachers of Christianity in Europe and Britain, the hate and wrath which had sent the proscribed and persecuted from Scrooby to Leyden across the sea to Plymouth, New England? Governor Bradford spoke and wrote it was "Antichrist, that man of sin, that old serpent."

One Lord's Day afternoon in December of 1628 Remember sat in her pew, the bottoms of her feet cold because the heat had gone out of the flat stone and the wool under her feet. And she could hear the northeast wind piling more snow after the other snows of that week and her ears caught the howling of that wind around the four corners of the fort and the cannon on the roof. Twice in the morning she had seen the Reverend Ralph Smith turn the hourglass amid repeated warnings of the Antichrist.

And now for the second time in his afternoon sermon, after dealing with further subtleties of Satan, the minister turned the hourglass. It was at that moment Remember came out of a half-sleep. She had almost dozed away. In a final swift instant of her dozing she saw herself turned upside down and the Devil slid out of her head and as she got to her feet again the Devil was standing before her clawing at her and trying to get back into her head again. Now she sat strictly awake, her head clear, the fantasy vanished.

Then a thin wisp of suspicion or foreshadowing came to her, "What if some day I forget about the Devil? What if I cast him out of my thoughts? What if I chase him from my brain and heart?"

This came to her. It would be another of her secrets. No word of it could she tell her father nor any of her church companions. To Hode

Latch and his wife she could mention it, and to Orton Wingate. To Peter Ladd it would be entertaining. But they didn't belong. They were outsiders, one a fugitive from justice, one merely an inhabitant, one a sojourner but not a citizen.

* * * * * * * * * *

Chapter 16

* * * * * * * * * *

Persons Plain and Flaunt-a-flaunt

PLYMOUTH stood lonesome. For ten years she stood by herself as a village while at Weymouth, at Wollaston, elsewhere came little settlements that stayed till the blue curl of their firesmoke faded and they were gone to leave a few bones on the ground and a line of phantoms on the horizon.

Plymouth stayed put, the hilltop community neither seagale nor landwind blew away nor did sickness nor famine nor massacre make to vanish. Neither outside savages nor internal dissension split her. There in her own harbor within the long protecting arm of Cape Cod she stood.

She was watched, Plymouth knew she was watched. Far over the sea white men watched her with anxiety and care and knew more of what was going on between her long double row of houses than the red-men neighbors who came visiting. Those Englishmen were upper and middle-class men, of position, money, education and university training—they had clocks, watches, books, inkhorns and devotions, views of life strictly devout. They were still, in a way of speaking, members of the Church of England, Nonconformist members, and they favored reforms and changes in that church, holding the Book of Common Prayer too formal and cut-and-dried, and seeing parts of the ritual taken over entire from the Roman Church as idolatrous or bordering on idolatry. And they were troubled over the new king of England, Charles the First, who thought highly of himself, who rated his regal authority and personal genius as grand and extraordinary, who from year to year refused to call Parliament into session, saying in effect that they were a bother to have around and he, Charles the First, would make the laws and rule the kingdom and put the conniving Puritans and Nonconformists in their place. At the right of the throne stood a short little cheerful man with piercing eyes who would nod his head for such a one to be hanged, again nod for such another one to have his ears cropped, and at another nod these and those men would go to the Clink or Fleet

214

Prison. This was Archbishop William Laud. His name carried terror. Laud made a list of the clergymen of the kingdom who favored Charles I and after each name either an O or a P. An O was Orthodox and needed no watching while any P for Puritan required attention, perhaps incarceration, and possibly obliteration. Archbishop Laud approved King Charles giving out a *Book of Sports* and he commanded that in pulpits of all parish churches should be published the King's declaration of his royal pleasure that the people of his kingdom having on the Sabbath Day first done their duty to God should then on the Sabbath engage in all manner of lawful games, recreations and sports. The King himself set an example by having in the royal court, on the Sabbath, balls, masquerades, and richly dressed lords and ladies, the nobles and ladies having wine, song, and follies. A clergyman marked P in Laud's book writing a work titled, *A Defence of the most Ancient and Sacred Ordinance of God, the Sabbath Day* found himself in jail. Laud put on trial and caused sentencing of a Scotch clergyman Alexander Leighton because of a book *Zion's Plea against Prelacy*. They fined him ten thousand pounds and they set Leighton in a pillory, lashed his bare back with a whip, cut off one of his ears, slit one side of his nose, branded on one cheek with a red-hot iron the letters "S.S." meaning Sower of Sedition. Then, to quote from the diary of Archbishop Laud, "On that day seven-night, his sores upon his back, ears, nose, and face, not yet being cured, he was whipped again at the pillory at Cheapside, and had the remainder of his sentence executed upon him, by cutting off the other ear, slitting the other side of his nose, and branding the other cheek." Then the rebel against enforced uniformity of worship was put in close confinement at Fleet Prison under a life sentence.

Not only in churches but among English soldiers and on English ships, Archbishop Laud decreed they must use the Book of Common Prayer of the Church of England. His jealousy and zeal it was that Lyford and Morton had tried to interest in their allegations that the Pilgrims at Plymouth neglected and spurned the Book of Common Prayer. It was Laud's work when ships loaded with emigrants to New England were stopped in the Thames River and not allowed to sail till the shipmasters solemnly bound themselves to use the Book of Common Prayer at morning and evening services. And it was taken at Plymouth as the act of Laud that Edward Winslow on landing in England was jailed four months on his admission that his marriage to Susanna White, three thousand miles across the sea at Plymouth, had been a *civil* ceremony by a magistrate, with no ordained minister of the church pronouncing the bonds of union in holy matrimony.

Laud of course could not know that it was written in the book of days to come that he would be sentenced to death for the crime of high treason and he would beg of the Lords and Commons to excuse him from the customary execution of sentence for that crime: he would shrink from being hanged, quartered, and ceremoniously having his bowels thrust over his face. He would ask a more decent death, requesting his head be cut off with an ax and no more ado, which would be done forthwith and the headsman not ashamed of his deft stroke.

Nor could the proud and royal Charles the First know it was written in the book of days to come that he would have his once authoritative head by an ax detached from his regal shoulders over issues fomented by Puritans and Nonconformists.

Revolution heaved and boiled in England under the surface of events. The coming civil war glimmered in the cold irreconcilable angers of men who hated each other's religion and way of life and came to loathe each other's faces.

In this air of worse woe to come in England it more than interested some of the Puritans that a little colony of Englishmen had fled England for Holland and later on the coast of New England had made a settlement that stood on its feet, earned its own way, had furthermore a church of its own making separate from the Church of England. Foremost of these Puritans so interested was the son of a rich clothworker, John Winthrop, writing his wife May 15, 1629: "My dear wife, I am veryly persuaded God will bringe some heavye Affliction upon this lande, and that speedylye: but be of good comfort, the hardest that can come shall be a meanes to mortifie this bodye of corruption, which is a thousand tymes more dangerous to us than any outward tribulation, and to bring us into nearer communion with our Lord Jesus Christ, and more assurance of his kingdome. If the Lord seeth it will be good for us, he will provide a shelter and a hidinge place for us and others, as a Zoar for Lott, Sarephtah for his prophet."

So it was that by plans set in motion in England the Plymouth Company sold a grant of land of its patent toward the north. And ships set sail from England and landed at Salem some two hundred persons to found a settlement and build the colony of "Massachusetts Bay in New England." Before the next spring eighty of the two hundred newcomers died.

The next year, in April 1630, four ships sailed from England landing at Salem in June with eight hundred people and their Governor, John Winthrop. In July came seven hundred more newcomers. Before the year end the bad or scant food, want, cold, poor shelter, sickness had brought death to two hundred members. And when Governor John Winthrop on July 23, 1630, wrote to his wife Margaret in England he named over things to protect her health and keep her in some measure of comfort on her voyage across the Atlantic to join him at Salem:

. . . Be sure to be warme clothed, & to have store of fresh provisions, meale, eggs putt up in salt or grounde mault, butter, ote meale, pease, & fruits, & large stronge chest or 2: well locked, to keep these provisions in; & be sure they be bestowed in the shippe where they may be readly come by, (wch the boatswaine wil see to & the quartermasters, if they be rewarded beforehande,) but for these thinges my sonne will take care, Be sure to have ready at sea 2: or 3: skilletts of severall syzes, a large fryinge panne, a small stewinge panne, & case to boyle a pudding in; store of linnen for use at sea, & sacke to bestowe among the saylors: some drinkinge vessells, & peuter & other vessels: & for phisick you shall need no other but a pound of Doctor Wright's Electuariu Lenitivu, & his direction to use it, a gallon of scirvy grasse to drinke a litle 5: or 6: morninges togither, wth some saltpeter dissolved in it, & a little grated or sliced nutmege. . . . Remember to come well furnished with linnen, wollen, some more beddinge, brasse, peuter, leather bottells, drinkings hornes &c; let my sonne provide 12: axes of severall sorts of the Braintree Smithe, or some other prime workman, whatever they coste, & some Augurs great & smale, & many other necessaryes wch I cant now thinke of, as candles, sope, & store of beife suett, &c: once againe farewell my deare wife.

Winthrop could picture his wife choosing and picking, buying and packing, cutting loose from many old things and places dear to her and saying words she had, "There is a time to plant and a time to pull up that which is planted, but the Lord knoweth what is best, and His will be done." In a later letter he advised her, "Remember to bring juice of lemons to sea with thee, for thee & thy company to eate wth y^{r} meate as sauce."

Even for the well-to-do, the voyage was not easy. His baby daughter, born in England since Winthrop left for America, died on the ship that carried the mother across. Year by year, more than a thousand persons a year made that voyage to Massachusetts. Scores of them were university graduates. Churches and town governments arose in the places forming Massachusetts Bay Colony, new towns with names: Boston, Charlestown, Roxbury, Watertown, Medford, Lynn, Dorchester.

Now with these added thousands who fled England for Massachusetts, there came officials, clergymen, delegates, relatives, visitors, traders, fishermen, hunters, trappers, drifters, some arriving in Plymouth and staying a long or short while. The population of Plymouth doubled in ten years. The houses spread out farther on its two streets, Leyden and Main. The First Comers had the roof thatches off their houses and there were second stories and more ground-floor rooms. Plymouth began to have more care and pride in what her visitors saw. With the fresh inflow of ships and people direct from the Old World there came to be seen more different specimens of upper and lower classes, more different kinds of clothes, finery, oddities of luxury.

Ruffs—when John Winthrop came to Plymouth on colony business, around his neck and above his black velvet cloak stood out stiff and flat a collar eight inches wide and ruffed about two inches. This was the first ruffing Remember Spong had seen. She walked barefoot and bareheaded to the wharf to see Governor Winthrop and his party step off a ship to the wharf, following them to Governor Bradford's house. The ruff, she thought, made Governor Winthrop look very important. She had decisions about the ruff, "I would of a certainty not choose the task of each week soaking, washing, starching and ironing such a ruff." She noticed too the trimmed black beard and mustache of Governor Winthrop. They covered the upper lip and all of the chin, with no scissor marks on the hair of his head like on her father's. So she guessed Governor Winthrop had the care of a barber clever with scissors. "I do believe his beard seems as smooth as the fur along the neck and back of Tamia." On the Governor's head his hair came down heavy and crinkly, falling thick below his ears, a mass of locks of hair resting on the snow-white flowery ruff. Remember worried a little about this. She was afraid if she came closer she might see oil from his hair on the immaculate, unimpeachable ruff. "His hair is so shiny I know it has some grease in it and I do hope none of it rubs off on such a spotless ruff."

One young man in the Winthrop party, Remember tried to guess who he might be. His dandy boots ran up nearly over his knees where the leather folded down in long crinkly cuffs. His sword had a silver hilt stuck in a belt inwoven with red and gold, silk and brocade. His scarlet satin coat with gold flowers on it, his blue breeches with gold stripes at the sides—these amazed Remember as did the young man's ruff, wider and thicker than Winthrop's, and his blue steeple hat with a wide band of gold. Remember had to wonder whether he dressed himself in the morning or had help. "His garb is gladsome and merry, if in a degree vain. Yet it must put him to trouble to get it on and keep it gladsome once it is on." She asked why this wonderfully dressed young man was in Plymouth. "He is a plenipotentiary," was the answer. And Remember didn't dare ask, What is a plenipotentiary? "I should have known without asking that he is a plenipotentiary. But what is it that plenipotentiaries do? I must know. Some quiet afternoon I shall go to Elder Brewster and he will tell me where plenipotentiaries come from and why they must take such trouble with their clothes."

Remember would like to have seen the plenipotentiary walk "flaunt-a-flaunt" side by side with a proud lady who had visited a cousin in Plymouth the month before. The lady wore a scarlet cloak, a black satin doublet, shoes with silver buckles and a glimpse of blue silk stockings at the ankles, a lawn whisk for neckwear. Her head nodded in a light silk knitted hood that folded back to leave a downflow of blond curls on each side.

"God should have those two marry and walk side by side," murmured Remember. Her memory flashed to a painting she had seen in Leyden when she was eleven years old, titled "Before the Temptation," Adam and Eve in the Garden of Eden and stark of all garments. "Nonetheless children of Adam, aye they be," murmured Remember of this amazingly clad man and woman visiting Plymouth, "with more to wear than Adam and Eve."

The lady had three fans, two of tortoise shell, one of feathers fixed to a silver handle. One finger sparkled with a diamond set in a gold ring, the first diamond Remember had ever seen. "She bedazzles others and is a bit bedazzled herself," Remember surmised. Twice during her stay in Plymouth the lady came, with her sister, to meeting on Lord's Day. Her entry and her steps moving down the middle aisle with her scarlet cloak, blue silk stockings, diamond ring and all else, set the congregation in a stir. She sat in her sister's pew, tenth from the front. Those to the rear fastened their eyes on her. Those in front of her one by one during the sermon turned sidewise or full turn of the head to have one or two looks at her. All except Ebenezer Fleharty who was old, deaf, and had lost the sight of one eye.

Plymouth breathed more freely when she was gone. "She was a rather quiet and agreeable woman," Remember told Orton Wingate. "I talked with her after meeting. And I heard from others what she is like. She made no bold advances. She had a little red mouth like a small ripe cherry and hesitant eyes like the one blue china dish we had in Leyden that broke. Does she have a secret? What could it be?"

Wingate's mouth widened, his brown eyes blinked, his eyebrows lifted and came down and, "She has no secret. Her husband has. He wants to show something to the world through her that he hasn't got. What it may be is his secret. His mother may have been frightened by a dolphin when she was carrying him. And nobody knows what a dolphin thinks and believes and wants. It could be her husband is racking his brain for what further he may pile on her to bring her more gazed at. He has made money in trade, goes to church because it is the custom, holds to no faith in a life hereafter, and believes that when we die we are very very dead and the day of resurrection is a false promise of wayward and deluded prophets. That is his secret, as I read him. His secret blossoms for him in the color and shine he puts on his wife and himself. I have seen him in Salem, visited his house, and spoken with others who knew him as a leading trader and merchant. They named over part of his clothes, a cloth coat trimmed with silver lace, a velvet coat, a tabby coat, an old-fashioned Dutch satin doublet, four coats of various kinds, two pairs of golden-topped gloves, one embroidered pair and a pair with black fringe—also a suit of fine broadcloth, one French serge suit, one stuff cassock, three pairs of red drawers, two yellow waistcoats. And my memory fails for the rest. He carries a silver-headed cane and is known as the only man in Salem with two silver watches. He is twenty years older than his little cherry-mouthed doll-woman and I would not put them asunder. They enjoy buying their kind of happiness. They need more to cover their nakedness than I do. And I wish them well so long as they harm no others."

Remember was shelling corn when this streak of conversation came into her ears. She shelled four ears not saying a word and then, "You do talk, Orton Wingate. You consider Satan as having no hand in this woman's scarlet cloak and sparkling diamond. You cannot know but the Evil One, who works little by little, who leads his victims on from the first excesses to worser excesses, you cannot gainsay me he has his designs on that doll-woman and her husband more vain than she is." With more ships, more people, towns and villages, had come more fabrics and more vanity, declared Remember. Fabrics beyond any need of woman were at hand in these newer days that had come. Calico, cambric, cheney, challis, darnex, dowlas, flannel, lawn, linen, genting, plush, lockram, essembrike, stammel, penistone, perpetuana, serge, velvet, sempiturnum, silk, water perigon—a few Remember had worn, others she had seen and touched, still other cloths and fabrics she knew only by hearsay.

Vanity, show, display, personal adornment—sermons were preached against them and laws passed forbidding "newe and immodest fashions." The Massachusetts Bay Colony laws, of course, were not made for Plymouth but their influence reached over into that town. The Bay Colony decreed the wearing of lace to be wrong—silver, gold and silk lace, girdles and hatbands were under prohibitions. "No garment shal bee made with short sleeves, whereby the nakedness of the arme may bee discovered," read one new prohibition. Yet large sleeves also were under prohibition and any maid or woman knew well enough at which moment a sleeve became a vanity and a show rather than a garment. One minister had a word for ungodly overdressed or underdressed women. They were "nugiperous gentledames." Any one of them to him was "the very gizzard of a trifle, the product of a quarter of a cypher, the epitome of nothing, fit to be kickt."

The bare skin of a woman's forearm between wrist and elbow—such an extent or beginning of nakedness—the General Court of Massachusetts passed an order: "No garment shall be made with short sleeves, and such as have garments already made with short sleeves shall not wear the same unless they cover the arm to the wrist; and hereafter no person whatever shall make any garment for women with sleeves more than half an ell wide." Forty-five inches made an ell. A sleeve half an ell would be twenty-two and a half inches in width. The new law gave warning to sleeve-makers. How wide can a woman wear sleeves? The lawmakers guessed half an ell should satisfy the decent woman.

Another new fashion regulated was "the slash." More and more the outer sleeves had been slashed—two, five, six slashes in the outer sleeve to show a fabric of another color worn beneath to please, baffle, tease, or mystify male beholders. The Bay Colony ministers decreed for decency one slash to a sleeve and one more slash down the back.

Chapter 17

Thieves in the Green Corn—and a Wild Dream

WAS it three or four years now since Remember Spong first met Peter Ladd? She was looking back counting the time, nearer four years than three. He would be gone from Plymouth two and four months at a time, once six months, on fishing boats at Boston and Salem, working at ship carpentry and repairs. Usually he had money. Once he flashed out a hand and laid six gold pieces in a row. He insisted that Remember hide and keep three of them for him, and for herself the other three. He kept stubbornly at her, and she gave in saying, "You are homeless. I will keep and hide the six for you and none for me." Then gone four months, one afternoon he came, his clothes rather worn and torn, his face pale, his blond hair straggling down his forehead. His usual swift sunburst of a smile over the whole of his face now came slow with an effort. He was asking Remember for one of the gold pieces left with her. She went up the ladder to her room, opened the leather-covered chest and untied a knot in a large white lawn kerchief, found the coin for him. He thanked her, sat by the fire and said he had been a damn fool, drinking day after day for a week. He should have quit at two days, he was saying, not clear on why he drank five more days after the first two. He talked on. He wouldn't do it again. A man out to make money, to get gold and land and a big house with servants for himself, such a man must not stay drunk a whole week— he must limit himself to two days.

John Spong came in and there was no more talk of drink. The three ate supper and with a little food in him Peter Ladd brightened into talk and smiles. John Spong, as usual, tried to frown and glower him down but Peter went on irrepressible about ships, fish catches, and news and affairs at Salem, Boston, and odd bits from Plymouth. "I gave my greetings last week to the good fellow who was haled into court and fined twenty shillings. You heard of him. He had gone about hither and yon telling of the whale he saw midafternoon, a huge black whale in the sea off Cape Cod, its mouth fourteen feet wide at least. No others had seen this whale at this time. Witnesses testified they could not see the whale he said he saw. Wherefore he was found guilty of a falsehood and fined twenty shillings for being a liar. He told me it was a good big whale, a fine wonder of a whale, and he was sure it did no harm to anyone that he had seen this whale that others couldn't see. He trusted me and said in confidence, 'It is my whale. I have made that whale my own. I will see it whensoever it pleases me to see it. If others wish a like whale, let them go seek one. They fined me twenty shillings and they convict me of being a liar but they cannot take away my whale.' "

"Incorrigible," glowered John Spong.

Peter Ladd talked through the supper, helped Remember clear the table and wash the dishes, took it on himself to scour an iron kettle while he talked on, after an hour or so leaving for his tavern. Peter had an eye for work to be done at the Spong place, chopping wood and bringing it in and piling it next the fireplace, mending a leak in the rain barrel, once borrowing a soldering kit and plugging the leaks in kitchenware. John Spong rated him "misbegotten and ungodly." Remember saw her father near the point of ordering him to stay away from their house. Twice on autumn afternoons she and Peter had gone to the woods and brought back sacks of hickory nuts, hazelnuts, red-haws, and John Spong had winced over rumors and questions about what his daughter and that young man might be doing in the woods. So he forbade it.

From then on what afternoon holidays Remember could snatch from her work for company with Peter Ladd, they went in sight of all Plymouth clam-digging, each with two buckets for mussels and shell-fish. At meeting on Lord's Day there would be Peter Ladd on the last bench to the rear reserved for sojourners and inhabitants as marked off from citizens and members of the church. After meeting Peter would walk alongside Remember to the Spong house.

John Spong threw out hints that Peter should change his habits, settle down into steady ways, submit himself for membership in the church, after which it would be more seemly and appropriate that he should so publicly walk with members on Lord's Day after meeting. This would start Peter talking and he was keenly interested in so many things he had seen and heard in the many places he had been that John Spong couldn't get a word in edgewise. He was going to do well by himself, the young man was sure. He would have first a fishing boat of his own, later a fleet of fishing boats of his own, and a big house with servants. Then he would join the church and they would be pleased to have him and he might consent to be a deacon and on Lord's Day sit facing the congregation in a velvet doublet with silver buttons and neatly made and fitted shoes, each shoe surmounted, where the laces tied, with a large quiet black rosette. For a time John Spong believed the young man might possibly have just such a future; his wit and confidence in himself seemed convincing.

Early in September one evening Remember had fixed a snack of food for her father's pocket and seen him out of the door and wished him a good night of it. She had done her after-supper work and gone to bed at dark. Her father had gone to stand watch over the nearly ripe corn. Here and there in the field well-ripened ears had been stripped off the stalks, husks torn off and ears carried away. Spong was to watch the north end of the field all night and Goodman Frank Childers the south end. They set themselves to catch and arrest whoever was stealing the corn. On this third night straight her father and Childers had kept watch and seen nothing of the thieves. It reminded her of earlier times when her father had stood watch all night over the fish put in the corn hills, three alewives to a hill, where foxes and wolves but for the watch would come and eat of the fish during the fifteen days in May that the fish rotted and became fertilizer for the corn. Then nothing had happened. And now again on this night watch for stealers of ripe corn, again might be no disturbers and nothing to happen.

A few hours Remember slept, waking to hear her name cried out loud below, her father's voice. She was out of bed, down the ladder in a hurry to see her father, in what scant light came from the fireplace. In the dark she could see him dazed and bedraggled. She ran for a candle, lighted it at the fire, put it on the table, led her father toward the light. Only his right eye looked at her, the left eye closed amid black-and-blue bruises. The right ear hung gnashed and raw. From rough broad gashes on his forehead and from other marks on his face ran down blood streaks. She looked at his hands—and saw blood and dirt on the knuckles and fingers. His hair stood tousled, matted a dark red in places. The breaks and rips in his coat, with one sleeve hanging loose at the shoulder seams, made Remember say to herself that someone had tried to tear the coat off him. He was not in all of his senses. Yet his lips were grim set and calm.

"Good God, father, what hap? Who? How?"

"Take not the name of the Lord in vain."

"The Evil One was about—the Black Shadow—his servants—brutish and bloody—who were they? How and whence came they?"

She helped seat him in a chair, threw wood on the fire and by fresh firelight and the candle she washed his face and head, helped get him out of his clothes and into bed. He swayed unsteadily going up the ladder. She brought an ointment for some of the cuts and bruises, made a poultice of raw meat for his left eye. While she was doing these helps for him he kept telling her in a disjointed way and rather calmly what had happened, and more of the action of the affair came clear to her when she heard the witnesses at the trial three days later.

Spong and Childers had been on watch about two hours when Childers came to Spong and asked him to come look. They were slow and quiet, moving with heads down and arms careful along the corn rows. They stopped and Childers pointed to an open space between the cornfield and the woods. The two of them watched five dark humps moving along the ground toward the corn. In a clear starlight they made out after a while three men and two women crawling on hands and knees to reach the corn.

Spong and Childers waited, drawing farther back in the corn rows as the prowlers came toward them. They could hear corn stripped from the stalks, then low giggles, titters and a mischievous laughter. They saw the five one by one stoop low and run for the woods. Having seen the fifth and last of the prowlers leave the cornfield, Spong and Childers at a spot farther south made a dash into the woods, and easily located the prowling five who were tittering and joking in undertones. Spong and Childers watched them, where they believed themselves safe, some three hundred yards away from the cornfield, in a clearing of hazel bushes sitting on the ground and eating of the green corn carried off. The kernels not yet begun to harden, the eaters laughed to each other their glee over a tender grain that to them was luscious eating. One of the men laughed, "The more we eat, the less the evidence we take home." To Spong and Childers it seemed that what they were doing they had done many times before and they considered themselves clever and it had become to them a laughing matter.

"A very pert and coppet taste it has," said one of the men, throwing away a cob and reaching for a fresh ear.

"Damned sweet corn," another man managed to say through a mouthful of corn.

Then one of the women, a large muscular woman, "Damned good corn and better than the lousy Plymouth Colony."

The third of the men looked young, a boy of eighteen perhaps. "I got six ears put away," he was saying. "And my belly is like to bust."

"All our bellies like to bust if we don't leave off eating corn soon," cautioned one of the women.

Then the other woman, "And I be telling you merry sparks, the time to eat green corn is when the corn is green and you can get it."

And a somewhat authoritative man stood up, "Our guts are better for this smack uh corn. This glut uh corn, I should say. What we're not eatin we stash near the edge uh the woods. No dumb constable uh Plymouth gets onto where we been tonight."

Now Spong and Childers stepped in and told the five of them they were under arrest and must go to the Plymouth jail.

"You the law?"

"Aye, we are the law."

"And you takin us in the name uh the law?"

"You are stealers of corn and you shall be tried on the charge of stealing corn."

"Yes?" came from the two men slow and defiant, and the two women, one after the other, "Yes?" and "Yes?" And then the youth's voice, "Yes?"

From that moment on the details of what happened came rather vague from all of the witnesses. A man and woman leaped on Childers, brought him down, twisted loose from his hands his hickory club. At the same time Spong went down with a man, a woman and a boy trying to pin him to the ground. Spong planted a terrific kick at the stomach of the man who reeled, fell, and lay moaning. The boy and the woman wrestled with Spong for his hickory club. The weight of the boy and the large muscular woman pinning him down, Spong let go his right hand on the club and gouged his fingers into the eyes of the youth, who fell away blinded and howling low. Spong swept the same hand to the throat of the woman and pressed his powerful fingers at her windpipe with a fierce grunt, "Get off me, get off me." She rolled off him and Spong sprang up to face the other man holding the club taken from Childers. The other woman leaped at Spong and ran her fingers like cat claws at his eyes and down his face. Spong backed away to see Childers rise dazed from the ground and leap from behind on the man who had taken his club.

By the time Childers had twisted his club loose from his opponent the boy with the gouged eyes had recovered enough sight to rush in on Spong and he was joined by the half-strangled woman who had gotten back her wind. The inrushing boy got Spong off balance so that the full wild swing of Spong's hickory struck lower than he had aimed and hit the man's shoulder. Man, woman and boy then tangled with Spong and brought him to the ground. Childers by now had managed to bring his hickory to the top of his opponent's head, the man slumping to the ground and lying perfectly quiet.

By now the three dealing with Spong had gouged his eyes, closed his left eye with fist blows, half-strangled him and landed glancing blows on his head with the club they had taken from him. Spong, however, was not so far gone but he could see, with his half-shut right eye from where he lay struggling against their holds on him, the swing of Childers' club to the man's head, who fell away and lay still. A second swift blow of Childers to the head of the boy laid him out quiet and motionless. This left Spong, his strength far spent, one eye closed, his face and hands bleeding, fighting against the heavy fierce woman who kept clawing at his face. Childers took careful aim and brought down his club on her head with what he guessed would knock her loose from Spong. She fell like a heavy sack off balance, still awake and conscious, suddenly aware that the other woman of their party had vanished. She was turning her head sidewise and sweeping the scene with her eyes and making sure the other woman was not there and had run away. "The lazy bitch, the dirty slut, I always said she couldn't cook nor frig nor fight."

As John Spong slowly raised his sore and pain-shotten body from the ground and sat up, there was yet a ringing in his ears and the hot breath of the woman on his face as she had spit at him, "Ye'll not be forgettin me nor my claws, ye'll be havin the fingernails of a fightin woman on yer goddam puke-face."

Childers arranged the four bodies so he could see them with one sweeping glance. When an eyelid quivered and opened he gave the warning, "Don't sit up," lifting his club and scowling. Spong hobbled and wobbled to the village for constables who put the four in jail.

The woman who had run away was rounded up. She was Hannah Horn, her husband Abel Horn, the first to go down under Childers' club. The Horns had come to Plymouth from the ruins of the Weymouth Colony and they hated Plymouth and had been trying to get away from it. The other three were Hutts, Alfred and Alice Hutts and their well-grown seventeen-year-old son, Benjamin Hutts. Both of the elder Hutts, it came out later, had been vagrants and petty thieves in London and there were London authorities who considered it good riddance to get them on a ship for America.

The trial was speedy and the next day the two women, Hannah Horn and Alice Hutts, also Benjamin Hutts, sat with feet and arms in the stocks while before their eyes at the whipping post thirty lashes were laid on the bare backs of Abel Horn and Alfred Hutts.

Remember Spong stood holding her father's arm and looked on as the lash hissed through the air and laid its mark on the bared flesh. She felt her father calm, justified, seeing stern and exact justice enacted, many eyes of the crowd on him as a wronged figure now witnessing retribution laid on the wrongdoers. Next to Spong stood Childers, the nearest either had ever come to standing before the Plymouth public as heroes though somehow the spectacle required some added quality for them to have high and heroic dignity.

Remember stood with her feet frozen in her foot tracks, noting the swing and hiss of the lash again and again. And she could only turn her thoughts to the Evil One. Who else than Satan could beguile fools into stealing corn with the end result that five figures of crime and two of justice should all have pain and anguish? Could God have any hand in this? Could the Christ who bore shame, humiliation and agony have any part in this? No, you could not look on this and give it a thought without feeling that back of it were the craft and seduction of the Great Mocker, the Head of Hell and his minions.

The whipping ended. The law had spoken. Tomorrow would be the second and final day of penance. Then the guilty five would be on view for the town, the two women and the boy in the stocks, the two men in the pillory.

Remember walked with her father into the jail. She stood with him and looked through the barred door at Alfred Hutts studying how to lie down and rest himself without touching his raw sore back to anything. Weak and dizzy, Hutts with weary eyes gave a casual glance toward the door and caught there the face of John Spong. Hutts walked toward the barred door, paused two steps from it, stood stooping and wriggling at his sore back, his feet wide apart, snarling, "We'll get away from Plymouth, John Spong. And we'll come back some day when it pleases us. And the people will be gone from the houses and the rats, the foxes and wolves, they will be the people of Plymouth

226

and no worse to look at than now. You Plymouth puke-faces don't know how to make a colony. I'm glad I bit your ear and chewed your ear, John Spong, the blood of your ear tasted good to me, I can taste it yet, I'm pleased I got your ear in my teeth."

Spong had expected this. He put his closed right hand through the door and flung into the face of Hutts a handful of mixed sand and ox dung. "Take that and shut your foul mouth. If you open it again I'll give you more."

Remember hardened. Across her early twenties the hardening inside of her went on not unlike the heavier calluses on her hands. As new skills came to her hands out of her varieties of labor, some added craft or cunning in the making of her way through life also went on. With the passing years her acquaintance with human evil grew. And with it came deepened resolves to sharpen her awareness and cunning in dealing with the ever-lurking Black Shadow. Along with this, of course, she never lacked for help from old friends and from good respectable church elders taking occasion to say, "Of a verity Satan lives and works and you can see him in the deeds of others round about you every day—and by searching your heart you can find the weak places, where the flesh is feeble in yourself, where he seeks to enter for possession of yourself."

On the night of the public whipping of the Hutts and Horns an unforgettable dream came to Remember. At supper she ate little more than two small early-autumn apples. It hurt that her father had had a pleasant and exultant day. She could find no mixture of sorrow in him. He exulted that justice had taken its toll. Remember knew it would be no use to tell him of one question that had flashed to her, "What if I had been born among the vagabond and vicious of London, England, and taught as a child to steal and to laugh with glee over my skill in stealing?"

She turned from side to side in her bed that night and sank into sleep with many repetitions of the line, "A worm of the dust am I, a worm of the dust am I." She awoke an hour later and after turning from side to side again, went to sleep to her own murmuring, "A worm of the dust am I, a worm of the dust am I."

Her dream began late in the night. She could hear the swing and hiss of a whip lash. Then she could hear the drum roll announcing Lord's Day services. Then was a silence, the smooth black silence of the sea when she stood alone on Plymouth hilltop in the fog of a cold northeast drizzle, when the sea could not be seen but she could swear it was there. Then came three low knocks on the front door below, long and slow knocks. A long pause and again those three knocks, louder this time, long and slow as before, and as though whoever knocked was sure the knocking would be heard. Again the three knocks, the timing as before, and this time the walls and floor of the whole house trembled.

Remember asked herself, "Should I wake father?" She answered herself, "No, the caller wishes to see me alone."

For a fleeting moment going down the ladder the faces of Hode Latch and his wife, the face of Peter Ladd, flashed to her and she said, "No, their knocking would be different—it is someone else."

The fire had sputtered low, only one thin smolder of an ember lighting the room. Her feet knew every inch of this room and in the dark she found her way to the door, hesitated a moment, thinking again perhaps to call her father. Then she unlatched the door and moved it slowly open perhaps the width of her face.

As she looked out through the narrowly opened door she was snatched through the door, heard it latch itself shut, and she was facing a tall lean black figure, two feet taller than herself, and he held her to him with smooth long arms that smelled of oil and felt to her touch like silk and leather both at once.

His ice-cold fingers, the slow rolls of smoke from his mouth with a grin showing long pointed teeth that came down over his lower lip—this she expected.

The flow of yellow sparks from his eyes, the yellow brows above the eyes, and the way the eyebrow hair came down in long droops that caught in his teeth and took fire from his darting tongue-end and burned with a yellow smoke—this she had not expected.

In her nostrils and throat the yellow smoke of the burning hair choked and suffocated her for a moment and she coughed and spewed. And as she writhed and wriggled in this coughing and spewing, she began shrinking and kept getting smaller and smaller as he clutched her to his breast and buried his face in her hair.

Then his first oily sleek words, "Too small, little pet, come longer." He tightened his fingerholds on her, a streak of pain shot through her from toe-bones to skull, a sharp wail of music ran through her— and she was very long and very thin—how long or how thin at this moment she could not say.

He whirled her round and round, gripping her ankles. Now she knew how long and how thin—as tall as himself and as thin as the house front door near by.

He stood her on her feet before him. His right hand in one sweep took off her linen nightgown and she stood bare and shivering, not from cold but from fear of what was coming next.

He seized her, put her flat form under his left arm and with an easy leap sat on the housetop straddling the roof.

A high wind roared in from the sea and a full moon sailed the sky and poured down floods of clear golden light.

A box on her right ear, a box on her left ear, and she was out of her long flat doorshape, back to her natural size, wearing a tight scarlet dress, tight as her very skin, tight as though this gleaming scarlet had grown on her and belonged to her for a long time.

The house began rocking like a slow-galloping horse or, she decided, more like the sinuous up and down of a snake length. Behind her came a vast furious mocking laugh that split the air. She lifted her head to the moon and laughed a great wild shriek herself.

The Devil had won her for his bride. What did she care? Was not this what she had waited for? Not till now did she know and realize it was like this she had wanted to be held and kept. Never before had she been proud of her nakedness.

When her lord and master behind her let out another long keen howling wail, she joined. The two mocking and exultant wails joined and went out over Plymouth and carried fright into every house. Soon all of Plymouth's people had gathered in a crowd. Fronting the house in the bright moonlight they stood gazing up, amazed, curious, shocked.

"What is it?" cried one. "Has John Spong's daughter sold herself to the Demon of Darkness?"

"Aye, the sweet wench Remember Spong is now the Devil's whore and consents to be seen shameless and naked with him."

Her master's voice cut the air. She turned and saw him pointing spears of fire toward three men who stood foremost in the crowd, Governor Bradford, Elder Brewster, and Edward Winslow, her master's voice piercing and mocking:

"Ye buzzards of God, ye thought to take her from me, but I have her and she is mine, every hair of her. I have made the skin of her scarlet and the very bones of her I have made scarlet. She is Plymouth's most dazzling scarlet daughter. You thought to make her a pale white lily of spotless purity. I have made her a flame flower of scarlet passion. You would have kept her low in the dust and ashamed of her flamerose. I have made her to ride and sing flaunt-a-flaunt and to show herself to all Plymouth as my bride of passion, naked and flaunt-a-flaunt."

And Remember knew that those who looked from below in the brilliant moonlight saw her as changed, saw the bony face of her gaunt with a new and defiant pride, her hair changing to a flame-chestnut, the apple-blush of her cheeks becoming a sunset-maroon smolder, her thick and tangled eyebrows now smooth as black silk lace, her blue eyes a fiery storm-green, her lithe lean body shining naked through a thin tight scarlet dress, tight as her very skin, tight as though this gleaming scarlet had grown on her and belonged as part of her.

Then faces stood out from the crowd, one her father's face mute with anguish, trying to speak and the words tongue-tied, hearing a deacon's outburst before the crowd, "Cry to your daughter and disown her forever, John Spong."

Now for the first time Remember found words. She howled in a defiant glee, a riotous mirth of triumph. "Tell my father he too is one of you buzzards of God and I defy him."

Then came two faces. She went limp a moment. Her tight scarlet gown pressed and choked her with ice. Beyond the edge of the crowd, and not really a part of it were these two faces. One was Peter Ladd, his face motionless as the dried head of Wituwamat on the fort, endless tears coursing from his eyes and down the face. Farther over was a tall young man with black hair, his face a blur and yet Remember knew this was the boy with the ax handle at the wharf of Plymouth, England, that boy grown to man size. And she knew he might be saying, "Queer people, you belong to the queer people!" And, "What if I should spit in your face now?"

The wind roared in from the sea. The high moon kept sailing, the house roof moving with snake-length undulations. Her eyes roved back to her father. Next to him loomed a face that smote her, a face infinitely gentle and understanding, infinitely soft and compassionate. This she saw was the face of one who had held her and given her suck from warm breasts. The memory came to her: this was the woman she had danced with in·Leyden when they stepped together the wild hate dance they called Sweep Out the Devil.

The next Remember knew she had let out two wild shrieks and was sitting up in her bed sobbing and her father with his arms around her, "What prank of the Evil One has troubled you?"

And she couldn't tell him, not a piece nor moment of it. He would hear it with silence and after days of his saying nothing she would hear from him that she must guard herself from lewd thoughts. In her own mind she tried to fathom why in her dream she had wanton, delirious delight such as never in her born days. Such keen pleasuring of herself, her fears told her, could be only that of a Bad Woman, an evil heart, possibly the beginning of a rot and corruption beyond control or discipline. She must watch herself. Cunning and insidious she felt the dream of this night. She came to a deep belief that the best way to guard herself against wanton folly was to join herself close to those others who were older, who knew Satan better than she, who knew the Black Shadow from experience and study. She must guard her thoughts, she must be sober, sedate, more solemn, more suspecting of any great happiness. Should too vivid and shining a happiness move her it was a sign Satan was near with his conjurations ready to seduce her feet with his diabolical designs. So she kept watch on her happiness. When she caught herself dancing she would stop in her foot tracks and say, "The foul Archdemon is hereabouts. I shall get the better of him." And when the urge to dance came hard to throw off, she would whirl herself in the hate quicksteps she and her mother did in Leyden, Sweep Out the Devil.

Hannah Horn, Alice Hutts and Ben Hutts sat in the stocks. The Hutts and Horn men stood in the pillory, their heads locked and bound so they could look only below and sidewise, their arms locked and the hands dangling from the wrists. The constables had clamped them in for the afternoon and gone away on other business.

A rain came down, a soaking rain, and a wind blowing rainsheets. Six minutes of icy hail pounded down. The rain slowly let down and was gone.

Amid the last sparse raindrops Remember Spong stepped from the meeting-house door. Not many steps and she could hear those in the stocks and pillory. Their backs to her, and a few raindrops still falling, Remember heard them accusing each other. Alice Hutts in a low sharp rasping with hot breath of speech: "It was your bright notion, out of your goddam fool head, your goddam stupid blockhead, that we should go and steal the corn and have a feast."

"No, fool woman, it was your goddam silly and idle tongue that first blathered what a gay prank it would be, you it was made our mouths water telling us how tender was the corn now, the white juice and milk of it not yet dry, and it would be a sweet night lark and we could be a lot of nightingales singing together, and it would be like all of us getting tight-drunk together."

"You lie, you link, you blow, you stink. Yes, I fell in with you after you first spilled it with your smooth fool tongue out of your rattling fool head. I would have better have known it was one more of your ape tricks. Ape, I said. Ape! Ape! Ape!"

"Be quiet, woman."

"I will not be quiet. I will make noise with my mouth for all Plymouth to hear."

"Be quiet, be quiet, woman, I said, ye'll wither yer tits with yer crazy hot ways."

"Crazy, mayhap, not hot. Wet to the skin I am, every hair of me wet and every hair shiverin, cold water to my skin and my clothes stickin cold and stinkin to me. I said I know you stink. You lie, you link, you blow, you stink. I hope yer cold and chilled to the bone more than I am here the first day I ever had hailstones of ice upon my head and shoulders peltin and poundin into the goddam bruises on my head and shoulders, ice meltin down into my ears, down my shoulders, chillin the tits and at last reachin my toes so numb my toes can't tell whether the water's cold nor warm."

"Quiet, ye slut."

"Slut, ye said. I know ye stink and I hope yer cold and I hope ye shake and shiver with chills fer lettin yer goddam silly wit bring us to that field for stealin corn."

"Quiet, woman. Shut yer goddam dirty mouth. If I ever get loose and get at ye, I'll slap it sore, I'll slap it black-and-blue."

The sparse raindrops had ended. People were coming. The spoken rasping snarls ended. Remember had heard enough. At first it was exciting, then her mouth dropped open and she stood amazed. She walked away and walked home alone saying, "It is some hard pitiless

231

game that man and woman play with each other. If she truly hated him and thought him an ape and a ninny she would cry it out before the people who came. So would he before all Plymouth be calling her a slut."

Then the cruelty of the punishment came over her. Too many of those she had seen pausing to jeer and mock at the two men, one boy, and the two women, took a queer pleasure in their jeering and mocking. Then recalling how her father looked when he came home after fighting with them, the ear that bled and kept on bleeding and soaking one linen bandage after another, the left eye that had as yet not come half open, she was sure some punishment was needed. She tried to make some kind of sense out of it all. But it stayed dark and tangled. The nearest she could come to straightening it a little was to go back to the Archdemon, the Most High Mocker. Men alone, God alone, could not make such a dark tangle of evil. The very words that man and woman hurled at each other in their misery and shame had been learned from Satan. "Their pride and their gluttony first brought them to this venture and pride is of the Devil and gluttony is of the Devil."

Having cleared the matter to that extent she repeated her resolutions to beware of pleasure: the plot of the Devil in snaring a godly person into sin was to lead one on. Such wanton godless fury as she heard between that man and woman had a skill in sin, a developed skill. "The Devil taught them, then they taught each other, then the Devil taught them more and they tried to outdo the Devil in their evil deeds and speech."

Remember told herself she must try to make her joys pure and innocent, holy and simple in the eyes of God. "Of any wantonness I will beware for Satan seeks ever from shallow wantonness into deeper till the sinner is entangled and lost beyond salvation."

* * * * * * * * * *

Chapter 18

* * * * * * * * * *

B.A.D. Women

JOHN CRAVE was starting on his day's work. On his face was expectancy or rather assurance. A sharp face, a pointed chin, large gray meditative eyes with a slow and changing brightness in them. He was about to open the door of the little room he made his workshop. The opening of the door on this particular late May morning had an exultation of holiness and zeal. The great dazzling disk of the sun, the most marvelous single creation of God the Maker and Shaper—the sun was about to be let into this dark room and flood it with the mystery of light. To him this threshold was an altar floor and he was performing a sacred service. He unlatched the door, stood breathless a moment with a heightened assurance on his face. Then he swiftly swung the door open full and wide. An oblong of white-gold struck the floor and held itself there. No broom and not any device from the world of men could sweep out this oblong of light nor scrub it away nor tear it up nor pound it loose. He stood in the doorway, gave one brief look toward that burning blinding ball of light, then closed his eyes, stood with his face to the sun and so standing with folded hands, he made a long silent morning prayer.

A little man, five feet three, silken light hair drawn in ringlets below his ears. This was a morning service he went through on the warmer days of the year when the sun shone and flies and mosquitoes not too thick. His prayer ended, with a sweep of his eyes to the arch of sky over the sun and a slow bow of his body toward that arch, he turned to his shop. A leather apron went round his middle and below his knees. Seating himself on a low-back, leather-bottom chair between racks and facing a bench of tools and materials he began his work. "What kind of feet has God given the people of Plymouth? Under the blessing of God and the fortuity of circumstance I know more about the feet of Plymouth than any other man in the colony."

And if you should ask John Crave about this "fortuity of circumstance" that he mentioned he could tell you he was one of the more patient and careful listeners to sermons and could recall an hour of preaching with twenty minutes given to an exposition of the word circumstance, another twenty to the word fortuity, then a further analysis and synthesis of fortuity joining circumstance.

Using different-length knife blades Crave shaped and fitted a pair of wooden heels and fastened them with wooden pegs to a pair of woman's shoes. He sang in a low voice two verses of a favorite hymn and went on in a low voice giving his sense of the meaning of the lines of the hymn. "He Jehovah made us, and not we. How could we make ourselves? And who but Jehovah could have made us? Are we not the folk and sheep of His feeding? And we shall enter the gates with confession and His courtyards with praising. How else should it be? By confessing to Him, blessing His name, we make known He is our joy, His mercy ever the same. Shouting triumph, singing gladness, we shall serve Jehovah and enter His gates and come before Him. To the unredeemed we shall bring word that Jehovah He is God. To the unredeemed we must say on and sing on that they too must be His people and sheep of His pasture."

A shadow moved on the oblong of light. Crave looked up to hear, "How is my heathen brother today?"

"The blessing of Jehovah on him and another day for the miracle of light."

"And have they yet proven you heathen?"

"The deacon came. They had heard I was a sun-worshiper, that I bowed and prayed to the sun and made an idol of it wherefore I was heathen and pagan. He was kindly and inquiring. People were talking. It might be idle talk. And he believed me and went away satisfied that my worship and prayer go to Jehovah who is God, the Maker and Shaper of the sun. His mighty hand could put out the sun and make another sun before I could drive one peg in a wooden heel. So I told him. And he told me there are vain tongues, idle fancies and more busybodies in church and out than he likes to see in Plymouth."

A bench, no back to it, stood against the wall. Wingate seated himself. Crave pegged away. Crave meditated aloud, "A sweet day for the miracle of light. My covenant with the Lord and His covenant with me it stands forth in light, in any light whatsoever. The new moon, the half-moon or full moon, the stars of evening or midnight or morning, they all speak this covenant. Likewise a row of candles or a single sputtering taper, likewise a fireplace blaze of oak and maple or the hissing plume of a burning pine knot. Each bring. to us the countenance of God and the mystery of His face."

Crave pegged away, once brushing back ringlets of hair that got in his eyes. He handed Wingate the shoes he had wooden-heeled. "Tell Remember Spong I miss her good face."

"Her message was she will be seeing you soon with no fear you are a heathen."

"How goes the affair of Remember and Peter Ladd? Or is it an affair?"

"She likes him much and wonders why she doesn't love him. She defends him. She will overlook any wrongdoing her father brings to light. Her father hunts and sniffs into the past and present doings of Peter Ladd."

"Has he time from his work for such hunting and sniffing? Is it idle talk that John Spong goes a deal with Ebba Hibbett?"

"More hours than he has given any woman since he came to Plymouth."

"Is she the short broad full-bosomed woman with smooth dark-brown hair like West Indian molasses? She is a brisk woman—beams and plays with her eyes—that is her?"

"Yes, you have seen her. A young widow from Boston, her husband lost in an Indian fight. She brushes her shoulder and bosom close to John Spong and makes apology it was not meant. She brings her face so near his face that he is befuddled, bashful, pleased and muddled. She has not failed at Lord's Day meeting since coming to know Spong. She is unfailing to be in the end of the middle aisle between him and the front door after meeting. What more there is between them I would not know. Remember mislikes talk of it. And I mislike talk of

Ebba Hibbett making free and loose with other men. I know not whether it be mischievous blab. We lack not such blab any day or hour in Plymouth. Ebba Hibbett may be a lively cat. She seeks a mouse husband. Or she may be a well-meaning woman who has sobered down in her course in life with honest intentions of entering the church."

Crave cut a round patch of leather, trimmed and thinned the outer edge of it, stitched heavy thread through a circle of holes made with his awl. "This should last you through the summer, Brother Wingate."

The door to the house opened. A young woman came into the shop. Wingate rose, shook her hand with a warm and cordial grin, "Mary Crave, good to see you, very good to see you." He looked into her smooth pale face, her handsomely homely and merry mouth, her straight nose a little crooked at the end, her eyes large, gray and melting like her father's, a head rather gay and commanding on her thick sturdy frame. Then there was much talk, at moments all three talking at once, a riotous and irresistible merriment in the air.

"You like it—both of you like it—then it has more good than bad in it!" cried Mary Crave, light-footed and neatly balanced drawn erect to full height, her right shoulder raised, her right arm thrust out in the gray sleeve of her gown with a large flame-colored Roman capital letter B.

Before stepping out into the street she turned to the two men, pulled her face into an unquestionable solemnity, "I shall walk strait-laced and straight-faced for Plymouth."

"Walk in the sun and be not afraid, daughter."

Wingate had heard of her trial and conviction the week before on the charge of blasphemy. The court considered the stocks for her and because of her father's standing and conduct relented. For a year, ran the decree, she must wear on her right sleeve the distinct and flagrant scarlet B.

"She's going to marry John Hobart," said her father. "You know how those fishermen are. When a man comes to own a vessel, if he was a cursing man before, he stays a cursing man unless the grace of God smites him. Thus far it has not smitten Johnny Hobart. And Mary Crave has the grace of God in her for all that she keep company with a cursing man who has spoken to her and her father for her hand in marriage. They are espoused. Johnny will be proud of her letter B.

"Two witnesses," Crave went on, "testified to her saying, as she did in fact say, having mentioned the name of Stephen Hopkins, a member of the Governor's Council, 'He wears a false face and God knows he is a hypocrite.' The two witnesses had then defended the name of Stephen Hopkins and reproached her with taking the name of the Lord in vain. And they angered her. They were cunning and meant to anger her. So Mary's final outburst of blasphemy, as the

235

court deems it, consisted of her saying, 'God knows him to be the wickedest hypocrite in Plymouth, and when he dies God will fling him into an everlasting hell where I hope to God he fries and roasts a thousand years and after that till the end of the world.'"

Mary Crave had rehearsed for her father the court decree and he could recite it word for word, sentenced "to wear a Roman B cut out of red cloth and sewed to her open garment on her right arm and if she shall be ever found without it so worn while she is in the government [of Plymouth Colony] to be forthwith publicly whipped."

The sentence of the court came clear-spoken and slow. The judge played with each word as though it were a jewel in a diadem, as though each word carved its own high importance and included was his own personal importance as a figure of due majesty. This Crave was telling Wingate. And Wingate knew that he was the only other man in Plymouth that Crave would let in on the confidence he now spoke. While the magistrate was pronouncing the sentence on her, Mary Crave had a thought or impression—it scampered across her brain with the speed of a mouse seeking an exit—and it ran in these words: "You may have a large heart but when I ask myself how large is your heart I answer it comes to the size of a mouse udder."

Crave handed Wingate a shoe with a finished patch. "Whether you walk upright in it or whether you stray is between you and God."

"Which manner of speech, Brother Crave, I would not deem blasphemy."

Remember Spong on yesterday had seen her first Roman Catholic, Wingate was telling. Down at the main wharf she watched unloading of a ship and saw a Portuguese sailor, a swarthy-skinned fellow with shining black eyes, a waggish fellow they called Santos. A heavy wooden chest slipped away and fell down at the end he was lifting, narrowly grazing his right foot. It could have crushed ankle and toes. He stood straight and sober-faced, crossed himself, touched forehead with the third finger, touched the lower breast, then the heart and then opposite the heart—the sign of the cross. Remember asked two church members standing by what they were seeing. "He's a Catholic, making the sign of the cross," said one, and the other, with a mischievously pleasant smile, "a papist, a benighted pagan." And Remember had told Wingate that morning, "Going to sleep last night I got to saying, millions of Catholics in the world, think of it, millions on millions of them and I have seen only one and I know nothing of him except he is Portuguese and a handsome wag who nearly lost his foot yesterday."

One day early in May it was that Remember Spong had seen the first Jew to meet her eyes since the landing of the *Mayflower*, Wingate went on. He was short, stoop-shouldered, black-haired, black eyes that snapped and sparkled, with an English accent direct from London. Into nearly every house in Plymouth he went with a pack he took off his back, polite and smiling as he showed what he had to sell, thread, needles, knives, ribbons, buttons, scissors, cords, braids, laces, a few thin garments that would not burden his pack, beads and modest jewelry that included a thin silver ring no one in Plymouth bought. He had come on a boat from Salem and was last seen walking the trail to Boston aiming to stop at a few fishing villages and trading posts on the way. Elder Brewster had talked with the Jew about his religion and had told Remember that he found it rather fascinating to talk with this man who kept to the rituals of his forefathers as outlined in the Old Testament. Only a few weeks before it happened that a French Jesuit priest from Canada stopped in Plymouth to see the colony and ask of its progress and methods. Governor Bradford entertained the priest, holding long discussions with him, and wrote of finding their discourse profitable and instructive.

"Live and wait long enough here in Plymouth and wanderers of all the faiths and breeds in the world will come to our streets and doors," smiled John Crave.

Crave began sewing a black rosette on a shoe. "They must bring me the rosettes. In my years here this is only the second time I have put rosettes on a pair of shoes." Crave's face sobered. The rosettes were so pretty and transient they sent him to the great depths and verities. The changeless marvels of light, the march of the chariots of the sun, the absolute stillness of a white sickle of a moon, the fidelity of the stars by which mariners chart their course—the trustworthiness of these apparitions of light haunted John Crave. Water was another marvel never to weary him. He talked of it to Wingate. The rivers, creeks and inlets finding their way to the mother, the sea —the many kinds of rain, summer showers of walking rain, sun showers, blowing rainsheets, cascades and foaming rapids where the water laughs and sings—Wingate felt at moments that John Crave himself had been part of the strange waters of which he had become a familiar. Wingate had heard Crave many times talking about light and water. Crave repeated himself—and then always had something new. "You grow," Wingate said to Crave. "You have roots going deeper into the ground of the earth and reaching up ever higher above the earth. Your roots below and your branches above go on reaching."

Each of us begins of a seed, ran Crave's meditation now. Some can grow and gain by struggle and endurance in any soil. Others are thwarted unless they find themselves in soil that favors them.

Crave brought out two seeds. They looked much the same. "This one if put in the ground would send up a tall stalk nearly as thick as your wrist and at the top of it a wide yellow-gold sunflower smiling to the blue sky and the sun, thankful to this little seed no longer than my thumbnail." He took the other seed between thumb and forefinger, turned his head from right to left looking at it with his large gray eyes. "This one put in the ground would slowly work its way up above ground and send out green vines and as the days and weeks went by the vines would put out those odd-shapen bulbs we call squash, at the core of each a heart filled with white seeds and each seed ready and willing the next year to bring a family of squash to the face of the earth."

The talk of Crave and Wingate, mostly Crave, ran on till the open doorway held someone. They looked up to see Mary Crave, with a laugh putting her hand to her lowest rib, her elbow thrust out and pointed. "Here I can make my letter B go flaunt-a-flaunt."

She took off her headkerchief. She seated herself alongside Wingate, on the low bench, leaned forward and put her elbows on her knees and began the news of her little journey over Plymouth with the Roman letter that published her as a sinner.

"Ebba Hibbett and John Spong—those names coupled—you have heard?" The men nodded. "I met Eliza Drew—and you know of her?" Again the men nodded.

"Eliza Drew with a Roman letter A for adultery in red cloth on her right arm and I with my B for blasphemy, as I say, we meet. And Eliza soberly asks, since A and B are here where be C D E F and the rest of the alphabet? Eliza comes from a talk with the constable, Brock Hodge. Him, says Eliza, being the one constable who has done me kindness and good deeds when he could do them without being seen, we tell each other doings and goings on."

Crave had finished getting the second black rosette on the second shoe. He raised his eyebrows as he swung the finished shoe into a rack as though to say, 'Tis as well that's done.

"From the other night constable," Mary was saying, "Brock Hodge had it that last night by a pale moon in a hazel thicket not a quarter-mile from the north palisade gate, Ebba Hibbett was arrested in the act which the law terms fornication."

"Who arrested her so?" John Crave's large eyes were soft and crossed with anxiety.

"Edward Emberton the night constable was one."

"And who else?"

"One other."

"And he was?"

"John Spong."

"And they will bear witness at the trial to her shame and she will walk Plymouth with a Roman letter V in red cloth to signify her viciousness?"

"We shall see."

"And the man taken with her?"

"George Orkney."

The blacksmith apprentice, young Orkney, slow to learn, twice a backslider and rejoining the church a second time after long probation, once in the pillory for drunkenness, and another time again he would

238

have been sentenced to the pillory but for the need in the colony at that time of more sickles, forks, hoes, metal edges on wooden shovels. Orkney, twenty-four years old, rather bovine, lusty, a brick-red face, slumbrous eyes, not lacking in a slow easy way with women, he had twice been reprimanded by the Governor's Council. On a Lord's Day it was he had drawn men from the church meeting by his performance in the blacksmith shop when he put a leather thong around a large cask of water, put his teeth into the thong and lifted the cask from the ground and stood erect with his head thrown back. Thereby he won his wagers with all present. Then too but for the colony need of sickles, forks, hoes, metal edges on wooden shovels he would have gotten the pillory and the whipping post, not merely for gambling, but gambling on the Lord's Day.

"John Spong will stand as a witness to testify to her guilt and shame?"

"Eliza Drew says nay. She says they will forget about having a trial. And this because Ebba Hibbett took John Spong one side and told him he was a low and foul beast of an informer. When her trial should come she would tell all Plymouth that it was John Spong who had first taken her to the place where she had now been found with George Orkney. 'I will point a finger at you and cry shame upon you and accuse you of the sin of fornication, and that before all of Plymouth, that before the public standing by to see me condemned and branded,' Ebba Hibbett cried to John Spong. The matter will be hushed, Eliza Drew is certain. And it is as well."

While Mary Crave stood further talking with Eliza Drew, there joined them Sarah Bairns, a slattern whose hair and clothes needed soap and care. Yet she was not empty of humor. She wore on her right arm the red-cloth letter D for drunkenness and without a smile, "Each of us has her letter. Do you notice we spell B-A-D? All the known bad women of Plymouth would be here could we now have Ebba Hibbett with a V for viciousness." Whereby Eliza Drew and Mary Crave saw that news could travel fast in Plymouth. After Sarah Bairns walked away from them with a rather tender good-by, they spoke of her on a fair warm day shivering as though cold, a broken woman, twice in the stocks with a sign on her, "Beastly Drunk," and a third time again given the stocks with the added penalty of a letter D to be publicly worn a year.

"To hell with their strong water," Eliza Drew said to Mary Crave as Sarah Bairns shambled away. "You pour it in your guts and lose your head. I am quits of it. It was vile Jamaica rum gave me this," as she touched her letter A. "Sober I wouldn't have done it. Drunk I let a man fool make me a woman fool. A little beer, a little ale, enough to be a wee tipsy and knowing every minute what you're doing, that's what I tell the little ones grown bold enough to ask me how to guard their maidenheads."

Now Mary Crave sat quiet, elbows on knees and bent in a kind of comfort, the two men silent, the design of the sunfall through the doorway having shifted a few inches while they were talking, the creak of a wooden oxcart coming through the door to their ears as a regular and familiar sound—John Crave with an exquisite caress in his voice, "You have had a day not unprofitable among Plymouth's bad women."

Wingate handed Remember her shoes. "Black rosettes, they lack one black rosette for each of your ankles." He told her of seeing Crave put on the second pair of black rosettes that had come to the colony.

Mary Crave's letter of shame and how it was neither shame nor pride but mainly a matter of laughter to her—of this Wingate told Remember, omitting the idea of the mouse udder.

"And your father—last night—you have heard?"

Remember had heard. Two of her neighbors had told her the same story Wingate had heard. On a walk over the town she met others who were tattling that it was John Spong and not George Orkney caught with Ebba Hibbett in a hazel thicket by starlight. Her father had lain abed till noon not sleeping, nothing to say, "Lying like a heavy log rather than a man." Through the night he had slept little and fitful.

Remember was sure her father studied what might come of the arrest and public trial of George Orkney and Ebba Hibbett. The whole truth—he would like to bring out the whole truth. Then what could be brought against his good name? At such a trial he would swear he had never gone out of Plymouth town, never once beyond the palisade stakes enclosing the town, not ever with any woman, except his daughter Remember, of a verity never with the woman Ebba Hibbett. Some would believe him and they would value Ebba Hibbett only as a bold and barefaced liar. Others would hear Ebba Hibbett swear that John Spong it was who first led her to that hazel thicket by starlight and it was on his beseeching her that she yielded herself to him and it was beyond midnight when they left the thicket. Some would believe this because the evil of fornication had a fascination for them and they liked to believe what they thought was most probable rather than plainly proven. And had not John Spong permitted himself at least three or four afternoon and evening visits with Ebba Hibbett, once having her hand held tight in his own hand as they stood spectators at the whipping post seeing a man lashed for his guilt of perjury? And even if John Spong were innocent of the act charged by Ebba Hibbett, did he not have somewhat the look of a jealous and angry man seeking revenge on a woman who had duped him? Such questions, tangled with many other slants and phases of the affair, ran in the gossip, the rumors, the tattlings. So John Spong lay heavy as a log

240

in his bed the hours from daybreak till noon, turning his face away and not answering his daughter willing to bring him food.

Early afternoon he ate a little, sent Remember for the constable Edward Emberton, showed Emberton what a helpless and tortured victim he was in the circumstances of the case, and convinced Emberton, who went straightway to one of the colony magistrates and made clear that he and Spong would refuse to testify or bring complaint and there must be no trial because it would inevitably smutch the good name of an honorable man. The magistrate agreed, on condition that blacksmith George Orkney be privately and sternly reprimanded, with notice to Ebba Hibbett that she must leave the colony forthwith and immediately on the first ship that could take her to Boston or there would be a public trial with all its complications and embarrassments, and it would end with not less than twenty lashes laid on her back at the public whipping post.

Wingate heard Remember telling it. He couldn't read what it was doing to her. She was so dry, so matter-of-fact, telling it. In an aside once she mentioned Peter Ladd. And Wingate made a dim guess she could not give her father now a complete sympathy because of his mistreatment of her and Peter Ladd.

Wingate took her right hand in his two hands, pressed it warmly and laughed. "Things never get better till they get worse."

Remember without a laugh, "A stupid old saying."

"Life can get so stupid only stupid proverbs will cover it." She knew he loved her and it seemed would never quit loving her and making no demands—he was too good to be true so she flung his proverb back at him as stupid and then relented in understanding again.

"Father and Emberton, I suppose, could better have been stupid last night instead of so pert and knowing. They could well have followed a proverb not entirely stupid, Let what thou seest of thy neighbors be as it were not."

The darkness of a Satan terribly real and marvelously cunning settled over the Spong house with a gloom thick and heavy. Only the instigations and maneuvers of a Supreme Mocker with an adoration of lust and a worship of evil for evil's own sake could have led John Spong's feet and heart into the trap that had been sprung on him, with a faint and hovering smutch on his name that he would have believed his eyes could never see.

Remember Spong let the weight of her father's gloom come down on her and clothe her with an odor near to a stench. It was as though a fate was on them to imprison themselves together and stand guard together against the Archdemon. Yet while so imprisoned and standing together she could not feel safe against the High Mocker using her own father to bring his daughter to harm. This last she came to when becoming aware that her father was asking questions and making a search for what he could find in the past of Peter Ladd. She and Peter could go out into Plymouth Harbor neither in a sailboat nor a rowboat. They could fish in no creek and walk in no woods. They had twice paid little visits to neighbor houses and this in the future was sternly forbidden by John Spong. The Spong house, Plymouth village and the beach so long as they were in sight of Plymouth—this was permitted them by the hard-faced John Spong.

And free-going Peter Ladd with his sun-bright face and his wavy blond locks, kept coming. He could yet be rich. "I would rather die early than live to be old and poor." The little finger of his left hand was gone, an accident with a piece of ship timber. "The other fingers, the hands, arms, legs, and the rest of me will follow that little finger," he laughed. Death had come close to him several times. Fever, scurvy, a drunken sailor with a long knife, a drunken ship carpenter with a hatchet, a furious, sober first mate who knocked him down, kicked him in the face, threw him in the brig for six days of bread and water, these and more chances and hardship near death he could mention with "I believe the Egyptian women in London, I paid them to read the lines of my hand. They told me death will brush by me close without touching me and I shall be rich and marry twice, the first time for love."

"I like him and I like his company," said Remember to her father, "better than any other man I have ever laid eyes on. What I have for him is deeply warm, cozy and snug, without fear. I tell him it is not love. I tell him it may become love. I tell him if another woman calls him, and he wishes to go to her, then go. He says love will surely follow, should we marry."

"Then he has gone so far as to ask you to marry him?"

"Not in so many words."

"In the name of decency and good order, in the name of all that is holy in wedlock, how else can it be read than a proposal of marriage when he tells you that love will follow should the two of you marry?"

"Of what are you thinking, father?"

"I am thinking this fresh-faced young interloper goes too far. I shall join myself with the fathers and the authorities of the colony who ask that soon there should be a law. We tire of these impudent and reckless young men who inveigle our daughters into promises of marriage and think to please themselves afterward by coming to the father and announcing they are espoused. The proposal must be made to the father before it is made to the daughter. We shall make it a law in Plymouth."

And it was made a law that no man should propose marriage to a maid without first getting consent of her parents—or of her master in case she were an indentured servant. And John Spong took a degree of pride in telling Peter Ladd he must come to the girl's father and the father say, "Yes, you may marry her," before there could be espousal or wedlock.

Her father saw to it that Peter Ladd was instructed regarding "unchastity." There had been several cases in the colony of marriages where the firstborn child arrived too soon after marriage. And in those cases the General Court sentenced the man fathering the child to be publicly whipped while his wife sat close by, in the stocks, as a witness of the punishment. Later the penalty of whipping had been changed to a fine of five pounds and unless the fine were paid the lash was laid on. On the colony records it was written that the child of one married couple had come "six weeks" too soon and another couple's first baby "five weeks and four days" before the allotted nine months of nature and God. The guilty couple were publicly admonished.

Peter Ladd came and went, his stays longer and less often. On one stay he helped build a one-room wing to the Spong house. He was drinking harder though he was never heavy with rum and brandy and Remember heard of no one seeing Peter Ladd drunk. What drink he had, she noticed, lit him up about his expectations and ambitions. He was more sure than ever he was going to be rich with land, gold, a big house and servants, and probably a seat as a deacon in church. Remember held suspicions that at times hope ran low in him and he reproached himself that so much time had gone by and he did not yet have his own fishing boat. Over one period he laid by much of his earnings, toward buying his boat, and with gay and laughing candor, his eyes sparkling about it, he told her of three days of drink and gambling that swept away his savings. Remember gave it out and her word was accepted that they were fast friends, good company, and they would go no farther than that.

"He kisses you?" asked John Spong once.

"On the forehead, gently, and he is kindly, thoughtful and even reverent, and I cannot tell him to stay away." Yet he would occasionally break a silence between them, with smiling eyes and a grimace of mouth, saying that should they marry she would grow to love him. In this mood once Peter Ladd turned serious, "If the time comes I won't ask your father. He doesn't own you. Now, your mother, you have told me of her. I should have liked to ask her if I could love you—but not him. Do you know he reminds me of the ship *Atlantis* I was on? In cross winds we drifted alongside an iceberg, a thick wall of ice, far through it, mayhap a mile of ice. That kind of cold thickness between him and me, I feel."

John Spong had gathered definitely that Peter Ladd gambled occasionally in Plymouth. Each time the constables entered, Ladd and the others had swept away and hidden the deck of cards. And Spong had gone farther, made his inquiries of Salem men, and confronted Peter Ladd in the Spong house one evening after supper.

"May I ask you, Peter Ladd, whether you have ever been brought before the magistrates of Salem and tried and convicted of an offense?"

"You may ask me," and Peter Ladd's boyish sunburst of a smile was turned on John Spong.

No fear in the air, no embarrassment. John Spong was puzzled.

"You heard me and I am asking you. Did it so happen?"

Again the smiling Peter Ladd and, "It did so happen—and you have so found by your searches and questions—and so what next are we to learn?"

Then John Spong let it be known and he was not lacking in a degree of pride and self-satisfaction about it. Twice in Salem—not once but twice—John Spong had the dates and the names of the magistrates —Peter Ladd had been brought to court on the charge of gambling, twice he had confessed his guilt, once his fine five pounds and the second ten pounds.

Peter Ladd came less often, the last year they saw him. After one four months' stay away he arrived looking sober and serious, new clothes and a new hat, quietly showing Remember a closed fist that he opened for her eyes to see a spread of gold and silver pieces. His open and gay candor had changed. By hints and indirect remarks, Remember felt his new prosperity of clothes and money came from less of fishing and more of gambling. Seated with Remember at the fireside he brought out a deck of cards, "I have been reading what your father and the deacons call the Devil's picturebook."

"The first time in our years here that the Spong house has ever seen the Devil's picturebook," said Remember.

Peter Ladd was shuffling the cards, his fingers nimble and skilled at it.

John Spong came in, spoke his scorn and loathing that a Devil's picturebook should be brought into his house.

Peter Ladd without his old-time smile, now with a half-wicked grin, flipped a card toward a firelog where it fell and burned to a crisp. A second and a third card he flipped to the fire—and one by one he flipped them till the last card on the bottom of the deck he handed to Remember.

Remember turned the card over—the ace of hearts. No word came from Peter Ladd but he gestured toward the fire with the palm of his right hand up and the look on his face telling her, "This one card in the deck, if it must burn you shall throw it in the fire."

The next morning being Lord's Day Peter Ladd was in one of the rear benches kept for sojourners and inhabitants, he being a sojourner. He walked home with Remember and her father. He stayed through the week, calling on Remember often, with his former open and gay candor changed into a reserve and a sobriety she could not read and for the first time she was not easy in his company. Now too some other change was working in him. For now he was saying, and she knew it was a heavy pain for him to be saying it, as he did once, "Should we marry, it would be a gamble and you might lose because the chances are you would not grow to love me."

"I have done my best," said Remember. "Ever have I been honest with you."

"I was never sure till the other night."

"And when and how could you be sure then?"

"When you threw the ace of hearts into the fire."

And Peter Ladd said he had one play left. On the next Lord's Day he would speak to John Spong about the hand of his daughter in marriage. Then with both John Spong and his daughter telling him, No, it could not be, then he would leave Plymouth and never afterward have any guilt over holding back when he should go forward.

Next Lord's Day came. No Peter Ladd at meeting, morning nor afternoon. Dusk it was when he knocked at the door of the Spong house and was let in. Remember could read what her father couldn't, that he was heavy in liquor, that he carried his liquor well, that an old brightness and a new impetuous daring, a bravery near to impudence, was on him.

Remember knew then that she had in her heart for him everything except a final great abandon. It was like she had known him all her life, had cared for him, and could weep over his ways of being handsome and wayward.

"You were not at meeting today," said Spong.

"No, I had other dealings."

"Not dealings with the Lord."

"Other dealings, yes," flashed Ladd. "And why not? Am I not in your judgment, in your book, a son of the Evil One—the Devil's own boy?"

"I could bring you before the magistrates tomorrow. Two nights this week, till far into the night, you were gambling and if I cared to take the time I could bring the witnesses who would tell what they lost to you with your smooth fingers taught by the Devil."

"I fear not you, John Spong," said Ladd, his teeth bared in a swift grin of scorn and defiance. "I fear not you," then lowering his voice to an ominous tone aware of the offense being committed, "Why should I fear you when I fear neither God nor the Devil?"

Remember put herself between the two men. Blasphemy under the law, blasphemy in the sight of God, had for the first time been committed in this house. Anger long held back in each of the men could bring a fight this night. She gentled them. She warned them. She told her father he must be quiet and go to his night's rest soon. "My heart and my bones tell me Peter Ladd is saying a long farewell tonight."

She and Peter Ladd sat before the fire with few words and those not easy to find. The old assurances came from Ladd, not so brightly spoken, and yet not gone from him. He would yet be rich. He was as good as any he had seen who owned land, gold, a big house.

The farewell was bitter because each knew it to be so incomplete, so much that each wanted to say that in the shape of things on this night could not get said.

A gong had rung. The time for him to go had come. He knew it. She knew it. It was too bitter to talk about, too tangled. So they left it unsaid. Her abiding affection for him when he wanted love, passion, how could either of them go into that and what end served if they did? His failure, as Remember put it to herself, "to constantly grow in inner grace of spirit," how could she add that to his own self-reproaches? The riches of land and gold that he thought so important, that came first with him, what use for her to repeat now the many quiet arguments she had given him about the vanity of material wealth beyond one's personal needs?

A handshake, a holding of hands, a light sweet kiss that made up for much that had gone unsaid—and Remember in the doorway saw Peter Ladd on Leyden Street vanish toward the fort and his tavern.

A year later came word from a friend at Salem that Peter Ladd, as first mate on a slave ship that had delivered two cargoes in Virginia— Peter Ladd had acquired gold, a small fortune. And it was more than two years later that the news came of his vessel in a hurricane foundering on a reef off the coast far below the James River. Another vessel blown near the same reef glimpsed the bodies of whites and blacks who had gone down with a ship that left no one alive to tell what had happened.

To Remember it was a sorrow. Had she not been sure of her heart about Peter Ladd it would have been a hard grief. To her father it was the work of the Devil who for his own designs led the ship to be broken on the reef. In black moments, brief but definitely black, Remember saw Peter Ladd as a clean and innocent victim of a dark and seductive Archdemon who soiled and polluted the heart and mind of a brave and handsome youth.

* * * * * * * * * *

Chapter 19

* * * * * * * * * *

A Finger of God at the Right Moment

BAREFOOTED and bareankled, her bare forearms sunburned, her hair disordered from milking a cow whose tail kept switching, Remember brought home one June morning a pail of milk for their house and a neighbor's. The wooden handle and a hoop of willow coming loose, she took the pail to an apprentice of John Alden at the cooper shop. She poured the milk in crocks and from a row of crocks in their cellar that week she would skim the cream. With a dash churn shared by neighbors she would pound the cream till butter chunks rose to be ladled out. Thus came buttermilk and a butter spread for corncakes.

Her father this June morning had finished a matter of church business with Eben Rank. They usually wasted no time in starting for their day's work. They paused now to see if each had heard all that the other had heard about reports from Charlestown about the witch Alice James. "She has a malignant touch, they say," said Spong. "Should her hands be laid on you with diabolical intent, your ears are stopped, you become stone-deaf, then comes vomiting and pains."

"So I heard it," said Eben Rank. "Though naught of the stopping of the ears. I heard further her husband took passage on a ship for the Barbadoes. The ship began to roll and toss. They arrested him and had him on his way to prison. With him gone, the roll and toss of the ship ceased."

"The Evil One, I doubt not, works such craft, through those disposed to him."

They walked away to their task of finishing that day a cowshed in a pasture some two miles out of the village.

Remember stood barefooted and barearmed in the doorway, luxuriating in the summer days before fly time, the front and back doors open letting in a fresh sea breeze. Her eyes glimpsed her father and Eben Rank as shoulders and then hats sank below a ridge of ground. Eben Rank puzzled her. Short, stout, well-fed, a chubby bloom to his face, he threw shoulders and head back as he walked. The church members accepted him, with reservations about his enjoyment of scuffling or wrestling with other men on a piece of work. At noontime after the meal he would stand and challenge any other man to hold both hands tight to the sides and not using hands, knock him off balance to the ground. Or he would call, "Who wants to knock off hats?" It was a form of boxing, and a sport not approved among church members. But Eben Rank was rather mild and pleasant about it, went to no excesses, and was rather generally commended for his devotion, zeal, punctuality, at Lord's Day meeting and at week-night gatherings for prayer and prophesying. When not scuffling or knocking off hats he moved slow, erect and easy, sudden in changes of pace at work or in fun.

On occasional days when the notion took him he would ask a man to shake hands and then give a swift hard grip to see the other fellow wince—and Eben Rank took it as fun when by a trick and a twist he brought another man to his knees. On John Spong and a few others with wrists and fists stronger than his own he had learned not to try his foolery. Spong and these others had brought him to his knees. After blowing his nose by pressing first the right thumb to the right nostril and then the left thumb to the left nostril, it might be Rank's humor to draw his sleeve along his nose, then running wrist, hand and forefinger along the nose to finally thumb nose and fingers, a twisted grin on his pink chubby face. Others usually laughed at his clowning and Rank went through the motions of it for them when his nose didn't need blowing.

As Eben Rank's head and hat faded from view below the hill ridge, Remember again asked herself what about him lately gave her an uneasy feeling. A stare he had now he didn't have a year ago, or two or four years ago when he came from Boston and his wife died leaving him with a nine-year-old boy and a twelve-year-old girl, and he had sent to Salem for a sister who was doing the housework and bringing along the children. Eben Rank and John Spong took to each other for company, both widowers and carpenters, unfailing in church attendance and doing their best to be truly devout. They had agreed with each other on those three remarkable men who headed the colony and the church, Brewster, Bradford and Winslow, how those three in their desires and strivings toward holiness, toward knowledge of Christ, as leaders deserved loyalty from church members. Spong and Rank gave the best loyalty they knew.

When signs arose of disunity or division, with murmurings against the leadership, Spong and Rank could be counted on. They had attended the meetings when the Reverend John Lyford tried to rouse malcontents to overthrow the colony government and set up their own. Spong and Rank reported faithfully and completely to Brewster, Bradford and Winslow what they saw and heard among the Lyford opposition. They had served the leadership well and were trusted with confidential errands and tasks.

As time passed, however, Spong and Rank moved into indulging themselves in criticisms of the leaders. It gave them a peculiar secret pleasure to pick imperfections. They would take a flaw or a personal defect, which any of the leaders would cheerfully and humbly admit, and magnify it. Spong and Rank knew well that such a spirit of deprecation and belittlement, if spread to a faction or group in the church, could work harm and might even split the congregation. It came over the two men, and they half-admitted it to each other in a sheepish sort of way, that what they were doing was to soothe themselves and each other. Each passing year had seen Brewster, Bradford and Winslow growing and ripening in mental reach and in grace of spirit—Spong and Rank would admit this and speak their praise. The next moment they would speak of how Bradford probably had pipe and tobacco hidden in the Governor's house and smoked on the sly—how Elder Brewster had bottles of rum stowed in a cellar corner and went to his cellar for drinking on the sly—how the handsome and lusty Edward Winslow probably had made his night visits to see Ebba Hibbett and other women. It got to be a habit with these two widowers and carpenters, Spong and Rank, to prattle of and dilate upon the imaginary sins and faults of leaders. Yet their loyalty to those leaders in any tasks and duties assigned them was constant. A silly game they played and a minor vice had grown on them.

Eben Rank on his visits to the Spong house began paying Remember excessive compliments. This was new to her and puzzling because so excessive. Rank was nearly her father's age and did not need to be repeating to her that she had the prettiest face, the prettiest eyes, the prettiest lips and hair in Plymouth. He became monotonous with his use of the word "prettiest." She pleasantly rebuffed him at first. Later she gave him several sharp rebukes. Had Eben Rank not been her father's close friend and loyal associate she would have burned him with her scorn, with insults held back on her tongue.

Then she took notice of her father actually making his first approaches toward winning her goodwill for Eben Rank. A gentleness rather unusual for her father colored his praise of Eben Rank and his intimations it would not be wrong for her to show favor to Rank. She was sure that her father did a good deal of thinking about how at home with her he could so present the merits and good points of Eben Rank that Remember herself would bring up the question of whether she ought to marry him, should Rank ask her. She tried to read behind her father's face and voice as he played at this odd little game with her, a new kind of game for both of them. She finally read rather clearly that he was acting and pleading in part for his good friend Eben Rank. And then equally his mind was occupied with getting her out of danger of marriage with a chance adventurer like Peter Ladd or worse than Peter.

Several times on Lord's Day, after meeting, Eben Rank joined Remember and her father in walking to their house, Rank at Remember's side. The Rank children and Rank's sister on those Sundays lacked their father and brother. A few months and a mild buzz of talk arose about Eben Rank going with Remember and seeking her hand. Remember dropped to the rear ten steps, then twenty steps behind her father and Eben Rank, in walking home from church on Lord's Day. The gossips were fascinated. The mild buzz of talk went on. It got to where some were saying that Eben Rank had been "too forehanded" and a clever young woman had outwitted him.

Eben Rank now found a gay and furtive whispering going the rounds about him. From unseen shadows a comic laughter mocked at him. His children and his sister had heard the gossip and the way they had of saying nothing about it at times made a terrible noise in his ears. His dignity at home and in the church was slipping. Worse yet, what Remember held at first for him had deepened into an obsession. It had not helped Eben Rank that John Spong had been rather overconfident and that Spong had gone too far in his hints of how often his daughter followed his wishes. It got to where Eben Rank couldn't keep her out of his mind nor stop himself even if he had wanted to from being swept into new and strange desires for Remember Spong. Though her torso was lean her breasts rounded full and rich, her ankles trim and neat as he saw them above her shoes, the glimpses of her neck and forearms in the warmer months when not covered, and the bright triumphant burnish of her chestnut hair—they haunted Eben Rank.

Spong once told Rank, when they were on carpenter work together, "Your mind seems far away, you are aloof and troubled."

"It is nothing. A man may want more than it is his due to want."

Once holding a board to a plane and not moving the plane, in his daze Eben Rank heard John Spong, "You are a dreamstruck man, Eben Rank."

"Oh—this board—yes, I should be smoothing this board."

Eben Rank came out of that daze. An hour later it happened again.

A day in late winter and John Spong had gone away with two other men to visit some friendly Indians and learn what amount of skins they had on hand to trade.

A day of fog and from the northeast a slow cold drizzle.

Orton Wingate, after ten days of being away from Plymouth, was bringing in three nice cuts of venison for friends. A day or two in Plymouth now and he could stay away another ten days or two weeks.

He came to the Spong house, knocked on the door his usual two quick raps with a little pause and then two quick raps again.

The door not opening, he waited a few minutes, then again gave the knock that nearly always opened the door. Again he stood waiting and the door not opening.

Inside he could hear a voice, hoarse and guttural, a voice he couldn't recognize as one he knew.

Then the voice twice broke from its hoarse and guttural tone and he knew on the instant it was Remember struggling in some sickness or misery.

Once more on the door, now more swiftly, he gave the raps that were his own.

The door not opening and a high howl in Remember's voice coming to his ears, Wingate dropped his pack of venison, lifted the latch and sprang through the doorway.

On a couch at the side of the room his eyes made out by the dim of the fire two figures in a struggle. He leaped toward them and saw Eben Rank with a knee bent and pressed down at Remember's middle, Rank with his left hand trying to loose her dress at the breasts, his right hand trying to keep her mouth closed while her body writhed and twisted and her hands fought to keep his hands off her.

Wingate's lurching run across the room ended in a leap with a clutch of his two hands at Eben Rank's throat. Rank's strength already much spent in his struggle with Remember, his hands loosened from her and he tried to get to his feet. But Wingate had him off balance, bent him back and the two of them went to the floor, Wingate on top. Rank pushed his hands against the clutch of Wingate's two hands on his throat, pressing his windpipe and jugular with a steady, relentless fury.

Soon Eben Rank slumped and lay limp and quiet. Wingate stood up. Remember fell on his right shoulder in tears. His hands spoke softly to her, to her own hands and to her face. She heard him saying it could have been worse, it could have been terrible, there was no harm done, nothing would be said of it, no one to hear a word of what had happened.

They turned looking toward Eben Rank on the floor. His eyelids flickered and moved open. His head moved, testing if his head were still on his shoulders.

"Give thanks you are alive," Rank heard Wingate. "I could have killed you."

The usual pink of Rank's chubby face was near a dark blood-color. He heard Wingate, "Go now. Say no word to anyone. We say nothing. If I hear of you tattling it, I shall come and put these two hands on your throat and choke you till the breath has gone to never come back."

Eben Rank, sore and spent, slowly rose from the floor with fear and shame on his face. He shambled toward the door, walking half-backward, head sidewise, slanting his eyes at Wingate and Remember, in no way clearheaded, dazed about what had happened, and he might be asking the two of them, "What happened? What was it? Did I do something? Did I lose my head? Did I hurl myself into an act unworthy of a sober and righteous citizen of Plymouth? Have I done harm to the good name of one not a sojourner nor an inhabitant but a citizen and one of the more exemplary citizens of Plymouth?"

Some such fright and bewilderment was on his face as he stood a moment at the door smoothing his clothes and hair, picking up his cap on a bench near the door, giving thought to how he might look to anyone he should meet, his hands at his throat in a swift prayer no fingermarks there would bring questions. So he was outside. They heard him latching the door and knew he was gone.

"I was scared," Remember was saying. "His face was terrible. He was out of his mind. He said he had for months burned with desire for me and he must have me, I must be his bride."

"Your father should long ago have told him he must stay away from you, from your house and home. The days came when he forgot everything about you except you were lush and fresh to be taken. He began wanting you till he lost his mind."

"He went on his knees on this floor. He wept with a never-ending cry, 'In the sight of God you are my bride and I can do no else than take you—it is a doom God has written between us.' He foamed at the mouth as he took hold of me and struggled to have his will, his eyes blazing and bloodshot. I do believe the poor man had no sleep

251

for nights and on this day, my father gone, it came to him that he must justify himself with moaning and crying to me over and again, 'In the sight of God you are my bride and I can do no else than take you—it is a doom God has written between us.'"

Remember took needles, thread, yarn, and swiftly repaired the damages to her dress, darned a hole in one stocking, washed a spot on the ankle where the foot of Eben Rank had scraped the skin off during their struggle.

Wingate as usual was a comfort. She laughed to him, "A finger of God pushed you out of your hut this morning and sent you to that door at the due and exact moment."

She was rearranging her hair, piling and coiling the gleaming chestnut mass of it. Wingate with all of his resources could think of nothing to say. His wide twisted slash of a mouth grinned what his tongue couldn't find of words. He adored her and was infinitely glad a scandal that would have shaken Plymouth for months had been averted. He nodded toward the door where Eben Rank had vanished and with raised eyebrows and a grimace, "He won't talk, we won't talk, your father won't know, and every malicious gossip in Plymouth is cheated. Some of their tongues would welcome this morsel with relish and gusto."

Wingate brought in the cuts of venison, left one for the Spongs and went away. John Spong came home two hours after dusk, his errand to the Indians a success. He asked if Remember had found the day pleasant.

"Pleasant enough and it could have been worse."

"What is your meaning, it could have been worse?"

"The house might have burned down, father."

"You have notions, daughter."

Then the days went by and Eben Rank managed to arrange his work so that less often he had John Spong for a working partner and companion. Spong couldn't understand it. He needed Eben Rank if only for their confidential exchanges on the colony leaders and others having ungodly faults and not being so holy as pretended. This byplay, this game or habit, had grown to be a need of Spong indulging himself in a sly pleasure—and he tried to begin the practice of it on Remember. He found she couldn't begin to join him in the half-malicious, half-playful sort of talk in which he and Eben Rank had evolved high skill. She felt a degree of sorrow and pity for him, and a thing she had rarely done to her father she did now in sharply warning him that there was a taint of the Evil One about such a practice and he would well watch himself. Her depths of affection and admiration for Brewster, Bradford and Winslow went far and she spoke her high praises of them.

On going back to Eben Rank, Spong found him a changed man who could not explain the change that had come over him. The nearest Eben Rank came to an explanation, "John Spong, my feet have trodden the valley of humiliation." Gossips for a time had their minds and tongues busy on why Eben Rank no more walked home from Lord's Day meeting with John Spong—and Remember twenty steps behind the two men. Now, as formerly, Remember walked with her father. And Eben Rank walked home with his sister, his two children well behaved in the rear, and Remember noticed a sharpening fear in her father that his daughter might in the course of the years become someone else than she had been and take a course of conduct leading her away from his roof and door.

* * * * * * * * *

Chapter 20

* * * * * * * * *

The Saga of Roger Williams

IN the womb of the future, the date of its birth unknown, the revolution in England slept and grew. In the book of days to come it was to leap forth with the demands of a storm and have its progressions of rising to full fury and going down. King Charles I took his fun where he found it and year by year played out a comedy of not calling Parliament into session. His satin and velvet breeches and coats, his lace ruffles and the sweeping ostrich plumes of his scarlet hat, they pleased him and his Cavaliers and their women and his. The farthingale—from their farthingales his women smiled at King Charles. A gown with wide hips was the farthingale, the hips run out so wide the lady must move sidewise through a door. The hips of woman must be stressed and glorified, said the farthingale. And the more of gay purple and green, of gold braid and hip emphasis, put on by the Cavaliers, the more strictly the Puritans wore dark and sober cloth, the material plain and cut simple. And the more the Cavaliers imitated the long hair and curling locks running below the shoulders of King Charles and the more they danced and swore, drank and laughed their ribald jests, the more the Puritans clung to their churches, heard long sermons, sang psalms in a nasal chanting, discussed the Bible, found new idolatries in the Church of England forms of worship, cut their hair short, deepened their hatred and fear of sin, of carnal indulgence, of all works of "the flesh and the Devil." King Charles could not know that far and high, heavy and bloody, hung the Puritan ax of doom, set for the hour his head was to roll. Nor could the little cheerful man with piercing eyes who stood next the throne nodding his head for one to be hanged and another to have his ears cropped—nor could Archbishop William Laud either look in a book or read the stars and gather the date of the year he would beg and plead for the ax rather than the rope, on account of dignity involved.

In the eye of Laud and Charles, a man was marked either an O or a P—Orthodox or Puritan. Among each were bigots. They nourished the revolution unaware, not knowing what they did, the Orthodox hugging a past cherished and dear to him, the Puritan repelling the past and favoring experiment and adventure towards a future. They were moving toward an hour when argument would be gone and language lost of meaning between them—and the dynamic of action would be on, the revolution full-born. And those to be harmed worst by the agony to come could not now foresee its shape.

Among those leaving England, a thousand and more a year, for Massachusetts Bay Colony, were ministers, scholars, merchants and traders, who smelled trouble in the air of the days to come in England —a faint moaning on the wind—the revolution. Governor John Winthrop's son had talked and sipped mild drinks, a spiced mead called metheglin, with a fair-haired young man who had later come over to Boston. Tall, with a tough frame, his blond hair falling below his ears made an oval of a face not easy to read. Storm was on his face—also peace. His face carried a soft gentle look, a quality of compassion for all men—and his face might carry another look of thongs of stubborn strength, challenging the deniers of human freedom, mocking at persecutors wearing robes of holiness. New England was to get acquainted with this strange face. He was to become its foremost lasting figure of high-howled controversy over the freedom of worship.

He came to Plymouth not yet thirty years of age and stayed more than two years. They saw him with his three goats and a heifer on good pasture allotted him. They saw him at the blacksmith shop having a hoe made and they saw him in a field hoeing his corn and beans. They saw his wife Mary carrying their firstborn child named Mary. They saw Indians come into Plymouth and seek out their friend and they saw this friend of the red man walk out of Plymouth and they heard of his fraternizing with the red men and they saw him becoming better learned in speech and understanding of the red men than any other white man they knew in Massachusetts. They heard his questions whether anyone had done a book giving a key to the Indian dialects and on his hearing there was none his hope that he might "dive into their language" and someday write such a book.

They knew in Plymouth he held services and discussions at his house of evenings and it was not quite clear what he was trying to do with himself and those who heard him. On the Lord's Day they heard him preach in the house of worship. He served as an assistant to the pastor Mr. Ralph Smith. He had begun his preaching in Salem in 1631, on his arrival from England where Archbishop Laud had him marked P for Puritan, and it was uncertain his ears would stay uncropped on his head. Colony authorities at Boston suspected him of unsound doctrine, had made interference so that he left Salem. The colony of Plymouth took him in. He was a teacher, holding no office in the church, not an ordained minister. He was learning how to farm, how to wring a living from the soil, how to talk with the Indians, trade with them yet keep them as friends—and the learning of these things in those two years at Plymouth was later to be a source of power for him.

He wore plain clothes in Plymouth—and walked very plain to the wigwams of the chiefs, sachems and sagamores of Indian tribes, where he sat amid their "powaks" or powwows and saw them, through most of the year each red man naked except for a loin girdle, using blankets and animal skins against the cold but trained and accustomed to live bare of garments. He could have stayed in London where his father, a well-to-do tailor, would have kept him in the men's apparel furnished to the nobility. He could have had position, honors, the luxuries, had he cared for them. Yet here he was earning his own living on the land, hoeing his corn and beans, tending his goats and heifer, becoming an accepted companion of red men regarded in circles of white men as primitive, pagan and filthy.

In England, the father had a prosperous shop and a membership in the Merchant Taylors' Company, his mother of the landed gentry and related to Sir James Pemberton, grocer and once Lord Mayor of London, being strictly loyal to the King, to Archbishop Laud, to the Church of England. They had seen their son at eleven years of age a Dissenter, later a Nonconformist, later a Puritan and a Separatist. They still loved him enough so that in their wills they were not quite ready to cut him off. When he had asked his mother about his marrying the wealthy Jane Whalley, his mother wrote him she would not throw any money into the venture. A jolt, a hard jolt of pain and humiliation he got out of the affair with Jane Whalley. He had taken honors and graduated from Pembroke College, Cambridge, prepared for the ministry, become a chaplain at Otes in Essex. Near by lived the aunt of Jane Whalley. And the aunt was the daughter of Sir Henry Cromwell, the "Golden Knight of Hinchingbrooke," and widow of Sir Francis Barrington. She was the aunt of Edward Whalley who in the course of time was to sign a death warrant to be executed on King Charles I. Another of her nephews John Hampden was to stand up and notoriously and flagrantly defy the authority of King Charles in ship-money matters, and another nephew, one Oliver Cromwell, was to lead armies that were to capture King Charles and strip him of civil and ecclesiastical authority. Seldom could an aunt look out on such a line of nephews distinguished in rebellion and insurrection.

Lady Barrington saw her niece Jane Whalley falling in love with the young chaplain. She stopped their seeing each other. She had a letter from the young chaplain asking her to let him have the hand of Jane Whalley in marriage. Lady Barrington had in mind what she believed a better match. She politely and decisively refused to let him have Jane Whalley. He sent her a letter, pious and polite, showing anxiety about her soul and whether she would go to heaven, and on a second reading of the letter it could be seen that he wished her to know that he and others he could name had fears she would go to hell. His first letter to her he had sealed with an emblem of a rose, the second with a fleur-de-lis. From then on he could call on neither Lady Barrington nor her niece. Lady Barrington fell sick and was moved from Otes to Harrow for a health cure. At the same time the young chaplain fell sick, "Very weak of a burning fever," one friend wrote.

The burning and twisting of him as he lay fevered came from a man who knew he had been too proud, overreaching for a marriage above him. Out of meditations and writhings a change came over him. A maid, a lady in waiting, serving as companion to one Judith Altham was in the house and often there came to his bedside the two young women. His eyes gathered the maid Mary Barnard as good for him. She had sober and devout stuff not to be seen in Jane Whalley. A comfort and a resource he saw her, a helpmeet. At the parish church near Otes came this entry on the church records: "Roger Williams, clergyman, and Mary Barnard were married the 15th day of December, anno domini, 1629."

Not quite a year later the couple moved out of London in flight cross-country, Williams writing later, "it was bitter as death to me when Bishop Laud pursued me out of this land, and my conscience was persuaded against the national church and ceremonies and bishops." On the ship *Lyon*, leaving Bristol December 1, 1630, with twenty passengers and about two hundred tons of goods, they saw the vessel battle through gales and ice sixty-seven days. They saw the son of a man named Way one day and the next they didn't see him, a record telling he "fell from the sprit-sail in a tempest and could not be recovered, though he kept in sight near a quarter of an hour."

At Nantasket near Boston Harbor February 5, 1631, moving through ice cakes, the ship *Lyon*, thick with frozen sea spray and hoarfrost, dropped anchor and Roger and Mary Williams landed in America.

Boston saw in him, at first, "a godly and zealous preacher." He stayed with them, talked it over, gave them the latest news from England, they reporting to him what they were doing. Then he refused their call to be a teacher in the Boston church. He was a Separatist and they were not. "Being unanimously chosen teacher at Boston," he wrote later, "I conscientiously refused and withdrew to Plymouth, because I durst not officiate to an unseparated people, as upon examination and conference I found them to be." He saw the Boston church still holding communion with the Church of England, which he couldn't go along with. And he must deny the power of the civil magistrates to punish any breach of the First Table of the Ten Commandments. The Second Table gives the duties between man and man and he would let the magistrates have authority there. The First Table tells the duty of man to God—and Roger Williams held that was a matter between man and God and not between man and human magistrates.

Salem church called him to the office of Teacher. There at Salem Roger Williams kept asking why the Boston congregation was having communion with the Church of England. Bad feeling against him began to spread among Massachusetts Bay Colony authorities. They worked against him. He went to Plymouth for peace of mind, study and meditation, having no "call," holding no office. It was seen at Plymouth and word of it reached Boston that the Indians liked and trusted Williams in trading and that he and Massasoit, sachem of the Wampanoags, became "great friends." Canonicus, great sachem of the Narragansett, was another good friend. One William Wood noted of Williams and the red men that he "hath spent much time in attaining to their Language, wherein he is so good a proficient that he can speake to their understanding, and they to his; much loving and respecting him for his love and counsell. It is hoped that he may be an instrument of good amongst them."

Amid bean rows and among Indians, in his home amid private discussions with invited neighbors or in the pulpit facing the Plymouth congregation, he was groping, inquiring, seeking. One English friend had called him "precipitate and passionate." So he was. Another termed him "divinely mad." So he was, in his way. Yet at first he gave Plymouth no trouble. He could take his part in a routine ceremony, as when Governor Winthrop came to Plymouth to repay a visit of Governor Bradford to Boston on the arrival of Winthrop's wife from England.

A shallop brought Winthrop and John Wilson from Boston to Weymouth and the two men struck through a forest, with a guide named Luddam, footing it on an Indian trail to Plymouth, twenty-five miles away. An Indian summer day wore on and their legs held good and at nightfall they saw lights of Plymouth and met Bradford, Brewster and others, come out to meet them. "Very kindly entertained and feasted every day at several houses," wrote Winthrop in his journal and recording: "On the Lord's Day there was a sacrament which they did partake in; and in the afternoon, Mr. Roger Williams, according to their custom, propounded a question to which the pastor Mr. Smith spoke briefly; then Mr. Williams prophesied; and after the governor of Plymouth spoke to the question; and after him the elder; then some two or three of the congregation. Then the elder desired the governor of Massachusetts and Mr. Wilson to speak to it, which they did. When this was ended, the deacon, Mr. Fuller, put the congregation in mind of their duty to contribution; whereupon the governor and all the rest went down to the deacon's seat and put into the box and then returned."

At one meeting during his visit Winthrop made a decision. The minister Ralph Smith with Roger Williams had argued against others who held it not right for any and all sinners to use the salute of address "Goodman." For the sinners Jones, Smith, Coddington, and Cuthbertson to each and all speak to each other as Goodman Jones, Goodman Smith, Goodman Coddington, and Goodman Cuthbertson was to assume there was no rascal among the four and they were all good men and true. Winthrop heard both sides of this debate and with a solemn Puritan face quoted the sheriff's summons to the jury, "Good men and true," holding it a way of speaking and no need for dispute about it. From then on it was safe for Goodman Jones to say, "Good morning, Goodman Smith," or Goodman Coddington to say, "Good evening, Goodman Cuthbertson."

"At Plymouth I spake on the Lord's Day and weekdays, and wrought hard at the hoe for my bread," wrote Williams later. He wrought hard too at his opinions, convictions, faiths. Had these fugitives from England fled that homeland because of Enforced Worship to practice now in the new country the same Enforced Worship they had fled from? At a later time he was to let out his cry, "Enforced Worship is a stink in the nostrils of God." He prized the 1611 Declaration of Faith of the Baptist's parent church at Amsterdam: "The magistrate is not to meddle with matters of religion or matters of conscience, nor compel men to this or that form of religion: because Christ is the Law Giver of the Church and of Conscience."

In the colonies of America Williams could see in miniature the same bigotry and contention, the same prejudice and intolerance, soon to drench England in civil war, already having fomented the devastation and slaughter raging on the continent of Europe, not half over yet, to be known later as the Thirty Years' War. A theocracy, Church and State joined in civil power to enforce uniformity, had not this arrived in New England? The Reverend John Cotton, the most eminent and fascinating pulpit voice in New England, could he not easily become to New England what Archbishop Laud was to Old England? A theocracy, the ministers of God in control of the government, was it not this advocated by John Cotton?

Roger Williams had known John Cotton in England, had once traveled a day with him and could understand John Cotton writing in a letter to Lord Say in England, "Democracy I do not conceive that ever did God ordain as a fit government, either for church or commonwealth. If the people be governors, who shall be the governed?"

Roger Williams amid his bean rows and goats, among Indians and whites, troubled himself about the trends and drifts he saw. Why cross the ocean for the same Enforced Uniformity they fled? He was a shaken soul. He spoke out sudden flashes of his mind he could not hold back—good men smelled danger in him. He accused no man in Plymouth or the Bay Colony and was "well accepted," a likable man personally, until as Bradford in Plymouth wrote, he began "by degrees

258

venting of divers of his own singular opinions, and seeking to impose them upon others, he not finding such a concurrence as he expected, he desired his dismission to the church of Salem."

The one most dangerous opinion of the young Teacher touched on the matter of who owned the land. The land belonged to the Indians, Williams held. Title to the land could come only from the Indians and not from the King of England. He denied that any "Christian Kings (so-called)" were invested with a right, "by virtue of their Christianity to take and give away the countries and lands of other men."

This was nearly breathtaking. They asked for his opinion in writing. In December 1632 he wrote a pamphlet. The King could grant the colonists trading rights, yes, but the King in blessing God that he was the first Christian Prince to discover this land and thereupon granting ownership to others was uttering "a solemn public lie." So there—King James I was a liar and King Charles I was a liar—and there it was in writing by the young Teacher of the church. So the Plymouth land patent was no good. So the Massachusetts Bay Colony land patent was no good. The land belonged to the Indians. Only a title from them was good. And Roger Williams was calling on the owners to set right the "sin of unjust usurpation upon others' possessions."

The few good men of Plymouth who read this pamphlet saw to it that not many got to read it though someone made a copy for Governor Winthrop at the Bay Colony and it figured in their future attitude and feeling about the writer of it. So the young Teacher was leaving Plymouth for Salem. He was moving. It was a bother. He sold to a Boston merchant and shipper, George Ludlow, a four-year-old heifer, three goats, a watch, "a new gown of my wife's, new come forth of England and cost between 40 and 50 shillings," also "mine own and my wife's better apparel put off to him at Plymouth." Years were to go by and he would be trying to collect from the rapscallion Ludlow for livestock and clothing that would overweight his journey to Salem.

Governor Bradford's impression of Williams ran in shadings. "A man godly and zealous, having many precious parts, but very unsettled in judgment." For Bradford to see a man as having "many precious parts" was extraordinary. The man must have something exceptional in personal integrity and in depth and quality of religious feeling, in order that the worldly shrewd and heaven-bound Bradford could see "many precious parts." Frugal in rich compliments and fine praise was Bradford and he measured Williams as though the man were his own brother. He saw how Williams "exercised his gifts" at Plymouth "and after some time was admitted a member of the church; and his teaching well approved, for the benefit whereof I still bless God and am thankful to him, even for his sharpest admonitions and reproofs, so far as they agreed with truth." The year 1633 Bradford saw Williams "began to fall into some strong opinion and from opinion to practice; which caused some controversy between the church and him, and in the end some discontent on his part, by occasion whereof he left them something abruptly." The gentle Elder Brewster had seen controversialists with conundrums and zealots with fagots, had himself in younger days written and published books that sent him into hiding from the King's officers with warrants, and he advised that Roger Williams' "continuance amongst them [at Plymouth] might cause division, and there being many abler men in the Bay [Colony], they would better deal with him."

The Bay men were able. They did deal with him. At Boston, at Salem, at other colony towns they were dealing with troublemakers. The General Court, with elected freemen from all the towns as deputies, had tried Thomas Morton, formerly of Merry Mount at Wollaston, "for his many injuries offered to the Indians," put him into the bilboes, the iron shackles, put him on a ship for England, and burned his house "in the sight of the Indians, for their satisfaction, for many wrongs he had done them, from time to time." The court ordered one Thomas Gray into banishment, "to remove himself out of the limits of this patent." Gray got drunk too often, kept a house where he sold drink to others who got drunk too often. "He was profane, and drew his knife, in a ruffianly way, in presence of the Court." Five others with Sir Christopher Gardiner, a cheater and killer of Indians, were found "Persons unmeet to inhabit here," were sent as prisoners to England. The court tried Thomas Walford of Charlestown and his wife "for his contempt of authority and confronting officers, Etc." and banished him "under pain of confiscation of his goods." One Philip Ratcliffe at Salem was fined forty pounds, his ears cut off, his ears made to vanish from the right and left sides of his head, "banished out of ye lymitts of this jurisdiccion, for uttering mallitious and scandulous speeches against the government & the church of Salem, etc." By court order Henry Lynn bared his back at the whipping post, took his lashes, and was banished "for writing into England falsely and maliciously against the government and execution of justice here." Nicholas Frost for stealing from the Indians and "sundry gross offences," was "fined, whipped, branded, banished." One Captain John Stone, adjudged a drunken and mutinous blackguard, after a heavy fine and notice if he ever came back it would be death, adjudged Mr. Justice Ludlow a "just-ass."

The Bay men dealt with Roger Williams too. They called him in about his pamphlet saying the land belonged to the Indians and no King of England could grant land title. What of this writing? He said that on request of others who wanted his complete thought on the matter he had written it. He didn't mean it for distribution. They asked for it. So he wrote it. Now the Bay men could burn it if they liked. He didn't care. They had his permission. He could think about it walking twenty miles from Boston back to Salem, where he was the Teacher and assistant to the Reverend Samuel Skelton.

The Reverend Mr. Skelton died in August 1634 and Salem Church called Rogers Williams to be pastor. The General Court did not like this. Salem Court knew very well the General Court would not like it. Salem Church did it anyhow and notwithstanding. Trouble was in the air.

On Lord's Day Roger Williams preached. Thrice a week at his house he held meetings. He was not an ordained preacher. He was not a Freeman nor a voter of the Bay Colony to which Salem belonged. He was a Resident. Of the five thousand members of the Bay Colony five hundred were Freemen, citizens, voters who elected deputies to the General Court which was the colony government. Residents having property and the approved moral character could become Freemen if they would join the Bay Colony churches—which churches were not Separatist but were Nonconformist, holding to the Church of England forms of worship with some omissions. What they omitted from the regular forms of worship of the Church of England they considered impure. By omitting such forms they purified the Church of England and so were Puritans, "Unspotted Lambs of God," and "visible saints."

Being a Separatist, Williams stood outside the Bay Colony churches. Not being a member of their church, he could not be a Freeman. Williams saw that a man not meeting their church membership requirement was stripped of more civil rights and property privileges than a Nonconformist by the same tests in England. He saw formality and hypocrisy, men joining the church not for love of God but for the privileges, advantages and conveniences that went to Freemen.

Now came the Resident's Oath of May 1634, which began, "I do here swear, and call God to witness," and which ended, "So help me God." Roger Williams preached against it, holding it in fact no civil function but a spiritual form and act of prayer.

He further pointed to the new oath dropping, omitting, lacking the phrase, "the faith and rule which I bear to our Sovereign Lord and King." Since they had made a point of his disloyalty to the King in the land-rights pamphlet, he was smashing back at them where he knew they were weak.

He further protested that the new oath accepted the right of magistrates to punish for breaches of the First Table and to rule in religious matters. Since there were far more Residents than Freemen in the Bay Colony he won friends as the spokesman of the Residents. The General Court had not yet begun to fight Roger Williams when they advised Salem Church "not to ordain him" a minister of the Lord.

The General Court, it was noted by Williams in sermon and discussion, was elected by the votes of church members through the fact that only a church member could be a Freeman. And yet, only about one out of four persons in the colony was a church member. This meant that when the court spoke, when the magistrates acted and decided, they did so with an authority vested in the Freemen who could vote

261

and not by the Residents barred from the ballot. To such of the Residents as there were who thought or cared about it, the lonely rebellious preacher at Salem was their mouthpiece.

Trouble in the air—from England messages and rumors that the King had ordered a General Governor to be sent over for the whole territory of New England. Two archbishops, ten others of the King's Privy Council, had been named by the King a Board to regulate all plantations, patents, laws, tithes for the ministers, to remove and punish governors, to hear and determine all causes, to measure out all punishments, with powers of life and death. The ship *Griffin* had arrived in September of 1634 with a copy of the King's commission and on it the Privy Seal, also the Great Seal for confirmation at the hands of the Lord Keeper.

What could this mean in its further working out? Some saw that it could mean the Freemen would become mere Residents and the Residents nothing but Inhabitants. Seriously, gravely, the Bay men saw their political independence, their church, their way of life threatened. New England would be to them in civil and ecclesiastical matters the same as Old England.

The Bay men took action—direct action. They built forts on Castle Island, at Charlestown, at Dorchester Heights. They formed companies of troops for drill and discipline. Muskets, bullets, cannon, ammunition, they collected and stored. From a tall mast on Beacon Hill at Boston hung a large iron skillet filled with combustibles, instantly ready to light the country for miles, in case of invasion.

"War may befall us," declared a Military Commission. Assembled ministers of the Bay Colony were asked by the Governor and his advisers, "What ought we to do if a General Governor should be sent out of England?" They agreed in replying: "We ought not to accept him, but defend our lawful possessions (if we were able); otherwise to avoid or protract."

A war against the mother country—they were ready should it come. The King's Governor General—they would meet him and his guards, troops and ships, with cannon, guns, bullets, swords, knives, hot fire and cold steel. They were ready to resist the King's authorized ruler over them with a war for their political independence and rights of religious determination.

The months passed. They strengthened their forts and piled higher arms and ammunition. The months passed. No General Governor for the King arrived. June of 1635 came a ship with good news. A great new ship, a vessel meant to be impressive under the King's colors carrying the new General Governor and his bodyguard with troops and supplies—this great new ship—God help us and God be thanked—His Majesty's grand and gleaming new ship had fallen to pieces in the launching of it.

The Bay men could now breathe easy and be glad. They joined with the pious John Winthrop: "The Lord frustrated their design."

Yet there were intricate politics and chicanery beyond solving in and around the King's court, with reports coming that the New England landholders might yet have to give up their titles and their new homes. Some of the Bay men had holdings of eight hundred acres, fifteen hundred acres. They had a thousand cattle grazing in the fields, four thousand goats on the hillsides. They were troubled, watchful, on edge.

In this foreboding air, this overcast of worry and fear, Roger Williams preached there were eleven sins of the Bay Colony and for these sins God was visiting punishment on them. Among these sins were: the King's patent claiming right to America by discovery and Christianity and the Bay's claim thereby to Indian lands—the magistrates punishing for breach of the First Table—enforced church attendance—enforced civil oaths—unseparated churches—an unjust treaty with the Pequot Indian tribe—collusions and dealings of the clergy in reaching for power.

July 1635 the General Court summoned Roger Williams. They charged him with "divers dangerous opinions." They judged him as having "a great contempt of authority." Time was given him and Salem Church to repent and change or else expect a sentence.

The same court gave answer to Salem asking the court for legal confirmation of Marblehead Neck, "the lande betwixte the Clifte and the Forest River, neere Marble Head." Definitely the court gave answer to the only insurgent and rebellious town in the Bay Colony. Definitely the court told the Salem people they would have to wait and see whether the court would do any validating of land claims for them. Roger Williams spoke in Salem Church and sent letters over the Bay Colony disputing and challenging the deeds and judgments of the General Court. "A hireling ministry" was seen by Williams in "merchandising of the gospel." He was one. They were many. They wore him down with replies, debates, slanders, threats. He fell sick, took to his bed, searched his Bible. "The Father of spirits is my witness of the upright and diligent search my Spirit made after Him . . . what gracious fruits I reaped from the sickness I hope my soul shall never forget."

The Bay men reached his flock with promises of land and other favors. Roger Williams drew out of the church, kept meetings at his own house on Lord's Day and weekdays, saw his devout wife go to Salem Church and hold communion. A good majority of the church still favored him personally, liked his ways and preaching, hoped he would throw in with them in joining with the other Bay Colony churches. He stubbornly held he must be a Separatist. The scholarly, suave and adroit John Cotton at Boston now rated Williams an "evil-worker" whose "head runneth round" and verily "it would weary a sober mind to pursue such whimsy fancies."

"It was mine own voluntary act," wrote Williams of his walking out from his Salem church. "Yea, I hope the act of the Lord Jesus sounding forth in me, a poor despised Ramshorn, the blast which in his own holy season shall cast down the strength and confidence of those inventions of men in worshipping of the true and living God: and lastly his act in me to be faithful in any measure to suffer such great and mighty trials for His name's sake."

October 8 and Roger Williams stood on trial before the fifty deputies and ministers of the General Court in Newtown. In a small, square wooden building, wooden benches, a dirt floor, Governor John Haynes presiding officer, prosecuting attorney and judge, pronounced sentence. In the front benches sat the fourteen ministers of the ten churches of the colony. They were trying the accused man on charges not written into the court records. Governor Haynes after the trial set forth four particulars or points of belief held by Williams. These four points Williams acknowledged as "rightly summed up," as follows:

> First, that we have not our land by Patent from the King but that the Natives are the true owners of it and that we ought to repent of such a receiving it by Patent.
> Secondly, that it is not lawful to call a wicked person to swear, to pray, as being actions of God's worship.
> Thirdly, that it is not lawful to hear any of the ministers of the parish assemblies in England.
> Fourthly, that the civil magistrate's power extends only to the bodies and goods and outward state of man, etc.

They started in the morning. They questioned him. He replied. They had further questions. He had more answers. Why had he written a letter to the Bay churches "complaining to the magistrates for justice" and a letter to his own church "to persuade them to renounce communion with all the churches of the Bay as full of anti-Christian pollution, etc."? He justified his letters. He would renounce no word, take nothing back. "So," wrote Winthrop, "Mr. Hooker was appointed to dispute with him but could not reduce him from any of his errors."

The room of the square wooden building grew dark. Sundown came and candles lighted. The questions, argument, dispute came to an end.

The next morning, October 9, 1635, they gave him their sentence of banishment. He was to be, as smart John Cotton put it, "enlarged out of Massachusetts Bay." Governor John Haynes intoned a scrawl of doom in words entered on the court record:

> Whereas Mr. Roger Williams, one of the elders of the church of Salem, hath broached and dyvulged dyvers newe & dangerous

opinions, against the aucthoritie of magistrates, as also writt lrs [letters] of defamacon, both of the magistrates and churches here, & that before any conviccon, & mainetaineth the same without retraccon, it is therefore ordered, that the said Mr. Williams shall depte out of this jurisdiccon within sixe weekes nowe nexte ensuing, wch if hee neglect to pforme, it shalbe lawfull for the Gour [Governour] & two of the magistrates to send him to some place out of this jurisdiccon, not to returne any more without licence from the Court.

What were the "new and dangerous opinions"? The record told nothing, except that whatever the court said they were, Mr. Williams agreed. Of what Mr. Williams' letters said, and in what respect they were defamatory of magistrates and churches, nothing was put in the record. Anyone at any later time wishing to see exactly what were the dangerous opinions and defamatory language of the convicted man, the text, his own words, must seek and find little or nothing, carrying the arguments, imagery, vivid appeals and decisive colors of the man himself speaking against their proposed banishment of him. He had on that day of trial "rockie strength," so he believed. John Cotton reported that the court members with all their pressure across hours failed to break "the rocky flintiness" of the man on trial.

Cotton, Winthrop and others reported that they doomed him to banishment mainly on two particular points: (1) He put in danger all land titles in New England except those of the Indians. (2) He so stubbornly and flagrantly resisted and defied the authority of the magistrates that either he had to go or they, if they were to keep face as a government, or, as John Cotton phrased the two particular points: (1) "his violent and tumultuous carriage against the Patent. (2) The Resident's Oath when it came abroad, he vehemently withstood it and disuaded sundry from it."

The Reverend William Hubbard, official Bay Colony historian, believed of Williams, "his too much zeal . . . made him beside himself." Hubbard had heard of those "wont to say in Essex, where he lived, that he was divinely mad." Yet Hubbard was to write later a matured judgment that they banished Williams because he demanded liberty of conscience and an "unlimited toleration of all religions."

Tenderly gazed Hubbard on Williams' course: "This child of Light had the root of the matter in him." The veering John Cotton had later to write, "His violent course did rather spring from scruple of conscience, though carried with an inordinate zeal, and not from a seditious principle." And it was later that John Winthrop was to write to Williams, "We have often tried your patience but could never conquer it."

Roger Williams had faced them, on the day they doomed him, prepared for death. A few members of the court would have voted to kill him for his opinions and arrogance. The Reverend Hugh Peters favored some kind of excommunication. But the others decided that when you have a man banished you have him better out of your way than merely excommunicated.

The smooth sophisticated butter-tongued John Cotton shed little light except on his own manners and intellectual status in explaining that Williams "looked upon himself as one that had received a clearer illumination and apprehension on the status of Christ's Kingdom and of the purity of church communion and all Christendom besides." Williams clung throughout to this demand for complete liberty of conscience and freedom of worship, "unlimited toleration for all religions," the civil magistrates to be shorn of all authority to punish men for their beliefs or unbeliefs in God or Christ Jesus.

"The world is scared of names," cried Williams. "What wonderful noise and sound have those three Greek names, Idolatry, Heresy, Blasphemy, made in the world, to the scaring and affrightment of the poor people?"

Williams saw John Cotton as "swimming with the stream of outward credit and profit." Cotton, Hooker, Peters, the fourteen ministers of the ten churches who sat in the front benches shaping the doom of Roger Williams to banishment October 8, 1635, did they know of the torments of questioning that had pressed in the mind and heart of Roger Williams before he came clear to himself on what he meant by liberty of conscience? Perhaps one did—he was the only member of the General Court not voting for banishment, his name not recorded.

One of them, two of them, might have stood up and told the assembled authorities something like, "I gather a faint gleam of sanity in what this wayward fellow telleth. Why not keep him with us and learn fully what he hath?"

Liberty of conscience, absolutely unlimited, no regulations, no restraints, no police powers—was that the proposal of Roger Williams? No—that was not his proposal at all. Then where limit and regulate? He knew where—well he knew. He had thought it out. And in his words it ran like this:

There goes many a ship to sea, with many hundred souls in one ship, whose weal and woe is common, and is a true picture of commonwealth, or a human combination of society.

It hath fallen out sometimes that both Papists and Protestants, Jews and Turks, may be embarked in one ship; upon which supposal I affirm, that all the liberty of conscience, that ever I pleaded for turns upon these two hinges: that none of the Papists, Protestants, Jews or Turks, be forced to come to the ship's prayer or worship, nor compelled from their own particular prayers or worship, if they practise any.

I further add, that I never denied, that notwithstanding this

266

liberty, the commander of this ship ought to command the ship's course, yea, and also command that justice, peace and sobriety be kept and practised, both among the seamen and all the passengers.

If any of the seamen refuse to perform their service, or passengers to pay their freight; if any refuse to help, in person or purse, towards the common charges or defence; if any refuse to obey the common laws and orders of the ship, concerning their common peace or preservation; if any shall mutiny or rise up against their commanders and officers; if any should preach or write that there ought to be no commanders or officers, because all are equal in Christ, therefore no masters nor officers, no laws nor orders, no corrections nor punishments; I say, I never denied, but in such cases, whatever is pretended, the commander or commanders may judge, resist, compel and punish such transgressors, according to their deserts and merits.

This, if seriously and honestly minded, may, if it so please the Father of Lights, let in some light to such as willingly shut not their eyes.

I remain studious of your common peace and liberty.

This freedom of worship voiced by Roger Williams in that little square wooden church, with its wooden benches and dirt floor, in Newtown, was held new, dangerous, defamatory.

Back to Salem he went. He could stay six weeks. The sentence read "the six weeks now next ensuing." He was worn and near sick, his wife Mary soon to become a mother. He and his friends petitioned the General Court which allowed he could "stay till spring" on condition "not to go about to draw others to his opinions."

Late October came Mary Williams' baby. They named her Freeborne. A pretty name, they thought. They prayed for a world of children "freeborne."

Winter came on. In his house, in his home, alongside of his wife and baby Freeborne, Roger Williams had his friends and neighbors, a score or more, in to see him and talk things over. He had to say, of course, what was in his mind and heart. He must have gone on saying the things he had been saying. The General Court at Boston took up his case again. They decided he was drawing others to his opinions. They would not wait till spring to see him leave. The Reverend John Cotton saw Williams as a spiritual plague: "The increase of concourse of people to him on the Lord's Day in private to the neglect and deserting of public ordinances and to the spreading of the leaven of his corrupt imaginations, provoked the magistrates rather than breed a winter's spiritual plague in the country to put upon him a winter's journey out of the country."

During those weeks of December and early January of 1636, Roger

Williams could have shut the door of his house in the face of tried and fast friends asking, "May we come in?" Or he could have let them in and told them, "We will talk about fish and deer, about chess, dice and playing cards, about farms, cows, carrots and the high merits of the Indian dish succotash. But we must be hushed and tongue-tied on all formal matters relating to the authority of magistrates, liberty of conscience and freedom of worship." He took neither course. Under his own roof he would not let his mouth be stopped.

Young Henry Vane, twenty-three years of age, son of Sir Henry Vane, comptroller of the King's house, had arrived at Boston in October. He took a liking to Roger Williams. He favored a plan of Williams for a settlement and colony down at Narragansett Bay. John Winthrop, too, favored the plan. Vane, Winthrop and others pleaded with Bay authorities to hold off any sudden action with Williams.

John Cotton and Thomas Hooker, however, got the Governor's Council to censure Winthrop for "his too much leniency to disaffected souls." That was January 4, 1636. Seven days and Governor Haynes and his assistants sent James Penn, Marshal of the Court, to serve a warrant on Roger Williams. They meant Williams must go to Boston. There he must go on a ship and be sent to England.

Williams refused to obey the summons. Two physicians gave affidavits Williams was too frail in health for a winter ocean voyage and he could not go to Boston "without hazard of his life," such was his illness. A committee from Salem made a like plea before the Council at Boston. And the Governor's Council took it as falsehood or folderol.

Governor Haynes and Council sent Captain John Underhill with fourteen men on a ship to Salem with orders to take Mr. Williams, carry him on the ship, bring him as their prisoner to Boston to be put aboard a vessel waiting for him to be shipped to England.

Underhill sailed with his fourteen men. Rough weather blew up, high seas. Their little ship, a pinnace, took four days reaching Salem.

Down the street went Captain Underhill and his men to the house and home of Roger Williams. They knocked on the door. The door opened. And what did they hear? Three days now Roger Williams had been gone. And whither had he gone? Nobody could say.

John Winthrop in Boston believed he knew in what direction Williams had headed but neither Winthrop nor Williams' wife nor any Salem friends who knew what direction he took could be sure he was alive. They knew he planned walking cross-country in the wilderness, steering clear of settlements, trails and beaten paths, in a blowing northeaster storm, the snow knee-deep, and at night for cooking or warmth no campfire that might bring settlers to a fugitive.

John Winthrop had affection for Williams, naturally liked the man and saw, as the vindictive John Cotton didn't, certain definite uses of Williams to the Bay Colony. The Bay men could feel safer, with their land titles safer, if a man known to the Indians as their trusted friend headed a settlement among the restless Narragansett Indians.

So Winthrop secretly sent a letter from Boston to Williams at Salem. He warned Williams of a ship starting from Boston to arrest him and deport him to England. Williams packed for an overland camping trip, packed letters and papers he thought important, embraced his wife, kissed the daughters Mary and Freeborne good-by, and with four friends struck for the woods and kept away from traveled roads and paths like true outlaws or hunted outcasts.

"In a mighty storm of snow as I have ever seen in the country, I was forced to depart," wrote Williams, "in the extremity of winter, yea, when the snow was up to the knees and rivers to wade through up to the middle and not so much as one of the Indians to be found in the extremity of weather to afford fire or harbor, such as themselves had, being retired into swamps and thickets where they are not to be found under any condition; we lay divers nights together and were constrained with the hazard of our lives to betake ourselves to Narragansett Bay."

The fugitive and snow-blown Roger Williams was to the smooth and zealous John Cotton a target for sarcasm. A very poor imitation of Christ it was now in hiding and flight out of the Bay Colony—as Cotton saw him. Was the banished man "such a transcendent light, as putteth out all the lights in the world besides"? Not quite. Rather he was "a man delivered up to Satan." The delicate touch of a righteous one, Cotton believed in his saying now, "No, we call not for Miracles at his hand!" and more scorn than wit ran through Cotton's mockery, "Let him call for fire from Heaven as Elijah did."

Like John Cotton it was to picture Roger Williams trying to escape from Bay Colony by calling on the Lord God to take him up out of Massachusetts in a chariot of fire. Cotton had no notion what Roger Williams would ask the good Lord to send down. Like Elijah in the wilderness Williams asked to be fed. And there were red men who took him in and saved his life and he got Biblical in writing about it: "The ravens fed me in the wilderness." John Cotton was preoccupied with ambition, power, the grand manner—leaving the earth and vanishing into the blue heaven in a streaking chariot of fire. Roger Williams, less proud, could be thankful he was alive and had a speaking acquaintance with a few red-men ravens. God was pleased to give him friendship with the Indians, he wrote later, and "a painful patient spirit to lodge with them in their filthy smokeholes." He couldn't have lasted much longer, what with plodding knee-deep in snow through the day, sleeping amid the snows without a fire by night, his packet of letters and papers lost in the snow and wind.

At last he reached the wigwams of a Wampanoag tribe of Indians at Sowams and his old friend of Plymouth days, Chief Massasoit. A four days' walk of steady travel on worn trails it was from Salem to

Sowams in good weather. In knee-deep snow and keeping away from the worn trails, it was twice as long a journey or double twice. The numbing cold, the grips and pains and chilblains of that cold had Williams weak and reeling. He warmed himself at wigwam fires but many years later he was to say he still felt in his bones the sinister creep of the cold of that winter journey.

Poles set in a circle and bent toward a center, covered with bark or plaited mats, a hole at the top to let out the smoke from the fire in the center—this was the wigwam. At the fire the squaws cooked corn, hominy, bear meat, beaver. Around the fire at night slept the family on bark spread with bearskins, plenty of other skins to cover their naked bodies. One and all—the smoke got in their eyes.

In Massasoit's wigwam Williams came back to a degree of strength. In other wigwams his companions made their recovery. Spring came. Massasoit granted land at Seekonk to Williams and his young colony. They had planted corn and beans. They made a start ón a place to be "a corner as a shelter for the poor and persecuted." Among his pioneer companions was one John Smith, a miller of Dorchester, banished "for divers dangerous opinions, which he holdeth and hath divulged."

Now came a letter from Edward Winslow, Governor of Plymouth. The new Seekonk colony had "fallen into the edge of their bounds and they were loath to displease the Bay." Should Williams move his colony to the other side of the water, wrote Winslow, he would have clear title land "and might be as free as themselves [at Plymouth] and we should be loving neighbors together." So he was banished again, decently and justly enough, perhaps, and yet banished.

So they canoed, Williams and the four other members of his colony, along an arm of Narragansett Bay till they came to the mouth of the Mooshasuc River. They worked their way upriver to a bubbling spring of sweet water on the east bank, later known as the Roger Williams Spring. They landed there late in May 1636 with a gay welcome from Indians camping there and an invitation to sit down to succotash and boiled bass.

At the mouth of two rivers, the Woonasquatucket and Mooshasuc flowing into an arm of Narragansett Bay named the Great Salt River —where the Seekonk and Mooshasuc rivers empty into the bay about one mile apart and form a peninsula—here in late spring of 1636 Roger Williams began his colony settlement. Through hard days he had come whole and alive by "Providences of the Most High and Only Wise." By Providence at last he was here. And he named the new settlement place Providence.

A hill sloped away and rose two hundred feet above the bubbling spring of clear water. Around lay meadows, farm and grazing lands, forest, clam and oyster beds, wild game haunts. They built houses of solid oak set on stone foundations, with large stone chimneys. Roger

Williams' own house stood large enough for fifty Indian guests to crowd in and have room for a powwow—and it was a house of worship, a public hall, a lodging for travelers—and here soon came the wife Mary and the little daughters Mary and Freeborne.

How came Roger Williams to own this land and peninsula? Through a grant made by verbal agreement between him and the Narragansett chiefs Canonicus and Miantonomo. They told him what had been theirs was now his. What did he pay them for the land? "Many kindnesses and services to them," in his own words. They liked his ways and what he had done for them. So they gave him a big stretch of land he wanted and they didn't need. "Canonicus was not to be stirred with money to sell his land to let in foreigners. 'Tis true he received presents and gratuities many from me . . . I never got anything out of Canonicus but by gifts."

The town of Providence took over, by arrangements soon made, the land Roger Williams had from the Indians. Allotments of land to private owners were made in town meetings. The agreement signed by twelve original settlers with Williams, which was really the constitution that created the town meeting and outlined its authority, read in its final form:

> We, whose names are here under-written, being desirous to inhabit in the town of Providence, do promise to submit ourselves, in active or passive obedience, to all such orders of agreement as shall be made for public good of the body, in an orderly way, by the major consent of the present inhabitants, masters of families, incorporated together in a township, and such others whom they shall admit unto the same, only in civil things.

A new thing had come. Among white men nothing else like it in New England, in America. Elsewhere, as in Providence, you had to be a landholder, a man of property, to sit in town meeting and vote and give your voice in government. And elsewhere, but not in Providence, you had to be a church member to sit in town meeting. Here in Providence you could be a church member or not—and you could sit in the town meeting and vote. You could belong to any faith or church or none at all—and sit in town meeting and vote. Elsewhere, among white men, you had to be a church member, and usually a particular, special, definitely restricted church member, or you couldn't vote, you couldn't sit in town meeting and say your say and give your voice about the government over you. Only civil things came before the Providence town meeting, nothing ecclesiastical.

Did this mean that a little heaven, a manner of paradise, a sort of a new Jerusalem, had arisen at Providence? Not quite—no, indeed. How well did Roger Williams know it from the very beginning. Disputes, difficulties, obstacles, politics, bickerings, gossip, backbiting, incessant and never-ending politics and the wrangling, trading, manipulation and skulduggery of politics—they were there because Providence was human. Well could Roger Williams write, "I have hitherto begged of the Lord an even spirit and I hope I ever shall." Without that "even spirit" he would have gone down and the colony with him.

An even spirit he had in journeying to Plymouth in 1636 to see Governor Bradford and magistrates to help clear their titles to land the Indians claimed. By his gifts to Massasoit and other Wampanoag warriors, he got them to give up their claims and straightened a matter that worried Plymouth men.

He saw his young friend Henry Vane, arrived from England, elected Governor of Massachusetts Bay Colony in May 1636. He heard of Henry Vane, wearied and borne down by disputes, accusations, slanders, colony disunity—resigning as governor—at the center of the tumult the woman Anne Hutchinson.

A woman of personal charm, exceptional mind, energy to burn, Mrs. Hutchinson found time to hold meetings in her home in Boston and give lectures on her opinions besides caring for her husband and fourteen children. Her opinions in the view of John Winthrop and others held "two dangerous errors: first, that the person of the Holy Ghost dwells in a justified person; second, that no sanctification can help to evidence to us our justification."

What her teaching came down to, the clergy saw, was at bottom near rebellious and almost like saying: You can grow your own religion by getting into your heart the right grace and love toward God or you can take the religion handed you by the laws and ordinances of the Church and State. She tore the Bay Colony in two and shook its foundations by insisting her "covenant of grace" was better than any of their "covenant of works." The effrontery and unholy ignorance of her to invite respectable women into her Boston home and tell them that the person of the Holy Ghost dwells in a justified person and furthermore that no sanctification can help to evidence to us our justification!

The clergy cried out against this bold unseemly woman. She cried back at them that the clergy, all except John Cotton and her brother-in-law the Reverend John Wheelwright, were "under a covenant of works." Cotton was for her, against her, for her. Cotton veered hither and yon. A synod of churches denounced her. The General Court tried her brother-in-law Wheelwright and banished him guilty of "sedition and contempt of the civil authority." Next they summoned Anne Hutchinson to trial, not on account of her religious beliefs, but "for traducing the ministers and their ministry." The General Court ordered her banished for "traducing," which is a kind of mean and malicious slandering. The Boston church took up her case and found her guilty, not of teaching religious beliefs contrary to the church, but of lying. Not as a heretic but as a liar they found her guilty.

She was excommunicated, besides being banished. In formally casting her out the Reverend John Wilson handed her over to Satan and called on her "as a leper" to take herself out of their congregation.

With her husband, her fourteen children and some thirty loyal followers, banished Anne Hutchinson journeyed overland to Providence, lodged in the house of the banished Roger Williams, and by ship moved to near-by Aquidneck Island to found a settlement. Young Henry Vane, who had shown ability and brilliant qualities, who had gone too far in toleration of opinion and discussion, Henry Vane sailed for England never to return to America.

Joshua Verin—the town meeting of Providence took up his case, charged him with "restraining liberty of conscience." What was wrong with him? Why did the town meeting disfranchise him, tell him he could no longer vote nor call himself a citizen of Providence? "A young man boisterous and desperate," Williams wrote of him, and, "he hath refused to hear the Word with us this twelve month." That is, for a year Verin wouldn't go to church. And for that, for refusing to hear the Bible read and discussed, did they throw him out? Not quite—that would have been exactly like the Bay Colony. Then what was it they proved against him? And what did he himself admit?

The case was simple. Because Verin didn't believe in going to church himself, and his wife did so believe, he beat his wife. Because she didn't agree with him in his non-belief, and she did go to church as a believer, he beat her and nearly killed her.

The first case in New England, it was, to set up a principle that a woman's freedom of worship should be equal to that of a man's—she could go to worship or not, as her conscience dictated, and if any man interfered with this liberty of conscience and restrained her by force, he would have the civil law on him and if found guilty suffer a penalty.

Roger Williams wrote of Joshua Verin: "Because he could not draw his wife, a gracious and modest woman, to the same ungodliness with him, he hath trodden her underfoot tyrannically and brutally . . . with his furious blows she went in danger of her life. At last a major vote discarded him from out civil freedom and disfranchised."

There was more to the Verin case. It would fill a book. Verin went back to Salem, taking his wife with him. And did Verin and those who listened to him make talk, tittle-tattle, scandal? They did. When Verin's versions, retold and losing nothing in the retelling, reached Boston, Dorchester, Roxbury, Plymouth, and other towns, they had it that Mrs. Verin wanted to stay at home with her husband but "Mr. Williams and others" enticed her to church.

The Verin affair—other affairs—some affairs made of whole cloth— inventions and fabrications—they were tattled and taken apart and put together again and blown on the winds of gossip over the Bay Colony and the not entirely godly town of Plymouth.

"The most extreme and outcast soul in America," one Englishman saw Williams, "a man of thirty-four, of bold and stout jaws, but with the richest and softest eyes." Yet the Reverend William Coddington at the Bay saw Roger Williams "a mere weather-cock, constant only in his inconstancy." And John Cotton, the jealous, the jaundiced, the jabbering, had a superlative for the most original teaching and preaching figure in New England: "the most prodigious Minter of Exorbitant Novelties in New England." The Reverend John Cotton, of Oxford education, having time to read and think things over, he could not know, because it was beyond his knowing, that he was the Past and Roger Williams the Future. It could be doubted that John Cotton had any definite and vivid understanding of history crowded and pack-jammed with instances like himself of the man proud of his learning and accumulations of knowledge whose foothold was completely in the past and who had no slightest tentacle or feeler stretching into the future and having there at least a slight hold.

Well did Roger Williams know, in a way the suave and garrulous John Cotton could never know, that neither Providence nor Boston had security against changes to come. The values of a great short poem, worth reading many times, stood gleaming in casual sentences of the Providence pioneer:

"I desire not to sleep in security and dream of a nest which no hand can reach. I cannot but expect changes . . . yet I dare not despise a liberty which the Lord seemeth to offer me, if for mine own or others' peace."

One exorbitant novelty Roger Williams gave New England in 1637 after a year in Providence. Did he in that year save the lives of hundreds, perhaps thousands, of the Bay Colony white settlers? A considerable argument was made that he so in truth did. The Pequot Indians had been murdering settlers, as many as seven at one time, burning their houses, and now forming a league with other Indian tribes. The Pequots wanted the Narragansetts in this league. Then they would be powerful enough, they believed, to sweep every last white man out of New England. Anxious words had come to Roger Williams from his friends John Winthrop and Governor Henry Vane at the Bay Colony. Williams stood as their only hope of stopping the Narragansetts joining a league with the Pequots. The Bay men urged him now to use his "utmost and speediest endeavors to break and hinder the league labored for by the Pequots."

At once, on getting this letter from Governor Henry Vane and his Council of Boston, hardly taking time to tell his wife what was doing, Williams put himself in a canoe and stroked his paddle to cut through a stormy wind and high waves, taking fearful chances, no time to be lost. He arrived in time to see the three-day powwow of Pequot ambassadors urging Narragansett chiefs and sachems to join with them and not to league with the whites. The Pequots, of course, had arguments. The whites had stolen Indian land. The whites took it that a King far across the sea owned the land, not the Indians, and it was the King who gave titles to lands that belonged to the Indians. This argument, of course, was one that Roger Williams understood so well that he had believed it, had written it, had spoken it before the General Court of Massachusetts Bay Colony. He was the one white man in New England who could stand in this three-day powwow and speak in their own Indian dialects, honestly and consistently, about Indian land rights. Three days and nights he stayed at this powwow, sometimes feeling his throat hardly safe from Pequot knives bloody with the killing of white men. Three days he stayed—and won. The Narragansetts threw in with him as against the Pequots. "God wonderfully preserved me and helped me to break to pieces the Pequotts' negotiation and design."

His leaving home with no delay on getting the Bay Colony letter crying help, his canoe trip over treacherous waters against storm winds, his facing of desperate Indian warriors and speaking to them in their own language, his stay of three days as a lone white man among red men brewing a war—this was an "exorbitant novelty." The safe and comfortable John Cotton and others who belittled and slandered him could not understand or appraise it or they would have been overwhelmed by it and called at once a session of the General Court to revoke forever the order of banishment on Roger Williams.

The war came. The Pequots wanted it. There were small fights. Then came the big one. Fort Mystic went down under an attack and strategy outlined by Williams. Five hundred Indians killed, women and children slaughtered by the score, their wigwams, corn, meat, smoked fish burned and made ashes. The Christian soldiers of Bay Colony cut off the hands of certain known Indian murderers and sent them to Boston. In that city the cold dead hands were gazed on as tokens and trophies. No John Cotton nor any John Wilson raised a voice against it. Roger Williams cried low. They heard him in a moaning of sorrow that white men after killing Indian women and children should cut off hands to be sent as trophies to Christian Boston.

White men with a land hunger, gone crazy for land, thirsting to have more land than they could use or need—Roger Williams saw this as a cause of present strife and of wars to come. Bay men were to come to him about land deals with the Narragansetts, to get more land for him and for them. "I refused all their proffers of land, and refused to interpret for them to the sachems."

He could see "a depraved appetite after the great vanities, dreams and shadows of this vanishing life, great portions of land, land in this wilderness, as if men were in as great necessity and danger for want of . . . great portions of land, as poor, hungry, thirsty seamen have, after a sick and stormy, a long and starving passage. This is one of the gods of New-England, which the living and most High Eternal will destroy and famish." In a letter to a friend he wrote sentences

to beat out his cadences of sorrow over those feverishly trying to
snatch from life more than can be gotten from it:

> Alas! Sir, in calm midnight thoughts,
> what are these leaves and flowers
> and smoke and shadows,
> and dreams of early nothings,
> about which we poor fools and children,
> as David saith, disquiet ourselves in vain?
> Alas! what is all this scuffling of this world for,
> but, "come, will you smoke it"?
> What the contentions and wars of this world
> but for greater dishes and bowls of porridge? . . .
> The new storm increaseth . . . the fire is like to try us. . . .
> Try all things. . . . Try all things. . . .
> Without search and trial
> no man attains this faith and right persuasion. . . .
> Esau will part with the heavenly birthright
> for his supping, after his hunting, for god belly;
> and Jacob will part with his porridge
> for an eternal inheritance.
> O Lord, give me to make Jacob's and Mary's choice,
> which shall never be taken from me. . . .
> Sweeter is the counsel of the Son of God,
> to mind first the matters of his kingdom;
> to take no care for tomorrow;
> to consider the ravens and the lilies
> whom a heavenly Father so clothes and feeds;
> to be content with food and raiment. . . .
> The rest is formality and picture. . . .
> > Neighbor, you shall find it rare
> > to meet with men of conscience,
> > men that for fear and love of God
> > dare not lie, nor be drunk,
> > nor be contentious, nor steal,
> > nor be covetous, nor voluptuous,
> > nor lazy-bodies, nor busy-bodies,
> > nor dare displease God
> > by omitting either service or suffering,
> > reproach, imprisonment, banishment, death,
> > because of the fear and love of God. . . .
> Must the nakedness of New-England,
> like some notorious strumpet, be prostituted
> to the blaspheming eyes of all nations?
> Must we be put to plead before his Majesty,
> and the Lord Bishops, our common enemies? . . .
> I design a civil, a humane and political medicine. . . .
> If the God of Heaven please to bless,
> you will find it effectual to all ends proposed. . . .
> I must crave your pardon, both parties of you . . .

I know you are both of you hot;
I fear myself, also. . . .
If it please God to frown upon us
that you should not like it,
I can but humbly mourn,
and say with the prophet,
that which must perish must perish.
And as to myself, in endeavoring
after your temporal and spiritual peace,
I humbly desire to say,
if I perish, I perish.
It is but a shadow vanished,
a bubble broke, a dream finished.
Eternity will pay for all. . . .
My study is to be swift to hear,
And slow to speak. . . .
Well beloved friends and neighbors,
I am like a man in a great fog.
I know not well how to steer . . .
I fear to run quite backward,
as men in a mist do, and undo all.

Having to be away from his wife and children on colony business, among the Indians, Roger Williams could write to her in singing lines: "My dear, love, since it pleaseth the Lord so to dispose of me, and of my affairs at present, that I cannot often see thee, I desire often to send to thee. . . . I send thee (though in winter) an handful of flowers made up in a little posy, for thy dear self and our dear children, to look and smell on."

A republic of free men doing their best in the practice of a disciplined democracy, this he hoped would come from the seeds planted at Providence. What he did and said went into news and discussion, up and down, over all of New England. He had planted seeds in the minds of men. And one Boston minister was to write it as history that the whole country of America was "like to be set on fire by the rapid motion of a windmill, in the head of one particular man."

Government, law and order, safeguards over life and property— these he studied and it was a help to Williams that in younger days he had been a shorthand reporter for the great jurist Sir Edward Coke, who took him as more than a student, and served as a friend and mentor.

"Not a man in the world, except robbers, pirates and rebels, but doth submit to government, no man is ordinarily sure of his house, goods, lands, cattle, wife, children or life," he wrote—and of Providence, "There is no man that hath a vote in town or colony, but he hath a hand in making the rates by himself or his deputies."

The ambitions, greeds and corruptions that ever menace a democracy Williams knew firsthand. Yet he would take his chances with the people, believing, "Kings and magistrates must be considered invested with no more power than the people betrust them with," also, "The sovereign power of all civil authority is founded in the consent of the people."

His book, *Key to the Indian Languages*, stood as the first written on the language, manners and beliefs of the American red men. The names of thirty-seven of their gods were given, their gods of the four winds, the sun, moon, sea and fire gods, the great southwest god Kautantowit "to whose house all souls go, and from whom come their corn and beans, as they say." In this book were first printed Williams' rhymed verses, including two:

> Boast not proud English
> Of thy birth and blood,
> Thy brother Indian
> Is by birth as good.
>
> If Nature's sons, both wild and tame,
> Humane and courteous be,
> How ill becomes it sons of God
> To want Humanity?

Learning and books, the fellowship of educated men, these Roger Williams prized. John Winthrop, Henry Vane, and other Bay Colony men read him as wanting ever fresh and deepening roots of the human mind and spirit over New England, over all the Western world. Salutations and prayers of hope for the future Williams gave to the newly rooted institution given the name of Harvard College. The General Court of Massachusetts Bay Colony in 1636 voted four hundred pounds toward "a schoale or colledge," at Cambridge near Boston. Young John Harvard, only thirty-one years of age, a Puritan minister just over from England, had lived at Cambridge hardly a year when he died of consumption. He had seen the new young college at work. He loved it for its promise. He left it more than four hundred pounds and his library of some four hundred volumes of classics, theology, general literature. Roger Williams' prayers ran that Harvard College as it grew and flourished might become a great fortress and watchtower for the cause of freedom of conscience.

A poet and politician, a statesman and businessman, a farmer and an athlete, a preacher and teacher, a man of silence and patience, a man of temper and fury and many challenging words—Roger Williams stood as a high portentous figure in New England, perhaps the most original and daring political adventurer in the Western world. At the head of the Colony of Rhode Island, the town of Providence its capital, he spoke welcome to the banished, the persecuted, the outcasts of conscience and belief. He termed himself a Seeker. Over the wide world he would ask to see more Seekers. The trails and footpaths leading into Providence were to see a wide variety of true Seekers, curiosity-hunters, babbling mystics, defiant rebels against all authority, troublemakers, conspirators, disturbers threatening to wreck the colony.

Roger Williams prayed for an even spirit and a rocky strength to stand through the days to come. He needed help. There might come more good men to be of help, men who would look at his tall tough frame of a body, his stout and well-set jaw, the blond wavy hair falling below his ears to his shoulders and framing his face with its rich and soft eyes—there might be men coming who would understand completely what he meant by liberty of conscience and freedom of worship and "a corner and shelter for the persecuted of all faiths."

They might join him in dry laughter at the wry twist of his large mouth saying, "I am like a man in a great fog." They might stand in loving awe of him and the way he could say with mingled wrath and patience, "In these flames about religion . . . there is no other prudent, Christian way of preserving peace in the world but by permission of differing consciences. . . . Forced worship stinks in God's nostrils."

* * * * * * * * * *

Chapter 21

* * * * * * * * * *

Human Issues—the Cleft Stick

REMEMBER SPONG from the first took a stand against Roger Williams. Half of Plymouth didn't care one way or the other about Williams and his ideas. They hardly knew he existed. The other half of Plymouth divided into those who loved the man or hated him. Remember was among the haters. More than once a creepy feeling came over her that Satan himself might come to Plymouth or Boston or Salem using the very methods of Roger Williams, handsome, persuasive, disputatious, setting men against each other, creating disunity, toward the end that he might be some manner of ruler or governor at the head of things as Roger Williams now was at Providence. He became an issue in her mind.

She must hate him and his teachings or he would take her captive and she become a follower of him. She heard of his standing alone, calm, defiant of the entire General Court of Massachusetts Bay Colony, pushing away their offer of place and honor if he would only take back what he had said, retract and repent. But he refused. He stood bold, alone. He stood ready to accept banishment, excommunication, any penalty, rather than take back what he had said and written. Remember's instincts told her she must beware of what he embodied.

Should his kind of fearless defiance take possession of her she would first rebel against her father and the law he laid down to her. Next she would defy the church and the magistrates. Next after that she would stand up and question all the land titles in Plymouth because they came from the King of England and not from the Indians.

Thus ran her explanations to herself of why she must go along with the haters of Roger Williams. Digging deeper and searching farther under these explanations, she found walls of darkness, rooms roofed and floored with darkness, places where her feet and her thoughts had never been. By dropping down into that darkness, by slowly and little on little finding it was not a total darkness and there were lights where at first she had not seen lights—she might come to know what Roger Williams was talking about—and again she might not. He had elements of fantasy and extravagance about liberty of conscience, freedom of worship. Those elements reminded her of her own easy and gay delights when dancing alone, when doing skips and steps that she didn't dare to show to others because they would suspect her a loose child of the Devil.

To Orton Wingate she burst out, "I understand Roger Williams so well that I must push him away from my thoughts. The less I hear of him, the better for my soul and its present peace with God. He is a born disturber. The more I hate him the more he disturbs me."

"Spoken like a woman," said Wingate. "I have been to Providence. I stayed three weeks in Roger Williams' house."

Then came Wingate's argument why Roger Williams was right and Remember wrong. The talk was pleasant. Wingate's great depth of regard for Remember would not allow him to get presumptuous with her or to fence her in with any embarrassment by his questionings. He didn't care to win an argument with her. He would no more have tried to change her than he would the south wind or a blue mist on the horizon. He let it go at telling her what he had seen and heard, no hearsay. He told her of the big room where he saw more than fifty Indians crowd in. "The worshipers I saw on Lord's Day came to that room of personal choice and free will. In Boston and the Bay Colony those staying away from Lord's Day meeting get fined five shillings and for repeating the offense are put in the stocks. In Boston and the Bay Colony the magistrates are the church and the church is the magistrate; Williams says they should be separated. He offers prayer, reads from the Scriptures, preaches, calls for discussion and testimonies. I believe him when he says he has no hate for those who banished him. The Indians trust him. They listen to him now as a brother or again as an uncle or father. It is rather lovely. I can't help liking the man. He is humble, no man humbler. Yet he hopes to do work that he can look at and be proud. Sweetness, nothing less than sweetness, a honey in his voice when he quoted to me from the time when he was a student with Sir Edward Coke and Coke saying to him, 'He that shall harrow what I have sown, must rise early.'"

Remember heard this and much more from Wingate, heard it all with interest. He read her face as taking it all in, enjoying it all.

Then when he had finished this fascinating firsthand report to her of all he had seen and heard of Roger Williams, she had no questions. She brought up no point where she wanted further light. And to Wingate it seemed that she pulled a tall iron door shut with a decisive clang and a bolt shot tight to hold the door shut. "I hate him. He disturbs me. I push him away. I want him out of my life and thoughts."

Wingate eased away from Williams. "William Blackstone—you should know him, Remember. He comes riding into Providence on the bare back of a bull. They let him preach in that town. And he may preach the Church of England and read from the Book of Common Prayer or offer very personal meditations of his own mystic faith and of no particular church. He graduated from Emmanuel College, Cambridge, and was the first white settler to build a house where Boston stands. That was seven years before the Bay Colony men came. They gave him fifty acres. He sold it back to them later for thirty pounds, bought cattle, moved to a river hill north of Providence. Now he brings in apples to Providence, the first apple-raiser with a true orchard in New England. He says he left England because he did not like the Lord Bishops and now he won't be under the Lord Brethren of Massachusetts. He named his place Study Hill and has shelves with nearly a hundred books. He disputes with Roger Williams about doctrines of God and forms of worship. They let him speak what is in his mind. He can read from the Book of Common Prayer in public, which, of course, he couldn't do in Plymouth."

"I like him," flashed Remember. "I like his apples. I like his loneliness. I like Study Hill. But Roger Williams—I fear him, I want him out of my life and thoughts."

Wingate eased away from Providence news and views. He had been delayed in Plymouth on his way to see Remember. He had stood in a circle of spectators watching a woman who had fallen to the ground near the corner of Leyden and Main streets. Before two constables came, lifted her up and half dragged her to the jail, she had raved. On her back and later sitting up, her hair down in disorder, her bosom blowsy, her eyes bloodshot, she let go ravings. On her breast was sewed the large letter D.

"It's Sarah Bairns—drunk again," men and women were saying.

"I'm drunk again—aye, drunk again," she moaned and blubbered on her back, her head to the ground. Then with a struggle she sat up, looked up and around, "They'll give me hell for this. Why don't you go away and let me sleep? Somebody hammers in my head. The Devil in my head keeps hammering."

281

Sarah Bairns wobbled and sank back to the ground again, wearily and thinly, "Lemme sleep—that hammer goes in my head—goddam that hammer." She was quiet. Then she sat up again with a mocking laugh, and a sort of squeal, "The Devil gets into me and I get drunk. The Devil got into the magistrates and they gave me this," laying a hand on the letter D. Then with a cunning leer, "Why did the magistrates let Ebba Hibbett go and no trial? It was fornication, I tell you, fornication," this with a triumphant howl. Then gazing from face to face with a drunken leer she had remarks about King Charles of England being no better than a Papist and having a shadowed maternal ancestry. And about then the constables came and took Sarah Bairns to the jail.

In Plymouth constable Edward Emberton cut a small piece from a rope. Handing it to John Spong he said it might work, it might not, no harm in trying. "When the ladder was kicked from under John Billington, this was the rope broke his neck." Emberton had heard of a piece of the rope that hanged a man, when touched where you have a pain or ache, it ends forthwith pain or ache. "No harm in trying," smiled Spong as he pocketed the piece of rope in his leather breeches.

Emberton took up whittling on a hazel stick thick as his thumb. The like of this whittling he had done before. The work was particular. Spong before leaving nodded his head toward it with a smile no less than ugly, "It will be good for her—an evil slut she is."

Emberton whittled. When his whittling should be finished he would have what the Plymouth magistrates termed a "cleft stick." He must cleave the stick so a woman's tongue could be fitted into the end of it and stay tight-fitted no matter how her tongue wagged. Yet it must not pain her to dizziness and fainting. The stick running out from her mouth, if carved somewhat wide and flat, would look at first like her tongue hanging out. Emberton would pin to her dress at one shoulder a paper with large letters reading "Liar" and "Slanderer."

And when the next day Sarah Bairns sat in the stocks with a cleft stick in her tongue and its end jutting from her mouth and lips, she was tired, dazed, far gone. She sat, with feet and hands in the hardwood clamps, neither comic nor tragic. What Plymouth people saw, who came to see, was a mute, soiled, drab image of what was once a woman.

Be hard, to endure. That was one Plymouth teaching. In the beyond, after death, would be a Heavenly City, no suffering, no weariness, no disgust. That was the hope.

Escape from the sin and wickedness of this world was sought by a child tired of it all, according to a gravestone on Burial Hill. Chiseled

in a stone were the implicative words giving their impress of what
went on in the mind of the elder who wrote these words:

> What did the little weary
> wayfarer find so disgustful
> in this lower world as to
> occasion so precipitous an
> exit?

* * * *.* * * * * *

Chapter 22

* * * * * * * * * *

Eyes Across the Church Aisle

THE new meeting house of Plymouth congregation was finished in
1638. Its steeple pointed upward with the lift of hands in prayer yearning
for the Heavenly City of the faithful. The pews inside had plain hard-
wood benches, high straight backs to encourage the listless to keep
awake through the two and three hour sermons. The preacher in the
high pulpit could be seen with no effort. The tops of heads could be
seen toward the front, faces and profiles toward the sides. To see
people toward the rear the neck had to stretch to lift the head above
the pew back to where the eyes could see who were in attendance.
The windowpanes—of heavy paper soaked in linseed oil—let in a gray
light and shut off outlooks on the land, houses, trees and sky.

The loyal and devout saw a shimmer of austere golden lights where
a brass chain held in fidelity their congregation's Geneva Bible. There
stood the Holy Writ in leather-board covers, pages of rag paper hard-
woven to the feel of the fingers, tracks of printed letters winding into
sentences to be read again and again for what they might tell of the
clay streets of Plymouth, Boston, London and farther beyond the
golden pavements of the Heavenly City.

On a Lord's Day in mid-November the prayer had been offered. All
present had stood up to sing. Their voices carried a favorite from the
book of psalms their Leyden member Henry Ainsworth had given them
in 1618 in Leyden. The First Comers had sung it on land, on sea,
on two continents. The lines ran:

> It's he that made us, & not we;
> his folk & sheep of his feeding.
> O with confession enter yee
> his gates, his courtyards with praising:
> Confess to him, bless ye his name.

Because Jehovah he good is:
His mercy ever is the same:
& his faith unto all ages.

At the singing of the line "his gates, his courtyards with praising," the large front door had swung open and closed. Several heads turned, as they sang the familiar tune, to see who was the late-comer to worship. Remember Spong turned her head. She saw a tall youngish-looking man in a leather doublet, his tall hat held by his two hands to his breast. He entered the pew opening across the middle aisle from her and two rows to the rear of her. She turned her head toward the pulpit to face the preacher again. But at the last line "& his faith unto all ages," she turned for another swift glance at the newcomer before resuming her seat. Her eyes met his, looking at her straight, cool and sure. She sank in her seat saying to herself she would not turn her head toward him again till the services were ending.

She heard the preacher announce he would consider verses from lines of the Twenty-fourth Psalm of David: "O let me not be confounded, lest mine enemies triumph over me. For all they that hope in thee shall not be ashamed, but such as become full despisers without a cause, they shall be put to confusion." From this the Reverend Ralph Smith went on to observe that it was a period of extreme misery and humiliation for the psalmist who had shortly before referred to his enemies and how "They have parted my garments among them, and cast lots upon my vesture."

This set a picture going in the mind of Remember. She was trying to see a man fallen among robber gamblers who take his every stitch of clothing, leaving him to stand naked while they draw numbers to see who wins his cloak, his shirt, his hat and shoes. Suddenly while this picture held her mind she found her head had turned and her eyes sought the face of the late-comer. Again there were his eyes looking straight, cool and sure into hers. This time her will said she must turn from him but nevertheless she was held to a long strange gaze into the steady eyes of this man.

Her skin tingled and a rush of feeling ran through her from skull to toe-bones. The preacher and his pulpit seemed a mile away, dim to see and very meaningless, his face a floating spot of gray. Had others seen? She asked herself. Was Patience Goodman's right arm gently nudging her left elbow as a reproof? She could not be sure. She sat fixed, wanting to turn her head again for another look. Her ears caught the preacher's voice saying words drenched with meaning for her and she could hear no more after the words, "Thou art he that took me out of my mother's womb; thou wast my hope when I hanged yet upon my mother's breasts." She sat rigid. Her image of perfection would be the steeple up over, keeping straight with no sign of a quiver in strong wind and storm.

She gave a look across the aisle to Governor Bradford's first son John. Many a time she had done this. She had grown up in Leyden, Holland, with John. She had seen John, a six-year-old, left behind in London when she sailed from England on the *Mayflower*, the same time her younger brothers Freeborn and Oliver were left behind in Plymouth. Then it was three years later word came that Freeborn and Oliver had been swept away in a smallpox scourge. Had her two brothers lived and crossed the sea like John Bradford, they might have married and by now had children and she, so ran Remember's fancy, would now be an aunt. She would have named her two nieces, if she had been asked, Beulah and Mercy, and if there had been two nephews of hers she would have named them Joshua and Jacob, if they had asked her. The name Jehoshaphat came to her mind for one of these imaginary nephews and went out as quick as it came.

Suddenly she was going to turn her head and look again. She saved herself by rehearsing from memory lines that ever had quiet power for her. "And they brought unto him all sick people, that were taken with divers diseases and gripings, and them that were possessed with devils, and those who were lunatic, and those that had the palsy: and he healed them. And there followed him a great number of people, from Galilee, from the ten cities, and from Jerusalem, and from the regions that lie beyond Jordan."

This helped. But not for long. Slowly and fatefully and helplessly, as though she might be falling into a deep blue pool of icy waters turning hot and changing to ice again, her head pivoted slowly to meet a face and eyes. There he was. Like her, she could read it, he wished to conduct himself otherwise on the Lord's Day, but he was helpless as she.

So there began between them this conversation, without words, by means of short abrupt glances, by means of long deep looks of question and wonder. His eyes were large and dark, a very dark blue, the deepest of sea-blue, danger-blue, Remember was saying. His wavy black hair came halfway down over his left ear and at the back fell below his broad white linen collar. His nose was straight, his mouth not too large and the lips, she said, "dreamy sad, mayhap too sad." His chin jutted out a little too far, she thought, "but it may improve with better light." And as she turned and tried to listen to the preacher she found herself saying, "He must have more faults than a chin that sticks out a little too far."

His eyes roving her had noted her cheeks, "Not rose bloom, but what? Not spring wildflower, but what?" and answering himself, "The winter apple, the fruit better for the first frost and the earliest snow biting and chilling it and giving it a flush to keep and endure." The faint burnish of her chestnut hair falling below her immaculate wide white linen collar, the dim sea-blue of her sea-wind eyes, the compulsion of bony and gaunt strength in her face—these troubled and pleased him as he sat straight, looking forward toward the preacher, yet always turning his head toward the left and across the middle aisle at the exact moment her head and eyes turned seeking him.

Half the congregation took to watching Remember Spong and the late-come visitor. What was this to which they were witness? Some were asking that, and more. Could it be that one of their unmarried women and a new-come man not a member of their church were conducting an outrageous sensuous affair of mortal and sinful flesh before their very eyes during Lord's Day services? some were asking. Remember saw their frowns, caught glowering faces rebuking her, felt Patience Goodman's hand take hers and press it till it stung with pain.

From new members came glances of righteous astonishment. To these Remember could rise superior. When, however, elder First Comers, *Mayflower* companions she respected, gave her their calm forbidding stare, her face shrank from them and her eyes gazed straight at the preacher and her mind ran over old verses she learned in Leyden from a John Robinson sermon: "I am poured out like water, all my bones are out of joint: my heart in the midst of my body is even like melting wax. My strength is dried up like potsherd, my cunning cleaveth to my gums, and thou hast brought me in to the dust of death."

In the second hour of the sermon she turned but twice to the new face across the middle aisle. And each time he seemed to know the instant her look was coming and turned to meet it.

The sermon ended. Her father met her in the aisle and she heard him in low voice, "You have given them a scandal. It was never thought a daughter of mine would bring such shame."

"I am abashed. I would give my oath I do not know how it happened nor why. As my father you know your eyes have never seen the like before this day. I beseech you to go to the visitor and make the proper inquiries why he joined so freely with me in this proceeding on the Lord's Day."

The visitor had sought various faces, found them cold and forbidding, had moved toward the door and when John Spong reached him he was outside standing quiet and looking at a fresh light snowfall. "I would have a word with you," said Spong. "What was the meaning of your bold and scandalous misbehavior toward my daughter on this Lord's Day?"

"I shall hope to clear myself of any evil intent, sir."

"He hath a face of brass," said a deacon to Spong. Another of the elders forming a small circle, "In what house of sin was the upbringing of this sojourner that he does not know conduct for the House of God?"

Hard words then John Spong poured on the sojourner who stood with his face and eyes plainly telling he was deeply moved. He gave them decent respect and even a true and polite deference. Yet there was no sign of cringing or fear and they began to see him a man of reasons, of a wish to deal soberly and solemnly with them, and they should give him the hearing due to him. He spoke as a man of education, and might be of the upper classes by the quality of his doublet and linen, perhaps a minister, and if so they hoped not of the Lyford breed.

"I wish to present my apology for conduct on my part that I would have desired to be otherwise than what you witnessed. It was a breach of good behavior and I was seized by some force beyond my understanding."

"The Evil One is ever present," came an elder's voice. "You should seek in yourself whether he cast his power over you."

"I have my shields of prayer and humility against the Evil One. Should there be any glint of high pride or vain desire or sensuous purpose in what I did this Lord's Day, the fault is in me to atone for it before my God and Creator, with no credit to a lurking Evil One having power over me."

They wondered a little at such a reply. William Bradford had joined the circle and his eyes lighted, for the answer Bradford heard had somewhat of John Robinson in it. "Your name and where from?"

"From a ship at Boston last month. I have heard much of you and I come among you as a sojourner. I may learn of you. I may go from here to Salem or Providence. My name is Resolved Wayfare and my last home in London, England. I was a Puritan, a Nonconformist. I am a pilgrim and a seeker."

"You are a pilgrim?"

"Should a pilgrim be one prepared to journey far seeking new light and ready to toil for his Master, for the Mediator sitting at the right hand of God, the Redeemer, then by such a reading I am a pilgrim."

They had relented toward him. That was on their faces. His look and tone carried a gravity, sorrow and reverence. He might yet be one of them.

"My plans wait. I seek lodging among you. I may stay the winter. My few belongings are in a seabag at your wharf where a fishing vessel landed me this morning before I hastened to your Lord's Day meeting."

"Till we consider further," said Bradford, "you can manage a space for him in your house, can you not, John Spong? There are only you two," and Bradford's glance shifted to Remember who had joined the circle.

"He will demean himself as is proper," urged Remember.

"And what of you?" asked her father. "You were as flagrant as he. What of your demeanor?"

"I have a name in Plymouth. I am no wench of folly and sin."

So Resolved Wayfare lodged at the Spong house and at early twilight of that Lord's Day joined Remember and her father in a supper of boiled carrots and salt mackerel, warm corn bread with butter and cheese, and homemade beer. "We brew it from our own barley and rye," said Spong. "Discomfort we had in years without it. Good beer is mild and wholesome. Those that drink it be healthful, fresh and lusty. When without it we did as best we could with a wine from wild grapes. Now there is cause to complain of the excess and abuse of wine through men's corruption. Ships come to Plymouth wharf laden with wines from Malaga and the Canaries. And we ask what is more plentiful than wine and that of the best? No want of the same now. And the sins and unthankfulness of man have led to drunkenness in this particular. Men must do more than drink friendly together."

Remember glanced from her father's face to Wayfare, and again back to her father, noticing that he was in a mood of goodwill and the freshly arrived Englishman was enjoying the talk he heard.

"Why should men drink beyond refreshing?" asked Spong who explained that in Plymouth men were admonished for going beyond "refreshing" in wine, rum or brandy. And four classes or categories of Plymouth law carried the punishments heavy or light according to the category. They were:

1. Plain drunk
2. Beastly drunk
3. Filthy drunk
4. Unmentionable drunk

Wayfare spoke for himself, a quart a day of beer was enough for him, a glass of wine would last him an afternoon or evening. He brought from a pouch his own pipe and joined Spong in crushing dried tobacco leaves and filling a pipe. "This is of our own Plymouth raising and not so sweet as we import from Virginia," said Spong of the first pipe, and, "This hath a coolness good to taste," of the second pipe, from Wayfare's pouch. He warned Wayfare not to smoke on the streets or highways nor in the meeting house or he would be arrested and fined. In a house or place of refreshment or in the fields or woods, it was lawful to smoke. On the Lord's Day card-playing anywhere, indoors or out, was against the law. Dancing, at any time and anywhere, also was forbidden. And on the Lord's Day one must rest and worship and the man who worked on that day, even in his own garden, was brought before the magistrates and it had happened there were cases.

Remember saw her father in rare mood as he blew a line of white smoke rings toward the roof planks and smiled slowly. "Each goes to follow the other and the last like the first ends in vanity and nothing." Wayfare raised the question of how much does the smoke weigh, saying the point had interested some good men.

"Have they solved it?" Spong would know.

"Of a certainty. How much smoke is in a pound of tobacco, the ashes will tell you. Let a pound be exactly weighed, and the ashes kept charily and weighed afterward, what wants of a pound weight in the ashes cannot be denied to have been smoke, which evaporated into air. They tell it in London that Sir Walter Raleigh won a wager with Queen Elizabeth on this neat issue."

Now Spong was the friendly listener while Wayfare rambled on, telling of the Spanish and Irish preferring their tobacco in a powder to be snuffed up the nose. "I have seen Irish men in the field at the plow, tired with labor, take out their boxes of smutchin, as they term it, and draw it into their nostrils with a quill, one of them saying to me, 'Smutchin! it mightily refreshes the brain!'"

They had relighted their pipes from sticks at the fireplace. Wayfare thought it a time to make undeniably clear his appreciation of their taking him in as a lodger and giving him their trust. "You shall not find me unthankful. A poor worm, dust and ashes, I am, a man full of infirmities, subject to all sins, changes and chances which befall the sons of men. How should I then promise thee or thy daughter any things of myself, or if I should, what credence couldst thou give thereto, seeing God only is true and every man a liar? Yet so far as a man may presume upon some experience, I may tell thee open and forthright I shall cheapen no pearl of comfort or fellowship you bestow on me. My prayer is that my stay, however long, may disclose good fruit."

On this the three sat silent and the perfect quiet of the room was broken only by the crackle and sputter of firelogs. After a time Remember spoke in a very low voice. "We are persuaded. The coming of thee is as a well-willer. Of that we know. Pride is not of your constitution. Of that too we know. The first work in the service of the Master, He has told us, is to deny thyself. We must be content to be underlings with Him to this worldly kingdom."

At the door was a sound that Remember's ear caught at once. She stepped to the door and opened it for a cat to come running in and chuzzle at her feet as she stooped and rubbed its fur in a long stroke from the head to the tail's end.

She picked it up and holding it in her arms came to her chair and seating herself spoke her fun to the pet, "Tamia, you have been out among the field mice again. You are late coming home. You deserve a scolding. You harry the mice of the fields too hard, Tamia."

Resolved Wayfare straightened in his chair, sat tensed, his face struck with lights.

"Tamia, Tamia?" He gave it as a loud cry.

They were startled. Only a cat had come and Remember had talked her usual fun to the cat.

Wayfare saw his excitement troubling them. Remember was stony-faced, her father glowering.

Wayfare lowered his voice, spoke so softly they could scarce hear him. "Tamia, did you say the name is Tamia?"

"Mesopotamia is the full name. Tamia for short."

"What can be happening this strange Lord's Day?" he asked. "Never since the morning my mother brought me to the light of day have I heard but once before of a cat named Mesopotamia and Tamia for short and the cat bright yellow with black spots on its haunches."

Remember, whose stony face had broken into ripples of light and her eyes blazing, "At a wharf? At a shed at the end of the wharf?"

"In Plymouth, England, it was, girl, and the year 1620 and a ship sailing and you on that ship sailed for this new Plymouth."

And he stepped from his chair and she rose from hers and he put his two hands to her shoulders and stood searching her face slow and long, moving to print a kiss on her forehead. Standing back and still keeping his arms to her shoulders, his eyes dwelt on her bony face with its changing blue sea-wind eyes and winter-apple skin.

Then his words came, "Queer people! You come from the queer people," and with a slow sadlike smile, "What if I should spit in your face?"

And Remember felt her mother inside of her dancing and singing and she was certain she was the child of Mary Windling as she murmured with dreaminess, "Where is your ax handle, boy?"

John Spong went to bed. The two by the fire talked. Mostly it was Wayfare talked. Remember insisted, asked questions, told him to go on and on.

He told her of his mistake or stupidity in not learning the name of the ship she sailed on from Plymouth, England, how his mother asked him the name and he answered, "I don't remember." His mother and a younger brother still were on that farm near Plymouth, England, devoted to the Church of England and troubled about him. For he had gone to London, worked hard in several occupations, reading books, many books, never enough. "How many books?" Remember asked. He said more than five hundred. Remember looked at him with open eyes. "You have read more books than there are in all of this Plymouth town." He had met writers of books, one of them young John Milton. He had served as a lawyer's clerk, as a copyist for a Nonconformist minister, had become involved in the organizations of extremist Separatists, with more secret work than he cared for because he liked to be outspoken. Twice he had been jailed, held for questioning and released by authorities who assured him they knew he was guilty and though this time they did not have the evidence against him, they would have it the next time. His decision to go to America came when he heard of the adventure of Roger Williams at Providence. It was what he himself would like to be doing. He must go to Providence and see for himself. It might be his lifework waited him there in Providence.

Chapter 23

Wilderness Winter—and Wild Hearts

SIX inches of snow had fallen on Monday night. Tuesday morning the sun came out and its light on the snow dazzled strong eyes and blinded the weak. The air glittered with the sheen of the snow that Tuesday afternoon. And on Tuesday night every star in the sky came out clean, clear and testifying.

Again on Wednesday morning the sun shone and over the dome of the sky not a flickering wisp of cloud in sight. The air tingled cold and sparkling, ice thickening in the ponds, with no sign of the snow becoming slush till many days should pass.

Fair weather it was, for wintertime, and the air what people meant by saying, "It is cold today. A door latch of iron could burn and blister a bare hand taking hold of it."

The two men went out that morning, each with gun on shoulder, to walk woods, hills, clearings, creek beds, looking for tracks in the snow, hunting for deer, wolf, fox, rabbit, hoping chiefly for deer. Noon came and for two hours they had been in tanglewood and timberland. In those two hours the sky had slowly turned to a noncommittal gray, shutting off the sun. The men spoke of it looking like more snow. They would go a little farther and they noted a light breeze changing into a strong wind bringing snow. They turned back to follow their own foot tracks homeward. After a mile of this the falling and blowing snow had covered their tracks and they tramped home by guess. Trees were bending lower and they knew from branches hurtling down and occasional dead trees falling, it was a storm wind of fury.

Hours passed as they fought and stumbled and picked themselves up and went on till evening twilight. The dusk before dark had come on. The older man, supposed to know the way, had to tell his companion none of the landmarks he expected had come in sight. The heavy and blowing snow, piling, drifting, and piling again, took away the old shape and face of the land. They were lost. He was slow to confess this. Worn and cold they were, leg muscles stiff and unwilling. They must plan how to spend the night, how to keep off the cold, how to be alive and able to walk when the light of morning should come. Their food had gone when at noon they ate their snack of corn bread and cold pork. Dried wood they found after patiently scraping away snow. They tried sparking flint but the wind and endless swirls of snow ended hope of a fire. The older man ran over in his memory other men lost in these woods outlying Plymouth, John Goodman and Peter Browne, John Billington, later Francis Billington—and others. A man must keep moving so his blood would keep running. If the cold should get through the skin and the frost bite into the bloodstream and harden it, that might cripple a man for life or bring fever and death as happened to young John Crackstone. They must go on, never resting, he told the younger man. If a hand, arm, foot or leg began feeling warm and cozy, that was danger, that was the frostbite setting in. No time to think or talk about how thick and cruel was the darkness, how dumb and weird the relentless and swirling snow. Their wit and strength must be given every moment to how they might keep their feet and when daylight came find a path back to Plymouth.

In the late evening twilight of that Wednesday Remember Spong looked for the men to come home. Dark came on and she sat by candlelight with a bowl of mutton stew before her, a favorite dish she had cooked lovingly for the two men. Little of it did she eat. They would come later and she would eat with them. That was her hope. The hours passed. She stood at the window listening, through the heavy paper soaked with linseed oil, listening to the howl of the storm. She walked back and forth, from the fireplace to the door and back to the fireplace. She unlatched the door and stood on the step outside and saw a starless sky and a merciless wind driving the snow into curves and huddles. And the cold had a wicked bite to it and she prayed for those who might not have shelter or fire this night. As she stepped back into the house she noticed a triangle of snow on the floor blown in by the swift and mocking wind. The fancy crossed her mind that the shriveling head of old Chief Wituwamat on a spike over the fort would in the morning have no such white hat as once she had seen after a windless night of quiet snow.

She fell on her knees in the middle of the room, held her hands high with interwoven fingers and spoke a passionate prayer to the everliving God to guide home the lost ones. She slept in fitful snatches, ate nothing. At daybreak she opened the door and stood on the step and saw the snow knee-high and still coming down and the fury of the wind giving no sign of going down. She swiftly stepped into the house and fastened the door. Not since she was seasick on the *Mayflower* had she scorned breakfast and felt too low to wash her face and comb her hair. She drew a chair before the fire, piled on logs, sat stony-faced and stiff an hour, two hours, longer yet. A few times came a mumbled half prayer and half challenge, "O thou beneficent God of the lost and forsaken, thou whose hand and will giveth the earth and sky its merciless wind and snow, hear my intercession as thou shouldst hear the plea of the helpless who ask thee to bring them through this peril."

Near noon she came out of this dumb and black mood. Out there somewhere in the cold and blowing snow they were making their fight, they were telling each other to be brave and struggle to the last breath and to use their every last flash of thought to outwit the demons of storm and death. She washed her face and hands slowly and calmly. She combed her hair and studied herself in the polished steel looking-glass, bringing out every wave and gleam of her hair and murmuring, "So should it look framing my pale face on the day when they gaze on me before carrying me to Burial Hill."

She put the mutton stew on to warm. She ate a full bowl of it and sat erect repeating in a low calm tone her mother's words, "Stay with them and fight, my love." She put her wits to work. It was time she did. She had been dreaming, fear-possessed, witless. She wrung her hands, and a short sobbing wail came from her. Had there been time for it she would have cursed herself for being so many hours witless. She ran to four neighbor houses, then to the Governor, and by midafternoon eight of the lustier young men were making a search that reached out and combed two miles and more in every landward direction. The wind had gone down to a light breeze, the snow falling lighter, the cold less piercing.

Early twilight it was that four of the searching crew brought to the Spong house the two men, John Spong able to stagger and lift heavy feet, Resolved Wayfare so far gone that he had to be carried part of the way and so completely given out that at the end he had to be carried head first through the Spong doorway.

What was the change in the two men? Remember could hardly believe her eyes as she saw what it was. At first her father looked swollen and Wayfare too lean. Then her eyes took note of her father wearing Wayfare's leather doublet, a wool-wadded garment. Sometime Wednesday night or Thursday morning Wayfare had seen his older companion so far gone from the cold that he took off his solid and comfortable outer coat and got Spong into it.

The days passed and it was seen that Spong's body and arms were mildly touched by the cold though his feet would suffer and he would limp for a long time. Likewise the feet of Wayfare would suffer and he too would limp for a long time but worse yet was the condition of his arms. They had numbed to where he couldn't move them. Remember was awe-struck at seeing him on a couch in a corner of the main living room, a man of strength and will, helpless to hold a spoon and take food. She must be cool of wit, with warm and lighted eyes, with a face of good cheer and hope every moment, she told herself as she saw his calm face suddenly twist when he writhed from streaks of flame zigzagging through his arms. Feeding him with a spoon she murmured, "I rejoice you are alive." When she repeated this, his eyes opened and he murmured, "Queer people! Queer people!"

Elders came, some of the First Comers, with advice from experience with frostbite, with cheer and choice victuals. Orton Wingate came and his quiet keen eyes made their observations. Plymouth had no phy-

sician at this time and Remember inclined to follow the hermit's coun-
sel: no rubbing with snow, no hot water, do not bring him near the
fire, wait and let the health of the rest of the body help coax, heal, and
restore. As the arms thawed and blisters came on the skin, Wingate
with a needle opened the larger ones, and from day to day for longer
periods lifted the arms vertical. Later yet, he seemed to know when,
he rubbed the arms and soothed the muscles and coaxed the lagging
blood circulation.

Day on day, after a long stretch of pain, sleep would come to Way-
fare and Remember saw him with his eyes closed in the rest that heals.
Then he would come out of it with a sharp moan from another zigzag
of fire leaping in an arm. As though it helped him to stand apart from
the pain, he would speak lines slowly, "I say unto thee, Arise, take up
thy bed, and go unto thy house. And he arose, and straightway took up
the bed, and went forth before them all; insomuch that they were all
amazed, and glorified God, saying, We never saw it on this fashion."
Once between spoons of a mutton broth, the words came, "O thou of
little faith, wherefore didst thou doubt?" On the instant seeing Remem-
ber uncertain whether it was a reproach of her, he added, "I, me—not
you, you." His few sentences giving his own thoughts were short and
what he spoke mostly was Scripture lines that came as though he kept
them for times of difficulty and they had become part of him. "The
Son of Man shall come in the glory of his Father with his angels; and
then shall he render unto every man according to his deeds," was one
of these and his favorite, often repeated, "Every one that exalteth him-
self shall be humbled; and he that humbleth himself shall be exalted."
And Remember was haunted by the meaningful glance he gave her
when having finished the last spoon of a savory rabbit stew, "O woman,
great is thy faith; be it done unto thee even as thou wilt."

Hard it was for her to watch him when Wingate took hold of his
arms and commanded himself to move them; at whatever cost he must
learn to make use of them; they would languish and wither unless used.
So Wayfare slowly moved his right-hand fingers toward their being a
fist and slowly brought the hand toward the shoulder while he set his
lips tight and winced with the pain of the reawakening muscles. He
told himself he must forget the pain or chase it from his mind a mo-
ment or two, reciting then with loose babbling lips: "Cursed is the
ground for thy sake; in toil shalt thou eat of it all the days of thy life;
thorns also and thistles shall it bring forth to thee; and thou shalt eat
the herb of the field; in the sweat of thy face shalt thou eat bread, till
thou return unto the ground; for out of it wast thou taken; for dust thou
art, and unto dust shalt return." And in the trial at making the left hand
and arm come alive for use, the words oozed slowly from him as with
bitter consolation: "This our bread we took hot for our provision; but
now behold it is dry, and is become mouldy: and these wine-skins
which we filled, were new; and, behold, they be rent: and these our

garments and our shoes are become old by reason of the very long journey."

When one day the hands had come fairly back into use, Remember laid between his two hands the cat Mesopotamia, saying in a soft clear undertone, "She is the great-granddaughter and the living image of the one we had on Plymouth wharf." His hands rested on Tamia's fur, his eyes closed, his lips pursed vaguely in silence and then, "Jephthah came to Mizpah unto his house, and behold, his daughter came out to meet him with timbrels and with dances: and she was his only child. And she said unto her father, Let this thing be done for me: let me alone two months, that I may depart and go down upon the mountains, and bewail my virginity, I and my companions."

These days of rambling and random utterance drew toward an end as the pain grew less and the blood vessels and muscles of the arms once more became obedient to their owner. On the left wrist stood forth a bracelet mark of healing blisters over raw skin. "That is an emblem," he smiled to Remember. "There the mitten failed to reach the end of the jacket sleeve and the cold and wind bit deeper."

Three weeks and John Spong was about, limping on sore feet, crying out loud from a sudden jerk of pain, then smiling, "That one had a bite to it." Slower came the time of Resolved Wayfare getting up and moving about, slowly stretching his arms toward the roof planks, and saying for the Spongs and Wingate, "God, we thank thee for good arms come back and fully restored," and turning to Wingate, "You knew when to pick each mischievous blister, when to lift the arms, when to rub them and tease and cajole them." And turning to Remember, "And you never once wearied of finding my large sad mouth with spoon after spoon till the bowl or the plate was empty."

Neither of the men cared to talk in detail or tell hour by hour what had happened to them. "After Wednesday twilight it was one long horrible monotony," said Wayfare. Spong told of how they picked an oak tree with a wide spread of branches, rounded by underbrush that gave slight protection from the wind, and there they had beaten a path and kept to the circle of that path, walking not to keep warm, but to keep the cold from numbing them. It was like to an hour before daybreak that Wayfare walking dumbly and monotonously, only half alive and awake, was suddenly amazed that he had gone twice, yes, three times around without seeing his companion. He was twenty years younger than Spong, heavier of build, and could stand more. He found Spong fallen near the path, given out. He picked the older man up, slapped him on the face, the sides and shoulders, arms, legs, woke him up, took off his own leather and wool-wadded doublet and made the older man get into it. Then they walked their path again. Each time around they must catch sight of each other once. Whoever might fall, the other must pound him awake and set him on his feet.

At daybreak Spong made his guess of what direction to take. They dragged heavy feet for hours. About noon Spong came to ground he knew, three miles from Plymouth. They dragged their numbing and stiffening feet, moving at a slower pace, Wayfare walking ahead, crunching the snow down for Spong to follow in his tracks. Less than two miles from Plymouth meeting the searchers, taking a few bites of bread and cold meat with a few swallows of rum, they had enough new hope and strength to go on most of the route home though Wayfare fell and had to be carried part of the way and more often than Spong.

Both knew their feet had swollen and there was pain from the tight hold of their boots or "buskins." Wayfare felt his jacket sleeves pressing so tightly he knew his arms were swollen. Shoes and sleeves had to be cut with a knife to get them off when they came home. When Remember or Wingate mentioned to Wayfare that he had made a sacrifice or been heroic he demurred to it. "I was under compulsion. I could do no else than I did."

Eight weeks Resolved Wayfare lay bedfast that winter, five weeks spoonfed by Remember Spong, till his arms and hands came back. Further weeks he was up limping, learning to stand and walk again, learning again what he used to do with his arms and hands. Through all these weeks Remember kept a lightness and cheer whenever in the presence of Wayfare. And alone in her room or outside the house she had at times heavy clutches at her heart and no lightness, no cheer. She was asking herself why she cared so for this man and why he took hold of her like nothing else ever entering her life. For him she knew she had the final abandon she lacked with Peter Ladd. Then she asked further, and this question pounded at her, "What is to come? What is written for the days to be?"

He had kissed her hand as she fed him and she knew it was more than thankfulness and ran off into a personal adoration beyond her fathoming. On his feet again he had kissed her, gathered her in his restored arms and held her bosom to bosom and afterward in a low fierce crying asked why he had so taken her and whether there was harm done.

Happiness to near bursting she knew when he in his lighter moods talked a learning of books, men, myths, odd stories of places and people, and when he would depart from the impersonal into flowing little praises of her face and hair, her swift feet, her skilled and kindly hands. "For weeks they were a part of me, your hands mine when my hands had gone away from me." In these moods she was one with him.

Then there were the darker moods that would run for hours, occasionally for two or three days with no words from him, matters beyond her knowing revolving in his mind. She noticed that his grave talk in moving out of one of these moods always had some reference to Roger Williams. He seemed to be shaping for himself something stern and shadowy that related to Roger Williams and Providence. Neither he nor she nor her father had ever spoken directly about how

296

Plymouth impressed him and whether he would make a long stay, whether he had any expectation of becoming a citizen and a member of their congregation.

All had run so kindly, even pleasant between them, that it was in the air and in a way accepted among them that he was their kind of a believer and as he joined with them and worked with them he might become one of the best and illustrious among them. This was partly because when he came among them he was not sure what in reality and deep down was their way of life and belief, what they had hold of in "things terrestrial and celestial." And of such things there could have been no talk in the long weeks when he hovered near the peril of being a tragic cripple for life, if he lived through. He had been powerless to dispel the impression that arose among the others that before long he would ask John Spong for the hand of his daughter, that he would follow the custom and law and make "proposal" to the father first and then the daughter. More than a trifle of guilt was in his mind about this after he had suddenly and irresistibly gathered her to his arms for a long deep kiss. But he could say that was no more to be helped or avoided than the way they had gazed at each other the first Lord's Day he came to Plymouth, no more to be foreseen than the storm change of weather that had struck him and her father in the woods.

His legs and arms were good as new again, spring and April a few weeks off. He began slowly unfolding to Remember the sealed determinations that had come to him out of groping, weighing, resolving, in the shadowy moods that had baffled her. He felt now as he did at first the worth and merits of the Plymouth settlement. Their zeal, courage, tenacity, he admired, especially the heroic material of the First Comers, the Leydeners, those who had first proven what could be done so that other colonizers had followed. But his resolve was made that he must go to Providence and join the work of Roger Williams. "I hope this will not stand between thee and me." He was asking her to go with him.

Knowing how deep her roots were in Plymouth, said Remember to herself, he was asking her to leave them all and go with him.

She said nothing. She sat thinking it over. She was near to saying Yes, though to break from Plymouth would be the hardest and loneliest step of her life.

The door opened and her father came in with a neighbor man and wife. The three of them were pleasant and dropped their remarks as though Resolved Wayfare inclined perfectly to be one of them, had looked them over and made his decision that he found them good and would stay and likely be one of those shining in piety. What their voices and faces said made more vivid to Remember what she would be leaving and what words she would have to find to tell them she must be leaving.

The three others went out the door. The two sat silent, Remember stony-faced. Wayfare stepped to her. He pulled her up from her chair, held her tight and looked in her face. She demurred to his will. He saw it in her sea-wind eyes. It was the first unkindly moment they had known. Remember pushed at his shoulders, broke away from him, pulled her chair near the fireplace, sat looking into the burnings logs, and began a flare of wrath at Roger Williams:

"The man was here. We know the man. Excellent in discourse, yea he is, and handsome, pleasing, yea he is. And again he is a fool, one of the proudest vain fools that ever walked the streets of Plymouth. Filled with delusions, this Roger Williams. Even a very child of the Evil One is this Roger Williams when you become aware of the snakes and worms that creep and writhe in the caverns of his mind and heart."

Long moments of silence then. Wayfare rose and walked back and forth. Remember sat stony-faced peering into the firelogs. Wayfare paused at her side, stood quietly, laid a hand on the head of chestnut hair he had praised, and it was as though he had touched an image of ice. He walked back and forth. He drew a chair alongside her and sat beside her with no word.

A knocking at the door and Remember rose to let in the neighbor man and wife who had come to borrow the spinning wheel till a carpenter had theirs repaired day after tomorrow. They sensed something out of the usual in the glum faces of Wayfare and Remember. They made remarks about what a good workman the carpenter is and what an excellent job he did with their broken door latch last month and how handily he repaired a window frame once. They got no response. They saw their remarks roused no sign of interest in the carpenter. They carried the spinning wheel away, pleased to be out of the house. They closed the door and about the room they had just been in the man was short-spoken to his wife, dismissing it entirely with, "Summat chill." When their spinning wheel should come back from the carpenter and be set in its place in working order again, he would say, "Summat better."

The wind rattling at the door they could hear. And the sputter of the firelogs they could hear. Each other's voices they did not hear for a time. Then Wayfare, "There is a time to plant and a time to pull up that which is planted. What I could desire might not be yet, but the Lord knoweth what is best and His will be done."

"It is dangerous," and Remember stood up with blazing eyes. "It is dangerous to gather flowers that grow on the brink of the pit of hell. You might fall into the pit itself while you think to pick pretty flowers."

She waited. No word from him. Then a soft moan as though to herself rather than to him, "A woman should be from her house three times; when she is christened, married—and buried."

The wind rattling at the door they could hear. And the sizzle of firewood with a snow damp on it they could hear. Then Remember with a straight glance at him and in a meditative voice infinitely gentle, "I remember long ago hearing my mother tell a bride, fresh in her virgin bloom, overconfident and overbright in her gleaming white linen, 'More belongs to marriage than four bare legs in a bed.' It is my wish she were here to give me her precious counsel on whether to go or stay, whether to put on my shoes of travel or be true to this house I helped build, this house I have swept and garnished these fleeting years of time, this house where I have tended the stricken and now am beset with the torment of the plea of the stricken made whole again."

Then with a rasp tinting her voice, "I remember a woman of evil pleasures and soft living going to her death with loud confession of her sins, and my mother having no pity and laughing, 'Having sold her skin to the Devil, she bequeaths her bones to God.' I would rather be the man who had nothing but from whom even that which he had was taken away. What availeth it to have quick feet and run swiftly on the wrong road? Few are they who understand the cunning of the Devil when he painted his tail a delicate sky-blue and looked at it, saying, 'Neat but not gaudy.' Ever the woman is the weaker vessel of the Lord. And I heard your vaunted Roger Williams himself say the fairest silk will soonest be soiled and a fair woman with foul conditions is like a sumptuous sepulcher full of rotten bones."

She paused. She had more to say but paused as though there were infinite time to say it in. Tamia had walked slowly from a corner and stood rubbing herself against Remember's foot and ankle. Remember picked up Tamia and held the bright yellow cat in her lap, her fingers quiet over the black spots on the haunches.

"Nothing happens for nothing and God works in moments," said Resolved Wayfare in a quiet tone of sealed determination. His eyes roved the ax sweeps of the hewn planks of the room ceiling. His eyes roved down to meet hers. Hard it was to say but now he was saying it. One day this week he must be going, tomorrow morning it seemed. He cherished her so truly that he could not consider taking her with him. Her doubts, the sincere shakings of her soul, would come again. "You have your sacred rights to live by the roots you have struck so deep in your beloved Plymouth."

Now a fear bit deep in her bosom, her heart. This was the first time he had ever spoken to her in a tone of deprecation, a sort of belittlement as though he could be sorry for her, as though his sorrow at what must be done moved with a purity above hers. She rose to her feet, dumping Tamia without care of where Tamia might be falling.

"You that take your self-willed course, you too have your sacred rights and what is the use you make of them? To speak taunts of the roots I have struck in Plymouth that hold me here while you go rootless over the earth wheresoever it pleases you to live rootless."

The words flashed from her, each word deliberate and each meant to reproach and sting, her head high, her impetuous hands making a talk of their own. Now he knew he had been guilty, at least to the extent that he had forgotten or not seen the range of her passionate loveliness. She too knew that things sleeping in her had come awake and she was the child of her mother dancing in the kitchen at Leyden. She went on. "I can take chaos in my bosom and I can eat it and drink it and smack my lips after it and dance it before a loved one. I know well those who marry with love and without money have sorry days but their nights shine with scarlet moons and the music of white sea-horses calling. Yet every moon is pressed by a time guide and the sea would be silly and inconceivable without a bottom. So love must have roots and time tries every troth."

"You are two persons, Remember Spong—a natural storm bird and a born homebody and they will fight in your bosom long as you live."

"It is a bold mouse that nestles in a cat's ear, Resolved Wayfare. Better, I have heard, for a man to have a violent shrew than a peaceable sheep ever obedient in all things—and better yet, I say, can he have both in his life for then he will never die of her tedious yea, yea, sir, and ever from day to day, yea, yea, sir. Yet pride can wreck them and sink them both and make them fitter to be loathed than loved. The Devil fetters them when they lose respect and belittle each other too far and with idle tongues of pompous wrath. Deck yourself with borrowed feathers and see how cheap is your comeliness. Stand in the shadow of Roger Williams and ask yourself is it he or you makes the shadow. Espouse him rather than yourself and wear his garments and find whether they be your own. Shoals and multitudes of people have walked the earth and few made a life their own. This world is like a great fair or market where those taking leave give way to those coming in, and of the living swarm the most part know not wherefore they are come together. Wicked fools, devious hypocrites, liars who have learned to tell their own lies to themselves and believe those lies, they may be seen to swim like bright crimson feathers in the waters of the sanctuary—and they like it and dote on it and think it their own creation—then they sink the same as stones and vanish forever from a world that was to them all the time they had it an illusion and a delusion. Mighty men shall stand trembling before the Supreme Judge, unable as they did on earth, with men, to outwit him with their bold subtleties. Delicate women, whose vanity overcame what little wisdom had been taught them, cast forth of their graves as abominable branches of wickedness, shall answer for their ungodly lives. None can escape. The strongest are but brittle earthen vessels, easily broken in shivers. We may dig down under the slabs to where all outward vestures are worm-eaten and moldered and our eyes cannot tell the knucklebones of servant and master one from the other. My own mother, on the *Mayflower*, weak and hearing another weak one spoken to harshly and no need for it, asked us, Why should those who puke into the sea together ever be enemies? She had her saying from the Song of Songs which is Solomon's, Love is a fire of God. Of a certainty love does teach eternity and is like a river that never dries up and has ever new water to succeed that which passeth. They who wear rings have an image of eternity on their fingers. They who handle a wheel have an emblem of eternity before them. For to what part soever of the ring or wheel one looks, one will still see another part beyond it."

Her first vehemence had gone down like a storm wind faded to whatever it is that moves in the spaces between quiet summer stars. Her speech amazed Wayfare. He saw new promptings at work in her. What he had seen and heard before were fragments and ripples alongside this relentless outpouring of wisdom and conjecture. Yet for all that might seem impersonal and abstract, the fear drove hard in him that she was clinging to the purpose of claiming her personal identity as an individual, the deep roots that fastened her life to Plymouth.

"You and I," he said, low-voiced with an utter anxiety and care, "you and I, before we give up hope, should search and scrutinize if there is a way for us to be buckled together as man and wife."

He told her that if she went with him tomorrow for the journey to Providence, their differences of belief would not trouble him, that he could never have aught but respect for her beliefs. "I would marry you, not your beliefs."

She was almost persuaded, saying she wondered if she could go with him and in time the two of them so weave their beliefs together that he could come back with her to Plymouth where was the grave of her mother whose last words were, "Stay with them, my love," where her father had toiled horny-handed, where she herself had planted and hoed and reaped corn and beans, where she had helped carry the hewn planks of their house. She mentioned the Great Sickness, trials past forgetting, her thorough inweaving with Plymouth congregation. She came to another plan for them to consider. Could he not stay for a time in Plymouth and throw in his strength and beneficence toward the end pleasing to him? Should he do so and after such a trial find it has not borne good fruit as he would like, then she would consider going elsewhere with him.

He had held a musket on his knee, cleaning it, laid it down and taken up a knife for polishing, and he heard her in a quiet finality. "You would then be my yokefellow. We would learn of each other. We would be better prepared if a day came there must be a going away."

He dropped his knife-polishing. He told her she did not know how deep ran his beliefs nor her own. A marriage and a later parting in Plymouth would be too cruel. He could not let his mind dwell on it. Away from Plymouth, with both of them as seekers together, they would stand a good chance of finding, nay it would be certain they would together find, garments of faith adjusted and fitted for them. He begged her to go with him tomorrow.

"Again I say," came her fierce outburst, "you speak taunts of the roots I have struck in Plymouth that hold me here while you go rootless over the earth wheresoever it pleases you to live rootless."

The door had opened while she spoke and John Spong had come in, to hear for the first time words of dispute and hot argument between them. He moved a chair between them. They told him the gist of the affair. They waited for his judgment. He waited and considered, then, "I am beholden to you, Resolved Wayfare, for life. It is true." He spoke slowly, his voice rose. "Were it not for you I would be a carcass with the meat eaten off the bones by the wolves, a sad pile of mere bones." He paused. "It is true. And yet—" He paused longer. Then with a low-spoken tenderness joined to absolute resolution, "And yet, what you teach and proclaim is from the Evil One and is the gospel of Satan as certainly as that of Roger Williams. Just as you saved my mortal and bodily life in the wilderness storm so we are giving our prayer and effort to rescue your spiritual life from destruction, your immortal soul from everlasting torment."

He had finished saying this slowly and with composure. The three sat silent. Then Wayfare saw tears down the face of John Spong and the man's throat gulping. Wayfare looked toward Remember and saw her eyes moist and her hands folding and unfolding the fingers. He tried to speak his own heart as he absently polished at a knife blade. "Tomorrow or the day after I must go and with a hurt in my heart harder to carry than any in all of my born days. Long hours in this room I studied it, long days I considered it, and I have infinite sorrow there should be this chasm between us related to Roger Williams. I go to that man not as a subject or a minion but one with him as a seeker, as one in fear of a faith that does not hold toleration of all other faiths."

★ ★ ★ ★ ★ ★ ★ ★ ★

Chapter 24

★ ★ ★ ★ ★ ★ ★ ★ ★

So Long as Grass Grows and Rivers Run

DOROTHY TEMPLE in the spring of 1638 kept company with Arthur Peach. And what happened between them, wild and intimate, set going a sequence of events that shocked and saddened Plymouth and all its neighboring communities of New England. When three white men are hanged for the killing of one Indian the circumstances must be far out of the ordinary, it was understood.

Arthur Peach at twenty years of age and "from a good family in

Ireland," in 1635 landed in Virginia from the ship *Plain John*. Two years later he was in New England fighting as a soldier in the war against the Pequot Indian tribe and, wrote Bradford, "had done as good service as the most there, and one of the forwardest in any attempt." The next year Peach was living at Plymouth in the employ of Edward Winslow. He was bold and smooth, "a lustie and desperate yonge man," short of money, bothered by debts, "loathe to worke," and furthermore "falling to idle courses and company."

Three other young men, Thomas Jackson, Richard Stinnings, and Daniel Cross, servants and apprentices, Peach interested in heading southward to the Dutch plantations. There, he said, they would find a better plenty of money, women and drink. His real reason for getting soon away from Plymouth, however, Peach kept a secret.

By night the four slipped out of Plymouth and ran away from the masters who had them indentured for services. They shied from traveled trails, took to the woods and creeks. The constables and searchers found no track of them. On their way they met a Narragansett Indian, Penowanyanquis, going to the Bay of Massachusetts to buy things wanted for head men of his tribe. The next day while hiding in their camp at the edge of a swamp, in bushes off a path several miles from Pawtucket, they saw the same Indian on his way back to his tribe, carrying a packsack of goods and valuables.

Gay and smiling Arthur Peach asked the Indian to come join them in a pipe of tobacco. And Penowanyanquis did so, sat down with them in fellowship. Peach in undertones told his partners now was the time to kill the Indian and take what he had. They were afraid. Peach said he had killed many an Indian and what was one more?

So they let him alone to do the killing. The Indian sat smoking when Peach sprang at him with a rapier. The Indian made a twist of his body and the rapier ran through part of his leg and up into the belly. Peach leaped back, sprang forward with another thrust of his weapon and missed his writhing victim. Another with a sword came at the Indian, missed and ran his sword into the ground.

Next the Indian took to his feet, running into the swamp. They chased him till he fell and when they thrust at him they couldn't run their swords into him for the way he twisted. Again he got to his feet and zigzagged through the bushes till they no longer followed him.

They thought him dead or dying from the first blade thrust reaching his belly. They went back to their camp, took three woolen coats and "five fathoms of wampum" as their loot from him, and went their way.

The weakened Indian managed to crawl to the Boston path and lie groaning and waiting for help. The Indians who found him set up a cry that it seemed to be the work of white men who wanted a general slaughter of red men. Roger Williams and two other men heard of the affair and came out to the Indians, took the stabbed Indian back to Providence and put him under the care of their two best physicians.

The Indian Penowanyanquis was far gone, had the strength to make a complete statement of what had happened to him, and soon died.

Williams had heard of four white men journeying from Plymouth, in need after losing their way near Weymouth, and had sent them provisions and rum. Now Williams sent messengers to arrest them. A panic had set in among Indian tribes. They sent word to Williams they would rise with their arms and fight against whites who wanted killings. Williams went out to them, told them he would see justice done.

Now word came to Williams at Providence that Arthur Peach and his three companions had asked some Indians for a canoe to take them to Aquidneck. And the Indians, knowing who the young wanderers were but not saying so, paddled them in a canoe over to Aquidneck where the colonists arrested Peach, Jackson and Stinnings, though Cross managed an escape and was not heard from again.

Williams reported the case to Governor Winthrop at Boston, remarking that while every "son of Adam is his keeper or avenger," Plymouth should give the men trial and punishment. Williams in a letter August 14, 1638, warned Winthrop "that the natives, friends of the slain, had consultation to kill an Englishman in revenge," and there were threatenings among the Indians though one friendly chief was spreading the word that Governor Williams had told him he would see justice done.

Plymouth put Peach, Jackson, Stinnings on trial. Among witnesses came Roger Williams, one physician who had attended the murdered Indian, and several grieving and anxious Narragansett tribe members. They testified. They heard the guilty confess to all of what the dying Indian had accused them. They stayed to hear a jury September 4, 1638, give a verdict finding the three white men guilty of murdering Penowanyanquis at Misquameece. They stayed to join the members of Plymouth Colony in seeing Peach, Jackson and Stinnings publicly hanged by the neck till they were dead dead dead for the wanton slaying of a red man who had done harm to no one. The Christian soul of Bradford wearied when "some of the rude and ignorant sort murmured that any English should be put to death for the Indians." Not only was it justice exacted for willful murder, in Bradford's view, but it gave the Narragansett Indians "good satisfaction" and staved off a war.

Resolved Wayfare in the early part of his stay at the Spong home had heard in many details of Plymouth's second and fearful public hanging. Remember and her father stood arm in arm to witness the hangings. When Arthur Peach was dead with his head slimpsing down as if trying to reach his right shoulder and lie in rest there, with his mouth twisted and black hair thick down his pale forehead, Remember could think only of what kind of a loving Irishwoman his mother might be, for the word had gone that he came "of a good family." She told Wayfare, "I saw enough broken necks for one day and shall never again go to see a man hanged till he is, by the language of the court sentence, dead dead dead."

Later came news whispered at first, then tattled with the shrewd faces and raised eyebrows of the knowing, then told aloud as known to everybody, then finally written down in the awful certainty of a court record. This news made it clear why Arthur Peach had sneaked by night out of Plymouth as and when he did. He it was who had been keeping company with Dorothy Temple in the spring of 1638 and as one of the meaner and more light-minded gossips had it, "gave her something to remember him by."

She could no longer keep her secret. The word was going round, "She is big with child, she is in the family way." This last held strictly true in the household and family of Stephen Hopkins where she was the maidservant indentured as yet for two more years of service. And when Dorothy Temple's boy child came, Hopkins gave it out that he could no longer shelter "such a slut and wanton" and he must put her out of his house where her taint might touch his five daughters and two sons, including the one named Oceanus born on the *Mayflower* in mid-Atlantic.

On one side Hopkins was a tender man and had put it in his will that when he died he must be laid near as convenient to his "godly and loving wife." Then too he was a hard man, boisterous with furies of energy and anger, independent, uncertain. His house stood opposite Governor Bradford's, on the easterly corner of Main and Leyden streets. At his land near Eel River, Plymouth, lay a wharf, the first mentioned in the colony records, which he built, owned, and in 1637 sold. His horse, cattle, oxen, cows, his farm near Yarmouth, his share of stock in a ship, his property and able management had earned him the name of "a man of enterprise." It was his two menservants Dotey and Lister who had been caught fighting with deadly weapons the first duel of the colony and it was in part Hopkins' pleading that got them off with only an hour of being tied head to heels when the court sentence called for twenty-four hours. In 1633 and three years following he served on the elected Governor's Council. His colleagues on that body had to put him on trial for beating up with his fists the fellow citizen John Tisdale. The jury included his old friends Miles Standish and John Howland and they found him guilty and sentenced him to pay Tisdale two pounds and the colony five pounds. Again in 1637 a jury of impartial friends fined Hopkins two pounds for allowing servants and others to sit in his house drinking and "playing shovel-board." In 1638 they fined him one pound each on five complaints for selling beer, wine, and strong liquors "at too great a profit." Later on being charged with selling "strong water" without a license and "frankly admitting" the fact, a fine of three pounds was laid on him. Later too he was brought before the magistrates charged with selling at sixteenpence a looking-glass "the like of which is bought at the Bay [Colony] for 9d." A fighter and hard worker, dependable in dangers the colony faced in earlier struggle, Hopkins was now of a doubtful element giving sorrow to Bradford who saw the congregation losing a "unity and love" that once held and nourished it.

Again Hopkins stood in court, information being that he refused to shelter or provide for Dorothy Temple and her infant child. This he admitted. But the court, finding that her contract or indentures had two years to run, gave its decision that Hopkins was entitled to her service for that time, and therefore he must clothe and board her in his family or elsewhere.

Hopkins in his day had sat on that bench as a judge. Now he was telling the judges, including his old *Mayflower* comrades, Bradford, Winslow, John Alden, that he must refuse to have anything further to do with the abominable woman who had shamed his household and cast reproach on his family. It was these old associates who ordered him to confinement for contempt of court. It was they who four days later ordered him released from custody on payment of three pounds to Master John Holmes who pledged to take charge of Dorothy Temple and her child for the next two years.

Then however came further action of the court. Having defied the powerful, ruthless and garrulous Stephen Hopkins, the judges in strict custom and the law as laid down in their book and their practice, took their course with regard to Dorothy Temple. Besides having to consider Hopkins and a drinking, lawless element he mixed with, the judges listened to that part of the church whose men and women hated sin and took a satisfying pleasure in exposing sin and punishing it.

What the judges did was to arraign Dorothy Temple on the charge and the crime of "unlawful maternity." They found her guilty on this charge and of this crime of "unlawful maternity."

They gave her a sentence. In the interest of justice, law and order, she must bare her back and stand at a whipping post and twice be "publicly whipped."

The law was the law. The judges had without mercy or favor put the eminent and respectable Master Hopkins in custody and forced him into a money payment because of a woman he held to be a "slut and a wanton."

Now without mercy or favor, by the book, by law and custom, regardless of sex, they must put into effect on the woman the same infliction of the same penalty common and customary over England and the colonies of England.

Twice at the whipping post she must stand fastened and receive on her bare back the lash of justice and punishment to bring penance.

Resolved Wayfare was making ready his packsack for his walk to Providence, to start the next day. The hours had not passed easy for him nor Remember and her father, since the decision was spoken that

Remember could not and must not go with Wayfare. The decision seemed to be past any recall and each was trying to make some sorry adjustment to living on, with a chill emptiness where had been warm pulses.

Orton Wingate came in, on his way to see the public whipping of Dorothy Temple that day, his first visit since he had helped bring Wayfare through the worst days. Wingate sensed a cool and changed air in the house, made his guess it was other than hate, too sad and shadowy a gloom for him to bring any ray of clarity. His slash of a mouth smiled its greeting and no flickering hint of a smile came from either of the Spongs or Wayfare. He said he would go soon, it was mostly he wished to see their good faces.

Then Wingate told of a king in Italy handed a rope knotted beyond untying. "After much trying the king could not untie the rope and gave it up, saying, 'If it is so much difficulty and misery to untie, what will it not do of evil if I once get it untied?'" The Spongs and Wayfare cared little for this. Wingate said he would be leaving. He recited sweet lines he had when a boy from his father in Norfolk, England:

"Matthew, Mark, Luke and John,
Bless the bed that I lie on.
Four corners to my bed,
Five angels there be spread,
Two at my head, two at my feet,
One at my heart my soul to keep."

He had said the lines last night, the better to sleep, having to think of the holiday in Plymouth today. "It was the doing of Steve Hopkins. He managed it. His loose mouth, his foul mouth, in its hate of this woman, spread a hate and scorn and detestation of her. He knows the overrighteous ones and the scandalmongers and those who lick scandal with their slithering tongues. By his complotting they threw fear into the judges. Wherefore we are to have a holy day of justice with raw, red flesh laid bare on a woman's back from the swing of a whiplash. For this the sanctified journeyed across the sea and fought the wilderness and made an example to the world."

And Orton Wingate was going. But he turned for a final word. "Once, Remember Spong, you showed me that bronze plaque from your bosom, on one side of it carved the Four Stumbling Blocks to Truth. And one of the stumbling blocks is made of a single word: Custom. What happens today when the lash comes whining down and cuts into the bare back of a woman, for a crowd to see? It is custom. Bradford, Winslow, Alden, they have let themselves be forced into the universal custom of cruel and besotted England and all of its cruel and besotted colonies where a child must live branded for all his days as having a criminal mother whose crime was the bringing of him into this fierce and roaring furnace we call life. I speak this to you. I cannot speak this to Plymouth. I am already taken for enough of a fool in Plymouth. They know me already as too good a friend of Roger Williams. They know well that no such infamy as shall be seen at the whipping post today in Plymouth could by any stretch be seen in Providence under Governor Roger Williams, the preacher with a burning heart." He had stood at the door ready to go. "Forget anything I say that might give hurt to your hearts. Your hearts are heavy enough without my laying added weight on them. God love you."

And he closed the door. But along Leyden Street on his way to see the show that would gather all of Plymouth around it, he mumbled lines his laughing father teased him with when a boy, "You limb of a spider, you leg of a toad, you little black devil, get out of my way."

Wayfare went on with getting his packsack ready. A little time passed and there was a knocking at the door. John Holmes entered, saying he knew well Dorothy Temple was no vile woman on whom should be visited so harsh a penalty. Holmes had heard others, good men and women, saying the same in their beloved Plymouth. Holmes did not care to see the procedure of whipping but meant to arrive when it was near over. He and John Spong left the house. Not so long after came a light knock on the door and Remember opened it to let in Wingate.

"It is over," he said in a voice of calm that they knew hid a surging wrath and scorn for the eminent and respectable men of Plymouth for their work today. "Only the sick and only those on necessary duties in Plymouth Colony were not there today. They saw her two wrists knotted with the cord that held her to the post. There was her bare back and its white skin gleaming and prepared for penalty. I saw the wife of Bradford look at him with eyes sad and lurking with rebuke for him. I passed near enough to hear one daughter of Stephen Hopkins saying to the youth with her, ' 'Tis a hellish game, I'd rather be home.' And Wrestling Fairfield, the man with the whip, he was trying to look official and play the role of a functionary. In him, he would have them know, did not reside the spirit and mind of justice. That was elsewhere, among elected, chosen and responsible men. They spoke the sentence of the law and he was to be its majestic executioner. But he knew he couldn't look majestic. Fearsome he might look or bloody but not majestic. I have seen him among the bean poles with his children in late summer harvesttime when he was truly pleasant to view. I have seen him with a child on his shoulders, its legs dangling down on his chest, and then by God he was majestic. Today with that child gazing at him, when he turned a moment and caught its eyes, he was a sad drab and he drew a sleeve across and under his nose not knowing he did it as a sign to himself wishing he were somewhere else than filling the high station of executioner of the sentence of the law. He saw to his long leather-woven whip, ran his fingers from the butt to the end of the lash, and spoke his hope to himself that he would show practice and skill with this peculiar instrument of justice, for one takes aim with a whip, and reaches the mark and target aimed at with a whip, no less than with a musket. So the moment came. He swung and let the leather thong go down cutting a strip of bruised scarlet crosswise on her back. He swung again with a different aim and had now shaped a large thin letter X of scarlet on the white skin. Then came two, three, four lashes that, where they crossed the earlier ones, brought little streaks of blood flowing. One could hear cries in the crowd, open and amazed cries of those startled who had never seen the like of this before. Other cries and moans from the onlookers came low and half-suppressed. Now many were looking into each other's faces and as much as asking, 'What is this to which we have come today? Even if this bloody business purifies the victim it can only harden us and the children and make all besotted.' That was on their faces. It was good to see. It became a moving unrest in them that found tongue. 'It is cruel, too hard,' was heard and, 'I did not think it would be so hard to look on.' When Wrestling Fairfield had laid on the ninth stroke of the lash, the white back of the woman was a mass of flesh with the look of raw beef to be hung over a fire and broiled. And Dorothy Temple had fainted and fallen and hung by the roped hands that fastened her to the post. 'Enough!' came the cry from many voices. And still others, 'You have gone too far,' 'She has fainted,' 'Let her go, all have seen enough.' The crowd pressed forward. Fierce cries of 'Shame! Shame!' Judges moved to the front and gave notice the first public whipping of a woman was ended and there would not be a second. It was over. And I came away saying, 'What is Plymouth? A little vain, squirming, vile, cruel image of hell where a pious mocker and fraud such as Stephen Hopkins can outwit good people toward the end of having justice raped at a public whipping post.' "

Remember pulled at Wingate's sleeve and motioned him to a chair. "Stay a little time." He seated himself and sat with folded hands and a face calm for all the burning inside him. Wayfare folded, fitted, wrapped, among shirts, books, hose, a cooking pan, keepsakes and supplies. No one spoke. The violence and pity of the day shaped new phases in their personal enigmas.

The door opened and John Holmes and John Spong came heaving in, a woman slimpsed between them. They were holding Dorothy Temple by the arms as she dragged herself with slow steps up and through the doorway to the middle of the room. Remember helped guide her to a couch near the fireplace where she lay face down. "A stop and rest here will be good for her before we go on to my house," said Holmes to Remember.

Remember brought a low stool and seated herself holding a hand of the beaten woman and heard the husky singing voice of Dorothy Temple, in a moaning husky tone, "Remember Spong, your hand in mine is so kind, so warm." A brief silence and then, "For the sake of a child, a wee breath of a child," this with a feathery dreaminess and a hushed

309

finality and she was accusing no one and asked no pity and was winding in her thoughts of "a pretty baby, a lovely boy to look on, well formed, no cripple, no blind or lame one, a sweet boy and he cries for milk, from these breasts" and with a rippling mockery of low running laughter "these breasts today put to nurse at a public whipping post" and shifting to another tone and very low, "Someone must tell him one of these fine days how they hanged his father for murder murder murder and whiplashed his mother for unlawful maternity unlawful maternity unlawful maternity and the name of it is Plymouth justice Plymouth justice Plymouth justice."

Remember dropped the hand she was holding and let Dorothy Temple go on in a joined song of babble and meditation that seemed to soothe the beaten woman for there was in it fantasy and elation, even a pride not at all beaten down by her terrific hour.

Remember consulted with Wingate. They made an ointment of goose grease and other ingredients they put on parts of the sore back. On the worst surface they poured lightly a lininent that burned a little. She winced. Then tenderly laying piece after piece of fresh-washed and immaculately clean linen they made a compress over the worst-wounded surface.

"You may sing soft to yourself if you like," said Wingate. "You are a strong woman and you should call on all your strength now. They have not conquered you. I believe you will conquer them. And time will help you to conquer them. Time works for you. They did it because of a living custom. And the living custom will die. Strong shoulders for burdens you have, and a strong back well shaped with a white loveliness of smooth grace that struck admiration in some eyes that I saw today."

He was tying bands around her body to hold the compress and his talk melted her and tears welled in her eyes. "You fared little worse than the woman whose child was born in wedlock here in Plymouth town and because it was the fifth month rather than the ninth month of wedlock the child was born the judges, the high and honorable judges, had the woman sit fastened in the stocks while she looked on to see her husband lashed on the bare back as you were today. It will pass. It is a custom. What horrible damned fools they were at Salem where they must follow a fashionable and cruel practice known in England where men of eminence and learning, heretic men, had their ears cut off for their beliefs. Therefore Salem must cut off some ears. But having no heretic of eminence and learning, what did they do? Nothing less than cut off the ears of a poor babbling lunatic who knew not whereof he spoke when he prattled what Salem termed heresy."

And this talk of Wingate that had begun with a tender solemnity had moved on, as he came near the end of wrapping and fastening the body bands, into the fantastic and preposterous. "Aye," he went on now with a foam-light mirth in his voice, "Salem was struck with humility when the lunatic reached England and word was sent back from the mother country, 'When we cut off ears in England, they are not lunatic ears.'"

The sore woman lay still for a time and all sat quiet in an air that had good and beneficence in it for they knew a soothing and a healing had begun to work. She stirred and started to say something. Remember took one of her hands and held it. Wingate laid a hand on her head of dark hair and they believed he had a touch of more than admiration for her in shaded tones of voice saying, "You are strong and you will conquer. You and the wellborn boy shall overcome fear and stand strong against all that would put you down and lessen you and keep you from deep roots and high flowering."

There was quiet again a long moment. Then Dorothy Temple twisted her head and face for sidelong and upward looks at Remember and Wingate. Then pillowing her head and after quiet a few moments, the slow words came in her husky contralto, with a dreaminess, "Your hands are kind and you will help me, I know you will help me study what to tell my baby when he grows up."

A rain blew up that night and near daybreak changed to snow, a gay wind blowing big flakes helter-skelter in the morning when John Spong and Resolved Wayfare looked out the door. Two inches had fallen and laid a white cover of slush on the road toward Providence. Wayfare would stay another day in Plymouth. By noon the sun came out, the snow vanished and the sky arched blue and warm. First Comers looked to their strawberry beds. Out of chinks here and there peeped a thin green line of early grass. Bird-knowers picked names for old friends returned to sing and chatter. Out from hiding and hibernating places came little green snakes with tawny stripes. They liked the sun and with many others alive and wriggling considered themselves part-owners of the sun.

A double misery had begun with John Spong, a racking neuralgia in his face, and shots of pain in his feet. He sat in a chair before the fire, his feet on a stool, occasionally rubbing liniment on his face and holding warm cloths to it.

Remember's face was sea-pale and thin with seamist in her eyes and her hair combed and plaited with skill and wisdom to frame her face. She busied herself with the meals, with scouring the pewter in a sideboard, with cleaning and tidying every part of the house inside and whisking with speed through the work of washing a shirt of Wayfare's and two of her father's. She ran a dusting cloth over a few stray corners she had missed and stood glancing as though she might be satisfied there was nothing more to be done. This was late afternoon. Wayfare came in from a walk with Wingate, and seeing her with arms on her hips sweeping her glances about the room, took his own look around, said he had seen the shirts drying outside, and,

"The house is swept and garnished as though it could go without care and tending for a long time." Her quick answer in an undertone: "Do me this help to say nothing till this night."

Wingate tried to comfort John Spong but the man was sore and said he knew all that could be done for him. And Wingate being in one of his reckless or garrulous moods and seeing no talk begin with Remember and Wayfare, he would be companionable. "Well it is we are not merely alive but in our right minds, for they are telling of a woman at Hartford, Connecticut, fallen into the infirmity, as they say, of losing her understanding and reason, the wife of a high official. And to what cause do they lay her infirmity? They are certain it has grown upon her over the years by occasion of her giving of herself wholly to reading and beyond reading going so far as to commit the folly of writing many books. Her husband sayeth ever he was tender and loving with her and loath to grieve her now it has come over him that he should have seen to it that she tended to her household affairs and not meddled in such things as are proper for men whose minds are stronger. By such a course, it is told in Hartford, she would have kept her wits and might have improved them usefully and honorably in the place God had set her. The husband brought her to Boston and left her with her brother, a merchant, though it is said no help can be had for her."

Remember had meant to keep still and now couldn't help blurting her swift fancy, "They might endeavor a search whether a device there be for having her unread the books she hath read and then to unwrite the books she hath writ."

"Which we might conceive to be no more difficult a manner of task than for Plymouth to bring Dorothy Temple to the whipping post and unwhip her." Wingate reasoned of men as questionable who estimate their own minds measurably to the minds of women. "It is one more custom that will die." A curious piece of gossip he would give. "In Watertown people had stood by to witness a combat between a mouse and a snake. So runs the tale as tattled. Until I have evidence I shall believe it was a large rat and a small snake who fought. It is one of those matters the oftener told, the larger grows the snake and the smaller the rat till he is a wee mouse. Yet a Boston pastor, one Mr. Wilson, they report to me, gave his church this interpretation: That the snake was the Devil; the mouse was a poor contemptible people, whom God had brought hither, who would overcome Satan here and dispossess him of his kingdom. I could make five or fifty interpretations and none of them more conclusive than his. He may next give his church the intention of the good Lord in the calf brought forth at Ipswich with one head and three mouths, three noses and six eyes."

"A bitterness lurks in you today, Orton Wingate," offered Remember.

"A bitterness lurks in all of us today, Remember Spong. It is the wrong done yesterday to a good and comely woman for the untimely fruit of her womb. It is the soon going away of a good and handsome man our eyes and ears shall miss."

"Let us still our tongues. We live at cost and on the mercy of the Lord."

Remember spoke with patience, Wingate noticed. She had been shaken by contemplations and had come through with a new light in her eyes, he believed. At the door he said he hoped to be with them in the morning to say farewell to Wayfare. Then he had gone away saying, "God love you all." And John Spong had not shifted nor looked and hearing the door close spoke only, "The man busieth his tongue too much."

A spare supper the three ate, John Spong feeling bitter and going to his bed. "Now I'll be telling you," said Remember, her voice grave yet her bony face having bright sea lights in its frame of plaited chestnut hair. She had made a bundle. She would go with him tomorrow for the foot journey to Providence. She would tell her father after their breakfast in the morning. The shock, shame and pity of the day before had kept her awake nearly the night through. Her Plymouth had lessened for her. They would have a civil marriage by the Governor and be two miles away before noon.

All of this tumbled from her smoothly, with no reservations, as though it could have no slips nor flaws as a plan. Resolved Wayfare in the sweep of this new turn, in the glow of the fresh blaze, let himself be whirled along in the rush and warmth of it.

He could have stretched a hand and pushed her away and talked arithmetic and practical possibilities. Instead he pulled her into his arms and held her close and they lost themselves and talked bold and flaming compliments and shaded into brief mysterious whispers and drifted into a silence broken by a thin music only they together could hear. They would see laurel and honeysuckle together, he was sure, and she added violets, the musk rose, the wild rose.

She went to her room dancing on stars. Resolved Wayfare in his corner couch of the living room slept deep and woke long before daybreak, puzzled, searching, praying.

Remember set warm porridge and milk, bread and butter, boiled eggs, cheese, beer, for a breakfast. They ate with few words. Then she told her father of her bundle, of her preparations, of the civil marriage to be, and then the foot journey to Providence. And John Spong knew she had no more to say. He waited. Long he waited. A knock at the door and Remember let in Orton Wingate. A few minutes later, another knock and Remember let in John Holmes and Dorothy Temple. "Tell them what you have told me," the father solemnly told his daughter. And briefly she did.

Then John Spong let loose with a wild tongue. A stranger had been taken in and given respect, affection, care, food, and drink, and repaid with mockery of their faith, violated their ordinance that a man must speak to the father before proposal of marriage to the daughter—a man vile and unclean, a thief, betrayer, seducer, loose-tongued servant of Satan. This moved Wayfare little. His face wore sorrow. He winced at hearing the questions shrieked at Remember, "How do you know where this man may leave you? How do you know he is not another Lyford? What do you know of life in a strange city with a husband not at all proven?" The father knew he had touched her deeper misgivings. Not that she feared betrayal or lapse on the part of Wayfare but that she had never made a life except among old roots, familiar and tested bonds.

Then the father went into a recital of Leyden, the *Mayflower*, the landing, the Great Sickness, the words of her dying mother, "Stay with them, my love," the very home and house where she had helped with carrying and hewing planks, carrying stones for their fireplace, the fields they owned where she had planted, weeded, hoed, and reaped, their keepsakes and memories, and her steadfast faith and works in their church they had come so far to build and cherish, the church that had made a name and commanded a regard and praise for what it had done in a wilderness and little to do with. He was driving his appeals at what he knew lay deep in her.

She wove shifting fingers in and out. She clenched her hands before her bosom and held them tight-closed in a beseeching for mercy, for a stay of time, for an escape from decision. She fell on her knees at the feet of Resolved Wayfare and, her hands and head on his knees, cried her broken and faltering outburst, "I am too weak a vessel of the Lord to hold what is poured on me and what runs over without mercy. There should be mercy in this valley of shadows and phantoms, this fiery trial in the furnace of life. Stay longer here. Consider what may be done. Time will find a way."

Resolved Wayfare put his hands on her head, looked in her face, stroked her hair, pulled her to her feet. "Tomorrow the Lord's Day— we go to meeting. We pray and worship together. We have one more talk. Then I go."

"You," and he took the hand of Dorothy Temple, "I shall not soon forget your strength and sweetness in heavy pain. Your days, I know, will brighten." And pressing firm and warm the hand of Orton Wingate standing close, and almost fondly close to Dorothy Temple, "Friend of mine! I shall miss your fellowship, your laughter and wisdom. I pray we meet again. You have many friends in Providence— you must come see them!"

Then his two hands holding the right hand of John Spong and Wayfare saying no word for a time as he gazed into Spong's unrelenting, unforgiving, hard face, "Tomorrow time will be pressing me and to make sure I do not forget I say now in the days to come I hope you will give me pardon. We have bonds. Did we for naught walk many hundred times around a tree in the blowing snow and bitter cold? Your kindness to me under your roof, your many thoughtfulnesses, will never be forgotten."

The others went away in twilight. The sun went down. Night came on. The Lord's Day had begun. The three ate little of supper. They were early to bed, wondering about tomorrow.

One more day Wayfare was waiting to start on his walk to Providence. He would go to the house of worship on the Lord's Day. He would show his face in public to Plymouth's men, women, children. They would see him—afraid of whom? "Ready to look any other man in the eye, I am," he said to himself. "The only danger is I might laugh in some of their faces." He was not skulking out of Plymouth.

After the sermon, the morning services, ending at noon, he would have his one last talk with Remember. To this she had agreed, saying, "Little is there to say we have as yet not said. Our parting may be for a long time enough. In that long time it would be well we have no regrets over a few hours of saying what we have said before. And if tomorrow we have only silence to share it may be a silence worth remembering over the long time."

And Wayfare soberly, "You say it well."

Spring rode the air that May morning of the next day, the Lord's Day, when the drum roll sounded for morning service. Spring had come again. The songbirds said so. The fresh flimmer of new grass peeping out, the whisper of buds on tree branches ready to soon leaf out, the stir of earth and air moving in the newborn—they all said: Listen and see. Give this Lord's Day to listening. And you may find a quiet mind and a singing heart.

Her father at her left and Resolved Wayfare at her right Remember Spong walked from home to the church. John Spong had the set, fixed face of a stopped clock. He cared to hear nothing and say nothing on this walk from home to church. Remember and Wayfare accommodated him. He probably didn't hear the remark of Wayfare moved by the weather, the many little springsongs, some shade of light over Remember's face and the insignificance of her five little freckles, Wayfare murmuring, "A gladsome day." They saw the procession of soldiers, magistrates, elders, the preacher, file into the house of worship, the new meeting house wherein they had pride. Now after many years of waiting were the windows of glass. Small they were, narrow and long, not clear as crystal, not letting in a full flow of sun, though having a solemn dignity and giving more light than the oil paper of Plymouth houses. When the windows had been put in there was guessing about whether it would be one hundred years or two hundred before all the houses of Plymouth would have windows of glass instead of oil paper.

The service began. The Scripture was read. The sermon began and came to its end. There was prophesying by elders and members. The sand of the hourglass had slowly run from the upper half into the lower and the preacher had turned it upside down and again the upper half had emptied into the lower and a third time the sand had nearly run out, nearly told the end of the third hour, when the dismissal benediction was intoned by the preacher.

Only once in those three hours had Remember and Wayfare exchanged glances. He had kept his face and eyes straight toward the preacher, except for that swift instant when he knew her face and eyes were turned toward him. A long slow look, a deep look at each other it was they had at the end of the first hour. It was not lost on the congregation. Half of them heard little of the sermon and prophesying in their watching of these two expecting they might see such a performance as when Wayfare first came. A few of the worst gossips were agog and hoping but nothing like the first time happened.

They could notice, gossips and nongossips, often for a long time Remember's right hand, then her left hand, rested in calm on her bosom. Her fingers, though seeming so quiet, were saying something to herself. Could she be talking in a sign language to Master Wayfare? No, that couldn't be—from where he sat he couldn't very well read her fingers. To Remember, however, it was an act of holiness, while the preacher spoke on, to feel under her dress, at her bosom, the bronze plaque she had from her dying mother. Engraved on her mind no less than on the bronze were the Four Stumbling Blocks to Truth as written by Roger Bacon. She could say them forward and backward with no help from the plaque. Once she had talked over their meaning with her father and he was so suspicious and superior that she had never again brought them up before him. Elder Brewster had smiled, discussed each Block, rated the Four as worthy instruction. Twice she and Wayfare had taken up the Four Blocks, one by one, and merrily, then soberly, asked each other which Block most often got in the way and made one stumble.

"Custom is the worst," said Wayfare. "To do what you do because others do it, and it is a custom, may be all very well and not harm you as a seeker of truth. To be afraid to do what you would like to do, when you have sought deep and your conscience tells you you ought to do it, to then hold back from doing it because it is not a custom and those who follow custom will mock at you or punish you, that indeed is where custom is a stumbling block to truth."

She knew she was not through with her study of the Four Blocks. Year by year she had seen a little more to each one. Resolved Wayfare had written them out in a large bold scrupulous well-wrought script on a small narrow oblong of parchment. "A tough piece of parchment and it will wear and keep well," he smiled. As she listened to the sermon she could see his script and recall her saying the parchment had the feel of tough thin leather. She had come near asking him to let her keep it, his personal shaping of those momentous admonitions:

The Four Stumbling Blocks to Truth

1. The influence of fragile or unworthy authority.
2. Custom.
3. The imperfection of undisciplined senses.
4. Concealment of ignorance by ostentation of seeming wisdom.

The sermon had run its course. The phrase "dearly beloved" in the dismissal benediction sounded sweeter than usual to Remember.

The members moved down the aisles to the front where, below the pulpit, two deacons stood alongside the contribution box with straight and sober faces, as became pillars of the church. The line moved into the middle aisle toward the front door, parts of it breaking into couples or groups, most of them staying a while for discussion, greetings, and the chatting of news and gossip.

Wayfare and Remember moved slow. Wayfare said good-by to certain ones he knew to be friendly, to some he had helped, to several who believed him queer and didn't hold it against him, to others who suspected him to be a menace to the church and community and were pleased they were to see no more of him.

After a time all had drifted away from the front of the church. Wayfare went inside, saw the sexton about to close the door. From the corner where he had thrown his pack, his musket and tall hat, Wayfare picked them up and stepped outside. From the church front he and Remember walked away in the soft May air over the smiling earth.

Out of the palisades gate at the town limits they walked, on the trail to Providence. They left the trail and their walk ended at a clump of pines with a tall solitary beech tree at its edge. They had been here before. A chapel, Wayfare had called it, their personal and private chapel. Their talk had been only in the press and the hold of their hands as they walked. They approved together of a light spring wind with mixed smells on it that came in to blend with the piny odor.

They seated themselves on an age-old moss-covered tree trunk, an oak predecessor of the circling pines.

"We have come rather in silence," gravely smiled Wayfare.

"Our silence becomes us this Lord's Day better than speech."

"Often I find I trust our silence more than I do our speech."

"Yet our speech has not been useless."

"I have valued so many a thought that came in swift speech on your tongue. And other moments when your long dark eyelashes had sweeps of meaning over your flashing eyes and words. I have had to marvel at speeches that lie hidden in you and are yet to come out."

"Please say little, say naught of how I look. A slattern I shall be,

317

I believe, after you go. What shall I care who sees me and what I present to their eyes?"

A wren quarrel began and ended in the beech tree. A scarlet tanager flashed to the end of a pine branch and was off and away to leave the branch swaying.

"Why be so final in this decision that you cannot go with me to Providence so we can make a life of it together? Why so final?"

"And you—why must you be so final in your plan to go today, to go now with no further waiting, as though Plymouth had kept you a prisoner and now being no longer a prisoner you must use your freedom to rush away, to break all bonds that have held you here?"

She spoke as a woman whose will was crossed, opposed by another will. She implied if he truly loved her he would take his chances, stay near and see what would happen, not imposing on her a decree that she must follow his will to go this day with no wait nor delay.

"Must we begin over?" His arms were around her. "Must we again at this parting dispute and argue and then return to dispute and argument?" And he babbled, "All words are a babbling and between lovers of no use."

His hold of her was fierce. The bones of their ribs pressed tight.

"You would crush me?" She said it slow between gritted teeth. She was mocking, merry, bitter, at once, and there was exultation in her tone. He caught it. She wanted him to hurt her with the fierce press of his body against hers. Her bony lean strength was such that she had no fear his embrace would break her any more than it would break him. "If I must be broken, it is you, sir, should do the breaking."

"Here we are the two sweetest companions in the New World." He laughed this and then somberly, "So we must go away from each other. So you must stay here while I leave you. And the two of us parted from each other should eat our hearts out for loneliness."

"And why? It is your will to be leaving. It is you who tells your legs they must bear you away from me. The action of leaving is yours. It arises from your stubborn heart and mind."

"You wrong me. You wrong yourself. Your heart knows we are not so simple as that."

"Why do you go? You go because it is your wish to go. And your wish is to be leaving me to whatever fate awaits me here."

"I go away alone because you do not wish to join me in leaving. I go away alone and without you because it is your wish not to go with me. It is by your desire you stay here and by your desire I sleep alone under the stars tonight on the trail to Providence."

These words had poured swiftly from them. Each had scarcely ended a sentence before the other had blazed in. They were terribly awake and alive. He clutched her tighter if that could be, printed a long kiss on her mouth and gathered a wild answer from her lips. He pushed her from him and held her at the shoulders, at arm's length.

They gazed at each other long, then Wayfare, "It means nothing and you may forget I ever said it now and here among these quiet pines this day of mild and holy May air."

His hands loosened at her shoulders, took a tighter hold. "Forget I ever said I held in my arms here a pearl beyond price, the Rose of Sharon, the pool of Bethesda, the road to Jericho, the lily of the field whose natural array surpasses that of Solomon in all his glory. Forget that I drank nothing and yet I was drunken with the look of her face and the shape of her clean and stark loveliness. Forget there were words crying out for the want of you. Forget a man desperate with desire on this Lord's Day had a lump and a strangling in his throat as he tried to tell you he would go away and you would not follow him and in the darkness of the night and at noonday for days on days and months on months his hands would reach out groping for the touch of her, reaching for the feel of her face."

And he moved toward her with his right hand gently and slowly coming down with its fingers in feathersoft sweeping caresses of her eyes and cheeks, saying, "her white poem of a throat," as his thumbs and fingers slid softly along her throat.

And Remember knew she wanted him for the rest of her life, for all the days of her life. She was trying to murmur something like that without making a plain confession of it. The palm of his right hand pushed gently under her chin and pressed back her head and then her husky, throaty words, "You are saying with that—you are saying I belong to you—I am yours to do with—as you please—and when you choose."

She shook loose from him, shook off his holds at her shoulders, though not moving out of her foot tracks. He took her by the elbows and pressed her to a seat again on the tree trunk with a moss heavy and clean as grass. He seated himself alongside her. They said nothing. They turned, looked deep and unafraid into each other's faces, and said nothing. The pine smell, the fragrance of leaf mold and of dry grass rising moist out of the loam, the slow light wind acquainted with the face of the earth—the mingling and subtle breaths of these came to them.

Plymouth was having its midday food, its spare Lord's Day meal. Plymouth was quiet. Now and again came a rooster crow, a hen cackle, the moo of a cow, and bird calls, bird conversations, with fast repartee and nothing settled. They sat in quiet studying the serene sway of pines with flat branches dipping and rising in a deliberation worth study. The carpeted pine needles, the brown and rusty under-carpet and the later cover of needles still green, the testamentary time sense of the place—each knew the other to be aware it was a sanctuary to them and they would live over again and again every moment of this session spent here.

How long this mood lasted neither could have told afterward. It had low music, consolation, strengthening, a communion of preparation for ordeals to come.

Wayfare rose, stretched his arms high over his head as though to limber them. He walked to his pack, took his favorite knife from under a strap, the knife a foot long with a narrow thick blade, a silver hilt and an embellished mahogany handle. He stepped over to the beech tree. On the trunk at about the height of his shoulders he scraped off the bark, cleared clean a space wide as his two hands, swiftly carved two hearts entwined. He moved away counting one for each of ten steps, "one step for each of the Ten Commandments." His left foot far to the front, the knife in his right hand back of his head and back of his right shoulder, the knife held by the blade point. This he did with the smooth and accomplished grace of a performance familiar and practiced to him. The knife slipped away from his thumb and three fingers, turned one clean somersault, made one smooth turnover in the air, and the point of the blade landed spang in the exact area where the two hearts joined, the hilt and blade trembling in a slowdown from shock and impact.

"That was for luck." Remember heard him in an undertone meant for her, meant to be precisely loud enough for her to hear. Again he stepped off ten paces and again the knife slipped from his thumb and fingers, again it streaked with a bright low whizzing sound. And again there it was spang exactly where those two carved hearts joined.

"That was for love, deep divine love." Remember heard his somber undertone.

And now Resolved Wayfare stepped off ten paces, then ten paces more. At those twenty paces she could see his face with care and eagerness on it though for all the depth of care on his face, he was cool, he would not miss his throw for not being cool. In the other throws he had been a little careless, carefree, debonair, as though he couldn't miss, as though he had done it thousands of times and what was once more? Now he was on his mettle. Now there was fate in the air. The last two were for luck and love. What would he say this one was for? Slowly he took his position. Very deliberately he measured with a look here and a look there the distance of his feet apart, the hang and balance of his body.

Now he was all set. He drew back shoulders, twisted slow in hip and foot. His right hand holding the knife drew back of the right ear, far back of the right shoulder, then the hand shot forward, fingers and thumb let the knife go and it began its fearful streak, its little arc and trajectory of a glittering path toward that target of two intertwined hearts.

As before it went spang and true, the blade driven deep, the haft and handle quivering long.

Then Remember heard him, "That was a prayer, that was the intercession of two hearts, that was a manifest and a plea."

He was going to pull the knife out. He turned to her, "To make it a joint prayer and a mutual plea you must come here and with your right hand draw it from where it has pierced."

She stood up, came hesitating. "If this is one of your own devising I will do it, if it is a form of pagan ceremonial I cannot have a hand in it."

"Spoken like your own father would have said it—your father is here telling you what to say, he has put his own fears and trembling into your blood and brain. Take that handle and hilt now with your right hand. Pull that knife out. And say with me the words, 'This is our joint prayer and mutual plea.'"

Slow, hesitant, stony-faced, Remember curled her fingers around the knife handle, pulled the blade out, her lips mumbling faintly after him the words, "This is our joint prayer and mutual plea."

They walked to their moss-wrought oak trunk and Remember, "Now you mock at me as though a mind of my own I have none, thoughts of my own I have none, as though I am a piece of baggage in my father's hands. I am not afraid to confront you. I am not scared by the skill you have which may be clever and yet betray you as being in league with an Evil Power, the Supreme Dark Power that never ceases its work against the ways of Light and the Supreme Genius of Light who is God Himself."

"Are you saying it is Satan, the Devil himself, who gave me lessons in throwing the knife? Do you believe it is the Devil's conjuration and not my own eyes and my own good right arm that guides the flying blade and sends it where I aim it, straight between our two hearts carved on that tree? Are you trying to say I could not have done this thing unless by covenant with the Devil?"

"Your ears have not heard all wrong. I will again make myself clear to you, if so can be. I say your skill is diabolical. It may be your own skill. Yet I am not sure but this and other gifts you have came to you by connivance beyond your own understanding. There have been handsome doers, sinners pleasant to look upon, who did not know in the smooth way they lived that the Evil One sought them for his own, and he bestowed his favors and charms on them without their knowing he was so doing. Before they were aware he was their friend and helper, he had seduced them into ways they could enjoy only by his consent and cunning."

"Listen, Remember Spong. You had better search farther in that dark tangled heart of yours. If you do so search, I believe you will find that you have a certain fear. It is a fear that has been there from the first. You thought once or twice you had driven it out, chased it away. But that fear is there yet. And what is it? It is the fear that the Devil himself brought us together, that Satan for his own purposes is working and conniving with diabolical cunning to throw us two into some crime or misdoing that will shame us before the world and bring us to degradation and ruin. Joy came into your life, a strange new joy, the like of it never before in your life. And because it was joy you were afraid of it. Because it was joy it smote you with fear. And you have nursed that fear. You have let that fear guide your decision. You say No—Yes—No—Yes—No by the control of that fear always moving and stirring in your dark and tangled heart."

He reached out a hand as he stood before her, patted softly the gleaming waves of chestnut hair over her ears. He took between thumb and finger an edging of the immaculate linen of her wide collar. She stood numb and dumb. Vaguely she handed him the knife. They had forgotten about the knife. She now spoke clearly enough but had a vague idea her tongue stuck and blurred her words. "This is your belonging," having handed him the knife. "It is yours by right of use. You should have some pride in it. You endow it with cunning."

Wayfare took the knife, moved a step away from her and standing some twelve paces from the double heart carved on the tree trunk, whirling on his toes three times and letting go the knife as if not taking aim, he sent the blade streaking again into the center of the target. The zing it made echoed dimly, lingered in the air as the hilt quivered.

Then Wayfare laughed, a ringing mocking laugh. He turned his head up toward the blue sky and laughed long and loud. "And you believe the Devil has some hand in that innocent knife going exactly where my good right arm sends it. You can think that Satan, the Prince of Darkness, has come here among these fragrance-of-balsam pines, here on this sweet May day, a Sabbath Day, the Lord's Day, here on this afternoon has come the Head of Hell, the Chief of the Imps and Demons of Hades—here he has come to help me throw a little innocent knife into a pleasant and noble beech tree for his own dark purposes in seducing me into his ranks."

He sprang forward, pulled the knife from the double-heart design, ran back ten paces, balanced himself for a throw, after bowing in mockery as he cried in mockery, sweeping his hand in a circle above and below him, "Somewhere around and about here is His Imperial Satanic Majesty. His craft and cunning, his black magic, will now guide this knife as it whirls through the air. Come now, Master of all the Devils of Hell, come now with your hellish magic, and help me to throw this knife exactly where I want it to go."

With a swish and a zing the blade again streaked through the air and again as before sank into the target. Wayfare bowed. To front and rear, right and left, he bowed, "Thank you, Master Devil, thank you, Chief of the Fiends of Hell, thank you a thousand thanks. I am now your obedient slave for life. I am now your complete possession and perfect plaything. I am now beholden to you for all the rest of the days of my life. My neck is your footstool."

322

And again Wayfare laughed, a ringing mocking laugh, turned his head up toward the blue sky and let go long and loud merry laughter.

Remember stood speechless. She saw his laughter cease, saw him sheath his knife. Then out came the knife and she saw him sway, stoop, and bend as he moved around in a circle crying, "Io Iah, Io Iah."

Now Remember could not keep back the beginning of a smile. Her own body began swaying a little as this tall lithe man, brandishing a knife as a tomahawk, executed part of a Wampanoag Indian dance she had seen performed with its stark punctuating cries of "Io Iah, Io Iah," a dance so interesting to her that she had done imitations of it for herself. In a brief glance he shot at her he noticed her perfect timing and saw she was murmuring the dance cries with him. He leaped toward her, had her in his arms, held her close and long, and she heard his mischievous whisper, "Now we have both gone to the pagans, now we are lost to the heathen."

Then the quiet of their pine chapel was broken. The yelping of a dog sounded near, a dog in pursuit of game, the sharp yelping of a dog near getting his teeth into his prey. Suddenly near their feet came a scurrying cat. Up the beech tree and over the double-heart design ran Tamia. And a mongrel hound, a mastiff somewhere among his ancestors, sat at the foot of the tree and barked, snapped, whined and yelped at the cat.

On a wide branch above Tamia sat cool and calm, blinking down at the shaking and cheated dog.

"Get out of here," growled Wayfare, throwing a stick at the dog. With sidelong eyes toward Wayfare it slunk away. Wayfare and Remember stepped over to the beech tree and talked to Tamia who came down to find comfort in Remember's arms. Then Wayfare sat alongside Remember on their mossed log.

Remember stroked the fur of Tamia, who settled into a serene and easy position, blinking her eyes as though she might take a sleep. Wayfare ran his eyes over this smooth cat figure, its hair running in yellow and tawny waves from nose to tail tip, its paws stretched yellow and tawny out on Remember's dark-brown skirt, at her knees like two affirmative prints, the haunches with those four identifying black and round spots. Wayfare leaned over, his bare head almost touching Remember's bosom, raising his head a little so her chin rested on his head. His fingers played softly on the fur between the ears of Tamia whose ears flicked a little in answer. Wayfare rose, stood facing Remember and Tamia, crouched on his knees and touched the four black spots one by one.

"Isn't it amazing?" he asked. "Her grandmother and her grandmother's grandmother had those same four spots—and back and back they all had that same yellow and tawny hair and those same four spots—all the way back to the Tamia you carried in your arms when you were a twelve-year-old girl there on the wharf of Plymouth, England. Those cats never changed. This is the same Tamia, in shape and color, as the one you held in your arms in 1620 across the Atlantic Ocean."

Wayfare straightened his legs, shot up in the air to his full height. "No change, my God, no change, the same, the same, the same now as then." The voice was sharp, rasping, harsh. Remember could see this outcry was not at her. He was hurling his words at forces of life that had him baffled and near torment. He caught himself. He slowed down. Now his low voice was rebuking himself for having been too high-keyed. Yet he was now speaking the depth of feeling that had struck him.

"I must say it to you. It comes hard to say. It is nonetheless so deep in me I must say it. I came near beginning to say it before this. But the time was not right. Now I must say it. It cannot be left unsaid for the time you and I will not be near enough to speak.

"Why did your Pilgrims here in Plymouth break from England? Why did they leave the old country, the land of their forefathers, to come here in this wilderness? Was it not because that old country was cruel and unjust and would not let them worship God as they chose? Did they not say they were leaving England for the reason that here they could in a new land, a hard and lonely land filled with savages, yet a new land and theirs to do with as they should order, here they would show the world what liberty of conscience, freedom of worship, could do?

"And now after these hard years of beginning what has come to pass? Did they leave the Devil behind in England? Not for a moment. They brought with them the same Devil they had in England. So sure and firm is their belief in this Evil One, so proudly do they prize this Prince of Darkness, that unless others believe in this Devil, those others must suffer for such a belief. And along with the Devil they brought hell from the old country, all that terrible distance from the old country they brought the same hell they had over there.

"They have instructions and laws, decrees and customs, saying that others must join them not only in worshiping their God but they must believe in their Devil and their hell. They have no more changed their Devil and their hell than the yellow hairs and the four black spots on the cats named Tamia have changed. In mid-sea crossing the Atlantic did they drop their hell overboard? No. Did they take their Devil and cast him out into the deep waters and say, That will be the end of you? No.

"In the cargo loaded that day, when I first saw you on the wharf at Plymouth, England, we didn't see them carry hell and the Devil on board for cargo. We didn't see it. But they did it. They didn't leave that part of the cargo in England. They took it on board. The ship was crowded with cargo but they made space for hell and the Devil. And arriving at Cape Cod and finding the place where they would land, they unloaded hell and the Devil with the food, the tools and the remaining cargo.

"It pleased them to do so. Each one of them had a clear right to his personal hell and his personal Devil. But why must they say all others must accept their hell, their Devil? Why must they force their particular hell, their particular Devil, on others?"

Wayfare had at one moment stooped with his face near Remember's and run his right hand stroking Tamia from head to tail. Now he turned and flashed out with his knife. "If I want a hell I want it to be my personal hell, my invention, my fate. If I want a Devil I don't want one handed to me by others. I want my Devil to be personal." He drew back his right arm and sent the speeding blade into the oval where the two hearts intertwined in the design carved on the tree ten paces away and went on, "I can make for myself a more terrible hell than I have heard any of them teaching in Massachusetts Bay Colony or here in Plymouth Colony. I can make a Devil for myself more terrible than any they have tried to frighten me with here in Plymouth or in Massachusetts Bay Colony. So can you. You have dreamed and visioned a Devil more cunning and oily and terrible than what they gave you to accept for a Prince of Darkness."

He turned to see Remember's face, a single tear coursing down each cheek, her eyes soft to him. Her mouth and lips twisted in a series of changes, she was laughing and crying at once—though crying more than laughing. She knew she had in her the same streak of gay mocking fantasy that he had been talking. She knew she could wait the rest of her lifetime in Plymouth or she might roam the world over and she would not meet another man with such inside streaks that matched her own. What went on inside him was like what went on inside of her.

At this she could laugh with joy. But the tears came because she knew there was a place where she left off, afraid to go farther, while he went on. He let himself have freedom she was afraid of. He went on and on. She was afraid to go on and on. And she was afraid both for him and for herself. She was afraid that if she let herself go farther it was the strength and lure of a Dark Power beyond her knowing and fathoming. In the end that Dark Power might come to possess her and ruin her life and slowly change her into a slattern, a strumpet, a loose evil woman. Likewise she was afraid that his skill and cunning, his brightness that she marveled at, came to him from an outside Dark Power. He was unbelievable. The gleams of him were "unnatural." That was the word she had heard so often—"unnatural." He was more than a natural man. And a Dark Power beyond the natural took possession of him and gave him the gleams that fascinated her. Her word for the Dark Power took many shapes, the Prince of Darkness, the Evil One, Satan, the Archdemon, the Head of Hell—yes—the Devil. For all the fascination and brightness of his fantasy and fooling, his mocking at the Dark Power—had he not slowly come into possession of the Devil? How did she or how could he know with any certainty?

Each of these two faces of Remember that kept shifting and mingling Wayfare had seen before, her joy face and her fear face. Not till this Lord's Day afternoon however had he seen the two of them on her at once. He saw her rise, dumping Tamia to the ground, and stand before him, putting her face near his, as though to say, "Read my faces."

He put his hands to her two arms and shoulders. "Your face is more than one face. Your sad mouth is trying to say things that fight and struggle in your blood and heart." He babbled this swiftly to her, high-tensed. Then with a low moan, "You will not believe it is I who can weep with your sorrow and shout laughter with your joy. You must go on believing I do nothing by myself—what I do comes by an Evil Conjurer, the Prince of Conjurers. And though I think I know what I do—it is not so at all—I have come into the possession of the Great Evil Shadow."

She saw his eyes moisten and his body shudder as the words came, "It is not I, Resolved Wayfare, you kissed with a long deep kiss today. It is not I at all. It is the Evil Shadow that has seduced me and bought me away from myself without my knowing I have sold myself for his price and charms."

He saw her face turn released from its torment of changes and questionings, her face turning white and calm and her eyes closing as her knees gave way and her body began to sink.

He caught her, took her in his arms, seated himself on the ground holding her head in his lap. When her eyes soon opened she said nothing, nor did he. His hands brushed her hair and forehead. The way he held her, the way his hands tried to talk to her, his care about her and his adoration of her—they swept through her and as her own words might have it, "came near to overwhelming and subduing me."

After a time she found words for him—and for herself. "I am strong yet. Believe me, I am strong yet. I have been sunk in darkness and have before this made my bed in thorns. I grope now. I grope in weariness. Believe me, it is a weariness. By the waters of Babylon we sat down and wept. Believe naught of what I say. Let me babble my nothings now of Babylon and the waters where we sat down and wept. The verses I say must have no meaning. My lips babble of what I must not lose. And what can I know of that which I must not lose? The verses are idle. If I forget thee, O Jerusalem: let my right hand forget her cunning. If I do not remember thee, let my tongue cleave to the roof of my mouth: yes, if I prefer not Jerusalem in my mirth. Who takes this daughter of Babylon, wasted and worn with misery, who takes her and says Down with her, down with her, who throweth her against the stones without remorse or compunction? What ointment can help these sores and wounds, what words of praise, what kisses on the mouth can help?"

She babbled on. It rested her. She knew she was babbling. There had been no one else in her life except her mother to whom she could babble as she now did. He saw it resting, smoothing her. It related to his own way of spilling his mind and heart. "I sat down under his shadow with great delight," she babbled on, "and his fruits were sweet to my taste. He brought me to the banqueting house, and his banner over me was love. Stay me with flagons, comfort me with apples: for I am sick of love."

At this last verse Remember sat up and laughed, a short rippling laugh, then she laid back with her head in his lap again, his hands at her hair and forehead again, as she repeated, "Stay me with flagons, comfort me with apples: for I am sick of love," and babbled on, "Being sick of love Solomon's dearest of women, his brightest dove of doves, she first drank one flagon of wine, then drank a second flagon, then it would seem more flagons, after which she comforted herself with apples. She was Solomon's dove of love, his love love love, his dove dove dove, and having drunk flagons of wine to forget her being sick of love love love, what does Solomon's dove dove dove then do for comfort? With apples she comforts herself, with apples."

Wayfare saw what she was doing, letting go of drolleries, small chaff or follies, bits and bubbles of thought and fancy that came to her mind, resting herself, drinking up thoughts of a freedom she could indulge herself in with him and him only. Her head in his lap she babbled on. "The black spots, the four black spots on the haunches of Tamia, Mcsopotamia, Tamia little one, the four spots, thou camest over on the *Mayflower*. Glad I am, good it is, we left not behind in England those four black spots. They belong on that yellow and tawny hair, yellow for the leaves of autumn, tawny for the last gold of the sunset. Shall I babble on, Master Resolved Wayfare, good master, shall I babble on? Aye was his answer, let her babble on. For the days are to pass and we are to drift and dawdle. The beeches may stand bold in the rain and the sea loom brighter yet with its marching dawn, its endless and repeating dawns that we shall not be gazing at together though with every dawn we shall speak the other's name and say Tomorrow will come beyond any lean shadow of a thin doubt, Tomorrow will come and when it comes we will call it Today and when Today is gone we will dub it Yesterday and say Farewell, Yesterday, my friend, my love, farewell and be kind to yourself and make for yourself fresh ropes of damask roses if you can, if so can be. And the nights will go on, the nights filled with echoes, an echo here and an echo there, large echoes with the slow sway of tall ships in smooth quiet harbors at anchor, even the echoes of deep hard anchors and the clank of them, the clank of two anchors of iron sworn to hold deep and fast, echoes, little echoes so frail you can

327

reach out your cupped hands and feel them fall into your two cupped hands and when you try to put them away for to keep they have melted into the air and when again you wish such a little frail echo you must listen and wait and again let it fall into your cupped hands, echoes of pines, tall commanding pines whereunder lovers stood and spoke of the journey they must not now take together and the journey farther beyond they may be taking, might be taking, could be taking, would wish to be taking, echoes of the zing, the zing of a knife through the air and the sping of it into the wood of a pine and the faint shudder of the haft and handle of it bracing itself after the sudden pause and stop of its wild flight, echoes—Oh God, the echoes we must keep in our hearts!"

And Remember turned on her side, raised her hand and pressed it to her shoulder as his answering arms and hands took her. Her left arm went over his right shoulder, her right arm under his left arm and up over him to hold on his shoulder. The strength of her arms made him glad. They answered to his own strength. On her closed eyes he put kisses. On her hair, then on her mouth, he put kisses and, "We must both be strong for the paths ahead of us."

Her still lips began to move, quivered, then her calm words, "My knees gave way under me and I could no longer stand. The fear in my mind ran down to my knees, the fear of the Evil One working his spell over you and you not knowing. You struck at that fear when you said in your mockery it was not you but the Evil One who has kissed me over and over again. You have been wise so often that now you make me ask myself if it could be that you are free of the Evil One and it is I am victim of his dark ways, that the Dark Conjurer, for his own ends, has planted in my mind that fear. I shall find as the days pass, I truly believe I shall find, that it is you who has kissed me. The tangles and confusions in my heart and mind shall yet come straight and clear."

In the moving of the sun they were now in a clear pool of light that became a tall bowl of silver and blue above them. She opened her eyes to see him in adoration of the play of light making a changing burnish on her braids and coils of chestnut hair.

"I will remember your hair." He paused. "And your eyes will not be forgotten—nor your mouth—nor the strength of your arms nor the strong will that runs in your blood."

He paused again. She closed her eyes, and heard him, "All I have named I will remember, my Remember, all I have named and much else, a vast deal, endless things out of your speech and silence—I will keep them, my Remember."

Her eyes still closed, she murmured in a slow singing dreaminess, "Resolved, my Resolved Wayfare."

On a carpet of pines, in a pool of light that rose into a tall bowl of silver and blue, the moments passed and they were lost to each other.

Each knew that the other had made a promise. They were to meet again. How, when, where they were to meet—this was not the time for the arrangements and details that would be taken care of since what had now happened between them had the seal of an oath neither had called for the other to speak.

"So long as grass grows and rivers run," he murmured low once as he stroked her face and hair.

"So long as grass grows and rivers run," she pronounced slowly, meeting his own finality.

On the air now came a sound with a threat, a pounding and insistent sound. For them, as they lifted their heads to get it clear and make sure of what it meant, it seemed for a moment to shake their pool of sunlight, to send ominous waves across their tall bowl of silver and blue stretching far to the limits of the sky.

They had heard that sound before. It was unmistakable. All Plymouth knew what it meant. It came from a drum. To the beat and pound of that drum, to the spaced march-steps of that drum, the doors of Plymouth houses opened to pour their people into the roadways. The military company of the colony, the men armed with muskets, led by their captain with a sword, their march headed by the Governor, the Civil Council, the elders, the ordained minister carrying a text and a syllabus —they followed that drum to the meeting house to open Lord's Day services. Except for the sick or disabled and except for the negligent or vagabond who had strayed to the woods and bypaths this afternoon, all of Plymouth was paying heed to that drum—they would assemble their psalms, hear Scripture reading and prayer, and hear a sermon through till the hourglass had to be turned once and then once again.

Those drumbeats, those march-steps pounded out on a drumhead in the inevitable and regular staccato of every other Lord's Day for years and years—it meant Remember Spong must go. She stood up, pulling Wayfare up with her. She threw her arms around him in a fierce embrace again. The strength of her—he measured it again in the lean muscles—and the warmth of her blood for him was there in kisses she rained on his face, on the hair of his head. She let go her arms, stepped over and picked up his tall hat and put it on his head, then stepped away from him and swept her eyes over him from head to foot as she let out a half-choked cry and a bitter laugh touched with an exquisite bittersweet in her words. She bowed low putting the tall hat on him, "Handsome is as handsome does."

They hid and covered his pack and musket in a clump of undergrowth near the Providence trail. They walked to the Plymouth meeting house together. They stood by a wide wind-worn cedar forty yards from the front door.

"They are less cruel, your people under that roof, less cruel than Boston, Salem and the others," he was saying. "They are less bigoted and less vainglorious and tyrannical than the others. Yet they have too few seekers. In times to come there will be more seekers, the young now growing. Those who rule and hold the power now are the Past. They brought over that Past from the shores of Europe. I am the Future. I go to seek and find. You have the Future in you. I have seen it. You are tied and fastened without mercy to a piece of the Past. It will not be ever so. We shall meet again. We shall walk together as seekers toward the Future."

She faced him, her shoulders shaken, not moving her hands to the tears that came down her face. "It is as you say."

Soon he would be on the trail for Providence, gone like a bell at the end of its ringing, and you could listen and what you heard would be a memory and not a bell. That was her thought. He saw a temptation wrestling in her for a moment, that she might now reverse her decisions and go with him. The code they had evolved forbade that he make any last plea that she go with him. He saw that temptation pass.

For this day and for a time that neither he nor she could measure in the future, here she must stay. These were the people she could not now leave. A thousand strange and deeply woven bonds dictated her choice. She must now go into that meeting house and—for a number of months or years not measurable—keep her place and follow her old ways. He too had said as much. They would be far from each other's faces but they would hold to that hope and light, as he had put it, "You are tied and fastened to a piece of the Past." She would not forget that nor, "It will not be ever so. We shall meet again. We shall walk together as seekers toward the Future." She repeated some of those words. She added her first answer to them, "It is as you say."

And Wayfare, brushing her mouth with a light meditative kiss, "So long as grass grows and rivers run."

And with her answering kiss in kind, "So long as grass grows and rivers run."

He stood under the wind-worn cedar and saw her walk to the meeting-house door, nod to the two sentries, and before unlatching the door, with her hand on the latch, her eyes met his and he read her face sad with a heartbreak she had never known before—not overcome, not lost, but groping and in her groping not lacking a thin silver-blue slant of light for her hands and feet.

She opened the door, went through and closed it. She walked neither proud nor humble, well aware of eyes on her, mildly dazed, down the middle aisle where her down-looking eyes seemed to know every plank and nail. Nearly every pair of eyes in pew after pew slanted toward her, tried for a glimpse of her face, tried to read why Remember Spong was late and what might have happened to her whose record for early attendance and promptness had been so good these many years.

She seated herself in the high-backed pew bench where she was expected. Many eyes sought her head and profile. Some of the keener ones, familiar with her face and ways, could read that a change had come to her. How deep lay that change and whether it would work to farther depths they could not tell. Only Remember herself under that roof could tell how deep was the change and report that it must grow and go deeper or life would shrivel for her and she would walk in Plymouth as one of the unburied dead. She heard the voice of the preacher droning on in expository elucidations of a text repeated several times. The text didn't come clear to her ears. She was weaving solemn instructions to herself around a text that kept recurring to her. "We shall walk together as seekers toward the Future."

The sermon came to its end. There were hearts it had reached in one part. The preacher had dwelt on the month of May in the human heart, the springsongs to be found in the Gospel of Luke, while from outside came dimly occasional bird calls and gay young twitterings, reminders of earthy odors on a light wind.

The sermon ended and in the aisles and outside at the front door there were hints and little queries that Remember warded off with hints and queries of her own or a baffling "We may speak of that another time."

She walked home with her father. They passed the stocks and pillory in front of the fort. And John Spong broke a long silence with a nod of his head toward the punishment devices and, "He was in good fortune he stood not there in the pillory with his head clamped down."

Remember's eyes blazed. No word came from her.

Then her father added as an afterthought that might bring her to her senses, "And you in the stocks alongside him."

Remember's face flashed. She stood still, as did he. They faced each other. Then her words hissed and spewed, "Have I, your daughter, been a slattern, that you should speak to me as though I am filth? Have I, your daughter and the fruit of your wife's womb, been a slut that you should spit on me as unclean? Am I a strumpet of foul and stinking sin who violates the memory of my mother and her archangels?"

They stood with a steady gaze into each other's eyes. The father was the first to turn and take up the walk homeward. The daughter walked alongside, with no further word.

They came to the house that had been home. He unlatched the door and went in. She followed. He threw off his hat, loosened a cord at his wide white linen collar and took himself to his big chair. She changed her brown skirt, her white bodice with its wide white linen collar and put on a dark loose dress, lighted a candle, set a table for two, got a fire going to warm a roast of pork, brought corn bread and cider, cuts of the warm meat to the table. And they ate little and said nothing. They went to their beds straight afterward without saying good night.

The father knew that a change beyond his understanding had come over this child of his loins. He could tell that it was a change not yet finished, that it was a change to go on and on and his wits and his strengths would be helpless against it as it grew and deepened. The nature and working of the change was her personal secret and beyond his fathoming. He would have to break and destroy the Past to understand it and be part of it. He was afraid she was the Future and he would have to be born again to be of the blood, will and vision of that Future.

Remember in her room was alone and not alone. Before getting into bed she lighted a candle and let her eyes linger and her fingers fondle a small narrow oblong thick parchment filled with a large bold scrupulous well-wrought script: the Four Stumbling Blocks to Truth. She blew out the candle. She slid into bed. She was alone and not alone.

Nine miles out, on the trail to Providence that night, with spring water near by his camp, and a smooth bed of pine twigs under him, looking up at a bowl of moving stars through branches of oak and beech, a man tucked his doublet and cloak around and under him before waving good night to the stars.

"I am the Future." He waved with an open palm of his hand toward the constellations. "And so likewise are you."

The walk with a sixty-pound pack and musket had worn him. "I'll sleep," he laughed, "I'll sleep like a baby." And he did, drifting into the sleep with lullaby words, "So long as grass grows and rivers run."

His fadeaway into sleep came with his fingers folded around a tiny bronze plaque graven with the Four Stumbling Blocks to Truth.

★ ★ ★ ★ ★ ★ ★ ★ ★
★   ★
★ *Book Two*   ★
★   ★
★ ★ ★ ★ ★ ★ ★ ★ ★

THE ARCH BEGINS

Stage-Wagon at Daybreak

IN the back room of John Biddle's tavern in Philadelphia on a March morning of the year 1775, it was not yet daylight. The wicks of the two lamps burning whale oil needed trimming but Ordway Winshore could make out the other faces in the room and they would come clearer yet with daylight. He had not shaken· sleep out of him and the faces over the room gave him half-thoughts. "Blessed are they who expect nothing: they shall not be disappointed. . . . A name you can change, your face you keep. . . . One face looks at another: 'I am me—who are you?' . . . Out of a deep hush, time long gone, came your face: try it a while yet."

In the rear courtyard outside he had heard the six horses, their hoofs on the cobblestones and gravel, the four wheels of the stage wagon coming to a stop with a grind and a clatter. His eyes had ranged faces, four women and six men, waiting the driver's call for them to step out the door and into the stage for the City of New York and points this side. Others of course had caught Winshore's face, harder than a second-frost pumpkin, a mystic harvest-moon twist on it. His mouth began far to the east of one nostril, ranged far west of the other, a slow long slash of a mouth half solemn and half comic, the upper lip thin, a heavy and mournful lower lip. His nose ran straight, dipped a little, ended in broad nostrils furbished inside with thick stubs of black hair. His jaw in its flowing width from ears to chin might have oaken-timber and anvil-steel quality—it could be. His deep-set brown eyes half-drowsed, the eyebrows a faded brown, a brick-dust hair straggling from under his fur cap. From in front, a steady look at him would note the two sides of his face different, one profile giving peace and calm, the other hinting at wrath and turmoil.

The heavy-muscled and somewhat hunched shoulders of Winshore sagged down in a high-backed chair, the head lowering between shoulder corners. He could be taken for the sleepiest, laziest man in Philadelphia. He slanted his eyes, one open and the other drawn to a thin slit, and began at the feet of the woman seated opposite him. A farm woman, by the leather of those shoes, and the hide of the cow slaughtered on their farm had been traded to a tanner for leather and the shoemaker had come to their house and stayed weeks making boots and shoes for the family, besides harness repairs. The coarse wool of her thick leggings had come from a sheep sheared on their land and she had carded, combed and spun the wool into yarn and knitted the leggings that from the instep and thick ankles kept her warm to above the knees. Her brown linen dress could have come from flax raised on their own acres that she spun herself, doing part of the work at "spinning parties" with neighbor women when they had coffee, cakes, and talk and gossip. At a neighborhood dyeing the linen got its brown, a color lighter than snuff-brown. It was her Sunday dress, her best, and she had worn it five, six or eight years and kept it neat, bare threads showing in places where the linen had worn into spots much washed and brushed. The yarn mittens laid across her knees were of the same blue as her leggings. The mittens narrowed long at the wrists; with the pair before these she had chapped wrists. Her cowhide overcoat she had draped over the chair before seating herself; many years of scuffing had in spots worn the hair off outside; summer insects and winter mice had eaten a few small holes; she had sewed the inner lining herself and kept it neatly patched; it hung baggy and warm on her; she still called this overcoat "Molly" after the cow she had milked for years and she didn't dare go help at the slaughtering because Molly was dear to her. Her wool-yarn hood was the same blue as leggings and mittens.

Around her neck hung in folds a noble white kerchief a yard square, of mixed silk, fringed, a Christmas present from her husband the year they had done so well with their sheep, some sixteen years back, when he had returned from driving the sheep to Philadelphia and for months until Christmas hid from her, hid in a basket of sweet corn in the garret, this kerchief. Sweeping curves at her hips and bosom, rounded with large breasts, a powerful torso, a woman off the land and at home on the land, her fingers having know-how in them, her hands saying they could take hold, a half-inch white scar on a middle finger, the knuckles gnarled, the fingernails rough and clean, the little fingernail gone. Her placid moon-face had the calm of cows amid late summer grass freshened by showers though her slow blinking eyes lurked with sagacity and devices far beyond the bovine.

Most of this Winshore gathered as his eyes moved from her feet to her face. "Elegant she is," he said to himself, "if the same can be said of new-mown hay and the smell of well-kept barns and kitchens. Her little mouth was once to some man a rich red cherry. She has changed thousands of diapers and washed them all herself with less than six regrets. Those hands can tell the exact instant in churning to dip out the butter chunks and pour off the buttermilk. She seldom fails to be in the family church pew on time on the Lord's Day. She believes most of what the preacher says and has heard him enough years so she catches him often repeating. With each lambing season, tending stricken ewes and unborn lambs, she has spoken her own little sermons to them. I would surmise she makes harsh judgments and then reverses them or forgets them."

In quick roving glances at him she had been measuring him, first for a man of good moral character, then for a lazy sloven, perhaps a hard drinker and gambler, then again perhaps a good enough man who could be terribly stubborn. She hoped it was the last. She was stubborn herself, "born stubborn and growing stubborner year by year," as she admitted to her husband. Her mother's grandfather had fought under Oliver Cromwell, an Old Ironsides man, a last-ditch no-compromise Puritan, of the faction that called for the head of King Charles till they got it. Of her eight children five had lived and her three living sons were in practice at shooting and marching, making ready for war when it should come, the youngest wailing and in tears because the father said he must stay at home to work the farm. To her the war, when it came, would be right and just. For her the time had passed for any longer begging their rights from the British King and his ministers: they must fight and for a union of colonies, a free and independent nation. Her husband agreed, with doubts the war would cost hard and might run long. She swept away doubts with "Better death than shame and ever more shame." The oldest boy told her, but not the father, of three days away once to erect a Liberty Pole in Elizabethtown, of joining a mob that forced a man on his knees to sign a paper favoring the colonies and against the Crown and still another mob that broke the windows and wrecked the store of a Tory merchant.

Such particulars, of course, Winshore could not read in the woman's placid face as her gnarled fingers folded over the blue mittens on her knees. He could only guess she would stand suffering and be long stubborn for a belief she could put in words few and plain.

Next to the farm woman sat two young women with the bloom off. Their green silk stockings glimmering between skirt bottom and overshoe top showed crude darning repairs. Their organdie gowns, trimmed with lace and black velvet, had seen better days, needed cleaning and ironing. On lace below the chin one had a grease spot, the other on her left sleeve finger daubs of rouge. The heavier one had gray shifting eyes and a bold plump sagging face. She dozed, her head slimpsing down and sidewise. Her breathing hoarse and near to a snore, she awoke with a jerk, crossed her knees that had swayed apart as she slept, smiled to the thin brunette leaning a head against her arm, brought from a small handbag a small bottle of rum. They took a swig each, brightened and looked around the room. The slight one had a starved look. Her face and body needed filling out. Her large black eyes drooped and her full lips hung slack. Tipsy at midnight she would go so far as to say to those drinking with her, "Men, money, and drink, that's all I want," and only to herself or her friend the next morning, "Christ, I'm tired of men and drink!"

"Not yet whores, perhaps," said Winshore to himself. "Birds of twilight, doves of a soiled midnight purple, forgotten daughters at the beck of forgotten men who need them and pay them, requisite tavern ornaments that ever take on more tarnish unless for the miracle that seldom comes."

Winshore pictured homes they could have run away from, work from daybreak and into the night, lusty men young and not so young, snug haymows in the winter, woodlands by summer moonlight, and in any neighborhood the complicated terrors of what was termed "a bastard child" or in courts of law "a bastardy case." The thin girl with her large black eyelids folded down in sleep, her mother might be saying, "She liked all the men and she was good to all of them and you can't say she didn't have good times." Such mothers and such daughters Winshore had known. "What they are is their personal secret and none of my business," he said. "Slammerkins I will call them, a slammerkin being a woman who doesn't know how to take care of herself, near to a slattern and kin to a strumpet."

What wind blew them into Philadelphia and was blowing them out Winshore would like to know. He saw them brightening toward a sailor in flapping wide-bottomed trousers and a thick pea jacket roomy on his bean-pole frame, a youth long-nosed, hawk-eyed, restless, smiling. He had sat for a time with a parrot on his left shoulder, a monkey in his lap. Then he tied the leash thong of the monkey to the chair and slowly strolled the room, the monkey on squirming haunches watching him. The slammerkins caught the sailor's eyes. The thin girl dropped her eyes. The blowzy blonde gave him a beckoning smile, then decided to doze. It was nearer bedtime for them than their noon or afternoon rising hour. Still, the sailor looked good to them with his reckless eyes and his voyage pay on him. The blonde managed one more glance at him before sinking into a doze with her mouth falling open, her breathing near to a snore, her knees slowly swaying apart, her left arm a soft pillow for her shut-eyed companion whose underlip thrust out in a grimace that could mean "Pity me and lemme sleep."

They slept and the farm woman sat serene, her hands on the blue mittens at her knees. She could help, if needed, her face said. Her look now, fancied Winshore, was the same as if she waited in a straw-bedded barn corner with a labor-pained ewe for the arrival of an unborn lamb.

Regularly all eyes in the room returned to the two figures at the door, standing ready for the stage. Greatcoats over their arms they stood impressive, even dazzling, in the full uniform of His Majesty's military establishment, first lieutenants in the Grenadiers. Well-mannered, correct, grave, men informed and thorough as to regulations, their particular missions, their personal responsibilities. The scarlet of their long-tailed coats, the bright gilt buttons in a double row down the front, the white breeches stuffed in glossy black leather boots to their knees, the wide white belt with its glittering square brass buckle—the two officers and their outfits dominated the room. Before arriving at New York Winshore would know them for brothers. One more lean and subtle-looking than the other, Lieutenant George Frame, after eight months' duty at the closed port of Boston, had joined his brother Francis on missions in Virginia and Philadelphia. Now they were traveling to the port of Boston to report to their commander General Thomas Gage. Fair-skinned, with clear blue eyes, light-brown hair neatly trimmed, straight noses, George Frame's face made a fine oval and Francis' a moonlike disk. "They represent authority," Winshore murmured to himself, "authority—with guns."

The stout woman in a chair next to the farm wife wore a smooth face, framed in a yarn hood she had knitted herself, as also three gray wool shawls in her lap, two for her shoulders, one to tuck around her knees, ready for this cold windy weather coming after the warm spell and thaw of last week. Slow to answer when spoken to she would likely shout her words as in conversation with her very deaf husband. Parting in their Philadelphia home he had warned in a soft even monotone, "Don't say anything against the King," and her shout at the top of her voice, "I won't say anything against anybody," brought a smiling nod of agreement from him before kissing her good-by.

She had eyes for no fellow passengers except the two officers of the Crown. This was her first real look at such men in such clothes. She sewed her own clothes and naturally puzzled over who had cut the patterns and plied the needles over the seams of their long scarlet coats and the white broadcloth breeches. She counted the gilt buttons on one coat, counted those on the other to see if they made the same number. She tried figuring how long it took them to dress and whether it bothered them they must put on these clothes every day and keep them spick-and-span. The belt at the middle of each officer had a special interest for her. She was sure her husband could make as good belts or better. He was a harness-maker and took pride in his bellybands. At first the two officers in their glittering array seemed more than human to her. Rather they stood as an institution. They betokened the guns, drums and marching might of the British Army Regulars with famous annals past and present. She went on studying them. It came over her they were not much more than a couple of naked, two-legged men wearing grand clothes for a special purpose. She thought of her husband's warning and assured herself, "While they are about there is no danger of my saying anything against the King."

In the chair next to her sat a lean man, pale as ashes, his body a bone-rack with skin pulled over it, his thin pursed lips seeming ready to speak to the sailor's monkey in the next chair. The monkey regularly screwed its head around so far it seemed about to fall off, twisting its neck to where its inquisitive face and eyes blinked and flashed straight up as though some nut or knickknack might drop from the thin pursed lips of the ashen-pale face. The pale man had a story of love with no wedding to tell Winshore before they got to Trenton. He turned his gaze off and on the furiously busy monkey as it scratched its buttocks and dug its paws into ribs and armpits. On his bench in the stage he would sit next the two British officers.

The driver in a quiet positive way had told off each passenger a seat. Of medium build, well-knit, measured and easy in his motions, the driver sometimes mentioned confidentially, "I think I know horses and men, but I don't claim to know women." To the banker and two merchants who owned the stage line he had pledged, "You'll hear of me beatin the horses only in a bad pinch. If I lash any horse it's desperate and I hate to do it. I'll never drink till off duty and then I won't get drunk. I'll try for no swearin. When I give horse or passenger profanity it'll be they have it comin."

The seat at the driver's right elbow went to a man six feet in height, long-legged and long-armed, overdressed, with a face "handsome at first sight and then it gets monotonous," said Winshore, who sized him up as more surface than content. "He would like to be reckoned bright as a whip and slick as a silver-belly eel." Later on the stage Winshore would find what his guess was worth, as to this long-legged lawyer.

At the lawyer's elbow would sit the odd number who on stepping through the door had stood wary and searched every face in the room, not with mere passing curiosity. Spare of build, well-muscled, he slouched with a smooth grace to his chair and sat in it. His swift light-gray eyes, under bushy eyebrows and long thick forehead bangs, seemed to take in faces, voices, atmosphere. He had asked the driver to give him a seat farther back as he had a bad cold, the driver saying he had come last and there could be no change. From the velvet wool-lined cap on his head he occasionally pressed down the rich brown bangs of hair that came nearly below his bushy eyebrows. His eyes had met those of the blonde slammerkin and he had winked at her. He was young too, and pinched, hard-worn. The only face to give him worry was Winshore who guessed, "He shies from light on his face, more anxious to start riding than anybody else in the room." His eyes flicked toward Winshore and flicked away.

"Cold ridin it'll be," called the driver. "Wrap warm if you can. We'll go now—step out, please." He had put their baggage under their benches. They were carrying wraps, shawls, blankets, and small bags or bundles to be held in their laps for journey requisites.

Outside the morning star Venus still glimmered faintly in the daybreak twilight near six o'clock of the morning. A cold wind swept the yard. The horses wanted to go, for the going would warm them. A champing sorrel brought the shoe of a forefoot down on the cobblestones, striking sparks. The driver helped the women put feet on the hub of the front wheel and step up into the wagon box. The ashen-pale man slipped on the hub and fell snugly into the arms of the watchful driver and on the second attempt made it nicely.

"All ready?" called the driver. "Here we go!" And he cracked his whip in the air, spoke to the horses sharply but with affection as between old acquaintances. And the New York-bound stage wagon moved out of the courtyard of John Biddle's tavern, swung into Market Street and headed toward the city limits and the open road, open and in spots rough.

* * * * * * * * *

Chapter 2

* * * * * * * * *

Frozen Roads and Tavern Fights

ALONG the cobblestoned city streets and a stretch of road topped with gravel, the riding went smooth. As the open front end of the stage wagon headed north and east, the full force of a driving cold wind swept in. The travelers on the front benches bent their heads and snuggled their faces deeper in shawls, scarfs, kerchiefs. Those seated back of the first benches could see little or nothing of the road, the sky, the land and country. The heavy curtains, leather wadded with wool, rolled down tightly at the sides, made a protection they were thankful for. From time to time they readjusted shawls, blankets, wraps at their shoulders and knees.

Winshore half-dozed as they rattled out of the city on smooth gravel. He took a long yawn of honest comfort. The yawn reached his toes snug in wool stockings under leather, copper-buckled shoes fitted in well-buttoned fur overshoes. He covered his mouth with a mittened hand; those at his elbows and any others could understand it was a personal affair and he couldn't help it was so public a yawn. He had missed sleep, packing bag and bundle till past midnight. In the smooth riding he drowsed, a vague murmuring in his head, "Faces —who wants to live without seeing faces? Your face yours, my face mine, Time brought them. And Time laughed to each of us and said, 'Here's yours—now go see what you can do with it.'"

His drowsing reverie, a yawn he had begun, stopped short. They had come to a frozen mudhole of ruts and bumps. A thaw of the week before softened the mud to where horses sank to their knees and wheels went two feet deep. Then the freezing days hardened the

341

mud as it lay. The driver called his horses by name, flicked them easy with his whip as they tried to dig their feet in and pull, as they slipped and slid and finally hauled the stage wagon over forty yards of humps and bumps that had the passengers lurching against each other and certainly getting familiar as fellow travelers. In the jolts and careenings Winshore at one moment found on his shoulder the head of the good woman with the deaf husband and with the next twist his head was on her bosom and from the right the sailor's head tumbled on his shoulder, the monkey was flung into his lap and the parrot from mid-air landed on the shoulder of a British officer, startling one and all with its raucous cry, "Caw crack caw crack kill him kill him." Then the sailor deftly removed the parrot to a section of the shawl in his lap.

Three times in this frozen mudhole the driver rested his horses. He hoped the harness would hold. Waiting for the puffing animals to get breath he talked as though it might be to the horses and if the passengers cared to listen, well and good. "A year ago this same place two tugs broke and we lost an hour splicin 'em. Froze hard like today she's bad but last week she was worse. The horses went knee-deep in mud, wheels in mud to the hubs. I gave the horses the whip. They couldn't pull her out. I asked the ladies and gentlemen to please get out and lighten the load and maybe the horses could pull her out. And would you believe it? What did they tell me? They had paid their fares. They had laid their cash payments down, six cents a mile, and were entitled to their seats. I told 'em they was right, they was correct, and they could have their seats and I wouldn't trouble 'em. I got out on the front wheel, jumped to the roadside and sat in the grass enjoyin the sun and the February thaw weather. The sky was blue. The sun came down warm. It was nice. I liked it. A little bird came along, an early spring bird, twitterin for my special benefit. It was pleasant. After a while the passengers began pokin their heads out front to see what I was doin. They told each other I was doin nothin, just sittin in the sun and listenin to an early bird. They poked their heads out front again and asked me what was I doin there and when would they begin ridin. I told 'em, 'The horses can't pull the load. It's too heavy. They might pull a lighter load— I don't know. Only one thing I see to do. *I'm goin to wait here till the mud dries up.*' Then they got common sense, horse sense, you might say. They climbed out. For the two ladies it wasn't so easy a jump off the front wheel to clear the mud and reach the roadside. But they did it. And I got pesky muddy climbin back to my seat. Well, those horses pulled her right out and fifty yards up the road they all got aboard happy as larks and we drove right on."

The road ran bumpy with misery, comfort, misery again. On bumps and hollows of frozen mud ran the road, successions of low bumps the wheels took in a regular timing, then a series of humps no two alike, often the front wheels tussling an upgrade hump as the hind wheels slid a downgrade so the driver's seat slanted a foot or two higher than the rear seat and the wheels snarled to the axles and the axles groaned to the wagon box and the wagon box mocked at the harness tugs and the tugs cried to the horses and driver, "Another hump like the last one and we go bust." Stretches of gravel and mire frozen smooth came. But mostly it was rough traveling. Those new to it found it more than they expected. The lawyer rubbed hip and buttock and spoke to the driver, "Rough on your bones." The driver chuckled, "I'm used to it. I got calluses where I sit."

One ten-yard mudhole came after a quarter-mile of fairly smooth riding with the horses on a slow trot. Then the wheels struck a line of humps. They hoisted wheels and wagon box off the ground into the air, sent the passengers up and off their seats to come down with a jolt and a tingle along spine to skull.

They rode smooth again. The sailor turned to the slammerkins back of him and grinned. "I been over it before. I knew it was time for that spot. Stormy weather—hey?"

They could see a bright sunshine pouring down on the lead horses on the road ahead. They glimpsed one-horse market carts taking milk, butter, farm produce to Philadelphia. They heard the driver muttering as he gave more than half the road to a slow ox team and a heavy cart holding four swine. They glimpsed a farmer afoot leading a cow and some guessed he had bought her to take home or he had decided to sell her and was leading her to Philadelphia. The guesses over, the sailor leaned to Winshore and whispered, "And maybe he's takin her to a bull."

At one rough piece of road the driver rested his horses. A skittish young bay shied from a farmer with two white geese flapping and hissing under his arms. "Now I got 'em, damn 'em," he cursed earnestly. The last two fowl had knocked his cap off and torn loose his red winding woolen scarf that blew in the wind like a banner.

To his one-horse cart the farmer slid and bounced with the runaway geese, pushed and squeezed them into a wicker basket, roped tight the wicker lids, and stood getting his breath. The lids had jolted loose of the ropes, the geese scrambling out and he was an hour in a windy field rounding up six white geese for the Philadelphia market.

Some five miles they had come, pleased one by one to step down over the front wheel and into a Frankfort tavern for breakfast near eight o'clock. A hostler helped the driver unhitch, stall, water, and feed the horses. The driver went in and handed the tavern-keeper several letters, saying of one, "Official and important."

In the big main room, near a fireplace with crackling logs, stood a table with breakfast waiting—heaps of hot corncakes, dishes of steaming corn mush with pitchers of fresh milk, codfish cakes, fried salt

343

pork, applesauce. The tavern-keeper, his wife and a maid, saw to it when empty dishes needed filling. The ride and the weather had sharpened hunger and travelers kept busy eating except for a few remarks brief as the sailor in starting to eat, low-toned to Winshore, "I could eat a raw cat." Winshore was going to answer, "My belly button is pressing against my backbone," and then let it pass. The ashen-pale man with the pursed lips picked lightly at his food and the driver said to himself, "Too bad, the ride was rough, he's off his feed."

The keeper's wife pointed to a large pitcher of cider to be passed round. Beer and ale could be ordered from the bar. A pot of coffee soon was coming. One of the British officers spoke for the two of them, "Could we order a pot of tea, if you would be so kind, on this cold morning?"

A bright look and lifted eyebrows came over the tavern-keeper's face: "We used to have tea here and it was always good tea that we served here but I am very sorry to inform you that at the present we have no supply of tea in the house, otherwise we should be pleased to serve it to you in any style you might indicate. When you should be traveling this way again it may be that we shall have on hand a supply of tea and meet your request. It is our aim and purpose to please our patrons."

Winshore during this reply munched a hot corncake thick-spread with butter. His eyes roved from face to face and when he had finished he said to himself, "Now I know who is Tory, Whig, half-and-half, don't care. Sarcasm and irony were there in the tavern-keeper's words and voice yet sheathed in good manners and a rather genuine tone of cordiality. He did truly wish that tea was not an issue and that he could serve it."

The spare-built young man, who could slouch with grace and ease, ate fast. While eating he dropped knife or spoon to press down the bangs of rich brown hair that came to his bushy eyebrows. Near his end of the table and next to a window two men had drawn chairs to a card table and begun a game. Between shuffling the deck, dealing and playing, they kept their eyes on this eating table, ranging from face to face. The young man with the distinctive brown hair down his forehead seemed to have finished, wouldn't wait for his coffee, stood up from his chair and turned to be leaving.

The two card-players rose. One of them stepped directly in front of the young fellow, the other to his side. The one facing him, "Your name is Henry Spoor of Chester County, Pennsylvania?"

"No," came an easy cool reply, "I am Edward Winters, a farmer out from Trenton."

"Would you swear to that?"

"On a stack of Bibles."

"You swear to that?"

"Why, of course."

As he said this the man at his side brought a swift hand up to his forehead and lifted the rich brown locks of hair. The full white forehead showed. Midway between bushy eyebrows and hair roots stood out two misshapen, plain, terrible letters—a brand—the letters once seared there with a hot iron—the letters H. T.

"You're a horse thief and we're taking you."

The constable saying this was hot as a stove lid but thought he looked cool as the ice sheet in a watering trough. He and the other constable expected they could handle their man. They hadn't counted on what came. Their man under arrest threw a swift and terrific uppercut to the jaw of the constable facing him who toppled and fell to the floor crumpled, cold, his white face twitching.

The other constable gave a hoarse low cry, "Brass knucks—the sonofabitch!" and made a wild leap, ending with his arms around the knees of the horse thief who had nearly reached the doorway. They were tangled in swift fury on the floor. The horse thief lay with his left arm pinned down. His right arm drew its hand out, from somewhere in his clothes, with a long knife. The other constable lay motionless, still crumpled and cold. Nearly everyone in the room stood scared, helpless and fixed. It had all happened in a few seconds. And the knife was raised and moving.

Winshore snapped out of his daze, made a fast calculation, took one spring forward and sent a kick into the horse thief's arm that nearly broke it. The knife flew up against a wall and fell to the floor.

When a little later the other constable came to, they took their prisoner to the tavern office where Henry Spoor sat in a chair handcuffed ready to go with the constables on the afternoon stage for Philadelphia and on to the Chester County jail where he had broken loose after his third conviction for horse-stealing. On his second conviction they had bound him fast and with a hot iron pressed on his forehead the letter H for horse and the letter T for thief. The envelope "official and important" from Philadelphia authorities had informed the constables to watch for a young fellow who would take strict care to keep his forehead covered.

"Staying with us?" the tavern-keeper's wife in a mild voice asked the woman with three gray shawls and the very deaf husband.

"No," the reply boomed loud. "I'm walking four miles out to my sister's. Her husband is a Patriot away for a week to the Committee of Observation and Prevention."

The stage wagon pulled out of Frankfort and the ashen-pale man sat at the left of Winshore. Up front with the driver a gaunt figure had smiling eyes. Even when his thin lips pulled down, a smile of some sort would be there in his eyes.

"Hiram Kester, you old hound dog, where you been since I saw you last?" had been the driver's greeting. He saw Kester two or three times a year, in from a cabin and family forty miles off in a hill wilderness, bringing in pelts and furs, buying supplies. Kester had shot the coon from which his coonskin cap was made, he had shot the buck and tanned the skin and helped his wife sew and fringe his buckskin shirt. He had killed the deer and tanned the hide and himself made the deerskin moccasins he wore and the same with the heavy fur leggings. He had shot the bear whose skin went into the greatcoat keeping him warm in all weathers. Repairs on his long firelock rifle and fresh supplies for his powder horn he had seen to in Philadelphia. He farmed a little, hunted and trapped more, his blood thirsted for independence and two years ago he had told the driver, "Any time I hear my neighbor's gunshot I'm goin to move further west."

"He's the wilderness, this Hiram Kester," murmured Winshore. "I doubt whether he can be tamed. If they do tame him they can't keep him tamed." He had seen Hiram Kester step up to the British officers and sort of talk to them like a father or an uncle. "You have my prayers, boys. We sure hope it won't come to shootin. If you'll go on travelin you'll find onhandy men in these colonies. To put down these people it'll take you a long time. Give them independence. Else they'll be goin to take it. You can't stop 'em."

Hiram Kester was a new figure to the officers, a piece of America they had never seen face to face. They returned the smile of his eyes, one saying, "We admire your plain speech. We thank you for your prayers. Time will tell whether you are correct."

"Out there," said Hiram Kester with a wave of his hand toward the Western wilderness, "out there you can find men stubborn as rocks and tough as tanglewood. They'll fight to the last against a government they got no part in. You can kill 'em or you can drive 'em further west, but you can't make 'em crawl, creep, cringe and submit."

He was saying this on the veranda of the tavern, his moccasins, coonskin cap and great shapeless coat of bearskin giving him a shaggy, earthy, mystic look. The British officers nodded to his smiling eyes and withheld any reply to the open menace of his words and the twisted turndown of his thin firm lips.

When he left the stage at Bristol that afternoon Winshore murmured to himself, "Good-by, we're sorry to be losing you, Old Wilderness. When the shooting begins we know where you'll be."

Strength and cheer from the hearty breakfast at Frankfort was needed for the fifteen-mile ride on to Bristol. There were nice smooth stretches of road when they could sit easy and talk or doze. And other times the holes and ruts seemed to get deeper and the bumps higher. The haul came hard on the horses, said the driver. "They'll be give out when we get to Bristol, if the harness holds or we don't get a broken wheel."

In one hard row of bumps the driver pulled in his horses. They

346

stopped and he talked quiet to them. Then he sat silent and the horses stood there on a lonely road with woods on the left and a long plain at the right with the cold northeast wind driving across it and sweeping its chill and fury through the front of the stage wagon. The minutes passed. One of the weary slammerkins touched a hand to the shoulder of the sailor, "Ask him what we're waiting for."

The driver heard. "These animals havin a rest spell, lady." Near the end of that particular stretch of ruts and bumps the wheels settled so deep they were stuck. The driver tried coaxing the nags, swore at a sorrel and lashed it, "Don't lay down on us here." The sorrel joined the others and gave the best it had. The driver called, "whoap" to the six horses and gave them a rest. He faced his passengers. Everybody would have to get out to lighten the load. If the men would put their shoulders to the rear wheels and the wagon box, "We might pull her out. Even then mebbe we're stuck."

Out they scrambled, one by one, over the front wheel and onto the ground. They all found places to throw their weight, except the blue-lipped, shivering slammerkins, who plainly had not brought along enough warm clothing. The farm wife smiled to Winshore as they threw their shoulders to the end of the wagon box at the word from the driver. The driver cried at the top of his voice to the horses, everyone hauled and heaved and slowly the front wheels climbed a little perpendicular of frozen mud that was ten inches rut and ten inches hump. On went the wagon across some twenty yards of this frozen mudhole and stopped. One by one they climbed over the front wheel, stepped over the benches, and found their packs, hand-bags, bundles, wraps, and again were traveling.

"You did pretty good, brother, mighty good," said Winshore to the ashen-pale man at his left. They got to talking. The man had misery to mention. Into the strangely comic yet solemn face of Winshore at his right he felt a comfort about reciting his misery. A smile flickered over his lips as he said once to Winshore, "Telling it to you is like telling it to a horse." He had come to Philadelphia to be married to a young woman and she and her father and mother had one and all told him there must be no wedding and he must leave their house and from then on must not be known as a friend or a speaking acquaintance of the family. "I can't get over it. The jolting of this stage wagon is pleasant after the jolting they gave me."

David Wardrobe his name, he had been teaching a school in the vestry house of Cople Parish in Westmoreland County, Virginia. On the night of June 30, 1774, he sat down and wrote a long letter to Archibald Provan of Glasgow, Scotland. Then the *Glasgow Journal*, August 18, 1774, published the letter, and on November 8, 1774, the Committee for the County of Westmoreland, representing the Continental Congress that had met in Philadelphia in September of 1774, called Wardrobe before them and asked him why he had written a letter false, scandalous, and inimical to America, a mischievous report intended to misrepresent the colonies and to deceive the people of Great Britain. He admitted writing the greater part of the said letter and concerning the rest of it, ran the Committee's statement, he "equivocated." So the Committee passed resolves that the said Wardrobe could no longer keep a school in the vestry house, "that all persons who have sent their children to school to the said Wardrobe do immediately take them away, and that he be regarded as a wicked enemy to America and be treated as such, and furthermore, that the said Wardrobe do forthwith write and publish a letter in Virginia newspapers, expressing to the world his remorse for having traduced the people here."

The Committee summoned Wardrobe to a later meeting. Instead of appearing, he sent them a letter they took as insulting. In a few days he had lost his schoolroom, pupils, income, respectable standing in the community. So he went to the Westmoreland County courthouse and before a large crowd humbled himself, wept tears of sorrow and repentance, signed a paper that he was "deeply affected with remorse for having traduced the good people of Virginia." And though he had groveled in the dust before them, he found a good name and place he had enjoyed were gone. He journeyed to Philadelphia to find full reports, highly colored, sent on to the bride he was to have taken for a spouse through life. Shocked he was to find they regarded him unclean and an outcast.

David Wardrobe told this in the stage in March of 1775 as though it was an old story and might have happened a thousand years ago in Mesopotamia. Now he would travel to Bristol, cross the river to Burlington, stay for a time with an uncle and try to open another school somewhere. "I can't tell my uncle what happened. He is neither Whig nor Tory, not sure what he is, like many others. If he leans to one side or the other, he won't say so, he won't let it be known, like many others. He would rage at me for writing a letter and putting my opinions in black and white on paper."

Wardrobe and Winshore were half in each other's laps over a piece of rough road. They rode into smoother going and David Wardrobe gave afterthoughts. "I could curse that young woman in Philadelphia. She led me on and betrayed me. We were betrothed as solemn as ever a man and woman." Here Winshore felt the story needed more about the young woman: she might naturally have changed her mind about marrying him if she could have met a handsomer younger man. Wardrobe told more of it as it seemed to him or as he wished it to seem to others. "Two years ago her father was Loyalist. Today he is a Rebel and she must forthwith be a Rebel too and they jointly cast me out." Wardrobe had one further and final afterthought: "If I had kept that letter and burned it instead of sending it to my friend Archibald Provan in Glasgow or if he had burned it or kept it secret, think where I would be now. I would be married into one of the best families in Philadelphia."

Winshore leaned against Wardrobe and in a sleepy tone of many bees murmuring, "Do you know what I shall remember longest out of the whole of this fascinating incident?" It would interest David Wardrobe to know and he heard, "That was where you said telling it to me was like telling it to a horse. I won't forget that, brother."

They arrived at Bristol, saw the wide majestic Delaware River and a glimpse of Burlington Village on the other side. They pitched into a pot roast of beef, boiled potatoes and gravy, carrots and peas, hot bread with helpings from deep dishes of butter, apple pie and as many cups of coffee as wanted. With changed horses they were bumping along toward Trenton in a half-hour.

Next to the driver sat a farmer with a three-weeks-old lamb in his lap. He covered it with a ragged old coat where it snuggled warm against the cold wind. Next to him a "bound boy," sixteen years old, was returning from a visit with his sister, a "bound girl" in service at Bristol. "He's proved up as a good worker," the farmer told the driver. "I'm going to be needin him when my own two boys go into the fightin to come." Next to the bound boy sat a thin furtive shivering Negro boy of fourteen. "Fellow farmin out from Bristol bought one for himself in Philadelphia, bought this one for a neighbor of mine. I'm takin him to his new home." Help would be more scarce on the farms with the younger men going to the war, the farmer expected. His own two boys in their early twenties, he couldn't figure 'em out. They knew their father's two year record of hard fighting and marching, with two wounds, in the French and Indian War. "I sometimes think they want to fight just for the sake of fightin. They're for Independence of course but they would like some fightin. Their older brother, married, got a farm of his own, he tells 'em they're damn fools to go to war, a heap of misery with nothin to pay for it when the shootin's over."

The wind drove roaring and slapping through the wagon front. The farmer to make sure the driver could hear him had spoken in a high shrill carrying voice. The British officers in the next seat behind caught every word, turned their faces toward each other with nods, as though, "Precisely how should this be reported to our commanding officer at Boston?" The long-legged lawyer, too, was all ears and permitted himself a smile as though "The American yeomanry, my good companions, has fighting quality of which you are yet to be informed."

A quarter-mile of bad ruts and bumps. Twice the driver rested his horses. Here in a deep mud of early December, he had lost two hours fixing harness breaks.

Then smoother riding. Winshore heard the two slammerkins passing a bottle of rum they bought in the Bristol tavern, heard them offering the sailor a drink he laughed off, "I've got my Philadelphia headache yet—no kill-devil till New York." The rum, it seemed, warmed them and made them very sociable, very conversational. They asked the sailor where he got the monkey, where he got the parrot, could the parrot talk more than one language, what tricks did the monkey have, and they must have names, so what were their names and what ship had he sailed on and had he seen any women in South America and if so were they nice to him and how did he like them? His ship was the *Hanshaw*, the cargo coffee and fruit, the name of the parrot Esmeralda, the name of the monkey Sir Jocko and he had met polite accommodating dark-skinned women that were all a man could ask and he had met others "as soon kill you as look at you for a gold piece." The slammerkins spoke in smoother voices. He was less an innocent, less a stranger to them, he might have known some of their own loneliness and desperation. Their voices caressed him just a little as they told their admiration of the way he took care of Esmeralda and Sir Jocko, of the way he mentioned his mother and a sweetheart waiting for him in his home village on Long Island. He felt a blithe charm about their asking him what was the most interesting day he had ever had as a sailor. He smiled, "Let me think," and rode in silence a minute or two. Then he told of the day leaving a South American port, directly homebound. And his best shipmate came up the gangplank in a zigzag walk, teetering with rum and brandy, on his shoulder a sack of bottles, a lot of rare old rum to take home. As he staggered and lurched to make the last step of the gangplank, the sack of bottles slid loose from his shoulder and dropped to the water below and sank. "You should have seen the look on his face." Then up the gangplank came the second mate fairly sober, carrying his liquor nice enough. In his arms was a bundle. He unwraps it for the captain. And what does the captain see before his eyes? A bright chunk of a six-months Negro baby. And the second mate laughing, "What do you think of that for one gold piece, one English pound?" He had been out over the town and had bought a Negro infant child for five dollars and thought it smart. "The captain puts the baby in my arms, orders another fellow to go with me into the town and give the baby back to its mother. We located the mother. She was glad to have her baby back and hug it. And would she tell us who was the sonofabitch that stole it and sold it? Nah!"

A man in clerical garb, at Bristol seated at the left of Winshore, heard Winshore, "We have worldly companions."

"Indeed."

"Buying a Negro baby for five dollars—you believe that?"

"Could well be. They sell them grown and half-grown every day in Philadelphia, sales advertised every week."

"You are a clergyman, sir?"

"Yes, sir."

"Might I ask you," and Winshore rather tender and appealing in this, "what would Christ do if he came to Philadelphia?"

350

"A rather extraordinary question on a stage wagon."

"In an extremity of humiliation Jesus rode on the back of an ass and without a doubt could endure this stage wagon over frozen roads. It is a relevant question. What would Christ do if he came to Philadelphia now today?"

"You are really asking a political question that includes spiritual issues."

"I think I know your meaning: If Christ came to Philadelphia now today would he be Tory or Whig, would he call himself Loyalist or Patriot?"

"In his own time Jesus was a rebel," said the clergyman. "If it were conceivable that this afternoon he should enter the City of Philadelphia, we might picture him standing in the market place and speaking a majestic scorn and irony. Woe unto ye scribes and Pharisees, ye rulers and governors, whose oppression is bringing a war on this people. Woe unto ye who have brought on this people the Stamp Act, the tea tax, the Boston Massacre, the closing of the port of Boston with warships and an army pointing their guns and threats at a people crying for liberty. Woe unto ye who are now provoking violence, for ye shall in due time come to awful punishment for your arrogance and greed."

This had come from his lips in a low intense whisper. Then he seemed to realize he had gone far and decided to go farther, "I have been dismissed as assistant pastor of one of the largest and richest congregations in Philadelphia. A committee of inquiry was put upon me. They reported my private opinions and public sermons as being continuously more colored with seditious doctrine. They resented my continuous use of the word 'combustibles.'"

"Combustibles?"

"Yes, you know, combustibles."

"Dry wood, dry grass or leaves, dry stuff a stray spark can set roaring into a conflagration?"

"Precisely—a conflagration. Terrible wildfire action is to come. The combustibles are at hand. The spark waits. From what wind we know not. But it will come."

A face somewhat drawn and ascetic the cleric had, a man of much solitude whose decisions arrived at in solitude gave unrest and fear of him to others never alone enough to arrive at definitely personal decisions in the area of spiritual issues. "I am no extremist, sir," his low whispering went on as his right shoulder pressed more closely that of his companion. "Edmund Burke in the British House of Commons or William Pitt, the Earl of Chatham, in the British House of Lords, have mentioned combustibles and spoken of explosions to come and given their solemn warnings that the American people must have the full rights of British subjects or there will be endless revolts and never-ending passive resistance. And coming back to your question I believe if

Christ came to Philadelphia today he would say what Burke and Pitt have been saying in the British Parliament."

"I am inclined to think," Winshore ventured softly and in a tone just low enough so that it would not trouble the ears of the British officers, "that if Christ came to New York he would visit the statue of Pitt before going to see that of King George III."

"We are agreed," came the cleric's reply as the stage wagon began tilting to the left and they wondered if they were going to be spilled out. The driver's clear cry came sharp to all of them, "Lean to the right! Lean to the right!" As the stage wagon again came to the level road the cleric leaned closer than ever at his companion's shoulder and, "It is a rather remarkable conversation we have had on this winter day in this odd vehicle. I have been completely confidential with you on matters I feel deeply. Do you know—" and his face screwed into a curious smile as though it had not known for some time the refreshment of any easy smile—"when I was a boy on a farm in Virginia I rode a bay horse with a roan face—or you might say he was a bay horse with a sandy-complexioned face sprinkled with salt—and I could tell that horse anything solemn or foolish in my mind. And I hope you will pardon me, sir, but you remind me of that horse." He had changed from whispering into a rather loud-spoken tone of voice as the stage wagon tussled into rougher road and the rattling of wheels and wagon box made a louder tone necessary, if he was to be heard. The heavy rattling ended as they came to smoother roadway, catching him unaware as he was saying in a tone that could be heard all over the stage wagon, "I could tell you are no king-kisser."

The two British officers turned and gave the cleric full in the face the benefit of stern glances to let him know that he had been heard in this very peculiar declaration that might yet require inquiry. The long-legged lawyer at the officer's left also turned and beamed with a light of recognition as though he had found a friend and a compatriot. Even the driver turned his eyes from the road and his six horses to twist his face around and award a large grin to the clergyman who had so clearly published himself as not belonging to the "king-kissers."

They could see the road ahead darkening. Twilight came on. They could barely make out six horsemen in British uniforms, riding in pairs. They could hear through the heavy rolled-down curtains the hoofbeats of the little squad of six horses.

"Couriers of His Majesty the King," came a voice as though the six horsemen were important.

"Couriers of His Majesty the King—haw! haw! haw!" came another voice from somewhere in the stage wagon, as though the six horsemen might not be so important after all, everything considered.

Silence now in the stage wagon as darkness enveloped the road. Little by little it was not darkness but a night of clear stars. The nearest faces vague in the wagon, there was a loneliness about riding now.

Each felt farther away from the other, unless they had pressed and huddled closer as did the cleric to Winshore, as did the Negro boy to the bound boy, as did the British officers to each other, as did the slammerkins who could be heard passing their rum bottle and who at last had coaxed the sailor to take, "for luck," one swig of rum. At one jolting place the parrot came loose from its wraps and until put back meditated for the benefit of all listening, "Caw crack, caw crack, damn your guts, damn your guts."

Once on the starlit road the wagon began tilting, more and more tilting, and they wondered if they were to be spilled out when the driver's keen shouts came, "Lean to the left! Lean to the left!"

By daylight, and then by starlight, they had been riding since daybreak over Pennsylvania. Now they had come to the Delaware River ferry for crossing over the New Jersey line at Trenton.

Out of a hut at the wharf came four men, captain and crew of the ferryboat. Not an hour ago they had brought across six British soldiers and six horses. They had seen worse ice on the river. The wind had changed to favor their spritsail. On the first trip they would ferry the twelve passengers, another trip for the stage wagon, six horses and driver.

"We've seen the ice worse than this," said the quiet-spoken captain, a thick hard riverman. He wore two pairs of wool stockings, shoes and overshoes, heavy underwear, two wool shirts, a leather waistcoat or "weskit" later known as a vest, a thick woolen scarf and a pea jacket windbreaker he had had six years, "a little threadbare but it fits all my curves and corners." Holding a lantern in one hand, throwing a shadow that dropped off the black wharf into vague floating ice and water, he was a shape, a voice, an authority, to the passengers, some of them fear-smitten and helpless over their choice of sleeping on frozen ground or crossing this river with its low plashes of water and the crunch and slide of ice at the sides of the boat, a flat-bottom scow with square ends. "We crossed four times today and I'll ask ye all to keep quiet till we're across and then ye can holler till your lungs bust."

The men walked on, the women followed, took places as told, stood waiting and heard the ice crunching at the sides of the boat and saw the spritsail unfurl and felt the wind moving the boat and three men with poles and oars taking orders from the captain and the scow gliding out in a lane between ice cakes and they had slow smooth sailing mid-river and the captain again saying he had seen the ice worse and they reached a lane between ice cakes and the other shore and they did say to themselves they were coming through nice and safe enough in this cold starlight crossing and they jumped out and they walked fast and they ran most of the way up to Mr. Williams' tavern.

A table waited them, hot barley broth, sliced cold roast pork, cheese with wheat bread, cider, weak hot coffee. Some ordered from the bar, beer and ale, hot slings. Past midnight the driver came in, passed word they would start four o'clock in the morning. A stageload of passengers Philadelphia-bound in the morning, other travelers riding their horses, a lady and gentleman with their own chaise and two horses, Mr. Williams' place was crowded. Winshore slept in the same bed with the cleric, the two British officers in their bed, the sailor and the long-legged lawyer bedded together—six men in three beds in one room—the farmer, the bound boy, the Negro slave boy, on the rag-carpeted floor with plenty of blankets and pillows, all at special rates—and one British officer cursed the parrot for its low clucking gabble, "Ram dam lamb sheep or mutton" as he was falling asleep.

Sleep in their eyes, their joints and muscles stiff and sore from the jolting of the day before, the passengers climbed up over the front wheel and stepped over the benches of the stage wagon for New York shortly after four o'clock in the morning. They could hear the driver crack his whip and the horses tugging in harness and the wheels rattling over stone and gravel and they knew there were morning stars up over them but they didn't care whether the morning stars were singing together and they wished they could sleep and they took catnaps and were jolted out of them and again tried to begin their catnaps where they left off.

They caught less of the cold wind than the day before. They dozed. They wondered how a body could be stiff and sore in so many places from the jolts and bumps of the day before. As the stage wagon now occasionally leaped from bump to bump, their stiffness eased under the pounding. It was still dark when they all had to scramble out and push wheels and wagon box to help the horses pull her out of a rut. The hours dragged. They dozed. No one talked. Even the parrot was subdued. They came to Princeton and warmed to a breakfast of fried pork, fried eggs, a sauce of dried apples and raisins sprinkled with cinnamon, cider, hot corncakes, and coffee. They had a snack of food in Jones' tavern at Ten Mile Inn and at Brunswick where they changed horses. It was dark and a spit of snow in the air when they drew up at Graham's tavern, Elizabethtown.

The supper of roast duck, mashed potatoes and gravy, assorted vegetables, finished with floating island. Winshore had a name since registering at Trenton: "Ordway Winshore, printer, Philadelphia," and one and another said at supper, "A punchbowl in the taproom this evening, Mr. Winshore." At a table in the taproom he drank with three other men who favored each his own way of making punch. Five things must go in the punchbowl. They agreed on pure water and sugar, argued the merits of lemon, orange, or lime for the best sour, whether two or four gills of rum gave potency, whether brandy or porter carried the right bouquet. "And nutmeg is trimming, just decoration, sometimes I forget it," said one.

On the wall near their table Winshore saw a large woodcut three feet long and half as wide, and pasted at its bottom a sheet of paper.

Winshore saw Lieutenant George Frame of His Majesty's Grenadiers stand before this picture and read the script below it. More closely Winshore saw the woodcut a portrait in black and white of His Majesty King George III, the royal head of Great Britain—and the picture right side wrong and turned upside down! He saw Lieutenant Frame leave the picture and walk with decision and no delay to his brother at the taproom bar. Winshore got up from his chair, stepped over to the upside-down portrait, read the bold handwriting of the lines:

> Behold the man, who had it in his power
> To make a kingdom tremble and adore,
> Intoxicate with folly. See his head
> Placed where the meanest of his subjects tread.
> Like Lucifer, the giddy tyrant fell;
> He lifts his heel to Heaven, but points his head to Hell.

Winshore turned to see the two scarlet-clad officers alongside him, Lieutenant Francis Frame stooping to read the insolent verse, so deliberately, so intentionally insolent. Winshore heard one low-toned "Extraordinary!" And the other, "Infamous!"

The officers strolled to the bar. Winshore followed. He heard Lieutenant George Frame, "*What* is the meaning of this?" Frame nodding his head toward the upside-down picture, giving the word "What" in a high stern tone and "isthemeaningofthis" in a low tone and as though it were all one word.

"That picture hung there on that wall right side up for years," said Mr. Graham, pouring a glass of New England rum for a bulking figure of a man with large hairy hands who had ambled in to stand easy as though he might be owning the place and saying softly the nickname for New England rum, "Kill-devil, Mr. Graham."

Yes, for years the picture had been right side up, Mr. Graham assured the officers. "Men of the Committee for Observation and Prevention came in one night. They thought it be better upside down."

"And you permit it to stay?"

"You should have it told to you and right quick, sir, this town is torn in two. You might near say the war in a way has commenced in Elizabethtown."

"The war has commenced? What war?"

And before answering, Mr. Graham spoke to Winshore leaning on the bar at the left of Lieutenant George Frame, "And you would like?"

"Porter, Mr. Graham," and having served Winshore and taken the pay Mr. Graham turned to the officers, speaking quietly and as though confidentially to the officers while his fresh-faced, beaming and chunky daughter, with an "I'm here," began serving a second drink of kill-devil to the bulking figure and plain beer to a couple of merry-faced men greeted, on their way to the bar, as constables. Winshore's eyes took in a hairy hand on the bar at the right of Lieutenant Francis Frame. At rest on the mahogany, it seemed a brute paw, then as the owner of the hand was saying something to the constables, the hand spoke, the fingers curving in swift quirks that went with his talk.

On Winshore's eyes tracing the hairy hand up along the arm to the face of the man, Winshore saw him a full head taller than Lieutenant Frame, black eyes and a head of glossy black curls, a broad-chested and thick-necked man. Winshore would learn this was a blacksmith's helper who had a late supper because of forging and welding a rim break in a wheel of the stage wagon. The giant was laughing and tossing his curls at some remark of the constables at his right and Mr. Graham's daughter at the beer tap had turned her head gaily to show them she was laughing with them, and Winshore could hear Mr. Graham quietly telling the lieutenants: "The war between those who call themselves Loyalists and those who name themselves Patriots though you give them the name of Rebels and when they feel polite they call you Tories and I could inform you that a half-dozen citizens in here tonight have referred to you two gentlemen as king-kissers and toadeaters and more than one has asked, on account of your uniforms, 'What are those lobster-backs doing here?' "

"You seem to be with them, keeping that piece of insolence on your wall there."

"I am trying to be what they call neutral. I take no sides. I serve a trade here and please any patrons who come. I have told you this town is torn in two. We had a riot last month. They dragged a man off his boat and took away his load of oysters and threatened to hang him for using his boat to haul from a British ship imported goods forbidden by the Continental Congress that met last year in Philadelphia."

"Who gives them these ideas here?"

"Some of it comes from a Justice of the Peace, a Judge of the County Court, chairman of the Committee for Observation and Prevention, Jonathan Hampton."

"We would like to lay our hands on him."

"You might lay your hands on him but if you put him in jail here the jail would be torn down. After dragging this oysterman around and pelting him and tearing his clothes, they put up a gallows in the middle of the town, with a rope dangling down from a crossbeam and they put his head in the noose and told him next time they caught him hauling forbidden imported British goods they would string him up and break his neck in that noose. Then next the gallows they put up a Liberty Pole and danced and drank around it, a big bonfire lighting up their jinks till late at night."

"Could we go out and see this gallows and this Liberty Pole?"

"No, the other side is not licked and they are putting up a fight. They have some aldermen and police with them. When the high jinks was over that night they tore down the gallows and the Liberty Pole."

"Could we go out and see this judge, this Jonathan Hampton?"

"If you could find him twould do you no good. He's a law to him-self, has men with him lacking fear of you, they are that kind here and it does seem the war has commenced in Elizabethtown or nearly so like it has in Boston and over near Brunswick where they tarred and feathered a man crying 'God bless King George!' and when they were all through with giving him his new-fashion suit of tar brushed over his naked body and a pillowcase of white feathers stuck and smudged into the tar, they told him he could go home and he turned to see his wife and children and he started off with them and while they were still laughing and catcalling at him and he was about fifty yards away he raised his hands over his head and yelled back at them, 'God bless King George!' I don't know what we're coming to but you would do well to go about any special business you have somewhere else than here in Elizabethtown. The war has come and it'll blaze higher."

Mr. Graham's daughter was now setting before the hairy-handed giant his third glass of kill-devil and a second mug of beer for each of the constables and a second glass of porter for Winshore. Mr. Graham himself set before the two officers their third glass of Madeira wine.

The blacksmith's helper looked along the bar, saw the line-up of glasses, lifted his own glass, looked along the faces at the bar, swung toward the faces at the tables, giving a special lift of his glass to the rouge-lipped slammerkins and the sailor at their table. His black eye-brows raised, a smile that might be gay or mocking in his eyes, a reck-less curl at the left side of his mouth.

"A toast," his voice crashed over the room. "We live only once—a toast!" Whatever he meant, it was terrific, for he was not shouting at the top of his voice and yet it seemed to shake the chandelier and the glass pendants around the oil lamps at the center of the room.

The toast was one he had heard when a delegate to the Continen-tal Congress had stayed overnight at Graham's last October. He gave the toast slow, carving each word, as though whatever you might think, for him they held bright and vital meaning, as a poem.

"May the fair dove of liberty," and his eyes swept about the room, "in this deluge of despotism," and his eyes found the faces of the two Lieutenants in scarlet and gilt and then bent with a smile of goodwill toward Mr. Graham and his now very solemn-faced daughter, "find rest to the sole of her foot in America."

The glasses of all had gone up as he spoke and at the end they drank the toast—only two glasses standing untouched. That toast the British officers were not drinking.

At his left Winshore felt a newcomer crowding in. "Judge Hamp-ton," said Mr. Graham in mild surprise.

"Kill-devil," said the angular, tall, stooped Judge with eyes far back in their sockets, queer sharp eyes. They took a slow gaze into the faces of the British officers, roved searching around those two faces. Judge Hampton lifted his glass toward them. His words came:

"May the sword of the parent never be stained with the blood of her children."

Alone Judge Hampton drank his glass. Not a finger of the officers moved toward their glasses.

Quiet over the room, silence at the taproom bar where Mr. Graham fussed with the beer tap and his daughter polished at a wineglass.

The two officers faced each other. They lifted their glasses of Madeira wine not yet touched by their lips.

"To the King!" said one with a slow singing inflection of the word "King." And with the same inflection and carrying challenge came the response from the brother, "To the King!"

The hulking blacksmith at the right of the officers had signaled for another glass of kill-devil, his fourth. He lifted it now and his voice crashed with a snarl not hinted at before. He stood erect, head raised and thrown back.

"Yes, the King!" his voice crashed with an ironic snarling of the word "King," repeating "Yes, to the King!" and then, "May he die tonight and be thrown into the darkest corner of hell and sit there picking hot cinders out of his eyes for a thousand years and after that to the end of the world!"

Then down his throat in one smooth easy gulp went the glass of New England rum. No one spoke. There was a perfect stillness. It seemed for a few seconds no one could think of anything to be saying that would fit till Mr. Graham in a low soothing tone, "Jack Mallon, watch yourself."

Jack Mallon was watching Lieutenant Francis Frame at his elbow, their arms touching, the Lieutenant's flushed face changing with the rages that heaved in him. The Lieutenant found the words he wanted, three words, in subdued guttural of anger and contempt: "You treasonable cur!"

And Jack Mallon, cool as a wrought-iron anvil in zero winter air, on the outside of him cool as anyone could ask: "A traitor I may be and I'll let you have it if you want it that what I talk is treason." Then flaring and swift with wrath and scorn: "And if I'm a cur I'm a sonofabitch and if I'm a sonofabitch I give you the back of my hand and the same to you, sir, and I hope you join your King in hell where both of you belong."

The words had hardly left him when Lieutenant Francis Frame spread his feet and swung his right fist at the face of Mallon. Mallon drew back his head. Frame's fist landed on the jaw, rocking Mallon to his heels.

And Frame gave a smothered cry and set his teeth at the stinging pain of two broken knucklebones of his right hand.

In a fraction of a second Mallon was holding Frame by the arms, his two hairy hands clutching him above the elbows. Then the hulking blacksmith, outweighing Frame by ninety or a hundred pounds, shook the man he held, shook him as an overpowering brute would a helpless victim, rattling the man's bones.

Lieutenant George Frame stepped fast to where he pulled at Mallon's left arm to get it loose, if he could. He found the arm fixed as a bar of iron welded to his brother.

Now the two constables pushed Lieutenant George Frame away. On each side of Mallon they tugged at his arms and called, "Come on, Jack, no fightin tonight, no sense in any fightin tonight. Come on, Jack, we'll all get out of here."

Judge Hampton joined the constables, "You've licked him, Jack, you've paid him back and what more do you want?"

The hairy hands let go their hold. Lieutenant Francis Frame's face twisted with the pain of his broken right-hand knuckles. His brother led him away to their room. The constables saw Mallon into his overcoat and walked out the door with him into a night of blowing snow. Winshore finishing his porter queried Mr. Graham, "Did I hear the officers asking you what war has commenced?"

"Yes, they asked me and I had to tell 'em it has for certain commenced in Elizabethtown, New Jersey."

"That was nice of one of them, what he said to you before going up."

"I didn't quite get it, what did he say?"

"He said, 'We regret this affair and desire you to know we should have preferred such an event did not occur in your establishment.'"

"They said that? Those were the words?"

"Yes, exactly."

"Say it again for me, I want to tell it correct to Mallon and Judge Hampton."

"And you're going to keep the portrait of King George upside down?"

"That depends on who wins the war."

* ★ * ★ * ★ * ★ * ★

Chapter 3

* ★ * ★ * ★ * ★ * ★

Winshore's Boys and Their Girls

WHITE gulls wheeled and cried their lonesome warnings, their hoarse announcements of a fish, a carcass, a scrap to eat. A morning mist hung on the air and over the rough waters a light wind carried salt-sea smells.

The two-masted ferryboat, a "periagua," had slid away nice enough from one and another jagged ice block that could have crushed in the boat. The captain in his time had seen one scow broken and a load of horses, cattle and three men go down and he could tell about seven men and two women leaping and clambering from an ice-crashed boat to floating ice they rode for hours before his and another periagua could gather all but the two men and one woman who slipped to their salt-water burials.

The shoreline now came clear to Winshore's eyes. "Manhattan Island—the Hudson River—the City of New York, a city of fifteen thousand people, the third largest city in America." Scows hauling cargo, brigs, sloops, a man-of-war, a frigate the sailor pointed to them, one he had sailed to Jamaica. His bundle he held himself and the two slammerkins had Sir Jocko and Esmeralda in their arms. Nodding toward the sailor, "We didn't take him," said one of the women. "You thought we would."

"You tried," smiled Winshore.

"He's too nice. We're goin to forget about him. If we think too much about him we'll cry. He's goin straight to that mother and sweetheart on Long Island. Harry Oates—what a name! Got a wild sister on the turf in Boston. He makes us cry unless we drink and then we laugh and it ain't him we're laughin at."

"I wish you well." And Winshore came near telling her he hoped his own boy over there in New York, if he was there, would be keeping as straight as the sailor and if the slammerkins met him they would be good to him.

The two British officers sat quiet. Lieutenant Francis Frame held his bandaged hand inside his greatcoat, his gauntlet too tight for the broken knuckles. From a few words Winshore caught he believed they had been surprised to find a spirit of rebellion in New Jersey, "arrogant and reckless as Boston and the country towns of Massachusetts." They were studying what they would advise a superior administrative officer. The faces, the insolence, the challenge they had met in Elizabethtown, would require discretion, no rash decisions, a ruthless hand if need be. "What can be the course of duty and policy with a man like that unless we kill him, hang him before the entire community?" Winshore heard once. The word "instigator" they repeated, probably meaning Judge Jonathan Hampton had given Jack Mallon wild ideas. The Frame brothers lightened a little as the boat neared a pier but the weight was on them of having to report to General Gage at Boston that war loomed and the sooner it came the shorter it would be. "The situation"—they would spend three or four days in New York among Loyalists and fellow officers seeking more light on the Situation.

Two days the father had with his boy, John Locke Winshore. Three nights they slept in the same bed in a long garret on the third floor of a tall narrow wooden house that rose out of lilac shrubbery and made conversation with a wise old elm and four young maples. Three nights the boy and the father talked an hour after going to bed and the boy fell into sleep first and the father went slower to sleep for what was called to his mind by this boy so like himself in so many ways. Not massive and roughhewn as the father but having the same brown eyes and the same trick of slitting the left eye at some quirk of thought either solemn or trifling, the same brick-dust hair and tangled rusty eyebrows and a mouth not so wide yet a slash of a mouth, sensitive, mournful, tender, gargoylish.

The father was at home in bed with this boy. He had visited a month ago the Negro woman Emmeline who had asked, "How is my boy doin, Mr. Winshore?" She had been wet nurse on the first day the boy came to the light of earthly life. The mother had brought the boy at great cost, his first day being her last. And the father had seen the baby sickly—and besides being anxious and helpful through croup, whooping cough, mumps and measles, he studied the boy; kept company with him, watched him, made two doctor friends take a personal interest. One year the child lost weight and pushed away his food. Two years he didn't grow. But he moved out of these phases. "After eleven years," the father would tell it, "he sort of shook loose, came to and never had a sick day since."

Now the father's memory ranged over those eleven years of the boy now sleeping next to him, breathing quiet and regular, a good sleeper. This well-formed and rather rugged young man of twenty years alongside him had been a bundle that he carried, that he tucked in, that he got up at midnight and daybreak to have a look at to see how he was coming along, whether he would grow man-size or be wizened and off-size.

He had tried to see the boy into good schooling, that what he got from the teachers was a help and not a fear or worry, that the boy heard the human mind is strange and a good education consists of learning first how to use books and second how and when to trust the workings of your mind which are reasoned and explicable and the deeper promptings of your heart and intuition which are mysterious and beyond language or logic. This was his chum sleeping next him in this tall narrow house on Bowery Lane in New York City amid lilac, elm and maples.

The mother too had been the father's chum. Not at first when they married but later. She was dark and sudden, a massive and vital woman with a quick tongue and lashing angers and afterward infinitely tender. Robert was her boy, the Robert the father would see up in Boston, four years older than John Locke Winshore sleeping now in this garret. Robert had her dark flowing wavy hair, her chin that jutted out, her deep-blue eyes, a deep sea-blue his eyes like hers, and her infinite tenderness along with her temper he had, a worse temper than hers perhaps

361

because fighting seemed to be in his blood. For years as a boy Robert would go out of his way to get fights, more than once coming home beaten and going back the next day to get beaten again by the same lad.

Robert had changed. The father and the younger brother had agreed on this three or four years back. They couldn't help seeing Robert going into books, getting lit up about "natural rights" and the other kinds of human rights, as Robert said, "handed to you on a platter and you are supposed to say, 'Thank you for what you are willing to give to me' and it will not be taken as bad form if you turn around, stoop and part your coattails, like a well-trained English butler and say, 'Kick me right here, sir.'" At first Robert read all the Independence pamphlets, scoured his way through the Whig newspapers, keeping a stack of them in his room. Then he began reading the other side, journals, pamphlets, speeches. "I want to know their arguments so when I meet a man calling himself Tory or Loyalist I will know what he is going to say before he begins speaking. Whenever I got into a fight it was handy to know what was coming next."

They had seen Robert ease away from fist fighting, saying he would save his fighting strength for the big fight ahead and he wanted to throw it against those he called "toadies and king-kissers." He had read the speeches of Pitt and Burke in the British Parliament over and over. They had become part of him and he could quote offhand entire paragraphs. When he came to New York three weeks ago, Locke had said, Robert must go see the statue of William Pitt erected by New York Whigs. He stood before the statue of Pitt, took off his hat and held it over his heart. "Think of this great man over there in London in British Parliament saying the same we rebels say here in the colonies," Robert smiled to his younger brother. Then Robert spoke sentences from a speech of Pitt, words that Robert repeated several times. Locke could say those sentences word for word as Pitt, and then Robert at Pitt's statue, and now Locke Winshore in a New York garret in bed with his father spoke them before falling into sleep:

"Sorry I am to hear the liberty of speech in this House imputed as a crime. But the imputation shall not discourage me. It is a liberty I mean to exercise. No gentleman ought to be afraid to exercise it. It is a liberty by which the gentleman who calumniates it might have profited. He ought to have desisted from his project. The gentleman tells us, America is obstinate; America is almost in open rebellion. I rejoice that America has resisted. Three millions of People so dead to all the feelings of liberty, as voluntarily to submit to be slaves, would have been fit instruments to make slaves of the rest. . . . The gentleman asks, when were the colonies emancipated? But I desire to know, when they were made slaves? . . . I am convinced the commercial system of America may be altered to advantage. You have prohibited where you ought to have encouraged, and encouraged where you ought to have prohibited. . . . The Americans have not acted in all things with prudence and temper. The Americans have been wronged. They have been driven to madness by injustice. Will you punish them for the madness you have occasioned? Rather let prudence and temper come first from this side."

And what was Robert doing in New York three weeks ago? This was the first the father had heard of it. "Business and errands for a Massachusetts Committee of Observation and Prevention and I am sure he is trusted with important and secret matters," said Locke.

"And he's got him a girl," Locke grinned. "They rode the stage from Boston to New York together. She came from a Boston dress shop to stay a few weeks and help open a dress shop here. Robert stayed four days and we didn't get talked out at all because he had to be seeing his girl."

"This sounds serious, Locke."

"It is. Wild about each other. Going to get married."

"Tush tush, Locke, on what is Robert going to get married and what time will he have for marriage that he can spare from the cause of Independence? He's already married to that, you might say."

"It's his affair. He didn't like to talk about details."

"It may be he'll learn there are a lot of details about marriage. What kind of a girl is she?"

"I wouldn't try to tell you, papa. You'll meet her in Boston. She's got beauty. You look twice to see it and it's there. And just between us she might be a little queer in the head sometimes."

"Well, it's about time I was going to Boston to see Robert."

"He keeps changing."

"Changing how?"

"Not easy to say. He keeps it hid."

"What does he keep hid?"

"I'm not sure. He would say one way and another, 'We want action now—the time for words is past.' I asked him if then my work is useless and I should drop it, print no more pamphlets, write no more handbills, no more mass meetings and crowds at the Fields where speakers pour out words, words and words. No, that must go on, he sees that. He put his arm around me and talked about action. He has talked with John Adams and others who know more than they dare publish about action that must come before any independence. When the Continental Congress met last September some delegates talked hopeless about the actions. They must see more action going and less talk. If these colonies are sovereign and independent, why don't we declare it? France and other nations ask that, Robert said. Indian sachems and sagamores laugh at us and say they will sign treaties when we are independent. On a fifteen-hundred-mile coast we must have forts and cannon to stand off attacks. Warships of our own we must have. We make guns and powder but we must have more from some-

363

where outside. There must be pay, food rations, officers and training for a standing army of at least 27,000 men. Little beginnings of all this go on. But too many talk independence and don't act. I think I could see Robert tangled up, deep-tangled and afraid he might talk too much and not act enough."

"Then he goes and gets tangled with a girl."

"I couldn't tell whether the girl helps. He's certainly tangled with her."

"Does she go along with him for a rebel, an incendiary, a ruffian, a plotter of treason against the Crown and, to use the phrase of that lieutenant of Grenadiers at Elizabethtown, a treasonable cur?"

"He didn't say, seemed touchy about her and I didn't ask." Locke Winshore yawned. "I'm sleepy, papa. You'll be talking to yourself if you say more."

"I hear you, my boy." He kissed the boy's forehead. "Now you go to sleep."

* * * * * * * * * *

Chapter 4

* * * * * * * * * *

Printer's Ink and Revolution

WINSHORE knew Rivington. He had bought books from Rivington when that elegant and often gaudy fellow, after reaping ten thousand pounds' profit from publishing Smollett's *History of England* and losing it on race horses, women and flashy living, quit London, crossed the Atlantic and opened a bookstore on Market Street, Philadelphia, the same year that Rivington opened another bookstore in Hanover Square, New York, and only two years before Rivington opened still another bookstore on King Street, Boston. Rivington, now in his fifty-first year, was not to be sneezed at nor ignored nor passed by. Rivington now had published for two years the most formidable Tory newspaper in America each week arriving to its thirty-six hundred subscribers with its high-coverage name: *Rivington's New York Gazetteer; or, the Connecticutt, New Jersey, Hudson's River, and Quebec Weekly Advertiser.* As a printer himself Winshore gave credit to this newspaper on its make-up, format, type, presswork, ornamental borders, woodcuts, alignment, agreeing with Isaiah Thomas, the famed Boston printer, "no newspaper in the colonies better printed or more copiously furnished with foreign intelligence." Rivington pledged he would never admit any matter "calculated to injure Virtue, Religion or other public Happiness, to wound a Neighbor's Reputation, or to raise a Blush in the face of Virgin Innocence." His policy would be "ever open and un-influenced," he announced continuously, and to begin with he had printed both sides of several minor questions, the speeches, letters and arguments of both sides. Then Rivington began lashing out at the Whigs and Rebels, pouring derision, contempt and hate on them, flicking them with satire, aiming to burn them with ridicule. They named his paper "Royal Gazetteer," "Lying Gazetteer." Violently angry Sons of Liberty had pledged they would "take" Rivington. Winshore had heard one delegate to the Continental Congress say to another, "If Rivington is taken, I must have one of his ears, you may have the other."

From Hanover Square to Wall Street Rivington had moved his book-store, and added his printery. Winshore saw him shortly after ten in the morning, a Negro footman in blue livery opening the mahogany door of a carriage with two bays and handing Mr. Rivington out to the brick sidewalk with an inch of snowfall on it, Mr. Rivington in a three-cornered hat, a long cloak of snuff-colored velvet, black silk stockings, silver-buckled shoes. His head turned to glimpse Winshore. At the doorway he turned for another look, tall, a little stooped, somewhat thin, his face having the extraordinary combination of a shrewdness nearly exquisite, a fox wariness, yet also good-fellowship and the sweet gravity of a man who enjoyed the company of good books, a man that Winshore read as did Isaiah Thomas: "He knew how to get money, and as well knew how to spend it; being facetious, companionable, and still fond of high living; but like a man acquainted with the world, he distinguished the guests who were his best customers."

Rivington in the doorway smiled to Winshore. "In Philadelphia years ago and you read books and you're a printerman."

"Winshore by name, Mr. Rivington."

"Ordway Winshore, I recollect, and are you still with that vilifying, calumniating William Bradford?"

And Rivington's face cracked and crinkled with a smile of swift changes, as though Bradford running the *Pennsylvania Gazette* "must like myself vilify and calumniate in my *Gazetteer* and we are brothers in the same queer amusing business."

Rivington favored the theater, played roles in amateur drama—and in real life.

Three or four questions they asked each other and their answers evasive of real information. Rivington smiled politely: he must go to his office and business. "We have a journal to publish."

"One question."

"As for example?"

"What, Mr. Rivington, do you think Christ would do if he came to New York today?"

"Why, I had never thought about that, Mr. Winshore, and at the moment I have no answer unless it should be that of a journalist."

"Which would be?"

"That if Christ on a summer Sunday afternoon should accommodate the people of New York City by walking on the water from our harbor to Staten Island, *Rivington's Gazetteer* would devote an entire issue to a narration of the event."

Winshore walked around the corner, went down a cellar dim-lighted by sidewalk windows. Here two men stood at type cases and a third man ran a small press. Locke Winshore went on with his typesetting, watched the greeting between his father and the other typesetter Henry Tozzer, owner of this little printery, who had learned his trade under Winshore at Philadelphia. The two printers talked till noon, Tozzer showing with pride some specimens of their Independence leaflets and handbills and grinning, "I hope you'll say they are inflammatory, we mean them to be."

Tozzer added that some of the handbills were less inflammatory than others, becoming confidential about it. A tobacco-seller who had helped finance the printery "likes to write inflammatory but he don't know how, he ain't got the trick, he goes too far and throws the words around too loose without giving the facts." One of these handbills, written by the tobacco-seller, began "To the Inhabitants of New York," addressed them as "My dear Friends and Fellow-Citizens" and then swept on:

At a time when Slavery is clanking her infernal chains, and Tyranny stands ready with goads and whips to enforce obedience to her despotick and cruel mandates; when Oppression, with gigantick strides is approaching your once happy retreats, and her tools and minions are eagerly grasping to seize the cup from the lip of Industry, will you supinely fold your arms, and calmly see your weapons of defence torn from you, by a band of ruffians? Ye, whose glorious and renowned ancestors, freely lavished their blood and treasure, to secure to you the full enjoyment of liberty, that greatest of temporal blessings; forbid it Heaven! Forbid it gratitude and honour! How long will ye patiently bear insult and wrong? Are ye so callous and dead to every sense of honour, as to disregard your reputation, and the taunts and scoffs of your fellow-subjects in the neighbouring Colonies? What is become of your former magnanimity and spirit, ye who dared to degrade the Governour of the Province, and exhibit his effigy, under the very muzzles of his Cannon? Are ye dwindled into such dastards and poltroons, as to suffer yourselves to be insulted, and robbed of your Arms, by a few petty Custom House Officers, with impunity? Methinks I hear you say it cannot, it must not be.

Then came two sentences alleging that firearms imported legally from Britain had been seized by a customs officer and put on board a man-of-war to be sent to General Gage at Boston—bare allegations with no particulars. After which the tobacconist thundered on in the special kind of thunder he relished:

Can ye bear such a thought? especially when ye have it in your power to prevent it; does not the bare idea of it harrow up your souls? In the name of Heaven, throw off your supineness; assemble together immediately, and go in a body to the Collector, insist upon the Arms being relanded, and that he must see them forthcoming, or abide the consequences; delays are dangerous; there is no time to be lost. It is not a season to be mealy-mouthed, or to mince matters; the times are precarious and perilous, and we do not know but that the Arms may be wanted tomorrow.

Some people may endeavour to persuade you that it would be improper to call upon the Collector in such a way, on account of his former polite behaviour to the mercantile body, but this objection has not the least weight in it, as he has shown himself inimical to the liberties of *America*, and has therefore cancelled every obligation.

"It's his way of gettin drunk," Tozzer laughed. "We can't print all the handbills he writes. He's a wife and six children and is neglectin them and his business. Of course, he's seen what a good handbill can do, like others of us. It was a handbill ten years ago cracked the town, when the Crown's stamp distributor refused to give up the stamps, when the handbills called for action and over a thousand men met in the Fields and a torchlight procession marched down Broadway to the Fort and hanged Governor Colden in effigy and dragged the Governor's fine coach to an open place, tore down the wooden fence around Bowling Green, piled it and set it on fire, then threw on the Governor's coach and the hanged effigy of him and burned them. I guess it was what you call a mob and they had to have more mob fun so they went to the fine country house of Major James of the Royal Artillery, tore his library to pieces, smashed his furniture and tore up his garden of rosebushes. We did go too far that night, I guess. And then again it might be we didn't. For the Governor gave up the stamps to the City of New York and they were put in the City Hall and never used. And the Colonial Assembly fixed payments for losses to property-owners. Then four years later came that handbill headed 'To the Betrayed Inhabitants of the City and Colony of New York' signed by a Son of Liberty. To the Fields that cold day in December came fourteen hundred people. Our rich young merchant John Lamb cut loose with a speech that reached the crowd and they passed resolves denouncing the Assembly for a trick bill to wring seven hundred thousand dollars in taxes to pay for keeping British troops here. It was a handbill raised hell then. Assemblymen called it an infamous and scandalous libel and they hunted out the printer of it, Alex McDougall, and had him in jail for months."

367

"Aren't you afraid of jail? Isn't Locke afraid you'll be caught for some of these handbills?"

"We are job printers. We do excellent printing for respectable merchants and we print religious tracts"—Tozzer squinted one eye— "and when we run off inflammatory literature we have Sons of Liberty keeping a watch outside, curtains over the windows and the door locked and bolted and no answer and only the quiet of the grave if anyone knocks to be let in."

Locke took the afternoon off, a clear day with a brilliant chill on the air, and they walked Wall Street, Broadway, Bowery Lane with its orchards, wide yards, lawns, gravel paths through shrubs and trees to elegant and spacious houses, on out to the mansion of James De Lancey. "America's foremost horseman, importer of Wildair, Lath, the Cub Mare and True Briton—by inheritance America's richest man, they say," Ordway Winshore gleamed at his son, who added, "And America's foremost Tory, the record telling us that on the resolution to approve the proceedings of the Continental Congress, the vote was 11 to 10 against approval and De Lancey was one of the 11, De Lancey managed it, damn De Lancey, damn his mansion and his city lots and his farms and his ships, damn his horses—"

"Oh no, Locke, not his horses, they are the most beautiful running horses I ever saw, sweet horses, don't damn his horses."

"We'll forget his horses then but we won't forget that 11 to 10 vote this January and he managed it."

They walked to the Fort and saw the equestrian statue of King George III where a few days before the Governor, Council, Assembly, Mayor, Aldermen, with military escort, after a procession and march to fife, bugle and drum-corps music, stood with heads uncovered, spoke orations and prayers for His Majesty. Here the father was solemn. "New York has great Loyalist strength, Locke. And the Patriots are split in factions. Perhaps we can only pray, hope, and stumble on in our present course."

They walked to the statue of the Earl of Chatham, William Pitt. "Robert stood here like this," said Locke with his hat off and held over his heart.

"There are two Englands, Locke," said the father. "The England of Pitt and the people he speaks for—and the England of a mad King and his ignorant, arrogant and selfish ministers."

They walked home, to the Tozzer house, to their garret, stopping to watch a lamplighter climb his little ladder, open a glass case and light the wick of an oil lamp. "When it's high wind and rain or a heavy snow they don't light 'em," said Locke.

Supper with the Tozzers, a table near the fireplace and the cooking smells, a tablecloth of red-and-white checks, two candles giving light, helpings of lamb stew from a large center dish, then Mrs. Tozzer bringing on Dutch potato pancakes. The five-year-old boy with smallpox pits on his face said nothing, ate well—a nephew of Mrs. Tozzer, Locke had told his father. An epidemic had taken the boy's father and mother and two children of the Tozzers.

Tozzer brought out a leaflet and read part of it that pleased him much. The Committee of Inspection at Newport had passed resolves in the Town Council chamber:

> " 'A certain James Rivington, a Printer and Stationer in the City of New York, impelled by the love of sordid pelf, and a haughty domineering spirit, hath for a long time, in the dirty *Gazetteer*, and in pamphlets, if possible, still more dirty, uniformly persisted in publishing every falsehood which his own wicked imagination, or the imagination of others ingenious in mischief as himself, could suggest and fabricate, having a tendency to spread jealousies, fear, discord, and disunions through this country; and by partial and false representations of facts, hath endeavored to pervert truth, and to deceive and mislead the incautious into wrong conceptions and wrong statements'—therefore the public was advised to have no dealings with the said Rivington, never to read his paper and to spread the word that his paper every week was 'an infamous liar, vilifier, a pedlar of calumny, a serpent's mouth of evil, a fomenter of violence who may yet come to his day of reckoning.' "

Tozzer interested Winshore who saw him as a Little Man, often puffed-up and swaggering, at times coughing as though he might be in the first stage of lung sickness, nothing original about him, a quiet ordinary mind. Yet from the outside were forces playing on Tozzer. They had come into possession of him. A deep trend, a slow tide, a human flow, a moving mass of personal forces rolling darkly toward ends no man could now tell. It had caught Tozzer. Its elements came natural to him. He was at home in it. Mystic fellowship it had. And if you happened to die for it you didn't vanish but part of you had entered something alive that was deathless. "I may be mistaken," thought Winshore, "but so I read the little fellow. He is important far beyond his little amiable yet indomitable self."

"England had her revolution," Tozzer was saying. "Rebels took up arms and fought the Government and captured the King and struck off his head. That was one of many rebellions in England. Out of it came religious liberty, freedom of worship, other rights. And does it please you, Winshore, that I have studied word for word a piece you reprinted in your *Pennsylvania Gazette* March first? I have it here. Let's go over it. I think we should have a leaflet made of it. Rivington can't answer it. De Lancey can't. It's the Independence cause in a nutshell. The next best statement I ever heard was a seventeen-year-old college boy, a King's University student, Alexander Hamilton, he spoke in the Fields to a big crowd July last summer, bright as a whip, he has promised to write us a leaflet.

369

"Now this piece," and Tozzer brought out the *Pennsylvania Gazette* and Winshore had a warm homelike feeling at the sight of that inanimate sheet of paper that to him embodied blood, thought, anger, love, and what not?

"The piece is signed Camillus," said the peering Tozzer. "And I have asked who the hell can Camillus be? I would like to meet Camillus."

"He's your own college boy Alexander Hamilton."

"No! Well, this is pleasant. He's a wonder. Take up these points with me, one by one." And they went over them as Camillus had written and signed them:

In England	In America
1. A trial by a jury of his country, in all cases of life and property.	1. A trial by jury only in some cases; subjected in others, to a single Judge, or a Board of Commissioners.
2. A trial where the offence was committed.	2. A trial, if a Governour pleases, three thousand miles from the place where the offence was committed.
3. The Civil authority supreme over the Military, and no Standing Army in time of peace kept up, but by the consent of the people.	3. The Military superior to the Civil authority, and *America* obliged to contribute to the support of a Standing Army, kept up without and against its consent.
4. The Judges independent of the Crown and people.	4. The Judges made independent of the people, but dependent on the Crown for the support and tenure of their commissions.
5. No tax or imposition laid, but by those who must partake of the burthen.	5. Taxes and impositions laid by those, who not only do not partake of the burthens, but who ease themselves by it.
6. A free trade to all the world, except the *East-Indies*.	6. A trade only to such places as *Great Britain* shall permit.
7. A free use and practise of all engines and other devices, for saving labour and promoting manufactures.	7. The use only of such engines as *Great Britain* has not prohibited.

370

In England	In America
8. A right to petition the King, and all prosecutions and commitments therefore illegal.	8. Promoting and encouraging petitions to the King declared the highest presumption, and the Legislative Assemblies of *America* dissolved therefore in 1768.
9. Freedom of debate and proceedings in their legislative deliberations.	9. Assemblies dissolved, and their legislative power suspended, for the free exercise of their reason and judgment, in their legislative capacity.
10. For redress of grievances, amending, strengthening, and preserving the laws, Parliaments to be held frequently.	10. To prevent the redress of grievances, or representations tending thereto, Assemblies postponed for a great length of time, and prevented meeting in the most critical times.

Above and below these ten points, they would have in bold blackface type, "breathing, like we mean it," smiled Tozzer, some language of Camillus that Tozzer thought "nice, very nice." He read it to Winshore:

" 'My dear fellow citizens, of what importance is it to us, that our fellow subjects, three thousand miles off, should be distinguished from the other Nations of the Earth, as free and happy, while we have no share in the distinction?'

"Now that's a question," said Tozzer, with a fierce glee. "Rivington will have an answer but he will wriggle and sweat writing it. And De Lancey will get someone to offer a reward for the names of the author and the printer of the leaflet."

Tozzer paused, mischief and fun on his face. "Who knows, Winshore, but Camillus and Tozzer may be sitting in jail together one of these days?"

They took a laugh together. Mrs. Tozzer laughed too, but Winshore noticed she laughed to be sociable, to join with them in their fun, rather than because she shared their interest in the ten points and the projected leaflet. She rose and left the room and returned with a washtub she set on two boxes in a corner of the living room. Then she brought a wooden bucket to Locke who busied himself with trips to a rain barrel outside till he had filled the tub so it would be there for Mrs. Tozzer to start her washing early in the morning. "I'll be in the garret, papa," said Locke, starting upstairs.

Tozzer excused himself, stepped out the back door and along a

371

trellised walk to a small wooden structure known in documents and private conversation as a privy.

Mrs. Tozzer looked at Winshore, pity and mixed feeling on her face, tears in her eyes. "Mr. Winshore, I don't know what we're comin to. He ain't like he used to be. This Independence, what he calls, this struggle for our rights, like he says it all the time, it is changin him. It's wearin him down. He don't have time to eat or to love like he used to. And he lets good pay work go by him. He is a good printer and he could get plenty of business, like he used to. The money don't come in the way it did a few years ago. He goes on credit too much. I hate to think he will end in the debtor's cell in jail. Some lay in the jail now for such little debts. He is too good a man to go to jail. Can you say a man has a good heart if he is so busy with politics he ain't got time to be goodhearted like he used to be?"

Mrs. Tozzer paused, not sure what had poured from her secret heart in this outburst. Winshore looked at her as she sat at the table opposite him, her forearms laid on the table where her folded hands rested, her lips mute, her eyes searching his.

He stretched an arm across the table, laid his right hand on her folded hands. "It is a time of trouble, Mrs. Tozzer. You are a brave woman, standing up to a hard struggle. You open your heart to me and I don't know what to say. Whatever I could think of to comfort you, you have already thought of, I am sure."

They sat in quiet, his right hand on her two folded hands, while a tall relentless clock went tick-tock and tick-tock, a well-made clock her father had scraped and saved to buy them for a wedding present, laughing and saying offhand and practical as he pointed at it on their wedding day, "A good clock tells you every day time is money and time is love and you better be careful with it."

"A time of trouble now," said Winshore slow and quiet, "trouble like never before, trouble we don't know how to meet because we never met it before. Thousands of families where they can't get away from this trouble. Families where brother is against brother, son against father, and even husband and wife snarling at each other over the Stamp Act, the tea tax, the quartering of troops. Thousands of good women like yourself, Mrs. Tozzer, can't make up their minds about this new thing in the air that has come along and made their husbands different."

Tozzer came in. The tall clock said it was nearly nine. Mrs. Tozzer put clothes to soak in the washtub. "The more I think about it, Winshore," said Tozzer, "I believe that will be the best leaflet we ever saw out of our press."

They said good night. Winshore went up to the garret. In bed he asked Locke about a little thing come up during supper, Mrs. Tozzer then telling Locke as a piece of news for him, "Tina was here to see me this afternoon. She never looked so fine. She had her hair fixed a new way that makes her so pretty, not like a country girl from up the Hudson River but a real New York girl. You should have seen her eyes shining, going to be married. So your chance is gone, Locke." And the way Mrs. Tozzer said, "Your chance is gone, Locke," half fooling and half meaning it that Locke had been serious about Tina, this had not been lost on Winshore.

"Who is Tina?" said the father. "This Tina, I never heard about her."

"Can you wait, papa? You slept four hours longer than I did this morning and that long walk made me sleepy."

"They spell it T-i-n-a, I believe, and pronounce it Teena and it is a nice name."

"Don't tease, papa. She means nothing to me and she's a nice girl and when we have our last walk around town tomorrow I'll tell you all about Tina and answer all questions."

"Get your sleep, my boy. You're a good boy," kissing him on the forehead, and soon the two were sunk in rest with eyelids closed down, the father fading away with that query of Mrs. Tozzer lingering and bothering him: "Can you say a man has a good heart if he is so busy with politics he ain't got time to be goodhearted like he used to be?"

The boy was gone at six in the morning. The father lay questioning. Why shouldn't Locke have told him about Tina? And again perhaps Tina meant little or nothing to the boy, so why bother about it? Yet come to think about it the boy hadn't mentioned any affairs with girls—and why shouldn't he mention one or two? Or could it be that he didn't care about girls and what would that mean? At this part the father took a laugh at himself. Hadn't the boy made it clear that when the war of the Revolution began he would enlist in the Continental Army and he was ready to be a free and willing soldier of the Revolution? This was the boy's own decision, what more could a father ask? What was any feeling, desire or decision of the boy about a girl compared with a devotion so deep in the boy that of his own free will he was going to fight for a free and independent America?

Yet the father knew he couldn't really laugh off more questions that kept coming up from under the others. First he had fathered his boy and after the boy was born he had done considerable mothering. For years the boy had talked free with him about nearly everything, even the first hairs of puberty when the father had laughed, "You're a man now, Locke, though not yet man-size," and then sober counsels where they talked about the vast mystic caverns and labyrinths of sex and over half the frank questions the boy plumped at his father, had the answer, "That you will have to decide for yourself. Nobody but yourself can tell you when you fall in love or fall out or how far to go with any girl any time."

Now the boy was man-size. It was his wish to leave Philadelphia six months ago and come to New York and see how life went when he was no longer "tied" to his father, as Locke had said, adding, "I don't mean you have tied me to you, I've had plenty of freedom but I want to see what'll happen when I'm away from you." And he had been with girls and probably a whore or two and didn't care to tell his father about it. And from a remark of Tozzer, Winshore knew that Locke had gone with other Sons of Liberty up into a Connecticut town and taken a hand in a brutal affair of putting tar and feathers on a Loyalist they regarded as "inimical."

And why should Locke use that word "inimical" so freely? And other words such as "tyrants," "despots," "varlets"? He had taken on a vocabulary. Walking away from the King George statue he had remarked with a smile his father thought silly, "We will yet make those tyrants tremble." There had been a little of this sheerly conventional blab before Locke had gone to New York but the company he kept and other influences in the air—had they affected Locke so that he was unduly parroting others and what he spoke was not from the roots of a growing mind and character? And why had Locke gotten into a habit of writing verse, rhymed and blank, losing sleep and wasting candlelight with writing a dozen sheets one night, "An Apostrophe to Liberty" with such lines as "On thy brow, O Goddess, we place this diadem of thy humble votaries"? It was neither a pamphlet nor a poem, "just another screed," the father had commented, then smoothed Locke's resentment, "It is practice, Locke, good practice. I wrote far worse poetry when I was your age."

It came over Winshore that he cared too much about the boy, that he was too sensitive about Locke, that years lay ahead for the youth, years of blundering to learn by blunders, and, "What the hell, I think I'll love that boy if he turns robber, murderer or—yes—idiot." And he tried to put away the incidental remark of Tozzer, "Some days Locke works good and other days he is slow and holds up the others." This was Locke's way in the Bradford printery in Philadelphia. He could be so slack, vague and dreamy. Those spells would come on him.

Winshore packed his bag, tied his bundle, went downstairs, heard Mrs. Tozzer as she turned from her washing, "I couldn't help talking like that last night. I know you won't tell Henry. You are right it is a time of trouble and we must make the best of it."

"You are a brave enough woman with what you have to face. The women have a harder time of it than the men. I often think they are stronger than the men." She wiped her right hand on her apron, shook his hand in good-by, he patted the little boy on the head, and was on the street walking to the inn where he would stay overnight and at three in the morning take the stage for Boston.

"Tina, you asked about Tina," said Locke as they walked that afternoon to the Fields and Locke pointed to where the Liberty Boys had set up a Liberty Pole and a Loyalist crowd had torn it down and it had again gone up and again come down. "I have had six girls since I came to New York."

"All serious?"

"Only one serious. Tina was the first, heavier than me, a round face and a wonderful milk-white skin."

"And you wrote poems to her."

"How could you know that?"

"Because if you could write twelve pages of apostrophes to the Goddess of Liberty you would write at least ten lines to Tina's milk-white skin."

"Yes, I wrote five different poems to Tina. And she laughed at them. She couldn't see anything in them, telling me to my face she was afraid I didn't have good sense, giggling I was a little silly. That was when I took up with a little spitfire I could lift with one arm. She could kiss terrible sweet. And she kept wanting more and more of my time, church on Sundays, parties and dances and walks weekday nights. And because I went with the Tozzers to an Independence meeting one night and she heard about it, she cut me off. If I would say I was sorry she would begin again but I wouldn't say I was sorry and she did cut me off with hard words."

They walked on. Locke was hesitating.

"And then?"

"Then came Leesa. I can't begin to tell you about Leesa, papa. She's the first girl I ever worshiped."

"Loyalist or Rebel?"

"Neither side, like her father. He rides a horse every day out to near Beekman's Swamp where he is one of the head men in Jacobus Roosevelt's tannery."

"You want to marry her? Is it like that?"

"When I hint at getting engaged she says we must wait and get to know each other better and then talk about it."

"And you worship her?"

"We are both the same weight, exactly one hundred and forty-five pounds. You should see us skating together. We look like a couple together. We talk easy together. Tina sometimes would not say a word for an hour. Leesa is a wonderful talker. And long braids of yellow hair far down her back. And blue eyes, such blue eyes! And we sing together. I have learned one song in Dutch from her." Locke paused. "Sometimes it is a hurt, what I feel about Leesa. Last week on the porch of her father's house when she said that just for once we mustn't kiss good night, we have been kissing too hard and must be more careful, when I walked home it was a terrible hurt and kept me awake half the night."

The father took Locke's hand as they walked, squeezed it, and they said nothing for blocks, stopped to say good-by to Tozzer in the printery, at the inn had a supper of shad roe with fried salt pork, and Locke saw his father to bed at eight o'clock.

"Tell Robert I'll be in the army and I know he will and I hope we meet and the best of luck to him always."

"I'll tell him that and I'll tell him you keep growing pretty fine and he can be proud of you for a brother."

* * * * * * * * * *

Chapter 5

* * * * * * * * * *

Kiss, Kiss the Cold Winter Away

A WHITE oval of a face she had and sea-pale it was, you might say, if it is agreed the sea-pale may hold deep strengths no one can fathom beforehand.

Under the oil lamp of the inn room where they waited at three in the morning to enter the New York stage for Boston, the others saw her with that face you might call sea-pale and some near her could see the skin of her cheeks touched ever so faintly with apple-blush, early apples of late June, you might say.

A hood of wool, light-gray and finespun with an oval of fur, framed her face where the cheekbones and the length of the face gave a hint of the gaunt and perhaps the lonely. Her blue eyes could look at you and you would be meeting her eyes with yours to find that it seemed she was looking through you and beyond you to matters that interested her more than you and they could be matters that would interest you if you could get her to tell you about them. And there were moments when a soft dreamgaze she had came crossed with a dark greenish storm-blue, a sea-horizon look that went with her sea-pale skin. The long smooth curves of her eyelashes swept with a perfection not there at all in the tangled and rough shags of her eyebrows.

Her cloak of light-gray wool with fur edgings, blue velvet embroidery, a cord of black silk at the collar and throat, her large brown fur muff, they did something to her being six feet tall. She stood six feet but didn't quite seem so.

Her legs under her overshoes and leggings must be limber and strong with obedient muscles, it was noticed when she climbed into the stage wagon in New York, for she sort of quickstepped to the hub and danced into the wagon box and was over the benches as though doing it to music or timebeats.

At breakfast halfway to Kingsbridge with her hood off they could see her chestnut hair in coils of a dim bronze burnish, plaits of it folding down as though if she wished she could put her ears under to be held back by' the plaits. Winshore considered stepping over and putting her ears back under those plaits and knew very well he would let it pass with merely considering it. Between her eyes and along the sides of her straight nose, he counted seven small freckles and an eighth still smaller in the hollow of her shapely chin. "Thin lips," said Winshore, "and a mouth you don't know is wide till she laughs."

He had waited to see whether she would laugh. She had smiled, she had puckered pleasantly, she had broken her gaunt gravity several times. Then she did break into a full and rippling laugh. But this laugh so widening her mouth that her rows of white even teeth came like a sudden burst of light, this laugh was slow in coming, preceded by one or two smiles and a medium laugh.

The Frame brothers faced her at the table, Lieutenant Francis Frame resting his bandaged hand on the table, handling his food with the other, having his buckwheat cakes cut by his brother. Lieutenant George Frame, it seemed clear, had known the young woman in Boston, had also known some of her friends and they used to pass along to each other "fresh a-*neck*-dotes," as they called them, odd stories picked up.

She had heard in New York of a young man on Staten Island who married a girl of plain face, ugly moods. On their wedding night she refused to please the groom. He begged her. She was stubborn. He pushed her in the face and gave her a few lashes with a whip. She ran out and up the street to her father who knew her well. He lashed her with a leather belt, led her to the door: "Go back now and tell your husband he beat my daughter but I am even with him for I have beat his wife."

"An incident true to fact, Miss Wilming?" smiled Lieutenant George Frame.

"I doubt it, Lieutenant. It's too maliciously clever."

"They report in Philadelphia of a certain gentleman who had long paid his attentions to a woman he desired to take in marriage. One day he was apprised she had married another man. The fellow who brought this startling news added with conviction, 'I have seen the bride and bridegroom.' 'Oh, have mercy,' came the answer. 'Don't use those names bride and bridegroom, I can't bear to hear them.' 'Then suppose I call them dog and cat?' 'Oh no, mercy no,' the poor loser rejoined, 'that sounds like man and wife and I can't bear it.'"

"A little cruel, that affair," mildly laughed Miss Wilming, smoothing butter on a buckwheat cake and doubling it.

"I agree," said Lieutenant Francis Frame. "For the pure comic with no dash of malice I prefer an incident of fact they tell in the King's Navy. It concerns a valiant officer who had lost a leg in battle.

As he commanded his ship one day in a fierce engagement, a cannon ball shot away his wooden leg. A seaman seeing him fall flat on the deck rushed in crying, 'I will call for the ship's surgeon, sir.' 'No, no,' shouted the commander. 'Send at once and no delay, send for the ship's carpenter.'"

It was then her full and rippling laugh came.

They had arrived in Stamford, washed, dressed and waiting the supper call. They heard the town crier's bell giving his news announcement in front of their inn and for the benefit of the inn lodgers:

"Hear ye, hear ye, at the tolling of the bells at eight o'clock this night, the assembled citizens at the market place will bear witness to the humility and contrition of two offenders against the unity of the colonies and the resolves of the Continental Congress, with pledges for their contrary behavior for the future, the ceremonies to be conducted with that regularity and decorum that ought to be observed in all public punishments."

The cheerful and gay Lieutenants of breakfast time were in a different mood through supper. They would answer "Yes indeed" or "Quite so" when asked if they did not find the pan oysters and roast duck excellent. Miss Wilming was aloof and the Frame brothers grave and, you might say, distant.

A farmer who had got on at New Rochelle found the man next him was a storekeeper from Sudbury, Massachusetts, and asked about an affair published in the *Massachusetts Spy*, whether the affair was reported correctly and did the storekeeper know the young man that figured in it?

Yes, he had sold the young man Hezekiah Ebell a saw and a pane of window glass just before the affair happened. "He asked for credit and I wrote it on the books because he was highly recommended, and I knew his father and I knew the family where he had just married the youngest daughter. He had bought him a piece of land in a new settlement and it took all his money. To help him get started, the selectmen recommended him to the parish for a contribution. They were goin to raise enough to get him a yoke of oxen, a plow, seed corn and a milch cow. The minister gave notice of the next Sabbath they would take up a collection and subscriptions for young Ebell and his bride. Well, ye know that tarnation fool on the Saturday before that Sabbath goes into a shop and buys a pound of Bohea tea promisin to pay for it with the Sabbath collection the next day. Of course the news flew around the town, everybody got talkin about it and the first thing ye knew a committee calls on the minister hot and mad about Hezekiah Ebell buyin imported *tea* with money they were goin to throw in for him and his farm. The upshot was the selectmen reconsidered their vote, refused to recommend him, and the minister gave it out from the pulpit there had been a change in plans and there wouldn't be any collection. And I don't know whether

378

I'll ever get my money for that saw and that pane of window glass I let him have on tick."

The Sudbury storekeeper had begun his story in a matter-of-fact tone of voice, then his enthusiasm began rising about it. The whole table listened and would have had to hear it whether or not they cared to listen, including the Frame brothers.

"That young fellow," said the New Rochelle farmer rather soberly, "must have felt pretty cheap, kind uh sheepish, and I guess him and his bride didn't care much for the taste uh that tea."

"No, he didn't look sheepish," said the storekeeper. "He acted like he didn't know what he had done and like they didn't know what they were doin to him. His pretty little wife took it hard. She went home to her folks and he had a hard time makin his persuasions on her to come back to him. The last I talked with him he was hirin out to a farmer near his land expectin to earn enough this year to start him next year with oxen, a plow, and seed corn. That little pound uh Bohea tea set him back a year."

The voice of the town crier could be heard outside, his last call and summons to those who desired to witness "public punishment" visited on offenders who had shown contempt for "the resolves of the Continental Congress." The Frame brothers went to their room. They had been gazed at, by several at the table, and by men stepping into the room as though to have a look at officers of His Majesty's military. The eyes the Lieutenants met had sometimes curiosity—and again curiosity with an added sullen glowering. Winshore noted Miss Wilming not easy about this, as though "anything can happen." The air cleared with the two Lieutenants gone to their room.

"I'm going over to the public punishment, Miss Wilming," offered Winshore, "and I think I could see no harm comes to you—that is, if you have any interest in going."

"Lost men howling to other lost men where to go," she said, looking through him and past him. "Mired men crying to others in the mire how to get foot-loose."

He was tempted to stay and ask her to go further with this thought of lost men, mired men. "We must talk sometime," he said as though he more than half understood what she was now talking about, and she saw depths of sorrow in his deep-set brown eyes, on his curving slash of a mouth. "And I think I must go over and see what they do. Sweet good night to you." He nodded, walked through the hall door and was opening the front door to the street. She had moved swiftly and softly and stood facing him, "I'll get my cloak and go with you."

They had heard a fife, drum and bugle corps playing funeral music. Now from the porch of Mr. Weed's tavern they saw it pass giving slow march music for a procession that had been winding in and out the central streets of Stamford. At the head were two captains of Connecticut militia in uniform. Next came six men with poles

379

over their shoulders and a chest slung with ropes from the poles. "That's the tea!" came crowd yells.

Then followed the guard, a militia company marching in fours, taking pride in their well-drilled ranks, bayonets fixed on their firelock muskets. Behind them two by two the Committee on Observation and their chairman marched followed by a miscellany of farmers and townsmen on horses, some with hunting rifles slung over their shoulders. Two blocks down the street they marched, turned and came back to the platform brought by a squad of men who set it in the middle of the street opposite Mr. Weed's tavern.

"We have privileged seats," said Winshore to Miss Wilming as they looked over the heads of the buzzing, milling crowd.

"We shall miss nothing."

"Nor will the Lieutenants—they can see all from their room window."

"Yes."

"Will it give them anguish?"

"Anger rather than anguish."

"Cold anger?"

"Hot and cold—mostly cool, probably—they have been in campaigns on the continent of Europe where they saw towns like Stamford burned to the ground—cool, I should say."

A man on the platform lifted a hand and brought a hush over the crowd of perhaps six hundred. They heard onlookers telling each other this was the chairman of the Committee for Observation and Prevention, Mr. Nicholas Gibbon. "Nick'll tell 'em," they heard a young man in working clothes whisper and titter. The young man was going to have a good time and was sure of it. He had come to see a performance, he had seen other like performances and thrived on them.

"Andrew Wentworth," called the chairman. And Wentworth came forward, a sturdily built man with a pink face, a well-to-do merchant who lived comfortably, one would guess by his greatcoat of fine wool, his three-cornered hat and shoes with silver buckles. "That's his wife," someone said in a low tone of the somber-faced woman in a wine-colored cloak and hood who had helped him up the platform.

"Kneel, Andrew Wentworth," said the chairman solemnly, to carry the meaning this was a life-and-death business. "And now say after me this pledge of contrition."

Then Chairman Gibbon read the pledge agreed on by the Committee, five to eight words at a time, with the kneeling man repeating in a tone reaching perhaps half the crowd who knew what he was saying because the chairman spoke the words loud, slow, clear:

"Before this company I confess I have been aiding and assisting in sending men to Boston to build barracks for the soldiers to live in, at which you have reason justly to be offended, which I am sorry for, and humbly ask your forgiveness; and I do confirm, that for the future,

I never will be aiding or assisting in anywise whatever, in act or deed, contrary to the resolves of the Continental Congress, as witness my hand."

The kneeling Andrew Wentworth rose to his feet, bent over a table, and with a quill pen handed him signed his name to the document, bowed humbly to the crowd and heard rousing cheers for what he had done, cries of "Good for you, Wentworth," and "Hurrah for the Continental Congress!" and a scattering of hoots and jeers, "Don't ever do it again, Wentworth, or we'll get ye."

"Nathaniel Horn," called Chairman Nicholas Gibbon. A slender, undersized, well-dressed man stepped to the platform, his hands and feet fidgeting, his three-cornered hat not sitting well on his head and his two hands setting it right. His hair graying, he seemed perhaps fifty or more years of age, yet his fidgets those of a sickly shy boy.

"Remove your hat in payment of respect to the Continental Congress, Nathaniel Horn," the chairman bade in a voice of command. The hat was snatched off and held between hands and he saw he was crushing it and immediately began uncrushing it and standing bewildered.

"The fifty pounds of tea which you, Nathaniel Horn, attempted to conceal from the Patriots of this community, and which was detected in your possession despite your two removals of it in fear of detection, an article of commerce forbidden by the resolves of the Continental Congress to be in your possession, those fifty pounds of that symbolic and detested article, now stand ready and prepared for destruction at your hands and by your act. By the mandate of the local Committee for Observation and Prevention, it is ordered that you are to take in your hands these two torches and commit to the consuming flames the chest containing the fifty pounds of an article of commerce, hated and hurtful, found in your guilty possession. And it is further ordered that you are to stand by and be silent witness until the consuming flames have removed from this community every sign and vestige of the forbidden article."

At his speaking the words "these two torches" Chairman Gibbon turned and received the torches made ready by another Committee member. Horn had dropped his hat to the floor, put out his hands for the torches, walked off the platform to where kindling and firewood were piled with a wooden chest on top. He held his torches to the kindling on one side, walked to the other side and there held the torches.

Soon the flames roared high, cheers and yells of elation, and a surge of laughter at a leather-lunged fellow, "Your tea is goin to hell, Mr. Horn."

Soon the boards of the chest fell away as the flames licked and ate and the tea spilled out and spread and then sank into ashes and was lost in the dwindling fire and the firewood ash and embers. An odor lingered, a tea-smoke smell reaching beyond the crowd.

"A good night's work, Mr. Horn," came the leather-lunged one again. "Now you can go home and get a good night's sleep."

Horn shuffled to the platform, still fidgeting somewhat, picked up his three-cornered hat, looked at the chairman and got a nod, slid off the platform, found a passageway through the crowd, meeting jokes and jeers and here and there an old friend who said, "You did the right thing, Nat," or "You won't be sorry, Nat, it had to be done."

Fresh firewood was piled on. Chairman Gibbon lifted a bundle of newspapers, loosely bunched. Chairman Gibbon with a face of scorn and menace, a look not seen on him before during the proceedings, shouted, "Rivington's Gazetteer!" the crowd giving a low growl, and, "Rivington's lying, detestable Gazetteer! Rivington's indecent and damnable Gazetteer that profanes the truth and befouls every community it enters!" And Gibbon handed the bundle of Gazetteers to a man who threw them on the fire. Came then the loudest mass shouting and cheering of approval and jubilation heard during the program. A punctuation from the leather-lungs, "Tar and feathers for Rivington!" was picked up by others here and there, the cry rising and falling, "Tar and feathers for Rivington!"

A sweep of laughter rose when a ragged, blear-eyed old fellow, tipsy and gay, did clumsy steps and capers around the fire while he howled in falsetto, "Hang Rivington, we're goin to hang Rivington!" This was the only time in the evening that Winshore saw Miss Wilming's face lighten a little. A wisp of a beginning of a smile was there. It faded when both of them heard a trio of stern-faced young men standing next to them in agreement with one saying low-voiced, "We'll wreck his place yet. He won't have a press nor type after we pay our call. His time has run too long." They were cool, these young men. They were terrible. They were, Winshore knew, Sons of Liberty, and they regarded themselves as instruments of vengeance in completely justifiable violence in behalf of a Cause they held holy.

"Good night, sir, you are very kind," said Miss Wilming in the lower hall, as she went to her room. Winshore went to the taproom for a glass of porter before going to bed.

"They make many noises and they walk lonely and they know nothing of how they are fugitives from themselves and how their food is black ice," Miss Wilming had said by way of comment on the evening's program. That was as far as she would commit herself. Could this be the same young woman who at breakfast halfway to Kingsbridge that morning had been so perfectly pleasant with stories and charming talk? Should he believe there was some bond between her and Lieutenant George Frame and she was gay or austere according to that officer's moods? No, he would have to go further and deeper than that. Was she profound and subtle—or merely soberly whimsical, with her "Lost men howling to other lost men where to go" and their being "fugitives from themselves" and the like? It struck him she was an extraordinary person.

"She has marvels of loveliness," Winshore said to himself finishing his porter and thinking about her contrasts, how suddenly and brilliantly her face could light and what an absolute stillness and composure she had of face and body when listening to others, no fuss or excess dignity. "And no gush about her," he said, knowing gushers too plenty. She could milk a cow or hitch horses to a wagon and had said as much in smiling cryptic remarks at the midday meal. She had leaped out brightly and joined the men in shoving with full strength against the stage-wagon box when the wheels stuck in a bad rut near East Chester. She seemed well read in Shakespeare, the New Testament, and in a discussion with a prim and excessively polite schoolmaster who rode the stage from Kingsbridge to Rye, she had quoted a woman in a Fielding play as saying of another woman, "I think her an ugly, ungenteel, squinting, flirting, impudent, odious, dirty puss." She had merrily claimed in the discussion that people can be overeducated in the use of words and the woman she quoted could better and more briefly have said, "I think her a dirty puss." She seemed to know the country around Boston and she and Lieutenant George Frame had met and talked on a number of occasions in Boston. "And she likes him and is decently gracious with him and there may or may not be more than that," considered Winshore.

At the midday meal sitting next to her, at a proper interlude he had softly asked her, "Your full name, Miss Wilming, is?" holding the "is" into an "is-uh" and finding he had to repeat "is-uh" and drawl it along while her eyes twinkled and with deliberation her answer came, "Marintha Wilming." She added there was a nickname for Marintha but it was "short and ridiculous" and they would get along if he called her Miss Wilming. This and more came to his mind before fading to sleep recalling her in a swift exchange telling the Frame brothers of a man to be hanged and his prison mates trying to break his cool way about it and he put them off with, "Damme, it's only a dance without music and no floor." She could say "Damme" as though it wasn't swearing at all. Winshore was practicing the way she said "Damme" when he dropped off into sleep with calm pulses.

"I'm not falling in love with her," he had said earlier with a smooth laugh. "I know better."

Four days later, with one day of rain, a delay with a broken wheel, they arrived in Providence, to hear before supper the town crier, ringing his hand bell as he walked, holding the bell quiet while he cried in a lusty voice, important though monotonous: "At eight o'clock this night in the market place a quantity of India tea will be hanged

383

from the gallows and afterward burned in detestation until every vestige of it has vanished from human view. All true friends of their country, lovers of freedom, and haters of shackles and handcuffs, are hereby invited to testify their good disposition, by bringing in and casting into the fire, a needless herb, which for a long time hath been highly detrimental to our liberty, interest, and health. Any good and worthy women, from a conviction of the evil tendency of continuing the habit of tea drinking, are invited to make free-will offerings of their respective stocks of the hurtful trash."

The shuffling of many feet outside on the cobblestoned street could be heard by the stage passengers at supper, reckless voices, some of them drunken. The Frame brothers spoke to each other in undertones. In the taproom afterward they drank their Madeira wine with no delay, seeing the looks of several men glancing toward them and talking about them. They went to their room and could hear shouts directed to them from the street, "To hell with your India tea!" and "To hell with King George and Lord North!"

"There will be gallows this evening," Winshore said to Miss Wilming. "You may wish to go to this gallows party with me."

They watched a crowd of two or three thousand people, mostly workingmen with an element of farmers, though not lacking prominent citizens, merchants and lawyers. They heard an importer-merchant read an apology and beseech pardon for having brought tea for sale into Providence, a paper written for him by the Committee of Observation. "My having drunk success to the Tories who oppose the American cause, which gave offence to the good people of this city, I desire to solemnly declare it was done inadvertently. In the most unfeigned sorrow for having made use of unguarded expressions, I beseech now your forgiveness and shall think myself extremely happy in being re-established in the good graces of my country." He read it as though he had been drunk and now sober was apologizing for what he had done drunk.

He stepped to the gallows. From an overhead beam hung a sack holding three hundred pounds of tea. The sack had been shaped into a body, a head, and a neck with a halter noosed around it. This effigy or dummy rested on a box.

The importer-merchant, as agreed, swung his right foot and sent a kick to the box and as it tumbled away the strangled sack of tea dangled midair from the gallows beam and a rocking applause of yells and laughter came from the crowd.

Again wild shouting rose when the sack of three hundred pounds of tea was thrown on the big bonfire. The blaze darkened a while and the shouting lowered, then rose again as the tea crackled and became flame and then ashes sending out a tea-smoke aroma. It was being done "in the name of those who are firm contenders for the true interest of the American people," a stern man of undoubted importance announced in a shrill carrying voice. Now a barrel of tar was thrown on the fire and a column of black smoke went winding, shifting its course once so that part of the crowd had to move back from its stench.

"The speeches of Lord North," cried the chairman as he lifted a handful of papers and handed them to a man who threw them on top of the burning tar. The crowd cheered. And again, a bundle of newspapers, and the crowd howled and there were sweeps of laughter and yells at a Boston Tory newspaper going up in flame.

Miss Wilming held Winshore's arm. There had been fantastic and comic moments when he smiled, even laughed a little. Not once did she join him. Not once did she offer any remark in answer to little things he said, no shade of thought she cared to give to his query, "What next, where is this leading?"

"The bells toll." Winshore heard her but it was as though she were talking to herself, as though she might be completely alone singing a sad song to herself. "The bells toll and for what are they tolling, I ask you, kind sir, for what are they tolling?" When once she repeated this and looked straight into his eyes, he felt she was looking past him and wanted no answer from him, "I ask you, kind sir, for what are they tolling?"

They moved to a circle of people making merry over a fellow with a brush and a bucket of lampblack. What had he been doing? they asked merrily. He answered merrily. "I am a Son of Liberty and I have painted out the word 'Tea' from every shop sign in Providence."

They went to their rooms. The stage for Boston would leave at three in the morning.

Three things stood out for Winshore in the stage ride from Stamford to Providence. He had asked Miss Wilming, "What would Christ do if he came to Boston now today?" and she had said, "Give me time on that, I must sleep on it," and the next day had answered, "Christ in Boston now this hour would find a way to rebuke the proud men who live for themselves and cherish personal selfish material interests. He would seek out the publicans, the Pharisees, the hypocrites, the whited sepulchers, and speak burning words to them before an immense mass meeting on the Common. Then time would pass and they would raise a rabble and haul him to the Common in a dung cart and instead of a crown of thorns they would give him a coat of tar and feathers and instead of a cross and crucifixion they would shackle him to the whipping post and flog him till they heard his words, 'It is finished.'"

And once she had smiled with a queer slant of her mouth, "Do you know you remind me of Old Charlie?"

"And he was?"

"A one-eyed white horse that lasted fourteen years on our farm.

385

A big white face sprinkled with freckles. I caught myself telling Old Charlie things I didn't know I knew before."

And as for the Frame brothers, Winshore had changed his impressions of them. He saw they considered themselves British aristocrats of good breeding and manners, in three generations of military men. They believed themselves to represent the might of the British monarchy, the authority of the Government centered at London to rule, to throw in troops where there was resistance and defiance as at Boston, to restore law and order and exact obedience.

"I came believing the acts of the Crown had perhaps been too severe and should be moderated," Winshore had heard Lieutenant George Frame saying to his brother. "I came to Boston highly prepossessed in favor of America. Then I found their behavior so mad, so inconsistent with that gratitude they owe Great Britain, that I have entirely changed my opinion of them. Though at the same time I do not entirely side with the Government in all their measures, I have come to agree with the sentiments of the best people at Boston that those who are making the greatest noise, the liberty side, should they get the better of things, it would end in the destruction of all the colonies, as New England wants to grind the other provinces. The sensible people of Boston, the people of property, and I suppose they are interested as much as any in the matter, hold that one master is better than a thousand and they would rather be oppressed by a King than by a rascally mob led by demagogues."

"Why hasn't there been more stern action to quell the rising disorders?" Francis Frame had asked.

"There is a considerable opinion that the ringleaders and Committee heads should have been seized many months ago. They are chiefly poor miscreants, of no affluence, who have come to enjoy the importance to which they are raised by their commotions. It is understood too they believe that when danger threatens they can abscond into the back country for safety."

"Has the clergy taken no stand for obedience and order?"

"The New England clergymen have been overwhelmingly mutinous and rebellious. They rise in their pulpits and affirm that the commands of God come first and the civil rulers' second, that what they preach is the politics of Christ."

"Does General Gage realize he should have applied a strong hand?"

"Loyalist leaders over Massachusetts are in fear night and day of the Committees that delight in the tar-and-feather procedure, and it is said General Gage now views the common people as mad, stung and provoked to their madness by demagogues and firebrands who should long ago have been killed, a few killings at first and then more and more if necessary to end mob rule. General Gage is now planning, I understand, to march troops out of Boston into the country towns to accustom the people to the sight of troops and the might and

386

authority of the King. Earl Percy, in command of the troops, estimates the Rebels as quick and violent yet at heart cowards who can be cruel and tyrannical. I am not so sure of that. They have desperate fanatics such as the vicious Jack Mallon at Elizabeth and that old hunter we saw at Bristol. I do not enjoy contemplating a long war with their armed forces. I believe we have underestimated the resistance strength of our opponents."

They were professional fighting men, trained to command troops in war. They made casual references to their service in Spain and their quick recoveries from slight wounds. They could stand where bullets were flying and be cool about it, Winshore guessed. They had asked for tea at Bristol, unaware that in New Jersey as in Massachusetts you could have tea at a Whig tavern only in secret. They had lifted their glasses in a toast to the King at Elizabeth because they felt challenged and in a like situation again they would not affront a roomful of Rebels. They had shown consideration for fellow passengers, with a courtesy that impressed Winshore. "They are men who can't help what they are doing. They have soft streaks in them, the way they talk about their father in England. They have humor and can laugh to their toes. They are not the despicable ruffians and murderers that my boy Locke terms them. Lieutenant George Frame actually had a queer sweetness on his face at times when talking to women and children. When he orders his platoons to shoot men down, he will do it with little hate and a large sense of duty."

Many hours since leaving Philadelphia, Winshore had sat behind, in front or alongside the two Lieutenants and they couldn't be guarded at all times in what they said to each other and Winshore considered himself no eavesdropper and it had merely happened that he came to know the two men in part as they knew each other. They were in their early thirties now but in their late teens in rollicking hours they had sung "Kiss the Cold Winter Away" and out of New Haven they had chased away gloom with the chorus:

> Sing rousy, tousy, rantum, scantum,
> Laugh and lie down is the play:
> We'll cuddle together,
> To keep out the weather,
> And kiss the cold winter away;
> Kiss, kiss the cold winter away,
> Kiss, kiss the cold winter away.

Softly and without giving the words they had hummed with a gay military precision the tune of "The British Grenadiers." And they had a capacity for silence and could sit for an hour next to each other and not a word. Francis, it would seem, had a wife and a boy in England and was vague about the wife and gravely tender about the boy. He joked about George's many women and ventured, "I deem

387

it entirely within possibility that you shall return to England with the daughter of a rich Massachusetts Loyalist."

"Such a daughter is not yet on the horizon, Francis."

"I have heard the Boston horizon is filled with them and they are eager for such a specimen as you."

"May Heaven grant that between combats and campaigns there will be time for that horizon. We have days of stern duty this year, by all signs and prognostications."

Francis sang a late song from London and his brother picked up the chorus and they sang together of Brother Bobby who first came to town a country clown "but now, to be sure, he's altered quite, can do anything but read and write" and:

> "He bows and struts with modish swing,
> And the ladies cry, Lord! he's quite the thing.
> He is neat the thing, and complete the thing,
> And the ladies cry, he is quite the thing.
> He bows and struts with modish swing,
> And the ladies cry, he is quite the thing."

They counted themselves modern men of a nation with high destiny for wide-flung modern empire, waging its wars with modern weapons and paraphernalia unknown to former generations. Low-voiced they recited to pass the time and for the fraternity of saying together the traditional lines of the famous military units of which they were officers: Hercules, Alexander, Miltiades, some talk of them "but of all the world's brave heroes there's none that can compare, with a tow, row, row, row, to the British Grenadiers." "All the gods celestial, descended from their spheres, Beheld with admiration the British Grenadiers," ran the gay extravagant lines—and verses:

> None of those ancient heroes e'er saw a cannon ball,
> Or knew the force of powder to slay their foes withal;
> But our brave boys do know it, and banish all their fears,
> With a tow, row, row, row, row, the British Grenadiers.
>
> Whene'er we are commanded to storm the Palisades,
> Our leaders march with fusees, and we with hand grenades,
> We throw them from the glacis about our enemies' ears,
> With a tow, row, row, row, row, the British Grenadiers.

Men of duty, orders, discipline, regimentation—men of barracks and journeys, marches and roll calls, weapons and discipline—men of traditions, possessed and dominated first of all by traditions, by the past. Gently and with delay and extended hesitations must any particular one of those traditions be questioned, be modified. Where a button was sewed yesterday it must be sewed likewise today. Life was regulations, pay, provisions, furloughs, active duty. Life was camp kettles, knapsacks, drills, active duty. Life was leaves, special missions, articles of war, evolutions and drill, communications and transport, drum and bugle alarms, marching and battle orders, names answering roll call, names of the wounded and missing, names of the dead— men of duty, routine, regime, men of fixed habits in thought, men instructed to believe and expected to hold to the persuasion that tried and established methods in the government, in the church, in trade or the arts, should be changed, if at all, very slowly, with hesitations, care and doubt.

So ran Winshore's impressions, fading toward sleep, after seeing a heavy sack of tea hanged on the gallows and then burned. Then there flitted across his mind the words of Lieutenant George Frame on being asked casually, out of Norwalk, "What would Christ do if he came to Boston now today?" and the Lieutenant brightly and offhand, "What an odd *in*quiry! I declare I had never given it any consideration, sir. It is rather out of my realm. Would you believe it, sir, I have not as yet permitted myself to indulge in speculations regarding what the Saviour would do if he entered the city of London, England, now today?" That was all. And Winshore could only draw the inference that the Lieutenant had a definite feeling that if Christ should come to earth now today, He would visit London first and Boston probably not at all.

In the mental blur before sleep Winshore instructed himself, "If I have a dream tonight it must begin in a conversation with Old Charlie, the one-eyed white horse."

* * * * * * * * * *

Chapter 6

* * * * * * * * * *

The Wilming Farm

"WHAT'S the trouble with Mim?" Agnes Wilming asked her sister Deborah.

"I don't know any more than you do, Aggie," said Deborah.

"Man trouble, Deb?"

"Might be."

"She's laughed and danced her way through every man trouble so far."

"But not this one."

"And is it only one? Who knows but it's two men she's tangled with?"

"You mean that Son of Liberty from Philadelphia, that reckless young devil, is taking her away from the British Lieutenant and she don't know how to smooth it over?"

"That might be it. "

"That would be too easy. We're just gossipin, Deb."

"She used to give us hints, Aggie. Now she keeps so still."

"More than a love affair she's hidin. That mind and heart of hers always had hidin places. That love she could manage. She'd find a way."

"That's what I've been sayin to myself. You remember how many times her mind would sort of go dark and her talk run off into a babble we was sure had sense to it if we could only figure it out."

"Maybe we love her too much. Maybe we're too anxious she ought to have everything like she wants it."

"And we know right well there have been the times she was a pig, she was selfish, she wanted more for herself than she had a right to."

The mother had come in. She heard part of what Agnes and Deborah were saying as they washed and wiped dishes and scoured copper and iron pots and pans in the kitchen corner of the big room in their house near Lexington off a by-lane from the Boston road. And the mother Ruth Wilming spoke sharp to her daughters and then relented.

"If I hadn't heard you say maybe you love her too much I'd be ashamed of you for callin up the few times she was a pig. It's no time now for goin back to her wantin more for herself than she had a right to. There was days when she did just that but if you'll look back you'll see in those days she was as hard on herself, as severe and mean on herself you might say, as she was on any of us."

"You referrin to Jabez Hunker, Ma, and those days."

"That's one time."

"And how do you mean?"

"She led him on, many people said, and she was aimin to live on one of the biggest farms around in the Concord neighborhood. Maybe she did lead him on. I wouldn't say. I think she knows if she did and she was sorry if she did mislead the first rich man that laid a proposal to her. Still and all he was ten years older than her and a widower with two children and he should've known what he was doin better than her. Then when everybody sees he ain't callin on her after him bein so regular and he ain't takin her home from church any more because she has quit goin to church on purpose to not be meetin him, the talk gets goin that she needn't have encouraged him as she did and we can't be sure Jabez Hunker didn't help that talk along, him puttin on a sorrow and a regret about it that was leastways and part a put-on."

"And she couldn't stand the talk," hurriedly spoke Aggie. "You'd've thought she had a child by Jabez Hunker and Pa was goin to bring a bastardy suit against Jabez."

"You're mean today, Aggie," the mother rebuked. "A mean heart you've got today for your sister."

"I'd do anything you could name for Mim and you know I would. When I talk mean it's what she hides from us. I get a helpless feelin."

"She's right, Ma, she would," said Deborah with a soft glance at her bothered mother.

"Course she's right, Ma," and Jake had come in and spoken, sixteen-year-old Jake with his overly bright smile, a twisting face, Jake dumping an armful of wood at the fireplace. He was their Jake and his pinched sweet smile now reminded them all that if what they had for Mim was deep affection or love, what he had was an adoration. In his blank or sullen moods she had been the only one who could bring him out of it, it was she could wake pride in him about coming to the table with his face washed and hair combed, and from her he had learned he could do more by gentling a horse than beating it.

Darius had come in with Jake and said nothing, twenty-one-year-old Darius, or as they said it, "Duh-rye'us," a year younger than Mim, heavy-lidded and melting brown eyes, a shaggy head of brown hair, sturdy of build, a slope to the shoulders and one higher than the other, his straight nose broken from the weight of an ox yoke he was under trying to wrangle into place when he was eleven and the ox yoke heavier than he; weather-beaten and rough-handed Darius had for three or four years done the larger share of the farm work, looked earthy, his ruddy face wearing sun and wind on it and a curious calm, the beneficence of a youth at peace with himself and as he would say, "with God." What is termed reverence, a sense of things seen and unseen being sacred, gave out from him. He sought fellowship for this at church and found it in degree among others who were seekers. One of his eight great-great-grandfathers had been born in Plymouth and moved to Providence and worked actively with the Seekers headed by Roger Williams. Darius liked quiet, tried to keep away from arguments, kept friendly with the Sons of Liberty and the Minute Men and couldn't join them as a sworn member. He had been the playmate, the chum, the trusted one of his sister Mim more than any other in the family.

They had seen the barn go up fifteen years ago, running together at daybreak rubbing sleep out of their eyes to see the carpenter and his two men helpers, except for the noon hour sawing and hammering until the "sunsetting" as they called it. Darius and Mim had driven cows and tugged at opening gates and letting down pasture bars and walked barefoot together to pick berries in the heat of summer and nuts in late October and early November, not putting on shoes till the second or third frost. They had pressed their faces at windowpanes and watched the blowing snow pile and whirl around the well sweep, the barn, the two oaks and five cedars near by and branches far and high where last summer they had sat and laughed to each other. They had set a ladder and crept up into the garret together only a few times to see the long rows of dried apples sliced and strung, to smell herbs and dusty, musty things sort of sickish, and to see the little belongings and reminders of the two little brothers and those syllables of fear "pu-trid sore throat." Darius and Mim had gone sledding, skating, sleigh-riding together, had churned butter, pitched hay, scrubbed the kitchen floor, carried a jug of cool water wrapped in a thick wet cloth to men in the fields and at the sound of the dinner horn raced to the house.

They could remember their grandmother on their mother's side. Her inheritance money had bought the farm and she wore a checked apron, a spotless white muslin cap, sitting summer afternoons by the back door with her spinning wheel drawing out threads that later on winter days she would weave, on a loom upstairs, into coverlets, tablecloths, towels. "She's like you, Darius, never hurries," Mim had said. They had stood holding hands gazing at her face on her burial day. "No more hurried than she was at her spinning wheel," said Darius. They cried because they would miss her, they agreed, not because they had any doubt where she had gone. They read aloud and together for a second time that winter a *Pilgrim's Progress* they owned, parts of the family Bible, and plays of *Hamlet* and *Macbeth* they borrowed.

Then Mim grew into sixteen, seventeen, eighteen and began "going with fellows," neighbor farmer boys, a storekeeper's son at Arlington, a gay spark from Salem who visited relatives. Not a flirt, was Mim, said the Wilmings. "The boys take to her, she likes their company and why shouldn't they the way she can dance, skate, sing?" At parties, picnics, hayrides, church socials, they would call on her for songs, especially "Green Grows the Laurel," and her contralto would give it low and smooth:

I once had a sweetheart, but now I have none.
He's gone and he's left me, he's left me alone.
But since he has left me, contented I'll be,
For he loves another far better than me.

Green grows the laurel and so falls the dew.
Lonely am I since I parted with you.
At our next meeting I hope you'll prove true.
We'll change the green laurel to the red, white and blue.

I wrote my love a letter with love between the lines.
He wrote me another all tangled with twine,
Saying, "Keep your love letters and I will keep mine,
Go write to your sweetheart, while I write to mine."

I passed my love's window both early and late.
The look that he gave me makes my poor heart ache;
The look that he gave me ten thousand would kill.
And those are the looks from the boy I love still.

Green grows the laurel and so falls the dew.
Lonely am I since I parted with you.
At our next meeting I hope you'll prove true.
We'll change the green laurel to the red, white and blue.

Twice it happened a young man said she had gone too far with him, that she oughtn't to have given him the kind of encouragement she did unless it was love and she had matrimony in mind. And Darius had answered for her to one of them, "You're thinking too much about matrimony and not enough about love or you would know she didn't consider you for either matrimony or love."

Darius saw less of her and his emptiness about her he filled with his great thanks that she had lived and was still alive and he could wonder about what she was doing and what would come of her doings. She did hurry too much, just naturally swift about anything she did, wearing herself out and then going into silent and sullen moods and everyone knew it was on her conscience she wasn't skipping and flying about, always Darius her comfort, mainstay, shield, when these spells came— or the other spells of days when she said, "My mind is dark," and nothing much more than just that or "I grope my way."

Her going away had been gradual. Her Aunt Ellen in Boston, the sister of her mother, with a modest estate left by her sea-captain husband, had lived alone, took Mim in one winter for a two-month visit, the next winter three months, had named Mim in her will to have a ten-acre farm two miles out of Boston. Then Mim had become fascinated with work she found and a new many-sided life she began in Boston.

Darius looked at his mother after Jake's "Course she's right, Ma," stepped over and put his arm around her shoulder and low-voiced, "You're right, Ma, and Aggie's right and it may be a strength and stay to remember there is an All-Seeing Eye."

Hard-worn looked the stout short mother, her dark-red hair graying, her plain wide face with lines coming on it these last years what with Noah Wilming turning the living room of their house into a Liberty Room serving coffee, beer, ale, food to those calling, an inn on the face of it but rather a meeting place for the Sons of Liberty and for Minute Men. Month by month the place grew more restless and late afternoons and evenings often Ma Wilming could see the Liberty Room crowded with men bent on trouble. She favored the Independence and Liberty they talked about and she feared the cost of it and she knew that Aggie and Deborah and Darius knew with her that Mim was being caught in some kind of a swirl that had to do with events yet to crash. Aggie and Deborah leaned to their father's way of looking at it, that there must be resistance, bloody fighting, men killed. Darius held off, went his own way, kept silence, seemed to have some serene counsel of his own, blaming nobody, his own resolves not clear to the others.

"He's a good man," Ruth Wilming would say of her husband though he had become careless about the farm work, leaving more and more of it to Darius and the girls, drinking more ale than was good for him in the excited discussions of the Minute Men late at night in the Liberty Room, and for a fairly pious and decent churchman swearing occasionally as he didn't used to, fearful oaths at "the lobster-backs" who had closed the port of Boston and swarmed by thousands into that city, throwing thousands of men out of work and making it what many called "a dead city." The father had hurt Mim before she went away. The way he talked to her they took as part of the reason why she felt more free to go away. He was the only one in the family who had hurt her. He gave her all the best-known and simple arguments there were for the colonies to resist, to make war if must be, to win Independence and Liberty and show the world a great new Republic of free men the like of which the earth had never seen. And Mim argued against him to the end that it wasn't as simple as he made out, that the cost would be terrible, that the Sons of Liberty and their mobs had done things so brutal and needless that she was afraid of what they would do with Independence and a new Republic.

* * * * * * * * * *

Chapter 7

* * * * * * * * * *

Tar and Feathers

THEY could have killed the man but they didn't. They wanted to kill him. They told each other before and after the action that killing him would have been fair and just payment. What they gave him instead of death however put scars on his dignity as a human being, put a bitter taste on his tongue that would be there till death. What they forgot, or did not know and therefore could not forget, was that they took risks on what they did to themselves.

When they set up a Liberty Pole and put on a celebration with roast pig and hard cider free for all, Reggs stayed away and, without raising a fuss, got others to stay away who might have come and who made excuses that they were owing to him or they might want a loan from him someday or for different reasons they didn't want him holding anything against them. After they had dedicated their Tree of Liberty it was known he had said they could stand under it and he would try not to and had considered the language of their sign under the tree "not well advised" and "a trifle vehement." The sign read: "The Tree of Liberty, and Cursed is he who cuts this Tree."

Erect, square-shouldered, short and thickset, pudgy-faced with pop-eyes and heavy jaws, Hobart Reggs was jolly, self-assertive, knew many standard jokes and liked to tell them, enjoyed high living. A fairly shrewd manager, he had inherited two farms, his wife another, and they did rather decently by the tenants who worked the farms. His wife was a friendly homebody, would have preferred less of high living than he went in for. She had hopes for her two daughters Sapphira and Abbie who had been to Boston under the best of tutors in language, music, dancing, manners.

They had merely threatened him so long as he was a passive Loyalist, openly against Independence for the colonies, a plain-spoken Tory whose farms and elegant village house had given him standing and influence. That he rode in a chaise to Boston and enjoyed parties and cotillions, with his daughters dancing with British officers, was held against him but nothing done about it except that once he had to forego a trip to Boston because the wheels of his chaise were missing and another time his favorite horse died of poison. The local authorities, selectmen, constables, the justice of the peace, and the county sheriff and his deputies, either mocked at him or with quiet sympathy told him they would like to be more active toward law and order but it would be no use till the excitement over Independence had passed.

Then came the incident of George Bromley, whose real name was William Fedger. He worked on Adam Wheeler's farm, a sturdy, good-natured fellow who seldom came to the village, drank little and minded his own business. Then one day came a British lieutenant with two sergeants and they arrested George Bromley and tried to examine Adam Wheeler who defied them and refused to answer questions and told them he would like to see them try to arrest him in that neighborhood. They identified George Bromley as William Fedger, a private in a company of British Fusiliers who had deserted, having two years and one month yet to serve of his enlistment period. They took him to Boston, and full reports were brought back to the village of what was done to William Fedger.

Year by year as more thousands of British troops had been poured into Boston, the struggle against them had taken many forms. One was to get a soldier drunk and haul him away and offer him work and pay at a distance where he would be safe—and there were such cases. Another was to argue and plead with a trooper, make him see the Independence cause and promise him protection in a solid Whig community. For these and other reasons Governor General Thomas Gage had given it out he could no longer be easy with deserters. They would take their punishment, no remissions of sentence.

Therefore as ordered by court-martial, William Fedger, shackled to a whipping post on Boston Common, took on his bare back two hundred lashes, each stinging, whining cut of the crimsoned leather thongs counted, witnessed so the count was correct, two hundred lashes, no more, no less. The witnesses included two regiments of soldiers spick-and-span in long-tailed red coats and white trousers, drawn up in dress-parade order, to see a deserter flogged—they all knew that technical term of the court-martial sentence—"flogged." They saw Private William Fedger slump and they knew when he had passed out of his senses and the pain faded. They heard the reports later that he would live but must linger months in hospital.

Adam Wheeler and other Minute Men and Sons of Liberty felt a challenge about the affair. The flogging lash had reached out and cut them a little with its indecency and cruelty. Twice a young man had come out from Boston to meet their Committee for Observation and Prevention. At the first meeting he said there were indications pointing to the informer, but they couldn't be certain. At the second meeting the matter was certain. The Boston organization had its way of getting at facts high in the military and political circles around the Governor General. And it was weeks after the flogging that the young man from Boston could tell them with certainty that the man Reggs, owner of two farms and the largest and most elegant home in the village, had been to a dancing and drinking party where he had casually mentioned a farm hand near his village who didn't come in often, hadn't been there long, and working for "the loud-mouthed incendiary Adam Wheeler," it might be the fellow was a deserter. The officers had asked Reggs to do his best, without prying or taking chances, to learn more about the fellow. And on a later trip to Boston, Hobart Reggs had told them he believed it worth while for them to send out men who could identify the deserter, if such he were. The case was clear that George Bromley would still be living a decent healthy life on Adam Wheeler's farm if, as Wheeler phrased it, "that goddam Reggs hadn't put his nose in where it didn't belong." A report from the bedside of William Fedger didn't soften anyone's feelings. Fedger slept face down and lay awake face down for weeks and then had moaned over the itches and twitchings of healing flesh and the beginnings of new skin.

At early candlelight one evening three men of the Committee called on Mr. Reggs, pulling the brass knocker on the front door as though they might tear it loose, walking through the door opened by the maid and striding past her as all three gave low growls, "We want Mr. Reggs." He had heard them, sensed their coming, led them into the big front room where one of his daughters quit her playing of "Drink to Me Only with Thine Eyes" at the spinet. The entering Committeemen glimpsed her pink flounces swishing and fading at another door.

They asked Mr. Reggs several blunt questions. They led up to their main question. They startled him with information, names and dates they had picked up somewhere.

"On your trips to Boston you have met officers of the British Fusiliers and Grenadiers?"

"I have."

"You know the names and faces of some of those officers?"

"Naturally I do."

"You know in particular one named Lieutenant George Frame?"

"I have met him, yes."

"Your daughters have danced with him, have they not?"

"I believe so."

"And you have sat at a table with Lieutenant George Frame and drunk punch and hot rum toddy with him, have you not?"

"I believe so."

"And you talked with him about deserters from the British Army?"

"He started talking about them."

"He said there were many more desertions lately than there used to be?"

"Yes."

"He talked about General Gage deciding on no more leniency for deserters, didn't he?"

"He did."

"He spoke of deserters sentenced to be flogged and then the sentence being remitted but this soft policy must be changed to a hard one—from then on every deserter caught would be flogged?"

"Y-yes."

"And several cases had been reported of deserters changing their names and settling down to another life in towns in western Massachusetts and eastern New York State?"

"Uh—yes."

"And twice they had nearly laid their hands on a deserter working on a farm near Boston, sticking close to the farm and keeping out of sight when anyone came—and in these two cases the deserter had got away because Rebels passed along the word of British soldiers coming to take him? Lieutenant Frame mentioned this to you?"

"He did—I believe that was in his talk."

"And was it about there you told him you couldn't be sure but you had your suspicions about a new hired man on a farm out from your village?"

"No, I don't remember saying anything like that."

"You had two glasses of punch and a hot rum toddy along about that time and your mind ain't clear on how you told Lieutenant Frame you just had suspicions, you wasn't sure, and still it might be you could help them catch a deserter and you wouldn't have any hand in it that anybody among your home folks would know about and it might be your way of getting back at the home folks for what you don't like about 'em."

"I would answer your questions if this was a court of law and I was on trial."

"You're on trial, sir, you're a witness before a pretty real court, we're telling you, Mr. Reggs."

The same question was asked in several different ways and each time Reggs made out he wasn't sure he could remember or he might give a better answer before a court of law.

"It's your hash, Mr. Reggs," said one of the three, rising to leave.

"Your hash and we're going to settle it," said another.

They took their hats and left. Mr. Reggs stood at the open front door and watched them fade into the chill of a November evening murk with a light drizzle neither rain nor mist. Reggs had Job the choreman shake up a big fire and sat before it with his wife and daughters talking about whether the time had come for them to move into Boston. Here and there over the province of Massachusetts a score of good Loyalists, after indignities or threats, had sold what they could of land and goods and moved for safety into Boston and the shelter of the British troops. The Reggses might go. They would think about it.

The daughter resumed playing "Drink to Me Only with Thine Eyes" at the spinet. She smiled merrily and it was more a matter of curiosity than anything else with her. She was naturally inquisitive. Her friends spoke of Sapphira Reggs as a born gossip and she was asking, "But tell us, father, were you the first or not the first to give Lieutenant Frame the information that a strange man was working on Adam Wheeler's farm?"

"If I did or if I did not, Sapphira, it is no concern of yours and entirely a confidential matter between myself and the British authorities of Boston."

She had hurt him. The question was a bitter one that coiled and recoiled in his heart and mind.

"I shouldn't have asked that, father. Forgive me and let it pass." And she played and sang "Drink to Me Only with Thine Eyes" as she had sung it with an octet of gay British officers at a Boston party and hoping one of the officers could see she wanted it to have special meaning for him.

The anxious mother and the less pretty sister Abbie let her sing and sat sorrowful and thought her light-minded. On feather mattresses in canopied four-poster beds they slept that night, a rather broken sleep for all but Sapphira who was born careless and a gossip. Her slight and well-formed body, her pale-blond curls and china-blue eyes, her pink cheeks and a mouth often puckering in sauciness, she rather prized herself and could look at a wiggling bare toe and say, "A fig for tomorrow."

They had seen to it, the local Committee for Observation and Prevention had, that Mr. Reggs should be at home awaiting a caller who wished to talk about buying one of his farms. They had further seen to it that the work of the evening, the very carefully planned work, should be done by outsiders with faces not known in the village and

398

neighborhood. These outsiders rode in from farms and near-by towns, tying their horses in scattered places, and meeting in the harness-maker's shop. Behind locked doors and shuttered windows, by the light of two small candles, they talked over the plan, then moved with speed. It was over in less than half an hour.

At the front and rear of the house they stationed watchmen. The brass knocker on the front door was slammed down three times, four, five and six times. The door opened and Mr. Reggs himself stood there expecting the prospective farm buyer. They took hold of him and put a gag over his mouth and led him into the big front room. They led Mrs. Reggs and the daughter Abbie into the next room, led in also the choreman and the maid, asked for Sapphira and heard she was in Boston. They warned the three women and the choreman to keep quiet, not a word, and no use trying to get out for the house was surrounded, blew out the two candles in the room, warned them not to relight those candles and to make no interference with what they might hear or see —then the doors of that room were closed and locked.

In the big front room they read a statement to the doomed man to the effect that he had betrayed the people of the Province of Massachusetts, that he had served the enemies of that people as a base and treacherous informer, that he had given himself to the service of a brutal and unwanted soldiery imposed on the people without their desire or consent, that his vile deed was worthy of a serpent and he should therefore be given punishment as though he were less than human. He would have talked and tried for an explanation or an apology, he would have tried to find out if he could reason with them or perhaps buy them off, if money could be any inducement. But the gag was tied fast and giving him pain, twisting his face out of its natural look.

The statement having been read, they told him to get out of his clothes, take 'em all off, everything. He hesitated, made signs with his hands, tried to send his voice through the gag. They told him once more. He stood helpless, swaying. A leather thong cut across his face, the right side, then the left. His coat came off, too slow, he was told, there was no time to lose. Again a thong stinging his neck and hands. Faster he moved and was out of his stock, waistcoat, trousers, shirt, footwear, undershirt and drawers. Naked and trembling he was led to near the fireplace where a black pot had been hung over the fire. He must now stand still, he was told. Unless he stood still a thong would be laid to his back two hundred times as happened to a certain British fusilier on Boston Common.

The faces around him were sober, grim, solemn, fierce—faces white with anger—they would as soon kill him as do what they were doing— so much he could read on them. When lips parted for anything like a smile—it was a leer of menace and terror.

The black pot was unhooked from over the fire. Two men dipped brushes into it and swiftly began coating his shoulders, chest, arms with a warm sticky black tar. They had covered him, all but the head, even lifting his feet to give the bottoms their tar soles.

Then came a touch of the ceremonial. The two men had finished their assignment. One of them handed his brush to a tall young fellow with a stuck-out chin, dark wavy hair flowing from under his slouch hat, troubled blue eyes. The local Committeemen would have recognized him as the Boston agent who had brought out the evidence against the doomed man. As some form of special tokening, as one from enemy-invested Boston, he was to coat the head of the victim. With sweeping strokes of the brush, leaving the nostrils open, up, down, and sideways, gag and all were smeared over, the eyes with their lids stuck fast beyond opening.

Now came a commotion and a shrill crying and the door to the hall opened and Sapphira Reggs stood there wrestling to get loose from the clutches of the front watch. She saw the figure she knew must be her father, saw the young man with the brush on tiptoes slapping a tight-fitting black cap of tar on her father's head of hair. Her knees wobbled and she fell in a faint and three men took her into the next room to join her mother and sisters. The head, excepting the nose, having been completely tar-covered, a feather mattress brought from upstairs was cut open and a thick coat of white feathers spread over the coat of tar. Over the Turkey carpet and rugs were spilled out paths and splotches in the emptying of the tar pot. Four men swiftly shook the slashed mattress till floating white feathers filled the room. One of the men, among the last to go, and as a farewell, lifted a log of wood and brought it down on the spinet, leaving the instrument splintered.

Before the fireplace they had set a large oaken chair, a massive piece of furniture, carved with royal emblems and fixed deep on both sides the lettering in antique as of the Geneva Bible style: "God Save the King."

To this chair they led the doomed man, dazed with shame and blinded with tight eyelids. In the chair they seated him. Then they moved into the hall and out the front door and away to their horses, the last man opening the door to the next room and calling in hoarse voice to the women and the choreman, "He's here—and now you can have him, what's left of him."

Chapter 8

Is Love a Necklace?

THE young man stayed overnight with a Whig farmer who knew him as "one of us." He slept poorly and began riding to Boston a little after daybreak. A light snow had fallen. The sun came out. The horse was a small dark bay, four years old, eager to travel. The hills shone, the pines stood grave with affirmations that life could be worse for him. And he wasn't easy in his mind. He had wrestled with the ins and outs of it during the night. Now in the daylight and the dazzling sun on the snow he was saying he had been a fool last night and he oughtn't have gone where he did and taken a hand in what was acting.

Two or three of the men had been wonderful. To know them was worth something. They hated the night's work. But they really meant it when they said they could have killed the man for his vile and low treachery, that what they were doing to him was less than exact justice. These men had lights on their faces and in their eyes that told of dedication. They were consecrated to the cause of Independence. They held no personal hate for Reggs. He meant so little to them as a person that they honestly hated to see him suffer. It was what he stood for, what he embodied and represented to them, it was that and the breath and shape of it they wanted to belittle and humiliate, to degrade and mutilate, to make it an image of the foul and unclean, utterly lacking in human sanctity. Those two or three men had something. They would be there with their dream of justice in the harder days yet to come. They were not the trouble of his heart this bright winter morning with a horse willing and somewhat skittish under his saddle.

Others in the acting were not so good to remember. Some had gone through with it too easily and too formally, as though in a hog-killing you know where to begin and where to end and you don't scrape the hair off till you've first scalded the hog. Others had definitely taken it as an adventure, serious enough, yet an affair where their wits and cleverness were pitted against the English troops in Boston and they would show they could win and have their laugh at the enemy. Still a few others had let themselves have moments of queer glee over seeing their victim twist, writhe, groan: their first motive was revenge: they would have favored giving Reggs exactly the same kind of a whip as that used on William Fedger's naked back on Boston Common. And at first two of the men had quivered with a peculiar satisfaction and it could be they hated the man having land, property, goods and a way of life they had a fear of because such barriers had always stood between their own hard cramped ways of life and his more smooth and soft way: this antagonism was gratified in those moments they saw him sink to less than dust with all his dignity smeared and smutted.

A tough well-knit body had this rider, six feet tall and the proportions there, his hair dark, wavy and thick hanging over his ears, a straight nose, a ruddy skin, a chin that jutted out somewhat irregular and overly bold, and deep-blue eyes, this morning deep-troubled blue eyes. Often enough his conscience bothered him about others and what they were doing wrong. Not often did he ask himself what it was stirring in him that was like a guilt he wanted to be rid of.

Those two or three men last night that he loved for what was on their faces—perhaps had he and those men alone done the deed—and no others present—then it would not be haunting him. It would then have had the air of clean justice, white and impersonal, Mr. Reggs being nobody in particular to begin with and the same at the end, and those visiting him with punishment not being persons with names and identities but swift anonymous archangels, duly authorized and perfectly humble agents of the holy cause of American Independence. It was those other men gave it the look, for him, of a mean sporting event, a game played for grim fun. He would rather have had it a holy ritual of awe and sacrifice betokening a grand dark dream for which men must dare and dare.

"It was a mob affair," he broke out to himself. "And I was one of the mob. They kept straight faces but was it fun for most of them to see me get the brush into my hand and give my personal touch as a representative from Boston, a visitor, a delegate, an ambassador? Why couldn't I be there as a witness? Why must they have it I should be a participant?"

He took note vaguely of shy peeps and dim whispers of spring among bushes and branches—April and spring waiting and hidden behind the bluster and snow of March. He thought of the girl he would soon be seeing and how he must keep back from her what was done last night and of how even though it should be right and no betrayal about his telling it to her, it would come hard to tell her of his own hand in it and the confusions and shames stirring in him. Nearly a year now he had been shaken by this girl, smitten deep, each wild about the other, each of them snared and swept, each of them beset with secrets they could not tell each other, each of them writhing and groaning under several kinds of pain and desolation.

Months ago it was, away last October and the autumn leaves blowing, she made up a dance for him, naming it: "Love Is a Two-face." She spoke her lines and then stepped and swayed and swirled them, arms, torso and feet in pantomime and moving with the shaded changes of thanks and horror on her face. He could remember those lines. She wrote them for him. He spoke them twice and once more as he rode along at a slow walk along an upgrade—those lines:

"Is love a necklace I can put on and take off? Is love a shoe I can slip on or kick off, if I please, to the moon?

"In a single hour, it would seem, love can be harder than the iron of a blacksmith's anvil—and that same hour be more thin and baffling than the blue shadow of a red rose thrown on a piece of white satin, more fine and tantalizing than a rainbow glimpsed in a bubble in the sun and in a flickering moment the seven prisms of mist in color vanishing.

"In five minutes by the clock, love can be a thrush pouring flights of song with scarlet numbers and dancing alphabets—and in that same five minutes before your eyes that triumphant wild thrush becomes a monkey scratching a louse at his ribs and a louse at his buttocks while he mocks at you with his jeering monkey-faces.

"Love is a great gleaming eagle that will sweep you for a ride to the top of the sky and a spread of green valleys and winding rivers for your eyes—it happens, it is an event—and love is a buzzard you can mistake for an eagle to ride, a scavenger who drops you to your death and takes its time to feed on you and pick your bones white and polished—this too happens and this too is an event."

Deep was the hold she had on him, deep with a loveliness touched with terror, only less deep than the hold of one other thing, what he most often termed the Cause. He spoke a prayer he might be able to adore and serve both her and the Cause. At the hilltop where his eyes met a mile of rolling plain of fields, pastures, orchards, farmhouses, he quoted from William Pitt speaking to the Parliament of Great Britain, shouting his favorite lines from the great Earl of Chatham:

"I am for toleration, that sacred right of nature and bulwark of truth. . . . Power without right is the most odious and detestable object that can be afforded the human imagination. . . . Where law ends, tyranny begins! . . . I can pronounce it an union solid, permanent and effectual. . . . The Americans are the sons, not the bastards of England. . . . I rejoice that America has resisted."

Months of elation he had had. It was good to be alive, to be in love with a wild dark-hearted girl, to be one joined to others serving the Cause, the great unfathomable Cause. Then he flashed back to the night before. He held up before his face the hand that had slapped the brush of tar back and forth over the face and the gag till the coating was thick with perfect black. And again his conscience gnawed at him. He had done right and he hadn't.

He wrestled with this in many phases as he jogged at a slow trot, walked the horse uphill and galloped an almost level downgrade. And he could come clear on one point. "If it was to do over again I wouldn't do it the way it was done. I would tell them before the acting began that I must be a silent witness only and not a participant, for the deed was of their thought and by their plan. When I walked into that house I did not know what the deed was to be. That was their secret to be unfolded to me. I expected to be a witness. They had not told me I was to be more than a witness. I could have refused and made a scene. That would have meant delay and risk besides spoiling their plan. I should have made them understand and agree, before I went with them, that they could not and must not call me to be aught else than a witness."

He rode at a slow trot with a singsong of "aught else and aught else and aught else" and then mocked bitterly, "And if you had told 'em that, would they or would they not have asked you what kind of a white-livered skunk the Minute Men of Boston had sent out as a representative?"

The mood of gloom was still on him when in Boston he put horse and saddle in the barn of the friend who lent him the nag and walked to the office of the *Massachusetts Spy* published and edited by Isaiah Thomas.

* * * * * * * * * *

Chapter 9

* * * * * * * * * *

At the *Massachusetts Spy*

PETER THOMAS kept a store in Boston and made a good living. His son Moses Thomas, who married Fidelity Grant, failed as a store-keeper, did poorly, died and left next to nothing to his wife and five children who included three-year-old Isaiah Thomas. They scrabbled a living however. Isaiah grew up and at seventeen rated a first-class printer. In 1770 Isaiah Thomas was a partner in starting the *Massachusetts Spy*, the foremost Whig newspaper of New England, the favorite and admired journal of the Sons of Liberty and the Minute Men. Now in 1775 Isaiah had been publishing Thomas's *New England Almanac* and started the *Royal American Magazine*. Twenty-six years old, he felt himself a beginner, colonial America likewise a beginner.

Tall, erect, neat, in his stock and wig Isaiah Thomas could be taken for a man of affairs, able and prosperous. Where his former archenemy Thomas Hutchinson had actually a face that could be termed ladylike, Isaiah Thomas ran to the other extreme and at first glance and later scrutiny was a man's man. Was his face ugly or just troublesome? You couldn't say for sure. As with Ordway Winshore the two sides of his face didn't match. His mouth with upslanted corners had fight, had hang-on and never-give-up to it, along with his bushy black eyebrows.

His large eyes had quest and decision in them, lurking with passion for the alphabet, printer's ink and what it could do to record and spread recorded thought. He was a demon for work at all hours day or night. His Mary Dill, the Bermuda girl he had married who gave him two children he was not sure he had fathered, his wife credited in gossip as sleeping with British officers and reputed a slut in reports he believed, she perhaps had her trials with him and he may have been a hard man to get along with. He would divorce her, though divorce was an ordeal, and end the gossip. A good printerman works better without gossip about who his wife is running with and especially if the gossip connects her with army officers, Isaiah Thomas reasoned.

As early as 1771 the Royal Government of the Province had ordered the Attorney General to prosecute Isaiah Thomas. This governor, Thomas Hutchinson, wanted to jail and fine Thomas. But the grand jury refused to find evidence of sedition or libel or treason. A watch was kept on him, as everybody knew. Now in early 1775 it was definitely understood that soon there would be action to clamp down on Isaiah Thomas and suppress the *Massachusetts Spy*.

At his office table this day of early March 1775 Isaiah Thomas sat with proof sheets, letters, papers, piled and scattered before him. Here at this table what he said, wrote, did, planned, had an interest for the enemy. Any day now he expected word from his spies that troops were to move in and seize his type, presses and equipment. He hoped that when such word came it would be early enough for him to call for the drays, wagons and Minute Men who had mapped the route they would take in hauling the establishment to Worcester. They would avoid the enemy guards at the Neck by crossing to Charlestown, over the Charles River with type and presses. Yes, here he was on this March morning with a business that had grown and prospered, with an excellent reputation and goodwill among the overwhelming majority of the people of New England, the foremost publisher and printer in America with the exception of Ben Franklin and possibly William Bradford of Philadelphia. And tomorrow or next week or certainly sometime next month he was sure he would have to move himself and his establishment out of Boston.

Street fights, robbery, murder, rape, clashes between troops and citizens and between Loyalists and Rebels, were on the increase. Governor General Gage and his Council blamed Isaiah Thomas as an instigator and fomentor of tumult, sedition, treason. Soon he would be an outlaw and a fugitive—that or their prisoner.

Two years younger than Isaiah Thomas was "the fellow from Philadelphia," as they called him at the printery. He was a first-rate printer, could set type, run a press, wrote news items, occasionally wrote an editorial, and at times went on errands and searches for Mr. Thomas and made confidential reports. Some rated this young fellow as a brawler who liked to drink, fight, dance, and go out with the girls.

Others discounted this as gossip and held such reputation given him by those he had beaten in fair fights and still others who would like to know more about affairs it was whispered he had a hand in and they didn't like it that he went his own way, kept his own counsel, had plenty of self-assurance and acted as though he could take care of himself in most any company.

This March morning he walked through the open door into the office with a smiling "Good morning, Mr. Thomas."

Thomas saw it was a forced smile, and rather gravely, "Good morning, Mr. Winshore. The affair last night was not entirely pleasant," which started Robert telling about it and his own mixed feelings.

"There is no perfect justice," said Thomas. "Always justice is complicated."

"We gave the man the wrath of God. Why should we then complicate it and befoul it with shaking feathers over the room and spilling tar over rugs and show a petty human anger by smashing a mahogany spinet?"

"You might look at it from another view and consider it fortunate that no man's anger went so far as to slide a knife across an informer's throat."

Robert Winshore thought a moment. "I see. It could have been murder. That has happened."

"In the days to come we shall have to expect more acting where justice is complicated with needless violence and petty anger and folly." And with a changed tone and interest, "You expect your father any day now?"

"Yes, Mr. Thomas."

"It will be good to see him. He will have news and messages from Ben Franklin and William Bradford, besides ideas from that boiling caldron of his brain."

"And I must show my father Boston so he can report back to Philadelphia. There is plenty to show."

"The American colonies and the overseas nations are all looking at Boston and wondering. We ourselves wonder where the first wild outbreak will come."

"It may come while father is here."

"If it does he will be at home in it—if I know him."

"I'm sure about that." And they talked of an editorial Robert was to write on the affair of Mr. Reggs, of several political errands for Mr. Thomas and various points where information might leak regarding the time and method by which the enemy should decide to clamp down and close up the successful, prosperous and popular publishing establishment of Isaiah Thomas.

Chapter 10

Mrs. Cavendish's Dress Shop

HER speech rolled loose and easy from her tongue, often so smooth and fast that part of what she was saying got lost. She could blur words and butter syllables. She was accustomed to hearing, "I *beg* your pardon, Mrs. Cavendish, but what *were* you saying?" She had no speech defect except high speed and was very pleasant about it and occasionally would say she was not as unfortunate as the Whig orator who enjoyed haranguing on John Locke's theory of natural rights and one said of him, "He always thickens the clear."

Her black silk gown, edged with wine-colored Manchester velvet, fitted her, was modish and quietly assertive. Her simple hairdress topped with a tuft of vague lavender feathers, known as an aigrette, affirmed fashion and the modish touch. Her latest announcement in the approved Loyalist weekly newspaper gave out that Rose Cavendish at the Sign of the Golden Ball on Front Street "makes and sells all sorts of Millinery, *viz*, Gauze caps, pungs, feathers, Italian breast flowers, shades, hats of all colours, ribbons, women's lamb and kid gloves and mitts, thread and blond laces, ivory fans, plain gauze, flowers ditto, figur'd modes, taffoties, sattins, palaneses, jockey caps, aigrets of all sorts, trimmings for shades, halters for ladies, skeleton wire, best pins, shoes, stay maker's trimmings, a variety of other Goods too tedious to mention."

From the cobblestoned sidewalk it was two steps up to the wide oak door with a brass-plate script: "Rose Cavendish." The narrow hallway or vestibule had a door with two small windows and entry into a large front room. From tall windows came light on dress goods, lace, ribbons, gauze, breast flowers, "of all shades and colours" as announced by Mrs. Cavendish. Her cheeks pink and round, stoutly built, richbosomed, she was an image of content and prosperity. Before her husband's death four years ago they had managed a shop for both ladies and gentlemen. Trade always good with her was now better than ever. With the arrival of five thousand troops and officers, social affairs, assemblies, parties, cotillions took new tones of gaiety, fashion, extravagance. Wives and daughters of well-to-do Loyalists of Boston, besides scores of other Loyalists who had moved from the country into the city for safety, seemed to be spending more freely for clothes, reckless and overly gay about it, a hint of fever and fear in the way they were throwing money into gowns, cloaks, dancing slippers and dress accessories.

Upstairs were Mrs. Cavendish's living quarters. To the rear of the front display room was a large workroom where each woman had a chair and worktable and there were chairs for patrons come to be measured or try fittings before a six-foot oval mirror in a gilt frame.

Of the three women in the room only Evelyn Trutt had been with Mrs. Cavendish from the beginning. Her husband had fought three years in the French and Indian War and it was fifteen years since he was killed in a night skirmish in Vermont and her earnings with needle and thimble had been the support of herself and a growing son. Since the closing of Boston port her son David had been out of work as a ropemaker, had done farm work and odd jobs, active beyond what he would tell her in what she termed "Liberty Boys' mischief." She was serious-minded, quietly religious, and with a casual sincerity, not thrusting her views on others, would make her references to "the Saviour" or "the Son of God," the shortness of life here and the certainty of a life hereafter. She had slowly come to believe out of her gropings that there was probably no hell in the hereafter, saying on occasion, "I sometimes believe the worst of us is not bad enough for everlasting punishment and even if we were, God, who created us, would stop the punishment before it went on time without end." Her views were regarded by her fellow members as extreme in the Congregational church she attended but she was modest and tentative about them.

David Trutt could swear at General Gage and vow that if there was a God he would punish King George III with hellfire and the mother would smile and say it was a matter between God and General Gage, between God and King George, and she would not presume to know what God would do. He would storm at her for not accepting his viewpoint and she would gently and gravely say she wished she could go with him in seeing one side as being entirely right and the other side as entirely wrong but she simply couldn't. She would agree that the King and his ministers and troops had done the colonies great wrong but she could not be sure how far the resistance of the Rebels should go. When she would urge, "The hand of God is working toward great unseen ends," her son would cry, "You leave it all to God. Suppose we left it all to God and made no resistance. There would never be any change. We would be slaves and our slavery get worse. How do you know but the hand of God is working through us Rebels?" And his mother would sweetly answer she didn't know. "You may be right, son. We shall know in God's good time." Once he had snorted at the end of a long argument where she kept smiling and he lost his temper, "You're too pious to please me. The preacher you listen to leads you around by the nose." He had rushed out of the house on her reply, "The preacher I hear every Sunday is a Rebel like you and talks against the King exactly like you and I often think he cannot know, nor can any man know, as much about the politics of Christ as he pretends to know." Her boy was at the door and opening it to leave as she was saying, "I don't blame him and I don't blame you." On the street he snorted to himself, "What can you do with a fool woman like that?" She wore well-chosen light-browns, thin fine laces at her neck. She was pale, slight, with mild gray eyes, a face of reserve and vast patience, and a cousin on her grandmother's side had once walked naked with dust and ashes strewn over her head and shoulders, down the middle aisle of a church full of worshipers at a Lord's Day noon hour in protest against five Quakers being held for weeks on a punishment diet in a foul jail for the offense of preaching their religion. Evelyn Trutt could sew and baste and fold and tuck for hours without saying a word and was the perfect listener to Jane Haddam and Amelia Gray.

Jane Haddam could talk streaks about nothing in particular. Her black hair folded neatly around her doll-face, small curved mouth, small black eyes. She liked men and among them had a way often of looking babyish and needing help and at times being offered more help than she could use. She had been with Mrs. Cavendish a year as also had Amelia Gray whose blond hair was thin and silken, her mouth in repose having a droop of melancholy, her hands long with tapering swift fingers, and she was being trusted more and more with pieces of work that Mrs. Cavendish said "must be of exquisite finish, nothing less than exquisite."

They had talked from day to day of the expected arrival of Marintha Wilming on the New York stage. "Mim," they called her, though if she was in certain moods, it was "Marintha." She had been with Mrs. Cavendish more than three years, tended to the front salesroom when Mrs. Cavendish was away, served as first assistant and consultant to Mrs. Cavendish. She and Mrs. Trutt were the only persons besides Mrs. Cavendish to have keys to the shop.

"Personal adornment is being carried too far, Captain Hupple," Mrs. Cavendish was telling her visitor. He gave her a mild boozy grin. "Something is being carried too far, my dear Mrs. Cavendish, and you must say it over so I may know what is being carried too far."

She spoke it slower. He understood the words now but couldn't agree. "It is well that personal embellishment goes as it does in Boston. I wish the ladies embellished. Not bedizened and bedaubed, mind you, no excess, but glitter and brilliancy—we cannot have too much of it in these troubled days. Would you believe that others who like myself have traveled are agreed that Boston has a gaiety now among its better people that compares favorably with London? Indeed I have met persons of discrimination who are of that opinion."

"You are a wee bit lush and free this afternoon, Captain Hupple."

"I am a ship captain on shore leave while his vessel lays up for repairs in Salem Harbor. Such a shore leave as I have not had in many a moon. I take it as a direct compliment that you estimate me as not lush but contrariwise only a wee bit lush."

They had met at a small dinner in the Red Lion Inn, had attended an assembly and danced together till it was remarked they were striking minuet partners. He was broad, thick, jolly, widely read, vain of his vocabulary, had been treating himself to high life and going places and enjoyed telling about it, allowing no interruptions and satisfied that his goings and doings should interest others as they did himself.

A careful half-moon dab of hair having the fixity of Cuban molasses curved along his forehead to bring attention to his looks saying he stood before you fresh-wiped and not lacking embellishment. The velvet of his waistcoat, the silk of his stockings, the ring of gold set with a ruby on one finger, meant to indicate successful voyages and paying cargoes. He puzzled some who could not solve his chatter and prattling. He had been known when along in his drinking to chuckle, "I may seem to overindulge myself in speech but I am telling you in confidence that I have the satisfaction I am not required to listen to such others as must continue to hear my valuable utterance."

"Much fatigued" he had been last Sunday with entertainment and discussions at the home of the painter John Singleton Copley. "You have seen their eleven-acre estate on Beacon Hill sloping to the Charles River. Mrs. Copley read a letter from her husband at Naples, sunny Italy, sunny but dirty he writes, streets dirty and people dirty, so offensive he was made ill, Mrs. Cavendish, at the sight of it. Mrs. Copley, like her husband, has been torn with doubts over whether to stay in America or flee. Her mother was an Elizabeth Winslow of the Plymouth Winslows who came over in the *Mayflower*. Her father is the Boston agent for the East India Company whose forty-eight thousand dollars' worth of tea was thrown into Boston Harbor two years ago. Her husband leans toward American Independence yet believes an artist should have no part in politics and he has had flattering offers from English friends who value him the equal of Van Dyck and Rubens in portrait-painting. Mrs. Copley said she will be in tears over leaving their beautiful home but soon she and the children must go to England. I assured her the hospitality of my own vessel would be at her disposal in three weeks should no other be available. She was disturbing in her conversation, Mrs. Cavendish. A growing spirit of violence on both sides she sees. Her husband seems to have made his decision a year ago. A mob swarmed up the hill to his house and demanded the person of one Colonel Watson, a Loyalist mandamus counselor. It happened that Colonel Watson had come and gone. They cried their threats they would have Mr. Copley's blood if he entertained such a villain again in the future. She remembered Mr. Copley's words, 'What a spirit! What if Colonel Watson had stayed, as I pressed him to, to spend the night. I must either have given up a friend to the insult of a mob or had my house pulled down and perhaps my family murdered.'"

"It is disturbing, Captain Hupple."

"You have met Mrs. Copley?"

"No."

"Then it is agreed that if possible on some salubrious evening we shall betake ourselves there. You should have a speaking acquaintance with her."

"I would enjoy meeting her. Several of my patrons have spoken of her poise and serenity."

"And have you met the Reverend Mather Byles?"

"No."

"He was there, a Tory, a wit and a scholar if ever I set eyes on one. Huge shoulders, an imposing presence, Dr. Byles, a Congregationalist with the heart of a true Episcopalian. Otherwise why should his son the Reverend Dr. Mather Byles, Jr., be the rector now seven years at Christ Church? A man of airy persiflage and puns when the mood takes him. A Whig constable guarding a British soldier under arrest he would term an 'Observe-a-Tory.' Isn't that good, Mrs. Cavendish? Pat and appropriate, I calls it. And now that the British soldiers in their scarlet uniforms have come to Boston, Dr. Byles will have it, at last the wrongs of the colony are 'redressed.' Not re-dressed, you understand, but red-ressed." And Captain Hupple chuckled and bumbled and was near choking.

Mrs. Cavendish beamed, "It is ridiculous. I like clever puns. I have heard a good pun is good fun."

"And so it is. A good pun is good fun. I must remember that, such as birds of a feather flock together and . . ."

"That is not a pun, my dear Captain Hupple. It is a rhymed proverb."

"But all proverbs are not rhymed, Mrs. Cavendish."

"Correct, Captain Hupple."

"Correct more often than I am incorrect, Mrs. Cavendish, far more correct with a reputation for the correct."

"Dr. Mather Byles is really Episcopalian, you believe?"

"His congregation may proceed against him because of his views favoring the King. He told Mrs. Copley he believes he will find the climate of England more genial and may meet her in London. Dr. Byles has prayed publicly that the colonies may submit to Great Britain. That is held against him. He associates with British officers, has them at his home for punch, and meets with other Loyalists at a King Street place called Tory Hall. For his straightforward and perfectly righteous conduct he hears that members of his Hollis Street church which is Congregational have made the blunt statement, extreme and unmannerly, with reference to Dr. Byles, 'We're going to shut his Tory mouth or throw him into Boston Harbor after the India tea.' He and Mrs. Copley indulged in some very melancholy conversation, I can assure you, Mrs. Cavendish."

"Naturally on Sunday you were fatigued."

"Naturally, no inclination to church, stayed at home overhauling papers, dined in the afternoon with three elegant gentlemen and three sparkling young ladies, attended ship matters the next day and in the evening did not forget my invitation to Mr. Hodges, a company of forty gentlemen. We dined in a very elegant manner upon turtle and so forth, drank a number of toasts and sang a number of songs and I may say we were indeed exceeding merry until three o'clock in the morning from whence we went upon the rake. Going past the Common on our way home, we surprised a company of country young men and women with a violin at a tavern dancing and making merry. Upon our entering the house the young women fled. We took possession of the room, having the fiddler with us and a young man with a keg of sugared dram. We were indeed very merry there and from thence went to Mr. Jacob Waycross who obliged us to drink punch and wine with him. About five in the morning we made our exit and went to bed."

"Are you not afraid you have been a little too much on the loose, Captain Hupple?"

"Too much on what, Mrs. Cavendish? I did not gather the word. Too much on what?"

Mrs. Cavendish made the effort and words came clear, "Too much on the loose." And Captain Hupple rambled on. "Lest you think me ungodly and not attentive to church duties, Mrs. Cavendish, I would beg you to know that on Sunday before last I dressed myself wearing a fresh-dressed and well-powdered wig and went with Mr. Abraham Orton to Parson Hilder's meeting. But he being at Rhode Island, Parson Henderson officiated for him, his text on the Psalms, 'O ye of little faith,' a very good discourse, dined at Captain Trusoe's and in the afternoon went to King's Chapel and was introduced by Mr. Gable into his pew and the parson Mr. Olworth gave us an excellent discourse on the text 'The fear of the Lord is the beginning of wisdom.' "

Mrs. Cavendish edged in with a smile. "I shall yet be convinced you are not a lost lamb, Captain Hupple."

King's Chapel, the Captain had noted as "very plain without, with large sash windows, but within very neat and commodious, the architecture modern, with a pair of neat little organs and gifts from King William and Queen Mary which Mr. Gable told me were a pulpit cloth, a cushion, a rich set of plate for the communion table and a painting from top to bottom of the east-end wall where you might read the Decalogue, the Lord's Prayer, and the Apostles' Creed. The walls and pillars hung with escutcheons of the King and the royal governors of the province. The Governor's pew opposite the pulpit vacant but the one near it, reserved for officers of the King's Army and Navy, filled. Sumptuous I consider those uniforms of our royal forces. You agree, Mrs. Cavendish?"

"Sumptuous indeed, sir."

"One lack of conformity I noted. Having no steeple the King's Chapel looks more like a Prespetarian meeting house."

"Prespetarian?"

"Precisely, Prespetarian."

And Mrs. Cavendish gathered that the Presbyterians care little for steeples but a good Episcopalian prefers his church with a spire pointing toward heaven. Captain Hupple was so well educated and widely read that Mrs. Cavendish, who rated herself no scholar, was pleased to catch him mauling Presbyterian into Prespetarian.

From the first, Mrs. Cavendish had found the Captain interesting. When his flow of speech had no special interest for her there was a charm about the way he could go on and on with no running out of things to talk about. In Boston and near-by towns he had been to parties of mixed company and played cards, cribbage, backgammon, battledore and shuttlecock, one night seeing a cockfight, "a royal pastime" he termed it, giving descriptions of the spurs or gaffs fitted to the feet of the birds in combat. Of music too he could report. "A brother of the Chief Deputy Collector invited me to join with his wife and her two daughters to go to a concert of which he was a member. I went accordingly and you may take my assurance the performance was as well as could be expected. It consisted of one indifferent small organ, one bass violin, one German flute, and four small violins."

Mrs. Cavendish had been trying to guess what lay in the changes of tone and mood in Captain Hupple's recitals of where he had been. She could see at moments that he was pleasing himself with how much he could remember of what he had seen and heard in his whirls around Boston. Again he would venture to the brink of somber matters and hold off from the leap into them because they involved his personal career and fortune, such questions for instance as what would become of shipping and commerce in American harbors if the present resistance spread into a long war. Or again he was giving her a series of self-portraits of Captain Hupple as a good fellow whose company was much enjoyed among the best people, as a scholar, a wit, a connoisseur. He knew she admired him. And she was asking whether the stolid glum look now on his face meant he wished more than admiration.

"The violins and the flute, Mrs. Cavendish, had their moments during the performance suggesting they were the creation of the most tender passion. The composer, it was evident, must have been a prey to tender anguish." He hesitated, mumbled the words low as his two hands took her by the wrists—"A prey to tender anguish"—his usual ease gone as he brought his face near to hers and repeating "a prey to tender anguish." Then came his hoarse whisper. He had to go on mumbling "a prey to tender anguish" or give his abrupt, silly, helpless plea, "Let's go upstairs."

Mrs. Cavendish tore loose her wrists, swiftly pushed him into a large chair, shook a finger in his face and gravely, "Captain Hupple,

413

you must not forget you are a gentleman and a shipmaster and this is a respectable public establishment for reputable patrons."

Captain Hupple looked worn. He knew he should have had a sleep after the noon victuals and the drinks that other laughing gentlemen had set before him. He couldn't remember where that was. He had been trying to remember and to tell Mrs. Cavendish of it, for they were men of worth and reputation like himself. He lifted his head, "Mrs. Cavendish, you should not be so companionable. You are the sweetest and most companionable woman in the world." His tongue had to struggle with the word "companionable" again as he took one of her hands in his two and looked up into her face, "Wunnaful companyanyaful."

"You should sleep, my dear."

"I go home'n shleep. Yes, I go home like a nice boy 'n shleep. 'N lissen—you lissenin?"

"Yes, Captain Hupple."

"Shall we dine tonight at the Red Lion?"

"Certainly, but I shall expect you to be a good boy."

"Your wishes respected, shall be respected. I condust myself, shall condust myself beccoming as becomes a genlemananashipmaster."

"The cold air and the walk will do you good." She helped him into his greatcoat, led him to the front door, they stood in the outside fresh sunny winter air and she saw it at once bracing him. "Now go straight home, get your sleep."

He began walking—fairly straight—and as she saw that he could find his way and he had gone a little way she called after him, "And where is it we dine tonight?"

He turned with a loose wave of one hand, a touch to his three-cornered hat and a smile, "The Red Lion, my dear." His head was clearing, his walk sturdy as his black silk stockings and silver buckles flashed. He had found his good sea legs again.

Mrs. Cavendish glimpsed a few doors down the street a chimney sweep, his face soot-black, moving with his brooms from a chimney he had cleaned to another he would climb inside and up with his broom. He seemed to know the man up on top of a passing hayrack loaded with hay and called, with a grin of white teeth from his sooted mouth, "Cold today."

"Cold, yes," called the driver from far up on his hayload, "but not cold as yesterday."

"Yesterday was cold."

"Hi-yi, cold enough to freeze the snot to your nose."

Mrs. Cavendish hurried into the dress shop shuddering. In the hallway she passed a sullen-faced young woman of twenty, with gray eyes blinking and flashing. Mrs. Cavendish nodded and went in.

Mrs. Trutt had come from the workroom. They tidied and arranged some bolts of satin, taffeta, lawn. Mrs. Trutt put fresh wood into the

Franklin stove, heard Mrs. Cavendish, "That girl who just left—haven't I seen her here before?"

"Ann Elwood. She lives neighbor to Jane Haddam and comes to visit and ask about the wild talk."

"The wild talk?"

"We think she has been wronged, Mrs. Cavendish."

"Who has wronged her and how?"

"You may have heard of the Rebel papers printing items, very curious, the like never seen before. They mention no names. But Ann Elwood is the girl. As the Rebels tell it her father goes into her bedroom one morning and finds in bed with her a British Grenadier sergeant. The father threatens to kill the sergeant. The sergeant coolly tells the father he and Ann are married. The father goes away and looks into the matter and hears there was a marriage ceremony in the Blue Anchor inn at midnight one night—and the officiating minister is proven to be another sergeant of Grenadiers wearing a false garb and performing a mock marriage."

"Who ever heard of the like?"

"It would seem it didn't happen as it is told and published. So Jane Haddam believes and she has never known Ann Elwood to be deceiving about such a thing. Ann says her father forbade the sergeant to see her at their house. They went to inns. They strolled streets and country roads. One night they go to a small inn and meet three other couples of grenadiers and their Boston girls. After many drinks it is proposed as a prank that there be a mock marriage of Ann and her sergeant. A sergeant has found a black coat at the inn, has a Book of Common Prayer with him, and reads the ceremony making Ann and her sergeant husband and wife, sealed with a ring. When they are sober a few days later her sergeant tells her that the grenadier who went through the ceremony had been an assistant rector of two churches in England and after dismissal for being beastly drunk and other improper conduct, had gone into the army.

" 'By English law and in the sight of God we are man and wife,' was the startling news Ann heard from her sergeant. Now she loves him and hates him and is all in a turmoil."

"Does he go to her house?"

"Twice he went. The first time, her father was at home. Together they told him the whole affair as it happened. The father blazed with wrath, left the room, came back with a pistol. The sergeant drew his pistol. She stood in front of her grenadier saying to her father if he shot it would be through her body. The sergeant moved to the door and went away. Then Ann Elwood heard from other grenadiers that the one who performed the marriage ceremony had only been a student for the ministry and never ordained. She sent word to the sergeant he must come to their house one evening when her father would be away at a meeting of Minute Men. The sergeant came, he denied he had fooled her. Ann's brother came in. He hadn't been expected home so early. He snatched away the sergeant's pistol, knocked him down with it and beat him over the head with it. The sergeant reeled out of the door and had a slow time finding his way along the street for the blood running into his eyes. Oates Elwood, Ann's brother, is known as a hard man in a fight. He had been in several brawls with the soldiers. He is a shipwright, has had no work for a year since the port was closed, and they say he is busy with the Liberty Boys and was likely one of those who threw the tea into the harbor."

"I wish I could read what is to come, Evelyn."

"On both sides more brawling every day, street fights, robberies. On both sides little respect for the Ten Commandments." Then lower-voiced as though perhaps it was her private meditation, "The sayings of the Saviour forgotten and the Son of God abandoned. When will they learn to be even-handed to everyone, even as God is even-handed to everyone?"

* * * * * * * * * *

Chapter 11

* * * * * * * * * *

Life Is an Onion You Peel

EIGHT bells and high in the steeple tower they hung. Eight bells, one weighing 1545 pounds, and the smallest 620, brought from England on ships. Eight bells with tongues of melody that rang out over Boston and could be heard in towns and villages miles away, reaching farther, it was said, than any other chimes in America.

Inside bell One the inscription: "This peal of eight bells is the gift of a number of generous persons to Christ Church in Boston, N.E., anno 1744, A.R." The "N.E." meant New England but what was the "A.R."? That you would gather away over at the bell Eight saying: "Abel Rudhall of Gloucester cast us all, anno 1744."

Bell Two informed of the church founded by the Rector Timothy Cutler, D.D. in 1723, nigh a hundred years after the landing of the *Mayflower* Pilgrims and the Boston first settlers who so hated the Church of England and all its works. Bell Three informed of itself and the others: "We are the first ring of bells cast for the British Empire in North America," and bell Four: "God preserve the Church of England." William Shirley, Governor of Massachusetts Bay in New England in 1744, gave bell Five. The cnurch wardens of 1743, John Hammock and Robert Temple, had begun the subscriptions, said

416

bell Six. And bell Seven breathed with melody: "Since Generosity has opened our mouths, our tongues shall ring aloud its praise, 1744."

The Bible, the prayer books, the communion service with the royal arms engraved on the silver, were gifts of King George II in 1733 to Christ Church. The priceless chandeliers and the wood-carved figures of child angels in front of the organ had been seized from a French ship by the English privateer *Queen of Hungary* and by its Captain Grushea presented to the church.

This lore and other matters of information inside Christ Church, Boston, had become familiar to Robert Winshore. He had gone to Christ Church to sit in a pew of this supposed sanctuary of the Loyalist and to consider how odd it was that his young friend, only a year older than himself, Robert Newman, the sexton of the church, was a Whig, a Rebel, and a Son of Liberty; that Robert Newman's brother of like belief sat in the organ loft of a Sabbath and played the airs of ancient royalist hymns; that the Christ Church vestryman Captain John Pulling belonged to the North Caucus and was a friend of Sam Adams and Joseph Warren and Paul Revere and others who met secretly at the Green Dragon inn to plot against those loyal to the King.

In former days Robert Winshore could visit his friend, the Christ Church sexton, at the Newman home across Salem Street from the church. Now the Newman house like many others in Boston was filled with strangers, British officers "billeted" on the Newman family. A billet was an order from the high military command that the family must take in as lodgers and boarders a certain number of officers or soldiers.

A block away Winshore boarded and in his room late this March afternoon he was meeting Robert Newman and hearing from Newman how that young fellow on the night before had climbed up the narrow winding stairway of Christ Church steeple, up beyond the eight bells, up to the highest window of the belfry. From that window he could see the Charles River and the hulls of British ships and their lights riding the tide. The two young men were old-time friends and often trusted each other with confidential matters. And Robert Winshore knew he was expected to guess why Robert Newman had made this climb of the night before. It wouldn't be right for Newman to tell it. And Winshore did make his guess that Pulling or Revere had lately come to Robert Newman and told him he must be practiced and familiar at this climb up the steeple because, as Revere would have put it, "because of what may be acting soon."

A knock at the door and it might mean anything. Newman and Winshore looked at each other. Winshore stepped to the door, opened it, saw a face and shoulders, and stepped into a pair of wide arms that held him close.

His father had come. They had questions after a year of not seeing each other's faces. They joked. They talked about the son and brother

John Locke Winshore and the Tozzers and Rivington and the bumps and ruts of the stage roads.

Outside now they heard shouts and cries, the scuffle of shoes on the cobblestones. Robert threw open a window, looked out and down and couldn't make out what was doing. He could hear "Tar and feathers" and "God save the King" and "The goddam lobster-backs" and "The *Massachusetts Spy*."

Robert led and they went down to the street and made their way to King Street, taking places with a surging crowd in front of the *Massachusetts Spy* building. There they saw a thing meant for a lesson, something to remember, a parade with an object of terror.

First came Lieutenant Colonel Nesbit, in command and proud of it, riding a sorrel horse, the same Nesbit seen by Robert marching a large fife-and-drum corps of noisemakers back and forth outside Old South Church on March fifth when the Sons of Liberty were holding their immense mass meeting inside, a yearly ceremony in memory of the men killed in the Boston Massacre five years before. Now came all twenty of the drums and fifes of the 47th Regulars, shrilling and pounding, shaking the frames of walls and telling Boston to come see what was doing. Then some forty soldiers, erect and brilliant scarlet in their uniforms, at their musket ends the bayonets fixed and gleaming. Bringing up the rear as a guard were files of officers, Negroes, seamen from His Majesty's Navy.

Between the two lines of shining fixed bayonets came a one-horse cart with four men on it, a driver and two seated guards with bayonets. These two guards saw to it with their bayonets that the fourth man did not sit or lie down. He must stand. Unless he did he was reminded by bayonet points. He must be on his feet up where the crowd could see him. For he was the Exhibit, the Example, the Image of Horror for all Rebels in Boston to see and remember.

What had happened to this Example was plain to see. His hat, clothes, shoes, had been taken off. Over his naked body had been smudged a thick garment of warm tar. The black surface of tar had been smeared with white feathers. What had been a man seemed no longer a man and less than human.

Robert and his father with Newman saw this procession pass with its pounding shuddering music, its arms and uniforms of authority, its mute and shadowy central image that you had to scan and scrutinize more than once to be sure you saw it. They read the mocking label stuck on the back of the image: AMERICAN LIBERTY, OR A SPECIMEN OF DEMOCRACY. They heard the music and made out it was first "The Rogue's March" then "Yankee Doodle" and back to "The Rogue's March."

They heard too the piercing cry, "The printer of the *Spy* will be the next to get this," and wondered if Isaiah Thomas was in the crowd and hearing it.

They moved to King Street and took places in a crowd about half-way between the British Coffee House and the Bunch of Grapes tavern. From men in the crowd Robert gathered that the victim in the cart was one Thomas Ditson of Billerica, a young farmer. Some said Ditson had been caught trying to coax a soldier of the 47th Regiment to desert. Others said he had tried to buy a musket from a soldier of the 47th. Some said he had been tried by British officers and condemned to tar and feathers, and public exhibition as a warning to Boston Rebels. Others said the soldiers of the 47th had caught Ditson and made their own decision what to give him.

Now came the parade again, Lieutenant Colonel Nesbit, on his sorrel, the shrilling fifes and the ear-splitting drums, the lines of bayonets, and at the pivot of it all the silent and smutted figure.

Robert and his father with Newman stood grim and somber rather than sorrowing. It was part of the drama of Boston and Massachusetts, one piece that related to other pieces. They knew that rather than striking terror to the Sons of Liberty and the Minute Men, it deepened fighting resolves already made and long sworn in solemn oaths.

Now it had moved up the street, turned a corner, and the high shrilling of "Yankee Doodle" and the thundering drums were fading.

They turned on the cobblestoned sidewalk to go to the Green Dragon inn. Suddenly Robert Winshore halted, fixed in his tracks. Farther over didn't he see Lieutenant George Frame, whom he knew by sight though Frame didn't know him? And on the arm of Lieutenant Frame who was it? Yes, wouldn't he know that head, that face? In a swift moment he was facing her, with a cry, "Mim!" and heard her answering cry and they stood with their arms holding each other tight after one kiss.

People stopped to look. People asked what this could be, for it was not customary in Boston. Lieutenant Frame had seen nothing in Marintha Wilming to prepare him for this. Robert's father was less surprised, for he would expect anything of Robert though he would not have predicted it from what he had seen of Miss Wilming.

After their wild and warm greeting Robert asked if she was going home to Aunt Ellen's and about her traveling bag. "You will pardon us," he said to Lieutenant Frame, Mim adding, after introducing Robert, "I shall hope to see you again, Lieutenant Frame, you have been very kind and thoughtful." To his father and Newman Robert explained he was taking Mim home and would be at his room later.

They walked crooked and narrow streets of two-story houses huddled close as if to protect each other against loneliness. They came to wider-spaced lots and the shrubbery path between two cedars and the home of Aunt Ellen with its first floor of combined kitchen and dining room at the rear and a small front parlor and a second floor of three sleeping rooms. Little Aunt Ellen heard them, came down

419

in a light-blue nightrobe, spoke her greetings of welcome home, and went back to her sleep.

They had said little in the walk. They said little on the settee beside the Franklin stove. They had different kinds of silences—Robert and Mim. This was one of the grateful ones. Their long kisses on the settee had no tint of reluctance, no misgivings. And they chatted swiftly an hour or more of things seen and heard since Robert parted from her in New York. She had been struck with pleased amazement at Robert presenting to her as his father the man she had come to like so much on her stage journey. With such a father it might be that Robert could have lights in him not known to her where now often in recurring mood she felt dark spots, areas where he was a complete stranger to her. She was warm and glowing about Ordway Winshore. "You must have further lights in you I have not seen, to have come from such a father."

Of the tea-burning affairs at Stamford and Providence she gave short mention and said his father would give him full details. She drifted and referred once to "men lost in mire beckoning to others the way out," checked herself. She spoke of getting Mrs. Cavendish's cousin nicely launched in the New York dress shop and the outlook for trade there better than Boston, fewer clashes and less of the spirit of violence, no such certainty of worse outbreaks to come. She mentioned the courtesies of the Frame brothers and the attentions of Lieutenant George Frame and his cool gaiety, read it on Robert's face that he could bear with little mention of the two Lieutenants.

Robert told of his work at the *Massachusetts Spy* briefly, though letting her know that it was more than a probability and seemed an unpleasant assurance that soon there would be soldiers arriving to take over and close down the printery, with Isaiah Thomas either a fugitive or a prisoner. This and its implications he couldn't carry far with her. It could send her into a mood with her hope low. Getting personal about her he was not brief. The sight of her face, the hold of her hand, the flow of her voice, they went deep in him beyond words. His hand was tender, shy and grave on her face and hair, on her wrists, at her shoulders. And she had her way of feeding on the look of him, the strengths and the modeling of him—and beyond that she knew she idolized him for bonds of companionship they had. She had her way now of saying what she had said before, "You could be homely to look at, homely as a barn made wrong and twisted by the wind, and my barriers wouldn't stand against you." Their songs, their many hours of singing together, their walks in the country, their skating and dancing as born partners, his complete joining with her in grasp of the dances she made up and performed and her extravagances of speech that some people feared half-mad, their many quiet hours with few words spoken, the silent comfort they could be to each other—this past of theirs had grown into something rare.

Yet little by little there had grown up between them a curious fabric of fear, a thin woven thing they couldn't touch and handle and bring out into the open between them because it had its roots in secrets neither of them could be free to tell. This film of foreboding they kept away from on this night. How could he tell her what he knew of Lieutenant George Frame and the hand of that Lieutenant in the seizure and flogging of a soldier near to death on Boston Common and his own hand in the ordeal given the informer? How could she tell him she was almost certain he was taking a hand in actions of dark shame it would not be easy for them to look at and speak of together?

Mim brought a small jug of cider she drew from a cask in the cellar, along with a plate of thin oatmeal cakes sweetened with maple sugar, after a recipe Aunt Ellen had from a Scotswoman. They had cheer and health. They were young yet. They chatted and laughed away their cares and forebodings.

Mim yawned once. Robert said it was the prettiest yawn in the world and would she yawn again for he liked her yawning face. For him only would she yawn, she said, and brought to her face a wide fresh yawn. Robert asked her to watch his imitation of it. He tried for the imitation.

"It does very well," said Mim, "but it is a man's yawn. I doubt any man alive could imitate a woman's yawn."

They discussed yawns, what health there is in a good long yawn at any time, how to yawn with insolence before someone who is talking too long, how to yawn properly in church holding a "handker" to the face as though to blow the nose, how there are people who yawn with a prolonged sigh of comfort at the end of it. They imitated this yawn with a long easing sigh at the end of it. They imitated a variety of yawns. Never before having practiced their yawns for each other, it was fun. They were good company for each other. They forgot themselves. They forgot the shrilling fifes, the ear-splitting drums, Nesbit on the sorrel, the awesome and muted Example in his garb of tar overlaid with feathers. They shared a long deep kiss. Robert would be seeing her at the dress shop late next afternoon.

Robert walking the dark twists of one crooked and narrow street tried his memory on slow-spoken words that had come from Mim after a rush of whimsical talk about practical matters. A soft dreamgaze had come into her eyes with the faintest flicker of storm-dark green and she seemed to be looking through him and beyond him. " 'A little and peace with it is the gift of God,' said my grandmother, sitting in the sun at a spinning wheel, speaking it gravely, then smiling, 'Life is an onion—you peel it year by year and sometimes cry.' And she, my grandmother, had heard from her grandmother, and that would be long ago, 'Miracles come only to those who believe in them.' She lived past eighty, my grandmother, and said it was like an old Dutchwoman told her when she was a girl, 'Grow twenty years, bloom twenty years, stand twenty years, fade twenty years.'"

Life rushing by, life made of time and ever the present gnawing into the future and becoming itself the future to be in turn eaten till the past was endless yesterdays and each one a tomorrow and a today before it became a yesterday—this and more haunted Mim. And she had herself and her Robert in mind in telling him that night, "Women and fine linen look best by candlelight, my grandmother liked to be telling us, and there are loves that come hushed in so finespun a fabric it is better they be not taken out into the noonday sun." What could he make of that? Robert asked. He loved her for it. It had the haze of the hazards they lived in with their strange and deep bonds. And again what could he make of it? he asked and answered himself, "Most anything."

He passed two men, just out of a tavern door, in leather breeches and aprons, brewery workers who loaded barrels into carts. They had enjoyed their drinks and were going to enjoy their wives, they were telling each other. And by comparison a ship's calker they knew was not so lucky, one of them putting it in a few words: "She is as thick as she is high. Gets drunk two and three times every week. It's disagreeable to him. She has valiant spirit and stands up to him when she's drunk. It's a great dispute in his mind what to do about her."

He crept into bed with his father.

"A good night of it, son?"

"Yes, papa."

And their sleepiness was gone. They talked long. Uppermost in his father's heart was a hope that the blessed Isaiah Thomas would have word beforehand and early enough to get away himself and take the best of his printery with him to a safer place. Robert said he worked on that every day and it was one of his cares and duties.

And someday soon Robert would take him to the wharf where the tea cargoes of three ships had been thrown overboard? "I want to see where that act of defiance and challenge took place." Yes, Robert would take him there. The father knew that act went on during a two-month stay of Robert in Boston that year of 1773. Once he had laughingly asked Robert if he had a hand in it. And Robert answered that if he did he couldn't tell, that all who had a hand in it were sworn never to tell it nor give the names of others in it.

"Miss Marintha Wilming, a rather wonderful young woman, Robert."

"Perhaps too wonderful for me, I sometimes think."

They actually reveled in their talk about her, each admired her so.

"We see the precious in her, Robert."

"Not many does she let see the precious."

"How many?"

"You and I, her brother Darius, and sometimes Evelyn Trutt, a woman at the dress shop. And perhaps her mother. Mim knows when to guard herself against what others would take to be wild meaningless talk."

"Mim?"

"Short for Marintha—her nickname on the farm ever since she was a baby."

The father told of Stamford and Providence, the bonfires, gallows and tea-burning ceremonies, and Mim saying, "Lost men howling to other lost men where to go" and "Mired men crying to others in the mire how to get foot-loose."

"That sounds like what I hear from her. And I study it and by God it isn't empty and sometimes afterward it gnaws in my heart though I don't know why."

"I've studied about it, Robert. You and I are partisans. We are making history. Only partisans can make the beginnings of history. Through us time and history work. But Mim is timeless. She has elements of the seer and the clairvoyant and she gives a terribly sensitive registration to everything human she meets and sees and hears. She is not afraid of how anything registers in her. With that at times goes an awful loneliness. When she gets too worn with the tragedy of life, as I see her, she shakes herself loose into a quizzical sanity by going folderol and flaunt-a-flaunt."

"That is her, papa, that is my Mim."

And the son told of their good times together, what partners they were whether dancing and skating or whether in long silences of mutual comfort. But when he came to the other silence, the film of foreboding between them, the area where they couldn't talk plain and free, where stood a box of secrets they couldn't unlock and didn't dare break open, the son couldn't go on. Not even to his father could he tell the affair of Mr. Reggs and still other affairs complicated and he oath-bound.

"Are you ever afraid of her, afraid of what she might do to you?"

"Perhaps, papa. I'm not sure. What few times she has given me pain even the pain had a touch of the exquisite. I think I could leave her if she said so, if she said it must be. She could say so if her heart told her it must be. She hides her strength. But it is always there. She is a law to herself. Neither the King nor the Continental Congress could sway her about any decision she made in the quiet of that slow and deep-burning heart of hers."

The son was a little sad about it. So was the father. But what was sad had a faint dark music about it they would rather have than not. He quoted for the father, "There are loves come hushed in so finespun a fabric it is better they be not taken out into the noonday sun."

"That will do to go to sleep on, son."

"It's my estimate you're correct there, papa."

And they slept without dreaming and saw no fantasy of a shadow-shape standing erect and tar-smutted between two ready and watching bayonet points.

* * * * * * * * * *

Chapter 12

* * * * * * * * * *

Prominent Persons and a Room of Smoke

ORDWAY WINSHORE and Robert were listening to Isaiah Thomas in his office. "As you know, Winshore," looking at Robert, "about the time they are going to whack down on the *Spy* and put me in jail for trial here, they confidently expect to have Sam on a ship bound for London and trial for high treason. Be sure Sam gets these papers," handing Robert a large envelope.

The Winshores walked toward Sam's home. Robert would know him. This was the third time Mr. Thomas had gravely told him to be sure to deliver the papers carried.

Sam's first wife dying in 1757 left him two children and he married Elizabeth Welles in 1764. Good women who called her "Betsy" also rated her "the best housekeeper in Boston." A Negro slave girl helped in the housekeeping. When Sam went away to conventions in New York or Philadelphia, Betsy could write him, "I am never more happy than when I am Reading your Letters or Scribbling to you my Self." They were a couple. Wasn't she afraid alone in the house with Sam away and organizing rebellion against the King? "No, I can take care of myself against the redcoats." She bowed her head with Sam as he said prayers at mealtime. She took turns with him reading pages from the Bible to the family at bedtime. She joined with him in their rule of no manual work on the Lord's Day. Sam had plenty of the old-time Puritan in him, didn't like the way each generation of the young had changed and moderated the old Puritan habits. He believed stage plays immoral and favored laws to forbid them, even Shakespeare too loose to suit Sam. Slavery—there were some two thousand Negro slaves in Massachusetts—he favored abolition of slavery by law but just now he couldn't say anything about that because the Southern colonies already were suspicious of New England about it, very sensitive, so he would say nothing and leave to his children and grandchildren the slavery matter. Often his hands shook, "not from fear but palsy," it was explained.

Sam was the most peculiar and widely known politician in all of New England, his chief maxim, "Put your adversary in the wrong and

424

keep him there." As town tax collector he had learned the face and name of every taxpayer in Boston. Before the brewery he inherited from his father went bankrupt he was nicknamed "Sammy the Malster" which, when he was elected head tax collector, the opposition wits changed to "Sammy the Publican." Foremost was Sam in organizing the Committees of Correspondence that spread over all the colonies, keeping all fighters for Independence in touch, Sam writing in 1771, "Our enemies would fain have us lie down on the bed of sloth and security and persuade ourselves that there is no danger: they are daily administering the opiate with multiplied arts and delusions." In that same year Governor Hutchinson said of him, "I doubt whether there is a greater incendiary in the King's dominion or a man of greater malignity of heart." Yet it came also to be written, "He had a genuine sympathy for men with leather aprons and hands browned by toil; he knew how to win confidence, and never abused it, for he was in no sense a demagogue." At times it may have been true of him, as one wrote, "He was feared by his enemies but too secret to be loved by his friends." Little doubt there was he enjoyed weaving plots and watching explosions he had arranged, though the fuse could not be traced to his hands. He it was, when Governor Hutchinson refused clearance for tea cargoes to return to England, on that gray and rainy day of December 16, 1773, when seven thousand people crowded Old South Church and milled around outside, had finally spoken the words, "This meeting can do no more to save the country," those words the signal for reckless men waiting and prepared in their Indian costumes, to board three ships and dump the tea cargoes overboard in Boston Harbor.

By coach and horse Sam rode in September 1775 to sit as a delegate in the First Continental Congress. Friends asked, "Why in Boston walk the streets alone, as you do, when there are those who wish you dead and out of their way?" He continued going alone on the streets and lived in his humble house with no guards. Sam was a failure in business, a mediocrity as an administrator, a poor manager of many personal affairs and debts. Unwilling to take high office with fat pay offered him, he was nevertheless a patient master strategist, a political marvel. His love of the people and his trust in them, his passion for representative popular government and the practice of democracy, lived as secrets of his personal bones and blood. Leaders of the far-branching Sons of Liberty trusted him beyond anyone else. He was humble, wanting nothing for himself, a Boston Socrates. So ran one view. The opposition called him false, evil, slimy, Boston's incarnation of the Devil.

"He looks a little foxy, papa, when you try to size him up the first time you meet him," said Robert. "And then you go on looking at him and he gets baffling. He's a fox, yes, and a bear and a weasel and a porcupine and I don't know what else. A snake the enemy call him but he's a farm horse for hard work, a cat at a mousehole for patience, and the way he's stood and walked and spoke where the enemy could get him I think he's been lionhearted."

They came to Winter Street at the corner of Winter Place and a two-story wooden house, a garden patch in the rear where Sam would be planting his vegetables and greens in a few weeks, should he then be staying in Boston.

They slammed a crude iron knocker on the front door. The door opened and there stood Sam himself, his coat off, his waistcoat with a row of buttons running far below the beltline and two roomy pockets with flaps at the bottom. The top button came near the throat to a carelessly tied and wrinkled stock of light-gray linen. His hair brushed straight back from the forehead came down thick and heavy below the ears they covered.

"Good morning, Mr. Adams," said Robert.

"How do you do, Mr. Winshore," smiled Samuel Adams.

They went in. He was pleased to meet the Philadelphia printer, had heard of him, asked a series of pointed questions about "the cause of Independence" and "the Patriots." Whigs they might have been, Rebels they might be now, but first of all they were Patriots, with a country to love and fight for, if need be, its voice and pivot for the present known as the Continental Congress where Sam Adams had been a delegate at its first meeting last September.

A fox face, yes, said Ordway Winshore to himself, and then still other faces, as Robert had said, the bear, the weasel, the porcupine and much else there. Possibly a fox mouth but a chin and a nose having more than wariness—large eyes that could melt with changing human themes that crossed his mind—at flickering moments a glow of warmth and passion and a touch of dreaminess.

"I've heard others say it with care and affection for you, Mr. Adams," Robert ventured, after delivering the papers from Isaiah Thomas, "that you are in danger and should not stay in Boston. They don't want you taken to London for a treason trial."

Sam Adams smiled. He would wait a little time yet before leaving this town of Boston where he had lived his fifty-two years. He seemed to think that if they should seize him and take him to London, it might "serve the cause." Such an act could raise excitement and stir blood as nothing hitherto of the blunders of the King's ministers.

Late in the afternoon Robert stopped in at the Cavendish dress shop. Mim was behind in her work, tired, tomorrow at the same time would be better. It was after dark when Robert sought a man who had just gone away from each place where Robert looked for him during the day. To this man must go a message from Isaiah Thomas. To the man's home went Robert, the first time he would have seen the man at his home.

A three-story house on Beacon Hill it was, overlooking the Common, the city, the harbor, and definitely known as the largest and finest mansion in Boston. Four dormers stood out from the sloping roof, two massive chimneys at each end and along the ridge of the gable an elaborate iron railing. Five tall windows gave outlooks from the second floor, the center window opening on a big square balcony. Two tall windows of the best imported English glass looked out on either side of the wide front door of mahogany with the proudest brass door-knocker in Boston. Two elms swaying branches higher than the house neatly spaced the front yard where shrubbery ranged around flower gardens. A stone ledge rose three feet above the street sidewalk level and over the ledge a fence of ornamental iron pickets. To the right ran a well-kept pavement to the elegant stone coachhouse with its three coach horses and nets for the summer flytime and harness bells for winter sleighing.

To this house came Robert Winshore to see his man. Not in Philadelphia, New York or Boston had he seen the inside of such an establishment. This house represented two generations of almost unlimited money, it seemed, and sustained continuous care and thought for comfort and the embellishment that ran into an evident and ripened luxury. Through the iron front gate and its nicely proportioned square-hewn oak posts Robert walked and on to the big front door and its ineffable and inextinguishable brass knocker.

This man he was going to see, he would note him well. He had seen him at a distance several times, and twice close-up. Now he would see the man in his home, in the most unimpeachable mansion in New England.

He took hold of the brass knocker, lifted it, laughed at himself. "What the hell is one brass knocker more or less? It's like all the other brass knockers, only bigger and brighter and better polished. I have an errand here. He wants to see me as much as I want to see him." He slammed the knocker down with a resounding bang. Shortly a maid in neat linen with a neat white cap opened the door. He gave his name and who sent him. The maid came back and with a smile let him in. She ushered him into a room that would have held the entire two-story house of Samuel Adams, bookshelves from floor to ceiling on one side, in the center a broad worktable strewn with papers, books, journals, ledgers.

A tall thin man with a narrow face and long straight nose stood up from a high straight-backed chair with upholstered armrests, with a worried face received the papers handed him and with a less worried face heard the verbal message Robert gave. Robert's eyes swept over the man and took note of the black velvet coat with gold trimmings and braid, silk stockings, white stock, white lace ruffles folded back at the wrists, an immaculate irreproachable white wig framing the lean forehead and covering the ears. Each wave of hair on the wig had its calculated curve and curl: it could be termed a triumphant achievement of the wigmaker's art. "The most elegantly dressed gentleman in New England," had been said of him. Also he was definitely the wealthiest man in all New England and the second wealthiest in America, an uncle having left him an estate valued at seventy thousand English pounds or upwards of three hundred thousand American dollars. Now thirty-nine years of age, his face lacked color and wore a pinched look; nervous, vain, easily annoyed, he often excused himself and lay down on account of headaches. His brocaded dressing gowns, jeweled buttons, his wigs, buckles, waistcoats, wine-coolers, also his gout, were part of his reputation. His wealth and investments, his ships, wharves, warehouses, establishments, reached to where it was estimated one thousand New England families were connected with him for the earning of their livings. His castoff brother, not recognized in the will of the rich uncle, wore his castoff clothes while at Harvard and he wrote his brother, "Don't wear them shoes of mine any longer, for they look scandalously." In his letters, "I have rote," was a frequent expression. A fire engine he gave to the town of Boston, steeples he gave to churches, also communion tables. Plain seats he provided for poor widows, bells, gowns, wigs, Bibles, mahogany seats for deacons. Firewood off his boats, rights to cut trees in his woods, he had given the poor and on special occasions barbecued oxen and barrels of rum on Boston Common.

New England's foremost smuggler he was and in 1768 his sloop the *Liberty*, loaded with Madeira wine, was taken ashore without payment of customs taxes, seized by Crown authorities. The event flared into street parades, mass meetings and wild riots from which the Royal Commissioners of Customs barely got away alive. After the Boston Massacre of 1770, with hour on hour of church bells in solemn tolling throughout Boston and neighboring towns, four hearses moved holding Crispus Attucks, a mulatto, and James Caldwell, Samuel Maverick, and Samuel Gray, three white men. In King Street on the spot where the four men were shot and killed the four hearses met. To the Granary Burying-ground moved the four hearses followed by an immense procession in column of six deep marching to where the four bodies were deposited in one tomb—this thin man with a stoop spoke the oration of the day, accusing the Crown soldiers of wanton murder and rebuking so as to offend Thomas Hutchinson, then Royal Governor of the Colony of Massachusetts. It was said his best speeches were written for him by Sam Adams but those who liked the speeches worried little about that. Elected to the General Court, he took a leading part in making public letters written by Governor Hutchinson and sent in secrecy to London, where Benjamin Franklin by some strange chance got hold of them, Governor Hutchinson being furious that his private and secretly expressed opinion of the people of Massachusetts did not accord with his publicly spoken views of the common folk. A delegate to the First Continental Congress in September 1774, a member of the Massachusetts Provincial Congress, this thin man had given services and money toward armed resistance of the King's soldiers, having his hand in the actions resulting in cannon, bullets, muskets, flour, and other supplies being stored at Concord, six miles from Lexington.

"Mr. Hancock," Robert addressed him respectfully several times. A hunted man was John Hancock, Robert knew. Not yet had the orders arrived from the King's ministers in London. But the orders were on the way. Isaiah Thomas and others had the information through sources they considered authentic. Soon the vessel now at sea would arrive and deliver the papers making it the duty of Governor General Gage, his officer, and troops, to seek out two men in Boston, two above all, to seize them and send them to London for trial on charges of high treason. These were the two men Robert had seen this day—Sam Adams and John Hancock.

Six years ago last November it was and in this house that the Marshal of the Court of Admiralty had called in this room and arrested John Hancock on charges of violating the customs laws, demanding three thousand pounds bail which Hancock furnished, and the trial had been delayed and dragged on with no result at the end except an indictment, for perjury, of the leading informer against Hancock. A smuggler Hancock was, defiant of what he considered infamous tax laws—a smuggler and an outlaw—soon to be a fugitive. To his agents in London, Haley & Hopkins, he had as long as five years ago sent an order for "fifty barrels of very best pistol powder" and shortly before the tea-dumping party two years ago had a letter from his friend John Andrews saying "'twould puzzle any person to purchase a pair of p—ls in town, as they are all bought up, with a full determination to repell force to force." So ran the lingo of the Revolution. Force would meet force. And in a letter you spelled pistols p—ls.

Mr. Hancock was scrutinizing one of the papers Robert had brought him when there came swishing into the room a trim, sprightly, chattering little mantelpiece of a woman. Robert saw her, knew her, caught the short nose, pointed chin, pointed fingers, every ruffle and flounce of her dress calculated, a young lady of quirks, polite, sudden, impudent. Talk about her in many circles was endless. She could be no other than Dolly Quincy, the youngest, keenest, most dashing of the five daughters of Squire Edmund Quincy of Braintree. She, perhaps, would marry John Hancock. She didn't know. Nor did he. Last year they had nearly married. Three years they had been seen together. Hancock's Aunt Lydia, a formidable woman known as "a very large girl," favored Dolly Quincy for her nephew and it might have been on her urging that Dolly had come to Boston for this evening. Neither Aunt Lydia nor Dolly nor John could feel sure about a wedding date already put off once. For ten years John Hancock had kept a sort of steady company with Miss Sally Jackson till one day he sat down and wrote with his long fingers in a large handwriting what was termed "a letter of dismission." On Miss Sally Jackson then immediately marrying Mr. Henderson Inches, and dying immediately thereafter, no one could say with certainty what had brought her sudden taking-away. Now Dolly was ten years younger than John and it seemed one time it was Dolly and again John who didn't care to set a wedding date and go through with a ceremony. She was coy, impulsive, her sparkling cherry lips half the time not pronouncing her mind or heart. She had tricks. And John had such money, finery, applause, matters of business and politics, headaches, that it was hard for him to find time enough to really think it over whether he loved Dolly Quincy enough to get knotted in matrimony with her for life.

"You have been called once and we do not wish to chide you, Mr. Hancock," Dolly Quincy burbled.

"Yes, my dear."

"The supper table is laid, they said I should inform you."

"Yes, my dear."

Her two hands took the sleeves of his forearms and she looked up at him. "Aunt Lydia waits. The guests wait."

"In a moment, my dear," smiling faintly, then turning, "Mr. Winshore, may I introduce Miss Quincy."

He shook hands with Robert and saw him to the door. At the square-hewn gateposts Robert stood gazing a moment at the most handsome and commodious home in Boston, and, "Will they get him? I hope not. Will he sit in a chair in London three thousand miles across the water on trial for high treason here where he was born and has always lived? They want it. I hope they don't get it."

In the White Cockade coffeehouse over a supper of baked blue-fish with salt pork fried to a crisp, Robert gave his father his impressions of John Hancock and the mansion. "I had a dreamlike feeling in that room with that man. I was asking myself what is real and what isn't. Between you and me, it was in my bones that John Hancock will be a wanderer outside of Boston and that mansion of his filled with laughing mocking enemy officers and soldiers. And by that time what will be happening outside of Boston and what will the Continental Congress and the other colonies be doing?"

As they were finishing with tarts and coffee, a young man joined them, a sturdily built fellow, heavier than Robert, a slow ease and grace in the way he carried himself, a scar on his left temple from a bayonet thrust during a struggle with British guards at the Neck early in the winter when he and two other men on a cart willingly opened barrels of molasses and refused to open several barrels of gunpowder they finally delivered at Concord. This was Oates Elwood, the ship-wright whose sister Ann had met trouble with a Grenadier sergeant.

Ann was not yet sure, he confided to Robert, whether the midnight marriage ceremony was mock or legal. He shouldn't have beaten the sergeant over the head as hard as he did with the pistol, said Elwood. "I lost my head about it."

"He's a fighter," Robert smiled to his father. "I think in my fighting days when I liked it just for the sake of fighting, he might have licked me."

Soon Elwood got up and moved toward the door. Robert rose and joined him. They talked briefly of something that Robert on returning to the table couldn't tell his father.

A mild clear night outside and the father and son walked to Old South Church. To their ears from open windows came the crowd tumult, roars, applause, outcries, a mass rumbling. Out from a window came words sheer and clear, as though the orator had studied them and rehearsed them in solitude and caressed them in quiet meditations. "The great Englishman William Pitt who understands our cause as do not the infamous King's ministers," it was Pitt he was quoting:

"'I am for toleration, that sacred right of nature and bulwark of truth. . . . Power without right is the most odious and detestable object that can be afforded the human imagination. . . . Where law ends, tyranny begins. . . . I can pronounce it an union solid, permanent and effectual. . . . The Americans are the sons, not the bastards of England.'"

And the preceding applause now rose to a mass shout and roar that rocked the building, as again when the orator went on, "I rejoice that America has resisted. Three millions of People so dead to all the feelings of liberty, as voluntarily to submit to be slaves, would have been fit instruments to make slaves of the rest. . . . The gentleman asks, when were the colonies emancipated? But I desire to know, when they were made slaves? . . . The Americans have been wronged. They have been driven to madness by injustice. Will you punish them for the madness you have occasioned? Rather let prudence and temper come first from this side. . . . The gentleman tells us, America is obstinate; America is almost in open rebellion. I rejoice that America has resisted."

The orator spoke warning and reproach to the well-to-do who prized too highly their well-being and creature comforts. "Who is he who boasteth of his patriotism? Has he vanquished luxury and subdued the worldly pride of his heart? He, who cannot conquer a little vanity of his heart, and deny the delicacy of a debauched palate, let him lay his hand upon his mouth, and his mouth in the dust."

No man could read what self-denial might be required of him, what personal sacrifices would be asked for their country, if they were to have a country their own. The speaker pointed to the Middlesex County convention of last year and the resolutions there passed by 146 yeas against 4 nays and the final sentence proclaiming:

431

"No danger shall affright, no difficulties intimidate us; and if in support of our rights we are called to encounter even death, we are yet undaunted, sensible that he can never die too soon, who lays down his life in support of the laws and liberty of his country."

Robert left his father at the Old South Church meeting, saying he would be late arriving at their room. It was one o'clock when his father heard him come in.

"You keep busy, Robert."

"Yes."

"I say my prayers your business is not too dangerous."

"It may be I need your prayers. I am glad I have them."

"It's late, get your sleep, son."

"God keep you in his care, papa."

The father was touched. Robert had little of formal piety. What he meant lay deep.

Neither was in a mood for talk. The father had a complete respect for the oath-bound secrets of his son. He made a little prayer that Marintha Wilming might grow toward some degree of a like respect. And the father thought of how like his mother was Robert. Her tempests were there. Often he might seem cool outside and yet anger writhed inside him. The father could read that like no one else. And he had seen Robert looking at Mim, touching her with a soft hand, and he believed he knew from Robert's mother how infinitely tender was the light of Robert's eyes and what a gentle reverence there was in his hand when he held it at Mim's arm.

Had the father known of the Ludgate affair in which Robert took a hand that night he would have seen in it the quiet deep-running anger of the mother. Could Robert have spoken he would have said the Ludgate affair satisfied him in a way the Reggs affair didn't. It had a rank bittersweet taste he liked and Robert crawled into bed and slept with no regrets.

The Committee had heard the evidence and found the man Silas Ludgate, a well-to-do merchant and importer, guilty. Two competent witnesses had heard him say toward the end of a pleasant drinking party of Loyalists that it was he whose suspicions were aroused and it was he who had sent men to search a small warehouse on the water front and under stacks of rope, lumber and canvas they had found six muskets and two barrels of gunpowder. One of the four men making the search had heard their leader say his instructions came from Ludgate. The seized muskets and powder were to have gone by boat on a dark night to Charlestown and by wagon to Concord for the use of Minute Men.

In the Committee discussion of what punishment should be given Ludgate a few favored tar and feathers. Robert Winshore and Oates Elwood had joined those who argued and prevailed that tar and feathers would mean too many details, take more time and heighten the risks: they favored another form of ceremony they believed would serve as well.

A few minutes after the town watch had walked the street calling "Twelve o'clock and all's well," the men had come two by two, had waited in the shrubbery on the two-acre place, and then gone to work. Entry into the various rooms was made at the same moment. Each of four women were seized, gagged, roped hand and foot, these being Mrs. Ludgate and her daughter Dora on the second floor and two maids on the third floor. Mr. Ludgate was given special treatment and swiftly, one of the men telling him, "We are executing a sentence on you as an informer. We have not come to pay a visit and you better give in and take your medicine and keep quiet." They wore black cloths over their faces and he tried to guess who were these Sons of Liberty. Oates Elwood tore the nightrobe off Ludgate in one ripping sweep. They gagged him, then trussed him with ropes, winding the ropes so tight as to leave marks when loosened, sat him naked and bound before his fireplace. They threw on fresh firewood, each stick carefully dampened. They stuffed the chimney so the smoke would slowly fill the room.

Toward the end of this came an interruption. In the doorway stood a young woman, too suddenly shocked for a loud outcry, moaning a low amazed "oh-h." There she stood shuddering. "She was in the spare room—we should have looked there," said Winshore as he and Elwood leaped toward her, struggled with her, gagged her, led her to the spare room and bound her hand and foot and locked the door. Robert Winshore saw the slight body, blond curls, a mouth fright-puckered. He couldn't be mistaken. It was Sapphira Reggs.

Then out of the lower-floor doors, locking each door and taking the keys away with them, two by two they went up the street less than a half-hour after the town watch had passed with his call "Twelve o'clock and all's well."

Elwood and Robert walked a few blocks together, saying little, crossing streets and turning corners and keeping clear of meeting others under street lamps. When they shook hands and parted, Elwood said, "After what my sister got from a lobster-back, it was a satisfaction tonight to hogtie that Tory bitch. Did you take notice she was scared we might rape her?"

Robert had taken notice.

Elwood slapped his heavy hand on Robert's shoulder and chuckled, "We're gentlemen, Winshore. That's a fact, by God. We're gentlemen. It's too bad I can't tell Sister Ann about it. Good night, me lad."

Through the night hours and until a choreman and a stableman in the morning had run to the town watch and the three of them heaved their bodies against the locked rear door to break it down—through those hours Silas Ludgate sat naked and numbed at his fireplace, in a smoke-thickened room, his eyes bloodshot and nostrils inflamed, his throat and lungs sore and racked with coughing, his meditations bitter, dents and blisters and raw flesh markings where the ropes had scraped.

* * * * * * * * * *

Chapter 13

* * * * * * * * * *

Wig-Boxes, Snow, and Gossip

WILLIAM PITT RINK walked knee-deep in snow, pulled and wriggled through drifts to his waist and shoulders. Twelve years old now, born in 1763 when the Stamp Act first came before the British Parliament, two years old when that Act was passed, a little older when his father who called him Bill gave him his middle name.

Bill had heard in detail of how when he was two years old, his two uncles on his mother's side worked in the night mob that burned and looted the North End mansion of the Royal Governor Thomas Hutchinson, and worse rioting Boston had never seen. They shattered the furniture, threw the library books into the street, drank or carried away every bottle of wine, rum and brandy in the cellar, stole what money was in the house and silver plate, emptied the clothes closets and danced around big bonfires on a sweltering hot August night in the hats, wigs and brocaded velvet coats of the Royal Governor.

A drunken mob it was and a mass meeting in Faneuil Hall of Whigs who hated Governor Hutchinson nevertheless passed resolves saying the mob went too far and acted improper, indecent and mustn't do it again. Two of Bill Rink's uncles on his mother's side were thrown into jail to wait trial. But another mob broke the jail doors and ran out with their friends, who never came to trial. In the Rink family and among the Rink folks it was no drunken mob. A few were drunk but most of them were sober decent citizens who gave a tyrant's tool what he had coming to him, held the Rinks.

Little Bill grew up a partisan Whig, a Tory-hater, a Rebel. Words too dirty to say before his mother and sister he had learned, curses for Tories, vile names rich with spit and he felt good rolling them off his tongue. In politics little Bill was at home. He heard one side, took it all in, ready to fight for it. What little he heard of the other side was either a lie or an argument his father could answer without stopping to think. His mother's two brothers, his two uncles, went to jail for shaming a "tyrant's tool." William Pitt Rink could say, "a tyrant's

434

tool—God damn his eyes." Far across the ocean in London sat King George III, a tyrant, and in Boston the Royal Governor Thomas Hutchinson, a tool of that tyrant. What was more simple and clear, once you saw it as little Bill?

His father had long hours and fair wages on a small ferryboat over the Charles River. With the port of Boston closed and troops to see it stayed closed, Bill's father was thrown out of work, the ferry forbidden. The family lived on short food supplies from the city and in payment his father worked on street and public-building repairs. Yesterday his father had helped kill and dress part of a herd of a hundred and thirty sheep that Colonel Israel Putnam of the Connecticut State Militia had driven into Boston to feed the people. Little Bill had helped, carrying in buckets of hot water, carrying out buckets of sheep guts. On Saturday and no school, Bill worked for himself and the pay from Joseph Ramsay, the barber. To Mr. Ramsay's shop during the week came the wigs of customers, wigs made personal for the head and face of each patron. Each wig worn a few times, got soiled and fussed up. So each wig in its own particular box was brought to Mr. Ramsay to be "dressed" so its owner could go to church on Sunday in a wig people could see neatly fresh-dressed, a nice white powder sifted and scattered over the hair, every hair in place.

Now on late Saturday afternoon and evening, Bill and the other boys working for Mr. Ramsay took these boxes, each holding a wig, and delivered them to the patrons who owned and wore them. On this March evening Bill had struggled and scrambled knee-deep in snow and delivered all his wigs but two. His arms felt easier now. He had started with three boxes roped under each arm. The boxes scraped and bumped on the snow as he roughed his way shoulder-deep in some drifts. The blustering wind whirled him and the boxes and nearly tussled them out of his hold on them.

Bill was glad to reach the London Book-Store. He went in and handed a wig box to the bookstore man who thanked him, gave him a penny, a pat on the head and, "Run home now and tell your mother she wants you."

Bill always noticed the man had two fingers gone, the third and fourth of his left hand. And Bill would walk home with the question bothering his little head, "How did he lose those two fingers? Were they bit off? And was it one bite or two?"

Over six feet tall the bookstore man, pink-skinned and pleasant-faced, his nose a little bulbous, he enjoyed life and weighed nearly three hundred pounds. He would sell a customer any available published book on military science and engineering. He had been three years a member of the crack Boston Grenadier Corps and was second in command. He walked like a soldier and was so anxious to look like he was walking like a soldier that some people called him pompous, vain, self-satisfied, which he really wasn't. His walk, the way that he could look like a soldier when walking, caught the eye of the woman he married. One of her friends said, "She married him for his martial bearing." She was Lucy Flucker, daughter of Thomas Flucker, Royal Secretary of the Province of Massachusetts, and it was June of the year before that he married her. She too was more than six feet tall and she too weighed nearly three hundred pounds. They were referred to as "the largest couple in Boston." He was free-handed, talked free but didn't care much about winning an argument. It hurt him when he had to speak sharp to his wife who had what people called "lofty manners." She was lively, breezy, and they were well mated and were to have, in all, nine children. But when among other people her tongue got too saucy and she gabbled too meddlesome in the affairs of other people, he would remind her she was drifting.

Once on a hunting trip a fowling piece had burst and mangled his left hand so the third and fourth fingers had to come off. A cool head in danger he had. At the Boston Massacre in 1770, before the muskets of a squad of British soldiers had laid four men horizontal and dead in the snow of a Boston street, this bookseller, Henry Knox, had done his best to keep the British Captain Preston from giving an order to his troops to fire on the mob. Had the squad commander that evening been as cool, there would have been no massacre, so Knox believed.

Bashful William Pitt Rink had been glad to get out of the book-store, for there were three men in velvet coats and two women gay in bright satin and they laughed at him and thought he was funny with his yarn cap pulled over his ears, snow over him head to foot. Bill heard one of the ladies say that it looked as though the boxes had brought the boy in on the wind. He saw a little old woman come in, shake the snow off her mittens, sweep the snow off her sleeves and shoulders with the mittens, take from a shelf *History of the Quakers* by Sewel, speak with Mr. Knox about how long she had put off getting the book. And she had a question. Could Mr. Knox show her what-ever was the book by one Roger Williams having the statement, "Forced worship is a stink in the nostrils of God"? Mr. Knox could not be sure. It sounded interesting, he would try and locate it for her, hoped she could come in again next week.

Roughing along Front Street with his last wig box, Bill puzzled over "forced worship." He wouldn't be sure what that was. A stink, though, he knew what a stink was, for every Tory was a stinker. And "the nostrils of God," he tried to picture that. It was the first he had heard of God having nostrils. And he made out that "forced worship" must be terribly rotten if it could reach up into heaven and make a smell so God would want to hold his nose. He was trying to imagine God holding his nose when he had to plow and scramble through snowdrifts "over my belly button," as he later told his father.

436

Then he came to the Sign of the Golden Ball, walked into the hall-
way, took off his yarn mittens, brushed off the snow from his shoulders
and sleeves, stamped his feet, scraped more snow from his yarn stock-
ings, took his last wig box and stepped in and delivered it to the
pleased shipmaster Captain Edelbert Hupple who gave him a silver
coin and a look of authority. Bill's feet were cold, his hands cold, and
would Mrs. Cavendish let him stand a while by the Franklin stove
and warm himself? She called him "little man" and told him to pull
a chair up to the stove.

As William Pitt Rink, twelve years old, sat there at the Franklin
stove he could see that what Captain Hupple was telling Mrs. Caven-
dish was something very special and particular and the Captain en-
joyed telling it even though it was so breathtaking he could hardly go
on with telling it. "Ravished," twice and three times Bill heard Captain
Hupple in a loud hoarse whisper. It was a new word to young Bill.
He wondered what it was to be ravished. One of his uncles on his
mother's side, Bill now remembered, had once said at a Thanksgiving
dinner, "I've got a ravishing appetite." But it didn't help him now
on why Captain Hupple three times had given the word "ravished" a
peculiar whispering twist. Bill had thawed out enough, pulled on his
yarn cap and mittens, said to Mrs. Cavendish, "I'm warm now, it's a
nice stove," and started for home.

What Bill would have heard had he been there earlier and had he
understood and believed what Captain Hupple was telling, would have
given him the shivers as it did Mrs. Cavendish.

"You will not hear of this being published, I am inclined to be-
lieve, Mrs. Cavendish," Captain Hupple had said to begin with. "It
is too brutal an affair, too foul and obscene, I regret to say, Mrs. Cav-
endish, and the intention of the miscreants and fiends who perpe-
trated it is that it shall strike terror to all Loyalists and more particu-
larly those Loyalists who have property and women."

Captain Hupple named for Mrs. Cavendish the man he had talked
with that day whose wife had talked with another woman whose hus-
band had personally and with his own eyes that day seen the interior
of the mansion of Silas Ludgate and Mr. Ludgate himself in bed with
his wounds and under the care of physicians who expected a slow
lingering death for Mr. Ludgate. A mob of no less than thirty of the
beasts in human form had taken possession of the Ludgate residence
shortly after midnight, according to Captain Hupple's informant. They
had ravished the wife of Mr. Ludgate and his daughter Dora and finding
a woman in the spare room they had ravished her. Then during the
long night hours they had tortured Mr. Ludgate, giving him knife jabs
and putting salt in each of the knife wounds. This torture having
failed to bring Mr. Ludgate to confess where he kept his hoard of
gold bullion and coins, they had put the soles of his feet to the fire,
repeating this till the flesh was burned raw and finally he cried aloud

where the treasure was secreted and half of them went and found it and returned and in his presence divided it among themselves. Then before his eyes they brought in the household silver and the jewels of the women and divided among themselves. Then they had stripped him of his nightrobe, adjusted a tightly bound gag over his mouth, bound him to a chair and seated him before an open window with the evident expectation that he would freeze to death if he did not die of his wounds and pains of torture.

"It is a startling and melancholy affair, Mrs. Cavendish," said Captain Hupple, showing a brass-handled, brass-barreled pistol he had begun carrying. "The physicians have counted no less than seventy separate knife wounds in Mr. Ludgate's body, so I am informed, and they have little expectation that he will survive alive. And the women, so it is told, are distraught and hysterical and it is said that by reason of the unspeakable indignities inflicted on them, they desire the affair should be kept hushed, at least until such time as they can make their decisions related to what would be proper action under the circumstances."

For two hours Captain Hupple had waited to deliver his morsels of extravagant report and malicious tattle. It was Saturday and the busiest afternoon and evening of the week, customers steadily coming in to brush off snow and stay to buy their yards of lawn, taffeta, satin, to buy feathers, pins, trimmings, to buy pung, Italian breast flowers. Miss Wilming and Mrs. Trutt were twice called in from the back room to help Mrs. Cavendish serve the buyers. While Mrs. Cavendish was still pressing her thumb ends and finger ends against each other, in her excitement over whatever it was that had happened in the Ludgate house, a few more of her old-time patrons came in. She waited on them and they went away. She excused herself to Captain Hupple, stayed a while with the women in the back workroom, returned to Captain Hupple as Robert Winshore entered and after greetings went back to help Mim on with her leggings and overshoes. They went out saying they would see Mrs. Cavendish and Captain Hupple later at the Knox bookstore. Mrs. Trutt and Jane Haddam helped straighten the stocks on shelf and counter, close the front window blinds and put out the oil lamps, then said good night. When Mrs. Cavendish locked the front door and walked away in the snow with Captain Hupple the week was over at the Sign of the Golden Ball.

When Mrs. Cavendish sneezed as she and Captain Hupple walked toward the Red Lion inn, she knew it wasn't that she was catching cold. She laughed with the Captain about it. Before putting out the last oil lamp he had drawn from a hip pocket his tortoise-shell, silver-rimmed snuffbox. And Mrs. Cavendish had permitted him to put a little pinch of it to each of her nostrils after which he snuffed a large pinch of it up his own nose. They sneezed together and laughed about it. The Captain said, "Snuff is designed for persons who are companionable that they may go farther in their companionability." He had a little pride and so did she that on this evening he could say "companionability" and not stumble over one syllable.

Marintha Wilming kept a tight hold of Robert Winshore's left arm as they walked toward the White Cockade coffeehouse. The hook of her elbow in his, the hold and touch of her mitten on his forearm, the brush of her shoulder against his, said about all she had to say as they plodded through the snow. Not now, possibly later she would tell him of this midafternoon when Lieutenant George Frame and his sister Elizabeth had come to the workroom and she had measured Miss Frame for a bodice of yellow velvet. They had held the fabric to Miss Frame's fair-skinned face and her very light-brown hair and had agreed it was as Mrs. Cavendish said "extraordinarily becoming" though Mrs. Cavendish blurred "extraordinarily" so fast she might be saying "wonderfully becoming." Miss Frame made her usual references to "the Puritans" being the cause of the trouble in the colonies. The same breed of irreverent Cromwellians who had murdered King Charles I were now stirring revolt against King George III with the same disregard of authority and the same rabble relish for violence. Mim could recall Miss Frame last year saying she was glad one of her great-grandfathers had been in the party that dug up the bones of Oliver Cromwell after his natural death and saw to it that he was publicly hanged by the neck to bring shame to the ruffian Puritans.

Except in this area of politics, Miss Frame was a merrymaking soul with a large mouthful of bright teeth. As to her brother George, however, Mim had her doubts. He had become too solemnly and broodingly attentive to her. His eyes played on her with a steady fixity reminding her of Jabez Hunker wanting to marry and own her. He had asked Mim to dine with him and his sister on Sunday and Mim had to say she had another engagement. The Lieutenant's considerate regard on the New York to Boston stage seemed to have moved into some desire for possession of her. If Robert had not come into her life, she said to herself, she might have gone along with George Frame to see further what this burning in him was, saying frankly too, "Perhaps I was something of a flirt before Robert came."

She had moved with Mrs. Cavendish to the front door to say good afternoon to the Frames, to say she was sure the yellow velvet bodice would be one of the shop's notable garments, to hear Mrs. Cavendish say it would look "hemmly" by which they inferred Mrs. Cavendish meant "heavenly."

In the workroom Jane Haddam had gone into a flourish of rambling gossip that ended with her saying, "I imagine Mim has been as pretty and free with Lieutenant Frame as she has with Robert Winshore— she went with one to New York and came back with the other."

439

As this flashed from Jane, Mrs. Trutt and Amelia Gray knew it was mild compared to the spite that ran in Jane's bosom. Once last summer Lieutenant George Frame had taken Jane to the Bunch of Grapes tavern for supper and again in late autumn to a small dancing party, each time the Lieutenant having asked Mim to go and Mim saying she had an engagement with Robert Winshore. It was rather plain that Jane believed Mim was seeing more of Lieutenant Frame than she let on and that if Mim could be out of the picture Lieutenant Frame would give her more of his time and the kind of glances she reveled in when coming from him.

Mrs. Trutt was trying to think of a kindly Christian rebuke for Jane. Amelia Gray flashed, "That's nasty, Jane Haddam. You're throwing dirty gossip today."

The three women turned their heads toward the back of the room and the door slamming, slamming hard. There stood Mim, rigid, cold. Still they all were. Then Mim swept to where she stood, arms on hips, facing Jane and in a low blaze, "Jane Haddam, I could give you the back of my hand across your foul blathering mouth—but I won't touch the vile filth of you."

Then they stitched and hemmed, fitted and basted, sewed in silence. Later Mrs. Trutt could hear and Amelia Gray could hear but it didn't quite reach the ears of Jane Haddam that Mim was saying she read a book last year where one woman called another "an ugly, ungenteel, squinting, flirting, impudent, odious, dirty puss," and that was "piling it on too thick."

Again they stitched and hemmed, fitted and basted, sewed in silence and the six-foot oval gilt mirror heard nothing, said nothing.

Marintha, her arm hooked in Robert's, plodding through snow, reviewed part of the midafternoon. "Sometime I may gabble it all to him—certainly not tonight."

* * * * * * * * *

Chapter 14

* * * * * * * * *

At the White Cockade

"IT'S in the air, Mim."

"Of course it's in the air, Robert."

"And when it comes, then what?"

"*You* ask *me*, then what?"

"Yes, what will it be like?"

440

"It will be like nothing you ever told me and it will not work out as you seem to think."

"But I have told you little of it, almost nothing, and I ask you please to know I see nothing certain about how it will work out."

They were eating at the White Cockade coffeehouse, a plain mutton stew with vegetables. The place had a Saturday-night crowd, mostly Whigs who had eaten their usual evening meal at home and were eating cakes with coffee or drinking beer and porter, some of them smoking their long pipes, a few having hot slings, slip, rum, and already slightly hilarious.

Mim had been silent with an edge to her so that Robert wasn't sure whether she was tired after days of hard work at the dress shop—or sullen. She could be sullen. He had seen that in her. When he said "it" was in the air, she knew he meant the end of the suspense Boston had been under for months. He would like to know if her mind and feeling had brought her any picture of how "it" would break, what would be the events and their shape, what she guessed she might be doing then, she in relation to him. And she didn't care to be specific. She talked as cryptic as he, in a tone with an undercurrent that baffled and troubled him.

They nodded and waved to friends at other tables. They watched four English sailors at one table, a Grenadier sergeant and two privates at another table. Robert mentioned their quiet behavior. "They don't act like they've come for some of their usual kind of pleasure."

"There *are* different kinds of pleasure, wouldn't you say so, Robert?"

"Why, of course, Mim."

"You have heard perhaps of the kind of pleasure there was at Silas Ludgate's house last night."

"What have you been hearing?"

"Oh, it may be just gossip. I don't think it will bear repeating."

"Then we will let it pass," said Robert, hiding from her what he read of her. He could see that she had rushed into her mention of Silas Ludgate against her intention not to let that name slip her tongue. What she had heard of Ludgate was a turmoil in her, so much so that she must guard her feeling about it because it had an edge against Robert in particular or the Sons of Liberty in general.

The front door of the White Cockade had opened and a young man stepped in, shook off snow, stamped his boots and looked around. Four tables away Mim saw him, sturdy with one shoulder sloping lower than the other, his face ruddy and weather-beaten, and as his hat came off Mim saw that shaggy head of brown hair and sprang toward him.

"Darius!" was her cry as her arms went around him and his around her and he laughed, "Mim, it's blessed to see you."

She took him to their table. His hand went out, "Robert, it's good to see you, too." They had met on visits of Robert to the farm last summer and fall.

Quiet, slow-spoken Darius told of riding in from Lexington that afternoon and errands that kept him so when he went to the dress shop it was closed and dark. "I ride back to the farm tonight. A short ride for a look at your blessed face, Mim."

Jake was well, yes. Mim had asked first about Jake. Cutting wood he had gashed his left foot a month ago but it was well in a week and he had laughed about it.

"And Ma?"

"She's well but worrying."

"I know, that Liberty Room crowd."

"Aggie and Deb cheer her, they're lively as spring lambs."

"That's good, I wish I could feel like a spring lamb these days."

Mim didn't ask about her father. Darius softly let her know, "He sees many kinds of men in the Liberty Room and I guess he'll drink more than is good for him till this excitement lets down." No one spoke. Darius added, "Seems worse than last year, the excitement, I wouldn't say why and I'm not sure I would know."

Oates Elwood came in, a young woman with him. "My sister Ann, Robert," said Elwood as they stopped for greetings and introductions and went to a near-by table.

"Ann Elwood, did I hear?"

"Yes, Mim."

"The girl Jane Haddam and Mrs. Trutt have been telling about who is trying to make certain whether she is legally married to a sergeant of Grenadiers?"

"Yes, hell to pay and may be more."

"A nice-looking girl and it *is* sad."

Elwood came over, sat alongside Robert speaking as though to him only. "I'm staying just long enough to tell you we have now found out for sure it was a fraud and a lousy game they played on Ann. That soldier who read off the marriage ceremony is a liar and a drunken no-good who never was ordained. If I didn't have other work you know about that counts for more, I think I'd hunt 'em out and kill the both of 'em." He rose, Robert with him, and they joined Ann Elwood.

Mim told Darius of the father finding the sergeant in bed with his daughter and the sergeant's claim they were married. They saw Robert's face grave and grim as he talked with the two Elwoods, saw his warm handshake with them as he left their table.

Robert noted changes in Mim. The sea-pale white of her oval face, some bright awareness that gave her gaunt lines a heightened strength, the deepening of the faint apple-blush of her cheeks, she had lost her sullen edge. It was being with Darius, that mainly, and it could be too that a compassion sometimes aroused in her had been lighted by the sight of Ann Elwood.

"She's no trollop for any man," said Mim. "She's rather handsome, when you look closer, with that heavy black hair and that full rich mouth."

Robert could say nothing. He listened and tried to look pleasant. Darius answered Mim's queries about the farm work, about neighbors, about Pussy Willow the yellow cat having her ninth basket of kittens, about Jabez Hunker having gone to Salem and married a fat young widow to bring home to Concord.

"What's she like?"

"Well-to-do in her own right and ever cheerful."

"The old hypocrite. It's good news. Now the talk can end that he had a broken heart over me."

Darius smiled gravely. "They are the laughingest pair in Middlesex County."

Darius had slowly put away three cups of coffee after his mutton stew. They went out into the snow and up the street to where the horse was stabled, saw Darius in the saddle with a kiss from Mim, and he rode away bound for the Neck and the road to Lexington.

As they walked to the London Book-Store they said no word and watched the snowfall ending. Robert pointed to one star then two between a ragged edge of clouds. Mim kept a tight hold on Robert's arm. She was saying to herself it seemed the only kind of talk left for her with Robert. Then she said it wasn't as bad as that though nearly so. Robert said to himself that she was telling him, Don't let me leave you, whatever I do, don't let me leave you. Then he said that would be too simple for Mim and, "I am wishing wishes." With Darius gone some of her brightness went. Robert could do better at guessing her mood if he could know what she had been told about Silas Ludgate. He was tired with this long week of so many whirling affairs. Mim rested him—and then she didn't. He wished more wishes and a useless feeling swayed him. Her tight hold on his arm—would it be there in the further whirls to come?

At a deserted street corner where the lamplighter hadn't come because of wind and snow they paused in drifts over their knees and looked up to see four stars, five, between the ragged edge of clouds. Robert pulled her to him, their mouths found each other in a long tight kiss that each of them knew meant prayer and hope, more of want and longing than of consolation.

Chapter 15

In the Bookstore

THEIR leggings and overshoes off at the London Book-Store, they found the crackling fire at a wide hearth very cozy as they stood there after greetings. Mr. and Mrs. Henry Knox had one kind of greeting, warm and easy, as was that of Mrs. Cavendish. Captain Hupple bowed to Mim, "Charmed, I assure you," and to Robert, "A pleasure to meet you again, sir." Lieutenant George Frame was polite with a smile half grim and his sister Elizabeth strictly self-possessed and aware of the exact middle point between the familiar and the reserved. Ordway Winshore was happy and jocular with spreading affectionate grins. The sleekly dressed and chunky Bliss Edmunds on close study had a furtive, bothered look on his face. Miss Mary Burton from the first interested Robert and Mim. Trim she was, very trim of structure and movement, hips too wide perhaps but they went with her wide face and the wide spread of her dark-brown hair out from the temples and her wide blue eyes. They noticed Ordway Winshore having a hard time keeping his eyes off her. Nodding his head toward her and speaking half-gay and for Robert only to hear, he said, "Unity, Robert, she's got unity."

Knox locked the front door after serving a customer who came in every year for a copy of Nathaniel Ames' *Almanack*, a hog-drover much pleased that his three-day journey with forty hogs had ended the day before the big snow began. He had his goad with him, a hardwood stick with a sharp steel-pointed end. He laughed, motioning with his goad, "You can't drive hogs mile on mile when they have to slide their bellies over the snow, Mr. Knox." Patting his newly bought *Almanack* with his fingers he said the rhymes of Ames got in his head and stayed there, quoting:

> "The honest Farmer now at Ease
> Regales himself with Cyder, Bread and Cheese
> And further to himself amuse
> He smokes his Pipe & reads the News."

And the rhyme was not so good but the lines made sense and he enjoyed reciting:

> "As Men salute a Prostitute
> At the Expence of Noses
> Some Ladies still their Tea do swill
> Tho' it ruin their Spouses."

444

And the early winter weather had been as Ames predicted in a line: "Puffing, belching, f—g Weather." He and his farmer neighbors laughed when it came true. The drover felt Ames went out of his way to be mischievous about women. He quoted from Ames: "Some sluts take advantage of that text of Scripture 'What goes into the body defiles not the body,' to poison all their acquaintance." The drover drawled his comment, "Sluts like that ain't so common they deserve a place in Ames' *Almanack*." Then he again quoted Ames, "The ladies should consider that when men view a nag they always look at the teeth." He had known good horses and good women that didn't have the best of teeth. Why should Ames bring up such a matter?

Ordway Winshore had strolled over. Knox introduced them. "He's got rather a drover's face, hasn't he, Mr. Knox?" The drover laughed and pulling the 1773 *Almanack* from a shelf, "I like it Ames made so bold as to print what has been told or read in every tavern and inn in New England," chuckling and reading:

> "The natives of this land are as witty and capable of improvement as they who boast their English extraction, as when Col. C—— ask'd the old Squaw 'how many Commandments are there?' 'Nine, Sir,' said she, 'since you and I broke one behind that bush.' "

"I must be going," laughed the drover as though he might have been making himself a ribald nuisance, first dipping into the 1775 *Almanack* at random and finding:

> "Rain, thunder, no! thunder first, then rain! so said Socrates when he received his wife's warm fragrant shower from a Window."

Mary Burton came up and was introduced. "Likely I wouldn't care about Ames if twan't for his politics. He's got nourishment for us all," the drover reading and quietly vehement about it:

> "Liberty is a more noble invigorating cordial than Madeira; think of this, ye splendid Slaves, Parasites and Pimps. . . . God has fitted our Constitutions to the Climate we live in, turn out, you Sluggard, and shake off the Scurvy. . . . It is astonishing to see how the Race of Spaniels encreases amongst us of late Years. . . . A servant of servants is too low for human nature. . . . Who can serve five hundred masters faithfully when they are three thousand miles off?"

With that the drover was going, with his jokes, his ribaldry, overlaid by curious resolves not entirely formulated. Mr. Knox and he were laughing good-by at the door.

"There goes the Revolution," said Winshore to Miss Burton.

"If King George or Lord North could know how little it is from them that they will not grant him, how different all would be," said Miss Burton.

"Yes. Pitt knows. Burke knows."

"The hog-drover understands the theory of natural rights without reading John Locke."

Winshore with a luminous quirk of his face, " 'I can no more know anything by another man's understanding than I can see by another man's eyes.' "

Miss Burton's wide blue eyes lighted, " 'Chains are but an ill wearing how much soever we gild and polish them.' "

Each knew one had spoken to the other a long-beloved sentence from John Locke. They felt magnets pulling them toward each other.

Miss Burton took from a shelf a book published in Boston in 1773, reprinted from an English text, titled *An Essay Concerning the True Original Extent and End of Civil Government*, the first American edition of a work that for a generation back had been read, studied, quoted, and used by leaders of the resistance movement.

Miss Frame and her brother came up to listen, joined by Robert and Mim. "The book I am holding," said Miss Burton, "was an accident. It came about in a curious way. John Locke met five friends one evening. They discussed morality and religion. Locke told them what he had to say of any value in the argument he could write it all on one sheet of paper. He burst out to them that evening with the sentence Mr. Winshore was just now quoting, 'I can no more know anything by another man's understanding than I can see by another man's eyes.' Then John Locke spent the next twenty years of his life writing a book to explain what he meant by that little sentence. A queer, stubborn, profound man he was and I was just quoting my favorite sentence from him, one of those quaint sentences that stick in your mind and on your tongue and you are not sure why. 'Chains are but an ill wearing how much soever we gild and polish them.' "

Robert saw a mingled look on Mim's face. The music of the sentence was like her own in those flashes she spoke for the few she trusted. It pleased her. Then too it bewildered her, for it faded hazily into the pivots of idea and feeling that moved Robert and others. So much Robert could guess. That Mim resented Miss Burton, well knowing her resentment was wrong and had some touch of jealousy of the scholarship, attainments, and distinctly of the serenity of Miss Burton —this was beyond Robert's guessing. Robert saw Mim take on a hard brilliance, welcoming Miss Frame suddenly showing all the handsome teeth of her large mouth, her chestnut hair at her forehead shaking, as she interposed, "Chains, Miss Burton? Are we not all born to chains? Is not each of our personal limitations a chain and we do the best we can through life at gilding and polishing it?"

Her mouth grave but her wide blue eyes dancing merrily Miss Burton replied, "I answer yes to your every question, Miss Frame. You are

446

correct. You would find John Locke saying you are correct. You wouldn't care now to hazard a surmise as to what Locke would mean by his sad little sentence, 'Chains are but an ill wearing how much soever we gild and polish them'?"

Miss Frame's merriment had receded. She would be debonair, blow the matter away like a flick of eiderdown. "Oh, some rainy day I shall read your friend Locke. What you speak of so earnestly is merely an abstraction."

"Merely an abstraction?"

"To be sure."

"Would you go so far as to say you now have a freedom of worship in England that formerly did not exist?"

"I suppose so."

"For a long time in England, for centuries in England, you went to one church and one church only. If you worshiped in any other faith than that church you did it in secret—would you say that is correct, Miss Frame?"

"I suppose so."

"You were chained to one form of worship in those earlier times—would it be correct to say that?"

"You are trying to trap me, Miss Burton. I suppose you will next be asking me to join you in admiration of Oliver Cromwell as a chain-breaker and a great noble hero."

"No, I would rather ask you if you have heard of the Magna Carta."

"Who hasn't?"

"One of the great documents of the human family, given to the world by the people of England."

"The barons of England."

"Correct, Miss Frame, the barons rather than the people of England. Yet a sublime document the nobles and their King John signed. They refused to gild and polish their chains. They compelled the King to remove them, take 'em away, off with 'em."

"You are getting quite colloquial, Miss Burton."

Miss Burton realized suddenly she *was* getting colloquial, blunt, and fiery. She thought of saying, "You must excuse my enthusiasm over your Magna Carta but I thought you might like it that I believe your Magna Carta a sublime contribution to human liberty." But that wouldn't do. She put out a hand, touching softly Miss Frame's shoulder. "I *am* sorry. I *do* talk colloquial and *too* much." It was a punctuation, Miss Burton knew, saying later to Ordway Winshore, "I could have beaten her in a verbal brawl she wanted and no good come of it."

Robert noted Mim's hard brilliance took on shadows. The atmosphere was unusual for Mim, abstractions, history, probings, the clash of ideas rooted and twining deep in a loam of emotions. She hadn't read Locke nor seen his reasoning come to life on living tongues. She could see that Miss Burton and Miss Frame knew they had clashed

447

and fought briefly in a realm of opposed ideas, that those ideas each stood for a way of life, that those two enemy ideas had made the war that Cromwell fought against King Charles I, that likewise two opposed ideas now raged over Boston and the American colonies, with Robert saying to her at the White Cockade, "It's in the air, Mim," and not sure what was in the air or what would come of it. She had suspicions of Miss Burton's sincerity. A sincere person couldn't be so damned clever. Then Mim accused herself of being slow rather than adroit in the realm of ideas. Robert saw her hard brilliance move into an oval of shadows crossing her face. He had never known so exciting and violent a week, nor Mim so hard to read nor his father so surprising—for here was his father with eyes ever roving over Miss Burton, hanging on her words with adoration. If his father was not falling in love, Robert would like to know what it was going on.

Mrs. Knox filled a doorway at the rear, spoke formal and buxom good cheer with her announcement that soon the punchbowl would be brought in "and various surprises." Mr. Knox said that pending the punchbowl they might look into a newly arrived volume titled *A New Select Collection of Epitaphs* by R. Well, a mischievous book that Mr. Edmunds probably would like to take home to his good.lady for their joint reading. Knox read:

> "Here Lies poor Ned Purdon, from Misery freed,
> Who long was a Bookseller's Hack,
> He led such a damnable Life in this World,
> I don't think he'll ever come back.

"Here, Mr. Edmunds, have a glance at it." And Edmunds turned to a random page and, "I couldn't take this home and let my good lady see it," and reading:

> "Here lies my poor wife, without Bed or Blanket,
> But dead as a Door-Nail, GOD be thanked.

"The more I peep and examine this work, the more certain I am it is not a book to take home," rambled on Edmunds, reading again:

> "Here lies a Woman—no man can deny it,
> She rests in Peace, altho' she liv'd unquiet;
> Her Husband prays, if by her Grave you walk,
> You'll gently tread, for if she wakes she'll talk."

Miss Frame gently removed the book from Edmunds' hands, "I am of a mind it is not a book for mixed company." She found four lines and pointed to them for the other women to read as they passed the book along; an epitaph for a profligate named Cromwell Lea:

> Here lieth old Cromwell,
> Who, living, loved the Bum well.
> When he dy'd, he gave nothing to the Poor,
> But half to his Bastards and half to his Whore.

"A sad little personal history, that is all," said Miss Burton, "and likewise these outrageously frank lines:

"Here Delia's buried at Fourscore;
When young, a lewd, rapacious Whore,
Vain, and expensive; but when old,
A pious, sordid, drunken Scold.

"In a Glasgow churchyard someone did well by a man whose life was given to digging coal underground," continued Miss Burton. And she read:

"Here lies the Collier, Jenkin Dashes,
By whom Death nothing gain'd, he swore;
For living he was Dust and Ashes,
And dead he was no more.

"An odd book," went on Miss Burton, her eyes dancing among its pages. "For here appears to be a man in Dundee, Scotland, who was entirely prepared to meet his God and Maker." She read:

"Here lies old John Hildibroad,
Have Mercy upon him, Good GOD;
As he would do, if he was GOD,
And thou wer't old John Hildibroad.

"Like many other books, much gabble, a little smutch, and a little to treasure," continued Miss Burton. "I choose you one more and it is precious. When Anne Green, a Quaker in Ramsbury, took her leave she was missed by someone:

"Here lies a Piece of Christ, a Star in Dust,
A Wedge of Gold, a China Dish, that must
Be us'd in Heav'n, when Christ does feed the Just."

They had heard someone rattling at the locked front door. This person now slid through the side door, stood with feet wide apart, crouching, wavering, peering from face to face. He took off his three-cornered hat, bowed his respects especially low to the ladies, shuffled toward Henry Knox, eyeballs rolling, the voice hoarse, "They are coming, Mr. Knox, they are after me again."

A tall man bent, a solid man shrunk, a handsome man twisted out of shape, what had once been there no longer all there, branches of him lightning-struck and blown away—this Knox saw and knew, this the elder Winshore guessed out of having seen the man years ago. A round face with finely spaced eyes that had lost a command they once had, a round mouth that had opened to let out mirth and wit, passion and eloquence, a mouth now of pity and broken bravado crying with shrewd narrowed eyes, "Unless I watch and foil them, they will get me, Mr. Knox."

"Who would be getting you?"

449

"They don't say. They come with unknown faces. They come without warrants to arrest me."

He spread his feet wider, clenched both hands, loosened one hand and flung it in gestured pride, his voice rising to falsetto. "Enemies of the human race they are. They want me because I have spoken. They seek me well aware I am not one of the minions of silence."

Marintha Wilming leaned forward, tensed, saying to herself, "He is beautiful and terrible. I wonder if it could happen to me." She felt herself almost inside of him with his pity and broken bravado. She was with him as he paused, his face softening as his eyes ranged the faces of the ladies, beseeching, "You should say prayers for me." Then with a gravity that could have hidden mirth, "Your lips should make intercessions at the throne of the Most High that I may watch and foil them."

He turned, "You heard of my deed yesterday, Mr. Knox, foiling them?"

"You faced them from the window of your house and fired your pistol at them, so I heard it told."

"That I did. The cowards ran."

He went with Knox to a table, picked through newspapers from London, chose one having a recent speech by Edmund Burke, paid for it, shambled to the door, made a long bow sweeping his hat toward the ladies, put on his hat, thanked Mr. Knox and slid out the door.

. A short silence, Ordway Winshore moving to a bookshelf, Elizabeth Frame abruptly, "A sign of the times—touched in the head, is he not?"

Winshore thumbing through a book and still looking into the book, absently, "A first-rate lawyer, young yet when he went as far as Halifax, defended three men accused as pirates, won their acquittal and the highest fee ever paid to a Boston lawyer."

"A first-rate lawyer indeed."

"Advocate General of the Royal Province of Massachusetts fourteen years ago."

"An honorable post."

"Dishonorable, he said, and resigned it, quit, washed his hands of it."

"And his reasons?"

"He gave them, publicly, in a courtroom. To hold the office he must join with officers of the Crown in compelling any citizen to assist in forcible search of any citizen's house. He said," and Winshore read from the book he had been thumbing:

"'To my dying day, I will oppose with all the faculties God has given me, all such instruments of slavery on the one hand, and villainy on the other, as this writ of assistance. . . . I despise all those whose guilt, malice, or folly has made them my foes. Let the consequences be what they will, I am determined to proceed.

450

The only principles of public conduct that are worthy of a gentle-man or a man are to sacrifice estate, ease, health, applause, and even life, to the sacred call of his country. . . . Our ancestors, as British subjects, and we their descendants, as British subjects, were entitled to all those rights, and we are not to be cheated out of them by any phantom of virtual representation or any other fiction of law and politics. *Taxation without representation is tyranny.*' "

"Could he have indulged himself," Miss Frame asked, "in the per-sonal vanity of making a bold front with seemingly brave words? One more Puritan enjoying his defiance of authority?"

"Two years later he spoke in Faneuil Hall as a Briton, a forthright Magna Carta Englishman, saying," and Winshore read from the book: "Every British subject in America is, of common right by Acts of Parliament, and by the laws of God and Nature, entitled to all the essential privileges of Britons."

"A true Briton, can you be certain?"

"I will read from the book, from his Faneuil Hall speech twelve years ago, and he might have taken the words out of your mouth, my good friend." All gave their ears. Winshore with a wry grin, his left eye a slit, read from the book: "The true interests of Great Britain and her Plantations are mutual; and what God in his Providence has united, let no man pull asunder."

"Hear, hear."

"He went farther, saying 'none but rebels, fools, or madmen' would contend for the colonies to be independent, writing a prophecy which I read," and Winshore looked in the book and read: "Were these colonies left to themselves, tomorrow, America would be a shambles of blood and confusion."

"Almost thou persuadest me." Miss Frame smiled, adding wryly, "The man tried to be completely loyal and perfectly disloyal at the same time and the double effort touched him in the head."

"Possibly that dismisses the case of James Otis."

"James Otis! I heard of him in London. Over the British Empire who has not heard of James Otis?"

"An angry man, a proud man swift to anger and he may have spoken the wrong words that night in the British Coffee House on King Street six years ago. A brawl began. An officer of the Crown, John Robinson, drew his cutlass and cut a gash fracturing the skull of James Otis."

"No." Miss Frame shuddered. "One shrinks from believing it."

"Whatever natural infirmity James Otis might have had in that head received no help, soothing or mitigation from a cutlass wound. His Loyalist wife, with her cold, placid and formal beauty, may or may not have been a help. He grew garrulous, chattered, gabbled trash, raved. The nickname came of Muddlehead Otis. No harm being near he shouted for protection. He broke windows in the State House, fired from his home at imaginary enemies. Four years ago the probate court found him *non compos mentis* and named a younger brother his guardian."

Winshore put the book back on the shelf. "I'm sorry if I haven't told it right. I suppose I wouldn't have told it at all if the man hadn't suddenly come tonight in his own tragic person with his infinite pathos."

"I thank you, Mr. Winshore. It is a strangely sobering story." Miss Frame meant it. Winshore liked her.

Mrs. Knox and a maid had brought in the punchbowl. "My own mix," said Mrs. Knox. "Pure water boiling hot poured into the sugar, then the lemon juice and a few peels for the souring, old dark-brown Jamaica rum, just the right whiff of brandy. Porter gives it the foam, nutmeg on top for decoration and for those who *do* prefer that nutmeg dust."

Robert and Mim sipped little, rather poured the punch down their throats. Captain Hupple drank likewise, pouring it down rather than sipping. The three of them had each emptied two glasses while the others sipped at their first. Mim didn't like the eyes of Lieutenant Frame, sober, caressing, demanding. Robert had come to notice it, which she saw, and that didn't help any. She still admired the Lieutenant but wished he could be rid of this new way of looking at her. Lieutenant Frame had a curious dominance over the room in his uniform conceived for dominance with its long-tailed coat of a scarlet insistent if not flagrant, the smooth and spotless white of the breeches, a wide belt with a large square brass buckle, the leather of the boots shining as black mirrors. He moved at ease, polite and agreeable, standing with feet well apart, erect and head high in a habit of military tradition. Some of his brief remarks could be taken to mean that he as a soldier didn't care about argument: the military would act when the time came and their acts would settle the arguments.

"I like you, Mr. Winshore," Lieutenant Frame had said, "though I have difficulty in solving you. You have an adroit quality similar to what I hear of your townsman Benjamin Franklin. You and he are acquainted?"

"Very well."

"Is there any basis, would you say, for the common reports that he has a way with frail women?"

Winshore more than smiled. He grinned and erased the question put to him. "It is my purpose this evening, Lieutenant Frame, to say nothing of Mr. Franklin's way nor mine nor yours, with frail women." He went on: "The peculiar love of liberty you find in these colonies, Lieutenant Frame—"

Frame interrupted. "You were there that night in Elizabeth, New

452

Jersey. Would you not say it was indeed a peculiar love of liberty that large hairy ape had when he drank a toast wishing the King of England in hell?"

"Edmund Burke touches on that. Have you read the speeches of Burke, Lieutenant Frame? Mr. Knox has them here. Might I present you with them?"

"No, I thank you, I have no intention of reading Mr. Burke."

"You must have excellent reasons."

"I do. He would probably fail to convince me and then I would have wasted my time on him."

"Yet suppose he should convince you, at least in part?"

"To whatever extent he did convince me he would then make my duties in America more difficult. An officer can't be loyal to his King and likewise loyal to rebels against his King."

He was smiling. So was Winshore. So was Mr. Knox who listened, who had made it understood it was an informal party of persons who enjoyed, used and bought books. "We know there will be no tavern brawling and howling," Mr. Knox had said. The Lieutenant had bought a book on artillery methods and thanked Mr. Knox for having it in stock. Miss Frame had bought two Fielding novels. Captain Hupple was showing Mrs. Cavendish and Miss Burton purchases for his ship library. "Dr. Samuel Johnson's *Dictionary of the English Language*, it is indispensable for any person wishing to acquire a valuable vocabulary. And these will pass the time, *The Memoirs of Madam Pompadour, Mistress of the French King, and Great Britain's Best Friend*, also *The Life of Cleveland, an Unfortunate Natural Son of Oliver Cromwell*."

A table was brought in. Mrs. Knox and a maid arranged sliced cold roast venison, Mr. Knox telling about his friend who had shot the deer. A neck of cold boiled mutton came in; Mr. Knox knew the farmer who had raised the sheep as an addict of Nathaniel Ames' *Almanack* and a reader of John Bunyan's *Pilgrim's Progress* aloud to his family. The long loaf of wheat bread was baked by a neighbor woman who quoted the Whig miller from whom she bought the flour as saying, "Books might help but what you do with a gun stays put." Mr. Knox shook with mirth telling this and Lieutenant Frame joined him, "I believe the miller is correct." The squares of cheese and the heaped platter of butter came from a farm the Knoxes visited every summer. They could name the cows on that farm. "One of the stubborn cows they call Free-and-Equal," Mr. Knox chuckled, "and the bull on a near-by farm they named Independence."

Coffee from the West Indies, Bordeaux claret, sherry, Madeira, a bottle of old Jamaica rum, stood ready for each to choose. At a smaller table against a wall of books waited a frosted gingercake and a large copper pot of coffee.

Captain Hupple poured claret, "A choice and rare old Bordeaux," he said and proposed the toast:

> "Here's a health to all those that we love.
> Here's a health to all those that love us.
> Here's a health to all those that love them that love those
> That love those that love them that love us."

They stood enjoying this ten-o'clock snack of food with drinks, keeping their talk and merriment away from politics and the shadowy vibrations of the Revolution that ever vaguely quivered under their feet. Then with no form nor agreement about it, they divided into groups, the Winshores, Miss Burton and Miss Wilming one side of the big hearth, the Frames, Captain Hupple and Mrs. Cavendish on the other side, with Bliss Edmunds at the table between them in conversation with the Knoxes about the wines and victuals.

The voice of Captain Hupple could be heard telling of pleasures and hospitality extended to him by excellent gentlemen including one Edward Hancy. "We halted at his country seat at Milton, remarkable rooms for size, a fine ancestral hall, a pleasure garden, a beautiful orchard and a beautiful canal. Would you believe it the canal is supplied by a brook, well stocked with silver eels? We caught a fine parcel and carried them home and had them for supper." Not quite so loud but enough so to be heard by the other groups Captain Hupple told of being in New York some months back and going to a boxing match. "I saw a mob of about two hundred men, near a Liberty Pole, roaring and cursing at a Tory fallen in their hands. They told him to go down on his knees and damn his King George and they would then set him free. On the contrary, he exclaimed, 'God bless King George!' They then dragged him through the common green, tore the clothes from his back, and robbed him of his watch. Had not peace officers arrived I verily believe they would have murdered him for the sole reason that he was a Tory."

Later Captain Hupple lowered his voice to a whisper. Robert Winshore noted him telling Lieutenant Frame something unusual and for their group only, and he had asked the Lieutenant three or four questions. Robert stepped around to the table for another pour of the old Jamaica rum, remarked about its flavor to Mr. Knox and Edmunds, kept an ear toward Frame and heard the words, "Oh no, Ludgate is well out of danger," and another sentence where Robert knew Frame was saying either, "We have *caught* one of the brutes" or "We have *track* of one of the brutes." Robert took a long sip of his rum, picked a small square of cheese, saying low-voiced to Mr. Knox he hoped some of the milk of the stubborn cow Free-and-Equal had gone into the cheese. Mr. Knox burbled merrily as between the two of them that they could be sure the cheese traced back in part to the noble herd sire Independence.

Robert poured his own glass full of rum again, filled another for Mim, took the chair next to her and they said nothing. Their agreement to say nothing was unspoken the same as their agreement to get a little boozy. They heard Miss Burton telling Ordway Winshore of a rumor that sped from mouth to mouth and valley to valley over Massachusetts last autumn, a report that General Gage had begun war by bombarding Boston. "Young and old crowded the roads to Boston with firelocks, fowling pieces, squirrel guns, pistols, pitchforks, hatchets—twenty thousand swarmed to Boston, found the rumor false. Yet they went back home satisfied. Who would have believed they could in a few hours send twenty thousand armed men to Boston ready to fight? They jubilated over their strength and spirit."

"What of Plymouth where my New England ancestry began?" asked Winshore.

"Peaceable and orderly, it seems—yet ready to erupt. Last October one day anxious Patriots thronged all roads to Plymouth. They dedicated a Forefathers' Rock and a Liberty Pole. Four thousand citizens pledged themselves to stand by each other against oppression by the mother country."

Miss Burton gave details about twelve thousand Minute Men in Massachusetts, ready for armed service any minute, about the Provincial Congress of Massachusetts organized at Salem and moving from town to town, a fugitive government, giving out proclamations and orders against the Royal Government at Boston. "How long can two such governments go on without some terrible open clash?"

The pace of the violence on both sides was increasing, Miss Burton was sure. "In the country towns and in Boston the Sons of Liberty punish and humiliate informers. They paraded Boston streets a while ago with one of their own members tarred and feathered. They had caught him informing. This week they went at midnight to the home of a wealthy Loyalist, an informer so the report goes, and gave him punishment so horrible the authorities are afraid to make it public. We don't know who the man is."

For the first time Ordway Winshore turned his face from the wide blue eyes of Miss Burton that he found so fascinating, and gave a casual look at Robert. Mim did not miss this look. Mim spoke. Except for conventional remarks and small talk, it was the first time she had anything to say at this evening party. She said it as though alone in the room: "Violence is an outlet for minds groping in dark labyrinths."

Lieutenant Frame had strolled over. He and his sister were getting ready to leave. He asked with courtesy and gravity, "How would you define violence, Miss Wilming?"

"I would not try to define it, sir," and she rose from her chair. "I can give you the well-known toast of the Sons of Liberty, if you wish."

"I am not certain I have heard it."

Mim lifted the glass of rum she had emptied, eyes flashing, lips quivering, a form of flame with a touch of anguish. All in the room had their eyes fastened on her. No one, perhaps not Mim herself, could have told the variety of intentions and promptings she had.

"The Liberty Boys," she cried clear and at near the top of her voice, "this is their toast as given in crowded public halls in Boston and the open fields and common greens of country towns and villages. The toast—" She paused long. Her eyes sought no face. She had moved through the doors and the packed bookshelves out to roads and fields where the toast carried its awful implications and realities. She pronounced the toast with her right arm straightened as high as it would reach:

"*Strong halters, firm blocks and sharp axes to such as deserve them.*"

Then Mim slumped to her chair. Robert stepped to the old Jamaica, came to her with another glass apiece for them.

There was a little uneasiness among all. It soon passed. The Frames, Captain Hupple and Mrs. Cavendish took leave with cordial words to all.

Bliss Edmunds had been fussing here and there among bookshelves, puzzling whether he should add this or that volume to his already large library. He was an importer, had a small fortune, since the closing of the port had seen his trade dwindle and had said to Mr. Knox, "The public meetings affect my temper. Likewise gatherings where they pretend to discuss the issues but chiefly talk to please themselves. Therefore I have tried by reading books to find a calm viewpoint. I seem to find there is none. For each calm viewpoint there is another bitterly hostile. If I do not find books that will give me relief it may become necessary for me to quit my reading. There have been occasions when I was furious at my books and all other books."

He was now saying to Mr. Knox, "I have looked into a hundred books tonight and not one of them tempts me. They disturb me here as they disturb me in my quiet home library."

Mr. Knox smiled, puzzled for an answer. Bliss Edmunds walked the room, turned, walked again, flinging his hands this way and that in an outburst: "Damn me if I can figure who is right. I hear Sam Adams and I say he is right. I read the proclamations of General Gage and His Majesty the King and I ask how we can have law and order unless Sam Adams obeys those proclamations. I hear men say they are on one side last week and another side this week." Bliss Edmunds walked, turned, walked. His fingers went tearing through his hair. "Damn me, why must I think, think, think? The war—is it coming? Or is the war all nonsense?" He wrung his hands. He seemed to have gone through this alone, perhaps before a mirror. Now he realized he was going through it before others with the face of a man tortured by thoughts that found no way out for him. He bent forward with a piteous face toward Miss Burton and Winshore. "I am for the war, I am against the war, and I hope to God the war comes soon so I will not die waiting for the war that I know will be less terrible for me than this waiting."

Winshore and Miss Burton tried to assure him that all truly alive were under a suspense somewhat like his. Bliss Edmunds thanked them, wished them to know he apologized if he had been rude and boisterous, slid into his greatcoat, said good night to all and walked out into the deep snow and winter night.

At ease in large oak chairs with wide armrests the others tried to go on from where Bliss Edmunds left off. The imprint of his desperate question hung over the room.

"A cornered rat can begin to understand him," said Mim in a tone so low it seemed she didn't care whether they heard her. Robert took it she was the cornered rat and Bliss Edmunds had spoken for her.

Miss Burton plucked a theme from the air and played it. "In the present howling of winds that howl higher from week to week, who can be absolutely correct, completely righteous? On both sides we have seen good minds fail, fine wits go dim and crack. If I should find myself in torment like Bliss Edmunds or taking a course like the splendid James Otis, I'm not sure but I would try joining the Sons of Liberty and see for myself what it is to strip a Tory informer, then tar him and throw on the feathers."

Again so low-voiced it would seem she didn't care whether she was heard, came Mim, repeating, "Violence is an outlet for minds groping in dark labyrinths."

"Speaking of good minds gone cracked and crazed, as we all are, it seems," said Ordway Winshore, "we know very little. Many still believe the insane have been touched by the Devil, Satan himself. We lock them in cellars and garrets. We chain them and feed them as though they are mad dogs. I have been interested to hear that John Hancock's father in his will left a large sum of money for better shelter and care of the insane."

He gave a side glance to Mim as he went on with a seriocomic face. He meant it for her too as he turned his head and went on: "Be silly, Miss Burton. Be silly often and don't be afraid of yourself being silly, Miss Burton. You have a rare mind and temperament, independent, searching and inquiring with no fear of where your inquiries may lead you. I feel quite sure that at intervals you have your impulses to be silly and you welcome those impulses and meet them more than halfway and issue from the mood saying to yourself, 'Excuse me, I had to be silly then because it was good for me.' And if the sorry Bliss Edmunds were here he would not understand the fellowship you and I have when I confirm you in a habit of yours by saying to you, Be silly, Miss Burton."

"I like your mood, Mr. Winshore. You are a trifle silly at this moment."

"Sam Adams, John Hancock, Sam Adams, John Hancock, I hear

457

those names over Boston, Sam Adams, John Hancock, as though if Sam Adams, John Hancock, struck dead now or had never been born, then Boston would not have its present turmoil. Yet in Rhode Island eight boatloads of armed men rode out to the ship *Gaspee*, shot the commander, overpowered and bound the crew and took them ashore, set fire to the ship and burned and sank it. They returned to Providence in broad daylight, having executed their revolt against a ship and an officer overzealous, obnoxious, hated in his enforcement of the King's Revenue Acts, no Sam Adams, John Hancock telling them what to do. They have seized powder stores of the Crown in Connecticut, burned the barns of Tories and tarred and feathered Tories, with no instructions from Sam Adams, John Hancock in Connecticut. They have published in the *New York Journal* a grim jest where one gentleman asks, 'Pray, Mr. Blank, what is a Tory?' And another replies, 'A Tory is a thing whose head is in England, and its body in America, and its neck ought to be stretched!'"

He looked toward Miss Burton. "Silly? Yes and also grim and portentous." Winshore went on: "No need in New York of the speeches they say here Sam Adams writes for John Hancock. In New Jersey they have rioted, erected gallows as a threat, and set up Liberty Poles. In Pennsylvania they have heard Ben Franklin and John Dickinson in their promotions of the American cause, in Virginia they have heard Patrick Henry as flaming in challenge as Sam Adams, in the Carolinas and Georgia they have defied the King's Revenue Acts, many of them never having heard of Sam Adams, John Hancock, Sam Adams, John Hancock. Something is happening in the minds and the hearts of the people. It precedes and portends some action to come. What form of war or revolution that action may take, no man can say now. It is a mystery. It gathers around an instinct. That instinct insists, for one thing, that Britain is an island of eight million inhabitants while the thirteen colonies with their nearly three million inhabitants are to become ten and twenty millions of people with a continent for a home."

"I like your portrait of our America, Mr. Winshore," beamed Miss Burton.

Robert had seen his father and Miss Burton drawing closer every moment of the evening. He was sure his father had told her of his errands in Boston, of his first marriage and his two sons. She had given him the personal data: "I live in a house on Beacon Street with my mother. My father, a carpenter and builder, died five years ago leaving a comfortable estate. My husband, a ship captain, during a stay in London fell into a dispute with an English naval officer who questioned his loyalty to the King. They drew pistols and both died of their wounds. Our marriage for various reasons had not yet been made known and I still go by my maiden name. Like Mr. Knox, I am studying and practicing for what may come. I hope I may be useful."

458

" 'Silly' means imbecile, idiotic, Mr. Winshore, I have been think-ing about it," Miss Burton was saying.

"When I tell you be silly I mean light-minded, loose and careless, like a wrestler who knows how to fall without punishing the ground under him. You can be silly and know what you are doing. You needn't be tipsy like two ropemakers I saw yesterday in the Black Horse tavern. One was saying, 'We can lick the lobsters,' the other, 'The bloody-backs—we'll drive 'em into the shea.' They were tipsy and kept re-peating it as a chant and response, 'We can lick the lobsters,' and, 'The bloody-backs—we'll drive 'em into the shea.' "

Henry Knox had squeezed his corpulent frame into a big chair, sat listening, his two-fingered hand dangling, looking up once in a while with bright eyes. "It is a time of storm," came from him now. "And you can't reason with a storm. You can't argue with it. You fight against it. Or you ride with it. You make yourself a part of it. I don't argue with anybody. I let any man have his say and his opinion. When the war comes I shall fight for America, for the Continental Congress, for Independence, so long as I can stand on my two legs. I study and practice with artillery. When the shooting begins I may be of some use in that branch of the service."

Knox excused himself to put back on their shelves some disorderly piles of books and blow out an oil lamp near the front door.

"Is he not choice?" Miss Burton asked. "They call him a fat man. Some laugh at him for walking military. And yet what is he? A rock, a pillar of granite faith. Tidal waves and cross winds may shake others. But not him. He banishes doubt and fear by knowing precisely what he will do when the storm breaks and the trial by fire is on. He leaves ideas and oratory to others. Another like him is Paul Revere, the silver-smith. Their phrase goes, 'What is acting?' "

"Robert, my boy."

"Yes, papa."

The father slid his hand below the son's shirt collar. "We must be going soon. Before we go I think they would all be interested to see it and read it."

For once Mim laughed. "Yes, Robert, bring it out. The only jewelry he wears he hides."

His great-grand-uncle had it from a family who came on the ship *Mayflower* to Plymouth in 1620, the father explained. Robert loosened two buttons, put in his hand and drew out a thin silver chain with a bronze plaque. They passed it around. "Read it aloud," said the father to Miss Burton, who gave slowly Roger Bacon's Four Stumbling Blocks to Truth:

"1. The influence of fragile or unworthy authority.
2. Custom.

459

3. The imperfection of undisciplined senses.
4. Concealment of ignorance by ostentation of seeming wisdom."

"Ancient words for our very modern times," said Miss Burton.
"Challenge, rebuke, consolation in them," said the elder Winshore.
"Deep love wrote those words and again deep love cut them into bronze. I would call it an act of high faith in God and mankind."

Miss Burton took it to Mr. Knox's desk and made copies for herself and him.

"I know the words by heart," said Mim. "Sometimes they help and again they are useless. Custom is the hardest of the four blocks to get over." With that she laid her eyes on Robert, meeting his eyes as though he should well know what more she could say.

All shook hands at the door and gave their thanks to the Knoxes for a fine evening party, in agreement with Mr. Knox that an end might come to such parties before long.

Robert and Mim felt the cold wind bracing them, their heads less sluggish. They had taken on punch and rum in plenty. Their mental haze cleared somewhat as they slogged through the snow.

The sky over Boston had a vast reach, not a wisp of cloud, a pale moon riding the wind in a shy blue space with a few white lonely stars.

At Aunt Ellen's doorway Mim said she was tired, it had been a heavy week. Robert kissed her and went away. Turning a corner he put a mitten to his mouth and wondered if it was the first cold kiss he had had from Mim.

Mary Burton nearing her home on Beacon Street, plodding with Ordway Winshore through the snow, had been saying with what Winshore regarded as grace of spirit, "Since you are to speak with the blessed old Benjamin Franklin, may I ask you to give him my respect and affection, even my reverence? If I do not see you again before you leave Boston, remember to tell Mr. Franklin I am only one of many who love him for his courage and wisdom."

"You will see me again before I leave Boston—that is, if you wish in the slightest to see me again."

"I do wish more than the slightest to see you again after this night."

"An evening of use and sweetness it has been," he said at her front door as he held her two hands in his, kissed her on two cheeks, said good night for the third or fourth time, and plodded away in the snow.

They had heard sleigh bells jingling. They had seen horses pass speeding with sleighs. And Mary Burton had said to him as she stopped and he saw a pale moonsheen glimmer on her face, "Do you know, you remind me of a sorrel horse I used to ride, sorrel with a blazing star in his forehead? I could talk sober to him or silly and he would nod back to me." She had said that. He wouldn't forget it.

460

Captain Hupple for the first time was permitted to watch the fire-logs in the grate of Mrs. Cavendish's room over her dress shop. He had asked for it very politely and very humbly. He said he would stay only a short time. When the short time had passed she reminded him very politely and very firmly. And he went with the promise that he could come again.

Marintha Wilming went to bed straight off but sleep wouldn't come to her. From her pillow she could see the snow on cedar branches swaying in the wind, a snow of white edged with blue in the moonfall. After a time she got out of bed and bent at the window for a look at the high moon with a pale silver flowing down into frost sparkles. She crept into bed saying, "It might be I am falling and sprawling over all four of Roger Bacon's stumbling blocks to truth—time will tell."

★ ★ ★ ★ ★ ★ ★ ★ ★

Chapter 16

★ ★ ★ ★ ★ ★ ★ ★ ★

The Blue Shadow of a Red Rose

DARIUS had brought in two plump chickens and left them with Aunt Ellen. At the White Cockade he had told Mim and Robert that one of the chickens would make "a nice dinner for the two of you after church tomorrow." Aunt Ellen and Mim had gone to their Congregational church. They had heard the preacher saying "the slavish doctrine of passive obedience and nonresistance" in England had brought Dissenters and Rebels who were accused by "interested politicians, contracted bigots, and hypocritical party zealots" of being "seditious and traitorous." This spirit of domination they had resisted, wherefore "God be thanked, one may, in any part of the British dominions, speak freely (if a decent regard be paid to those in authority) both of government and religion."

Mim rather liked this preaching. Her mind worked on those words "bigot" and "zealot." Among Whigs and Tories she could name several who were bigots, "so completely self-righteous about their own beliefs that they would like to kill off those who don't agree with them." She repeated that phrase from the preacher, "hypocritical party zealots." It was rich. She rolled it over her tongue and prized it. Week in and week out now for three years, where she worked and had the most of her life, the Cavendish dress shop, she had heard the Tories praised and the Whigs cursed, and she couldn't quite fish up from the index of her memory the names and faces of "hypocritical party zealots"

461

among Tories. But among the Whigs she could name them. At the dress shop she had heard scorn and vituperation poured on them. And deeper than any of the dress-shop gabble ran her personally evolved aversions and fears of John Hancock and Sam Adams. Certainly they were party men, zealots and hypocrites. "And my Robert, as I have these months for nearly a year called him, my Robert, can it be he is a bigot? A zealot he is, a party zealot, though I must not believe he is a hypocrite. Here on this Sabbath in this pew I must not believe him a hypocrite."

"Tyranny brings ignorance and brutality along with it," she heard the preacher. She hung on his words. They struck deep in her. He went on. "Tyranny degrades men from their just rank into the class of brutes. It damps their spirits. It suppresses arts. It extinguishes every spark of noble ardor and generosity in the breasts of those who are enslaved by it. It makes naturally strong and great minds feeble and little; and triumphs over the ruins of virtue and humanity. This is true of tyranny in every shape. There can be nothing great or good where its influence reaches. For which reason it becomes every friend to truth and humankind, every lover of God and the Christian religion, to bear a part in opposing this hateful monster. It was a desire to contribute a mite toward carrying on a war against this common enemy that produced this discourse. And if it serve in any measure to keep up a spirit of civil and religious liberty amongst us, my end is answered. . . . There are virtuous and candid men in all sects; all such are to be esteemed. There are also vicious men and bigots in all sects; and all such ought to be despised."

To Mim this was freshening. Wasn't this her own mind the preacher was speaking? A glow came over her. She would listen on. It was like good news. Soon the preacher quoted St. Paul, "Let every soul be subject unto the higher powers," and gave it as sound doctrine that resistance to tyranny and oppression is "in nowise contrary to Holy Writ."

Then Mim reminded herself the preacher was Whig and his congregation by a large majority Whig. Her glow began to fade and was gone as she heard him swing through a passage that fascinated her with its smooth anger: "If we calmly consider the nature of the thing itself, nothing can well be imagined more directly contrary to common sense than to suppose that millions of people should be subjected to the arbitrary, precarious pleasure of one single man (who has *naturally* no superiority over them in point of authority), so that their estates, and everything that is valuable in life, and even their lives also, shall be absolutely at his disposal, if he happens to be wanton and capricious enough to demand them. What unprejudiced man can think that God made *all* to be thus subservient to the lawless pleasure and frenzy of *one*, so that it shall always be a sin to resist him! Nothing but the most plain and express revelation from heaven could make a sober impartial man believe such a monstrous, unaccountable doctrine, and, indeed, the thing itself appears so shocking—so out of all proportion—that it may be questioned whether all the miracles that ever were wrought could make it credible that this doctrine really came from God. At present there is not the least syllable in Scripture which gives any countenance to it. The hereditary, indefeasible, divine right of kings, and the doctrine of nonresistance, which is built upon the supposition of such a right, are altogether as fabulous and chimerical as transubstantiation or any of the most absurd reveries of ancient or modern visionaries."

Now Mim knew that Robert would feel justified if he sat alongside her in this pew hearing the preacher go on with exultation: "We may very safely assert, without undermining government, that no civil rulers are to be obeyed when they enjoin things that are inconsistent with the commands of God; all such disobedience is lawful and glorious."

So here Robert probably considered what he was doing to be very lawful and somewhat glorious. Then she roved back to that first passage that had moved her so deeply, giving her a glow. It was still true for her. Tyranny does degrade men to brutes, "tyranny in every shape." And the preacher was no rank and stinking bigot or he couldn't have said, "There are virtuous and candid men in all sects; all such are to be esteemed. There are also vicious men and bigots in all sects; and all such men ought to be despised."

Home went Mim and Aunt Ellen in a warmish air and a sun beginning to turn the snow to slush. They had taken the chicken and potatoes from the oven and crisp pies with a crust holding dried apples water-soaked overnight.

Robert arrived. He shoveled snow, saw the wood running low, brought in several armfuls from the woodshed. He mended a chair, going to the cellar and the woodshed for things needed. "Ten minutes yet," said Aunt Ellen and Mim. Robert gave the house a looking over, at the end of the second-story hallway found two rungs loose and nailed them tight in the ladder for reaching the garret. A few times before he had busied himself about this house in this way summer and winter, when there was delay about seeing Mim. He had laughed about it, "It's my opinion, being as how you didn't ask me for my opinion, I go puttering around like this just to show you I'm not a bad handyman to have on the place."

The dinner went well. There were jokes about the chicken, the potatoes, the pie, the tough chicken that Aunt Ellen once had boiled for a week and then had to use it for soup and throw away the mess of strings, potatoes so small that when peeled they were gone, pie with a crust hard and elastic so rather than eat it the farmer used it for harness repairs.

Robert and Mim were so enjoying each other that they tried vaguely to get at what in the party the evening before had roiled them. Somehow it was Lieutenant Frame and his sister. They were strangers in Boston and America, aliens in a land to them foreign. They spoke with their own accent from England. They were fully accredited British subjects and should they become Americans they would not be so fully accredited. After their duties and visits in America they would return to the England that was their home. Both Robert and Mim if asked, "Why did you do it?" could answer for fun in New England colloquial, "I was sot on't." The Frames would require the translation, "I was set on it," which might call for further interpretation, "I was determined on it."

Then too the party was made up of their elders by from ten to twenty years. Had there been more of their own age Robert might have given songs and Mim dances. James Otis, a great and fine mind gone to ruin, was a shock. The bookshelves pressed on both Robert and Mim with reminders that they wished they could have read more of those volumes that beckoned and half-reproached them.

Parts of this Robert and Mim talked frankly and with good humor, omitting Lieutenant Frame. Their talk ran smooth till each suddenly was aware the name Ludgate had been mentioned at the White Cockade and Robert had heard it at Knox's and it had foreboding and they would steer away from it at this pleasant Sunday dinner.

The table cleared, Aunt Ellen and Mim washed and Robert wiped dishes. Robert could let a dish fall and when it seemed about to smash on the floor swiftly pluck it to safety. They had seen him at this trick often enough without his being asked. Now he waited till Mim said, "Time to break a dish, Robert."

They sang together in the front room at the cozy Franklin stove, a song Robert had from his father:

> "Contented I am, and contented I'll be;
> Resolved, in this life, to live happy and free.
> With the cares of this world I'm seldom perplex'd;
> I'm sometimes uneasy, but I never am vex'd:
> Some higher, some lower, I own there may be;
> But there's more who live worse than live better than me.

> "My life is a compound of freedom and ease;
> I go where I will, and return when I please;
> I live above envy, also above strife;
> And wish I had judgment to choose a good wife;
> I'm neither so high nor so low in degree,
> But ambition and want are both strangers to me."

They were not contented. They were vexed. But the song had a mutual comfort. They sang it soberly looking into each other's eyes, catching at each other's faces.

The night before, while waiting long for sleep to arrive, Mim had

464

a dance come to her. She had written the words, danced it twice and gone to bed shivering, to find sleep. She named it "There Are Loves," and this Sunday afternoon standing to face Robert she spoke the first sequence of it:

"There are loves worn for show and the longer they are so worn for vanity without inner merit, the more secrets they acquire. And each secret is a rat that gnaws and breeds, that hides and feeds and scampers, till the days when the outward vestige of such a love is a garment of shreds and holes where the teeth of the rats have taken their fill and had their rat holidays and not so much thankful as to squeak a rat farewell to the abode that nourished them."

She stood preening herself, plucking herself sleek with vanity and show. She stood motionless, with her face in serial contortions of the ugly. Her body and arms swayed in awkward and ugly wantings, her teeth alive with a faint quiver. She paused, spoke again:

"There are loves like potted plants with thwarted seeds and a few weeks sees them finished and wilted like a name not easy to remember and gone out of mind because not worth remembering."

Robert saw her tall lithe body stand as a form to thrive and bloom. Then it wilted, faded, bloom and hope gone, eyes closed, mouth dumb, face blank. She waited, then spoke again:

"And there are loves not unlike certain tall cedars that clutch their roots around great underground rocks and they welcome storms, taking storm as a test and a witness."

Robert did believe she made herself one tall cedar and her knees, ankles and feet took root deep around a great underground rock. Far above swayed her lean quivering torso, her arms stretched high in topmost branches tremulous as they bent and gave to the fury of the winds.

She saw Robert moved, inwardly shaken, his eyes holding a faint moist film. He took her in his arms. He had never before so wanted to hold her. She was light in his arms, featherfoam light. They could curve and blend. Their very low joy laughter became dim moaning. They were lost in fog. They whirled in spokes of silver light.

Her chestnut hair with its thin sheen of bronze had fallen in ripples to her shoulders and on down. They were each fighting, Robert against being overwhelmed with his will broken by the gaunt sweet loveliness of her enveloping him, by her sea-gray sea-wind eyes that melted him, by an aura of lights around her oval face, by the shades of meaning that trembled on her sensitive mouth. His own mouth after the press of a long kiss was saying to her the words he had heard from her lips away last autumn when they had piled leaves of maroon over each other's feet and watched leaves of gold blowing against a late October sky and a slow sundown. "More thin and baffling than the blue shadow of a red rose thrown on a piece of white satin," he was whispering, "more fine and tantalizing than a rainbow seen in a bubble in the sun and the seven prisms of light and color vanishing in a moment."

She was fighting against the need she would have for a listener like him if she lost him. He had told her she had "an aura" for him. She wanted to have an aura. If they should part could she ever find one who would see her as having an aura? She wasn't sure what an aura is. An aura, the way he told it to her, was more decorative than anything in Mrs. Cavendish's shop and you couldn't buy one and it was more personal and distinctive and more closely and durably fitting to you than anything money could buy. A red rose you could choose and pluck. A piece of white satin you could pick up anywhere. But the blue shadow thrown by the rose on the white fabric, you couldn't pluck that or pick it up and make something of it. Like an aura it was.

What he had whispered to her, the words of last autumn, they were made of a deepening fear that had come to her and her sad wondering over love and how it can't be fixed nor fastened down, how it can't be locked in a box and hid away like a memento to keep, how it is like an air for breathing and the two of them must breathe the air together. Her breath of last autumn was in those words.

Part of this she said to him. Then her eyes were looking through him and beyond him and she was saying, "There are sentences in the language of love that you can erase and everything is as before and the sentences are forgotten and whatever harm there was becomes forgotten and the faces turn into faces beyond remembering—it is smooth and wiped out and clean as dry leaves fire-burnt and wind-blown."

Robert felt strengths in her past any measuring. She went on. "And there are phrases and fragments of sentences, speeches of five or six syllables, and they get hammered deep and chiseled hard to where no storms of driving wind, no beating and repeated lightning forks of fire can erase them, can change them or dent them or mutilate them into something other than they were when first spoken from lips carrying the breath and seeds of life, with blooms and blossoms of hope."

He had told his father she was a woman who could not be broken. She would take suffering if she had to and come through it. He wished that in one or two particulars of understanding him she could be different. Outside of that she was so amazing and dazzling to him that he asked if it could be a trance or spell he would come out of open-eyed. He had heard that could be.

At dinner she had quoted from the preacher that tyranny "in every shape" degrades men to brutes and in opposite parties and sects there are good and virtuous men and likewise bigots and, she remembered the phrase, "hypocritical party zealots." He agreed with this. He could tell too that she had reserves about what the preacher had further said of Holy Writ justifying disobedience against tyranny in

466

authority. She had sensed precisely where to quit. To have gone further would have brought up the old barriers and a guarded give-and-take between them.

On a solid oak settee this afternoon they sat curled and tangled. Their hands and arms had run along the smooth wooden back, their fingers and elbows along the wide armrests of the sturdy old settee. Between talks and silences they had become familiar with the skilled wood-joining of it, the strokes and sanding of the carpenter on the oak. The five oak chairs were good company. They could speak to the two chairs that had loose legs and ought to be fixed or those legs might give way with someone of importance in them. The small center table with two thick stubs of candles and a worn calf-bound Bible with brass clasps had become personal to Robert and Mim. The low ceiling of hewn timbers, the clapboard walls, the square front and side windows, the two long narrow rag rugs and the two smaller square ones and their placing so your foot seldom touched the oak floor with its three boards starting to warp—this had come to be their room.

Aunt Ellen was up in her own room strewn with comforts and keep-sakes. Her husband had been a hard man, had been acquainted with the drink customs and the women of many seaports, had managed his ship well and in another five years would have retired to his Boston home, a hard man dealing with others but never hard with her. He could lift her with one hand gripping her cloak between the shoulder blades and holding her at arm's length, he weighing two hundred and ten and she half that. She was shy, reserved, taken as a woman with a very still tongue, among most people. To Mim however and her sister, Mim's mother, and to Darius, she could talk streaks. Mim leaned on her a little more than Mim was aware. Three children had come to Aunt Ellen, a girl who had died at ten in a smallpox epidemic, a boy stillborn, a boy who at twelve in six weeks wasted away with a lung malady they called quick consumption.

Aunt Ellen had shown Mim her will which would divide her estate equally among the members of the Wilming family, except that she gave, bequeathed and devised to Marintha Wilming the ten-acre farm two miles from the Boston Neck. Robert and Mim had walked to it of a Sunday afternoon, talked with the neighbor farmer who pastured his cows in part of it, sowed corn on a few acres, and tended the little orchard. Once they had stayed late and stood under branches of apple blossoms in moonlight and they could not be sure what happened and what vows were spoken—they were that lost in finding each other. The little solid old house of hewn clapboards would do for them, they were sure, if time should be kind. That was Mim's phrase, "if time should be kind."

Aunt Ellen called from the top of the stairway. "You were going for a walk, you said, and before you go," Aunt Ellen warned, "I shall read you a few lines my husband liked to read to friends." She was coming down the stairs, holding a small book, "a rather foolish little book he chose in a London bookshop, I haven't opened it in two years." Aunt Ellen joined them on the settee and read:

"A fool seeing a carpenter lying asleep in his Yard, with his Axe by him, took it up and cut off his Head; and then run into the House laughing; 'I wonder,' said he, 'what the Carpenter will say when he wakes and misses his Head.'"

Robert laughed, joining Aunt Ellen. Mim forced a smile. Her own brother Jake couldn't have done what this particular fool had done. Yet Jake had done things nearly as queer. And she loved Jake and repelled and rejected humor touching half-wits. This of course she couldn't mention this pleasant Sunday afternoon. She put on a smile meaningless as a thumbprint on a piecrust. Then she welcomed, and asked Aunt Ellen to repeat from the book, the last words of François Rabelais:

"I am going to take a leap in the Dark: let fall the Curtain for the Farce is over." And the last will and testament of Rabelais, so brief and without parallel: "I am not worth a single Sou; I am over Head and Ears in Debt; the Remainder I bequeathe to Pious Uses."

They walked in the crisp air of late afternoon, through and out of crooked and narrow streets, passing so often soldiers on furlough and sailors on shore leave, seeing guard mounted among the tents and baggage wagons on the Common and the ranks of scarlet-clad men bright against the snow, passing the Hancock mansion and Robert telling Mim of how the inside of it looked to him though neither of them venturing any personal opinion on whether John Hancock was a vain creature of low ambitions playing a sordid game with the rabble or Boston's wealthiest citizen risking his fortune in behalf of an outraged people. They wandered and passed Christ Church and strolled into the Copp's Hill Burying-Ground and read headstone inscriptions.

They walked back to Aunt Ellen's. Robert after a few moments on the settee with Mim kissed her good-by till "probably next Tuesday." He had work this night. Mim wouldn't ask. He could have told her he was going to see two persons at two different places and learn whether any information had come to them about how or when the officers and troops expected to take over the Isaiah Thomas printery and the *Massachusetts Spy.*

Late dusk it was and he had joined her in a procedure. He brought a lighted piece of kindling from the kitchen fireplace. He put the kindling to one and she the other of the two candles on the two-foot-square center table.

"I light one candle, you the other," said Robert as he had said it before when they did this. "It may bring us luck."

This time Mim had a fresh rejoinder. "You go while I stay and watch them burn lower and lower."

Often they had mentioned the sturdy workmanship of those two candlesticks, made for short thick candles, of a heavy brass kept well polished with no fleck of tarnish, of Arabian make. Aunt Ellen's husband had brought them from Algiers. Hammer strokes had dented a script with many sweeping curves. Those loops and scrolls said something in Arabic.

Mim's fingers ran over the brass hieroglyphics. "We can't read it, Robert. Until we know more about Arabic letters it is what they call indecipherable. That's a pretty good word, indecipherable. Say indecipherable, Robert."

He did. He was glum doing it, as though swallowing a drink with a touch of rancid.

"Tell you what, Robert," Mim beamed. "We will just let those candlesticks stay right here and," she beamed less, "two or three hundred years from now when we go to Arabia we'll take them along and get the writing translated and bring them home to the little farm beyond the Neck and when visitors come we'll tell them how we got the indecipherable deciphered."

Robert stayed glum, went away puzzled. His memory strayed to Aunt Ellen once quoting two Arabian proverbs her husband brought home with the candlesticks:

> One vinegar seller does not like another vinegar seller.

> They who are lean but not from hunger are hard as brass.

* * * * * * * * * *
Chapter 17
* * * * * * * * * *

Hole in a Yarn Stocking

A REPUTATION for "a rough place" had the Roebuck coffeehouse near the Faneuil Market House. It smelled of fish, served raw clams, meat stews, and at high noon the crowd and the cookery gave the air a thick odor.

Two British fusiliers strayed in, carrying a few drinks and wanting more of the same. The two redcoats would better have not taken chairs at the same table with the huge, muscular, earth-bound Ebenezer MacIntosh who sat in consultation with Robert Winshore. MacIntosh it was who had led the mob that burned and looted the Hutchinson mansion and later took a hand in opening the jail doors for men charged with that burning and looting. "A wild bull of a man," he

469

had been described, and rumor had it he once killed a man with a blow of his bare fist. Not being seen in public places as often as formerly, he seemed to respect the wishes of Whig leaders who hoped he would not again serve their cause as a mob tactician since he so distinctly preferred physical force to wordy appeals.

"The worst of luck to yuh," said MacIntosh, lifting a mug of beer to the two redcoats.

"A fight you're callin for?" leered one of the soldiers.

"From all I hear you're better at friggin than fightin," was the level-eyed jeer of MacIntosh.

The three of them tangled. One soldier reeled to a near-by table and fell to the floor, knocked cold. Robert and two others managed to wrangle loose the hold MacIntosh had on the other soldier's throat but Robert came out of it with his shirt collar torn, the top button gone, and a wide tear in one stocking showing bare skin below the knee. Robert ate a beef stew with MacIntosh and learned that MacIntosh was in Boston for only two days and his old friends among the leaders needn't worry about his raising hell in Boston again. He could be just as useful out in the country towns. This was what Robert had been sent to ask about.

A bright warm day, the snow mostly shoveled from the walks, pools of slush here and there as Robert midafternoon walked to the Sign of the Golden Ball to tell Mim he couldn't come on Tuesday and they would make it Wednesday noon and he hoped she could have a full hour or more at noon on Wednesday in the White Cockade.

He had opened the front door, stepped into the little hallway, his hand on the knob of the door leading into the front sales and display room. Through the little pane of glass he saw Mrs. Cavendish bringing Mim into the front room from the back workroom. At a table spread with dress goods he saw Captain Hupple speaking with Lieutenant George Frame and a man whose face he couldn't make out because it was turned in about one-quarter profile. Hand on doorknob Robert waited till the man's head turned and he saw it was Silas Ludgate. Two women farther over at the end of the table had their backs to him, looking toward a group of new spring hats. As they faced toward the others he saw a head with pale-blond curls falling to the shoulders, recognized Sapphira Reggs definitely, and made his guess the other was the sister Abbie Reggs.

Robert's hand fell away from the doorknob. He would come later when these people were gone. His hand was on the knob of the outside door and he expected in less than one second to be on the street. Instead he found he was opening the door as if politely and attentively to help Miss Elizabeth Frame to enter.

"I thank you and we will now enter as though you have been my escort," said Miss Frame in a waggish mood.

To tell her he was leaving and have her go in and tell them she met

470

him in the hallway without his having been inside the front room—
that wouldn't do. He opened the inside door for Miss Frame. He
followed her in.

Robert had clean forgotten about his torn shirt collar, the top
button gone, a stocking tear showing a large patch of bare skin where
a yarn hole yawned and said, "Look, how come this?" Had he known
how long he must wait for a word with Mim, he would have excused
himself and gone to the back room to wait. As it was, he watched his
chance to edge in, while Sapphira Reggs, with Mim and Mrs. Caven-
dish helping, looked over shades of blue, pink, lavender, various silks
and velvets, some satins and foulards that had arrived only the week
before at the port of Salem and come by wagon to Boston.

Mrs. Cavendish and Mim were agreeing that the outfitting of
Sapphira Reggs would be a distinguished work in which the shop
could take pride. Miss Reggs' father, shaken by the ordeal she had
gone through, had given her carte blanche as to a new wardrobe,
limited only to the goods now on display at the Sign of the Golden
Ball.

"It will be the talk of the town," she now burbled. "The dress of
laylock satin edged with gold, with a blue girdle, long sleeves with
white satin cuffs and a cape, the frock high-waisted with short puffed
shoulder sleeves and the tiniest of ruffles clinging like flower petals to
the throat and bosom, lavender ribbon circles at the waist, a white
taffeta cap with a spreading bow to sit smart on my powdered hair."

While Robert waited, he found Mr. Ludgate's eye roving him.
He saw the elbow of Mr. Ludgate nudge Abbie while he spoke to
her in an undertone. Captain Hupple and Lieutenant Frame were
trying to summarize their views of the local and colonial "situation."
It was "growing increasingly grave," Captain Hupple believed and
Lieutenant Frame agreed. Lieutenant Frame's quick and shifting
glances at Mim indicated he liked to look at her without staring.
Robert trying to stand quiet and shy, with his hands folded loose
behind his back, found his fingers doubling into fists as he saw how
neatly Frame could look and look at Mim without staring. Ludgate
moved over toward Frame. They spoke. After that Robert had both
Ludgate and Frame roving him with their eyes. Suddenly he became
aware of his shirt collar, the top button off, a stocking gap showing
bare skin, torn yarn hanging loose. He wished he hadn't come in.
He wished he had gone to the back door. He could have seen Mim
some other way. He said he was a fool. Some shade of that registered
on his face and the hang of his body when the worst of all came.
Sapphira Reggs in some casual slanting glance away from the fabrics
she was handling, caught a look of him, fixed her eyes on him, her
face getting into a tension as a breathless little "Oh!" came from her.

Mim at that moment started to skip to the back room for a measur-
ing tape and some dress designs. Robert followed her into the back

room. What with the customer-service excitement and Robert's hurried speech, Mim was a trifle astonished furthermore at her usually neat Robert being tousled and ill-kept of shirt and stocking. She hesitated, her face very sober, then, "Come at noon Wednesday. No, don't come. I'll go to the White Cockade and meet you there Wednesday noon."

As Robert swept through the front room, giving a brief silent bow to all present before ushering himself out, he had all eyes on him and felt a creep in those eyes. Along the street he brushed at his ribs and head with both hands as though he might scrape away queer glances that had been put on him.

Before arriving at the *Massachusetts Spy* office, he had worked out for himself the consolation that Ebenezer MacIntosh, the wild bull of a man, had gotten better men than him into embarrassment, chagrin, befuddlement and difficult dilemmas.

★ ★ ★ ★ ★ ★ ★ ★ ★

Chapter 18

★ ★ ★ ★ ★ ★ ★ ★ ★

Follies and Sorrow at the White Cockade

JONATHAN SWAY ran the White Cockade coffeehouse with the help of two daughters and a Negro slave boy. His stiff walk and his limp came from a hip wound and much sleeping on snow and the cold damp ground in three years of service in the French and Indian War. He had fought to take Canada from the French and put it under the British flag. He was one of thousands of Americans who had fought and taken wounds under the British flag in America. To the Whigs the White Cockade was a place to go for fellowship and friendly faces. The Tories held it "a Whig pesthole."

A physician had called on Sway in the late forenoon, a youngish man to look at, not yet thirty-five, a rounded face with pleasant curves when not in anger, neat and clean, extra careful to look neat and clean, and his patients liked that and it was partly why he had a reputation as one of the best doctors in Boston. Blond with light-blue eyes, his changes of face going with what he said, his clear voice and man-to-man way of talking had won him many friends—among the Whigs—among the Rebels—for he was Whig and Rebel—or Patriot, as he styled himself, a Lover of America, an orator at great mass meetings, signing articles in Whig journals "True Patriot," and a poet, author of the "Liberty Song," seven verses that had his heart's blood in them, his words telling what he and his compatriots were willing to fight and die for.

Sway spoke to him of how several times young Robert Winshore had sung the "Liberty Song" in the White Cockade. "They ask him for it, Dr. Warren, and they listen like it tells them what they want to hear." Sway asked about reports they were going to arrest Warren and send him to England for a treason trial and didn't he feel he would be safer to leave Boston? No, he would stay. Another physician, of Warren's own age, Thomas Young, had come near being killed by political enemies, had made a speech in Old South Church in 1773 and from the church had gone without Indian make-up to the tea ships and helped throw the tea into the harbor, and on his friends bringing him fair evidence he was to be seized and sent to England for treason trial, he had moved from Boston to Philadelphia. They might try it on Warren. But he would stay and see what happened. Sway had heard that on the Neck where the British held their hangings Warren rode past three officers and heard one calling, "Go ahead, Warren, you'll soon come to the gallows," and Warren turned his horse, rode back and asked which one had spoken and none of them would answer. Yes, it was told, it happened like that.

Had Paul Revere, the engraver and silversmith, been in? Warren asked. Yes, but only for a look to see who was around and then Revere had gone, said Sway. They were close friends, Warren occasionally taking off his coat and pitching in with Revere and his fifty workmen in the foundry. Warren liked Sway as an old proven soldier and Patriot and he knew Sway admired Revere and before leaving Warren opened his mouth and showed Sway where he had lost two teeth, one an eyetooth, and Paul Revere had cut a piece of ivory in two and shaped two artificial teeth and wired them in so Warren could look natural when he spoke or smiled and no wheeze or whistle when he talked.

Warren went out. Sway stood looking at the door. Out of it he had seen this man go who had married Elizabeth Hooton, the daughter of Richard Hooton, and they had two sons and two daughters, comforts and wealth in their stylish home near Faneuil Hall, and he was talking about quitting his medical practice and going into the army the Continental Congress was raising. "I guess he means fight and struggle in that 'Liberty Song' he wrote that young Winshore sings," said Sway. "Part of it sounds highfalutin and part of it has fire and steel."

Sway's daughter Ellen had come to his side. She had noticed and was saying, "Kind of lovely, isn't he, that Joseph Warren?"

"Lovely? Might be. I can't think of any other man in Boston can be called lovely."

"They say he'll be taken most any day."

"Young fellows studying medicine under him told him to visit only day patients, no more night calls on the sick. He said no, showed them two pistols he carries. He's ready to shoot. Someone told him a British officer said the Rebels won't fight. Warren blazed he hopes to die up to his knees in blood."

The father and daughter went on looking at the door, then Ellen, "Pa, should a fine man like him with so much to live for talk about dying up to his knees in blood?"

"Near as you can get, it's in that 'Liberty Song' he wrote. We've heard young Winshore sing it here."

"I'll listen closer when he sings it again."

"Part of it's highfalutin mimity-nimity, just mishmash out of the books of poetry he's been reading. And some of it is big, wild, grand. He sees away past this little America we got now. You can tell he expects the continent of North America to get settled up with people, three million now growing into thirty or sixty million, God only knows how many, ready to fight the rest of the world for what he calls liberty, ready to welcome any people who want to come here and try what we've got. If you believe the last verse of Warren's 'Liberty Song,' a time is coming when we'll be a nation and the terror of the world, the old countries scared to death of us."

"Sounds like I don't know what," smiled Ellen.

The midday crowd had begun drifting in, city folk with a sprinkling of farmers, clerks and tradespeople mixed with workmen whose leather breeches had lasted them five to ten years and were good for another five or ten.

Ordway Winshore and Mary Burton had a corner table near a chunky pumpkin-faced farmer lean with a radish face and alongside him his wife with a broad pleasant turnip smile and corn-tossel hair piled high on her head. Farther over two hickory-framed wagoners with wind-bitten faces smacked with enjoyment over their fish and beer, and with them two hog-drovers tousled and weathered of hair and hide.

"Blessed are they who expect nothing, for they shall not be disappointed," said Ordway Winshore to Mary Burton. "Your name you can change. Your face you keep. Each face looking at another says, 'I am me—who are you?'"

"Go on," said Miss Burton. "These faces move you."

"Any one of us can say alone before a mirror: Out of the deep hush of time long gone came your face."

"Go on. I like your mood."

"The face of America—who can read it? A few years ago it stood all wilderness. The First Comers plowed and hammered at the wilderness face of America and made it something else. Now those early strugglers are gone, their faces vanished. Now along the east coastline nigh three million faces, add them up and get the sum total. Read that mass face, if you can. The good faces and the bad, the best faces of all and the worst, they make the face of America. Neither America itself nor the world across the wide wild sea can read this face—can tell the meaning of America. Look to any horizon where fog hangs heavy. There in that fog, clearing away into sunlight in the times to come, there you will find the face of America."

They had noticed a lone man at the table next to them, so quiet he seemed hardly to be there. Ellen Sway had set a brandy before him, then a hot sling, then coffee. Each time he paid without looking at her, kept to what was occupying his mind, if anything. A thick stub of a man, freckles from ear to ear, eyes bloodshot, yet deliberate in the way he sat with far-off eyes in a faraway face.

The babble of the White Cockade slowed down. The front door opened to let in the scarlets of a soldier and a sergeant in uniform. From table to table they politely asked names. They turned from Miss Burton and Winshore to ask the lone man his name. He refused, shook his head, no use to try to get his name. In loud anger they threatened to arrest him.

A farmer came over, stoop-shouldered, bony, beak-faced, tight-lipped. "He might uh forgot his name—how'd you know?" Another farmer put in, "Whyn't he keep his name to himself if he wants he should?" A hunking sailor put his face in with a jeer, "How'd you know he ain't forgot his name?"

"We'll go," the sergeant glowered. The babble took up again. Was a man hunt on? Who for? What had he done?

Soon again the front door opened to yield the crackling illumination of six scarlet-clad troopers heading straight to the lone broad stub of a man finishing his cup of coffee. The sergeant gave it as final: Either he tells his name or they take him away. With no flurry the man rose to his feet, spread his arms wide, his eyes ranging the troopers, his voice cool slow respectful. "My initials, perhaps I inform you first of my initials, E. E. E., three names each beginning with an E, two Christian names beginning with an E, then a family surname beginning with an E. They form the monogram I shall put on my coach when the time arrives I shall be having a coach and I have considered that when I have horses for my coach, on the gleaming harness of each harness of each coach horse there shall be my silver monogram: E. E. E.

"The name is Edward Ebenezer Edgington. You may have heard the last name, if you are acquainted with English history, for my great-grandfather's uncle was hanged for high treason, the only one of the Edgingtons to be honored with a special grant from the King that he be hanged with a silken noose about his neck, the silk betokening quality, sir, as there has ever been quality in the name of Edgington."

Edgington lifted a hand, eyed the sergeant about to leave. "Stay, my good sir, I am a loyal subject of His Majesty the King and have never hitherto been honored with a communication so direct from him as you have given me today. You may report to His Majesty that my father was a hatter and ceased being a hatter. For the same reason that he ceased being a hatter I never became one, the cause thereof being the enactment of Parliament that no hats of felt, dyed or undyed, finished or unfinished, shall be put on board any vessel, in any place within any British plantation, nor be laden upon any horse or other carriage, with the intent to be exported from there to any other plantation, or to any other place whatever, upon forfeiture thereof; and the offender shall likewise pay five hundred pounds for every such offense."

Again the troopers turned to go, again they heard Edgington in mummery, in a mocking added severity of tone, preceded by a coarse and studied hiccup and a hand over the mouth as though to hold back a second hiccup, "Stay, honorable sir, I have but one more request before you depart from the White Cockade. May I petition that you communicate to His Majesty the King my urgent message that he delegate his ministers to inquire into the administrative results following enactments of the Sugar Act, the Stamp Act, the Declaratory Act, the Townshend Duty Act, the Act quartering a large body of troops in this city of Boston. Send the word, if it is within possibility, to the ears of His Majesty the King that all who are loyal to him in this city of Boston cannot sufficiently thank him for his regard of them, for the protection accorded to them by his ships of war and their cannon that meet our eyes in the harbor. For his illustrious battalions and jubilant drums in our streets, we thank the King and for such devoted and gracious servants of duty as yourselves, who as direct representatives of the King can pay your attentions and direct deliberative inquiries to so humble and loyal a subject as Edward Ebenezer Edgington."

The sergeant shrugged, put a forefinger to the end of his nose, looked his troopers over, saw them puzzled as himself. The highflown language sounded important. Maybe it was sarcasm. First the sergeant was going to say to the squad, "We can't waste time with this damn · fool." Instead he mumbled, "Thank yuh," and marched out.

Robert Winshore and Marintha Wilming had come in as Edgington began his speech, had nodded to Ordway Winshore and Miss Burton, had stood so as to miss no word or move of Edgington. Ordway Winshore let his eyes rove from head to feet over Robert and Mim. His eyes reveled over what a couple they were just to look at, flame and fight in them, Robert perhaps a half-inch taller than Mim's six feet, both lean and sinewy with some fine bodily accord between them, Mim in a gown of pale gray sheathing her narrow hips and rounded breasts perfectly, in a V-shaped area below her neck a quiet arrangement of white ruffles and a black velvet border. No dreamgaze about her eyes now, she was in one of her keen and wary moods, gathering every shade and accent of Edgington's mummery and personality.

476

Throwing her cloak over the back of a chair, she swung her eyes to all three and rested them on Robert while saying, "I like him. He's a clown. I like clowns."

Robert knew by this he himself was a clown and she too and they could both do with more clowning than they had of late. The best he could do now was to make a long slow yawn and take out a handkerchief and put the yawn in it and tie and knot the yawn and fold it back neatly in a waistcoat pocket. His blank face as he finished this caught the equally blank face of Edgington, who, setting down his coffee cup with a left hand, raised the other hand and wiggled fingers of greeting and approval. Catching Mim's eyes in a sparkling look at him, Edgington nodded to her, wiggled his fingers, almost smiled, with the back of his hand wiped off the threat of a smile from his mouth, and sat again with his bloodshot eyes gazing far off into nowhere in particular.

They were finishing their pork pie and coffee. Ellen Sway brought a pot and poured second cups for them, Robert asking, "Your father keeps well?"

"Spry as ever."

"Anyone been in?"

"Joseph Warren a few minutes this forenoon." Then she stooped to Robert's ear and whispered about the two teeth Paul Revere put in.

"Would your father come to this corner, Ellen, and sing just one verse of that soldier song?"

"How stands the glass around?—Why, soldiers, why?"

"That's it."

"I think he might, he does take after that song."

Jonathan Sway came limping, weaving amid chairs and tables toward their corner, Mim saying, "What a curious dignity his body has, every motion perfect."

Robert felt his blood warm and glowing. This was the Mim he adored. She had crept inside of Jonathan Sway, who wanted no one's pity, who knew precisely what to do with his body, whose walk had the ease, grace and practiced calculation of a well-wrought eccentric dance. She warmed to it and could gush over it as she did over certain failings of Jake and Darius. She had seen some of their supposed failings develop into what to her were perfections. She resented the word "half-wit" for Jake and once scratched four finger-lines across the face of a woman who had smirked out with the name "half-wit" for Jake. "That woman couldn't have trained a wild black crow to eat out of her hand and sit on her shoulder like Jake did." And Darius, there were those who called him "slow" or "dumb," rattle-headed people who didn't know how to keep still and manage their own minds like dear Darius.

Sway came weaving along, Ellen bringing to Robert a lute-shaped six-stringed instrument Robert called "a git-tar'" and he had seen it

spelled guittarre and gitterne. Robert tuned it, swept the strings, and
Sway in a chair alongside, gave with a rough and throaty gusto the
famous lines:

"How stands the glass around?
For shame, ye take no care, my boys;
How stands the glass around?
Let mirth and wine abound,
The trumpets sound!
The colors flying are, my boys,
To fight, kill or wound;
Content with our hard fare, my boys,
On the cold ground.

"Why, soldiers, why
Should we be melancholy, boys?
Why, soldiers, why?
Whose business 'tis to die.
What? Sighing? Fie!
Drink on; drown fear; be jolly, boys;
'Tis he, you, or I;
Cold, hot, wet, or dry,
We're always bound to follow, boys,
And scorn to fly.

"Tis but vain
(I mean not to upbraid you, boys),
Tis but vain
For soldiers to complain;
Should next campaign
Send us to Him that made you, boys,
We're free from pain;
But should we remain
A bottle and a kind landlady
Cures all again."

There were faces like still pools, the whole room hushed. The man
singing had known the hard fare, the cold ground, the campaigns,
and the reason for naming the song "Why, Soldiers, Why?"

Now, said Ellen Sway, Robert must give the "Liberty Song," "if
only that Joseph Warren was in the White Cockade this forenoon."
This had been printed in the *Massachusetts Spy* in May, '74, and was
sung with rough variations to the tune of "The British Grenadiers."

Robert swept the strings, tensed, slowed down his tension, and as
he got going in the verses he lost himself, lost the room, the faces
around him, and was outside and ranging wide over America, Free
America ("Amerikay"), among its people of today and in a mystic
tomorrow beyond any man's reading. The first verse ran:

"That seat of science, Athens, and earth's proud mistress, Rome,
Where now are all their glories? We scarce can find their tomb.

478

Then guard your rights, Americans, nor stoop to lawless sway;
Oppose, oppose, oppose, oppose for North America."

People had come up to hear. Some would eat their fish or pork pie cold rather than miss this. That about Athens and Rome, you could see, didn't interest the wagoners but those words "guard your rights, Americans" and "Oppose, oppose, oppose, oppose for North America," they had a call.

Who is Albion? What is a Pict? And is a venal sycophant a fish you eat or a beast of prey or a breed of politicians bought like sheep or swine at current market prices? Joseph Warren put his scorn and defiance of them in his next verse. Robert sang:

"Proud Albion bowed to Caesar, and numerous hosts before;
To Picts, to Danes, to Normans, and many masters more;
But we can boast Americans have never fallen a prey:
Huzza! huzza! huzza! huzza for free America!"

In the third verse the first four lines were too fancy, but the last four had fifes shrilling and drums pounding:

"We led fair Freedom hither, and lo! the desert smiled;
A paradise of pleasure now opened in the wild:
Your harvest, bold Americans, no power shall snatch away;
Preserve, preserve, preserve, preserve your rights in free America."

Swinging into the fourth verse Robert glimpsed on the outer ring of listeners two new-come faces, Lieutenant George Frame and Sapphira Reggs, and their faces might have been pieces of paper blown in a high wind as his smooth fighting baritone carved the line, "The world shall own we're freemen here"—

"Torn from a world of tyrants, beneath the western sky
We formed a new dominion, a land of liberty:
The world shall own we're freemen here, and such will ever be.
Huzza! huzza! huzza! huzza for love and liberty!"

More defiance followed:

"God bless this maiden climate, and through her vast domain
May hosts of heroes cluster that scorn to wear a chain,
And blast the venal sycophants who dare our rights betray:
Assert yourselves, yourselves, yourselves for brave America."

With the last two verses Robert caught for a moment the face of Henry Knox and forgot it, flashed an instant into the depths of Marintha Wilming's sea-gray and storm-green eyes, glimpsed a moment Mary Burton's wide blue eyes and his father's curving slash of a mouth sad and comic, then forgot all faces, became blank to all small personal causes and lost himself in the granite determinations Joseph Warren carved in the lines:

"Lift up your hearts, my heroes, and swear, with proud disdain,
The wretch that would ensnare you shall spread his net in vain:

479

Should Europe empty all her force, we'd meet them in array,
And shout huzza! huzza! huzza! huzza for brave America!

"The land where Freedom reigns shall still be masters of the main,
In giving laws and freedom to subject France and Spain;
And all the isles o'er ocean spread shall tremble and obey
The prince who rules by Freedom's laws in North America."

The listeners lingered, shifted on their feet, stood looking at each other and shifted again. One churchgoing farmer spoke a reverent "Amen amen," and his wife "It *is* like a psalm, isn't it?" and a wagoner, "Kind of moves along, don't it?" and one of the hog-drovers, under his breath, "Goddam, there's trouble in that song," and his broad freckled face utterly sober E. E. Edgington raised a hand near his chin and gravely wiggled every finger, and Ordway Winshore thought Marintha Wilming's face no longer sea-pale but a snake-belly white.

They drifted back to their tables, food, drinks and talk. Ellen Sway took the guitar to her father who hung it on the wall alongside the woodcut of General James Wolfe who sixteen years ago commanded at Quebec and planted the British flag there and died at thirty-three of his wounds.

Lieutenant Frame three tables away nodded greetings to his four acquaintances, kept a conversation going with Sapphira Reggs, Robert aware he got their eyes regularly and that Sapphira would know him again if she met him and the light was poor.

The sergeant strolled in, ambled to Edgington, insisted on buying a drink, explained he had been under orders to get the names of everybody in the White Cockade, and he liked the speech that Mr. Edgington had made and the way it was respectful to the King and he wouldn't have liked to take Mr. Edgington into custody because he had heard about another sergeant making an arrest in the White Cockade and how the Rebels massed at the door and wouldn't let him out with his prisoner and now he had noticed Lieutenant Frame at a table, a strict officer, and the sergeant would finish his drink and be going, which he did, with a polite bow and smile.

The unaccountable Edgington too was leaving. He arose and with an easy distant gaze directed perhaps at the woodcut of General Wolfe, stretched his arms to shoulder level inviting the wide world to come hear him, and opened his freckled lugubrious face with goodwill to all men. "I bid you farewell. It has been a mellifluous midday. On future occasions when the enigmas of life are insufferable and the tortuous handwriting of the gods baffles the interpreters, I shall revert to the distinctive pleasures of this day with the citizens of Boston and the soldiers of the King."

With a hiccup not intended and for which he apologized, he proceeded, "On the tablets of memory these hours of fellowship shall be emblazoned in postulates beyond destruction by the mightiest cannon that encumber the vessels of the British Empire riding at anchor in the beleaguered and distraught Boston Harbor."

Edgington paused, as did the passing Henry Knox who had sold Edgington whatever there was of Thomas Browne, Addison, Steele, Pitt and Burke.

"Nothing further you wish to add, Mr. Edgington?"

"In sooth, my friend, I am in peril now of speaking beyond my depth. They come unbidden, these attacks of verbosity, these seizures of circumlocution. Tomorrow I shall speak, when the attack has passed, with the sparse address of a carpenter whose front teeth hold five nails. Adieu. Farewell." Then waddling to the door, with a sweep of a three-cornered hat and bowing to the room, he waddled out.

Henry Knox pulled a chair and seated himself with the Winshore group. They smiled and their smiles flicked away on account of Knox's eyes with no twinkle and his mouth drooped sad. Mrs. Bliss Edmunds had come to him at noon from a talk with the coroner. In a coat of claret-dark velvet with gold buttons, silk stockings and a gold-brocaded waistcoat, white silk stockings, lay a body she identified as that of her husband. The rumpled clothing, the spattered head, the weird and twisted face fixed and changeless, the sudden news and shock, Mrs. Edmunds spoke of it all to Mr. and Mrs. Knox in broken sentences, in spells of sobbing and wailing her grief. An empty rowboat was seen offshore near Charlestown yesterday afternoon and later a body found near the shoreline with a lead ball through the right temple and a pistol near by.

Whatever made him do it began months ago when he complained his books failed him, when she heard him curse the books, when he said till then his books either brought him comfort or passed the time so he forgot his miseries. Then in the last month had come news and letters. His twenty-two-year-old son he had been training to join him and later take over his shipping and import business, a boy of promise, had gone to Philadelphia and flung himself into the work of organizing arms and supplies for the army being shaped by the Continental Congress. He had loved the boy. They were chums. The boy had acted without asking his father about it. And there was the daughter two years younger than her brother. In New York City three weeks ago she had married a British officer ten years older than herself and now favored plenty of hanging and shooting for Rebels against the Crown. She was frivolous about it, seemed to welcome violence to come.

No timid man was Bliss Edmunds, Knox was certain. In two years of service in the French and Indian War Edmunds became a captain, at close quarters once killed a man with his pistol and sabered another to death, and himself took wounds. "A proven warrior," said Knox, "though he allowed his manners and speech to give no indication of it." He seemed to have held a court-martial, sentenced himself to death and executed the sentence himself, Knox believed. "If any counselor could have told him how by his death he could avert the war he would willingly have given his life."

To General Gage and to Loyalist leaders Edmunds had gone that winter to ask plain questions and to find they were resolved on force to the limit, preparing to shoot down enough Rebels to maintain authority and to crush for all time the rival provincial government. Then to John Hancock, to Sam Adams and to John Adams, Edmunds had gone to find them, too, resolved on force, resistance to the limit, with a view to establishing a nation independent of Great Britain. Edmunds offered them no plans, no arguments. He saw both sides certain and absolute they must fight and kill, fight more and more and kill more and more yet, and wear each other down till one of the two should win the struggle and enact his will and rule.

He loved his books, learned how to use them. They became his companions. They could offer him wisdom or make him forget his personal misery. So he told Knox as he went on building his library, his long shelves filled with personal companions that could advise or rebuke him, entertain and cheer him. "I saw his mind affected when he broke into curses on his own books and all other books," said Knox.

For weeks Bliss Edmunds had been haunted. He saw a war coming, a struggle more bitter and bloody than the one when he killed other men in hand-to-hand fighting. He would come to the White Cockade, said Knox, to talk with Sway about old times when they slept in the snow around a fire and couldn't keep the blankets dry nor the smoke out of their eyes. "Till I met Bliss Edmunds I wouldn't have believed a first-rate fighting man could be so gentle and sensitive."

Mrs. Edmunds had said she would keep the claret-dark velvet coat with gold buttons, the white stockings, the gold-brocaded waistcoat. His burial would be in the new wig, the white stock, and a simple black coat and gray wool stockings he wore among his books. The pistol, she couldn't think who might want the long-barreled brass pistol.

Robert Winshore sat uneasy, recalling his remark that Edmunds was "a cornered rat." He glanced sidewise at Mim, saw every tint of color leave Mim's face and her skin pale to a weird white not snow but the ash of burning beachwood long water-soaked and sun-dried, a glistening gray-white. She closed her eyes, her lips trembled, her eyelids wavered and opened and she was saying with infinite pity, "I remember his words last Saturday night, Mr. Knox, and they will stay with me long as I live, that outburst. The agony was on him then. They are with me now, those words as he writhed before us and went away apologizing if he had offended us, those words like each was a thorn cutting deep in him," and Mim half-closed her eyes and repeated the words: "I am for the war, I am against the war, and I hope to God the war comes soon so I will not die waiting for the war that I know will be less terrible for me than this waiting." She checked herself, held back from repeating now what she had said then when she saw the press of death coming on Bliss Edmunds: "Violence is an outlet for minds groping in dark labyrinths."

* * * * * * * * * *

Chapter 19

* * * * * * * * * *

Walk in the Moon

THE scud of the moon between clouds, a high wind blowing, silver streaks of mist hanging to the moon and then blown away and the moon gliding clear and alone again, then a slow smoke of cloud rolling over the moon and again the scud of the moon in an illusion of the wind driving and tossing it—this was the night sky over Boston that Robert and Mim saw. It was a help. They were tired, mentally restless with the packed turmoils of the week. The clean wind, the changing sky, helped as they walked around the Common, up and around Beacon Hill, fields where cows were pastured in summer.

Mim ran ahead and slid along a strip of ice, her foot hitting a rough spot that sent her into the air. Robert rushed toward her, saw her make a quick marvelous twist of her body and legs, lighting on her feet. He held her close. They laughed together.

Robert was reminded of her dancing for him one time and saying, "My feet were made glad." And did she remember what else she said then? She didn't and Robert recalled her proud words: "When I die my feet will be so glad they will carry me through the Gate of Heaven whoever tries to stop me."

"Too proud, I must have had vanity of the feet when I said that. I'm not sure tonight that I'm going to heaven even though I'm inclined to agree with Evelyn Trutt that God is too good to damn us all. Do you know, Robert—"

"Yes."

"If there is a hell I wouldn't be surprised you and I will meet there."

"You've been thinking about that?"

"Yes, and I have a toast for us."

"How does it go?"

Mim hopped on a small boulder, lifted toward the scudding moon an arm holding high an imaginary glass and spoke her toast: "Here's to hell! May our stay there be pleasant as our way there!"

This was Wednesday. Next Saturday night he would see her and then leave Boston to be gone for weeks, "God only knows how long." And of what he would be doing while gone he didn't say and left it in the air that he was under pledge or oath not to tell.

She had seen decisions and motives in him deepening. Lights of devotion to her she could see there yet—with an added shadowy abandon she couldn't fathom. Those lights of devotion in his eyes, the touch of adoration in his hands on her, the depths of desire in his kisses, they were there as of old and she counted them her belongings. Could it be they were being overshadowed by this new and growing abandon she couldn't quite place? At moments a fright came over her that he might love some crazy movement or organization among men more than he loved her. Were shades of the passion once reserved for her being transferred to the ventures of which he could tell her nothing?

Of the new reckless flair in him she was jealous. This change in him and whatever brought it she hated. She doubted she would be able to hold her tongue about it. When she twisted it around in her mind and tried to pluck deeper into this motive and find more to it because it seemed too simple, she had found herself asking, "Have you, Robert, with all these new errands and secrets, become some manner of a sneak?" Then she slowed down and called herself a poor desperate fool and cautioned herself never to be that sort of a fool before Robert.

They had walked in one of their silences. Mim began talking. Mrs. Eliphalet Slater, a richly dressed woman who was a steady customer of Mrs. Cavendish, the wife of a Loyalist who owned four farms and stock shares in shipping companies, had come into the dress shop. She and her husband had returned from Providence on the stage the night before. And Mrs. Slater told Mrs. Cavendish, "A pretty state of affairs we met at home. A scamp of a carpenter apprentice had run away with our hired maid. The old Negro woman had gone to our wine and liquor cellar, got drunk and fallen into the fire and burnt out one of her eyes. And our best china bowl was broken, smashed beyond repair."

Then, Mim went on, Mrs. Slater and Mrs. Cavendish talked and talked about that big china bowl, the size of it, the inlays and designs on it, the cost of it, how impossible to get another, how visitors always spoke of it as precious and nothing like it in New England. "On and on they prattled about that damned china bowl," said Mim. "How fragile, how delicate, how choice and bee-yoo-oo-ootiful. And not a word about the failing old Negro woman they bought fifteen years ago and she fell in the fire and burned her face and lost an eye and will go blind in that eye the rest of her life."

"It is sad," said Robert. "And what to you is the import of it?"

"Import, you ask, Robert, import?"

"Yes, what do you make of it?"

484

"I can't make anything of it. I have no import for you. It's too silly and cruel to think about, I say, and then I go on thinking about it."

"Do you hate those two women?"

"No, but they scare me."

"How could that be?"

"They scare me with the thought that they are helpless, they don't know in the least how silly and cruel they are, and it could happen, I suppose, that I might someday come awake to what I had been doing and see it as silly and cruel—and if I shouldn't come awake that would be more tragic yet."

"I could tell you," said Robert in a burst of candor, "of my being silly and cruel, nothing less, and it would be terribly involved. And one of these days, if we live, I will tell it to you."

"That's a sweet confession. Don't soften me, Robert, when I need hardening."

Some vague and inquiring remark of Robert about what a time it was of hate and hard judgments sent Mim into a spin of feeling and what she had to say was for Robert, for herself, and perhaps the scudding moon she turned her face up to twice as she spoke. "Why should I hate John Hancock? I did once. I don't now. He is only a two-legged man who will come to an end and be less than dust. Or why should I hate His Majesty King George the Third? I don't. He too is a man on weak legs to get weaker till his end comes and you could burn him to ashes and put it all in a tortoise-shell snuffbox with bright-gold script on the cover and the script reading: 'This *was* a man.' Power crumbles. Riches take flight. The gold men get more often gets them. The finest silk or wool cannot stave off moth and rot. What stands? What lasts? What stays when all these others go? What is proof against death and the rot of dissolution? Could it be love? Could it be a dream softer than fine mist and you could no more take hold of it and say, 'Now I surely have it,' than you could wash your hands in a wind-blown winter moonlight?"

By indirection she was saying in part, Robert gathered, that she couldn't go along with him in his zeal for a cause and the kind of hate that must mix with the zeal. She might even hold that their love came first and what he called patriotism second, though of this he wouldn't be so sure. Certain he was however that she was declaring herself a free human spirit with a sacred heart: she could never be like him a Whig, a Patriot and a Rebel, merely on his telling her so to be and their love so required. What she would be in the changes to come she would work out for herself. That was Robert's guess on what lay behind her words. He knew himself on the danger line when he spoke. "We're young, Mim. We didn't begin this awful trouble that's come on us. It began long before you and I were born. Now we have to take it as it is, as they left it to us. They put a fort and cannon on Beacon Hill, drilled with troops, ready to shoot one hundred and forty years ago, when

485

messages arrived that a new Royal Governor they didn't want was coming. Later they revolted against that Royal Governor named Andros and threw him out. You and I were babies and in our teen-ages when there was high howling and hate piled on hate over the Writs of Assistance, the Declaratory Act, the Townshend Duties Act. Then seven years ago came the Stamp Act, five years ago the Boston Massacre, two years ago the Tea Party. Do you see that another older generation made the war a younger generation will fight? We have had no voice, no vote on the war coming to us. Tangled it is, too tangled for us to untie all the knots and unravel all the snarls. All we can do is make a beginning toward ends that seem fantastic to me sometimes, this pattern and model, this vision that Dr. Warren put into the 'Liberty Song' with its great promises that look impossible. He and the Continental Congress leaders think we can give the world something never seen before. We can't be sure but we can raise a hope that an American Republic of free men is possible. It could become the light of the world. Liberty of conscience, freedom of worship, we now have, bought with struggle. Further liberties, still other freedoms, we must have. They will be bought with struggle. They will cost."

They walked in silence. They came to crooked and narrow streets. The water front opened before them, harbor lights. Under the now clouded moon the sea horizon stood black. "You have spoken tonight," said Mim. "And I could speak. It would come heavy. Let it wait. I might say it better Saturday night before you leave."

Robert clenched a fist. He thought of when he put a mitten over his mouth a few nights ago and asked himself if he had just had the first cold kiss from Mim.

They stood on a wharf. Out along the water level they could see ships riding at anchor with hull lights. The sight of them hit Robert of a sudden. Yes, these were the enemy frigates. They shook him loose from his tangled thoughts of Mim and himself. He put out a stiff arm and pointing finger, an excited voice, "Yes, there they are, the enemy warships. There they stand keeping the port of Boston closed and dead. There they wait with their guns telling us Americans, On your knees—submit or we shoot you down! They and their guns come three thousand miles to tell us what we can do or can't—ugh!"

In his grunted and loathing "ugh!" Mim heard the new abandon, the fresh reckless flair she hated so.

"Yes," and she put out an arm and pointed a forefinger of her own toward the scene of the Boston Tea Party. "Yes, and over there three hundred and forty-two chests of good tea flung into salt water to spoil and rot—the criminal rabble—the filthy vile scum."

And out of Robert's mouth came words only she could have pulled. Not fully knowing what he was doing he had cried back at her: "And I was one of them!"

Now they said nothing. Now they walked back to Aunt Ellen's saying nothing. Now Robert at the door said she must understand he was sworn never to tell of his own hand or any other man's hand on that night of a wild deed that rocked the Western world and London.

"It is locked in me as a secret till death," said Mim.

He went away with her kiss on his lips. It was no cold kiss. It was a warm desperate kiss.

What could Saturday night and its leavetaking bring? Each tried to guess and gave up guessing. Each did take note of a wide space among clouds where the moon was riding free. The wind had gone down. The moon rode high and serene. It was later and while they slept and unbeknownst to them that a slow wind arose and a slow smoke rolled over the moon and a fog moved in from the sea and when morning came it was a gray day with a monotonous meaningless anonymous drizzle of rain.

* * * * * * * * * *

Chapter 20

* * * * * * * * * *

Brass Clasps of a Heavy Bible

PORK and beans baked to the right minute for a Saturday-night supper make a perfect Sunday breakfast, Aunt Ellen was saying to Robert and Mim. "You can eat 'em cold and they have flavor." Pickled herring from a keg in the cellar, the Indian dish called succotash made with corn and beans from the Wilming farm last October, cider from a barrel in the cellar, apple pie with coffee and the pie having Mim's fingerprints on the crust—it was a tasty, pleasant supper, and, said Aunt Ellen, "It's filling."

Mim had worn a calico dress getting supper and then slid into a gown of white linen with a wide starched collar.

"It looks quite the thing," said Aunt Ellen who could manage slang of the day. Aunt Ellen went further. "I am of the opinion, Robert, that you can say tonight like the man I heard once about his young wife."

"And he said?"

"The pootiest, purtiest gal in all Massachusetts."

"He said that?"

"I heard him."

"I'll go further. I'll say, with you as a witness, Aunt Ellen, that Mim is the pootiest and purtiest gal in all New England and Philadelphia."

"No more than that?"

"Oh, I'd say the pootiest and purtiest gal in the world if I'd ever seen any outside of New England and Philadelphia."

"This is enough," Mim cut in. "I'd be satisfied to be just plain pooty and purty without any comparisons. I don't want to be like the woman so damned proud of her face who, as the years passed, became a squat bag of guts and a draggletail."

"A what?" Aunt Ellen rippled.

"I should say it again?"

"It was funny and I want to be sure I heard it rightly."

"She was a face-proud woman with the pride that goeth before a fall and she was vain, priggish and piggish and after a time she had flaps under her chin, pouches under her eyes and became a squat bag of guts and a draggletail."

"Mim, you *do* lay it on that woman."

They cleared the table, washed the dishes, and Aunt Ellen brought out a pair of pure-gold earrings her husband had picked up in Constantinople, long ovals with luminous blue stones in them. "Mim likes these bangles but she won't wear 'em."

"Not now. Perhaps two or three hundred years from now when Robert and I make our trip to Persia, Afghanistan and Mesopotamia."

"Especially Mesopotamia," said Robert.

Aunt Ellen said good night holding a hand on the newel post of the stairway and they saw her hand along up the stairway banister to near the top when she turned and with a quiet gravity, "Good luck to thee, Robert. May the good Lord return thee safe again here."

"She feels something in the air," said Mim. "About once a year she says *thee*. She got it from a Quaker woman she likes. They have long sweet talks saying nothing."

"I knew one in Philadelphia who had a prayer," said Robert. " 'Solitude, give me solitude, but in my solitude give me one friend to whom I can murmur, Solitude is sweet.' "

"Something in the air there is. Aunt Ellen sniffs it."

"So do you and I."

"And many others."

"It gets more shaky," said Robert, clenching his hands, unclenching, and taking one of Mim's hands as they sat close on the oak settee and watched the two heavy stub candles in the sturdy Arabian brass candlesticks. "Action will come soon. We don't know where. I don't know when I see you again. It may be two weeks or two months."

"We have never had trials, real tests, Robert."

"They are to come, I suppose."

"Indeed they are to come, you must know that."

"You've seen changes come over me the last year, Mim, and especially the last three or four months. I've done things hard to tell you about if I were free to tell you."

"Blinding the bound and gagged Hobart Reggs, coating his head and hair and filling his eyes with a brush of warm tar, it would not come easy to tell."

So she knew. Robert loosed his hand from hers, folded his two hands, wove the fingers.

It hurt Mim to go on. But she did. "Sapphira Reggs blabbed it all to Mrs. Cavendish and me. She recognized you, said she would swear it was you she saw that night before she fainted."

"I am ashamed of my hand in that. But I wouldn't try to tell you how or why I am ashamed. I was tricked but you wouldn't believe how I was tricked."

Mim's hurt was eased a little. Robert was telling some kind of truth that might come more clear later.

"The affair of Silas Ludgate," Mim went on, "I am sure, without definite proof, you had a hand in that. You meant to throw terror into the Loyalists."

"That affair, if I had a hand in it, I would defend. The man was an informer. An informer is a rat. A rat should be killed. He was mercifully allowed to live."

Here was the new abandon, the reckless flair.

"I can't make up my mind how you Sons of Liberty look on what you do and call it good. In the books and the teachings, in the commandments of God and man, these deeds are crimes. Men sharing in these deeds are criminals."

"If it was as easy as that my conscience would be very easy."

"Would your father, would good old Ordway Winshore, take a hand as the Liberty Boys did with Reggs and with Ludgate?"

"I rather think not."

"Do Sam Adams, John Hancock, John Adams, go in for such deeds in person?"

"No, they are leaders."

"Why don't you be a leader and *not* do them?"

"*Someone* must do them or *they* wouldn't be leaders. Reggs and Ludgate were caught in specific acts of treachery that had to be answered with violence and terror. You talk when talk helps. You act when only action counts."

They said nothing. Robert still folded his hands and wove the fingers. He found his voice, very low-spoken in somewhat of Mim's way of speaking beyond those hearing. "The noble words are good. They serve. But with no actions to illustrate them and enforce their meaning, the words are dead. The Boston Tea Party was better than ten thousand orations full of bright abstract arguments."

Again they said nothing. Then Mim mentioned having seen Lieutenant George Frame and Sapphira Reggs together too much lately. She would guess it was just as well Robert was leaving. They might be looking for him.

Robert agreed. Then he asked her what it was the other night she had held off from telling, hoping to tell it better this Saturday night at his leavetaking.

She began. It came hard. She couldn't have gone on with it if she hadn't lived with it and turned it around and in and out and learned how to hold it as a controlled pain that came and went:

"I think I know exactly why Bliss Edmunds pulled a curtain and took a leap into the dark. I could do it and laugh doing it. But I won't. And I won't crack in the brain and go babbling and helpless while still alive like James Otis, peace to him. I may writhe and swing near the door of death but I shall not swing in. That other door Otis slid through, I may slide near it and then come back for the good reason I can be silly as your father told Miss Burton to be silly. You don't know how silly I can be."

"I do know, I thank God for it," mumbled Robert and Mim liked hearing it.

"I must go a certain path alone. After going it alone I may come to you, if you live, and tell you what I know then. I don't know it now. I will then," and she measured off hard words. "Now I have slowly come to see you a fool, a bigot, a brute who sees merit in his crimes and most of all you are what the preacher meant by a hypocritical party zealot. I think so now. Yet I do not fully trust what I think. It is you who has that kind of full trust and that is why you are zealot, bigot, and hypocrite. You cannot reason with me about it. I cannot reason with myself about it. I must wait. I must go my way alone. Life will teach me while you are gone from me and inexorably life will teach you while I am gone from you."

"I follow you," came Robert's contrapuntal baritone. "I know it costs you to say it."

"We are young yet. You said that the other night. It is our hope. In the worse blood and terror to come we will learn. I can see they will shake me near to death. I will be swept near the gates of the lost mind." Mim trembled, her body and voice trembled. Robert put an arm around her, took one of her hands lightly in his. She went on. "They will not get me, those dooms that reach for me, those fates that reach out and hawk at the sensitively alive. My strength will be a fine thin cord drawn tight and near breaking but it will hold."

"So I told my father the first time we talked about you," Robert murmured with dreaminess. Perhaps they should have had this candor earlier, thought Robert. It came hard now, yet there was cleansing in it.

Mim went on. "I loathe your deeds and your excuses and justifications of them. And I love the companion you have been and the boy you are, my boy, my only lover, my hope for a home in the hills, for the bright day," and Mim choked a little at this, "the June day we pictured for the ceremony and the words 'until death do us part' and Darius would be an usher and he would drive us to the house and before going in we would stand under apple blossoms in the moonlight, under the same trees where last year we had a long deep kiss."

She waited before going on. "My arms will reach for you. My mouth will seek yours. And I will put away the wanting of you. Relentless and whirling events will tell me what I want to know without doubts or reservations. What I see now may be right. If something else is right life will press and burn it into me. Till then I put away from me the want of you, the need of you. And often it will howl and swirl about me and near crush me, the want and need of you."

Robert had seen her face pale to the same weird white as when Henry Knox told of Bliss Edmunds' leap into the dark, a faint tremor of blue on her lips.

They said nothing now. They sat in a long silence now. They had each a nameless gratitude for the silence they could keep now. They were long in a fierce interlock of caresses and Mim cried low and Robert felt his eyes too soft. And their mouths were close and they heard the breathing of one another and they were saying by no spoken words that such a farewell should have this kind of bittersweet, this sort of earth tang. The two thick stub candles, the five oak chairs, the two with loose legs, the worn calf-bound Bible with brass clasps on the center table, the long narrow rag rugs placed just so in their accustomed places —they too belonged in the bittersweet ritual of parting.

Robert in his "Liberty Song" at the White Cockade and his words to her under the scudding moon of Wednesday night—he had said the most of it—little could be added. Mim in her straightaway and poignant talk this night had come to an end of words. So their silence on the oak settee in the low-ceilinged room became them as a garment they had made together.

Rather early in the evening it was for them though they couldn't have told and didn't care whether it was late or early.

In this quiet room of this still house they could not mistake it there were footfalls and voices outside, feet coming along on the two-plank-wide walk from the gate to the front door, voices that had spoken and then let down.

A rough knock at the front door, nothing timid about it, rather like a pounding. Mim strode to the door, Robert standing a few steps behind her.

At the door Mim opened were the voice and face of Lieutenant George Frame. Might he be permitted to enter? Certainly, a little unusual but come in, said Mim. And at his right elbow Sapphira Reggs, "My guest, I presume she may enter?"

"Your call is unexpected, but you are welcome," said Mim.

Would they have chairs? Mim asked.

Miss Reggs might like a chair. Lieutenant Frame would come to his errand standing, he believed.

"Without further ado," said Frame, as though already there had been a lot of ado and he preferred as little ado as possible, and facing Robert, "my duty here is to put you, Mr. Robert Winshore, under ar-

491

rest for a criminal assault on the person of Hobart Reggs, who with his daughter here will be the principal witnesses against you. I can further notify you that the evidence is nearly complete for your conviction of participation in a criminal assault on the person of Silas Ludgate."

While Frame spoke Robert moved slowly to where the center table stood between him and Frame, whose back was to the front door and his feet on one of the long narrow rag rugs.

"No tricks, none of your monkeyshines will help you tonight, Mr. Winshore," said Frame, even-voiced, with a stern face and eyes as he drew a pistol. "You are coming with us. Four of my men are outside. They will take you in custody."

"By what authority is all of this?" Robert asked, looking Frame straight in the eye and with no fluster and as though he had a right to ask the question and it was customary in Boston.

"By the authority of the Governor General of the Royal Province of Massachusetts and I have the signed warrant for your arrest here in my pocket but you are the extreme and dangerous case where we do not go through the formality of reading or showing the warrant."

"I am to be your prisoner how long?"

"Till your trial when your punishment will be determined."

"A court-martial will try me?"

"Yes, and they will be more just and considerate than you were with Mr. Hobart Reggs."

For a fleeting flash of a moment Robert wondered how Mim's face looked and whether Sapphira Reggs had taken a chair and how she looked and he laughed at his fool curiosity and kept himself strictly to measuring every one of five or six chances that ran through his head as he played for a few priceless seconds in which to think out the best of the chances.

"May I ask—" he began.

"No, you may not ask and there will be no more palaver." This now came from Lieutenant Frame with a bark and a snarl as he lifted the pistol and held it toward Robert's heart.

"My hat and overcoat," said Robert.

"You walk to that front door and step out and we'll bring your hat and overcoat," said Frame.

"A step at a time, one step and then another, that will be obeying your orders?" asked Robert as he moved one small step. Frame was puzzled about what this could mean but hesitated and seemed inclined to accept it as an admission from Robert that he was ready to go along.

"While I am going along with you one step at a time," said Robert as he moved another small step, "may I ask—"

"You may not ask one more question and you're going to learn to keep your damned Rebel mouth shut," barked Frame.

At the word "shut" the room went dark and the two brass candlesticks clattered to the floor and there was a sound of a body falling, followed by a crackling thump, after which came a bang at the top of the stairway and a rolling rattle down the stairs.

Frame's three grenadiers in front of the house came rushing in, falling tangled and cursing in a chair at the foot of the stairway. After Mim had lighted the candles, they made out what had happened. With a sweep of one hand Robert had sent the two candles and candlesticks to the floor, stooped and with a swift pull at the long narrow rag rug had Frame reeling and toppling to the floor, had hurled the center table over Frame, and then flung one of the loose-legged oak chairs up to the top of the stairway for whatever confusion might follow from its bang and its roll and rattling down the stairs.

A minute, two minutes, a third minute passed. Frame with an effort and a groan sat up and felt of a bump on his forehead where the brass clasp of the heavy calf-bound Bible had struck him. Frame came out of his daze to cry, "Out the back door, you two, look to the back door!" he ordered and to another grenadier, "Up the stairway and search every corner!"

One whisked up the stairway to find his way blocked by a little one-hundred-and-five-pound woman with a dignified scowl and a righteous voice asking, "Is it murder or robbery come this night to a peaceful house of decent citizens?"

"Did he run this way?" the soldier shouted at her.

"Did who run this way?"

"Robert Winshore, he's under arrest," cried Frame, before dashing to the kitchen and the back door. Through the back door he went to see two of his men working on a third man who lay alongside a sawbuck next the woodshed. This third man Frame saw was the grenadier assigned to watch the rear of the house. When he came to his senses the grenadier remembered a man rushed at him and pushed him over the sawbuck and then brained him with a billet of wood and he forgot where he was.

In the house Mim had comforted Aunt Ellen and put her to bed, had moved the center table where it belonged with the candles in their usual place and picked up the old calf-bound Bible and fastened the brass clasp that had come loose and had heard Sapphira Reggs shake out moans that it was a shame if "that ruffian, that beast," had got away.

Lieutenant Frame had recovered, spoke to Mim with a fine gravity and consideration. "I regret it was necessary to inconvenience you, Miss Wilming. We had allowed Winshore his freedom in the hope of learning more of his associates and accomplices. When we were informed this afternoon that it was certain he planned to leave Boston tomorrow to be absent indefinitely, we made our decision to seek him here."

"He will not trouble you in Boston in the immediate future, you may be sure," said Mim, cool and level-eyed.

"You give me your word of honor, Miss Wilming, that is to your best knowledge and belief?"

"I do, Lieutenant Frame."

"That is sufficient for me. I apologize again for disturbing you and wish you good night."

The house was still again. Mim rested back in the solid oak settee. Could it be only some twenty minutes ago she and Robert wore a garment of silence together and shared a strange, earthy bittersweet?

She looked to the two candlesticks and spoke a blessing to them. She rose and walked to the kitchen and out of the back door, looked up at a gray noncommittal sky, walked over to the woodshed and touched the sawbuck and spoke a little blessing on it.

In the front room she blew out the candles, sat for a while in the dark on the settee, went up the stairs, peeped in on Aunt Ellen asleep, got into her nightrobe and stood at the window wondering what way and route Robert might have taken, thought of Ordway Winshore sleeping alone this night, and crept into bed saying, "It will be hard but I will learn."

* * * * * * * * * *

Chapter 21

* * * * * * * * * *

April the Nineteenth

ROBERT NEWMAN in his home across the street from Christ Church had yawned so the billeted British officers in the house could see him yawn, had told his mother loud enough for the officers to hear it, that he was going to bed. They had got used to his habit of going to bed early. This night he lay abed, hearing in the room under him the laughter and banter of the drinking and card-playing officers. He had not yet dozed off into sleep when he heard a sound on the window-panes, once, again and a third time. It sounded like fine gravel thrown to the glass. He slid out of bed and made for the window to see Robert Winshore crawling up the shingled roof. "He wants in," said Newman, opening the window for Winshore. He heard from Winshore of Frame, the arrest and the escape. Over the grenadiers tangled in the chair at the foot of the stairway Newman laughed loud; Robert clapped a hand over Newman's mouth. They slept two in the bed that night. A block away Ordway Winshore slept alone and guessed why two soldiers stood in the street below and were there yet in the morning. They were still there at noon of the next day when Ordway Winshore and Robert Newman made a bundle of changes of clothing, kerchiefs, a pistol and other things for Robert's traveling.

Near midnight of April 15 Robert waited with two men and a wagon on the bank of the Charles River near Charlestown. Two hours they had waited and at last came the expected boat with Isaiah Thomas and four men. On the boat they had one printing press, a few fonts of type and the paper stock of the Thomas printery, only part of it because hauling all the type and presses would have meant added risk. They loaded the wagon. Isaiah Thomas with one other man rowed back to Boston. Robert with a pistol ready rode past a point where at times British guards stood watch and searched wagons.

Thus New England's foremost Whig journal, the *Massachusetts Spy*, moved in the night forty-eight miles to Worcester, fled with speed from the enemy soon to take over the remaining presses and type, borders and ornaments, stocks of books and pamphlets.

Three nights later Robert at a farmhouse beyond Charlestown stood outdoors and kept a watching eye on the Boston skyline. When his eyes caught for two or three minutes a clear gleam and glimmer of two lights high in the steeple of Christ Church he went in the house and told the Whig farmer of it, and saddled a horse and rode away.

Other men watching for it had seen that brief glimmer of two lanterns in Christ Church steeple. One lantern would have meant troops marching by the land route over the Neck. Two lanterns told they would move by the more secret route, in boats over the Charles River. To Robert that moment when the lanterns spoke their signal was very personal. Away across the Charles River and in the heart of Boston miles off he could hear the chuckle of his friend Robert Newman. It was many weeks later Newman told of how on this night of April 18 he had again stretched and yawned for the benefit of the billeted officers, yawned he would go to bed early. And looked out the window of his room to see no one below, took note of the full moon that had come up after nine o'clock. Then Newman opened the window, slid along the sloping shingled roof and let himself down to meet in the street the Christ Church vestryman John Pulling. They crossed to Christ Church, the big front door, where Newman took out his key and let himself in, Pulling locking the door and standing watch in the street. Out of a closet Newman took two lanterns and went winding and climbing up the bell-tower stairs, groping with his hands and feeling with his feet, passing the eight great bells whose bong and boom could be heard for miles, massive bells silent as the moon that hung in the sky to slant its white patterns among the bell shapes. At the top window of the belfry Newman lighted the two lanterns, hung them out of the window, held them and waited, making the wait just long enough for watchers to see, and not so long as to alarm the enemy. Then on down the belfry stairway in pitch-black dark, and suspicious of the street, Newman slipped out a rear window of the church, took a roundabout way home, then up over the shingled roof and into his bedroom window. In bed he could hear the chatter of card-playing

British officers in the room below and wondered what they had to laugh at.

Along the highway he rode Robert Winshore felt familiar. He had come this way with Mim to visit the Wilming farm. He had come again riding alone this road going to the first Provincial Congress meeting in Concord, eighteen miles from Boston, last October, and again when the second Provincial Congress met in Concord February 1, writing part of the resolves and actions for the *Massachusetts Spy* and reporting to Isaiah Thomas what could not be made public. Again three days ago, on April 15, he had attended the meeting of the Provincial Congress in Concord. He had performed errands, helped guard wagons and locate arms and supplies for the Committee of Safety and the Committee of Supplies who were seeking to buy "military stores sufficient for an army of 15,000 men," specifying there should be stored at Worcester and Concord ready for campaigns and battles "at least 335 barrels of pork, 700 barrels of flour, 20 tierces of rice, 300 bushels of peas." Toward the army not yet raised which was to use the arms and supplies not yet half collected, Robert had given time and efforts in co-operation with Artemas Ward and Jedediah Preble, the commanders elected by the Provincial Congress. Robert had won the trust of Committee members Azor Orne, David Cheever, John Pigeon, Benjamin Lincoln, and Elbridge Gerry, the well-to-do Marblehead trader who shipped dried codfish to the Barbadoes in exchange for Spanish goods. Robert had come to like Gerry who surprised elders and classmates at Harvard in 1765 with a Master's-degree address that lambasted the British Government for "oppressive measures." Gerry kept his politics close to Sam Adams, taught younger men the value of "obstinacy that will risk great things to secure small ones."

A trim, thin-built, clean-dressed man, Gerry was one of the Committee of Supplies who had met this day of April 18 in Menotomy at the Black Horse tavern.

Robert riding through Menotomy stopped at the Black Horse and talked with Gerry, Azor Orne and Charles Lee. They were staying overnight. They had heard the British might be marching. Robert told them of the signal in Christ Church steeple. "We'll stay overnight and run the chance," said Gerry.

And if anywhere on the road to Lexington and Concord Robert could find John Hancock and Sam Adams and tell them the British Regulars were out and marching toward those towns, it might be a help, thought Gerry, who had already sent to those two men, sought for treason to the King, a written message that he wanted surely to reach them.

Low rolling hills, slopes and knolls, pasture land, fields with fresh-plowed furrows, stony barren acres scattered with boulders, fences where patient hands had piled stone on stone from the near-by soil, strips of bog and marsh, lanes and cow paths—over and across, around and about, Robert rode his horse, sometimes at a slow gallop, more often a walk or an easy trot.

An hour or more of this, it seemed, and he shifted his direction toward the road, not sure he was keeping parallel to it. He made a guess it was just beyond a low wide ridge ahead. It wouldn't do to ride up on that ridge in a full clear moon. He tied his horse where three small pines threw shadows, walked keeping his head and shoulders below patches of bush, moving fast in the open moonlit spaces from one patch to another. Reaching the ridge he stood in the shadow of a hawthorn tree and sighted the track of the main road to the village. He wasn't lost. He turned back, walked stooping and made his way to the last patch of bush, an open space of forty yards to the three pines where he could see his horse. He would wait a minute, get a good deep breath and then run for the horse. While he waited he heard a swish and crackle and saw moving out of the bushes off to his left perhaps twenty yards, a redcoat officer running toward the horse. He waited and saw the officer draw a pistol and stand on the lookout alongside the horse.

Crouching and guarding against swish of twig overhead and crackle of dry branch underfoot, watching that bushes stood between him and the horse when he ran from one patch to another, he got to the ridge and moved along to where he saw two British troopers standing at a roadside clump of underbrush. "Guarding the road and keeping it clear for the army marching this way," said Robert to himself. Zigzagging and making use of cover he reached a stone fence that screened him to the end of a field where in the fence corner he took a long look toward the three pines and his lost horse. Then he began his walk to the village of Lexington, keeping off the road.

Some in homespun wool shirts and stockings from their own sheep, some in leather breeches of home-tanned hide, men living so close to the land that they cherished that land—they had stood in company formation on the common and answered roll call. They had heard an army of British Regulars might be marching from Boston and might try to march through the village. What they might do to stop that army they didn't know. They had no plan. They would stand, perhaps shoot, in some kind of a showing. They would decide what when the time came. They were independent farmers every day making quick independent decisions. Most of them had an idea they were taking a stand against interference with the way they wanted to live. At least a few had a curiosity about how it would feel to be in the shooting, if there was any. If it came to fighting, what kind of men would they be shooting at? The "Regulars," that was the word, the regularly trained soldiers of the regularly uniformed British Army, homeless men, landless men who had come three thousand miles to enforce the will of their King on the little landowners of the Royal Province of Massachusetts.

Something like that Robert thought he saw in the faces of the men who had come in from the outdoor chill to stand around the big fireplace of the Buckman tavern. Their Captain John Parker had gone to his home two miles away: they should call him when needed.

On some of the faces Robert could read a mystery he loved. He had met it before. He saw this night in the eyes and the shaded determinations on those faces he met what lay back of the words in the resolve passed in the village town meeting a few weeks after the Boston Tea Party, a pledge they stood ready to sacrifice "everything dear in life, yea, and life itself, in support of the common cause." Land, property, cattle, sheep, wool, cargoes, ships, trading and manufacturing rights—these figured second and came after the mystery beyond all the tangibles of arithmetic and accounting, as set forth in their Middlesex County convention resolve:

"No danger shall affright, no difficulties intimidate us; and if in support of our rights we are called to encounter even death, we are yet undaunted, sensible that he can never die too soon, who lays down his life in support of the laws and liberty of his country."

The moonlight fell soft and white on the land, the trees still, the houses quiet, and the night seemed to be the same as a thousand other nights when you could listen and hear nothing, when you could stand on the village common where three roads fork away, one to Boston, one to Concord, one to Bedford, and you could listen beyond eyesight on each of those roads and hear nothing.

In this still of the night Robert walked the quarter-mile to the parsonage of the Reverend Jonas Clarke. Under that roof he would seek John Hancock and Sam Adams and give them the message he had for them. As he walked in the quiet he could hear only the scruff of his shoes on the gravel. Then he heard hoofbeats. A man rode past him. He made his guess who the man was. He saw him get off the horse at the Clarke parsonage, saw the eight men on guard there press around the man, and came up to recognize an old friend and they were telling him he was talking too loud, making too much noise.

The new-come rider answered, "Noise! You'll have noise enough before long. The Regulars are out," and began pounding on the front door of the parsonage.

Out of an upper window came the head of the Reverend Jonas Clarke and he was saying he couldn't let strangers in this time of night. Then came the invitation of John Hancock who recognized a voice, "Come in, Revere, we are not afraid of you." They let him in and Robert followed, to hear Revere tell of riding from Charlestown and at nearly every house giving "the alarum" and warning, "The Regulars are out!"

Candles were lighted. The house came alive. Hancock, Adams, Dolly Quincy, her Aunt Lydia, Clarke, heard the news. Revere himself had seen the British troops crossing the Charles River at ten o'clock, "over a thousand," perhaps. Soon arrived William Dawes, who had rode out of Boston through the Neck, and he had the same news. Revere and Dawes ate and drank, then rode away to get the news to Concord. John Hancock cleaned his sword and pistol and talked about fighting. There was discussion whether Hancock and Adams should take their places in fighting ranks.

Sam Adams argued. It became a wrangle when Dolly Quincy and Aunt Lydia insisted Hancock must not "go to battle." Hancock polished his sword and insisted he must. Robert came near putting in his say and joining with Sam Adams in the point that Hancock and Adams were delegates to the Continental Congress and they shouldn't accommodate and please the enemy by risking capture and trial for treason. Robert did quote the Tory threat in crude rhyme:

> "As for their King, John Hancock,
> And Adams, if they're taken,
> Their heads for signs shall hang on high
> Upon that hill called 'Beacon.'"

Paul Revere returned, bedraggled but cool. A British patrol had taken him prisoner, questioned him, threatened to shoot him, taken his horse and let him go, and he had made his way across back fields.

Word came that Captain John Parker had been summoned, had arrived at the common, his company having roll call. They could hear from the parsonage the drum roll beaten by twenty-year-old William Diamond and the gay air of "The White Cockade" shrilled on the fife by seventeen-year-old Jonathan Harrington. Through the Clarke parsonage windows came that drum roll and fife shrilling—and the first slants of daybreak—in a clear sky of sunrise soon to come. And from the old belfry alongside the common came over and over the klong-klong of the bell—a harsh daybreak jangle of drum, fife and bell crying to the hills and houses it was no time for sleep.

A chaise drew up in front of the parsonage, the horse pricking his ears at the bell-drum-fife noise. Dolly Quincy and Aunt Lydia had decided to go to Boston, John Hancock saying, "No, madam, you shall not return as long as there is a bayonet in Boston," and Dolly pertly, "Recollect, Mr. Hancock, I am not under your control yet." The two women did decide to stay. The other decision was that Hancock and Adams would ride in the chaise to Woburn or farther, with Revere for guard and escort.

In the chaise with them must go John Hancock's big leather-covered trunk. The enemy would like that trunk with its papers in conclusive evidence of treason. Paul Revere and Hancock's clerk John Lowell would go to Buckman's tavern and bring the trunk in the chaise. Then Hancock and Adams would start their ride to get away from the enemy now reaching to clutch them.

Robert would follow Revere and Lowell and be on hand for whatever might happen till the trunk arrived safely in the chaise. Up to the second floor of Buckman's tavern went Revere and Lowell. Out of the front door they came with the trunk, Robert following them some fifty yards to the rear. On up the Bedford Road that quarter-mile to the Clarke parsonage carrying that trunk went Revere and Lowell turning for a few backward glances toward the village common. Robert took more of these looks back.

The moon had paled, the daybreak eased into daylight, the red-dawn glimmers of sunrise shoved up the eastern sky. Down the slope of the Boston road into the village Robert saw them. The two lanterns Robert Newman had lighted in Christ Church steeple had foretold this. There they were. "God, what a sight!" Robert grunted. Now he thought of a remark of a British officer reported to Dr. Warren the day before, "There will be hell to pay tomorrow." Down the long slope in steady marching order came six companies of light infantry, a stream of scarlet cloth flicked with brass buttons glittering in the fresh dawnlight, marching men, trained professional marching men with horsemen in the lead and alongside guiding, officers astraddle their big horses picked for parade and show.

The morning mist mingled with a film of dust that rose from the road. Somewhat dreamlike, a touch of fantasy to it, a flicker of the unbelievable about it. Robert was thinking and Captain Parker's men on the common, some of them, "No, it can't be true that this moment has come. Do we see what we see? Yes, there they are. We have never seen it before and so we look twice and three times and more and—yes—it is true, there they are, the marching British Regulars, eleven miles out of Boston, all night marching in the moonlight, all night marching and for what? Soon we will know. This day and the hours of this day will tell what they get for coming. No mistake, the more you look the more sure you are it is them."

Robert following Revere and Lowell with the trunk couldn't make out the words but he saw a scarlet-clad major gallop to maybe six rods from Parker's ranks of Minute Men. He heard the major yell and learned afterward that the major was crying, "Lay down your arms, you damned rebels, and disperse," and that Parker told his men, "Don't fire unless fired on, but if they mean to have a war let it begin here," or as Paul Revere heard it, "Let the troops pass by and don't molest them without they begin first."

Robert could see Parker's men breaking ranks. Parker saw they would be swept away if they tried to fight what was sliding down that slope toward them.

As they broke ranks the Minute Men carried with them their guns. Robert could hear the major on his big horse snarling and heard afterward that the major was crying, "Damn you, why don't you lay down your arms?"

Robert for a moment had been tempted to run to the common and stand in line with Captain Parker's men. There they stood on that neat clean green common, two ranks of them, some sixty men, in farm clothes of homespun and leather, with their firelocks, their flintlocks, their shotguns never yet aimed at living men, never yet tried on human targets. They were Minute Men and this was the minute they had waited for.

Half the time Robert looked back toward the common, and the other half kept his eyes on Revere and Lowell with the trunk. At last he turned for a look at the Clarke parsonage and saw coming out of the house the two men for whom the long arm of Great Britain had reached clean across the Atlantic Ocean to take them for treason trials, Hancock and Adams. Any two or three of a dozen enemy horsemen in the village a quarter-mile away could in a minute of riding have captured the two foremost leaders of rebellion in New England, the two Continental Congress delegates.

The wheels turned. The horses jogged away, with Revere as guard and escort. The chaise moved on to Woburn and beyond. Hancock and Adams on the way heard church bells ringing alarms, drums calling Minute Men, and two sharp crackles of gunshot volleys. Adams felt good and smiled and exclaimed, "Oh, what a glorious morning is this!" And Hancock thought Adams was talking about the weather—a fine, clear, coolish, windy day, and everything underfoot a little dry or dusty from weeks of no rain.

Robert left the road, ran across back fields to where among lilac bushes in a lot back between the blacksmith shop and the Jonathan Harrington house, he could see the common. Shooting had begun. The two loud blasts he had heard were volleys the enemy invaders had sent into Captain Parker's line-up of Minute Men. Off the common they had scattered, some shooting from behind fences and trees, from corners of the Buckman tavern. Some in the scattering couldn't run. One lay sprawled on the turf as if he had run and then dropped face down and arms spread. Another lay still with his face to the morning sky, another sidewise and crumpled as though trying to sleep, hugging his firelock. Others, three, four, five of them lay writhing with their wounds, another sitting up and twisting himself to find a position to ease his wound.

Robert set his teeth, clenched his fists, took out his pistol to aim at bunches of redcoats crossing the green, decided to wait, wished he had a musket, wished he was forty men with forty muskets.

Coming straight toward him he saw one of the Minute Men zig-zagging, half-stumbling, guiding his feet somehow straight toward the Harrington house. On and on, stopping to double himself with pain, raise himself again, and go on. Out of the front door of the Harrington house came a woman who saw him trying to reach her. She would help him walk. At the front steps he sagged and fell. Her hands and arms were round him, she tugged at lifting him on into his home. Jonathan Harrington, Jr. had come home to die before his wife's arms could reach him.

One moment Robert felt desperate and wilted, wishing for a gun to try a shot at a trooper rushing to bayonet a Minute Man kneeling and wobbling. This was Jonas Parker, a cousin of Captain John Parker. He stood his ground, this Jonas Parker. A bullet had torn through the middle of him. Robert saw him sag to his knees while his hands worked at reloading his firelock, his hands fumbled among bullets and extra flints in his hat on the ground before him. Jonas Parker would on his knees reload and fire. He would send a last bullet into the oncoming line. Then a trooper had sighted what Jonas Parker was doing, rushed on him and stretched him flat on the green turf with one straight thrust of the polished steel. Bleeding, defiant, stubborn as any granite boulder in Middlesex County, Jonas Parker single-handed had tried to stop a marching army.

"Huzza!" and "Huzza!" came the cheers of the enemy in a long line of eight hundred marching men in and out of the village and on along the road to Concord, leaving eight dead Minute Men and nine wounded for the village to remember them by. "Huzza!" and "Huzza!" Robert heard them. Their victory had come cheap, one man shot in the thigh, another in the hand, and two bullets nicking the commander's horse, "Huzza!" and "Huzza!" Let the village go bury Jonas Parker, Jonathan Harrington, Jr., Robert Munroe, Isaac Muzzy, John Brown, Samuel Hadley and Asahel Porter. Let them tend the wounds of Francis Brown, Joseph Comee, Nathaniel Farmer, Ebenezer Munroe, Jr., Jedediah Munroe, Timothy Munroe, Solomon Pierce, John Robbins, John Tidd, Thomas Winship and the mulatto Prince Estabrook. "Huzza!" and "Huzza!" rang in Robert's ears.

Was he seeing what he thought his eyes told him, hearing what his ears told him? Was there a drum beating as though of more action to come and what he had seen was only a beginning? Again the klong-klong of the belfry bell on the common and off toward Lincoln, Bedford, Menotomy, rang bells and on the air the sound of gunshots—and those men limping and wobbling toward houses where women were running out from doorways—Robert saw these realities and couldn't get at the queer dreaminess that had him in a soft daze, he who had told brother John Locke in New York there must be more action and less talk.

Then it came over him that two things surged in his blood, pressed deep in his brain, for the moment held back his will to action. One was the awful fact that the long-talked-of war had begun. There could be no going back. Whatever resulted from this day the news of it would go wild and flaming over the other twelve colonies. The deed was done. The fire would spread and run wild. Now would come soldiers, guns, supplies to the army the Continental Congress was raising. Now would come the terrors and the hard grinding that Bliss Edmunds foresaw and rather than live to see it made his exit. Now too the fears, agony and shames that haunted Mim. Yes, Mim, he had not so completely forgotten Mim in a long time. She was the second part of what surged in him. For out there just about where Jonas Parker sagged to his knees and tried to reload his firelock and send one more shot with his dying curse on foreign invaders—just about there on that same spot of turf, Robert had stood with Mim last December in clear moonlight, such a sweet clean moonlight, and their skates slung over their shoulders and their warm blood coursing as their arms held each other tight and they kissed once and they kissed again and they held hands and looked up at the winter moon. They had spoken of the light snow on the ground having an infinite hush near to low music and if you listened you could hear the slow going down of a wind that an hour before had roared at them as their skates curved over the moonlit thin snow on the pond.

Robert shook himself out of this, ran to the common, helped carry two of the dead to their homes, and three of the wounded into Buckman's tavern. There he met Isaiah Thomas who had ridden out from Cambridge. He agreed with Thomas there would be fighting at Concord and the enemy would that afternoon come marching back from Concord and there would be Minute Men by the hundreds firing at the marching troops from roadside fences, rocks, trees, logs, hillocks, hedges, trees. He agreed with Thomas that some of those men, perhaps many of them, would run out of powder, bullets, flints. Robert knew of several hide-outs of ammunition and why shouldn't he take Thomas' horse and ride the back fields and supply men run out of reloading? Eating a slice of cold roast pork with bread, Robert rode away on Thomas' horse.

Hardly beyond the village limits Robert looked toward a pasture corner, near a thicket of briers, and riding up saw two men on the ground. One was a redcoat, both of them still, the one in homespun lying face down. He turned the body over, saw the face and brown hair of Darius Wilming. An eyelid quivered, the two eyes half-opened, and a throaty mumble, "You, Robert?"

"Yes, Darius, what happened, what shall I do?"

The two men had met here, Robert gathered from Darius' slow broken moanings. Neither had seen the other till they came out of different ends of the thicket. They shot. "I killed him . . . I dunno if he killed me . . . I can't stand—"

Robert rode toward the village, overtook tall rawboned Gamaliel Meader carrying a firelock and wondering when he would shoot and how many this day. They went to the nearest house, hitched to a one-horse cart, drove it to the roadside near the thicket, carried Darius to the cart, Meader driving, Robert seated in the cart holding Darius' head and shoulders.

Jake had run out to meet them, had tied the horse, had run up to walk alongside them, no slightest cry from him, tears down his face.

In the doorway of the Liberty Room stood Ruth Wilming and the two daughters, crying, "Oh God, our Darius."

They carried him into the ground-floor bedroom of his father and mother. They loosened his clothes. Robert took off his shoes. The little sounds from him were now a faint moan of pain and again an expulsion of breath as though with relief. Ruth Wilming stood by, once with low hoarse whisper, "Our Darius, merciful God, our Darius." Darius had heard. His eyes didn't open but faintly his voice, "Mother, yes, mother." He was going to lift a hand toward her but the hand dropped. Water, would he like water? The fingers of his right hand lifted and came down—no water now.

Gamaliel Meader came in with young Lemuel Cartwright, indentured for a year as a student under Dr. Joseph Warren. He looked closely at the bullet hole in the outer jacket. "An abdominal wound." He unbuttoned the shirt, slashed an undershirt deftly, and was pushing back the blood-soaked garment that adhered to the area of the wound.

The youth's eyes slowly opened, fluttered and stared, and the slow words, with his turning head, "Mother, it is you. Aggie, Deb, Jake, it happened quick. I kill him. He kills me. So quick. Both of us, him and me."

He sank back, the eyes closed, a white quiver over his face, locks of brown hair down to his eyebrows. Cartwright again tried to get to work on the wound, to examine and make his decisions. At the touch of the groping, probing hands, the body writhed and shuddered.

Suddenly Darius seemed gathering himself. The body stiffened, rose, and he sat erect, wild-eyed yet calm-spoken. "The bosom of God, I am ready for the bosom of God. Father and Mim, tell father and Mim now we must fight. It has come."

He crumpled backward, horizontal again, with a sighing and sleepy moan. "A pleasant valley, mother. . . . In the bosom of God many pleasant valleys. . . . You'll be there, mother, we'll all be there. . . . Even Mim will be there."

A long sleepy moan and, "Kiss me, mother." Ruth Wilming bent over and touched her lips softly to his. The first faint flicker of a smile came over his mouth. "Now I can rest me, mother. The pain is gone. Tell Mim I will go far down the pleasant valley and meet her with a kiss when—"

There his words ended. His shut eyes held fast. "It is the end," murmured Cartwright.

Then quick-spoken but with reverence Cartwright said, "He is beyond my care, others need me this hour," as he picked up his instrument and supply bag.

"You did your best," said Ruth Wilming at the door of the room. "You know you have our thanks."

They stood in quiet at the bed, at the cold silent figure of Darius and his white face with the peace of a great rock across it. They stood a long moment of no one saying anything—the mother, the two sisters, Robert Winshore, and the man everyone knew as a friend and somewhat of a teacher or exemplar of Darius, this tall rawboned Gamaliel Meader, thirty years older than Darius, as faithful as Darius in attendance at their Congregational church. The mother had heard Darius often mention the two of them as "seekers together," Darius saying he would go in snow or rain to the midweek prayer meeting, "if it should be for the sake of hearing the blessed Meader speak one of his prayers."

Ruth Wilming looked toward the gray-headed Meader, a farmer with a wind-bitten face and a wide sculptured mouth, quiet communions in his eyes and composure. He read her as having tidal waves beating in her and she wouldn't break under them.

"Gamaliel Meader," she was saying, "speak a prayer." She knelt on the rag-carpeted floor, with bowed head and closed eyes. The others went to their knees, bent their heads low, their eyes closed. In a sonorous voice husky with earth strength Gamaliel Meader gave forth with the meditations he believed his young friend would have wanted spoken for this hour:

"O God of Hosts, we came to this wilderness and gave it the hard oak and hickory of our plows and the iron of our axes and the sweat of our toil, till in due time we came to call it our own hard-won land. Now we are told by proud men who know not what they do—vain men lacking vision of what we have done, with no understanding of what manner of men we are, not knowing we are freeborn and asking that our children be freeborn—that they must fix their rule over us.

"O God of Hosts, it was our prayer that strife be kept away from us that we might enjoy our hills and rolling acres in peace, that the test of steel, fire and blood be kept away from us. Now they have come three thousand miles across a sea to tell us we are strangers and they will instruct and command us in our way of life.

"O God of Hosts, this youth, this lad of valor and fortitude, stood his ground today as a man, as one freeborn. On an altar of freedom his lifeblood was poured out today and our hearts will remember him and the day of his passing, remember long."

Outside the sky was a dome of clear blue. On the winding road from Lexington to Boston rose dust whirls from the feet of horses and men. Ruth Wilming steadied her knees on the rag carpet, moaned softly, "Yes, remember long," and heard Gamaliel Meader's voice:

"Grant our conduct may be such in thine eyes that we may meet him again in thy eternal arms. Grant that when fiery trial comes to us we shall meet it full-front and dauntless as young Darius Wilming. Be with the grieving father and mother. Let their sorrow be a garment of consecration to them. Let thy tokens visible and thy sacraments invisible be with all hearts that understand his heart and unite themselves with his vision of men freeborn maintaining their freedom.

"Beget wisdom in us as we struggle toward the light. Hammer us into fresh fortitude and steel resolution on thy ancient anvils of trial and fire.

"O infinitely wise Maker of the sky and the land we love, thou who devised the sunfall and the rainfall of peace and the storm bolts of lightning, be thou with us now. Vouchsafe us that liberty may never be a possession profaned by idle mouths, by creatures of vanity, by the devious self-seekers. Pour into us thy grace and fellowship. Give thy great and deep consolations to those who loved this youth as they love life itself. Bestow on us the strength to hold fast. Make us humble and calm for our difficult undertakings in the heavy days to come. We petition thee in Christ's name. Amen."

Alongside the road four miles toward Concord Robert rode the back fields, seeking men run out of powder and bullets for reloading. The enemy had met heavy fire at Concord and had seen men pouring in every direction. And having destroyed what he could find of stores and munitions, the enemy was marching back to Boston, back to safety. As they marched no one could tell from where the next shot would come laying one of their grenadiers dead or wounded in the dusty road. He sent out flanking parties to rove the back fields and search out the sharpshooters. These parties were Robert's main worry and his second worry was the regular fire from the marching troops toward any puff of smoke from behind a fence or tree. Twice he heard the zing of bullets meant for him, rode to cover, and had the luck to keep going till near Lexington his horse gave out and he left it with the bridle off in a friendly cow pasture, walking a mile or more to near Lexington where he saw scurrying Minute Men shooting at the enemy, dodging in and out, some alone, some in couples, others in little bunches, climbing walls and fences, running from woodsheds and barns, from smokehouses and rain barrels to clumps of bushes, then to a tree for a shot and after a shot back behind the tree to reload or to scamper to the rear to reload and then return toward the enemy.

"There's more to shoot at now," grinned one Minute Man to Robert. A fresh army of eight hundred troops had marched in from Boston. The new arrivals were holding the day while those of the other army rested, the army that had started from Boston by moonlight and marched all of last night and after fighting at Concord had marched since noon the dusty six miles back to Lexington.

"We was in the meeting house, the House of God," this Minute Man went on. "A cannon ball crashed in and we made for cover."

Two six-pounder cannon had wheeled to an elevation where they could send fire into anything on the Boston highway for a mile out of Lexington. Black smoke rolled where the home had stood of

Deacon Joseph Loring, now seventy-three years old and not in the fighting, his mansion house, his barn seventy-five feet long and his cornhouse, all going up in smoke.

The Minute Man pointed toward the Loring place. "A nice piece uh proputty, hell of a business to burn it." He had finished reloading his firelock, pointed where the new commander, arrived with the fresh troops, was riding and giving orders, a lean, high-set man on a white horse, his scarlet coat and white breeches "wonderful to shoot at," said the Minute Man, and going on with a grin, "I tried for him twice and got one button. Fellow next to me tried three times and all he got was a button. That general on that horse I bet he's got a bargain with the Devil himself. We shoot five times and get two buttons. I be dingdanged if I'd believe it if I hadn't seen it." He started for a fence corner he had picked, "We'll get him yet, mebbe."

With a dead man's firelock and powder and bullets for thirty reloadings, Robert joined the scurrying hundreds of Minute Men who ranged the back fields and kept up a fire on the enemy troops that began marching to Boston midafternoon. Now for the first time in his life Robert ran his eye along a gun barrel sighting it at another man, aiming to kill. Once he saw his man drop and once again a redcoat falling out of the marching line and Robert couldn't know for sure whether yet he had killed a man. It became dizzy and wearing work to fire, reload, fire again, run ahead and find another place of cover from which to shoot, always with an eye out for flanking parties the enemy sent roving the back fields. There was a monotony about it, at times an exultation, or at moments Robert was dizzy and dreamy.

Near the road he would take a chance on firing from between the slits of a hewn-log hogpen, he decided. The trees and bushes of a lane would cover him as he ran for it, hide him from the line of men slogging along the road in the dust and the sun, men tired and worn as he.

He made it safe in a move to the hogpen, stopped for a long breath and a cooling off before he would pick his target and shoot. Around the corner of a barn he saw two hands and two forearm sleeves moving along the ground. Next came a blue-cockade hat and a red coat and white breeches—a wounded British officer crawling to the shade. Reaching the shade the officer groaned and lay trying to rest, shifting position to ease himself.

Robert leaped to the man, took away a pistol, pulled him into the barn, looked through the blood, mud and dust on the man's face and cried, "Lieutenant George Frame!"

"Yes, Winshore," groaned Frame between set teeth that had parted and set to grinding again.

"You're in pain."

"A ball in the right leg. Broke a bone, I believe." He set his teeth and there came an escape of breath, a high thin shrill of a moan. Robert caught it as the man's amazement that pain could be so exquisite while he still kept his head.

He hated Frame. He had believed he could kill Frame. Now he pitied the man and admired him. This was a fighting man. The darts and quivers of pain slowed down a few moments and Frame twisted to ease himself, then lay calm and closed his eyes as though to rest himself for the next torment.

Robert waited, wondering that his legs didn't carry him straight out the barn door and down the field to safety, for any second of time might see a searching party at the barn door. The dust, mud and blood had come on the face from the man's hands wiping away sweat, Robert saw. Under the crisscross of grime the man's usual fair and florid skin ran in streaks sickly pale.

"You've lost blood."

"Too much."

"Try to bind it?"

"Couldn't, too weak."

The pain came again. He writhed, set his teeth, the high thin shrill of a moan came again.

Robert cut a tie rope in a horse stall, wrapped it tight above the big blotch of red on the white breeches that indicated where the wound oozed. He brought a dipper of water from a bucket on a shelf, offered it, "Not cold but the best there is." Frame nodded. Robert poured more than half the dipper down the eager man's mouth, took a kerchief and washed the face, spoke a "God help you." Then at the crack below the upper hinge of the door Robert scanned the ground toward the road, ran for the hogpen shelter, between a slit saw four men leaving the road and coming up the lane.

At the house the four of them went in at the back door, one coming out to stay at the half-closed door holding his musket, keeping a lookout toward the barn and the back fields, little more than his head, right shoulder and his musket barrel showing. A minute, two or three minutes passed. The door moved full-open and he stood with his musket held careless as though if there were danger it would have showed by now. Robert took a long steady aim, fired, felt the heavy jolt at his shoulder, saw the trooper drop his musket, fling one arm wild and then fall the four steps down from the door.

Robert made for the same winding lane by which he had come, with its fair cover of bush clumps and trees. At the lane end he leaped a fence and ran straightway from the road and soon was farther from the road than any searching party or flanking columns went that day. As he ran the dizziness and dreaminess that had come over him in spells during the afternoon was on him. Over one more fence into another field he would go and then stop to think what next.

His foot caught leaving the fence top. He couldn't make his feet behave as earlier in the day. He made a clumsy fall to the ground and lay there. A flow of comfort ran over him. He would lie here and do his thinking about what next.

Robert hoped it wasn't sleepiness, creeping over him, stealing through him sleepiness, sleepiness. "God, I'm sleepy," he yawned and heard the humming of bees in clover, and in a swift processional saw the horse he lost last night, Revere and Lowell carrying Hancock's trunk, Jonas Parker sagging to his knees on the common, the white face of Darius dying, two redcoats dropping, Frame with set teeth of pain, the redcoat tumbling down the doorstep, bees in clover, and he hoped it wasn't sleepiness. Yet he slept. In the dry thin grass and weeds there, he slept. When he awoke it was past sunset and the stars had come out on the evening of April 19, 1775.

Her man had gone to the fighting and a woman heard alarm bells, the roll of drums and shooting—the shooting had begun. She could see the smoke of a burning house. Next they would be at her house, she said. She must take her three children and run to the woods and hide till the fighting let down. She was thinking which way to go, which woods the best hiding place. Before going she would put on a checked apron. The neat woman wore a clean checked apron and she had that kind of pride. She pulled a bureau drawer where she had seven checked aprons. She put an apron on, carried the baby, told the others to follow. They reached the woods. They lived through the day and came home safe. Hiding in the woods however she had to laugh and the children laughed with her. For she found when she reached the woods she had put on all seven of her checked aprons. One after another while thinking about the fighting, the shooting, the burning, she put on every last one of her aprons and wondered how many she would have put on if she had had seven more aprons.

In the Liberty Room of the Wilming house this was the only thing Robert heard that night to give him a real laugh. Two small stones under his left hip were easy when he first slept but after a while began to grind and he woke hungry. In the Liberty Room he ate six thick slices of wheat bread and fair hunks of cheese, with ale.

In and out the room went people talking of the day, the fighting, the sorrow, the victory. To the Minute Men and the Sons of Liberty the victory called for a jubilee. They would have danced, sung and made merry, only they were tired and there was sorrow. They could be vehement however about the British Regulars, professional troops under officers who had campaigned over Europe, trained soldiers with tried and approved weapons, being defeated and sent reeling from Concord, and their dead and wounded scattered on the dusty road from Lexington to Charlestown. The news of it would go to the other colonies, to London, to the wide world. Long there had been talk of the war. "Now the war has begun."

Over at Menotomy the night before, shortly after Robert left there, the troops had come marching, a searching party knocking at the door of the Black Horse tavern, Elbridge Gerry and two others in their nightshirts running out the back door and lying on the ground in a field of corn stubble that hid them. In the damp night chill with only a linen nightshirt between them and the cold ground they lay an hour or more, crept with caution and quiet back to the tavern. The house had been searched. They would have been taken. It was a hurried search. "It warn't no slow time they was searching," said the Minute Man telling it to Robert, "for under his pillow Mr. Gerry found his timepiece, his nice solid-gold watch, ticking like it knew he would be back soon."

A thousand men had been on the way from Worcester, as the fighting ended at Charlestown. Hundreds of other companies from scattered towns and villages had been on the way. From hill to hill and town to town that morning and afternoon had gone the gunshot signals, the ringing church bells, giving the alarm. At Concord the cannon had been laid in a field and furrows plowed over them, bullets had been thrown into soap barrels, into the bottoms of barrels of feathers. The sixteen-mile march out from Boston and back had failed to reach and destroy the stores they sought. The enemy had lost heavy in dead and wounded and more important to the Patriots, the enemy pride had suffered.

By candlelight, it was told, a shoemaker and his wife in Menotomy were melting pewter plates and running them into bullets. The marching troops saw their light through front window shutters. A soldier knocked at the door, asked what they were doing up so late in the night. The wife answered, "The old man is sick and I'm making him some herb tea." The soldier looked in to see the "old man" who had leaped into bed and didn't take time to stir the fireplace ashes where the wife had dumped the molten pewter.

Gamaliel Meader stopped briefly, saying, "The old men did tolerable well today. Sam Whittemore down near Menotomy River he's eighty years old. His wife asked him to go with her and the children late afternoon so to not be home when the Regulars came back. He went on oiling his flintlock and cleaning two pistols, wouldn't go with her, walked off and picked him a stone wall near Medford, waited till they came marching along. He pulled trigger and saw his man go down. They saw his smoke and rushed on him. He killed another with his pistol. By then they stunned him with a bullet in the head, clubbed him with their musket butts and gave him the bayonet. Now a fellow was here saying he talked with Dr. Tufts who fixed his wounds up in Cooper Tavern and old Sam Whittemore is saying pert as you please he'll live many a year yet. His wife asking him if he ain't sorry he answers, 'No! I would run the same chance again!'"

Deacon Josiah Haynes of Acton was another, said Meader. "He's going on seventy-nine years and he walked from home to Concord and on to Lexington, shooting and reloading. Between Fiske Hill and Lexington common they got him. An earnest man, they tell me, Deacon Haynes was, in his farm work and his church work, and terribly earnest today about driving the British back to Boston.

"And James Hayward from Acton, one foot part cut off, you know," Meader went on. "He comes up to the little Fiske farmhouse south of the road and down the east slope of Fiske Hill. The family was gone and the Regulars had been in the house and took what loot they wanted. And Hayward after a drink from the well going to the house meets a Regular who had stayed. 'You're a dead man!' says the Regular. 'And so are you!' says Hayward. They both shoot. They both fall. The Regular is dead. Hayward they say won't live. The ball went through his powder horn and drove splinters into his side. In his bed he calls for his powder horn and bullet pouch and shows them. A pound of powder and forty bullets he started with and the powder about gone and only two or three bullets left. 'You see,' he told them. 'I am not sorry. I die willingly for my country.' Who would have believed it, limping on that foot part cut off, miles and miles shooting and reloading?"

The Minute Man of earlier in the day came up to Robert with a grin. He had met another sharpshooter who aimed at the commander on the white horse. "And like me and the other fellow all he got was a button. Three good men try their guns three times to knock him off that white horse. And all we get is three buttons off his coat." He had learned that the man on the white horse was Earl Percy who headed the second army from Boston and took command at Lexington. "I hear he rode on into Charlestown, the luckiest man and horse in America today. Mebbe we should've shot at the horse stead of him. But somebody else than us would have to do it. A purty white horse, with a shine. I could kill him but not that horse."

Agnes had sat at the table as Robert munched endless bread and cheese. She told of the burial late in the afternoon. The body of Darius had gone with the others into a broad grave that received all of Lexington's dead. No sermon or preaching, just a simple short prayer by the Reverend Jonas Clarke as a service. Off in a corner was the trench, near the woods, and the horse carts came with the boxes made of four large boards nailed together and "the slain were let down, one by one, and we waited to see them covered up with clods, and then for fear the British should find them, Reverend Clarke thought some of the men had best cut some pine and oak boughs and spread them on the place of burial so it looked like a heap of brush."

It came harder for Agnes to tell of Deb's grief. The young farmer at Lincoln between Concord and Lexington, who was going to marry Deb—he had been caught by flankers and lingered and died. Deb had run two miles to his home, where they had taken him, and he died holding her hands and saying he was sure he would get well.

What of Jake? Robert was asking. Agnes lighted with glee about Jake. It was his own idea to go to the back fields with two jugs of water. From time to time came Minute Men desperate with thirst and "here was this boy beckoning them to come drink the water he brought for them."

"I haven't seen Ma tonight," said Robert.

"Plumb tuckered, she just fell on a bed and went to sleep."

"And Deb?"

"She's with Pa."

"And he—he?"

"It's hard to tell about him."

"Where is he?"

"In the room there." Aggie nodded her head toward it. "On the same bed where you saw Darius this morning."

"You can tell me the worst, Aggie."

"He's suffering—"

"Then he is alive, thank God."

"Alive, yes, but God, in what a way! He wriggles and twists and moans with the pain of it."

"He was shot, then?"

"Him too, down toward Menotomy late afternoon, behind a pile of rails and his right arm raised up over the rails. Says he was a damned fool to let that arm get up there. They got his arm, shot a ball through it, splintered the bone. The doctor says it will be summer and fall healing, if all goes well. After that the arm will be crooked, no use."

"Ma said if you came to wake her before you went away," Aggie went on. "She didn't have a chance this morning to ask you about Mim."

"I don't know where I go from here, don't know where I'm staying tonight."

"Stay in Darius' room. Darius won't mind." Aggie rose. "I'll wake Ma."

The crowd had been thinning out and the last stragglers were going while Ruth Wilming and Robert talked of the Wilming home and farm and the press of fate on it this day.

"He suffers, the pain won't let him sleep," she said with a nod of her head toward the room. "Once he gnashed his teeth and said anybody that ever hated him was welcome to see him now and it might be that Mim would like to come in. Cruel to say but he was part out of his right mind with the pain.

"Mim should know about today, soon as we can get word to her," she went on after a pause and Robert with nothing to say. "I suppose we can't ask her to come back here and help put us on our feet again. But she ought to know. At least it might be she can come out here and advise with us. I know she'd want to have a look at where Darius is under the ground."

The last came with a quick stifled choke. Robert drank half the mug of fresh ale before him, put his two hands over the two of Ruth Wilming that lay folded on the table. "You are a brave woman."

"She's wonderful," said Jake, sliding into a chair at the table with a gentle and sly smile. "She's wonderful like Mim is."

"I'll get the news to Mim," said Robert. "I mean, I'll try." The town of Boston would be triple-guarded now, they knew. Ruth Wilming eyed Robert as though he could be somewhat her own.

Jake's pointed face took a shine, his lips and eyes fluttered with a smile. "Tell Mim it was like she said, hell to pay. Then tell her the blue sky didn't come down and the stars was out like usual."

"I'll tell her that, Jake, your words exact."

Ruth Wilming quietly opened the door and held it for Robert to step into the room. On the bed lay Noah Wilming, the right sleeve cut from his gray wool shirt, his right arm in splints and bandages laid on a pillow. Deb sat in a chair, her body sloped downward, her eyes closed. She awoke a minute later when her father let out a moan in a sliding gamut from high to low. Then Noah Wilming saw his wife and Robert, closed his eyes, twisted all his body except the right arm on the pillow, and spoke with closed eyes after settling quiet again. "It can't last ever, Robert. Nothing lasts ever. It will end. Everything ends."

"It's hard, Mr. Wilming. We know it's hard."

They stood a minute or two, saw Deb falling to her sleep again. Ruth Wilming took Robert to Darius' room and before leaving, "How is Mim? There wasn't time to ask this day."

He told her briefly of Saturday night, his escape from Frame and the Regulars, and, "Mim is restless. She don't know which way to turn. She's fighting her way through herself and a lot of enemies outside of herself. But she isn't weakening under it. She's strong, Ma, she's got terrible strengths in her, good as any of us, I guess, and it may take time but I think she'll come through." And Robert kissed the mother on the cheek, "Good night, Ma. I'll try to make it into Boston tomorrow night."

Sleepy though he was Robert before getting into bed thumbed casually in a candlelight through two books of sermons Darius had dogeared, then more slowly in the pages of three other books, the Bible, *The Pilgrim's Progress*, and a tattered copy of the play of *Hamlet* that three generations had passed along to a fourth. Mim liked to imitate a deacon who said, "What I make of it is that right handsome young feller Hamlet saw so much sin he got teched in the head." Mim would add, "Hamlet was mad, in a way, but not so mad as the scheme of life where he couldn't fit himself in."

Folded in *The Pilgrim's Progress* was a sheet in Mim's handwriting, a poem, "credited to one Thomas Dekker, the year I know not but very old." Robert could hear her voice as she had said the poem that afternoon when they had walked to Aunt Ellen's little farm and seen autumn leaves whirl scurrying toward the sunset:

> Art thou poor, yet hast thou golden slumbers?
> O sweet content!
> Art thou rich, yet is thy mind perplexed?
> O punishment!
> Dost thou laugh to see how fools are vexed
> To add to golden numbers, golden numbers?
> O sweet content! O sweet, O sweet content!
> Work apace, apace, apace, apace;
> Honest labour bears a lovely face.
> Then hey nonny nonny, hey nonny nonny!

In the Bible as a marker of the Sermon on the Mount, Robert met a small leaf whereon Mim had shaped in exquisite miniature letters Roger Bacon's The Four Stumbling Blocks to Truth. Folded with it was a scrap of rough wrapping paper where Darius had written in big letters: "I have studied these much with myself and with Gamaliel Meader. We are sure only we have not stumbled over Number Four." Of this Robert was certain, Darius was one who had never tripped and fallen as one more fool over "concealment of ignorance by ostentation of seeming wisdom."

Once in the night Robert woke out of a swift dream when he heard Mim in the room whispering, "Darius, you haven't really gone, have you? Darius, you didn't mean to leave us, did you?"

* * * * * * * * * *

Chapter 22

* * * * * * * * * *

I Must Forget You

LAND arrivals into Boston came by the Neck road. Men afoot and mounted, men on carts and wagons with women or families, came over the Neck every day. Now after April 19, 1775, they were stopped by the officers and guards and questioned more closely about who they were, where going and what doing when they got there. Yet the guard couldn't be too strict in some cases. Boston had to eat, provisions were not plenty, and carts and wagons loaded with livestock, poultry, vegetables, by the scores came through with little search unless something roused suspicion.

A load of hay for the horses of majors and colonels was more than welcome, hay being scarce, Whig farmers bringing in hay only to Whig friends. Midafternoon the officer of the guard liked it that the driver of a load of hay whistled to his horses and himself the good old tune of "The British Grenadiers."

The driver having passed through drove his load to the barn of a Whig, waited to see who might be looking as he forked the hay into the loft. And no one saw a man slide out of the hay and into the barn. What followed was complicated. The Whig barn-owner was a Minute Man and a Son of Liberty, twice arrested as a rioter, often under suspicion, one of the men in the Silas Ludgate affair. They had often come to his house to question him and at times had his house and barn watched. He brought food to Robert Winshore in the barn while it was still daylight near sunset. He went to Aunt Ellen's and learned that Marintha Wilming, because of her associations with Robert, was under suspicion and they had called several times to press her in questionings of Robert, of the secret organizations, of his work for them. When Robert came to Aunt Ellen's it must be after dark, keeping to the alley and entering by the back door, as he did.

Aunt Ellen had come down for a greeting and returned to her room, and halfway up the stairs, rather softly, "You'll be safer to make it a short stay, children."

Their arms went around each other and they kissed and Robert didn't want to make anything of it but noticed Mim didn't rub her ear lightly below his collarbone. "And she took my kisses without returning kiss for kiss," ran a blur in his head and blood, a misgiving he could have no time for now. She had slipped out of his arms without being abrupt and yet too soon and too smoothly she did it. That too was a blur in his head and blood and no time now to look back at it.

He seated himself on their old settee, bent forward with elbows on knees and one hand wrapped around fingers of his other hand. Mim pulled a chair and sat opposite him, elbows on knees, one hand curling its hold on the other hand's thumb.

"It broke yesterday," he said.

"Yes, the war has begun."

"And it comes hard."

"You wanted it to come hard. You can't have a war not hard."

"I have a message for you—and news."

"I'd as lief you brought me no messages. Enough news there was when we met last."

"What is wrong, Mim?"

"The war is wrong, Robert."

"You know what you're saying, Mim, and you know my answer."

"Agony, dead men, cripples, waste, ruin, women and children waiting for those who never come home."

He looked into her face, a deep and long look.

She went on, her faint smile hard and mocking. "The wedding was to have been in June. Whatever year it was the wedding in June, the blossom month. In my father's house the wedding and Jake to fill the big Liberty Room with flowers and Darius with his brown hair and brown eyes would usher the few invited to their chairs. Then after the words 'until death do us part' and the rest of it, Darius would drive us to our own little ten-acre place. By then the moon would be up and before going into the house we would stand under an apple tree and look up at the moon through a latticework of white apple blossoms. And once we joked that the first baby would be a boy with brown hair and brown eyes the same as Darius."

The faint smile had faded. Her lips stretched wide over the gaunt bone structure of her face. It was a mask rather than a face. "Apple blossoms—pooh—and the moonlight a mishmash with the stink of stale cheese. What do you and your rabble care? Ashes and blood now —and good women crying for their lost ones."

"You may yet understand better the hearts of your friends and kinfolk. The sorrow may come less bitter."

Her words sprang. "I know more now than I can understand. The more I know the deeper twists the bitterness. I trust no one, not even myself. Tories and Rebels, they both lie and lie how noble they are, how sacred their causes. On both sides false and cunning trickeries, crazy hate and defiance. Both sides wanted this war. Now they have it. Your Sam Adams wanted it. You followed him wanting it. Now you've both got it."

"A terrible sincerity you have, Mim."

"So you *say*."

"A storm has come. It began far back. Sam Adams couldn't bring it. It began before he was born. A voice, that's all Sam Adams is. He says what we want said." Robert put out a hand, clutched one of her wrists. "Before giving you the message and news I came to deliver, I'm telling you the days to come will bring you lessons. I have no lesson for you. I leave it to time. I'm not throwing any persuasions at you. I still value beyond price that fine sincerity of yours."

"So you say and it may be you know what you say and mean it."

Feet scuffing the plank walk outside, and Robert ran on tiptoe to the kitchen, and Mim answered the doorknock, in enough clear moonlight to know the face.

"Lieutenant Frame! Would you come in?"

"Thank you."

"I was just going upstairs. Enough of the moon comes in for you to see this chair. Seat yourself and I will go to the kitchen for candlelight."

She returned with the two stub candles lighted, set them on the table. "And now?"

"I have come on two matters. The first is official." And Francis

516

Frame was grave with a touch of severity though he had the peculiar moon-round face that puts on severity with effort. His having an acquaintance with her was the reason his superiors had sent him to get her solemn word that she was not playing the role of an informer, making reports to the Rebels of intelligence picked up among her Loyalist friends. She gave him as solemn word as he wanted that she was no informer.

"Your association with the lawless and incendiary Robert Winshore has been intimate, has it not? In fact, it has been rather generally accepted that you were bespoken to him for marriage, has it not?"

"That is true."

"Naturally it gave rise to suspicion, to uneasiness, to a feeling—you will pardon me for being so candid—to a feeling that you might be a colaborer with him in his designs of violence and treason."

"If Mr. Winshore were here, he would testify that I have opposed his views and designs and have tried to prevail on him toward a different course of conduct."

"You may be assured, Miss Wilming, that it will be a pleasure for me to report that you have made these declarations and avowals."

"Avowals?"

"Is it not a solemn enough hour to term them avowals?"

"I presume so. I am not yet accustomed to these strict examinations." He saw her his full equal in severity. Her eyes held austerity and she wasn't trying. She now asked, "And what was the second matter, Lieutenant Frame?"

Now she felt sorry for him. This was the grief of a man hit hard. His voice shook. "A ball in the leg . . . my brother . . . yesterday . . . above the knee . . . no course but amputation, said the surgeons—"

His lower lip hung loose. That and his moist eyes held the sorrow and pity, that and his thick voice. "Death, Miss Wilming, I am not sure but I would rather witness death than a major amputation. You may know the procedure, the ordeal, we might say. They bind him down fast with leather straps none of his struggles can break. They proceed with their knives for the flesh and the saw for the bone. In the beginning he moans and screams with the pain. Then he faints away and awakes to go through an agony of healing and then a cripple for life.

"Before the operation"—and now Francis Frame was soft and tender, with no trace of severity—"my brother spoke of you. He said he might not come through. He wished to be remembered to you. He requested me to present to you his compliments and to say to you for him, 'Assure her that I hold her ever in the highest regard.' Those were his words."

"It is sad to hear, deeply sad. You must convey to him my respect and my affection. Give him the message that I speak prayers for his recovery and his future. And I should be asking now, he will recover?"

"The surgeons believe so. They value his high courage, they say."

"And his future?"

"He leaves shortly for England. The fabrication of a substitute limb when amputation is above the knee has added difficulties. We hope now for his recovery. The plans for his career after that can wait."

Now Lieutenant Francis Frame paused. Mim said nothing. She saw on his face the fading of sorrow and pity and again the official look, his moon-round cheeks and chin trying for severity, accuracy, dispatch.

"You have heard, Miss Wilming, that Robert Winshore was in the fighting yesterday?"

"No, it is news to me."

"As near as we gather it Winshore was the first to find my brother. He dragged him into a barn, perhaps gave him some slight assistance, then ran out of the barn, shot and killed one of our men and disappeared into the back fields. We have learned too that he was active in riding fields and woods between Lexington and Concord with powder and bullets for Rebels whose supplies were exhausted. We consider him a dangerous man."

He paused. The nub of it was coming, Mim saw. His question came simple and direct as she might please. He was asking, "May I have your word, Miss Wilming, that if you hear or know of his return to Boston you will thereupon immediately notify us?"

"You speak with candor and with courtesy, Lieutenant Frame. And I appreciate that what you do is in line of duty. Yet you must know there is a stern severity and there are sharp implications underlying your words. What manner of a character have I become that you must pay an official call on me at my home in night hours to require a pledge from me that I shall serve you as an informer?"

"A war began yesterday, Miss Wilming. Boston from this day is under the strictest martial law. The Rebels who killed our men yesterday want to kill more of us. It is our lives or theirs. They hunt down our spies and informers and we must hunt down theirs. This must be evident to you, Miss Wilming. It is nothing extreme under the circumstances that we require of you."

"I shall think it over, Lieutenant Frame, in every turn and viewpoint. You will find, I believe, that I shall not be lacking in due and solemn appreciation of what it is you desire."

"It is a matter where we cannot stand on delay, Miss Wilming."

Mim rose and moved toward the door. Lieutenant Frame stood up, moved with her till they stood at the door.

"I am asking you, Lieutenant Frame, I must ask you, to be so good as to come to this house tomorrow night. I shall then give you my decision. Your request is abrupt. I do not refuse it. I ask a day of time. It may be that I shall give you exactly the pledge you ask and give you the fullest possible accommodation. Or it may be that I must follow some other course. It is a matter I must consider."

"I regret I must report to my superiors that I find you hesitant and quibbling. I had higher opinion of you. However I shall call on you at this house and the same hour tomorrow evening."

He bowed himself out the door and his polished high boots scrunched on the plank walk in the moonlight.

On shadow feet Robert joined Mim at the shutters watching the black boots, the scarlet coattails, the blue three-cornered hat, turn off the gravel path and move up the street. Mim after a minute or two stepped out, walked to both corners, went round the house and up the alley in two directions, returned to the front room, to the chair opposite Robert on the settee. "We are safe now, I think, for what little further we have to say."

"Do you remember, Mim," Robert began, as much to himself as to her, and as though both of them were tired, bedazzled, worn in the whirl of circumstance and what he was saying might help, "Do you remember the night on the green at Lexington in a sweet clean moonlight and we kissed once and kissed again, and later we stood still listening to the slow going down of a wind that an hour before had roared and whined around us as our skates curved on the moonlit pond? Do you remember?"

Like the thud of a flat stone falling plunk into a quiet pool came Mim's voice, "Is this your message? Time counts. Is this the news you bring?"

Now he couldn't fathom her. He had seen her step away from him more than once though never so far away.

"I guess you're right, Mim. I guess I oughtn't be dreamy and maybe instead," here his voice rasped, "I ought be asking you what's got into you? What the hell's the matter with you?"

She too couldn't quite fathom him. Now she said he had never been so far away from her. It was too far. It hurt enough for her to say, "You could be cruel to me, Robert. Once I thought nothing could ever happen where you could be cruel to me. That was before the Reggs affair and the Ludgate atrocity."

This he wouldn't meet. She could go farther with this and he would sit dumb.

"Of course," and she spoke loud now, she didn't care who heard her or who might come, "of course I remember the kisses on Lexington green and the hush on the snow that was a whisper of music only we two standing still in the moonlight could hear. That's a memory," she went on, "and when both of us clean forget it it will be a hell of a memory.

"Now this little folly here," as she crossed the room and came back with one hand in a clasp, "I did it for the sake of memories. There was an hour in a hazel thicket when we stood tiptoe together and plucked stars from the meadows of the sky and that was a memory. There was another hour we snuggled close in a wagon and tried to bring down a ring of brass chains circling the moon." Now she was crying her words in a low swift murmur and Robert sat awe-struck and swept away by her.

"Wear it, keep it in all weathers," she said, her hand opening as she reached over, thrust a hand inside his coat and into his wool-shirt pocket. "I began making it weeks ago and went through with it and couldn't think of keeping it for myself having you and the memories in mind every moment of stitching it."

His hands took it, unfolded and rolled it, clutched and caressed it, a large kerchief of thin blue silk.

"A trifle—keep it—keep it to forget me by," she was saying.

"To live pleasant, to skip the hard places with a light hurt, I might be able to do it, Mim."

"So that's the message you came at danger to yourself to deliver."

"If you care to take it as a message—and I wish I hadn't had to come."

"If there is more, tell it. You can't pile grief too high this night."

His pause was long. He would have liked to be whisked away. He should have made excuses to her mother and not promised. And it was baffling she hadn't rushed questions at him about the reports flying over Boston of the fighting at Lexington and Concord yesterday, why she wasn't asking who, what, when, where, and how did it happen among the neighbors of her youth and childhood. That perhaps was her pride, her clinging to her notion that he shouldn't have gone, he shouldn't have had any part in it. And the press of suspicion and official questioning of her had done something.

Her guess ran he had some last plea for her to join in works for the Sons of Liberty. She knew there was a light dash of evil in her now mocking, "We have heard of a man risking his life to bring a message to be spoken and then at the final moment forgetting the words," adding as he still sat in his long pause, "There were evenings less dangerous when we said, 'We can't stay here all night.'"

"Marintha." It was both a whisper and a groan. She caught herself sobered and awed, threw it off, and mocked, "Yes, that's the name, you remember the name."

"Marintha," and Robert found himself trying to speak with a disembodied voice, in words detached, monotonous as the regular pendulum of an impersonal clock telling the time to the just and the unjust. "Marintha, yesterday morning the goddam foreign invaders of Middlesex County with a bullet of hate shattered the right arm of your father and with another lead ball of evil aim they killed your brother Darius."

In the dim light of the moon through the shutters, she couldn't read his face as she arose, as she stopped in her pacing to and fro. It was too amazing and shocking to be true. It was one more lie flung into the tangles and turmoils of illusion with which her brain had wrestled in days just passed.

She stood before him, dazed, not certain she heard. He gave it to her again, shorter as a statement, and again detached, monotonous as the inevitable brass pendulum of time to the just and the unjust:

"They crippled your good father for life and they murdered your sweet and brave brother Darius. I stood at the bedside and saw him d e and heard his last words and what he said was, 'The pain is gone. Tell Mim I will go far down the pleasant valley and meet her with a kiss.' "

She turned and walked five slow steps to the front window. She stood looking and half seeing through the shutters and half seeing the moonwhite on the grass, on the plank walk, on the cedar branches.

She turned, walked two steps feeling the way with slow feet, stood silent toward Robert a long moment. Then he saw her sway and crumple to the rag rug on the floor before he could reach her.

He ran to the kitchen for a dipper of water, laid a wet kerchief over her forehead, eyes and face, saw her eyelids flutter and slowly open, saw her coming to, heard her faintly, "Take me home, Robert Winshore, take me home. You took me too far away. Now take me back." The eyes settled in quiet, little bars of moonlight from the shutters marking her face, the eyelashes still, her tongue moistening the lower lip, and her words Robert couldn't get clear till at the end of a pleading, "You wouldn't fool me, Robert, you wouldn't fool me, Robert," five times and more, "You wouldn't fool me, Robert."

She lifted her head, raised her shoulders, sank back, with closed eyes seemed to rest, seemed near sleep.

Then she pushed at him, wanting him away and not touching her, sat up, straightened herself and shook her head and held it high, gave a ripple of wild laughter as she faced the ceiling.

Then came her words spinning out in ripples. She was laughing it. "Now Marintha Wilming is herself again, Robert Winshore. Marintha the bright child with her skates on Lexington green listening to the wind go down, the tall proud howling stallion of a wind become a wee mouse of a vanishing zephyr, we heard it and what of it, sir, I ask, what of it?"

She moved into a heady mockery, a tipsy groping. "What a delightful evening, sir. What a marvelous night we have had, sir, what conversations with the shadows of barn rats and man-killers. A pleasant valley he said and he would go far down the pleasant valley and meet his sister with a kiss. And an arm off here and a leg off there and an arm off here and a leg off there—it's like you can drum it on drums of fate—dead in the morning still dead in the afternoon and when the evening stars creep out and look down dead and still dead—an arm off here and a leg off there and when a leg comes off he screams till he forgets his leg is coming off, he can't see, he can't hear his leg is coming off. And if your lover comes it is your duty to tell us your lover has come. He is a dangerous man, a lawless incendiary, and we want our hand on him, tell us when he comes so we may put our hands on him, the rat, the foul and squeaking rat. What smooth and conniving silhouette of warships on the horizon brought them? And whither goest thou, me lad, and thinkest thee thou knowest whither thou goest?"

In swift ripples of a tipsy abandon it came from her. She paused and it came slow with a shiver of amazement at her bones. "What sweet angels of fathomless doom have overheard our kind words to each other this night, sir?"

Then again swiftly. "Apples, how many the times Darius and I picked a big red apple, so handsome an apple, and put our teeth into it to find it a mushy wallow of neither taste nor content. And again we met windfalls of scrawny little pippins with no reputation and we filled our mouths with them and glutted ourselves with their scrawny little perfections."

Small moonbars through the shutters rested on her head and Robert saw the burnish of her chestnut hair as airy slats of fine bronze. Her hair had come loose on one side and broken ropes of it lay on the wide white linen collar of her left shoulder.

Now she was far beyond him. He would hesitate at touching her. She was so far away, he said to himself, that if he should reach out a hand she wouldn't be there and his hand would be still reaching toward her into empty air.

Time counted. And it didn't. What did they have more of than time for speaking the finalities that hung in the air, for saying what they could not say in the long time, the looming stretch of time ahead of them?

Mim scrambled to her feet, stood at the window, looked out. "Here we can see who might come to listen to our chitchat, our elegant and amusing chitchat."

She bowed, curtsied in mimicry of courtesy and went on smooth and broken, broken and smooth. "Having broken a heart, would you care to pick up the pieces, sir, and put them in a little snuffbox to carry away, to gaze at early or late standing perhaps among yellow pie-eyed daisies, pigweed, ragweed, sow thistle in a cow-pasture fence corner? Or you might give them to an auctioneer and hear him, What can I get to start this? A broken heart—a little mending and it's good as new—what am I bid? Yes, all the pieces of a broken heart in a little oblong of silver and you can take it in your hand and say with sea music, if you can manage it, I remember her, I do, I do, I do, remember remember her and the bits of shadowcreep woven in her thistledown hair, I remember a warm lingering kiss she gave me on Lexington green one night when a brass moonfall came down and a white snowfall drifted on our shoulders."

In her pause she made a grotesque mouth. "I'm a clown, always a clown you have found me. How can there be a brass moonfall and a white snowfall at the same time? There must be a mistake somewhere. Yes, there must be a grave error, some figure in the arithmetic of Boston streets and Lexington green got lost and wasn't there when they added, subtracted, multiplied and divided and especially divided." It was wearing her down, losing its weave and timebeat. She was asking, "Or was it a cipher, sir, a naught, a zero, a goose egg, an oval of no promise, no crimson or folly, no bright seduction, deaths instead of weddings, deaths on deaths instead of wedding after wedding?"

She took three quick steps toward the center table, staggered, stood heady and swaying. Robert stepped toward her. She drew back and away, her hands out as though she would push him away. What of fantasy rushed from her now he afterward saw in a dream as a relentless line of white flame destroying itself, eaten, going and gone as it reached an equally relentless black pool of green scum. She would have it so.

"Listen, sir. Let your ears gather my farewell to you, sir. In the sacred name of all the crowning apple blossoms of next June, I promise to forget you. So completely will I put you out of my mind you may know you will not be the least of my thoughts because you will not be among any of my thoughts. I shall kiss my father's crippled arm. I shall stand at the grave of my brother on a Sabbath of gray rain and blowing mist and I shall bless his name and bless his curly brown head of hair and bless his slow brown eyes of faith that never betrayed man, woman, nor beast of burden. But you, sir, I shall forget. Letter by letter I shall forget your name till I cannot remember how to spell it."

Robert saw the very tumult and rioting freedom of her speech had its music of consolation for her, had eased awful and inexplicable thorns piercing her. She now measured slow words. "A dark and tangled wonder has happened that can never be solved. I would have brought you flagons and chasubles, moonmist and rainbows. Instead I brought you the trifle of a kerchief of blue silk, silk for you to remember my heart was made soft as moonmist, and the blue of it blue as a blue moon shining on a blue sea for you to remember me by. And you, what did you bring me, for exchange, by way of barter, by way of a bargain? Why, you brought me the pains of death and the aches of hell."

She swayed. Robert caught her fall. He held her in his arms on the settee. She sobbed in his arms. He went because there was no mistaking her command. "Don't pity me. I'll do my own pitying. Go now, Robert Winshore. Go and stay gone. I must forget you. The forgetting will come hard but I will forget."

* * * * * * * * * *

PART TWO

Chapter 23

* * * * * * * * * *

You Cannot Conquer a Map

MICHAEL McGILLICUDDY had come to the back door of the house, knocked softly, and Jean Shepherd had let him in. She had given him a cut of pork pie, a warm swig from a bottle of rum without letting him have the bottle, and sent him to the cellar. He would eat and wait there while she finished cooking and serving the supper.

It was ten days since she had seen him. "Michael my man, where for God's sake have you been?" she had asked. And his story was that for being drunk, disorderly and fighting with a night watchman, he was arrested and given ten days in Philadelphia city prison, the jail. That was all. The rest of it he would tell her after supper when he helped her wash the dishes. Down the cellar he went.

Jean Shepherd believed him. His pockmarked and ruddy face looked thin, his gray eyes wild and bloodshot. His blue-and-white worsted stockings were torn and hung in tatters. His new shoes were gone and in their place a scuffed pair full of holes. Worse yet his buckskin breeches were gone and in their place a cloth pair in tatters. Either he had been in the city jail or some corner of Philadelphia as evil, thought Jean. Most likely it was the jail. She believed him. He would tell her later. "It's a God's shame, the way the poor man looks," she was saying.

Jean cut the pork pie in portions so it could hardly be told that a piece had been sliced out, set it on the table for the two men and two women, set dishes of carrots, buttered parsnips, wheat bread, cheese, cider. When they had finished these victuals, helping themselves, Jean brought on an apple pie and coffee. When they had gone to the front room Jean called down the cellar and Michael McGillicuddy came up.

They were a couple, each five feet three inches in height. He was a thick ranting man and she plump and lusty. He drank hard and amazed her at the liquor he could carry. She smoked a clay pipe, bowl after bowl every day, and took snuff between-times, and her black underteeth didn't show when she smiled.

The jail had a big stone-walled room with iron doors, Michael told her, all prisoners packed in this one room. No sooner had the watch pushed him through the door of this room than they rushed him. "Like a pack of hungering dogs they hurled themselves on me, showing their teeth like dogs." They tore the clothes off him, hat, shoes and all. They stood him naked in a corner by himself. His clothes would come to him after he said they could have his few coins for the jailkeeper to bring in rum and gin. He said Yes and would like now to kill the two fellows who brought him his clothes and let him know his buckskin breeches and new pair of shoes were good for drink money and he would get along with the old shoes and tattered breeches they handed him. He could have fought them one by one "but they were in league against me and I would have to fight them all to oncet—so now, Jean, I look like a beggar, I know I do and it's the will of God."

His hands trembled, his eyes had fear, remembering the big room with young men and old, boys and girls, wrecks of women, crowded together, with straw over the stone floor to sleep on and scarce room for all to lie down at night and creepers, bedbugs and lice everywhere, you couldn't get away from them. In wide leather buckets they voided excrement, at daybreak those not in favor with the jailkeeper took their turns at emptying the buckets.

The farthest end of the room, in the lingo of inmates hardened to the place, was termed "the stink corner" or "the shit stall." There night and day lay a woman who had been in nearly a year and two men who had served a year and a half. Under their rotting ragged clothes could be seen scabs and gray-backed lice, cracks of yellow flesh open with filth, and a heavy odor, a reek and stench.

"You should meet the likes of the same in any other place," Michael was saying, "you would puke at the sight and not berate yourself for pukin. But in jail you kept yourself from pukin unless it would be you wanted them to kick you in the backsides for a faintheart and for lackin the guts of a man."

Michael talked between mouthfuls of more pork pie, of vegetables, apple pie and coffee. He wolfed his food before Jean. Ten days of hard foul bread morning and evening, a thin soup at noon, "rather made me forget the taste of food." Jean told him: "Now beware of overfillin, twould make ye sick."

Those three in the corner, the woman and the two men in their filth and misery, said Michael, there were some of the others who would look at them as though they were many many miles below somewhere. "They looked so low you believed men and women couldn't sink lower and not be in hell itself." The woman sat up to the extent of her head on an elbow one day and Michael heard a bloat-faced younger woman ask her what she was in for. The answer came, "I'm a slut men don't want any more, you bitch you," and she tried to spit at the questioner. "Her mouth drooled having lost the strength to spit," said Michael.

"You've had your fill, you'll be sick, Michael," said Jean.

"I do be thinkin, Jean," said Michael, a smile with a warm glow over him.

"You'll be a new man soon."

"I'm a new man now, Jean, what with you and the food." He put an arm around her, gave her a thumping kiss and a slap on a buttock, took a dishtowel and joined her at wiping dishes, prancing to put them in place on a cupboard shelf.

The door to the kitchen opened and the man of the house and his woman stepped in.

"You near scairt me, Mrs. Winshore," said Jean who now couldn't be scared at the pleasantly mischievous faces that had come, and asking, "Did you hear? Did you listen to us?"

"No, we came to say good night and didn't know you had company."

"You've seen Michael here before, you know how the two of us are."

"But he looks different now from the other times."

"If you'd listened you'd know why the likes of him is so different."

Then Ordway Winshore and his wife Mary Burton Winshore brought in chairs and seated themselves while Jean and Michael went on with the dishwiping and Michael saying a sorry fool he was that he did get drunk and that he did act disorderly and he shouldn't have struck the watchman a blow that felled him—but the city prison, had Mr. Winshore ever seen that room where they keeps 'em?

"Only from the outside, Michael, though I'm not sure but I will see it or a place like it one of these days."

Michael told his story, with the comment once, "I'm not a man to shrink from evil, Mr. Winshore. I've seen much of evil that wasn't all evil by far. But that big room with the young and old, menfolk and women, two girls just off the streets and runnin sores on their faces, it had a rot to it, rottin those who were in the room and goin out to rot the jailkeeper, the town watchman, and fine folk who have never seen the place. The deep rot I smelled there, Mr. Winshore, Mrs. Winshore, I know it spreads beyond our knowin." He had forgotten about his dishtowel and the drying, his gray eyes wild and bloodshot, tears in his shrill swift voice.

There was more. He might find work to his liking. Yet even if he did he might think it better to go northward and fight with the army of General Washington. Part of it was he liked the idea of America being free and independent. And the other part, he spoke it more directly toward Jean, "I think I'll end in the fightin, macushla. My father was a fightin man and his father. The McGillicuddys have ever been fightin men."

The Winshores said good night. They would talk of it further tomorrow. Mrs. Winshore was sure she could find shoes and breeches "more becoming" to Michael. "Mr. Winshore doesn't need them."

"I'll see he has a place to sleep," said Jean with a nod toward Michael and looking Mrs. Winshore straight in the eyes. "And I'll do my best at comfortin him." With that Jean reached for tobacco leaves, crushed them to fill her clay pipe and began sucking at her good-night smoke.

Henry Tozzer and his wife were the couple having supper with the Winshores that evening. It was a year and more since Ordway and Mary Burton Winshore, newly married in Boston, had visited the Tozzers in New York.

A year now and there were names come out of nowhere to burn with meaning, words that meant death and scars and the letters of them spelled as with scarlet on snow and with black embers in spotless white ashes. Names—Bunker Hill, where the farmers met the Regulars and stood their ground till their powder and shot ran out and Joseph Warren died swearing "the proud disdain" he had sung in his verses of "free Americkay"—names on a scroll: the names Lexington, Concord, Boston, the Continental Army—and George Washington strange, quiet, solid, responsible, the Commander-in-Chief of the Continental Army, his name a hope, not yet written in blood color.

The Continental Army, authorized by the Continental Congress, swarmed to Boston, for months pinning the enemy army prisoner in that city, at last planting its cannon where they could sweep the enemy warships. The Continental Army in March of 1776 moved nearer and fortified and again moved up and fortified till the enemy saw it must surrender or sail away and it chose to sail away taking a thousand New England Loyalists to Canada.

Now the fighting was to come around New York to see who would hold that city. Around that port the Continental Army was moving to meet the enemy.

"Your boy Locke is with them," Tozzer had said.

"And my boy Robert," Winshore had added softly.

"I saw Locke after what they did to Rivington, he was in it," said Tozzer.

"He was?"

"Oh yes. He is a courier and on some duty came down from the Boston siege on his horse. You should see Locke on a horse. He's a good one. You could think he had been on horses all his life, the way he rides. His face has the outdoor weather on it. Maybe he shouldn't be a printer."

"And you say he was in the Rivington affair?"

"In Connecticut riding back to Boston he meets Captain Sears, Captain Isaac Sears you know, the Sons of Liberty leader Rivington was always picking at. And Locke rides with Sears and seventy-five men on horses, with guns and pistols. They ride on down to Manhattan Island, on into New York till they line up in front of Rivington's place. 'What are you going to do?' people asked. One man on a horse yelled, 'We're going to wreck the damned lying *Gazetteer* and then we're going to hang Rivington.' Rivington was away. He had heard about it.

They smashed the press. They broke the furniture and Mr. Rivington's personal walnut desk. And they carried away every font of type in the place—by now that lead is run off into bullets. And they say Rivington is not showing himself and some say he is gone back to England. Locke was one of the men who went into the building. He said he was glad to give Rivington such a dose but he is a good enough printer so he didn't like to see a good press smashed."

Tozzer had come to Philadelphia, after selling his press and type in New York "to pay my debts or go to the debtor's cell in the jail," as he said, and done well with the printer Bell in Philadelphia. The press-work had been heavy on a pamphlet which was really a small-sized book. On its publication in January thousands of copies had been sold, passed around, "read to pieces." More and more editions had been run off the press of R. Bell and by summer they knew it would break all records for sales, circulation, for talk and tumultuous excited discussion, by summer it would go to a hundred thousand copies. Tozzer had enjoyed the heavy work of getting out one edition after another. "The book says what I wanted somebody to say and it is like a miracle such a book could come now so terribly needed."

"*The cause of America is in a great measure the cause of all mankind,*" said the introduction. "*The principles of all lovers of mankind are affected, and . . . their affections interested.*" The eyes of the world were on America and what she did had "universal" rather than "local" interest. The outside world, neither Britain nor Europe, could conquer America, "if she does not conquer herself by *delay* and *timidity.*" The writer quoted Milton: "Never can true reconcilement grow where wounds of deadly hate have pierced so deep." And was it absurd or not to suppose a continent to be perpetually governed by an island? He was certain "if they cannot conquer us, they cannot govern us." He was tired of "always running three or four thousand miles with a tale or a petition, waiting four or five months for an answer, which, when obtained, requires five or six more to explain it in." This method of America conducting its trade and politics "will in a few years be looked upon as folly and childishness. There was a time when it was proper, and there is a proper time for it to cease." They belonged to different systems, "England to Europe; America to itself."

He had wished for reconciliation, the author of this little book. Then came "the fatal nineteenth of April, 1775." From then on he was through with the King of England. "I rejected the hardened, sullen-tempered Pharaoh of England for ever; and disdain the wretch, that with the pretended title of FATHER OF HIS PEOPLE, can unfeelingly hear of their slaughter . . . is he, or is he not, a proper person to say to these colonies, '*You shall make no laws but what I please!*'?"

Then again came the writer's recurring theme. He began and finished with it. America now could set herself free and show to the world its first great republic of free men—the same vision Joseph Warren sang in his verses and then dying at Bunker Hill to prove he meant them. "Every spot of the old world is overrun with oppression. Freedom hath been hunted round the Globe. Asia and Africa have long expelled her. Europe regards her like a stranger, and England hath given her warning to depart. O! receive the fugitive, and prepare in time an asylum for mankind."

The religious liberty to be seen in America foreshadowed farther and wider liberty. "I fully and conscientiously believe, that it is the will of the Almighty, that there should be a diversity of religious opinions among us. It affords a larger field for our Christian kindness. . . . I look on the various denominations among us, to be like children of the same family, differing only in what is called their Christian names."

As between reconciliation and war for independence he could see no other course than the war. "Our backwardness tends only to prolong the war."

Tozzer had been reading some of these pages and sentences. The Winshores agreed with him that the wide reading of the book, copies passed around and "read to pieces," the Tories angered by it, the Rebels pleased at seeing their case and their arguments as beyond the enemy's answering—this had helped make opinion and lay the way for the colonies to stand up before the world and through their Continental Congress declare themselves free and independent states. Till this was done the Americans still, in law, stood before other nations as subjects of Britain and therefore rebels. "Until an independance is declared," said the book, "the Continent will feel itself like a man who continues putting off some unpleasant business from day to day, yet knows it must be done, hates to set about it, wishes it over, and is continually haunted with the thoughts of its necessity."

"God, how true are those words!" said Winshore as Tozzer read them. The long curving slash of his mouth had a twist that made Tozzer say, "I never saw you look so sad, Mr. Winshore."

"It's a sad business. Until we speak out and tell the world we are a free people and an independent nation we are fooling ourselves. Other nations believe our faith in ourselves slack."

The February edition of the little book came with an appendix that Winshore liked. Taking the pamphlet from Tozzer he read a paragraph that he said had deeply moved him. Should independence arrive by the legal voice of the people in the elected Continental Congress, then:

"We have every opportunity and every encouragement before us, to form the noblest, purest constitution on the face of the earth. We have it in our power to begin the world over again. A situation, similar to the present, hath not happened since the days of Noah until now. The birthday of a new world is at hand, and a race of men, perhaps as numerous as all Europe contains, are to receive their portion of freedom."

The two printers laughed over Winshore's copy of the first edition of the book with its title page reading

COMMON SENSE

addressed to the

INHABITANTS

of

AMERICA

written by an ENGLISHMAN

"Later he thought it would be better to have his name on it," laughed Tozzer. " 'Thomas Paine' went on those later editions. He don't like it, Mr. Winshore. Peak-faced, lean like he was hungry, and his face like he had come from his books and his thinking and would never get to write it all. His dark-blue eyes, I think it is them that has him, deep eyes with funny shadows like you might kill him but couldn't change his mind if he made it up. He smokes and drinks and he can talk like a streak but my guess is he is a dreamer and dreams much."

"I would venture," put in Mrs. Winshore, "that he says to himself he would like to put on paper dreams so immense that men would say they could fight and die for such dreams."

"That is the gist of it, Mary," said Winshore. "He dreams of an America that could stand as a light and an example to the rest of the world. Of course those are dream sentences no hard and practical man could write. They hold the vision of a zealot writing a testament."

"I believe he has with his dreams reached dreamers who will fight," Winshore went on. "But he is not all dreams. Cold hard logic too he has. His pamphlet is not mishmash or we wouldn't hear of Ben Franklin and General Washington saying it has worked to good effects."

After the Tozzers had gone and after the talk with Jean and Michael in the kitchen, Winshore spoke to Mary of his wish that the Paine pamphlet could have mentioned the people in America having no hate for the people of Britain, that it was the King and his ministers making the strife. He hunted out a copy of a letter Ben Franklin wrote last October to a friend in England. "No one has put the American cause of the past year so clearly, in so few words," he said to Mary as he read her the letter:

"We have as yet resolved only on defensive measures. If you would recall your forces and stay at home, we should meditate nothing to injure you. A little time so given for cooling on both sides would have excellent effects. But you will goad and provoke us. You despise us too much; and you are insensible of the Italian adage, that there is no little enemy. I am persuaded that the body of the British people are our friends, but they are changeable, and by your lying gazettes may soon be made our enemies. Our respect for them will proportionably diminish, and

I see clearly we are on the high road to mutual family hatred and detestation. A separation of course will be inevitable. It is a million of pities so fair a plan as we have hitherto been engaged in, for increasing strength and empire with public felicity, would be destroyed by the mangling hands of a few blundering ministers. It will not be destroyed; God will protect and prosper it, you will only exclude yourselves from any share in it. We hear, that more ships and troops are coming out. We know, that you may do us a great deal of mischief, and are determined to bear it patiently as long as we can. But, if you flatter yourselves with beating us into submission, you know neither the people nor the country.

"Two phrases in that letter haunt me," said Winshore. "They carry terrible meanings. 'Your lying gazettes' is one. They will use language and print to make their people hate our people. Whether we win or lose the war the poison of hate spread by the lying gazettes will last for generations and play its part in still more wars. And that other phrase, 'the mangling hands of a few blundering ministers.' A few men in high places say Yes, say No, say Wait, say Don't. They dilly-dally, mangle and blunder—and the war comes."

Winshore spoke of John Adams rating the First Continental Congress "one-third Whig; another Tory; the rest mongrel." Washington's troops at Boston had only five rounds of ammunition apiece against sixty of the enemy, he had learned. And toward the end of the siege of Boston, of twenty-one thousand men in the Continental Army, twenty-seven hundred were sick and unfit for duty. After taking Boston, thousands quit the army as though the war for them was over, went home or drifted here and there. For the march to New York Washington had only eight thousand men.

"I'm with you in your gloom," said Mary. "We'll see what we'll see."

She reminded him of their brief call on Ben Franklin one evening and how the seventy-year-old man had spoken in gloom of the obstacles ahead, sat with a grave face under the bald top of his head and the hair falling down over his ears to the coat collar, his shrewd and kindly eyes suddenly twinkling from behind the spectacles. Either in the history of nations or in personal lives, one must consider the role of completely unexpected events, said Franklin, "like the proud girl who wished and resolved not to marry a parson, nor a Presbyterian, nor an Irishman, and at length found herself married to an Irish Presbyterian parson."

A rain blew up and they could hear it beating on the slope of the shingled roof so near their pillows. They were slow going to sleep. And their sleep was not easy. He had two boys out with the Continental Army. For years he had brought them along, closer to them

531

than any others. And those boys loved this human cause, they were ready to give all for this American Revolution. Like a boiling caldron was this Revolution into which had been poured many elements and materials. What would be there when the fire died down and after one crisis following another there were no more crises, no more tests of flame and heat? Not even the wisest could tell. The Winshores listening to the blowing rain on the shingles had the same wonder and humility, the same hope and philosophy as John Adams of Massachusetts, delegate to the Continental Congress sitting then in Philadelphia, who wrote that month:

"Such mighty revolutions make a deep impression on the minds of men, and set many violent passions at work. Hope, fear, joy, sorrow, love, hatred, malice, envy, revenge, jealousy, ambition, avarice, resentment, gratitude, and every other passion, feeling, sentiment, principle, and imagination, were never in more lively exercise than they are now, from Florida to Canada inclusively. May God in His providence overrule the whole for the good of mankind. It requires more serenity of temper, a deeper understanding, and more courage than fell to the lot of Marlborough, to ride this whirlwind."

One great vague hope they had. They could sense that hope in every seafog from the east, every landwind from the west. A hope rooted in an instinct born òf knowing those fogs and winds, and living with them, breathing them, tasting them, on American shores and hills. Geography, ai ai, geography and time might yet win them the war. A continent they had to fight on—and centuries of time, as much of time as there was in the future. Land, they had land enough for six or eight Europes. Pitt in telling it to Parliament and the King's ministers, packed it in five words: "You cannot conquer a map." The ministers laughed it off as though, "This laconic ass makes brevity ridiculous." He was brilliant and this was one more of his epigrams. The ministers rated him, Pitt, an astute politician jockeying for place rather than a historian trying to tell them a portentous geographic and military fact: "You cannot conquer a map."

Was it the wind and the rain or did he hear a knocking at the front door below? Winshore listened and couldn't be sure he heard knuckles on that front door downstairs. It might be either Locke or Robert. He slid out of bed and went down, opened the door and saw—no one. He slept and two dream flashes came to him. In one he saw Locke bent low over a horse riding in the night, riding in rain and wind. In the other he saw Robert, lean and down to hard bone, worn and pale, sleeping by a fire, wrapped in his blanket sleeping and his hat and blanket covered by the white snowfall.

Chapter 24

An Army Finding Itself

THEY were tall sun-browned hard fellows and the bigger one had said, "Bobby me lad, we've got a country, haven't we?"

"Sure, that's what we're fightin for, our country."

"But we haven't told the world we're a country, have we?"

"Not yet but that's comin. They can't hold it off much longer. The Continental Congress has *got* to declare us an independent nation and a free people."

"They're slow."

"Molasses in January, says I."

"New England has a flag with a lone pine tree in a corner."

"And South Carolina," chimed Bobby, "has a flag with a coiled rattlesnake ready to bite and a sign under him, 'Don't Tread on Me.'"

"And America has no flag."

"That's what we're laughin about, is it, Bobby?"

"Yes, Oat, and more like it we can laugh about."

"Like what?"

"Like havin an army and no uniforms," said Bobby.

"That's better than uniforms and no army."

"I'll laugh with you about that," and Bobby did.

Then a glum Bobby, "An army without powder? Can we laugh about that?"

"No, it worries the General. We lost Bunker Hill when we ran out of powder and didn't even have bayonets to meet theirs."

"How do we hang on?" asked Bobby. "No country yet, no flag, no uniforms, Bunker Hill with no powder, no bayonets. How do we do it?"

Oat grinned. "We're just naturally pestiferous, thorny, and stubborn, even among ourselves. I heard one fellow say, 'We'll hang on till we drop and then look around to see what hit us.' It's our ignorance scares the enemy. We was ignorant at Lexington and Concord and killed nearly double of them what they did of us and we did the same at Bunker Hill. If they came out of Boston now they could shoot till we had no more to shoot. They don't know that. They're ignorant. We're ignorant. And our ignorance so far works out better than theirs."

"Could we have a laugh at General Henry Knox, the artillery chief who lacks nothing but artillery?"

"Jolly, reliable three-hundred-pound Henry Knox, he'll get cannon, my bones tell me. And he'll plant 'em ready to sweep the lobster-backs into the sea."

"Can that be more of our ignorance, Oat?"

"Time is on our side, Bobby."

"How much time have we?"

"Heard an Indian say once, we've got all the time there is."

These two on the headquarters staff of General George Washington at Cambridge, Massachusetts, Sergeant Robert Winshore and Sergeant Oates Elwood, in the summer of 1775 had been well over the lines and camps of the Continental Army that half-circled Boston and hemmed in the enemy army.

They had seen twenty thousand men arrive in the towns and country outlying Boston, only the Rhode Island volunteers in tents, some with their firelocks and blankets sleeping in Harvard College buildings, in the Episcopal Church and private homes of Cambridge, but the most of them dotting the fields and hidden in woods in shelters their own hands made, huts from boards picked up and sailcloth canvas, shanties of stone and of sod, still others of logs and twisted branches and withes.

They had laughed together over a handbill some joker had printed reading:

American Army	English Army
1. Seven dollars a month.	1. Threepence a day.
2. Fresh provisions in plenty.	2. Rotten salt pork.
3. Health.	3. The scurvy.
4. Freedom, ease, affluence, and a good farm.	4. Slavery, beggary, and want.

Pickets had thrown this handbill, wrapped in a stone, over to enemy pickets. Deserters came from the enemy. The British commander put a stop to it by shooting one they caught trying to desert.

Sergeants Elwood and Winshore laughed.

"Why do we laugh?" asked Sergeant Elwood.

"Because we don't get seven dollars a month unless it's paid and we hear troops cursing because it isn't paid. Because one day we get fresh provisions and another day we don't. Because our camp fever spreads and about one man in ten is on the sick list and the army health grows worse. Because none of us will have 'freedom, ease, affluence, and a good farm.' "

"That isn't funny—why do we laugh?"

"We laugh because we might do our cryin later, Oat. And we laugh because the enemy lies to us and we show we can lie as good as the enemy."

"Might be that's it. They're good liars and we're better."

"That's war, Oat."

They laughed too over ragged barefooted American soldiers deserting to the enemy and slipping back into the Continental Army lines and you could see them now here and there in long-tailed red coats and new shoes and nobody cared and it was taken as comical that they wore the uniform of the enemy they were fighting though of course there was a curiosity about whether in a battle they wouldn't get shot at by Americans who took them for redcoats inasmuch as they wore red coats. As one of them smeared his red coat with juice of walnut and butternut hulls, his Yankee nasal singsong ran, "I dye for my country."

They sobered talking about General George Washington. Men could mock at Washington, jeer at him, call him names but the names wouldn't be funny. Sergeants Winshore and Elwood slept in a third-floor room with a dormer, Washington on the second floor, the headquarters on the ground floor. They had seen Washington pour water from a china pitcher into a china washbowl and rub his face with soaped hands. Robert once brought him a mug of hot water and saw him lather his face, strop a razor and shave. Both had heard him curse when he knocked over a bottle of ink and it ran on a document, hearing him at once recover himself and apologize to them.

"Sometimes I think," said Elwood, "when he looks so wonderful frozen-faced he tries to act more frozen-faced because he can't let loose the fire of wrath burnin away under in him."

"What is there about him you know it isn't cold but you wouldn't touch him, you wouldn't dare get familiar, and you can be in the same room with him and he seems far off, but he can give you an order and look you in the eye and you go out and risk your neck for him?"

"We've both done that, Bobby, haven't we?"

"He stays with you when you go away from him."

"When I look at him he seems to be saying something without talking. I don't get tired lookin at him."

Washington stood six foot three, compact, well built, with his two hundred and twenty pounds of weight, naturally erect like a straight-grown tree, moving with the ease of a man who had been around horses all his life, had broken wild colts and owned stallions that guaranteed foal.

"Owns a hundred slaves and more land than any other man in the colonies," said Robert. "That's what they say. And he wasn't sure about fighting for Independence till months after Lexington. He came to it slow."

"When he did he came with all he had."

"Just like John Hancock."

"Yes."

"And I hear Hancock is sore as a boiled owl at John Adams for not nominating Hancock to be Commander-in-Chief."

535

"What I hear, too," said Elwood, "Hancock never heard a bullet whiz in his life and never slept on the ground, never was ambushed by Indians, like Washington."

"Did you hear the General first week when a brigadier talked about what he calls our problem of vermin?"

"And the General said he once slept on straw in a backwoods hut and the lice and fleas weighed more than the blanket."

"Yes, the General nearly smiled. He meant we are a lousy army but he has seen lousier conditions."

"And he *nearly* smiled. That's peculiar in his make-up, ain't it? I've never seen him smile and many times I've seen him nearly smile." And Robert saying it tried to put on a near-smile like the General's.

"Sentencin a private to sit straddle a rail for hours where the other privates came to mock at him—that's no smilin matter." Elwood was grim as the General.

"And the gantlet, makin a man run the gantlet, two lines of soldiers givin his ass their gun butts—you can't smile about that."

"The General don't like it. He sees days we're more a mob than an army. I heard him say every private in this army thinks he's a general."

"We're lucky to be on headquarters duty sleepin in a feather bed with clean sheets." Robert felt guilty about his comfort. "If our post was out among Liberty Boys we know, fellows that tarred and feathered Tory king-kissers and toadeaters, it might be we'd join them in what they call mutiny when those old Liberty Boys can't have what they want. When they say 'liberty' they mean it and to hell with officers, even their own army officers. Discipline ain't for them yet. Restrictions, they say to hell with restrictions, and what we're fightin for is freedom."

Rather stained and worn, certainly not bright, new and flashy, was the uniform of the Commander-in-Chief. A cocked hat of blue with a black cockade on it, high top boots, buff breeches he wore, a blue coat with buff trimmings, five buttons running down each side and of those ten buttons only two, on the left side, in use as buttons, the other eight for decoration, the other eight to look at. On epaulettes fastened to the shoulders fringes of gilt hung down.

Faded and drab from years of wear this uniform didn't tell for sure who was in it. So headquarters announced you would know the Commander-in-Chief by "a light blue ribband wore across his breast between his Coat and Waistcoat," while major and brigadier generals would be seen each with a pink ribband. When you met a pink cockade in a hat, it was a field officer, yellow or buff meant a captain. This was the time Winshore and Elwood sewed a stripe of red cloth to the right shoulders. That ought to tell anyone they were sergeants.

Officers on trial, officers found guilty of cowardice at Bunker Hill, General Washington signing his approval of the court-martial findings that an officer "be cashiered for cowardice," the General writing he did it "with inexpressible concern," these troubles added to what the enemy gave. The General had to break men as he had broken horses in his time. He mentioned two officers he "broke," their names "Captain Parker of Massachusetts for Frauds both in Pay, and Provisions, and Captain Gardiner of Rhode Island for Cowardice in running away from his Guard on an Alarm." A captain "abusing" his major drew a reprimand, a captain guilty of throwing his men into the guardhouse and snarling at them without proper cause, not to mention his drawing more provisions than he was entitled to, another captain letting civilians and most anybody pass through his lines—General Washington approved the court-martial findings. A sergeant with disrespect for the Continental Congress, who lifted a glass in a toast to the enemy commander, what should be done with the likes of him? Washington approved the penalty. The sergeant rode in a cart with a rope around his neck and an escort of drummers and soldiers who hooted him out of the camp and told him never show his face again among Americans.

Soldiers of New England regiments left camp, without leave, to work on their own farms or the farms of their officers. At headquarters they knew Washington termed this "base and pernicious" and the men "infamous deserters and defrauders." The General gave it out publicly that this was unbelievable conduct, scandalous, and he would pay no attention to "insinuations" but from now on if he caught any of them at it he would "show no favor to any officer guilty of such iniquitous practices." From headquarters later went the order of the Commander-in-Chief taking notice of "repeated instances of officers, who, lost to every sense of honor and virtue, are seeking by dirty and base means, the promotion of their own dishonest gain, to the eternal disgrace of themselves and dishonor of their country," with the warning "Practices of this sort will never be overlooked."

Sergeant Winshore found himself coming under a quiet influence he had met before. In the presence of Washington or in thinking about the man and remembering his face, his ways and his silence rather than his speech, Robert felt the same thing he had seen on the faces of certain Minute Men, a certain section of the Sons of Liberty. He told Elwood, "You could say it's a divine zeal on his face or unconquerable will or absolute and holy resolves—and that sounds like gab talk and you're huntin for words to say something that can't be said. I haven't seen the man warm to me yet I warm to him. And so do you, Oat. You'd go out and do things that look crazy and impossible because he told you to. And I guess you do it because you know he'd do the same thing if somebody could take his place as the Chief."

"Not a crooked bone in his body. I get suspicious he's slow and not bright. I end up thinkin he knows he's slow and he knows he's not bright. And that I say is an advantage. I'd rather have him where he is than a man too sure he's fast and satisfied he's bright."

"Oat, you've been thinkin. That's part of why we trust him so. He'll make one mistake after another before we give him up."

From the country around flocked in relatives and friends, curiosity·seekers come to see warriors. One day came Ann Elwood, having left Boston at risk, taking on duties as a cook and mending woman for ragged soldiers.

When there was spare time Robert Winshore sought Ann, enjoyed company with her, came to admire her shadowy hair, her deep and wide-open gray eyes. He kissed her, found soothing and warmth in her kisses. He made her no promises, felt he owed it to her and her brother there should be no promises. He dug into himself saying the companionship had loveliness yet was not love and he must beware and be more careful. Yet what she gave him softened a bitter loneliness that ran in him, and his telling himself he would stay away from her didn't work out, and his saying he would make no promises began to take on a color of wrong and it hurt him and he felt tangled with a shade of shame to the tangle.

They had a three-hour walk one moonlight night ending in a clump of underbrush where he came so near to wild promises that afterward he cursed himself and talked plain to himself, "You're a fool, your kisses are promises and her answering kisses are her promises, and you're a weak muttonheaded fool if you don't make a clean breakaway." He woke out of a sleep saying, "It's lovely but it isn't love and you're a rat and a louse, you're a rat and a louse, that's what you are, rat, louse, rat, louse, and you know it."

* * * * * * * * * *

Chapter 25

* * * * * * * * * *

Over Wilderness to the Unknown Mountain

SEPTEMBER and flicks of brown and spots of yellow over the woods. And they slung their knapsacks and began marching on September 13 and footed it through Medford, through Malden, and camped at Beverly overnight and the next day marched into Newburyport where they slept in the Presbyterian meeting house Friday and Saturday nights. Sunday in that same meeting house they heard the Reverend Mr. Parsons preach a sermon, then they marched to the wharves

538

where thirteen companies of eleven hundred men in all boarded a fleet of seventeen ships, sailed down the river out to sea and steered east.

One morning and another and they steered into the Kennebec River, sailed to the waiting boats at Gardiner, heavy boats made of green wood and leaky, often called "batteaux" from the French colonists to the north. Into the boats they loaded barrels of pork, flour, sugar, salt. They took turns at the oars and up the river rowed the heavy boats five miles to Fort Western, on to Fort Halifax at a river mouth the Indians called Sebasticook.

They unloaded the boats. They carried the barrels of pork, flour, sugar, salt, some eighty rods past the falls. They came back, roped the boats, pulled them up from the river and carried them, two men to a boat, to be loaded again with the barrels of pork, flour, sugar, salt.

They rowed upriver again. Sergeants Winshore and Elwood and their squads of men dropped out of the boats and waded waist-deep and higher tussling to lift the boats over rocks. Night came and they slung together shelters of brush and built roaring fires and stood drying their clothes while eating their pancakes and pork before going to sleep in their still wet clothes and waking to shiver in the early frosts of the northern colony of Maine.

The next day came colder and the river more rough and twisting. They could see the boat leaks getting worse and the water seeping in to reach flour and sugar. Night came. It turned colder. Their clothes froze on them.

They were picked and hard men. They could still laugh. While it was night yet they unloaded their boats, carried the barrels of pork and flour up a steep ledge. After that they dragged their boats past the boiling and foaming Skowhegan Falls.

Seven miles of smoother going the next day took them to Norridgewock Falls. Here sleds and oxen waited. They loaded barrels and boats on the sleds and prodded the oxen a mile and a quarter through woods, opening a few soaked barrels of flour to find it spoiled.

Thirteen miles to the Devil's Falls, a sixteen-foot leap of the river, they came to the next day, unloaded the boats, lugged barrels, dragged the boats, reloaded.

Seven miles upriver the next day again they packed their boats and barrels on ox sleds, slogged through the woods in a cold four miles passing the last human settlement. From there on no roads, paths, trails, no mark or sign of men, women, people. From there on wilderness and only one white man, a British officer, had ever made the trip.

Here they shot a moose. Here they broiled big steaks on the fire coals and joked and capered, though they capered less than they joked.

Were they not going to Canada? Were they not a secret expedition aimed to surprise Quebec and drive out the British and make friends with the French and seal all of North America to the North Pole in a common fate with the Thirteen United Colonies? Were they not chosen woodsmen, hunters, and sharpshooters, including even a battalion from Virginia that General Washington viewed with special pride?

The next day some of the oxen and sleds had given out. At the next unloading the men opened pork barrels, shouldered poles slung with pork slabs, staggered in underbrush, moss, over fallen trees. Hard going yet trout thick in the streams here made them a fried-trout supper.

The seventh carrying place they came to the next day, over a bog. They sank in slippery mud and mire. Sergeant Winshore kept standing, to rest and get his wind, more than once mired to his knees with a pole of pork slabs on his shoulder.

The days passed, getting colder, the frosts heavier, the damp of their clothes slower to dry. The days passed and it was a month since they slung their knapsacks just outside Boston and started for nobody knew where. They were moving up Dead River now and could see a mountain far off snow-white.

The fifth week, flour running low and one day no flour and the pork ration small. They began to know hunger and the pull in the guts when weak from hunger and marching with a heavy pack. One night that week came all-night rain, endless water pouring from the sky. The river filled and flooded over its low banks and ground into their blankets. They stood up in water halfway to their knees, all around them water and in the dark they couldn't tell where was the river and where away from it. In water up to their knees near daylight they groped guided by shouts and yells to where men had found ground free from swirling raging waters.

The sixth week and they came to the eleventh carrying place early in the morning, wrangled past that with boats and shoulder packs, rowing two miles upriver to the twelfth carrying place, then a half-mile to the thirteenth carrying place. Then in falling snow to meet ice and driftwood as they tugged against a flood-swollen stream, the men underweight from hunger and worn with lack of sleep, they saw six of their hard-worn boats go to pieces on rocks, saw the last of their salt wash away.

Wet to the skin, their shoes, stockings, breeches, full of holes from wear and tear, their feet and legs black-and-blue, their ankle joints swollen, Sergeants Winshore and Elwood went to sleep that night by a roaring fire and woke in the morning damp, sore, stiff in every muscle, their bones aching, each with his personal and particular misery, the same grinding exquisite pain for Robert when he tried to move his right knee joint, for Elwood when he tried to move his left shoulder joint.

"A week ago, Oat, and we had the last flitch of pork, was it?"

"Yes, Bobby," smiled Oat in return, "and yesterday we killed the last ox to roast and put it into our bellies as though between here and Quebec we'll meet more oxen every mile."

They snuggled in their clothes and blankets, careful to hoard what was inside. Not warmth was it inside but a few layers of protection against worse chill from the cold air they could see as a smoke when they blew their breath into it. They had a question and answer for morning, noon and night. They comforted each other awake or worn and half-awake:

"How in the hell did we get here?"

"On our legs."

"And how'll we get back?"

"On our legs."

Now Robert asked, "Oat, can you see that mountain far off snow-white? I can just see it without turnin my head."

"I twist my neck a little, Bobby, and out the corner of my eyes I see it. Kind uh purty and kind uh terrible, ain't it, Bobby?"

"Yes, like us. We're purty and we're terrible, Oat."

"Might be."

"I'm thinkin, Oat."

"Don't think too hard, Bobby, no place to be thinkin."

"Then you don't want my thinkin?"

"Tell me your thinkin, Bobby, leastways make it easy if you can, no dark thinkin."

It was a half-dreamtalk that eased them. The others sleeping or dozing round the fire could take it for the wind in the trees mingled with firelog sputter and crackle.

"I had my mind on why we came, why we stuck, why a thousand other men came and why they stuck."

"They ain't all stuck. There's plenty want to go back."

"I know—and there's a plenty ready to go on to starve and die in the snow before they'll give up."

"You can have it—but why?"

"That's what I been thinkin on."

With his father, with Isaiah Thomas or the Frames or Mim, Robert would say "thinking" but with Elwood and the rank and file he talked like them and said "thinkin."

"And the thinkin goes like this. There are men so made they see a thing to go through with and they go through with it. They can't see the end. The end is too far off to see. And they go on and on as far as they can toward that end of a thing they got to go through with and no other way to it than go far as they can."

"Might be." Elwood meant he should go on.

"They wonder what's over there that ain't there. They wonder what it's like. They start toward it and keep goin. And what keeps 'em goin is the wonder. When the wonder wears too thin they hesitate.

When the wonder dies down and they lose it then they can't keep goin. That's when they stop. Sometimes they keep that wonder alive by lookin at themselves as wonders, not proud about it, not braggin, but goin on because already they've gone farther than they ever believed they could go."

"That sizes up this expedition, Bobby. I never expected to be part of uh expedition nor yet more any expedition like this."

"And my thinkin ran on, Oat, to where I had the united American colonies, the Continental Congress and the Continental Army and the American people, all off on uh expedition. They can't see the end of it. The end is far off, further off than the white snow on that mountain they say is forty fifty miles away and they don't know how far exactly. And those holdin the wonder in 'em, those who'll never let the wonder die down in 'em, they're the ones that'll keep on. They are men and women so made they see a thing to go through with and so long as their legs and their will lasts, and the wonder stays with 'em, so long they'll go on and on. If they could be sure exactly what's at the end, like as not they wouldn't want to go on."

"Never heard you like this of a mornin, Bobby."

"Been thinkin. This expedition the American people is on, it aims a country across the Continent. So they name the Congress Continental and the Army Continental. Ten million people after a while, then twenty million, a big new country, one of the biggest in the world. We're makin one America. The children will make another. Their children and the children's children will make other Americas. Change, all the time change. Under all the sufferin, shame and struggle, enough hope and wonder to keep it goin, from one America to another. The people uh one time will look back and wonder how the people in uh time earlier stuck it out and stayed through and went on."

"Danged if I see how you do it, Bobby. You're too danged cheerful in your misery this mornin."

And Sergeant Winshore mumbled on, afraid to come fully awake and slide out of his clothes and blanket, he mumbled on, near a caressing tone. "And you're a danged fool this mornin, Oat, or you'd know danged well I been talkin about you in what I been thinkin. You wouldn't uh come on this danged expedition if you'd uh knowed what you had to go through. And you wouldn't uh believed you had it in you to stand up against what you been through at the thirteen carryin places and what lay between 'em on the Kennebec River and the Dead River till you come where you see a mountain far off snow-white and nobody knows its name and I hear it might be us the first to give it a name. There she stands with a shine and a glitter and we've come to the Unknown Mountain and that's all we know."

"I tell you again, Bobby, you're too flighty and cheerful this mornin and I'll live to see you change your tune."

This day again the same as other days just passed these two chums stuck it out and in grinding pain kept on with their units. They were slowing down, others saw, falling behind, and yet keeping on and arriving after dark to join their command. Aches all over their bodies most of the men had but Robert did his slogging with that never-ending grind of pain in a knee joint and Oat with the same endless misery in an arm joint. It was the next morning Oat heard Robert, "Why did we ever start on this God-forsaken expedition? What god-damned fools ever took it into their heads any man could make this march and at the end of it stand on their legs and fight? We're gone, Oat. I'm gone, you're gone, we're just a lot of lost sonsabitches, the whole lot of us, the sick and the well, the rank and file and the officers."

Oat spoke softly. "Bobby, you're out uh your head. You're tired and sick and you don't know what you're talkin."

"A lot uh poor sick starvin sonsabitches lost in the wilderness—that's us."

"Shut your mouth, Bobby, you're wastin what strength you got left. I'm tellin you now you got more strength than you think for."

This was the morning they tried to stand up. Oat stood a minute or two longer than Bobby. And what both of them did was to wobble and sink to the ground and lie there. They were sick and dazed though not so far gone their eyes and instincts didn't tell they were under suspicion from the other men looking them over as though they were as good as any of the others only they were soft and afraid and what they lacked to go on was guts for one thing and will for another. Worse than their weakness and pain for both of them was this suspicion from the others. They had belonged to a fellowship of hard unbreakable men. Now they were being thrown out of that fellowship. They didn't belong.

They were dragged rather than carried to the boat they lay in to the next carrying place where again they were dragged rather than carried to their boat. They were alive and dimly conscious enough to see others like themselves burdening the command. They numbered forty the late October morning when they were loaded into boats, the forty sick men who couldn't stand, put in charge of three hundred who could stand but who said it was death to go on and they were backtracking to where they came from.

Oates Elwood saw Robert try to push them away when they came to drag him to the homebound boats, heard Robert, "I can go on. All I crave you to do is let me go on with you. I'm not quittin."

"Me the same," cried Sergeant Elwood. "I'm not quittin."

A colonel stepped in with an order. "Stand 'em on their legs, we'll see."

Up on their feet they were stood like two long wavering sacks. Their eyes, their grim mouths, said they would stand, they would show what they could do. A few flickering seconds they stood. They

543

had pride about it. They would call up hidden strengths and move on with the main command. They were not turning back. Then the fibers by which men stand slackened, their frames sagged. Elwood pitched forward on his face. Winshore drooped and fell to the ground with his knees near his chin, his eyes closed, his lips trembling.

Their boat on a downslide of foaming wild water crashed on a rock. They were spilled into whirling waters. They could thank the two men who took the risk of bringing them through raging shoulder-high water to the riverbank. They could not later reproach those two men for going on with the main party.

Two days they lay in bright warm sunlight and rested. Two nights of the first real sleep they had in many days. The aching weariness of their bodies let down a little and their ankles throbbed less and the swelling went down so they could notice it. Elwood could move his right shoulder joint a little easier though the rheumatic pains of Robert's left knee made him howl if he tried to stand and move on that left leg.

They lay on dry grass in the morning sun and turned their bodies and caught the smell of their clothes drying and made sure the powder for the gun left to them got good and dry. Was it two days or four they stayed there, heaping leaves and dry grass over them at night, and spreading the last of their wet flour on a heated flat rock and making fire-cakes that stayed their hunger? Was it two days or four that Elwood dragged Winshore along on a crude combination of a sledge and a litter? They could remember it was Robert's eyes that caught sight of a deer and it was Robert who lay waiting alone and wondering for four hours while Elwood stalked the deer and wounded it and chased it and reloaded and killed it. He dragged cuts of the animal to where he and Robert with their knives trimmed it and cut hunks of it to roast and to eat as the most nourishing food they had tasted in many days, even though salt was lacking and neither dared mention salt to the other when they so keenly missed it.

On the third day Elwood brought branches and withes and they made an improved sledge-litter for Robert. On the fourth day they started in a light drizzle of rain, with cold roast deer meat they believed would last them ten days. It did last them the ten days and they went on another day and another with nothing to eat except redhaw berries and hazelnuts.

Elwood followed a small creek that ran into the Kennebec and found a still pool that looked good to him. He dragged Robert to it and they camped there three days using bent pins for hooks and several kinds of twine and string from their pockets and knapsacks for line, catching carp, bass and pickerel, traveling on with smoked fish that lasted them five days. Then it was hard faring again, few fish or none in the pools they tried.

Was it two miles a day or ten they were traveling? They couldn't tell. Sometimes Elwood gave out before noon. If it was raining they built a lean-to and spent the time near a fire though there were the two days that set them back when Elwood couldn't scare up any dry wood.

Was it late November or early December by now? They couldn't know. The rain turned into sleet and then snow one day. Then had come a two-inch snowfall. Their clothes hung in rags, the bare skin showing in many places. Their rheumatic pains shook them and by word and by silent looks and gestures they told each other they would go on till death took one and then the other would lie down alongside and join him in the long sleep.

They could never be clear afterward about how those last staggering five days brought them to a hut where they lay fevered and spent on pine boughs with dry ground under them, a fireplace with a clay chimney near by, roast deer meat and corncakes brought to them by a hunter and trapper who never smiled, talked little, and seemed to be saying, "I think you'll die here but mebbe you won't and I'm curious whether you will and you're welcome to what I've got if you can show me you'll come through."

That was Elwood's guess as to what the man's eyes and other signs said. Robert's guess was that the man had had some great trouble in his life and the man believed his trouble would sit easier on him if he could bring life to two men nearly dead.

With shelter and warmth, with rest and food that were rich comforts after what they had been through, the days came when though weak they could stand and walk without pain. They reached Newburyport and the home of a Minute Man still limping from a wound he took at Bunker Hill where he had fought alongside Winshore and Elwood and seen them among the last to retreat.

The feather bed with white sheets, they stood before it and laughed. They crept into it. They found their bones resented it. They slept on the rag carpet on the floor. They tasted milk, wheat bread with butter, cabbage and carrots from a root cellar. They felt a shame creep over them when the news came back of half the expedition to Quebec arriving alive and able to stand, living skeletons making a brave fight and losing, high officers killed and wounded, the entire body made prisoner. They talked about this shame that crept over and through them. They fought against it but it came back. Their Bunker Hill comrade told them, "You were sick men that couldn't stand, you were half-dead when you turned back, now you're a couple of crybabies about it." And this shame, this sense of guilt in not being there at Quebec among the living skeletons that fought to the last, this bored in on them and was harder to get over than the rheumatic pains that still kept at them in occasional twinges and flashes. They had fairly gotten over it when at the end of January they again slept in the dormer and had been put on light duty at General Washington's headquarters.

"He's put us straight," said Elwood as he and Robert came away from their little talk with General Washington. Their record at Bunker Hill, in hand-to-hand fighting that covered the flight of those who had run out of powder and had no bayonets to meet enemy bayonets, Elwood taking two minor flesh wounds in the course of killing three of the enemy, Robert stunned and senseless for five hours from a cannon ball that scraped his breast and carried away one coat button—Washington had that record clear in his head and spoke of it. He seemed to read their faces and flickers of the shame and guilt that had been an awful load to them. Now the load went away for all time. The Commander said that with men like them the common cause couldn't lose. He spoke of each man learning to face his own conscience. They knew he was misread, his motives attacked, lies gabbed about him—and he wasn't letting it bear down on him and weaken him.

The Commander used the word "calumny," a cold fearsome word meaning malicious gossip aimed to break a man down. The blame that would be laid on him for the failure of the Quebec expedition would be worse than any put on the two sergeants for not reaching Quebec to be in the fighting there. They saw his load so far heavier than theirs that they went away lighthearted. They felt important and ready for anything. "Yes, he's put us straight," echoed Robert. They had taken to themselves part of the calm and patience that was Washington. "You know," said Robert, "he makes me think of that snow-white mountain we never reached."

"That mornin I said you was too flighty and cheerful."

"That mornin."

"And the next mornin you took it all back and damned whoever it was got up the expedition."

"Out of my head, crazy with the rheumatism."

"I know. We did fair and well, Bobby, never on the long way back, not one goddam."

"We was too near either heaven or hell, we didn't know which."

The evening came when Elwood said, "I told her, Bobby."

"She can see how it is?"

"Yes. It hurts. But Ann sees. She covers the hurt. And I wouldn't be sure. With a woman you can't tell. She cried at first. Then she talked about how there's nobody like you and she wants you so."

"What could you say there?"

"I told her things you don't know about yourself."

"How would you mean that, Oat?"

"How I heard you out of your head with fever and pain and you would babble over and over, 'Mim, where are you?' and words I couldn't

546

make out but that name Mim runnin through them and one time, 'Mim, come close, I need you, Christ, I need you.'"

"Jesus, I didn't know I did that."

"And that blue silk kerchief, I told her about that, how every stitch on you went ragged but you kept that clean without a tear in it, how you would touch and handle it, how one time I saw you kiss it and I wouldn't be sure you hadn't been cryin."

"And you told her that."

"Then came the worst. She said you never told her about this other girl, this Mim."

"It would be too crazy to tell, Oat, too crazy I say. This Mim, this other girl told me to go to hell, never to show my face around her again, goin to forget every last letter of my name, and I was low as the lowest."

"She gave you the blue kerchief?"

"Yes and I should keep it to forget her by. Is that somethin to talk about?"

"I think I see, Bobby."

"It's as crazy as the Kennebec River rheumatism."

"That's crazy enough." Oat crushed tobacco between his fingers and filled a long clay pipe.

"Give me a suck when you get it lighted, Oat."

"Twould uh been handy on the Kennebec."

"Twould uh killed the rheumatism and us with it."

"Ann is one of the loveliest women there ever was, Bobby."

"She is and I know it. That's part of the tangle and the hurt."

"I mean inside lovely, too. At first she blamed you. She said you led her on. She cried about that. Then she got straightened out uh that and I'll be damned if she wasn't sayin she led you on as much as you did her and maybe more."

"I know what you mean, inside lovely, Oat. She is."

"She said you had suffered enough if anybody wanted revenge on you. And she said she's so glad the two of us are alive and you have saved her brother's life as much as he saved yours and the rest of it she'll try to forget and she'll know how to take it that you don't come to see her any more because you hold a fear some wrong or harm might come of it."

A silence came over the two of them. Oat smoked and saying no word now and then passed the pipe to Bobby for a suck. Soon they put out the candle lighting their dormer room and went to sleep on a Turkish rug knowing their bones would be restless in the feather bed.

547

Chapter 26

Every Girl I Had in New York Turned Out
Flighty

HORSES and oxen, sleds and men, between mountains and along valleys, up to the hilltops then down the grades, forty-two sleds and eighty oxen, hauling, all winter long hauling, stopped by rain when the oxen couldn't drag the sleds over the wet ground. Yet over bare frozen ground they hauled, over thin layers of snow and through drifts piled to the oxen bellies, on trails through forests where they had to chop a pathway, across creeks and rivers where the ice had to be thick enough to hold the heavy loads they were hauling. From far up at Lake Champlain and near the Canadian frontier where American troops had seized Fort Ticonderoga and Crown Point, they had hauled their heavy loads, with eighty oxen to feed and squads of men and their horses.

Far down at Boston Washington waited for what they were hauling. If they came through, Washington could pound Boston to pieces and drive the enemy into the sea. The Continental Congress at Philadelphia had studied whether Washington should have permission to pound Boston to pieces and after debate had decided, Yes they would let him wreck and smash Boston if he could, even John Hancock standing up and saying Washington could knock down the walls and roof of his mansion and they wouldn't hear a whimper from Hancock.

Guns lay on those forty-two sleds, thirteen brass and twenty-six iron cannon, eight brass and six iron mortars, two iron howitzers, twenty-three hundred pounds of powder, and a barrel of flints—fifty-five big guns in all. They made a long silent clumsy parade winding their way through the wilderness. Washington prayed and hoped they would come through. If they did, he could take Boston. If they didn't, God only knew how long the siege of Boston might run. Weeks had passed and the news came back to him of difficulties, obstacles, weather conditions, hindering and hampering.

At the head of this procession of slow oxen and heavy guns—or at the tail end of it, if needed—rode a heavy man. He weighed nearly three hundred pounds. After the battle of Bunker Hill he was named a colonel. Before that he was a Boston bookseller, a militia grenadier, studying artillery, trajectories and range finding. This was the Colonel Henry Knox who came to Washington with the idea of this winter haul. Over frozen rivers and lakes you could bring sleds where wagons couldn't make it winter or summer. Washington hesitated till he talked it over with Knox. He liked Knox. He told Knox to go to it. They were taking chances, both knew well enough. "Hazardous," they called it.

Down to Albany and across the Hudson River and on into the Berkshire Hills the ox teams had now come. And again as twice before there came the young express rider from General Washington to see and talk with Knox, to look at the sleds, guns and oxen, to ride away again and this time to report to Washington the chances looked fair, the worst hazards over. And when late in January the word flew around in the army at Boston that the big guns were coming and it was a sight to see, every man not on strict duty went to see them pull in, lining the road by thousands and cheering to see enough big guns to blow Boston off the map.

That was the day Sergeant Robert Winshore saw Colonel Henry Knox walk into Washington's headquarters with General Nathanael Greene and alongside General Greene a young fellow Robert had to look at twice to make sure who he was. Robert didn't know then that the young fellow was an aide on the staff of General Greene and had been "lent" by Greene to Washington for the rides to New York and up into Vermont to see how Knox and the cannon were coming along. But Robert with a long slow second look did figure out who the young fellow was. He had changed, this young fellow, and now stood hard and brawny, walked with an easy swing, tan and windburn on his face.

"By the Everlasting," muttered Robert with glee. He had slept in the same bed with this young fellow, he had kicked him around and slapped his face in play.

"It's Locke, the little devil," said Robert. Later Locke had him meeting Colonel Knox and General Greene. They were brothers, hadn't met in a year, and could they visit an hour? General Greene told Locke, Yes but no more than an hour, there was work to do.

And they visited, telling what had come in letters from their father, Robert giving Locke assurance that their new stepmother was a rare woman and he hadn't a worry about that.

"You look peak-ed," Locke said with an anxious closer glance at Robert, who told of being stunned and unconscious four hours at Bunker Hill, losing one button, and then of the Kennebec River, briefly sketching it, and ending, "I wouldn't like to think back and tell all of it. I was that dazed and half-awake through it I guess I don't know the half of what happened.

"I'm proud of you, Locke," Robert went on. "You're good for sore eyes to look at. You don't know how sweet you are for my eyes to see. A little more weight and your face wider and you'd be the image of papa."

This hit Locke deep, went to his bones, for his father was to him the man of men. Leaving the Tozzer printery Locke had gone to Jamaica Plain and enlisted with the Rhode Island volunteers under General Greene and had gone up from private to corporal to sergeant and for "valor" at Bunker Hill up to second lieutenant.

When Robert shyly mentioned the "Leesa" he had met with Locke in New York, Locke followed with a gay laugh. "I wouldn't trust her like I do the horse General Greene gives me for important messages that must be delivered. Leesa's father turned Tory and she turned with him and tried to take me with her and I came near calling her a dirty baggage."

"Locke, I've heard good men say a good horse is more dependable than the best woman."

"I don't go so far as that. What I'd say now is I know plenty of horses I'd trust farther than I would Leesa. Her father went Tory for comfort and to please some bigwigs he hopes will make him a bigwig some day. And Leesa went right along with all his reasons, no mind of her own, looking for a man can give her comforts and finery. That's enough of Leesa. What of that girl you came to New York with? You went around New York so much with her you couldn't give me the time I wanted."

Robert's answer came slow. "I can't talk easy about her, Locke. I went with another girl, and a fine girl, but I couldn't forget that first one. She told me never to come back, said she'd forget every letter of my name. But I can't tell why. I'm not sure I know why. I'm not sure she knows why she sent me away like she did. It may be I'll forget her and take up with another. And then, Locke, there's this war to fight. What is love when a war is on? It can be anything. I've met men glad the war came because they could break away from their wives. It's tangled, Locke."

"You was in a state about that girl, I calkerlate," said Locke in mimicry of the New England dialect they had picked up.

"A woman'll go with you if she's sot her mind on't," mimicked Robert in return.

"I hain't met such a woman yet, leastways that I know of," said Locke.

"You might alter your mind about it and if you should think to come away with me, let it be soon," said Robert, quoting from Jabez Hunker's farewell to Mim.

"A woman a bit flighty in the upper story can get a man most beat out till, la fer me, he's in the twitters," laughed Locke.

"He'd better've gotten him an uncommon woman with takin ways," said Robert.

"Nonetheless she might threaten to wring his nose," said Locke, adding that it wasn't particularly Yankee.

Robert had heard a Virginian on the Kennebec, one of the Morgan outfit that had marched in three weeks the six hundred miles from where they started in Virginia to Cambridge, Massachusetts, "We care no more for our lives than three straws," and newly arrived troops not yet sheltered telling visitors, "We sleep on the soft side of the hard ground without straw."

Both had heard of the father and son at Bunker Hill moving toward the action, not sure what was going on, and the father feeling the sting and scrape of a bullet in the calf of his leg, crying, "They're shootin bullets, son, and we got to shoot bullets back at 'em."

They were taking a slow walk around and among seven houses circling headquarters where seven well-to-do Tory families had for many years enjoyed fellowship as good neighbors. Now those houses swarmed with American officers and troops. The seven Tory families, after the bloodspill of Lexington and Concord, had moved into Boston to live that winter in want and cold they had never known before. Locke had heard from a man out of Boston about a woman with chilblains "not only in her feet, her hands had chilblains too." Houses and good furniture had gone for firewood, Locke had heard, and hundreds of good trees.

"Our grand old Liberty Tree was cut down to the roots," added Robert. "The only satisfaction we have was that one lobster-back climbed the tree to show 'em he wasn't as drunk as they thought and what did he do but get too far out on a limb and crash down to a fall that killed him."

"You might near call that an act of God," said Locke. Robert looked tenderly at Locke saying this. He could see his brother having found something that, if not a religion, lay in him as a genuine reverence, something they had always felt deep in their father. Robert had felt it moving and growing in him. He made a prayer it would grow in him as he saw it had in Locke. Had Locke laughed about the enemy soldier falling to death from the Liberty Tree Robert would have joined in the laugh. As it was, he said softly and gravely, "You're right, Locke, it was an act of God."

Locke had heard two officers from Boston talking of a third officer, one saying, "They report his finances warn't rather low than otherways," and the other, "He sustains the fairest character."

This would go for their heroes, they agreed. Of Washington Robert would say, "He sustains the fairest character," and Locke would say it of Nathanael Greene. Among many of the generals and colonels there was jealousy, spite, bickering, low gossip and intrigue, "like cats and dogs," Washington had said. Robert could tell of Washington's moments when he was vexed enough to say of the New Englanders that their officers and troops didn't deserve their reputations, "they are exceeding dirty and nasty people," and of their greed for money and profit, "the Massachusetts people suffer nothing to go by them that they can lay their hands on."

To this Locke had an answer fresh from General Greene who saw Washington as not having "had time to make himself thoroughly acquainted with the genius of this people." You couldn't expect veterans in a raw militia of a few months' service nor Yankee traders naturally commercial to drop their lifetime habits to be good soldiers right off. "His Excellency," Greene had written of Washington, "has been taught to believe the People here a Superior Race of Mortals, and finding them of the same temper and disposition, passion and Prejudices, Virtues and Vices of the Common People of other Governments they sink in his Esteem."

The young brothers saw Washington and Greene as two great generals helping each other with fine understanding though they came out of different conditions of life. Washington was a Virginia aristocrat, a country gentleman, planter, sportsman, one-time card-player and gambler, a proven Indian fighter. Greene was a Yankee of Quaker training, his ancestors following Roger Williams to Rhode Island for religious freedom, the fourth son in a family of eight boys and one girl. Greene had swung a hammer in his father's forge at Coventry, Rhode Island, read the books of Locke, Watts, Swift and other authors under the guidance of the Reverend Ezra Stiles who had become president of Yale College. Why shouldn't his sentences be correct since he had wormed his way through the famous grammar of Lindley Murray and talked personally with Murray?

Greene it was who had been picked to face the new Commander-in-Chief under a wide elm tree and speak the welcome of New England. Greene it was who brought to the Continental Army the only regiments in uniform, with tents, camp kitchens, better than usual order and discipline. Greene had a slight limp, a stiff knee from boyhood.

"On a horse you can't see the limp and when he is afoot he's where needed," said Locke. "You might not believe two years ago when his home neighborhood organized a militia company they wouldn't elect him a lieutenant and they hesitated at letting him join as a private. After doubting he would make a soldier, because of that slight limp, they at last did let him in. He drove to Boston and passed out of the town through the guards in a wagon loaded with straw that covered a complete military outfit for himself and a deserter from a British regiment who served them in Rhode Island as a drillmaster. The Quakers read him out of their church. And he says now with a sober face he's still a good Quaker and that's his religion and he believes the hush of silence is good for a man and he can be the most wonderful say-nothing I ever saw. He's against war but he can't be against this war."

"If all the officers could understand each other and put away personal jealousy and know when to say nothing like Washington and Greene, the war would move faster," said Robert.

They were finishing their talk in a corner of the headquarters front room when Oates Elwood came in and joined them briefly, his face rippled with pleasure at meeting Robert's younger brother and finding him such a fine specimen.

"A little heavier and the face widened a little and he'd be wonderfully like his father," said Robert.

Elwood before leaving spoke of his sister. She was lately mending officers' shirts and uniforms besides working on bandages and other hospital needs. Two officers had brought her a ham and he was joining her this evening in a ham supper.

"Your brother might like to go along with me," said Elwood to Robert and with a nod toward Locke.

"Why me and not him?" asked Locke with a nod toward Robert.

"I'm on special duty," said Robert.

"Ought to be a pleasant supper," said Elwood to Locke. "With you there will be four of us. A woman working with Ann, just come last week, will be with us eating the ham. She's been with some relatives on a farm and she's a first-class sewing woman. Used to be in one of the stylish dress shops in Boston."

Robert held back, with an effort, his question, "Who is she?"

Robert was restless that evening. He rode past a mile of campfires and made inquiries for a headquarters officer on matters where Washington wanted assurance that all was going well with the newly arrived artillery. He was very much awake in their dormer room when Elwood came in at nine o'clock saying the evening was perfect and he didn't expect such another in a long time.

The new woman at work with Ann, the Boston dress-shop woman, turned out to be Mrs. Evelyn Trutt. And she had looked so kindly, so gracious, so sweet and understanding to Elwood that on leaving he dared to put his two hands to her arms just above the elbows and smack her a kiss on the cheek.

"I didn't think I'd dare do it to a decent woman," said Elwood with a half-bashful grin.

"I knew her at that dress shop where she worked," said Robert. "A quiet woman and something lovely about the way her gray eyes would take in what was going on and she wouldn't say a word when all the other women were gabbing."

"Quiet and lovely, that's her," said Elwood. "Older than me, I suppose, but I like her and I'll be thinkin about her."

And Mrs. Trutt had spoken of the Cavendish dress shop being completely empty of customers for many days after the fighting at Lexington and Concord. And in tears and bitterness a few days before the battle of Bunker Hill Mrs. Cavendish pulled the curtains, locked the door, and told the girls the place was closed.

"And the Wilming girl, that Marintha Wilming you met with me at the White Cockade coffeehouse nearly a year ago, did she mention her?"

"The last heard of her the enemy sent her through the lines to get to her home folks out Lexington way."

And that was all, the first scrap of news Robert had of Mim near ten months.

The days pressed fast with heavy duties for all. They worked on getting the big guns to where they could sweep Boston. Then if the enemy didn't leave Boston they would open fire.

Yet an hour or two could be snatched now and then for the lively quartet that met at the house where Ann Elwood and Evelyn Trutt lived and worked. Locke and Ann, Elwood and Evelyn Trutt, those were the couples. With each of them a serious affair was developing.

"Every girl I had in New York turned out flighty," said Locke to Robert once. "Ann isn't the flighty kind. I feel I can depend on her like no other girl I ever met."

Locke knew by Robert's face that Robert was pleased and couldn't quite find the words for what pleased him so.

"She is open, Robert," added Locke. "She wouldn't hide what she thinks I ought to know."

And it came out Locke had learned that neither his brother nor Ann's brother thought fit to tell him about Ann's going with Robert nor about Ann's fraudulent marriage with a British sergeant who had slept with her in her own home and later taken a fearful beating from Oates Elwood.

But Ann had told it all to Locke. Not at first but later when she said that sometime he would find out all about it and it was better she should tell him everything before others who might tell it wrong. She had had enough sorrows. And if Locke was going to be another sorrow in her life it would not be through suddenly finding out things it was better he should know to begin with.

"And I'll be danged if I don't love her more than ever since she told everything like it happened," said Locke. "I asked Oat about it and he says she's a brave woman with a big heart or she'd be suspicious of all men forever from now on. But she ain't suspicious of me. I look at her and I say she's made for love, the kind of love I can give her."

"Have you told her that?"

"I don't have to tell her. She's the first girl I've had where I feel it's there between us and it's going to last and we just ought to be near each other and not talk too much about it."

Chapter 27

A City Taken

SIR WILLIAM HOWE, chief in command of the British troops at Boston, was a brave man in battle. He had shown that at Bunker Hill in 1775 and at Wolfe's Cove and the Plains of Abraham fifteen years before. His younger brother George Augustus Howe had come to like the Americans in that war against France for Canada and after this younger brother was killed in action at Ticonderoga there were Americans who loved and revered him enough to put up statues of him.

And when General Sir William Howe came to Boston at forty-six years of age and replaced General Gage he was under the difficulty that the Americans loved his brother and hated him. He was under still more difficulties. He didn't agree with King George III and the King's ministers on how they were managing America; they didn't need to bear down so hard. They named him to go to America and bring the Rebels into submission because on his brilliant record as an officer and strategist he looked good and could do the job, so they believed.

Now these months General Howe had stayed in Boston having at times more guns, powder and troops than Washington. He could have run ships up the Charles River and split Washington's army. His ships could have pounded American fortifications to pieces to be followed by infantry assaults as at Bunker Hill and again run the Americans out of powder. Howe tried none of these. At times he didn't seem interested in what he had come for. An Englishman loyal to Great Britain was to write of Sir William Howe that he "liked his glass, his lass, and his game of cards." He had time, with other officers, for pleasant parties, drink and cards—and time too for a woman who came to be known as an attachment, if not a belonging, of his. She gambled like no other fine lady in Boston, had a name for more than once having lost at a sitting three hundred of the gold coins known as guineas. Her husband had been mayor of Hingham, Massachusetts, had been high sheriff of the royal province of Massachusetts, had been among the foremost of Loyalists. General Howe was to name this man Commissary of Prisoners and the man's wife was to win a name, even among Loyalists, as "a Delilah," an "Illustrious courtesan," a handsome, extravagant woman, a Massachusetts-born girl from Dorchester, whose play and byplay with General Howe figured in why he was slow and why one English letter-writer should say, ". . . the harlot's eyes glistened with wanton pleasure at the general's table when the brightness of his sword should have reflected terror on the face of the rebels."

The rousing good song "Kiss the Cold Winter Away" could have been sung that winter of 1775-76 in Boston when hundreds of houses of absent rebels were torn down for firewood and the well-to-do Whig John Andrews, having sent his delicate wife to Marblehead and safety while he stayed to watch the six houses he owned, could write to a chum, "if you'll believe me, Bill, I was necessitated to burn *horse dung*," underlining two words.

In a bright moon the March night came when hay stood piled one side of the steep road up to Dorchester Heights, enough hay to screen from enemy view the three hundred carts, ox teams and horses, thousands of men with pick and shovel, wisps of hay around the wheel felloes so to make no noise, not a word above a whisper spoken to ox, horse or man, while all night long men toiled at making the fortifications from which, with those cannon and mortars hauled on ox sleds from Ticonderoga and Crown Point, they could bombard Boston and the enemy ships and troops.

General Howe's first thought was to attack, as at Bunker Hill, to march his men up those steep hills and take those freshly fortified positions. His second thought was more slow and sober; the cost would figure high. It would be the bloodiest battle fought on American soil and he wasn't sure he could win it.

Boats to carry more than two thousand troops had been made ready. The boats would take them near the fortified heights where American cannon commanded the harbor. Wave after wave of troops would be hurled up. More reinforcements would be brought over in boats and hurled up the heights. The war of the American rebellion would be over. Boston lost, the war was lost—that would be the feeling over the other colonies. So General Howe planned and hoped.

Then a storm wind began blowing and with it a lashing rain. On Dorchester Neck and up and around the Heights rode Sergeants Winshore and Elwood. The moment came when soaked to the skin they could ride back and report at headquarters that it was clear the enemy had given up and American officers were sure the boat crossing couldn't be made and the attack was called off.

Then came what was ever after called the Evacuation of Boston by the British, Sir William Howe moving out of Boston Harbor with every last man and gun he had—and along with them more than a thousand Loyalists who couldn't think of staying in Boston.

When Robert, the next morning after a night in cold rain, tried to get up and stand he did it on one leg. The rheumatism had come back. The pain of it was grinding him as he rode into Boston on March 17 with the Continental Army. But what he saw and heard that day took the edge off the pain in his knee joint.

Never had Boston Harbor been so thick with sails, so white with sail canvas. They were a city by themselves, those ships with nearly eight thousand British troops and eleven hundred Loyalists bound for Halifax.

"Some good men on those ships," said Robert to Elwood. "Doctors, merchants, a ship designer, two carpenters I knew well, and they went along on their work and never made any trouble as informers or in any other way, peaceable men who just naturally love the King of England and can't see a war against the King. But the most of them on those ships, let 'em go, good riddance, we can be glad they're gone."

Robert waved his hand toward the ships on the horizon. "You're out there, Hobart Reggs, I suppose, and your evil daughter Sapphira and I hope you never come back." Another sweeping gesture of farewell, and, "You're out there too, Silas Ludgate, you tattler, you betrayer, and I hope you never come back."

He had heard of the miseries of the Loyalists but his heart was hardened toward them and he luxuriated in an evil glee over what he heard. So little room was to be allowed them on the ships that they had to pick and choose among their belongings, many a one leaving behind for the detested Rebels a cherished coat or gown, a chair or clock, books and paintings. To the ships they hauled by cart or personally lugged their hurriedly chosen goods of life, necessaries, keepsakes, treasures. Some brought cats, dogs, birds and bird cages, furniture, bedding, violins, harpsichords. From many of these came wailing, howling, cursing, when it was found more space for more refugees had to be made on the overcrowded ships and no time lost about it. Overboard went cats, dogs, furniture, a spinet around which a respectable family had often gathered, and bird cages from which fluttering canaries, macaws, cockatoos and parakeets had been released. And as one ship hoisted sail and drew out of the harbor those who had seen it told of the man who couldn't part with his dog and leaped off the ship and went to sea bottom with his beloved pet.

While Oates Elwood rode to find his home torn down for firewood and no news of his father and mother, Robert rode toward Aunt Ellen's house, saw it standing, tied his horse in front, and went toward what seemed the front door standing open. Reaching it he found the front door gone. Every other door of the house he found gone. Every piece and stick of furniture in the house was gone. At the rear and sides boards had been ripped away. The rag rugs were gone from every room, the stubby Arabian brass candlesticks, the Franklin stove, the andirons, pokers, shovels of the kitchen fireplace, no article of fond memory left. The ax and saw he knew could not be in the woodshed as he looked out the back door and saw the woodshed vanished, every chip and splinter of wood picked up from the bare earth oblong that stood marked off in back-yard dry grass.

He must leave this place in a rush. The hurt of looking at it stabbed dark and soft in him. Before leaving he leaned at a wall in the front room corner and sent his hands groping toward where the oak settee had stood, where he and Mim had touched with their feet and heads both heaven and hell. He leaned there half-spent and the tears near came and he shook in a series of dry sobs and thin moans.

"We been pitched on for to go to New York," said Elwood to Robert early in April.

"Must need us," smiled Robert.

On a three-day ride to New York they met here and there among others the same comfort, the same fear, they themselves held this month of April, 1776. The comfort was definite. They had driven the enemy out of Boston after eight months of siege. They had beaten the enemy at Bunker Hill till they ran out of powder. They had killed two for one and driven the enemy from Lexington and Concord to Charlestown a year ago when the war began. This was a string of victories. They could look at it with pride; a few more victories would see independence won for the American colonies. This hope and comfort had spread wide over all the colonies, with more unity, more confidence, from Maine down to Georgia.

Their fear too was definite. More than half of General Washington's army had melted away. Men had gone back to their farms and towns, gone for many reasons. They were needed at home, they said. Or they had had enough of fighting, enough for a while anyhow. Some were tired of discipline, camp-life monotony, irregular and bad food, and the conditions that at one time had more than two thousand soldiers around Boston on the sick list. For some of them Washington couldn't hold back his disgust and contempt. He spoke and wrote of these as "chimney-corner heroes," even mentioning one prominent officer who resigned as dreading to leave "the smoke of his own chimney." This was the fear. Enough of that slack and careless spirit could lose the war.

Sergeants Winshore and Elwood had threshed over the comfort and the fear that in a way canceled each other.

"What we got out of this war so far, Bobby, shall I tell you?"

"What's on your mind?"

"What we got so far out of the war is hard work and the rheumatism and neither of us expects to get any more from now on except more hard work and more rheumatism."

"That's right, Oat. You had time for a little love with Evelyn Trutt and now you kissed her good-by and you know well your luck will be good if you ever see her again."

"And you, Bobby, you don't tell me and I ain't askin but I think I can see it that you had some kind of a love and you lost it and if we win the war you don't know whether you got a love to go to."

558

"It's a little like that, Oat, but if I talk about it I think about it and I got no call to think about it, for when I think about it it makes me go soft and you can't be soft in a war."

* * * * * * * * * *

Chapter 28

* * * * * * * * * *

Betrayals and Wavering Faith

MICHAEL McGILLICUDDY'S sister Maureen entered the Blue Anchor tavern and many eyes turned on her. Some spoke greetings, the keeper said, "Good to see yez, Maureen." She was short, stout and hard-muscled like her brother. When she spoke or smiled her wide mouth brought into view one black tooth and the gaps of two missing teeth. A scattering of large rusty freckles on her face made the creamy skin look more fair. Her blue eyes, she had been told, had the lakes of Killarney in them.

The man who had told her this, her Dan Shannon, came in carrying his blacksnake horsewhip, a worn-looking and tall bone-rack of a man, his clothes wet from driving a cart in the afternoon drizzle of rain, and soon as they had eaten a bit of food he would be going home for a change of clothes. The Blue Anchor was about halfway between where Maureen worked and stayed as a house servant and the little upstairs room where Dan slept. His seven-year indenture to a brewery owner would run out in the fall and hers to a merchant next January when Dan and Maureen planned to be married.

Michael McGillicuddy came in, joined them in ale, fish, vegetables. And before Dan was to go home and change out of his wet clothes Michael, who himself had been loading kegs and barrels into carts during the day and his clothes not dry, thought they should have a good glass of hot rum. They were tilting their glasses and having slow sips of the hot rum when a tipsy fellow stopped at their table and scraped his shoes on the sanded floor and leered at Maureen and called her his macushla. He was not Irish, they noticed, or he wouldn't be saying it as "meecooshaler." Dan told him to go away. Michael told him he was making a monkey of himself and to be gone. Still he stayed leering and calling Maureen his "meecooshaler." With a silly face he reached toward Maureen and patted her face with one hand. Then Dan Shannon stood up and gave him a shove under the chin that sent him sprawling on the floor.

Now another man had left the bar and came heaving at Dan Shan-

559

non, who didn't see him. He swung a blow that sent Shannon cold to the floor. Michael stood up, saw Shannon on the floor, senseless, not a move in his body. Michael picked up Shannon's whip, felt the stock of it heavy-leaded, swung a fearful blow at the man who stood over Dan Shannon and seemed pleased over his smooth fast knockout of Shannon.

The blow Michael swung cracked the man's skull. The doctor who came a half-hour later called it a fracture. When the man died the next day his friends saw to it that the police made a search for Michael McGillicuddy.

Jean Shepherd hid Michael for three days in the cellar of the Winshore house, not even telling the Winshores. It was after that third day when the police had come and questioned Jean and the Winshores about Michael, that Jean told the Winshores where she was keeping Michael. It was two days later that men recruiting for the Continental Army arranged for Michael to wait at the house of a farmer, a patriot, a few miles out of Philadelphia, and there join, as he did, an outfit of raw recruits marching overland to join the forces of General Washington up at Long Island, New York.

"'Tis well Michael has gone to the army," said Jean Shepherd to the Winshores. "He was born to fightin. It was only me cryin to him not to go held him away. Had he let the man have it with his bare fist in place of a whipstock heavy with lead, he wouldn't have killed the man and why he did as he did he swore to me he could never tell from searchin his heart. He killed a man not meanin to and now he's gone where he means to kill men and it's his duty to kill and the more he kills the better a soldier he is."

Then came her confession that she and Michael were indentured servants at York Town, Pennsylvania. Each had three years yet to serve. And they had run away, hoping to marry the next year and move to a distance where they could not be taken by the law.

"Then came his wish to go to the army and fight," sobbed Jean. "Only the warm love between us kept him from goin. And now he's got the first wish he had and I am a woman more lonely than any in all Philadelphia. He may go to hunger and death and he may go to strange women."

The Winshores had her bring a pitcher of cider to the front room. They sat her between them and comforted her and partly persuaded her that Michael had gone to a great army fighting in a holy cause of human freedom, that if he died from fighting or camp fever it would be alongside some of the truest men that ever walked the earth.

Winshore pointed to William Bradford. "He owns the printery where I work. He owns the bookstore next to the printery and the coffeeshop next to that. He is no young and brawny man like your Michael. He is fifty-four years old. And where do you find him now? He's with that same army of Washington your Michael has gone to.

He's an officer, a major, heading a battalion of Pennsylvania militia he helped organize. They need him. He knows they need him. His wife, sons and daughters here in Philadelphia, knowing him to be a man who will be in the front of the fighting like your own Michael, they too have heavy hearts."

Winshore pointed to Robert Morris, supposed to be the richest man in Philadelphia. "He was no Rebel till the news came of the bloodshed at Lexington and Concord. Then he said it must be war. Now he is risking his fortune in this cause your Michael fights for. He gives all his time to getting cash for guns and powder. He could have comfort and ease by not taking a hand in the war and he says he must refuse that kind of comfort and ease."

Jean's eyes lighted at Winshore saying, "I have two boys I love as my own flesh and blood. They are with that army. They may sleep on the cold ground with your Michael next winter."

The wide curves of Winshore's mouth trembled and his voice was a half-whisper.

"I shouldn't have been talkin so," said Jean. "It was my first cryin over Michael goin. I'll cry again but I'll cry soft so you won't hear me and I'll try not make it a selfish cryin."

Jean went to her room saying she was sure she would sleep better than the nights just passed.

Winshore spoke to Mary of the force that Michael marched with. He had seen in their Philadelphia recruiting office the hunter and frontiersman Hiram Kester, the tall spare man he had once seen on the stage wagon to Bristol and then nicknamed him Old Wilderness. A fifteen-year-old boy and "the old ooman," said Kester, would take care of the five smaller ones while he would try his firelock at any sharpshooting Washington wanted done.

From an Elizabethtown man who came to the printery one day Winshore had learned that Jack Mallon—the hairy giant he had seen clash with the two British officers in Mr. Graham's tavern—had gone to the army.

"Some hard men, wild brute fighters in that army, what with Mallon and Kester and Michael McGillicuddy," he said to his wife.

"And your own boys, they have become hard," said Mary.

"Yes, to endure in war they must grow hard."

"And what these hard men fight for is a dream and a hope."

"Yes, Mary, a thing as airy and insubstantial as the mist and color weave of the rainbow. They fight for a future and what they believe they can make of that future. Beyond that they know nothing. That future may fail them."

"They want to take the chance that it won't."

His right hand rested softly and lifted and shifted on her hair and head, at the sides and over the forehead, as he said, "Yes, Mary, they want a future where they can take the risk of making a nation that will be a light to the world."

"A terrible risk, isn't it?"

"So terrible it fascinates men with its possibilities. If they win they know the like of such an adventure has seldom if ever been seen in the world."

He rode a horse and turned into the roadway leading to the shed where the Winshores used to keep a horse. A knock came loud on the back door and they heard Jean Shepherd's voice, "Why, it's Mr. Robert!"

In his uniform of buff and blue, throwing his cocked hat to a corner, his arms went around his father who held him tight and said no word.

A pale face, the cheeks sunken, the cheekbones and jaw standing out, and his eyes seemed to have drawn farther back into the sockets, his clothes hanging loose for he had lost thirty of his hundred and eighty pounds of weight. The lines crinkled here and there on his face told the father his boy was ten years older than when he had last seen him scarcely more than a year ago.

Headquarters had sent him on several rides to forges and shops making muskets and powder. They wanted immediate reports on what they could expect and when, no time to be lost. Their campaign plans depended on what powder, guns, flints, they might be sure of at certain dates in the future. On the last ride he had pushed on through driving rains that soaked him, had forded two swollen streams, and had ridden two days in the grinding pain of his rheumatism come back worse than ever.

Headquarters saw him a sick man, a case for the hospital. There he rested and improved enough to make the ride from New York to Philadelphia, to try for a complete recovery before return to duty.

In the tumult and confusion of his service at the headquarters, shaping crude militia into an army while they held the enemy in Boston, seldom had Robert known anything like rest and nourishing food at proper hours. Now beginning this mid-May of 1776 he had it. He rested, loafed, luxuriated in a clean bed with white sheets that sometimes mocked at him with their accusations of what he had that other good men he knew didn't have. Now Jean Shepherd set before him the fat of the land and as the weeks passed of evenings and Sundays he had the healing companionship of his father and a stepmother he called blessings on. She did housework of mornings and went to the printery and filled in on many kinds of jobs during the afternoons. She saw Robert rounding into better physical condition, his weight on the increase, his cheeks filling out, care lines of his face filling and smoothing a little. But his talk didn't come back to its old light and warmth. His eyes didn't change. Back in the sockets lurked a mockery that came and went. He would brighten, then lapse into silences Mary couldn't fathom.

Once he quoted a Boston Tory he had heard saying of the Loyalist magistrates of Massachusetts, "They haven't the spirit of a louse," and added freely with a bitter twist of a smile, "I am like that now. I haven't the spirit of a louse."

With a few days of rest the rheumatic pains had gone. And he had groped for a new strength and in part that had come. But he spoke of his weakness and his lack of worth and the failure of his body to return soon enough to the old fiber and fire he had in the days when he was on an instant's notice ready for anything.

Worst of all signs they saw in him was a recurring mood when his faith in the Revolution sagged and sank low. In one of these moods in mid-June and days lazy and pleasant to his body, he said, "I'm going back and I'll fight to the end and I won't live through it. But I'm not sure what the war will bring even if we win it. I used to believe. Now I don't believe. I've seen in our own ranks too much greed, jealousy, fear, hate, petty bickering and low spite."

He looked at his startled father on the evening he said this. He saw in his father's eyes and face only silence and anguish. He could read that his father pitied him as a sick weakling and for the moment an irresponsible. He saw an easing of stress move on his father's face when after a long pause Robert said, "My body is coming back but something inside me that was there doesn't come back. Till it does come back you must forgive me for what may seem to you a slack faith. It has run darker and more slack in me than I have told you. It may be nothing will bring back my full faith but the army, where I can every day see men under harder trials and worse betrayals than I have known."

"Betrayals?" asked the father.

"Isn't there betrayal somewhere in this country when brave men must fight without powder, without the small pay promised them, without the food and equipment they deserve? We won at Boston because the enemy didn't know how low we were in powder. He could have routed us any day he had chosen to attack and go on with the attack till our short powder supply was gone. Washington was betrayed by those who didn't care, those who could have seen to the powder supply and didn't."

A long pause and the father asking, "Do you think, son, that perhaps it can be worth our time to try to stand up under these wrongs and betrayals so long as the head of the army doesn't go down under their almost crushing weight?"

Another long pause and the son saying, as something like muted sorrow crossed his face, "You understand it, father. You too have groaned and tossed over it. Washington it is and men like Nathanael

Greene and others fastened to him in a loyalty beyond death—it is they will bring the war and the Revolution through. It is they haunt me and rebuke me and pull me back toward the Continental Army."

They said little more that evening and spoke good night aware there had been a cleansing of hearts and a glimmer across the bitter darkness in the house.

A little action, some degree of responsibility without heavy work, was what Robert needed now, the father saw. And as Bradford was a printer for the Continental Congress, an arrangement was made that Robert should attend afternoon sessions and serve when needed as a clerk or messenger for committees and members of the Congress.

Often the tonic of new hope ran through Robert watching those fifty-six men of the Congress in Carpenter's Hall, twenty-five lawyers, eight merchants, six physicians, five farmers. And again he felt slack over slow and self-important delegates, fidgeting, nibbling and quibbling. Toward the end of June on warm afternoons flies came swarming in from the livery stable next door and the sweltering delegates did their best at being deliberate and dignified while fly-bitten or brushing away flies.

Robert knew the presiding officer John Hancock welcomed news that the enemy had used his house in Boston and left it in fairly good condition and yet Hancock still let it rankle in his heart that he had not been chosen Commander-in-Chief of the army. Sam Adams, John Adams, Robert recognized in their seats—and Elbridge Gerry who had lain chilled to the bone in a cornfield at Menotomy wearing only a nightshirt, Gerry with his long pointed nose and wide-open frank eyes. Three Philadelphia men he knew, the eminent young physician Benjamin Rush, Robert Morris the financier, Ben Franklin the world-famed scientist who until the last week in June was kept to his home with an attack of the gout while recovering from boils and dropsy that set in on his long journey up to Montreal. There Franklin, a freethinker, and Charles Carroll, a Maryland Catholic, simply got nowhere at persuading the French Canadians to come join in a war against Great Britain.

Most of the delegates dressed as gentlemen of the propertied classes. Even Sam Adams and those of little or no property wore finer clothes than at home, some of them like Sam in suits and silk stockings presented by the home folks who believed it would add dignity to the Congress as well as to the colony their delegate represented. Many wore wigs though Benjamin Franklin got along with a black skullcap to cover his bald dome. Several had their silver snuffboxes and exchanged snuff and sneezes in courtesy and fellowship. The soft melodious drawl of delegates from the Southern colonies stood sharp alongside the New England keen nasal twang. From the Middle colonies were spokesmen of neither drawl nor twang. Many Southern and Middle-colony delegates had their suspicions of New England. More especially Southerners slanted their eyes in doubt of New England motives. This was partly suspicion of "the shrewd Yankee trader," partly that New England was and had been fiercely Puritan.

Robert didn't know it nor did the Southern gentlemen who were suspicious of New England know it and John Adams, the Massachusetts delegate, wouldn't for the world have spoken nor published what he wrote to his wife April 14, 1776:

"The gentry [of Virginia] are very rich, and the common people very poor. This inequality of property gives an aristocratical turn to all their proceedings, and occasions a strong aversion in their patricians to *Common Sense* [the Thomas Paine pamphlet]. But the spirit of these Barons is coming down and must submit."

Yet this same John Adams had nominated George Washington, of the Virginia gentry, to be Commander-in-Chief. And this same John Adams was saying in June of '76 to the delegates one and all that when the Continental Congress should be ready to pass a Declaration of Independence, the one man to write that declaration was Thomas Jefferson of the Virginia gentry.

There were good men and great men from all sections, not sure of each other, thought Robert. They hadn't worked together long enough to know what they could and might do together. Sometimes a desperation came over him when he heard a cheap and garrulous speech from a self-important delegate. "Gabber, good only at gabber," said Robert. For they were debating in this June of '76 in Carpenter's Hall the phrases and ideas for a document to tell the world that the thirteen colonies were formally entering the nations of the world under the name of the United States of America.

Every delegate had personal viewpoints. Every sectional group of delegates had political secrets they couldn't bring into the open, for doing so would threaten the unity of the colonies. This impression Robert discussed with his father who said, "We can be thankful for what unity there is. The common cause has thus far overridden the meaner motives of the smaller men."

When Washington walked into the hall there was applause and all eyes studied him. Was he not their shield and spearhead? What authority could the Continental Congress have without the Continental Army to back it up? The Commander had been asking for more to fight with than they gave him. He would go on asking for more guns, powder, supplies and equipment than they would give him. And between them they would have disagreements and hard trials without losing faith.

The delegates spoke, nibbled and quibbled, and brushed away the livery-stable flies biting through black silk stockings. They spoke, voted and transacted momentous business of world-wide interest this

June and early July of 1776, reaching a long arm of hope far into a hazardous future.

Two men rode up to the Winshore house one evening, tied their horses, went into the house and made it ring with glad babbling and high laughter.

John Locke Winshore and Oates Elwood were these two, with messages from General Nathanael Greene for General Washington. They expected to ride back to New York in a day or two. General Greene had told Locke the messages were important and he should pick a rider to accompany him in case anything happened to either one of them.

Locke had filled out, grown harder and more sunbrowned, outweighing Robert now, and his deep-set brown eyes a little moist at seeing Robert and knowing why Robert looked ten years older than his age.

The tears rolled down Ordway Winshore's face as he held in his arms the boy that now looked more than ever like himself.

"Good Lord, I've never seen you so happy," said Mary.

There were moments that night in the Winshore house when the four men and one woman held their peace and said not a word. There was so much to say they were aware they couldn't get it said. They felt so utterly solemn over the issues and events of the hour that they were shy about laughing; they were so glad to be alive and whole for such a coming together that they sat quiet with faces shining at each other.

There did come the little stroll of Robert and Elwood up the street a few blocks while they talked about their rheumatism, how Robert's seemed to have gone away for the time being, how Oat had been on his back four days with one attack and a week with another. Ann Elwood and Evelyn Trutt had taken smallpox inoculations in Boston and were coming down to New York to join the Medical Corps. "We hope to see our girls in camp on Long Island this July," said Oat. And very tenderly Oat asked, "No word from Miss Wilming?" and heard Robert's brief "No," and that was all of that.

The father that evening saw a touch of color come to Robert's cheeks, his eyes for the first time losing the furtive gleam that he seemed to hold deep back in the sockets. The Congress and its talk had been tonic for him but it was the Continental Army and its action that woke the heart's blood of Robert, so the father thought. The two comrades, Locke and Oat, their faces and voices reached deep into Robert.

As Locke got going, to his father and Mary he was swift and vivid with more than enthusiasm. Adoration it was the father saw moving this son, two adorations that gave him strength, glow and zest for life, Ann Elwood for one, Nathanael Greene for the other.

"I liked her face the time I saw her at the White Cockade and I can see yet the loveliness of her gray eyes and the smooth rich black of her hair thick around her white face," said Mary.

"She knows just when to be cool and when to be warm," said Locke.

Later Locke talked of General Greene's information that the enemy would land in heavy force under warship guns at some point around New York. And the General had his doubts about letting the enemy choose the New York neighborhood for a campaign. The General seemed to favor burning New York City, blotting it off the earth, and forcing the enemy to come to ground more favorable for the Continental Army. Of two things Locke was certain, first that General Greene would join in no mutterings or complaints about the Commander-in-Chief and would give all he had in loyal support of any plan of campaign that Washington decided on, and second that the year would see terrific fighting and put the Continental Army to harder tests.

Mary had asked Jean Shepherd to bring a bottle of sherry and glasses. Mary poured a glass for Jean. They joined in Mary's good-night toast: "Here's to Michael McGillicuddy and may he be brave and health and good luck go with him." And Jean gave an answering toast: "Good luck before ye, bad luck behind ye, and the grace of God to guide and guard ye."

It was later, before going to their night's sleep, later after quiet talk and the shadowed glow of being together, that the father called on Robert to speak a toast to end the rare evening. They held their glasses long and saw Robert's face white, drawn, strange yet calm. And the waiting troubled no one. Then with a finality each one understood came his words: "To the common cause—so dear to us it is, dearer than life itself."

The father and Mary went upstairs saying good night. Robert before going up spoke to Locke and Oat about their sleep on the front-room carpet being a soldier's luxury. As he turned to go upstairs Locke's two hands took Robert's right hand and pressed it tightly as he said, "Jesus, I'm proud of you, Robert."

* * * * * * * * * *

Chapter 29

* * * * * * * * * *

The Moon Sees Death

THE moonlight made an oblong on the rag rug of the upstairs room. Then with the moving of the moon, far, high and lonely on the sky, the oblong slowly slanted into another shape with sharper triangles at the end. And these triangles shifted smoothly and relentlessly into a thin straight inch-line on the rag rug.

The man and woman in the bed saw nothing of this moonlit oblong and its pale mark that soon fluttered faintly and went away leaving no print of what it had been. The man and woman in the bed slept on as they had many another night when the moon had put those same inevitable changing patterns on the same rag rug.

They had picked several pails of blackberries that day. The man had taken a look at his hayfield and sharpened two scythes to be ready for hay-cutting if the fair and warm weather kept up.

The man stirring in his sleep, suddenly sat up. The woman too sat straight.

"Thee heard?"

"Shots, Jacob."

"Five or six shots?"

"Four, five, mayhap six."

Jacob Drayton was out of bed and into his clothes. He stood at the front door. Off toward the north he heard galloping horse hoofs, heard them slowly fade. His wife was at his elbow. The two young girls and their sixteen-year-old brother came. They listened. The horseman who came into view rode at a slow walk. They went out toward him. He turned his horse toward their gate, stopped and waited. Jacob Drayton had run out to the gate. In front of the rider, slung over the saddle and the horse's shoulders, he saw what seemed the body of a young man.

They let the rider in. They helped carry the body into the front room of the house. Mrs. Drayton sent the girls up for quilts they spread on the floor. They laid the young man's body on a pile of quilts, saw the breath was gone from him, some tension of struggle still marked on his face, a bullet hole nearly over the heart, another bullet hole lower down.

The family cast glances occasionally on the face of the dead youth. The straight massive figure of him they could see had been lithe and swift, while the strange rider gave his name and that of the other one, and how where the road went through the woods a half-mile away two enemy horsemen had wheeled and pointing pistols cried they must hand over their pistols and consider themselves prisoners of the King. In an instant all had emptied their pistols. One of the enemy fell to the ground, his horse running away. "He, too," pointing toward the white face, "fell off his horse that took fright and ran. Thankful I am the nearest house was not Tory."

"Neither are we Whig. We have no part of this war, either side, no hand in the killing of man by man."

And yet could not they do the errand of mercy to take the body of this youth to his father in Philadelphia?

568

"Thee should, it is a work of mercy in the name of the Lord," said Mrs. Drayton.

So the rider soon went on. He had to be going. The orders were that if one of them was stopped the other must go on. The message they carried might mean life or death for some good men that General Washington valued.

Toward the north and New York went the horseman. Toward the south and Philadelphia went a farm wagon, Jacob Drayton driving, at his side his son Enoch. They halted for a look in the underbrush at the face of a trooper in a scarlet coat, with gilt buttons, a white belt and a brass buckle glittering. The moon came out from a fluff of cloud and suddenly lighted the profiled face.

"Not a bad man," said Jacob Drayton, "not a bad face. A mother, a sister, will weep for his not coming home. He could not know what he was doing, to go out and seek to kill other men a sweet summer night like this."

He straightened the body for decency's sake, moved the head so the face turned toward the sky, stood in a silent prayer.

They drove on. Neither the father nor Enoch spoke as the wagon lumbered on. The hush of silence, it was their doctrine and practice, could bring the benefit of calm amid turmoil.

They found the street and the house. They knocked. They saw the father in the doorway holding a candle that lighted his face. The father helped them carry the quilt-wrapped body into a front room to a couch. They were asked to come again sometime to this house where they would always be counted good neighbors. They drove away.

The father sat with his hand in a woman's hand for an hour, two hours, at the couch and the face with the tight-closed lids. He studied the mouth whose tongue had made clear he was prepared for this; if the lips could now speak they would be saying there must be no regrets.

To his other son sleep was so precious now that it would be best to wait until morning before he should know what had happened. In the morning would be the time to say, "Robert, Locke came home last night."

He sent the woman to bed and sleep. "You must have your rest." He sat alone another hour. Then he went to his sleep as though he had done some of his mourning before the sudden bloodshed of the early night. Though he slept deep, twice he awoke and came again to the couch and the lovable bright brown head and the mouth not unlike his own.

****

Chapter 30

****

A Shroud, a Document, a Meeting

A LIFE, even the longest, is a short one. The oldest man that ever lived died at last. Nothing more certain than death and nothing so uncertain as the time and the hour.

These ancient proverbs Ordway Winshore murmured as he walked Philadelphia streets early this July morning on an errand that comes perhaps in each lifetime. He had walked along blocks where the stone houses stood three stories high with four tall windows on each side of the big front door with its shining brass knocker, sixteen windows to the two lower floors and four large dormers on the third floor—and between the house front and the iron picket fence a garden space for roses, for beds of pansies, for winding paths lined with bushes and bordered with mulberry and magnolia. He had walked other blocks where the two-story houses had only a wall between them, stood flush with the sidewalk, and the neighbors always near if not dear to each other. He had walked alleys where through open doors he could see knee-high children taking care of babies that crawled the floor and the mother bent over a washtub and summer flies everywhere in and out of the house. Here along these alleys he expected, for he had been here before, the smell and sight of the chicken house or pigpen so often at the rear of the small lot—and here and there he stepped around a comfortable bleary-eyed hog wallowing in a mudhole.

More than two thousand houses now in this year of 1776 standing in the city named Philadelphia—and exactly ninety-four years ago, a little over nine short decades, not a street nor an alley, not a house big or little. That was when William Penn and the Quakers came in 1682 naming their first settlement with a Latin word meaning "The City of Brotherly Love" though now it was a city split with anger and hate between Tory and Whig, between those who called themselves Loyalists and Patriots. Yet this generation would pass and time would heal old wounds and bring new ones and the birth rate would go on and the babies and the newcomers keep coming and instead of Philadelphia having two thousand houses it would have ten thousand, twenty and forty thousand houses.

"Perhaps so," said Winshore to himself, "I won't see it. The dear boy Locke won't see it. But the children and the children's children of these people in these houses this morning, they will see it."

The future had hold of him. In a grief that he was pressing down and would not let have full sway over him, he reached into the future, the Philadelphia to come, the America to be. It soothed him to do this. The boy Locke in the past two or three years had always been reaching out into that future, talking about it and dreaming of it when he would not talk of it.

"I suppose," said Winshore, "we might write on Locke's gravestone: He died for a future America in which he had complete faith. He was first of all a good soldier, trained under Nathanael Greene so that he would have gone to any death ordered by his general. Yet he couldn't have been that kind of a soldier without the compulsions of his dream of an America to be a great nation lighting the world."

He passed on Sixth Street near Catherine the Four Alls tavern with a painting, on its big sign, of a palace. On the steps stood a king in his crown and robes, an army officer in uniform, a clergyman in gown and bands, a laborer in crinkled leather breeches. What each of these four had to say for himself read:

> King—I govern all.
> General—I fight for all.
> Clergyman—I pray for all.
> Laborer—And I pay for all.

At the store of Attmore & Hellings, on the wharf a few doors below Chestnut Street, he stopped to read a sheet of paper on the door: it told him what loads wagons hauled to Philadelphia from many corners of America, what cargo ships carried from many seas to this American port. "Bar iron, American blister, spring and square steel, sheet and rod iron, bake plates, iron tea kettles, Dutch ovens, pots, kettles and skellets." He read this and said, "We Americans are born ironmongers," and read further, "Tea at the price limited by Congress." Now you could drink tea and you were a good Patriot if you bought it or sold it "at the price limited by Congress." Also Attmore & Hellings were ready to sell you "loaf and brown sugars, molasses, French brandy, Fyal wine, nutmegs, spermaceti and whale oil, mackerel, &c &c &c."

In a store on Water Street, the fifth door above Market, Isaac Hazelhurst was offering "coffee of the best quality, Muscovado sugar in hogsheads, tierces and barrels, molasses, cinnamon, powder blue, and a few hogsheads of exceeding good Jamaica spirits five years old." How many years back was it that Isaac Hazelhurst had come out to pat knee-high Locke on the head and ask him into the store for a helping of Muscovado sugar?

Another store near by always brought him the same thought: After the war and the Revolution there would be generations of Americans who would have peace between wars and they would go far in their work on the earth, in the variety of fascinating forms they would coax

571

from the land. "I think I could have a life given over entirely to peas and beans when I read this announcement of Marson Paddock":

Early Golden Hotspur, early Charlton, Dwarf Marrow-fat, and Dwarf Sugar, with some other Sorts of Pease; broad Windsor beans, broad White Pole, dwarf Yellow and dwarf Speckled beans, with a general assortment of Garden Seeds.

Winshore had a hunger for land, curiosity over what he might do with trees and bushes, with Marson Paddock offering young "grafted and inoculated trees" such as "Cherries, Pears, Peaches, Plumbs, Apricots, Nectarines, Apples, Quinces, Lime Trees, English Elm Trees, &c. Grape Vines of all Sorts, red and White Dutch Currant Bushes, English Gooseberry Bushes of all Sorts, Asparagus Plants of the large early Sorts, Box for Edging of Walks."

Winshore's ignorance of plants and spices came over him. With more time and a little land, of which he had neither, he would open the door and talk with Marson Paddock about "all sorts of Plants in their Season, as Cabbage and Cauliflower, Savoy, Cellery, Endive, Marjoram, Thyme, Savory, Baum, Rue, Sives, Sage, Mint, Sorrel, also Garlick and Horse Radish, all Sorts of Dried Sweet Herbs, all at the very lowest Prices, by Wholesale or Retail, for Cash."

Here Locke and he had paused once and Locke had said that after a time it might be they would have the little farm they had talked of and then they would go into Mr. Paddock's store and get one each of all the interesting seeds, plants, slips and shrubs announced by Mr. Paddock.

On Second Street between Market and Arch streets he came to where Hyns Taylor "begs leave to inform his friends and the public in general, that he makes up all kinds of furniture in the newest fashing, *viz.* dome, teaster; drapery, Venetian, Gothic, canopy, four-poster and couch beds, also field and camp beds, all sorts of mattresses, Venetian and festoon window curtains, and every other article of household furniture, terms most reasonable."

Next door was the place he had his errand. "Cynthia George, Milaner and Mantua Maker," read the first large-letter lines of her announcement, which continued, "makes up all sorts of milanery goods, *viz.* childbed linen, children's robes, jams, frocks, vests and tunics, gentlemen's shirts, stocks, gloves and all kinds of needlework, in the very latest manner."

Cynthia George had just opened the store for the day's trade, it seemed, and two women could be seen in the rear room making ready for their day's needlework. A short stout blond woman in an orange bodice and a triangle with foam-white ruffs that gave a fleeting view of her well-rounded breasts. A plump face with a full underlip and they were very cool, calm, grayish-blue eyes that Winshore looked into. An independent woman with no excess of courtesy, not troubled about ad-

572

dress and manners, saying, "Yes, sir, what might be your good wish this morning?"

"A peculiar errand I have with you."

"You are not a lawyer come to collect a bill, I hope."

A woman of humor, not afraid of lawyers though she knew persons who were—that was her little joke.

"You could be taken for a lawyer, sir," she added with so bright and pleasant a look that he saw she mistook his load of grief for ordinary gloom, his breakfast not sitting well perhaps.

"There are many kinds of lawyers. I hope I look like one you could trust."

He wanted her trust. Whatever he had come in for she must give him trust. Now she knew that and her underlip was very grave, and her eyes flawless as they gazed into his deep-set eyes with shadowy quivers of brown moving in them.

"You do have a peculiar errand, no common business you come on early this morning," she said.

"You are Miss George?"

"Yes."

"I am Mr. Winshore, Ordway Winshore of the Bradford printery." He reached a hand toward her and they shook hands warmly. "William Bradford, as you may know, has left his shop, his bookstore, his coffee-house and his insurance company, and is away with General Washington's army."

"I had heard of that."

"The printery he has left in my charge, though of course the business I came on has nothing to do with printing."

He hesitated, not over what to say, but in a sudden remembrance of the figure of Locke lying silent and cold out at the house.

"Yes?" said Miss George softly.

"It's my boy I come about. He looks like me, same eyes and hair, same cut of face. His mother died when he was born and I brought him up—the Negro woman Emmeline and I, we brought him up though perhaps some credit should go to a brother just a little older who is a fine specimen of a man now.

"A little more than a year now since my boy Locke went into the army and General Nathanael Greene, you've heard of him I suppose, took a liking to the boy, found he could trust him. They could put him on a horse and send him with orders and messages and he would get through. He seemed to know when to be cautious and when to be reckless. And it was only last night he rode out of Philadelphia with another horseman. They both had copies of important papers they must get to General Washington's headquarters. If one didn't get through the other would. Whatever happened one of them must get through. And it wasn't as far as eleven miles out of Philadelphia where the road ran through heavy woods, two enemy horsemen tried to stop them and there was a fight and all four emptied out their pistols. One of the enemy rode away wounded, another lay dead, and Locke's companion brought his body slung over a horse to a Quaker farmer who hitched a cart and brought Locke's body to our house only six or seven hours ago."

"God help us," said Cynthia George in amazement and in affectionate response to this father who had drifted into her store with this wild tale early of a morning.

"Now he's out there in the front room of our house, a white sheet over all of him but the face and the embalmer is to come this morning and tomorrow we will have short services and the burial."

"And your errand with me? I would like to help, Mr. Winshore. I can assure you I would like to help."

"I'm coming to that. He was a fine figure of a boy. And now we're going to lay him in the cold ground after our last look at his face and his earthly frame of a body."

He had brushed his hands together as though to rid them of any dust and ran his fingers tenderly over a bolt of white linen, a strong and thick fabric, immaculate and gleaming.

"Yes? and now?" Miss George was the image of attention.

"I've been thinking it would be nice, no, it would be utterly appropriate, for you to make a shroud, a winding sheet of some material like this, and you would make it very plain and simple and you might put on it any slight touches that you would think right. I would leave it to you. Any ornament should be so slight it could hardly be seen."

"You would trust me for that, Mr. Winshore?"

"From what I had heard of you I believed you could do it, now that I have met you and talked with you about it, I have no doubt you can do this service."

Winshore saw her eyes glistening. She brought a chair for him, saying he had had a hard night, brought another chair for herself, seated herself, leaned far toward his face. "I will work on this today and my two good women will give it their time. One of them is far from common with the needle."

Now Miss George gave him a close scrutinizing glance, and went on to say, "You should know a year ago or two years ago I would have served you as one more ordinary patron of this store. I cared for neither side. I said to the Tory and the Whig, It's as far from here to there as it is from there to here and I'm not going to join in your wrangling. A Tory called me a mongrel. A Whig called me a king-kisser. Then my boy went in. He's a short thickset staunch boy, nineteen years old, the same big dark eyes as his father who was killed at Ticonderoga in the French and Indian War. He enlisted in New York where I had my store then and I went out to the camp where he was drilling and training and he came in a few times to see me. Now no one could have argued me into joining the Rebels. But he burned with something inside him and it got into me and burns there now. I have letters from him. The last I saw him he was on a horse with a company that rode into New York and wrecked the printery of *Rivington's Gazetteer*."

"No! Who would believe it?" broke in Winshore. "My boy out in the house there now, my boy was in that affair. Your boy and mine rode together that day."

"And I have my boy yet," she said with a choke and a shrug. She rose. "Time passes. How tall was your boy?"

"About a half-inch taller than me and I am five feet eight inches." She took a pencil and noted this. "And his weight?"

"Near to one hundred and sixty pounds. He actually gained weight in the army. He always worked indoors in a printery and the outdoor life of the army, he took to it."

"I'll hope my boy does that. Now this very linen here that you touched and admired, we'll make it out of this. You'll be going to your home or your day's work now. We'll begin on this right off. I'll try to come myself to the Bradford printery by six o'clock and show it to you and leave it to you to take home."

Winshore walked home to the house in a curious glow of dark solemnity mingled with an exaltation. Over coffee, bread and butter and a boiled egg, he told Mary of the shroud and of Cynthia George and her boy. After the embalmer had finished, they went with him and viewed Locke's body, told the embalmer he had done well and saw him out the door. In two large chairs gazing at the body with a white bed sheet drawn to the chin, they sat keeping company with Locke's head and face.

"Mortal remains," said Winshore. "He was mortal and had breath in him. Now the breath is gone and here are the remains—a husk, a shell, an outer vestige, a garment of clay that will molder with worms eating their way through it till they come to the bones. They will leave the bones to time and when enough years go by time will have eaten the bones to a thin white ash, a very fine dust."

"A process of the elements," chimed Mary in a soft contralto. "It will come to you and to me and to every one of the millions who now walk the earth. King George will be laid away in silk and regalia in a marble tomb and it will count no more than with Locke in his plain linen winding sheet."

"A husk, a shell," said Winshore. "Speech gone, thought gone, and the dreams gone. Yet the dream Locke died for, the dream that Joseph Warren died for, the dream that sent Robert to agony on the Kennebec River—all of them held that dream to be deathless. There are men thankful they can live in a time when great dreams take hold of men."

"Yes, God help us," said Mary. "There are men who go stalking

575

through life to end in magnificent tombs without once being shaken by enduring flame, eight white horses in plumes and spangles hauling a cadaver in resplendent garb, a husk and a shell, as you say, never in all its days touched by a great human dream, a vision and a hope incalculably greater than any lone individual, any shovel of dust held and moved in the possession of the dream."

Robert had entered and seated himself and said no word through their murmurings. Now he did say swiftly, "You people, you two, in your quiet conversation that I could hardly catch, you have spoken Locke's funeral oration, so far as I am concerned. I hope you limit the preacher tomorrow to some favorite passages from the Bible and perhaps one or two paragraphs from Tom Paine."

They said nothing now, resting their eyes occasionally on Locke's head with the thick brown hair neatly parted, a heavy straggle of it down his forehead as he usually had it, and the wide slash of his mouth composed and utterly grave as though "I have said it all and there will be no more from me."

Soon Ordway Winshore's head sloped forward. His unrest had been quieted by the hush of peace on Locke's face and mouth. In his final sleep he too would look so. Now he drowsed. Robert tiptoed to the front door and out, on his way to the town and an important session of the Continental Congress. Mary took up household duties. And the father in his bent posture in the chair breathed heavily and sonorously in his sleep while his son lay with no stir in a stillness of lips that the mightiest hammers and the most colossal sledges of earth couldn't break.

The mahogany secretary at the printery where Winshore wrote letters and handled ledgers, bills, orders, complaints, stood battered, nicked, scratched and scrawled, and as sturdy as ten years ago when new. In one corner of the secretary stood a small square of thick paper and on it the first piece of printing wherein Locke six years ago set the type and ran it off a press and took pride in it. The text was from Ben Franklin and read:

> Printers indeed should be very careful how they omit a Figure or Letter; For by such Means Sometimes a terrible Alteration is made in the Sense. I have heard, that once, in a new edition of the *Common Prayer*, the following Sentence, "We shall all be chang'd in a Moment, in the Twinkling of an Eye," by the Omission of a Single Letter, became, "We shall all be hang'd in a Moment, &c," to the no small Surprise of the first Congregation it was read to.

The father reached for this, read it, and recalled Locke's joking that "the great Art and Mystery of Printing" was a great art true enough but no mystery to him for he would soon be able to stand at the type case with his eyes shut and pick out letters, capitals, numbers, italics, punctuation marks, initials, flowers, plumes and headpieces. Double pica Roman, English Roman, French Canon Roman, the boy babbled his early pride in having learned these "founts" of type. Time had since shown, the father was thinking, that Locke was no natural-born printer but had caught a surface enthusiasm from his father's deep devotion to the printing craft.

Now today the father would stand at the type case in a leather apron and pick the letters and make the type arrangement for the document expected this day from the Continental Congress. In these later years it was only on special work that Winshore took a hand at the type case. He had in his day set up newspaper intelligence items, editorials, advertisements, and almanacs, hymnbooks, collections of sermons and political speeches, pamphlets, tracts, title pages, woodcuts with and without plumes. He felt interest, even challenge, about the work to come today.

Late in the afternoon came Robert, somewhat breathless, for he had walked as fast as he dared.

"It is to be read aloud to all the armed forces authorized by the Continental Congress," said Robert in catches of breath, "on all our warships and privateers—and in all churches, mass meetings, and gatherings of men who are for the Cause."

Mary had quit writing a letter at the mahogany secretary and come to hear Robert adding, "It is the first announcement to go from the Continental Congress to all the governments of all the other nations of the world."

"The long-waited Declaration! My God!" cried the father, reading the title and heading he was to set: "In Congress, July 4, 1776. The Unanimous Declaration of the thirteen united States of America." Then he read on, the cadenced opening paragraph:

> When in the course of human events
> it becomes necessary for one people
> to dissolve the political bonds
> which have connected them with another,
> and to assume
> among the powers of the earth,
> the separate and equal station
> to which the Laws of Nature
> and of Nature's God
> entitle them,
> a decent respect to the opinions of mankind requires
> that they should declare the causes
> which impel them to the separation.

He read on. It was meat and drink to him. It was a mystic music to him. It had the laughter of Locke when he said good-by yesterday afternoon and went away with his brown eyes bold and confident. The words ran:

> We hold these truths
> to be self-evident,
> that all men are created equal,
> that they are endowed by their Creator
> with inherent and unalienable rights,
> that among these
> are Life, Liberty, and the pursuit of Happiness.—
> That to secure these rights,
> Governments are instituted among Men,
> deriving their just powers
> from the consent of the governed.—
> That whenever any Form of Government
> becomes destructive of these ends,
> it is the right of the People
> to alter or to abolish it,
> and to institute
> new Government,
> laying its foundation on such principles,
> and organising its powers in such form
> as to them shall seem most likely to effect
> their Safety and Happiness.

He scanned it swiftly and picked out the austere and momentous pledge that closed the document:

> And for the support
> of this Declaration,
> we mutually pledge
> to each other
> our Lives,
> our Fortunes,
> and our Sacred Honour.

Winshore's eyes had been screwed to this paper, this document. Now raising them he saw Robert's face white, his body with a queer hang to it. "I would like to send you home and put you to bed, Robert. You are a trifle limp. Now you go straight back to that bookbinder's table in the corner and stretch out there and get you a good rest right now."

Robert straightened, gave his father a tipsy gaze. The unknowing might have thought he had had one drink too many.

"Come along now, Robert, it will be good for you," said Mary, locking an arm in his and walking him to the corner, hanging his

578

coat on a wall peg, loosening his top shirt buttons, laying one blanket over the table and fixing a pillow of another blanket, making him stretch out with a sigh of relief, and easing his shoes off. She left him with his eyes closed and on her way to the mahogany secretary said to her husband, "He's better right off."

Robert was near asleep when two flies began crawling over his face and one that had located his hand sunk a bite into him that brought him up sitting.

Now he took a quiet laugh for himself. Did he know this breed of flies? He did. He knew them well. On hot afternoons lately they had honored the delegates of the Continental Congress and now it was a distinction that they should pick on him, a lone weak person in this printery corner. He looked at one that came through the window and sat on his big toe to reconnoiter the field. "The same size, the same impudence, the same sharp bite you give the delegates," he laughed. Here the flies were few, however, while over there at Carpenter's Hall, with a livery stable next door and horses and dung piles for feeding grounds, the flies bred and thrived and swarmed through the windows and bit through silk stockings and thin shirts. One Virginia delegate agreed with others that the momentous resolutions that week would have been delayed in passage but for the incessant operations of persistent and bloodthirsty insects keeping the delegates completely awake and ready to pass on long-unfinished business.

Robert got up and pulled down the window and stretched out again with a newspaper over his face and another over his hands, and soon fell into sleep.

Through the front door of the shop had come a woman with a bundle under an arm. Her eyes ranged over the shop and she walked straight to Winshore at the type case. She held out the bundle for him to see it as it lay on her two flat hands. He didn't see her for the bundle. He could see they had cared, they had anxiety to make it look precious in a smooth thick pale-gray paper bound in blue-and-buff cords of silk.

His eyes followed the bundle as she stepped to a near-by table and unwrapped it, and tenderly and with skilled hands that seemed to know every fold of it, smoothed out to full length the garment that would shroud Locke for his last earthly journey.

Winshore's eyes ran the length of the winding sheet. Then his hands went smooth along it. He had never been a man for ceremonial and regalia, punctilio of form, and his assurance to himself now was that this final vesture for that boy was fitting. The fabric had luster without gloss. Shrewd eyes and hands had seen to its strength of fiber and delicacy of texture at a hand loom, then bleached and dressed it with a sagacity out of long experience with linen. So it was both rugged and fine—the perfect sheathing for a bare body to lie in final repose in a small oblong of cold earth.

He saw a fine thin braid of blue-and-gold edging had been hemmed in so delicately that it took a second close study to notice it. While his eyes still roved over the winding sheet, Winshore said, "Cynthia George gave great care to this."

"She instructed me to make it sweet and reverent, those were her very words, sweet and reverent."

His hands again ran softly over it, the finger ends touching the blue-and-gold edging. "It was your handiwork?"

"My day's work and you might say a holy day. I am instructed by Miss George to remind you that she has a boy of her own in the Continental Army and she wishes it understood that she cannot think of accepting any remuneration for this piece of goods. Her exact words were, 'Tell Mr. Winshore that I am a Christian, a mother and a Patriot first of all before I am a mantuamaker.'"

The excitement of the night before, the sorrow and the inevitable duties, the further impact of exultation over the Declaration of Independence arriving to his hands, had brought Winshore to where he was moving bodily and mentally not in a daze or trance but in profound preoccupations. His mind and spirit had been sent groping and clutching amid all the abstractions his life had accumulated around the immense themes of death and love, immortality and faith, human freedom and dreams worth dying for.

Now for the first time he turned for a full look into the face of the woman who had brought the shroud, whose fingers had caressed it with a gracious and breathing handiwork. Now as he looked into her face he saw it was one he had met before. It had changed since he met it, the oval of it slightly more narrow, the gaunt quality of it having more of the gaunt, and he thought he could remember a reckless flair of pride that now had become something else. He dug down into his index of faces and the name to go with this face and then, "I am correct, am I not, and you are Miss Wilming, Marintha Wilming?"

"We saw tea burn, we saw tea hanged on the gallows."

"We did, more than a year ago, and now the war has surged up from where it lay waiting to break on us, and you have come four hundred miles from Boston down to Philadelphia."

"I went to New York, you remember, to help a woman open her new dress shop. That was Cynthia George. I worked with her in New York this spring and helped her move down here."

Mary had come over to listen to part of this, then to shake hands with Mim. And Mary was going to ask Mim where she had been and what doing. Then she read in Mim's face and eyes a dark turmoil, that only by an effort was Mim holding herself together. Mary laid a hand on the quiet burial garment, "Did I hear you did the work on this today?"

"Yes," came from Mim with a faint tremolo Winshore didn't hear but Mary did. That same tremolo was in the face and eyes though not so definitely.

Mary took Mim to one side. Winshore stood over the shroud, giving it final glances and touches before going to the type case. "You can see he's lost in his grief," said Mary, "not broken, but bowed down. He tells me he would rather have died himself than have this boy go. It may be you can come and see what an impressive splendid face he has even cold with the life gone."

"Yes, I must have one long look at that face," said Mim in a faltering voice.

"There is something of pitiless beauty, something stark and melting," Mary went on, a little shaken herself yet finding relief in telling another woman an impression that haunted her, "about seeing the father's face and head alongside that boy's face and head. They looked alike in life and in death the boy looks still more like his father."

"My God! It is Locke then who was killed!"

"You didn't know?"

"I had no chance to know. I heard nothing more than that it was his son."

And Mary's keen ear got it that the tremolo was still there in Mim's voice but now it was an excitement of the knowledge that Robert still lived. She saw Mim's face and eyes shade into a strange glow. Mary read clear that whatever had happened between Mim and Robert in the past Robert now meant the world to her.

Mary spoke softly. What she said made Mim close her eyes and slowly clench her hands while her even white teeth moved over lower lip and then upper lip, biting the pale lips scarlet.

"Robert Winshore," said Mary, "is in the back of the printery on a bookbinder's worktable. He is sleeping or resting there. Hard-worn he is, you should know. He came here to his father's house early in June, rather a shadow of what he once was and he has been making a recovery but it has come slowly."

"I'll go see him. I'll go softly. I'll not wake him, you may depend."

"You'll take every care? He needs rest, God he needs rest. You believe you'll rest him?"

"If I can't, if I don't," and Mary thought it was an inexplicable and marvelous shadow of loveliness that crossed Mim's face, "then tomorrow I'll want to sew a shroud for myself of black linen with two black roses stitched at the breasts small and fine and I can't think of a nightshade black of cloth that would be too dark for such a shroud."

Mary believed her. Mary walked with Mim to where they saw

Robert on his back, the window light dim in the corner, a newspaper over his hands, another newspaper having slid away from most of his face, and his eyes closed. Mary went away, giving a fierce pinch to Mim's arm as though to say, "My prayers go for the two of you."

Mim glided as a frame of shadow on feet of mist to where she stood in reach of the sleeper. She felt herself a sort of ghost and him another ghost, though she asked if a ghost could have a curiosity like hers near to a hunger, and if a ghost could have such thick dark hair as she saw flowing away from his forehead and then tousled as though her fingers had run through it. High hope she had now. He was alive. She mourned that death had come to Locke. She exulted, not sure why, over Robert among the living. His eyes were closed. He hadn't heard her. He might be sleeping or dozing half-awake, his chin, that jutting and determined chin, shifting to point in a new direction.

She stood with her right hand folded tight over the fingers of her left hand. She ran her eyes from his face to his feet where one bare toe stuck out on the left-foot stocking and three on the right. She wanted to reach and touch him. She held back. The first this was she had seen him in uniform. Her right foot touched his three-cornered hat that had fallen off the table. She glanced to the long coat of blue with buff trimmings that hung on a peg above the table. His wool shirt had the same worn look as the stockings, with holes, stains and splotches. Two small holes in a shirt sleeve had been burnt, perhaps from fire sparks while he slept.

Her right hand pressed hard the left-hand fingers as it dawned on her more vividly that toil, exposure to raw weather, cares, duties and battle fatigue had worn his rugged body to frail edges. The pathos of that shirt, hanging so loose on him about his torso, smote her. The shrinking that torso had undergone, that body her arms had so many times encircled, she saw it and a guilt came over her. She put away the guilt with a single eyeblink. That could wait. If he was now better than when he had come home then at that time he must have been emaciated.

He was stirring. He raised his right leg, laid the right ankle onto the left, gave a slow delicious sigh of ease.

His eyelids parted and through the slit he looked at his feet, wagged the three bare toes back and forth as though they might be telling him, "We're here and you're here and it does seem as though if we call the roll we're all here."

Now his eyes came full-open. The pivot of his head brought his eyes around to where they fell on Mim. His eyes dwelt on her face, peered straight into her eyes as his mouth screwed itself into a comic twist and the tip of his tongue came out and Mim half-expected he was going to stick out his tongue at her. His face smoothed down and his eyes ranged the length of her from head to toes and then back to her face and eyes.

He shook his head sharply to make sure he was awake, again ran his eyes over her, blinked and looked again. He then dropped his head to a complete resting position, gazed at the ceiling, closed his eyes fast and tight, held them so a few moments, then opened them wide and flashed them full on Mim, and seeing precisely what he had seen before, he spoke as casually as a man in a dream, "I've seen the ghost of you so many times I'll burn my boots if you're not a ghost now."

Mim stood in her foot tracks. She couldn't move. She couldn't be sure what to do if she moved. She saw in his eyes an unfathomable final something that his father saw and feared. Her shoulders shook. When her eyes closed an instant and opened, two or three large tears slowly draggled down her cheeks.

He raised his shoulders, drew himself to a sitting position, and with a curious soft mockery, "But the ghosts I saw never cried. They were too proud to cry. They wouldn't cry if the sky should come falling down. They wouldn't cry if all the stars in the night sky were crying."

He turned his head toward the ceiling, laughed a hollow ha-ha with a peculiarly merry chuckle in it, then turned to her with an appeal not loud but deep-toned, beseeching her with a grotesque mouth, "Jesus, good lady, have a little pity on me. I've had my share of spells with hallucinations. That's the name for 'em—hallucinations. You see 'em. You reach. They're gone. And you're a fool. I've seen you before. I put my hand out for you. And what I got was nothing, a bubble, a bauble, a whiff and a whoof of phantasmagoria and you can look at it and say 'Good evening, my sweet phantasmagoria, how do you fare today and will you walk a piece with me?' and you get no answer and you come out of it with a splitting headache and you poke the fire and pile on wood and roll into your blanket again praying in Sweet Jesus' name for no more phantasmagoria."

His eyes left her. He meditated aloud. "Up on the Kennebec River sleeping in the snow near the Canadian line I had some of the dangdest meals of roast duck with plum pudding and grape-jelly tarts with strong hot coffee, food as fancy as ever a man threw into his belly, and when I came out of it and sat up shiverin in my wet clothes, it was just one more of those tricks, a cheat, a bubble, a bauble."

His head pivoted swiftly to see if she were still there, and, "Stop your danged cryin. Step over here and put your hand in my hand. I'll be danged if I'll reach for you."

Their hands met. Their mouths met. His feet swung to the floor and they stood locked and interlocked in moaning and quavers.

Something struck the floor near them. They looked and saw Robert's father and Mary gesturing. They were leaving and had thrown the front door key to Robert and Mim, who plainly wouldn't be leaving.

Suddenly Robert had lifted Mim and seated her on the table with her feet dangling. Himself he seated on the table with his back to the wall and his legs crossed under him tailorwise. Then she saw his face cold and he was asking, "How do we know? Can it be we are making a beginning that will have the same end as the last beginning? How do we know?"

A flash of pain crossed her face as he saw it in profile and as it lingered when her face turned toward him. She would have that flash, he thought, if her arm ever had his rheumatism. He was less cold saying, "I wouldn't bring you pain, Mim. You're the last person in the world I would bring pain to."

"Not now, Robert, please don't be ice now. Another time be ice if you must—not now."

"Who taught me I must teach myself to be ice? It was you."

"I didn't know what I was doing that night. I was out of my head. I was daft. I was crazy with grief. I was tangled head and foot."

"So I said to myself over and over. You didn't mean it, I said. Up on the Kennebec River your ghost would keep coming to me and I would talk with your ghost about it. I was down to skin and bone. There was one night they cooked a dog for supper. They boiled the guts of that dog and tried eating it and spit it out. That was about when I said I must forget you because I began saying to your ghost, 'You did mean it, Mim, and how could you, how could you mean it?' I had enough bitterness without remembering you told me you would forget my name and every letter of my name and I could do the same for you."

His hand went to a pocket and brought out a small fistful that he unfolded and he spread on the table the blue silk kerchief. Now the tears poured down Mim's face. He went on, " 'I give you this to forget me by.' Those were your words. 'I give you this to forget me by.' Remembering you began to hurt so much and was such a pain that I decided it was good advice you gave me and I should try to make myself forget you. I was forgetting warm clothes, pleasant firesides, because it hurt to think of them. I was blotting out memories of good food and clean beds because that hurt. And of all memories yours hurt the worst, yours gave the hardest pain. And it got after a while that I could forget you a whole day and sometimes two or three days not a thought of you."

Mim winced and thrust out her two hands to press his left hand and drop it.

"I practiced at learning to forget you," he went on. "With practice I improved at forgetting you. As time went by I said you must have spoken wisdom and it was important to forget you, never to see you again, never to let there be a beginning again, for another beginning could have an end like the last beginning had."

He was tired. His head slumping sidewise said so, his head leaning at the brick wall, as words came from him in a dreaminess of song murmur: "Is love a necklace I can put on and take off? Is love a shoe

I can slip on or kick off, if I please, to the moon? In five minutes by the clock, love can be a thrush pouring flights of song with scarlet numbers and dancing alphabets—and in that same five minutes before your eyes that triumphant wild thrush becomes a monkey scratching a louse at his ribs and a louse at his buttocks while he mocks at you with his jeering monkey-faces."

He could remember, after all that had passed, the lines she spoke to her dance named "Love Is a Two-face." He was whispering, "The jeering monkey-faces, I saw many of them, I hope you saw a few." He wasn't looking at her and he went on as though she were not there and listening: "Love is a great gleaming eagle that will sweep you for a ride to the top of the sky and a spread of green valleys and winding rivers for your eyes—it happens, it is an event—and love is a buzzard you can mistake for an eagle to ride, a scavenger who drops you to your death and takes its time to feed on you and pick your bones white and polished—this too happens and this too is an event."

He had paused for exact remembering, had hesitated and fumbled a moment and then gone on, his memorizing of her lines perfect.

"I couldn't say them," said Mim. "I've lost them. I found them when I found you. I lost them when I lost you, when one of my dreams ran that you wrote me a long letter of pride and anger and laid it on a fire and watched it burn and then in the middle of a sheet of foolscap, having sharpened a quill to write very fine, you wrote:

'My once dearest Mim—Since
it is thy spoken wish, I
cross thee quite out of my
book.   Robert Winshore'

The dream ended there. I like to think if it had gone on you would have laid this second letter in the fire."

"I could have written it and I could have sent it from the Kennebec River when there was health and strength in forgetting you. I did anything that would help forget. I used to make a list in my mind of all your faults, the faults you yourself admit to and especially the faults mean gossips give you. That helped, like it helped to repeat an old saying in one of my father's books: Whosoever hath her hath a wet eel by the tail."

"That was unclean, Robert."

"And unjust. But it helped me forget."

Were they getting anywhere? What was happening between them? Mim was asking herself. The answers, for the immediate moment, came to her.

"Forgive me, Robert, forgive me not for all time nor forever. Only a few days now forgive me. And listen to me for one or two minutes."

"Tell it. I have talked too much. I could better have slept than talk like I have. Or I could have listened while you told me where in hell you have been since I saw you last." He laughed. It came rather thin and hollow, not full-blooded.

"I was getting to exactly that. We have been prattling here. Since we saw each other you have been to hell and so have I and we haven't begun to tell it. You have done hard duty and met heavy grief today and you are worn. I didn't know you were in Philadelphia. I came here with Cynthia George when she moved her shop from New York. I intended to seek out your father sometime and ask him about you. And I asked Cynthia to let me deliver the shroud I worked on all day so I might learn which son of your father had gone to the Great Valley."

And Robert saw a gray-blue seadrench in her eyes, ominous resolves beyond his reading now. She slid off the table. She pulled out his feet and straightened him and made a pillow and told him she would bring a chair and sit quietly by him for ten minutes or longer, when she would see him home. "You must do this. Tomorrow, later, we can talk. Another time we can report to each other what we saw, you in your hell and I in mine."

She took his head between her hands and touched his lips with a long foam-light kiss, stood by him with her hands softly alive over his eyes, whispering he must rest and sleep. Then she brought a chair and sat in quiet, watching him ease away into the rest his body and mind sought.

★ ★ ★ ★ ★ ★ ★ ★ ★ ★

Chapter 31

★ ★ ★ ★ ★ ★ ★ ★ ★ ★

Robert Hears the Saga of Mim

IN a wide cone of blue paper Marintha Wilming brought an armful of white roses and a handful of pansies and two crimson damask roses. With these heavy white roses, a fall and a droop to their leaves and a fold over fold of the petal curves, she made a long thin oval around the body of Locke in his shroud. Here and there a black-and-gold pansy set its punctuation in the white-leafed oval. Above the two hands and touching the first-finger knuckles she laid the blush-red damask roses.

She took a chair next to Robert and her voice reminded him of the thin blue silk of the token kerchief. She was saying as between the two of them, "A long journey—no harm in a few emblems—black and gold for midnight and dawn—white and endless white for the immortal part of him that's gone and can never molder."

586

Till midnight they kept that room alive with their stillness and their sudden snatches of talk, remembering this and that of him, Winshore, Robert, Mary and Mim, and for a time Jean Shepherd mutely sobbing—and Emmeline, the Negro woman who wet-nursed him and brought him along and now wept and cried, "He was purty fer a baby and he purty now fer a man. Gawd, he nevah look so like his fathah."

Cynthia George came for a while and vanished as quietly as she came, having kept her chair to the wall, seeming to be aware precisely what the evening was about, seeming to represent many of like sorrow who couldn't come.

Occasionally one or two rose to stand at the coffin and gaze on the face, to marvel at the fixity of the eyes never to open again and the mouth never again to give forth a syllable of speech, in awe at the irrevocable fact of death.

Robert sat as a grave changeless stone when the father told of Locke at the statue of Pitt in New York giving an imitation of his brother declaiming Pitt's famous lines in sympathy with the American colonies.

Later Mim sensed a complicated tenderness in Robert's telling of the deep and sure bonds that had grown between Locke and Ann Elwood and how hard it would be for Ann to hear the news.

A subdued woe came from the father in pointing to the strides and growths he had seen in Locke since the boy went into the army. In time he would have been a colonel with his own regiment and later a general. The family had lost a rare boy, the country a great soldier.

They buried Locke early the next morning in a grave next to his mother's, between two small cedar trees in a square marked by four Lombardy poplars. The minister read from the Bible favorite passages of Locke and his father including the verses, "Charity vaunteth not itself, is not puffed up," and "Blessed are the meek, for they shall inherit the earth." From a worn and much-thumbed copy of *Common Sense* the minister read paragraphs that Locke knew by heart, then two verses from the "Liberty Song":

"Torn from a world of tyrants, beneath the western sky
We formed a new dominion, a land of liberty:
The world shall own we're freemen here, and such will ever be.
Huzza! huzza! huzza! huzza for love and liberty! . . .

"The land where Freedom reigns shall still be masters of the main,
In giving laws and freedom to subject France and Spain,
And all the isles o'er ocean spread shall tremble and obey
The prince who rules by Freedom's laws in North America."

"Two years of storm—and he is ten years older—his face scraped and furrowed ten years older—his knees and elbows older and his right knee joint with its pitiless flashes that still keep coming, the bone

587

joint a hundred and two hundred years older than when I first met him in Boston two years ago."

This was Mim talking to herself about Robert as she saw him in the days after Locke's death. "His kisses are less swift and lingering," she said. "Yet I have had slow long kisses from him now that hold the pity of night stars and seadrench in them. Yes, kisses I have had from him now with a lasting tang of bittersweet I would rather have on my mouth than highly praised honey or candy sweet."

The father saw to it. So did Mary. Robert must have care, attention, rest, sleep, no wearing excitement, so they told Mim, no long visits, no long talks, rest, sleep, and whatever might give his mind quiet and his heart consolation. "You are thoughtful," said Mim, letting them know she had earlier considered seeking out Robert but she had kept from going to him afraid of what the shock and tumult of their meeting would do to him. When she did go to him it was not of her planning. When she sewed a shroud on the day of July 4, "I couldn't always see the work I was doing half-expecting it was to wrap Robert." They should understand, too, that she had heard Robert tell, and the telling eased him or she wouldn't have let him go on with it, of his hard and humble service at Washington's headquarters and the shaping of an army that after the evacuation of Boston melted half away, of his escape from starvation and death in snow and ice on the Kennebec. When he became too graphic in the mean, the scrawny, the devastating details of what he went through on the Kennebec she would interrupt and lead him away.

"He was out of his mind for some days, I'm sure," said Mim. "And when you try to tell someone else how it happened and how you came out of it, you can make desperate work of it."

Mim saw Winshore and Mary look in each other's eyes with meaning, enough for Mim to know they understood she herself had probably gone out of her mind and if she were to tell Robert about it she would do so gently and delicately, with healing rather than hurt for him.

That Robert had told her of his meetings and walks with Ann Elwood and how close he had held Ann and how at cost he broke away—of this Mim couldn't speak to Winshore and Mary.

Winshore's full-throated laugh was gone in these days. At meals or in his chair at a writing table Mary and Mim had noticed him drop his hands and stare at nothing in particular for a while. His talk had less of banter and fantasy. He sought out in her alley cabin the old Negro woman Emmeline one afternoon and mentioned this visit casually at home, "I wanted to talk with her about how it felt to handle Locke and throw him around when he was a baby learning to walk."

In two weeks he would be going, said Robert. The way he said it had finality. He had been where hard decisions are made and men accept those decisions and do the best they can by what of necessity and fate follows. The others in the house, including Jean Shepherd and Mim who came to stay two and three hours every evening, offered their gentle hints to Robert that another two months of rest and regular meals, with a dry corner to sleep in, would bring him back to complete health and he would return to the army a better soldier for heavy duty. They gathered by his quiet answers that he had thought it all over.

The shame was on him of half the army leaving General Washington after the siege of Boston, leaving for comfort and fun and grudges against officers and discipline, leaving after months of sleeping on the cold ground again to slide into the clean sheets of a bed with a rainproof roof and again to put arms around a wanted and cherished woman. In that kind of shame, the result of seeking personal pleasures and gratifications, he was going to have no part. The longer he put off a decision and lived at ease and "resting," the more would be the danger he might take the course of others who had meant to stay home for a few weeks and had never come back to the army. An edge of sarcasm had come into the way he could say the word "resting."

"If his scorn of rest, which is near to a fear of rest, deepens much more," said the father to Mary and Mim, "you can see he will probably get more true rest with the army than here."

The women agreed. He came from a world with its own secrets, the army of men whose world was shock and tumult and blood when it wasn't dreary monotony or camp fever or a variety of disorders of men without women, the longing for home, the heaviness of no escape from the pettiness and arrogance of supposed "superiors," the hurt of seeing good men go to pieces.

A shirt of finespun gray wool Mim was sewing for Robert, and she said, "I make it loose expecting you will gain twenty pounds."

"Shrewd enough," said Robert.

At the house while they chatted of evenings Mim made complete repairs of neat patches and restitchings on his uniform. She had asked to replace his old stockings with a new pair from an assortment at Cynthia George's store and Robert preferred she would darn the holes and tears in the old pair. "I'll begin where those toes stick out," she said.

This evening, as often before, Robert's eyes drew to her face and held to a steady gaze as he tried to fix his mind on what was the change that had come over her. More thin, more gaunt she was, more down to bare bones yet nothing sickly or weak about her as with him. She seemed to have some sure strength not there in the old days. She seemed tireless of body and mind and perhaps never so quick and clever with her hands and so ready-witted at any given moment. Her mouth lay as a vivid wafer of pale plum blossom wind-blown and held firm on the day-white bone structure of her face. When her full wide smile came over the even white teeth the lips spread tighter and more round and full. Her head of chestnut hair, done with skill in plaits and ropes, shone rich as ever with the same changing slight burnish of bronze as the light on it varied. The eyebrows hung thick and twisted in comic shags, the one feature reporting definitely her stubborn will, thought Robert. The eyes as before varied, from a deep sea-blue to a stormish green. The impression came to him she had been hard-worn and haggard, everything failing her except those clear unfailing eyes.

This was the evening he wouldn't be put off. "I can stand it if you can. The dark journey you called my story when I told it. Now I must hear your dark journey, even if it hurts you a little to tell it."

"It's part of my bones and blood now. I'll make it short as I can and pray it won't hurt you." She smiled faintly, a mild swift grimace over her face, the odd stretch of skin made luminous by the white bone curves underneath. Robert read it, or believed he did, and it sent a glad streak through him, for that look in the old days cried a proud abandon. Now it still held abandon, a reckless flair, with a touch, more than a touch, of austerity. "Your dark journey—tell it," he said.

She had never before been hunted. She had been watched, innocently unaware she was watched. And suddenly she found herself looking into eyes of quiet contempt shading to anger when they questioned her and got nothing of what they wanted, the voices of Lieutenant Francis Frame and two other officers coaxing her and keeping perfect manners and later with harsh reprimands asking her if she knew what was the penalty for a spy in wartime and did she know that a spy was a treacherous rat that met no mercy. This began on the day after Robert made his escape from Aunt Ellen's house, the afternoon when she told Lieutenant Frame under no conditions could she give a pledge to inform them at any time she learned of a return of Robert Winshore to Boston. Where was she on the night that Sapphira Reggs saw Robert Winshore participating in an infamous crime on the person and property of Hobart Reggs? What did Robert Winshore tell her of that affair? How could she lie and repeat her lie that when she took Winshore into her home, ate and made merry with him, walked over Boston with him, frequented with him "that Rebel pesthole" the White Cockade and the bookstore of that Rebel Henry Knox, yet in all of this Winshore gave her no hint of the Reggs atrocity? How could she likewise falsely declare she continued an intimacy with this dastardly traitor and she learned from him no fact nor detail of the criminal act perpetrated on the respectable Loyalist Silas Ludgate? Had she not stationed herself in the Cavendish dress shop with its distinctive British and Loyalist patrons with the expectation of there gathering information of service to the outlaws and incendiaries who termed themselves Sons of Liberty and her intimate friend Robert Winshore one of its most active members?

"They seemed to know everything about who came and went and what I said in the shop and who I went with and where." And it came out they believed Mim had pressed and pried the wives and daughters of British officers and Loyalists seeking military information. It came out further that they had this information from little dollfaced Jane Haddam. "On her testimony, if it could be supported, we could hang you," Lieutenant Frame had told Mim very gravely.

Robert's eyes held a queer dull blaze and Mim said, "Now I think I know how your eyes looked when you sighted your musket at the first enemy soldier you killed. You mustn't get mad now. What I'm telling you is over and past and part of it is funny. Don't you think it's funny that little odious draggletail puss Jane Haddam should have been chosen for a spy, she with her spite and jealousy and naturally a liar even when talking to herself?"

Robert grinned. The queer dull blaze was gone. He admired her for what she wasn't telling. For a person of her extraordinary pride and sensitivity to be hauled before accusers who questioned her every act and word, and this being her first experience in such an ordeal, she could have mentioned it but wouldn't trouble him. She could have said there was anguish in her attempt to answer their questions, "What is this Robert Winshore to you and how many nights has he slept with you in your Aunt Ellen's house?" She had hesitated and finally answered, "I refuse to reply to unwarranted questions deliberately intended to be insolent."

Mim had finished the stocking where one big toe stuck out and begun on the other where three toes could wriggle through.

They had questioned her six hours straight the first day, the officers taking turns at trying to wear her to a breakdown. They seated her on a chair with no back to it. They wanted the names of any and all persons she associated with and what she had learned from those persons of the membership of the Sons of Liberty, of guns, powder and provisions being procured and where stored. Her answers they took as those of a liar who couldn't be so completely ignorant as she pretended. It was beyond their belief she could have been so close to Robert Winshore for so many months, with so many endearments between them noticed by others, and not be in possession of one of his many secrets of the underhanded Sons of Liberty.

Overnight she had a small room with a guard outside the door, permission to send word to Aunt Ellen refused. The second day six hours without food, again the chair with no back to it, again the officers taking turns at questioning her. They brought in a Bible, tried to put her under oath in her statements and she refused. "What is the Bible and God between you and me? You wouldn't believe me today if I should swear to every word of it on a stack of Bibles."

They wanted to use her to bait and trap Robert Winshore and others. Finding they couldn't use her they told her she must leave Boston. They gave her a pass allowing her and Aunt Ellen on a cart with some goods to go through the lines.

Parting with Mrs. Cavendish came easy. Mrs. Cavendish was frank to say, "I'm afraid, my dear, you gave our place a bad name. I have had my own loyalty to the King's cause questioned because of your conduct. The shop stands empty. Not a new piece of work in three days, the Rebels surrounding Boston. It is as well you are going, my dear."

Mim kissed Amelia Gray, put her arms around Evelyn Trutt to hear her "We will meet again, my boy outside sends word they will take the city."

Then Mim looked Jane Haddam in the face. "And, would you believe it, I hesitated whether I should call her an odious draggle-tailed puss or merely a nasty little bitch, and then I did manage to lock my lips and turn away from her and walk out forever and ever from the Sign of the Golden Ball."

The spring weeks and summer months went by on the farm in the by-lane near Lexington. The work of the farm fell on Jake, Deb, Aggie and Mim, with Aunt Ellen tending the lightest of household duties. The father suffered with his arm and shaky nerves. The few days he didn't suffer he sat sullen or he moped. They rode for the doctor twice to reset the splints, the doctor saying the second time there had been no need for him to call, and to the girls, "He is a little peevish, I would say, it's mental with him, he's too queasy." And Noah Wilming persisted over the summer that his arm wasn't healing, it hurt for him to walk with it; he must lie quiet or sit still.

Weeding among the carrots and cabbages, in the bean rows and the turnip patch, the daughters and Jake stooped and knelt day after day, taking turns at the farm work and the housework and kitchen chores. In the potato field and among the corn rows Mim blistered her hands on a hoe handle and went on and grew calluses, winning a burst of laughter from Deb and Aggie as one afternoon she stood in checked gingham and with sweat running over the sunburn of her face, "I'll be blamed if there ain't a difference between a hoe and a needle, burn my boots if there ain't!" Deb and Aggie in previous years had helped Darius and were not the strangers like Mim to spells of work near-backbreaking. Her bones sore and her muscles stiff, their vibrations woke Mim and put her to sleep again in the first days of weeding and hoeing. She said she would get used to it and she did. She ate supper after sunset and right off went to her room to slide out of her clothes and fall onto the bed fairly asleep before she was in the sheets.

In the plowing not finished by Darius, in the sorting of seeds and planting over May and early June, the mother worked harder than any of the others, saying as she had for many a year, "Work is good for whatever ails you." They saw Ma struggle to go on when an attack of dysentery came in early June. They saw that malady wear her down and overcome her strong will. For a week or two she managed to make a pretense of helping around the kitchen and they heard her say bitterly from her bed or a chair on the days she was up, "I'm give out. *You* know me. I'm give *out*."

Mim let down gate bars, drove cows from pasture, pulled at the teats with a pail between her knees, put the milk in crocks in the cellar, skimmed off the cream and churned it to butter under an apple tree near the cellar door, padded the butter into a small bucket she let down the well to keep cool, carried part of the skim milk to the two calves, poured the buttermilk in two pitchers for the supper and breakfast tables. When the flies swarmed thick in the cow stalls, she expected every so often a kick in the shins or knees and a pail of warm milk spilled.

At haymaking time she joined with Jake, Deb and Aggie in handling a pitchfork, her calico dress sweat-soaked on sweltering July days, hayseed in her hair and down her sweating neck and back.

Mim left the others one Sunday morning in June to go alone and stand where Darius lay covered over with the other battle dead of Lexington. Below her feet there his earthly frame had moldered and corruption worked at the shag of brown hair down his forehead and the sockets where the brown eyes held no more the liquid glow she could never forget. There was this dust of him underground mute, corrupt. There was another dust of him, a thin invisible impossible dreamdust that lived on in her and that would live on beyond her little life. How this could be ran over and up and down her mind as she heard the sonorous and valiant Jonas Parker in his pulpit.

"In church that Sunday," Mim was saying to Robert as her knitting needles progressed at the stocking toe hole, "on my knees weeding the carrots and bending with the hoe along the corn rows, I began to see what had happened to me those three years in Boston. You can't help what people do to you. You can't be proof against the people you see every day. They have their ideas, beliefs, rumors, notions. What runs in their blood and talk may yet get into your blood and talk. I saw early that neither side, Tory or Whig, could be as high and holy, as pure and perfect, as righteous and straightforward, as they pretended to be. And I told myself I would be as holy and pure a spectator as they were participants. There grew in me, though I didn't know it, a comfort and self-satisfaction about sitting on my pleasant perch above the strife and bickering, a witness of the hate and scorn yet not a part of it. I got smug. I didn't realize how smug and superior I had become after two years of it when I first met you. You were the first Rebel to throw Rebel ideas straight in my face. I didn't like the evangel in you. That's what you were, an evangel of American Independence and freedom. You saw I didn't like it at first and still more later when it was plain, though you wouldn't talk about it, that you had a hand in secret doings of the abominable Sons of Liberty. They were a threat to my dream and hope, snuggled in my heart and fastened with deep roots, a place of our own, a sweet home for us two. I had a jealousy I didn't dare show of anything that meant danger to that home. I made a hoard of happiness, you might say, of our future happiness, the things we would do and have after a wedding. I took that hoard out to count it and fondle it like a crazy miser handling his gold he will never spend. I saw you were moving in the works of the oath-bound Sons of Liberty, secret works. Those works shook you deep. They aimed to terrify the enemy and show him your will stronger than his. I saw this shook you far deeper than our little love. A fright came over me that you could love a secret organization, working in blood and terror, more than you loved me. Fright and jealousy ate in me and wore me. I began to throw away that little hoard of future happiness. I recoiled in myself and writhed and twisted and flung paradoxes, follies and taunts, at you.

"At Darius' grave, on my knees weeding carrots, with a hoe in the corn rows, this began to come clear to me. Lexington, Concord and Bunker Hill, they helped, of course. Men who could fight like that against the world-famous British Regulars, I said they must have something not reported by the patrons of Mrs. Cavendish and the Sign of the Golden Ball. I had heard too much gabble of no meaning in that dress shop, not merely political gabble but endless prattle of style and fashion, women peacocks and ape men who believed in money and show like a religion, who didn't know for all the finery and spangles they put in their parties and cotillions they were still peacocks and apes. 'Vanity of vanities, thy name is vanity,' I babbled to myself once looking at the hoe-handle blisters on my pretty hands and taking a fierce joy in those blisters and then the calluses."

She held out an open hand toward Robert. "They're not gone yet, you see." He had already noticed, he said. He liked them.

Early September Noah Wilming died. He seemed to want to go. "Useless," they had heard from him that summer, over and again, "so useless," with an arm no good when it should heal, worries and vagaries on his mind. Bunker Hill should have been won and held. The Americans should have stayed and slaughtered the enemy and held the hill. Then his last three days he brightened, his face and eyes with exaltation in them. "Noah Wilming, died in the Battle of Lexington fighting for his country, died of his wounds September 8, 1775." They could put that on his gravestone, he said.

They suddenly loved and admired him, all of him, those last three days. They kissed his face. He asked to kiss them each on the lips. He lay with eyes closed and a murmuring mouth, "The Revolution, it will go on long, longer than they think yet it will win because, in the name of God, you can't conquer unconquerable men."

Then a pause and, "Am I one of the unconquerable men?" Dreamily he asked it as though it might be and as though it would please him, not much but a little.

Then his eyes opened again, "Mim, am I one of the unconquerable men?"

"You are, papa, we all say you are."

His eyes closed. "Kiss me, Mim." She touched her lips gently to his and whispered, "Dear papa."

Then a long pause, his breath coming slower, and they believed their ears caught him saying, "Her hair always so pretty, far back when she was a little girl I liked Mim's hair." And they heard no more from him.

The spring weeks and early summer months had gone fast for Mim. Blue sky, drifting clouds softer and whiter than any satin in the Cavendish shop, they helped, so did clouds piled and rolled taller than mountains, growing corn ears with rusty brown silk curling out, leaves with a changing rustle as the vivid fresh green of mid-July shifted to pale sun-dried green in late August. She remembered again farmers she had heard, "I can hear things grow," and she tried her ears and believed she did hear the hay, the corn growing, and especially the pumpkin and squash hills.

"You pitch in pretty good, Mim," her mother said one day. "Deb and Aggie like it. They've come to approve of you like never before."

"You wouldn't say that, Ma, without I had," Mim replied and was pleased. "I guessed maybe only Jake would be sure to approve."

Jake adored her as before, perhaps more, Mim saw, for it was she who had always spoken up for him, always Mim who said she would rather have his peculiar kind of brightness than what some other smart people had.

With his pinched sweet smile on a twisted face Jake had said to her the first day she was back, "Things here just like they was before the war, now they're inside out and upside down." He had been once to Boston and had his opinion, "Boston is purty to look at if you like to see the twitters." They hurried too much in Boston. "It gives them the twitters, and when they get what they want, they want more of it." His mind working alone had reached around to some certainties. "If you know too much it makes you sick and if you don't know what it is you're sick with, that's bad and you might as well be plain ignorant." He told Mim he had learned how and when to keep his mouth shut. "If I'm going to say something and it doesn't sound right in my head I don't let it get to my tongue. I notice most men have a respect for a man with a still tongue, he might be dangerous, and they never know what he knows till he gabbles." He was seventeen now. With Darius and the father gone, he was the man of the place, not rugged and tireless as Darius, "but he's takin hold and gettin to man-size in a way I'm proud of," said the mother to Mim.

The orchard near the house was a sort of book that Mim and Jake read and shared. Half the trees, slowly dying, took their time. Two gnarled and spreading trees hadn't blossomed in three years and this year they burst into a flowering white cloud and red apples that ripened soon and fell early and when Jake and Mim bit into them they were a flat pulp of no taste and they spit it out. One small old tree in a corner with currant bushes and rhubarb for neighbors gave small sour apples that set the teeth on edge but when those apples lay yellowed in the sun ten days they had a wild and racy tang and Jake and Mim watched every windfall from that tree. There were apples with shrunken skin worth two bites for their queer flavor, worm-eaten apples so fresh and tasty you ate all but the worm and its path, and not often enough came the apple so perfect you ate all but the core, seeds and stem. Red-cheek, pudding-sweet, long-nose, were names Jake had for some odd ones. Along a cow-pasture path where wild crab apples fell to the sod it pleased Jake to hand one to Mim begging her to take one bite so he could enjoy the quizzical pucker of her face.

Summer had eased into autumn, more chill and haze in the air, plant leaves wilting and turning brown and crackling, spots and splashes of umber, yellow and crimson over the trees and woodland. The earth had laughed a harvest but the reapers couldn't take a real glad laugh till it was gathered and dug. The mother was still weak and couldn't join but the others were up early and going late with cutting corn, digging potatoes, turnips, carrots, heaping the pumpkins, squash and cabbage in the cellar and in barn corners and bins.

Ten-minute snatches of time for reading, a half-hour once in a while on weekdays, two or three hours on Sunday with her books, for that much Mim had been thankful. With the crops in came more time with her beloved books and her occasional scribbling. Mim at one holiday gathering with neighbors picked up from a fellow who sang it forty times for the girl he was to marry:

> Oh, the fox and the hare,
> And the badger and the bear,
> And the birds in the greenwood tree,
> And the pretty little rabbits
> So engaging in their habits,
> Have all got a mate but me.

Toward November's end Mim gave nearly all of her time to her mother. The summer attack of dysentery had returned, the doctor said, in a more malignant form. It had been epidemic in some parts of New England. Ruth Wilming wasted away and became a mildewed reminiscence of the strong woman who through life had never wanted others to do for her, as she said. She had a terror of being a bother, a care and hindrance, to others. "I've never learned how to complain and it hurts me to."

An early December night it was and snow all day in a driving wind gone down at dusk. From the house windows they could see the five cedars snow-mantled in a still starbright gloaming. Ruth Wilming made her weak gestures, pushing away food offered her, opened and closed her eyes in the only speech left her. By the light of two candles on a table near her pillow and a rigid shiver of a moment that came to the body, they knew she had gone at about the hour she wanted to go.

They had all seen woe and grief come to the house but nothing like this. Ma Wilming had become part of every door, window and floorboard of the house. Here under this roof she had borne each of these children who now wailed, fell on each other's shoulders, wept and shook. Darius could go this year, the father could go, and they could think of the house and the land and themselves as having a root center, a wheel with a hub, a clock with a mainspring. They were her brood. She was gone. And now they accused themselves, each feeling a guilt about words and deeds they could have spoken and done for her while she lived. Now they knew they had leaned on her more than they could have believed and they held depths of affection for her that could well have been spoken more often. When they sobbed, "Oh, Ma," and called to her now it was like nothing before in their lives. Jake perhaps had better hold of himself than any of the other children. They found it soothing to see him in a chair at her pillow, sometimes leaning forward to lay a hand on her icy forehead, then with an utter quiet on his face and a new solemn look on it, near a whisper, "She's better off, she suffered so."

Aunt Ellen kept hid except for an hour late at night when she sat by her sister, two years younger than herself, and kissed the mouth and brow and went away, dry-eyed and at no time wailing. "She hides it," said Deb, and Aggie agreed, "Yes, dear Aunt Ellen, it's there but she won't let on it is."

They buried her next to the father and near the ground that held Darius. They came home to a house where every doorway kept her shadow, every corner and utensil echoes of her voice.

Mim would eat little, talk little, on the third day after the burial kept to her room, telling Jake in the late afternoon when he asked what he could do for her, "Leave me alone, Jake, I have to work it out for myself." To Deb and Aggie, Jake said, "Mim is takin it harder than any of us." He couldn't go further and tell how Mim had hinted to him when Ma's suffering was at its worst in the summer that it was crossing her mind she had done a great wrong to Ma in leaving when she went away to Boston and in staying away so long and in not coming out more often to the farm where Ma always said her visits did a world of good. Jake could remember Mim's words back there in the summer, "I wonder if I've got into a habit of going out of my way to do wrong to people I love." Jake had rolled that over in his mind for a few days and then said to himself, "There must be others too she thinks she's done wrong to and she don't want to talk about it."

Jake had gone to the barn to tend a sick calf and to finish shoveling a path to the barn in the foot-deep snow. He was walking back to the house, taking notice it was like to an hour till sunset and a clear sky for the stars to move out on. His eyes near the house caught foot tracks leading off through the orchard and over toward woodland. He looked at them, wondering what animal could have made those tracks. Then suddenly he made a dash for Mim's room, broke through the door, saw she wasn't in her room, and ran down to tell Deb and Aggie to come along and Aunt Ellen to stay on watch at the house. Jake ran back for a lantern and a flint, ran and caught up with Deb and Aggie following the tracks Mim had left in the snow.

The trail ran on fairly straight across pasture land, into thickets where no path led, zigzagging through woodland. She had leaped a brook, hesitated there, walked back and forth by swift waters sliding over flat rocks with streaks of rust and moss-green. They were going to shout, all their voices together crying, "Mim! O Mim, where are you?" but decided it might not be for the best. They followed the aimless winding foot tracks and suddenly came into a clump of pines, no snow on the ground, a thick matting of pine needles.

There was Mim, rising from her seat at the foot of a pine, rising to her full six feet of height and pride, Mim in a cloak of finespun gray wool with fur edging and a fur collar and below they could see it was over a gown of blue satin, then black silk stockings and fur-lined overshoes, her Boston dress for cotillions and parties—and her bare head of chestnut hair gleaming with a few fluffs of snow on it from thicket branches. They had never seen her in these fine clothes. They didn't know she had such clothes. That she could run away as she had was strange enough and that they should track her down to meet her in such a costume was equally strange.

What did they want? Didn't they know all she asked was to be let alone? Her questions came in a swift babble, a little thick-tongued.

They drew to within two and three feet from her and her warning came, "Don't you dare touch me." They stood waiting. They saw her tremble. It could be her mood and the excitement. And it could be the cold too, the December air that had frozen a thick ice on ponds.

Jake spoke, coaxing and tender, "You're shivering, Mim, come home with us where it's warm and you can eat something."

She wouldn't. "Don't come near me. Don't you touch me."

They waited in the cold winter silence, Mim cold and mute, and dusk coming on.

"You've got to go with us, Mim. You can't stay here and catch your death uh cold." This was Jake, less coaxing and more firm of tone, a note of command in it.

"You must come, please, Mim, please, Sis, you must." This was Deb and Aggie pleading, tears in their voices.

"Don't come near," came the terrible words. "Don't you dare touch me."

"Then we'll have to take you and drag you, by God," came the fierce cry of Jake. "We can't let you stay here. It's gettin dark and we got a mile to go and we can't let it be on our conscience we let you freeze to death." Then no word from Mim. She stood dumb and defiant. "Will you come along or will we have to drag you?" came Jake's fierce cry again.

No answer coming he stooped toward her and tried to take her by the hands. She pushed him in the face with a furious shove that sent him reeling back.

"Come on, Deb, come on, Aggie," yelled Jake as he threw himself at Mim and brought her to the level of the pine matting.

How long it took from then on, how long the fight lasted, how long the wrestle and the struggle before Jake had brought twine out from a pocket and tied her wrists while she struck, pounded, bit and scratched, none of them could tell afterward. Nor how Mim was pushed and led and dragged and at times carried that distance of near a mile to the house and home.

"It was the next afternoon I awoke," said Mim to Robert as she laid aside the stockings and the needles, having darned the toe holes and various large and small holes, holding the stockings up and laughing, "They're nearly as good as new," and going on, "Yes, the next afternoon I awoke. They had poured hot rum into me and a sleeping drug that Aunt Ellen had. I was in a warm room with a blaze in the fireplace going and in the bed where you saw Darius die, the same bed where my father and mother had died that year. It came over me I was alive though I'm not sure but I had meant to join them. Jake sat in a chair by the bed. He had a pan of parched sweet corn. He enjoyed the grinding noise his teeth could make on parched corn. Not a word did he say, he just went on grinding corn with his teeth and a beautiful mischievous smile on his face. I asked him, 'What happened, Jake?' He answered, 'We're proud of you, Mim.' Then my eyes caught scratches on his face and what seemed dry blood on one ear. I looked at my wrists and they had been scraped raw and ointment put on them. I held up my arms to see black-and-blue spots and bruises. My head ached and there were aches over my body.

"I tried to sit up and I fell back. I was too weak to sit up. I closed my eyes and I could hear Jake grinding parched corn with his teeth and I could hear him very softly, 'We're proud of you, Mim,' and if I should open my eyes I would see that sweet mischievous smile on his face. It used to be a pinched smile but now the pinch was out of it.

599

As I rested wondering what he meant by their being proud of me, a prong of pain ran around in my head and the dull aches spread over my body. Yet there was a dim light and a soft glow I had not known in months. I had come out of something that had a hold on me. I had crossed a bridge. I had come out of a winding dark passage.

"My eyes still closed I asked, 'Why proud of me, Jake?' and the grinding of his teeth on corn stopped and, 'Shall I tell it now, Mim, or wait till you're rested more?' I asked him to tell it slow and easy and I would be listening. He had told the most of it when Deb and Aggie came in, their hair like mine not yet smoothed out from the night before, their faces covered with wildcat scratches and Aggie with a bad bloodshot eye where my thumb had gouged her. They were saying the same as Jake. They had agreed on it. 'We're proud of you, Mim.' Then it all faded from me and they waited and I came conscious again and felt the shots of chilblains in my feet and they took off the loose heavy stockings and the warm brick they had placed there the night before when they were afraid my feet might be frostbitten. My fur-lined overshoes got pulled and kicked off in the fighting.

"We all talked a little about what a wonder it was that the last I remembered was telling Jake to leave me alone and I didn't know how or when I got out of bed and put on my Boston dress-shop finery and sneaked downstairs and out into the snow. I had gone out of my head, lost my mind, what there was to lose. They said I got my teeth into Jake's ear. They heard me yell, 'You say you're Jake Wilming but I know you're Robert Winshore.' "

Mim and Robert sat in one of their old-time silences for a while.

"Robert, did you ever go out of your head?"

"Two days up on the Kennebec. The least I did was to curse Oates Elwood and tell him I would travel better alone. And I saw a deer he didn't see and cursed him for not killing it so we could eat."

Again a silence and what was between them couldn't be told. Then Mim, "My need, I saw then, was for only a little to believe in but that little must be strong and fastened with unbreakable thongs. It must be hard beyond any destroying and it must be soft too, thin as a dream. You can't put out your hand and touch the air and filaments of it. And if you clutch it and keep it to hoard and fondle like a miser, it will turn on you and bring you down. You give and give from that little and it always renews itself. There is always more of it. I don't know that what I'm saying makes common sense. I do know I have two great passionate loves and I can live for them or die for them, either one or both of the loves. One is for you, the other is one that I join with you in, a consecration of ourselves to dreamdust, to the mystic lighted dreamdust of Joseph Warren, of Darius Wilming, of Noah and Ruth Wilming, of John Locke Winshore, of a dream so deep in your eyes it is beyond fathoming."

She arose, leaned over and put a tight kiss on his mouth. "Now I must go. The little more there is of my story can wait till tomorrow night. The command is you must rest."

"A night worth having, so much to remember, my darling," said Robert, lifting his head toward her. "One more kiss before you go."

She put fierce lips to his a brief moment and swept away without another word.

The next night Mim went on with her story. In the spring they sold the farm and moved to Aunt Ellen's house in Boston, a week after the enemy sailed away. Aggie took up with a merchant, the wedding sudden, and she moved with him to Salem. Deb began working in the White Cockade. Jake was proving himself as a city teamster and saying he might next year go into the army. Mim helped as she could on the repairs and the remaking of Aunt Ellen's house and did her thinking over a letter from Cynthia George who had heard of Mrs. Cavendish leaving her shop and sailing for Halifax with the other refugee Loyalists. Cynthia George was soon moving to Philadelphia and Mim might like a place with her.

"Philadelphia, the Continental Congress, your father and your home there," said Mim. "I would go there. I wouldn't get in your way. I would see what might happen. And now in God's good time, see what has happened."

"It isn't over yet. Hard days to come," put in Robert.

"I am ready for them. I have been tried by fire. We have both been to hell and back. We know what the climate and weather is in hell. We'll be at home in whatever is to come."

"Mim, I'm afraid you're too good to be true."

"I met an old withered man in Boston, no firewood all winter and miserable scraps to eat and the scurvy wearing at him, and he said, 'How'll I know it from Boston when I get to hell after I die?'"

With a mild grin Robert was asking, "Whatever became of that queer loud-mouthed rascal Captain Edelbert Hupple?"

"A rascal he was. He had no ship at Salem. He had fine clothes and a deal of gab. He went through a wedding with Mrs. Cavendish and got his hands on her money and took a ship for the West Indies."

"No!"

"Yes."

"And Mr. Hobart Reggs and his daughter Sapphira?"

"They sailed away nicely with the others. The mahogany spinet your Sons of Liberty broke, they had repaired that and they took it on board ship and to make room for others they had to throw it overboard."

"Which was worse than our smashing it."

"Yes. Sapphira's baby you may be sure they didn't throw overboard."

"Sapphira's baby?"

"She married the British officer she wanted. He was killed at Bunker Hill."

"A wild time we live in, Mim."

"A time of storm."

"Storm and dream," said Robert. "I wouldn't let the storm whirl me, kick me, punish me, unless for the dream beyond the storm. It may be, in Tom Paine's words, the birthday of a new world. And it may not."

The father had come in, fussing with the latch so they could hear him coming, and he was saying, "Hazard and risk—we are born, every child, every man and woman of us, to hazard and risk, from womb to tomb, birth-bed to burying-ground. Some live so careful, so prudent and anxious over their little hoards of money or love or power they clutch, that they die without having lived and you could write an epitaph for many of them and it would read:

"HE WAS A PRACTICAL MAN
WHO LIVED DREAMLESS.
NOW HE SLEEPS HERE
AS HE LIVED—DREAMLESS.

"Nations too live at hazard and risk and when their rulers dream only of themselves and not their people you might say their soldiers die for a dreamless flag. Our American dream began years ago, its flag came into adoption late, and its Declaration to the world that it is an independent nation among the world states came only this month. It is the freshest young dream in the world. It is so daring a dream it will have to live by storm, inside its growing and lusty young body storm, and from outside forces storm."

"Papa."

"Yes, son."

"Talk on, you're talking what ran low in me last month and is now come alive again."

"Enough I've said perhaps for us to think about. It's your bedtime, son."

Robert kissed Mim and went upstairs. The father and Mim talked an hour.

"The wonder of the dream keeps him," said Mim. "He has that word 'wonder' for what keeps him going. We will pray he keeps it."

"And we'll pray we ourselves keep it. Love of country is a holiness that comes and goes and those too sure of it better beware. It exists as a wonder. It lives by vision, prayer and works. With high words and no works it is a hypocrisy and blasphemy. I tremble at calling myself a Patriot when I consider Joseph Warren and our boy Locke—and our boy Robert."

They stepped outside the front door. The summer stars hung low and timeless. She held his right hand in her two hands and on leaving said, "You have a heart of storm and dream. Pray for Robert and me."

Before Robert's going away one incident broke the smooth flow of his recovery. He was writing copies of several involved resolutions passed by the Congress and from his chair at a table in a front corner of Carpenter's Hall he saw Mim standing by herself far at a rear corner. When he looked several minutes later she was talking with a sprightly uniformed captain, a rather handsome pink-faced fellow. There was more than admiration on her face, thought Robert, and on his too. He could see Mim in bright laughter at what she was hearing. Then later her face was serious and she seemed deeply moved.

All of this that he had seen, he flung at her that evening, suddenly flung it in a burst of suspicion and jealousy. Why this pleased her Mim couldn't tell. Nor could she let on she was pleased.

"He will be here this evening," she said. "He wishes to see you. He comes from Boston."

When he came Mim had the visitor tell again what he was telling her that afternoon. "Captain Edmunds, Roger Edmunds, the son of Bliss Edmunds," she introduced him to Robert. He had visited his sister in New York last winter and they couldn't get along on his first call and on his second and farewell call he was giving her a piece of his mind and telling her she was a snob and one of the lowest breed of Tories he had ever met. Then her husband in full British-officer uniform came in and they had words that ended in a brawl, a fist fight where they bloodied each other's noses, stocks and shirts and neither was winner and Captain Edmunds backed out of the front door hurling curses in reply to his brother-in-law's vile epithets.

Robert exploded in a rollicking belly laughter. Captain Edmunds, still on duty in procurement of munitions and supplies, told Robert of powder and provisions, how there was more than there had been yet there ought to be more for coming actions. The clash of Captain Edmunds with his sister and brother-in-law reminded Robert of two brothers in a well-to-do New York family, arriving home on the same afternoon, one in American and the other in British officer's uniforms, and they drew swords and fought till each had brought blood on the other and a mother and sister separated them and ordered them out of the house.

The night before Robert's going away, the Tozzers came to the house and Cynthia George joined them. Tozzer had brought a guitar and Robert sang "Come, Swallow Your Bumpers, Ye Tories," to begin a merry evening. Robert had regained more than half his lost weight. The grayish clay pallor of his face had changed to a clean white and then taken on a hint of the old ruddy color. They had led him into staying a week longer than he planned. Now when they spoke of his staying yet another week he would repeat General Washington's phrase "chimney-corner heroes." He had not been useless on "light duty" at the Continental Congress but now he must go.

The father pulled a cork from a bottle of Madeira wine to go with oatmeal cakes Mim had made by Aunt Ellen's recipe. Mim read lines copied from a letter of a son of Silas Ludgate, one of the hundreds of young Loyalists who had gone into enemy uniform. From his winter of duty isolated at Halifax the bright young Ludgate had written confidentially to a Boston friend: "A cursed cold wintry place. Nothing to eat and less to drink. Bad times, my friend. The displeasure I feel from the very small share I have in our present insignificancy is so great that I do not know the thing so desperate I would not undertake to change our situation."

Mim did her new Declaration of Independence dance, precise and military with right-face, left-face, about-face and drumbeat clicks of heel and toe, then signatures, name signing with a pen, reverent slow shifts from one posture of prayer to another, exultation in a variety of fierce whirls, ending with an enigma of closed eyes, folded hands, her bony face with a plum-blossom mouth fixed mute and grim in acceptance of whatever fate lay ahead.

Robert strummed the guitar and she sang of "the pretty little rabbits, so engaging in their habits," and sang it again because they called for it and there was no second verse. Cynthia George merrily read a verse by one "Bob Jingle," from a letter of her boy. "Meant to be sarcastical," she laughed, "but our boys in camp find fun in it," and read:

"With anxious cares and grief oppressed
Our inmost bowels rumble,
And truly we are so oppressed
Our very guts they grumble."

Tozzer asked Robert to sing the "Liberty Song" of Joseph Warren. The father said, "It is exciting the way you give it, Robert. You know whether you should."

"That song tells why I'm leaving tomorrow." And he sang it defiant, vibrant, envisioning. Mim trembled, her plum-blossom lips a day-white pale.

He finished and they waited a while hearing the clock tick. Then Ordway Winshore, "We are a fellowship of outlaws, carrying on a bloody rebellion. At least so they will write it if we lose. And if we win there will be, along this Atlantic coast and over the continent, statues and bronze memorials to those who fought it and won."

"You talk history, Mr. Winshore," laughed Mary.

"Yes and I must be careful. Those who *talk* history too much *make* none of it. They can't see it in the making before their own eyes."

On a rested horse whose flanks had filled out, saddlebags packed, with a blanket, a pouch of roast pork, smoked fish, wheat bread and apples, Robert rode away in the morning. It was a laughing farewell, crackling with jokes and nonsense. They all wanted it that way. He turned a corner waving a blue silk kerchief. In the house Mary Winshore put her arms around Marintha Wilming as the salt tears ran down a face still laughing.

* * * * * * * * *

Chapter 32

* * * * * * * * *

The 1777 Twitters

THE summer months of 1776 had gone by and the winds of autumn blown away the leaves of yellow hills turning gray. Early December it was when a Philadelphia merchant called on Cynthia George and handed her two letters, one for herself from her son, the other for Mim from Robert.

"We haven't made much progress," ran one sentence of Robert's dry letter. "Our satisfaction is that while beaten we are not destroyed." Mim laughed—inside of herself a laughter no others could see. She could read that Robert himself laughed at such a letter telling her what everybody knew, what the whole world knew, that the enemy had arrived at New York and Long Island with the largest expedition ever sent out from England, 35,000 troops with 1200 cannon on 400 transports convoyed by 10 line-of-battle frigates manned by 1000 seamen, that as the weeks passed the enemy had pushed Washington's army off Long Island, off Manhattan Island, out of New York and over across northern New Jersey.

"When I see you, blessed day, I will tell you much more than can be put in a letter," sounded more like the Robert she wanted to hear from, as did the ending sentence, "My whole love to you, always and ever and always." Those words had to last in her heart many long weeks before she heard from him again.

On the day Robert had swiftly written this letter and got it into the hands of the merchant going to Philadelphia, he had awakened from his night's sleep in a pasture corner where he and Oates Elwood on scout duty had snuggled in overcoats and blankets among weeds and fence boards. The frost lay thick and white over their blankets at daybreak. They joked about their rheumatism being easier when they had plenty of wool cover.

The sun hadn't come up when Robert awoke and lapsed into a doze wherein a letter to Mim ran through his head. "Dearest Mim:

Oat and I rode our horses where we saw the enemy transports crowded with men and cannon. It will be a long war, sweetheart. Don't try to be cheerful. Make yourself hard and patient, if you can. This enemy can't be beaten in one campaign or two. We had double 8000 men, then we had 8000 in this army, now we've got not quite 4000 and half of them under suspicion. To be in the field and see an army melt away with desertions and men's enlistment terms running out, it gives you heartbreak. General Washington I am sure has died of heartbreak several times this autumn and where he gets a new heart every time an old one goes to pieces, I'd like to hear. We have held on and how God only knows. It must be God who gives Washington a new heart when the old one breaks. We would have gone under months ago but for his heart and will. Oat and I can't figure out how it is Washington makes the army hang on and never give up. You can hear good officers say it's more a mob than an army. We've done some fighting, I wish to assure you. I saw hills lost in gun smoke at White Plains and felt the ground shake with the heavy guns going.

"A ball took my horse in the neck and he sank under me and I slid off and it wasn't easy to see him quiver and die, a middling horse that had shared a mess of trouble with me and I cried taking my overcoat, blanket and saddlebag off him before I ran for a piece of woods. The next week I crept across an orchard with men who surrounded a farmhouse, killed ten Hessians in the house, set a barn afire and shot two Hessians that came running out. We came where a cannon had been captured, two British officers, three British soldiers, two Hessians, piled around each other this way and that, all dead, all quiet. One of the officers glassy-eyed, his hands yet clutched a saber and a pistol, his eyes staring up as if he would like to get whoever ran a bayonet through his neck. Last week Oat and I riding along saw strips of cloth caught in bushes. We got off our horses and looked. We saw the body of a good-looking young woman, heavy-set with strong arms, hair like oat straw crisscrossed with blood, streaks of blood on her face. The men who killed her could have been our men or the enemy. There wasn't time for us to look into what had happened. They had had their way with her. One man couldn't have mussed her up like she was. She had fought them—black-and-blue where they had bruised her when she fought. And the dirty bastards cut off the third finger of the right hand. The ring on that finger wouldn't come off so they took along the whole finger."

About there in his dozing Robert came fully awake. He shook the frost off his blue three-cornered hat and laid it back over his head, snuggled deeper into his blanket and called, "Oat."

"Yes, Bobby."

"Have you ever tried writing a letter telling the whole truth about this dirty war?"

"I'd never try unless I was obliged to. How could you tell folks

that's got a clean dry warm privy about the camp vaults we use? the
flies in summer, the ice in winter? How could you tell about the poor
devils with the quickstep and every day some of them do it in their
pants before they reach the vault? And the pogies with barrel fever
—and the bleary they have to eat—and the scuffs every day caught
and thrown in the crib, the poor scuffs that want to go home to
mamma and the girls and a roof over their heads."

"That's enough from you, Oat, don't tell any more."

Dozing a while longer Robert thought of how he could put in a
letter to Mim: "Oat is keeping something from me, I can't guess
what. It is a secret with him and when he tells it to me at the proper
time it will be a surprise and very interesting. Oat is solid. Oat is
good. I value him."

A letter from Mim came to him and he wrote a letter answering,
"It snuggles in my heart and sings there when I am wet or dry, hungry
or filled." And while he was waiting the chance of someone going to
Philadelphia who would take his letter to her, a rainstorm came up
one day and soaked his clothes and blurred the ink and he threw the
letter into the next campfire he sat by. He would write it again and
put the fresh letter wrapped in canvas in a saddlebag. Then he read
her letter to him again though he could nearly say it by heart. It read:

> I have moved to the house of your father and they have given
> me your room and I talk with the ghost of you and the echo of
> your voice kept here between these four walls. In the dark of the
> night and a rainfall on the roof I have come awake and heard
> your voice, "Mim, is that you?" and I have answered, "Yes, my
> Robert."
>
> Your father is in good health. There are now more days when
> he is short-spoken. He reproaches himself that he cannot do
> more for the Cause. And he is sad because there are so many
> people indifferent about who wins the war and worse yet so many
> who like to make money by trading with either side and men
> supposed to be on our side who are not queasy about "frauds,
> cheats, and peculations" that will bring them money. He heard
> John Adams say one night and he repeats it for us: "Unfaithful-
> ness in public stations is deeply criminal. But there is no encour-
> agement to be faithful. Neither profit, nor honor, nor applause
> is acquired by faithfulness. But I know by what. There is too
> much corruption even in this infant age of the republic. Virtue
> is not in fashion. Vice is not infamous." Terrible words: I would
> not dare send them to you did I not know you are more bitterly
> aware of them than we—and that you should know your father
> and John Adams are aware. One night when he was in a gloomy
> mood Mary and I talked and talked trying to draw him out of
> it and the only part he took in the talk that night was to remind

us of the cathedral in Spain where a big clock on the front of it has the inscription: "Each hour wounds; the last one kills." Yet the next night he was laughing about how pleased John Adams is with the landlady he has found, Adams saying, "She has buried four husbands, one a tailor, two shoemakers and Gilbert Tenant, the last and the fourth, and still is ready for the fifth husband and well deserves him too." Your father is often gloomy now but please know his health is good and we have no fears about him. Mary, of course, is his precious one, always food for him. I imagine he would be rather lost without her, and she understands him so completely and knows what to do for him.

I remember you and I never stop remembering you and I make a business and a ritual of remembering you and I can't help myself in what I do in this remembering of you. If my body should of a sudden turn into a tall wisp of smoke blown away on the horizon I am sure even then I would be remembering you. I send you remembrance woven of our many flamesongs together. We have been shaped in a fiery furnace for each other. You, I know, are harder outside and more beautifully soft inside than you have ever been. Think of me and please let it be often you think of me as part of you, our lives interlaced by thongs invisible and unbreakable. Please know what I am writing you here trying to end this letter. I would rather dance it for you or sing it for you, my precious, my only, my daystar by day and my voice at night in the dark.

Mim could have added a postscript to this letter. She thought about that. But she didn't write it. Through her head the unwritten postscript ran:

"A dish of squash, tender boiled yellow squash it was, made the trouble. I passed it to your father saying, 'The Indians gave it the name of squash.' He took the dish saying, 'The Indians grow strong on it and so will I.' Then he gave my hand a little pat to go with his joke. We turned to hear Mary saying, and her eyes blazing, 'Do you think that was called for?' During the rest of the meal the three of us merely looked at our victuals and did the best we could at eating, finally Mary rising to leave the table saying in a choked voice, 'I hope it never happens again.' She came to my room hours later and lay down beside me in bed that night crying it was the first time she had ever been jealous of him and asking me, 'Did I do wrong? What was the matter with me? Was there anything to it?' I got out of bed and lighted a candle and brought her the letter I wrote to you this Sunday afternoon. She smiled and was her old self. Things are the same again except I am sure he would never again dare to pat the back of my hand when I pass him a dish of tender boiled yellow squash or any other victual. I couldn't quite begin to understand it till I got to imagining what I would have done if you were your father and I was Mary and some other young thing was in my place, I am that fond of you, Robert, and she is that fond of him. And in these gloomy days the best of us have the war twitters. When I said that to Mary everything was like before. Peace be to you, sweet soldier love of mine."

Thus ran through Mim's head the postscript she didn't write, except for that last sentence. She did put that in, saying to herself, "It sounds sentimental," and decided to add still another sentence that ran: "Of course I'm sentimental about you, Robert, God, I'm sentimental about you and you only."

"The Rebels are everywhere moldering away like a rope of sand." Robert and Oat enjoyed quoting this to each other. A New York Tory newspaper, the *Mercury*, had printed it, with much else about Washington losing battles, forts, supplies, recruits, the confidence of Congress. Then out of nowhere Washington struck on Christmas night at Trenton, New Jersey, taking a thousand prisoners and piles of supplies, powder and guns. Then again eight days later out of nowhere Washington marched his army all night and struck at sunrise the enemy at Princeton, sent him flying with heavy loss, and then settled down in winter quarters at Morristown.

"Looks like we intend to be in the way of the British if they try to move on Philadelphia," said Oat.

"The Rebels are everywhere moldering away like a rope of sand," grinned Robert.

They had seen in November an odd piece of a man serving as a volunteer aide on the staff of General Greene, a man five feet nine, a mobile mouth, a long curved nose, thick hair brushed straight back and not parted, and eyes that flashed and burned. A rather careless-looking man except for those blazing dark-blue eyes.

"So that's the fellow who wrote *Common Sense*," said Robert.

"Yes," said Oat, "so we know what is acting behind those eyes."

"We need more of his writing."

"Then we'll get it."

In late December it came, a pamphlet titled *The Crisis*.

" 'What we obtain too cheap, we esteem too lightly; it is dearness only that gives every thing its value,' " quoted Robert.

" 'It would be strange indeed if so celestial an article as FREEDOM should not be highly rated,' " added Oat. " ' 'Tis the business of little minds to shrink.' "

" 'But he whose heart is firm, and whose conscience approves his conduct, will pursue his principles unto death.' "

One paragraph they knew by heart and on Oat saying, " 'These are the times that try men's souls,' " he would hear Robert. " 'The summer soldier and the sunshine patriot will, in this crisis, shrink from the service of their country; but he that stands it *now* deserves the love and thanks of man and woman.' "

Then Oat's stern guttural, " 'The harder the conflict, the more glorious the triumph.' "

Their clothes, overcoats and blankets had seen wear and tear but Robert agreed with Oat, "We'll try to go through the winter with what we've got. When I look at the hundreds of men in rags and strings of clothes, bare feet sticking out from holes showing through shoe leather and stockings, I feel like I don't want to go among 'em with a new overcoat." They did manage to draw new blankets, saying, "It'll help our rheumatism," which it did.

Robert heard a soldier read a letter about New York Tories saying this year of 1777 was a bad number for the Rebels, "the year of the three sevens," each seven a post with an arm, a gallows, wherefore this was to be for the Rebels, "the Year of the Three Gallows."

Oat said, "Years ago in Boston they had the answer to that joke. I was a boy when I heard people saying the big year for American independence would be the first year with three sevens in it. It could be this is the year, Bobby. I'm not scared of three sevens. It was just a saying and old men and women said it with a smile as though they hoped so leastways and it ought to come true."

Mid-March it was that Robert noticed Oat sort of anxious. "Or is he anxious? Sometimes he seems glad enough to choke about this thing he won't tell me."

They were sent on several scouting assignments that plainly annoyed Oat, so much so that Robert had to ask once, "You haven't got the twitters, have you, Oat?"

"You'll know all about it, if you'll wait," said Oat, "but it's not easy for me to wait."

A pleasant day the first week of April it was they rode their horses at a slow walk some five or six miles out of Morristown. "They ain't had the best of feed and we'll walk our nags," said Oat. "It's spring and you can see the grass peepin out."

"I can't wait to see what I'm to see," said Robert.

"It might be afore the day is over you'll know better why I've had the twitters."

Oat would pull in his horse and ask, "Where is Henry Ingleside's place?"

"Two miles mebbe," came one reply. "You turn right at the second road, then to the left at the first road and it's the fifth house."

Oat counted a by-lane for a road and they lost an hour before at last arriving at a two-story house of clapboards with a shingled roof and a big barn and a fat corncrib.

They went in. It was noon and Henry Ingleside had come in from

610

plowing and they were having dinner. Both Henry Ingleside and his wife were very pleasant.

"We ain't got so much but what there is you're welcome to it," said Mrs. Ingleside as Robert's eyes caught the face of another woman about to seat herself at the table.

"Evelyn Trutt, our old Boston friend!" laughed Robert and it was a laugh of joy.

So this was what Oat had been keeping from him. Here and now before his eyes was the sweetheart of his army chum.

And Robert saw Oat and Evelyn Trutt step over to a corner and hold a little talk between themselves. This was natural and Robert would have expected it. She was a rare woman. She was good for Oat. Beyond that Robert cared to know nothing. It was a great day. And Robert knew that Oat was enjoying this day.

Then a door opened and in came—who were they? Robert could hardly believe his eyes. This was Henry Tozzer, pale white, skin and bones; a coughing spell shook him after he had weakly greeted Robert and before he had taken his chair. With him was Mrs. Tozzer, a sister of Henry Ingleside, and they had come here—Robert felt smitten and half-guilty about it—for Henry Tozzer, the Patriot, the revolutionary, slowly to pass away. And yet, said Robert to himself, there were grace and human sweetness beyond words that they should take in their kinsman and make his last days as easy as possible. On the faces of the others he could see only affection for the wraith of the far-gone hero who used to shake New York City with his handbills. They sat at a table eating a tenderly boiled ham smelling of hickory smoke, boiled cabbage, boiled potatoes, pie made from dried apples, and Robert a little bewildered that he should be stowing away such tasty food before the wraith of Henry Tozzer and the baffling glances he saw running between Oat and Evelyn Trutt, faint smiles and knowing looks between the others.

"I feel queer," said Robert to himself. "There seems to be more here than they tell me. Or is my brain in a spin?"

Dinner over, the smiles and the knowing looks went around from face to face again. Then Mrs. Ingleside led the way, opened a door and they went into a room where a bed had an outlook on apple trees and rolling hills. Robert's hands took hold of the arms of Oat and Evelyn Trutt as he stood gazing down at a face on a pillow and still another face alongside the first one his eyes caught.

"Ann!" cried Robert in a low unbelievable moan.

"Our Ann, my sister Ann!" Oat Elwood was moaning.

"You here—Ann Elwood," said Robert, half-choking.

"Ann Elwood Winshore," came the sharp and almost delirious cry of Oates Elwood.

"Your baby," said Robert, staring with wild and glad surprise into

611

the large gray eyes of Ann. "Your baby and Locke's baby! and my nephew baby! and my father's grandchild!"

And Robert fastened his eyes on the baby, half-asleep and its blinking eyes a vague gray-blue with a faint hint of brown, its hair red, a brick-dust red, Locke's hair, Ordway Winshore's hair.

"Jesus, Ann, I'm glad, God, I'm glad."

And Ann knew she might never have another moment like this in all her life. For here were these two hardened veterans of the Continental Army and their eyes wet and slow large tears running down their faces.

Ann smiled. "Oh, you are all so kind I don't know what to do."

She had a marvelous loveliness, thought Robert, her face day-white amid tosses of black hair.

"For your sake and for Locke's sake, Jesus, I'm glad, Ann," Robert faltered and fumbled.

"I think he'll be a real man," smiled Ann with a nod toward the little fellow who seemed ready to doze off. "He may become a great American and carry on the fight you and Oat are in."

All of them drew chairs. They visited. They talked. It was all too good to be true. They laughed. They cried. Certainly Oat and Robert laughed and cried and felt in a way dazed, drunk and delirious. The baby three weeks old, Oat had fretted that he couldn't get to see his nephew sooner.

"What's his name?" asked Robert.

"John Locke Winshore, Jr.," said Ann with a pride about it.

The tears welled up in Robert's eyes, ran down his face. "I'm not ashamed," he said. "I'll cry about this and the most of it is a glad crying and I don't care who knows it. And I believe Locke would cry with me about the wonder of it if he could be here."

Before sunset they must be in camp. They shook hands with Henry Tozzer as with a ghost for Henry Tozzer kept to his bed with his flickering flame of life and had got up from his bed for this special occasion. They couldn't forget the fading fire of his eyes and his faraway voice saying, "The war may go long, boys, but the Revolution will win." He was not a live flame, rather a burned-out ember of the Revolution. But his faith they couldn't forget. "The Revolution," Robert said to Tozzer, "now depends on Washington and we can tell you that Washington has what we need."

"I'm glad you told me that, I like to think about it," said Tozzer, a low ember light on his face.

Oat and Evelyn Trutt begged for a little talk between themselves before going. They went to Evelyn's room. Robert talked with Ann. Nearly strong enough to get up, she said. Three weeks ago the little one came. The doctor said the baby came easy and she was a fine mother. Only once did Ann become solemn and strange. "Oat will tell my feeling," she said. "He understands, he will tell you."

The two soldiers rode away. They said nothing for a time. Then Oat, "You understand, Bobby, you mustn't tell this to your father. Ann has some feeling I don't quite understand. But you mustn't tell him till she gives the word. You know how women are. They have their own ways. And Ann has a right to command us in this. Not a word to your father till she says so."

"It's been a wonderful day, Oat. Of course, I do what you and Ann say."

"We couldn't help it, Bobby, we was all so sweet on each other we went and got married May last year, the four of us, Ann to Locke, me to Evelyn."

"Sweet days you had."

"Two days' honeymoon then back to the war."

"That was all?"

"Another day in June for Locke and Ann then Locke and me made that ride to Philadelphia."

They rode along saying nothing, the spring sun kind, the hills and slopes coming out of winter sleep, a few robins flashing copper feathers, a pair of cardinals giving notice they welcomed spring.

"Look like any marrying for you, Bobby?" Oat broke in casually.

"Might be after next winter the way I figure it now. I think so, hope so."

* * * * * * * * *

Chapter 33

* * * * * * * * *

Visible Flesh and Invisible Faith

GENERAL SIR WILLIAM HOWE, commanding the British forces in New York, for months had a pleasant time in that city. Mrs. Loring, the Hingham woman who had become well known as his friend, had come along from Boston. He had time for parties, dances, social affairs. He seemed to have decided that a swift brutal war at all cost crushing the American forces might work out but a better course would be slowly and gently to extinguish the rebellion, sort of suffocating it into submission rather than hammering and crushing it to a quick bloody death.

A plan—or perhaps a whim—came to him. He put an army on transports in New York Harbor, 16,000 to 18,000 troops. They sailed away out of the harbor.

The scouts, spies, informers of General Washington couldn't tell him where this fleet of troops was sailing. What was their aim?

Where would they land? Who were they going to fight and where? Robert and Oat were among those who tried to get the answers for General Washington, tried and failed. For days across that summer of 1777, "the Year of the Three Gallows," Washington and his generals puzzled, guessed, worried over the fact and point "Howe is moving his army—but where to?"

The answer came. Howe's army was sighted off Delaware Bay. Could he be aiming at anything else than Philadelphia, the capital city of the Rebels, where the Continental Congress sat, where the big decisions came of the pretended government of the newly announced United States of America, where the Rebels had stores of ammunition and supplies at near-by Reading?

To the south, to Philadelphia Washington marched his army to meet Howe and battle for Philadelphia. On the way he would show Philadelphia his army, the people in that city more than a third Tory, less than a third Rebel, the rest neutral or mongrel. He would show them his army. They could see for themselves his marching thousands of veterans and raw recruits and make of it what they would. It might correct the impression in some quarters that his army had melted into thin air, existed on paper. They would march on Front Street alongside the Delaware River and wheel into Market Street, the General sent word ahead, almost with the delicate ironic implication to the Tories, the neutrals, the mongrels, as though, "My phantom Army, you have heard of it, my pale ghosts of rebellion and treason, you have heard of them, they will march for you, before your eyes they will march along Front and turn at Market, and you may witness for yourself how airy and insubstantial they are, what figments of imagination, what figures of fantasy and rumor the battalions reported as fighting for American freedom and independence."

On the day of this march, early in the morning, two hours for each other had Robert and Mim, two hours, short, swift and breathless, so much to say, so little time for it, after one hour with the father and Mary.

"Never so danged wild happy in my life when I saw them," said Robert to Oat, "never so low-down dreary sad about going away."

They had wondered at Robert. He was underweight but all of him looked hard and they saw his eyes blue steel with unquenchable purpose.

On a doorstep near the corner of Front and Market streets, Ordway Winshore, Mary and Mim, with Jean Shepherd, stood waiting, stood two hours watching the army march by, the wheeling columns of an army the world was wondering about, an army that came and went to return after it vanished, an army that lost in afternoon fog had hammered its attack at sunrise, an apparition army in tatters and makeshifts, an army lacking nearly every essential but visible flesh and invisible faith and vision, a paradoxical army of tatterdemalions

614

who could take defeat after defeat and come on for more, an army more barefoot than well-shod, an army with slim rations and great expectations in its knapsacks, an army that lived on hope and that hope kept alive by one dreamer in ten who saw a continent and a world republic of free men to be won by fighting, by the will to resist till the enemy gave in—an array of nationalities, breeds and crossbreeds where the native-born shared with English, Scotch, Welsh, Yorkshiremen, Irish, Germans, Dutch, Swedes, Jews, Poles, Bohemians, Negroes, Protestants, Catholics, Lutherans—an array of farmers, mechanics, hunters and trappers, fishermen, day laborers, indentured servants, vagabonds, looters and criminal plunderers who had been published and warned by the headquarters command, pious descendants of Puritans who fought under Cromwell against King Charles I, drifters and rollicking men who wanted to taste fighting and blood, landless men who wanted the hundred-acre farm promised them by the Continental Congress, men holding title to wide fabulous tracts of land—dreamers and desperadoes with dawn in their eyes—chimney-corner heroes who wished they were home and wondered whatever got them into the army—they marched—they wheeled in the column that turned the corner of Front and Market streets that day.

Marching they came with drums beating and the fifers shrilling "Yankee Doodle" and "The White Cockade"—

Marching four abreast and spaced out with dignity, sprigs of green on many a hat and twigs of pine that gave out like little songs—

Ragged marching men with here and there a British or Hessian uniform stripped from prisoners or battlefield dead and wounded—

Marching farm boys in homemade jackets without sleeves and black-and-white checked shirts torn and splotched and over the shoulder the squirrel rifle from home—

Marching lean and worn men, middle-aged and old, hard and battered, slouching at a gait that wasted no muscle or breath—

Marching rough men with nameless gleams in their eyes, men of drink and carousal who had nevertheless proven they could fight, kill, and stand hunger, rain, snow and the sleep on the cold ground—

Marching barefoot men and men with shoes tied and bandaged to their feet, men with shoes patched and repatched and bound and rebound with thongs and strings till the wonder was they didn't drop off the feet—

Marching raw recruits who couldn't keep step, their fresh clothes from home standing out against the rags of veterans—

Marching they came with drums beating and the fifers shrilling "Yankee Doodle" and "The White Cockade"—

Horsemen there were with sabers and pistols, teamsters and the commissary wagons, brass and iron cannon with the huge figure of General Henry Knox heading his artillerymen—

Marching, they were more than two hours marching around that corner of Front and Market streets—

615

At their head with other horsemen rode the Commander-in-Chief, the responsible head, General George Washington—a man, a legend, a hope, a bulwark, a threat and a promise—a born rider, he and his horse one piece, a unit—Washington in his faded buff-and-blue giving the people of Philadelphia and the delegates to the Continental Congress a good long look at the Continental Army of the United States of America—

Soon were to come his words: "The time is now near at hand which must probably determine, whether Americans are to be Freemen, or Slaves, whether they are to have any property they call their own. . . . The fate of unknown millions will now depend, under God, on the Courage and Conduct of this Army. . . . We have therefore to resolve to conquer or die."

"Oh, there he is!" Jean Shepherd had sobbed as a wagon train passed and they saw on a wagon seat and holding the reins none other than Michael McGillicuddy, alive and important, with no fear of any authorities in Philadelphia.

Faces that seemed familiar and couldn't be placed, many such faces had passed. Winshore picked out Hiram Kester, "Old Wilderness," in buckskin shirt and coonskin cap—and Jack Mallon, the Elizabethtown blacksmith. Mim thought she saw a teamster who used to bring wood to the Cavendish dress shop and was sure of the face of a Boston chimney sweep. And of course the high moment of the marching for all of them was when Robert Winshore and Oates Elwood, who had been told where to look for them, raised their arms and fluttered their hands and put on their widest smiles showing all their teeth.

As the ranks on ranks passed by for an hour Marintha Wilming shuddered, laughed, and shuddered again. She had heard a Tory merchant farther along the sidewalk and of his jeering words caught only "half-naked lousy ragtag and bobtail, they call it an army." The shudder came again and she suddenly felt the world to be very old and too many people with a queer pride in its shabbiness of which they were a part with a hand in the making of the shabbiness. Then an icy-cold wave of strength ran through her and she was saying to herself, "This half-naked and lousy army marches through black night believing in a dawn, a bright flaming dawn to come. Suppose that dawn fails them—what then? I would rather be Robert Winshore dead and cold for the dream of that dawn than not to have nad that dream. So far have I come. So near am I to the red blood of his heart, his army and Cause."

Her eyes touched this day the lurking indefinable quality of the elemental brute—a strange factor of hair and blood and will to win—that must underlie unconquerable armed forces. In such a human swirl moved her Robert day on day, the camp earth their bed at night, the sky their roof, cooking their own spare meals, picking vermin from shirts and breeches, at home in filth, profanity and scabs among the fever-smitten and bullet-torn—this for the sake of a moonwhite dream, for the faint scarlet filaments of a dreamdawn to come.

Out of Philadelphia marched the Continental Army, on to Brandywine Creek and defeat, back to Germantown and another defeat.

And Howe took Philadelphia and the British Army settled down in it for triumph and contemplation, for rest and comfort and pleasure.

The Bradford printery and Ordway Winshore took on another tone and color, printing no more Rebel pamphlets, tracts and handbills except at night with guards on watch. Mary and Mim and Cynthia George and a thousand other Rebels in Philadelphia led double lives and stilled their tongues and kept aware that walls have ears.

* * * * * * * * * *

Chapter 34

* * * * * * * * * *

Incalculable Bethlehem and Valley Forge

SINCE the day that Robert came for his precious two-hour visit, since the day Marintha Wilming saw the march and measured the dream of the Continental Army, they saw a certain calm and determination take shape in her. At the Cynthia George shop Mim's weekly pay ran above her highest in Boston. Business was brisk. The British officers and troops, the Tory fashion leaders of Philadelphia, feeling a new security and the war about to end as they wished, were spending freely and it was plain the city would see a winter of social whirl, gaiety and extravaganza. The customers with their talk and manners now annoyed Mim. "I am here to serve them," she said. "Why should I let them annoy me? But they do." A wealthy Tory matron's son came in with his mother, saw Mim and took to her, asked to see her of evenings and was told there were reasons it wasn't proper, and her son came of afternoons to chat with Mim as she worked at sewing and at directing others. The young fellow was soon going into the British Army with an officer's commission. He was respectful enough, somewhat stolid and decent. Yet Cynthia George heard his mother one day blutter the words of a plain-spoken haughty dame, "You should well know, Miss George, that at least it is not *my* intention that my son shall marry a mantuamaker."

The day came when Mim saw that it wasn't the annoying customers that bored her deep with discontent. She felt out of place, with the streaks of awe and reverence in her, at times feeling a blasphemy in

617

the vanity and furbelows, the trimmings and chitchat of life that drifted in and out of the dress shop.

Winshore and Mary understood when they saw her one morning in a sturdy gray wool gown, stockings of thick wool, and a warm but shabby and worn black cloak, a small bundle of traveling needs. They helped her to the farmer wagon that went out of Philadelphia and began her trip that ended some forty miles away in Bethlehem, Pennsylvania.

It was dusk and a snow falling on the second day of her rides in farm wagons and carts when she set foot in Bethlehem. Around three sides of a quadrangle that made the center of the town stood stone buildings, one of them eighty-three feet long by fifty feet wide, three stories high. This building, known as the "Single Brethren's House" of the communal brotherhood of the Moravian Church, had been set aside for the unmarried men and youth of the church. Now it served as a General Hospital of the Continental Army.

Marintha Wilming walked toward it, bundle in hand, feeling herself one of many people, one of hundreds moving on work and errands in and around this dark quadrangle. She was prepared for confusion and scurrying here and was to learn that in one building two hundred British prisoners had been held under Continental Army guards, that sixteen delegates of the Continental Congress in flight from Philadelphia to their new capital at Yorktown, Pennsylvania, stopped here, that a wagon train had arrived bringing Philadelphia church bells where they couldn't be made into lead for enemy bullets, that the archives and treasury of the Continental Congress had been brought from Philadelphia via Trenton here under guard of fifty infantrymen in wagons with an escort of fifty armed horsemen, that the Church Store opposite the cemetery held in its deep cellars commissary and medical stores for the hospital, that this quiet country town of some five hundred people whose creed opposed war suddenly became a wild swarming pit of the fury and onrush of war.

Wagons, two, ten, twenty wagons, and at least twenty more, at least forty wagons she counted, wagons and horses in a falling snow waiting, moving up, waiting again, the teamsters sitting silent, shaking off snow, some speaking to their horses occasionally, a few cursing the long wait.

From these open wagons, from men lying on the straw-bedded floorboards of the wagons, Mim heard murmuring and mumbling, the questions "Where are we?" and "How far yet to go?" and "Goddamit, the time seems long," and occasional moans of pain and twice the piercing and prolonged shrieks of wounded men calling to be put out of their pain, hoarse mad cries from one, "I want to die, I want to die!"

Of this and much more Mim had heard after she walked into the General Hospital and began her service at whatever was ordered by whatever doctor or steward she was assigned to from day to day. The one hundred and twenty-two beds vacated by the Single Brethren had long ago been filled—and since there were no more beds, no linen, no pillows, the sick and wounded lay on straw and took what came and there were seven hundred of these sick and wounded and they were packed close to each other in November and December of 1777 and upward of one hundred died each of those months. Dysentery cut men down to shadows. A rotting of blood and bone, a disease baffling to the doctors, wore men to death. Worst of all was the toll of what they named the "putrid fever." Where the victims of that plague died the litter was pollution and filth. Yet such was the overcrowding, so pitiful and merciless the lack of space and the number of victims, that it happened sometimes that one died and still another and four and five died on the same pallet before it could be changed and made clean for the next one. This was the malady that crept into Mim's lean hard body after weeks of endless duties and services that had won her the praise of doctors and stewards.

They gave her a bed with clean linen in a corner where two stewards had died of the "putrid fever." She lay weak and foul of odor, her memory serving her only dimly as to Robert, his father and Mary, as to Cynthia George, Rose Cavendish, and far back there, so far she could only faintly touch it, the farm at Lexington, the graves of Darius, her father and mother, and the living sisters Deb and Aggie wherever they might be.

A December day and a thin drizzle of rain blowing and the man driving the small strong woolly horse pulling the two-wheeled cart wore Quaker clothes, a broad-brim hat, a gray scarf wrapped around his neck and chin.

The floor of the car held eighteen inches of straw to cushion in degree the body swathed in thick wool blankets.

What food the Quaker-clad man ate that day and night until midnight he ate while driving, while on the move. About every two hours he pulled in the horse, stopped the cart, and got out for a good look at the face of the woman in the blankets, saw the eyelids open, gave her one or two spoons of a twenty-year-old rum from Dutch Guiana, and three times at taverns brought her warm broth and spooned it to her, and believed on his soul that once he saw the faint flicker of a smile of thanks to him for bothering with her.

The patrols at Philadelphia took him for a Quaker on an urgent errand of mercy, which was correct.

The drive from the Single Brethren's House in Bethlehem to the Winshore home in Philadelphia took from daybreak till midnight.

The weeks went by. Marintha Wilming came out of the "putrid fever." Having made her recovery she was long weeks winning back her strength. Ordway Winshore wouldn't listen to her thanks and gratitude.

"Leastways," she smiled to him and Mary, "you will allow me to say it was bright of you to be alarmed at the death rate in Bethlehem and go prepared to haul me back in case I was down with what they correctly name the putrid fever."

The days passed into weeks, the "putrid fever" gone. Then coughing spells set in. The doctor called it "inflammation of the lungs." If she had been handling scores of the sick at Bethlehem, it was not strange she should have the beginnings of "galloping consumption," ran the doctor's opinion. More weeks went by. The coughing spells stayed on but lessening in violence. Days came with no coughing. The doctor said she had "a wonderful constitution" and "a stoical spirit."

To Mary and Winshore she said, "I have tried to cast out fear." She could remember and bring into play the same icy-cold wave of calm and determination that swept her when she stood at Front and Market streets and watched the Continental Army march.

"I was born and made to live skinny," she smiled to Mary when taking a first look at herself in the long oval gilt mirror of the room. "It shouldn't take long to put a little meat on these bones."

Two letters from Robert had come for her in the months she was away at Bethlehem. They were handed to her one morning when the signs looked good for her to climb back to strength, her grayish-pale face become a clean white-pale, and the last rank odors of the fever aired out of the room.

The letter paper had a dusty feel. In a grain sack a farmer had driven it to a gristmill near Philadelphia where the miller had brought it to town in a sack of flour he had ground. The paper carried a smell of wheat and flour dust—Mim liked the smell.

"I read them, I smell them, I forget them," she smiled to Mary. "Then I come back and smell again."

The longer letter, the earlier one, his October letter, was not long but was rich, sweet, wild, like a dream come true. The other, the late December letter, was short, cryptic, a little dazed, thought Mim.

Days passed when she stayed in bed most of the time though going downstairs to join Winshore and Mary at meals, bringing up wood for the fireplace, sweeping and tidying her own room, dipping into books, writing occasional lines, talking to a pair of cardinals that came and went in elm branches that brushed the window.

A visitor dropped in one night, began coming every night for an hour or two. They talked about the scandals of high living in Philadelphia that winter, the parties, the drinking, the swagger and show— and twenty miles away their sweethearts with the Rebel army in Valley Forge. Evelyn Trutt had come to Philadelphia to be nearer Oates Elwood and her son David, both at Valley Forge, and to help them and others with her good evenings at Cynthia George's dress shop.

As in the old days in the Cavendish shop Evelyn was a better listener than talker. She still wore well-chosen, light-brown dresses with neat and thin austere lace at her neck. Her pale narrow face, her slight body and mild gray eyes, still had invisible strengths that again impressed Mim.

"You don't look a moment older than those days when you were sewing that costly gown for Sapphira Reggs," said Mim. Mim herself, Robert, the father, Mary, all had aged from five to ten years in the two years that had passed, Mim would guess. "Time and this terrible storm we are living in doesn't press its marks on your face." And Mim heard some deep strength in what now came from Evelyn, words Mim had heard a hundred times: "The hand of God is working toward great unseen ends."

Mim couldn't define it. She was sure that she herself out of trial and grief had come to some faith akin to that of Evelyn.

"We may have different words for it, Evelyn, but far under we lean on the same rock and in rare moments touch the same finger of God. You are health for me and you must come often. If I seem low at any time just sit quiet by me and we'll listen together."

Now too as in the old days Mim felt vast reserves and patience about Evelyn. And now more than before she would like to know what were the keepers and watchers in the head and heart of Evelyn so that she could move through tumult and hideous affairs that left no hammer dents on her face. There was no hate in Evelyn. She still saw good people and bad on both sides of the Revolution. When she said, "I seek the inheritance that fadeth not away," in her smooth deliberate contralto, Mim took it and dug at it and made something of it. An eye for the droll underlay the solemn in Evelyn as saying, "You egg me on," she would bring one oddity after another of what she had seen and heard, the harried mother calling to her boy on a doorstep, "Don't sit there pickin your nose, we must go now," the two respectable-looking men she passed coming out of a tavern, one of them lush with liquor saying, "I've had one woman lawfully and forty women unlawfully and never one of them cried over me," and the powder horn Oates Elwood had seen where the owner had cut the words in 1759:

> The rose is red, the grass is green,
> such days is past which we have seen,

and for the year 1776 the record:

> My horn and I have wandered far,
> for lobsters, redskins, deer and bar.

"In New York one night, windy and snowing, I passed two men, Evelyn, and heard one of them curse a woman and cry out, 'I'll never see her again, I'd as lief sleep with her as the scrag end of a neck of mutton.' "

This was byplay. They allowed themselves a little of it. Evelyn's boy David had stumbled out of woodland on Long Island one autumn night to see a harvest moon come down in quiet and peace on two brass cannon, seven dead Hessians in a heap and on top of them a big bass drum. "Who could make either sense or nonsense of that?" Evelyn asked. From a piece of paper where she had copied the words, Evelyn read a sentence from a speech of William Pitt a few weeks before to the British Parliament. "He was on crutches, a sick man with the gout, and he rebuked the government for using Hessians and Indians in the war here." Evelyn read the sentence she had copied:

"If I were an American, as I am an Englishman, while a foreign troop was landed in my country, I never would lay down my arms— never, never, never!"

When they spoke of the American Army, their men twenty miles away in Valley Forge winter quarters, they hushed their tones. What they had heard at first they didn't believe, taking it as war rumor. It came over Mim that she had been shut away from rumors and that Winshore and Mary had put on good cheer to help her get well. At Cynthia George's, over the town, from people who had met drifters out of Valley Forge, Evelyn had impressions she could mention only in subdued awe. "You don't like to tell yourself you're coming to believe something too dark and terrible to believe."

The men of the army at Valley Forge for days had slept on the ground in December-cold rain till tents came mid-month, Evelyn knew for certain. They slept on frozen ground in those tents for weeks while they took axes and went to near-by woods and cut and hauled logs to build huts, horses so scarce that the men themselves buckled into rope harnesses they made to haul their logs. The huts sixteen feet by fourteen had twelve men to the hut. "Can you see them crowded into one of those huts?" Evelyn in her chair asked in a slow voice that barely carried to Mim in bed. "Each man hardly room to turn over, for the fireplace and the wood must have room, too. . . . Smoke in their eyes, they curse the smoke, the goddam smoke that has all of them with bloodshot eyes, never an end to the smoke what with only green wood or wood damp from rain and snow. . . . And shoes, more than a thousand men with no shoes, barefoot except for the rags they tie around their feet, the strips of blanket they wind around their feet and keep wearing out till they have no blankets, blood on the snow from feet swollen and cracked . . . and blood runs if they pick the scabs."

Now for the first time Mim saw Evelyn's serenity gone. Her voice had choked on the last she was saying and now she whispered, "My David is one of the barefoot, my boy Dave and his feet with big cracks that break and bleed and he can't stand on his feet and he is in one of the hospitals."

She waited a few moments, then spoke with her old serenity. "Eleven hospitals they have, the floors bare damp ground with straw shaken over it—they are even short of straw for their beds, no linen, no extra blankets, and the man lacking a blanket goes without and shivers as best he can. And those eleven hospitals all filled so that some of the sick must stay in their log huts. . . . The sick and the well have seen days go by with no meat, no vegetables, nothing to eat but a lump of dough baked in fire embers, fire-cake they call it, no coffee, tea, rum—plain water and a muddy polluted water at that to wash down fire-cake is the meal . . . morning, noon and night fire-cake and water for days on days.

"Clothes in rags and strings, why not? They have marched hundreds of miles, fighting in woods and underbrush, sleeping where night found them, wearing and tearing their clothes to pieces. Now the bare knees, shoulders and legs show unless they can be covered by an overcoat or blanket likewise not in rags and strings.

"Hundreds lacking blankets huddle around their hut fires and sleep sitting up and a headquarters order says they would get better sleep if they stretched out but if they stretch out they get cold so they sleep sitting up. To run a hundred yards in knee-deep snow and cold wind and ease themselves at an outdoor vault is too much for some of them and they don't do it and a headquarters order is read to the regiments that guards will fire on any man easing elsewhere than in the vaults. The filth and stench in the crowded huts gets thick and they burn pitch to fumigate and change the air."

Mim was listening, the back of her hand on a pillow, her ropes of hair glinting in the light from a candle at the bedside table, her eyes closing and then opening on Evelyn. Her long acquaintance with Evelyn, her trust in her as never an idle talker, had Mim saying to herself, "It is all probably true, if Evelyn says so, and if half of it were true, then what?" Mim had put her hands under the quilts, her fingers winding and twining. What she was hearing, Mim believed, was a sane account of matters cruel and sordid for the mind to hold and consider. And Evelyn was piling it out and moving it around for Mim to see and know with the hope that the two of them could join in sanity and grief. Behind her mask of serenity Evelyn seemed to say that she must tell it and the two of them could share the bitter knowledge.

"The drums beat and the men crawl out of their huts for grand parade ten o'clock in the morning," Evelyn went on. "They hear orders read. Dead horses must be buried or removed from camp, too many dead horses, bone-racks, starved horses. Gaming with cards and dice has become a vicious custom, punishment is ordered for either card-playing or dice gaming. Soap not yet on hand but a soft soap made from wood ash expected soon. Huts will be inspected regularly for filth. Clothes get stolen. Men going to hospital are warned they must have their company officers make a full list of all their articles of clothing to be kept by the acting surgeon. Men unfit for duty by reason of the itch must report at certain huts and be anointed. Women from Philadelphia claiming they must visit friends or relatives in the army are hereafter forbidden to enter camp as too many of them have sought to induce soldiers to desert. The orders are read at grand parade in the morning. One man called it a raggedy-assed grand parade."

"Evelyn."

"Yes, Mim."

"You said that last as though you had been there."

"I was there."

"You have been to Valley Forge?!"

"I had to see Oates Elwood and my boy David. I rode out with a farmer Cynthia George has known for years. I stayed two days and I left the day of February fourth when they published that order. I saw my David in what they term a hospital and I have wept over what I can't do for him he needs done."

"Did you see Robert?"

"He was away on some three or four day expedition, as they called it."

"Did you hear how he is?"

"Alive and hard, Oat said, somewhat weak like all of them.

"Two or three times a week," Evelyn went on, "the afternoon grand parade sees a soldier led out and flogged with thirty lashes or a hundred on the bare back, for stealing clothes, food or money from other soldiers, for stealing provisions from the commissary, for stealing a horse from an officer, for talking desertion to the other soldiers, for disobedience of orders, for going out of camp and plundering farmers, and always one hundred lashes, well laid on, as the sentence reads, for attempting to desert. Desertion—would you believe it, they are saying three thousand men have deserted over the winter, many to their homes, hundreds to the enemy here in Philadelphia. One morning in January they hanged a man. They had caught him deserting and taking with him two prisoners in irons. The troops formed a circle around the gallows, heard the man make a little speech that he didn't mean to do what he had done. The rope from the gallows was fastened around the man's neck as he stood in the wagon. An officer gave the signal, the wagon drove off and the man hung a moment and the rope broke. They lifted him into the wagon again and a doubled rope was noosed around his neck and when the wagon drove off he hung there till he strangled. They dug a hole in the ground just under him, and while he swung there they cut the rope and he dropped into the hole and was shoveled over. I don't know why I tell you this, Mim, except it was told to me just so. Oat said he supposes perhaps three thousand men have deserted, another three thousand lie sick or unfit for duty, and if the enemy came Washington wouldn't have three thousand good and able men to meet an attack."

"General Washington, do they blame him?"

"You might near say they worship him, that is, Oat and Robert do and they say the main part of the army is like them. The General lives plain in a common farmhouse, seems to be on duty day and night."

"But don't they blame him? Why doesn't he get food, blankets and clothes for his men?"

"He has done everything that can be done, the men believe. They believe that the Continental Congress did fix it for some clothes and blankets to be sent. And those supplies either didn't get started or horses were lacking or the teamsters didn't get paid. They saw a report of the Commander-in-Chief to the Congress, Oat and Robert did. They could remember sentences out of it. Oat was proud of them: 'It adds not a little to my other difficulties and distress to find, that much more is expected of me than is possible to be performed, and upon the ground of safety and policy I am obliged to conceal the true state of the army from public view, and thereby expose myself to calumny and detraction.' The other was two sentences. Let me think." Slowly Evelyn spoke. " 'Perhaps by midsummer the soldier may receive thick stockings, shoes, and blankets, which he will contrive to get rid of in the most expeditious manner. By an eternal round of the most stupid management the public treasure is expended to no kind of purpose, while the men have been left to perish by inches with cold nakedness.' "

"An eternal round of the most stupid management," Mim repeated.

"More than that," said Evelyn Trutt, coming nearer hate in her eyes than Mim had ever seen. "Corruption is in it, politics, trickery, stealing, pilfering, pelf, rascality of the lowest order." Evelyn paused, regained herself, "I mustn't go on like this, my very dear Mim. Perhaps I have talked too much."

"No." And Mim's sad smile had meaning for Evelyn.

"The men at Valley Forge, they see the Commander as hard with officers as with men, for the sake of discipline and order. One court-martial after another has found officers guilty of perjury, of stealing from the men and from each other, of disobedience and mutiny and disrespect of authority, of neglect of their men. Those officers have been cashiered with infamy. A commissary officer in General Greene's division they found guilty of theft of two hundred dollars from two men and they made him pay the money back and then—this we might have enjoyed seeing, Mim—they mounted him on a horse without a saddle, faced him to the rear of the horse, his coat turned wrong side out and his hands tied behind him. Then all the drums of his division followed the horse and drummed him out of the army lines never to return and the court-martial order said the sentence and its execution should be published in the newspapers."

"The army does laugh a little for all its misery and woe."

"A little—Oat chuckled over an officer looking into a pot a soldier had over a fire and asking wasn't it a stone there in the pot. 'Are you boiling the stone to eat?' the officer asked, and the soldier grinned, 'I don't know, sir, but I'll try anything. They do say there is great strength in a stone if you can manage to get it out.'

"Half-naked, cold, hungry, eyes bloodshot from smoke, and then, Mim, I saw chapped hands and beards tangled with dirt and scabs everywhere, cracks in the skin filled with dirt and dried blood and if they had the soap they don't have they wouldn't wash the dirt out of those cracks because it would start them bleeding again. And vermin—the little time I talked with David, half the time he had to keep scratching. 'My shirt is full of 'em,' he said. 'I take it off and pick 'em out of the seams, wide flat graybacks, and crush 'em with my fingernail and watch the blood come out and then I say there's the blood I'm shedding for my country. I've had my armpits bleed from scratching 'em. I have nourished more of 'em in my two armpits than there are people in Boston. The head lice are not so bad but the crabs are worse than the graybacks. When they really want your blood you can't sleep for the way they bite.' Like that my David talked, brave and trying to comfort his mother. He saw me begin to cry when I looked at his cracked and bleeding feet, the left foot more swollen and purple than the right. He smiled and said, 'Ma, next summer you'll see me runnin like a rabbit scared up in a cabbage patch.'"

Evelyn didn't break as Mim expected. Evelyn sat composed and quiet with tears streaming down her face, wiping away her tears and sitting composed and quiet.

She kissed Mim on going away that night, said she wasn't much of a comforter but she had to talk out what she did to someone and Mim would better say nothing of what she had heard.

The next three nights Evelyn Trutt didn't come to see Mim, not even for one of her pleasant five-minute greetings.

Chapter 35

Mim's Foretokening Dream

FROM her window Mim had watched a short morning snowfall cover the horse-shed roof, fill crotches and corners of the elm trunk and branches, and the afternoon sun melt it away and the blue sky high over looking rested and fresh-washed.

The letter she was writing to Robert came slow and she felt cramped in writing it. She would like to give him cheer and consolation besides her love. She suddenly felt empty and worthless and wouldn't dare trust any words she could send him. She tore to pieces the letter she had written and threw it in the fire. She would do better tomorrow, she hoped, and her mood was fog-gray. She drifted into sleep that night in a fog-gray, her hands groping, her mind fumbling.

Mim wakened near midnight to hear footsteps and hushed voices, hushed and tense. They seemed to be coming up the stairs. She was out of bed and opened the room door to look down the hallway. From the door of Locke's old room came a slant of light. She could see Mary and Evelyn Trutt entering that room and she heard a quiet moving about of feet and soft shufflings and a few words she couldn't make out spoken low and tender.

Mim lighted a candle, left her door open, lay back in her bed wondering and listening. Mary had seen her light and came in and stood over Mim's white and awed face.

"It is sad yet it could be far worse," said Mary.

"Yes?"

"It is David Trutt. Oat Elwood started with him from Valley Forge at daybreak, got him through the Philadelphia lines with British gold pieces Evelyn gave him, and he is here with his left foot cut off and we believe we can bring him through. His foot turned black and the surgeons said it must come off. Oat and Mr. Winshore carried him from the wagon in front of the house and up the stairs as easy for him as they could make it. The wagon jolting on the road hasn't been good for him. He is still in a stupor from hot rum they poured in him."

Mary's wide-set blue eyes blinked away at a moist film. "Mim, they are getting him out of his sad and filthy rags. When they pulled away our blankets they had rolled him in for the wagon journey, I couldn't have believed it, you might as well say he lay half-naked in that Valley Forge hospital, cracks in his chapped hands and his beard tangled with dirt and scabs. Soon as we can we will wash him. Tonight we are putting him in clean linen. When he wakes he may cry with pain. You must not be troubled at what you hear."

Mim shuddered at the knees. "I know. It will be like Bethlehem and what I heard in the House of the Single Brethren. Go now, Mary. You are one of God's own. Go now. Close the door after you. Good night."

Before sleep came her memory ran back to Lieutenant George Frame with a whole leg gone, and she tried to picture him somewhere in England, a bright and fascinating man on a crutch, living on a government pension, perhaps with a wife and a house of his own. Perhaps his suffering has broken his pride and made a difference in his voice and face. She slept and woke to hear a low keen moaning from David Trutt. She slept again and a dream came to her, so vivid and strange a dream that when she awoke to a sharp piercing cry from down the hallway, she reviewed the dream again and again and clutched for its meaning.

She saw David Trutt the next morning, his small black eyes luminous, his eyeballs watery and bloodshot. Mim flashed to a hut with twelve men crowded on a square of sixteen by fourteen feet around a fire of snow and rain-damped wood, smoke in their eyes and day in and day out and night and day smoke in their eyes. His dark-brown hair had been combed yet it was so scraggly and tangled that a comb couldn't do much with it till it was washed. In the scrabble of beard over his face mingled dirt and the dry blood from fissures in the skin, with a fresh tiny trickle of blood from one that had cracked open. His shirt of tatters and his ragged breeches had been taken off but there were still habitants in a right armpit at which he scratched with his left hand. "We'll wash his armpits today," Evelyn was saying low-voiced to Mary. Now he had finished his scratching and his two arms lay quiet over a quilt of white with blue checks.

A hint of a smile came to his pale mouth partly hidden in the scraggly beard. They could tell that for him there was a touch of gay revelry over the utterly clean linen that encased him. Mim's eyes ran along the immaculate sleeves of scrupulous white. Her eye came at what stuck out at the ends of the sleeves. Those were hands, chapped in weeks of winter cold, gnarled and fissured hands, cracks over the fingers and the backs of the hands, streaks of dirt and dry blood. A hint of a smile came again from his wry, shy mouth as he heard his mother saying low-voiced to Mim, "He would have died out there. They have nothing to do with out there. We have every hope he will come through."

Mim went back to her room and her bed, hearing afterward that a doctor came, on the amputated stump put clean bandages and cursed the unwashed and putrid ones he had taken off. Jean Shepherd had come up with two pails of lukewarm water and they had given him a bath, skipping the many fissures where it hurt him to be touched. David said he could stand scalding water at his armpits if it would kill the creepers there, which it did, though it gave David pain because the skin had been torn with his scratching. With fine-toothed combs they went over his head for the breed of creepers there. The ache of his leg came sharper after the doctor's washing of it and then eased. On the fifth day of these attentions David was saying, "I'll be a new man soon, mamma."

There came two days when Mim wouldn't eat or talk and the letter to Robert wouldn't get written. They felt she was sweet, patient and aware in telling them she wished to be left alone and would come out whole and well. On the third day she was saying, "The dream came again and I can't tell it to you as yet."

On that same third day a coughing spell seized her. The doctor joined them in warning her she was letting care and anxiety wear her down. The thick shags of her eyebrows lifted and on her slowly parted lips came a pitiless smile. "You will know when it comes that I have now been through the worst. When the word comes I will be the strongest of you."

In four days came the word and they knew what she meant. It was a note Oates Elwood sent to Evelyn: "Bobby died last night they had to take off both his legs and he didn't have blood enough to carry him through the doctors said. I held his right hand through part of it and never saw a man braver. His last words I could make out he wished he might have seen more of Mim and papa this last year. Before he went on the expedition where his legs froze I heard him say, 'I hope the people to come after will understand what it costs to win a war' and he was sure we were going to win it."

Winshore and Mary sat on Mim's bed and studied her thin and now somewhat pinched oval of a white face with a peace on it.

"I crossed a bridge and walked a dark valley before you," Mim said.

"You knew beforehand," said Winshore, "and a peace has come to you."

"A peace with long roots winding around in dreamdust. There was Darius, then my father and mother, and now Robert—and now Robert —all given to a dream thin as the air around and over the elm branches," moving a thumb toward the tree outside.

"I tried to write him a letter," Mim went on. "Something kept telling me I couldn't write him a letter to do any good. And the dream kept coming—three nights in a row the dream."

Winshore moved toward her and held her hand. She was dry-eyed and the stronger. He blinked his eyes but couldn't blink away the wet film that came.

"I wept for you too, Ordway Winshore, you who have now given your two sons and have no more sons to give having given all."

His soft brown eyes seemed deeper-set and past fathoming. He asked, "And your dream?"

"Three times it came and no time different. A man walks an open plain toward the sunset. He walks straight into the sunset flare, no pride, no fear, an unbreakable man. He wades into sunset flame. He struggles knee-deep and then waist-high in the moving and changing sundown fire, blood-color fire. He makes a slow turn to face where he has been and he raises his right hand three times to his three-cornered hat as he speaks clear slow words:

"Some go soon and some go late into the sunset. I am one of those chosen to go soon. I have kept my faith in the storm and dream that must ever move in the blood of the American people. Now before going I give my three salutes, one to the American flag, one to my Valley Forge comrades, one to the undaunted and enduring Commander George Washington.

"Then he bowed low again and turned and walked into sheets of blazing maroon cloud. And that was all. The earth dropped away from him and he vanished. That was all."

She paused, then went on. "What could I do with such a dream? I couldn't write it to Robert. I took it as a foretokening. Those days I wouldn't eat or talk with you, those days I wept till I had no more tears. Then it came over me if I was ever to live and laugh again I must keep the wonder of the storm and dream that is on us. We can't see the end. Away off on a mountain forty miles away you can see the white snow glisten and the blue mist change but like Robert and Oat far up in Maine you don't even know the mountain and it's for you to give it a name. Those who never let the wonder die down about what is beyond, they're the ones that'll keep on. Robert died with the wonder still in him, I know. He gave me enough of it for me to keep on.

"And this," Mim went on after a pause in which she reached under a pillow and brought out a closed hand, "this by right belongs to you. I forgot to give it to him when he was here and I couldn't put it in a letter."

She opened her hand. Winshore took from it the bronze plaque and ran his thumb over the Four Stumbling Blocks to Truth. "They don't age, they are timeless," he said as he read:

1. The influence of fragile or unworthy authority.
2. Custom.
3. The imperfection of undisciplined senses.
4. Concealment of ignorance by ostentation of seeming wisdom.

"Aunt Ellen found it near the woodshed door the morning after Robert's furious rush that took him away from Lieutenant Frame and the soldiers who tried to capture him. The silver chain broke."

"It is yours," said Winshore, handing it to her. "I may borrow it from you. It is your keepsake."

She hung it around her neck and put a kiss on it, "One I was saving for Robert."

She read from Robert's last short letter: "Your face and your name they never leave me. When I wrap my blanket around me in a tent or on the bare ground before I sleep I see the hang of your hair around your good face and I hear the ripple of your laugh. The days go by and never a day I don't want you. Keep one kiss I send you now. Keep four more kisses I send you and tie each one in the corner of a handkerchief. The blue silk kerchief you gave me has only one little tear in it. Be lonely for me as I am lonely for you. We must make our loneliness warm with its promises till our spring day. A shining spring with one great day we will have. Keep it tight and keep it sure this one long kiss I send you now."

There was a choke in Mim's throat as she came to the end of the letter. And Mary, as her hand stroked Mim's hair, "You don't weep but you have dry tears."

"Yes, Mary," as the choke in the throat came again.

* * * * * * * * * *

Chapter 36

* * * * * * * * * *

Dawns, Many Dawns

THE huddled men of the huts of Valley Forge stayed through into spring and June. In Philadelphia, New York, Charleston, Boston, in London and Paris, the question came often, "Did the American Army last through the winter and if so where is it?" and had the answer, "Yes, it held through at Valley Forge and will march and fight this summer with added fresh forces."

Good news came. The French Government had signed a paper. France was joining America as an ally. France was sending warships, troops, arms to America.

General Washington writing to a friend said, in his own formal style, he would like to know when and where an army of half-naked, shivering, hungry, lousy, unbreakable men had done more or done better for their country during a winter of icy rain and knee-deep snow.

Out of Valley Forge they marched in June to meet in northern New Jersey the enemy army that had quit Philadelphia.

Again in Philadelphia the Rebels could speak, write, print for the American Cause.

The fourth day of July came. Over the Winshore house-front doorway hung an American flag that had lain folded and creased under the straw mattress where Mim came through fever and a lung malady and other grief.

In the front room of the house Winshore noticed a festoon of red, white and blue ribbons, sweeps of pink and white peonies, here and there sprigs of white syringa—and a table set with nine plates, at either end of the oak board a tall glass vase from which rose spires of blue delphinium—and at the table center a bowl smiling with clusters of the flower known as baby's breath, sprays of flowerets in which hovered stars and mist.

"This is your day," Mary had laughed to her husband, smoothing and straightening his yellow linen stock and pinning a tiny rosebud on his coat lapel. "And what is acting you will soon learn."

Mary, with Mim and Cynthia George, seemed to be in charge of these arrangements that pleased and puzzled him, for he had noticed Mim do two or three dance steps he hadn't seen in a year. And Jean Shepherd's short thick body moved in quicksteps, for she had as her helper Michael McGillicuddy who scuffled with his right foot and could explain, with a merry grin, "Wouldn't you believe that such a God-fearing man as me would leave only three of his toes at Valley Forge?"

"Your toes ran away to the same hole my foot went," laughed David Trutt from a shaven and shining face.

At noon Mary answered a doorknock and let in Oates Elwood who said, "They will be here soon." Oat further mystified Winshore with telling him, "It's high time you had this day, sir." Oat and Mary seated Winshore in his large chair at the far corner of the room and Oat went out the front door. Evelyn Trutt came in, wearing a fresh light-brown bodice that sang gaily as it set off her well-rounded little breasts. Evelyn and Cynthia, with singing pink fluffs at her throat, were seated in chairs at either side of Winshore.

"They are waiting," said Mary who had stepped in and closed the door and stood with her hand on the knob.

"Send them in," called Evelyn.

The door opened. A woman walked in, of medium height, full-bosomed, melting gray eyes, a head of rich glossy black hair, and a smooth neat gown of soft cornflower-blue. Winshore had never seen her before. Mim and Cynthia knew who she was, Oat Elwood's sister Ann. Those who knew her face saw that she couldn't tell whether she ought to laugh or break into tears.

She faced Winshore, bowed her head low and lifted it to look Winshore straight in the eyes and to say, clear-voiced and with no faltering, "Mr. Winshore, I have been queer and I have acted stubborn and I don't know why I have done so. I give you my word now that

I am sorry for what I have done that might have been unfair to you. I am sorry about it in a thousand ways." She looked toward Mary standing at the door, then turned again to Winshore. "What more there is to say of any wrong doings you can hear from your grandson."

Winshore drew in his chin, gripped tighter the armrests of his chair, the wide slash of his mouth in a grimace both tragic and comic.

Mary opened the door and Oat Elwood strode in with an easy solemnity, in his arms a bundle of white batiste, and Winshore made out a pink-white foot at one end of the bundle and at the other end a child face, a child head, a baby boy.

Oat put him slowly and tenderly on Winshore's knees saying calmly, with a touch of austerity, "The name of this child is John Locke Winshore, Jr."

At his right Winshore could hear Evelyn Trutt saying, "Born March 16, 1777, the Year of the Three Gallows."

And at his left Cynthia George, as though she were ringing merry little chimes, "The child of John Locke Winshore and Ann Elwood, married May 26, 1776, the year of the proclamation of American Independence."

The big hands of Ordway Winshore were roving around the little body he held. Both Mim and Mary flashed to the same guess in their minds. They saw his hands wondering if this was the same feel the hands had when they had roved around the other body, the baby legs and arms, the baby torso and backside of its father.

Now the grandfather peered and was lost at looking into the deep-set and liquid brown eyes, at searching the strands of vivid brick-dust hair, at the wide mouth and the long curve of it. Then Winshore closed his eyes. And Mary and Mim knew he was using the trick he worked to keep back the tears.

No one dared say a word. No one could think of a fitting word. His eyes came open and he gazed from face to face in the room. They saw it was a faraway look that swept out beyond this little room.

"Tomorrow has come to this room and the Future is here," he said, running a hand along the brick-dust hair and searching the soft brown eyes so deep-set, so much like him that they were part of him. "He will see many dawns and one will be the coming true of the dawn his father died for. We shall pray that like his father he will be at home in storm and dream."

He beckoned to Ann, pulled her to a seat on an armrest, put an arm around her and said, "Now tell me more about this wonderful young one."

"He's trying to pull off that rosebud," laughed Ann as she pushed away the mischievous fumbling baby fingers.

"His eyes," Ann went on, "month after month they kept changing a deeper brown till now they're exactly like yours and I couldn't keep him from you."

"How does he walk?"

"You'll see."

Their four hands slid him to the floor. He toddled and wobbled across the room to where Mim crouched and waited and when he did fall it was into her warm arms.

Mim hugged Locke's son, the dying words of Robert flashing to her: "I hope the people to come after will understand what it costs to win a war."

With her arms in a tighter hug around the little one, Mim cried to Ordway Winshore across the room, "He *will* see dawns, *many* dawns."

```
* * * * * * * * * *
*                  *
*   Book Three     *
*                  *
* * * * * * * * * *
```

THE ARCH HOLDS

PART ONE

Chapter 1

Erie Canal Sweethearts

"I DON'T own the Canal, not a bit's worth of it, not two bits. Yet I look at it every day and say I belong to part of it and part of it belongs to me."

Such words Joel Wimbler had written in a letter from Arpa, New York, to his sixteen-year-old sweetheart Brooksany in Springfield, Massachusetts, in the year 1825. In the four years of waiting for her he wrote often of the Erie Canal. "The Big Ditch is paying for itself. It cost seven million dollars and the tolls will have it paid for in ten years." And Brooks wrote in reply, "I want to see you in Arpa. Next after that I want to see with you the Ditch that cost seven million dollars."

She didn't need the information he sent her. She had seen it in the newspapers and heard her father and mother telling it, how it took eight years to dig the canal and it was a big day when Governor DeWitt Clinton in 1817 struck down and brought up the first shovel of dirt and how eight years later they had the 363-mile ditch finished from Albany to Buffalo and a long flotilla of canalboats meeting flags, music and cheers traveled from Buffalo to Albany and then down the Hudson River to the port of New York, where a procession of bands of music, fife-and-drum corps, carriages, wagons and floats, prominent citizens and plain people made a procession five miles long, and thousands stood in glee and shouted when Governor Clinton poured a keg of fresh water from Lake Erie into the salt waves of the Atlantic.

Joel put it in his letters as if it would be new to her, though she had seen it in print and had heard it from elders and it seemed the whole world knew about it and had the figures down pat, that before the new marvelous waterway came it took *twenty* days to haul corn, wheat, cattle, hogs, farm produce, furs, from Buffalo to New York—and now, think of it, the trip took only *six* days—and more dazzling yet, where it used to cost one hundred dollars a ton by river and wagon routes now the cost on the Erie Canal was only five dollars a ton—put that in your pipe and smoke it—ninety-five dollars cheaper than it used to be.

Along with this information, however, Joel wrote Brooks about something new. She caught it from him. His eyes were seeing on the canal-

637

boats the corn, wheat, cattle, packed meat, hogs, bundles and boxes of furs from farther west, from the states west of the Allegheny Mountains. Now they could ship straight to New York, part of the cargo bound for Europe, quicker and cheaper than by the old route down the Mississippi River to New Orleans. "This hauling," Joel wrote her, "once ran north and south, now it runs east and west. Every day in late spring and summer the wagons pour through Arpa, movers going West, thousands every year. The Great West is going to fill up with settlers and I tell you, Brooks, after a while the people out there in the West will run the country, I do believe, I can see it coming in your lifetime and mine."

When their wedding date was set for a few months ahead, he had written, "You may find me changed a little in appearance when I come for you and I am not certain you will like it." She guessed he was raising a beard of some kind, and he was, a stubby affair on the chin only, an experiment. Brooks replied, "My hope is it will have no sharp sticky bristles, for I have always liked your soft cheek against mine. Pa has bristles. I don't like them. Ma had to get used to them." Joel from then on shaved his chin.

Brooks believed from his letters that he was more steady in church-going and in Christian practice than he had been in Springfield. He kept a strict Sabbath, he wrote her, not going to the harness shop on that day except once when a tug needed splicing and another time when a bridle had to have a new section of strap so a deacon could drive home to his farm. The folks he boarded with forgot to give him one of her letters that came on a Saturday. They handed it to him on Sunday morning.

"I saw it was your handwriting," he wrote Brooks. "The sight of your handwriting ran right through me. I dashed upstairs and read it before I knew what I was doing. The letter made me forget it was the Sabbath Day till I was halfway through the letter where you tell about the sermon you heard the Sabbath before. I reminded myself I ought not to read it. It was against good Christian practice. Yet I went on reading. Your sweet words were there on the paper I touched to my lips before I began reading what was written on it. It might be I should have put it in my pocket and carried it with me through the day and waited till Monday or past midnight to read it. During the sermon that morning and in Sunday-school class afterward I kept asking if I should have waited. I answered it would have been like I had seen you come into church and I would sit in my pew and never once dare turn my eyes to your pew for your face. We did not call that a sin in Springfield. If I had denied myself reading the letter my mind would have been filled with thoughts of you instead of listening to the sermon. Even so, my dearest Brooks, often I find myself thinking of you when I am supposed to be listening to the sermon. This may be ungodly yet it does not lay heavy on my conscience. You are in my

638

prayers whenever I pray and I suppose I couldn't deny myself reading your letter any more than a boy could keep a red apple in his pocket all day. If our love is sacred, why should it be wrong for me to read a letter from you on the Sacred Day of the week? You have become so a part of me that I think of you when I think of myself."

One week a long letter might come to Brooks, the next week another of no more than two lines: "Would enjoy this evening to be side by side with you holding your dear ·hand," or a rhyme copied from a candy heart:

> Together let us faithful twine
> A wreath that will our hearts combine.

In those early years in Arpa, Joel had been troubled about fine points in theology and church practice. When he was alone, and before Brooks came, those troubles had weighed on him. He favored religious revivals —and he didn't. People ought to be shook up and get hot and cold and hot again and scream their salvation—and then again religion should be a matter of calm faith and no wild excitement. Females should not pray publicly in church—yet women were made of finer stuff than men and Joel had heard of a Scotchman asked why he had married a woman: "To have something to look at on Sunday." A church convention at New Lebanon went into an uproar of a debate between the revivalists and those who moved a resolve "that audible groaning in prayer is to be discouraged." Joel favored those who wanted to groan and especially those who groaned because they couldn't help it—yet he didn't like to hear groans with prayer.

Late spring, summer and the early fall months of each year, Joel wrote back to her, he had more than plenty of work at making and repairing harness. Twelve to fourteen hours a day in summer he had worked. "I need you for company when loneliness creeps over me and I need you for a helpmeet and I need you because I crave affection," he wrote to Brooks. "Please write letters. I need your letters. And more I need the light of your eyes and the touch of your hand."

But she couldn't come. Not till she was twenty did her parents let him come on and marry her in Springfield. Her father, a schoolteacher and a deacon of the Congregational church, had said the young man must prove himself, as he had, what with his own harness shop, a four-room house and barn, a horse, a cow, chickens, a large garden, a well and sweep of their own, besides a few small pieces of land he was still holding, having made profits on others as the town grew when the canal began operating.

Soon the smell of leather had become part of Brooksany's life. Joel's hands and his clothes had the odor of reins and tugs, of bellybands and hames, of thread and twine he slicked with beeswax and that became leatherish as he passed it through the holes his awl drilled. When she stopped in to see him at his workbench, he was short-spoken. "I have to be particular about this," usually naming the farmer who wanted him to be particular whether it was a repair job or a new set of harness, sometimes saying merely, "Cowhide," or "Horsehide," or "Bullhide," as though he knew what he could do or expect from the look and feel of the leather, sometimes praising or blaming the tanner for the quality of the leather. A saddle he would make only when business was slack, telling the customer, "I can make anything in the harness line, plain or fancy. When it comes to a saddle I can make a plain one that will wear you, but don't expect it fancy. For a fancy one you better go to Utica and pick what'll satisfy you."

And again Brooks would see her husband drawing a sharp curve-ended knife across a fresh heavy hide and he would mention a "piece of land," the owner moving West "and he'll sell it for a song and where it lays it's sure due for a rise, and I'm dickering with him." She saw he had a knack, a peculiar sniffing sense about land that a year or two later he would feel "on the rise," as he said.

Once Brooks had told him, "Nobody ever wrote such long letters that were long and such short letters that were short as you did to me." Which was about the same as her telling him another time, "There never was such a talking man when he gets to talking nor ever such a still-tongued man when he wants to be still." He could talk streaks by the hour. He could sit silent an hour or two of a Sunday afternoon, then hoe potatoes or weed a garden bed till evening and eat supper and walk to and from church without a word. He had done that. And his working on Sunday, where other Presbyterians could see him, seemed rather flagrant to the church trustees and they had discussions about it and one of them came saying, "Mr. Wimbler, I've been elected to take up with you this matter of your working in your garden on the Sabbath."

"Did God make the potato?"

"He did."

"And God made the earth the potato grows in?"

"Yes, that's good doctrine."

"And God made the weeds?"

"Yes, I suppose that's good doctrine though there have been those who say that Satan created the weeds."

"Well, I take it as good doctrine that if I plant potatoes for the subsistence of my body, God is willing I should choke with a hoe the weeds trying to choke the growing potato."

"But doesn't God say you should rest on the Seventh Day which is the Sabbath?"

"And wouldn't God believe me if I should give Him solemn testimony that it rested me to hoe those potatoes last Sunday? It could be that God heard me among the potato rows last Sunday saying each potato plant rising from the earth was a miracle from His blessed hands."

The deacon could do little with Mr. Wimbler. The trustees took no action and agreed with their chairman, "The man is a good Presbyterian in all matters, it would seem, except potatoes."

About his life and days before he met her, Joel had been still-tongued. She knew little more than that his grandfather and three or four of his great-grandfathers had been ministers, on back to the ministers' council that banished Roger Williams, where one of his ancestors had been among the foremost to throw the heretic and rebel out of the colony. His father had broken from the ministerial line saying, "I'm not a good enough man to stand up before people and tell them how to live now and where they will go in the hereafter." And his father, failing as a storekeeper, worked in a cutlery factory at fork-making. The grinding and filing in the finish of shaping a fork sent a fine iron dust into the air, which explained why wages were higher and the death rate higher and the fork shop had a bad name as "not so healthy" compared with the other rooms where table knives, pocket and pen knives, butcher knives, scissors, axes and scythes, were shaped and finished. "In two years he was taken down with consumption and after three months died," said Joel. "Mother took it from him and died a year later. I was ten years old and went to live with my mother's brother in Springfield. He saw to it I had some schooling, apprenticed me to him as a harness-maker and raised me up in the Presbyterian church where I met you."

Not much beyond that little would Joel go. There had been a sister and a brother older than himself and he couldn't bring himself to tell how they both died the year he was born. He gave Brooks the impression his father and mother gave him great love and fond care and that he tried to grope back and find meanings around them and why out of a family of five, the hand of God swept out all but him before he was eleven. Once he had come out of a long silence to say, "I was the third child and I lived."

* * * * * * * * * *

Chapter 2

* * * * * * * * * *

Three Babies—and a Fugitive

A SMALL wood stove kept the bedroom warm and Brooksany Wimbler "snug as a bug in a rug," she said. Through the open door to the big living room she could see the front door. Late this January night of 1837, she waited to hear footsteps. She hoped soon that front door

641

would open. She could hear, from where she lay, the quiet sputter and hiss of firelogs in the big stone hearth of the living room. Her ears gathered the blur and thud of a log burned through in the middle and its collapse with a shower of sparks and a shuffle of embers.

She could hear the clock tick, a timepiece serene in a cabinet of shadowy mahogany, taller than herself by a foot. She talked to it on lonely days, smiling at times, with a wry smile, "Mr. Clock, I guess I tell you things I wouldn't bother my husband's ears with."

Thirty dollars it had cost them, half paid in harness repairs by her husband, and thrown into the bargain a horsewhip and a fly net for the young gelding driven by the clock-peddler. "We're just dickerin to pass the time," the clock-peddler had said one day in late July, but the next day the gelding had fretted and stamped in the hot sun, at a hitching post for three hours tormented by horseflies, and at last in a fury had kicked part of the shafts to splinters. The fly net was wanted, "right off," said the peddler.

"Vanity of vanities, thy name is vanity," she had said to her husband as he stood the clock in the place she pointed to, laughing, "It looks too elegant for us."

Since then the clock had become part of the house and part of them. The first and only time it had stopped was also the first time the house had seen a small white box lined with white satin holding a child. They had wondered if the stopped clock was a sign and a mystery till they joined in remembering that in their sorrow they had forgotten to wind the clock. In her bed now she could hear the clock and across the dark see the antique script on its face: *Peace Be unto You*. This afternoon she had nodded her response to it, "And peace be unto *you*."

"Let me wind it," she had said to her husband once. And he had lifted her in his arms and held her as she turned the big brass key winding the spring to keep the clock going eight days.

"You know, Brooksany, what that clock says?" her husband had asked.

"Tell me."

"It says: Forget me, leave me alone with no attention, no care, and I refuse you, my pendulum stops, my hour and minute hands stop, and I am dumb and dead to you."

"Yes, Joel, so it says," she had answered, adding, "Obedient, I call that clock, obedient."

"*Sweet* and obedient, I call it," he had said. "Like you, *sweet* and obedient."

"So then, I am like a clock you wind every eight days with a brass key."

"Excepting," he had said with a solemn smile as she laid the brass key on the top of the clock, "excepting never yet a clock gave the world a beautiful baby." Then he had carried her to this bed where she now lay. And that was before their first child came.

642

She had not forgotten his words. Occasionally instead of "What time is it?" she would ask, "What does Sweet and Obedient say?" They had discussed a storekeeper, having woman trouble in his home, saying, "You can trust a clock but not a woman." And they would not soon forget a fugitive slave quoting a Negro field hand on a Tennessee plantation: "I don't trust the living and I walk carefully among the dead."

Her ears caught outside the branches of pine and maple trees creaking, once in a while a branch splitting and crashing to the ground from the weight of a two-day ice storm. She could hear too that the frozen rain had turned to snow, or so she believed, and to make sure had got out of bed and looked through the one blind with shutters open and had seen it was true, ground and trees whitening under a heavy quiet snowfall. It was a trouble, her husband late in coming home and now more of it, walks and roads slippery and treacherous, ice under snow.

She had made supper ready and sat at a window sewing, had seen the dark come on, lighted a candle and eaten alone, then to bed. The doctor had said plenty of moving around, with long sleeps at night and many rests during the day, were best for her till the baby came in perhaps two months. Bent a moment on her knees in prayer before getting into bed, she had lain in the dark speaking more low prayers. "Let him be well-born, O Lord, and let him live long. If it be a girl, let her be well-born, O Lord, and let her live long."

Why the first child, a girl, seemed well-born and then had died in a week, the doctor said he couldn't explain; babies can't answer when you ask where the pain is. The second child, a boy, born lusty, never saw a sick day—and what came was like a dream she wanted to forget. She and her husband drove a gig with a skittish horse one night, the road bright with moonlight. A bundle of shining weed suddenly blown across the road by a high wind had given the horse a fright that sent it wild and shying to the side of the road, on into a crash against a stone fence, the horse out of the broken shafts running away, the father badly bruised, the mother not harmed at all, and the two-year-old boy looking alive and asleep yet growing cold and gone into his last sleep.

Since then she had become known as a woman still of tongue and face. In earlier years at the Bethesda Presbyterian Church she had lifted her voice in song with the others, at the Friday Sewing Circle gossiped merrily with the others. Now she stood in church holding the songbook with her husband and never opening her lips. The Sewing Circle saw her seldom and heard little from her. Her face took on more of the still look and she named her favorite verse, "He maketh me to lie down beside still waters." Asked why she once came regular to Wednesday-night prayer meeting and now hadn't been seen in a year, she answered, "When I try to talk with God now I do it alone. What there is between Him and me, I don't know for certain—only God knows."

643

Her husband, a rather silent man, complained often that people talked too much and didn't "meditate" enough. If he ever quit the Bethesda Presbyterian Church, which wasn't likely, he said, it would be to join the Friends, and, "I think I might make a pretty good Quaker." Once before the crackling fire on a winter night, an hour without a word, she had broken in with a quiet voice, "There's nothin the matter with ye, Joel, is there? You're all right, ain't ye?" he had replied in her own kind of quiet, "Just havin my meditations, Brooksany. If anything comes of 'em I'll be tellin ye."

Twice he had been to the local branch of the Anti-Slavery Society of America and had come home to say, "Brooksany, they mean well. I wouldn't for the world try to stop 'em in what they're doin. But they talk too much and I'm afraid they scold too much and I suppose I'll have to do what I can against slavery in my own way and I don't know what that way will be."

Brooksany, on this night of ice storm and snow, faded into sleep murmuring, "Let him be well-born, O Lord, and let him live long." She awoke refreshed, wondered why her fears were gone and why she was saying now, "The Lord will guide his feet home safe and well." She lighted a candle, went to the clock, held up the candle to read five minutes past two in the morning. She went to bed and fell asleep. A dream came to her, the same she had known before. In a sky, bright and soft with moonlight, floats a horse and he winds downward in circles and in figure-eight patterns. When at last his feet touch the earth, his legs and his body fade away and there is a slow wagging horse face looking at her and the eyes of the horse infinitely sad. And she hears the horse saying something about God. She can make out the word "God" but what the horse has to say about God never comes clear. She comes out of this dream very alive and awake trying to coax her mind and memory to tell her what it was the horse tried to say about God.

Did she hear the front gate hinge squeak? Out of bed and at the window in a flash, she saw through the shutters a man and woman walking in the snow toward the house, the man catching the woman once as she slipped and near fell. She stood at the front door as a knocking came and her shout, "Who is it?" had the answer, "It's Joel, Brooksany." She unlocked the door, fell into Joel's arms and half-cried, "I'm so glad you've come."

He kissed her quickly, held his hands at her shoulders, saying, "We must fix something to eat for this woman and then get her out of here quick. Caleb Meadows is coming with a bobsled. He'll take her where the law can't get her."

Brooksany lighted a candle, held it in her left hand toward the woman, put out her right hand as Joel was saying, "Susan Gilmore, this is my wife." Brooksany for the first time in her life shook the hand of a Negro woman. "Susan, I will do the best I can for you."

644

Susan's black and gleaming face came out from a scarf and hood. She looked down at Brooksany, who came only to her shoulders. Susan still kept a tight hold on the blanket around her upper body and with a curiously sober smile, a soft voice, "My feet is cold and my knees knock with the cold but I'm thankful to you, God knows I'm thankful."

Brooksany went to the pantry, Joel stirred up the fire, put on fresh sticks of wood, seated Susan to warm, then gave his help to Brooksany. They brought bread and butter, cuts of cold meat, warmed a pan of meat stew with vegetables, brewed a pot of tea. In less than an hour, when Caleb Meadows arrived, Susan said her feet and knees were comfortable, she was thankful to be fed. Her voice shook and both her hands went around theirs as she said she hoped "the grace of God abounding" would be with them forever for what they had done for her. As she went out the door, their eyes followed her to the sled, where she vanished into one of the five or six boxes and barrels in the sled. And Caleb Meadows untied his horses, shook the reins over them and they moved up the street in the falling snow.

"They'll be in Utica by morning," said Joel Wimbler to his wife as he bit into the first mouthful of food he had eaten since noon of the day before. "And they never catch 'em in Utica. Tunnels from houses to barns and barns to houses in Utica. They thrive on the excitement of it."

He had dropped his work midafternoon to drive fifteen miles with the ice on the roads getting worse and the return drive on the same ice with a snow cover. Caleb Meadows had come to him saying it was a case of a slave woman who claimed her "free papers" had been taken away from her and she jailed in a town in lower New York, her two children taken from her; friends had broken her out of the jail and "passed her along."

"The Constitution says she's property," Joel had said to Meadows.

"When the Constitution says she's property, the Constitution is a liar and you know it, Joel Wimbler, by God you well know it," Caleb Meadows had hissed.

"I'm goin to meditate about it," said Joel to Brooksany, as her head snuggled in his right arm and they were falling asleep. "As yet, my conscience don't hurt me." He chuckled. "Caleb Meadows' wife don't know what he's hauling to Utica—it's secret. I don't know who told Caleb about the runaway Susan Gilmore—it's secret. And I won't tell nor you who came here this night—it's secret. Caleb don't belong to the Anti-Slavery Society and neither do I and everybody knows that ain't secret."

He drifted into sleep after Brooksany thought she heard him, "The abolitionists talk too much, worst of it is they like to hear themselves talking."

The constable who woke them with knocking on the door at early daylight had a stranger with him who had come horseback and said the footprints in the snow looked to him like evidence. Joel Wimbler told them to search the house and the barn, if that would satisfy them, even though they didn't have a search warrant. "I have a warrant for the arrest of Susan Gilmore," said the stranger, pulling from an inside pocket the paper he considered important, legal, correct.

Joel huffed in a quiet tone, "I don't know where the woman is you claim or the property you're seeking. Make your search. Let us alone is all we ask."

The two men went to the cellar, peered into every corner, box and barrel, put a ladder to the garret floor, went up through the trapdoor and crawled on hands and knees with a lantern, then to the barn and in the loft tossed hay around and stabbed into the hay with a pitchfork.

On their leaving the constable explained to Joel he was only doing his duty as an officer, the stranger was a United States Marshal and on the capture of a fugitive slave "he gets his cut." Joel shook hands with the constable, and, "I wish you *well*," and with a sidelong glance at the United States Marshal, "And I wish *you* well."

The days passed and Joel went to his work at his harness shop, things much as usual. He saw Caleb Meadows nearly every day and not a word passed between them about their winter night's work together. A month passed and Joel came home one night to tell Brooksany, "Caleb walked into the shop today, put his face close to mine and whispered, 'She made it into Canada, thought you might like to know,' then Caleb walked out, turning around at the door to show me his face and a smile of mischief on it if ever I saw one, a dangerous smile."

* * * * * * * * * *

Chapter 3

* * * * * * * * * *

In a Grand and Awful Time

BROOKSANY WIMBLER walked down the center aisle of Bethesda Church on the last Sunday of January in 1837 with many eyes turned for a look at her. They knew of the first baby, how Brooksany didn't come to the church for months afterward, how again and later when sudden death came so casually and cruelly to the second child, then too it was months before Brooksany cared to be present at Sabbath services.

Now they could read that again the Wimblers were "committed to

646

the trust of the Lord." Anxious eyes rested on Brooksany, the eyes of mothers who spoke silent prayers that what was to happen should have health, life, grace and kindliness. Others there were, the thoughtless, the garrulous and gossipy, female and male, whose minds ran around the questions, "When will it come? How far gone is she? Will she have a midwife or a doctor?"

A smallish woman, at first glance, because Brooksany's narrow face had the peculiar still look on it. "I can wait while you go first," her shy thin lips seemed to say. Yet her straight nose and decisively the deep blue of her eyes held the glow of no timid mousy woman. A will of her own she had. When humble, as nearly always, it was her idea of good manners. She stood below her husband's shoulders and his inch or two over six feet of height, his thick chest and broad shoulders emphasized the "smallish" about her. The natural quiet of her face as a girl and a young woman had, under tragedy, taken on a pale keen shade of the mystic, rather baffling to people who valued comfort, as most of them did. A small minority element in the Bethesda Church, acquainted with grief, could read in her a reverence for life with as sure roots as any other heart in the church. These could see she had worked out some new basis as between herself and God. In Joel Wimbler they saw a somewhat like change had come, though of no like depth. They were a much talked-about couple in the little town of Arpa because neither of them could be led into familiar details of what they had between them of relish for the gossips. And the tongues of gossip had their questions and guesses as to why God sent two crushing losses on such a couple. The woman kept her house in order, did well by the few who came there, no lazybones, no gadabout. The man ran a harness shop, in a pinch could make wagon repairs, fix a pump or cider press, hang a door, shape a barrel stave or once in a while turn a lathe and round out a wooden bowl from a maple-tree stump.

Her grandfather had spent the last two years of his life with them, staying indoors except on pleasant summer days. He had fought at Bunker Hill, at Trenton, Princeton, Long Island, Brandywine, Germantown, had been in the House of the Single Brethren at Bethlehem with a light wound and on recovery had gone to Valley Forge where, as his own words had it, "My feet give out." Joel's people went back to Massachusetts Bay Colony Puritans, and Joel said of them, "Solemn men, all the time solemn, one thing I pray God is I won't be solemn all the time."

Together Joel and Brooksany had stood up as members of the church and repeated a pledge required of all members: trusting in God, they would abstain from the use of intoxicating liquors, never cease nor relent in their efforts till the ruinous and murderous traffic in liquor was abolished in the town, the country, the state and the nation. One after another the speakers against alcohol had come to Bethesda to hurl their curses on whisky, rum, wine, beer. The tavern barroom, and the grocery selling liquor, they named them "the Devil's Workshop." Like other towns Arpa had its Temperance Society, members pledged "to abstain from the use of intoxicating liquor as a beverage, wine, beer and cider included, and to further abstain from all profanity and from the use of tobacco in all its forms." At intervals some member of the church was "read out" from the pulpit, his name stricken off; after repeated warnings he had again fallen, was again caught drinking alcoholic liquor.

On the Sunday that Joel and Brooksany stood up as members in good standing to repeat the pledge, a little man muttering words that didn't come clear walked out of his pew and along the aisle out of the church. A grocer, for years he had kept a barrel of rum and a keg of whisky to sell by the pint, quart or gallon to customers whose faces he had known for years. "I put myself out of the church," he said, "before they could put me out." Then later came the powerful speaker who four evenings straight argued that rum was a wrecker of homes and the barroom a highwayman robbing the workingman of wages and the farmer of crop money; the drunkard drank because the liquor was sold and those who sold drink to the drunkard made him what he was, a grief and a cruel load to his wife and children. And the little man who had walked out of the church listened the first night, came back for more and on the fourth night stood up to take the pledge and afterward led a committee of churchmen to his grocery, where he rolled out the rum barrel and the keg of whisky, broke them with an ax and poured them into the gutter and as the liquor slid along the stones he joined others with their hats off while the temperance speaker offered a prayer of thanks and jubilation and the little man's wife rushed in to throw her arms around him and cry.

The temperance movement, as they called it, had swept the Mohawk Valley, memberships and pledges growing at first by hundreds and then by thousands. When the rum and whisky had slid along the gutter stones of Arpa, leaving an odor or bouquet in the air for days, the temperance speaker had shouted, before offering prayer, "May God smite the conscience of every rum-seller to go and do likewise. In ten years, mark you, people of Arpa, in ten years every barrel of rum in the nation will be poured away, evil in the sight of God as we have witnessed tonight."

"Ten years and the liquor traffic abolished for all time," said men of the churches as the antiliquor movement grew.

"Ten years," said schoolchildren who had taken the pledge.

"Ten years?" said drinking men in the Arpa tavern barroom as they hoisted schooners of beer and roared their laughter. "Ten years? Not in fifty or a hundred years, not till hell freezes over and we skate on the ice."

Then another movement gaining more powerful headway had slowed down the temperance cause. There was a pledge Joel and Brooksany stood up and spoke with the rest of the congregation as required of all members, the solemn promise to toil and advocate without ceasing to the end that slavery be recognized as a sin in the sight of God and that the duty, safety, and best interests of all concerned required its immediate abandonment, that the duty of every Christian was to proclaim that whoever holds his fellow man in bondage is guilty of a grievous wrong, that religion and justice teach that man cannot hold property in man.

In this pledge for the abolition of slavery was a fierce taste and a fury surpassing any flare of the temperance movement. The drunkard being helped by his ragged and pinch-faced daughter out of the muddy ditch where he had fallen, this and other pictures of the drunkard and his family, gave shock after shock to those who listened to speakers and read the printed tracts. But those shocks were nothing to compare with the terrors aroused by the abolitionist speeches, tracts, weekly journals and personal conversations. Negro slave families broken as the auctioneer sold away father and mother from children, husband from wife; slave gangs chained and driven under the lash in cotton and rice fields; mulatto, quadroon or octoroon sold away sometimes by her own father; Negroes who had managed to buy their freedom having their "free papers" taken away from them and sold back into the slave market; the slave mother who took an ax and killed her twin boys rather than see them sold into slavery; the naked slave woman strung up by her wrists while a white overseer flogged her till the flesh lay raw and bleeding; incidents of violence and shame, atrocities piled high and higher from lecture to lecture, from journal and tract that came week by week with fresh news and ever more horrifying affairs of slavery in the Southern states below the Ohio River, besides the riots, mobs, fights, clashes north across the Free states followed by officers of the law claiming them as property sanctioned by the Constitution, which they were.

For the drunkard it could be said that he himself did the drinking and no one owned him and lashed him into getting drunk. There was an Irishman in Arpa who would step up to the tavern bar and smile gaily to the bartender, "Unchain the sarpint," meaning he had no fear of the Great Snake symbolized by potent liquor. There had been men at that bar lifting glasses to each other with the challenge, "If we drink we die, if we don't drink we die, so—it's better to drink."

The drunkards among them in that town of Arpa, they could name them, they could classify the hard drinkers, including one who had died a few years before. He had to get drunk, it was told, Saturday night without fail and on his way to the barroom, hearing, "Well, John, goin down to get drunk again?" answered, "Yes, and how I dread it!"

But the million and more slaves of the South, what the Mohawk Valley people had learned of them was mainly hearsay and not what they had seen for themselves. Yet they did know that down there Man could own Man. The slave was born a slave, born the property of his owner, listed on the tax books with the other assessable livestock such as horses, mules, cattle, sheep. The law had a word: chattels. The slave was a piece of movable property, a chattel.

Joel and Brooksany had held the songbook in church and she had stood shut-mouthed and heard him sing with the congregation the lines that later he heard her at home singing and she wished she knew the full meaning:

> We are living, we are dwelling,
> In a grand and awful time,
> In an age on ages telling,
> To be living is sublime.

They talked about it how not so long back the church was a place to hear about the Heavenly City in the sky, the mansions of rest to be given them after this life. Then occasional excitement rose over issues, "causes," in the church and nation—but not like now in this year of 1837. Now the leaders who preached, speakers who came to pound the pulpit desk and stare with blazing eyes at their listeners, they were calling to battle, they were summoning Christian soldiers to be ready for action here on earth. What the action was to be did not come clear. The shape of the war against the rum-sellers had not been made clear nor how they should free the slaves if the Christian slave-owners refused to look at slavery as a sin in the sight of God.

"What will be the end of this anger ever in the air?" Joel and Brooksany asked each other. They had spoken their doubts to each other about this anger taking form in movements, societies, clubs, leagues. Then they decided that the passion, the zeal, the vitality of the church and the movements that gathered about it, had some kind of dark meaning beyond them. They would stay in the church and do their best though they would stay out of the many societies that beckoned, pleaded and threatened.

Often doubts came to the harness-maker and his shy little wife. They felt their faith slipping. They said to each other, "Remember Theodore Weld" and knew they couldn't forget him. Only two hours had Weld talked in Arpa but in Utica it was three hours the first night and four hours the second night. Tall, long-haired, swarthy, face and eyes with "the severity of a streak of lightning." Earlier he had spent years going from town to town in western New York and Ohio in the temperance cause, then measuring the antislavery movement as far more greatly needed, he had thrown himself into it and given all he had. Mobs had broken up his meetings and he had come back the next night to face them again, returning till the mobs no longer tried rushing at him to beat him, no longer put out the meeting-hall lights nor burned cayenne pepper to inflame the nostrils and half-blind the eyes of those who stayed to listen. Rotten eggs had crashed on his face, shirt and coat. Stones thrown at him in the street had welted his head and body. Meeting street rowdies who told him, "We'll beat the living whey out of you," he had folded his arms, stood quiet, looked them in the eye from face to face and talked a plain calm talk without a sign of fear till they walked away from him.

Hour on hour could Weld talk, never loud, no howling, no tricks, piling up facts and asking what the facts might mean, moving into deductions and logic, then setting the logic ablaze with storm and dream, letting it cool to a quiet glow, then sending the flame higher than before. A newspaper editor night after night for three weeks heard Weld and didn't write a note, line or word of what Weld said and explained himself, "How can you print on paper the rolling of thunder?" Man after man, ten, fifteen and twenty of the foremost fighting figures in the antislavery movement had been converted to their work by Weld. They talked long with him, and he changed their lives. They quit what they were doing, as lawyers, physicians, merchants, teachers, ministers, to throw in with all they had to give of their lives to a new work, a fresh deep purpose caught from what they heard Weld say and from something else, for Weld was a presence and came near having an aura. "Eloquent as an angel and powerful as thunder," said a famous Boston preacher of Weld. Joel and Brooksany heard one Arpa woman say, "There be archangels and in this life I will never see one, but Mr. Weld comes near to such shine and strength as I expect archangels have."

And did such praise please Mr. Weld? When he heard anything bordering on it, he shrank from it. He had the name of being modest, a shrinking violet. He stayed away from the big cities: when the small towns and villages awoke, the big cities would follow. He wrote letters and reports to the antislavery journals and refused to sign his name. He wrote tracts and had other names than his own or no name at all on the covers. Stateliness, pomp, circumstance, show-off, these he said, "I loathe in my inmost soul."

At a pleasant after-meeting in Bethesda Church, someone mentioned the great personal reputations, big names of the antislavery movement, with a reference to Weld's modesty. His rich smooth voice rolled out his confession: he made it a principle never to accept an office of authority or honor and to keep away from speechmaking at conventions and functions. "Pride," he went on, "is the great besetment of my soul, pride the poisoned thorn that festers and corrodes. I am too proud to be ambitious, too proud to seek applause, too proud to tolerate it when lavished upon me—proud as Lucifer that I can and do scorn applause and spurn flattery."

On the mention of famous or notorious names, of dramatic figures of the antislavery movement, names of men quoted, accused, jailed, men who welcomed stress on their sacrifices as though they had achieved martyrdom, they had seen Weld's eyes flash and his mouth twist in a moment of anxiety and pain. Glorifying men instead of measures, encouraging the itch of men for distinction, fame or martyrdom, he called this "one of the greatest perils of the cause." He could see rivalries coming, clashes and factions, good enough men sunk in "one of the basest sediments of human depravity." In a mourning voice he quoted, "He that flattereth his neighbor spreadeth a net for his feet," and spoke his sorrow, "We abolitionists have dreadfully entangled our own and each other's feet."

One remark of Weld stayed with Brooksany. Up till this time no woman in Arpa had ever stood up to pray and speak in public meeting. The rule had always been that men could rise, speak, pray and testify while the women kept silence. The accepted custom was for women to sit quiet and let their ears gather whatever the men chose to deliver. A church authority told Weld this came out of regard for "the modesty of woman's unperverted nature." Weld argued that if women were more "unperverted" than men, the men ought to hear them and if the men didn't care perhaps God did. Weld had noticed that where this matter was discussed beforehand the women were generally shut out to keep silence as before. But when women took the lead and stood up and spoke out their hearts in testimony and prayer the men accepted it as a new and worthy custom.

Brooksany said nothing to Joel but it lay in her heart that in the next "protracted meetings," if her heart was moved, she would speak. She would lift a prayer to the throne of God in behalf of herself and a child.

"He's soft as lamb wool," said Brooksany as they walked home that night. "And hard as hickory," added Joel. They had heard him say he would like to be "always ready to shake hands with Toil and call Peril by his middle name."

The two sat by the big stone fireplace till past midnight. Weld had made them feel less lonely, less off by themselves, more a part of some great stream of human struggle.

"The only abolitionist I never heard talk too much," said Joel. "If I could talk like him, I'd talk."

Brooksany quoted, "To help the helpless, be eyes to the blind, feet to the lame, a tongue to the dumb, to raise up the fallen, bind up the bruised and guide the wandering."

Joel sang softly and she joined him:

> "We are living, we are dwelling,
> In a grand and awful time,
> In an age on ages telling,
> To be living is sublime."

She moved from her chair to seat herself on the armrest of his chair, leaning over in ease and comfort close to him, her head on his shoulder. She spoke of any child born in this year of 1837, how its eyes would live to see ends finished and wonders completed that their eyes would never see.

"Yes," murmured Joel, "and she may hear drums pounding and roaring and see the shedding of blood. God has His ways."

"She? It is to be a girl?"

"That is my prayer, as I have told you."

"Then I wish it to be a girl."

They held each other in a silence in the room lighted only by the firelog glow.

"I think I feel her kicking and squirming in me," said Brooksany.

She put his hand where he might feel the quiver of the oncoming life.

"I think I do. It's very faint but I get it. She will live, Brooks, she will come strong and live to see ends we never dreamed of."

"I believe, I believe, I have a perfect faith, Joel."

Their sleep had depths of peace. At daybreak they knelt at their bedside and bent their heads in a long silent prayer of thanks for what was to come.

★ ★ ★ ★ ★ ★ ★ ★ ★ ★

Chapter 4

★ ★ ★ ★ ★ ★ ★ ★ ★ ★

Omri Winwold, Gambler, Visits in Arpa

ONE early October afternoon three years before stood out for Brooksany. The maples tossed gold out of green, the oaks from day to day threw wider slashes of rust-brown and yellow. The sunlight straggled with films of orange and silver in the autumn haze.

"A day fresh from the hand of God, sky and trees manifest of the Lord," Brooks had said as she stepped out with a basket, went to the carrot bed, dug her hands in the dirt and pulled carrots, twisted off the tops, threw them in the basket, taking it easy, taking a look now and then at the trees and the open sky.

She didn't hear the front-door knocker. She didn't see the man there at the front door. He was about her own height, a strong-shouldered man, the shoulders rounded and hunched, his head rather massive, the face covered with a beard and mustache neatly trimmed, his hair and beard a brick-dust color, his eyes a liquid brown. His stylish shoes were made to order of kid leather. His black coat fitted him, tailor-made, measured for him. Stiff round white cuffs stood out from the coat sleeves. A spotless white shirt with a flowing roll collar set off the broad band of a green silk cravat tied in a flaring bow. A ruffled shirt front was rounded with a low-cut two-button vest of green satin, its wide lapels of a darker green satin, a frail garment intended to gleam and shine. The large cuff buttons, if not of solid gold, were meant to be so taken, as were the flat round engraved studs in the shirt front.

He slammed the knocker down five times, waited long before the sixth knock, stood with his hands folded and looked at the flaring trees and the dreamy autumn drift in the air. Then as though he had all the time there is, he went down the steps, walked to the corner of the house, and there saw the woman in the carrots, digging her hands in the dirt and like himself in no hurry. He watched her a while, then walked toward her.

She was quitting the dirt and carrots for another look at the proud trees and sky as he came near her. She stood to her feet. Her eyes swept him head to foot, getting the walk and shape of him. She cried out with mingled glee and surprise as he came near and they shook hands: "You can't hide your face from me with those whiskers, Omri Winwold. I'd know your walk and your shoulders anywhere. What brings you here?"

That was the beginning of his overnight visit with Brooks and Joel. They talked half the night and most of the morning till the noon stage for Utica.

"Cousin Omri" was one name Brooks had for him. She rehearsed for Joel what her mother had told her long ago and what she had told Joel too years ago and was now going over it again to show how clear she kept it in mind. Her mother had stumbled through it at first and then repeated it to make sure: "Your grandfather's grandfather on your mother's side was a full brother to Omri's grandfather's grandmother on his mother's side."

Brooks was the same age as Omri, somewhat shorter. She had seen him work as a chore boy at the Maple Leaf Tavern in Springfield, going to school six months in the year, learning to read books, plowing his way through all kinds of books, moving into good wages as a barkeep at the Maple Leaf and, as he admitted to Brooks, taking on more of "choice imported and domestic liquors" than was good for him. Those last two years she waited for the wedding with Joel, Omri had called three or four times a year and each time her mother made it clear they mustn't let it get out that a Maple Leaf barkeep paid evening visits at the home of a respectable Presbyterian family. Once in the last of those four years Omri had said to her, cool and matter-of-fact, "Joel is the man for you, Brooks. He'll do good by you, I think. And I want you to remember, if anything happens not right for you, I'll be around if you say so."

"I'm pleased the barkeep doesn't call often," Brooks' mother said after one of his evenings.

"He has read four Shakespeare plays, a whole book of poems of

Robert Burns, a book of the essays of Francis Bacon, and he says he's read the Constitution of the United States and the Declaration of Independence five times from beginning to end, trying to make sure what they mean. I don't understand him. He is deep. And he is a fool and I can't make him out."

"He tells you jokes and stories from the Maple Leaf bar, I suppose."

"Says he can't tell me some he hears. Those he does tell are funny."

"Does he go in for the profanity they are so free with at the Maple Leaf?"

"Never to me. Half of the Old Testament he's read and all of the New Testament. Recites verses he likes."

"And why doesn't he join the church?"

"Ma, how could a Maple Leaf barkeep join the Presbyterian church of Springfield, Massachusetts?"

Ma waited a moment, dismissed the matter. "I'm glad our distant cousin doesn't call often."

Brooks couldn't tell her mother nor Joel of an evening when Omri arrived with liquor on his breath, tipsy, loose-tongued, profane, his wide slash of a mouth in comic twists as he mimicked various patrons of the Maple Leaf bar. When his mouth subsided into stillness she noticed more vividly than before the two sides of his face different, one with a storm toss on it and the other utterly at peace. Brooks mentioned on this evening that she knew almost nothing of what he was before coming to Springfield. "You come to us out of Nowhere. You know my folks and I don't know yours."

He took this as a reproach. It stung him. He rose from his chair, walked back and forth, ran a hand through his hair, flicked with a finger at his vest lapel, pulled at his straight bow tie to make it straighter, stood for a long look down into her grave upturned face, saying, "You have New Testament verses on your face and the azure of a cool summer sky in your eyes."

He turned, walked again, paused. "You want me to talk. Good—I'll talk." He walked to the door, tried the knob as though to open the door, as though to hear whether any listener moved away. He paced slowly before her, speaking swiftly. She sat with both feet on the floor, erect and tense, her eyes and face following him, sometimes keeping a timebeat with a foot wagging to and fro, up and down.

A year before coming to Springfield he had worked as a bobbin boy in a cotton mill. At 4:30 in the morning a bell rang for the town to hear and he was out of bed into his clothes and inside the mill gates before they closed at 4:45. A bell rang for breakfast at 6:35 and rang for work again at 7:00. At 12 noon the bell rang for dinner and at 12:25 for work again. At 6:00 o'clock a bell rang for supper and at 6:25 for work again. At 8:15 a bell rang and mill gates opened to let him go to his boardinghouse and his room where six cots stood in a row and he could creep between blankets and sleep till a bell rang again at daybreak in summer, in darkness on winter mornings. If any boy didn't hear a bell at 4:30 in the morning, the others pulled him out and hauled him along to the mill gates. His pay of $2.00 a week was better than the six-year-old girls paid 90 cents a week or the ten- and twelve-year-olds getting $1.40 and $1.50 a week. His nights from 8:30 till 4:30 in the morning he had free. His Sundays he had free. He heard it explained how the mill used to have a fifteen-hour workday but now it was only fourteen hours and twenty-five minutes. Once he heard a man say to a mechanical loom, "You've got it better than I have, damn ye, you don't have to sleep nor eat."

He had left his Boston home, such as it was, for this mill town. His younger sister had died, his older sister, "a man-chaser," as he said, had gone to New York City smiling, "I can get along wherever there's men want women." His father, a lawyer, drank harder from year to year, lost his practice, and drifted into a peculiar way of earning a living. Omri overheard, from two callers at their house, enough to know his father was a collector of money from a row of cheap brothels, known as "two-bit houses" and from the streetwalkers of a designated district of low-priced hotels and rooming houses. For a time the family had a burst of prosperity with new furniture, his father dressing spick-and-span, his mother splurging into gay clothes, drinking and dancing with other men at night in fashionable taverns, coming home late in the night somewhat tipsy to laugh in the face of her more tipsy husband. There had been three Sunday mornings the last year in Boston when his parents were sufficiently sober and inclined and the family marched sedately to services in the Episcopal church where they had once kept a pew they paid for. A Sunday morning came when Omri's father was brought home with a bullet hole in his neck and the police said it was one more saloon brawl and they couldn't be sure who fired the shot and Omri was sure his father had been careless about money collected and a brawl in the saloon was a renewal of an angry dispute about money Omri had overheard late at night when he had made a quick trip to the back-yard privy. He had heard a voice, "You kept out this time. Another time and you'll get it." His father had answered in a scared voice and stayed sober for a week afterward.

Then a month after the father's funeral, Omri's older sister went to New York and his mother didn't come home for three days and Omri searched and found her in a water-front saloon. He had stepped in the door, his eyes catching his mother at a corner table drinking with three men and he had stepped out into the night and gone home and the next day made a bundle and walked two days to the mill town that advertised in the Boston daily papers for "hands."

One day in the mill the question struck him, "Would I be any worse off in jail than I am here?" He had kept the names of very distant relatives in Springfield. He wouldn't trouble them. He would only call on them. What he would say to them he didn't know. He might get a job and then look them up. He had laid by $6.90 when summer came. He made a bundle and tramped west over Massachusetts, sleeping in barns and haystacks, working for his meals, earning a little at wood-chopping and in hay harvest for his meals and a few bits of money, arriving in Springfield "with five dollars and more hope than I ever had in my life." He got a job as chore boy at the Maple Leaf before he looked up his very distant kin. When at last he did get to their house and they asked him about his folks, he said they were all dead and he would tell them later the whole sad story. "If I should tell you about it you would think I wanted you to be sorry for me and I don't want that."

Brooks had seen tears in his eyes at one moment. He had seen that her eyes were not dry. She saw too that he had completely sobered under the telling of his story. She saw a lush extravagance that he carried when he first arrived was gone. She would have liked to hear him say again, for the words would haunt her, "You have New Testament verses on your face and the azure of a cool summer sky in your eyes." Sudden thoughts of Joel came to her and flushes of feeling that told her "Joel is the man for me but if there were no Joel I would go far with this distant kinsman, this Omri Winwold, this barkeep my mother would shut the door on."

She had asked him, after an interlude of silence, "What is a two-bit house?"

It was as though he had sunk far in a black pool and she wanted him to go down again. "Forget about it, Brooks. Some other time ask me anything like this and I'll answer."

"Have you ever been in a two-bit house yourself?"

"Yes, since you ask me. But we won't talk about it."

The door opened and Brooks' mother put her head in. "Lemonade is made for you and Mr. Winwold."

And Brooks had brought in a pitcher with glasses and a plate of cookies. She poured him a glass and he sipped. "That's better lemonade than I can make."

In the years since that evening so unforgettable to Brooks, her rehearsals of his story left her doubting no detail. He wanted no pity, too proud for that. She had never before that evening asked him to tell about his folks. And she saw how the telling of it sobered him, sent him to a pool of memory from which he shrank.

Since she had married Joel and settled in Arpa, news had come of Omri through letters and a few visitors from Springfield, his going to Albany to clerk in a law office and read lawbooks, his dropping law and being seen around Albany in prosperous and even flashy clothes, his name appearing in the papers when he was arrested and fined as a gambling-house keeper, his vanishing from Albany and little heard of him in two or three years.

At supper with Brooks and Joel this October evening in 1834 he said he had been in Utica six weeks. "I'll last about three weeks more, might be a month."

"And what are you doing in Utica?"

"It's a proper question, Brooks, though I'd as soon you hadn't brought it up." This with a smile, then abruptly, "I'm running a game in Utica."

His voice ran cool, with a hidden warmth. In this house, he implied, he would meet trust and perhaps understanding. Brooks saw Joel wince slightly and then peer with a look of interest and good humor into Omri's face, as though he recognized candor without limit.

"You run a gambling house in Utica, you mean?" asked Brooks.

"Yes."

"Isn't it against the law?"

"A law on the books, of course. Yet you might say the police are the law and as we run the game the police know what the take is and they, as a lawyer might say, they share and share alike with me. Nobody loses except those who come of their own free will to buck the tiger and try to pull its claws and teeth."

"And why do you leave Utica so soon?"

"A game can run about so long. Then the shorn lambs begin to cry. It gets around there is gambling. The police know it is time for them to close us down. The police read the weather signs. They tell us and we flit. We have the name, you know, of fly-by-nights."

Next after Utica Omri would go to Buffalo, after that perhaps Syracuse, Rochester, Schenectady, choosing his time of going by what he learned of the police, the mayors, the townspeople and their feeling about gamblers.

"And that is enough about my career and what we might call my position in society."

He had gone on with his books and reading. Brooks could tell it. He had somehow grown, she believed. She plopped out with the leading question in her mind. "Surely you don't aim at being a gambler all your life?"

They were rising from the table. "I'll clear the dishes and we'll talk," said Brooks. The two men drew chairs to a front window of the living room, Joel saying it would be light for an hour yet this fall evening, and they talked about the canal and the trade it had brought and the railroads to come and the wagons always going west in the Mohawk Valley.

When Brooks came in and took a chair Omri Winwold began talking. "You asked a question, Brooks. I'll answer it. I'm laying by a stake. Before long I go West and farm. That sounds silly. Yet it's the God's truth. I quit drinking my first year of gambling. And I'll quit gambling. I may quit smoking though I doubt it." He pulled two fat black cigars from a vest pocket, insisted Joel take one for sometime when he might wish to start smoking, struck a phosphorus match, watched the blue flame of it burn. When it turned white he lighted his cigar and puffed—and talked.

"I wouldn't talk so free here tonight if it wasn't I felt good about you two. I was afraid I might trouble you or find you in trouble. You've had your sorrows, miseries, tangles. But I can tell two people decent and happy together. It was worth coming out here to see you.

"I heard about a man who sits down to a breakfast table and when his wife comes in to join him, he stands up like she surprised him and breaks out with a big smile and says, 'Heaven has broke loose again.' I can tell Joel is like that. You don't see it in many houses. There are houses where a wife is scared to come in to a breakfast table. There are rooms where a wife is scared to creep into bed with her husband. In some houses marriage is a sacrament, in others it is a tired dishrag, in more yet love is only an accommodation to a necessity. Many a wife wants to love, cherish and obey but the man she drew in the marriage game of chance is a deuce for her, not an ace, king or jack but a two-spot. She obeys and forgets to love or cherish, and the reverse goes. A man thinks he is drawing a Queen of Hearts from a deck and finds it is a dirty trey, a soiled three of clubs."

"The deck of cards is a book to you, isn't it, Omri?" said Joel.

"I work with it from early candlelight till daybreak. I have to know it like a preacher does his Bible."

He had his theory of gambling as a business. "Life is a series of chances. You take a chance on life when you get born. A baby is a gamble, for the father and mother, for the child. They all gamble it will live yet it may flicker out like a candle in an eyeblink or a sudden gust of wind, a door opening and closing. Death is a card in a deck and when it will turn up for you only God, who knows the cards, can tell. An old saying has it, 'Nothing so certain as death and nothing more uncertain than the hour,' and the Christians have it, 'The Lord giveth and the Lord taketh away.'"

A change Omri couldn't read came to the faces of Brooks and Joel, he noticed. He made his surmise, "They lost a child they gambled on."

He went on, "Why do we hear that marriage is a lottery? Why do good Christians say a child was born under a lucky star? Why do they say, 'We'll do well if we have luck'? They're talking gamblers' talk."

Brooks and Joel wanted him to go on and on. He could see their wish. He went on. "Gambling under the law in the books isn't a crime, you know. The gambler who plays a straight game, no marked decks, no loaded dice, taking his percentage of the winnings, he matches his skill against the ignorance and passion of customers who come to him for a service. They want luck. They hope for luck. They bet on their luck against his experience and sagacity. In the long run they lose and he wins. When a beginner knows too much and is just naturally a keen and skilled gambler, we don't go far with him and we can generally get him to play for the house at a percentage."

"And you're sure you'll quit when you get enough for a farm?" said Brooks.

"I don't like the nightwork. I hate the greedy and suspicious police. I hate to see young fools lose their last dollar and begin to blubber and threaten to shoot. I try to forget a farmer's son in Rochester. He tried to shoot himself. We pried his brass pistol out of his crazy fingers, gave him back half the money he lost and kept his pistol."

"Why keep half his money?"

"For a lesson to him."

The three sat at the window in a quiet and a last slow flare of sungold haze before dusk.

Omri spoke. "A strange evening for me. I see little of your kind. Or rather you are a new kind. You loosen me. The farm out West, I will have it, Brooks. And with luck I'll take a wife to it."

"A wife?" said Brooks.

"A woman who troubles me, I'm not sure of her, no telling what a wife she'd make, and I'm enough gambler I wouldn't want a woman I was too sure of. She's a ball of fire, this woman I want. She scorches. She may burn me to ashes. I can't get away from her, don't try to, don't want to."

"Ball of fire?" queried Brooks.

"A woman out of nowhere, like myself. A bluebird and a wildcat— can a woman be both?"

Again no one spoke. The dark had come on. Stars picked points in the haze. Brooks lighted two candles on the fireplace mantel. Two men rode past, their horses on a slow walk. A horse team and a wagon jolted by.

It was a one-sided visit. Omri could have asked them questions about the increasing population of Arpa, Utica, Syracuse, discussed national politics, gardening, flowers, new styles in clothes, the harness trade and the price of leather. He knew they poured themselves out to each other, that they had a gift for listening, that a chasm stretched between their world and his, that they had some exceptional trust in him. What talking they had done was to get him to talk more. He went on:

"I'm a lost man now, a wanderer and a stumbler. A seeker, like Roger Williams was, has some glimmer of light he moves toward. I haven't. I grope. I go down one pitch-dark road and come back and start on another as black and winding. Not that I have a sick body nor am I torn with melancholy brooding like Hamlet. But the soul, or the inner light of me, sputters low. I search in the great books and I read the journals and I go to lectures and I go to halls where famous speakers declare their causes and make their pleadings.

"Were there ever so many writers using up such vast tons of paper

660

for the reforming of men and women? Was there ever such lung exercise by such immense squadrons of public exhorters telling us what we must do to be saved, telling mankind what it must do or be damned? Was there ever a time when a poor bewildered sinner had his ears beset with such a variety of voices instructing him what to do about national sin in general and his personal sin in particular?

"How can you abolish gambling unless you abolish a passion in men's blood for taking a chance? I've seen men bet whether it rains tomorrow, whether a coin comes head or tail, whether the seeds in a melon come odd or even, whether a bay horse named Scuttle can beat a black horse named Scrabble, whether the next woman at the post-office window is a blonde or a brunette. In a mill where I worked two boys with head lice used to bet a penny at noon which could pick the most off his own head before the bell rang for work.

"Mr. Satan is around, they tell us. Up and down the Mohawk Valley goes the Devil. Sometimes people after a day's work play cards for fun. It is the Devil's doing. A boy and a girl sashay back and forth in a square dance and swing at the corners and a fiddler plays 'Money Musk.' It is the Devil at work. I saw a preacher sweat and pound the pulpit calling damnation on a candy drop that hides a wee whiff of rum in it, Mr. Satan at work. A girl gets in the family way and the man won't marry her and the finger of shame is pointed at her and the child is a bastard other children mock at as unclean. 'Baseborn,' say the elders, the Devil's stepchild.

"The homeopaths say we take too much medicine. The hydropaths say water will cure you. The mesmerists pass their hands before our eyes and tell us we'll forget whatever ails us. The phrenologists feel the bumps on our heads and if a man has Amativeness he can love a woman and if he has Philoprogenitiveness he will love his children.

"The lawyers are to blame. Wherever you find skulduggery there they are, and some way should be found to kill all the lawyers. The merchants are to blame. Stop buying and selling and go back to barter, these reformers tell us.

"I heard a lecture on Free Love. Any marriage is a mistake. If after matrimony comes divorce, why matrimony? In New York City one church elder has seen to it that they have for communion a sacramental wine from which the alcohol has been extracted. I see a man in Schenectady vain of his white linen clothes, proud that no sheep has been robbed of its wool and that no cotton from slave labor has gone into his garments. Vegetables give you long life and meat poisons you, if you believe one of the lecturers. Pure wheat bread, made without yeast or fermentation, is your only hope for health, says another of the lecturers.

"The Negro slave, the African bought and sold in the open market, we hear about him. Of course, it's wrong and it's infamous. But that

661

mill town in Massachusetts, where we worked fourteen hours a day, is a slavery of white men, white women and children, under the unseen lash of hunger and need."

Wrapped in what he was saying Winwold forgot to flick the ash off his cigar into the saucer Brooks had set before him on the window sill. A cone of it fell into his beard and his two hands swiftly brushed it off. He went on.

"The Magdalen Society—there is a summons to brave men. They have issued the Magdalen Report which finds in New York City not less than ten thousand whores. Of the one hundred thousand women in the city, one in ten is abandoned to virtue and selling her body, they find. So bold have these fallen women become that they flaunt their wares at the doors of churches when the congregations are dismissed on the Sabbath Day. They become fleshwise, sinwise, manwise, in the sense that there is an evil wisdom of rot and corruption. They drink to forget. They drink to wipe out night and day and forget when their time began. They drink to forget faces, to forget promises, to forget whether they ever nourished one small withered hope. They last on the average, it is computed, five years. After that span of time there is nothing they can offer in their market that men will pay for."

He saw his cigar ash this time, bent forward and touched it loose in the saucer, took three slow puffs, the cigar end a spot of red that Brooks and Joel could see in the dark now come on, Brooks in an undertone near a whisper, "It is *too* sad." Winwold went on.

"I wouldn't mock at the Christian reformers who opened the place they named an Asylum for Females Who Have Deviated from the Paths of Virtue. They nursed sick and broken women. They tried to bring back lights that had gone out. I went into the place and saw a woman I had known as a girl. She was dealt with kindly, in a strait jacket for her own protection, a room or cell to herself. She didn't remember me. She babbled vaguely of jewels and money, fine clothes she once had and was going to have again. Then she would go quiet, search me with sharp brown eyes, and ask me, 'Why did I do it?' over and over that question, 'Why did I do it?' Then after a quiet spell again the babble of jewels, money, gowns and furs till she seemed tired, rested herself, hushed herself and came out of it again to peer in my face and ask, 'Why did I do it?' "

He took a puff at his cigar to see if it was still lighted. He drew a long slow filling of it and sent it out in a spiral winding gray and vague.

"Was she asking why she had led a life that burned her out too soon? That could be. Or was she asking why she had lost her mind, why she had stepped out of a room of light where she knew what she was doing and seeing and hearing, into another room where unaccountable bats and rats kept her company? Did she open a door from that belfry and get a slit of daylight and the sun for one flickering

662

instant so she could ask with reason and sense one terrible little question, 'Why did I do it?'"

He paused long now. He knew Brooks would be saying to herself, "It was that older sister of his who left Boston telling him she could get along wherever there were men wanting women." He wondered whether Brooks had ever told Joel. He would sooner she hadn't. His guess was that she hadn't.

He tried his cigar. It had gone out. He struck a phosphorus match, held it till the blue flame changed to white, lighted the short stub with care not to singe beard or mustache. They saw he had practiced with many matches, many cigars. He went on:

"Brooks and Joel, you are kind to listen here in the dark this October night to my chatterings. I told you I grope, I am a lost man trying to find his way. I wish I could be as sure of myself as some of the people who go every Sunday into the sixteen houses of worship in Utica. The sun rises on the Sabbath Day to see the doors open for Presbyterians, Scotch Presbyterians, Episcopalians, Methodists, Baptists, Roman Catholics, Universalists, Dutch Reformed, Quakers, and still more, five churches to one gambling house. There is a Young Men's Association for Mutual Improvement. I like that for a name. Shouldn't we all associate for mutual improvement?

"After a sermon on gambling, they tell it in Utica, a deacon with a mischievous eye said to the preacher, 'How could you describe a gambling hell so accurately unless you had been in one?' and the preacher with equal mischief in his eye asked the deacon, 'How could you know the description was so accurate unless you had been in a gambling hell?' They shook hands. It was a draw. They probably played a game of pinochle to see who had won.

"I grope now. Someday I shall come out of it, like a tumblebug I saw on a Massachusetts road one hot summer day. He must have worked a long time shaping the ball of dung that he rolled into the dust of the road to give it a coating. That ball he pushed was many times taller than he and outweighed him a hundred times. You've seen it, I'm sure you've watched it. He pushed it straight ahead, to the right, to the left, along ruts and up slopes and downhill and out of holes and sloughs. He digs himself into the front of it and pulls, coaxes, wheedles the ball to where an egg planted in it can brood and hatch. The wide earth and the hills and grass and trees stretching miles away on either side, the open blue sky and the dazzling white unsearchable noon sun millions of miles away, they were nothing. One cause, one service, one single aim, had the tumblebug captured, controlled, enthralled. The dust-coated and sacred ball of dung must be transported from where he shaped it to where it would enact its role of giving birth to more tumblebugs who in turn would push, dig, pull, haul and toil with endless devotion given to endless balls of dung to be rolled in dust and hauled to their sanctuary.

"I studied about it and I am still studying. I look at the devotion and humility of the tumblebug and I bow before it. I look at its ignorance and fixed habits and it has me saying, 'What of your own vast ignorance and your own fixed habits?' I know, for instance, that you and I and the sun and the moon and the earth are made of atoms. It is a fact. I read it in the books. Therefore I know more than a tumblebug. He is ignorant. He has never heard of an atom. Yet suppose he should ask me, 'What, Mr. Man, is an atom?' I would answer, 'I don't know. The wise men of science in their experiments and laboratories have never yet broken an atom to pieces and told me what they found. My ignorance, Mr. Tumblebug, about what is inside an atom is the same as your ignorance. As ignoramuses in the field of the atom we are equals. There is, however, one difference between your ignorance and mine. I read and see and know that the men of science have a restless, deathless curiosity to find what is inside the atom. If they ever find out while I am alive, they will tell me. And if I should bring news of it to you, you would say, "Excuse me, I'm not interested, and if you will permit me I will now proceed to push and pull this ball of dung till it has the proper coat of dust as established by my ancestors generations without end and to them, my blessed forefathers, be the power and the glory. Amen."'"

Brooks stepped away to light a fresh candle after one had sputtered out as he was saying to Joel, "I'm getting ridiculous and fantastic."

"Did you ever hear Theodore Weld?" asked Brooks as she seated herself and her eyes roved over his shadowy massive hunched shoulders.

"I heard him in Troy. He came near getting me, had me hot and cold by turns. He tempted me. Why not follow him and be a regular fighting abolitionist? Then I asked, What about the mill town in Massachusetts where I was a slave for a year?"

"They didn't put bloodhounds and sheriffs on your trail when you ran away," Joel put in.

"No, I wasn't a chattel slave, I was free to run away. You're correct there, Joel. What I mean is that Theodore Weld tells the awful truth about the sin of slavery in the South and forgets about awful sins in the North. Who dug the Erie Canal? Mostly the Irish, twelve hours a day, sixty-two and a half cents a day up to eighty-seven and a half cents a day. Who is shoveling the right of way and laying the rails for a new railroad coming this way? Paddy, twelve hours a day and less than six dollars a week. Of course, he's free to quit, free to go hunting another shovel job at six dollars a week, twelve hours a day. Do you wonder there is drinking and fighting? They drink to forget and they fight because they drink, we've seen that happen. When they want to gamble with their mean little savings I let them in and give them back half what they lose."

"Did you ever see the like," said Joel, "of how when people try to have a nice quiet talk nowadays it always ends up with abolition?"

"Yes, in polite society they try to keep away from it and then they come back to whether you're for the nigger or against."

"Going to be that way a long time."

"I guess so, Joel. The fourth night I heard Weld in Troy he came to the platform limping on one knee where a stone had hit. A black-and-blue lump stood out on one side of his face where another stone had welted him. He didn't mention a mob that hooted and stoned him. He didn't offer to die for what he was saying. But you could tell he would. He had thought about it. They could kill him but he wouldn't shut up. And they did nearly kill him there in Troy. They welted his body and broke him so for a long time he couldn't speak or write. And I'm sure one thing hurt him there in Troy, hurt him as much as the stones of the mob. The church where he spoke had one of the loud-mouthed kind, the blatherskite abolitionist, for a preacher. He talked to hear himself talk. He had become a pompous, self-right-eous nuisance. When Weld came from out of town they took Weld for a target. His quiet yet powerful attacks on slavery shook up and stung an opposition that had always laughed at the local preacher. Some pretty respectable people in Troy egged on the mobs that near killed Weld. I hear people call him Christlike and I wouldn't argue he isn't. If I should talk with him I'd ask him if he isn't suit of a Lost Man, not in the way I'm lost, but sort of groping in the wilderness."

Brooks and Joel told of an after-meeting where they saw Weld shy and shrinking about any personal fame or glory.

"What I would expect," said Omri. "A clean man in an unclean world. If I had his gifts I would talk and talk."

"That's what Joel said," laughed Brooks.

What had the three of them together? This had flitted through their minds this evening. They could be somber, sad, and laugh together. Omri edged into praise of them as "seekers." They reminded him of Roger Williams in regard for other believers in other doctrines. "You let them alone and ask them to let you alone."

They gave him a candle and showed him to a small "spare room" with a bed, washstand, pitcher and bowl. He stood in the doorway to bid them good night. Their laughter rang and Brooks chirped, "You *have* got mischief in you," on his telling of the far-famed evangelist Lorenzo Dow, "Bearer of the Word," tall, lean-faced, a beard flowing to his waist, locks of hair down over his stooped shoulders, losing his first wife and three months afterward holding a meeting on Bean Hill near Norwich, Connecticut. To the hundreds of men, women and children under a great elm Dow preached from a text, "So then, they are no more twain, but one flesh. What therefore God hath

665

joined together, let not man put asunder." They heard Dow favor matrimony as ordained of God and going farther he spoke of his first wife Peggy Holcomb Dow who had "shared viscissitudes" with him for fifteen years and died at the age of thirty-nine, prepared to meet her Creator, buried sitting upright so as to spring forward more swiftly on the day the Archangel Gabriel should blow his horn. What God had said to Ezekiel had happened to Lorenzo Dow, "Behold I take away the desire of thine eyes with a stroke." A divine flower of purity and fidelity she was. The people of Connecticut had never heard richer praise showered on a dead woman. It was only three months since her burial and his memories of her were vivid. "And yet it is a world of the living in which we find ourselves," Lorenzo Dow announced and after a pause his eyes roved the congregation and they heard him: "I am now a candidate for matrimony. If there is any woman in this audience who is willing to marry me, I would thank her to rise."

Two women stood up, one near the pulpit, the other far back. His eyes ranged from one to the other.

"There are two," he said in a solemn voice as the necks of the audience twisted to see the one up front and the one far back.

Which of the two would he take for a life partner? What decision would come from him when he had finished looking from one to the other?

Slowly and again with solemnity came his words: "There are two. I think this one near me rose first. At any rate, I will have her."

She was Lucy Dolbeare, daughter of a well-off farmer to the south of Hebron. But she hung back. He had to plead with her. It took him hours to argue her into going with him at midnight to the parsonage of a minister friend of Dow who heard a knocking and put his head out of an upper window with "Who's there?"

"It's Lorenzo and she says she's willing."

The ceremony went as usual till the minister was asking the bride if she would evermore love, cherish and obey her husband. Her answer flashed, "No, I will be a thorn in his flesh and a Satan to buffet him as long as I live."

That was the way Omri had heard it in Utica only last week, he said to Brooks and Joel. They laughed their amazement at such a bond of matrimony. Brooks caught the twinkling of Omri's soft brown eyes, bearded lips drawn back from a set of uneven yellow teeth. Brooks chirped, "You *have* got mischief in you," then sobered. "Could there be any lesson in this funny midnight marriage?" She put a hand over her mouth for a yawn. It was two hours past their bedtime.

"Oh yes," said Omri.

"Tell us," said Joel with a yawn he didn't bother to cover.

"Some women act sudden and you can't tell what they're going to do next," laughed Omri. "Good night now," and very gravely, "It's been a sweet evening, good night."

Joel had finished breakfast, gone to his shop and put in an hour on stitching and splicing a saddle girth before Omri came down to his oatmeal, fried pork chops, and two yellowed and mellow russet apples, windfalls from a tree you could see from the breakfast table, as Brooks pointed out.

She poured from a copper coffeepot three cups of coffee that he drank in sips as she ate honey off a spoon and sipped from a cup of pure black coffee. He said he couldn't be light-minded about this visit. And he wouldn't have talked so much last night unless they had led him on. He didn't mean to impress them with any of his personal miseries. He could see that both of them, Brooks especially, had been acquainted with chastening sorrow. She told of the little one who had lived only a week. She hoped the woman Omri had his eyes on, "bluebird and wildcat," would meet his wishes. He said, "I know her well enough to know if we stand before a minister, she will promise to love, cherish and obey and in her own mind be saying what Lorenzo Dow's wife said openly, I will be a thorn in his flesh and a Satan to buffet him as long as I live."

"And yet you love her and would marry her, knowing that?"

"Yes, for I love her more than any woman I know who is free to marry me."

His quiet solemnity as he said this, the convincing reverence in his face and voice, stayed with her long after he had shaken her right hand with his and given a touch and light caress with his other hand to the black hair smoothed down over her right ear, long after he had said good-by to Joel bending over a saddle girth, and taken the stage to Utica.

"We will see him again, I know it," said Brooks that noon as she passed Joel a plate of dumplings with apples from their own russet tree in their own back yard.

* * * * * * * * * *

Chapter 5

* * * * * * * * * *

Valley Forge Veteran and Wagons West

ON the death of Brooks' mother the grandfather had come to stay till his death two years later. Friendly visitors came, sometimes schoolchildren with a teacher, to see a soldier who had fought under Gen-

667

eral Washington. Brooks let them in, sometimes on condition, saying, "He is far along, you know, can't talk with you, and you must stay only a minute for a look." And they would step in to see in an arm-chair a man sitting erect and quiet before a window, the daylight falling on snowy hair in tufts out over his ears and a spare lock down across his forehead, his cheeks sunken, a hawk nose, quiet thin lips, a bleached white skin, a deep crease running from the nostril to the mouth corner, the face pulled tight over cheekbones and jawbone, his head set on wide bony shoulders, a loose black coat folded in comfort over a white linen shirt. He might turn his head toward them with an unconcerned look from light-blue eyes set far back in the sockets. Brooks would be saying, "You should be going now," and they would leave. Or again after handshaking, he would answer questions, though because of his failing memory Brooks wished less of this.

"You saw General Washington?" came a query once.

"Many a time and all weathers."

"What was he like?"

"A good man, a beautiful man, always pleasant, never changed countenance, wore the same face in defeat and retreat as victory."

"Did you ever see him smile?"

"Once only, he smiled but didn't laugh out. They say he never once did laugh out."

"Did you see General Greene?"

"When he joined us in Virginia. Had the awfullest set of men you ever see. Some, I should presume, had a pint of lice on 'em, a ragged lot, no shoes."

"How was Valley Forge?"

"Cold and filthy, I couldn't say which was the worse, the cold or the filth. Most of us had bloody feet."

A young man came saying, "I walked eleven miles to see you."

"You're a fool, twasn't worth it. Now you're here you can see I'm cheap to look at."

His eight-dollars-a-month pension from the Federal Government he turned over to Brooks, who sewed, washed, cooked, ran errands and wrote letters for him to his kin.

A few times in fair weather he shuffled on his ailing feet to the canal to sit watching the boats go by loaded and crowded. When he heard Joel say the twenty-day haul from Buffalo to New York had been cut to six days and the hundred dollars a ton hauling cost brought down to five dollars, he asked Joel to repeat the figures for him, then shook his head and asked again for the figures. After his first weeks of watching from a window or the front steps the wagons moving west and ever west he asked Brooks, "How long this been?"

"How long what, Grandpa?"

"These wagons all the time, all going west."

"Ever since we came here, more and more every year. I suppose I've seen thousands of those wagons."

"Where they going?"

"Ohio, Indiana, Michigan, Illinois, Iowa, some won't stop till Nebraska or Kansas."

Several times later he asked her, "Where did you say those wagons go?" and had the same answer. It seemed to Brooks that he had heard and read more or less about the country to the west getting settled up, and the wagons he saw gave it a sharp new impact on his mind.

At supper one evening he deliberated over his spare portions of mashed potatoes, meat chopped fine for his toothless mouth, finished the light meal he preferred, and then spoke with a tension curious and unusual for him. "Brooks, Joel, a new America is coming, sooner than we thought. The country is going to be more the other side of the Alleghenies than this side. A great new country, it will make changes we can't see now. A new people on a new land must have changes. They will make a new America. How they will do it my poor eyes can't see now. They will dig more canals and lay more railroads. Along the new water routes and railroads you will see cities big as Springfield, Boston, New York and Philadelphia, by God, bigger than London and Paris. Washington saw it coming and so did Jefferson, this settlement from the Atlantic to the Pacific, but they expected it in five hundred years, maybe a thousand years. We talked about it in the army. The Continental Army was fighting for the continent and we expected it would take about a thousand years to settle up the continent. Now it's coming in a hundred years, less than that. And there will be trouble. The country will get so rich and richer there will be rich men quarreling, not because they are rich but because they are human and enjoy power and like to have their own way. Trouble—I feel it in the air. Too many people excited about too many different ideas."

He paused, his wide bony shoulders uneasy, his grim thin lips trembling. "I can read *my* America. *You* can't read *yours*, Brooks, and I tell you, Joel, *you* can't read this new America coming. You'll be part of it, both of you, hidden so deep in it, both of you, you won't know what's outside of your little hiding place."

They saw that neither he nor they had expected such a burst of speech from him. They saw him with his teeth gone and cheeks sunken under a bleached skin of a faded and sepulchral white, his voice under the excitement cracking. The tufts of hair out over his ears hung as snow with late afternoon sunslants on it. The high cheekbones and the jawbone curves stood out as a mask beyond changes of fate. The deep-set eyes had blazed with a slow blue light in their sockets. Then he subsided and sat erect and silent as though no one had said anything. His slightly palsied hand trembled as he lifted a glass of milk. Brooks and Joel looked at each other and at him and

669

spoke no word. A spike of maroon sunset light crossed the room from corner to corner, widened into a horizontal band of crimson-gold dust and vanished in no time. Brooks helped Grandpa to his big armchair and he sat there with closed eyes, the bony mask of his face half-luminous in the dusk, his feet stirring occasionally with the itch of bygone frostbite and chilblains. The mood he had spoken came no more. The Past was enough for his strength. The Future, the America of others tomorrow, rattled his bones when he tried to reach into it.

* * * * * * * * * *

Chapter 6

* * * * * * * * * *

The Woman He Called Wildcat and Bluebird

GRAVEL CREEK on the edge of Arpa crossed the corner of a farm that hadn't been worked for some years and that lay waiting a buyer with more belief in it than the former owner, who had one October day held an auction and sold off what couldn't be piled in the two wagons he and his son drove away the next day. "Streakin it for Ohio," he had laughed to a horseshoer. "Got a young brother gettin rich on a big farm near Ashtabula. Got a Cousin Defiance with a sawmill and six hundred acres, makin money hand over fist. He comes through last year, says if I stay putterin here the day'll come I won't have a pot to piss in nor a window to throw it out of. I'll be back one of these days and lift the mortgages. I'm tired layin awake nights to hear rats gnawin a mortgage."

Gravel Creek had its merits for the movers, clear water to dip for cooking or washing, wide oaks and friendly pines, and near by a clump of timber and thickets where firewood for a quick meal or a cold night could be had. There was shade and cool water in hot weather. Around a small clearing with a stone fireplace for cooking, the pines made a fair windbreak. In rain or storm the horses were not bad off among pines that wove a roof not perfect but shedding the worst of the rain. The stores of Arpa, the horseshoer, blacksmith, harness-maker, post office, apothecary, taverns, churches, were less than a ten-minute walk.

The camp had usually two or three wagons. It might be empty a few days straight running. And again, and more often of a Sunday, it had six or eight wagons and as many as twenty or thirty people. Mostly came a plain four-wheeled lumber wagon that had done farm hauling, a wagon topped with a framework of three or four pieces of arched wood over which a canvas or muslin cover was pulled tight and fastened

670

with ropes. No special covered wagon was on the market. Each man or family worked out their own. They could roll up the canvas in warm weather or keep it down against a cold wind or dust or mosquitoes. At the camp they usually slept in their wagons, though on mild nights it could be a luxury to spread blankets on a clean carpet of pine needles. The wagon was their house on wheels. It held under its canvas or muslin roof their meager possessions and their mighty hopes.

There had been single men, bachelor brothers, married couples with no children, but mostly the movers were a family ranging from three or four to a record-breaking Presbyterian set of Heptonstalls, all twelve of them marching into the Bethesda Church one June morning, and the next day jogging along through Arpa behind two yoke of oxen that had worked their New Hampshire farm. They were a pageant, an independent proliferant nation in themselves.

Every breed and variety of horse had come along to the Gravel Creek camp though mostly they were like their owners, slow, patient, hopeful, a little dusty, a little tired of the monotony of being crowded and keeping house in a wagon.

On a day in mid-May of 1836 the camp had held two wagons and five people. The two bachelor brothers had arrived about noon. One of them was long-legged, thin-faced, sharp-eyed, talkative, smooth and lazy, Robert Kelway, Bob for short. The other was not so tall, more trim of build, and his hair a fair or pale brown against his brother's oily black hair; and he wasn't skittish and restless like his brother, nor so lazy, and he did most of the work, unhitching the horses and tying them in a pine clump and seeing to their corn and going to Arpa for a mess of meat, potatoes and carrots for an evening stew, besides corn meal, lard, and salt. This was Elbert, or Bert for short, and he sort of pleaded with his brother to get a pail of water from Gravel Creek while he made a hunt for firewood. Bob had a way of acting and talking superior and Bert accepted it. Bert more than half believed when they settled in some Indiana or Illinois town that Bob would marry the daughter of a rich farmer and someday be mayor or governor. Bob had a way with women and men seemed to like his loose-flung talk, what he had done and could do. "Spreads it on too thick," some men would say but others had a suspicion Bob might be important, he was so sure of himself. Bert liked to work, liked to manage, and Bob let him though Bob could tell when a certain look came in Bert's eye that he had better pitch in and help. Bob had sometimes been able to wheedle Bert into washing both their shirts but he had come to understand it when Bert said, "You wash your own." He saw that look this day when Bert had said to him, "You made too free with that woman yesterday. You'll be in a peck of trouble next you know."

In the other wagon at the Gravel Creek camp at Arpa was Omri Winwold, his wife Bee, and their year-and-a-half-old baby Andrew Marvel Winwold. They had shared a camp at Schlossville with the Kelway brothers only yesterday.

At Schlossville, a three-hour drive away, and on the day before, it was, only yesterday that Bob had "made free" with a woman and his brother Bert was anxious about it.

The Winwolds had driven into the Schlossville camp at noon to find no other movers there. Omri had started a fire and cooked dinner while Bee made a beginning at washing the baby blankets from a wicker basket. She had put it off for days and Omri had to beg and argue with her; the little wool covers were messy with grime, dust, diaper marks, the washing wouldn't take long, he had done it the last time and the time before, she'd feel better for a piece of work like that. She finally said she would. In saying so she seemed to think it more of a favor to him than the baby.

After their noon meal he had piled out of the wagon some things Bee and the baby might need, including the wicker basket. It was a mild day, the sun falling through clear air, branches leafing out with a fresh green. Omri smiled to Bee that she could really enjoy herself this afternoon, standing in the sun doing the wash in the big tin pan, rinsing it in the tin pail and spreading the wash to dry on a dwarfed locust tree.

"I think you'll enjoy the afternoon," he had said as he drove downstream into the creek where it widened and was shallow and he could water the horses, unhitch and tether them on a spot where grass was coming green. Then with his leather boots and wool socks off, his pants rolled to his knees, he had washed off the mud too long caked on the wheels, wagon box, tongue and whiffletrees. His feet were cold and he felt comfort about getting out of the water to wash the harness with the sun on his feet and legs. Then he had thrown the harness on the horses, led them out to the wagon in the creek and hitched them, led them out of the water to the slope of clay bank. There he talked soft to the horses while he rolled down his pants, drew on his socks and boots, felt grateful at the warmth coming back on the blue skin. He sneezed, told the horses he hoped he wouldn't get a dodgasted cold. They were middling-sized horses, a bay and a dun he had bought at auction in Albany. The bay he had found a more willing puller, but the dun had a white blaze in its forehead, a white stocking over its left foot, and it flicked an ear when he said he hoped he wouldn't get a dodgasted cold.

"I'm finding myself," he had said two months ago after he quit gambling. He had laid by a regular percentage of his winnings. He had more and more taken care to run a game only in towns where the public understood him, lighting out before "the crusade against gambling hells" got under way in earnest. His hope of a farm out West in "the new country" deepened and kept him cautious. His two green satin vests he had traded to a pawnbroker for a long sheath knife and a leather belt to wear it in. He caught himself having vanity about his wool shirt of black-and-white checks, his soft felt hat with a nice brim neither wide nor narrow. He had walked over dozens of farms, talked with the farmers, put in a few spring days at milking, hauling manure, plowing and planting with a farmer friend near Albany. He had no fears or doubts about what he could do with that rich Western soil once he got on it. "A little sound mother wit, willingness to work hard, and your farm will keep you," he had heard and now believed. Having made a neat pile of money out of winnings from players in games of chance where he had the benefit of skill and experience, this weighed somewhat on his conscience. "It only balances that year I put in at the cotton mill fourteen hours a day six days a week," he would say, though it didn't always still the voice of an insistent conscience.

Bee was now his main trouble. "The most uncertain woman in the world," he had said. Slim, swift, clean and lovely, he had seen her—before she moved into one of her streaks when she was reckless, dirty and often lazy, mean, biting, and drunk. Her father had died in a Massachusetts mill town of long hours of work and lungs that rotted. When her mother "got played out" with the millwork and was sent to a county hospital to die of "complications," five-year-old Bee was sent to her grandparents in Albany. Had she been a year older she could have gone to work in the mill, and, as the phrase had it, "supported herself." Her grandparents had moved to "somewhere in Pennsylvania," leaving her in an orphan asylum. At twelve she was bound out, the papers signed, to housework in a family that treated her kindly, gave her schooling, kept her as one of their own. She ran away to Schenectady, then to Troy, reappearing in Albany to wait on table in a hotel, to meet theater people, to hear she had looks and gifts and might become a singer or dancer.

She had fallen in with a set known as the Haymakers, with a slogan, "We make hay while the moon shines," a fast-and-loose set who went in for barn dances on the outskirts of Albany and occasional sprees at city taverns. At one of these tavern affairs she had caught Omri's eye—in a blue lawn gown tight around her slender waist and smooth elegant hips, a long straight nose of fine dignity coming down to a small mouth of heavily rounded lips rich with impudence and laughter when she was feeling good. Small narrowed eyes flashing black from wide sockets, the eyelids and eyebrows a faint purple, and sleek black hair folded close and neat over long white ears that lay close to the head. Omri saw her as motion, curves, grace, speed, "a ball of fire." He saw her swing in the arms of a "canawler" or canal boatman, a Hudson River boat pilot, a railroad construction gang straw boss, two flashy fellows who had been repeatedly arrested and fined for selling liquor without a license, two loud-mouthed sons of well-to-do farmers, a cook from one of the river-front taverns, an upstanding bare-knuckle prize fighter who had a reputation, an undersized garrulous joker who managed cock-fights, several lusty farm hands who were getting rid of a month's wages and wouldn't be back for another month.

The other women dancing and drinking were an assorted lot that didn't interest Omri. He put up with the Haymakers because Bee was a part of them. It got so that he brought her to them and took her away and was, in a fashion, accepted as Bee's man. He clashed with her over her going with other men while he was running his game in Albany and later away on trips working other towns and the canal-boats. Once at a barn dance and again at a tavern party he got into a knockdown and drag-out fight over other men too familiar with Bee. He saw, to his surprise, that she took a fierce enjoyment in watching him wade into another man and win a fight over her even though he might have a black eye "with a shanty over it" for a week or a torn ear that pained him for months. Their sudden quarrels usually ended with her telling him to go to hell-and-gone and she was meeting plenty of men who told her, "Follow me and you'll wear diamonds." She admired a strength, will and wit she believed she saw in him—and the fighter stuff in him. And she said, "I love you and I don't," more often than "I love you." He shaved every last hair of beard and mustache from his face, on her imperative command and derisive insults. She met his kisses riding wild, hated his books and steered him away from book talk, mocked impudent unbelief at half his compliments and covered him with caresses when he paid for a Christmas blue silk dress for her and brought her what she had stipulated for an engagement ring, of solid gold set with a "gen-you-wine" red effulgent guaranteed ruby.

"Tranquillity," said Omri, looking up from a book he read one after-noon. "That's a hell of a word for me. Since I've known Bee I haven't had tranquillity and if I marry her it will be the same. Yet I want her. She's bluebird and wildcat and I'll tie to her for the bluebird and see what comes of the wildcat."

So they were married. And his work of nights at his game and his occasional trips away saw her making free with other men and he heard about it and clung to his fantastic hope that when a child came and they went West to the new country, a change would come over her.

Parts of these past days with Bee flitted through Omri's mind as he started to drive toward the Schlossville camp with the wagon washed, the harness cleaned, and his feet cozy.

Then he remembered an errand. He turned toward a farmhouse a third of a mile away, jumped from the wagon, unhitched the horses, tied one, took the harness off the other except the bridle. He led the horse alongside the wagon, rummaged around with a hand and brought out a two-quart wicker-covered jug. Bridle rein in one hand, the jug in the other, he rode bareback across the creek and over to the farm-house, where they said they had only two cows and one was dry and they didn't have milk to spare. "It's for a baby, a year-and-a-half-old

674

baby living in a wagon. We're movers." They smiled, gave him the milk, and refused pay for it. "I thank you. My heart's full of thanks, you know that." He rode back to the wagon, hitched again and drove up the slope from the creek.

Omri Winwold took it cool when he drove up to the camp and saw that another wagon had arrived with two men, one of the men repairing harness and the other, the long-legged one with his hat off and his black oily hair shining, sitting under a haw tree with an arm around Bee, who was handing him a bottle and Bee's hair mussed with part of it straggling down one cheek, her dress above her shoe tops and showing her slim shapely legs to the knees. They hadn't heard the horses scraping through underbrush and the squeak and lumbering of the wagon, either hadn't heard or didn't care.

Omri was off the wagon, tied the horses, and came over, taking it cool. They saw him, had themselves somewhat straightened. The bottle toppled among leaves and ran empty. Omri stood over them and said not a word. The moment was different from any of their turmoils in Albany, said Bee to herself as she rose tipsily. This chill in the glitter of Omri's brown eyes was new to her. Bob Kelway reached for his hat, rose to his feet, stood swaying slightly, brushed leaves from his shirt and his trouser waist. Bob Kelway felt the play of steady eyes boring into his face. He knew he was being called and would need trumps. He summoned to his face a grin lacking final reality. He brought words to his lagging tongue, any words would do, something must be said and it must come from him. "It's a nice day, pleasant weather as a man could ask, pleasant weather for movers." Bob Kelway could have gone on about the weather. The man boring him with brown eyes was a heavy solid chunk of a man. He would summon up a better grin yet. Didn't he always have a way with women and often with men? He was trying for the grin when a fist crashed into his jaw and he sank to the ground and lay crumpled on one side with his eyes closed, one leg hooked upward like a half-open jackknife and the lean fingers of one hand resting on it.

Omri turned to Bee. "Get your things and the baby—into the wagon —we're going to light out from here."

"You can't make me." Her head was up, her eyes defiant of him.

Omri walked away to gather up their things and put them in the wagon, bending over for a deliberate look of pity at the baby just out of a good sleep and smiling to him. He couldn't smile back. He carried the wicker basket to the wagon. He paused before Bert Kelway, who stood over his brother and said to Omri, "It's too bad. I'm sorry it happened. He didn't know what he was doing."

"You must be the decent one of the two of you," said Omri. Alongside him now stood Bee, who had been sort of wandering and half-

675

following Omri, interlacing the fingers of her hands and slicking down her clothes. He said to her, "We're lighting out."

"I told you, you can't make me."

He took hold of her and carried her kicking and squealing her repeated cry, "You'll be sorry for this, Omri Winwold." He put her on the wagon seat with a hoist and a thrust saying, "I don't wanna give you what I gave him." He ran to untie the horses, climbed to the seat and drove away.

The baby began crying. For a mile and two miles the baby crying. The wagon took a bump in the road with a jolt and Bee awoke to mumble to Omri, "Marvel is crying, don't you hear him?" Omri drove to the roadside, pulled in the horses, hunted up a biscuit, leaned over from the wagon seat and gave it to the baby, speaking to him as though he wanted his voice or any voice, "Here you are, Marvel, here you are, it's going to be all right, Marvel, it's going to be all right."

On a tumult of sheep-wool clouds the sunset threw runners of pink and then billows of crimson that fell away into a monotone of slate-gray and the stars came out with poise and no hesitations, wearing assumptions they had no misgivings room would be lacking for the least of them, the stars wearing the faces of serene travelers who had bought their serenity at cost.

The monotonous jolting of the wagon and the liquor she carried had Bee asleep sitting up on the wagon seat. Omri kept an eye on her. She fell against his side, awoke, straightened up mumbling and was asleep again. She fell the other way the next time, her head hanging over the front wheel as Omri's right arm snatched her back. She mumbled. He didn't quite get it. She was mumbling it again. He got part of it. "Drunk as a fiddler's bitch yeanh drunk as a *blind* fiddler's bitch yeanh and you knocked him down drunk, him dumb cold and him drunk as a fiddler's bitch yeanh drunk as a *blind* fiddler's bitch dumb cold dumb cold." She put herself to sleep with this mumble song.

They arrived at the Gravel Creek camp on the edge of Arpa two hours after sunset.

Noon of the next day it was that the Kelway brothers drove in and halted their wagon, made their cook fire some forty yards from the Winwolds. Bert Kelway had come over to say with quiet respect that they would be pulling out that afternoon or evening, so they expected, so they were aiming to.

Omri had been saying to Bee, "I told you about these kinfolk of mine here in Arpa."

"I guess you won't let me forget about 'em, especially Brooks Wimbler, a *good* woman, *such* a good woman."

"They're way distant kin, yet the only ones I know in the world. We're going way West and I might never see 'em again."

"Go see 'em. I'm not the one to hinder you."

"I thought you might like to come along and see 'em. They're nice folks and would like to see you."

"I've heard enough about what nice folks they are, especially how nice Brooks is."

Omri made guesses. He might have let on more than he intended sometime when talking about Brooks. More than likely, though, Bee was crazy jealous or was up to one of her tricks of taking a point and trying to make something of it. He said as much to her. And no, she wouldn't go along. "They're your kin, not mine."

Would Bee do him a favor? He was riding one of the horses to Arpa to get it shod while he greased the wagon and someone helped put a new sideboard on the wagon. After that he would stay with the Wimblers for supper, a visit and talk. He would have a crowded day. Would Bee go to the farmhouse for milk for the baby? They might be out of milk for Marvel if he woke at midnight. No, Bee wouldn't. He asked it as a favor. She wouldn't. She had the wash yet to tend to that he wouldn't do yesterday and that she hadn't finished. That wouldn't take an hour, he was sure. But she wouldn't go for milk. That was for him to do. He went for it, came back to see her nearly finished with the wash, spreading the last pieces on an elderberry bush. The Kelway brothers had gone to Arpa. Yet Omri was uneasy. "I'd light out now with a shoe loose on the horse and the sideboard rattling ready to fall off and the wheels squeaky, I'd light out now if it wasn't for these kinfolk."

In a piercing voice near a scream Bee answered, "Go see 'em! Go see your *nice good* kinfolk. I wouldn't hinder you if you give me the Erie Canal and every last goddam boat on it."

The visit with Brooks and Joel had its pleasant side. They searched each other's faces to find a fellowship and an indefinable common bond still there. They told of their sorrows rather tenderly and indirectly, of the child in the gig and the runaway horse, of the woman who had proved more wildcat than bluebird. Omri was through with drink and cards, moving into a new life. Joel had property, money laid by, and they too might go to Illinois, were talking it over. Brooks stared open-eyed at the money belt of fine thin leather that Joel had made for Omri that afternoon.

"He's got eight hundred dollars," Joel said low-voiced to Brooks. "He figures half of it for Illinois land and half for tools and improvements. I pray the Lord he's as good a farmer as gambler."

"My heart will be in farming like it never was in gambling," said Omri as he stepped in their bedroom, closed the door, fitted each of twenty twenty-dollar gold pieces into its little pocket, laid a line of paper bills smooth and even, buttoned six buttons, buckled the belt around his waist next to the skin, finished dressing, and came out to ask the Wimblers whether it looked suspicious and they said it didn't.

They lighted a lantern and went with him to the barn to see him off, to see him leap on his bareback horse that got a new shoe that afternoon, to see him reach down for handshakes, and then ride away laughing. "I'll see your good faces again tomorrow before I go." He walked his horse, slow, he would take his time. Whatever cards he held as against those Fate might play wouldn't be helped by any speed of horse or man. Being loose with other men, that side of Bee didn't hurt him so much as her indifference and neglect of the baby. Those streaks had come to her like the phases of the moon, when she drank hard at home and went out and came home drunk saying she had a right to a little fun in life. He could see a way to meet that, if the baby hadn't come. He could have gone along with her and tried living together a while longer and then parted, if that had to be. But little Andrew Marvel made a complication. She loved Marvel, in her way. He had her black eyes and hair. But she couldn't mother him, had almost no sense of responsibility about him. She took to one of her drinking spells when Andrew Marvel had whooping cough and the father had come home to find Marvel alone. He had called in a neighbor woman, stopped to send a doctor home, and then made the rounds to find Bee in a bad-smelling dram shop in a cellar on the water front, Bee with a partner and three other couples around a table drinking hot slings, Bee heavy-eyed and sullen cursing an overdressed young farmer whose hands had been hunting for the buttons to loosen her dress front. Omri had taken her home. She cried that night and spoke sorry and sat for hours at Marvel's cradle. He had asked her that week, "You like to lead men on, do you, Bee?"

"Yes, Omri, but that's as far as it goes. I play a game and they play it and nobody loses and we have fun."

Had he expected too much of her? Was leaving Albany and her liquor when she wanted it and her drinking companions when she wanted them, was it asking too much? She had her personal loveliness, wit, magnets, and some kind of a flare of genius. She had a right to her life. He could go his way, if it had to be, but what of Marvel? Didn't Marvel have rights? What would become of Marvel with a mother that was loving and anxious enough three weeks of the month and then went into one of her reckless streaks?

He came this night to a curve of road near the camp. Should he slide off his horse and walk in quiet? Yes, he would play that card. He tied the animal and walked the side of the road, turned into the camp, made his way half-groping in quiet to the wagon and found the bed of blankets where he and Bee had slept last night, the wicker basket alongside and Marvel nicely asleep and a jug of milk near by.

Omri stepped out, took a look at a sky of no stars. He could make out the dim flicker of an ember off toward where the Kelways last had their wagon and cook fire at noon. He moved toward it with slow and sure feet on the pine needles. His whispered "Damn!" came when there loomed before him the shape of the Kelway wagon. They hadn't gone, after all. He walked beyond it, wanting for the moment to get away from the camp and to slow down the surges in his blood. He crossed the piece of open ground on a line taken by campers going for the plentiful variety of firewood in the oval clump of timber and underbrush. Should he circle it and get around to the road and on to where he tied his horse? Vaguely, his brain pounding, he thought he would do that, as he stood still a while and took a look at the sky and again saw no stars and vaguely mocked at himself as though he and the stars were playing a game and a patch of cloud might move off and a few stars sneak into the open space and win the game on him.

Suddenly he stood cold as ice with fire shooting through it. He could swear he heard a man's voice begging, "Once more, honey lamb, only once more, we live only once," and he couldn't swear it was Bee's voice in the subdued words that sounded like, "My God, what a night!"

Omri dropped to his hands and knees, feeling his way so as to snap no twig or branch. He crept in the black night to where he could hear them, their moans and abrupt exclamations. He stood up and leaned against a tree. Now his thought and will operated. He would rush in and pound the man to death. His gambler's canniness came to him and he countered the impulse. Let them have what they had. Whatever they had he couldn't take away from them by murder. And one chance in a thousand it could be another couple than Bee and the oily-haired Kelway. Then came a quiet broken by a clear voice and he knew it was Bee's and she couldn't be stopped because she was saying, "It's late, I'm going now, we've had our night of it." Maybe he should rush in. But he didn't. He stayed fast in his foot tracks. He heard them in a final long kiss. He felt weak, faint. He clutched a tree branch his hand had a loose hold on. He took a new hold, a hard handhold and drew himself to his tiptoes and came slow to his heels. His breath was coming easier, the tightening in his throat slacked. He had nearly crossed over the line, nearly let himself go into a delirious rage with the single purpose of getting his hands on another man and killing that man.

He heard them go away. Their whispers he heard but not their words. "Tomorrow" and "again," he thought perhaps he heard whispered. He was afraid his brain conjured those words. He sat with his back to a tree, looking up for stars and there were no stars, and he was still winning the game of no stars, no hope, no place to go. He saw now it was a deep darkness, a pitch-black night with a shrouding mist that had made them sure they could not be found. Chance had led him to their tryst. And they had been lost in their tryst and not keeping watch or they would have seen him crossing the two hundred yards of open field. He sat dazed, an hour, it might have been two hours. He skirted an oval piece of woods to the road coming from Arpa, led his horse to the camp. He found Bee asleep, the baby alongside of Bee and asleep. He took off his boots and slid softly under the blanket, next to Bee. He slept an hour or two, his mind restless and toiling at what he should do. How could he right the wrong? He wished he had sprung on them and in wild action and crazy words had it all over with somehow. Should he forgive her? Was there any such way out? Perhaps it was one wild night for her and there would never be another. Bee was impulsive. He had heard her say and he loved her for it, "I'll do anything once!" He would wait. He must go careful.

He saw daybreak come, he saw the morning mist creep over the open field beyond, he could glimpse the border, the clump of woods, timber and thickets where last night he couldn't see his hand held out at arm's length. Next to him they slept on, Bee's face with a flush on the skin of her cheeks, the mouth calm and the lips fixed with a curious silence as though she might suddenly break the silence. Omri made a wish. He wished to God she might suddenly open her eyes and look at him with tears in them and then cry and say all must be forgiven and then forgotten. He had lost this wish as he studied the profile of her head that he had always adored, as his eyes fed for the thousandth time on the length and the faint purple gloss of her eyelashes as they lay so silent over her closed eyes. Then again he was wishing to God she would slowly open her eyes and fall on his shoulder sobbing for him to forgive and forget, for she didn't know what she was doing.

He was leaning on an elbow and staring down at her as her eyelids quivered and slowly and lazily came open. She saw him staring down. She blinked twice and again. She had before this of a morning opened her eyes to find him in a smiling adoration of her.

"Why, Omri," now came her hoarse whisper, "what's the matter?"

"Nothing."

"Nothing?"

"I had a bad dream, I guess."

"You had a bad dream?"

"I dreamed the world came to an end last night."

She gave a troubled laugh, faltered, "And what was the next world like?"

She was trying to be gay. Her laugh had an edge of puzzlement. She would like to know what had happened that for the first time of a morning he should be staring at her with a baffling grief and pain in his eyes.

"Where were you last night?" she asked. "You came late. Marvel and I went to sleep early without you."

"How early?"

"Away before ten o'clock. What were you doing? Are you questioning me?"

"No."

"Where were you last night? Why did you stay so long and leave us alone here? Who were you with?"

"Why don't you ask one little question at a time?"

680

"I have the right to know where you were last night and who you were with last night so late."

"I wish you could have woke up dumb and just shut your eyes and lay there acting dumb instead of asking me lawyer questions."

"I'm not asking you lawyer questions. I'm asking you wife questions. Where *were* you last night and *who* kept you so late?"

Then a resolve, till then sleeping in Omri, became awake. If she was going to put on this kind of a face and hold herself as right and clean and lay the blame and the wrong all on him, he could have no hope.

"I'll answer nothing you ask me, Bee: And I'm asking you to take notice I haven't asked you a question, not one, no lawyer question, no husband-to-wife question, and I guess I'm not going to ask you to answer anything. I wouldn't ask where you were last night nor how early or late you came back."

His eyes now troubled her, he knew something and he wouldn't ask her about it. In small matters it was usual for her at such a point to insult him, to flare up and threaten to leave him or tell him to go, he could do the leaving. She couldn't think now of an insult or a flaring and flagrant remark that she felt sure would fit in with what he seemed to know. She asked herself, "What can he know? No one could have seen us in the dark and he wasn't here when I came back." It must be he had only suspicions, no knowledge. Jealousy, she suddenly decided. He had gone queer and was acting strange because he was afraid of losing her. Yet he looked as though he could kill her. The look she had never seen on him before. She had seen him a little jealous, enough jealous to be mean and talk hard and threaten, but never before the silent look of pain she saw in his eyes now that left her no words and his face and breath coming close to her as though he could reach out his hands and put them on her throat and hold his hands there till breath was gone. She said nothing more. Nor did he.

Omri built a fire, led his horses to the creek for water, tethering them in a spot of grass hardly worth their cropping when they should finish the corn ears he laid on the ground. He patted the bay's neck, stroked with his fingers the white blaze in the dun's forehead, thinking, "You're good company to movers."

As he walked toward the camp with a pail of water he could see the Kelways around their fire and moving nearer he heard Marvel crying. He came up to see the baby refusing his cup of milk, screwing up his face and bawling. He picked up the baby and held it toward Bee's arms. She hesitated about raising her arms to the wriggling inconsolable squealer. Omri said, "Take him and try to rock him a little while I fix breakfast." The baby began easing down. "Wanted somebody to hold him close," said Omri under his breath. He went to the wagon, reached in for bags and packages, stepped around the stone fireplace and before long had a tin plate of fried corncakes, pork chops and two eggs, a tin quart cup of hot coffee in Bee's reach, a like plate for himself, and offering Marvel sips of warm milk from a cup, pieces of corncake.

The damp daybreak chill was gone and the sun poured down on another fine May day. Omri said as much. Bee wasn't interested except for a clipped grunt, "Yeanh."

Omri had a bad moment halfway through his victuals. "There's going to be hell to pay and I eat like it was any other nice morning." He came out of it. He must keep cool and he must hold to all his strength and wait for this day. Desperately, mournfully, he tried to read Bee. If she could suddenly be saying, "Let's light out, Omri, let's get out of here right away this morning," that would have helped. That could be the beginning of something. Yet it seemed she wanted to stay or was in one of her lazy spells when, as Omri had heard her drawl and yawn, "I'm not one of these fuss-and-feather housewives sayin work is good for you. I wait to see what'll happen to me. When it happens I don't blame myself nor take credit. All I did was wait and see it happen."

Omri had washed the breakfast dishes, washed his shirt and socks that morning, mended a tear in the shirt, took the baby in his arms when he had a crying spell, walked around the wagon with him, made faces at him, rattled a tin cup with four coins in it, gave him another cup of milk and saw him sleeping at noon in his wicker basket. Bee had moved the blankets from under the wagon into the sun and had slept and dozed part of the morning, had sewed repairs on rips in her blue wool skirt and her black wool cloak, had cleaned her blue velvet cap and the orange silk bandanna.

After the noon meal Omri told Bee he was going to Arpa on several different errands and would she like him to come at evening and bring her along to the Wimblers for supper? A hoarse throaty "No" with a flavor of disgust cut that proposal short and Omri said, "I'll be back about the same time tonight as last night. Tomorrow we can leave early and never come back to Arpa."

Her black eyes searched and queried his face and eyes, with no word from her mouth that had now a fixed mutiny on it.

He was walking to Arpa. Bee followed him a piece of the road, stood with her head out from a bush, her eyes following to see him turn a curve of the road. The checked shirt, the coat slung over the left arm, the steady swinging stride and never a look back, he was in Arpa on his errands. Bee picked up her feet and ran hotfoot back to the Gravel Creek camp.

682

Chapter 7

Murder and a Hellcat .

THE banners of dawn smote the Mohawk Valley and streaked over Arpa and flung blood-red filaments across the rolling mist.

On the Erie Canal the westbound boats met the eastbound and bells rang as men navigated and met the new day with salutations and fresh hot coffee.

Grace had been spoken at the breakfast table in the Wimbler home. "And in thy wisdom and beneficence, bless this food to its proper uses, we ask it in Christ's name. Amen." They were about to eat when they heard a knocking at the front door, a knocking with no pauses. Whoever was there wanted to be let in and no time lost about it.

Brooks went with Joel who opened the door. They saw a woman, her face white, not a white-linen white but an ivory-pale white. A blue velvet cap on her head, an orange silk bandanna at her neck, she strode in on their invitation, the words rushing from her as she crossed the doorway, "I am the wife of Omri Winwold and I am looking for my husband."

Her flaunting and insolent tone of accusation had both Joel and Brooks near to saying in unison, "We haven't got your husband and you're welcome to search the house and premises if it'll do you any good."

They saw her shaken, sick of mind if not body, her lips twitching, her underlip running in and out, desperation and danger lighting her small black eyes in their wide sockets.

"Did he leave a baby with you?" she asked Brooks.

"No, we know nothing of a baby. We would like to have seen the baby."

"You would, would you? Did he leave anything with you for me?"

"He left nothing with us for anybody except a few kind words as between friends and distant kinfolks," said Joel.

"Did he come here for supper and a visit with you night before last?"

"He did."

"Did he come again yesterday or last night?"

"For early supper last night, leaving right away afterward."

"What did he say?"

"He said it was good to have the visit and it might be a long time before we meet again, if ever."

"And he left nothing with you?"

"Only good words and kind wishes."

"I mean did he leave anything with you for *me?*"

"No."

"He didn't tell you he was driving away with my baby last night, that he was stealing that baby from me, that he's a thief and a kidnapper?" She looked at Brooks.

"He didn't," came Brooks' voice gently.

"Not a word about who he'd leave the baby with?"

"Not a word."

"Did you know he had eight hundred dollars on him?" looking toward Joel.

"Yes."

"And he left none of it with you for me?"

"No."

"Did he leave any of it with you for the baby or anybody else?"

"No."

Bee's twitching had slowed down. The talking, the questioning, the excitement of flaunting herself and showing her wrath to people she suspected, had brought her nearer her normal condition when she had a specific objective. She had stood with hands on her hips, occasionally loosing both hands to wriggle the fingers. She had expected to overwhelm them, knock them endways with fear of the law, fear of their reputations. And nothing was happening.

"He said you were *good* people, Christian people. He laid it on what a *good* woman you are, Mrs. Wimbler."

"He did?" said Brooks soberly and gently, with an inner smile.

Then looking from one to the other Bee said, "I don't see you good Christian people have any pity for a woman whose husband has run away with money that part belongs to her and a baby that belongs to her more than to him."

"We haven't had breakfast yet," said Joel. "It might be you'd join us in breakfast and feel better about us. We were just sitting down to it when you knocked on the door."

"I'd see you in hell before I'd eat with you hypocrites. You're lying to me, lying about my baby and lying about my money. You know where *he* is and the *baby* and the *money.*"

Brooks and Joel looked at each other, looked at Bee, again at each other, their eyes saying, "Let us see if this strange and disturbed woman can add anything to her already vehement remarks."

They waited, eying her with calm. Bee waited, shifting her eyes from one face to the other, thumbs on her hips and slowly wriggling the fingers. Bee tried to think of more to say and found she had just about said it all.

"You'll be damned sorry before this is over and so will your relative, a thief, a kidnapper," was the best Bee could do as she swept out of the house and down the steps and into the side path leading toward Gravel Creek camp.

Brooks and Joel out on the steps saw her walk and stride away. "She is a ball of fire," they remembered Omri saying. She struck them into a mingled admiration and pity, vivid, unforgettable. They better understood what fate had shaken and drawn Omri Winwold. He had told them the evening before of her flagrance, how it outran anything of previous days, of how if leaving her he must take the baby with him, and how he must leave her if on returning early this night to the camp he should again find her gone from his wagon and bed. Omri saw it as no matter for the courts of law, no friendly discussion of rights and equity involved. "When I go out there tonight if she isn't around that wagon, close to that baby and the bed under the wagon, if she isn't there, I go. I don't tell you where I'm going and you can tell anyone who asks where I went that I didn't tell you."

That was all. And now Omri was gone, heading West, they were sure, to that Illinois farm, heading West to "the new country." They remembered him in their prayers, him and the baby often in their prayers.

Joel went out to the Gravel Creek camp the next day, a Sunday afternoon, finding four families and wagons there. Two of the families were returning from church. One of them had arrived the day before and the man said, "Yes, we saw the two brothers, name of Kelway, they said. One of them sober, kept to himself. The other had a woman. They drank and kind of acted up, pulled out this morning, said they was headin for Buffalo."

Two weeks later when Brooks walked home from the post office, part of the way she read their weekly copy of the *Mohawk Valley Transcript*. Nearing home she had turned to an inside page. Her eyes met a paragraph, an item. It stopped her. She stood still and read it rather breathless. She hurried to Joel's shop where they read it together:

Sheriff George Aberdeen of Axminster County gave out the information this week regarding the man who gives his name as Elbert Kelway and who has been in the county hospital for two weeks recovering from stab wounds. According to the man's story he and his brother Robert Kelway and a woman who went by the name of Bee were movers going to Indiana and had made a three-day halt at Upson Hill camp. Elbert Kelway alleges that his brother Robert treated the woman with indignities that finally became cruelties he forbade his brother to repeat. When they were repeated he struck his brother a severe blow with his fist. His brother thereupon drew a knife on him. He ran for a knife of his own and a duel with knives ensued. They fought for half an hour, inflicting dire wounds on each other, at the conclusion Elbert driving his weapon into the jugular vein of his opponent, who died shortly thereafter. New arrivals at the Upson Hill camp found Elbert Kelway prostrate and exhausted from his wounds and loss of blood. The woman known as Bee had disappeared and her whereabouts have not to date been discovered. At the coroner's inquest no witnesses of the affray were heard and a verdict was rendered to the effect that death had resulted from knife stabs inflicted by a party or parties unknown. Elbert Kelway, according to the sheriff, has the marks of thirty-six incisions and slashes on his body, and when sufficiently recovered to appear in court, will stand trial on a charge of murder. It is reported that he will give strange testimony regarding the conduct of the woman in whose behalf he had interfered, this being to the effect that she stood by throughout as a spectator, crying her delight in the spectacle, making no attempt to part them, and continuously shouting her approval of any successful knife thrust by Robert Kelway, and at the end of the tragic affair reproaching Elbert Kelway as a murderer who would deserve the hanging he would get. Strange to relate, Kelway has a distinct recollection, it is reported, of the woman known as Bee standing over him after he had fallen to the ground exhausted and bleeding, and glaring into his face, she had used the expression, "You're going to marry a widow with wooden legs." This, says Sheriff Aberdeen, is an expression from the gypsy vernacular, "a widow with wooden legs" being a gallows and the ceremonial of formally fastening a noose about a man's neck before breaking the neck constituting the nuptial knot that binds him to the aforesaid widow for eternity. It is believed the woman may be of gypsy blood. She is described as slender, below medium height, long straight nose, black eyes and black hair, when last seen wearing a blue velvet cap, a black cloak, and an orange silk bandanna about her neck and shoulders.

Three weeks later Joel read aloud to Brooks from their copy of the *Mohawk Valley Transcript*:

The verdict of the jury in the case of Elbert Kelway found him guilty of manslaughter with a recommendation for leniency. The court in pronouncing a sentence of one year in state prison adverted to the main evidence being the testimony of the accused man and the fact not being established as to who was the first to draw a deadly weapon. Kelway testified that the woman Bee had a husband in their camp area at Arpa where the husband discovered her in the act of adultery and thereupon deserted her, taking with him their eighteen-month-old child. Kelway alleged further that the woman claimed her husband had $800 in cash on him, declaring, "She kept at Bob egging him on to kill her husband and get the money on him but Bob wouldn't believe the man was carrying any such amount on him and when we came to Upson Hill and she said he had slipped the chance to get all of $800 and when she blazed sharp and mad at him he took a horsewhip and brought blood you could see on her neck and arms. I know now I shouldn't have stepped in then and better have lit out like the husband did and let them rassle their own hash." Kelway made an excellent impression as a witness in his own behalf and it is expected that sympathizers will intercede with the state Governor for a pardon before his term expires.

"She stood and watched 'em fight—you believe that, Joel?"

"She's a sick woman, sick in her mind, moments she don't know what she's doing, crazy."

"She would have got Omri killed for his money—you believe that?"

"She'd do anything that came into her sick mind. You could see it the way she about spit in our faces when we asked her to sit breakfast with us. She ain't in her right mind, wherever she is now."

"I'm glad Omri is alive," said Brooks, "alive and the baby with him."

"That baby we never got a sight of."

"Yes."

"Will we see Omri again you think, Brooks?"

"I don't feel like prophecies, Joel. The present now is enough without trying to peek into the future."

"Brooks, you remember Omri in the doorway of the spare room telling of the wedding of Lorenzo Dow to his second wife?"

"Yes, and how the bride said, 'No, I'll be a thorn in his flesh and a Satan to buffet him as long as I live.'"

"I believe he wasn't just telling a funny story then."

"No, he was studying about that kind of a woman."

"With Lorenzo Dow it worked out to advantage."

"And with Omri he's lucky to be alive and out of her clutches."

"More wildcat than bluebird, eh, Brooks?"

"More hellcat than wildcat—though I shouldn't be saying it. She's not of her right mind. In the Bible times they'd have said she was possessed of devils that required to be cast out before she could be saved. We won't talk about her any more or I'll cry."

* * * * * * * * * *

Chapter 8

* * * * * * * * * *

Prayer for a Child to Come

WESTWARD went the wagons, week on week the westward wagons till freezing roads and the first snow slowed them down. Joel and Brooks asked whether this or that wagon would pass by Omri and the baby so often in their prayers.

Westward their own thoughts had turned definitely that autumn and winter of 1836. At meetings in Arpa and Utica they heard speakers explain the Plan, heard of the Mississippi, the world's greatest river, hundreds of miles on both sides rich with prairie and timberland. Crops? You could raise anything on a virgin soil needing no fertilizer, a black loam six feet deep, a few thousand pioneer settlers already there. They would become pilgrims, movers heading west to take up land at $1.25 an acre and make an empire, a new country, a Mesopotamian domain. "And who," asked a speaker, "is to sway and govern this new domain? Is it to be Christ or Satan?" They heard his appeal, swept along with it:

"On a rich tract of land between Lake Michigan and the Mississippi, we shall see the settlement grow into a city. From the beginning we shall have a college and train young men for duty as citizens, teachers, ministers. Their lives will go to saving the Great Valley for Christ, against the rum traffic, for the abolition of slavery."

A lust for change, a passion for a holy crusade, a vision of Christian farmers and citizens shaping local and national affairs, yea, even world affairs—this was in the air and the breath of speakers and listeners that autumn and winter of 1836 and 1837. With history in the making, they were to be makers and shapers, not idlers, onlookers, not gazers from afar. The details and specifications of what they would shape and do by will and example, this they left to the future, in the main. They were to fight and overcome "ignorance and sin," ancient foes before which nations and peoples had gone down. They would vanquish ignorance with knowledge and sin with Christian living and discipline. One speaker had words: "The Great Valley of the Mississippi is a cradle in which a giant in his swaddling clothes is sleeping. These swaddling clothes he will soon burst. And the time is not distant when he will sway the world! It lies with the present generation to decide whether he shall tread down the nations in blood or whether his march shall be the march of resurrection over the graves of ignorance and sin."

Over the autumn and winter the Plan took form. Eleven wagons would start in the spring for the chosen land tract in Illinois. Down

688

payments on the land had already been made. At the same time the Boat would go. Next May, Joel and Brooks made their plans, they would step aboard the Boat with their baby. Their trust was complete that God by then would have given them their baby for this journey by water route to the Great Valley. They had lived along the canal, they knew the captain of the Boat, they and the baby would be safer with more comfort on the Boat. They had joined thirty and more others from towns and farms forty miles roundabout in signing papers and making payments to the committee in charge. On the Erie Canal to Buffalo, was the route, from Buffalo on Lake Erie to Cleveland, then down on the Ohio Canal to Portsmouth and down the Ohio River to the Mississippi and up the Mississippi to the Illinois River and up the Illinois to Phantom Creek. Then by wagon overland forty miles to their town of New Era that would grow into a city. Joel would take along his harness tools and a supply of leather. He had found buyers for some of his Arpa properties and was dickering about the others.

Busy as he was, Joel went with Brooks night after night to the revival, "the protracted meetings," in that January of 1837. The evangelist was a thin bean-pole of a figure, stooped at the shoulders, with a long right arm and skinny lengths of bony fingers he shook at his audience. His hands flung glittering digits and raised wonder the bones didn't crack and the fingers drop off as they twisted and writhed to his cry, "Hell is real, hell is deep, and the flames there wrap you in garments of fire and you howl and beg for mercy and you can't shake off those garments. You burn and you suffer and time goes by and your torment never ends because hell is eternal." He bent low with arms stretched out, crouched with his hands close to the floor, then he shot up to his full straight bean-pole height to cry, "God, smite these sinners, crack their heads and open their hearts and bring them burning with conviction of their sins. Pour down on them the guilt of their sins. Let it rain, let it rain guilt on them. Let them know they are, before You, worms in the dust. Let them believe, believe, believe. Let them come forward tonight saying, 'I believe, O Lord, I believe.' "

His long pale face flushed as he accused and denounced. His veins turned purple on his large well-shaped nose, his eyeballs bulged as he threatened, then stood still to ask in sarcasm, "Unduly excited over this work of the Lord, are we? We vociferate and expostulate, do we? Shout and cry as though men and women stand on the flaming brink of hell and the bottomless lake of fire, do we? Let it pass and say we do. We warn them they will go to hell unless they believe, and hell is eternal."

Little he said was new to Joel and Brooks. They had heard parts of it many times over. Yet they were moved. His scrawny face with its contortions, his anger when he wrenched a chair to pieces as no comparison of how God would wreck and tear to pieces the world after Judgment Day, his pantomime in pious quiet posture representing the calm sea after storm, these struck deep to some hearts and to others were seriocomic theater. He had, too, his occasional moments when it was plain that he was repeating himself, saying what he had said many times before to other audiences before he came to Arpa. Yet he gave outcries and he stood listening and humble in long pauses and Joel and Brooks made their guess he had suffered torments in past days and that now he was heavy with anxiety, possibly anguish.

"Peace don't come natural to him," said Brooks. "He'll never be easy till he settles what is on him now, whatever it is."

"He don't believe the hell he preaches," said Joel. "Or else he has sin on his soul and he's afraid he'll go to a hell exactly like he preaches."

"Might be a little of both," said Brooks.

"He didn't give me a scare when he nearly broke his finger-bones shaking them over hell and those garments of fire. I can't see people wearing garments of fire in eternity as punishment because they couldn't see their way to believe like he does."

"Joel, you're not moving over to the Universalists, are you?"

"No, I'm not turning Universalist. I'm just studying in my mind what hell really is. There don't any of them know enough about hell to tell me anything I can be sure of. Everlasting punishment, torment and no end to it, for millions of sinners—and what do they do while they suffer? All we hear is they weep and wail and gnash their teeth. That's too easy, Brooks. You can't burn and burn and go on burning a million years and after that more millions of years. I don't see how God could go that far. Everlasting is a long time, too long. A year of wearing those garments of fire would be enough, a month, a week would be enough."

"Are we getting to be doubters, Joel?"

"What they call doctrine, teaching, I suppose. But not the church itself. We must have a church. Where the church is wrong it rights itself in the end. Take slavery. It is a terrible wrong, a monster of evil. And the cry against it has come out of the church. The abolitionists begin with the churches. Unless the church goes out into the Great Valley and spreads everywhere, the slaveholders will take over the West as they have the South."

"It's tangly, isn't it, Joel?"

"It won't be tangly if we do our work right and save the Great Valley for Christ."

"Will the baby live to see the end of slavery, do you think, Joel?"

"We may see it end, you and I. But if we don't, she will."

"Sometimes I feel it is going to be an awful cost to get rid of slavery."

"What awful cost?"

"Fighting, anger, blood and no end to it. Mobs in Boston, mobs on the Ohio River, mobs here in the Mohawk Valley, mobs ready to kill the abolitionists they call nigger-lovers. Mobs with fist, clubs and stones now. What if they go to fighting with guns?"

"There won't be a war. Something will stop a war coming, I think. And then you may be right, Brooks, a war could come. It is in the eyes of men on both sides. They are ready to kill and kill for what they believe right."

"You turned lawbreaker one night, Joel. You went straight against the law."

"And why shouldn't I? It was right. My conscience don't hurt about it."

"When enough men turn lawbreaker like that, the war comes soon."

"You may be right, Brooks."

"And she will see the war?"

"The baby, you mean?"

"Our baby, she will see a war? I tremble inside me thinking about it."

"Let's not talk about it. We thank the good Lord you're in health and strength and the signs are good."

The last night of the protracted meetings came. The long arms stretched out with shaken fingers, the face of torment writhed, the evangelist cried aloud and moaned low. Sinners in tears groaned as they testified and prayed. One by one, men and women went forward to the mourner's bench and sank to their knees.

"Is there a Christian here who will stand and testify and pray for these lost sheep who have come to the sheepfold of Christ?" the evangelist asked, and man after man stood up to pray for the converts. There was a pause and again the evangelist asked for prayer and fellowship. No one rising, Brooks Wimbler, big with child, slowly rose to her feet. In some quarters there was surprise, amazement at this forward woman. It had never happened before in this Bethesda Church, Arpa, New York. As far back as the oldest elders could remember no woman had made so bold. What was she saying? She was speaking low-voiced. There was a hush wherein the words came clear from her:

"Dear Lord, we speak to Thee with overflowing thankfulness for the hearts that have been changed, for the new grace of life that has come to those who have heard the call to Christ." And Brooks poured and went on pouring out her grateful heart. She came to the end. "Thy will be done, O God, the great Giver of all good things. Thy will be done in the affairs of the high and the low, the rich and the poor, the strong and the weak. May they bow to Thy will, may they bow humbly before Thy will as true Christians accepting Thy decrees and decisions. We are mortal creatures made of dust and given birth by the cunning of the great hands and wise spirit of the Creator, the Maker. Our heads are in the dust before Thee. We bow low and request of Thee great kindness, only great kindness. It is Thou alone who knowest whether great kindness or hard judgment should be measured out. It is Thy heart and pity and love, Thine all-seeing eye, that knows best. We thank

Thee for what has been given us and taken away. We thank Thee for gifts to come, for what is given not to be taken away. We are wanderers in a dark world, pilgrims in a wilderness, stumblers over the hard and weary road. Thou must be our guide and counselor, reaching down Thy great hand to help us when we fall, to sustain us. when we sink and cry. Be with us when old lives go. Be with us when new life comes. We ask it in Christ's name and Thine be the glory. Amen."

They listened closely for Brooksany's every word. To some it was a fresh-flowing Christian prayer, as true and fitting as any man ever spoke from Bethesda pews. To a few it was as though she had stood up and held a private and personal conversation with God about her unborn baby. It was talked about for a long time, how she seated herself quietly alongside her husband, her hands folded, an elbow touching him fondly. Two other women stood up and spoke. Then a third arose. They spoke briefly. Yet it was done. And it seemed natural. In fact it seemed as though it had been done for a long time and it was no longer the law and rule that the woman in church must keep silence and only man lift his voice to God on high.

* * * * * * * * * *

Chapter 9

* * * * * * * * * *

The Time Is Near

THE horses on the towpath of the Erie Canal slipped and slid in the slush of the February thaw. The sun came down welcome. After the heavy snow and days of sleds and sleighing, the shoveled paths had melted and in the center of the roads the sled tracks were now showing the press of wagon wheels in half-frozen mud. Next door to the Wimbler house, Joel and Brooks laughed to see a snow man with a stick in his mouth that had pointed up now drooping and one of his eyes of charred wood sliding down the left cheek.

"The time is near," Brooks had said to Joel that week. Of a morning Joel would wait, wouldn't start for the shop till the girl came who helped with the housework, and the girl didn't leave in the evening till Joel came home.

"Kiss me again, Joel," Brooks would murmur as she clung to him before he went away of a morning.

It was this bright day of February thaw that late in the afternoon a man came in and said Joel must go with him to where surveyors were finishing their work and setting the markers on a two-acre piece of land the man was buying from Joel if the markers and everything looked right. The man was anxious to close the deal and had to drive to Utica that night. They spent time in the justice-of-the-peace office looking over title papers and getting an agreement signed with earnest money down.

Joel, two hours later than usual reaching home, asked himself why he was in a sweat. "You ran part of the way and you're in a fret over being late, no wonder you're in a sweat."

Light came from the front and side windows of the house. The house looked anxious. Why should the house look so anxious? What were the candles in the house seeing?

In a burst of speed he ran through the open gate and along the path, leaped to the porch, checked himself and quietly but swiftly unlatched the front door and stood inside.

The girl came ambling toward him, a mute-faced farm girl, dough-faced, her small eyes blinking and starry, two big fingers on her mouth as her eyes went on blinking, then starry.

Joel felt his knees shaking. He was afraid and wondered a moment if he could go under and fall.

Then came a loud whisper from the girl and he could have cursed her for what came from her in a guttural whisper. "Be quiet. They are all in there and it is all over now. The doctor and the granny woman I run for, they are all in there and it is all over. They have been working and Missus Wimbler take it hard, oh, so hard she cry, and it is all over now."

Till then Joel could have cursed her. Then came more of the whispers and Joel could have kissed her for an angel of light and music. "The baby has come and it is a good baby, a nice big girl. The baby is all right. And Missus Wimbler she put on a smile and she cry and she put on a smile again and she looks white so white on her face and she ask to look at the baby and they hold the baby to her face and she put on a smile and cry and then smile again. She is all right. The baby is all right. The doctor says it is good. The granny woman says it is good. And you must not come in. They say No, you must not come in, not now. They are cleaning up and finishing."

Joel put out a hand, patted the girl's cheek, with "God bless you" to her. He sank in a chair, bent with his head over his knees and moaned, "God bless all, all in this house, God be praised."

Would he have a little supper? the girl asked. No, he couldn't eat now. He moved his chair near the fireplace, watched the logs flicker, stood up and walked back and forth, took a dishtowel and helped the girl dry dishes, sat again by the fire, stood up in a flash when the bedroom door opened and the doctor came out.

"Was she in pain? Did she take it hard, Doc?"

"Usual, Joel, just about usual. She's doing fine, the baby as perfect as I ever saw delivered."

The girl had gone home, the doctor had left saying he would call early in the morning, and it was past midnight when the granny woman stole in to say, "She is awake," and he could go in. "She asks for you but you must stay only a minute and let her sleep, no excitement, you know."

Brooks' eyes opened large, her lips spread to their widest smile, as he gave her a feathersoft kiss, as he pulled back the cover and studied the face of the sleeping baby with a long look, as he turned before leaving, to say, "Rest and sleep, darling. God has heard your prayers."

This was a fresh calendar date, Joel Wimbler was saying before he slept on the living-room couch, ready for any call. Arpa, New York, Springfield, Massachusetts, Albany, Rochester, Syracuse, the Mohawk Valley, this baby might never see them. She was going soon to the Great Valley, to Illinois, to the prairie domain they were to establish for Christ as against Satan. What was this little one to see that would never come before the eyes of her mother and father? The name Millicent picked for her, would she like the name? Would she prefer some nickname made from it? Would she marry a man? Would she marry early or late? Would a man come to him and ask if he could have her? Would it be a lucky marriage or unlucky? Would there be grandchildren? Would his grandchildren look anything like him or Brooks? His final hazy thought was, "You're a fool—if you could know those things beforehand you wouldn't have curiosity enough to live—go to sleep and let Providence and Millicent work it out."

694

Chapter 10

Two Skaters and a Cradle Moon

HE had come at Friday noon to tell her, "I'll go with you this afternoon."

"That's pleasant of you," she had said.

Before turning to leave and as though he needed no answer from her, he had said, "I am doing as you bid me."

It was in her mind but she checked her lips from saying to him, "I *do* hope you're not grumpy about it but you do *say* it as though you're a little grumpy."

He would be back for her after his class at the college in Greek from one till two o'clock and his class in Latin from two till three o'clock. And before the one-o'clock class he would try to find some farmer who was going to the Wahomah neighborhood eight miles away to let them know he could not keep the date for a Saturday-night meeting in the Wahomah schoolhouse. He had been the first abolitionist speaker there, had started its branch of the American Anti-Slavery Society, nursed it along and seen it grow from his personal efforts.

"They think highly of me there and I see them high in devotion to the cause," he had been on the point of telling her.

"You can go to Wahomah any other Saturday," she would probably have answered. "You know there are more than fifty other Saturdays in the year." She had already told him that.

And he hesitated about telling her that when on Saturday he would walk with her past the stores, the depot, the hotel, the blacksmith shop, the wagon teams hitched along Main Street, they would meet people to see the skates slung over their shoulders, people to say, "So you're going skating?" or "So you're going to try the ice?" or "The ice is hard today, don't slip and fall." He could name the gossips whose tongues would relish what they could do with it. "A gay skylarking couple they seem to be, just the two of them going for an afternoon at Pine Flats Pond, I hope they're not up to any mischief."

Another couple was to have gone with them, in a party of four. Each couple would safeguard the other, something like that, anyhow they would be safer against mischievous talk. But the girl in the other couple had brought word, "We had a tiff, it wouldn't be fun and I can't go."

Worse yet, ran a mild fear in him, what would they be saying at Wahomah? It would reach them that he, dedicated to the cause of emancipation, had forsaken them for a merry afternoon of pleasure with a pretty girl on skates. They would ask him about it, some with a solemn doubt of him, sorry for him, others with mischief in their eyes hinting they would like to know if he was going to marry the pretty girl that was taking his time from the cause he had told them he would give his life for. They rated him an earnest Christian. "No softie," one farmer's wife had said, her husband smiling, "Hard as nails," the night a quartet of Hickory Grove farm hands, whisky on their breaths, had ridden up to the schoolhouse, tied their horses, opened the front door and stalked down the center aisle to stand a few feet from the speaker and let him have eggs in a spatter over his face and coat while they yelled, "Nigger-lover! Nigger-lover!" Two had run past him to leap out of windows they opened back of the platform. He had hooked an arm around the neck of one and dragged him six or eight feet to the other window where he locked an arm around the leg of one halfway out of the window, holding them till others came to his help—and the Wahomah constable had hauled them to the calaboose at New Era, where the justice of the peace fined them ten dollars and costs for disorderly conduct, disturbing the peace and assault and battery, and they lay in the calaboose two days till the money to pay their fines was brought in by Hickory Grove friends. Out of this rough play the professor of Latin and Greek at New Era College had come with one black eye, long fingernail scratches on his left cheek, a sharp pain in his crotch from a knee joust, his coat ripped up the back and his clothes and face egg-spattered. "The eggs are fresh, it's not so bad," he had said as he wiped his clothes with his own and borrowed handkerchiefs. "Broken eggs are better than broken heads. And I suppose before this is over there will be many bleeding heads."

Now the mild fear ran in him that from Wahomah the report would spread farther to other towns, villages and crossroads neighborhoods with schoolhouses where he had spoken for the antislavery cause. He had forsaken "the cause" and called off an important meeting with others of "the movement." The report would reach to Galesburg and Peoria and come back to New Era. "It seems that his habits are not steady and he will break a promise to go on high jinks with a girl who twists him around her little finger."

In New Era it wouldn't be so bad. There they knew he had grown up with the girl and he and she had been chums and he had never gone with any other girl. On this Saturday night when he would like to have been speaking at Wahomah, her father and mother were giving a birthday supper for her. She would be twenty years old. He was twenty-four. He had held back from asking her when they should be married. Her folks had hinted the wedding shouldn't be till she was

696

twenty-one. "We don't want her leaving us till she's twenty-one, that's young enough for a woman to get married." They had told him this as though a string of young men were keeping company with her. He didn't quite know what to make of it. They said it a little as though she might have told them to say it. He wasn't sure what was happening inside of her. She was a true abolitionist, of that he was certain. But she wasn't exactly his kind of an abolitionist or she would have let him go to the meeting at Wahomah instead of insisting he must go skating with her Friday afternoon and then come to her birthday supper at her home Saturday evening.

She was so sweet about asking him to come to the dinner that he felt safe in saying to himself, "The affections of her heart are wholly mine and she is destined to be my life companion." When he had repeated this to himself forty times, he knew he was saying it to comfort himself. He recalled one of the two barbers in New Era, snipping with the scissors, blabbing, "There's two kinds of men, one understands women and the other don't." It was about that easy. The barber said he understood women, good and bad, and he liked the bad.

She liked his brown hair and he followed her wish it should grow long and fall over the tips of his ears with tall shags of it combed back from his forehead. And she was fond of his hazel-gray eyes, said she liked them as she peered into them, far back in years when her skirts came to her knees only. He had never tasted whisky, rum, wine, beer or any intoxicating beverage, nor had she. He had never smoked nor chewed tobacco, nor had she. He was twenty-four and in school and college he had been four years ahead of her. She was proud of his record as a class leader, winning prizes in oratory and debate, but when he talked with her about his studying for the ministry, she sort of drew away from him about it and said she wouldn't help him decide. "I'm not good enough to help decide, it's for you to decide." He could see it pleased her more that he was to be a professor. And she had agreed with him that his work as an abolitionist speaker might attract the attention of the American Anti-Slavery Society when he spoke his ambition, "It may be they will call me into the national field." He was sober, stubborn, a wide sensitive mouth, a strong arched nose, a man of books and the platform. His reading and study by an oil lamp till past midnight and rising at daybreak to again read and study had sometimes worn him thin and pale. Then he would pledge himself to early sleeping hours and three hours a day at a sawbuck, coming back to rugged health and hard muscles. For three years he had not failed at every other Saturday and Sunday driving a gig or sleigh to some place miles away where he proclaimed that as Jesus drove the money-changers out of the Temple thus now the aroused Christians of America must purge the nation of the sin of slavery.

There was a mood came over him three or four times a year. He could feel it coming, tried to shut it away from him, and yet it came.

It might last a week. In this mood or series of spells, he felt himself not one man but two men and they fought against each other with arguments. Two voices kept clashing in him. One voice said: "You think for yourself and act for yourself. You are an abolitionist because you have worked it out for yourself in this age and this time. What you do and what you say is purely out of your own mind, your own heart and will. You read and hear what others write and say. Then you form your view, your course of action. It is you who have made yourself an abolitionist prepared for toil, sacrifice or death in a holy cause."

Then the second voice came mocking, "You are a puppet and a creature. You think with your blood and the passion flowing in and from that blood. Where did that blood of yours come from? From your forefathers and dim grandmothers far back. They had to have a holy cause to fight for so they fought under Cromwell and drenched England with blood. They came to America with zeal against sin. They fought against the sins of King George III. Where they found sin they fought it. Every sin they fought against they magnified. It was in their blood. Likewise you have found a sin, slavery, and you have magnified it beyond all fact, truth and common sense. It is in your bloodstream. You are an abolitionist because you can't help yourself. You think you know why you say what you say and why you do what you do. And it is pleasant for you to so think. It has become so great a pleasure to you that it is an indulgence and a sin."

In some spells the first voice would have an answer that gave him comfort. At other moments the second voice would send him leaping out of bed into his clothes to walk miles out into the country at night or in the daytime to a woodpile and a sawbuck and a fury of hard work that cooled his blood.

This mood and these spells he kept a secret from her. And he believed she too had labyrinths of her mind where things went on she didn't care to tell him. If he had talked freely with her he would have told her that these spells seemed in the passing of time to come less often and with less of the anguish there used to be. When he was out crusading, getting subscriptions to antislavery papers, stopping at houses in farms and villages inviting them to come to the meeting where he would speak that night, hunting out important men who leaned to abolition but hadn't come out for it and quietly arguing with them that they ought not to hang back, the dark twisted moods didn't come. It was when he caught himself reading a book for mere pastime or when he was swept into fun and gaiety at a social gathering, a picnic, a hayride party or pitching horseshoes, or singing light-minded songs such as "Captain Jinks of the Horse Marines"—when he caught himself in any sheer joy of living, then the black twists and the groping and that mocking second voice might come pulling him down into

698

searching himself as to why he was doing and saying what he did and said.

Today was the second time she had said to him with a grave mouth and clear eyes, "I'm for abolition, Hornsby, believe me." Then her thin wide lips had parted for a line of white even teeth and her blue eyes had laughed and it seemed to him a laugh came in odd shimmers from the very coils and plaits of her head of chestnut hair as her voice rippled low, "And I'm for a little fun skating this afternoon and a little more fun at my birthday supper tomorrow evening." He had walked away asking whether Millicent was changing or was it himself?

She pulled on heavy wool stockings that came far above her knees. Over these she pulled thick wool leggings fitting snug at the shoe tops of her ankles. Over a wool gown she put on a light jacket and then a heavy one of wool. She ran downstairs to greet Hornsby. He helped buckle her fur-lined overshoes, held her sheepskin coat for her to slide into, watched her put on her fur cap and wind a long red woolen scarf around her neck. He got into his overshoes and cowhide overcoat, stepped out the front door and pulled it tight shut and pulled on the knob again to make sure it was fastened against the wind that roared in the maples and the eaves. She took a peep at the thermometer alongside the door. "Getting colder, five below this morning, fifteen below now, it says."

She skipped to the front gate to open it and wait for him and bowed, smiling for him to come through. She closed the gate and they began their walk of two blocks to the row of stores and the depot and past the blacksmith shop. They saw faces at store windows. They spoke to a farmer who came out to blanket his horses. They walked to where the town houses stopped and the farms began. It was here she began to run at a slow jog—and he joined her.

The wind roared and whirled out of a blue sky brilliant with sun and whimsical with a few flicks of cloud. The bare ground lay frozen and what was left of the last snow two weeks before showed only where the sun couldn't reach, in ditches and rail-fence corners and the north side of sheds and strawstacks.

Half of the mile from the town's edge to Pine Flats Pond they ran at a slow jog. They pulled their scarfs over their faces. They talked small talk or none. She put her red mittens to her face, the first time saying to him with a gurgle through the wool, "Don't get your nose frozen, watch your nose, Hornsby."

They climbed a rail fence, crossed a pasture, a clearing with many stumps, climbed another rail fence, and then through hazel brush and under haw trees, past a clump of walnut trees and then into Pine Flats, where a farmer who drove a wagon and four horses from Maine to Illinois in 1836 wanted to see pines on his place. "They're scraggly," he had said of them, "but they're pines, the spruce and hemlock seem to do best."

There lay the oval of slate-blue, sixty yards long and half as wide, the little pines slung round it moaning as though the wind talked too loud and should learn to be quiet. They stood sweeping their eyes gently over and around it.

"You could hold services here, Hornsby."

"Yes, you could, Millicent."

"It seems old as time and young as this morning when the sun came up."

"Yes, it does seem so."

He put his arms around her and held a kiss hard to her lips. She broke from the kiss sooner than he wished. She took off her overshoes and began putting on her skates. He offered to help. She said they would both be skating sooner if he put his skates on while she put hers on. She was quick at it and had skated the length of the pond before he had his skates on.

The shadow line from the sun crept out over the pond. They skated solo and as partners. The girl whirled and danced, tried for daring feats and fell and slid and laughed about it. Her cap came off after a wild tumble on her head and a long slide. He brought her the cap, sat alongside her, put an arm around her as she fitted the cap on and lifted her face to the sky with a rippling gushing laugh.

"You are a pagan this afternoon," he said.

"And a pagan is one who adores the earth?"

"Adores and worships the earth."

"You can have it," she laughed as she leaped to her feet and was off in a series of whirls.

He found her baffling. He called on his will power. Much can be done by the power of the will, he had heard and read. He would whirl and take breakneck chances and be gay and match her laughter and speed. For this hour he would be her equal in hilarity, joy, abandon. And it was no use. He and she knew it was a forced effort on his part.

They took off their skates, made their way back to the road, and went up a ridge for a look at New Era a mile away. In the last of the sunset they saw the town off to the west in a burning maroon and a creep of dusk and gloaming. The evening lights had come in New Era and they could pick out windows of houses and stores they knew, spots of flame at the brickyard kiln on the edge of town and in the blacksmith-shop forge near the depot.

There it lay before them, a collection of houses, barns, sheds, of horses, cattle, cows, chickens, a railroad depot, with a stockyard and loading platform for steers and hogs, a flour mill, a weekly newspaper and printshop—and men, women and children. It was their town. They had come here as children and seen the empty prairie blocked out in squares of sections and all roads, except two old trails, running at right angles, the main street longer year by year, new cross streets year by year.

They had talked about a mystery that lay before them. Often they had talked about it. Now they stood silent before it. That huddle of people and houses before their eyes had come in twenty years. The little pioneer settlement of strugglers had become in twenty years a town on a railroad with a telegraph operator who would send over "the lightning wires" a message to Chicago, to Buffalo, to Boston, to New York, Philadelphia, Charleston, New Orleans, with sacks of mail thrown off every day for delivery of letters and newspapers at the post office to any who called, letters written only a day or a few days before by people hundreds of miles away, Chicago morning newspapers arriving on the afternoon train, New York and Boston papers three or four days later, New Era in communication touch with all America. Before the railroad and telegraph came in 1854 New Era felt itself a place of loneliness, solitude, an isolation now gone. Less than eight hours by railroad to Chicago now instead of eight days by wagon and team, less than three days to New York instead of thirty days by horse and canal and river routes. When at the national capital proslavery and antislavery Congressmen shook their fists in each other's faces and threatened to shoot and kill each other, the telegraph carried it from Washington to Chicago. What happened the day before was there in the afternoon mail at the New Era railroad depot, with one version in the proslavery *Chicago Times* and another version in the antislavery *Chicago Tribune.*

What happened far beyond New Era came reported so soon after it happened that New Era felt itself part of what was happening far beyond. With the railroad and the telegraph what used to be "far off" was now "near by." Did the honorable United States Senator from Illinois, Stephen A. Douglas, make a four-hour speech in Washington yesterday calling for a bill that would let the people in the Territories of Kansas and Nebraska "vote slavery up or down" as they chose? New Era had the speech on the evening mail today. Did the Springfield lawyer and politician Abraham Lincoln make a reply to Douglas in a two-hour speech at Peoria? New Era soon had the speech. Was there a civil war blazing out in Kansas, abolitionists shooting and sabering proslavery men to death and proslavery forces burning antislavery settlements to the last house, fighting over whether Kansas be voted free soil or slave? The daily newspapers, weekly journals, monthly magazines, the *Congressional Globe*, books and pamphlets arriving on the afternoon mail train, gave New Era as much essential information as New York or Boston.

Part of this the young couple on the hilltop with skates over their shoulders saw as a mystery. In their short lifetime these things had come on the empty prairie with them as living witnesses, with many years to come, they hoped, for them to live as witnesses of a future beyond their reckoning. For the soil, the climate, the people, foretold to them that New Era would stand, thrive, grow, change for centuries, for a thousand years and more, as they believed.

Vaster yet what they saw as mystery lay in the fact that New Era stood as a single specimen, one town, and in these same twenty years New Era had seen companion towns, larger and smaller, by the hundreds arise among the prairies and timberlands west of the Allegheny Mountains and running west into Kansas and Nebraska, running north to the upper limits of Michigan and Minnesota. The voters of New Era, Illinois, and their companioning hundreds of towns with their country neighborhoods, had sent men to Congress in Washington who formed a new balance of power in national politics. Out of the swirl and fury of the seething politics of the time, out of the speed and restless turmoil in the minds of men as carried alive and clashing in the mail sacks flung from the afternoon train at the depot, out of this broiling and crying had come the new Republican party organized the year before to challenge and combat the old established respectable powerful Democratic party.

In this mystery that moved the young man and woman as they watched the town fade in a maroon burning sunset and a creep of dusk and gloaming, followed by the evening lights that picked off windows a mile away, in this mystery the town had a past and present that stood ridiculous, almost silly, alongside the future it was moving into. The past of New Era was so short, so brief a page of chronicles, so easily in the memory of the first hundred settlers, so measurable. Ahead stretched a Future, poignant with echoes on the horizon, faint purple voices in the prairie horizon haze, murmurings shaken with deeds of the Great Unknown, vast and immeasurable foreshadowings.

Before she was born her mother had heard a preacher say, "The Great Valley of the Mississippi will yet burst its swaddling clothes and become a giant that will sway the world!"

They stood a while looking, his right arm around her shoulder, her left arm around his, his mittened left hand holding her right. About themselves they had misgivings that had been growing, uncertain and indefinable. About the town, the prairie, the hundreds of other like towns, the roaring panorama of life that made their country, their America, they had no misgivings. They had their deep-rooted vague personal hopes and schemes but deeper yet ran wonder and dream about their country, their America. Three million people in Washington's time had become near thirty millions now. They expected, if they lived, to see an America of sixty or eighty million people and railroads from the Atlantic to the Pacific. Once he had brought her sentences copied from a letter of John Adams to Thomas Jefferson in 1818:

The American Revolution was not a common event. Its effects and consequences have already been awful over a great part of the globe. And when and where are they to cease?

Again he had copied and brought her sentences from one John Luzac writing from Leyden, Holland in 1780: *"If America becomes free, she will someday give the law to Europe."* They puzzled about that and over words from Barnaby's *Travels through the Middle Settlements of North America, in 1759 and 1760,* reading: "An idea, strange as it is visionary, has entered into the minds of the generality of mankind, that empire is traveling westward: and everyone is looking forward with eager and impatient expectation to that destined moment when America is to give the law to the rest of the world."

This and much else they had talked over, getting nowhere in particular except in wonder and dream about America growing fast and becoming a world power, and for all of her stains, sins and enormities, taking place as a light and an example to the rest of the world. Her great-grandfather had fought in five battles of the American Revolution and ruined his feet at Valley Forge and to the end of his long life had kept his wonder and dream that she now had: it was so rooted and tangled in her that she stilled her tongue as she started to tell what it was like. And as for him, his dim ancestor of the *Mayflower* voyage had helped cut the clapboards for the house of Governor William Bradford at Plymouth, so the family told it, and they were men and women willing to live on ground corn and boiled clams if they could have only the one desire that had made them quit Europe: freedom to worship God according to their own consciences. To him the phrase "human freedom" had a wild delirious taste. On his tongue had been that taste last year when he drove to Rock Island with six shotguns to be sent on farther west in Iowa for an abolitionist named John Brown to use in the fighting and killing in Kansas.

He could sing, with quavers of melody, verses of the Quaker poet Whittier, "Kansas Emigrants," to him a Pilgrim chant and a crusader's oath. He had learned it from stern, bearded men amid their wagons and cook fires, camped outside New Era, Kansas-bound. The tune was "Auld Lang Syne" and they stroked their rifles and lifted their voices:

"We cross the prairie as of old
 The pilgrims crossed the sea,
To make the West, as they the East,
 The homestead of the free!

"We go to rear a wall of men
 On Freedom's southern line,
And plant beside the cotton-tree
 The rugged Northern pine!"

This and much else lurked in their silence as the young couple stood in the dusk and watched the window lights come on in the

703

town. The wind roared around them, a driving wind pitiless with cold. They were still warm from the skating and the walk up the ridge but knew they must soon go.

"No night for driving without plenty of heavy blankets," he said.

"And hot bricks for the feet," she added.

Suddenly she pointed a mitten up at a sky of bluish-white frost sparkles. "Look!"

The prairie moon hung in the sky as a baby canoe, a silver moccasin, perhaps a token of youth and hope.

They were young, they took the moon as young. They ran down the ridge and halfway to town. They stopped for another look at the floating crescent, the phantom cradle of light, perhaps a token of youth and hope.

"Tomorrow," she said when she kissed him as they stood on the doorstep. "Tomorrow I'm twenty."

* * * * * * * * * *

Chapter 11

* * * * * * * * * *

Mibs' Twentieth Birthday

SHE opened her eyes in the morning daylight and lay snug, warm and cozy on a feather mattress that had fitted itself to her body. Over the quilts and blankets she had thrown her sheepskin overcoat. She had pulled the covers up over her chin and lips, leaving her nose free to the air. She reached out a hand and rubbed her nose, the only part of her that was cold. She drew her hand in and put it to warm between an arm and her side.

She listened to the wind sweep and growl under the wide eaves, the wild song of it both hoarse and gay in the cedars and oaks, the slap and brush of one or two branches against the house. The west-window blinds hung open and rattled. The window frames and casings squeaked and shook.

She turned her head for looks at the tall north and west windows with long panes of glass. She studied the tapestry and lace, the flowing and winding lines, woven of frost over the glass.

"It's twenty below, I'll bet," she said. She drew herself down under the covers, got her neck warm, then reached out a hand, rubbed the nose once more, put her hand back between arm and side. Then she closed her eyes and lay completely awake and very alive, asking, "What thoughts should a young woman of twenty have on her first day of being twenty?"

She quoted, "Vanity, thy name is woman," as she found herself asking, "How do I look this day and what will people be saying about my looks?" She quoted, believing it was perhaps from Sir Walter Scott, "Her form was exceedingly fair," and made her guess no one would say that about her and some might have the fancy and not speak it, "Her form was exceedingly *long.*" She stood six feet in height and her hips could curve wider to advantage and her neck might be shorter and no harm done and her eyebrows were rough shags of shiny reddish brown that sort of startled persons who had been smitten with admiration at the smooth white of her pale face and the deep sea-blue of her eyes that could suddenly change to a storm-green. She could name one or two women who would paraphrase Sir Walter Scott, "Her form was exceedingly skinny and when she lifts her eyebrows in that independent way of hers she does seem a little gawky." She chuckled over this in such glee that she found her mouth getting into the hairs of the sheepskin coat collar.

What few times she had gone to church, to prayer meetings, to church "sociables," to parties with other young men, was it too readily accepted and understood that her "steady company" was Hornsby Meadows?

"My looks are good enough for him," she said. And then she asked the question that had been coming to her more often, "But do I want him?" Into what were they moving? What was happening between him and her? His mind was solid, even brilliant, in a way hers never was. He could work out things she couldn't begin on in mathematics, in Latin and Greek. He was, with his many Saturday and Sunday speaking trips over the country, improving in his ideas and the way he put them from the platform and he might yet become a leader and orator of national fame. In his chosen work he steadily improved, that was plain.

A practical man, too, Hornsby could be. He could put a leather sucker on a pump. He could toil hours savagely at a sawbuck and enjoy it. With trousers rolled above his knees he could stand barefooted in a cistern and shovel silt and mud into a bucket for another man to haul up. In a pinch she had seen him make wagon and harness repairs. He had delved into books on chemistry and physics and held long discussions with the professor of those branches at the New Era College. His range of ideas, the grasp of his mind, often amazed her, and she had said more than once, "It may be that I shrink with humility from him and I am not good enough and bright enough to be the life partner he wants and he is mistaken in what he reads in me about what I can give him."

Well she knew that body of his with its massive bear hug. He was six feet three inches, barrel-chested and round-shouldered, with a straight thin-lipped horizontal mouth, his face framed by sideburns. Late every Wednesday afternoon he went to the barber for trimming. Two years now since he had grown those sideburns. He believed he looked too young with a smooth face. He looked older, as a teacher, professor and public speaker should, commanding more respect and a better hearing, with sideburns. He had asked her about them. "If you say so, off they'll go." She was about to say, "Very well, off with 'em, Hornsby, off with 'em." She checked her tongue, saying to herself, "He wants 'em, they're his vanity." Later she had corrected herself on this. The sideburns were not vanity on his part. It seemed worse than that. It seemed that he wanted life to have a more somber dignity than she cared for.

She had overheard a bright cynical student saying, "The professor certainly does appreciate his lilacs." He would stroke them with his hands, fondle them with his fingers, when mentally abstracted during class sessions. He had learned the students regarded this as comical. He had resolved to quit the habit and no longer amuse them. Yet it seemed that when his mind roamed into abstractions of thought, one of his hands would stray to the sideburns and muss them and then straighten them again. He had told her of seeing a daguerreotype of Longfellow and he had modeled his sideburns on those of the New England poet. He had considered a throat muffler with sideburns, like Theodore Parker, the Boston abolitionist preacher. He had considered a full long beard, never to be touched with a scissors, like the New Era hotelkeeper. He had considered chin whiskers, the whole face smooth except the chin. And he had made comparisons of the short well-curled mustache as against the long waxed Texas-longhorn style of the depot agent of New Era. Longfellow suited him best.

He could flare with wrath at the sin of slavery, the sins of rum-drinking and rum-selling, the sins of dancing and card-playing, but he had kept himself from quarrels with her. She had opened the way for tiffs with him. She had been mean and petty at times, she admitted it to herself, in her invitations to him for a clashing argument, a sharp dispute. He had brushed her off with quiet answers, with reasonable questions. He had been so smoothly generous, so sure of himself, that she had sunk into a cold anger, a chill of courtesy to him, for weeks brushing him away from the good-night kiss.

She admired him, and affection, yes, she had affection for him. And she adored the strength of him. Then she asked what was lacking, what was she groping for? Was it some wild call of blood that he didn't arouse and that she was seeking? Had they been these many years so close, cordial and familiar that there was lacking some element of the wild Unknown that she wanted summoning her farther into unpredictable fate? Or could it be that at once and in the same moment he was not enough of a Stranger and then again too much of a Stranger?

These searchings went on till she was saying, "If I go on like this, I'll have a headache along with a heartache on my birthday."

She heard the door of her room open and close and saw her mother, shy and smallish with a narrow face that had a peculiar still look on it. Her mother bent down and kissed her on the cheek and she took her mother's hand and looked up into deep-blue eyes with a dark glow in them and the shy, thin lips parted, saying, "Mibs."

"Yes, Ma."

"You're twenty today."

"Thanks to you."

"I'm glad you say thanks. It means you're not sorry."

The mother turned to a basket of kindling wood, laid pieces in the stove, piled large sticks in, struck a friction match, lighted a fire, then returned to the bedside.

"Have you decided to tell Hornsby you'll marry him a year from now?"

"No, Ma, I can't make up my mind. I'm afraid but I don't know what I'm afraid of."

"It can wait. It's your say-so."

And she patted Mibs' cheek and went out of the room, quiet as the stillness of her face.

The fire in the stove was Ma's birthday present. Usually Mibs was expected to make her own and did.

"Mibs," that had been her baby-talk way of saying Millicent. She had forgotten the names of her two brothers. The one that lived only a week would have been twenty-five years old now and perhaps able to advise her about Hornsby Meadows. The one that died when the runaway horse dashed into a stone fence would have been twenty-three years old. And what would he have been like now, today?

She had been the only child, "much cared for and a little spoiled," said her mother, and "much cared for and hardly spoiled at all," said her father.

On her account, because she was no more than three months grown, they had come near putting off the Boat Trip. Joel Wimbler had said he would chance it but not unless Brooksany was glad and willing to go. "There may be dangers but we'll chance it," Brooksany had said.

In snatches and fragments Mibs had heard of the Boat Trip, and on her fourteenth birthday her mother told her the full long story of it:

They went on board the boat at Utica, taking along horses, wagons, cows and a bull, sows and a boar, plows, tools, cooking outfits, clothes, blankets and pillows, no furniture, no bedding. Their own horses took turns on the Erie Canal towpaths hauling the boat some eighty miles every twenty-four hours. By land on the wagon route it was near six hundred miles and by the water route more than a thousand miles to where they were going to build the town of New Era and set up New Era College. "Human slavery and human liberty cannot coexist in the American Republic," their pastor had declared in the first sermon preached on the Boat. Each weekday afternoon they held prayer meeting in the cabin, "though it was dreadfully crowded." Sunday mornings at daylight they tied up the Boat and attended services at some church or held their own on the Boat.

Thirty-two people in all, they were, twelve of them small children. "The two smallest," said the mother, "were a boy nearly four years old and that was Hornsby Meadows. The other was a wee thing, a babe in arms that cried for nursing at night sometimes, and that was you, Mibs. I remember the first time Hornsby came with his mother and he was shy and she had him reach his chubby hand out and chuck you under the chin just for fun."

At first they were scared when at night the Boat took a thundering thump and there was a grinding noise, but they learned it was only another boat going the other way and the boats would scrape each other. "The Erie Canal is made wonderful," said the mother. "Would you believe once we rode in our boat on the canal high over a wide foaming river that ran under us? Would you believe we rode under a bridge and could see a stagecoach on the bridge over us and the horses galloping full speed? Sometimes we rode between walls of rock sixty feet high on both sides. Once we left you with Mrs. Meadows and Pa and I walked and ran on the towpath alongside the horses pulling our boat."

"Were you good company for each other on the Boat?" Mibs had asked.

"The captain said it was remarkable that so many people who were strangers could make so happy a family. I suppose we all had the same object in view, which was to help settle a new country for Christ.

"Plenty to talk about, with the cities and places we floated past, Rome, Oneida Creek, Syracuse, Otisco, Jordan, Montezuma, Palmyra, the Great Embankment, Pittsfield, Rochester, Lockport, Tonnewanta Creek, and at last Buffalo on Lake Erie. There at Buffalo our canalboat was fastened to a lake steamboat. Our trunks, clothes, cooking outfits, we moved onto the steamer, leaving the captain and pilot on our canalboat.

"The steamboat whistled, I'll never forget the cry of that whistle, and how we moved out of Buffalo on the big blue Lake Erie till we were out of sight of land, the first time your father and me ever got out of sight of land, around us water to the skyline in every direction."

"I want that sometime," Mibs had chimed in. "The most water I've ever seen at once is Pine Flats Pond here and the Spoon River over at London Mills."

Smooth and blue, clear sailing they had over Lake Erie till off Ashtabula. A strong wind began blowing, the sky clouded green and black, a wild rain poured down in sheets, and the steamboat climbed and lifted out of one trough of waves into another. The passengers

708

crowded the little cabin, anxious, kneeling, praying. The canalboat in a twist of a high wash of waters clashed against the stern of the steamer. The captain ordered the canalboat with its captain and pilot cut loose. They sailed on, the canalboat they had bought "on shares" with hard-earned money faded out of sight—gone where?

They weathered the storm, put into the harbor of Cleveland, saw their trunks, clothes and cooking outfits dumped on a wharf rain-soaked. They hunted up fellow churchmen and abolitionists, told their story and heard, "We can take you in if you'll put up with what we've got."

Sad faces they wore waiting the first day, the second day and no news of their canalboat, of their livestock, of their axes, hammers and adzes on that boat, of their plows that were to break the prairie soil of Illinois. Sad faces again on the third and fourth days and no news of their boat they had last seen rising and falling in the high waters and galloping winds of that storm. They were giving up hope and talking whether to go on or turn back.

On the sixth day they knelt in prayer and shouted jubilee hosannahs and again knelt in prayers of thanks and some of them with tears of joy at the sight of their canalboat moving into Cleveland Harbor, the captain saying, "Providence and favorable winds were with us."

Again their horses pulled along a towpath, along the Ohio and Erie Canal, up the Cuyahoga Valley, on through the center of Akron and its twelve locks, over a lake with a bridge for the tow horses. They could see the beginnings of the Great West, the Great Valley, corn rows leafing out in longer and wider fields than they had ever seen, smooth flat prairie land. The oriole warbled summer would come soon, the kingfisher and the redheaded woodpecker swept by on errands of the June month. They moved down the Muskingum Valley into the Scioto. Through Licking Summit they rode, through a cut where the banks rose thirty feet high and the towline ran far and the horses shrank to pony-size before their eyes. Then Circleville, a village in a ring of Indian mounds twelve to twenty feet high, its public square a circle, its brick courthouse built round. Then through Chillicothe and on to Portsmouth where the canal ends and pours into the Ohio River and far up on an eighty-foot bank they could see the wide dirt-bottomed streets of Portsmouth.

And what did Portsmouth say about their coming? Portsmouth was divided. Some said, "Here's that damned Abolition Boat we heard was comin." Seven years before, the prominent citizens of Portsmouth had made a public ceremonial of driving eighty free Negroes out of town with warnings never to return if they wished to live. Along the route across Ohio they had been tagged with that nickname, the Abolition Boat. In one town came men whose leader said, "We're a committee," in a tone as though if you were a committee without a doubt you had authority. The hip-pocket bulge of the leader and two others perhaps meant revolvers. One wore a belt with a leather sheath and a knife handle sticking out from it. "There's some people stole a nigger and we're lookin for the nigger and the people who stole him," said the leader. They searched the Boat and went away scowling as though what they hunted might yet be hidden on the Boat.

Twice they had been warned that in a town ahead there was a mob getting ready to swoop on the Boat and put everybody ashore and sink the craft. In each of those towns a gathering of men, women and small boys had met them with jeers of "Nigger-lovers" but no violence. Some of the men held rocks in their hands, others had clubs, but the hour passed with a few insults that fell on the air like a bad odor to blow away on the next fresh breeze.

The float down the Ohio River went slow. At one stop three ministers called to warn them. At Cincinnati they would get a public reception. A meeting had been arranged for them at the river front. One leader had said, "We'll never let that boatload of damned Yankee abolitionists set a foot in our city." So they kept their eyes out nearing Cincinnati. When they tied up the Boat they sent the women and children ashore to stay with friends while the men kept watch on the Boat and stood ready to fight. They found it was a false alarm. They met ugly looks, here and there a few threats, but no blows struck.

Now came another trouble. Abner Henshaw, who had put more into the Boat from the beginning, the only man of them left with any money, was quitting them. He had been down two days with malarial fever. At Portsmouth they had buried a woman, the first to die. Halfway to Cincinnati they had buried a man and a boy. The overcrowding, the bad food, the change to a climate they weren't used to, the worry over going so slow, the bitter disappointment that it was taking them twice as long as by wagon on the land route—from this Abner Henshaw figured that worse lay ahead and more deaths than he cared to see.

They had decided that when they came to the Mississippi River going upstream they would need a propeller on the stern, worked by a horse on board in a treadmill. And Abner Henshaw was the only man on board who had any money left to pay for this propeller. The others had put their last dollars into buying the Boat and provisions. They pleaded with him. They prayed with him. He was hard to win. In the end they won him. And they might not have won him but for the help of Andrew Biddings, a wheelwright in Cincinnati, a convinced and fighting abolitionist.

During the several days' stay, while the new propeller was being rigged on the Boat, Henshaw had his horse and buggy unloaded off the Boat and drove around Cincinnati with his wife and daughter. One of the buggy shafts broke and to get it fixed Henshaw hunted up a wheelwright who was more than pleased to hear about the scheme to settle a town and build a college on virgin prairie in north-central

Illinois and "save the Great Valley for Christ and human freedom." The more Henshaw told about it the more interested was Biddings. Mrs. Henshaw was taken to Mrs. Biddings and they visited and talked and Mrs. Biddings rated it "a grand plan."

"You ought to go on with your boat," said Biddings. "You're working for God and the freedom of man. I will sell out in Cincinnati and join you next year with my four sons, my daughter, my adopted daughter, and the woman who helps at our house. You're on the right track. I'll be with you next year and you'll see me building houses and ready for business with a wagon and carriage shop."

"And you mean," Mibs interrupted her mother telling this, "you mean if Mr. Henshaw's buggy shaft hadn't broken in Cincinnati he wouldn't have seen Mr. Biddings and the Biddings family would never have come to New Era and they might be down there in Cincinnati yet?"

"Exactly, Mibs. It's what they call Providence and circumstance.

"Some of us were too outspoken, I suppose," the mother went on. A steamboat on a Sunday morning had unloaded passengers next to their canalboat and three ministers, delegates from Southern states to a church convention in Cincinnati, came on board and invited the Yankees from New York to attend services. A Utica woman asked in a sharp voice, "We see you arrive this Sabbath Day on that steamboat?"

"True enough you did," smiled a cordial pastor.

"We do not attend meetings conducted by men who travel on the Sabbath Day," came the high-toned voice of the Utica woman in reply and rebuke.

Brooksany Wimbler felt at the time, "She was too superior. She needn't have thrown that in their faces on a pleasant Sunday morning."

"We're not Yankees, we're from New York," a woman had corrected a Southern delegate moving off the boat.

"We always heard New York Yankees are the meanest," came a soft answer with a faint smile.

Down the Ohio River and the water low, the air miasmic, they moved, passed by steamboats, meeting steamboats, passing flatboats, "broadhorns," and rowboats, the monotonous summer sun scorching them by day, mosquitoes a pest and a plague at night, fever and ague bringing more than half of them down disabled or sick.

"Most of us able to stand were half-sick, weak and give out," said Brooksany Wimbler to her daughter. "You too looked pale and puny, sort of give-out, like you didn't care to live. I knew many a day I didn't have the right kind of milk for you. I never before nor since had fear about you like I did those days. I prayed God, not out loud so the others could hear me, of course, that He would forgive me for taking you on such a journey."

The sun poured down sultry and blistering on the crowded boat and midday they tied up on shore and took the shade of friendly trees and what river breeze there was. Those who could stand and walk did their best at helping those who couldn't. They traversed a canal around rapids at Louisville, reached the miasmic bottom lands of Illinois and moved upstream on the Mississippi River.

The new propeller worked at first. Then it didn't. A part of it fell in the river. Danny Hilton, a bright boy of sixteen and one of the few on the Boat still rugged and healthy, got out of his clothes and dived into the mud three times and brought up the missing part. The Boat moved on. Again another part of the propeller fell off and again Danny dived and they could navigate. The captain's watch fell out of his pocket into the river and Danny brought that up. A little girl fell overboard and Danny leaped to the water and brought her alongside.

"A handsome boy and not only ornamental but useful," said the captain to Danny's mother.

"I want him useful," said the mother, "but if he can be ornamental too that's so much extra I thank the good Lord for."

The Boat snagged on a sandbar and they were two days getting off it. Again they were snagged two days on a sandbar and had to wait till they could signal a steamboat to pull them off. Again a propeller part fell off and Danny Hilton dived and brought it up.

By now more than two out of three were sick in their bunks and some of those who could stand and walk were shadows of what they had been when they boarded the Boat on the Erie Canal at Utica, New York, ten weeks back. The four biggest men on the Boat, heavy-boned and muscular men, six-footers, lay yellow-faced and helpless.

They came to St. Louis, took on stores of better food, and called in the best of doctors, who helped with medicine and advice.

A man came on board and made an offer of a thousand dollars cash for the Boat. The answer was No. They were now so near to the end, they must go on according to the Plan.

Before making their turn into the Illinois River they stopped one day to bury a husband and father and the next day the wife and mother, leaving two little ones orphaned.

Up the Illinois River they steered their course, scorching sun by day, cool mist and ravenous swarming mosquitoes by night.

"That was when you were weaned of me, Mibs. My milk had give out. When the Boat made stops Danny Hilton ran to one house after another till he got cow's milk for you. Some days it didn't keep. I spooned the clabber to you and you spit half of it out. I said at that you were plucky."

Again on a sandbar the Boat lay snagged two days. A child died and they buried it there in the sand, the pastor rising from a bunk, white and tottering, to say the last sacred words the father and mother too weak and far-gone to witness the burial.

They had one hope left. They waited for a steamboat that would tow them to Phantom Creek. The hours went by. And at last around

712

a bend, her smokestacks puffing, came their hope, and the word was, "Yes, we'll tow you."

The last ten miles of more than a thousand, the last day of the last and eleventh week of boat travel came to an end, came to its evening shadows when the few who could stand and walk had barely the strength to carry and lay under the sod two of the big men who had wasted away.

They were at Phantom Creek, the point aimed for, there at last and only one among them willing to say he could sit a horse and not fall off. This was Danny Hilton. He was lightheaded and had dizzy spells but he was sure he could sit a horse and make the forty-mile ride to the settlement of New Era.

The next day came a procession of teams and wagons, men to help, women to nurse, blankets, food, medicine. The sick were lifted into wagons. The drivers did their best for smooth riding and few jolts to those who lay on blankets spread over the wagon floor and the hot sun of near mid-August pouring down on them.

Ten miles from Knoxville they lifted out the cold body of Abner Henshaw and buried it under a haw tree, his wife and daughter in the same wagon too weak to rise, hardly aware of their loss. At Knoxville the captain of the Boat breathed his last and was laid in the village burying-ground.

At New Era a one-room cabin had been made ready for those worse off to be laid on pole beds laced with ropes to hold mattress ticking stuffed with straw. Others of the sick were laid on chests that held clothing and towels and the sick had to be moved when the chests were opened. A large box stove for cooking, in the center of the room, added to the heat of the August sun on the roof and walls. Over the open windows hung cheesecloth to keep out flies and mosquitoes; the night breeze came grateful and in the quiet they could hear in the corn rows the rustle of dry leaves among ripening ears of corn turning yellow and hard and they could hear it as half a promise.

"A few more died but most of us lived," ran the end of Brooksany's story to her daughter. "The suffering, the mistakes, the way death reached its claws and came so near taking you and your father and me, the skinny thing you were when we lay in that first bed in New Era, I don't like to go back to it for the dark thoughts that came."

That was twenty years ago, the Boat Trip, and it was last summer, at the county Old Settlers Picnic, Mibs had heard the wife of the professor of rhetoric and declamation read a paper on how the Boat was named the *Argo* and they were supposed to be Argonauts as in an old Greek story where the sailors never knew what was coming next and when it came it was another storm or another murder, or as Mibs had heard Hoosiers from Hickory Grove say, "A power of bad luck and a heap of hard times."

"The story of our boat," read the professor's wife, "commissioned to carry Christian settlements, churches and colleges into the Empire of the New West, is a nobler theme for a classic and immortal epic. The trials and troubles that befell the crew and passengers of the modern *Argo* were almost equal to those met by the crew of the ancient *Argo*."

The woman reading had been a six-year-old girl on the Boat and had sometimes asked if she might hold Mibs in her arms because her doll had fallen overboard. Mibs saw her mother's eyes close and her shoulders cramp forward when the woman read: "Their long, tedious journey through malarial regions in the hottest and most unwholesome period of the year, brought them to their destined port a company of invalids, some of them so sick that they passed almost directly from the decks of their ship to the Golden Shore, while others were conveyed in extemporized ambulances to New Era, where they received a warm but sad welcome to their new home."

Mibs later found herself saying, "Extemporized ambulances, extemporized ambulances, what did she mean?" and suddenly answering, "She meant wagons with blankets. Then why didn't she say so?" with a later afterthought, "I'll bet the professor *did* write the paper for her like the gabmouths say." And once sitting between her father and mother on a wagon ride she cocked an eye at her mother, and, "I *do* like a ride in this extemporized ambulance."

And Ma had spoken sharp, "I know it's funny, Mibs, and I could laugh with you if tweren't for a thing I remember." And Ma spoke more soft. "It was one of the hard early years, the ground wet and soggy so many weeks the corn and wheat came poorly. One winter day we had run complete out of flour, scraped the bottom. And I went to that girl's mother to borrow. And she was near to scraping the bottom too. And she offered to divide what little she had. I refused. And that woman pressed on me the half of what she had of flour. She put the backs of her two hands together and pushed them toward me and parted them with a sweep and spoke like a summer shower in dry time, 'The good Lord knows I don't want to live if my neighbors don't.'"

From then on whenever the phrase "extemporized ambulances" came to Mibs, as it would regularly, she would be saying right after it, "The good Lord knows I don't want to live if my neighbors don't."

The wood in the stove crackled, a sheet of iron went slambang as its metal expanded with the heat. Mibs could feel the first little wave of heat come to her face. She would pile in more wood. By noon there would be a trickle of water from the center of one windowpane and a hole of clear glass giving her a look at the sky, the five cedars and two oak trees her father planted years ago.

On this morning of the twentieth birthday, an old feeling again ran in her, an old resolve shaped itself in a rebirth. She went over again the Boat Trip as told by her mother. She knew that her mother had in the telling skipped misery and filth hard to remember and not easy to

714

tell. She saw her mother shake in the telling, cutting the end short, with tears in her eyes. The words "mistakes," "suffering" stayed deep with Mibs. They had known there were going to be mistakes and suffering and they were not afraid. And Mibs was shaping again her old resolve: "I shall live the life ahead of me expecting mistakes and suffering and I shall not be afraid."

She had been given every care and affection, the spoken fear of Pa and Ma being that they might spoil her but would take their chances. "You can have your way," her mother could remark. "If people say you're spoiled it will be you that's spoiled yourself. I wouldn't go so far as to say you're pretty to look at. You may be. You'll find out about that soon enough. I'd like to teach you, if I could, that what's under the looks is what counts most. The looks change and wither in time. What's under the looks, if you pray and grow and do rightly, that will keep like evergreen, never betray you, never make a fool of you."

From Pa and Ma she had heard for years the phrase "work for work's sake." It was part of Pa and Ma. There was a natural health and righteousness about work for work's sake. Of course, wood had to be cut and carried in, the cow had to be milked, the horse fed, the barn stable cleaned, the manure piles hauled away, the privy cleaned out once a year, water pumped and carried into the house from the well for drinking and cooking, rain water pulled up with a bucket from the cistern for washing faces, clothes, dishes. Of course, chamber pots had to be carried out, chickens killed and dressed, eggs hunted, rats and mice trapped, weeds cut, leaves raked, washing, ironing, mending, walks shoveled after a snow, the horses combed and curried, the cows in summer driven to pasture, the garden rows of sweet corn, potatoes and cabbage hoed and the beds of onion and carrots weeded, and in the house sweeping and scrubbing, the cookstove fire started every morning, the wood-stove fires kept going in the sitting room and other rooms in winter, trips run to the cellar for vegetables, apples, preserves, jellies, cider and the tub of brown apple butter that had been put up in the fall, trips to the garret in late winter and spring for the dried apples that hung strung on twine in the peak of the garret roof besides hazelnuts, hickory nuts and walnuts in sacks on the garret floor. Helping hands were called for when a fresh calf was dropped or a new colt foaled.

In many of these chores Mibs, as she had grown, had shared more and more. She could remember the harder earlier days when they worked with neighbors at making soap from wood ashes they saved, when her mother carded wool and spun cloth for their clothes, when before the first butcher shop had opened for trade the neighbors joined in a hog-killing and she had carried home "cracklings" and a pail of thick red fluid from which Ma had made "blood pudding."

What home chores Pa did were before and after his work at the harness shop, where often he had spent his time from a little after daybreak till sunset. Then Pa had thrown in with Biddings and others on buying land tracts they sold at big profits. They had seen contracts of a dollar and a quarter an acre of land go to six dollars in three years and rise to twenty dollars. And Pa had many days left the harness shop to his apprentice while he had filled a contract with the railroad for ties cut from a piece of timber he had bought cheap from a farmer joining an outfit known as the Jayhawkers and headed for the Great Plains, California and gold. In the brickyard and in a sawmill near Pine Flats Pond, Pa had small interests paying well on the money he put in.

"I guess we can say we're well-off now," said Pa at supper one evening.

"You seem a little worried about it, Joel," said Ma.

"I am. We're well-off, sure enough, but I'll be damned if we're going to get proud about it."

"Why, Joel, you're swearing. Is it a swearing matter?"

"Why isn't it? Haven't we seen two of our deacons losing whatever peace of God they ever had because they don't know what-all to do with the land, money, investments and schemes they've got into that keeps them awake nights? I believe it what they say about one of 'em, that he heard it told he was greedy about land and he answered, 'Why, I'm not greedy about land, I only want what joins mine.' And he couldn't get along with the harness we make here in New Era. He had to go to Chicago and get harness with brass rings and fancy brass spangles and a new team of glossy black horses to pull a carriage he bought in Chicago that has curtains and little glass windows."

Pa went on further about the two deacons getting suits of broadcloth, the coat corners coming to their knees. "And silk stovepipe hats and studs in their boiled shirts. And to think we saw 'em skinny and yellow and near dead when we took 'em off the Boat at Phantom Creek."

There was a long silence. Mibs' face had the stillness of her mother's.

"What I mean is," Pa went on, "I'm not going to talk scandal. They're putting on the agony. That's what people say. I'll talk about it here but not outside my home. And what I say here is we're well-off but just because we're well-off I'll be damned if we're going to get proud, I'll be damned if we're going to put on the agony."

"It's the most profane evening we've ever had in this house," said Ma. "And when I well think about it I guess it might be you're justified, Joel. We're going to look out and not be proud."

"I heard them talking one day," said Pa. And he mimicked them. " 'It's a good piece uh proputty, say I, and I'm goin to hold on to it.' "
" 'That proputty you got over on Haw Creek, has it got a right smart uh black walnut on it?' "

"Proputty! Proputty!" Joel wailed in shrill falsetto, screwing up his face in derision.

There was further silence and they drifted into more pleasant talk after his subdued declaration, "We'll make out without getting crazy

716

over property and finery and show-off. I'm praying we'll never forget the first of the Seven Deadly Sins is Pride."

She had heard Ma say, "Pa can be strict when he has to." This was when Pa had spoken and voted for a man to be read out of the church for "timber-taking," or "hooking timber," as it was called. For this offense more members had been read out of the church than for drinking, profanity, or any other doing counted wrong. A member caught one time at cutting wood and hauling it off another man's land was warned and when caught a second time, out of the church he went.

In this case where Pa was "strict" he had caught the man once and joked about it, for the man said he needed firewood at home. Again, the second time, Pa was easy with the man and didn't report him to the church. But when Pa found out the man was really cutting railroad ties and getting cash for them, the third time he caught him he brought the case before the church trustees. "It's time to throw him out. He's hooking timber and selling it. He's a timber thief." And Pa warned the man, "If I ever catch you on my land again I'll beat seven bells out of you."

Another time Pa was strict was when he saw his lawyer and had him foreclose a mortgage on a small farm near Rolling Prairie and make out a deed to Joel Wimbler. Ma noticed Joel sort of moping for some days afterward. She said to Mibs, "It don't sit well with him." She had learned as Joel had that the farmer, a Welshman with six children too young to help work the farm, had lost half his hogs from cholera, a storm had flattened his wheat and a smut ruined most of the crop. Ma would have spoken to Pa about it but she saw what was working in him. He came home one day, cheerful and lit-up. He waited till near the end of supper before he said careless-like, "I wasn't satisfied in my conscience with what the lawyer called my equity in that Rolling Prairie farm. The lawyer is fixing to turn the damned farm back to the Welshman. He needs it worse'n I do. He'll pay me, but I'll sleep better if he never pays."

Ma smiled. "I guess it was a damned farm, after all," which was the first and only time Mibs had heard her mother say "damned."

"Is Pa brave?" Mibs at nine years of age had asked after Ma had been reading to her from Sir Walter Scott. Ma said it was six years ago Pa was riding from Wahomah with another man driving a bobsled and they saw a wolf jogging along in the sled tracks ahead of them. They agreed they would drive fast and when they came up with the wolf, Pa was to jump out and hit it over the head with an ax handle. The driver put the whip to the horses. They came up to the wolf and Pa jumped out and ran to where the wolf sat in the snow tuckered-out. The nearer Pa came to the wolf, the more he didn't like the way the wolf was showing his teeth. Pa slowed down, looked at the wolf awhile and then walked to the road and walked two miles home because the bobsled horses had run away. "It wasn't what you would call a real adventure," said Ma, "yet I think Pa did pretty good to even think he could kill a wolf with an ax handle."

Two years later it was, as Ma told it, that Pa a mile out of New Era, driving a team and wagon, saw a big wolf near the road digging away at a gopher hole or rabbit nest. Pa stopped the team and hollered at the wolf but the wolf went scratching away and didn't notice Pa. "So, Mr. Wolf, you won't look or listen?" said Pa. And he jumped out, stripped the harness except the bridle off one of the horses, jumped on her back and made straight for Mr. Wolf. The wolf gave Pa a hard run across a field toward a slough and Pa with a pitchfork ready to jab when he should come alongside the wolf. Pa was gaining and expected to win. But the wolf knew his slough. Pa came to a dead stop when the horse began sinking in mire over the fetlocks.

And Mibs had asked for more stories about Pa and the prairie wolf and Ma had said that since those two wolf hunts Pa wasn't interested in the animal. "When he meets one now he gives it a look you'd call funny rather than ugly and drives on."

* * * * * * * * * *

Chapter 12

* * * * * * * * * *

Prairie Town and People

THE chill had come off the room. The wind rattled the blinds. Mibs could see from her open mouth only a faint smoke mist of her breath. She slid out of bed, flung off her light-gray woolen nightrobe, whirled on two feet, whirled on one foot, touched the low ceiling with the flat of her hands, stooped and touched the floor rug with the flat of her two hands, did her best at reaching the ceiling plaster with a high kick that brought her toe about the height of her head. She had heard of dancing women doing this rigamarole of a morning, worked it out as fun to start the day and wake up from head to toes. Ma would ask how she was feeling and hear "Tiptop, Ma, tiptop."

She was no time getting into underclothes, high wool stockings, shoes lacing above the ankles, a thick wool skirt and a blouse of fine blue wool cloth that she had sewed herself and Ma had been pleased to say, "You're clever, Mibs, it fits your shape and you couldn't have done better at the Boston Store in Chicago."

She stepped to a window, breathed at the center of a small window-pane, rubbed her fingers on it, peeped out through the glass with one eye and saw snow falling, a light cover of it on the ground, skirls of snow blowing in a rough wind. "Tiptop for my birthday," she said. "Snow on your birthday and you marry in a year, I've heard, but I don't believe it."

She skipped downstairs to the kitchen, peeped into the oven and sniffed at the ham baking, heard her mother say everything for the supper had come straight out of New Era except the coffee and the spices for the ham and that she and Pa "thought it would be a kind of a novelty" if they could have some escalloped oysters. Pa had seen a five-gallon tub of oysters unloaded at the depot and they couldn't have been more than six or seven days coming from New York and in this weather they certainly kept good. So Mibs with a gallon tin pail started for the grocery store in her fur-lined overshoes, sheepskin overcoat, red scarf and white woolen hood, red yarn mittens, feeling very snug.

She near stumbled on a snow-covered nail sticking up from the three-plank sidewalk. Two weeks ago it had torn a hole in one side of an overshoe and sewing the split edges together as neat as she could she said, "Dodgast that nail, I'll get a hammer and knock it into place," and then it had slipped her mind. Later this very day she must see to it.

She waited for a large hog of sagging flanks to pass in front of her. He had finished ears of corn in the road and was foraging further the same as other hogs loose around the town raising talk the town should have an ordinance compelling, yes sir, compelling owners to keep hogs in pens where hogs belong. Mibs saw the wagon from which the corn ears had spilled over into the road. The driver had turned in the driveway to a barn where he was going to unload it for the two horses, six hens and a rooster, and a hog they kept at that house. Before swinging his big scoop shovel into the corn the man warmed himself with throwing his arms wide apart and hitting his chest with his hands. Mibs recognized the man. On his farm near town she had seen in the stubble the scattered piles of corn he hadn't room for in his crib and the corn lay through rain and snow without spoiling, for it was that kind of a winter for corn.

Now it crossed her mind she had seen that hog and met him before. He belonged to an Irish family across the tracks, Paddy Whalen who worked on the railroad section in all weathers seeing the rail joints kept together and no spikes loose in the ties and the roadbed smooth so the passengers wouldn't be jolted too rough. "A little joltin is good for 'em but not too much," Paddy would say. His stout wife did the washing and ironing for the Wimblers, Paddy coming with a wheelbarrow for the big wicker basket of washing, the section boss letting him have the railroad wheelbarrow for this weekly chore. Mibs had seen Paddy point at the wheelbarrow and laugh, "She's a help in the time uh need. I've pushed gravel and stone and sand in her and spikes and tools and dinner buckets. The house I live in, that's one home, and the wheelbarrow that's my other home and it's between these two handles I spind my life. You can see on those handles the smoothin my hands give 'em."

719

The Whalens had a fifteen-year-old boy Tim the schools of New Era couldn't help much. Two years behind in his classes, Tim mocked at book learning, reading and arithmetic, liked fighting better than any other boy in the schoolyard and took on fellows bigger than himself. His thirteen-year-old sister Maureen, the Wimblers had her at the house often of Saturdays for light housework and for her company, a freckle-faced, carrot-headed, skimpily bodied girl with bright dancing hazel eyes, a nose with a slight upturn and a mouth of a mournful sweetness and a sudden lovely smile. Once Mibs had crossed the tracks and made her way to the block of one-story houses of two to three rooms each where common laborers and later arrivals in New Era lived. She was going to ask if Maureen could come over to help her and Ma at some spring housecleaning. The front door of the three-room Whalen house was open that mild April evening and Mibs stood in the open doorway and stood still and didn't make herself heard for what was going on. The voice of Maureen came clear and precise, even emphatic, and the words from Maureen ran, "Senator Douglas arose and demanded an immediate roll call, declaring that the issue was of such vast moment that it could no longer be postponed."

Mibs threw her head one side and looked in to see the profile of Maureen, with her feet on the rung of a chair, Maureen's eyes fixed straight on a newspaper she clutched with her two hands, her neck tensed and her head thrust forward as though she might any moment leap through the newspaper. Facing Maureen sat her father and mother leaning forward, wrapped and enthralled in their child who could read to them from the printed page they had not had the time nor the chance to learn to read, who could give them the latest report of the deeds and words of their political hero, that fearless leader of men, United States Senator Stephen A. Douglas. Maureen read on, sometimes swiftly and again halting over the words Douglas spoke. "Leave the people—perfectly free—to form and regulate their—domestic in—do-mes-tic in-sti-tu-tions—in their own way—"

"In their own way," came the father's guttural approval, with a nod of the head and his eyes shining. Paddy Whalen had his shoes off, a stub clay pipe held out from his face, his left elbow jutting out, knuckles and a clenched fist pressed to his leg, very alive.

"Subject only to the—only to the—" Here Maureen paused stiff and tense and then with near a shout, "to the Constitution of the United States."

"That's it," came the father's keen and caressing voice, "the Constitution!"

"That is all there is of the Nebraska Bill," Maureen read on. "That is—that is—the doctrine of popular sovereignty," Maureen knowing that she had sort of slurred and mangled "sovereignty," and she would have to look that up in the dictionary or ask somebody about it. "It's a crazy word to look at, that sover—sov—" and she refused to tackle again those messy syllables "eignty." Then came smooth going, Maureen proud of herself as were her two listeners, Senator Douglas saying, "I know the Democrats of Illinois. I know they always do their duty. I am not afraid they will be led off by a handful of traitors into a Negro-worshiping, Negro-equality community. Illinois has always been, and always will be, true to the Constitution and the Union."

"That's it—the Constitution and the Union," Paddy Whalen repeated.

And about there Mibs had spoken her pleasant inquiring, "Hello? Hello? Could I come in?" and arranged for Maureen to be on hand the next day, learning from Maureen that nearly every day she read to her father and mother a column or two from the weekly Chicago Times and on Sundays two or three columns. Mibs had told Hornsby Meadows of this remarkable little reading circle where the literate child read to the illiterate parents the latest political news as printed in a violently partisan organ. Hornsby had thereupon subscribed for the weekly antislavery Chicago Tribune to keep company in the Whalen house with the proslavery weekly Chicago Times over the summer and fall months of 1856 before the election in November. "He may vote Republican, he may vote for Frémont," said Hornsby. But Paddy Whalen didn't. He voted Democratic, for James Buchanan for President, and Mibs heard Maureen, "My father said we were wasting our time with that Republican paper, it was all lies and a waste of time."

"Did you read it for yourself, the Republican paper?" Mibs asked.

"Yes."

"And what did you find out?"

"There's two sides to all this politics and it's so mixed up I don't know who I'd have voted for in November."

A keen bright girl, thought Mibs, for Maureen had been the first person to make her curious about what was in the Constitution of the United States and one Saturday afternoon they had read it aloud together, Mibs frankly telling Maureen she wasn't sure what it meant and they would read it together again and talk with lawyers and older people about it.

Mibs crossed the tracks and went to the Whalen home to make sure Maureen could come in the afternoon and evening and help with the supper.

"And it's twenty you are today," said Mrs. Whalen. "And you'll find it's soon enough you'll be forty." She left her ironing board to shake Mibs' hand and say Maureen had gone out with a sled to join another girl at a romp in the snow. "She'll be along quick now. It's cold. The pump froze last night. We had to pour a wash boiler of hot water down it to get it going." A short, stout, cheery woman whose eyes snapped when she talked. Smoking was not a habit with her but she liked a pipe now and then and Mibs had seen her sucking at a clay stem with a clay bowl and curling her lips as she puffed. Of other women in New Era who smoked, the folks knew only one, a widow of a veteran of the War of 1812 and she sat on the front porch summer evenings calmly puffing, a seventy-year-old white-haired woman puffing in a rocking chair, an image of contemplation. Mibs when years younger would join another girl and they would walk slow and pass the house looking out of the corners of their eyes to see the curiosity of a woman smoking, saying at home and at school, "We saw her, we passed Mrs. Ilbersee's house and saw her with a pipe in her mouth and the smoke coming out when she puffed."

Beyond the depot Mibs saw men in the snowfall driving hogs up from the stock pen onto a loading platform where the hogs were pushed into a railroad stock car, squealing and grunting, to be "picked up by the local freight," as the depot agent would say. Mibs had seen the foot tracks of those hogs on Main Street and one of the men loading the hogs she knew for a farmer six miles out who must have started about daybreak afoot to drive them in for shipping. He was a deacon in the Presbyterian church and people said he always did well with hogs, his advice worth hearing on what to feed swine and when to sell. For a year he had been a teacher in the Bible class in Sunday school and Mibs liked the friendly way he would read a chapter and give his interpretation and then ask others in the class for their interpretation. Mibs resented the cheap humor, the petty and malicious fun of people saying, "If John Ankers knowed the Bible like he knows hogs he'd be a pretty good Bible-class teacher." Someone brought this to John Ankers and he said he drove over to Galesburg one rainy night and heard Ralph Waldo Emerson lecture and one sentence had stuck in his mind, "The hog never looks at the stars." Ankers had thought about it, and, "I wouldn't be so proud as to say I knew what Mr. Emerson meant but I think I could name New Era church members who think he meant something else than I think."

Mibs had been in the same classes in New Era College with Mr. Ankers' daughter Rebecca and they had graduated the same year and Rebecca right off married a classmate and went East to help him finish his studies and go to China as a missionary. Mr. Ankers had pleaded with the couple to stay in the United States and help Christianize their own country but the young husband said "the call to work among the heathen" pressed too deep on his soul. Mibs had heard Mr. Ankers say to her father, "I try to tell that son-in-law of mine there's enough heathen to work on in Illinois and New Era without traveling months on months clean over to the other side of the globe where they don't know his language and by the time he knows theirs he's played out." Over there now loading his hogs, the stalwart man in a stocking cap, boots and leather mittens, with a hurt that ran sharp in him because of his six children his eldest and favorite was going to China and would stay years and he'd probably never see her again and it was almost like she was dead while living. That was the way he had talked to Joel Wimbler that night. Mibs said to herself, "A hog never looks at the stars," and her eyes caught the depot agent with icicles hanging from the ends of his drooping Texas-longhorn mustache.

The store and shop buildings that faced Main Street had every one of them human faces and stories for Mibs. The shoemaker Jacob Dilley, the time had been he made boots and shoes from start to finish. "I'd measure the feet and then I needed only the leather and my tools." Now he would go into sad streaks about how in Boston and Philadelphia they had machines making boots and shoes by the millions. "My brother learned the trade with me and did nice in Ohio till the machine shoes come. Then he gets tired puttin on half-soles and patches like I do now. He goes to Philadelphia and stands at a machine drivin pegs into shoe soles fourteen of them a second—would you believe it— fourteen a second. Next to him another machine makes pegs fast as they're wanted. Upstairs his wife stands at a stitchin machine. She watches the machine so it don't go wrong and feeds it what it needs. From the first floor to the third they just feed leather and thread and wood to the machines and it comes out boots and shoes. The real shoemakers are all dead, I tell you, Miss Wimbler." And he had brushed a hand along his leather apron and repeated it in case she hadn't heard him the first time, "Dead, dead, dead." The shoe customers now went to a corner of the big dry-goods store and picked their sizes and styles and if what they wanted wasn't in, it could be ordered and soon on the way from Chicago or St. Louis jobbers. The sad streaks of Jacob Dilley didn't last long, however. He read his Bible and preached Jesus to all who came into his shop. His inflamed eyelids glowed around bulging eyeballs as he stitched or drove pegs and testified to the customer or caller, "Jesus saves. I know it. He has saved me. I am ready for the day I will meet my Jesus." Gently he would add for the unconverted, "You should read the Good Word. You should prepare your heart to meet Jesus, who died for you. He is waiting for you. He made sacrifice for you and asks only that you believe on Him so you may have everlasting life."

And so on, along the little Main Street, there were the store and shop fronts of varying voices and faces for Mibs. There was Mr. Biddings, the wagonmaker of Cincinnati before he came to New Era and became a trustee of New Era College. It was Mr. Biddings more than anyone else who had encouraged Hornsby Meadows to go beyond New Era and spread the gospel of antislavery and organize local societies. When Hornsby's hope ran low, which wasn't often, Mr. Biddings was his comfort and consolation. It didn't worry Mr. Biddings that "G. & D. Cooke & Company of New Haven, Conn." and other concerns were making wagons cheaper and better than he could. He was now their agent. He didn't have to worry about wheels, hubs, spokes, felloes except on repair jobs. He had a catalogue and could show you lumber wagons, drays, and rigs of all makes, light four-wheeled rigs named the Jagger, the Gazelle, the Cricket, buggies with a top that folded back, buggies named the Box Jump Seat, the Eureka Jump Seat, the Crescent City, the Champion, one with many fancy curves named the Prince of Wales. Also Mr. Biddings had the agency for the new McCormick Harvester Reapers that lightened the work of getting in the wheat, oats and barley.

Next door to Biddings' place was very special to Mibs' eye, the sign over it reading: Joel Wimbler, Harness Shop: All Kinds of Repairs: Hides Bought and Sold. Next came a place that needed no sign, the livery stable where Fred Shamp had two men working for him who regularly got blind-drunk, "but never both of them at once on the same day or I wouldn't keep 'em," said Mr. Shamp. One of them on a hot July afternoon had driven a fast sorrel full-speed up and down the length of Main Street several times till at one lurch of the buggy, the chunky woman in a pink dress, tipsy as she was, got spilled into the street and it took four men to hoist her back into the buggy. That seemed to have been the one time a woman was publicly drunk in New Era. She was the daughter of a farmer at near-by Hickory Grove, a settlement known to New Era as "a foul nest of Steve Douglas Democrats."

Mibs saw through a window Mr. Biddings holding a man by the coat lapel and Mr. Biddings' face serious and his lips moving fast from one word to another. He was talking abolition, Mibs could see, it was his abolitionist face. Mibs had seen Mr. Biddings' name in the *Chicago Tribune,* "one of the most active freedom men in north-central Illinois," and in the *Chicago Times,* "a leader in the abolitionist pesthole misnamed New Era." Mibs had heard her father say, "He talks too much, he talks 'em into abolition and then talks 'em out." When two of the prosperous and prominent Presbyterian deacons had gone to Chicago for their new two-seated carriages with curtained glass windows, they meant to show Biddings he was going too far with his talk and it was his kind of blather (they called it blather and him a blatherskite) that had split in two the Presbyterian Church, the Methodist Church, the Baptist Church and more churches yet so now you had a Presbyterian Church North and a Presbyterian Church South, a Methodist Church North and a Methodist Church South, and they hated each other worse than they hated the Catholics, who hadn't split though there were Catholic bishops North and South who disputed about slavery and Christ in letters the newspapers printed. "Biddings don't care if he loses customers," said Joel Wimbler. "With him abolition comes first and buggies second." Fixing a surcingle for a farmer with a new buggy, Joel had heard the man, "It's all I can do to run my farm and I don't give a damn about slavery one way or the other. I believe in minding your own business and when Biddings went at me and liked to talk my arm off about the Nebraska Bill and the war in Kansas and it's time for us to wake up, I backed away from him and dogged if I didn't go on over

724

to Monmouth and buy me a buggy slick as any Biddings could show me."

Next to the livery stable a hammer hit an anvil and Mibs could see dimly through a smoky window the sparks from a horseshoe getting shaped. At the anvil would be the face of Al Dunnigan, Al for Aloysius, the best-shaped man in New Era, a flat head with a squarish mouth, curly black hair, weighing two hundred and ten pounds, with a magnificent well-proportioned torso and shoulders. Twice he had gone over to Hickory Grove for a bare-knuckle fight in a timber clearing, meeting the Grove champion, the two men stripped to their waists and given the word to start they pounded each other, with no letup, no rest, till the last blow had one of them fagged out and senseless on the ground. Al Dunnigan had won both the fights and was going to take on another, so the gossip ran, but when the next fight would come off no one could tell though it would be some day next summer and the purse was being raised of $100 to go to the winner. "Pete the Slugger and he's got a reputation," ran the gossip, "he'll come from Chicago and it might be we'll have to go over the line in Fulton County where the sheriff is friendly and the damned Presbyterians of New Era can't stick their noses in." An excitement simmering here and seething there over whether Al Dunnigan would lick Pete the Slugger. Mibs had caught a little of it herself from the Whalens, for she joined with them in an admiration for the clean brawny looks of Al Dunnigan and the way he walked, "afraid of no man or beast," as Paddy Whalen put it. Mibs had her misgivings about seeing one of those fights, "bare-knuckle and to the finish." It would be cruel to see. She had noticed a twist in Al's nose and the tip of one ear hanging limp. "I'd rather see wrestling," she said to Paddy, who answered, "So would I but they tell me there's no blood in rasslin and it's blood the crowd wants to see."

Al puzzled various good people in New Era, keeping company with men who smoked and drank and swore and he himself never touched tobacco nor hard liquor and said out of his cool squarish mouth very quietly at times, as a man of few words, "A cursin man loses his head and loses the fight." A bartender at the Wild Buckhorn tavern at Hickory Grove didn't ask Al, "What's yours?" but drew it and shoved it toward him with "A short beer for you, Al, and here it is." In the course of an evening with the wild boys who idolized him he would have "five or six short beers and no harm done." His little wife he had brought along when he came from Peoria four years ago. On occasion she had, before others, spoken sharp words to him about his bloody bare-knuckle fights and he had let her go the limit, saying, "Give it to your husband, lay it on, macushla," then swinging her over his head to brush the ceiling and plumping her gently into a rocking chair. To the big front room of the Dunnigan two-story house came once a month a priest to celebrate Mass and speak admonitions of faith to the Catholics of New Era. When their number should double they would build their own church in New Era, they expected.

"I hear they say Mass," Mibs had said to Ma. "What do they do when they say Mass?"

"They worship images, Mibs. That's the way I heard it when I was a girl. They bow before images. I used to worry about them. I heard they were pagans. But time went by and now I don't worry about the Catholics and their Mass. Whatever they do and whatever they worship, they can have it so long as they let the Protestants alone. Pa and I decided long ago there's good people in all the churches and we've seen unbelievers and backsliders no worse than some of the pious hypocrites regular in their pews every Sunday. The meanest gossips in New Era belong to the church and some of the most stuck-up proud men and women actually go to church to show off their fancy broadcloth and the new satins fresh from Chicago."

"Hypocrites, ain't that a word?" Mibs had laughed.

"An awful word—you pretend to be holy and humble before the Lord and you know it's more pretend than real and you haven't got the sense nor wisdom to search your own heart and you feel superior to those who do study and care about what we call the Human Family."

That was October of last year and Mibs had told Ma of stepping in to hear Mr. Biddings tell Al Dunnigan why he should vote the Republican ticket for Frémont for President. The Nebraska Bill, the civil war in Kansas, Mr. Biddings explained it all and made it clear as it was to himself that the spread of slavery into newly made states must be stopped. When Biddings finished, and asked, "Do you see, Al, where it's your bounden duty to vote for Frémont?" the brawny horseshoer looked him cold in the eye and clipped the words, "I'm a Democrat, Mr. Biddings. You can't get up an argument with me. I'm a Democrat and I vote for Buchanan."

Twenty years, lacking a few months, twenty years Mibs had seen of this town of New Era. Out of those years she now carried in her heart, in her head and imagination, an album, a folio of faces and voices, stiff and fixed people of habits and she knew their habits better than they did, and here and there people who kept taking new roots and growing and still others who faded or shrank under the press of time.

She would be double twenty, she would be forty soon enough, Molly Whalen had promised. And what would her album, her folio, be holding then?

She had walked in the falling snow along past the two blocks of stores to a cross street, cutting across the New Era College campus and passing the two-story brick building where she knew every desk, table, shelf and banister, and the little chapel where she had joined in hymns and heard student debates and orations, prayers and counsel from elders, and where one morning the exercise had to be delayed for the reason that prankish youths had somehow during the night brought through the front door and up the stairs and into the chapel a pleasant and innocent brindle cow that faced the college president when he opened the door.

What was the college? A seat of learning, that was the phrase. She had heard that a thousand times, "a seat of learning." Yet what kind of learning was it that had the New Era board-of-trustees members about evenly divided in a dispute and publicly calling each other men of low principles, double-dyed deceivers, scoundrels, liars and skunks? The new president, Andrew Brench, a solid muscular man, breezy and vehement, with a full-faced set of brown whiskers, was a valiant and heroic crusader who came straight out for immediate abolition of slavery. So said four of the trustees. Another four said President Brench was using his high position to besmirch the good name of the college by incendiary utterances calculated to bring war or disunion to the nation. The ninth trustee with the deciding vote had climbed a perch he straddled to proclaim, "I am for a peaceable adjustment of the difficulty. We should compose our differences." The chairman of the board, credited as the founder of the college, pastor of the New Era Presbyterian church for twenty years, now aged, dyspeptic, crabbed, yet his smooth-shaven face still carrying in its shaggy eyebrows and thrust-out underlip some of an earlier Puritan austerity, Jonas Fry had allowed a dispute over issues to become a personal quarrel having the tones of a tavern brawl among spittoons and the smell of stale beer. When Fry heard of the ninth trustee hoping to "compose our differences," he queried in dyspeptic falsetto, "What can you compose with a crossbreed of rattlesnake and polecat?"

Mibs stood with arms akimbo looking at the college. She snorted, "Seat of learning!" Then she let out a syllable she had picked up from a Swede who worked at the sawmill, "Ish!" It was a spewing syllable. She repeated it before walking on. "Ish!"

She went on three blocks to the brickyard, watched two men loading a wagon, taking six bricks at a time squeezed between their hands. A beginner took four bricks. A good man could handle seven or eight.

"What's become of Hod Willis?" Mibs asked the loaders. She had seen Hod Willis take ten bricks between his big paws. He had strength and a sense of balance.

"Oh, Hod," said one of the men, "he saved his money and went to Chicago. He's a house-mover."

And the other man with a laugh, "Ain't any house in Chicago Hod won't move."

Back on Main Street she passed the new little Methodist church. The Methodists had been meeting in the Masonic Hall over Biddings' store. Now they had their little boxed frame with a tall oblong tower that sprawled over the lower structure. When Mibs first saw it she

727

spoke a hope the tower wouldn't fall and crash through the roof when the Methodists were holding services.

The gallon tin pail in one hand had steadily reminded her that her errand was oysters. She went to the James Parkinson General Merchandise Store and bought the oysters, two quarts, and showing them to her mother, "Here's some of the Atlantic Ocean we're going to eat, every one guaranteed fresh and ready to slide down your gullet like a greased lizard."

"You're sprightly today, little girl."

Mibs looked into her mother's still face, depths of care and affection in the solemn eyes, a smile lurking not on the lips but in the eyes.

"Oh, I've got my troubles, Ma."

And Ma knew part of that meant Hornsby Meadows—part Danny Hilton.

* * * * * * * * * *

Chapter 13

* * * * * * * * * *

Birthday Supper, Travelers and Lawbreakers

ABOUT an hour before suppertime Mibs went down the cellar stairs to a corner and a bench strewn with tools, found a hammer, went to the outside cellar door, raised the door and felt snow sliding off the door down her ears and neck, stepped out and let the door down and rushed out front to the three-plank sidewalk. Under the snow she located the loose upthrust nail, whacked it down with the hammer, and ran into the house, telling her mother, "I fixed that, the nail I ripped my overshoe on."

The Meadows family arrived first, Caleb, Mrs. Meadows, their son Hornsby. "It's fit you should come first," said Joel. "The only other people from Arpa, New York."

The Henshaw widow and her daughter came next. Their husband and father had given the money to bring the Boat through and had died and was buried near by at Knoxville, as they said, "like Moses just in sight of the Promised Land." Then came the wife of the professor of rhetoric and declamation and her mother.

Danny Hilton arrived, the sixteen-year-old boy who had dived and brought up the propeller part each of three times it came loose, who had fished out two children who would have drowned but for him, not to mention the captain's gold watch that he dove for time and again till his fingers located it in the slippery mud and brought it up and holding it to one ear, "It's ticking, Captain, ain't lost a minute." Danny

728

Hilton, who had made the forty-mile ride to New Era when no other man of the company could stand up to get on a horse, Danny who had seen the captain die midway of that forty-mile span, the bachelor captain handing his wallet to the Presbyterian pastor and fumbling his gold watch out of a pocket, his tongue thick and his eyes and his weakly stretched hand saying the watch should truly belong to Danny. They had asked Danny to bring it this evening. Before sitting to supper they passed the watch around and held it as a token that in a way belonged to each of them. Each felt too that the Wimbler clock had a friendship, for it had stood the journey from Arpa to Utica and Utica to New Era, its mahogany scratched and dented but the works still going and the face telling time, often slow, but fairly regular if they didn't miss winding it.

Danny Hilton, thirty-six years old now, lean and wiry, apple cheeks overlaid with a ruddy sun and wind tan, wavy dark-brown hair, teasing gray eyes, a carpenter-contractor who could build a frame house from the ground up, living on a small farm just outside New Era, a bachelor "handy with the girls but not caught yet," the top of his head on a level with Mibs' eyes. He was the acknowledged best horseman in New Era, with three saddle nags, one of them a rangy Kentucky bay that had sooner or later thrown anyone trying to ride him, except Danny. He had come this evening on Mibs' invitation, Ma and Pa letting her have her way though saying it wouldn't look so good and might raise talk they should have present a man who had raced his horses weekdays and Sabbath and gone swimming in Pine Flats Pond on the Sabbath Day and after repeated warnings and no improvement in his conduct had been read out of the church fellowship.

Hornsby Meadows towering bear-shaped over Danny had a feeling that in Danny's being there Mibs had intended it somehow as a flaunting of him. Mibs nodded her head sidewise toward Danny and said to Hornsby, "The Boat couldn't have gone on but for him." Hornsby had heard this before.

"Shet up, Mibs," leered Danny. Mibs knew Danny was aware that "Shut up," was correct but he was being horsy and more yet did he deeply resent any reference to himself as a hero. His modesty took refuge in comic vulgarity. He dragged and slurred his pronunciation of the first word of "Shet up." It was quizzical and Mibs with a screwed-up mouth mimicked him, "All right, I'll s-h-e-t up," and changing the subject swiftly, "How's Rambo?" This was the Kentucky bay.

"Prime—full of the devil—tied him in a warm stall at Shamp's. Still think you'll try to ride him?"

"I do, I'll take that very notion one of these days."

"Well, when you're ready I won't let you get on Rambo. You're too pretty to be picked up with broken bones."

"You wouldn't mean I'm pretty enough to be picked up with *no* broken bones?"

And Mibs no sooner said it than she was sorry. She was no flirt but she knew this was a straight-out flirty remark. She saw Hornsby blink and wince. She knew she had said it to flaunt Hornsby and his pretense of having a hold on her. And she knew now for certain that she liked Danny Hilton better than she did Hornsby. She had gone riding with him three or four times, had learned about horses from him, had feared she was too easy, warm and comfortable with him, had refused his later invitations to ride.

They turned toward the eating table with Mibs trying to clear the air. "I haven't stopped being a fool because I'm twenty. Molly Whalen said I'll be forty soon enough and before I know it. Maureen is here tonight. Speak to her about her going to college. She ought to, and she will if we get her lit up about it."

Pickles large and small, slaw with whatever touch of vinegar you liked on it, wheat bread or corn to be spread with a yellow fresh-churned butter, from the milk of two cows, were among the spread of the table. The two cows were brown-and-white Priscilla Alden in the Wimbler barn and the black one in the Biddings barn named by Mr. Biddings Free-and-Equal. The platter of baked ham, well spiced and smoothed thinly with maple sugar, came from a barrel-shaped, short-legged, black China hog that the Wimblers in their pen alongside the barn had fed and fattened from a pig and they had named him Acropolis, "not because the Apostle Paul preached there but because it sounds like a nice hog name," said Pa Wimbler. Christmas week two men had hauled Acropolis to a slaughterhouse beyond town and killed and dressed him.

Maureen brought in the deep dish of escalloped oysters and there was agreement with Danny Hilton that they were a nice change from Spoon River clams and Mississippi River mussels. Mashed potatoes with gravy, carrots with a cream sauce, were passed along for helpings. "I think I seen you hoein them taters and weedin them carrots last summer," Danny ventured and Mibs had a suspicion Danny was being unusually ungrammatical this evening for the benefit of the correct Hornsby Meadows.

Danny had an off eye on Mibs when he spooned himself a helping of oysters and showed the influence of the only poet he enjoyed reading. He recited:

"The oysters are properly scalloped,
Said the horseman who into them galloped."

Mibs laughed, "That's a challenge, Hornsby," who by the time the oysters had traveled around the table to him was prepared, a broad smile between his brown sideburns as he recited:

"There once was a hard-working oysterer
Who quit and became quite a roisterer."

A cheese sent in by John Ankers as a remembrance, and from his orchard apples that had been baked brown, were passed along with a pitcher of thick cream to be ladled with a big spoon rather than poured over the apple.

The big copper coffeepot arrived and with it a brown cake chock-full of black-walnut meats Maureen had cracked that morning. Over the top was the figure in white frosting: "20." Mibs took a knife and cut through the figure and divided the cake amid laughter and banter.

The women pitched in, cleared the table and washed and dried the dishes in no time, to join the men in more coffee, nut cake and a nut taffy. They were not really eating any more, just lingering and passing the time. They talked about the Boat journey and what it had cost to get New Era started. They talked about the loss of life and the human wreckage that had gone into the settling of the Midwest and the plains farther west. In January of '54 the Mississippi River froze so that two steamboats carrying two thousand Irish and German immigrants were ice-locked near Cairo and they ran out of food and there were many deaths from hunger and cold, from cholera and fever. Their sufferings had come when they were near the end of their journey, rather different from a shipload of sixty immigrants from Sweden, aiming to settle in Illinois, ship and all sinking mid-sea in an Atlantic storm.

The wrangle of the New Era trustees came up. Hornsby threw in a defense of President Brench and immediate abolition. Joel Wimbler couldn't agree. "President Brench talks too much." Hornsby went into an elaborate argument, one of his abolition speeches. They let him talk, not an interruption. It dawned on Hornsby he was turning a pleasant birthday party into one of his meetings for the unconverted. He said there was more to say but it could go till another time but it would be appropriate that some of his questions should be answered. There was a silence. It lasted till Joel Wimbler ended it with his first remark, "President Brench talks too much."

Danny Hilton went to an overcoat pocket and unwrapped from a newspaper fold a fist-sized chunk of black, "Tisn't slate nor stone." They passed it around from hand to hand. "Coal," said Hornsby Meadows.

"Two miles out of New Era," said Danny.

"Coal," repeated one and another, looking into each other's faces.

"It'll take the place of wood in all stoves before long," said Danny.

"They are using it on some of the Eastern railroads," said Hornsby. "Firing the engine boilers with it. Chicago and other cities make illuminating gas from it. They run the gas through underground pipes for miles."

Caleb Meadows in Chicago, buying needed sizes of stock for his lumberyard, had seen a pile of coal used to fire the boiler of a stationary engine. "It's coming to stay, they told me, soft coal and hard. You put a half-bushel of hard coal in your stove today and it burns slow and lasts till tomorrow. Coal is coming to stay."

"Will the eight-hour day come with it?" Mrs. Meadows asked. "Tell them about the eight-hour day, Caleb."

Carpenters, bricklayers, house-painters, paperhangers, plumbers, printers, were holding meetings and had speakers calling for an end to the ten-hour workday six days a week. "Eight hours for work, eight hours for sleep and eight hours for education and recreation," was their motto.

"And in New Era the carpenters work sunup to sundown satisfied if they get the work," put in Danny. "And they quit when they don't like it."

"What is the difference between a free workman of the North and a slave worker of the South?" Hornsby couldn't help putting in and was off again on immediate abolition, speaking tenderly and sadly, in a mood of finality beyond any thought of self or self-pity, the mood that softened Mibs and of a tone for which she had great respect. She knew he had a like quality with antislavery leaders who had come to despair of ending slavery by peaceable measures. "It will go down in blood," was their saying among themselves of a belief they couldn't speak openly, publicly, giving their reasons for the belief.

This mood of Hornsby had humility. The arrogance that sustained him most of the time would not permit a patience with other viewpoints. But now he was naming those other viewpoints. His own father was a Garrisonian abolitionist: preach, cry, shout aloud the monster wrong and sin of slavery—but no violence, no resistance except by moral appeal. There were abolitionists like Mr. Wimbler: Let slavery alone where it is but stop the spread of it into the Territories of Nebraska and Kansas. Then there was the faint shadowy hope of those antislavery men who held to the American Colonization Society and would like to believe it possible to send all the Negroes back to Africa. Still others were against slavery, saying it was infamous, saying in a confidential whisper it was so vast, dark and complicated that we would never be rid of it except by an act of God. There were the extremely decent people, the perfectly polite persons who said, "Let sleeping dogs lie," and accepted it as the rule of good society and respectable position for the well-behaved person to shun slavery and abolition as topics of conversation. These persons had evolved phrases of service. Hornsby had heard one of them say, "To discuss the domestic institutions of the South is in bad taste and bad form," and had replied, "The very word 'slavery' has a nasty touch on your tongue, so you have coined a comfortable phrase for it, 'domestic institutions of the South.'"

The man had grown, Mibs saw. In strengths of purpose beyond her knowing and in mental reach and grasp, in some sort of dumb and groping prayers that kept him alive, he was not the familiar and the playmate of earlier days. The others respected Hornsby Meadows in

732

this mood, and listened to him. They could go along with him only part of the way. But in his confessions and fumblings this evening he represented a haze and a hush of destiny over the country, indefinable threats that hovered at all horizons and could take shape in they knew not what.

As persons, as individuals, they had seen lives of change, incessant change. In wave after wave, pioneers had swept westward in the breath of change. The country, the nation, had always moved on from the known into the unknown, taking its chances. Slavery, the Constitution, the Union, each had been one thing in one period and something else as time pressed on. Of what they were to see of history in the making they could not foretell. They were certain only of change.

They had heard in New Era the gentle Ralph Waldo Emerson in their Presbyterian-church lecture course, the crashing and angular Theodore Parker of Boston, and a score of the nation's famous speakers, writers, educators, ministers, who got off the five-o'clock afternoon train from Chicago. And those men of the platform were all troubled and shaken over slavery, some of them trying to subdue a wrath they did not dare to explode in public. Each had his own affiliations, plans and measures related to what should be done immediately with slavery. But how to do away with it, how to destroy slavery root and branch without in the process destroying the American Union of States, in the face of that indescribably enormous problem they lapsed into silence or they recoiled in horror before the hazards and the cost of violence involved or they could only refer the future to the inscrutable designs of Divine Providence.

They drifted into reminiscences. Caleb Meadows could remember when eleven years ago he first saw George W. Brown over at Tylersville, a thirty-one-year-old farmer living with his wife in a scrabbled one-room log house. "He was barefoot, only clothes he had on was a straw hat, a hickory shirt and brown jean pants. He was considered queer, working on a corn-planter. He kept at it and at it for all they laughed at him letting his farm work go and running into debt trying first this and then that. Time came howsoever when he did have a machine where two men and a team could plant sixteen to twenty acres of corn in a day. Last year in his shop over at Galesburg he made and sold six hundred of his corn-planters. This year of 1857 they say he figures on making and selling a thousand."

"The Methodists are proud of him and they got a right to be," said Mrs. Henshaw.

"Like the Presbyterians are proud of Cyrus McCormick for inventing the reaper," smiled Danny Hilton.

"And the Catholics proud of Columbus for discovering America," said Joel Wimbler.

"And the Jews pointing to the Bible and correctly saying their people wrote it," Hornsby threw in.

Danny Hilton by some twist got a discussion going about what happened "when two gentlemen fought themselves out of their overcoats into each other's." He had led up to it with telling of a Yankee lawyer in Peoria challenged to a duel by a Kentuckian and being asked what weapons he would choose, sent back word, "Cornstalks."

A stomping of feet was heard at the front door and a sharp knocking. Joel went to the door and opened it to hear a man in a cowskin overcoat asking for Hornsby Meadows. Joel asked the man in. Hornsby smiled to the man, "Oh, it's you," without speaking the man's name. Hornsby opened the door into a bedroom, the two of them stepped in, and the door swung closed.

The party went on but the going was slow. They thought of jokes and foolery about this interruption and then couldn't bring themselves to speak in any easy and light-minded way about this affair of secrecy. They guessed it must be "some kind of abolition business" and perhaps very serious.

The door opened. Hornsby asked Mr. Wimbler for a word with him. Mr. Wimbler went into the bedroom and the door again closed. After a few minutes the door opened and Joel came out to say he was sorry but the party was over and it was nice they didn't have to end it sooner and it was near bedtime anyhow.

They put on their overcoats, cloaks and wraps, spoke merry good wishes to Mibs for many more birthdays of health and cheer and thanks to Brooksany Wimbler for an elegant supper, "a scrumptious supper."

Danny Hilton took Mibs to a corner of the room and spoke low, "It's none of my business and you know I wouldn't cut in where I'm not wanted. But if it should be an Underground Railroad move they're on, I'd be willing to take the place of your father rather than him make a long cold drive a night like this. I can get a sled if you want and that team of blacks I haul with and they're good, you know."

Danny was sixteen years younger than Joel Wimbler, handy on roads with horses, something of a fighter in an emergency, Mibs mentioned to her father and Hornsby.

"Can we *trust* him?" said Pa.

"I think so."

"You *think* so, Mibs. This is breaking the law and mocking at the Constitution. You *think* so."

"I *know* you can trust Danny."

Through a door came two Wahomah men, the snow still falling, a northwest wind piling it in high drifts. They had stuck in drifts, some "nearly horse-high," had shoveled their way out and the horses and themselves couldn't last through the trip to Galesburg as expected. They would stop the night with a friendly farmer, "one of us," two miles out from New Era on the Wahomah road. They shook hands and were gone.

734

Two bundles had walked in and before the fireplace began unbundling, straw from a sled bottom flying about the room, dropping on the floor, straw chaff from blankets, cloaks, scarfs, caps. One was a massive black woman, perhaps taller than Hornsby, a strange woman with steady eyes of blue-tinted pupils and a lurking fire in them, her small mouth heavy-lipped, cool and composed, once flashing a smile from a wide set of even teeth, and her skin, Mibs noted, a blue-black with a shine of polished stone. She had been a house servant in St. Louis and a month ago her master and owner, a widower, had brought home a new purchase from the slave yard, a fresh arrival from Memphis that had been advertised at two thousand dollars and sold for that price. This one had come out of the other bundle brought through the snow from Wahomah. She had gone to sleep and the straw and blanket folds over her feet had jolted loose and she was moaning over the pain in her feet, the blood trying to circulate more freely since she stood on her feet and walked and brought them close to the fire. Brooks went for a pail of cold water. She and Mibs took off the shoes and stockings and insisted on the feet going into cold water though it hurt at first, Brooks saying, "Poor thing, she ought to have had overshoes." From the other woman they heard a somber mockery, "Do the best you can by her, she sell for two thousand dollars, she come high. Only sixteen, she got huh life ahaid of huh. Octoroon, what they calls it, uh eighth of huh nigguh and duh res' wite as yuh please."

A slim miniature, her bare feet and legs slender and shapely, hips and shoulders of proportion in a flame-yellow blouse soiled and torn with travel, lips of the red maple leaf, eyes of a hazy violet, an arched small nose, and her cheeks with a flush of brown, "an infinitely light brown that's lovely," said Mibs to herself later.

The heat from an armful of small dry sticks Joel had thrown on the fire was now reaching them with more than they needed. The big woman, who said she answered to the name of Hetty, moved her chair back. The octoroon had help in moving back her chair and the pail of cold water now becoming easier to her feet. "It's grateful," she said in a soft voice. "You are kind to me. You are thoughtful. My name is Marova." She said the last as though it was understood South and in the North too that she had no parental name and Marova was enough.

Pa Wimbler and Hornsby brought in warm baked ham with hot coffee. The two women ate, they smiled to each other, then turned slowly smiling to the other faces about them. Hetty paused in a mouthful of the savory ham, let out an irresistible hilarious chuckle, her broad shoulders and ample breasts shaking, as she bent her head forward and looked Marova full in the face with an inquiring twist of her own face. It was as though she were asking Marova whether what was happening in this room was a dream or a fantastic procedure without meaning: "Are we here, alive, warm, eatin sweet baked ham, and white folks waitin on us?"

Then Hetty lapsed into inscrutable calm, her face with its blue-black skin holding a faint gleam of polished stone, her face a stolid mask.

Now the front door burst open with no knocking. Danny Hilton came in with decision, brushed off snow from his sleeves and shoulders, shook snow off his fur cap, while he gave his message, not breathless yet swiftly, no time to be lost. Bringing his team and sled past the hotel he noticed two horses tied in the shed alongside the hotel. He pulled in his own team, tied them, went back and took notice he had never seen those two horses in New Era before and they were the kind of horses he could recognize if they belonged anywhere around New Era. He went into the front room where George Spitzer kept the register book and stayed up till midnight in case travelers should arrive. George said two men had come in and asked for a room and asked further whether any people had come into the town from Galesburg or Wahomah this evening. They had gone out saying, "Going to take a look around town. We'll be back and help you put up the horses." A few minutes later the two men had come in, warmed themselves at the stove and talked so they couldn't be heard, talked standing and holding their overcoats. Then they had come over and signed the register and swept Danny from head to foot with their eyes, comfortable-looking men, maybe well-off.

"I can't help smellin they're officers," Danny rushed on. "They saw my team and sled and they signed the register as a blind. They'll follow my team and sled sure as shootin." Danny was talking against time. "We'll be takin chances to hunt up another team and sled. You hide these two women and quick, where they can't be located. I'll go back to the hotel and talk with George Spitzer again and tell him before those two officers—I smell they're officers, I can't help it I smell they're officers—tell Spitzer that I'm drivin away on important business and I'll see him when I get back and those two owls they'll follow me a windin route that'll end up in my barn and home where I'm an independent American citizen—damn their dirty man-huntin necks, and huntin women is a damn sight dirtier."

All were tensed and solemn, except Hornsby, who wore a grim smile, for here was the easy-going and accommodating Danny Hilton, never picking quarrels, never meddling in politics, and for the hour here was Danny Hilton as wild and fighting an abolitionist as any.

Hetty had stood up and gathered her cloak and made ready with her blankets and wraps. Mibs and Ma Wimbler had brought towels and dried Marova's feet and helped pull on the stockings and put on the shoes, Mibs running for a pair of her own overshoes. Danny had left saying he would drive his sled the other side of the tracks and out around that way, smiling with his eyes slit, "I'll be drivin miles away from any New Era churches."

Out into the blowing snow hurried Danny, into the hotel front room he walked to see the "two owls" at a writing table and he chattered with George Spitzer about what a crazy cold night it was for a drive to Galesburg and he considered himself lucky he didn't have to make that drive tonight and he'd bet there was drifts the horses couldn't pull through till you got out and shoveled a way for 'em. And Danny talked loud and misleading and he mumbled in a low tone what was of no importance in George Spitzer's ear but when he was through with his noisy prattle and his mysterious undertone confabulations with the now mystified hotel clerk, the "two owls" knew him for their suspicious party to follow. Which they did. Danny was not out of the New Era town limits when he looked back to see them on their horses crossing the railroad tracks. He drove out two miles straight, hit the Monmouth road winding through timber for two miles, turned into a straight road where after a half-mile the horses stuck in a drift. Danny worked with his shovel a half-hour, drove through, stuck again, shoveled more, made two more turns and ended up at his own barn.

He lighted a lantern, watered and fed the two blacks, petted them, came out carrying the lantern and saw two men sliding off their horses at his own barn door, moving to where Danny held the lantern to their faces with his left hand and a six-shooter revolver in his right.

"Who the hell are you two nighthawks that follow me around a crazy night like this?" Danny burst out. "How do I know you ain't a pair of horse thieves? I'm ready for yuh. If you don't make clear what you're up to I'll order you off this property. This is my farm. I got my eye on yuh. Better not either of yuh move. What are you sayin?"

The two men looked at each other, one of them clearing his throat. It hadn't dawned on them till now that they were not on their home grounds and possibly their actions as suspicious as Danny's. One of them in the lantern light tall and thin-faced, the other of Danny's own height, chunky, his overcoat out at the middle as if pot-bellied. Danny backed toward a wagon shed alongside the barn. "Let's get out of this wind, if you got anythin to say. I'm not goin to hold this gun on yuh all night."

They moved out of the wind and blowing snow and began talking streaks. One was a deputy sheriff from Quincy, the other a United States Marshal from St. Louis. They were hunting two Negroes and the kidnappers of those Negroes. They had evidence the stolen property had been taken out of Wahomah that afternoon in a sled going in the direction of New Era. Only one team and sled in sight in New Era, they had followed that one team and sled on the chance it might be the one taking the stolen property to Galesburg.

"What were you up to?" said the Marshal, the pot-bellied one, with a pleasant grin. "'You drove a funny route to get from New Era to your farm.'"

"You come on my own property and ask me where I been and what I'm doin. For two cents I'd tell you to go to hell and bring me into a court of law to answer your damned silly question."

"I was only saying," said the Marshal, keeping his pleasant grin, "that you drove a funny route to get from New Era to your farm."

"All right," said Danny, hard-faced and still playing with the six-shooter. "You say you're this and that. How do I know? I say again you might be a couple uh horse thieves, for all I know." He paused. He went on. "I'll tell you this much and then you'll get off these premises I own. These premises are my property by law just as much as the property you say you're huntin.

"Now," said Danny, leering at them in a flashing impudence. "It couldn't be, could it, that I have business regular over at Monmouth? It couldn't be I started for Monmouth and after I shoveled the horses out of one bastard snowdrift I decided I wasn't goin to shovel any more and the thing for me to do was head straight home till the weather clears up? You couldn't think of that, could yuh?"

They thought about that. They thought long. They were still thinking when Danny put the lantern on the ground and suddenly hurled swift words low and menacing, as he pointed his revolver at the United States Marshal and held his shoulders at a sort of ready crouch. "You're standin between me and the doorway of my house, my property. Now you'll get on your horses and ride off my property or I'm goin to shoot my way to the door of my house that's my home and my property. Get along, get on those horses!"

Slowly they turned, slowly they moved on, put feet in stirrups, the Marshal calling back, "You may be hearing from us again, sir."

Danny picked up his lantern and went into the house.

Each night an hour or two after dark Mibs Wimbler had left home with a wicker basket on one arm. And three times she would walk around the block where the Methodist church stood, turning suddenly to see if anyone might be following her. Then she would run up the church steps, key in hand, unlock the big front door, enter and lock the door.

The third day she did this, the word was, "They're still here, they haven't gone." The two officers had come to the Wimbler house and asked for names. "Who came to your birthday supper party?" Mibs gave the names, and they called and questioned each one. Of New Era people only the three Wimblers, Hornsby Meadows, and Danny Hilton, those five, had with their own eyes seen the two fugitive slaves. The polite and patient questioning of the United States Marshal with a pleasant grin had brought him no results. The two officers seemed to be waiting in the hope of clues or informers turning up.

They had run down all trails, and didn't like to head south empty-handed.

On the third day Danny called at the New Era Hotel, was sent up to their room, knocked on the door. The Marshal opened the door and invited Danny in. Entering, Danny saw the Quincy deputy finish shuffling a deck of cards and lay them on a table as he leaned back and took a stretch and a yawn.

"You're at home here, you think so?" Danny asked the deputy.

"Sure," as his head tilted back and he took a short stretch and yawn just to show how at home he was.

"I came to tell you, whether you're at home here or not," said Danny, hard-faced. New Era had not believed Danny had among his faces one so hard as he wore this week. "I came to give you information," Danny went on.

The deputy straightened stiff. The Marshal brightened and a glitter came in his eyes.

"You're certainly welcome," said the Marshal. "It's information we're waiting for."

"Here's my information for you. You need to be informed this town and this county ain't southern Illinois and it ain't Missouri. You can do things down there you can't do here. You know you ain't welcome here. You know that much. You don't know there's talk goin round, bad feelin, and the longer you stay the worse it gets. I'm not sayin there'll be trouble. I'm not sayin if you stay you'll be run out of town. I don't threaten you. I don't warn you. I give you the information there's bad feelin and the longer you stay the worse it gets."

Danny backed toward the door, stood with his back to it. The Marshal said this was important, he'd like to talk it over. Couldn't Danny sit down and go into details? The Marshal opened a carpetbag, fished around in it and brought out a quart bottle of whisky. "Wouldn't you like to sit down here and talk it over sociable?"

"You haven't got the sense God gave a mudworm," snorted Danny. "This ain't St. Louis. This is New Era. They don't drink whisky here if they want to get anywhere and it's against the law to sell it. A stubborn God-fearin lot of people run this town. They don't like interference. When you get back to St. Louis you tell 'em I said you ain't got the sense God gave a mudworm. I'm leavin and you won't hear from me again. The information I bring you is there's bad feelin and the longer you stay the worse it gets."

The Marshal had kept his grin but now it crept away and looked like an effort worn for effect. He picked his teeth with a wood sliver, pursed his lips as Danny opened the door. The two officers saw the door close and heard Danny clumping down the hall in his riding boots.

On the fourth day since their arrival the officers left New Era, riding toward Quincy.

✦

739

The cold wave passed after the first night but it was two more nights before the frostbite pains of her foot went away from Marova. Mibs noticed Marova in spells of silent weeping, held in fears that Hetty understood and could soothe. Hetty took the four days in a dark corner of the sprawling Methodist-church tower with a sort of gladness that increased as the days passed, an elation over their chances of escape to freedom. Hetty gradually brought Marova out of the fear and melancholy, nursed the girl as a child of her own, said often to Mibs, "What dat chile been t'rough," till finally Mibs' curiosity overcame her and she asked to know more and Hetty answered in a moan, "You wouldn't believe it if I tole yuh, where dat baby come from, high life she had and den low life and mizry on top uh mizry."

Mibs had come to know her way in the dark, every board and turning place in the climb up with the wicker basket to the loose planks of the bell-tower corner where the two slept, ate, talked, dozed, waited their fate five nights and four days, Saturday night till Wednesday night midnight. Food, coffee, a water bottle and a chamber pot were in a wicker basket Mibs brought near Saturday midnight. Humble services Mibs performed, singing it to her mother at home, "Ma, I never in my life felt so useful."

On the night of the fifth day a team and wagon took Hetty and Marova to Galesburg for transport by the Underground Railway to Chicago and north to the Canada line and freedom.

Over the town, those days they were hiding two fugitives from the outstretched arm of the Federal Government spread a vague unrest mixed with a suppressed glee. The raging national issue of slavery had come straight into their midst in concrete form. Hundreds asked the question, "Where do you suppose they're hiding them?" The *New Era Enterprise* printed an editorial mocking at the Fugitive Slave Law with no hint of the exciting news event that New Era had in this week flagrantly given that Federal Act what Danny Hilton termed "a big horse laugh." Maureen Whalen had noticed the wicker basket being prepared Monday evening and with a laugh mentioned her suspicions to her mother, who passed them on to Paddy Whalen at the supper table. Paddy asked what was the law coming to if it didn't mean anything and why should they pass the law if it wasn't to be a law?

"I'm with you a good Steve Douglas Democrat," said Mrs. Whalen, "but if it was for me to say and they're hidin away two black women here I wouldn't say the word to send them back where they come from, I'd keep my hands off."

"Me too," chirped Maureen.

"Let it be, we'll forget it," said Paddy. "I buy whisky payday and the man sells it to me he breaks the law and I tell him he's keen to break the law for me to have a breath of the sarpint. We'll forget it. The law is the law—or tisn't."

✦

Mibs Wimbler felt the town a pool of wild currents this week past, at the vortex two hunted creatures, one of them seven-eighths white blood with a small capital R branded on the lobe of one ear and the same capital R branded on the inside of one knee, as Hetty had shown them to Mibs during the wait near Wednesday midnight before the sled came to the Wimbler house. Mibs had passed her hand over their faces, she had held their hands and their talk had been as the blind and dumb talk except for snatches and whispered conversation mainly about immediate needs, requirements, strategy and hopes. Now those two creatures, a woman and a girl, had been swept off toward nowhere and she would probably never see them again nor hear of them. For them she had been a lawbreaker, secretive and furtive as though she were herself hunted. Her intimacy with them had been like none other she had known. She took their hands, she ran her own hands over their faces and asked them to do the same with her so they might know there was an outside world where they were not forgotten. She told her mother of this. "They're my children of darkness," said Mibs. Her mother had asked Thursday morning, "Are you sleeping good, Mibs?"

"I get in bed, Ma, and my head goes around with this and that for an hour, then I sleep like a hired man in haytime."

"That's good, I hope our sisters in the bell tower can say the same."

And Mibs had found the query recurring to her, "Are they sisters of mine?" and she recalled Hetty whispering the phrase "our little sister in Christ" a couple of times and Mibs had caught her tongue repeating the lines "sisters in Christ, sisters in the dark, sisters in Christ, sisters in the dark."

Weeks had passed and in early April came a soft Saturday afternoon with spring smells on the air and a tall white cloud rolling and changing in the west. The evening saw rain that shifted to hail and then snow but Mibs and Danny Hilton had the afternoon on horses and had seen birds skittering over Pine Flats Pond and Danny had told her for the first time of his drive the night he misled the two officers and of the words that passed at his barn and later in the New Era Hotel. And Mibs had told him of the trips to the church, the groping climb to the bell tower, the vocal snatches of speech and the stranger speech of hands and faces in the dark.

Danny had this day given Mibs a look before they got on their horses. The look told Mibs if they had such a meeting as this day again he might not be able to keep his hands off her. He kept his eyes on her in a way new to her. She wasn't afraid of him. She was a little uneasy about any beginning that would have to lead into a middle that ran on farther to an end she couldn't see clear. Hornsby was still known as her steady company. The two week ends each month that he wasn't off organizing for antislavery he saw her home from Sunday-morning church services, took her to and from evening services, took her perhaps once a month to Wednesday-evening prayer meetings, to lectures, concerts, taffy pulls, social parties, bobbing for apples at Halloween, the county fair at Knoxville in the first week of September, the annual fife-and-drum-corps celebration when one veteran of the War of 1812 and two veterans of the Mexican War sat on the platform with their medals and decorations for valor.

"Duty," said Mibs to her mother the next Saturday. "That's Hornsby. He's duty from head to toe. He duties me this and duties me that. It's my duty to go to church, his duty to go with me. I'm tired of this damned duty business."

"Why, Mibs!" The mother was shocked. The first profanity she had ever heard from her daughter, this was.

"I've told Hornsby that next Sunday it isn't my duty to go to church and I'm staying home to meditate on the thousands of sermons I've already heard and to read my Bible and meditate. I've seen Pa meditate, hours and not a word from him, just meditating by himself. You and I know he's the sweeter for it."

Since the affair of the two fugitive slaves Mibs had changed sharply toward Hornsby, the mother had read. A rift between them had been widening, and since the events of that hushed and somber week, gone deeper. Hornsby had been so coldly logical about what happened, seemed to take on a fresh arrogance about the dominance and the destiny of the antislavery movement, with little imagination or curiosity about the two vivid and contrasting creatures at the vortex. "They're just two figures to him, Ma. He adds and subtracts 'em. They're not people to him. They're straws in the wind, proofs of the awful righteousness of the cause of abolition. He didn't want to know and didn't ask me what kind of people they were I talked with in the dark like the blind and the dumb talk. And I wouldn't tell him, I wouldn't try to interest him. If it makes talk I'm not sitting with him in the same pew next Sunday, after these years of it, let 'em talk, let the fools talk and see what it'll get 'em."

And Mibs fell on her mother's shoulder in tears that came and came.

* * * * * * * * * *

Chapter 14

* * * * * * * * * *

Politics and the Heart of Mibs Wimbler

A FEW times that year of 1857 Hornsby and Mibs sat together at church. His will and pride, his depth of persistence in any purpose he shaped definitely in his own mind, kept him coming back to her, recalling the past and telling her she didn't know her own mind. There had been a long past with so many happy days, so much of the familiar and endearing, as he saw it, that he hesitated about going along with her view that for a time, and they would let events tell how long a time, they wouldn't keep on as steady company.

Her twenty-first birthday came in January of 1858 and at the birthday supper were only the three Wimblers. In the spring of that year Hornsby told her it had come to him and was common talk that she was oftener riding of Saturday afternoons with Danny Hilton, and, "What's he to you?"

"No more than you, so far as promises go."

"So there are no promises?"

"Not to you nor him."

"He's sixteen years older than you."

"And by the same token I'm sixteen years younger than him."

The months ran on into early October and on the seventh day of that month, early in the morning, people of New Era and hundreds of farmers roundabout piled into wagons and buggies, drove along roads that streamed with thousands of people riding to the same central attraction. The rain had poured down the night before, the air was damp and a sour northwest wind blowing with chill on it and those who brought along their overcoats and cloaks were glad of it.

Hornsby had asked Mibs to let him drive her that day. So had Danny. Mibs said she would leave it to chance. She would let them flip a coin. "Heads I go with Danny and tails I go with you." That, said Hornsby, would be gambling and he would have no part in it. He walked out of the Wimbler house calm, dignified, and as he believed, somewhat austere. Wherefore on this morning of October 7, Anno Domini 1858, Mibs sat gaily alongside of Danny handling the reins of a span of black trotters eager to show their gloss and speed.

Twenty thousand people streamed into Galesburg that day. A few hundred had seats but most of them stood in that raw northwest wind, stood on the Knox College campus three hours listening to the words of two men on a platform at the east side of the college main building. The speakers knew and so did the audience, the whole country was listening, millions would read the speeches in newspapers.

Hayracks, floats, banners, flags, buggies and wagons, saddled horses, peddlers and hawkers with balloons and candy, brass bands, fife-and-drum corps, formed a scene around the audience that stood in quiet and good order to hear the first speaker, the Democrat. He was at home among crowds, that man was, you could see it, Mibs was saying in half-whispers to Danny, by his face, by the tilt of his head, by the cool way he laid his cigar on the chair as he stood up after the introduction, by the easy way he took off his high white silk hat, slid out of his overcoat and stepped forward to wait till the cheers, handclapping and shouts slowed down, raising his right hand with the palm

743

of it toward the audience meaning there was no time to waste and it was a cold day and the men buttoned their overcoats to the throat and the women tightened their shawls and cloaks. A man of fame, the foremost son of the State of Illinois in national affairs at Washington. He would speak an hour. Then the other man, the Republican, would speak an hour and a half and the first speaker be allowed a half-hour to answer.

He stood there letting the last of the applause and cheering die down before he spoke a word. He had been through the ordeal of having his voice go husky and his throat hoarse and sore so he had to quit. He would go slow with each word and sentence, aiming exactly to reach the far-off rim of the audience. He had practiced this. He was confident his voice wouldn't give out. He stood there like nothing else in American politics, a storm figure, a bold and daring player of the game, short in stature, having to look up in the face of the medium-sized chairman who introduced him. He was somewhat taller than a tall dwarf, it could be said and had been. Then Mibs and Danny looked again to the torso of him, thick and well rounded, shoulders broad in proportion, an erect well-set frame topped with a magnificently molded large head and tall brow with smooth wavy black hair brushed back and he could toss that head with defiance, disdain, triumphant pronouncements. Admirers nicknamed him the Little Giant. Republican editors belittled him as the Shortboy Senator.

Mibs caught a glimpse of the Paddy Whalens on the edge of the crowd, Maureen lifted to a shoulder of her father. On Paddy's face she saw smiling admiration change to a light of adoration and Maureen with a solemn unutterable curiosity as her eyes kept fastened on the man she had heard her father swear was the greatest living fighter that walked and talked for human freedom in the arena of American politics. At last had come the day her eyes could rove and play on the breathing speaking man himself, United States Senator from Illinois, Stephen A. Douglas.

They could see on the platform the opponent, till now practically unknown nationally outside of Illinois, the man who when Senator Douglas had finished his argument would have to stand up and answer it, answer the readiest and most adroit debater in the United States Senate. There he sat, listening to every word, missing not a phrase, his knees reaching up higher than the seat of his chair, occasionally crossing one knee over the other, giving idle absent jogs to the boot held up from the floor. A long man, the length of him in his legs mainly, his bony shoulders sort of drawn in, his chin at times sunk deep in his overcoat collar and his head bent forward, his right elbow at times resting on a lifted left hand and his half-hidden face dropped into the right hand. For whatever effect he chose, he wore a silk stovepipe hat, a hat tall as they were made. He had challenged Senator Douglas to this debate. If he did well and stood strong against the arguments of Douglas he would have a national reputation and might go far, that was the guess among Republicans. And everywhere East and West Republicans hoped that in the Illinois Legislature in November this man in the stovepipe hat would win election over Douglas as United States Senator. He represented the Unknown. He embodied shadowy elements of the Unseen yet to be unfolded and disclosed by events.

Four times before this day these two speakers had stood on platforms before big outdoor crowds in discussions and wrangles over the Kansas Nebraska Bill, Squatter Sovereignty, whether the people of a new state should "vote slavery up or down," the Dred Scott decision, the Constitution, the Declaration of Independence and what the great Democrat Thomas Jefferson meant by the sentence, "All men are created equal." They had started in August in two Illinois cities far north, swung to farthest south in Illinois, come north again and would end nearer the center of the state. What had stirred up excitement West and East lay in the fact that the Unknown had stood up to Douglas and made a showing that amazed and pleased many people who wanted to see Douglas trimmed, smitten and, if it could be, struck down and shorn of political power.

Douglas began his speech and moved into claiming that for himself he was saying the same thing north and south in Illinois while his shifty and tricky opponent was saying one thing north and something else in the south, that northward his opponent played to the antislavery element and southward kept an eye out for the voters of Kentucky and Tennessee connections who hated abolitionists as snakes in the grass. "He is to be voted for in the south as a proslavery man and he is to be voted for in the north as an abolitionist," said Douglas. From his opponent's speech of last June Douglas read:

> " 'A house divided against itself cannot stand.' I believe this government cannot endure permanently, half slave and half free. I do not expect the Union to be dissolved—I do not expect the house to fall; but I do expect it will cease to be divided. It will become all one thing, or all the other."

Mibs wondered what Douglas, having read this, would do with it. She had heard her father read it aloud from the *Chicago Tribune* last June. She now heard Douglas saying that when the Constitution was framed more than sixty years ago there were twelve slaveholding States against one free State. "Thus you see that the doctrine he now advocates, if proclaimed at the beginning of the government, would have established slavery everywhere throughout the American continent; and are you willing, now that we have the majority section, to exercise a power which we never would have submitted to when we were in the minority? . . . Are you willing, now that we have become the strongest under that great principle of self-government that allows each

State to do as it pleases, to attempt to control the Southern institutions?"

"Clear as mud," said Mibs once, and again on hearing, "There is but one path of peace in this republic, and that is to administer this government as our fathers made it, divided into free and slave States, allowing each State to decide for itself whether it wants slavery or not. If Illinois will settle the slavery question for herself, and mind her own business, and let her neighbors alone, we will be at peace with Kentucky, and every other Southern State. If every other State in the Union will do the same, there will be peace between the North and South, and in the whole Union."

Cheers and applause broke for the speaker as he closed, and those last two sentences stayed with Mibs. She caught a finality of sincerity about them and about the voice of Douglas as he gave them. For a moment the mask of the political actor dropped off and a man spoke a simple hope that echoed with millions of his followers.

Mibs saw the long man, now out of his overcoat, his stovepipe hat on a chair, bowing to the tremendous shouts and hurrahs after the chairman had said, "The Honorable Abraham Lincoln of Illinois."

He stood before them as the Unknown Contender against the distinguished Champion. Over his face flitted a smile of mirth as though he and the assembly might have fun today. It was an antislavery audience, about two Republicans to one Democrat at the polls in that section of Illinois. He was Kentucky-born, with a dash of Pennsylvania Quaker blood in him, a Springfield lawyer who ten years ago served two years in Congress at Washington. The smile vanished and he stood gaunt and lonesome till the cheering let down:

"When the Judge says that I make speeches of one sort for the people of the northern end of the State, and a different sort for the southern people, he assumes that I do not understand that my speeches will be put in print and read north and south. I knew all the while that the speech that I made at Chicago and the one I made at Jonesboro and the one at Charleston would all be put in print, and all the reading and intelligent men in the community would see them and know all about my opinions; and I have not supposed, and do not now suppose, that there is any conflict whatever between them."

A high-keyed voice, a clear and far-carrying treble that reached the rim of the crowd, the tone pressing, hauling and hewing around one point, hammering it home: "I believe the entire records of the world, from the date of the Declaration of Independence up to within three years ago, may be searched in vain for one single affirmation, from one single man, that the Negro was not included in the Declaration of Independence; I think I may defy Judge Douglas to show that he ever said so, that Washington ever said so, that any President ever said so, that any member of Congress ever said so, or that any living man upon the whole earth ever said so, until the necessities of the

746

Democratic party, in regard to slavery, had to invent that affirmation. And I will remind Judge Douglas and this audience that while Mr. Jefferson was the owner of slaves, as undoubtedly he was, in speaking upon this very subject, he used the strong language that 'he trembled for his country when he remembered that God was just'; and I will offer the highest premium in my power to Judge Douglas if he will show that he, in all his life, ever uttered a sentiment at all akin to that of Jefferson."

A horse was property. A Negro was property. And Judge Douglas was neither logical nor moral in assuming there was no difference between the two species of property, a horse and a Negro. Mibs memorized, to carry away and mull over till she would read the speech, two sentences: "He is blowing out the moral lights around us, when he contends that whoever wants slaves has the right to hold them. . . He is in every possible way preparing the public mind, by his vast influence, for making the institution of slavery perpetual and national."

Douglas replied with denials, four times walking over and shaking his fist in Lincoln's face. Douglas in ending said, "I stand by the laws of the land. I stand by the Constitution as our fathers made it."

When the people in front seats arose Mibs caught sight of Hornsby and a woman alongside of him. He had her arm, taking care of her, guiding her through the crowd.

Mibs made her way with Danny along the crowded street toward the railroad depot, where a block west of the depot Danny had tied his horses. They walked out of their way a little for a look at the George W. Brown corn-planter works. Near the depot they met a swarming mass of people heading toward the Knox College campus, part of two thousand passengers who had left Peoria in the morning on a special train of twenty-two cars. What with locomotive breakdowns and cars uncoupled, they arrived just as the debate was over and many decided at least to run over and have a look at the speakers' platform.

Driving to New Era they passed with nods and smiles Hornsby and his companion in a buggy that needed washing and a farm work horse on a slow jog. Mibs wondered how her nod and smile looked. She recognized the woman, Fidelia Englehart, a sturdily built woman of twenty-two, plain of dress and manner, the fourth-grade teacher in the New Era school, scrupulous and unfailing at the Sunday-school class she had conducted for five years. Her father was head man at the sawmill. Her black hair came down prim around a face of milk-white skin that people liked for its notable contrast with the black accent of her hair. Her straight-lipped mouth with a slight downward pull at the corners gave her a mute look of patience and exactitude. She was known as "dependable in whatever she set her mind to."

There had been a Sunday two years ago, Mibs recollected, when Hornsby called a little meeting after evening church services and reported that on the two successive Sunday nights before, he saw as he was going home, a house with no curtains drawn and through the windows he could see eight persons at card-playing. On the night of the Sabbath these persons sat at two tables laughing and playing cards. Hornsby favored a plan that he and those he had called into consultation should go to this house as witnesses and afterward go before the grand jury then meeting and get indictments of the card-players. "It is the duty of good citizens to exert themselves for the suppression of such things," Mibs remembered Hornsby saying. Some had demurred pleasantly to Hornsby's proposal, others disagreed rather positively that no good would come of it. Mibs had said nothing and resented Hornsby's not having told her about his scheme beforehand. But he had at this little meeting one firm supporter in Fidelia Englehart. She considered it a mockery of the church that those people should before lighted windows play cards flagrantly in view of passers-by. "Maybe they were so interested in their playing that they forgot the curtains," had been suggested. Hornsby couldn't see it. Nor could Fidelia. They were outvoted and the matter dropped.

Mibs and Danny had seen two men in a fist fight with bloody faces, a crowd around them, a block from the Knox College campus. Both men were from the Maple Hill crossroads, Danny learned, and one of them, a Buchanan Democrat, had been appointed postmaster, winning the place over a Douglas Democrat. The loser had galloped past the winner crying, "Stinkfingers!" And the other man had speeded his horse and challenged the other to fight it out.

"There they were," said Mibs as they drove in the dark that had come on, Danny letting the horses find the way at an easy trot. "There they were, spattered and cursing, snarling like two animals, like two dogs that would rather fight than eat. What do you make of it, Danny?"

Danny mulled it over. "There's some men take to fightin just like dogs. It's nature to 'em."

"But one was sore because he didn't get to be postmaster of Maple Hill, wasn't he?"

"That was part of it, and there was more. The Douglas fellows thought their man ought to have been nominated and elected President two years ago instead of Buchanan. Southern Democrats that don't like Douglas swung the nomination to Buchanan. Bad blood between the Douglas Democrats and the Buchanan Democrats. They hate each other as they hate the abolitionists and the abolitionists hate the both of them."

"They were fighting about politics, after all?"

"You could tell they liked the fightin too. They'd put off the fight so long it did 'em good at last to get into it."

"They wanted to kill each other, don't you think, the way their faces looked?"

"Yes."

748

"But not over a little post office."

"A post office—*and* politics."

Politics is queer, Danny went on, telling of some Iowa Republicans he had talked with. "They're against the spread of slavery but that isn't the half of it. They're afraid if the South secedes from the Union the Southern states will control the Mississippi River from Keokuk down to the Gulf. It's their river, the east line of their state. They don't want to see it divided up. More yet, they want a railroad to the Pacific. The South has been blockin it in Washington. And there's a clique peggin away on the quiet to get a Republican President and Congress that'll put that railroad through. They have their eye on that railroad more than slavery, not regular abolitionists by a long shot. Over in that little corn-fed State of Iowa now they've got double the white population of South Carolina. They've grown so fast that South Carolina is scared of what they'll be in another ten years. Yet Iowa only a few years ago had Senators and Congressmen that was straight out for slavery. That's been changed and South Carolina is scared of more changes."

"Do you suppose, Danny, there could be a war between the North and the South?"

"I can't see it now. Might be, though. My guess is if the North fights it'll be a short war, over in no time."

"Hornsby some years back was for letting the South go, if it wanted to. Then he shifted. If there was no war the South would keep its slaves. Now Hornsby won't tell all of it but I think he wants a war and believes it will be the end of slavery."

"I don't like to think about it, Mibs. Whatever comes will be different from what we think now. War comes hard on men and horses."

"And women and children?"

"Yes, they stay at home and suffer."

They drove on, the road ahead a vague gray line between the dark rise of the Osage-orange hedge fences or the zigzag rail fences almost invisible. Occasionally came an upland ridge where corn shocks stood as dumb and patient silhouettes.

"The brave man who knows he's going to lose, is he braver than one who knows he's going to win?" asked Mibs.

"Why do you bring that up?"

"Thinking about Chief Black Hawk nearly thirty years back. After the whites won the war and took him prisoner they hauled him on to Washington and he told President Jackson, as I remember reading it, and the way they translated it, 'We did not expect to conquer the whites. They had too many houses, too many men. I took up the tomahawk to pay them back for wrongs my people could no longer endure. Had I borne them longer without striking, my people would have said, Black Hawk is a woman, too old to be a chief.'"

"He *was* brave, I guess."

749

"He came home to Iowa, to a cabin on the Des Moines River, died at seventy-one, buried sitting up, his left hand holding a cane given him in Washington by Henry Clay, and in reach of his dead hands enough corn and tobacco to last him three days' travel to the spirit land."

"Say anything about how the whites done him?"

"Made a Fourth of July speech. Part of it comes back to me, the way I read it. 'Rock River,' said Black Hawk, 'was a beautiful country. I liked my town, my cornfields, and the homes of my people. I fought for it. Now it is yours. Keep it, as we did. It will produce you good crops.'"

"Gosh, he was a good loser. You can't beat that."

They jogged past a hayrack load of people, saw Pa and Ma Wimbler, drove on and about had supper ready when Pa and Ma came in.

On the front steps saying good night to Danny, Mibs kissed him and then had to keep him away. He wanted more of her than she could bring her heart and mind to give. It was getting complicated. Danny was tangled in her heart but not deep. She had wondered how much longer they could go on. There was his house and farm and horses for her when she cared to join him. A married couple did most of the farm and house work. It beckoned to her. Danny was much her kind even though he had been read out of the church fellowship.

Hornsby dropped in one Friday afternoon to let her know he was starting for a rousing antislavery rally at Maple Hill in the evening and another at Monmouth on Saturday night when he was to be the principal speaker for resolutions demanding that Illinois repeal its law against free Negroes entering the state.

"Is that still on the books?" asked Mibs. "How did I get the idea that had been repealed?"

"It's still there, I told you sometime ago about it."

"It didn't sink in. What do they do with a free Negro caught entering the State of Illinois?"

"The law says they must jail him and if no owner claims him he must be sold to the highest bidder."

"They have done that? It has happened?"

"More than once."

Hornsby gave her part of his Monmouth speech as it lay in his mind. A burst of warm feeling came over her. She held one of his hands in both of hers and wished him the best of luck at his meetings. He turned to go, faced her again, "Millicent, I wish you to know it is my desire that our old relationship of so long a standing could be resumed."

Following a habit, he stroked his brown sideburns, first with one hand, then the other. In his eyes and on his mouth she read granite purpose, his life ordered by a relentless will, by a mind which she had seen grow with turmoils and accumulations. She pressed his hand. "Let's not talk about it." And he had gone away to his Friday-night Maple Hill and Saturday-night Monmouth meetings. And it haunted her that in the State of Illinois the law said that a free Negro coming into the state should be jailed and if no owner claimed him, then sold to the highest bidder.

Saturday night Mibs was three miles out from New Era, halfway to Hickory Grove, couples from both those towns joining in a barn dance, her first one. She had waltzed at home occasionally, just practicing or to see what it was like, with Danny Hilton. Now there was a fiddle and an accordion playing waltzes between the square dances and Mibs giving way to it, finding herself at home in the sinuous steps and winding whirls of the interthreading couples.

She had heard one evangelist term the waltz "a hugging match set to music with shame lost and modesty abandoned." That was true enough for two of the Hickory Grove couples whose bodies pressed close and tight, the women close-up with hands on the shoulders of their partners, moving their feet in short shuffles rather than the wide one-two-three steps, swings and glides of the true waltz. She and Danny agreed these couples went too far. There was a table with small glasses for those who chose to pour from a jug of Peoria whisky and pottery mugs for those who cared to pour from a keg of St. Louis beer. Mibs kept away from the drinks till Danny said before the "Home, Sweet Home" waltz that maybe one beer would do no harm. And Mibs drank her first glass of beer and out of politeness said it wasn't so bad, though she didn't like the smell nor taste of it and her unspoken thought was she still would prefer cider or lemonade.

During this good-night drink and while the fiddle and accordion were fooling with bars of "Home, Sweet Home," a fight suddenly started. A Hickory Grove man didn't like it that a New Era boy had kissed his girl. The Hickory Grove man had taken on too many drinks and the New Era boy had him on the floor, had set the man's lower lip bleeding with one fist blow and was swinging again when others tore them apart. The Hickory Grove man had pulled a knife and was babbling and shrieking, "I'll cut the sonofabitch to pieces." Al Dunnigan made him hand over the knife, carried him outside and put him into his buggy driving away with his girl. And the "Home, Sweet Home" was played and danced but it was the least merry of the evening.

Mibs wasn't sure why she had gone to this dance. It was in part curiosity. She had heard so much of barn dances and never been to one. And she was not mistaken, she told herself, that the waltz was a creation that would always have grace and lure for her. Her father and mother were rather stern in warnings she must go careful, must watch herself about going in for a life of dancing. She couldn't bring to them the question in her mind, "Since you have never waltzed, how can you know what is wrong in it?" But when Hornsby came

751

the next Wednesday she knew she had gone to the barn dance partly with him in mind, a vague expectation of a certain result which now did follow.

Hornsby had heard rumors. They might be gossip and tittle-tattle. He had sought out people who were there. He heard from their own lips, two, three, four witnesses. "Yes, the Wimbler girl was there with Danny Hilton. She danced half the waltzes with him and went around the rest with the other boys. She's handy with her feet, born to the waltz." And the drinks, did she go in for a few glasses? No, she kept away from the redeye, just one mug of beer before the "Home, Sweet Home." And they told of the fight and how a drunken Hickory Grove man threatened to cut a New Era boy to pieces and it was straightened out.

The depths of self-righteous wrath in Hornsby were stirred. He didn't go into details in telling Mibs, "I have gathered a full knowledge of the melancholy affair, Millicent. It is proper for me to express my regrets, my deep regrets. You will permit me to say that our relationship has arrived at a point where the bonds of long standing are broken. It is perhaps needless for me to inform you that I shall not in the future beset you with further difficulties. I wish you happiness and I earnestly beg of you that you hearken to the counsels that I know proceed from your father and mother regarding the new course of life on which you seem to be entering. I would not presume to lay down precepts nor recall to you the teachings of a Gospel with which you are familiar enough in the abstract. It is with fervent prayers that you may have guidance from on high that I say farewell."

He was gone. Out the door of Mibs' home Hornsby was gone—for good. Mibs laughed. "He studied it out beforehand. He rehearsed it." Then the peculiar strengths of him lingered with her, the bear hugs of those powerful shoulders, and still more his doing the best he could last Saturday night at Monmouth for any newly arrived free Negro entering Illinois unaware he could be jailed and sold. She laughed about his set speech. Then her eyes were moist about an old playmate who did have his rare qualities.

Danny kept pressing her with questions. The night came that she sobbed on his shoulder and told him to go, he must go, she had a love for him but it wasn't the love he would want for the long run, for the years on years. He loved her the more for a candor that he knew came true from her and that in the long run would be best for both of them.

It was April when Danny arranged his affairs on the farm and in the town and gave out word he was going to Chicago for a year. It was April too when the word came that Hornsby Meadows and Fidelia Englehart were engaged and it was Fidelia he now brought to and from Sunday-evening services. Regularly to the morning and evening Sunday services Mibs went, with her father and mother.

Mibs puzzled over whether to go to the wedding in June. A card of ornamental design had come with the names of the three Wimblers written on it, inviting them to the church and to the Meadows home afterward for a dinner. Mibs went to the church ceremony in a blue silk bodice and a wide blue satin bow that fell from her throat as a cascade, her chestnut hair in the most sober and sedate arrangement she could think of. She went straight home after seeing and hearing the two pronounced man and wife.

She went to her room, an anger tossing in her. What of it that the sky shone a flawless blue and the glints of the sun came on the oak leaves as a bright music? What of it that a young catalpa cried with fresh and immaculate white blossoms and her heart never failed to wonder at the lines of quiet brown rust laid even and absolute inside of each blossom? The anger tossed in her and slid reckless from her tongue, ending, "She's the one woman for him, the one *good* woman he ought to have, a good good good woman. She'll drop him children like a cow drops calves." Then her clenched left fist drove into her open right hand. "O God, forgive me. God, wipe those words away."

She knew she wouldn't have taken Hornsby back if he had begged it of her. Yet now it was on her that she had broken old bonds for all time—and it cost. As between Hornsby and Danny she would have taken Danny. And she had told Danny to go, with anguish told Danny to go. And in her bitterness she had swept into low, cruel and earthy prattle about a plain and good woman.

She untied and flung off the cascading satin bow, kicked off her slippers, fell on the bed and sobbed. Her shaken grief slowed down into a quiet that found halting snatches of sentences. "Let me pray to Thee, O Lord. I who would be a lamb of God, I have been a swine. Help me."

She lifted her head to see her slim strong legs from knees to feet against the blue-and-white checked coverlet. She lifted one of them, then the other. "Give them strength, O Lord, strength to go on and if they stumble let them go on again unafraid."

As she lay there the flawless blue of the June sky came closer to her from the open window and the glint of the sun on the oak leaves had ministrations. Later she would go out to the young catalpa and look again into the heart of a white bell-shape of a blossom and study the traceries of quiet brown rust.

She read more books that summer and fall, put in more hard work, and had more fun in the kitchen and among the potatoes, carrots, tomatoes and cucumbers, than any other year her father and mother had watched over her. She had lost standing in New Era and now went to church only once a month, "the less to trouble those who have misgivings about me." To the Paddy Whalens she went oftener than to any other house for warmth and human cheer, listening to Maureen read aloud from the *Chicago Times,* asking questions but not trying to instruct unless it was in the pronunciation or meaning of words.

Her mother on a September day of 1859 asked her, "Are you happy, Mibs, or how is it with you?"

"I'm better off than Hetty or Marova, if you think about it, wherever they are."

In the potato-digging days the mother was pleased at her daughter's tireless strength in forking out bushel after bushel and carrying them to the cellar bin. The mother brushed the loose black dirt from a potato with her apron and a smile on her still face, "I really don't know what to make of you, Mibs."

"Nor do I, Ma," as her face came close and she put a light kiss on the still lips that ever had meaning and sweetness for her.

The leaves were turning, with every day new sneaks of yellow and gold on the branches, spots of utterly weary and crackling brown, slashes of unspeakable scarlet crying hosannahs, shifting maroons sending the faint whisper, "And thou too goest whither?"

Scrolls of wild geese had crossed the sky with a scurrying whirr that after it passed left the impression you might have listened closer and learned something.

Now as in early summer and late spring Mibs put in an hour or two every day with a banjo she had not before taken seriously. Over the town and in the country among odd people and at Paddy Whalen's she picked up new songs and plucked accompaniments and variations on her banjo.

A melodeon, a small reed organ with black and white keys, she could have had or even, said the father and mother, even a Chickering piano, though it would be extravagant and make talk. They would go that far for their girl. She had considered a violin or an accordion and hesitated between a guitar and a banjo. Friendly and simple, intended to go with singing, she took the banjo saying later she might try the guitar. She picked out the chords from a book, *The Famous New York Banjo Instructor,* "containing easy lessons for beginners, popular songs and approved compositions." The chords were what she wanted. She learned them and worked hard and practiced many hours at strumming the chords to go with her songs. She then had the queer satisfaction of being the only banjo-player in New Era. There were two over at Galesburg. She must look them up sometime to see what they might have for each other. Near Hickory Grove was a family from Kentucky that had a dulcimer, a wooden box with four wire strings. She had heard them once at a Fourth of July picnic singing "Barbara Allen" and other ballads and odd little folk songs, one with two verses she must learn:

754

> Hello girls, listen to my voice,
> Don't you never marry no good-for-nothing boys.
> If you do your doom shall be
> Hoecake, hominy and sassafras tea!
>
> When a young man falls in love
> First it's honey and then turtledove.
> After he's married no such thing,
> "Get up and get my breakfast, you good-for-nothing thing."

Of the man who sang this song for her five times so she knew it for sure, she asked if he had written out any of his songs. He said, "The whole of my endurin life I never learnt to write and never needed to." He could read a little, he said, but what he needed was to learn how to use what he already had of knowledge. Once a week he went to Baptist preaching and the country and the world could be saved if they'd follow the Bible. He had a dozen verses to one song and liked best the lines:

> You may boast o' your knowledge
> En brag o' your sense,
> Twill all be forgotten
> A hundred years hence.

"I'm right proud to give you-all one uh my songs," he had said to Mibs. "A little somethin like that won't bring you harm." To him a horse was a "critter" and Kentucky "a far piece off." He could meditate that "the soil uh ol Kaintuck ain't just yaller, it's the yallerest kind o' yaller." For emphasis he could say, "Dang my darnicks," whatever that meant. Of his half-section of land that he "took up" long ago, two forty-acre pieces had gone each to a son and daughter who married. When his twenty-year-old son brought home a sixteen-year-old bride the young husband most often called her "my old woman." It was a custom. The old man's wife had died and two boys and four girls were working the farm with him. "Land worth a man's sweat," he said of the farm, taking pride in the six-room log house they had built from trees they themselves cut down and logs their own axes had hewn. "A strong house the wind can't shake and the rain can't beat into."

Mibs made three trips to see this Hickory Grove old man named Robert Emmet Crittenden who on being asked if he was related to the distinguished United States Senator from Kentucky, John J. Crittenden, answered, "Distant kin, so distant we don't claim him and he's so right busy on the slavery question he ain't got time to claim us." He enjoyed quoting a neighbor, "I'm a leading citizen of Hickory Grove because every man here is a leading citizen." He had been on a horse and carried a Douglas banner to Galesburg on the day of the debate, "fifty of us a-horseback for the Little Giant."

Mibs brooded over Robert Emmet Crittenden. The South had

secrets the North knew little or nothing of. That was certain. And it was equally certain that the North had its secrets the South hadn't fathomed.

"Either they must know each other's secrets better," said Mibs, "either that or they must somehow love each other more."

She said this to herself again, forgot it and came back to it and asked herself if she knew what she was talking about. She repeated it and added, "It's as true as there is a living God—even though I can't prove it. Either they've got to dig deeper in each other's hearts for what they'll find there or somehow they've got to love each other more in order to get at what they don't understand now. Otherwise there'll be a holiday of pride and hate, a storm bloody to look at."

She had heard of an Illinois man saying, "We must not only convince the South that we will let them alone but we must convince them that we are sincere in letting them alone." This haunted her. It was the obverse, the other face, of what she had been telling herself. When she had mentioned it to Hornsby he had said it was silly and, "The North and the South don't talk the same language." This was bitter and appalling to Mibs. She held back from giving Hornsby the answer on her tongue, "If there are not enough men in the two sections who understand the same language the Union will go to hell and it ought to." A comfort vague and with a brackish taste was there in the lines she sang:

"You may boast o' your knowledge
En brag o' your sense,
Twill all be forgotten
A hundred years hence."

* * * * * * * * * *

Chapter 15

* * * * * * * * * *

New Riders into New Era

FOUR men rode into New Era on the afternoon of October 20, 1859. They had made the ride out of Galesburg on good speaking terms. Then a coolness sprang up between them. And they rode apart, two by two.

One was a man in his early fifties, a rugged, chunkily built man with a bristling chin beard, a full-lipped positive mouth, popeyes, and his hair, when he took off his wide-brimmed hat, "every way for Sunday," as the saying went. His nineteen-year-old son had a spindling

756

frame of a body, was slightly taller than his father, and his pale face had an intensity seen in the active bulging eyes of his father. A mile out of Galesburg that morning, with a light frost shining over pasture grass and corn stubble, they had turned their eyes on two young men past the middle twenties who overtook them. There were greetings and mention of what a good corn year it had been in Illinois and how it was something to think about that Galesburg and New Era and every farmhouse and barn between those two towns hadn't been there less than thirty years ago and the road they were riding hadn't been there and the lonesome prairie then stretched away far as the eye could see with nothing human in it. In the course of the talk the elderly man was saying, "This is a great country, this America we live in, never anything like it, never a country with so many independent farmers ownin their land, and cities full of prosperous factories and workingmen that when they don't like it can go out on the land and be independent."

"It *is* a great country," said one of the young men.

"Could be the greatest nation in the world, givin the law to the rest of the world, except for what's workin against it."

"What's workin against it?"

"Two things."

"And those are?"

"First, the damned abolitionists, workin night and day to bust the Union apart. Some of them want a Union with the South and slavery left out. Others want a war with the South. This John Brown they caught at Harper's Ferry last Monday, shootin and killin, he wanted a war. I say goddam the likes of a man like that, tryin to start a war between the states. They'll hang him and they ought to."

"Hangin would be good for him," said another of the young men. They were in agreement. It was a rather pleasant morning.

The elderly man chewed at a half-smoked cigar, spat to one side, and went on. "But this vicious rascal John Brown, he's only half the trouble. Another element's workin against the Union and they're as bad as the damned abolitionists." He slanted an eye toward the two young strangers.

"And what's that other element?"

"That's the fellows talkin secession, the states-rights fellows. Why, I heard a while ago about a family somewhere down South named Gist and they gave one son the name of States Rights and he signs his name States Rights Gist. That's a hell of a name."

"Have you read the Constitution of the United States?"

"Course I have."

"Is there any place in it says anything against a state seceding if it wants to? Any place where it says the Federal Government has the power to stop a sovereign state from leaving the Union?"

"So you're one of those states-rights fellows?"

"I'm for the Union, mister. I love this old Union. I want to see the states hold together and go on united. But I'm clear on one point. Any state can go out of the Union when it pleases. Each state is sovereign."

"Is that so?"

"Now I'll tell you, mister, it's no use our going into an argument. You know, don't you, that some of the best lawyers in the country have been arguing for years about states rights and what the Constitution says. I'll bet it won't be settled in the end by talk."

"You're maybe right there. Maybe it won't be settled till they fight it out."

"And maybe if the whole South goes out they'll let 'em go. Then after the South goes these states in the Northwest can make a country of their own and tell abolition New England to go to hell by herself."

"It won't go that way, young man. There's too many up North here and out on the West coast where I come from, too many ready to fight, ready for war, ready to fight in blood up to the horses' bridles before they'll let the Union go to pieces. There's too much invested that'll be lost if the Union breaks. You can't divide up and parcel out the rivers and plains, mountains and coasts, of this country. God put 'em together for the whole American people to enjoy and use in peace and union."

"Then why did God make the abolitionists to go around howling, writing and printing, 'No Union with Slaveholders'? Why did God make John Brown?"

"When God did that He used the same kind of mud He used for makin those states-rights fellows—" And the chunky elder man didn't get to finish the sentence, for the young fellow broke into a rollicking laugh, "That includes me, mister," clucked to his horse and the two young strangers galloped into a long lead. They registered at the New Era Hotel and stayed for two weeks that neither they nor New Era would forget in a long time.

The elderly man, Amos Hines, registered his son at New Era College. That was part of his errand. Of his four sons three were of his own views and active with the Republicans of California. The youngest, Herbert, had fallen in with Democrats of Southern sympathies, favored states rights, had joined in mobbing an abolitionist speaker, had been on the loose with girls. The father believed the radical air and strict discipline of New Era College couldn't harm and might help Herbert. Of this he hadn't spoken to Herbert, not a hint. Herbert believed he was locating in New Era mainly on account of his father owning one thousand acres of land in near-by townships and it was his assignment to report to his father on land sales, farming prospects, possible veins of coal, and whether to sell or to rent the land on shares and hold it for a rise.

The arrival of Amos Hines in New Era was an event. He and

Herbert were made welcome at the home of Silas Higby, who owned the controlling shares of the New Era steam sawmill. Amos Hines had long ago put some money into it and had helped install the machinery and get it going. He was known as New Era's first millionaire. He had lost half of the million but enough was left so it had been said, "Amos Hines could buy and sell the whole of New Era if he had a mind to." They knew him as a hard man, hard in driving himself and hard in driving the two women who had struggled with him through the early days and who had died before he headed West in 1849. From San Francisco the reports had come definitely back to New Era that his fortune was up in dizzy figures, that on the ground early he had made big strikes in gold and then operated shrewdly in real estate, steamships, and mining machinery, that he had married a wild girl he picked up in a saloon concert hall where she sang and danced.

The old settlers of New Era had praise for Amos Hines. He had arrived from Ohio in 1836, bringing his wife, two children, a half-brother, a neighbor and wife, in a nineteen-day drive when it rained every day, their household goods and blankets soaked in fording flooded streams. "The horses and harness never dried." For six years he had gone to school two months each year and that was his education. His one-room log cabin, cow shed and covered hogpen, gave way in 1841 to a big barn he painted red and in 1842 the first brick house in the county. He had started the first brickyard in 1840 and the next year the first sawmill with creek power and had taken up more than a thousand acres of land in Wahomah township and in two other townships the thousand acres that Herbert was now to oversee.

Out of New Era in 1849 drove Amos Hines with fifteen other men. They had three wagons and painted in big letters on the Canvas: "California or Death." For six of them it had been death and of the ten that were left, three came back to New Era in shattered health.

Amos Hines had twice sent a thousand dollars to the New Era College. He didn't like the news that President Brench and his abolition faction had won over the hesitant neutral trustee. He went with Jonas Fry, the chairman of the board, to the office of President Brench and exploded, "I don't give a damn about slavery where it is. Let 'em have it. It's only the spread of it I'm against. And I think I'd be willing to let it spread if that would save the Union. If those secessionists pull their states out of the Union and a war comes I'll blame you abolitionists as much as those states-rights bastards. You egg 'em on. You leave 'em no peace. You lay awake nights thinkin up new insults."

The ascetic and dyspeptic Jonas Fry enjoyed it. The burly President Brench tried to find words of decent protest or mild reproof that would correct the raging Californian who contributed liberally to the college and was registering a son as a student. And Amos Hines, by way of summary, in case he had not been understood, shook his fist in the face of President Brench and closed his case. "They're stink-

fingers down there, those states-rights secessionist rats—and you aboli-
tionists, you're the same kind of stinkfingers, the same kind of rats,
tryin to sink the good old Union ship of state."

Hornsby Meadows, not knowing who was with President Brench,
had entered the room to hear this last outburst. He stepped out
quietly and unseen. An elation he had that week rose higher in him.
Hornsby had helped raise a fund of twenty thousand dollars from anti-
slavery men of Illinois for the works and schemes of John Brown,
Osawatomie John Brown of Kansas, soon to be given a fair trial in
Virginia and according to law hanged by the neck till he was dead as
his doom for the crimes of murder and treason.

Hornsby felt himself a member of a sacred brotherhood and this
week, with the violent and mad deed of John Brown flaming before
the world, Hornsby touched many unseen hands of that brotherhood.
The members of it were resolved and irreconcilable, prepared in their
hearts for the ordeal of war, if need be, to destroy slavery root and
branch. Opposed to them, they knew, was an open brotherhood of
equally resolved and irreconcilable Southern men also prepared for
the last resort of the test by blood and steel. Hornsby believed in this
month of October 1859 that there was in the air something like the
hush that precedes a hurricane. Had he thought it permissible for him
to stay in the office of President Brench he would have heard Amos
Hines in a hoarse low voice and with eyeballs bulging put a statement
and a query. "You're an abolitionist out-and-outer, Mr. Brench, and
some of 'em haven't got much at the end of the backbone where the
brain begins but you're the head of this college, and you're supposed
to have more than ordinary. Has the idea crossed what passes for a
brain in that headpan of yours that the way you fellows carry on
you're liable to have this country where you'll have to send every
able-bodied student in this college out on battlefields where men shove
cold bayonets into other men's guts?"

The undisturbed, resolved and irreconcilable Mr. Brench tried to
be cordial yet precise. "There may arrive, Mr. Hines, I regret to say,
exactly the manner of crisis you describe, and we shall have to meet it
with resolute hearts and minds."

"Poof! I don't think you see it," said Hines with a sniff, turning
the talk to college and local affairs. He stayed three days in New Era,
rode out with Herbert to look over his one-thousand-acre tract, inquired
about his local investments in the sawmill and the brickyard, let it
be known that he and others who had subscribed for stock to help
bring the railroad through New Era need have no regrets, even though
the stock was quoted low and had been "watered." His advice was,
"I'm freezin onto mine. It'll go up for all the jobbery in it. We'll have
to wait for the Pacific Railway boom. It's comin, that Pacific Railway,
if it takes a war to clear the way for it."

The Wimblers heard Mr. Hines say this. On his last evening in

New Era Silas Higby gave a supper to the four families that had put money into the sawmill. They heard Mr. Hines chuckle and then laugh to his boot bottoms describing his first sawmill with creek power at Wahomah. They got the impression he was a man who sat in with other men of money and power discussing investments and prospects, reports on national conditions in finance and politics. "Politics is in trade and trade is in politics all the time," he said in a pause after the Wimblers had told of the outpouring of twenty thousand people over at Galesburg to hear Douglas and Lincoln. "Douglas is a good man, has the advantage over Lincoln, knows *politics* and where it ties in with *trade* and *finance*. If he'd been elected instead of Buchanan he might have saved the Union. Lincoln has tricked him into some answers that have lost Douglas friends in the South. I remember when Bob Toombs, the Georgia Senator, said Douglas was 'the greatest apostle since St. Paul' and now comes word that Toombs would like to see Douglas hanged on a high gibbet."

They could see Mr. Hines was troubled about the immediate future of the country yet earnest and calm about the farther future. "It's too big a country, too young and strong, to lose out in the long run. It can be she'll have to go through an awful fever that'll burn her bowels and bring her near death, but she'll come through it and be stronger than ever."

Mibs was sliding into her cloak when Herbert Hines asked if he might see her home. Having seen her home he asked if he might see her to church next Sunday evening. Mibs said yes, wished him good night with thanks and a handclasp. Then in the house she told her mother of it.

"He looks sort of skinny and dried-up, doesn't he, Mibs?"

"He talks fresh, too fresh. I should have told him I had another engagement."

"They'll buzz about it, Mibs, you and him alongside in a pew, they'll buzz."

* * * * * * * * * *

Chapter 16

* * * * * * * * * *

Rod and Doss Arrive: The Arch

THE two young men who had galloped away from Amos Hines, cutting off conversation with a buzz-saw finality, put up their horses at the New Era Hotel stable, saw personally to the feeding of their nags, then signed the hotel register. "Nack J. Doss, New Orleans, La." wrote the short one. He would have been a tall man if his legs were in proportion to the bodily trunk. He seemed to waddle, at first look, then it could be seen he was handy enough with feet and legs. His arms, pivoting head and glancing eyes were swift in motion and he might be taken as nervous and jerky but for the slow ease of any turn he gave his thickset torso. Over his gray eyes his light-brown hair fell tumbled on the forehead with no intention to hide a scar that curved white and deep around the left temple and down to near the brown hair of the left eyebrow.

"Now you make your bird tracks," he said, handing the pen to his six-foot companion with an upward look into a face with a jutting chin, dark-blue eyes and a forehead with black hair combed back in waves and crinkles. The hotel clerk knew that look the shorter man gave to the taller one, a face blank and mocking rather than solemn, with a quirk in the gray eyes that held affection, loyalty and merriment. They had known each other long, maybe had been in tight places together, and they had signals and jokes rather beyond others fully understanding. Nack J. Doss of New Orleans turned to the clerk and made a remark not meant for the clerk in particular, nodding a head sidewise to the man signing his name, "He never learned to write, he just picked it up." The man signed, "Rodney Wayman, Atlas, Ill.," and made the counter-remark to the clerk, "Atlas ain't as big as New Orleans but it's more respectable."

They ate a hotel meal of T-bone steak, fried and dripping with grease, boiled potatoes with the jackets on, tender potatoes out of the ground less than a week, peas, carrots, beans, cabbage in platters and bowls to be reached, wheat bread from loaves just out of the oven and a golden butter churned yesterday, applesauce with thick cream from a big pitcher, and three cups of coffee apiece.

"You honor these victuals the way you eat," said Mr. Wayman.

"I'm hungry, your honor, hongry, if you please," said Mr. Doss with a stress on "hongry," and adding, "I notice with a knife and fork yourself you're not so clumsy."

Between mouthfuls Wayman had said with a satisfied subdued baritone grunt, "Good grub," and Doss in a responsive basso harumph, "No shanks and necks, no chitterlings."

They put away the food, said nothing to the five others at the oblong table, except when requesting or passing the sugar bowl, the cream pitcher, the butter plate. They walked out and took a slow stroll around the town. They took it easy. They had never been here before but they were at home—in the sense that they would have been at home most anywhere in the United States. They had been up and down the East coast where the ships came in with emigrants from Europe and the outlook was across the Atlantic. They had seen half of California where the outlook was across the Pacific to Asia and cargoes of Chinese coolie labor were unloaded at the Golden Gate.

They were each twenty-six years of age, their faces fresh and boyish at first glance, later scrutiny finding lines and twists of hammer indentation and anvil tests.

They asked the depot agent about passenger trains to Chicago, timetable and fares, and about the local freight and how long shipments took to Chicago, rates on merchandise and livestock. They knew they had no intentions of shipping freight or buying tickets to Chicago. They had seen the depot agent hustling express on the platform, his Texas-longhorn mustache interested them and they wanted to look him over. When they stopped in at the livery stable and talked with Shamp it was mainly curiosity over what was doing in horses. They heard that the best horseman in New Era, Danny Hilton, had gone away for a year and maybe longer and there would be less excitement in horses with Danny gone.

"Why would a man go away and leave a bunch of horses he'd raised?" asked Wayman.

"Account of a girl wouldn't marry him, they say," said Shamp.

"I've knowed girls would've married him for the horses and taken a chance on him."

"This girl liked the horses, all right. She got boots her own size and put on her father's pants and rode with Danny Hilton around the county. Scandalized the town. Her father's the harness-maker here, Presbyterian deacon, laughed at the scandal, thinks the sun rises and sets in that girl's eyes—only child, you know."

A woman drove into the stable in a light open buggy with a finely built champing trotter in a sweat. A hostler began unhitching the horse to blanket him and put him in a box stall. The woman jumped out of the buggy, looked at Shamp as though she was about to cry, and walked away.

"The best trotter we ever had in the stable," said Shamp. "That's my wife, takin her last spins with him. She'd like to renege now. She agreed with me when a Chicago buyer came through and offered one figger and then another till he bid three hundred dollars. I gave her the hundred-and-fifty down payment and she's spent it for a sealskin coat and other wear she looks good in."

Wayman stepped nearer the horse and ran his eyes over the sleek body and slim long legs. He gave his opinion it was one of a breed of fast trotters that had some mixture of the Kentucky thoroughbred running horse.

"Could be," said Shamp. "Jesus, I hate to see her go. It's the drift now. The cities have more fast horseflesh than the country. The farmers can't stand those prices the city buyers offer." And as they were leaving, "Come in again, gentlemen. If you need a rig I've got it. If you don't, we'll talk about hosses," and he chuckled as though "hosses" was a password.

"In your line," came the basso profundo of N. J. Doss, "I guess you hear it that some hosses knows more'n some people."

"I hear that about as regular as I hear you can trust a horse sooner'n a woman."

"We'll look into your establishment again, and pleased to make your acquaintance."

They walked away. Shamp had termed them "gentlemen." He had taken notice of the quality of their felt hats, the flexible blue-black leather of their boots, the plain durable weave of their gray trousers and coats, the peculiar though noiseless assertiveness of their blue satin shirts, Doss with a blue-and-white checked narrow strip of a silk necktie, Wayman with a red-maple-leaf silk cravat that flowed and crinkled down to the third shirt button. They dressed in harmony till it came to neckties. Then they defied each other.

They went into Joel Wimbler's harness shop. Wayman asked, "If I bring you a saddlebag with a broken buckle, do you think you could fix it or put in a new one?"

"I think so. I've got different kinds of buckles."

"I'll be in," and they were out of the shop and Doss saying, "You got no buckle wrong."

"I didn't say so. I asked if there should be a buckle wrong could he fix it or put in a new one."

They had walked to the brickyard and out to the sawmill and back along the blocks of the two- and three-story houses where the well-off lived and across the tracks and along the blocks of two-room and three-room one-story houses. They had watched a cow tethered on a long rope in a vacant lot near an apple tree. Two boys had come along, one grinning, "She's a hookin cow, I tell ye," and he had pranced around the cow and kept her worried and away from the windfall apples while the other tightened a rope around his waist and filled his shirt with apples. They met two college students swinging strapped books, one of them vehemently declaring to the other, "Unless we go heavy on why Hamilton favored a strongly centralized government, we can't win."

They had nearly reached the hotel when Doss stopped, pulled Wayman to face him and in a grand gruff mockery in a low tone, "You snake-in-the-grass galoot, you're aimin to be a customer and talk slick to that harness-maker and find out about his hoss-ridin daughter. That's why you're goin to bust a buckle."

They laughed. They went to bed shortly after dark and a little after sunrise rode to Maple Hill and stayed overnight there, returning to New Era the next day.

At Maple Hill they looked over a quarter-section farm, a hundred acres of rich level prairie and sixty acres of timbered upland. There was a two-story frame house in run-down condition, weeds crowding the path to the ramshackle barn, corncrib, and sheds empty of tools, machinery, vehicles, except a buggy without wheels that hung inside a

764

barn wall, affirming that in its old age the world had gone topsy-turvy.

A plague had struck here, as it had in hundreds of neighborhoods over the land. When it came to a house it often dealt death in a few days to all in the house. A communicable disease, brought from across the Pacific, named Asiatic cholera and the word passing with fright, "It's catching, anybody can catch it." A family of four had gone to death here in as many days. That threw the property to the man's mother in Cincinnati. She had wrestled with sickness and no time to manage. On her death two years ago the farm passed to N. J. Doss, as next of kin. At last the owner of title to this abandoned and desolate place had come to see what it looked like.

On Saturday Doss was seeing various persons who could give him information that might help him decide whether to make some immediate disposal of the Maple Hill farm or to hold it. Rodney Wayman was up early for a ride to Hickory Grove and a visit with a fifth cousin of his father. This cousin was of a branch that had been among the earliest to migrate West from Virginia and Zadock Wayman, whom Rodney was seeking, had built and drifted away from his land and log cabins in Tennessee, Kentucky, southern Illinois, making his fourth remove to north-central Illinois at Hickory Grove. What few letters the children had written for Zadock told little and both Rodney Wayman and his father had a curiosity about Zadock. Three miles out from the Hickory Grove settlement he located Zadock, husking among the corn rows and throwing the ears into a wagon. Helping him were two of his married sons, three sons not yet married and of voting age, a twelve-year-old boy on the wagon seat driving and alongside him a five-year-old son who seemed to be there for luck. At the house for the noon meal Rodney met three daughters in their twenties and upper teens, saw a girl baby in a cradle and was told of the two married daughters and the two near-by farms of the married sons and their wives. The farm was heavily timbered and hilly, about a third of its four hundred acres cleared for cultivation. Zadock was what the people of New Era and Galesburg, who had come from the Eastern states, called a "Hoosier," meaning they had come up from Kentucky and Tennessee; they preferred timberland with game for food, and wood for fuel and building, as against prairie, an instinct in them about personal privacy and independence going with plenty of trees.

Rodney had, as they drove toward the house, somehow formed a quick impression that Zadock's wife would be a worn woman with a thin white face. What he saw as he shook hands with her was a formidable muscular woman with a face blank rather than solemn. He saw her speaking harsh commands to snarling sons ready to fight each other for a turn at the washbasin and she gave infinitely tender words to Zadock as she passed him victuals and asked him about his rheumatism, her face the same whether she spoke hard or soft.

They laid suspicious eyes on Rodney at first. Zadock asked him to stay to dinner as though it was a duty between relatives and they would have it over with. Then as Rodney had stepped along the corn rows and done some brisk husking himself, keeping up with Zadock, they began to warm to him. Rodney had a laughing way about him that caught them. About the middle of the field Zadock told them to go on while he and the newcomer talked and would meet them coming back.

"How is Randolph?" Zadock Wayman asked, naming Rodney's father. "I've heerd Randolph was uppity but I can see you ain't." Then Rodney explained that the big farm Randolph had from his father in the Shenandoah Valley had run down, there had been bad luck in the Negroes running away, dying or growing old and useless, and when an uncle in St. Louis, a lawyer who had got a six-hundred-acre farm in Pike County, Illinois, as a fee, offered it to Randolph for the price of two dollars an acre, just so it wouldn't look like a free gift, Randolph had accepted. Randolph's wife, the younger son and the daughter were doing well, helping work the farm. As for himself, when Zadock questioned him, Rodney about let it go with saying, "Uncle Zadock, I'm a kind of a good-for-nothing, I guess. I wouldn't begin to tell you how many things I've failed at. You better believe me, your cousin Randolph will be glad to get the letter I'll write him about how you've acquitted yourself of your responsibilities."

"How was that last again?" asked Zadock.

"You've done what's right by yourself and the country, working hard and raising a big family and owning a farm you can be proud of."

"Tell Randolph I had a good woman helpin and the thirteen children all seem to be in their right minds and we ain't ashamed of what we brought in the world and," his voice sank quite low, "there was only three we lost and one of them was an accident with a horse."

Riding back to New Era Rodney felt one impression outstanding from this visit with distant kin. They were all more than admirers of Stephen A. Douglas. They worshiped Douglas. They had hoped he would be President by now. They hoped he would win next year at the 1860 election. "He's for lettin the people vote slavery up or down in Nebraska and Kansas," said one of the married sons. "And he's against making the nigger the ekal of the white man." That, to all of them, was the gist of the matter, except for one added point where their faces had a zeal just short of religious frenzy. "Douglas is the only man can hold the Union together and this'll be a hell of a country if the Union don't hold."

A memory came to Rodney Wayman of a fog night in San Francisco when he and Doss had watched a young man die. On a cot in a room next to theirs, in a hotel of new lumber not yet painted, the young man lay. Wayman could feel in his nostrils now the lumber smell of that room. They had heard the moans of this young man through the thin wall and had gone to help him as best they could through the torments of his sobering-up after going stone-blind drunk. They had heard him in marvelously convivial streaks when he seemed to be babbling his every last secret. He was pure Scotch for generations back with a strong face that had girlish contours and delicacy, a tall forehead with curls of a straw-colored hair over it. He had a mind retentive and brilliant, with unpredictable wild offshoots when he was well liquored. He would turn from the wrongs he said the rich put on the poor and go into the wrongs the rich men and women put on each other. He recited Thomas Hood's "The Song of the Shirt":

> "With fingers weary and worn,
> With eyelids heavy and red,
> A woman sat in unwomanly rags,
> Plying her needle and thread.
> Stitch! stitch! stitch!
> In poverty, hunger, and dirt,
> And still with a voice of dolorous pitch
> She sang 'The song of the shirt.' "

He babbled of a young woman. "She was chaste as the snow, yes, by Jesus she was chaste as the snow and when the time came she was all snow, all ice, her head, feet and bosom, all snow, all ice." He was a university graduate with a complete devotion to architecture. And on this day, what Rodney Wayman recollected was the young man's frequent and repeated speeches about the Arch. Between him and the young woman the Arch had failed. He quoted the poignant sentence from the ancients, "The arch never sleeps. When the arch holds, all else holds. Love stands and hangs by an arch. Hate breaks the arch. The rainbow is an arch. Where you find truth, love, harmony and lasting strength, an arch bends and curves over it as a blessing and an oath. Unity, union, you get it only with an arch. Hate and pride break arches. Love and understanding build unbreakable arches." He could wander till his boozy words were repetitive and silly in praise of the Arch. Once he had ended a flight of declamation, "I assure you, gentlemen, I have never yet been so foozled with redeye and tanglefoot that I couldn't lift a glass of the amber fluid to the inexpressible worth and mystery of the Arch."

Rodney Wayman rode on with a dilemma teasing at his brain, as it was likewise tossing in the minds of millions of Americans North and South. This dilemma had again come alive in him. The right of secession, the legal prerogative of a state to step out of the Union and go it alone as a sovereign commonwealth, this to him was clear and undeniable as the October sunlight falling around his shoulders, saddle and horse. Yet what? The breaking of an Arch, the crash of a great curve of strength and affection that hitherto had held through all stresses? In the voices and faces of his kin, the Zadock Waymans, he had read it: They would take as blasphemy and obscenity any acts of men aiming to break the Arch that held the United States as one sovereign nation facing the world.

He shook himself loose and out of this mood. "If the worst is yet to come let 'er come," he told his horse and asked, "What do you want? The earth with a ribbon around it?" Then he sang lines:

"Oh, what was your name in the States?
Was it Thompson or Johnson or Bates?
Did you murder your wife
and fly for your life?
Say, what was your name in the States?"

To the field of Illinois stubble and the marching corn shocks of an upland, to the final yellow and maroon flamings of maple and ash, to October and its films of haze and fine harvest dust, he repeated as though trying his voice:

"Ho boys ho, for Californy oh!
There's plenty of gold
so I've been told
On the banks of the Sacramento oh.

"Ho boys ho, for Californy oh!
There's plenty of stones
and dead men's bones
On the banks of the Sacramento oh."

He didn't care who heard him sing those verses. But the third verse he gave low-voiced. It was the creation of hard and lonely men without women, men mocking at their getting nothing out of considerable hardship:

"Ho boys ho, for Californy oh!
There's plenty of grass
to wipe your ass
On the banks of the Sacramento oh."

* * * * * * * * *

Chapter 17

* * * * * * * * *

Mibs Finds a Lost Minstrel Man

JOEL WIMBLER had finished repairs on a crupper and hames for a farmer whose buggy and harness had been in a runaway. Mr. Biddings had been in to say that the John Brown excitement would keep on till Brown was hanged and go on with no letdown. "Galesburg man in today," said Biddings. "Says man fightin with Brown, name of Jeremiah Goldsmith Anderson, went to school over in Galesburg a few years ago. I guess that won't help the reputation of Galesburg in some quarters.

Twenty-seven years old and they say he worked in a sawmill after he left Galesburg. Wonder if it could be our mill in New Era. Hornsby used to go out there to talk with a young fellow he said would be a fighter for the cause. Anderson was one of the last of Brown's men to be killed. He refused to surrender and made a rush and got caught on a bayonet."

"The whole country shook up about it," said Joel.

"Never anything like it."

"Every harness shop in the country they're talkin like you and me, this and that about John Brown and what'll come of it, like a big wind blew over the people and bent 'em where they'd been still."

"You always said the abolitionists talked too much, Joel. You've seen action now."

"Too much, too bloody. Wouldn't have done it myself and can't say I favor another man doin a thing I wouldn't do myself. This John Brown excitement, we'll hear about it a long time. Looks like Brown was a little crazy. Still, I've heard good preachers say the blood of the martyrs is the seed of the church. They'd burn a martyr or put his eyes out with the idea he was crazy and good riddance of bad rubbish. Maybe Brown is a martyr. They'll hang him and time will tell."

"You think they'll hang him?"

"By the neck till he is dead. And then reach up North and try to get at the men who gave him money and rifles for his work."

The two men had now edged into an angle of the matter where it was not advisable to speak freely before Rodney Wayman, who had come in about where Joel was saying, "Every harness shop in the country they're talkin like you and me, this and that about John Brown." Wayman hadn't seemed anxious or in a hurry, had held back as though they should have their talk out. Joel spoke to him with a nod and a smile, "That's the buckle went bust, is it?" as he reached for the saddlebag and eyed the buckle.

Biddings left. The door closed after him. Joel Wimbler, at his bench facing a front window next to the door, hunted in a box of buckles for the right size. Then he worked swiftly at shaping a new leather clasp for the buckle end and stitching it to the strap end. Wayman made no interruption except to say, "I like to watch a good workman."

The door had opened silently at a hand familiar with it and had closed with no sound. The young woman who had entered, carrying a banjo case, stood four or five feet from them, glanced around her father's back with a bend of her head to see what he was doing, then rested her eyes on the quarter-profile of the stranger's head, the six-foot length of him, the thick hair black and wavy under the pearl-gray felt hat, the straight nose and slightly jutting chin. The hazy afternoon sunlight came through the window sharpening the lines of his back and shoulders and she wondered if her fancy were playing or did her eyes feel an unusual proportion and grace about the lines of him. He turned

769

now, half-aware she was there, turned and so shifted that a flow of sun fell clear on her face and hair for a moment before she moved enough to get the sun out of her eyes.

She stood as she had been standing, having moved only her right leg and foot. She dropped her eyes and for two or three seconds his gaze caught the long curves of her eyelashes cool on a sea-pale skin overlaid with a sun and wind tan. She lifted her eyes to his and saw them caught a moment later at her rough and tangled eyebrows, then back to her own eyes with a steady gaze into them. He may have seen there depths of pool-blue change to the slightest shade of a storm-green. They were swift roving glances he took at the straight line of her nose down to her wide mouth of lips neither full nor thin. Then meeting his eyes again and holding them two or three seconds she knew that the hair under the narrow-brimmed hat had come under scrutiny and he was a little startled at the play of the sunlight heightening the natural burnish of the back wave of chestnut over her ears and the coiled braids of chestnut hair. Then his eyes were back in hers and seemed troubled over a sea-wind gray or some lurk of shadows he found there, dropping toward the general sweep of the gaunt and bony frame of the structure of her head and a dim blush of winter apples creeping over her face and cheekbones. And perhaps there was a moment he glimpsed her eyes as wide apart with to him a suggestion of distance and long valleys with thin echoes.

Each made a guess whether they had met before. Each had a definite wonder whether now they were not strangely familiar though their names were not yet known to each other. His large dark eyes of the deepest sea-blue, a danger-blue, held no threat to her. Her response to them was that she must know more of them. She trusted them now but must peer farther into them for more shadings of the blue and the dark. His black hair stood out in tufts of wave and crinkle around the upper half of each ear and she had to hold back from reaching out a hand and brushing one of them to see if it would fall into the same tuft again. The chin stood out a little stubborn, she thought, yes, decidedly stubborn. His straight nose had wide nostrils with black hairs curling in them. The mouth was full-lipped, the lower lip heavy and rounded, a mouth of dreaminess, somewhat sad and it might be cruel, and somehow the impression sank deep in her that the mouth held a wealth of laughter and that there were mockery and song hidden in it.

They agreed afterward that they had held a long conversation in silence before a word was spoken. The gist of the understanding arrived at with no exchange of words was to the effect that they must know more of each other, that they must go into certain basic essentials, arisen as their eyes met, roved, and came back to meet after every roving. They couldn't have told whether it was two minutes or five or ten they held their foot tracks, breathed deep, drew a chin in now and then, her head tilted one side for a minute, his right shoulder lifting in a

770

small slow shrug that could mean anything, while their eyes went on in a silent mystic speech new to both of them.

Joel Wimbler with knife, awl, needle, twine and beeswax went through his motions unaware Mibs had come, aware chiefly that this job this Saturday afternoon would be the last of the week and he would have accommodated one more random customer of the many he had served well.

Wayman moved the end of his left arm and wrist, dangled a careless left hand with a brushing motion and she heard his velvet-soft baritone, "A banjo." She saw his lips shape the syllables, the "A" as an "uh," and the "ban" not exactly "bahn" nor yet as flat and nasal as the Northern "ban."

Mibs waited. She replied. She heard herself saying, "Yes, a banjo," starting the "Yes" away high and sliding down, giving "a ban" on her highest soprano and the "jo" the nearest she could pitch her voice to a contralto. It came closer to guttural than contralto.

There was a pause. For the life of her she would like to guess what was coming. It came. His imitation of her was perfection. He too could start away high and arrive at a stop in a comic guttural. "Yes-a-ba-a-a-nnn—" at the ladder top and then the cutoff and at the ladder bottom "jo-o-o—."

He was cheap. She had been mistaken. He was like some farm hand known as a "cutup" who could pick up your intonation and throw it back at you and think it was funny. Did he see something like that in the flash of her eyes and the upward wriggle of her tangled eyebrows? He had expected it. The words came tumbling from him, "Of all the instruments that God in His infinite wisdom permitted the creative genius of man to shape, devise and bring forth, of all the sweet contrivances born from the brain of man for the provocation of innocent pleasure and the incitation of rollicking mirth, of all the humble instruments that knock for admission at the higher gates of musical art, what you have here and now, what you have there in your hands, is a banjo, nothing more and nothing less, here and now in New Era, Illinois, a banjo."

He kept his face straight through these tumbling words. She too kept a straight face. She saw one of his eyelids flicker, the corners of his mouth not keeping as straight as they had. She could read now that behind his sober mask he was laughing to his toe-bones and heel-bones.

Her lips parted, her lines of even white teeth shone, and the smile spread to her eyes. Then he smiled open-mouthed and she caught cross-plays of light in the dark and the blue of his eyes.

The father had seen that Mibs wanted to ask the fellow to the house that evening and that the fellow wanted to be asked without getting presumptuous. "You'll take potluck with us, I don't know what'll be on the table," said Joel. Then he fitted, delicately whittled and chipped, fitted again the wooden bridge for holding the banjo strings and told Mibs it was better than the old one.

The supper turned out to be baked beans with well-browned side-pork slices, vegetables, baked sour apples glazed with brown sugar and freshly skimmed cream that poured from the pitcher like a thick gravy. Wayman did most of the talking. Joel encouraged him. So did Mibs. On Mibs saying, "I'll dry the dishes for Ma and help straighten things," Joel and Wayman sat in the living room and again Wayman did most of the talking while he tuned the banjo and plucked various snatches of idle airs. He had decided that the next week he would go out in the country and buy a carload of cattle to ship to Chicago. Joel did most of the talking as Wayman plied him with questions about the most likely places for him to look over cattle for the Chicago market. He rated himself a good cattleman, said he had driven one herd of eight hundred up from Texas for feeding on his father's farm near Atlas, Illinois. And what times he had gone out buying to ship to the Chicago market he had made a profit. When Mibs and her mother came in all this was explained to them.

Mibs blinked her eyes and caught her heart jumping. A fear had smoldered in her that in a day or two he would ride out of town and never be seen again. Now there would be a week or ten days or more he would be in New Era.

In the next two hours were ten or fifteen minutes that Mibs took the banjo, on Wayman's urging, played her chords and few tunes, hearing from him, "You have a knack with it, you ought to go on." The rest of the two hours Rodney Wayman took in stride. From one "instrumental selection" to another on the banjo and from song to song they pressed him for more. Joel had started a fire and threw on a small stick now and then to take from the room the chill of the late October frost. The tang of that frost was familiar to them and meant that for miles around the last tomato, the last melon and pumpkin, had been brought into a cozy cellar or barn.

They had their suspicions of Wayman as no amateur, some kind of a professional, a teacher maybe and more likely a concert performer or a minstrel man. The speed of his right-hand fingers at picking and strumming, the smooth and swift movements of his left-hand fingers at the frets, the Wimblers saw his skill had come from long practice, from many days of intimate fooling with the instrument. He fondled, coaxed, cajoled, even caressed the banjo.

The Wimblers had heard "Sweet Alice, Ben Bolt." Ten years ago it had swept the country. At perhaps half of the concerts on the lyceum courses in New Era it had been on the program. At amateur concerts in New Era, Galesburg and Monmouth, they had heard it overdone and underdone. Wayman first played it on the banjo smoothly and simply, then with variations, and then sang three verses of her hair so brown, and how she wept with delight when you gave her a smile and trembled with fear at your frown, and:

> " 'Do you mind of the cabin of logs, Ben Bolt,
>   At the edge of the pathless wood,
> And the button-ball tree with its motley limbs,
>   Which nigh by the doorstep stood?
> The cabin to ruin has gone, Ben Bolt,
>   The tree you would seek in vain;
> And where once the lords of the forest waved
>   Are grass and the golden grain.' "

So softly he couldn't have been heard beyond his three listeners he gave the four lines:

> " 'There is change in the things I loved, Ben Bolt,
>   They have changed from the old to the new;
> But I feel in the depths of my spirit the truth,
>   There never was change in you.' "

He said it might interest them to know, if they hadn't heard, that a practicing physician at Fort Lee, New Jersey, Dr. Thomas Dunn English, had written the words. For years it had been just a sad and sweet little poem often published in newspapers and even reprinted in England. Then in 1848 a play was put on in Pittsburgh, *The Battle of Buena Vista*, and an Englishman named A. M. Hunt thought the "Ben Bolt" poem put to music would make a good song for the play. Nobody had a copy of the poem, however, and Hunt racked his memory for the lines as he had read them in an English newspaper, filling in with lines he made up where he couldn't recall what he had read.

"Then Nelson Kneass wrote the music, using an old German melody he liked," said Wayman. "The play went bust and never came back but the song lived on and went everywhere, the first American song to sweep England. I met a man who heard it whistled in Edinburgh and hand organs grinding it in London where street hawkers were selling broadside prints of it. And in cases it's been a hoodoo. A Mississippi River steamboat named *Ben Bolt* blew up with its boilers and a ship out of New York with the same name was wrecked. Name your cat or cow anything but Ben Bolt. It's a hoodoo. Nelson Kneass wrote the music to it and didn't get enough out of it to buy a secondhand suit of clothes."

"The way you mention Nelson Kneass I think you must have seen him and known him," said Mibs very soberly.

"For months we were in a minstrel show together and I feel like I knowed him a hundred years."

Mibs' long legs shifted and crossed the right knee over the left. Her eyes tried for sharper searching of Wayman's face. He saw her surprised, if not startled. He didn't believe it could be the sudden information to her ears that he had been a blackface minstrel. It was something else that connected with him or with minstrels. Perhaps it aroused some memory of a minstrel.

He played "We Have Lived and Loved Together" with intricate variations and the shadings of melancholy on his face varied with the music. Mibs said to herself, "He can be sad in many different ways and there are times he can tell his sadness only with music." Then he gave the words, how two had shared each other's gladness and wept each other's tears, and,

> "I have never known a sorrow
> That was long unsoothed by thee,
> For thy smile can make a summer
> Where darkness else would be."

As though life was very whimsical, he told of these lines and the air. "You can never tell how a song is born," he explained. A man named Charles Jeffreys one day brought home groceries and found a musical score on the wrapping paper. He liked the tune, asked his musical friends what it was and they didn't know. He wrote words for the tune and years afterward located it in the opera *Joconde* by Nicolo.

Wayman's eyes were slit and his mouth puckered as he plucked swiftly a medley of "Money Musk," "Irish Washerwoman," "Pop Goes the Weasel," ending with "Arkansaw Traveler" and a man on a horse asking a settler at a cabin door, "Where does this road go to?" and hearing, "It don't go nowhere—just stays right here," the settler fiddling a tune, the rider asking why he didn't play the rest of it and on his horse the traveler fiddling the rest of it, and then being told, "Stranger, git off yer hoss and come right in! You kin lodge with us a month free of charge if you'll just teach me the turn of that tune." The period of happy-go-lucky pieces closed with four lines:

> "Reuben, Reuben, I been thinkin
> 'Bout this matrimony sea.
> If the ship should start to sinkin,
> What in the world becomes of me?"

Mibs had her feet to the floor, sat erect with folded hands, closed her eyes through Wayman's dreamy talk about Stephen Collins Foster. He had hunted up the song-writer in Pittsburgh. "And he wouldn't talk. He had had a few drinks. He was in a sad mood and wouldn't talk. We told him millions of people thank him, millions who love him. And his face turned a gloom you could cut with a knife and he didn't want to talk about it. We told him we had seen audiences of thousands laugh and cry over his songs. He called for more drinks and looked at us as though he was tired of hearing what we were telling him and some kind of wrong had been done him that he didn't care to mention or hint at. Heartbreak in his face, heartbreak plain on the face of America's greatest song-writer." Then Wayman sang "Hard Times Come Again No

More," "Open Thy Lattice, Love, Listen to Me"—and of Jeanie with the light-brown hair borne like a vapor on the summer air, Jeanie with the gay dawn smile.

The earlier searching and puzzled look came over Mibs' face as Wayman sang "Jeanie with the Light Brown Hair." The look moved into a flash of exultation when he began singing "In the Bright Mohawk Valley." He had become aware of it and kept his eyes on the mask of her gaunt face. She had muted an instrument, come to a punctuation, as his voice called to her from the lines:

"I have waited a long time, my darling,
    For the words that you never would say;
    And at last my poor heart now is breaking,
    For they tell me you're going away.

"From the valley they tell me you're leaving,
    I shall miss your bright eyes and sweet smile,
    For you're taking all of the sunshine
    That has brightened my life for a while.

"Just consider a while ere you leave me,
    Do not hasten to bid me adieu,
    And remember the bright Mohawk Valley
    And the one who has loved you so true."

Mibs saw a single tear go down on her mother's still white face and saw her laugh a brave laugh. "We had lovely days in the Mohawk Valley. With all our trials they were lovely days." And Mibs saw too that it was more than sweet memories of those days moving her mother and later she would hear what it was. She saw her father too, under his sober face, stirred as was the mother. For Wayman it was the nearest to an embarrassing moment during the evening. He murmured he would be leaving soon. "Of all things, please understand, I don't want to wear out my welcome."

Joel and Brooks said good night to Wayman rather absently, their pleasantries as they shook hands with him sounding as though they could be thinking of much more than they were saying and if it were their thought that he had made himself too welcome under their roof this was no time to speak such a thought. They went to their room, leaving Millicent Wimbler and Rodney Wayman for the first time facing each other alone—alone for whatever speech and communication they might have.

Mibs went for a pitcher of apple cider and a plate of brown molasses cookies. She set them on the table before Wayman without a smile or a word, poured a glass and handed it to him, a droop at the corners of her mouth, a faint storm-green in her eyes, the sweeping and riotous elation of late afternoon and early evening faded away.

"Thank you, Miss Wimbler." He too was utterly grave, the air of the happy-go-lucky songs gone.

She took her chair, moved it nearer him, their knees almost touching. Their eyes met for a long clean steady gaze. Could it be that each had a grief and it was a like grief and their eyes so told each other?

Mibs spoke. It was a nickname she spoke. "Pickup Charley." And with it she smiled at him a tight queer smile.

Wayman straightened, drew in his chin. "Pickup Charley, did you say?"

"Charley Amberson," said Mibs, saying it in slow syllables, measuring it as a name.

"Charley Amberson, yes," said Wayman in perfect repetition of her slow measurement of the syllables of the name, adding, "And Pickup Charley, that was me and that *is* me."

"I'm pleased to meet you again," said Mibs, her smile less tight, less queer.

"I never met you before, I couldn't have forgotten your face if I had ever met it."

"I suppose it *was* a case of where I met you and you didn't meet me." It was some four years back, she told him, and a fellow named Danny Hilton had driven a party of five to Galesburg in a surrey, on a cold night with the curtains buttoned tight and hot bricks to keep their feet warm, and for all of them except Danny Hilton it was the first time they had ever been to a blackface minstrel show and for Mibs one of the unforgettable nights of her life, the one when she saw and heard Haverstraw's Mammoth Minstrels. And she had gone away with curiosity and wonder, more curiosity than wonder and yet definitely with a peculiar lingering wonder about what might be alive with joy and pain, hate and love, back of one of the burnt-cork faces and the voice that went with it. This was the face and voice of Pickup Charley, the Marvel King of the Banjo, also Charley Amberson, also Mr. Charles Amberson, in various announcements of the middleman, the interlocutor who sat with three men on each side of him rattling the bones and beating the tambourines.

"George Hoagly," said Wayman, naming the interlocutor.

"George Wainwright Hoagly, the papers said," Mibs corrected and went on. " 'We will now proceed to witness Mr. Charles Amberson, better known as Pickup Charley, in his demonstration of how to pick up your pedal extremities and travel fast in a soft-shoe dance'—wasn't that the way he introduced you early in the program?" It was. And by his dance she merely knew he was nimble and had clever feet. It was his instrumental solo, "We Have Lived and Loved Together," the smooth and surprising variation on an old Italian opera melody, that first made her curious about him.

Then later he had sung "Jeanie with the Light Brown Hair" and it gave her wonder and when his voice traveled through the lines and low quavers of "In the Bright Mohawk Valley," "It was as though I was the girl in the valley and it was me they were telling he was going away

776

and it was me would stay in the valley after he was gone." And many a time since she had laughed about the burnt-cork face that covered another face she would never meet and wouldn't know if she did meet it. "But the voice that sang of the Mohawk Valley girl, that voice I had snared in my ears to keep and if I ever met it again my ears would tell me, they couldn't go wrong."

She paused. He sipped the last of his cider, ran his eyes to her prim white lace collar, over the black satin bodice which sheathed a spare bosom that seemed to have small and well-rounded breasts, down the loose folds of her satin dress to her small and gleaming button shoes. Instead of helping Ma dry the dishes she could have run upstairs and slid into a light sky-blue silk crinoline, of medium balloonish width, the more modest type of hoop skirt. She had worn it six times in two years. It was for parties and occasions where appeared the other fourteen women in New Era who could wear crinoline. He had bitten into the cookie but didn't finish the bite. She was saying, "Did you hear, Mr. Locutor, about the peculiar individual that went into a lager-beer saloon in Chicago and walked out with a gallon of beer in a paper sack?"

And Wayman straight-faced, laying the cookie back on the plate, "No, Mr. Bones, it has not been my pleasure to hear about the peculiar individual who went into a lager-beer saloon in Chicago and walked out with a gallon of beer in a paper sack. Would you be kind enough, Mr. Bones, to inform us what happened to this peculiar individual?"

Then Mibs in a burst of cackling laughter, "Well, Mr. Locutor, I'd be glad to tell you what happened to the gallon of beer in a paper sack —only it ain't leaked out yet!"

Mibs poured herself a glass of cider. They both sipped, looking at each other, then Wayman, "I have an interrogatory to direct to you, Mr. Locutor."

Mibs tried to keep back the twinkle in her eyes and the mirth in her mouth corners as she said pompously, "You may direct your interrogatory, Mr. Bones."

"The interrogatory, Mr. Locutor, is: What is more noiseless than the most noiseless?"

"The important reply to such an important interrogatory, Mr. Bones, I shall leave entirely to your omnivorous wisdom. What, then, is more noiseless than the most noiseless?"

"A boneless skeleton, sir, a boneless skeleton, kyah! kyah! kyah!" And Mibs knew it was a subdued and suppressed "kyah-kyah" and had it been given as she first heard it four years ago it might have disturbed sleepers in the house or passers-by outside.

"Surely," said Wayman, "you don't remember all those jokes."

"Nearly all. Try me."

"What is the difference between a cat and a legal contract?"

"One has paws and claws and the other has pauses and clauses."

"Perfect—and what is the difference between a sewing machine and a kiss?"

"One sews seams nice and the other seems so nice."

"You'll do. You're too perfect."

Each ate a cookie and finished the glass of cider. Mibs looked at the tall mahogany clock that had traveled from Arpa. "The hour hand says it is ten o'clock."

"That's a notice you serve on me." Gravely he said, "I don't know when I've had so pleasant an evening," and added with a slow dreaminess, "I could stay till the clock says midnight and I could stay on till the light through the windows said daybreak."

"You're staying over all next week?"

"Yes."

"Then we can have other evenings before you leave the Mohawk Valley again."

"It would be sudden and presumptuous for me to go to Presbyterian-church services with you tomorrow night?"

"I made an engagement with a new college student who just arrived this week."

Monday evening, then, he would call. Mibs stepped out on the shadowed front porch with him. He took her two hands, pressed them in a tight hold, suddenly pulled her toward him, put a light kiss on her mouth, broke away, and on the steps going down heard from her a hoarse "Good night."

* * * * * * * * * *

Chapter 18

* * * * * * * * * *

Jonas Fry Preaches from Jeremy Taylor

HIS black sack coat, of finespun wool, Joel Wimbler had worn five years on Sundays, holidays and occasions, the sleeves and back now shiny. A year ago he came near buying a new suit, then made his decision to go along somewhat shabby, his protest against splendor in clothes put on by New Era churchmen in English broadcloth and silk stovepipe hats. A wide bow tie of black thrust out from the lightly starched collar of his white linen shirt, the tie a gift last Christmas from his wife and daughter. Every Christmas they gave him a new one. He regarded this tie as near extravagance along with the solid-gold watch in his vest left pocket and the solid-gold link watch chain running to its clasp at the right pocket. His wife sat alongside him in their pew this Sunday in the same

778

black satin dress she had worn four years, neckpiece and edgings of white lace fresh as new. The stillness on Brooksany's white face was there as always and no one but the daughter alongside her could read in it this Sunday morning a flicker of trouble, a faint breeze setting a light ripple over a smooth blue pool.

The daughter wore a bodice of black velvet, a white collar halfway up her neck with a string tie of black velvet, puffed satin sleeves with long white cuffs. In the coils of her chestnut braids of hair ran glints of gold and sorrel changing in the sunslants from tall windows. From all but her father and mother she hid in her face an elation and a tension running in her blood. She was at home as she had always been in this church. Yet she was wondering why it was not the same as last Sunday or any of the hundreds of other Sundays she had set foot in it and taken her place in a high-backed pew of black walnut. She could remember the dedication of the building twelve years ago when it was new with smells of oak and walnut and fresh plaster and before that how for two years the long oak logs had lain piled in the public square while dispute raged among the deacons over whether Congregationalists could worship under the same roof with Presbyterians.

Here she had made her entry and seated herself with Hornsby Meadows more times than she cared to remember. Here she had sat and heard warnings delivered that swimming and horse-racing were defile ment of the Sabbath Day and later heard Danny Hilton read out of the church fellowship. Here she had joined the church and taken communion in the church and repeated the creed she had memorized to every article of faith, later to have her questionings of which she was never free-spoken. For the church to her was made of living men and women on a hard pilgrimage and a thousand loyalties held her to membership.

To her as to others the pastor Jonas Fry spoke for the church. Yet the church stood for more by far than he could speak. His hundreds of sermons had flowed through her ears, "in one ear and out the other," for the larger part. Yet there were times he was illuminated, sometimes giving the best he found in a great preacher out of the past. This day he was quoting liberally from Jeremy Taylor, one-time chaplain to King Charles I of England. He quoted the Greek proverb, "A man is a bubble," St. James saying "life is even a vapor," Homer calling man "a leaf," Pindar seeing him as "the dream of a shadow," and still another "the dream of a shadow of smoke."

Whatever was to happen that phrase-poem would be a comfort to remember, said Mibs to herself. "Each of us is the dream of a shadow of smoke. Every face in this church today, every face in my album of memory, what is it but the dream of a shadow of smoke?" She came out of a reverie to hear the preacher: "Man is born in vanity and sin. He comes into the world like morning mushrooms, soon thrusting up their heads into the air, and conversing with their kindred of the same production, and as soon they turn into dust and forgetfulness; some of them without any other interest in the affairs of the world but that they made their parents a little glad, and very sorrowful." She saw her mother's right hand slowly clench its fingers at this.

"Life is short, death sweeps out one generation to make way for another, and measured by what went before you and what comes after you life is but an eyeblink of time," the preacher was saying. The deacons bent on money-getting, on fine clothes and carriages, on showy harness sets brought from Chicago, could the words of the preacher sober them ever so little? Mibs asked. The preacher went on in a psalm from Jeremy Taylor. "Death reigns in all the portions of our time. The autumn with its fruits provides disorders for us, and the winter's cold turns them into sharp diseases, and the spring brings flowers to strew our hearse, and the summer gives green turf and brambles to bind upon our graves. Deliriums and surfeit, cold and ague, are the four quarters of the year, and all minister to death; you can go no whither but you tread upon a dead man's bones."

Why be proud? What is more foolish and treacherous than pride? the preacher asked and went on to tell of a rich young German gentleman. Handsome he was and they told him he should have his portrait painted. He cut them off and later told them a few months after his death they could open his casket and put the image of him on canvas. "They did so and found his face half-eaten and his midriff and backbone full of serpents; and so he stands pictured amongst his armed ancestors."

When the preacher came to hypocrisy and hypocrites Mibs wished that he could have named names and pointed to those in the congregation who were meant. Then on naming the names to herself she saw that the church would be split and broken and the preacher himself thrown out of the house of worship if he named names. "There is a universal crust of hypocrisy that covers the greatest part of mankind," he was saying. "Their religion consists in forms and outsides, and serves reputation or a design, but does not serve God. Their promises are but fair language, and disband and untie like the air that beats upon their teeth when they speak the delicious and helpful words. Their oaths are snares to catch men, and make them confident; their contracts are arts and stratagems to deceive, measured by profit and possibility; and everything is lawful that is gainful." What followed for a few sentences Mibs missed because of thinking over what wrong can be done by men whose rule goes, "Everything is lawful that is gainful."

Then she heard a terror tale of an ancient evil woman. It was blurred and softened in the telling. Mibs wondered how the story of Leporina would have been told if it happened in New Era, Galesburg or Monmouth.

"First she lied to him about how she loved him. To show him she didn't want his money she would drink a glass of poison and die right there before him. He says this is so lovely of her that he'll join her and drink half the glass and they'll die together. Can you see her face as she drinks the top half of that glass knowing the poison has sunk to the bottom? Can you see his face as he drinks and his guts burn and he tumbles down dead? Then can you see her weeping at his funeral and coming into his money and marrying the man she was after all the time? And where was the law and who did she buy off and what kind of a second husband did she get?"

Mibs let it pass to hear of the Doomsday "when God shall lift us from the dust, when the trumpet of the archangel shall sound and millions of men and women at the same instant shall cry aloud with great fear." This didn't interest her. She had heard it many times. "The bowels of the earth shall be rent with convulsions and the graves shall open and give up their dead." It was too easy, too meager, said Mibs. Jonas Fry was honest about it. He believed he knew what the end of the world would be like, but Mibs for years had found herself saying, "Why should God make all the dead come out of their graves so He can pick out those who go to Him and send the rest to hell? Why not leave in their graves those He is sending to hell? Why not leave them dead and quiet in the dust with the worms? Why not forget about them and let them sleep where the flesh has rotted off their bones and they can never again sin and do harm to others and themselves?"

She warmed to the counsels, "A lazy prayer never won a single secret of the kingdom. Be not cold and tame in your prayers. Be as a lark rising from the grass toward the sun."

She puzzled and wove in and out with her own shadowings of what she heard. "They that enter into a state of marriage open a gate of peril. Happiness may follow, or sorrow. He rules her by authority and she rules him by love." Mibs inwardly protested, "He does and he doesn't and she does and she doesn't—it all depends." But she inclined to agree on hearing, "It is the woman who ventures most. The man can flee his home in the course of his labors and projects but the woman must stay at home. For her there is no flight to sanctuary."

The preacher mentioned Jeremy Taylor as "a comforter of men." It dawned on Mibs that she had never heard so comforting a sermon from Jonas Fry. She made her guess that he was trying to smooth the anger still in the air between the Brench and anti-Brench factions. She could see the president of New Era College, in a pew up front, his bearded and tousled head tilting on his massive shoulders, wagging a little, as though instead of giving comfort the preacher should be voicing an outcry against John Brown being hanged, with a demand for immediate abolition of slavery.

Of the hour-and-a-half sermon Mibs heard perhaps a third. For her there had been interruptions. Before the organist had begun playing the music of the first hymn, in the broken quiet of the last comers moving

781

down the aisles to their pews, she had turned her head to see Rodney Wayman and Nack J. Doss seat themselves in a pew two rows to the rear of her and just across the aisle. She couldn't keep her eyes off this man she had seen for the first time only yesterday. A score of times during the sermon she turned her head for a look at his face, twice meeting his eyes for a long steady irresistible search into the deep-blue, the shadowy immeasurable blue of his eyes. It would make talk, she was aware, and there had been a time she could have been troubled about the kind of talk it would make but that time was long gone. However, it did hurt her father and mother. She could see they regarded her as flagrant and near wanton. This gave her sharp pain. Between her and them now had arisen a barrier. From now on they would guard their words to her and she would guard hers to them. Each would hold back words not worth saying because they could not be carried over the barrier. And the feel of the barrier was sometimes immovable granite and again impenetrable fog.

* * * * * * * * * *

Chapter 19

* * * * * * * * * *

The New Era Melting Pot Boils

DURING the ten years Max Mutter had published, edited, and written the *New Era Enterprise*, setting the type and running off the paper on a hand press with the help of an apprentice, he had been drunk only three times and each time he had picked a fight with a Know-Nothing. His score was about even. The first fight was a draw, each man too worn to hit the other. In the second Max Mutter had been near killed and in the third had nearly killed his opponent.

The Know-Nothings had once had a national political party, the American party, with representation in the Congress at Washington. When in their secret lodges members had been through the initiation the president announced to them, "Brothers, you are members in full fellowship of the Supreme Order of the Star-spangled Banner." When outsiders should ask what the secret order stood for, the answer was, "I know nothing." Their slogan was, "Americans should rule America." Each member, in secret session, had laid his right hand on the Holy Bible and the Cross, to swear he was twenty-one and Protestant, believed in God, was American-born and neither he nor his father nor mother nor wife was Roman Catholic. He further swore to vote for only Protestants and American-born for public office. He could be a

782

member in good standing only if he hated all Catholics and all foreign-born.

Max Mutter was known in New Era as peculiar in one thing, genealogy, with candid notes and data. He had a diagram of his four grandparents, his eight great-grandparents, his sixteen great-great-grandparents, showing his blood and breed. He had in his veins English, Cornish, Welsh, Irish and Scotch-Moorish blood. Into this had streamed Dutch, Danish, Polish, Slovenian, Bavarian, Württemberger blood. "This great-grandmother," he would say, "had one-quarter French Basque. My mother's grandfather was one-quarter Jewish. My father's great-grandfather was one-quarter Cherokee Indian. I wouldn't be surprised to find one sixty-fourth Negro in me somewhere. And you can see, if you go back three generations, there were Lutherans, Catholics, Huguenots and freethinkers. Their blood runs in me. I'm so foreign-born that I'm the most American citizen in New Era. That's why I favor killing all the Know-Nothings."

The few friends to whom Max Mutter had shown this diagram knew him for a man of humor, even fantasy. They couldn't be sure about him. He might be fooling. Yet they could see that he had done some thinking and much brooding about the variety of breeds and blood that composed the American people and he hated the sham aristocracy and the genuine snobbery of the Know-Nothings who swore to vote for no Congressman or county supervisor, no county clerk or coroner, who was foreign-born. "Why must a coroner handling corpses be so extra-pure?" he would ask.

Max Mutter's wife had died after bearing him nine children, of whom three had died. The eldest of three daughters, now twenty-six years of age, was stout and high-bosomed with large soft brown eyes and corn-gold hair. The young men were drawn to her. Joel Wimbler had heard her father say, "She's turned down three proposals I know of and I suppose others she didn't tell me about." The father couldn't quite bring himself to tell the whole of it but he had his belief that this eldest daughter, doing much of the housework and being near at hand to help when four or five of the babies arrived, had come to shrink at the thought of the pain, the toil, the endless details of childbirth and child care. "She's afraid of fading and withering like her mother did."

When Mibs Wimbler heard her father telling this softly and inquiringly, as something to think about, Mibs had begun questioning herself and ended her questioning with a resolve to herself. "When I marry I will want children by my husband. I shall marry no man until I am deeply sure he is what I want for a husband. I shall marry him for love and babies, for love and for one love child after another." Having said this swiftly and on impulse, she slowly and gravely asked herself what it was she had been saying. Then she repeated it to make sure it was no abrupt impulse.

Then she brooded over it. She searched herself with the resulting later decisions that to marry Hornsby would have been a matter of habit and convention, taking the easiest way, while marrying Danny Hilton would be too much an affair of convenience and pleasure. Her mother had waited and married for love and babies and she would do likewise. That is, if she married at all. "And I must not and shall not marry unless for love and babies."

Max Mutter was long-shanked, bony, loose-limbed, hatchet-faced and hawk-nosed, halting of speech, often licking saliva from the corners of his mouth, his bulging eyes bleary and sometimes bloodshot. Yet his eyes were canny at seeing. He could go on writing an item or an editorial for the paper and carry on a conversation with someone who had come into the office without turning his face and if it was someone he knew he would call the name on hearing the voice. Earlier he had seen hard work, long hours, lean years. When he had ridden into what was prosperity compared to former years, he had what he called "my sarcastic years, when I wrote mean pieces and put them in the paper to make people wriggle under my thumb and let them know I had the power to do it." Then sorrows that came with the children who came sent him into a corner of honest meditation one day. "The more devilish I get by making people squirm the more I feed on it and my heart gets harder and they see it on me in my own home and I can't play with my own children like I want to." He studied himself, looked back through the files and saw scores of "mean pieces" that he had written merely to exercise his own sense of power and, as he said, "to please some cantankerous streak in me." He came out of this meditation with a decision to write meaner and more cantankerous pieces than ever before—and then not print them. Where, too, in former days he had written gossip and suspicion and printed it, now he would write it and not print it. Into a tin box that he kept locked in the bottom drawer of his desk he put sheets of paper week after week, filled with fact, gossip, surmise, suspicion and comment that he wouldn't have dared to publish in any of the six columns of the four pages of the weekly *New Era Enterprise*. He wrote for the tin box:

> *Sunday.* Who are the two men who strode into the Presbyterian church for morning services wearing blue satin shirts? Who was the young woman of a respectable New Era family who kept turning her head and making eyes at one of the men and why did she scandalize that part of the congregation who saw her performance? Would the scandal take on a different color if it should be generally known that the man at whom she was making eyes was entertained at supper by her parents on Saturday evening and it is known that he left their home at a late hour? Does it add interest to the affair that the young woman has earned a reputation for being a heartbreaker and has twice this year rejected the proposals of two thoroughly reputable men whom she led to her feet with

her many wiles? Is it now her purpose to show that she can snare a handsome stranger by the same charms she employed on old New Era acquaintances? What can be the source of the rumor that the handsome stranger is a thoroughgoing Southerner and has boasted of the number of slaves he owns? And why did the young woman attend evening-church services in the company of a wealthy young man newly registered at New Era College? Is this part of her strategy to make the handsome stranger jealous? And what sort of a character is this newly come college student with his loud attire and his open flagrant flirting with another young woman who did not respond to his advances? Has there ever been another instance in New Era of a youth at church service so bold as to wink an eye at a young woman across the aisle from him whom he had never met before and who coldly stared him down? Why should we not accept the word of another young couple who distinctly observed the wealthy new student, on escorting his companion to her home, suddenly found himself deserted and alone at her doorstep after she skipped into the house and without a good night shut the door on him?

Having so written Max Mutter looked at it and chuckled. "It is a mess of truths, half-truths, dirty gossip, falsehood. Mibs Wimbler did turn her head for a look at that fellow. I saw her do it over and again. She started it. And he didn't want to keep looking into her eyes but he couldn't help himself. She's a pretty straight girl, Mibs. Came to our house one night and played her banjo and sang her songs for the whole family and was like one of us. Now why does she take up with this Herbert Hines the same time she has this handsome stranger on the string? Herbie Hines, he ain't properly the son of his tough rough father, with his face white as a catfish belly. I can see Joel Wimbler and Brooks worried. They won't talk about it. I never saw them with so sad eyes." And again he wrote:

Tuesday. Is the handsome stranger really a cattle-buyer for the Chicago market or is that a stall so he can stay on and make his play with the young New Era woman he has his eye on? What is there to the reports that he is a vagabond of the stage world, formerly a blackface minstrel who turned gambler and then went to the California gold fields and made a failure there? Has there ever been more gabble, gossip and conjecture in New Era about a couple of people seeing each other evenings? What happened on Monday evening when he went to her home for supper at six o'clock and the sounds of banjo-playing and singing came from the house and it was past midnight he returned to his room at the New Era Hotel?

Thursday. Where did our new-come cattle-buyer in the blue satin shirt stay overnight on Tuesday? Will he prove up as a cattle-buyer or is he a bilk? Why did he return on Wednesday evening just in time to go to prayer meeting with the young woman he so persistently attends? Was there ever so peculiar an astonishment at a New Era Wednesday-night prayer meeting as when the handsome stranger spoke a prayer like they had never heard before? Why should some old-timers be saying it was one of the best prayers ever heard in New Era? Does he really want the kind of brotherhood between men that he beseeched the good Lord to bring through a change in the hearts of men? To whom was he alluding in his prayer when he cried out that it was the hope of many good men that the nation should not be rent asunder through the designs of men not evil at heart who might not know what they were doing? Did he detect in the later prayer of an abolitionist with sideburns a rebuke and a denunciation of himself as a mouthpiece of monstrous and iniquitous men who hold the detestable doctrine that there can be property in men? Is there anything in the report that the two men met in front of the New Era Hotel and had a brief sharp wrangle in which there were insults and threats of violence? If it comes to a fight between the two men, will it be strictly as between two men who hate each other's politics or does it figure that one of them seems to be courting the woman who rejected the other?

Saturday. Was there ever a courtship set New Era by the ears as this one of the handsome cattle-buyer who comes here a total stranger and pays his devotions to a young woman brought here as a babe in arms who saw the town grow up on the empty prairie? Will they marry? Can it be they will have to elope to marry? Was there some finality about their riding their horses to a branch of Hickory Creek yesterday and in a clump of redhaws amid hazel brush making their campfire and lingering among the embers till past midnight?

Monday. Why, since it is known he was in New Era yesterday, was the abolitionist with sideburns absent from morning church services? Would it not seem this is the first occasion he has thus been absent? And why likewise was the handsome cattle-buyer absent at morning services though the object of his endless attentions was there? And why, at evening services, when one appeared with his wife and the other with his inamorata, should they have discolorations and the marks of heavy fist fighting on their faces? What is there to the talk that the pastor and one of his deacons crossing the college campus saw two men weakly striking at each other and both fell to the ground and the pastor and deacon carried the New Era man to the college dormitory and on returning found the other one gone? Will we hear later what kind of a fight it was? Could it be they slugged each other through a series of

786

knockdowns ending in a draw where each had the other laid out cold? Could it be?

Wednesday. Where and whither and for how long has the handsome cattle-buyer left our midst? Can we take it as a fact that with his companion, who owns a Maple Hill farm, he has departed and that his companion will not return to New Era but that he will? How often has it not turned out that the handsome stranger, having had his way with the comely and juicy country girl, has not again been seen? Will he come back to New Era with nice profits from his carload of cattle? And if so what will be his course of conduct inasmuch as there is not available another carload of market cattle at this time? If he returns and tries to marry the girl and take her away, what will be the story? Where would he be taking her? Was there ever a more sad-faced couple of old folks in New Era than her father and mother? Is it not rather decent and considerate the way their old friends have not the heart to ask them any kind of a question about what is happening or to happen in their home?

Friday. What is an editor to do when he has with care and scruples avoided mention in his paper of an affair that has shaken the town with rumors and reports yet finally the affair has reached the point where it becomes a matter of public record that the leading man concerned, the handsome stranger, the cattle-buyer, has returned from Chicago and proceeded to the county seat at Knoxville and taken out a license for him to marry the New Era girl, who, with her family, have hitherto been given every consideration of decent privacy in their personal dealings and doings?

Having thus made a memorandum to go into his tin-box journal, Max Mutter at noon on Friday wrote an item to be set up that afternoon and run in the paper which would go to press Saturday morning. The item read:

A marriage license was issued at the county clerk's office in Knoxville on Thursday to Millicent Wimbler of New Era and Rodney Wayman of Atlas, Ill.

Having so written, Mutter studied it and said, "I could add, but I won't, other paragraphs to read," and he wrote:

We met the presumptive bride early Friday morning, only two doors from the post office, in a heavy downpour of rain. She was under an umbrella. So were we. We could have asked her when and where her wedding takes place. But we didn't. If she had volunteered that information we would give it to our readers. We chatted briefly with the bride and then both went on with our umbrellas keeping off the rain.

In Shamp's livery stable we learned, through an informant we cannot name, that on Thursday evening the bride and groom presented themselves at the parsonage of Jonas Fry, exhibited to him their license, and requested of him that he tie the nuptial knot then and there. To this request the pastor made his reply directly to the bride, "A young woman may pay a fearful price if she does not thoroughly inform herself of the moral antecedents of the man she is to marry," and thereupon abruptly terminated the interview with a refusal to perform the ceremony.

These the editor dropped in the bottom drawer of his desk, then gazed out at a downpour of rain and said to himself that he must write an item about the heavy rains of the week. Out the window he saw a man pull in his horse, slide off the saddle, tie the horse at a hitching post in front of the *Enterprise* office and come in to say hello.

"Hello, you white crow!" said Mutter, shaking hands with the man, who happened to be one of the few Republicans over in the Hickory Grove settlement of Steve Douglas Democrats.

Before joining his lawyer to drive over to Knoxville on a case being tried in county court there, the man had to stop and tell Mutter the funniest thing to happen in Hickory Grove parts for a long time. After the man had gone Max Mutter wrote the item that ran in the *Enterprise* when it came off the press Saturday. It read:

Justice of the Peace William Orkney of Hickory Grove came to his office about ten o'clock Friday morning to learn that a couple had been in to see him and get a marriage ceremony performed. On hearing that he was at his home and small farm two miles away the couple had got on their horses and ridden out to his place. They missed meeting him when he was on his way in because he stopped at a farmer's house on business. So the justice of the peace got on his horse to ride out to his home and accommodate the couple by splicing them.

About halfway to his home the justice came to the bridge over Hickory Creek. For two years the bridge has been shaky and an appropriation has been made by the county board of supervisors for a new bridge but the building of it has been put off from time to time. It interested Judge Orkney to now see that the rising, raging waters of Hickory Creek had swept away the bridge.

The justice was sitting his horse in a light drizzle and figuring to himself whether it was two miles or three to the next bridge over the Hickory Creek. As he sat his horse and studied his predicament, he saw two horses coming down the long slope of the road, the riders walking their horses easy on account of the slippery mud and slush. As they came near he made out they were a man and woman, the woman in man's pants and wearing a rubber coat and a slouch hat.

They called hello to the justice and stopped their horses at the creek edge and laughed as though they were having a good time. The justice hollered back his hello. The woman hollered, "We're trying to find Mr. Orkney, the justice of the peace."

"I'm Mr. Orkney, the justice," he hollered.

"We want you to marry us," the woman hollered.

"Have you got the license?" the justice called, but the last word didn't carry clear over the crazy rushing flood of Hickory Creek.

"Have we got what?" cried the woman, cupping one ear with a hand.

"The license," called the justice, "the license."

"Sure we got the license," the woman laughed and hollered.

And the man fussed at his inside pocket and pulled out a paper and held his one hand over it to protect it from the drizzle of rain.

"Read it," hollered the justice of the peace.

And the man read the paper and the justice of the peace sat his horse studying and the light drizzle of rain began coming into a heavy downpour and the woman had a big smile on her face as she hollered, "Come on, Mr. Orkney, marry us right here and now and you'll never be sorry for it."

"Give me the names again," Mr. Orkney called.

"Give you what again?" the woman cried.

"The names," he called. "I can't marry you without your names."

The man smiled as he took out the license again and hollered the names clear and clean over the yellow roaring onrush of Hickory Creek.

The justice repeated the names twice to make sure he had them correct. Then came the voice of the justice, clear as you could ask, over the tumultuous babbling waters: "Do you, Rodney Wayman, take this woman Millicent Wimbler to be your lawful wedded wife?"

"I do," said the man as he stretched out his right hand and took hold of the woman's hand.

"And," called the justice, "do you, Millicent Wimbler, take this man Rodney Wayman to be your lawful wedded husband?"

"I do," came her very sober reply.

"Then," cried the justice of the peace in a high-keyed tone that was his supreme effort at making himself clear, "I pronounce you man and wife and may God bless the both of you as long as you live."

Mr. Orkney was about to turn his horse and ride away when he saw the bridegroom out of the saddle, handing the reins to the woman, pick up a stone, wrap something around it and then throw it across the creek. Mr. Orkney off his horse picked it up to find a ten-dollar bill wrapped around the stone.

Mr. Orkney got on his horse, threw two kisses with a loving hand to the bride, and rode to Hickory Grove saying such a thing as had happened would never happen again, "Not in my lifetime."

Wet to the skin, singing in the rain, reckless and gay, the newly married couple rode their horses, with detours because of washed-out bridges, till they were a mile or so from New Era. The young woman was saying, "If the justice had asked me whether I promised to love, honor, cherish and obey my lawful wedded husband, do you know what I would have said?"

"No, Mr. Bones, what would you have said?"

"To the question, 'Do you promise to love, honor, cherish and obey?' I would have cried out loud and clear, 'No, I will be a thorn in his flesh and a Satan to buffet him as long as I live.'"

"You would, would you?"

Then she told him, as she had it from her mother, of the gambler's story of Lorenzo Dow's second wedding. She added that the gambler had married a wild woman, quit gambling, stopped at Arpa, New York, to see her father and mother before driving on west to buy a farm and settle down in Illinois. "He caught his wife sleeping with another man and what did he do but drive away in the dead of night leaving her with the other man and taking with him their year-and-a-half-old baby. And not a word of news about him has ever come back to my father and mother. They took a liking to him. More than once my mother had a queer sweet pleased look in her eyes and mouth when she tried to repeat some of his ideas."

"That was long ago he ran off with that baby."

"Year of 1836, a few months before I was born."

"And no word of him since?"

"Not a word."

"What was his name?"

"Omri Winwold."

"I wouldn't be sure but it seems to me I've heard the name somewhere, but I can't fish it up now."

"And the baby, gosh, the baby would be twenty-three years old, just a year older than me. Rack your memory, Rodney. If you can fish up Omri Winwold for the folks they'll forgive us. He'll make them forgive."

In the dark before daybreak the wagon moved out of New Era on the Tuesday following the Friday that Mibs and Rodney were married across a flooded creek.

There had been hours of silent picking, packing, sorting of her things to go in trunks and boxes for this sudden honeymoon trip to the home of her husband. It wasn't that her father and mother had changed from love of her to hate. That they still loved her was plain. It was the love of her that made them fear the future, the unknown, the fate that might be awaiting her when they could not be at hand to see, to help. And the emptiness that would be there with her gone, that gnawed at them. And, too, what was plain, they could not so quickly accept Rod as she did.

"You jumped at him too quick," said the mother. "You can't know a man in a few days."

"I knew him in the first few minutes better than I know Hornsby after all these years."

"What harm in waiting a little?"

"He said eternity to me that first Saturday night we had him here. And on Monday night when he sang 'Ever of Thee I'm Fondly Dreaming' he said love and babies, love and babies, to me though I didn't dare tell him."

"You're so sure, Mibs, so awful sure that it helps some with me. It eases my hurt a little that you're so sure."

"You'll never hear me whimper, Ma. Whatever comes you won't hear a note of sorrow out of me."

"And that's what hurts, my young one. You might be needing me so bad and your pride won't let you tell me to come and give you the help I want to."

"We can write letters. There will be news, Ma. Don't be so sad about it. Maybe it's near time you were a grandmother with a baby you can look at and say it's got some of the loveliness of your own sweet face."

At this Ma smiled, her eyes luminous, and it was an hour before again she guarded her words and held her fears unspoken.

They had loaded the wagon the night before and Rodney had come in the dark and opened the unlocked front door and gone to Mibs' bed and wakened her. And she had gone to the room of her father and mother and they had both held her tight in their arms and wept and she had wept with them and then Rodney had gone in and held their hands and spoken words they could never forget and that had small crumbs and tiny grains of comfort. "I promise you before God I'll try to be a good and faithful husband to your precious child." That was all he had said except "Good-by." He had rehearsed it. He believed he meant it. They said maybe he did know what it meant and would try to keep to the meaning of "good and faithful husband." The days were to come and go for them, with an emptiness they were under compulsion to fit into the pattern of their lives, with whatever grim comfort lay in the curt wisdom of "Wait and see" or "Time will tell."

Among pictures that kept coming back to the mother was one of the day Mibs' face and voice were twisted with lights and tones. Mibs had seen Fidelia, Mrs. Hornsby Meadows, across the street from her, near the post office. And she had nodded her head, with a little wave of one hand, in greeting to Hornsby's wife. And she gave long sidewise looks at Fidelia and had given her mother the news, "A baby—and I don't know why I'm so glad for them—and at the same time why I should feel sort of hurt and sorry for myself."

Then there came the face and voice of Mibs on the morning she told her mother of the evening campfire on a branch of Hickory Creek and her stay with Rodney Wayman till past midnight. There was the straightaway flash of Mibs' eyes as she said to her mother, "You don't want to die without being a grandmother once." And there had been a radiance, a feverishly happy radiance, glowing and changing on Mibs' face as later she said, "If he leaves me—or if he stays with me and beats me—I'd rather a baby by him than any other man in the world." This had come not as an outcry but rather like a slow-spoken oath.

Mibs had brought a chair and some sewing work near the chair in the kitchen where her mother sat peeling potatoes. And the mother's pale still face had tightened and Mibs had seen a series of faint blue shadows move over it as for a long time her mother said nothing, and then, "From the way you talk, darling, a body might almost think you were already married or as good as married." And the needle of the daughter had stitched on and the paring knife of the mother cut curleycues of potato peelings and after a time the daughter spoke, "It may be, it may be, mother dear, in the sight of God I am as good as married."

And then since that wagon had rolled away in a darkness before daybreak there had been the return of Danny Hilton to New Era with a plump, stanch, homely young woman he had married in Chicago. And he had tied his horse in front of the Wimbler house one evening after supper and talked freely as between old friends. "I made up with a dozen different women in Chicago. It was like I shook a sieve and after a time only two left. I had to decide between 'em. One was purty as a pitcher. I asked what would I say about her if she was a horse. She's got style, I said, but she can't stand grief. I took the other one." And Danny drawled in his horsy way with a soft light on his face, "She isn't what they call five-gaited but she's dependable, a real homebody." Then he whispered with a smile, "Baby already on the way." Mrs. Hilton's mother was an Irish Catholic whose father had done shovel work on the Erie Canal. Her father was a German Lutheran authority on lager beer in a Chicago brewery where he rated as brewmaster. "I looked over the sire and dam," said Danny. "They get along fine, and so will we."

When Joel crept into bed alongside Brooks that night and her head rested on his arm she was saying, "You can never tell who is going to marry what."

"Nor why," yawned Joel.

PART THREE

Chapter 20

Pieces of a Prairie Saga

IN the five-room log house of Robert Prindle they were to have the double wedding on the afternoon of December 20, 1836. The house, with the barn and sheds, stood on a farm edging off from the town of Atlas, in Pike County, Illinois, about halfway between Springfield and St. Louis. Prindle, a widower near fifty, worked the farm with a son and two daughters helping. The daughter Anne was slight of build, with bright russet hair, a bright freckled face, sparkling brown eyes, and a small rather flowerlike face with a tiny mouth. She was twenty-five and it was four years since her husband of ten months had marched away to the Black Hawk War and not returned. When last seen by those who wrote letters about him he had lain fever-smitten with other soldiers in a settlement in southern Wisconsin. Since so long a time had passed with no word from John Creed, Anne Prindle Creed took it as certain her husband had died. For two years Greenleaf Moore had been keeping steady company with Anne. He was the son of a neighboring farmer and it was planned that after marrying Anne he should make his home on the Prindle place.

Anne's younger sister Sarah of twenty-two was of sturdier build, her shoulders curved where Anne's were squarish, black hair, black eyes, smooth rich black eyebrows, a large full-lipped mouth, her pale face somewhat sallow. Sarah was to marry on this day of December 20, 1836, a newcomer to Atlas who had arrived last June. He had taken up some four hundred acres, half of it timber on rolling prairie, had hired two men to help him and had a three-room log house, a log barn, livestock, supplies of salt meat and vegetables in a cellar, awaiting his bride. He had made a name as a hard worker, people saying, "He makes things git," and Robert Prindle noticing, "That man knows how to work to a purpose." Except for three or four Sundays when livestock was ailing or astray, he had ridden in to the Methodist-church services every Sunday. The Prindles were Methodist and toward summer's end he went on Sunday to their house for dinner and stayed the afternoon, coming to know Sarah, making his proposal and being accepted.

"You want a woman," he had said over and again to himself before he proposed to Sarah. He knew too that he had said this definitely with a sharp wanting even before he considered proposing to Sarah. He examined himself about it after he had proposed. "Can it be that the need of a woman is so hard on me, a necessity like food or drink, that most any kind of a woman, just so she is a woman, will do for me?" He asked himself whether he wouldn't just as soon have married Anne as Sarah. And his honest answer was that Anne too would have suited him for a bride. Then trying further to clear the matter in his mind he ranged over a dozen of women in and around Atlas and found that he wasn't sure he would go so far as to marry any one of them except either Sarah or Anne. This comforted him and it also set him thinking about what common flame the two Prindle sisters had that it should be a tossup with him which of the two he would marry. He and Sarah had held long talks about whether Anne should marry Greenleaf Moore. "She likes him," said Sarah, "but I can tell she isn't dead-gone on him the way she lets on and the way I'm dead-gone on you," which brought her a fierce sudden kiss from her betrothed. Sarah spoke too of Anne's husband, John Creed, his laziness, his mental quirks and odd ways and how Anne understood them.

About the newcomer who had arrived in Atlas that summer there was in the town and its neighborhood a mingled curiosity and tenderness. Though it was a common remark, "His wife died," the man himself had never made any such statement. What he had actually said, if they had taken particular notice and had reason to be suspicious of him, was that he had been married and his wife, "She went out of my life," or "She faded away from me." On his arrival with a team and wagon after dusk of a June evening he had camped for the night under a spreading oak on the bank of a creek near the Prindle farmhouse. Sarah Prindle, early the next morning, had just come from the barn with two pails of milk and had gone up the steps and had put one of the pails down to open the kitchen door when she turned to see a stranger come round the corner of the house with a baby in his arms. The baby was crying and the three farm dogs, one of them a large crossbreed with a strain of mastiff in him, barked and yelped, the largest one for a moment standing in the path of the man snarling and showing all of his teeth. The man held the crying baby in his arms, cast a glance at the snarling dog, nodded with a smile toward Sarah Prindle, who dropped the other milk pail and ran down to call off the dogs. Anne Prindle stepped out of the door to see what was going on, followed by her father with a towel in his hands drying the brown beard over his face after his washing up for breakfast. They heard from the stranger of his driving from New York State, his camp and team and wagon near by at the creek, and of how he wouldn't have troubled them this morning but for the baby. They asked him in to breakfast. They gave the baby a cup of fresh warm milk and saw his crying go down as he sat and gurgled on a quilt they laid for him on the floor. "His mother went out of his life just before we started on our trip West," said the stranger, who soon became less of a stranger as he talked and joked and seemed to make himself at home and gave his name as Omri Winwold as he asked for their names and bowed to each of them his pleasure at meeting them, his thanks for their asking him and the baby in.

Three days later Winwold had found a tract of land that was just what he wanted, about what he had pictured. The Prindle girls took over the baby like it was one of their own, while Omri Winwold worked from daylight till dark, sweating in heat and dust, making the rainy days count with jobs put off for that kind of weather. He grew sunburned, harder-muscled, blisters turning to thick calluses on his hands, his leg and shoulder muscles thickening, and there had been a few nights of moonlight when planting or getting in crops he worked several hours after supper. The Prindles heard him say more than once, "It's going to be a sweet farm after I've had it a little. The more I rassle that land the better it'll be."

December 20, 1836—a date fixed and fastened in the memories of many thousands of people—was a day of weather. People said afterward of the weather that day, when trying to tell about it, "You wouldn't believe it—the craziest thing that ever happened in Illinois weather, never anything like it before or since." It was wild, colossal, misbegotten, fateful.

Omri Winwold that morning was riding in toward Atlas, starting well before noon so he wouldn't fail to be at hand for his wedding at four o'clock in the afternoon at the Prindle farmhouse on the edge of Atlas. Several inches of snow lay on the ground from the days before. And the snow had turned to slush and a slow rain was falling. The feet of the horse sank into slush and mud and sent out splashes on all sides. The basket Omri held had scared the horse at first and then the horse slowed down and got used to it. Omri's wool overcoat ran down nearly to his feet in the stirrups. He was riding along about a quarter of a mile from his house when he sensed the northwest wind coming stronger. Farther back he saw a black cloud moving toward him with a strange deep swoosh of sound. The rumbling rolling swoosh came harder. He threw away the basket and with both hands on the bridle he did his best at holding down a horse that shied, reared, came down and broke into a full wild gallop. Then on the suddenly frozen clumpy road the horse slowed down. As the cold wave struck, Omri saw ice slithering off his leather gloves and ice rattling from the bridle, the horse's mane and ears. In a few seconds a shining thin garment of ice came on his overcoat, on his hat that he pulled lower over his eyes. There was ice on the hair of the horse, on the rail fence, on the fields and trees.

Slowly the horse picked his way over the uneven icy surface, Omri coaxing, "Come on, boy, this is my wedding day." Omri looked down and around at himself with a grim smile at the garment of ice that clothed him and held him tight into the saddle. The horse slipped and made quick twists and Omri never felt more safely balanced and fastened in the saddle. He soon began shivering with the cold, a chill that ran to his bones, his fingers and hands getting numb so he fumbled at the bridle and couldn't be sure what he was doing with his hands. His loud and repeated "Whoa!" rather than his pull at the ice-stiff bridle stopped his horse in front of Ed Houseworth's store. He tried to turn part-way around toward the store front but found himself ice-locked. He shouted, "Ed, Ed, help, help!" He heard a door open and the running of feet and out of the corner of an eye could see men coming. One of them held the horse. He heard Ed Houseworth's voice, half-laughing, "You're stuck, Winwold, you're in a tight fix."

As many a time before and always easy to do, Winwold started to swing a leg for the crouch and the slide off the horse and out of the stirrups. The leg wouldn't move, he couldn't begin to swing it. He sat there in his saddle helpless and shackled, the ice binding him with sheet-iron strength. The other men picked up stones and knocked loose the ice along edges of the saddle and the bellyband. Then with a lot of hewing and hauling they managed to pull saddle-and-man off the horse. They carried saddle-and-man into the store, alongside the stove. He slowly melted loose, shook and brushed ice and slush from his clothes.

A half-hour later Winwold, nicely thawed out and dry, saw a wagon stop in front of the store and the man on the wagon seat call for help. It was the work of four men for several minutes to pry loose a man stretched on the floor of the wagon box and bring him in by the stove. The driver explained that he had had a wagonload of hogs when the cold wave struck. On the rough slippery roadway the ice-covered horses couldn't pull the wagon. He had opened the end gate, goaded the hogs out and driven on. His companion he had picked up on the road, walking to Atlas, a half-sick man afraid he might faint and fall off the seat, so he had stretched out on the wagon-box bottom.

Ed Houseworth brought his favorite big chair with long armrests for the man to sit by the stove and warm. A little later Ed and the two other Atlas men did some whispering by themselves and then beckoned Winwold. He heard Ed Houseworth's hoarse whisper, "My God, Winwold, we don't know what to do about it but we're certain that man is John Creed. He ain't the size he was when he went away into the Black Hawk War and he looks twenty years older, but that's him." One of the other men whispered, "That's Creed, I knowed him, worked with him, it's John Creed." The questions ran in the minds and hovered in the faces of the four men: "What now? What next? The whole country round they expect John Creed's widow who ain't a widow to be married this afternoon—what ought we do? What can we do? What about Anne Prindle and Greenleaf Moore, what can they do instead of getting married?"

They saw the man in the chair stirring, shaking himself under the prickles and the mild streaks of pain in his warming thawing flesh. They saw a smile come on his wizened face and he nodded to himself in approval of something. Wimwold walked over to him and he said half to Winwold and half to himself, "Jesus, many a day I never thought I'd get back to Atlas." A medium-sized man worn down to skin and bone, his breeches ragged with gaps and tears, and through the larger of these could be seen the red flannel drawers with several small gaps and the naked skin underneath. On the face of the man Winwold thought the nose nicely arched, a sweetness to the well-formed and expressive mouth, the chin receding and possibly weak, the Adam's apple large and scrawny. The long white thin face had an utter weariness, it seemed to Winwold, till he caught a dim fire in the hazel-green eyes that seemed to say the man had come afoot a thousand miles and was ready for the second thousand if it had to be.

"What's your name, if I might be asking?" said Winwold.

"John Creed," came the slowly pronounced name, and, "I do pretty good to remember my name, don't I?" Then a shrewd awareness, an amused assurance, came over his face as he gestured with half of a weak hand, four fingers uncrooking toward the three men up near the front door. "They know me. They know I'm John Creed. I come back to see if my wife is alive."

A shiver ran through the man. Then came his first little yawn. "Rest," he said, "I need a long rest." He blinked his eyes slowly and took three or four little yawns that seemed to please him and bring an added calm to his face.

Winwold had Ed Houseworth pour a small glass of whisky. Winwold handed it to Creed. "Take it in long slow sips, don't drink it all at once, sip it." At the third long sip John Creed yawned again, a long yawn, slid his feet along the floor and looked up at Winwold from half-shut eyes, "Annie, where's my Annie? I'm sleepy, Annie, Jesus, I'm sleepy," with more mumbling of words Winwold couldn't make out. His feet slid a little further along the floor, his head tilted back with closed eyes and it was plain he had gone into a sleep and in desperate need of that sleep.

An hour later it was that Winwold came with Anne and Sarah and they stood at a bed in Houseworth's living room back of the store. After a while they drew chairs to the bedside and watched. Once and again another time Anne shuddered and a quick sharp moan came from her, "Oh, Johnny, I waited and waited for you, oh, Johnny, my Johnny." They waited perhaps two hours, saw his eyelids flutter and open, then open wider yet as his eyes rested on Anne and with a slow weak smile, "Don't you fool me, Annie, it's you, I got to you at last." He tried to sit up. He sank back. Anne bent over him and put her lips to his in a long kiss and again her lips to his eyes and forehead. "Where did you go? What happened to you? It was so long, Johnny, and it was hard for you, I know it was hard, my Johnny."

He lay quiet a while. Then came his murmur, before his eyes opened, "What happened? Yes, what happened?" Then with his eyes sometimes closed or again open and turned toward Anne, Winwold noticing in the hazel-green eyes the same dim fire he had noted earlier, John Creed began a mumbling disconnected statement of his four long years away from his wife since the Black Hawk War. His company had marched away leaving him down with a fever in a southern-Wisconsin settlement. What happened when he came out of the fever he wasn't sure except that when his mind was clear again he was living with an Indian tribe near the Canadian line and they had sold or traded him to another tribe that was good to him and said he was one of them. At about this point the man's statement became cloudy and muddled to those listening, his tongue rolling off peculiar gutturals and resounding vowels. It dawned suddenly on those listening that he had learned some Indian language, its words familiar and natural to him. Again he was speaking English and saying that he got away from the Indian tribe that adopted him, taking a canoe that brought him to the upper Mississippi River. He came to rapids that whirled him into the air and twisted away from him his canoe with its supply of corn and jerked meat. After two days he reached a white settlement half-starved and the fever came back on him and he was there months. They were good to him. The fever passed. He was weak. They told him to wait and they might get him some kind of canoe, yet he started on a walk overland keeping close to the river. He couldn't bring his story to an end because he wasn't sure just how he had begged food and shelter and walked on and on, with a ride now and then on a boat or wagon, till he reached Atlas on this day of the sudden change to cold weather. Once in a while he had broken his story to half-smile and half-cry, "It was like this, Annie, I had to get to you, I kept saying I had to get back to you, Annie."

His eyes closed and he lay still a long time, then his body shook and his eyes came open and his white lips moved faintly to say, "I got to you, Annie, kiss me good-by." Anne was on her knees and her lips touched his softly. As she drew away his lips murmured weakly what they took to be "Sweet Annie, sweet Annie." Then his face and body sank back into the final sleep.

Anne laid her head alongside the face of her dead husband. Winwold saw the frame of her shaken from head to toe yet not a sound coming from her. He knew it was some special secret grief that no one else could understand any more than anyone else could ever have understood John Creed as she did. When she suddenly rose and faced them, Winwold had a notion her little face was like a white flower bending before a driving rainwind, near broken yet holding.

The doctor who during these hours had twice come in to give the best he had, said later, "He was just plumb worn-out, exhaustion they call it, a fighter with nothing left in him to fight with."

At the Prindle home it was left to Sarah to tell Greenleaf Moore that Anne couldn't marry him on this day of December 20, 1836, that after this day she must wait a year before she could marry again.

Sarah Prindle, in a cream-white dress of taffeta, thin and glossy, setting off her black hair and smooth black eyebrows as almost startling, stood up and joined hands with Omri Winwold and heard the Methodist minister pronounce them man and wife.

At the supper they enjoyed Winwold telling of Lorenzo Dow's second wife being asked in the marriage ceremony whether she would love, honor, cherish, and obey, answering, "No, I will be a thorn in his flesh and a Satan to buffet him as long as I live." Sarah's father chimed in with an incident of fact about a young doctor in a near-by county in a marriage ceremony on an Illinois River ferryboat. They had seen a young blacksmith they all knew rowing toward the ferryboat. He climbed aboard and reached the ceremony at about where the minister was saying that if any person knew reasons why the said parties should not be united in the holy bonds of matrimony to let it be known or forever after hold his peace. The young blacksmith at this point rose to shout, "I object! I object!" The minister asked him what his objection was. He shouted seriously, earnestly, righteously and as though it was the most proper thing in the world, "I want the girl myself! I want the girl myself!"

Sarah confessed that she and the groom had practiced a little on the lines of the marriage ceremony. Winwold told of a young farmer near Springfield, Massachusetts, who was scared he might make a mistake in the ceremony. Hunting through a book that had the lines to be said, the young farmer memorized the lines for the baptism of elders. At the altar in the church the minister asked him, "Wilt thou have this woman to be thy wedded wife?" The bridegroom, sure of himself, for he had rehearsed it, gave the response in a solemn tone, "I renounce them all." The minister at once believed it was the cheap joke of a country bumpkin who wished to make a dignified affair ridiculous, the minister busting out, "It would appear that you are playing a fool here." And to this came the blank-faced response in solemn tone, "All this I steadfastly believe."

Few such light-minded moments however did they have at the supper or throughout the evening. Anne had witnessed the wedding ceremony and gone to her bedroom wanting no supper. At the burial the next afternoon of John Creed in a heavy box of rough pine boards, Anne stood quiet and white-faced till the minister dropped clods of earth on the box in the grave, saying, "Dust to dust, ashes to ashes, earth to earth, thou returnest." Then a curving wild cry shrilled from her and her shoulders shook and from her tight-closed lips came not another sound.

The next morning Winwold kissed the baby Andrew Marvel as Anne held him in her arms, telling Anne he was sure Marvel would be safe with her till he and Sarah got better settled. Then Winwold rode out to his farm on the icy roads, alongside him his bride on a solidly built iron-gray work horse that the affectionate father had given them for a wedding present. They had many chores, "much to do to get this farm running right," as Winwold put it. It was at supper one evening that week that Sarah asked him, "Does Marvel look like his mother?"

"He's got her dark eyes and hair."

"Did she take her last sickness hard?"

"When she went away it was hard for all of us."

Weeks ago he had said to himself, "If you marry again, and Bee is alive, before the law you're a bigamist." Then he had laughed. "I'll take the chance. There's a wee drop of gambling blood left in me."

The years had gone by—one and a one and a one—two and a two, five and a five—and there had been slow dragging years he thought would never end. There had been rushing years that had swept by him and Omri Winwold hardly knew their numbers.

Now in the onrush of the years they had stopped, as they do ever and always, at a number, a specific unalterable number, the year 1857. What had happened in the years before this inexorable number one-eight-five-seven, Eighteen Hundred and Fifty-Seven, was largely in a haze, a mist, a confusion of vast small interacting events, completely beyond any one man's knowledge. And out of this haze and mist stood a few significant years when the smaller events had piled high and erected a landmark number—1492—1776—1787—1812—fixed in the minds of all who could read or listen and particularly the mirthful and the contemplative, who repeated as no idle proverb, "God exercises a special providence over children, drunkards, idiots, and the United States of America."

Omri Winwold particularly liked this proverb as he considered in this year of 1857 the numbers of the years to come after that number. The next five years to come, the numbers between 1857 and 1862, the five years to come after that with the numbers between 1862 and 1867, he saw these in a crimson haze and a blood-color mist, with insoluble triangles of shadow and incalculable tumbling silhouettes of action and interplay.

For eleven years now since the first anniversary of Sarah's death Anne had been his wife. Nearly every day this year he read to her from newspapers as she sat in a wheel chair, meditating aloud to her as she asked him to do, she insisting that the national chaos was no harder to think about than her personal misery. He and she had been riding one day the year before in a light, open spring wagon, with a seat that had come loose and should have been repaired and tightened. It was a downhill side road, the horses running free, and they were suddenly hurdling several ruts and bumps. The seat coming loose, Winwold landed sprawling on the bottom of the wagon box but his wife was thrown on her back across the sideboard of the wagon box. Two physicians had pronounced it a permanent spinal injury, with paralysis that decreed she would never walk again. And the physicians were gravely sober in telling Winwold that a cure was beyond possibility, her life definitely shortened. A skilled nurse brought from St. Louis was in constant attendance on the disabled woman except for the hours she was not needed when Winwold and his wife shared the news of the day and the surge of memories they had out of the past.

The first log house on the farm was now an implement shed with a McCormick reaper and binder, with the latest George W. Brown corn-planter, with other machines that made one man able to do the work of ten or twenty men of twenty years back. The brick house built five years ago had living room, parlor, library, dining room, kitchen, an end bedroom for Winwold and his wife with large windows east, west and south. In the upstairs rooms, the sons and daughters, the second generation, had their beds and belongings. On the long and wide front porch, overlooking the two-hundred-yard maple-lined lane that led to the highway, the woman in her wheel chair, the man seated alongside of her in a cushioned heavy chair with a back of arched saplings or the man pacing to and fro in hearing of the woman, they had watched together the processionals of late spring, summer, and early autumn. It was now one of those drowsy hazy early October days, a film of dreaminess on the air. The flies and mosquitoes were not so bad but the man with a swatter made of shingle wood could deal with them.

The news of the day was that a wild financial storm, "the Panic," had broken on the country the last week in August and across September, banks stopping payments to depositors, thousands of factories closing down, workless men marching in the big cities, troops and police on guard against bread riots, over five thousand banks and stores gone up in bankruptcy. American and British naval frigates had laid the wires for the first Atlantic Ocean cable, had met in mid-ocean and spliced the wires, then heavy swells had broken the wire and the day for instantaneous messages to flash between America and Europe must wait. James Buchanan of Pennsylvania, a lifelong politician, a polite and quiet bachelor who looked toward the past and hoped that the present and the future would be the same, had been sworn in as President of the United States on the fourth of March, '57. Anti-slavery factions had dramatized with fierce outcries the United States Supreme Court decision on March 6 wherein Chief Justice Taney for the court majority had declared in the case of Dred Scott an opinion that slaves have no rights which the white man is bound to respect, that in law they are never thought or spoken of except as property, and that free Negroes whose ancestors were slaves cannot become citizens.

Then in April Baltimore & Ohio Railroad workers had given the country its first big railroad strike, with stubborn fighting of police guards over railroad property and troops called to put down riots. The steamer *Central America* leaving Havana for New York with six hundred persons on board sprang a leak in weathering a storm, losing over four hundred passengers and crewmen along with two million dollars in gold that went to sea bottom. The reputable New York dentist Dr. Harvey Burdell had been murdered in his bedroom but nothing could be proved against the widow Mrs. Cunningham, from whom he rented the furnished room and who claimed to have been privately married to him. Out of the reeking and stench-laden slums of New York City came days of street fighting between two gangs, the Dead Rabbits and the Bowery Boys, with rioters barricading the streets and driving off the police till the Seventh Regiment Militia rifles arrived. At Mountain Meadow south of the Salt Lake Valley in Utah, this September, a camp of a hundred and thirty-six white immigrants, attacked by Indians and by whites reported to be Mormons, gave over their guns and farming tools and on their way to Cedar City met a surprise attack wherein more than one hundred of their number were killed. Between the violence of New York City and of Salt Lake Valley lay Kansas, where politics was wilder, more tangled and violent, than in any other American arena, with proslavery and antislavery forces from outside pouring in men and guns to force a decision whether the Territory of Kansas, on being admitted to the Union, should be a free state or slave.

There was the national scene to contemplate, Omri keenly, poignantly interested, and the woman swayed by what deeply moved him. He had seen the early years when it was one mile, two and three, between neighbors' farmhouses. He had seen year by year the wagons of "the movers," ever going west, over into Missouri, up into Iowa, out into Kansas, Nebraska, Colorado, and there were still the California-bound wagons. America, still in the making, and the three million inhabitants of George Washington's day, in a narrow strip hugging the Atlantic coast, now spread out between the two oceans and numbering near thirty millions.

He was fifty-two now, surging with personal memories that shook him, personal circumstances that still held wonder for him. There had been those first six years on the land with Sarah Prindle for helpmeet and he had been ruthless with himself, and with her, his endless saying, "I'm going to make a go of it, by God, I've got to." He drove himself hard, daylight till dark, often by moonlight and lantern.

There were periods he was fear-driven. The loneliness of the great wide sky over the rolling prairie that lay in one direction from his house, the other loneliness that hovered in film and shadow in thickets, tree clumps and trails of the timbers that stretched away in another direction—these were kinds of loneliness he had never known in Boston as a boy, nor in the mill town as a bobbin hand, nor as a barkeep at the Maple Leaf inn at Springfield, nor as a gambler in Albany and along the Erie Canal to Buffalo. Only on that short walking trip of a few weeks from the mill town to Springfield had he known the true loneliness of the open sky over the bare earth and himself the one witness. Slowly it had come over him as the years passed that he had a vague determination to eventually work out companionships at some of the points where loneliness first smote him on the measured piece of earth he had bought and to which he held a registered deed of clear title as owner.

The fear drove him that he might fail as a farmer, and having failed would go straight to St. Louis and set up as a gambler there or up and down the Mississippi and Ohio rivers on steamboats that always had games going. This fear so rode him one week that he came out of a nightmare, in a sweat and crying out, over shooting a man who had rung in a marked deck on him and it turned out the man was a younger brother of the county sheriff and he had been tried for murder and he was standing in a wagon and they had put the noose around his neck and were about to drive the wagon away to leave him with his feet trying to walk on empty air and his neck writhing in a noose, and that was when he woke in a sweat and crying out. It had scared Sarah, who was then six months gone with their first baby. And it was one of the things that sent him searching into himself on how to overcome the fears that rode him. He found too that he had a vague fear of the unknown and part of that fear connected with the chance that Bee might locate him and there would be no telling what desperate and vindictive Bee might do. Most of all however what drove him day and night was the desire, a hunger and thirst that never left him, to make a go of it as a farmer, first of all to sink the roots deep to hold himself and his family against poverty and mean living across the future.

During those first years he stayed on the farm and hoed corn or cut hay or cradled wheat or salted down the pork of the hog neighbors had helped him kill and dress or split rails for fences or swung his scythe to weeds. These chores he did rather than go on a Saturday to a political barbecue in Atlas or Pittsfield. There and then a speaker, who was not a milk-and-water Jackson man but what they called a whole-hog Jackson man, would tear the hide off the opposition and nail the hide on a barn door, metaphorically speaking, after which the ponies would be untied from fences and trees and their well-liquored riders would gallop over the town from end to end, cursing the opposition candidates, flinging their arms high in hoorahs for their own favorite candidate, inviting anybody that wanted a fight. Young wild fellows most of them were, variously called the "barefoot boys," the "flatfoot boys," the "butcher-knife boys," and a few vociferous fighters known to each other as the "half-horse half-alligator men." Among candidates it was understood these "butcher-knife boys" swung a balance of power and the winners in politics most often had these boys with them.

Winwold once overcame the temptation to go in of a Saturday to a barbecue where the speaker was a candidate for lieutenant governor, a former Baptist preacher of whom it was said that he went among voters "with a Bible in one pocket and a bottle of whisky in the other," this candidate saying he was "armed with the sword of the Lord and the spirit," preaching to one set of men and drinking with another and garnering the votes. Winwold stayed away though his curiosity was keen; later when better fixed he would go to town more. A few Sundays there had been that he had stayed on the farm and got in his hay. But he aimed every Sunday it was possible for the family to go to church, one day in the week to be clean, to wear clothes with no barn smell or kitchen grease, to try to think about the soul of man and what he may owe to God and his fellow man. He had noticed that as a general rule the churchgoing people were cleaner and had a certain sense of decency not to be seen among some of those who stayed away. Riding over the county on various errands and for his own purposes, he had seen neighborhoods where the people reminded him of certain blocks of tenement houses he had seen in Boston as a boy, too many of them pale, stooped, shiftless, sort of hopeless. He told Sarah, "Hopeless people have the same dirty pale look and the same stink whether you find them in a crowded big city or a lonesome country crossroads."

There had been a week of days in December of 1837 when every morning he was up before sunrise, lugged baskets of corn from a crib over a path in four inches of snow, threw corn into the hogpen and into the boxes of the horse stalls in the barn, climbed to the loft and pitched down hay to the mangers of horses and cows, with fork and shovel cleaned the stalls and bedded them with fresh straw, milked two cows and gave a pan of milk to a calf, carried the milk to the house on a path in the snow, glanced at the sunrise and went into the house. This was the week Sarah was sick with ague and headache and he brought to her bed a corn-meal mush with milk. She was nursing at her breast their two-month boy baby Milton, said she was feeling a little better and would try to eat. He took Andrew Marvel, then three years old, to the kitchen and they had mush and milk followed by fried potatoes with pork chops and one fried egg apiece. Marvel was saying as he smiled and munched his chop, "I yike duh chitchen," by which Omri knew the boy was saying, "I like the kitchen." He washed and wiped the dishes, bundled Marvel into warm clothes with deer-skin overshoes he had cut and sewed, carried Marvel to the barn, hitched a team to the wagon, put Marvel on the seat and on a clear day of mild sunshine hauled two loads of horse and cow manure to be spread over a field of corn stubble. At noon he cooked and served more food, washed and dried the dishes, then cut and sewed half-soles on his boots and Sarah's shoes. He chopped wood for an hour, made a salt lick for the cows, took his gun and went to the creek bottom and shot a wild turkey, came to the house and found Sarah improving, though it worried her that Marvel had made a team of horses out of two chairs and was using the fireplace shovel to throw imaginary manure around the floor of the room. He took Marvel and a lantern for after sundown with him to the barn, fed the stock again, milked the cows, carried the milk to the house with Marvel following and once slipping in the slush and falling face first in the snow. He carried milk down into the clean dry earth-smelling cellar and poured it into crocks where the cream would rise for the buttermaking tomorrow. He cooked supper for all, washed the dishes, had Marvel help him dry a few of them. He cut the head off the wild turkey, picked off its feathers, dressed it, held it over the fire to burn the pinfeathers, carried it down cellar for roasting later in the week. He took a spare piece of canvas and sat alongside Sarah's bed and talked with her when she felt like it while he sewed patches on three grain sacks. For three days more that week he had done a round of regular chores with a variety of odd jobs between.

Then Anne had come out for a three-day stay with them and they had gone over with Anne again the ins and outs of Greenleaf Moore going to church with her every Sunday, seeing her one or two evenings during the week, and his arriving one evening in August finding only the father at the house and his saying to the father, "I've got the license and the justice of the peace here and I want Anne to marry me right off without any waiting." Robert Prindle had said, "Anne is out in the field milking. We'll go see what she says." They went out in the pasture where Anne sat milking and Greenleaf said, "Anne, I've got the license for us to marry and the justice of the peace is at the house waiting to marry us." Anne went on pulling the teats of the cow and sending streams of milk into the pail, turning her head to look up and say, "You men go back to the house and I'll be there soon as I milk this cow." Then, as Anne told it, "They went back to the house. I milked the cow of every drop in her udder, and went to the house and got married."

The second day of Anne's stay he had ridden over to a neighbor two miles away and helped with the killing of two hogs. In the afternoon he hauled corn to the mill at Atlas, ground his two corn knives and an ax, bought the twenty nails which were the last the store had, and shot a turkey and two wild ducks before sundown. The next day after morning chores he started away with his gun, walked three miles of timber, ate a cold pork chop with corncakes, walked back and about three-quarters of a mile from the house killed a buck deer, dragged it a ways, that night skinned and dressed it and the next morning sold four quarters of venison for $3.18 in Atlas. Early in the afternoon he dug up a bushel of turnips he had in October buried below the frost line and brought them to the house. A light snow was falling when he left the house with his gun. About a mile away, along a creek, he met deer tracks, followed them and after a quarter-mile, sighting the animal, shot it in the ham, saw it fall and jump up and run. It was about four hundred yards farther on that he got his second shot at the weakening animal and killed it. It was a big specimen and he skinned it that afternoon and the next day carried home cuts from it. The three evenings Anne was there he had held a stone on his knees and with a hammer cracked hazelnuts, walnuts and hickory nuts for Anne to make nut cakes for his home and hers. Betweenwhiles he peeled raw turnips for Anne, Marvel, and himself to eat, saying, "In a few years we'll have our own orchard and it will be apples instead of turnips."

Sarah got out of bed the second day Anne was there and on the third day was helping with the housework. The two sisters were good for each other, Winwold saw, and though the outsides of them were different, far inside of them there was a likeness. He remembered the day he had said, after puzzling about it, that it was a tossup and he could marry either of them.

The day came five years later when he was thankful Sarah had a sister Anne and the two of them had inside likeness even though one was a carrot-head with brown eyes and the other so smashingly decisive a brunette. Those five years were filled with a fury for gain. Near to avarice, rather than mere acquisition, this motive ran through Winwold. Often it was almost a sheer sensual pleasure, like that of a fabulous miser endlessly piling his gold coins and knocking them down and piling them again piece by piece, a sensuous music of possession giving him gratification. The land he owned in perpetuity in a pyramid down to the center of the earth and in another geometric form up to the zenith of the sky, this land he could waste or spoil, if he chose, or use and profit by, if it pleased him; he didn't actually rub his hands as though washing them in contemplation of this little empire where he was the emperor—yet his greedy eyes and the possessor's mind that had grown in him did in their way perform that little pantomime. He would have let his hands say it but for his instinct that it was a secret and saying it with a sign language of hands would be a procedure like writing it on paper as a confession. And he had not grown so deeply into it as a fixed and unchangeable habit that he cared for any free confession of it.

The house had a front porch added, with a nice large kitchen addition, with a smokehouse for hickory-cured ham, with a barn six times the size of the first one, with two hundred more acres added and most of it pasture land for feeding herds of cattle brought up from the plains of the Southwest for fattening and selling to the Chicago and Cincinnati meat-packing plants. These and other acquisitions had resulted from his fierce concentrated activity. A certain rasp came more often in his voice. He rasped at himself, at the growing and impressionable boy Marvel, at horses that he once gentled and coaxed. There were occasional hours when his high-riding self-assurance left him and he was back in his old Erie Canal mood, "I'm a lost man, groping, groping." At no time however in such hours did he get back into the cold icy shrewdness, the mood of arctic frigidity, when he got at himself with a genuine humility and a curious kind of dim-lighted laughter, an inaudible laughter woven of irrefutable logic and utterly naïve prayer. He had lost what he had of gift and habit for invoking this mood. The compulsions of that repeated and incessant line, "I'll make a go of it, by God, I've got to," had almost broken and swept out of him an earlier gift and habit that had swung the big decisions of his life.

An October day of gray drizzle in 1842, a season of big potato yield on his farm, he was hauling half a wagonload of them to sell in Atlas along with a few baskets of windfall apples. He had rasped at breakfast about a good cow he had found sick in a pasture slough three days before and he had tried to move her up to a shed near the barn and the cow wouldn't budge and he had made a dozen trips to the far end of the farm and this morning had found her dead. "She would have brought twenty dollars if I'd had the sense to sell her a week ago," he rasped, looking at Sarah as though it was her fault as much as his.

Twenty dollars—maybe a twenty-dollar gold piece—five of them he had left yet out of the money belt Joel Wimbler made for him in Arpa—five—he counted them again last night, piled them five in a pile, spread them out with his fingers and counted five, piled them in a neat snug pile and counted them, five. He had toiled and fought off every force that could take these away from him. They were a backlog of security that he measured, fondled, and aside from what they were as realities and bulwarks against need and want, he luxuriated in the look of them as symbols. Vaguely and darkly he had suddenly caught himself with a suspicion of himself that wouldn't come clear, except that he muttered, "Thou shalt not make unto thyself any graven image."

He had his hand on the doorknob of the living room, ready to hitch up and go to town, when Sarah smiled and her wide smooth black eyebrows arched as she patted his left arm at the shoulder and said gaily, "Wait a minute." She vanished into the bedroom and came out wearing a piece of headgear that amazed her husband. It began about a third of the way back on her head, leaving a good width of her parted black hair showing and it had, on a slight framework that fitted her head neatly, an arrangement of purple satin, lavender lace, and strips of black velvet. She had bought it with chicken-and-egg-money savings yesterday in Atlas from the latest St. Louis arrivals. "Anne helped me pick it out. We think it's nice." The quiet half-smile of her large mouth with its large white teeth and one upper tooth gone, the hazy blue dust sifting in her very black eyes, it had little personal vanity. "Sarah isn't much of a girl for showing off," had been one of the first remarks about her that Winwold had heard from Anne. The main idea now was to please her husband. His wife perhaps needed a little brightening for him to look at. That was her feeling, and he shuttered his eyelids, and colder than a long woodshed icicle in January came what was both rasp and grunt, "That's a gaudy thing. You think you're purty in it, purty. You look like a half-wit in it."

He turned, his hand on the doorknob, pulled the door toward him, took a step and stood in the half-open doorway to see her eyes blazing and to hear from her large mouth a cry of clearly carved words: "Go on to town. Go sell your potatoes. Get out of this house." Her two hands lifted with palms facing toward him, they shushed him as she cried, "Be gone, out of the house, be gone!"

He was going, he was pulling the door closed, when he opened it wider to see her snatch the offending hat off her head, throw it on the floor and stamp on it, with one foot, with another foot, with both feet. He closed the door and was gone.

Three days of rain had soaked the roads, the mud slithery, the ruts in places deep, uneven, treacherous. Once and again another time the front wagon wheels sank nearly to the hubs. And Winwold did what he wouldn't have done two or four years ago. Instead of resting the horses after their first tugging and pulling and failing to lift those wheels out of the rut, he swung a blacksnake whip on them and let fly curses. A half-mile out of town the front wheels were in a rut, to the hubs in mud, and the right hind wheel in a water puddle above the hub, the wagon end tilted. Winwold gave the horses no rest. He lashed at them and cursed. They both tried, they both pulled. Then the gee horse balked. The lash came down, the rasping curses fell, the horse didn't move, didn't try, wouldn't budge.

Fury grew on the man as he let the reins drop, and he swung the leather thongs, aiming at one place, deepening the line of a cut as he laid welt on welt. His head roared and his curses came hoarse and muffled from a worn throat as the blood oozed out in dark-red areas over the sorrel horse coat of hair. He was now nearly spent, his right arm muscles used up. In a daze of exhaustion, and feeling a little silly, he was wondering what to do next. He needn't have wondered. The horses decided for him. With a leap and a wild snort the balking horse sprang forward, the other horse joining. With a terrific jolt they had the lurching wagon out of the mudhole and water puddle. The reins had fallen alongside the left front wheel. The hind wheels jolted with a crazy lurch out of the front mudhole as Winwold stood up and bent over trying to reach the reins. The swift zigzags of the wagon were too much for him. He fell off into the road. He sat up in a puddle of mud to see horses and wagon vanish at runaway speed, vanish on a downhill road, saw them again on an upgrade. Turning a corner in Atlas, they were out of sight.

He looked around. No one on the road or in field or house had seen what happened. So it seemed. At arm's length in a puddle of mud was his hat. He reached for it and bringing it before his eyes saw the inside of it, the band, lined with black slush and ooze. He wouldn't put it on. He was tired, worn. A streak of pain throbbed in his head. His right shoulder ached. He would find it swollen and bruised, black-and-blue, when he took his shirt off. He had landed on that shoulder. The whole weight of his body had driven that shoulder down through mud into solid ground. He sat in the mud, trying to think. Suddenly he was pleased with a little of his thinking. He smiled for the first time that day. How many days back was it since he had smiled? he asked. He couldn't remember. Now he was smiling. He was lucky. On two points he was lucky. The nice soft oozy mud had cushioned his fall. And he had a good right shoulder. He thanked his right shoulder for not breaking.

He slid his feet and legs around in the mud, got a footing and slowly and lamely rose and stood. Then he stepped to the side of the road, climbed a rail fence, and by a roundabout walk without going into the town he reached the house on the Prindle farm. His head cleared somewhat with the walking. He wouldn't believe it, at first, what had happened. As he walked on he was sure it had happened. A certain Omri Winwold had died over on that road. It wasn't elation, ecstasy, or exultation over victory. There was no particular radiance or burst of illumination about what had happened. He had been a certain kind of fool, driven by hopes, illusions and delusions that had served well enough in his first two or three years on the farm—and now he had shed them. "I'm going to be a fool," he said, "but not again the same kind of a fool."

The sun had come out and at the Prindle farm Anne was helping the hired girl hang out the week's wash for drying. Her father and her husband were helping a neighbor shock corn. Winwold had thought he looked miserable but he knew from the way Anne laughed at him and joked that he looked funny. She led him before a mirror and he saw his head of reddish hair mud-soaked on the right side and the most of his hair as though it had been dyed with gray slush. His right ear could have been a large gray mouse flattened out. The right half of the reddish muffler beard that ran along under jaws and chin had many small chunks of half-dried grayish mud clinging to the hairs. The sleeve of his right arm could have been sewed by a tailor who measured him for a mud sleeve. The back of the coat and its bottom, along with his pant legs and shoes, were mud-daubed and mud-caked.

"You're a sight to see, Omri Winwold," chirruped Anne.

"How are you, Mr. Mud?" Winwold bowed to his face in the mirror, his yellow uneven teeth smiling through an area of dried muddy water that was like a map of North America and Greenland. Anne helped him out of his overcoat and started getting the inside of his hat cleaned, after she had helped him to a basin of rain water and soap and towels on the back porch.

"It's good you're here alone," he said.

"What happened?"

"Tell you later," as he soaped the reddish muffler of whiskers that ran under his jaws from ear to ear.

Later in the living room she gave him the large rocking chair and sat sidewise on a chair. She faced him with her hands on the back of the chair, her white face peering at him with mischief in it, her brown eyes sparkling, her mouth puckered at him as though he were still somewhat funny. "Now, what happened? You're mussed up, Omri."

"I've been a goddam fool and know it." He was glowering, ugly. Anne knew that the veering thrust outward of his underlip and the savage curl of his wide slashed mouth were at himself and not at her.

"*What* happened, Omri?"

"Today it happened. Today at last after these hellish years of making that farm a go, today I learned about it."

"You learned *what*, Omri?" And he could have kissed her for a sweetness in the way her eyes lingered on him and a wind-in-the-willows murmur in her voice as she went along with him and asked him to go on.

"There was an Omri Winwold died today."

"One of him died and another of him is pert and keen before me now." ·

"He died and he's going to stay dead."

"Yes, let him be dead, dead as a dead dog, dead as a dead hog. And *how* did he die?"

"A skinflint I was and a miser. They're dead. You'll see. A nagger I was, an evil-mouthed scold with a vile tongue, meaner than a barn rat, worse than a chicken-house weasel, and this morning I had the slime and malice of a copperhead snake. And they're dead. You'll see, Anne, they're dead."

"It's sudden, Omri. I believe you. They're dead and they're going to stay dead. But *how* did it come this October day like a crash of lightning? Saul of Tarsus went down on his knees when something hit him, the Good Book says. What hit you?"

He began five years back, telling it short, how the fever of getting more and more had grown on him and he didn't notice how it had grown. The gold pieces last night he had piled and spread under idolatrous fingers and piled again for his eyes of adoration to behold, the sick cow that had died and his rasping at Sarah, Sarah's beautiful new hat that she and Anne had picked and his crazy insult to her, the balking horse and the runaway team and wagon. "And if I'd landed on my head instead of this shoulder, I'd have been folded up on the road with a broken neck."

He set his teeth together and grimaced with pain as he reached toward a throbbing that went on in the right shoulder. "You'll have to help me, Anne." She did her best at helping him out of his shirt and out of the right sleeve of his red flannel undershirt. She brought arnica and was skilled and tenderly understanding in applications of it to the swollen area of the shoulder where the skin was bruised, black-and-blue with a fine crisscross of red lines.

"My God, this looks awful, you could have had a broken neck, Omri, you can thank your stars you're alive," had been Anne's first outburst and then she had worked in quiet.

"I'm glad it happened like it did and no different. Walking over the fields to get here it was like some heavy load slid off me. That heavy load was the carcass of Omri Winwold that's dead, and he'll never come back."

"Sounds good to me," said Anne, stepping away a moment and looking at him. She gave a laugh that had silver bells in it. "You can tell me more, Omri. I'll believe all of it." She peered with level eyes at him. "Your face is good. I'll take your face on it."

She helped him into the red flannel sleeve, into his shirt and coat. Again he was in the rocker and she sidewise on a chair facing him, her arms on the chair back, her chin on an arm. They sat gazing deep in each other's eyes and no word spoken. Her darting humor and straightaway merriment, Sarah had it too, only Anne was swifter with it. Or in his incessant driving of himself, and of Sarah along with himself, had he in some degree held down and choked back that readiness for laughter in Sarah? Yes, he had. He would admit it. He was guilty. Anne saw the ease and cheer of him fade off into a glum dumb look, a gargoyle melancholy on the long gash of his mouth, a traverse of shadow lines crossing in his liquid brown eyes.

"What next?" Anne asked. He saw her face in light quivers of anxiety. He roved to a timber clearing where he had seen white windflowers tremulous in a ripple of breeze. She went on. "What next? Now what? Five or six dirty low-down Omri Winwolds are dead and you have buried them so deep they can never be dug up. Now what next?"

His gloom face dropped off him, slid away with the finality of a snake shedding an old skin for new.

She went to the barn with him. She saddled and bridled the horse, helped him with his lame shoulder to mount, holding the reins in his left hand. In the town he met curious, suspicious faces, queer smiles, as he asked about his wagon and horses. Already a buzz had run from mouth to ear and from mouth to ear that the steady industrious Omri Winwold, the man who kept by himself and went it alone and worked his farm like a barn afire, the sober churchgoing Omri Winwold had gone drunk as a fiddler's bitch and fell off his wagon and the scared horses ran away. For the changed man in Winwold this was easy to take. What he had actually done, and of which they knew nothing, was worse by far than what they buzzed and gossiped. He could stand it and be glad.

The horses had "run hell-bent through town," he was told, making into a road that led to the farm where the balking horse was foaled as a colt. The team had made this turn so sharp that the tongue broke loose from the wagon and the whiffletrees kept hitting the horses' heels and legs. A farmer had left his cornhusking and tied them to a fence. Winwold petted them, talked coaxing, loosed the whiffletrees, in town hired a man to lead the horses to the Prindle barn and to see that his potatoes and apples reached a produce trader and buyer.

Later at the Prindle farm he told Anne: "I can't face Sarah alone. She'll laugh sooner if you come. You'll talk to her first. Then all three of us'll talk. Then you can go."

"I like it," said Anne. "We'll go, right off."

Two on a horse, blankets instead of a saddle, Anne behind Winwold, they rode to town and on out to the farm. Anne went in first, took Sarah to the bedroom. Ten minutes later the two of them came out. Sarah wore the new hat, battered, flat, mussed-up. She wore too a sunburst of a smile. So did Anne. Winwold's mouth widened into a harvest-moon effulgence though the corners of the mouth twitched and they saw by a moist shading in his eyes that he was near crying. Sarah fell into his long winding left arm with a tight kiss on his mouth and when they loosened he was saying, "It's a damned lovely hat and we'll keep it long as we live."

"I'm going now," said Anne to Winwold. "You said there was a special surprise I could see you give Sarah."

"I forgot about it. Yes, the special surprise." He climbed the ladder to the loft, came down with a sober face, nodded them to the table where he stood with a closed fist. He opened the fist and raised the palm of his hand from where it covered five gold pieces. The sisters bent over them, their breath coming fast, their faces questioning. "Gold," he said to Sarah. "Yours and mine. You keep it. And if you want to buy fifty more hats to look more purty for me, I say throw it away. You won't hear a mumble or a moan out of me. I want you purty. Till today I cared more for the damned farm than I did for you. From now on you and the children come first and then the property. The gold is trash."

He saw tears flooding Anne's eyes just before Sarah fell on his shoulder with a long soprano wail that cut the air like a silver blade.

They walked out with Anne to the horse, both kissed her, and Winwold held a strong left hand as a stirrup to help her mount. Anne gave a long look from face to face, then her eyes resting on Winwold and her head nodding toward Sarah, "She'll put the arnica on good for you," Anne galloped away.

* * * * * * * * * *

Chapter 21

* * * * * * * * * *

The Saga Moves On

THERE are monotone years with a pendulum regularity of clock ticks and the healthy rhythms of deep sleep coming after hard work, where every interruption and interference with set programs and intended schedules has its pleasant side, often with something to laugh at afterward.

And there are years crossed over with unforgettable dates on the calendar, the day of the month with a ring of blood-color around it, the midnights when there could be a crimson thumbprint on the front doorknob and what must be spoken in the house goes in hushed tones.

At the Winwold place and likewise at the Prindle farmhouse, they were crowded and moving years, those three years from 1842 on. A three-year-old child of the Winwolds' died. A six-weeks baby died. The boy they named Holliday lived, and that made three boys in '42 under their roof, Marvel who was seven, Milton who was five, and Holliday not yet weaned. And they counted it some kind of justice that Anne's two babies lived, a boy and a girl, smoothing somewhat the matter of her first baby stillborn and her second, perfect to look at, lusty and promising, dying in its second month. Then in a third year typhoid fever took Anne's father in August and her husband in September.

The same year it was that Sarah lingered for eight months with an intestinal tumor, shrank to a skeletonized figure of white, her face snow-pale and her thin hands the color of a blue-tinted snow; her large black eyes luminous and speaking crept farther back in their sockets. Her vivid black hair took on streaks of gray but the smooth black velvet curves of her eyebrows stayed. To the last the nightstar smolder of her eyes spoke some language of infinite care and thought to her husband and children. In a mild delirium of her last week, she told Omri where she kept the five gold pieces and had him bring them to her. Taking one coin in her right hand she whispered, "I will be holding this when I cross over. Bury it with me. Tell Anne I took it with me for her sake, for your sake," and after a little wait for the strength of another whisper, "and for sweet Christ's sake."

The living had managed, had kept going across the year of '46. In November of that year, on the anniversary day of Sarah's crossing over, Omri and Anne were married. And there had been benedictions and blossoms, for their baby Patrick Henry lived and the girl Hope lived though Esther died, and little Robert Prindle had never a sick day.

They sold the Prindle farm, they bought more acres next to what they had, they kept taking on larger herds out of the Southwest for feeding and sale to ready markets. They built additions to the house. They had a hired girl and two hired men. They put in new pumps and windmills, the new machines that came, plows, cultivators, mowers, rakes, reapers, and threshers. They saw a new generation with blooded cattle, pedigreed hogs and sheep, railway transportation to market, daily newspapers, agricultural weekly journals with the latest scientific findings as to soil, seeds, ditches, fences. Toward the east for a thousand miles and more, toward the west across the Mississippi River for hundred of miles and northward toward the Great Lakes and the Canadian line, the same changes, the same "march of improvements," as it was called, going on in thousands of neighborhoods—the new young American nation still building and growing, still in the making.

Omri and Anne had seen this series of changes that made the new generation and they had glimpsed the generation of men before them, the frontiersmen, hunters and trappers who had fought the Indians and trodden the earliest wilderness trails and laid out highways still traveled. They had a few times given a chair at their eating table to one of these old-timers in a coonskin cap, a linsey hunting shirt, fringed buckskin breeches and moccasins, belt around the waist with a butcher knife and hatchet stuck in it, a long squirrel rifle and the independence that went with their saying, "When you kin hear yer neighbor's rooster a-crowin, it's time to call up the dogs, piss out the fire and move on." Horse thieves of the earlier generation when caught were hanged by a mob or had their ears cropped and letters put on the forehead with a hot branding iron by the sheriff. Omri had talked with a man who in 1832 stood in a crowd on the public square in Carrollton and saw a horse thief naked to the hips, his hands roped to the cross piece of the public whipping post, the sheriff swinging a rawhide whip laying fifteen lashes on the bare back, resting while someone put a tumbler of whisky to the horse thief's mouth, the sheriff then laying on the other fifteen lashes as ordered by the court. Now, the whipping post gone, when the new law had its way, a horse thief went to the state penitentiary at hard labor.

Year by year with no letup of movers in their westbound wagons covered with canvas or muslin, Omri and Anne saw a wide variety of American citizens, some of them college-educated, others with no use for reading and writing. Four wagons from North Carolina, bound for western Missouri, to start a new settlement, stopped on the public square in Atlas. Each man's work laid out for him, one said he was to open a store, another to run a blacksmith shop, two others to raise hogs and sheep. In one wagon sat a rack-boned, white-haired, half-bald, feeble man who croaked that he had seen eighty-six summers in his life. A young fellow was asked what possible use the old-timer would be. "Oh, we'll use him all right. We're taking the old man along to start a graveyard with."

Omri had helped a barefoot six-footer of a man, a mover, water his skin-and-bones horse. Along with the woman and boy in the wagon were an old straw bed, a skillet and a spinning wheel. The man wore only ragged tow trousers, a torn tow shirt and a hat with holes in it. Where was he from? "Hiwassee Purchase, McMinn County, State of Tennessee, off the roaring fork of Grindstone." And where going? "Missouri." But why not stay in Illinois? Didn't he like Illinois? His answer edged with a snarl, "Well, sir, your *sile* is mighty *fartil*, but a man can't own niggers here, God-durn yuh."

Since Omri quit his hard driving of himself he had made trips up the Mississippi to Rock Island and over to Chicago by rail, by boat to St. Louis, Louisville and Cincinnati, overland trips horseback over southern Illinois. The farther north in Illinois he went the thicker the abolitionists and the farther south the fewer. He met people out of Kentucky, Tennessee and Virginia who had themselves owned slaves or their kinfolk and friends did. On the abolitionists they poured hate and vituperation only equaled by the vehement loathing of the abolitionists for slaveholders. Omri had ridden for miles through pretty hill country along the Mississippi River, where a man by turning his eyes could lift them back and forth across the river from the free-state soil of Illinois to the slave-state ground of Missouri.

There was a good neighbor William Hoon, of Swiss parents, a fine cheesemaker, and he was like many another antislavery man in southern Illinois when saying to Omri, whom he trusted, "I don't talk about it, you notice. I like to get along with my neighbors. Why should I stir up trouble? They have their ways and I have mine and it is best for us to let each other alone. If I had been born a little different, maybe I would go around and tell every man to his face that slavery is a curse and a sin against God and man and before the rest of the world we ought to be ashamed of it. I catch myself saying the abolitionists are crazy and then I ask how can they be crazy if they are right and what they say is terrible truth, so terrible men turn away from looking at it. If I was a slave they could come and take my wife Lisa and my boy Hans and my baby Lena and sell them to different owners. Slavery says to hell with marriage and the family. A baby born to a slave woman is like another calf dropped, another pig farrowed for the market. If you own a nigger you can sell him for cash or trade him for a horse or borrow money and sign a mortgage on him. You can write it in a will he belongs to whoever you want to have him when you are dead. You can ship him in a crate or handcuffed without a crate. He is your property and you can clip his ear like a hog, harness and drive him like a horse, break one of his legs so he won't run away a second time and put a rawhide whip to him leaving scars on the back or even the face for life. That is the law. He is your property. From the top of his head to the bottom of his heels the law says he is yours." And Hoon had paused, lowering his voice. "Excuse my talking like that, Mr. Winwold. I think about it so much and talk about it so little, it helps to say it to you, and I know you will not pass it on I have such ways."

And one day Winwold and William Hoon rode over to John Walker's place near Cool Bank, a farm of four hundred and sixty acres with cattle, hogs, sheep, poultry, a McCormick Reaper, a horse rake and other machines, and they talked with John Walker, the owner, a free Negro. Born a slave in Virginia in 1802, he had been sold several times, he said, and liked each of his masters and best of all the last of his owners, David Van Aue. "One of the nicest men ever lived, Mr. Van Aue. Let me have time to myself, work for other people, earn a little money. I save three hundred dollars. He let me buy my freedom. I rent a piece of land and go to work for myself." Saying this, John Walker's shrewd cool eyes glistened, Winwold noticed. In rather neat blue jeans and a cotton shirt he was of medium build, unusually well-muscled, an easy way of standing or moving, no fret about him; he wasted no motions in whatever he was doing. His skin near black, his face, his nose and mouth in shape and proportions that had Winwold guessing, "Possibly quadroon, more likely mulatto or at least a mulatto father or mother, at least one-sixteenth, perhaps one-eighth white, could be he had a white grandfather, or a grandfather and grandmother on one side mulattoes or forty other crossbreeds I'll figure out later."

On his rented land in Virginia, the newly freed Negro John Walker learned his freedom had a catch in it. Virginia law said a free Negro could stay in the state only a year—free Negroes could make trouble and did better out of sight of slave Negroes. John Walker, however, had a friend in the legislature, a white man who thought well of John Walker and got a permit for him to stay in Virginia three years. As to whether he stayed the full three years he wasn't clear. "I disremember ceptin I worked hard, saved money, bought a team of horses cheap and sold 'em in 1838 and went West with William R. Dusen." He mentioned the Dusen name as one fixed deep in him, and a name known to many others. John Walker could never forget Mr. William R. Dusen, the man who owned, with clear title of possession, the wife and children of John Walker. It would be a long story, he said, how with the money from selling his team in Virginia he bought fifty

816

acres of land in Randolph County, Missouri, and went to raising tobacco, corn and hogs, and how after a time, with hard work and saving, he bought from Mr. Dusen the freedom of his two children, Peter and Letty, and still later bought from Mr. Dusen his wife Lucy and his son Oregon, the two for eleven hundred dollars. The wife and children came on his farm and they worked and saved and after a time he was able to buy from Mr. Dusen for six hundred dollars the freedom of his daughter Louise and her two children, Charles and William. Of his sixteen children three were living with him now, Oregon, Archy and Peter, and exactly how many were dead and precisely where all the others had drifted, he wasn't sure. Did he read or write? "No suh, had'n been time."

"Are you for slavery or against it?" said Hoon, gently, respect and depths of curiosity in his tone.

John Walker slanted a wary left eye at Hoon. "It's been here a long time and I don' know how I'd change it. I don' study about it, suh. My folks, some of 'em, would'n know what to do with freedom if they got it. Used to havin white folks look after 'em. I look out I take care uh my own. I make no trouble for othuhs. The Lord has been good to me and mine. If slavery is a sin in the eyes of the Lord, like some say, the Lord will do what is wise. The Lord God Almighty seeth and knoweth all and it's in His mighty hands."

"Ever whipped?" Hoon asked softly.

"Nevuh had the lash laid to me."

"Get hard words?"

"When I did'n do my work right or marster drunk or feelin mean. I got no complaints. Course, Mr. Dusen was a little high, what he made me pay for my wife and Oregon. I ain't got time for complaint and makin trouble."

Hoon and Winwold thanked him as he went to helping Oregon oil the McCormick Reaper. They had other questions but they could see he wanted to be by himself, to shut off the outside world, to say and do nothing that could bring trouble to him from that outside world. As they rode away Winwold said, "He's a wonder. He can drive himself harder than I did myself my first years in Pike County and it don't wear him to pieces like it did me."

They rode a mile, nothing to say and plenty to think. Hoon smiled and in a thin sarcasm, "I hope Mr. Dusen is doing well. It would be too bad if Mr. Dusen had to go to the poorhouse."

They rode further in silence, then Hoon, "You can talk easy with me any time, Mr. Winwold, any time about this damned slavery mix-up and I tell nobody." Hoon heard rumors that Winwold had come under suspicion of hiding on his place two Negro women slaves from St. Louis one winter night. Hoon spoke of it to Winwold. "People *will* talk. You know that *talk* is going around. I'm sure you do. Anyhow, in these times, you ought to know such talk is going around.

Those two women Marova and Hetty, like it said in the St. Louis papers, one of them a big black woman and the other a pretty little yellow girl. You have heard the talk you hid them on your place and drove away with them toward Quincy?"

"I've heard it. People *will* talk." That was all, from Winwold. And Hoon later was saying, "I talk free with you because you are a man I can trust. When you want to talk free with me you will see me listen and you can trust me and maybe you can help me on this damned slavery thing that hurts all of us who have to think about it. I talk to you about it the same as I tell it to the horses, only they never answer me."

"You're a troubled man, Mr. Hoon. So am I. So is John Walker. So are the President of the United States and Steve Douglas. So were those two Irishmen who came through here from Peoria and they don't want the 'naygers' free because then the black man would be the equal, the ache-ul as they said, of the white man, and worse yet, said these ninety-cents-a-day workingmen, if the 'naygers' down South got free they would swarm up into the North and work cheap and take the jobs of white workingmen. They were troubled, Mr. Hoon, the same as you and me. So is every living man who tries to find a way through the misery and fog of this slavery issue. I get the creeps over it. There will be hell to pay. I don't know how it will come, but there will be hell to pay. It's a fog. I haven't heard of a man who can see through this fog. It's fog thicker than pea soup, thicker than a bunch of black cats in midnight mist. I heard long ago about an Englishman telling a sailor, 'London is the foggiest place in the world.' 'Oh, no,' says the sailor, 'I been in a place a lot foggier than London.' 'Where was that?' 'I don't know where it was, it was so foggy.' "

Sometime they must have a long talk, said Winwold to Hoon. They parted with smiles and warm handshakes. "I trust him," said Omri to Anne. "But why should I trust him with secrets that even you would rather I didn't tell you so you'll never have to swear to a lie? You can swear any day I'm no abolitionist and it's the truth."

"I can swear you don't *talk* abolition," laughed Anne.

"Yes, and you can swear that I go straight along with the free Negro John Walker telling me if slavery is a sin in the eyes of the Lord, like some say, the Lord will do what is wise, for the Lord God Almighty seeth and knoweth all and it's in His mighty hands. I read once about a fellow in the French Revolution arguing if God didn't exist they would have to invent God to take the credit and blame for what they were doing. It's handy to have a great All-wise God to lean on now. Only God can straighten out this slavery tangle. And God will make it cost. It won't be easy when God really and at last begins to work on it."

And Anne said it was a shame that all over southern Illinois were so many good neighbors hiding from each other what was in their hearts and minds. Two cases they had heard of and probably others not heard of where a man's barn was burned in the night by men who called him a nigger-lover after he had come straight out and said all Negroes everywhere ought to be set free now and at once. And Anne was saying she didn't like it that Ed Houseworth's wife heard a Pittsfield storekeeper say of Omri, "He's either an abolitionist or a little crazy or both."

Omri said, "We'll go to England sometime, Anne, and hunt up a fellow there named Charles Babbage. He's about finished now a machine that will work out for you any problem in arithmetic or mathematics. You feed the numbers into the machine and it spills out the answer."

"What's that got to do with people saying you're crazy?"

"Babbage has set up a little club, very exclusive, for men of science. You can't get in unless you have six certificates, three that you are sane, and three that you are insane."

"You can get the six here in Pike County, Illinois, sure enough," laughed Anne.

It was about this time that Winwold came home one day and told Anne he had a session with his lawyer in Pittsfield, and, "I made a new will."

"And I'll be disinherited, I suppose."

"It's a good will," said Winwold. "I made a copy for you. And left the original in a safe." He handed her the copy and she read:

> Unto my beloved wife—
> All my worldly goods I have in store
> I give my beloved wife and hers forevermore;
> I give all truly, I no limit fix;
> This is my will; she my executrix.

And whatever the year and crops, market demand and prices for cattle, in their home as in so many others was an instinct about the future, changes to come, America of today something else tomorrow. Ever the mover wagons by hundreds going west and ever the crying out loud there must be a transcontinental railway to the Pacific, added fury from year to year of an endless political seething, abolitionists calling "No Union with Slaveholders," Southern men predicting the old Union of States would go to pieces, the American Republic wrecked and broken and the Old World smiling in triumph, "We told you so."

The future? Did it not romp and howl, fight and make up, prank and howl, and go storming and laughing upstairs and down over the house and around the farm? Eight children at the eating table and some meals quiet and orderly, others with pleasant talk and news of the day, and occasionally a dinner or supper that was a tumult of accusations and grievances, eight children taking sides and divided on who was wrong and what to do about it. Eight sons and daughters.

There was Andrew Marvel now, in 1857, twenty-two years old, the luck child brought overland from New York. There were Sarah's boys, Milton now twenty and Holliday seventeen years old. There were Anne's two children, the girl Cedora now seventeen and Peter Moore who was sixteen. And three who were the very own of Omri and Anne—the three littlest—Patrick Henry who was ten, Hope, now eight years old, and the seven-year-old who could say his name distinctly and was proud of it, "Robert Prindle Winwold."

* * * * * * * * * *

Chapter 22

* * * * * * * * * *

Two Women

AS the years had passed the memory of Bee had dimmed, months sliding by when she was out of Omri's thought. Or again her shadow rose before him and his phrase for her, "bluebird and wildcat," returned. He would like to know how far and where she had gone with Bob Kelway, who could no more have stayed by her than she could have stayed by him, they were that sort. With what other men had she gone on? And who was kissing her now? And the way she was burning herself away, how many years could her gloss and gleam last? And with her particular pride and vanity, what would she do with herself as a flower of faded and drooping leaves?

In St. Louis one afternoon on the street he saw ahead of him a woman of Bee's figure, the same swift dancing grace, glossy black hair. He followed her, saw her into a dry-goods store, caught her profile— and the face wasn't Bee at all, too young and fresh-looking.

Noon the next day he was having fried catfish with lager beer in a water-front place overlooking the river wharf. And it was another woman than Bee who saw him through the street window and came in and sat opposite him and spoke to him. He had to look at her twice and twice again to be sure it was Bee and she had become another woman. Heavily bodied, she faced him, the heaviness, it seemed to Omri, having an element of sag and bloat to it. Omri was reminded of the opposite, of Mrs. Sylvanus Goforth near Pittsfield whose fat flesh color had a peony-pink with enough good muscle in and around it for Mrs. Goforth, who also had knack and know-how, to have a reputation as the best housekeeper in the neighborhood.

The tawny smooth skin of Bee, luminous with shadings of light and tint that once had fascinated Omri, now it had powder and paint in

820

excess, the rouge daubed too thick on the lips. It was a little startling to him. A woman so painted and rouged usually belonged in the theater or the bawdyhouse—either that or she was reckless with her reputation. "Painted woman" was an epithet, and it meant a woman on the loose. There were respectable women who could use a few pinches of white or creamy powder, along with the faintest tinges of paint and rouge, and they might be suspect but no one could say they were "bedizened." Bee *was* bedizened, somehow desperate, and her flaunted silk bow of lavender at her neck couldn't hide the folds and wrinkles in the flesh of her chin and jaws. Her once straight and firm underlip had a helpless hang to it. She ordered whisky and drank it straight without a chaser. She joined him in food, taking roast wild turkey and cleaning her plate of a large helping of mashed potatoes and gravy. She had had three or four drinks that morning, Omri guessed, from the way she drooped and flounced into her chair rather than seated herself, and from a vague look on her face, half-maudlin. After ordering another straight whisky and while it was on the way, she blurted at Omri in a throaty tone, with a huskiness of muffled quality not there in the Erie Canal days, "I guess I've changed more than you have. Damned if you don't look like the same old gay boy for all the hayseed rig you come to St. Louis in." He asked her to say it again, he wasn't sure he got it. She blurted rather than spoke again and it seemed the same and he hoped he got it.

Omri worked on his fried catfish and beer and said nothing. Between bites of her roast wild turkey Bee asked him, "Is it straight you're a hayseed? If it ain't, what's the bilk? And what's your lay in St. Louis?" With the drink and food she spoke in a clearer voice, her wits and face now alive. He began getting her eyes. The gloss of her hair had turned somewhat drab and over her ears lay stringy hair and ill-kept. But her eyes held much of the early brilliance, still quivered with a black flame that came and went. It hurt him. A rush of memories cut through him. Then his guard of wit began its work on her. He was running a gambling house in Chicago. "Took a little sashay down to St. Louis to look around." How was *she* doing? "You live in St. Louis or goin somewhere?" he asked.

Bee was married to a storekeeper, a groceryman. "He's retail and wholesale, spondoolix to burn, stuck on me and jealous as a catfish in spring." She said this meaning it to be spoken fondly and Omri saw it as the frail flutter of a dying bluebird. Then she summoned her wary wildcat strength and part of it came and was there in her saying, "You better keep hands off. We're respectable people, him and me. He won't pay hush and I won't. You stick to your deck of cards and your dice."

"What's he like?"

"He's jug-shape, comes about to your elbows, wider than you, hard as nails, chews tobacco, drinks beer and nothing else, gets the gilt, goes to bed with me four nights a week and he'll kill any duffer lays a finger on me and," her eyes flamed black, "you hold up the ace of hearts and he can put a bullet through the ace and it'll be a clean hole." Her words came clear now and the blurt was gone and the voice carried flickers of the former wild flaring Bee. And she slowed down and softened and was saying, "If tweren't"—and Omri was puzzled where she had picked up the "tweren't" that came so natural—"if tweren't for a streak of decency you always had, I'd do somethin, I don't know what, but I'd stop you comin between me and my husband."

"I'm leavin St. Louis tomorrow, Bee. I might be back a year from now, but I don't think so. I give you my solemn promise I'll never make trouble for you unless you try to make trouble for me."

A hard glitter crossed the black flame of her eyes, softened to a steel-blue and was gone.

"If you mean it and you're leavin town tomorrow for a year and maybe always, Omri, you can come out and have supper with me and my husband tonight, Omri. I'll tell him you're a gay old blade that wouldn't harm a flea." She had had four whiskies by now and was blurting again and on asking her to repeat, Omri made out what she was saying.

Omri took supper with Mr. and Mrs. Henry Flack that evening, pig's knuckles and sauerkraut, a roast quail apiece, musty ale, watermelon, chocolate cake with black coffee. Mr. Flack was jug-shaped, as Bee had said, wide-shouldered and thickset, earthy and fleshy, round-faced, with small sharp eyes, big fists still hard from considerable handling of boxes, barrels, baskets, hampers, kegs, merchandise in and out of containers. And he knew his merchandise, made good money, had respect for himself as a merchant and for other merchants of whom he would remark, "He's on the square," or "You can count on him." He told a St. Louis story, "Two nice young brothers have a coalyard and one of them says he is goin to join the church and tells his brother he should join the church too and the brother wants to know, 'If both of us join the church, who is goin to weigh the coal?' " Mr. Flack's eyes often ran over Bee from head to feet and once when his big hands had pawed over her back and hips and he had flourished light fingers over her breasts, he half-apologized with a smile, "You see, Mr. Winwold, I think Mrs. Flack is a whole team and the dog under the wagon."

Mr. Flack had a Tyrolese father and an Alsatian mother, played the zither and could yodel, and he enjoyed seeing Bee put away old brandy and chartreuse though when she poured he would sometimes give her a pleasant giggle and a warning finger and a pat on the cheek, "Too much and you'll be tight, my darling Bee." And when Mr. Flack said "tweren't" a couple of times, Omri knew where Bee had taken it. There was a brief moment of politics when Mr. Flack said, "Why do they make such a noise in the North about slavery? Let the nigger stay where he is. The noise is bad for business. St. Louis buys from New

Orleans and sells there. When New Orleans says maybe she goes out of the Union if the noise about slavery don't stop, it's bad for business. The Mississippi River is the Union and we don't want to break it up."

It was between two pieces on the zither that Mr. Flack told of Jenny Lind in St. Louis and a brewer who gave her a big reception saying "Efery note you sing, Miss Lind, iss a pearl." And she asked the brewer for his hat and into the hat she sang a little song and handed him the hat with a smiling "Now, sir, you have a hatful of pearls."

A caller dropped in for ten minutes' conversation with Mr. Flack on a business matter. About halfway in the interlude Bee's hanging underlip quivered and Omri heard a hoarse whisper, "How's the kid, my little one?"

"Coming nice, you couldn't ask better." Had they been alone she might have cried and put on a scene about her baby, Omri believed. But he was sure part of it would have been play-acting. When he took his hat to go away, Mr. and Mrs. Flack went out on the porch and said good-by pleasantly and said he must call again, and he went down a gravel walk lined with rosebushes and lilac shrubs and reaching the sidewalk saw Mr. and Mrs. Flack each with an arm on the other's shoulder and they waved him good-by with their free hands and arms not twined around their shoulders.

That was in 1852 and it was not the next year but the year after that Omri went to St. Louis again. His business finished, he called on Henry Flack and asked how things were going and Mr. Flack asked if he didn't read the papers. Omri explained that in Chicago he didn't read the St. Louis papers. And Flack was searching, peering with a long steady look, after which he poured himself out to Omri. He could let himself go before this Chicago gambler with a big crooked comic mouth, liquid brown eyes and a crisscrossed face. Here he could talk straight with a kind of comfort.

"That woman, Mr. Winwold," said Flack, "I picked her up, you know. Some of my old-time friends, their wives they wouldn't let her come to their homes. She was slick and slim when I meet her first in a ten-dollar house, girls and everything extra-special. In her room, looking-glasses on the walls, a looking-glass on the ceiling over her bed. She got into fights, carried a funny knife to hold her hair, stabbed a man one night, and had to change to a five-dollar house. I kept going back to her. She kind of liked me and I fell in love with her and married her. Drink, it was always drink and more drink. And I guess she took up with other men sometimes, trying to be careful. I went shooting ducks down the river two weeks one fall and she had other men drinking at the house and I couldn't tell her about it, she could act up so terrible when she wanted to make a fuss. Then six months ago it happened and got into all the papers. I go home one morning eleven o'clock and there she is in bed with a cheap sonofabitch gambler and I get my gun and

823

kill him and they give me a trial and the jury is out only two minutes and gives me acquittal. After that she is hard to live with, so sweet two or three days, then so damned ugly for a week. One morning she gets out of bed and comes at me with a knife."

Flack rolled up the sleeve of his right forearm showing a three-inch twisted white scar. "She cut me here but I got the knife from her. I told her that was the end, Mr. Winwold. She was discouraged with St. Louis. She took up with an outfit going to California for gold, some pretty rough fellows in it. I hope she gets out there and does better for herself."

His lips worked from one pucker to another and one eye squinted as he gazed solemnly into Winwold's eyes and said, "You know, Mr. Winwold, I think soft about her yet. I think she ain't strictly what you would call a bad woman. She is a good woman with crazy spells."

"You are right, Mr. Flack. I sized her up like that myself."

"And you know, Mr. Winwold, I believe if she could have had a baby or two, early in life, by some man who could love her proper, she might have been different."

"That might have helped, Mr. Flack. That's one way of looking at it though it might have turned out she wasn't a natural mother and would have left the baby home while she went out for a good time. I knew one woman like that. The baby had whooping cough and the husband came home to find his wife gone and the baby alone and when he hunted her out she was in a cellar groggery drinking with a low lot of men and women."

"Jesus, that was tough on that husband. I'd like to talk with him. He'd understand my case."

"He was a good friend of mine. You'd like each other."

"Did she ever try to kill him?"

"He hinted to me he didn't trust her."

"Do you know, Mr. Winwold, if my wife hadn't tried to kill me, if she hadn't gone that crazy, we might be living together yet? I look at it and I guess I could pass by any mistake she made except trying to kill me. She had been as loving as a man could ask that morning. Then she gets out of bed, not a stitch on her, for her drink to start the day. Every bottle in the house was empty. She swore she hadn't poured the last half of the last quart of whisky the night before. She cursed me for saying too many times she was drinking more than good for her. She cried and yelled I was trying to change her ways. I tried to slow her down. I didn't argue with her and I meant it when I told her I loved her more than ever. Then you know what she did? She opened a bottom bureau drawer and pulled out a six-inch ebony-handle knife, French make from New Orleans, holding it about her right breast, a terrible screwed-up face, and it came through her teeth, what she said: 'I've had enough of your goddam sweet talk.' Then she came at me and I sat up and got the knife away from her. I s'pose we'd be living together yet, fighting and making up and kissing again, if she hadn't pulled that knife on me."

Flack saw a lucid amber mist in the eyes of Winwold. A friendship had begun. On his St. Louis visit two years later Omri told Flack he was farming and where. Flack said one of the outfit had come back from California and Mrs. Flack had got a divorce and she seemed in better health than ever, wearing finer clothes and jewels like never before, and doing a good business.

"What business?" Omri asked.

"Eight girls working for her."

"Girls? In San Francisco in the gold rush? Girls?"

"Of course some of them not so young as they used to be."

Then Omri's business and errands brought him once or twice a year to St. Louis. Each time he and Flack visited, exchanged the news, drank beer with good food.

"Any word from San Francisco?" Winwold would ask.

"Not a word, no news," Flack had always answered.

Before the accident that crippled Anne, Omri was about ready to tell her of his first marriage, of his first wife still living and of his being technically before the law a bigamist, of the unpleasant talk that would arise from his divorcing a first wife while living with a third— and he would change his plans in any way that would suit her.

Now as he sat with Anne in the warm early afternoon hours of a rare October day, the air soft as the best of summer now filtering in an autumn haze, sashes of flame and saffrons of farewell running over hill timbers, Omri had no regrets over what he had told or hadn't told of his years before Illinois. A gambler he had been, and a barkeep, he admitted, and, "I'm not proud about it, nor ashamed. It happened, like my red hair." Of his shadowed boyhood he said little except of the year as bobbin boy in a cotton mill.

In these months of Anne in the wheel chair Omri held himself to everything bright and happy they had ever had together. Anne knew well however that a certain fury surged in him and he wouldn't trust himself at voicing it or trying to find tongue for it. To him it was cruel and tragic that thousands of grown men and women had a fourteen-hour work day, six days a week, and it was an infamy, beyond language and past any words of indictment or damnation, that skinny and thwarted children of six and eight years of age should perform routine clockwork automatic motions twelve and fourteen hours a day for ninety cents a week, six days a week, "Year on year, world without end, Amen and God bless you, and in the name of Christ, why?" Anne had heard Omri cry out. She had seen him tear his red hair in relentless questions. "Am I crazy or what? How can those New England abolitionists keep their eyes always fastened on the monstrous sin of slavery in the South and never turn their eyes on the infamies and sins under the roofs of the near-by New England mills? I can't join the abolitionists because I couldn't enjoy being so damned self-righteous. Am I crazy or what?" And at that particular outburst, Anne had put her two hands to his cheeks and he heard her cool voice, "Couldn't I get you a glass of cider, Mr. Winwold? And then you'll go on and on, I wouldn't stop you for the world."

Now they sat sharing their best hoards of memory. They could see pumpkins laughing yellow spots along a slope where they remembered riding in horse-high prairie grass, about the time she had asked, "What made you come out to this lonesome country?" when he answered, "I wanted to buy a farm and own a chunk of the earth." And Anne had plucked from her memory a moment he had clean forgotten, an evening of the first week they were married, when she was knitting, and bringing her chair toward him she had said, "How close do you want me to sit to you?" And his drawling, "I want you far from me, far as I could kick a red-hot anvil barefoot."

And he had stayed away from the county fair in the fall of that year of '57 and he had given up going to church for that year and he went to no public meetings or neighborhood gatherings and let others do the errands to town. The doctor was sure Anne's days were numbered and Omri wanted to miss no hours with her.

There came a night in late November when the last leaves had blown away in orchard and timber, the fields brown, dark and lonely, in wait for the first white shapes of gay and whirling snow. The youngest children were asleep upstairs and the older ones had gone to a Methodist-church oyster supper that night. Omri had said over, for Anne, various lines she enjoyed hearing from him, one old favorite, "Solitude, give me solitude, but in my solitude give me one friend to whom I can murmur, 'Solitude is sweet.' " Anne had closed her eyes and fallen asleep and Omri by a new kerosene-oil lamp had fumbled among three or four books and wondered if he cared to read. Then he had noticed Anne somewhat restless, her lips moving in disconnected words that made no sense. He saw she was again in a mild delirium that had come twice before that month. Then with open eyes turned toward him, her white flower-like face in one of its rarest smiles, with a faint touch of sweet mischief in the slight arch of her brown eyebrows and an odd twist of her little mouth, she was saying, "It will be sweet to die, Omri, when the time comes." Then her eyes closed, her little mouth and the cherry lips utterly still, and Omri's hands told him she was going cold, that her body had moved out into the ice, the dust and the dissolution, sometimes called eternity.

They buried Anne in a plot of ground with Sarah, and between her and Sarah the graves of their five children who had crossed over before them. At the old house and home Omri gave the required care and daily water to an oleander that Anne had planted in a tub of black loam Omri brought her. Sometimes he spoke to the living oleander, low-voiced, "It will be sweet to die, Oleander, when the time comes."

Now Omri had three gold pieces of the five he had given Sarah, of the four that had been in the keeping of Anne. One had been, as she wanted it, in the clench of Anne's right hand when they lowered her below the grassroots. And Omri had these three token coins left. They could be symbols, he said, as he looked at the three in his right-hand palm. They could mean either the Father, the Son and the Holy Ghost, he said, or Faith, Hope and Charity.

* * * * * * * * *

Chapter 23

* * * * * * * * *

Sons of Winwold; Storm Horizons

THE Winwold house shook with the roar and surge of youth, of young America, of the coming America. They wore the stairways with denting feet, splintered banister railings chasing each other, loosened the doorknobs they yanked in a hurry. In '58 handsome Marvel Winwold changed girls, quit one "steady company" for another, so the first girl's father came over to ask Marvel's father why his daughter was, as she said, "frozen out for another." Omri listened in patience and heard him out and asked, "You wouldn't mean he promised to marry her and your daughter is in the family way?"

"Oh no, I didn't come for a bastardy case."

"Then don't you see that my boy is doing just what you did and I did? He's going from one girl to another. When he finds the right one he'll marry her, or try to. Either that or he's a crabby old bachelor for life. Don't you think so?"

"I guess you're right, but my girl is pretty mad about being frozen out all of a sudden."

"How many girls did you go with, steady company, before you got the one you married?"

"Three or four."

"And I went with nine or ten."

"I'll try to straighten it out with the girl. She cries and cries."

"The more she cries today the less she'll cry tomorrow. She'll get through crying and she wouldn't marry him for a house with ten lightning rods. Tell her if he don't love her he'd make a poor husband. He's gone and it's good riddance of bad rubbish."

"I gave her a good talking-to, Mr. Winwold. I told her I never did want him around anyhow, and if he tries to make up to her again I will chase him away with a shotgun."

827

"Tell her the boy don't know his own mind and he's what they call a heartbreaker and he will just go on breaking one heart after another."

"I'll tell her that, too, Mr. Winwold. I have five girls, you know, and this is the oldest one, twenty years old and the prettiest one, our first baby, you know, and it don't come easy to scold her."

"And this boy of mine, Mr. Hofnagle, I took care of him when his mother was sick. I changed his diapers and washed 'em. I worried about him like you did with your girl. Maybe I overlook his faults too much now. You are a father and I am a father and we are both trying to do the best we can to get along, isn't that so, Mr. Hofnagle?"

And there was more talk and they parted good neighbors. Marvel had overheard the talk and came in to say, "Sorry I put you to trouble, papa."

"You ought to be sorry. How far did you go with this girl?"

"Not as far as I could have."

"You kissed her?"

"That was all."

"You never tumbled her?"

"I'll swear I didn't, papa."

"Just a nice home girl you got tired of?"

"We had nice times. I found out I didn't love her and took up with another."

"Be careful, Marvel. If you have to get wicked, let it be with some older woman who knows about heartbreak and knows it's useless to cry. Will you remember that?"

"I will, papa."

They talked more and Marvel went away laughing. They had over the years kept going fairly well as good chums. Marvel at twenty-three was still "the boy," five feet eleven, with glossy black hair, a handsome regular-featured face, with some of the flame-smolder of his mother's black eyes. He was hard-muscled, had learned to work alongside his father, threw in with more than his share of the farmwork in spring, summer and fall, was a leader in winter at parties, "shindigs," barn dances. He had been on two or three wild sprees that worried his father, twice had ridden drinking and yelling with the "butcher-knife boys." He was having his flings and the father believed he would find the right girl and before long settle down. He had found that when he had to be away a few days or weeks Marvel could be trusted to run the farm and make the decisions, the father saying once, "When I put you on your own, you're good. Why do you wait till I get home to go skylarking?"

"Wildcatting, you mean, papa. Maybe it's in my blood and I take after the sire."

"Shush, boy. Watch your tongue."

"Well, you seem to know what I'm doing about like I know it myself."

And the father slow-spoken, in a grave low tone, "You won't forget the books, Marvel—the books."

"I've caught it. It's a habit now."

They had read a dozen timeworn classics together and several current works, the father constantly saying, "You can get some instruction and a little wisdom from the books, but the main thing is companionship. The good books give you the company of men who help you find your own answers to the great questions that shake every real and true man."

He had seen the reading habit grow on Marvel and had hopes. Milton, two years younger than Marvel, held his reading mostly to the Bible and newspapers, taught a Sunday-school class and went to mid-week prayer meeting. "He's steady, if you'll notice, Marvel," the father had said. "There'll be times you can lean on Milton. The church is good for him. He's pious but it's a genuine piety so you don't notice it and it's like they say you don't notice particularly what the well-dressed man wears."

Milton was chunky of build, rounded shoulders, rounded nose and mouth and a rounded apple-face. He had had a sunstroke in hay harvest once, the doctor warning him about working too long in a hot sun. At fourteen a vicious horse had kicked him in the head and he had lain unconscious a good part of two days, with a wandering mind, and then made a recovery and growth into exceptional strength. He could take care of a crying baby or a sick calf a little better than anyone else around. Sometimes for a day or two, at meals and between, and of evenings, not a word came from him unless a short mild-spoken answer to a question that he asked to have repeated. "Serenity, reverence, a sweetness like the wild honey John the Baptist ate," the father said. "I wish I had more of the best qualities of my boy Milton."

The father had more to learn from Milton than Marvel but it was Marvel who was his chum. It was Marvel and he who rode to Quincy and heard Lincoln and Douglas debate October 13, 1858, and then two days later down to Alton to hear the seventh and last of those debates. Acres of listening people, acres of faces turned in one direction to catch the words borne on the air from the mouths of speakers, acres of faces that blended into one mass face of the People—this haunted Omri. "Those people listening, Marvel, they said more to me than the speakers on the platform."

"What did they say, papa?"

"I can't make it come clear. They want to go but they don't know where to."

"I'm that way myself," said Marvel. He recited from Lincoln's Quincy speech:

" 'You say it [slavery] must not be opposed in the free States, because slavery is not there; it must not be opposed in the slave States, because it is there; it must not be opposed in politics, because that will make a fuss; it must not be opposed in the pulpit, because it is not religion. Then where is the place to oppose it? There is no suitable place to oppose it.' "

Marvel remembered the quizzical face of Lincoln speaking: "The Bible says somewhere that we are desperately selfish. I think we would have discovered that fact without the Bible."

Omri didn't like seeing an abolitionist spit in disgust and let out a groan when Douglas said, "I hold that the people of the slave-holding States are civilized men as well as ourselves; that they bear consciences as well as we, and that they are accountable to God and their posterity, and not to us." And Omri knew that Douglas was looking partly toward his powerful block of friends and supporters in the Southern states in saying, "I think there are objects of charity enough in the free States to excite the sympathies and open the pockets of all the benevolence we have amongst us, without going abroad in search of Negroes, of whose condition we know nothing. We have enough objects of charity at home, and it is our duty to take care of our own poor, and our own suffering, before we go abroad to intermeddle with other people's business."

Omri went on, "In politics, what is not spoken, what men hardly dare speak, counts for more than the loud words tumbling from their mouths."

"What's in your mind there?" said Marvel with a keen look at his father.

"Well, you and I ride away up to these two towns and we hear two famous speakers go on and on for six hours, three hours apiece. And they talked up, down and around a big question. And they did pretty good on that question. Yet neither of them dared to come out on a still bigger question."

"How do you mean?"

"I talked with a delegate to the first Republican-party state convention in Illinois, held in Bloomington. And he said this man Lincoln stood up and made a wild hair-raising speech, like to have torn the roof off. The speech struck everybody dumb and fascinated and nobody wrote a report of it. This delegate remembered one sentence of Lincoln: 'We will say to the Southern disunionists, *We won't go out of the Union, and you shan't!*' Now this week, Marvel, you and I hear Lincoln talk three hours and we don't hear him say that or anything like it. We don't hear Douglas say where he would be if Southern states went out of the Union. They don't say what they would have the Government at Washington do if Southern states secede and kiss good-by to the good old Union of States."

"Well," and Marvel squinted with a pleasant leer at his father, "what would you do if you were running the Government at Washington and the slave states of the South seceded and kissed good-by to the good old Union?"

"I don't know, Marvel. I'd hate to see the old Union of States go to smash. Those grand old Virginians, George Washington and Thomas Jefferson, those two slaveholders who wanted to get rid of slavery, they had a dream of a great American Republic that would be a light and an example to the rest of the world, able to fight off any power or combination of powers from the Old World. That dream would be gone. I'd hate to see it go. Worse yet, I'd hate to start a war on the Southern states that went out of the Union. It would be a wild crazy bloody war, a war of brothers. I can name men in our Pike County and other counties over southern Illinois who would refuse to fight against the South. I can name some who would leave Illinois to fight for the South. It would be a hell of a war. I don't have a doubt Douglas and Lincoln both know what a terrible war it would be. And that's why both of them in these debates have kept away from that awful question Lincoln raised at the Bloomington convention when he swept them off their feet and had them cheering till they were hoarse. If the decision was up to me I don't know what I would do. Either way I could take would be agony and misery. Maybe something like that was on the faces of those acres of people at Quincy and Alton when I tried to read them. They want to go but they don't know what way. Either way, any way, we'll pay a fearful price."

"I haven't heard you talk like this before, papa. Those debates bring it on?"

"Brought it to a head, boy. It's come over me, like never before, the North don't understand the South, don't know what the South is up to. Down there plenty of men love the old Union and they'd like to see it last a thousand years and then to the end of the world, as the Irishman said. But they've always stood together against the North on two points. They want to handle the Negro their own way. And they want each state sovereign, running its own house and no Federal Government telling it how, each state under the Constitution having the right to step out as an independent nation any time it doesn't want to belong to the Union. In the South that idea runs in the blood, as natural as independence did in Washington and Jefferson. Your state comes first and the Union second. I heard a Yale student from Charleston say, 'South Carolina is a sovereign state, a nation by itself: the United States of America is a confederacy, an association, a league of states each of itself under the Constitution a sovereign nation.' He hoped the time would never come he would have to fight for that idea, but if the time came, he said, he would fight."

"I get your points, papa. A storm coming, and you saw on those faces the quiet, the still air, before the storm."

"I don't know. Blood up to the boot tops, blood up to the bridles of the horses, it may be, Marvel."

Chapter 24

A Wagon at Late Evening

A YEAR later John Brown crashed into the depths of the national conscience—telling the judge who sentenced him to be hanged he could stand it if they could, and God would remember and rivers of blood would run.

In this November before the fixed day of December 9 John Brown was to tread the gallows and meet his Maker, Omri rode home from the Atlas post office and read in four different semiweekly newspapers about the excitement South and North over John Brown. He wondered if this was a single spurt of flame that had broken up from a pit where a vast accumulation of flame waited for the time it would blow the entire top crust off.

A walk of an hour and he would sleep better, so shaking off his carpet slippers and getting into his boots with the trousers tucked in, a pea jacket and thin buckskin gloves, he stepped out into a night of stars and galaxies, familiar planets that he called by names and nicknames, misty patterns and spatters of stars that were strangers and dangerous aliens. He walked a mile toward Atlas, turned and came back. At the highway gate to his house he saw a fire alongside the highway and it could be a mile or a half-mile away. He walked toward it. It kept getting farther away, that or the fire was going more dim. Then slowly the fire went out, winked away into darkness.

Omri walked on enjoying the keen frosty air, the flimsy shimmer of moist silver sparkles. He came to where the fire had been, dusky maroons of it fading in black charred wood. Near by were two horses tied to a tree. Near by another horse stood tied, a saddle leaning against the tree. Then his eyes lighted on a wagon and he stood in the middle of the road listening. Voices came to his ears and he made out two voices, coming from under the wagon, a man and a woman. He stood still and heard them babbling and laughing, the words not coming clear. Then a short silence and a confusion of low sounds, one of them perhaps a kiss, and the only words coming clear were the man's voice once, "Sweet girl," and the woman's low moan, "Oh, darling," and a prolonged, "Oh-h—"

Omri walked on a quarter-mile, came back, again stood in the middle of the road, heard no sound except one of the horses cropping grass and saying something in horse language with its teeth and resonant nostrils. Omri moved over to the wagon, saw the iron rim of the left hind wheel loose, half off. They were camping here because, with another quarter-mile, the wheel rim would have come off.

Omri stooped a little and saw a man and a woman in blankets, the woman sleeping, the man open-eyed, awake and wary, low-voiced, "What do you want?" At Omri's beckoning, the man slid from between the blankets without waking the woman, a Colt six-shooter in his right hand. Omri walked to the middle of the road, the man following, sliding into a coat and below that wearing only drawers and socks. Again he asked, as his right hand swung lightly the six-shooter, "What do you want?"

"Wheel rim nearly off?"

"Yes."

"I live the next house, my farm, less'n a mile."

"Yes."

"We got room and could put you up tonight, if you want, if you need. Or you stay here and come morning we got breakfast for you and maybe help on the wheel."

The man put the six-shooter in his left hand, put out his right to shake with Omri, while his face broke into a big smile and in the starlight Omri could make out a line of white even teeth. "You're good for sore eyes," said the man, and he went on, "I belong hereabouts. My name's Rodney Wayman. You might know my folks the other side of Atlas."

"My name is Omri Winwold. I've met your folks and I've heard of you."

"We're on a honeymoon. My wife under the wagon. Married up in Knox County ten days ago. Drove to Oquawka and took steamer and got off the landing over here this morning."

"You'll get chilly in just those drawers. We'll be looking for you in the morning."

"If you'd come an hour sooner we'd have gone to your house for the night. I wouldn't think now of waking my nice partner there under the wagon."

"And you picked a girl away up there in Knox County, maybe a Yankee."

"New York Yankee."

"Around here they say a New York Yankee's the meanest there is."

"I've heard that. I don't scare." And with a nod of his head toward the wagon, "She's a wonder. We got married out in the rain. Tell you about that in the morning."

"What was her name?" And Omri had no sooner plopped that question than he was half-afraid he was indecently inquisitive.

"Family named Wimbler, her name Millicent Wimbler."

"You'll excuse me, Mr. Wayman," and Omri's breath came fast and his words swift, "what's the name of her folks?"

"Joel Wimbler and Brooksany Wimbler."

833

"Good God!"

And Rodney's memory flashed. "Yes, good God, I remember now she mentioned your name the day we rode back from our wedding in the rain. Her mother told her about you."

"You're shivering, young fellow. Back to bed with your wife and come early for breakfast."

* * * * * * * * * *

Chapter 25

* * * * * * * * * *

A Saturday in St. Louis

SIX miles ran the water front of the City of St. Louis along the Mississippi River. Three to four miles inland the city had spread and now in January of 1860 numbered over a hundred and sixty thousand people. You could hear it in talk and you could read it in newspapers and almanacs, that where this rushing tumultuous city now stood, forty years ago there was only a little village of fur-traders, and riding a scow, skiff or canoe downriver you had to look sharp and then you couldn't be sure you were seeing the village named St. Louis. Railroads east and west out of St. Louis now and five thousand vessels a year loading or unloading cargo at her wharves. On one point St. Louis was overly sensitive, not sure of herself. Chicago twitted her. Chicago bragged and blustered. In thirty years Chicago had come from nothing of a village into a roaring metropolis of a hundred and ten thousand saying that St. Louis was a mudhole that lacked enterprise and strategic location.

The saloon and restaurant of Bill Morissey on one street overlooking the river had changed with the times. The small oblong box-shape of it first was of rough lumber from a near-by sawmill. The customers of that day spit on the floor. Later Bill Morissey put in boxes of sand and part of that idea was to protect the stove, which too often was the target of tobacco-chewers. Morissey in 1850 built an addition that doubled the floor space, running the bar at a right angle to accommodate double the customers. Then in a few years came a building bigger yet, of stylish red brick, a mahogany bar brought upriver twelve hundred miles from New Orleans, brass fixtures, polished brass spittoons that stood two feet high, a brass rail for either foot of a sociable customer, mirrors the length of the bar so that any customer standing at the bar could without turning his head and by merely gazing into the mirror see the line of faces at the bar or other faces over the room. The tables where German waiters brought food and drinks stood heavy with solid oak. A side door had over it the sign and strict notice: "Ladies' Entrance." Morissey tried to be particular about what kind of women came through this entrance, and in his words, "We try to keep a high-class respectable place." Along the front and side walls ranged a line of booths or stalls, with oak tables and high-backed benches, horsehair cushions lined with black leather at bottom and back of the benches.

Women with escorts could come in at the Ladies' Entrance for drinks and food in a booth. Women without partners or a lone woman were under watch from the first. A woman too free with her eyes or smiles, if Morissey didn't like the looks of it, he would step over to her and kindly, firm, sober, with a jerk of his head toward the Ladies' Entrance, "*I'm* sorry." If, as rarely happened, the woman insisted, "I'm a respectable lady," Morissey in turn insisted, "*I'm* sorry" and usually convinced the woman that no matter how respectable, he was nevertheless so sorry that it was up to her to leave without further words.

On a day in late January of 1860, two men came into Bill Morissey's place, shook light snow off their overcoats and took seats in a booth, each laying his overcoat in a bench corner with hat on top. It was early afternoon and after a dinner they ordered steins of beer, one then another. They sipped beer and talked brightly. At moments a keen interest on their faces rose into surprise and astonishment. They talked about their health and prosperity, not having seen each other in two years. They let go their feelings about the hanging of John Brown last month, the excitement not yet over, and what a wild year in politics lay ahead. One set down his empty stein, and in an undertone, "Any word from San Francisco?"

"A man comes back, he saw her out there. She has taken on flesh, so much she waddles. Her girls sell whisky, champagne, she hardly ever touches it. She eats and eats. A twenty-dollar house. Money coming in hand over fist. Silk dresses made special and big fancy hats she wears, and jewels, pearl ropes on her neck and shoulders, a diamond ring and an emerald on one hand, a diamond ring and a ruby on the other. Married, by gosh. She is forty-six and married to a Portuguese boy who is twenty-four and calls himself a prince of some kind while other people say he used to be a pimp. When they take a box in a theater or when they go to a big saloon with music, singers and dancers, everybody looks at them and says, 'Here they come,' or 'There they are.' They take the air, drive the streets in an open carriage."

"That is all?"

"About all. If I think of more I'll tell you."

"So that is the latest."

"Yes, she will never come this way and trouble us again."

"You can't tell about her, most uncertain woman ever lived." And Omri Winwold took a letter out of his pocket and read part of it to Henry Flack. And out of the envelope he brought newspaper clippings, the *Mohawk Valley Transcript* account of Elbert Kelway's killing his brother Bob near twenty-four years ago. Not until this last month had these clippings and this news come to him, Winwold explained. He had heard nothing of the Kelway brothers since he last saw them at Gravel Creek camp on the edge of Arpa, New York, in 1836.

The two men sat silent for several minutes. They looked each other in the eye, Flack would drop his eyes from Winwold's, and Flack would study a while whatever he saw in the dinner dishes and the oak table surface, and then Flack would again look up and keep his gaze in Winwold's eyes.

At last Flack said, "So you had eight hundred dollars on you and Bee was trying to get Kelway to kill you for that eight hundred dollars."

"It looks that way."

"And she really didn't care a damn about her baby."

"I know she didn't."

"And you took care of that baby on that long hard wagon trip from Arpa, New York, out here to Illinois."

"Yes."

"Jesus, you're a real man, Omri Winwold."

There was fellowship between the two men. Hadn't each escaped any one of several sinister fates that the Lost Woman might have brought on them? And didn't each of them feel and believe deeply in some basic underlying loveliness in the woman that never came to blossom and fruitage? Didn't they have a common bond of understanding that though they drank and talked and half-laughed about her, they were more nearly ready to weep over the latest swine phase of her development and degeneracy?

"Why shouldn't we have one drink and then another?" asked Flack with a smile edging on the tipsy when, late in the afternoon, they had covered many topics, including cases of insanity, jealousy, greed, avarice, and what the law says about the difference between manslaughter and premeditated murder, about kidnapping and bigamy.

Two women came in through the Ladies' Entrance and took a booth diagonal to theirs. They wore slightly balloonish skirts, one blue and the other a dark lavender, their hats small, odd and a little too natty. One was of medium size and build, ample of bosom, hair a light brown near blond. She seemed the decisive one of the two who had brought along the neat doll-faced one in lavender. A lawyer having a Tom and Jerry before he should go home studied her in a mirror, wiped a touch of cream froth from his heavy mustache, and said with a lift of one eyebrow, "Petite, eh? Quite a bijou," finished his drink and went out. The faces of the two women, in the light of the chandeliered kerosene-oil lamps, were rather charming. They had used precisely enough powder, paint and rouge, little of the obvious or overdone.

"Good-lookers," Flack, who faced them, said to Winwold, with a nod toward the women. "Good style and getup."

Omri waited, turned his head for a glance, and, "Not bad, not bad."

836

The face of the petite one, he could carve it on a hazelnut with four quick knife strokes for eyes, nose, mouth. He took a second look and the perfect regularity of her face pleased him. With a third glance he saw the face monotonous as a high-priced Christmas doll. "Press your hand to her belly and her mouth squeaks 'Ma-ma' forty times the same way over and over, forty times 'Ma-ma.'" Then he shamed himself. "If she was my own child I'd say she was sister to a black-and-gold pansy in that garden Anne kept."

He heard Flack, "You are thinking. *Why* do we think? This afternoon we *don't* think. What *is* it you think?"

"I was thinking about buying some of the new paper collars. Twenty-five cents a box and a dozen to the box. They look like linen. You wear one dirty and throw it away and put on a clean one, twenty-five cents a dozen for paper collars."

Flack nodded toward the two women. "I'll ask them to have supper with us."

Omri thought a moment and eyed Flack. "It's you that lives in St. Louis. It's you got a reputation here."

Flack stepped over and with a cordial grin, "We have been waiting for you all afternoon."

"What for?" asked the one in blue.

"To invite you to come over and join us in supper now."

They came over. The four had Napoleon brandy, an Irish whisky Flack guaranteed thirty years old, after which he ordered a supper with two bottles of champagne. Flack had given two or three toasts to health and long life for those present. And in a tone heard well over the place, now fairly crowded, a touch of wrath was in Flack's usually even and pleasant voice as he lifted a glass of bubbling champagne, and reverting to the Swiss-immigrant accent of his father, "Here's to deh dam ablishnists—may dey hang t' edge of moon wid fingers greased."

Bill Morissey had come shortly after to stand quietly saying, "Supper satisfactory, Mr. Flack?" and Mr. Flack, sobering a trifle, "Best in St. Louis, Bill."

It was not much later that Mr. Flack was chucking under the chin the blonde woman in blue, who went so far as to chuck him under the chin in return. It was about then that Bill Morissey came over, nodded his head toward the Ladies' Entrance, and said, "Mr. Flack, *I'm* sorry."

"'S all right, Bill, 's great 'stablishmun yuh got." And Flack stood up, took hold of a coat lapel of Morissey, and beamed, "You're merchant your line, I'm merchant my line, an never goin be hard feelins you an me." This won an eye twinkle and a hint of a smile from Morissey's forbidding face.

The four went out. Flack called a one-horse hack. And the four rode to the Straight Ticket saloon, drank whisky sours made with Straight Ticket whisky while they watched four women in black tights and black slippers do a high-kick dance followed by a little bald man in a checked suit of clothes who had two new songs and five jokes Omri had heard long ago on the Erie Canal and one that was new to him, about the wife who caught her husband kissing another woman and she said to him, "You're as glad to see me as though you'd run a nail through your foot."

They went next door to the Possum Trot, where a dozen couples, mostly rivermen with assorted women, were waltzing to the music pounded out by a downcast man with a drooping mustache, wearing a Prince Albert coat, seated at a piano out of tune. A drink of Monongahela whisky was served to them by a young woman in a red satin blouse, a black skirt to her knees and tight black stockings that ran to her black and shining slippers. Then Flack tried to waltz with the blonde woman in blue, got tangled in her balloonish skirt, and quit, saying his feet were not as good as they used to be.

They went out and Flack called a one-horse hack that took them to his home. On the way the blonde woman, now known to Flack as Sally, spoke to him in a warning tone, "We haven't got all night," and heard from the uproarious Flack, "Just what we have got is all night. If it ain't all night we got, what is it?"

On entering his house, Flack pulled at his hair and cried, "I forgot the whisky, not a drop in the house." Then he livened with a grin. "But the cellar is full uh beer. We can go on a beer bust." Beer it was they drank, pouring it into tall glass steins with pewter covers that lifted to a thumb-push. Flack got out the zither about midnight and tried for a few songs and a yodel or two but his tongue was thick and his throat wouldn't tighten for the high-note climbs and slides of the yodel and he quit about the time Sally was saying again, "We haven't got all night, I told you before." It was shortly after that Omri tangled in an India rug while trying for a waltz with the bijou in lavender. He tripped, fell on his face, dragged the girl down with him, on a chair gashed his left temple so it streaked blood, and suddenly found himself somewhat sober. The pain throbbed in his head. And he sobered.

"You lay down, Henry," he said to Flack, pushing him over and straightening him on a sofa. "You need a sleep, old boy. You stay here and I'll see to the ladies and come back here."

Flack was willing. The walls of the room were already closing in and down on his brain as he closed his eyes for sleep. Omri, with a handkerchief occasionally stanching the ooze at his temple, walked with Sally and petite, dark-haired, violet-eyed Annabell a few blocks, hailed a hack, handed them a ten-dollar bill each, pressed their hands and wished them good luck and good night.

Annabell sprang at him, put her arms around his neck and hung there as she kissed at his mouth and nearly reached it. He bundled her tight in his arms and the kiss he gave her pushed back her head till she was looking skyward. Her ribs hurt as he put her on her feet, and she swung an open hand that smacked him on the cheek, howling a laugh. "You near broke my ribs." He opened the hack door, lifted her in as she put a kiss on one cheek, set her alongside Sally: "Take my address," she insisted. He wrote it in a pocket notebook. "And the last name?"

"Ponder, Annabell Ponder, come see me." He was closing the hack door when her hands pushed against it, opened it wider as her head came part-way out. Omri put hands to her shoulders, jolted her back into the seat, slammed the door, called to the hackman to drive on, saw through the glass window Annabell's little red mouth and her dimpled fingers touching it and throwing the fingers toward him.

He walked to the house, put a pillow under Henry Flack's head on the sofa, went to his upstairs room that was once Bee's private chamber, poured water from a pitcher into a porcelain bowl, washed and wiped his face, lifted the lid off the porcelain jar and emptied the bowl into it. He found a sticking plaster for the cut on his temple. He slid into the wide commodious four-poster mahogany bed, the pain in his head fairly eased away, and fell into a deep sleep with occasional vague dream flurries of a large glass window moving away from him and through the window five little red mouths and many dimpled fingers touching the lips and then the fingers thrown straight at him and a fading voice that repeated, "Take my address, come see me."

* * * * * * * * * *

Chapter 26

* * * * * * * * * *

Sabbath Morning and Long Thoughts

THE six massive bells in the steeple of the Catholic cathedral rang out in Sabbath bong and boom, in reverberated punctuations that floated over the Missouri side and across the river to Illinois. The swinging tones hung in the air with summons and appeal.

Omri lay awake in reverie. He and Henry would probably never get drunk again because not again would they meet on a day when each had news for the other about such twists of fate. This was the bed where Henry had killed a man. This was the bed where a woman leaped at Henry with a knife. And twenty-four years ago she tried to get a man to knife him, Omri Winwold, to death for a belt of gold pieces and paper bills. And her swift lithe body as he knew it the year before that, the grace and cunning of her motions, the changeable flashes of her black-flamed eyes, the exquisite fire and whimsical quality of some of her sudden bursts of anger, it hurt him now that neither he nor she could work any change for the better in her and she had to go on and

839

on in a zigzag course driven by quirks of brain and taints of blood beyond the healing of any physician or the help of friends or lovers.

Then too, Omri felt like drinking out of a moodiness that had grown in him, that he couldn't shake off. He could see a war coming. Others couldn't. He would like to know, "Is it me that's crackpot or is it them?" He wouldn't trust himself to spill the full turmoil that surged in his mind. After helping Rodney Wayman and his wife to a new wagon wheel, he had driven with them to their home with Rodney's folks, and had visited them several times. Four years ago the Waymans had sold in Virginia their six slaves, two house servants and four field hands, a four-hundred-acre farm of soil that had been worked for two hundred years, and bought in Illinois six hundred acres of timberland and rich virgin soil. The father, Randolph Rutledge Wayman, was tall, cadaverous, pleasant-spoken, with an endless sense of humor, and a pride in the State of Virginia, the Old Dominion, the Mother of Presidents, so quenchless and distinct a pride that he often seemed a Virginian rather than an Illinoisian. Over Pike County were twice as many Democrats as Republicans and not so far away Randolph Wayman had met a score of farmers born and raised in Kentucky, Tennessee and Virginia and in politics they understood each other's language. He had been a red-hot Douglas man and then cooled off toward Douglas, going along with Southern Democratic-party men. They had favored Douglas for President, and now they wanted no part of him.

"He's for shutting out slavery, for all time, wherever the people vote against it," Omri heard Wayman. "He's for letting Kansas into the Union as a state the minute Kansas has enough population for a congressional district, and then he would be willing for someone like John Brown to be the Congressman if the people elect him." Wayman predicted, "Douglas will split the Democratic party in two. The South won't have him, they'll have their own candidate. He'll get the nomination from a Northern Democratic party. Then the Republicans, with their abolitionists, with their hungry office-seekers, may come into power."

Wayman had paused, had slowly and gravely pulled at the curving hair of his mustache, then smoothed it, then softly drummed on it with three fingers, hearing Mibs say, "And then?"

"Disunion." More drumming of the three fingers on the mustache, and, "Secession."

Another pause—and Mibs' low shaken voice, "Then the war?"

And as though speaking long thoughts, well mulled over, with no doubts or hesitations Wayman spoke. "I can't see any war coming. And if I'm wrong and they do start a war on the South, I can't see how they'll raise big enough armies to go down into the Southern states and conquer them. From the Potomac River in Virginia to the Rio Grande down in Texas is a long stretch. It would take millions of men for the job. They would have to cut their way to the Gulf and then hold what they had taken. It can't be done. I can see a war that might last three months and then the North would give up. If the North was all solid for the Union and everybody abolitionist, they might do it, they might conquer the South, though it would take many years. It does seem most of the abolitionists want the South to go off by itself. Then take the southern half of Ohio and Indiana and they're like Illinois, thousands of men born in Kentucky, Tennessee and Virginia and they wouldn't fight a war to free the niggers."

This was a revelation to young Marvel, with open bright eyes, saying, "So there won't be a war after all. You mean, Mr. Wayman, the North is about ready to let the South go and make a separate country of its own?"

Mr. Wayman raised his rack of bones out of his chair and stood up. Mibs, watching this, always thought the joints ought to snap or at least creak a little, but they didn't. Mr. Wayman stepped to an heirloom, a rosewood secretary in the corner, and took from a drawer some newspaper clippings, and stepped back to his chair. As his collapsible frame let itself down into the chair and the bones got themselves accommodated, Mibs smiled inwardly at herself because at this feat she half-expected joints to creak at least a little. Mr. Wayman started with the year 1842, citizens of New England petitioning Congress for "measures peaceably to dissolve the Union," Congressman John Quincy Adams requesting a committee to report on it. Mr. Wayman read from a speech of Wendell Phillips in 1854 that the North and the South were "essentially two nations," that the Union was "accursed of God" and "the whole South is one great magazine of cowards." Mr. Wayman could go on and on, taking hours, he said, with quotations from hundreds of speeches and editorials in the North calling for disunion, saying, "Let us withdraw," saying, "Disunion is our destiny," saying, "The South is a shrew to whom the North is wedded and the time has come for parting," and the shrew described as "thriftless, idle, drunken, dirty, lewd, shrill-voiced, feeble-bodied, and ugly to look upon."

Mr. Wayman passed around a New York Tribune Almanac opened at the correct page. He was saying, "In politics the South is off by itself, walls up, bristling barriers, watchtowers with watch guards. Notice the vote in the South in 1856 in Alabama, Arkansas, Florida, Georgia, not one vote cast and counted for the Republican candidate for President. In Louisiana, Mississippi, Missouri, North Carolina, South Carolina, Tennessee, Texas, not one vote cast and counted for the Republican-party candidate for President," and Mr. Wayman leaned over Mibs' shoulder to read "who got in the North 1,342,164 votes. In my beloved and scrupulous State of Virginia they did count 291 Republican votes, in Maryland 281, in Kentucky 314, in little old absent-minded Delaware 308." Mr. Wayman was back in his chair. "She is a section, the South, off by herself, isolated, misunderstood, alone, and part of the North points at her as a monstrous and ill-born outcast. What kind of patience do they want from her when she hears those voices in the North year after year crying, 'We welcome disunion! Speed the day!'?"

"They're *tired*," began Mrs. Wayman, Barbara Billy Wayman, and she put a burden of woe into that word. "They're tired of the nigger and the rights of the nigger served up to them morning, noon and night, from Northern hypocrites and professional word merchants. The niggers —they eat you poor, they beg you poor, they steal you poor. And suppose by some miracle of finance, politics and religion they could all be set free, who would take care of them, feed them, police them? I have seen the free nigger, seen enough and plenty of him. Every free nigger is a danger, when he is around every minute he is a danger."

Barbara Billy Wayman began naming slave Negroes she had known as persons, Silas and his wife Mary and their sons Paul and John and their daughter Rose. Mr. Wayman had sold the family, not on the auction block, not to one of those slave-traders, but to a planter with a good name for taking care of his Negroes. The black woman Ada at whose breasts she had been wet-nursed when a baby, Ada's grandchild that she had helped watch through a sickness and bring back to health, she named these with many details. She took pride in the personal relationships, the warm human bonds, that she had seen among slaveowners and their Negroes. Most of the black folk, she was certain, had better food and living quarters than the factory, shop and mill workers you could see in the crowded sections of the cities in the North. She recited from Thomas Hood's "Song of the Shirt."

"Those desperately driven sewing women of London," she said, "you can go to Philadelphia, New York and Boston and there they are by the thousands. They are worse-used than our Negro slave women. We take care of our sick and old slave workers. That is put on us. It is our responsibility. In the North they are forgotten."

She had spoken rather mildly, in a thin high voice, well controlled, with a certainty of her ground. The others caught the first tremor in her voice saying, "They lie and lie about us, they pile lie on lie. Their only question about any lie is, Will it be believed? I can see a day of reckoning to come. The South will go out of the Union, as it ought to. And if the North wants a war, the South will give it and whether the war ends soon or goes a long time, the South will win."

To Mibs, to Omri and Marvel, the woman was amazing, sort of breathtaking, partly because she gave them an insight into what vehemence and intensity, what peculiar sincerity and passion, could be seen toiling and weaving as motives and justifications underlying what was termed the Southern Cause.

Mr. Wayman shifted his bones around in his chair and gave low-spoken assurance, "There'll be no war. Take those glad to see the South go, then take those who don't want to leave their homes to sleep in rain and snow on the cold ground and die of gangrene or fever, and

842

add them to the millions who either love the South as we do or else can't find it in their hearts to hate the Southerners enough to kill them. Take those three and what have you left in the North to make war on a solid determined people?" He shifted his bones and sat easy. "Won't be a war, no, can't be a war."

Mrs. Wayman spoke sharply. "R. R."—her abbreviation of Randolph Rutledge—"don't forget you're dealing with some crazy men. And you can't say beforehand what crazy men will do."

Mibs had been in the Wayman home several weeks before this evening when the two elderly Virginians unburdened their hearts. What they were saying this evening they did not care to make public nor proclaim among their neighbors. Their convictions were so intense, and to them so deeply sacred, that in their own house they seldom spoke as freely as this evening. Mibs caught her own father re-echoed in Mr. Wayman's, "Talk, there's been too much talk on all sides." She saw Rod's mother move with a dignity cold and icy, rather than merely cool, among neighbors and outsiders.

In her own family and among accepted friends, Barbara Wayman could loosen up and sing weird old ballads and irresistibly comic ditties she had from a Scotch grandfather. Urged and led on by the family or by company, she would recite verses serious or light, and cut capers, even to getting into kilties and dancing a Highland fling learned from the grandfather whose kilties and bagpipes were family heirlooms. She was of medium height, rather spare of flesh, lean-bosomed, a rather long pointed nose, lips straight and thin, her dark-brown hair not abundant and combed primly so that it did not touch her ears, and her gray-hazel eyes had a gamut of glances from proud to funny and back. She was distinctly a person. She was born human before being born Virginian. She had, as an instance, gathered her impressions across the years that went to form her definite judgments about an upper-class set in the city of Richmond and elsewhere:

"I have seen a clique in Richmond, exclusive, very exclusive, so stuck on themselves that I have sometimes thought they are a worse influence in the South than the free niggers. I have seen them calculating, cruel, coarse, inconceivably coarse-mannered in the way they snubbed and maliciously gossiped about good women whom they mistakenly believed had a desire to enter their exclusive circle." Omri's wide brown eyes flickered with elation and Mibs caught her jaw dropped gaping and she closed it. "The calculating woman in silk crinoline, the cruel woman with jewels in her hair and French satin slippers, I find her less difficult than the woman whose essentially coarse manners stick out from her fine clothes like the bones of a spavined horse. Apes—I heard my mother say—apes may put on finery but they are still apes." Her ears had a bluntly pointed look and if you saw them hazily they had somewhat the cupped curve of white foxglove. She was Presbyterian, her husband Episcopalian, and they attended together the Presbyterian church of Atlas, she going with him two or three times a year to the little chapel in Pittsfield where the Established Church of England, in spite of two hundred years of onslaught by the Puritans, still held sway.

Coming from Presbyterian services in Atlas Mr. Wayman would mutter sometimes that the preacher did it all, that the congregation never kneeled, that the worshipers never crossed themselves, and the affair lacked ceremonial. Yet Mr. Wayman, as the family and others well knew, though he appreciated ceremonial and panoply, hated the Roman Catholic Church, mistrusted all Catholics that he didn't hate, had his fears of the Irish, the German, the Catholic vote in national and state elections. Mr. Wayman, in other words, was a Know-Nothing, and nearly a million like him had voted in 1856 for Millard Fillmore, the American-party candidate for President. Mibs saw him wag his head with a glum face over "the foreign influx," "the alien horde mingling its un-American blood with ours." She puzzled a bit on how Max Mutter would take Mr. Wayman and agreed with herself, "Max would insult Mr. Wayman and pick a fight with him."

Long talks, big and free and confidential talks, Omri and Mibs had. The curious mistrust in the air, the furtive uncertainty of noncommittal faces whose mouths came out with nothing to indicate what way they leaned, the huddles of antislavery men who quit talking when others came near in any public place, the huddles of pro-Southern men who did likewise, the free and outspoken opinions men and women could deliver to a small select company under their own roof and the understanding of all present that it would be more convenient, if not safer, to keep those opinions within their own select small company—of these matters and much else Omri and Mibs talked. What they sensed, a chill suspense in the air, a sound that to Omri had the faint silly far-off and almost inaudible swoosh of the oncoming northeast wind on the day he froze to his saddle—out of what Omri and Mibs exchanged they steadied each other.

"Rod goes his own way, he's pretty independent," Mibs had said. "In his minstrel days he met fellows he forgot were Irish and Catholic because they were openhearted, two of them in particular, one that nursed him when sick and another that lent him money. They were laughing men and singers. So he quietly tells his Know-Nothing father, 'You go too far,' and he tells me, as between the two of us, that the Know-Nothings are an ignorant and besotted lot. He goes along with his father that the North can never whip the South, that if the South goes out of the Union she has a right to and she ought to. When his mother says there are crazy men in the North and they may try to start a war, he laughs at her and says the crazy men in the North will not be that crazy."

"Don't you and Rod ever dispute and clash about these awful questions?" Omri had asked.

"From the first, and I know it sounds a little ridiculous, we put a guard on our tongues. Those awful questions—if we examined each other and got into regular arguments, after a while it would be like the fight in the New Era College board of trustees between those who cried for immediate abolition and those who wanted it gradual. When either of us gets too earnest before the other, the other is expected to say, 'Fleas or Presbyterians, which?'" She had heard an Oquawka barber, visiting New Era relatives, telling it: "The fleas got so bad in Oquawka that I went to Monmouth and after a while in Monmouth the Presbyterians got so bad that I went back to Oquawka. The fleas were worse than ever in Oquawka so I went to Monmouth again and tried it a while but the Presbyterians were worse than ever. So now I'm back with the fleas in Oquawka."

Omri's keen eyes had roved over Rod and Mibs as a couple, as young persons with their wagon honeymoon over. In their house and his own, on a sleigh ride to Pittsfield and back, at a lecture in the Presbyterian church by a missionary returned from India, Omri had watched their open conversation and jokes, their covert and almost invisible signals, the curious and quietly accepted understandings between them. Though they completely disagreed in viewpoint on whether slavery was a monstrous wrong, on whether a war was coming, outside of such areas or spheres of national controversy the two of them ran spiritually, mentally and temperamentally in an extraordinary harmony. And as physical mates they gave one surprise after another to Omri's searching and pondering eyes. "I'd guess it's near to the same thing Bee and I had in what few weeks she didn't have one of her spells," said Omri to himself. "Whether they walk across a room together, or she passes him the butter at table, or he helps her into her cloak, it's always got a touch of style and grace. Their bodies bend and wind and flow together, careless, easy and natural as a stand of wheat in midsummer curving in wave on wave before a soft rainwind." He had seen them waltz in his home and their own, humming themselves the three-four time for their feet, in precisions of glide and maneuver that spun a gossamer web of exact numbers in a mutual pattern, and again in the partnership of their bodies they had forgotten pattern or design and there was no more scheme or exactitude in what they were doing than in the float of thistledown over green pastures into summer horizons. "We can waltz," he heard Rod in a cool beam of eyes. And Mibs, "The two best waltzers in the good old U.S.A."

"Is that all?" asked Rod in a mummery of shuttered eyes.

"The two best waltzers in the whole wide world, God bless you."

His fourteen months as a banjo king and soft-shoe dancer with Haverstraw's Mammoth Minstrels, with a gay garrulity he told much of it to Mibs. Of the six months with a wagon show in California and nearly two years of prospecting and mining with Nack J. Doss, Rod talked little, implied the memories were bitter, what with rotten food, endless hard work, ten months straight not getting a sight of one woman, a fight with two robbers they killed and Doss laid up and suffering six weeks with a head wound, drinking and gambling days in San Francisco when Doss won nearly as much as Rod lost and they made the six-weeks stage trip across the plains to Illinois with something over twelve thousand dollars in gold apiece. Last year Rod with other cowmen had driven eight hundred Texas longhorns up from the Southwest, fed them for market on the Wayman farm, and said he was sure his profit ran somewhere over two thousand dollars and he needed a bookkeeper.

"I wouldn't ask you what's his worst fault, I'd be afraid you might tell," Omri had said.

"I'll tell you. He gets moods. For hours he won't talk. Once, two days, not a word, he'd just *look*—at me or anyone trying to get a word out of him. I think he's groping, reaching for some kind of footholds, or as my father would say, harness buckles you can put faith in."

"Sounds a little like me," Omri had said, "exactly like me, dear child. I have been a groper and I'm not over it."

Mibs had become sort of precious to Omri. He had caught himself studying her as she talked. "So this was the third child. The first two died and it was heart-wrenching to see them die. And I remember Brooksany's face and she wouldn't say outright this third little one was on the way. Then it came and they loved it and they never ceased loving it and I'd like to know what combination of freedom and discipline they used to bring her along. Now they eat out their hearts in loneliness with her gone."

And in his first letter to Joel and Brooksany, Omri had poured out his praise of Rod and Mibs as a couple, "one couple in a million," and it was a clean vital blameless impulse that had sent Mibs into the arms of Rod. He gave them his judgment and surmise that the match would work out. Then had come a long letter from Brooksany and it was "Dear Omri" and not "Dear Mr. Winwold" as he had feared. And Brooks wrote, "You throw light into our gloom, you take the curse off our loneliness," and she enclosed the *Mohawk Valley Transcript* clippings which he had last night handed to Henry Flack and which had played a part in their first joint reverie and Henry Flack insisting, "High jinks, my friend, high jinks, tonight it is our right and our duty to have high jinks."

Omri hadn't told Mibs of his own life when a boy, as he had told it to her mother. He did confess to Mibs that he was the Maple Leaf tavern barkeep and had come to the Wimbler home "a little tight, a little jingled," and Brooksany had shamed him out of his silence about his life before coming to Springfield. He had told part of that boyhood to Mibs, saying at a later time he would tell more. He told Mibs his father was no success as a businessman, omitting reference to the business of a go-between collector of police-protection money from the lower level of bawdyhouses. He referred to his mother and sister as "taking things too easy," with no particulars as to the water-front saloon where he last saw his mother after his father had been killed for holding out protection money on the police, nor of how he had had no word from his sister since he last saw her in a strait jacket in an asylum for Magdalens and her piteous query, "*Why* did I do it?" He told Mibs of working a year in a cotton mill as a bobbin boy and it was monotonous and suffocating but he considered it better to wait and perhaps at a later time tell her of the curses that came to his tongue.

Omri wanted no pity, as such, from Mibs. And furthermore, he couldn't trust himself in one area of human contemplation. He could never shed his impression that more than half the chattel slaves of the South were better off and only slightly more hopeless than most of the New England mill workers. He held it against the abolitionists that they so truthfully cried out over instances of atrocity inflicted on slaves in the South with a policy of complete silence about misery and degradation inflicted on white wage workers by the New England mill owners and managers. He didn't like it furthermore that the largest fortunes and profits that had been made out of hauling black people from the Gold Coast of Africa and selling those black people into slavery at points in the West Indies and the South—these fortunes and profits had come to New England shipowners. "When you get enough passionate extremists blind to their own sin and guilt, completely silent on their own sin and guilt, while they make it a habit and a custom to accuse an opposition of its sin and guilt, the opposition having the same habit and custom," Omri had been saying—

"Then you get war," Mibs finished the sentence for him.

"Yes," said Omri. "Bigots begin wars. Long before the guns start shooting the bigots begin the war."

"What *is* a bigot?"

"A bigot is a proud man who enjoys his pride and can gloat over how good he is. A bigot can see only one side, his side, of a human issue. He will not admit that the other side can be partly right and he is no more right than they. The bigot says *they* are completely wrong and *he* is completely right. The bigot is a mole, living in the dark, and you mention to him a blue sky and white clouds and he says 'There is no blue sky and there are no white clouds, for I have never seen them.' The bigot is a fish who refuses to believe in birds because birds prefer to fly rather than swim. The bigot is a bundle of black-and-white habits and any other human bundle with different habits, blood-scarlet or fog-gray, is under suspicion without one question asked. The bigot hates for the joy of hating. The bigot needs our understanding without sympathy or pity. He stands before the mirror and shakes hands with himself, saying, 'I am my best friend.'"

"What you don't know about bigots!" Mibs smiled.

"Once a bigot died and they threw him in the river and he floated upstream. Another bigot died, and reaching Heaven went straight to the Great White Throne and began an argument with God."

"I nearly married a bigot," said the very sober Mibs, her wide thin lips parted over the white even teeth, her blue eyes edged with a faint green mist. And she told of Hornsby. "I like him yet. I suppose I would have married him if it wasn't that in time he would have made me some kind of a weak imitation of himself. And I look at him closer and think more about him and it's not fair to call him a bigot. He crusaded against strong drink and the liquor-sellers and though he was overrighteous about it, he wasn't all wrong in crying that too many good men go to ruin by what they pour through a hole in the face. He never played cards, he never waltzed nor sashayed in a quadrille, nor right-and-left-hand in a Virginia reel, and he never had any teaching that card-players and dancers are like fish and birds, of infinite variety. A zealot, not a bigot, I guess that's Hornsby now. You can't name any hard work or suffering, or even death, he wouldn't be willing to go through for abolition of slavery, immediate or gradual. I told Rod and the other Waymans once, and I won't trouble to tell it again, when they were saying there won't be a war, they're sure there won't be a war, I told 'em, 'You don't know Hornsby Meadows.' A Wednesday-night prayer meeting in New Era, Rod and Hornsby, you should have heard it, they prayed against each other. Then the next Saturday night they happened to meet crossing the college campus. And without a word they started fighting and they hit each other and knocked each other down and stood up to fight again and kept it up till both of them were stretched out flat and half-senseless on the ground. I'm not sure but Hornsby learned the South can fight and the war he wants will be a little longer than he used to figure. We grew up together. I can read Hornsby. The last two years it kept coming over him: The way to end slavery is to get a war with the South and in the welter and confusion somehow the slaves will be set free, every last one of 'em."

And Mibs had shrugged her shoulders or rather lifted them both and sunk her chin deep between them. She went on. "I remember when I decided I couldn't marry Hornsby. I had been a witness over four or five years of something dying in him and he didn't know it was dying. His sense of humor that he once had, quizzical and odd and yet it was there, you could say he had poisoned and buried it. It could be that when Rod came along he hit me the harder for the way he could laugh and the way he needs fun as a baby does milk. The liveryman Fred Shamp, in New Era, I heard him say about Hornsby, 'I've never seen him smile of his own accord.' It was in Shamp's place I first heard Rod give the three-card-monte palaver."

Omri had heard this palaver which Rod picked up in a St. Louis gambling house from a man in a starched shirt with white stiff cuffs, no coat, a black silk vest with two buttons, the stiff shirt bosom a-sparkle with two diamond studs, the man pausing in whatever he was doing, at times, to click and twist upward the ends of his little dapper black mustache. Standing behind his little table the gambler takes out three cards from the deck, shows their faces to the crowd, and then smooth as you like, for his tongue has rolled it off thousands of times, he goes into his palaver:

"Here you are, gentlemen; this ace of hearts is the winning card. Watch it closely. Follow it with your eye as I shuffle. Here it is, and now here, now here and now" (laying the three on the table with faces down) "where? If you point it out the first time you win; but if you miss you lose. Here it is, you see" (turning it up). "Now watch it again" (shuffling). "This ace of hearts, gentlemen, is the winning card. I take no bets from paupers, cripples or orphan children. The ace of hearts. It is my regular trade, gentlemen—to move my hands quicker than your eyes. I always have two chances to your one. The ace of hearts. If your sight is quick enough, you beat me and I pay; if not, I beat you and take your money. The ace of hearts—who will go me twenty?"

Three times a country boy in a new oversized suit of clothes looked puzzled and sheepish, then covered with a laugh meant to show that he was a good sport, having lost three twenty-dollar gold pieces, three straight, each time having the ace of hearts spotted by a raised corner. How that corner was smoothed out and a raised corner put on another card not the ace of hearts, his eyes couldn't see, nor the swift hands that did the trick. The country boy stood by and watched older and smarter men than himself lose a gold piece or two. The three-card man, in the midst of a palaver, pointed a finger at Rod's face, and, "May I inquire of you, sir, why the white sheep eat more than the black sheep?" The little crowd around the table was further puzzled at Rod's response, "You wish an immediate reply, sir, to the interrogatory you propound?"

"It will gratify me exceedingly if you will accommodate me with an immediate reply and no delay, sir."

"Then I desire to inform you, honorable sir, to your interrogatory why the white sheep eat more than the black sheep, my answer is, and you will have trouble to deny the answer, sir, the reason the white sheep eat more than the black sheep is simply because there are more of 'em. Kyah! kyah! kyah!"

Billy Rockingham and Charley Amberson, two former members of Haverstraw's Mammoth Minstrels, had recognized each other. Later, at supper, Rockingham told of taking a wagon show around mining camps in Colorado, of winnings and losses as a real-estate speculator in Denver, how he couldn't solve the hog and grain market in Chicago and lost more than he won, the roulette wheel he had got tired of running in a place in Cincinnati, the bullet that grazed his ear when he was dealer in a house in Louisville, and he had found no sure thing that brought him in such money as three-card monte. In a single day now he raked in a week's pay with Haverstraw.

"Rod takes up with people, they talk easy with him," Mibs had said. "He's full of people that walk around in him and they sort of live and talk inside of him." Rod as a growing boy had knocked on the door of a Negro cabin on a neighboring farm. The gaunt six-foot-two woman who let him in stood in the door for a long look at a sunset of banners and flares. She closed the door and built a fire against the February chill.

"Yuh come fo sompn, I know dat," she said. "Yuh come fo bread. Yuh want some uh duh livin bread, enty?" She went into report, meditation, exhortation. "I tell yuh when duh sperrit in me I struts. Duh sperrit come fum Jedus. It Jedus in duh sun." Young Rod went along with her, seeing her as a Christian with a touch of fire-worshiper. "It Jedus in duh sun. By duh sun Jedus tell me good report or evil report." A flicker of ecstasy, of delights of revelation given her, was on her face. "Evy one on us got uh baby inside duh body. Wen duh rest uh duh body shuffle off, dis baby go tuh Jedus. Dere is wings waitin tuh be hitch on. Atter dat yuh is angel." She was sleeping in her bed and a travel came to her. "It cum to me lak uh dream, dis travel. Train come toward muh bed, fas it come, an it jes eased in, jes eased in, not a choo-choo choo-choo, jes eased in an out. Twarnt uh real train, yuh unstan. It jes eased out an it say, 'Set yuh clock by duh sun.' Well, I know it don mean dis clock yere, tuh set dat by duh sun. It mean muh heaht, yere in muh body, tuh set dat by duh sun. Fo duh sun is Jedus' sign. Jedus make evyting, duh yearth, duh flowahs, evyting grow, duh birds, duh buzzard. Set yuh clock by duh sun. Dat mean keep muh heaht right wid Jedus."

And Rod had thanked her, put twenty cents in her hand, and, "A contribution, like it's a church here and you preaching. You do give out the living bread, Hester." She lived alone in this cabin, worked in the fields, her husband dead and her nine children scattered.

Then there was the young man Rod and Doss had seen die in the San Francisco hotel of the fresh-lumber smell, the floor and wall boards not yet painted and new from the sawmill. Of nothing else he had met in California, it seemed, would Rod talk as freely and repeatedly as this hard-drinking Scotch-blooded youth whose white face had strength and valor along with his fair and girlish quality, his tall forehead with a fall of hair the color of oat straw.

"What kind of a young woman was it that fooled him?" Rod asked. "She was probably a pretty thing and at heart very practical without the slightest notion of the irony in him on his deathbed mocking at her, 'She was chaste as the snow and when the time came she was all snow, all ice, her head, feet and bosom all snow and ice.' She thought him queer in his worship of the Arch, his never-ending quotation from away back, 'The arch never sleeps.' He oughtn't to have died. It was too soon. It'll stick with me long as I live, that boy, he wasn't much more than a boy, on a lumber bedstead with wooden slats and a straw mattress, and him saying, 'Love stands and hangs by an arch. Hate breaks the arch. The rainbow is an arch. Where you find truth, love, harmony and lasting strength, there an arch bends and curves over it as a blessing and an oath. Unity, union, you get it only with an arch. Hate and pride break the arch. Love and understanding build an unbreakable arch.' "

Omri had seen tears come to Mibs' eyes on this. "Rod loved that boy. He couldn't any more pity or blame that boy than he could himself. That boy is part of Rod now. Those moody spells of his, when he won't talk to me nor anyone, I think it's these other people alive in him and he's too near them." Mibs brightened and told of a matter as she had it from Mother Wayman in confidence. Others in the Wayman family were sometimes cold, often strictly reserved, seldom suspicious though there were the occasions, but Mrs. Wayman, Rod's mother, accepted Mibs in a curious inclusive way. From the first, Mother Wayman gave extra efforts and went out of her way to make things cozy, agreeable and homelike for Mibs. She and Mibs were alike in one particular: under the cold impersonal look often on their faces ran laughter, a readiness for mirth and even clowning, natural gifts of singing, vehemence of speech when needed, each having a wild streak that had led into unaccountable ventures.

A day in mid-January it was, Mibs standing at an ironing board and talking with Barbara Wayman, who was tearing a variety of cast-off clothes into strips for weaving a rag carpet, and Mibs asked what a woman generally does when she is going to have a baby. "I think it will be in August or September," said Mibs. And after the older woman had given her advice, their talk ran on to Rod and his ways with girls and women. Several had offered themselves to him, said the mother, "only one of them open and flagrant," she said, "and you had to know her very well to catch her at being flagrant." Her father owned a bank, a shingle mill, and an interest in a short-line railroad to which he had sold ties cut from his extensive timber holdings. His daughter Maude Humberton stood out as the brilliant and resourceful figure in social and cultural affairs in a small town near the Wayman farm in Virginia. She was "looked up to." Those wishing to go up the invisible yet definable ladder for entrance into the most exclusive inner social circle of the town had heard, "Maude Humberton can make you or unmake you." She was tall, blonde, blooming, sort of overwhelming physically in her proportions. Some persons who relished their acquaintance with Roman sculpture said her form was Junoesque.

Well educated, a ready conversationalist with a large library and many current periodicals, an excellent horsewoman, an active Presbyterian with a driving and almost furious enthusiasm for the temperance movement, for the utmost moderation and preferably total abstinence everywhere, Maude Humberton had brought temperance lecturers to the town. She had a little personal list of drunkards she had helped "to redeem from the demon," her phrase. And Maude and Rod had gone to school together. To her own parties and to the social events of others, she saw that Rod was invited. She was pleasant company. Rod liked her vitality and endless drive. She had her way of parading him, showing him off with satisfaction and pride. "She's smitten on Rod," ran gossip. How it got around and who started it, Rod wasn't sure, but soon the rumors were definite of Rod and Maude engaged and soon now there would be a ring on Maude's finger. Rod suspected Maude herself started the rumor. Months went by and he saw Maude assuming they were engaged; if not, it was for him to speak up. People spoke to him as if Maude Humberton had verified it by not denying it.

"Rod got scared about marrying her and told her so," said Barbara Wayman. She could be resplendent, as Sir Walter Scott would say, "and she put on a radiance she could take off and put on." His honor as a gentleman—what of that? She couldn't believe he would "demean himself." Then she wept for her pride to be crushed. Rod stayed away and she sent for him. It got to where Rod was desperate because she spread the word they hadn't broken and everything was sweet. Rod solved it. He swept the deck and threw the broom in the sea. He went to a lawn party at Miss Humberton's one summer evening, first taking two stiff drinks of rare old whisky. For the guests to see, from a pint bottle on his hip he poured freely into his lemonade glass. Then he acted the lush blabbing fool who has taken too much, ever polite in telling one and all how happy he was, busting in to tell how happy he was, and purposely clumsy in his pawing at the shoulders and bosom of Maude Humberton and messing up her orange and cream-tinted organdie gown. The engagement was off.

Rod came home perfectly sober, grim and sober, "I swept the deck and threw the broom in the sea." Then an appointment to West Point Military Academy soon after and eight months later a letter from him and he liked everything at the Academy except mathematics, chemistry, tactics, drill and discipline. "And you know he then quit and joined the minstrels."

"He decides quick," Mibs had smiled.

"He decided quick on you."

"We both decided quick," and Mibs told of Hornsby Meadows, the root-and-branch abolitionist, his hold on her till she went to a barn dance and drank her first mug of beer.

Barbara spoke her horror over "such a creature" as Hornsby. Mibs couldn't tell Barbara of Hornsby shuddering in horror over her, Barbara, his unspeakable loathing of her. Mibs became the agreeable listener, the patient hearer, feeling it useless to explain, nothing she could say would inform, correct or modify. Earlier that afternoon they had talked of the baby to come August or September. As a phrase of sacred music to Mibs came Barbara's low voice, "That baby, my first grandchild, it may be I will love you and Rod and the little one all the same, all one."

And Mibs, "We'll mother the little fellow together."

"The little fellow? A boy?"

"Sure."

"How do you know it will be a boy?"

"My mother knew I was going to be a girl."

"And my mother knew I was going to be a *boy*. What can you do about that?"

"If it's a boy, I want him like Rod, if it's a girl, I want her like you."

Sweetnesses grew between them, these two women, much of underlying likeness. The daughter Rosalind Wayman had no such likeness. Of medium height, buxom, a wonderful mass of black curls falling over her ears down to her shoulders, a face regular and rather pretty, her thin-lipped mouth drew back too far between nose and chin. It was Rod's jutting chin carried out farther. Rosalind held back any open dislike for Mibs, didn't seem easy when Mibs was around. She could refer to the "skinny" woman of fashion in dress aimed to make her look less skinny. And Mibs, free to admit she was skinny rather than plump, didn't like the insinuation Rosalind put on the word "skinny." Rosalind rated a year at a girl's school in Shelbyville, Kentucky, and overrated the way she could thank you in French. Nineteen now, across three years she had gone out occasionally with Marvel Winwold and didn't like it that someone said, "Marvel sees her between his regular girls."

A year older than Rosalind was Brock Wayman, not so tall as Rod, straight brown hair with none of the waviness of Rod's, a squarish head and face, a ruddy look to him, rather enjoyed all kinds of farm work, a hunter and fisherman, quick-tempered and quick to fight, riding alongside Marvel with the "butcher-knife boys," with high records for ringers in pitching horseshoes. Brock had put in a year at Transylvania College in Lexington, Kentucky. Mibs saw him as pleasant, vital, with a hint of country bumpkin about him and little of Rod's wit and awareness. His face overlaid with sun and wind tan, the skin at the cheekbones had a glint of copper leather.

Brock had been keeping steady company with Cedora Winwold, now eighteen, lean, smallish and moon-faced. Both took to farm work, seemed to belong among those who naturally like farming, the land, the crops, seedtime and harvest, the animals, the ancient procedures of breeding and birthing, the chances of weather, the gossip with other farmers about stock, seed, the crop outlook. Cedora had told Omri, "I've heard every good farm wife knows the creak of her husband's wagon and I want that husband and wagon."

They had walked with Omri over the hundred acres to be their farm, Omri's gift, after the wedding. He noticed they went to church as a habit, with no troubles of belief or doubt. Likewise political issues of

853

the hour swept in fury and never touched them: their immediate personal plans and private affairs filled their minds and shut out slavery, disunion, Kansas, John Brown. Brock rode and drank with the "butcher-knife boys" for the fun, the excitement, the fellowship, politics to him a dim notion of a fight between two sides where the slickest liars won. Brock would rather listen to the cackle of a hen who had just laid an egg or the whinny of a horse saying it was lonesome. Brock and Cedora had an instinct about land: it would be there, waiting and willing, when the latest church dispute or political wrangle ran back out of the memory of living men.

The well-off Winwolds and Waymans many a Pike County farm struggler referred to as "rich," as "big bugs." A few termed them "the bon ton." The ground-floor bathrooms of the Winwold and Wayman houses had a long tin tub they filled with warm water carried from the kitchen-stove "reservoir." Now lately with a system of pipes and a heater installed, they turned faucets for hot or cold water. Over the county, however, in most houses it was a custom that they still took their baths in the family washtub. Tall and wide glass windows gave outlooks from the Winwold and Wayman houses while greased paper as in pioneer and colonial days still served the many farmhouses where they couldn't afford glass.

Every year came the cases, like clockwork, like phases of the moon, the county authorities dealing with crime, insanity, incest, cohabitation, pauperism. Omri took pork, hominy and potatoes to a house of filth, the floor unswept, the roof leaking, hairs of mangy dogs and soiled cats on chairs and table. The lone woman had bent shoulders, sly eyes in a thin face, weeks since soap and water touched her neck and ears. Omri had come partly out of curiosity to see this widow, the mother of a twenty-year-old boy caught by the sheriff's men riding a stolen horse. They had him off the horse, disarmed of revolver and knife, when he made a breakaway into a cornfield and they were near the whole afternoon getting him again. They lashed him to the back of a mule, roped his feet tight under the belly of the mule. They came to a flooded creek, high water, dangerous to swim their horses across, and they decided to turn back to another route. Suddenly the boy got action and had his mule floundering in the high rushing waters. "You'll be drowned!" man after man yelled to the boy. He yelled back, "I'll go to hell and kick the gate open for you." Two days later they found boy and mule washed up on a bank downstream. "He's my boy, he's dead, he never was scairt in his life," said the mother to Omri, having little more to say except, in a finger wag to the pork, hominy and potatoes, "Since you brung 'em, I'll keep 'em."

Should Mibs get real homesick for some abolitionists, Omri once told her, "You could run over to Griggsville and see a few come-outers there." Far back as 1838, he told her, a Democrat named Key, running for constable, was beaten by a Whig named Coffey and the Democrats

854

cried "dirty work." When a Key man hit a Coffey man from behind, the free-for-all fighting between Whigs and Democrats came near to a riot. A few weeks later arrived an educated gentleman holding anti-slavery meetings. In the Methodist church he brought out a paper, a petition to the United States Congress, calling for slavery abolishment in the District of Columbia and slave-soil Texas to be kept out of the Union. When citizens walked up and signed their names to this radical petition, parties in the audience stood up and howled it was no way to do in a church. Around a stove in a grocery near by, with corn liquor fresh from the burnt wood, the Democrats passed resolutions calling for signers of the petition to erase their names. The next morning the Democrats rode their horses out to the farmhouse of a deacon where they found the visiting abolitionist and made him hand over the signed petition. They rode back to Griggsville and called on the signers—some would erase and others wouldn't. Those who wouldn't erase began organizing, met in the hotel, with guns and powder, farmers pouring in from the country. They elected a captain named Blood, and sent a committee to the other crowd—if they wanted slaughter they could have it and they better forget the petition. "That was all," said Omri. "From then on you could talk abolition in and around Griggsville without feeling exactly like a toad under a harrow."

Mibs now brought herself to tell Omri of Marova and Hetty and how she had carried food and water to them while officers sought their arrest in New Era. She saw in Omri's brown eyes a shifting color of moonglow in a mirror of pond water at night. He too had waited on the slim octoroon and the heavy black woman. A Griggsville man had come to him at his house before daybreak saying they couldn't chance the drive toward Barry, on the way to Quincy, in daylight. "He thought he could call on me because I had done my best to help him catch two men who had kidnapped a couple of black boys, free Negroes, handcuffed them and took them down to New Orleans and sold them." And Omri puzzled the family and the hired men by the amount of work and odd jobs he must tend to in the barn and the hayloft that day when Marova and Hetty stayed over and kept hidden till another Griggsville man with a different wagon came at night. Mibs agreed with Omri about Marova, "like a plant grown under glass, you can't be sure what it'll do set out in the rain, the wind, and the cold."

"Aren't you near an abolitionist when you help run the Underground Railway?" Mibs had asked and Omri, "I'm human, and I can't stop my ears to any human cry."

"My mother teased my father about helping the runaways and then denying he was an abolitionist. He'd say if he *was* one he wasn't a *talking* one."

At the mention of her mother to Omri, Mibs noticed his eyes picked up with a peculiar interest. The eyes kept that interest as he plied her with questions whether Brooksany had had a happy life, how she carried her years, and had her face held to its look of stillness that meant an inner life of quiet meditation with resulting humility and strength. Omri liked Mibs' answers. His wide-stretching sensitive lips took on a sober twist and he pushed one hand around the curve of brick-dust muffler beard under his chin and jaws.

Omri's eyes on Mibs' face searched and queried. From the mouth up it had lines of the mother and at moments the still look. He had spoken to Rod once of Mibs' face as mystifying and beautiful—and her long and winding frame "skinny" till she moved. "She's a poem of motion, Mr. Winwold," Rod had said. "I told her that the second night I called on her." And Omri in bed that night had caught himself praying, "Take 'em through, O God. Be with 'em, O God. They'll need you, God. Bring 'em through." He had studied Rod. With a singing and rollicking grace, with enjoyment of fun, music and dancing, with whimsical capers and ditties, was Rod soft, would he crack under disaster and hard trial? "No," said Omri, "he isn't soft. I've seen him handling men and steers, mean horses and broken wagons, sick cows and hogs with cholera and a dog that killed three sheep. He's made for Mibs and she's made for him and all they need is a little kindly consideration and help from Almighty God."

Omri couldn't help adding, "Which is what the free black man John Walker says is all the United States needs." Then he spoke another of his little prayers that Mibs and Rod would not be forgotten in the Divine mercies.

* * * * * * * * * *

Chapter 27

* * * * * * * * * *

Holy Day for Two Men

GRATITUDE ran deep in Omri on this Sunday morning in St. Louis in late January of 1860. The peal and bong of the cathedral bells rolling in tone waves over city and river, what they were saying had the solemnity of his gratitude. He was drunk enough last night, and so was Flack. Morning and daylight could have brought regrets, headaches and a bitter ash taste on the tongue. He was snuggled in white sheets, with feather pillows and a bolster, two light wool blankets and a down quilt scrolled and brocaded over in silk. The two tall windows had lace curtains and wine-red velvet draperies. Only when occasionally glimpsing the quilt and the draperies did he have a fleeting thought of Bee. The Winwold boys and girls, the Waymans and their children, Mibs and Rod, Mibs' mother whom he probably would have married but for the chance event and random circumstance of her having met Joel Wimbler—these and the war to come—aye, the war to come—these had crowded his calm wakeful reverie. He speculated on why none of these had come to him in dreams while he slept. The nearest he had to a dream was an apparition of a large glass window always moving away from him, and through the window a little red mouth and white dimpled fingers touching the mouth and then being flung toward him, while a fading voice kept repeating, "Take my address, come see me."

Weeks ago he had a dream, on a night of flying snow that went down for a clear sky and a moon to come out and lay its added white on the feather and plume shapes of snow in the five cedars and two oaks framed in his window. And why after such a beneficent good night from the world outside should a dream come in his sleep, of Rod with a fourteen-foot blacksnake whip, swinging it with speed and accuracy, taking off the head of first one rattlesnake and then another and another, each snake coiled ready to leap and its red fangs darting from the open mouth as its rattles shook warning? Why such a dream then? Rod was handy and keen with a fourteen-foot blacksnake whip and last year had killed two rattlesnakes with one. But why should he, Omri Winwold, have a dream about it many months later? Maybe time would tell.

In the dining room below a free Negro woman brought the breakfast dishes from the kitchen where the cook was her slave sister earning the money to buy freedom. Buckwheat cakes with comb honey and farm-churned butter, with fried salt pork and fresh eggs fried on one side, preserved plums, coffee with thick cream and brown sugar, and Omri saying, "I guess we'll make out a breakfast, ain't it, Henry?" Henry tried to meet this in the nice way it was given. "Um-humpf," came his grunt he tried to make genial. The kitchen door had closed on the black serving woman when Henry was saying, "If tweren't for these damned abolitionists, Omri."

"Henry," and Omri's wide mouth had a harvest-moon grin, "don't you know, Henry, no sensible man nowadays begins the day, and especially Sunday, with thinking about the damned abolitionists?"

"I can't help it, they're bad for business, they're bad for the country."

"Now, Henry, see this," and Omri put a finger to the sticking plaster on his right temple. "One of your chairs last night, the corner of a chair, cut me here and drew blood. Now I don't know whether it's a good chair or a bad chair that likes to get in the way of people and cut them and draw blood. I'll forget the chair if you'll forget the damned abolitionists this morning and go with me to the Catholic-church services for the good of our souls."

"Gosh, Omri, I haven't been there since I went a couple of times with Bee."

"It was Bee's idea?"

"She kind uh liked it. They put on quite a show, you know, sort of mysterious what they call it and you never know what's coming next. Bee hinted she might join 'em and go regular. I told her go ahead. I think, Omri, it might have been good for her, you never can tell."

Their clothes and hats brushed, shaved and clean in fresh linen shirts, the massive Omri Winwold with his shags of scraggly red hair falling over his ears and the bright muffler of brick-dust beard around and under his jaws, his massive shoulders rounded and hunched with muscles, he with his short jug-shaped waddling friend Henry Flack, with reverence and curiosity in about equal parts, entered one of the most impressively conceived and wrought pieces of church architecture north of New Orleans and west of the Alleghenies. On the way, walking the wooden sidewalks a little sloppy from a bright warm sun melting a three-inch snow of the two days before, Henry losing one overshoe that got stuck in the mud at one street crossing and hiring a newsboy to bring it to him, Omri told Henry he had friends in and around Salem near Pike County and they were Universalists.

"Those are the people believe there is no hell to go to?"

"Yes—and they got more than a half-million members in this country."

"That's a lot of people not to go to hell."

And Omri told Henry of drinking beer with a Pittsfield Irishman who joked, "Them Universalists won't squeeze through the Gates of Heaven till all hell freezes over and they can skate in on the ice." This mildly interested Henry. He didn't get the picture. So Omri told Henry of a Peoria Irishman driving through Atlas a six-mule team hauling whisky to Peoria, getting into a fight with a Know-Nothing who called him a papist, voting like the Pope told him. They fought free-for-all, with pounding fists, fingernails clawing faces, knees gouging, teeth tearing at noses and ears. When the bystanders felt it had gone far enough and broke them apart, the two fighters needed tender care. Omri helped wash and tend the Irish teamster, ate a snack of food with him at the tavern before seeing him up on the wagon seat. Omri asked the teamster, "Why must the Catholics and Protestants be fighting all the time? Why can't we all become atheists and live together like good Christians?"

Omri noticed Henry keenly interested but puzzled. "Henry," he asked, "you know Unitarians?"

"They're for God only and can't use Jesus nor the Holy Ghost."

"Well, Henry, I heard one of those laughing joking Universalists over at Salem tell what is the difference between a Universalist and

858

a Unitarian. A Universalist believes God is too good to damn us all and a Unitarian believes we are too good to be damned by God."

They had come to another street crossing, where the broken planks sagged around in mud, and Henry watched his overshoes at every step. Safely across, Henry showed that his mind too, on this bright and pleasant Sabbath morning, dwelt on hell and damnation. "About six blocks from my store used to be a ten-dollar house and a woman, a Spanish Mexican, black eyes and oily black hair, long gold earrings, silver slippers and always a knife in one slipper. Well, one time we was havin Napoleon brandy and talkin like old friends and I asked her where she got a dandy thick gold bracelet with two rubies in it. And I could see she took it for an insult. I oughtn't to asked such a question, I told her right off. Then she says like she was thinkin to herself, 'Sins have different prices in hell.' I had her say it again and let it go at that. It was more to think about than I ever heard in a whorehouse. 'Sins have different prices in hell.' A price list telling what you pay for different kinds of sins, high-priced sins and low-priced sins, nice little ten-cent sins, three-for-a-dollar sins, a thousand-dollar sin that will get a woman on her wrist a dandy thick gold bracelet with two rubies."

The two men took far rear pews in the cathedral. They went on their knees occasionally with the other worshipers. The music, the lights, the stained-glass windows, the intricate garments and traditional symbols, the investitures of flowing robes and sacred utensils, the cadenced ritual pronounced in the same ancient language in thousands of other churches in other lands, the solemn announcements of the actual presence of the living Body of Christ—Omri sat somber and let these carry him along. The responses between priest and choir, the pling of a bell across an impurpled silence, carried mystery. His eyes would close and faces moved before him, each of his children, the faces of Sarah and Anne, of Rod and Mibs, of Joel and Brooksany Wimbler—and suddenly and hazily the little face with the cherry lips and violet eyes swaying through the glass door of the hack, Annabell Ponder, "Take my address, come see me."

Omri roused himself, kept his eyes open, bent his head in humility and devotion, followed every accent of the services, tried to join himself to all seekers of the Great Unseen. His ears lost no word of the sermon and he tried for the essence of wisdom or revelation in the sentences spoken by the earnest composed figure in the pulpit. He heard a reference to Ember days and learned for the first time they are "days of fast and abstinence in each season of the year, to thank God for the benefit received during that season, and also to pray to God for good priests, because on Ember days is usually held the ordination of priests." Omri heard for the first time why certain "holy days" have their names, how on Ash Wednesday the priest blesses ashes he then places on the heads of the faithful. Of what do such ashes remind us? That we are mortal of body, the priest saying as he places the ashes on the head, "Remember, man, that thou art dust, and to dust thou shalt return."

Good Friday, Holy Saturday, Whitsunday, Omri had become rusty on their meanings and now was refurbished. He had forgotten the Catholic farmer near Albany who explained to him that Rogation days are for prayers and processions "to implore God's blessing on the crops in the fields." And Omri had somehow kept his thought away from the war to come, when again it struck him with its familiar grinding impact, at the priest quoting the counsel of St. Paul to the Romans, "Salute one another with a holy kiss." Omri didn't hear the next few sentences for a rush of ideas that ended in his saying, "I don't ask the extremists on both sides to kiss each other. I'd be satisfied if they made an honest trial at understanding that every great war turns out to be different from what is planned and expected by those who begin it."

Omri returned to hearing the sermon. His eyes roved occasionally among heads and faces he could see without turning his own head and staring. He saw grave serene faces to whom the services were as healing waters. He saw thwarted hungry faces seeking fresh springs that had been denied them. He saw noncommittal anonymous faces that live in twilight, afraid of the sun, afraid of sinking their roots deeper, unaware "The standing stalk rots." He saw the faces of women who might be house servants, "hired girls," and he knew them for teachers, educators, instructors in behavior and manners to the children of the families where they worked, some of them tending to the upbringing of children more than the parents. He saw one somewhat shadowed face white as clean-scraped bone in a bright sun, and as his eyes stayed fixed on it, it took on a startling resemblance to Brooks Wimbler. Beyond this face was another, also shadowed somewhat, and in the blend of color rays from a stained-glass window he was saying the face could be a black-and-gold pansy in a moonmist and he couldn't be sure it wasn't the face of Annabell Ponder. When he turned his eyes toward his jug-shaped friend next to him, he had seen Henry keeping his eyes open, always interested, and at one point Henry crossed himself in unison with the other worshipers.

The services over, they moved with the stream of people thronging the center aisle, stepped out under the four majestic Doric columns, Omri pulling Henry toward the descending steps at the right, and lifting a hand toward a hackman at the sidewalk edge. Omri pushed Henry in, got in himself, pulled shut the door with its glass window. The hackman had just got his horse going at a walk and the hack was slowly moving along when Omri saw a woman at the sidewalk edge. She had come to a standstill for a straight-away look through the hack window. She caught Omri's eyes, she bowed very slowly and very gravely. It was Annabell Ponder, alone. Omri couldn't take his eyes off her. He took off his hat slowly and returned her very grave look. And the horse went into a slow trot and took them to Henry's home.

At dinner Henry made it clear that he would hate to see secession come but if it did he wouldn't blame the South. Henry had heard about an Irish couple snarling at each other and a priest rebuking them, "Your cat and dog get along better than you do." And the Irishman, the husband, "Yes, but tie them together and see what happens." Omri then mentioned Rodney Wayman once saying that a sovereign state could no more surrender part of its sovereignty to the Federal Union than a woman could surrender part of her chastity. Omri stayed overnight and before starting the ride home the next morning, he said to Henry, "Next time I see you will be November or December, after the election, and I'll tell you then about when the war will begin."

"There won't be a war," said Henry. "They'll find some way to fix it. There's always a way."

"I like you, Henry, it's been a good visit." They shook hands. Omri rode away. He did like Henry but he was troubled about Henry and so many other people being certain about matters uncertain, being careless, offhand and easy, about death and taxes around the turn of the road, about that faint and nearly inaudible swoosh Omri could hear beyond the horizon.

Where would Henry be when the war came? Omri couldn't figure him. Henry loved the Mississippi River, had five times ridden on it from St. Louis down to New Orleans and back. "It would be wrong, dirty wrong, to cut up the Mississippi River and give it out to different states," Henry had said. Yet Henry leaned to the South, had many friends there and liked Southern ways, saw them as good fighters. "Might be a little shootin, some kind of a blowup, and then it will all simmer down," Henry had said. "The North can't raise big enough armies to go down there and make those people free their niggers and behave like the North wants to those niggers. They can fight down there. They can ride and shoot, got a good record when it comes to fightin. They sing and drink and have more fun down there than the North. They can make a hell of a war before they give up. And you know, Omri, they have plenty uh good fine friends up here in the North. No, you look at it up and down and there won't be a war."

Omri had led his horse on a gangplank to a steamer and he had watched the vessel take the big bend of the river around Madison and Greene counties in Illinois and again the long curve of the river that bordered Calhoun County, Illinois. "Calhoun," said Omri, "the first settlers there came up from the South and named their county after John C. Calhoun, United States Senator from South Carolina, the great defender of states rights, the fellow Rod had it from when he said for a state to surrender part of its sovereignty is like a woman surrendering part of her chastity."

861

At Louisiana Landing on the Missouri side he led his horse off the boat, was ferried over the Father of Waters and back again in Pike County. He rode on in the late afternoon and he couldn't get out of his ears that faint and nearly inaudible swoosh beyond the horizon.

* * * * * * * * * *

Chapter 28

* * * * * * * * * *

Events, Seasons, Children, a Boy Baby

THE days fled by into weeks. The months marched on across the year of 1860. Punctuations came, days when what happened seemed like nothing before. The Winwolds and the Waymans read of national and world affairs in a Republican weekly at Pittsfield, with further details from dailies and semiweeklies out of Springfield and St. Louis. There were days Omri came out of reading a pile of journals to say, "The more you know the less and vice versa."

For the first time, in that year of 1860, the Emperor of Japan sent ambassadors to the United States Government, and arriving in San Francisco Harbor in the USS *Powhatan* they proceeded to the port of New York in the USS *Roanoke*, then to Washington and the Executive Mansion and the Department of State and a series of receptions. The Nipponese ambassadors saw New York, parties and receptions, a National Guard escort to the Hotel Astor, a grand ball at Niblo's Garden, embarking for Tokyo on the USS *Niagara*. It had never happened before. A small island empire that had always kept to itself, with pride, culture, art, folkways, swords and tsubas, an elaborate ceremonial for tea-drinking, sleepy-eyed Japan was beginning to look out over the world with vague ideas of accommodating a modern world of trade, expansion, wider markets. Omri told Rod and Mibs of one of the Tokyo embassy at his first glimpse of a ballroom filled with waltzing couples. "The efforts and monotonous motions he saw them going through, it looked to him like hard labor for small pay, and he asked, 'Why don't they leave it to the servants?'" And Mibs, "I wouldn't doubt the Japanese have some nice dances they like that would seem to us hard work."

For the first time and for whatever it could mean, it was this year of 1860 that a Prince of Wales, a direct heir to the throne of England, after touring Canada made a triumphal tour of the United States, winning goodwill for Great Britain, in Washington the guest of the President at the Executive Mansion, reviewing the cadets of the West

Point Military Academy, visiting the Governor at Albany, escorted down New York streets by seven thousand troops and an immense torchlight procession and meeting "everybody who was anybody" at a grand ball, and after salutes and fireworks at Boston leaving Portland, Maine, on a British man-of-war. The event of the Prince's friendly visit couldn't have happened twenty or thirty years before, and earlier than that he would have been hooted off the streets of New York and Boston, a target of eggs and vegetables not strictly fresh. The little coastwise remnant of three million American people who had won independence now had spread across a continent and numbered thirty million, known abroad as the American Union of States and the question often asked abroad, "Is it written in the book of manifest destiny that this people and their nation will take a place and hold a position among leading world powers?"

Omri said to Marvel one day, "Some of the figures make a fellow dizzy. If you believe these men who are neither drunk nor silly, this country in a hundred years will have more than two hundred million people." Omri showed Marvel a copy of *Blackwood's Magazine*, a serious, sober and almost funereal publication, saying in thirty years the population of the United States would double and in 1940 reach more than three hundred millions of people. Marvel had taken *Blackwood's* to Rod and Mibs for them to be amazed. Mibs remembered her mother quoting some preacher: "The Great Valley of the Mississippi will yet burst its swaddling clothes and become a giant that will sway the world!" Then Mibs hunted out the sentences copied for her by Hornsby, John Luzac, writing from Leyden, Holland, in 1780, "If America becomes free, she will someday give the law to Europe," and the words of Barnaby, the traveler over North America in 1760, "An idea, strange as it is visionary, has entered into the minds of the generality of mankind, that empire is traveling westward: and everyone is looking forward with eager and impatient expectation to that destined moment when America is to give the law to the rest of the world."

A pang of memory shot through Mibs as they read this aloud twice. In the week she first read it was the evening she stood with skates on one shoulder on a hilltop overlooking New Era and up among bluish-white frost sparkles came a prairie moon to hang in the sky as a baby canoe, a silver moccasin, a phantom cradle. The world, so young then, seemed to her even younger now in this year when she believed come summer she would give and bestow more youth on the world.

Omri wouldn't trust himself to say a word after the accounts he read early that year of the main building of the Pemberton Cotton Mills at Lawrence, Massachusetts, being so built and so managed that one day, on the fated instant some inaudible signal clanged, the whole structure collapsed, fell to the ground in ruins, bringing down in

863

wreck and death looms, spindles, machines, people; after the fire that spread and ran wild they pulled out the burned and mutilated bodies of exactly one hundred and seventeen men, women and children, finding one hundred and twelve badly scorched or crippled for life while eighty-nine others, young and old, couldn't be found and were never heard of. Omri wouldn't trust himself on the affair. Somebody didn't care, he didn't know who. He was sure it was none of the eight- or nine-year-old bobbin boys whose mangled and burned bodies he could see laid in rows alongside men and women who had suddenly felt floors giving way under their feet and that was the last they knew.

Omri long ago had driven his wagon with baby Marvel over one corner of Pennsylvania where they now had the new oil wells pumping and farther down in Pennsylvania miles on miles of derricks. From now on, petroleum, kerosene oil for the lamps in millions of homes, better light than sperm oil from whales or from tallow candles, better light for housework and for the readers of books and journals.

And precisely why the United States Navy should break into the activities it showed in the West Indies this year wasn't clear. It did seem that the Navy rounded up slave ships and landed cargoes of some seventeen hundred Negroes at Key West for reshipment to the Negro Republic of Liberia in Africa. The USS *Mohican*, off the coast of Africa, took over a ship with a cargo of eight hundred Negroes bound for the West Indies. And in this year, in Southern and Northern journals, could be read the speech of Gaulden, the largest slaveholder in Georgia, saying, "I am a Southern states-rights man. I am an African slave-trader. I am one of those Southern men who believe that slavery is right, morally, religiously, socially, and politically. I believe that the institution of slavery has done more for this country, more for civilization, than all other interests put together. . . . We can never make another slave state with our present supply of slaves. . . . I would ask my friends of the South to come up in a proper spirit, ask our Northern friends to give us all our rights, and take off the ruthless restrictions which cut off the supply of slaves from foreign lands. . . . I tell you, fellow Democrats, that the African slave-trader is the true Union man. . . . If any of you Northern Democrats will go home with me to my plantation in Georgia, I will show you some darkies that I bought in Maryland, some that I bought in Virginia, some in Delaware, some in Florida, some in North Carolina, and I will also show you the pure African, the noblest Roman of them all."

Omri and Marvel read this together and Marvel said, "I think I understand every one of his words, papa, and yet it seems to me I have a funny feeling he's talking in some language I haven't learned."

"He is talking about his property in particular and property rights in general," said the father. "The South has something like three billion dollars invested in slaves. That's an awful lot of money. They have a right to be sensitive about it." Marvel saw his father break off there, sit quiet a while, run his fingers along the curve of his muffler beard, put a finger alongside his nose and bring it down, and then, "The American people—you can never tell what they're going to do next. The most contrary, ornery, contradictory people on earth. They go after the dollar, leave it for dreams and often impossible dreams, then they swing back to dollars, but the first thing you know they are back chasing a dream and ready to fight and sacrifice for it."

"Have you ever figured how the war will come when it does?" Marvel asked with a sweet seriousness that had his father's eyes very soft.

"The future is always packed with surprises. It unfolds one scene after another and seems to say, 'This one, now you didn't expect this one,' and mocking, 'or if you did you expected it different, it came from under and from over and it came sidewise in shapes and explosions you didn't expect.' It does seem, Marvel, that every big war and every great revolution slides in, sneaks in, and has begun before most of those who are in it know it is there. There are no rules, laws, precedents, that can tell you how and when the next big war begins and how it will go after it starts. The Thirty Years' War *nearly* came to an end each one of the thirty years and at last *did* come to an end because they were so dog-tired of fighting, and about all the slaughter accomplished was that Catholics and Protestants had a little more tolerance of each other. The British had George Washington licked a dozen times and the surprise was he always came back. Napoleon gave Europe one surprise after another and then met his own final surprise in Russia. Santa Anna had four to one against us and we drove him across desert and valley to where we signed terms in his capital city. The French Revolution shook all Europe with one surprise after another. The Puritans who began war on King Charles I didn't expect when they got him they'd cut his head off, nor did they expect a counter-revolution to put King Charles II on the throne and Cromwell dug up from his grave to be hanged on a gallows because he had died naturally and decently." Omri paused and gave his son the best he had. "We are a swift and furious people when we get going, Marvel. We are the most original, inventive, unpredictable people in the world. When the war comes it will be full of surprises, from start to finish, some of them grand and wild to look at, most of them rather sad.

"I must get hold of a book I've read about," Omri went on. "Written by some Englishman who thinks he makes out a case that a nation can go insane, plumb daft and crazy, the same as any man or woman. And what you get then is war. They do tell, among Illinois politicians, about Justin Butterfield, the Chicago lawyer, who was appointed some kind of land commissioner by President Taylor, and held some other office that he lost when the War of 1812 was on. Asked if he was opposed to the war with Mexico he said, 'No, by God, I oppose no wars. I opposed one war and it ruined me and henceforth I am for

War, Pestilence and Famine.' I wouldn't say a nation can go crazy, but we do know when the storm wind of war comes blowing, many people say and do crazy and cruel things they would never do in the days of peace." At the words "crazy and cruel" the voice had dropped and faltered and he was looking Marvel level in the eye.

In his father's eyes Marvel caught a late-sunset-ember brown and at the inner circle of it a hint of seamist and the unfathomable.

The surprises came, the unpredictable events riding high and wide that year in the field of politics. Crash followed crash as old and buttressed walls fell down, as old and timeworn bastions slid away.

"Who would have believed it, and now what?" cried many an onlooker, as though a Doomsday trumpet had sounded, when late in April the solid and formidable Democratic party, the party of Jefferson and Jackson, the party entrenched in control at Washington, this party was torn in two, split wide open, with delegates from Southern states walking out in a secession from the party's national convention at Charleston, in a revolt against nominating Douglas for President, in a protest against the party's failure to approve of slavery extension. Their orator Yancey of Alabama, his voice of velvet and flame, had said:

"We came here with one great purpose . . . to save our constitutional rights. . . . We are in the minority, as we have been taunted. . . . In the progress of civilization, the Northwest has grown up from an infant in swaddling clothes into the free proportions of a giant people. We therefore, as the minority, take the rights, the mission, and the position of the minority. . . . The proposition you make would bankrupt us of the South. Ours is the property invaded—ours the interests at stake. . . . You would make a great seething caldron of passion and crime if you were able to consummate your measures. . . . When I was a schoolboy in the Northern states, abolitionists were pelted with rotten eggs. But now this band of abolitionists has spread and grown into three bands—the Black Republicans, the Free-Soilers, and squatter-sovereignty [Douglas] men—all representing the common sentiment that slavery is wrong." Then they had walked out.

Never before had they walked out. It was no custom or habit. There was no book of rules to tell what to do about it. So the convention adjourned to meet again in Baltimore in June while the seceders met and held their own convention that decided it too would adjourn to Baltimore in June.

Then in convention in May met the Republican party, new and young, only four years old, composed of enthusiasts and zealots at one extreme and at the other of politicians seeking victory, offices, contracts, practical favors. In Chicago at Lake and Market streets, in the new barnlike lumber affair named the Wigwam, holding five hundred delegates and ten thousand spectators, with some thirty thousand

866

strangers and visitors to Chicago milling around outside and trying to get in—there the champing snorting new party came up with a platform saying nothing in particular against slavery except that it ought not to be allowed to spread. Then came the naming of a candidate for President of the United States. The predictions and the betting for months had favored Seward of New York. Shrewd men who knew their way around telegraphed home, wired to New York and Cincinnati, to Boston and Washington, that it was Seward for sure on the first or second ballot, nothing else to it. The first ballot came. Seward led big, with not quite enough. The second ballot came. Seward was losing. For a long time he had been too far out front with his faults made known and his party enemies many. The dark horse, his faults and failings not known and his enemies few, the dark horse was gaining on him. The third ballot came. The dark horse, the newcomer, the runner unknown to national fame till two years ago, passed Seward by a big lead, so much so that the convention made unanimous the nomination of Abraham Lincoln for President. A Griggsville man came home telling neighbors he never heard the like of the noise made by the Lincoln shouters before the balloting began. "They packed the place and they sounded like a thousand stuck pigs and I don't know how many whooping Indians and crazy steamboat whistles."

The unexpected, the unknown, a country lawyer up at Springfield, Illinois, nominated for President of the United States, two years a Congressman and that was all—never a governor, never a United States Senator, no experience at touching and handling that immense machine called the Federal Government at Washington—what would *he* do if elected? What would he say now? What speeches would he make about what he would do?

The months went by and he said nothing. Or rather, what little he did say amounted to his saying he had already said enough. They could go to his speech at Cooper Union in New York the past winter, to his debates with Douglas, many thousands of words, plenty and enough for those who wished to know where he stood or didn't stand. "Excuse me, you know my position," would about summarize his campaign speeches, his answers to letter-writers.

In Baltimore the broken sections of the Democratic party held their conventions in June, sort of looking in on each other to see what was doing, a few of the quiet-footed on both sides meeting for hushed conversations on whether anything could be done. Douglas sent messages he didn't want the nomination for President if it was going to split the party. Some who believed Douglas didn't mean it were sure no other man than Douglas had a chance to win. The Southern seceders of course had washed their hands of Douglas and didn't care. Discussions, in hope of unity, failed. A professor, a man of learning, a Greek scholar, had three sons, one favoring the South and the other two the North, and he wrote to the Southern son quoting the historian

867

Thucydides on the Greek nation split in two before the Peloponnesian War. "The Greeks," wrote Thucydides, "did not understand each other any longer, though they spoke the same language; words received a different meaning in different parts."

The Northern Democrats could deny and deny they were out to rule and bankrupt the South and the men around Yancey of Alabama and Gaulden of Georgia couldn't make sense of what they heard. The Northern Democrats nominated Douglas of Illinois for President with a running mate from Georgia, Herschel V. Johnson. The Southern Democrats nominated John C. Breckinridge of Kentucky for President and for a running mate reached as far north as you please, up into the new West-coast State of Oregon, naming United States Senator Joseph Lane. Douglas stepped out. North and South he spoke. On the point Omri had mentioned to Marvel, the question that Lincoln and Douglas in their debates had kept away from, the question of what the Federal Government should do if or when states seceded from the Union, on this Douglas stepped out bold, clear. He lost old supporters and won fresh haters in the South, and he won Union men to him in the North by saying, in about so many words, that the next President of the United States should meet attempts to break up the Union by calling for troops to put down treason.

Season moved into season and there was dry weather and rainfall. Earth and sky had the same speech and interchange as any other year. The political storm, anxiety and wrath in the hearts of men, could not be read in the sky. Over the crops planted in the spring, corn growing tall across summer, came the same bend of the kindly and familiar blue sky. Rod, with two other men, arrived at Atlas in mid-July with a herd of cattle from Texas, Arkansas and Missouri.

He was sunburned, his wavy black hair grown long and tumbled, a little under his regular weight of a hundred and eighty pounds, hard and lean. He kept watch over the locations and feeding of the cattle for market, riding to the house two or three times daily, when he could, to see Mibs, to be near her, to laugh with her, when she was in a light mood, about what was to come in August. They had their own big room at the end of the house and of evenings they brought out the two guitars they now preferred to the banjos, though there were times when a certain impetuous hammering gaiety called for the banjos. The guitar could better decorate and stress the lines and phrases, promises and allegations, of the extravagant song Mibs called for often—

> Ever of thee I'm fondly dreaming,
> Thy gentle voice my spirit can cheer,
> Thou wert the star so mildly beaming,
> Shone o'er my path when all was dark and drear.

Still in my heart thy form I cherish,
Every kind thought like a bird flies to thee;
Ah!—Never, till life and memory perish,
Can I forget how dear thou art to me.
Morn, noon and night, where'er I may be—
Fondly I'm dreaming ever of thee.

"If you really think about it, that's a long time," Mibs said. "Never, till life and memory perish."

"Only as long as I live, my girl," Rod breezed.

"And you cherish my form now? When I stick out in front so we can't really hold each other for a waltz?"

"Yes, and isn't it going to be nice to have around a little form I can cherish holding it in my two hands?" And he spread his open palms the length of a fresh-born baby. "I will love it as God's kiss."

"Give me that," said Mibs. "Say it again." They had been to a camp meeting and heard a preacher. "He's got the power," Rod said and Rod remembered part of the preaching and liked to repeat it for Mibs. "It's good for us in this time, this summer." And he gave it as she asked:

"We hain't all got the same cross—oh, no! Thar's no two jes like no more than our eyes or noses. The same pattern wouldn't fit us all, but thar's nary rale child of God but has his cross made a purpose fer him and no other. And let him love it as God's kiss, not endurin it a-whinin, and grudgin, an a-draggin it 'long in the dust. Let him bear it proudly, as a soldier carries his gun, and tenderly, as the lover holds the rosebud given by his sweetheart.

"The Lord will say, 'What's your cross, stranger?' And when you show him the battered old thing he'll answer, 'All right,' and turn to an angel and say, 'Angel, give this brother or this sister a crown.' And, bretheren, the heavier, the crookeder, the uglier the cross, jes so much brighter'll be the crown. Pr'aps 'twas a thorny cross, tearin your flesh, and spotted with your blood. Well, every blood drop'll turn to a costly jewel in your splendid crown, and will shine like the sun while you dance in silver slippers above. So you see you must endure it to the end. You can't get shet of it fornenst a steep hill or a deep river. You'd a heap better never teched it if you don't endure clear to the end."

And Mibs carried the tune and Rod sang alto to "In the Bright Mohawk Valley" verses:

"From this valley they say you are going . . .
Do not hasten to bid me adieu,
But remember the bright Mohawk Valley
And the girl who has loved you so true."

They had a group of favorite songs they had begun singing those first flaming days in New Era and they had by now worked out their duo parts to fine points. Omri told them the first week in August, half-joking but more in truth, "You two wind yourselves around each other singing like you do when you waltz."

"That's good for a woman to hear when she's not in waltzing trim," laughed Mibs.

They asked Omri if it would help that the mother and father were agreed the baby must be a boy. Omri said, "I think wishing helps and I make all my wishes it's a boy," adding for good measure, "and to have its mother's chestnut hair and changing dangerous eyes and its father's mouth and jaw."

Rod told of a boy witness in court in Missouri, asked about his parents and saying he had none, "I'm just a camp-meeting baby." Omri then recalled the Reverend Christopher Toppan in Newburyport, Massachusetts, how a man and his wife presented to him a child for baptism. The minister, while performing the rite, incidentally informed the congregation, "Not having confidence in the man's sincerity, I baptize this child wholly on the woman's account."

On leaving, Omri was deeply moved, more so than ever, at what he saw between Rod and Mibs, a clairvoyance of lovers there, likeness in gravity and mirth. In a brief chat with Rod's mother he said, "There ought to be a law against such happiness as those two people have."

"What's wrong with great happiness?"

"When it's too perfect they're not prepared for the time they can't have it."

"That's bosh, Mr. Winwold, and you know it. Great happiness can't bring future harm."

"You're right, Mrs. Wayman. I'd like to see happiness like theirs last forever and I was wriggling around about it."

Rod was helping the men put in a fence of Osage-orange hedge when he was called one afternoon in late August. It was Brock on a sorrel pony, riding down a lane and cutting across a meadow on a fast lope, calling as he came near, "Rod, you got to come up to the house, they want you." Hearing it the second time Rod ran to his black mare, leaped into the saddle and made the house about even with Brock.

At the house, though, there was nothing Rod could do. In the room with Mibs were a doctor and nurse, and Rod's mother. For a time Rod sat in the big living room and shut his eyes and clenched his hands as the screams came from his wife. He had never heard her scream unless in fun or mimicry. She had been sick and in pain once or twice, he could remember, and always found a way to joke about it or forget it. They had agreed they heard too much complaining about personal miseries and it was no help to recite aches and glooms constantly. Now she screamed. There was a lift and an abandon to her screams. Or again they were long wavering high-pitched moans. Rod went out on the front porch and sank in a chair. He wondered how long the screams had been going on, how long they could last, what they might mean. Then came a series of low sobs, hushed moans scarcely reaching his ears, they were such soft quavers. He first thought she had grown weaker and was worn, her strength spent. Then his hands loosened a clench they were in. A grim smile came to his mouth with the lips pressed hard to each other. His lips parted to half-groan in joy, "I can't be wrong about my Mibs. She's made a fight and she's won it and glad she won it."

Ten minutes later his mother took him in where he saw Mibs and her face whiter than the pillowcase. Her eyes slowly opened to look straight into his as though on opening they couldn't have met any other eyes. Her right arm turned over with the palm up for him to say nothing for now except in the touch and hold of their two hands. He let it go at that. He couldn't think of words and no more could she. Then after this little message of the hands they let him peep into the cradle at a bundle neatly wrapped and his eyes got only the red raw impudent mouth and nose of the newcomer.

"A boy," came the clear whisper of his mother. And he went out and got his fourteen-foot blacksnake whip and whirled it and whanged it at anything and at nothing.

A week later, when Mibs had finished nursing the baby and laid it in the cradle and wiped the milk off its chin, she stood erect to her full height, bent her head and looked down at the little one closing its eyes in sleep. Rod came in, said nothing and joined Mibs in gazing down at the raw pink body, on this sweltering August day wearing only a diaper. "Know what it is?" said Mibs.

Rod lifted his eyebrows, glanced down. "A dream of a shadow."

"Yes," said Mibs, "or a dream of a shadow of smoke."

"A wisp, a bubble, a leaf," said Rod.

"And so are we all," she agreed. And he repeated in agreement with her, "And so are we all."

"And he's God's kiss," Rod remembered.

"We'll keep to that like we said. We'll love him as God's kiss to us."

At the christening, as the sprinkled ritual water fell on his head, his name was pronounced to be Clayborn Joel Wayman. The first name was after a brother of Rod's mother and the second for Mibs' father.

. In September came the wedding of Brock Wayman and Cedora Winwold. It was a merry event, held outdoors at a pioneer picnic where old men with cracked voices forgathered before the younglings. One of the hoary and venerable ones, bald and toothless, needing for support the crooked blackthorn stick in his right hand, spoke to the crowd in a voice that went shrill on him when he was afraid the younglings wouldn't get the picture. "Pike County now's got more'n seven thousand inhabitants. When I came to what is now Pike County she didn't have seven inhabitants. If they didn't speak to each other twas cause they lived so fur apart. Later was seventy inhabitants and you could drive a day or two thout seein a cabin or a wagon. I lived fifty years without a nightshirt and when my daughters give me

871

one for Christmas I didn't know what to do with it. I'm alive, you can see that, but I've quit kickin." They loved him. They cheered him. A few didn't hold back from printing a kiss on his withered and furrowed cheeks.

The marriage of Brock and Cedora drew the Waymans and Winwolds closer. Omri deeded the hundred-acre piece of land to the couple. For the time, for another year at least, the couple would live with Brock's folks because Brock now knew the run of the Wayman farm better than anyone else.

The march of the seasons went on. The leaves turned yellow and rusty, turned brown and gold, fell and scattered before wind, rain, frost. The same as any other year the leaves did this. And not the same as any other year, and not at all like any autumn before, the drama of politics was played out act by act with players and audience wondering and troubled over what next. For the first time the South had, in effect, one solid monolithic party and any rival of it unthinkable. In the North the race was between Douglas and Lincoln. One of the two would be the next President. For the first time the Republican party marched in immense torchlight processions of citizens and voters with a new organization, the Wide-Awakes, young men uniformed and drilled, young men supposed to be wide-awake and ready for possible danger not mentioned.

The standing corn had mostly been husked, the last of the leaves blown away from ash and maple, oak and sycamore, when in November the American voter spoke. Marvel rode in and was at hand when the postmaster gave out the first newspapers printing the election count. Marvel glanced over them, made a fast ride home, and read the figures to his father and others. Lincoln was elected. His vote in round numbers, of 1,800,000, gave him nearly a half-million more than Douglas. Ten Southern states reported no vote, not a single ballot cast, for Lincoln. In a total of 4,700,000 votes the other candidates combined had nearly a million more votes than Lincoln. "We'll hear," said Omri, "that Lincoln got only a plurality and not a majority of votes. We'll hear that he's a sectional man elected by sectional votes. Which he is."

The snowfalls came that winter about like any other. Out of the same sky fell the snow and over the same land lay hushed in quiet or went whirling and wind-driven about the same as any other winter. Yet to Omri Winwold and to Mibs Wayman it wasn't the same snow and the winter had no likeness to any other they had known. The news came. Week by week it came. As by clockwork, as by signals and arrangements, the mechanism was sprung with its coils and recoils prepared. State by state seceded. State by state in the South called up troops, laid out money for guns and supplies, took over forts, ships, mints and other properties of the Federal Government.

Omri was in some degree afraid of himself. "The war has begun," he said to himself. "The war is here. The shooting will begin soon after the new President is sworn in." He would say this and then wonder why he didn't hear others saying it. For the first time he couldn't talk freely with Mibs. If her talk drifted in that direction, he wouldn't go along with it. She was hearing so often that there would be no war, and she herself had such dread of a war that she had gotten into the habit of mildly agreeing with what she heard. She surprised Omri one day with the information that Brock and Cedora had several times pleasantly argued, with no hard feelings, against Rod. Brock and Cedora had decided between them that the South was both right and wrong and the North was both right and wrong and they were not taking sides. Rod seemed to be having more "say-nothing days," as Mibs called them. "And they weigh on him heavier," said Mibs. Omri could see that under the Wayman roof all were more sensitive as to current events, the drift of the country. They might be having turmoils like his own, he admitted to himself, saying little or nothing of anxieties that continuously gimleted deeper.

Mibs told Omri of one day when about all she heard from Rod was "Last night I was going to ask father, 'Do you still think there'll be no war?' and instead I asked myself, 'What happens when you try to pat a porcupine?' " Then Rod let out an uproarious laugh, a ringing and rollicking laugh. "He shut off the laugh, choked it off, and his face turned solemn sudden as you'd chop the head off a chicken," said Mibs. And Omri saw they had troubles, as persons, as individuals, troubles each was fated to carry alone.

"There are burdens and crosses you have to carry yourself," said Mibs to Omri. "They're your own and no one else can get under them with you. You stagger and groan by yourself and it's terribly personal, just like each of us has secrets no one else can ever know, can ever understand." Her wide red lips drew back showing the line of smooth even white teeth and the mouth ends moved into a rather comic down-pull. "How could Rod ever come to understand Hornsby Meadows? You don't know Hornsby, but sometime my mother will visit here and she'll tell you about him. Rod is sure the best thing to do about Hornsby is to kill him and cover the carcass right off. It is his secret why he would kill Hornsby, it is my secret why I would let Hornsby live."

Omri believed he saw the bonds between Rod and Mibs over months striking deeper roots. It looked so good to him that twice on riding over to see them he said to himself, "I will glue my most suspicious eyes on them. I'll be cold as a pawnbroker, skeptical as a horse-trader, mean as an Erie Canal gambler." And he peered aloof and slit-eyed at them, listened for hidden motives and implications in their tones and shadings of speech, relentless as a cross-examining lawyer hunting traps for a witness. And Omri came away a little ashamed of himself. They had talked crops, cattle, various cattle feeds, a new hogpen, how and why you could be serious and solemn with a guitar better than a banjo, the gossip about the rival Republican-party factions pulling wires to get offices from the new Administration in Washington next March. They had brought out the squirming red-faced Clayborn Joel Wayman and had their quiet jokes about Rod a couple of times helping Mibs wash and hang out Clayborn's diapers, Rod saying it was a trifle of a chore for a man who had washed his shirt two years in California, "once a month whether it needed it or not." Omri saw them having a dark reverence for each other and he wondered what would come of it and caught himself speaking little prayers that it would last.

On this visit Omri had seen his stepdaughter Cedora, Anne's girl, with her husband Brock Wayman. He was pleased to see them healthy, contented, somewhat assured and satisfied with themselves and the world in general. The unrest of Rod and Mibs, the mystery, the ascents into mirth and mimicry, the poignant moments of music falling with endless shadows, of these Brock and Cedora had little. Omri could read them as having satisfactions in their not being as restless, uncertain, sort of groping, out of the ordinary run of people, as Rod and Mibs. When they heard Rod sing "Ever of Thee I'm Fondly Dreaming," it was not an oath but rather "a lot of fancy words" to Brock and to merry Cedora "extra-big promises for sure." They had their suspicions, didn't quite gather the mock pomposity of Rod asking Mibs, "What is the difference between an attempted homicide and a hog butchery?" and Mibs' mock pompous answer, "One is an assault with attempt to kill and the other is a kill with attempt to salt." Brock preferred Rod's rambling anecdote of a druggist at Pittsfield serving a short overweight farmer who had gone out the door, and another customer saying of the farmer that he was kind of roly-poly, and the druggist, "Stick a pin in him and he squirts fat for three miles."

A newly arrived settler called himself a Christadelphian and after a discussion nearly all agreed the word meant "a brother of Christ," though Brock with a pleasant foxy smile said, "Why can't we just let him be a Christadelphian without knowing what it means?"

* * * * * * * * * *

Chapter 29

* * * * * * * * * *

Despair, Drink, Poems and a Prayer

IN the last week of February 1861 Henry Flack, in the second-floor office of his three-story building where he conducted his wholesale and retail grocery and dry-goods business, sat facing the pigeonholes of his large walnut desk, filing letters, bills, invoices. He heard someone come through the open door and heard the footsteps pause alongside his chair. He finished reading a lengthy invoice, put it in its proper pigeon-hole, then turned his round owl face and popeyes up toward whoever it was had come. Then his jug-shaped body shot upward from the chair and his thick calloused fingers were giving a warm handshake as he said, "Omri, good to see you, over a year since you been in St. Louis." He smelled liquor on Omri, whose face had a variety of puzzles on it. "Got your business done?" said Flack.

"Yes, Henry, now I'm starting on my *real* business."

"Like what?"

"I'm going to get drunk."

"What for?"

"You can drink till you forget. Then when you sober up and begin to remember you can drink again and forget."

"You just drinkin by yourself, Omri?"

"I might take on a woman to get drunk with me. Got the address of a damn sweet woman last time I saw her said, 'Come see me.' "

Flack said it was a busy day, dinner at noon with other merchants to discuss why trade was slow, no confidence in the business world, and a full afternoon on inventories.

"You can have supper at my house tonight. Or come along any time tonight." Flack dug a hand into one of his pockets. "If you don't get tied up with a woman and if you're sober enough to find your way, here's the key to the house." Henry sat down, wrote on a card, stood up and put the card in the inside pocket of Omri's overcoat. "That's the address. If you forget it, tell any hack-driver it's in your inside pocket." His eyes went up and down over Omri. "Don't get too drunk, my friend. Just enough to feel good. Not so much you forget but just enough so you don't remember."

Omri walked a few blocks along brick sidewalks with a bare spit of snow on them, in a sunshine that straggled thin and hazy from between gray clouds. He stopped to watch and listen to the driver of a load of hay. In a rut about one foot deep among the cobblestones, the front left wheel got locked. The driver sat high on top of the tall hayload with a long blacksnake whip he swung on the mule team. As he swung the whip, Omri heard him, "Git up, you sonsabitches, you goddam sonsabitches." Omri stood watching and listening. What he heard from the teamster's mouth was the same thing over and over again. He hoped there would be a break in the monotony. He walked away, sorry for the teamster, for he had heard mule-drivers who could vary the monotony of what they had to say to the mules.

Omri walked on to the address, one of a row of narrow two-story brick houses, and at this house curtains down at all front windows on both floors. He knocked and no one came and he knocked again louder. The door opened and a woman in a loose pink gown, curlpapers or pins holding her hair tight to her head, the hair having a bleached light that went with a bleach on her face, looked at Omri with large inquiring wary eyes. Omri asked for Miss Annabell Ponder.

"She don't live here any more."

"She gave me this address."

"She's gone, I'm telling you."

"Gone far?"

"So far she'll never come back here and I wouldn't tell you where she is, she wouldn't want me to tell you, she wouldn't want you to know."

"She gave me this address and said come see me."

"She wouldn't say that now and you better leave Miss Ponder be."

"Not for a five-dollar bill you wouldn't tell?"

"No."

"Not for a ten-dollar bill?"

"Not for a million dollars, mister."

"Is it good news or bad about her?"

"Not so good, not so bad, I ain't sayin."

"You ever to see her?"

"Might be."

"Well, when you see her you tell her the man with the red whiskers, she called 'em purty red lilacs when she ran her fingers through 'em, tell her he was here and he sent her his best regards, that's all."

"I'll tell her, mister."

Omri handed her a silver dollar. She took it, saying, "And listen, mister."

"I'm hearin every word."

"Can I tell her you'll never bother her?"

"Sure, when I'm a friend, I'm a *good* friend."

"All right, you run along with you, mister, I'll tell her."

There had been one interruption. A well-dressed man in polished boots, a long stylish overcoat, a white-brimmed hat and a shoe-brush beard had got out of a hack, and the woman at the door smiled. "You want Miss Brimley?" The man nodded with a low-spoken "Yes." She had opened the door for him, saying, "I'll call her in a minute."

Omri walked down the street, turned a corner and walked a few blocks to find himself alongside a team of mules with a hayload and the same driver up on top with a satisfied face. Omri nodded smiling to the man, who nodded with a quick grin. He had seen Omri watching him when he was stuck and his quick grin now meant, "You've heard me sing."

Omri walked on to the Planters' Hotel. At the bar he had two brandy smashes and a whisky cocktail. He walked into the lobby and met Henry Flack, who said, "I don't want to be short with you, Omri, but this meeting here in a side room, I have to go to it. Trade is slack and getting worse. It's my business to talk it over with them."

Omri bought an armful of newspapers, went into the dining room of the Planters', ordered a steak dinner and ate it with draught beer and a bottle of porter. He opened his newspapers and rambled through them. President-elect Lincoln was on his way to Washington, making vague speeches here and there, rumors from some quarters he would never be inaugurated. The *New York Tribune* and its editor Horace Greeley had asked what was the use of a Union of States "pinned together by bayonets," and saying as to the seceded states, "Let the erring sisters depart in peace." That sounded like the Waymans. There would be no war and the South would go out of the Union with the best wishes of Greeley and others who didn't care for a Union "pinned together by bayonets." At the same time the *New York Herald* and its editor James Gordon Bennett had said in a long editorial and forty ways that Lincoln ought to resign, that Lincoln ought to know he was a second-rate man and by resigning he could let Congress choose some man of experience and competence who would know what to do. Omri dropped the papers on the floor, saying, "They don't make me feel I ought not to get drunk. They make me want to forget or at least not remember, like Henry said."

At the bar he had another brandy smash, put his foot on the brass rail, straightened the slouch hat on his head, rearranged the wide black bow tie in his wide linen shirt collar, ran his hand around his curve of whiskers, said to the bartender, "You don't s'pose anybody will take me for a Congressman?"

"You never can tell, there's a lot of different-lookin Congressmen. You can't tell one by the cut of his jib."

He saw two men meet at the bar and heard them in slang greetings of the day, the first one, "Pull down your vest," and the other, "Wipe that egg off your chin."

Midafternoon Omri found himself in a large saloon, Hipple's Concert Room, listening to singers and watching dancers in short skirts. He drank Monongahela straight with two blowsy women whose faces he found empty and their talk more so. He paid for the drinks, with a half-dollar to each of the women, and went to a side room that had been pointed out to him by a furtive whispering long-faced pale youth. The youth was at the door of the side room and Omri paid him the twenty-five-cent admission and with six or eight other men watched a woman on a table dance the cancan in a black skirt that covered her lower middle. The furtive young man then told the little audience, sort of special and confidential, that the little lady would next dance the cancan "completely disrobed," and for those to whom this might not be clear he added, "Not a stitch on her." He added further, "You can stay and see it for a half-dollar."

Omri watched the naked woman on the table go through steps, high kicks and mild wiggles, and found himself muttering, "Let the erring sisters depart in peace—like hell they will." He found he couldn't see the nude dancer for the newspapers he had read. He went out and sat alone at a table and drank more Monongahela straight. A compactly built young fellow with shifty eyes, a drooping mouth and a partly broken nose, sidled next to him and said, "If you're interested I can take you to a couple of classy ladies. You can take your pick of 'em or stay with both of 'em long as you want." Omri gazed without a word into the face before him. Omri was going to say, "I'd clean forgot there are pimps in this world. Away back on the Erie Canal I saw a few and I clean forgot that where there are women who sell themselves there are men who share." From the face before him came the words, "They're classy, they got style." The face floated away as Omri grunted, "I'm fixed for today."

Omri finished his drink and went out on the street. The fresh air tasted good. It was getting colder, a bright sun shining from a clear sky. He turned up his overcoat collar, buttoned the top button, put on his yellow buckskin gloves, and walked block after block at an easy saunter. The faces passed him, laughing faces ready for fun, serious mouths and eyes on serious errands, a rare and sudden face sacred with both peace and sorrow, evil faces with slants of cunning, smug and satisfied faces that seemed to have been copied from still other copies of smug and satisfied faces, empty faces staring at nothing and going nowhere, unfinished faces waiting for what was to happen to them and hoping it would be good, late afternoon sunfall on the human stream of faces.

Omri went into a reverie as he walked, as the float of faces and voices passed him, and he was going to ask a corner policeman, "Where are all these people going?" and then changed his mind. He walked on past Bill Morissey's place and went into the Straight Ticket saloon, found it rather empty. A woman at a table told him the crowd didn't begin coming till seven or eight o'clock. On a close second look at her face he asked her if she wasn't one of the four dancing girls he had seen in black tights and black slippers last year. She was. Now there were six of them, she said, and they would come on at eight o'clock in pink tights and golden slippers. She joined Omri in two whisky sours. She gave him quick flip answers to nearly every question he asked. "I just want to be sociable and you think I'm nosy, I s'pose," said Omri. And she flipped, "You're all nosy, never yet saw a man wasn't." She gave a laugh meant to be gay but it was hard, reckless, bitter. Omri had heard a laugh like it from Bee. He ordered a third drink for her, thanked her for her company, heard her, "The same to you and many of 'em," and went out.

In Morissey's Omri ate oyster pie with black coffee, walked eight or ten blocks passing dark store fronts between the gas lamps on street corners, taking a look up to see if the evening stars were out, which they were, seeing faces more furtive and scurrying than they had been in the afternoon. He strolled back, keeping a hand in his right overcoat pocket as though he might have a weapon with which to meet any of the thieves who liked the nighttime along this street. He went into the Possum Trot, spoke to a man at a table having a stein of beer, wiping the foam off the black droop of his mustache, his face and Prince Albert coat looking more battered and worn than when last year Omri had seen him playing the Chickering piano for the dancing rivermen and their women.

"Sit down and join us," said one of two women at the table, with a nod toward the pianist. "Professor Montgomery will begin playing soon." Omri ordered drinks, the Professor taking beer and saying his doctor had warned him against hard liquor. The women and Omri took hot rum with brandy and a touch of lemon. The Professor sat empty-faced. The two women put on a brightness that for Omri faded the more he looked at it. They were overly agreeable. They threw out remarks about Omri being just the kind of a prosperous farmer that needed a good time in the city and they could show it to him.

"They can see I'm a wee bit come-you-so," said Omri to himself, "and it's a hundred to one they'd like to get me to a room where a few more and I'd be a jackroll." The Professor had begun to work on the piano. Omri went around in a waltz apiece with the women. He told the women he was a Peoria gambler and a reform wave had hit the town and he was seeing what he could do in St. Louis till Peoria opened up again. He asked them what they had heard about the Peoria boy who came home from St. Louis with a diamond ring and when the home folks told him it wasn't "genooine" the boy said, "If that diamond ain't genooine then I've been skun out of seventy-five cents." They liked this.

"You're a hell of a farmer," said one of them. He lifted a warning forefinger, "Be good girls now," stepped out of the Possum Trot, walked around the block breathing deep of the cold night air and taking one look at overhead evening stars that rebuked him, and came back into the Straight Ticket for two whisky cocktails as he watched six jaded women in pink tights and golden slippers going through drab attempts at being light and fantastic on their feet.

"You're alone." She spoke the word "alone" as though he should know better than to be alone when he could have her company. Her chubby painted face had sags in it, blue pouches under her watery brown eyes and a pathetic violence in the dye of her extremely auburn hair. "A strawberry blonde," said Omri pleasantly to her as she seated herself, saying to himself, "She will tell me she's more to be pitied than censured." Omri asked what he should order. She asked what he was having.

"Straight Ticket whisky with a short beer."

"I'll have the same."

"I'm aimin to get drunk. Are you with me?"

"Not stone-blind drunk, do you mean?"

"No, just how-come-you-so."

"I'll go you how-come-you-so," and with a laugh meant to be merrily mischievous and an open palm pushed toward him, "but not stone-blind, sir."

At the first Straight Ticket with short beer she had covered her aristocratic birth and childhood in Louisville, her two years of convent schooling, her debut, her dayboo, the blooded horses her father kept in the Blue Grass region and the sweepstakes they had won. At the second Straight Ticket with short beer she wouldn't tell the family name, not for the world, it being so well known and distinguished a name. She had language. On her own, no slang, no profanity.

"You speak a chaste Addisonian English," Omri said, his tongue stumbling a little on "Addisonian." The reply came, "I am not as chaste as I once was, but I sank you for compliment." Omri's mumbled and polite return to this was "And I sank you, madam, I sank you." At the third Straight Ticket with a dwarf beer she recited in a diction derived from *Ivanhoe* how she had married, against her father's wishes, a handsome devil of a race-track gambler whom her father had unmasked as an ex-convict, her father declaring that unless she divorced this interloper he would cut her off in his will and bid her never again darken his doorsill, Omri mumbling, to show he was listening, "doorshill doorshill." They were divorced with the fourth Straight Ticket and diminutive beer and her second husband was a rich lawyer who took up with another woman, a low and despicable woman, Omri murmuring, "deshdubble." She drove him out of the house at the point of a revolver and he won a divorce, with no alimony to her, on the ground she was an irresponsible woman of violent temper. With the fifth drink came her third husband, a drunkard who beat her.

Omri had casually noticed the six dancers in pink tights bow and fade and a heavy woman in black crinoline and a bodice cut very low at her bosom toiling in a treacherous soprano through two famous opera arias, followed by a comedian who was exploding in Dutch-dialect stories. Omri blinked his eyes at moments when the one comedian seemed to be several comedians bobbing and weaving in a blur. And on her reaching the third husband, Omri rose slowly from the table. "My wife shpecksh me, Strawberry." He laid a five-dollar bill in her hand. "Besht regards, Strawberry." And he went out.

He walked straight, with no lurch, past Morissey's to the corner, and no hack in sight. A feathery snow was falling, big lonesome flakes that fell softly on the brick sidewalk under the street lamp. Out of a near alley came two men with a policeman between them and five or six onlookers. Under the street lamp the policeman gave each of the two fighters an inspection. One had a bloody nose and a red blotch over the left eye. The other had a cut lip and a right eye partly closed. The policeman seemed to know them. "This is the second time in a year I ketch you fellows fightin." He had them promise that the next time he could arrest them. They went their ways. Omri asked one of the party how the fight started. "Same as the first time. The one with the cut lip he calls the one with the bloody nose a sonofabitch and the one with the bloody nose he calls the one with the cut lip an abolitionist and they have it back and forth sonofabitch and abolitionist till first thing you know they're fightin and right while they're fightin they go on gruntin and hissin sonofabitch and abolitionist."

In front of Morissey's two couples were getting out of a hack. Omri got the hack, wasn't sure he remembered the address of Henry Flack, dug into his overcoat pocket for the paper Henry had put there in the morning, and read it to the hackman. As the hack rolled over the cobblestones Omri wrangled his hand under overcoat and coat to his vest pocket for his watch, for the gold chain running from the watch and fastened in a vest buttonhole. As they passed a corner with two street lamps Omri pulled the watch toward his eyes and found he would have to stoop much lower to read the dial. He bent shoulders and head low and lower till his eyes made out the slim Roman numerals saying it was ten minutes to midnight. A bump and a lurch of the hack, catching him off balance, sent him sprawling with his face flat on the leather of the opposite seat. He pushed, wriggled and scrambled back to his first position, his fingers following the gold chain to the dangling watch at the end, which he slowly slid back into its customary vest pocket. He spoke confidentially to hear himself saying, "I got drunk all right. Wouldn't been thrown like that cept I was drunk."

Out of the hack at Flack's address, he paid his fare, watched the hack wheels glide away in a thin mud over frozen ground. Inside the gate, standing on the gravel walk, he saw against a lighted window the large airy and lonesome snowflakes. It was a light snow, the flakes few, wavering and hesitant about coming down, Omri gazing at them and muttering, "Few and far between like angels in human form." He walked the gravel path between leafless lilac and rose bushes. Up the steps and at the door with fumbling he found the bell-cord handle and pulled it. He would use the key given him if nobody answered. He heard footsteps in a hallway, the wide oak door opened and Henry Flack saying, "Omri, it's good to see you, you look sober. Come in and hang up your hat."

Omri walked in, threw his hat five or six feet so it caught on a hall-rack hook. Henry grinned. "A man can do that is sober." Henry went on, as he took Omri's arm and went down the hall a few steps, "We waited up for you, Omri, my wife said we must wait up for you."

There wasn't time for Omri to say he didn't know there was a wife and his first dim flash was whether by chance or possibility Bee was around the corner, in which case he would prefer to be stone-blind drunk. The door was open and they turned into the room where Omri's first glance took in one wall of the room lined with bookshelves filled with books. His next glance caught a massive rosewood center table, not unlike a pulpit, and on it an immense Bible with heavy leather covers and thick shining metal clasps. Farther beyond and toward a corner stood a tall straight-backed chair with wide armrests, the black wood spotted with brass-stud designs in circles and triangles. Out of this chair a woman had slowly risen. As Henry walked arm in arm with Omri toward her, he said, "Sure I got a wife, Omri," and as they stood before her, "Meet Mrs. Flack."

Omri had glimpsed her crinoline gown, a flowing bell-shape giving an impression of immensity in size yet light and airy in the hang and placement of it. Brief, too, was his glimpse of her bodice, with a first impression it was a daring low-necked affair coming below the upper curves of her breasts. Brief, too, was his momentary amazement that this was a close-fitted arrangement of some fascinating white fabric that clad her smoothly with its surface blending in a small collar that vanished somewhere in the white skin of her neck. It was later Omri said to himself, "Suddenly when you were going to feed on how voluptuous she was, there she stood ascetic as a nun in a coif."

Her hand was out to him. They shook hands. They held their hands together longer and warmer than for an ordinary handshake. She was saying, "Yes, I said we must wait up for you." Her violet eyes were larger than he remembered them. Her mouth, not tiny, was a cherry mouth, a well-rounded crimson cherry. The arrangement of her black hair gathered well over both ears gave a frame of dignity to her face. A small brooch with a garnet spoke of sunset-flame dusk in her hair.

"Henry tell you my business today?"

She had not smiled and she answered now with her grave cherry mouth, "Yes."

"I tell Annabell everything," said Henry.

"Henry is a good man." She had nodded her head toward Henry. "Henry is worth having for a friend." The cherry mouth was very grave with a hint of tremor on the lips, a faint quaver in the voice overheard rather than heard.

She pointed to chairs for Omri and Henry and seated herself in the tall black brass-studded chair. Henry moved a commodious lounging chair alongside her, placed another one opposite the two for Omri.

Omri was restless, not yet sober, his mind not yet working clear, surprise and amazement near to shock running along his bones, overtones in the air that had him baffled, that by paradox sobered him yet added to a loose and reckless tipsiness. He sank in the chair offered him. He ran his hand along the curve of his muffler beard. He ran his fingers through tangled thickets of the brick-dust hair that came down and covered half his ears. Henry sank deeper in his chair for a more comfortable slouch. Henry straightened up. "I can bring you a drink, Omri, if you want." Annabell spoke. "Or we could offer you some tender cold roast pork we had for supper and coffee with it if you like."

Henry went to the kitchen. Annabell sat grave, composed, as though

882

she were part of the tall fixed immobile chair. Omri sat with his brain in turmoil, not knowing what part of the turmoil to bring out for her. A minute or two before Henry came in with a tray, Annabell spoke three words and Omri replied with four.

"You remembered me." It came low-toned yet deep-spoken.

"I dreamed of you." He spoke matter-of-factly. The fact was enough. The matter had import. He saw the smooth black lines of her eyebrows rise and her violet eyes held ever so little a smile while the rich rounded cherry mouth kept the same cool gravity.

From the tray Henry set on a low table between them, Omri ate a cut of the tender pork with a slice of buttered bread and took two cups of black coffee. Henry and Annabell ate lightly for old acquaintance' sake and drank half a cup of coffee apiece. Omri put questions so Henry kept going on trade being slack, on the merchants' dinner meeting at noon bringing out nothing practical, on the hard work with inventories through the afternoon, on how St. Louis would always lead Chicago in everything.

Omri rose from his chair. He walked the width of the room, with fleeting side glances into the faces of Annabell and Henry. Would he pour out some of the turmoil of his mind now? What else could he do? The silence in the air had inanity, hung meaningless. He would break it and look at the pieces. Part of the time he walked eight or ten steps back and forth in his talk or again he stood before them and looked at them, often being held longer by the inquiry and wonder in the eyes of Annabell.

"Why did I come to St. Louis to get drunk?" As he rambled on in his answer, it took on a quality of mockery from the very nature of it and an element of fantasy out of his knowing very well he was still drunk and it was a long series of drinks and a wide variety of liquors he had put away after the first whiskies he had with breakfast that morning and the hot rum and brandy smash he had stopped for on his way to Henry's office.

"Why did I come to St. Louis to get drunk? Because first of all my friends and neighbors at home, should they see me drunk they would say, 'He wanted to get drunk and therefore he is drunk and there is no importance to his being drunk and it was not thinking that brought him to drinking and he is merely one more drinking fool, one more besotted tippler who may yet become a broken fool with a big red nose, a beet-colored beak for an insignia, a bulging encrimsoned nose hung on his face for a warning of the doom that comes to topers, a choice and fiery organ of smell that misled him to the redeye, to the demon's essence of corn, to the distilled extract of corn that has the curses and the mocking laughter of the Devil himself in the lure of its amber light dancing through the glass of the bottle. Yes,' they would say, 'nothing of portent or significance attaches to what he pours through a hole in his face and of a certainty twas not thinking that brought him to drinking.'

"Therefore I came to St. Louis to do my drinking. Nor would I declare that here in St. Louis they say, 'Ah, he is drinking and therefore he is thinking.' Rather am I well aware that in St. Louis they say, 'Ah, he is drinking and whether he has reasons to drink or no reasons, we will go about our errands and let him drink, reasons or no reasons.' Should I have told the bartenders my reasons for drinking, they would have listened with courtesy as do all bartenders and believed me one more of the distraught and befuddled who stand with one foot on a brass rail and deliver their vacant minds while the bartender wipes the drip from the mahogany bar and asks what the next will be. Therefore I kept a worthy silence before the bartenders and they respected my silence as I did theirs.

"To you, Annabell, and to you, Henry, my dear friends, to you I can say a thousand years ago it was that a Turk was brought before the Sultan for speaking in disrespect of the Government. And the Sultan informed him that at sunrise the ax of the government headsman would neatly and officially lop off his head. He bargained with the Sultan, saying, 'Your official palace baboon speaks only French and English, but give me a year and I will teach him to speak Turkish so you can understand him. Will it not be an advantage to you to have a baboon who can take what the French and English say and translate it for your ears into your own dear familiar Turkish speech?' The Sultan twirled and twiddled the slick black mustache that reached near to his ears like two streaks of blackstrap molasses and said with a voice out of a cistern, 'And if you fail?' The man promised, 'If I fail you may stick long splinters of kindling wood into my naked body and set them afire and burn me to a crisp.' The Sultan said, 'It is a bargain and you have a year to teach the baboon to speak Turkish so I can understand what he says.' A friend said to the man, 'Why have you invited yourself to a slow and horrible death?' The man said, 'I have three chances. In a year either the baboon will die or the Sultan will die or I will die.'

"Now you, my good friends Annabell and Henry, may ask why I have introduced this ancient and grisly anecdote of life among the Moslems. And I can only reply this month of February 1861 that I wish to God I could think that the American Union of States had two or three chances as good for its life. I have put to myself the pertinent inquiry whether I am making a cheese of myself. I have directed to myself the interrogatory whether my speech and actions bear resemblance to the pathos of a blind dog in a butcher shop.

"I had one small tremulous dream that came to me in the dark of the moon and in that dream I saw five virgins, and they stood knee-deep in a snowdrift and they mocked at me for moaning to myself, 'Am I my brother's keeper?' And they went away and I came awake and I was repeating a sermon I heard twenty years ago and the preacher took for his text the sentence, 'She was pure and her chaste bosom was filled with snow,' and he vociferated on the purity and expostulated on the chastity of the woman and the desire grew in me that he would discourse and expound on the probability that there are different kinds of purity and many varieties of chastity. Yet the hour grew into two hours and when he had finished, we, his hearers, were like him in our ignorance of the essence of purity and the quality, in addition to the mere negative one of abstinence and denial, that constitutes true chastity. He thundered it at us, 'She was pure and her chaste bosom filled with snow,' till the suspicion crept over me and became a certainty that, in some slight and nameless degree, she was *afraid* of the snow, that there were moments she was shaken with fright and wouldn't dare look out from her window at a soft and dreamy snowfall beckoning her to come out and be tested in the actual realities of snow. To that preacher purity and chastity were abstractions, tumbling from his mouth like the word 'liberty' we hear from the orators North and South. The South will go to war for its ideal of liberty and the North will slay and burn and fight for its idea of liberty. And neither understands what the other means by liberty. I came to St. Louis to get drunk to see whether drunk I would know more about liberty than sober.

"While drinking I have been thinking and one thought is there are too many of the leaders of the people sick with their own shilly-shally, sick with their own pride, sick over property, and they have no slightest glimmering of the fact that they are sick and their sickness is a form of delusion and insanity and their sick desires will bring the war.

"They toss the word 'liberty' back and forth. They pound the word 'liberty' as though it were a pulpit. They squeeze the word 'liberty' as though the harder it is squeezed the more it will yield of some unknown substance. They blow it full of air as they would a bladder and the more air it holds, the more there is of liberty. They bawl the word 'liberty' open-mouthed and the louder the bawling and the wider the open mouth the greater their attestation of the holiness of liberty and what they know about it.

"In this regard, I wish again to refer to Moslem lore, to Hadji the Hacha. He walked up the high winding stairs in his robes of white silk and in the pulpit with his hands laid in reverence on the Koran spoke to the congregation, 'O true believers, do you know what I am going to say to you?' The congregation answered, 'No.' And they heard Hadji the Hacha, 'Then truly there is no use in my speaking to you.' And he walked down the high winding stairway in his white silk robes. On a later day they saw him walk up the high winding stairway and facing the congregation, 'O true believers, do you know what I am going to say to you?' The congregation responded in one voice, 'We know, we know.' Then they heard Hadji the Hacha, 'Truly, since you know, why should I take the trouble of telling you?' And they saw him go down the high winding stairs in his white robes of shining silk. Then for the last time he came to preach and the congregation had made preparations for him. He faced them from the pulpit and asked again the same question, 'O true believers, do you know what I am going to say to you?' From the congregation came shouts and cries, 'Some of us know, and some of us do not know.' And Hadji the Hacha waited till the silence was beyond question, a quiet in which you could hear only an imaginary pin drop on a theoretical floor. And Hadji the Hacha said, 'It is well in the sight of Allah, O true believers, that some of you know what I am going to say to you and some of you do not. Truly, therefore, *let those who know tell those who do not know.*'

"What is the lesson of this ancient fable? Well it would be, sweet and fine it would be, if in our country today we could sift out those who know and have them tell it to those who do not know. That would be a spectacle of impressive grandeur. Not yet however can we go out and pick those who know from those who do not know. I could go over St. Louis or to Chicago and walk the streets like Diogenes holding a lantern up in the face of this man and that man, asking him, 'Are you one of those who know or one of those who do not know?' And the police would take me to the lockup and the newspapers would say, 'Police are still trying to fathom the mystery of the lunatic who has been going around poking a lantern in people's faces and asking, 'Are you one of those who know or one of those who do not know?'

"The men of books, the learned men, the educated men North and South, they have all had a hand in the making of the war. It is up in the realm of conflicting ideas that the preparations have been laid for years. The half-stupid men of the educated classes, they are to blame. The completely stupid man, he is blameless. Look at him. Gaze on him. There he is and he has the same ideas from year to year and they are the same ideas he has had all his life. All the powers above the earth and under it cannot put a new idea in his head. There he is, the completely stupid man, and I sing his praises. His skull will resist the most powerful gimlets that come to drill a new idea in him. But the half-stupid man, educated at the seats of learning, what can we do with him when he reads the books and does not know, and worse yet does not know that he knows not?"

When Omri had begun these spills of utterance, which he said were intended to explain if possible why he had come to St. Louis to get drunk, he would have puzzled the shrewdest of bartenders as to how many drinks he had had. He had seen a cattleman in high boots and sombrero, swaying like a lilac bush in a light wind, ask the Planters' Hotel bartender, "Am I drunk, bartender, am I drunk?" And the bartender, cold and impassive, went on polishing a rare small goblet used only for an old Dutch Guiana rum. "I might swear to it but I wouldn't bet on it."

Whatever of lush and voluble barroom manner there was in the be-

886

ginning had vanished. Omri knew it. The woman in the tall black chair, his listener, she knew it. She had sat awake, alive, her torso and erect shoulders never moving, her violet eyes following him and her face turning slightly at such few times as his steps took him the width of the room.

Henry had, somewhere in Omri's discourse, closed his eyes and fallen asleep. Omri had half-expected to hear snores from Henry. There was something about Henry's popeyes and loose mouth that had given Omri the impression that any moment the mouth would fall open and there would begin the curious unorganized concerto of a saw progressing through wood and meeting unexpected knots. Omri was mistaken. Henry didn't have a loose mouth. He sat fairly erect with his head slumped to one side, his mouth closed, his breathing even and regular. With a little forefinger sweep toward Henry, Omri said, "He had a hard long day of it."

The violet eyes peered into his, the head nodded just by the narrow fraction that could be taken for a nod. He knew her to be aware he was intoxicated in the realm of ideas, that his hard massive well-knit and smooth-moving body carried a seeker groping and questing. He was strictly enough sober yet he couldn't keep cool, couldn't keep from being somewhat dizzy gazing at the human scene where city streets and country roads soon were to hear crashing drums and crying bugles. He wasn't looking at her, his eyes ranged from one of her white hands to the other on the armrests and up to a triangle of brass studs above her hair and a circle of brass just beyond the garnet. She closed her eyes midway of his saying:

"Each time is a time of its own and the time before and the time after can never know any other than its own.

"Each time has its own hopes, visions and illusions, its own plans, follies and vanities, and the time before and the time after can never know them as its own.

"Each time has its own heroes and martyrs yet often they are not known as heroic or martyred till another and later time.

"Each time has its own proud fools and not until another and sad later time is their pride measured and the mad inanity of their folly understood.

"Each time has its plain people and humble folk, lacking both the guile and the desire to lay false exactions upon others, asking only a fair chance, and across the generations they speak to each other, for they are the same in all times, the plain people and the humble folk."

Her wide violet eyes had come slowly open. He could see a momentary flicker of her black eyelashes. He knew her to be aware that whatever it was he was saying, whatever sense it might make in recalling it next week, it was in his blood and bones, haunted him, and it had cost him to work it out for himself.

887

He took out his watch. "Five past one." He stepped toward her, held the watch close to her eyes, saw her face with her eyes near to it.

"A half-hour and we go to our sleep. Tomorrow afternoon I go home. When I see you again, if ever, the storm will be blowing." He moved away from her. "Brother against brother, blood up to the bridles of the horses, rats gnawing cadavers the sun has rotted in dry grass."

He went on. "I say I must shake myself loose from it. I walk a river-front street in St. Louis and I speak a psalm of riches any man can have for the taking. The gold of tawny feathers fallen from afternoon ashes of the sun wheeling into sundown—I gather such gold. I pick such feathers. I watch the wheel of that sun. I follow that fall into sundown."

She was murmuring, almost unheard, "The gold of tawny skyfeathers, I caught some once, it was a dust I streaked over my hair and people said I looked funny." It was nearly as though she hadn't spoken. She saw a twist come over the width of his gargoyle mouth and a liquid light in his deep-set brown eyes as he was saying, "I instruct myself with nonsense. I meet a drunken wharf rat who has slept in the rain under a board sidewalk and he is a member and I am a member with him when he speaks his psalm 'Slong me bedoodle. Flibtwist my crawdad. And I shall meet you hongworbed, lamooshed.'"

"I walk past the cathedral and look up at the bells—"

"Six big bells," came a murmur from the tall chair.

"Six bells, with marvels of punctuation. I look up at them and I walk on and instruct myself with ancient wisdom: Better leave undone the act requiring haste. Let it lay. Be shallow. Be deep. Let it lay. Be slow and deliberate. What is fated for you will come to your hands unsought, unasked, like weather and rainwinds. Take your time. The leaves do, the roots do, the long strong oak branches do."

He reached for his watch, looked at her and then at the calm sleeping Henry with his head tilted sidewise on a broad shoulder, then back to her face with a moment of memory that once he had said it came and went before his eyes as a sunlit black-and-gold pansy coming out of a raindrench. He looked at the watch, put it in the vest pocket, and went on. "Time is to give us lessons. Time, for those who wait and listen, always accommodates. Time will not fail us. Time will be sure to tell us what we ought to have done that we didn't do. And beyond time looms eternity. Over the triple doors of a cathedral in Italy three inscriptions span the arches. Over one with a carved wreath of roses and over one with a sculptured cross you read 'All that which pleases is but for a moment.' Underneath the great central entrance to the main aisle they carved 'That only is important which is eternal.'"

Omri seated himself. She heard him talking low to himself and for her to hear too. "She lets me pour it out. Blood and ashes, roses and potatoes, flamingoes and wharf rats, she lets me pour it out." He reached to an inside coat pocket, brought out two small sheets of paper.

"Antiques, you sit in a chair two or three hundred years old. Here are sentences older than the dark chair you sit in." He read:

"Woe unto him who believes nothing.
Always the impossible happens.
God works in moments.
For a web begun God sends a thread.
Nothing happens for nothing.
Everything has belonged to others and in time returns to others.
The glutted understand little of the hungry.
Many a famous prince has at last been put to bed with a dusty shovel.
We are born crying, live complaining, die disappointed.
When the heart is full of lust the mouth is full of lies.
The praise of self gives forth a stench.
Wait long enough and the most evil gossip dies.
No one so long he must not stretch, no one so short he must not bend.
Habit is a shirt we wear till death.
Either a man or a woman may say Yes shaking the head sidewise or No shaking the head up and down.
Even a great river's glory ends at the sea.
The morning mist goes and life goes.
The moon waxes, the moon wanes, the world goes by and life goes by."

Omri looked up. She was stone-still, the mouth and eyes utterly grave. From the mouth came a murmur. "Old as the hills. I like 'em. Jawbones drying in the sun. Blue smoke and bird feathers." She saw Omri hesitating with the second small sheet of paper. "Read it. Read on." He explained, "I haven't looked at it since I wrote it after the second brandy smash this morning." He glanced over his shoulder to the elaborate chandelier of glass pendants that covered two burning gas jets. He turned to the paper and read once, and at her "Read it again" a second time the lines

> "Pour from the sea
> one hand of salt.
> Take from a star
> one finger of mist.
> Pick from a heart
> one cry of silver.
>
> "Let be, give over
> to the ease of gongs,
> to the might of gongs.
>
> "Share with the flamewon,
> choose from your thorns,
> for God to be near you,
> for God to be witness."

The even murmur came, "Please make a copy for me." Omri rose from his chair to find his glance meet the open and wide-awake eyes of Henry, who smiled. It was the only smile the room had seen at this midnight party. Henry smiled. "Kind of prayer meeting we're having, Omri?"

"I'm going to pray, Henry," and turning to her, "I'm going to pray, Annabell, and then we will go to our sleep. Why shouldn't I pray? There's no law against praying. And sometimes it helps." He looked down at his plain gray suit. "Suppose I had a black broadcloth coat to my knees. And my hair, instead of every way for Sunday, as they say, was combed down proper. And I was a preacher standing before a big congregation in one of the fashionable churches where the silk rustles when the women come down the aisles. How would I pray? I don't know, for sure. I think maybe I would pray something like this." And he stepped back, interlaced the fingers of his two hands, letting the arms hang loose, gave a slight upward lift of his face, and most of the time keeping his eyes closed, he began his prayer. His lips seemed to carve and chisel at some of the words and phrases, dwelling and lingering on them as though they had further meanings than his voice could give them. His prayer came:

"Thou, O Lord of Hosts, Thou who watchest over us in the noon sun at meridian and again in the still midnight and the first flush of dawn, Thou whose identifying prints are on the faces one and all we meet in streets and houses, in barns and in open fields and meadows, help us to chasten our hearts and be humble before all that meets us visible to our eyes in the domain of matter, and all that comes to us invisible in the dominions of the mind.

"Thou hast in earlier times gathered a proud people and broken their pride and swept them in a whirlwind as burnt stubble in the wind. Grant that our people have Thy mercy and are not to be given the uttermost of fiery trial ending in destruction. Give us storm for chastening and leave us still with the bright dream of wider freedom for all human strugglers.

"Into Thy ken it has come, jesters have declared it, that ever Thou watchest with a special Providence over children, drunkards, and the United States of America, and in Thy indulgence and wisdom Thou knowest it was spoken as a prayer to Thee rather than as babbling of idle wit.

"Thy decree went forth long ago that on good land in a fair year the planted corn shall ripen and the shocks stand waiting for the huskers to strip the ears and gather the harvest, that likewise grapes shall ripen and the purple bunches be flung over-measured in baskets, that likewise wool shall thicken on the valley sheep for the spring shearing, that everywhere the same sun moves to shine over the same Family of Man and brings at evening

890

the same spread of stars over that same Family, and that likewise Thou hast made it so in Ohio and China, in Michigan and Russia, in the Carolinas and in England, in Massachusetts and in Bavaria.

"Everywhere among the habitations of man and the familiars of the earth Thou hast written they shall know meanings of frost and rain, the miracle of sprouting seed and potato-blossom promise and the laughing harvest wagons, the music of leaves in tremulous talk with the morning wind, the mystery of storm and dream entering the soul of man with songs born to die and be reborn.

"Of the seven deadly sins Thou hast, O Lord, made pride the first and deadliest, wherefore first of all we ask Thee to teach us the requirements and needs of the humble. We ask it in Christ's name. Amen."

Omri stood silent a while. His eyes turned toward the tall chair. She sat silent and fixed as a bell of bronze. He glanced to Henry's face and saw him sober, puzzled, a shade of tenderness there. He took Henry by the hand and raised him from the chair. "You have been kind to me, Henry, when I needed it. I told Annabell I'm leaving St. Louis tomorrow and I'll be long gone, long gone." He stepped to Annabell, took her hand from an armrest and held it to his lips, turned from her, and, "Now show me to my room, Henry."

He saw Annabell move and stand as a bell-shape with a half-torso and head risen from the crinoline cavern and a coif white at her neck and shoulders. She bowed her head. "Thank you, Mr. Winwold. It was good." Again Omri flashed to a memory that humbled him. In this room he had waltzed with her and they were both tipsy and he fell and got a cut on the head that sobered him. He was going to make a joke of it now and mention it and point at her and say, "She always sobers me, Henry." And he held back, thinking this was no night for such a joke. He bowed his head to her. And somehow it seemed all right to him that during the evening neither of them had once smiled to the other.

Henry lighted a small kerosene lamp, went up the hall stairs with Omri and showed him his room, with one of Henry's nightshirts hung over a chair. "Anything else of mine around you're welcome to, Omri," and pointing under the bed with a laugh, "A thundermug, if you're caught short." Henry was at the door and turned at Omri's call, "Wait, come back." And Omri whispered, "Any word from out West, San Francisco?" Henry wagged his head. "No news, not a word. She must be dead by this time the way she was going it."

Henry turned away, came back, and in a whisper, with a nod toward the hall, "Ain't she something, my wife?"

"She's a wonder."

"And she's straight, I'll be goddamned if she ain't straight, not a

891

crook in her. Did she tell you about," and Henry hesitated, "did she tell you we joined the church?"

"No."

"Yes, we're both good Catholics now. We go regular. We like it, keeps us steady." And Henry smiled. "I know when to kneel now better than that Sunday you and me went. She was born and raised in it, knows the rigamarole better than I do, but I'm learning it. Twelve-year-old boy she had when she was eighteen, he's kind of sickly and we got him in a school where he's improving. She was married to a shyster lawyer in Chicago. He mistreated her and ran away from her and was killed in a gambling fight in Denver. She came here to St. Louis to find a brother and sister but the sister had died and the brother gone West somewhere nobody knew. And she had hard times."

Henry had led Omri to the corner of the room farthest from the door. Omri saw a light he believed hardly short of ecstasy on Henry's face as the man was saying, "She's strong, Omri, a tough wiry body. And before we're through we'll have five or six little ones hollerin up and down the stairs and halls. You'll come to see them, my old friend, won't you?"

"I'll come when it's two, when it's four, when it's six, the even numbers," and Omri smiled for the first time in this visit to this house. At the door he said, "Good night, Henry, and God bless you."

Sleep came slow to Omri's eyes. He had aches that rang and split and rang again in his head. "Inevitable payment received," he moaned to his pillow, "for excellent inexorable liquor overused by an inexperienced glutton." Yet there was ease in benedictions he sensed floating around the house. Before finally falling into sleep he promised himself that if the same quick dream kept recurring to him as the last time he slept in this house, the face in the hack window would be to him lovelier than ever, but the fingers at the cherry mouth, instead of throwing him kisses, would be holding an open palm of a hand pushed toward him, and the words, instead of "Take my address, come see me," would be "Hands off, stay away."

Vague flutters of dream and memory ran in his sleep. He had come tipsy to a house where he saw a young woman's face that smote him with adoration and he had said to her, "You have New Testament verses on your face and the azure of a cool summer sky in your eyes." And a rebuke she gave him that night sobered him. Again he saw a woman who was a relic with bygones scrawled over her face and she was in a strait jacket and asking him, "*Why* did I do it?" Again he was riding in a wagon along the Erie Canal and the night stars clear and a drunken woman on the wagon seat putting herself to sleep with a mumble song, "Drunk as a fiddler's bitch, yeanh drunk as a *blind* fiddler's bitch and you knocked him down drunk, him dumb cold and him drunk." There came drifting the picture of a woman in a bright new funny hat smiling at him with depths of affection in her eyes and his snarling, "You think it's purty, you look like a half-wit in it," and he awoke from this shuddering, with hands clenched. Later in a soothing dreaminess he tasted the salt of tears at a brave woman voice, "It will be sweet to die, Omri, when the time comes." And at his bedside, near by, and more like a living voice, came the words, "Please make a copy for me." He was awake and restless. He got out of bed, lighted a lamp, wrapped a blanket around him, and with his newly patented Indelible Pencil, writing a violet tint, he copied the lines ending

> Share with the flamewon,
> choose from your thorns,
> for God to be near you,
> for God to be witness.

With his head on the pillow again, stray moments of the past day and night kept coming back. Henry jerking a thumb toward the woman, "Ain't she purty, Omri?" And the answer, "She's a wonder." And again another moment, Henry tilting his head toward her, "Ain't she beautiful, Omri?" And again the answer, "She's a wonder." The cold slit-mouth of the bartender when the drunk asked if he was drunk, "I might swear to it but I wouldn't bet on it." Two travelers from the Ozarks, one telling of two men in a fight over a girl, the first blow struck after the casual remark, "I say, stranger, do you make purtensions to this gal?" The other had heard of a cabin where the mother called, "Look out there, Sal, you're standin on a coal of fire," and then, "Which foot, Ma?" And his friend Henry, jug-shaped, owl-faced, with the eyes of a wall-eyed pike, who in this house had once killed a man over a woman, who in this house had been slashed with a knife by a madwoman, Henry could be swift, quicker in action than expected. "Simple, rugged, honest," said Omri, "he isn't what's wrong with the country. I'm going to pray with him there'll be five or six little ones hollerin up and down the stairs and halls of this house." The aches that rang and split and rang again in his head, they were slowing down. He repeated sentences that eased him. . . . "Thou whose identifying prints are on the faces one and all we meet in streets and houses, in barns and in open fields and meadows, help us to chasten our hearts and be humble . . . everywhere the same sun moves to shine over the same Family of Man and brings at evening the same spread of stars over that same Family, and likewise Thou hast made it so in Ohio and China, in Michigan and Russia, in the Carolinas and in England, and in Massachusetts and in Bavaria . . . the mystery of storm and dream entering the soul of man with songs born to die and be reborn." He fell into deep refreshing sleep.

The morning sun ranged high and slanted through a window, a zig-zag box of flimmering yellow light on the blue Turkish carpet. His watch said ten o'clock. He was out of bed, poured from a small pitcher of green glass two tumblers of drinking water his dry raw throat welcomed. He poured from the porcelain pitcher into the porcelain bowl, doused his face in it, washed his hands and neck with soap and water, emptied the bowl, poured a second for rinsing himself, dried with a long white linen towel, dressed in a hurry, and then walked down the stairs taking his time, the most deliberate man in St. Louis, he said, adding, "Unless it might be that wharf rat I saw yesterday who says 'Slong me bedoodle.' "

He went along the hall and the door of the big living room opened and Annabell stood there, in a black gown with a slight hoop-skirt effect, a large blue satin bow at her neck, her hair as the night before but without the garnet. She bowed to him, put out her hand, they shook hands lightly, and she said, "You slept well, that's good."

Neither of them smiled. She led him to the breakfast table. As last time the same free Negro woman brought in the food and he asked about the one who had been in the kitchen, the slave woman earning and saving to buy her freedom. "Came last Christmas," said Annabell, "she needed exactly sixty dollars more to buy herself free. Henry gave her the sixty Christmas morning before we went to early Mass."

Annabell sipped at black coffee while Omri put away a bowl of corn mush with cream, two fried eggs and a crisp pork chop, an apple strudel and two cups of coffee. He could see she was on guard. He could read that she wanted barriers between him and her and she had hope, perhaps even faith, that he understood why.

"Henry told me about your boy at school."

"A spindling, one time had what the doctor called rickets. I couldn't give him the time I wanted to. Now I want to make up for it."

"What's his name?"

"Edward Joshua Ponder. We call him Josh."

"I ask so if ever I meet him."

"You'd be good for him."

"Jesus, last night was a beautiful night."

"You can't have a night like last night but once in a lifetime."

"It was you said to wait up for me."

"I was eaten with curiosity about what you looked like."

"And now you've seen me you want me to get out of here and be quick."

"Yes." She said no more, took a last sip of black coffee, and they went to a parlor fronting the house, with a large bay window hung with blue plush draperies. She pulled aside the draperies of the large center window and the morning sun flooded in.

They stood in this bright sunpour. Her right sleeve had touched his left once. She was keeping to her barriers. Omri wondered what he would have done if she had given him one inviting smile or a touch of an insinuating hand. He recalled Henry's words of last night, "a tough wiry body." Swift she had been, and definitely tough and wiry, the time he was putting her in a hack and she made a leap in the air, and her hands tightened at the back of his neck and brought his head and face down to meet her mouth. Now she spoke, with her two hands in a tight clutch almost to her chin, with eyes she wanted to look cold though Omri could see them burning.

"Do you know, sir, we have to be careful? Do you know you go out of here to stay out, never come back, never again?"

"I knew it last night the first look."

"Henry Flack, he's an honest man in business. You know they're not common." The words rushed from her tongue. "He says he worships the ground I walk on. The way he backs it up, no humbug, no bogus, eighteen-carat. He's got terrible strength. He can kiss without slobbering. I don't want to lose him. You're the only man for a minute could make me think of running away from him. You know what that means?"

"I keep off the premises. I make myself scarce. I vamoose, like they say, and make it a permanent vamoose."

"Exactly."

Omri's hands hung in front of him with the fingers interlaced as in the prayer the night before. "Jesus, last night was a beautiful night." And he added, "A night of holiness I'd call it."

Her clutched hands swung back and forth under her chin and the words tumbled and rushed. "You get me like nobody ever came along. It's a feeling. I can't help I've got it. I like your smooth warm mess of whiskers, your ugly kind face, and your big catfish mouth and the way you can talk, and I could lay my head on your shoulder and cry and cry and you've got to get out of here and never come back."

"I dreamed of you."

"How did it go?"

"Your face in a hack window, five mouths and every mouth your mouth, a round red-cherry mouth, and your white fingers touching the lips and then thrown straight at me, over and over."

"No dream at all. Only remembering what happened." Then in a choked voice, near to a sob, "Oh God, Omri Winwold, you got to go."

He turned to go. She walked to the hall with him, helped him into his overcoat, handed him his hat, with a whispered moan, "Oh Lord, I hate to see you go."

"Last night I promised Henry I'd come back three more times. We named the dates I was to come back."

"When? How do you mean?"

"Henry says there'll be two, four, six little ones hollerin up and down the stairs here. I told him I'd come back after the second, the fourth, the sixth, the even numbers."

"Come back after the first one and watch me nursing it." Her eyes were dancing, her arms flung wide apart, and her smile had a thousand pent-up smiles. She made a leap that had her hands tight clasped at the back of his neck and his arms held her and their mouths met in a long wild kiss. He let her down to the floor. She picked up his hat, stood on her toes, gave a little jump and put it on his head. She was saying with a rich smile, her arm in his, as they went to the door, "Go now, go now, it's time."

She stood in the open doorway. They both drank the air of a cold sunny day. He was saying, "You'll remember two things I'm telling you now?"

"I'll keep them and wear them like two secret precious garnets in my hair."

"Remember I said when I come again there'll be an awful storm blowing and a million houses will have on the front doorknob a bloody thumbprint."

"Yes."

"And I'm saying I know you trust me and it's beautiful you trust me the way you do and you're one of the loveliest blossoms God ever dropped on the earth."

"Go now, go now."

She watched him along the gravel path between the lilac and rose bushes, heard his boots crunching the gravel, saw him turn on the sidewalk and fade without looking back.

PART FOUR

Chapter 30

When Conflict Broke

EARLY in the morning Rodney Wayman and Nack J. Doss had laughed and chuckled with others to see a lone woman bring into camp seven enemy soldiers. A revolver in each hand she had marched her prisoners ahead of her near a mile. Yesterday nine in Union blue had taken over and slept the night on her front-room carpet, ordered breakfast, eaten corncakes and fried ham she set before them. Muskets, revolvers, haversacks, they had thrown around the front room. The nine who sat at her kitchen table suddenly heard her in the doorway with two six-shooters, "Up your hands, I'll shoot any man don't!" One sprang toward her, she pulled the trigger, he reeled and fell. A second yelling, "You bitch!" plunged on and fell with a bullet through the neck. The seven with hands up saw her for sure a wild woman and a dead shot. With no looking back they walked as she commanded. Short, stanchly built, broad-shouldered with thick muscular arms, she stood mute in the camp laughter and glee. Some read the mute shapely mouth in her round face as one time having laughter, cheeks with dimples. Her lips now stiff and relentless, her light-gray eyes hard, she packed her grief in few words. Her husband had gone to town with two sons, to see them enlist and march away. "He got into an argument about the war, a fight with knives, and he killed a man. I didn't see him again till I step out the back door in the morning. There he hung from an apple tree, a rope around his neck." She walked away, her lips still stiff and relentless.

Rodney Wayman and Nack J. Doss rode out of the camp, wearing farmer clothes, boots and hats.

"War changes people, hey, Nack?"

"Before she laid eyes on her man dangled from an apple tree she couldn't uh pulled trigger to kill a man."

"What if one of 'em had got the gun away from her?"

"They'd have laid her."

"She'd have fought 'em tooth and claw."

"And they'd have taken their way with her."

"Hell of a breakfast, wasn't it?"

"She returned their hospitality, you might say."

They rode in a sultry air under a hot sun, turned in at a brick farmhouse for water, knocked at the front door to speak thanks for the water and ask for information. A woman and her two daughters came out and met the question, "Confederate or Union?" The mother answered, "Both." A widow, two sons in the Confederate Army, one in the Union Army, and a fourth hiding in the mountains to keep out of either army, she pointed to an eighteen-year-old daughter, "Confederate," to a twenty-year-old daughter, "Union." She fingered a curling ringlet at her right temple. "I've gone old and gray about it." She turned to the girls, "They might like to see the flags." The girls went into the house to come out, one unfurling the Stars and Stripes, the other the Stars and Bars.

The two scouts rode away, "to feel out the sentiment of the people," report enlistments, locate small enemy detachments rumored on the move.

They had, one day of that week, turned their horses off the road into a shallow creek lined with underbrush and thickets. On one side lay a level cornfield, on the other a slope of orchard and pasture with a farmhouse, barns and sheds at the ridge. They stopped at an open grassy piece of ground, watered the horses and tethered them for grazing, ate corncake and cold fried ham. Nack started washing his shirt in the creek. Rod went away saying, "I might come back with a hat full of peaches."

Nack worried two hours, had the horses saddled and ready to go when Rod came out of underbrush, dusty and sweating, clothes torn and hat gone. He was biting into a luscious peach when down the slope from the farmhouse he saw a horse and rider coming straight toward him. He set on the ground his hat half-filled with peaches—and waited. The rider slid off her horse and faced him, two upper teeth missing in the wide queer grin she gave him, her small eyes peering at him with a peculiar squeezed look. "A big powerful woman, big breasts and fine curving hips, and a face that would stop a clock." She was saying, "Come up to the house yonder. We got better than those," pointing to the hat, "peach brandy my father made." She added, "You're Rebel, of course, I'm s'pos'n you're Rebel." He said yes, he was Rebel. She led her horse and they walked to the house. Her father brought homemade peach brandy and she set out roast lamb, boiled cabbage, boiled potatoes with gravy, coffee. Their talk often disconnected, jumped from one thing to another. Rod had finished, said he must be going to his horse down the roadside, "Got a long ride ahead of me."

The young woman brought out a big revolver and pointed it. "You sure have got a long ride ahead. I'm taking you to the Union Army lines." The father shook a bony finger at him and with a cleaving shriek, "You Rebs hung my boy week afore last. You strung him up cause he was goin to 'list Union." They took his two revolvers out of the holsters, marched him to the barn, had him mount a barebacked slab sided horse, roped his legs and feet tight under the horse's belly.

The young woman on her mount ordered her prisoner to ride a little ahead. Two miles or so by a backwoods trail, branches hitting their faces, they came to a stream where Rod begged her for a drink of water.

She untied him. He leaned over the cool water running clear over gravel. And this was the first time he dared reach his hand into his shirt bosom for a small revolver he always carried there. His hand touched the butt of it as he turned his head to see her eyes on him and her revolver pointed at him. A swift sidewise roll to his body, the back of his head on gravel, running water to his ears, he pulled trigger and sent a bullet into her arm that dropped her revolver he snatched in a hurry. She fell to the ground, raised herself to sit up moaning with pain, rolling up her sleeve to where blood oozed over the pink flesh.

"I didn't want to do it, I had to," Rod said three times as he washed her wound, bandaged it with his handkerchief and told her it was soon healing. Pleased enough with his care, once for a moment she gave him her wide queer grin and the peculiar squeezed look of her small eyes. In telling it he said, "I wouldn't have minded being near her fine big figure if it wasn't for her face." He commanded her, "Now you ride the crowbait." He tied her feet and legs together under the horse. They rode back the trail. He sent her through the open gate and saw her father come rushing out on a side porch crying to her. He galloped past the creek where he had turned in hours before and around a curve of the road to the cornfield end. There he got off the horse, turned it to-ward the farmhouse, knicked it in the belly, yelled for it to go, and dashed into the cornfield.

The two scouts moved for a night camp farther up the creek. Under starlight Rod found his hat of peaches, turned for a final look at a dim light from the farmhouse window, soberly grunted, "By God, I don't know whether to laugh or cry."

The talk of these two men, riding lonely roads of Tennessee in 1861, ran often to failed expectations. March and April they expected no war, sure it couldn't last long if it came. "Three months and it's over." Now after five months Kentucky and Missouri still didn't secede, their state governments taken over by Unionists. And this Tennessee, where they rode their horses, scouting, was split wide-open, the mountains and valleys of East Tennessee lighted with Union bonfires, Confeder-ate journals now telling their readers what to do with any man talking Union: hang him. They met wagons of poor bedraggled families driv-ing overland, hoping to reach Cincinnati and escape the noosed rope or torch at work in East and middle Tennessee. A Confederate general at Memphis, organizing "to invade Kentucky," might want the two scouts in the forefront of his army.

Rod and Nack looked back on green days, the funny first days of the war. Could they forget those women and girls crowding the sidewalks, the depot throngs of women and girls with flowers and smiles, Testa-ments and handkerchiefs? That fellow kissing his girl good-by, arm out from a car window and his hand holding hers, then tears in her eyes and a big flashing smile as the train moved and her cry, "Oh, you'll come back. You're too homely to get shot"; on the train a woman in a fury, ready to claw a guard's face, "I'm going through that door if I have to kill you," and the guard, "Are you a man in woman's clothes?" her saying No and, as he let her in, "I'll be damned if I'll fight a woman or be killed by one"; the chevalier lawyer commanding a company, "Fall in, gentlemen, please fall in with as little delay as possible"; the clergyman commissioned captain, drilling his troops, "By the grace of God, right wheel, march!"; the colonel's wife who pitied the rain-soaked picket on guard duty, saying, "I know it's his duty, but, dear, couldn't you at least let him have an umbrella?"; the drafted man who wrote in his personal description, "one leg too short," the next man writing, "both legs too short"; the conscript writing, "I am entirely dependent on my mother for support," an officer informing him, "We'll relieve your mother of that responsibility." These matters were now of the green days, the funny first days.

Back in uniform six days and nights on a cavalry dash up into Kentucky they slept only in snatches, never out of their clothes. They dozed in the saddle, Rod once brushed out of his saddle by a tree branch in his face. The sun one morning hadn't as yet melted the frost on grass and stubble when they met on a curve of country road the first horsemen of an enemy troop. They fired at each other, saw men drop from saddles, one horse falling dead. The main fight then followed in a village two miles away. After twenty minutes of shooting and saber work they rode out of the village by the road they came, without the enemy following, leaving seven dead and more wounded and captured.

Rod came through without a scratch, Nack getting a bullet through his hat, one coat button cut away by a lead ball, and nearly knocked out of his saddle by a saber cut into the flesh of the shoulder. Two miles from where the fighting began, they dismounted and Rod took off Nack's coat and shirt, washed the wound with canteen water and gave it a makeshift bandage, helped Nack in the saddle, was about mounting himself, when he noticed the body of the first man fallen that morning. Over the face and shoulders lay the head of a horse. He ran a halter around the horse's neck, and pulling with all his strength, he managed to haul the horse head off the face and shoulders. Two holes in the coat, one over the heart, he saw death had come to this youth on the instant. The face wore a look of peace, the wavy brown hair parted and falling down the forehead about as combed that morning. Only the open eyes were disturbing. The white eyeballs stared, not glassy and cold, light-blue eyes staring in surprise at the blue sky. Nack called they must be going. Rod thrust a hand under the upper bullet hole in the coat and brought out an ambrotype case, bullet-nicked in one corner.

They rode away and two days later, toward evening, twenty miles away made camp for the night. Loyal friends, with two sons in the service, lived in a farmhouse a quarter-mile away. Those with light wounds there found warm water, clean linen for bandages, ointments, various simple medicines, the best of food. The farmer, his wife and two daughters, four Negroes, gave every help and attention to fifteen men somewhat disabled in their first combat duty in what the records would term "a minor engagement."

As Rod helped one of the daughters bind clean linen over the shoulder wound of Nack, the two men suddenly found themselves glancing and blinking at each other in eye talk. Each knew the other to be saying this must be the girl in the ambrotype. When she spoke or gravely smiled, they couldn't be sure. But their eyes on her face in repose, they said that was the face and no mistake. They had memorized that round face, full underlip, somewhat aquiline nose, wide forehead, cheeks rather chubby, a fun-loving face, they had decided, except for the grave mouth. "If it wasn't for that mouth," Rod said to himself, "I'd say she could trifle with men." In his breast pocket, only a foot from her living face, he had the camera register of her face, bullet-nicked in one corner and a brown blood-soak along one edge. He could take it out and hand it to her, telling her where he got it, telling her of right it belonged to her. And afterward shame and guilt might ride him. Nor later in talk with her mother did he dare to think of handing her the ambrotype.

The mother poured out her heart to him. The sight of the wounded, their laughter and patience, their thanks and affection, had moved her. The house had never seen the like before, she said, the nearest to it the day a recruiting officer met a dozen of the neighborhood's young men. And one of her daughters had given the recruiting officer every help he could ask. She buttonholed the young men and told them of the Cause, of honor and self-respect and how to win the regard of all true men and women. One by one they signed the enlistment papers, went out of the big front room into the long hallway and out the front door to the portico where tall white columns put shadows from a south moon. One youth stayed in the big front room. His arms went around the daughter who had told them all to fight. He kissed her long. He turned from her with a tremulous mouth and moist eyes. She tried for a smile as he stood in the doorway with a final hand-wave. His step could be heard down the hallway. "Then," said the mother, "she fell to the floor in a dead faint. When she came to she babbled and kept on babbling she was glad, oh, so glad, no one but her mother had seen her faint away." And Rod put his hand inside his coat and fingered the ambrotype case to be certain it was there and by no mistake fallen into other hands in this house.

"Charley," said Nack on their way to camp, "that was her, wasn't it."

"Nack," said Rod, "we'd both swear it was her."

"She'll get the news soon enough without our breakin it to her."

"And she'll cry her eyes out."

"Can't tell about a woman these days. Some have dry tears."

"Yes, like that woman steps out the door to see her husband dangled from an apple tree."

"That girl ought to have the picture, Charley, his lifeblood on it."

"I'll send it to her—later. But I'll never tell her I pulled a horse head off a face she kissed many a time."

Nack's wound healed fast. Again in farmer clothes, days of hard complicated work came. "We're not soldiers, we're man-hunters," said Rod to Nack one day.

"Yeah," said Nack. "Started soldier, tried scout, now we're detectives, a kind of bloodhound."

They reported to Memphis headquarters more and more wagons heading up into Kentucky, after the proclamation that East Tennesseeans must move out or take the Confederate oath of loyalty.

Then came the burning of five bridges on three different railroads, cutting transport of troops and supplies. Rod and Nack helped to fill the Knoxville jail with suspects. They saw two bridge-burners, father and son, hanged outdoors before a large crowd and a troop guard.

"Satisfied now?" Rod muttered to Nack.

"Satisfied like you are," grunted Nack.

They had helped gather the evidence to hang the men. Each knew the other felt his own hands at the roped necks of the father and son who swung limp on the gallows. It was duty. "I would do it again, if it was orders," said Nack, "but I don't hanker after it."

At the same gallows another day they were to see one more bridge-burner hanged. It happened a girl arrived on the day set for the hanging and a man helped her write a telegram to the President of the Confederacy: "My father, Harrison Self, is sentenced to hang at four o'clock this evening, on a charge of bridge-burning. As he remains my earthly all, and all my hopes of happiness center in him, I implore you to pardon him. Elizabeth Self." Back from Richmond on the wires came a pardon.

"I'm a little pleased," said Rod, "that part of the public expecting to enjoy a hanging this afternoon is disappointed."

Nack ran a hand over the full brown beard that covered his face and pulled at the triangle end of it five or six inches below his chin, saying, "Same here." Rod ran a hand over the full black beard of hair that ran in wavelines and curved in a half-circle, saying, "Don't feel like soldiering, what we're doin these days." They had started smooth-faced, then tried mustaches with chin beards, let the face hair grow full with no tending. They felt themselves getting anonymous, their clothes likewise. Their scruffed farmer boots with worn dark trousers tucked in, their checked shirts after many rough washings losing the bright first pattern, their cotton coats rumpled and crinkled, their felt hats with low crowns fitting tight and five-inch brims that flopped—in their line of duty they had so often tried to look indistinguishable, impersonal and nobody in particular that it had done something to them. They hoped to get back into their captains' uniforms and feel themselves part of the army.

They shook hands early one April morning, a Sabbath morning of clean air, a daybreak of birds in tall timber and thicket tangle, branches leafing out and new smells of fresh-planted earth. Before the attack they shook hands. As captains of foot soldiers they might lose sight of each other. It was that kind of an attack. Nack and Rod, two captains, shook hands.

The enemy had pushed down through Kentucky and across Tennessee, taken Nashville, moved on down near the Mississippi state line. Now that enemy camped with the Tennessee River at his back, and the daybreak attack meant to press him for the river, death, capture, surrender, forty thousand hurled in surprise on the enemy's thirty-three thousand, their commander saying to staff men this April morning, "Tonight we will water our horses in the Tennessee River. I would fight them if they were a million." He saw his rank-and-file boys ready and eager to fight, and the feeling might pass. Boys they were—in both armies—the average twenty years of age—most of them greenhorns at battle combat—some of them never till this Sabbath morning pulled trigger on a gun, let alone killed a man with a gun.

"If I never see you again, don't think the time long," Nack had said with a slow smile as they shook hands.

"I'll be seeing you," Rod had smiled back. "Like that girl told her feller, you're too homely to get shot."

They did meet again, on Monday after the Sabbath and a two-day battle, evening and dusk with a steady downpour of rain, Rod ankle-deep in mud, one of thousands of men and boys waiting for the blocked road to untangle for cavalry, infantry, artillery, wounded in wagons, wounded walking. Horses and wheels had softened the mud to a slush and mire in places knee-deep and over the wagon hubs. The rain fell to worsen ruts, puddles, mudholes. Pitch-dark and strict orders said no lantern or torch. Of foot soldiers answering roll call yesterday at daybreak perhaps half were dead, wounded or missing back toward the Tennessee River.

Here in the dark slogged boys and men after two days of shooting from tree to tree, creeping through underbrush or from rock to rock up wooded ravines, lost from their units. To Rod's tired eyes and mind they were humps and blobs of shadow, each a vague man-shape with the line of a musket barrel slanted over the shoulder. The suck and pull of their shoes in mud and mire, the patient and hunched shoulders of utterly weary men wasting nothing in their stride, it came monotonous to Rod's eyes and ears. Then three sounds and Rod's ears told him what his eyes couldn't make out—a blubbery spludge off in the dark, a string of curses from a man sprawling into a mud bath, and along the halted column voices grumbling and cursing the delay. The man sprawled in the mud, musket, blanket and all, had a name, thought Rod, a mother, a home. And down the line, each voice had a name, a mother, a home somewhere. Last night the rain blew in torrents and these plodding shadows slept on the bare ground, taking the rain. Some had slept in enemy tents, for in the first sweep of the daybreak attack they took over part of the enemy's camp. Sunday morning and the long afternoon, ground taken, lost, retaken, on both sides.

One acre Rod saw with dead and wounded so thick and close you couldn't walk without stepping on a body. He saw two boys perhaps eighteen years old, heads touching as though they had gone to sleep together, one hand laid on another, peace on their mouths and eyes, one in Union blue, the other in Confederate gray. Then a body five feet away, a foot gone, a hand gone, and Rod's eyes reaching the head saw the face gone. Ten feet away stood a bloody shoe with a foot in it, near the shoe three fingers. A shellfire-wrecked battery he saw, the cannon barrels dismounted amid broken wheels, splintered ammunition chests, an overturned carriage with its tongue erect in the air and pole yokes swinging high, four dead horses, one with four feet pointing toward the sky, six dead artillerymen and one sprawled with dangling arms over a dead horse. Of his own company Rod reckoned eleven dead, twice as many wounded, litter-bearers taking most of the wounded to wagons, these men now a mile or two up the road crowded like sacks of grain on the floor of a wagon, some without blankets, clothes rain-soaked, rain from the open sky as the wagons jolted and lurched on. Their names and faces, home towns, favorite card games, Rod knew them, those who carried New Testaments, those backward in battle action, those without fear and those fear-shaken who nevertheless fought well. He had gone with the wagon of his wounded the first mile. Out of the wagon to the roadside he threw the bodies of two who died and took on two lighter-wounded men who had been walking. As wagons now moved past him he heard men who still had strength to cry, ravings of men in final extremities of pain, the disjointed babbling of men out of their senses. Voices of character pierced the dark, one man's shrilled and repeated, "O God, *why* did you do this to me?"

Rod's mind worked idly and vaguely on what he was seeing and hearing. Can the limit of human suffering hold a final dignity clothing it? That man back there in a peach orchard with a hand, a foot, his face blown away, what was there sacred about him? That man on a wagon floor in the cold open rain up the road now, still crying, "O God, *why* did you do this to me?"—what of his agony had lonely unfathomable majesty?

Among the shadows far up the column plodded one of his own men, walking wounded. With no aid in sight that afternoon, Rod cut off the

904

lower quarter of his shirt to bandage this man's arm and the man smiled thanks and patience. Rod saw him start for the rear, a quaint grin as his free hand touched the bad arm. "I don't mind this, Captain, but I shore do hate leavin this fight." Another idle and vague thought of Rod ran to his luck. His finger touched where a bullet took off a button. His right hand up over a shoulder could feel the little hole where a shell fragment had zipped. Above his left knee he could finger holes in pants leg and drawers, a grazing bullet, a minute's trickle of blood and nothing to think about. The army commander, however, after calling "I will lead you" to hesitant men, on Sunday afternoon took a leg wound, went riding on, a half-hour later taken off his horse with a boot full of blood and a death regret he couldn't go on fighting. Luck is what? Divine Providence, who can explain it? Rod was asking. In a bloody battle he had bled more from brier scratches on face and hands than from three bullets that only nicked him.

Nack too was in luck. Rod had helped a surgeon bandage Nack's leg wound and put Nack in an ambulance reserved for officers. "You said I was too homely to get shot," Nack had greeted Rod, and pointed to a hole in his hat, another in his left sleeve, and a bullet path through the beard an inch under his chin. Nack smiled to an officer waiting attention to a right hand, three fingers off, a gambler who said to Nack, "I'll never be able to hold a full hand again." The cold rain poured down. On leaving, Rod heard Nack, "You know, Charley, I'd feel like a hero if I wasn't so damned wet."

The black night broke into gray day. They came to the new headquarters town, the floors of schoolhouses, churches, hotel and depot covered with sick and wounded, railroad trains loaded with cases for Memphis and other cities. Rod gathered his men for a roll call, less than half answering "Here." He brought Nack the official news of why they lost the battle: an army of twenty thousand fresh enemy troops had come on the field for the second day's fighting. "We'll remember Shiloh," said Nack.

Ten days went by to see Nack up and ready for duty, he and Rod on horses, assigned to reconnaissance. The enemy, moving down into Mississippi, dug trenches as he came, feeling his way, siege operations, this enemy having two men to their one.

Two days Nack and Rod rode near the advancing entrenching enemy lines, sought wooded hills and underbrush where for hours their field glasses tried to gather enemy intentions. They rode a third day over a long stretch of open ground, making for another ridge, their horses side by side, Nack on the side toward the enemy. They rode at a slow gallop.

Rod's eyes searched a clump of trees down the slope a quarter-mile away. He was going to raise an arm, point it out to Nack and ask whether he saw bluecoats skulking around a huddle of pines. Next he heard a "zing" and saw Nack's horse go down and sink into quiet after a few shudders. Rod pulled in his horse, wheeled around, slid off the saddle, saw his own horse go down, roll over and then lie quiet, while three or four bullets went sping past him and another bullet zipped through his left sleeve.

He threw himself on the ground behind Nack's horse. He lay still and heard only an oriole call, the caws of two crows, faintly the cackling of farm hens. The time passed and he could smell red clover and the hair of the sorrel horse and saddle leather. He could see a mullein leaf almost touching his nose and turning his eyes a film of sunset pink on a great rolling white cloud. And he could see on the head of Nack J. Doss a bullet hole in the left temple exactly where a white scar began. In California the bullet tore a path and glanced off. Today the bullet went through, into the brain of Nack J. Doss, instant death for his chum, his long-time friend who had once saved his life. A low groan, despair and hate mingling, "Sharpshooters—the sonsabitches."

Rod saw the sunset pink on the cloud fade to dark maroon and vanish, the cloud itself moving into a slow spread of white feathers and flecks of wool. Then twilight, then the dark and a few stars between cloud rims. He lay nearly as still as the three dead, the man and two horses near him.

The two men with long rifles silhouetted above Rod took him for dead, took it they had killed two horses and two men and it was a good day's work. Rod knew as he swung his six-shooter he couldn't miss the one stooping over him. He saw in a flash that the other one made an instant decision he couldn't swing his long rifle and aim in time and so made a rush at Rod, who waited till the fellow was almost on him and then sent a ball straight into the left eye. Rod rushed to a saddlebag and took out a canteen, cold salt beef and hardtack, lifted Nack's body to his right shoulder and struggled up the low slope of the ridge two hundred yards, rested, climbed on, with pauses to get his breath, till he was a mile nearer his own lines and a mile from where two dead horses and two dead men lay in the pale light of a half-moon now come out between two clouds.

He sat with his back to a tree, ate a little beef and hardtack, dozed a while, then studied the patch of moonlight that moved along the brown beard, the nose, eyes and forehead. They had been thrown out of West Point together, had gone into Haverstraw's Mammoth Minstrels together. This silent one had picked for him the minstrel name of Charley Amberson, saying it had more fun in it than the name of Rodney Wayman. Death had come near and passed them by in California. From the young architect who adored the Arch, Nack had learned a line and Rod had heard it this morning as they rode out of camp, "To every man, be he who he may, there comes a last happiness and a last day." He knew his friend would have preferred it that his body should be a shield between Charley Amberson and hidden sharpshooters. He imagined Nack in a conscious minute before his last breath saying, "Better me than you, Charley old hoss."

Early in March of last year, near fourteen months ago, Rodney had kissed good-by to Mibs, had thrown high in the air the baby Clayborn Joel Wayman, had gone back to kiss Mibs and Clayborn again. From the buggy his brother Brock was driving him in to a steamer landing, he had thrown kisses to his father and mother, his sister Rosalind, Mibs and Clayborn standing on the front porch of the house. He was going to New Orleans for a visit, long put off, with Nack, then to Texas, where he intended to buy a mustang and a herd of cattle to drive North for feeding for market on their farm, a business in the cattle trade that he had done before and made it pay well. He himself believed no war was to come and so did those on the porch who threw him good-by kisses, all except Mibs. She couldn't say it, though he half-guessed it from a fear that danced in her eyes as they changed from sea-blue to storm-green and he noticed her brave effort to chase it away.

He had found Nack well-off as a cotton trader, worrying about the cotton future. He couldn't forget the wrath he saw in Nack's eyes and voice over an affair in the shipping trade. Nack and two other men each owned a one-third interest in two ships. The other two had seen fortunes made in the slave trade. They favored sending the two ships to Africa for slave cargo to pay enormous profits on the capital invested. Nack refused his consent to this, refused to sell his interest when they offered to buy him out at a profit to him; in plain words Nack gave warning that if they overrode him and went through with their scheme, he would kill the two of them and take the penalty.

April had come, the South and North armed and marching. Nack J. Doss and Rodney Wayman took commissions as captains in the Confederate Army, little doubting, with many others, the war would be over in sixty or ninety days. A guilt lay in Rodney's mind that in those exciting weeks of drill and preparation he sent no letter to Mibs. And when one day in May he had a letter written to her, mail service North and South no longer operated. In Tennessee he had handed a letter to a man with family and wagon heading for Cincinnati and had paid the man to see the letter mailed in that Ohio city. He had written the news of himself, his hope the war would end soon. then home again to see the little one born last August. Never a day, he wrote, but he wondered whether it was a boy or a girl and its eyes and hair like father or mother. His postscript to Mibs he could remember: "I went out and counted the stars. Every star I counted had your name on it. Does that make sense?"

After the terrific April battle had come his first shivers of mistrust that the South could win the war. Dark the hour for him and Nack when late in April came news of the forts guarding New Orleans surrendered to the Union fleet and land forces. There was left the Cause.

There was left "honor," a word, an invisible reality, a phantom of meaning. For the Cause, for "honor," he would go on. If his name was on some bullet of destiny marked for him he would meet it, with only the single and bitter regret that he couldn't have had more bright days and songs with his children and the one woman who never faded from his visions and hopes.

The patch of white moonlight had moved off Nack's face. He stepped over and knelt for a long look at the face. He wiped away a splatter at the left temple, brushed the hair back from the forehead, stroked the beard once. He took from the pockets a silk handkerchief, a large bandanna, and bundled in them a wallet, a jackknife, a box of matches, a pipe and pouch of tobacco, a few coins, a small round chunk of pure-gold bullion out of California days carried as a luck-piece. The watch, still ticking, still telling the time, he put into a vest pocket. The associations of these familiar and sacred pocket articles somehow threw him back to a hospital visit when Nack said, "Death is a funny customer anyway you look at him, Charley." And he was sure Nack wouldn't mind that now suddenly he ran back to a sunny afternoon in California when he and Nack had washed their only shirts and hung them to dry. He had asked Nack, "How would you prefer to die?" And Nack had drawled, "Since you ask me, Charley, I'll tell you. What I'd like would be this, I'd like on my ninety-eighth birthday to be hanged for rape."

He located a little depression of ground, dug out leaves and sticks from it and heaped them at the side. He went back to the body, and remembering a man in his company whose shoes had given out so he fought barefoot in the big battle, Rod took off the boots and socks. The gray uniform, others could use it, but reverence commanded burial in it. He laid the body in the prepared place, hunted out the silk handkerchief to cover the face, then heaped leaves, sticks, a few handfuls of earth for ritual, then piled heavy branches over and around. Alongside this shallow grave he slept, awoke soon and was long in falling to sleep again. Then came a short flash of a dream that repeated and came always the same, of a man riding a horse in the sky straight at the sun and singing. Into the blinding inconceivable light of the sun the man rode singing and was gone.

Chapter 31

Home Fires Burning

SNOW had fallen two days. The path shoveled to the barn in the morning had filled in with blowing snow. The stars shone clear on the white snow and Omri Winwold didn't need the lantern he carried as he lifted his boots step by step and heard the crunch of them in the quiet night. The ailing sow he had tended looked better. He would see her again about sunrise. Her dam had once taken a blue ribbon at the Pike County Fair and he didn't want to lose her.

In the house he blew out the lantern, hung it on the kitchen wall, got out of his boots into carpet slippers, took a chair under a kerosene lamp and picked up a letter on the table. "Dear Papa," it began, "Your son went from captain to major since I last wrote. Now since the battle of Shiloh I can tell you the sad news of our colonel killed and two majors wounded and sent to the rear. It devolved on me to command the regiment through the second day of the battle. I had two horses shot from under me during the fighting and a third horse sank under me and died just as I reached headquarters. I lost a hat and a bullet scraped my left arm to no injury. I have been promoted colonel, not brevetted, but promoted. I think you'll be pleased to know this." There was more to the letter, signed, "Your affectionate son, Marvel."

Of other letters in the little box on the table, one was after Murfreesboro, Tennessee, where on the last day of 1862 and the first two days of 1863 two armies fought in rain and fog, on wet ground and over mud, the weather changing to cold and freezing, one man out of four on the field killed or wounded, each army losing more than eleven thousand men. Marvel's division saw seventy officers killed, two of them brigadiers. "A cannon ball grazed my hat rim and then took off the head of a major riding alongside me. I saw one horse torn to pieces in a shell burst. I did my best for wounded men. They lay frozen to the ground in pools of their own blood." Marvel in this letter mentioned nothing of his own wound. He came home for recovery, a six-week furlough. Later arrived notice he was brevetted a brigadier general.

Omri Winwold was almost afraid of his pride in this boy, of his love for this son that he had tended and cared for as a baby. In Kentucky the boy had met a Missouri girl visiting relatives there. "At last I've got the one I'm sure I want, papa," he had said. Her father had a big farm out of Springfield, Missouri, owned six Negroes who worked the farm, yet he had fought with the Union Army in one

909

battle while his son fought with the other side. "She's got a mind of her own, honey-colored hair, and she writes poetry," said Marvel in one long enumeration of her qualities. And now the last letter Omri didn't care to read again before going to bed. Marvel, transferred East, saw his army in its last action smashed, routed, outwitted, sent reeling in shame with twelve thousand killed and wounded as against half that number of the enemy. "This army seethes with politics, with personal ambitions and petty jealousies among officers," Marvel wrote. "Near by we have the national capital seething with political treacheries, contractors getting away with scandalous profits, the politicians openly saying the war is a horrible mistake and no harm in breaking up the Union." Marvel quoted an officer praying, "O God, if there be a God, save my country, if my country is worth saving!" Across the Rappahannock River Marvel had heard fraternizing pickets of the two enemy armies, one, "Hello, Bluebelly," and the answer, "Hello, Butternut."

Omri piled the letters tenderly in the box and put it on a high shelf. Before going to his bedroom Omri looked in on Milton and saw him nicely asleep. In the morning Milton would be helped into the wheel chair that stood alongside his bed, the same wheel chair his stepmother Anne had used in her last months. Up till June of 1861 Milton had been going along as in the years before, keen and steady at the farm work, regular with his Sunday-school class and his Bible readings at home, with a peculiar touch of understanding with children, animals, land and weather. Then two weeks later the book *Uncle Tom's Cabin* came his way. He spent another two weeks reading it again to make sure he hadn't misread it. The next Sunday at church he spent the session teaching his class to sing "The Battle Hymn of the Republic" with its awesome religious solemnity, its lines, "In the beauty of the lilies Christ was born across the sea, As He died to make men holy, let us die to make men free." At barn-cleaning, cow-milking, corn-planting, manure-spreading, Milton sang now with gusto and elation, now softly and sadly:

Mine eyes have seen the glory of the coming of the Lord:
He is trampling out the vintage where the grapes of wrath are stored:
He hath loosed the fateful lightning of His terrible swift sword;
His truth is marching on.

I have seen Him in the watch-fires of an hundred circling camps;
They have builded Him an altar in the evening dews and damps;
I can read His righteous sentence by the dim and flaring lamps:
His day is marching on.

The next they knew Milton came home late one afternoon from Pittsfield. He had joined the army, signed enlistment papers, twenty-four years of age and his own man. To him the war was a holy war. Omri's eyes moistened and he would never forget this first son of

Sarah saying, "I could do no otherwise, father. The call was on me. It is a holy cause." He wore sergeant chevrons won at Shiloh, at one time firing and reloading only a half-mile from where Marvel had the first horse shot from under him, neither of the boys knowing the other was on the field.

A bullet through Milton's side, lodged near the spine. Sent by hospital steamer to Cincinnati, there after a few weeks the surgeons ordered him home as "permanently disabled," his left arm paralyzed, his two legs paralyzed. At times during the day in his wheel chair in the big sitting room his mind wandered. He would be saying something that made sense and then suddenly break off, "That's all right, my dear friend, we'll forget about it." Often they found him a cheerful presence that rebuked them. He read the Bible an hour or two daily, seemed to read *Uncle Tom's Cabin* backward and forward, occasionally singing "The Battle Hymn of the Republic." He would smile his appreciation to those who listened to his reading aloud a favorite chapter from the Bible. To Omri alone had he told of moments fateful to him. "It was like this, father, they charged and he wasn't eight feet from me when he let me have it and I knew I was going down. Before going down I let him have it and the next was there we lay on the rainy ground arm's length from each other. I saw his eyes go glassy and then shut before he went to his Maker. And that wasn't all. It was what he said to me before he went to his Maker. He said in a voice sweet as you like, 'I'm from Georgia, I'm a Christian, are you?' I told him yes and then, God help me, he had strength to reach a hand out to hold my hand and say to me, 'We ought to be friends rather than kill each other.'" Milton paused. Omri waited. Milton finished, "The Good Book says 'Thou shalt not kill,' but there we were, I killed him and he crippled me for life."

Working the farm now were Holliday, who was twenty-one and saying next fall when the crops were in it was time he went into the army, Peter, who was twenty and saying that in the summer of '64 he would be twenty-one and enlist, Patrick Henry, who was sixteen and hoping the war would not be over before somehow he had his chance to show himself a real man among the flying bullets. The girl Hope at fourteen years of age and the boy Robert Prindle at thirteen were not sure what they could do for the war except help raise corn and hogs to feed the Union armies. Omri was deeply moved, as the months went by, that one and all of these young people in the house had no mere kindly affection for Milton, what they had for him was reverence. To them Milton had been somewhere, an indescribably wild country. It was as though he had been wherever it is you go when you die and he had managed to crawl back. Holliday at table one evening, when Milton had been put to bed early, burst out to the others, "He went to hell, looked out, yelled 'Hurrah for the Union!' then jumped out."

Spring came, May arrived, peach and plum blossoms rioting white and pink, and a letter from Marvel. He had handled his regiment in a terrific two-day battle, the first day getting a light flesh wound on the right cheek, the second day his horse shot from under him pinned his leg to the ground so he couldn't rise. "An Illinois colonel got off his horse, pulled me from under and ordered two men to help me limp back to a field hospital. I've heard a lot about this colonel. His regimental officers say they doubt any other man in the army has killed more men with the saber. He's a funny duck, solemn as an owl, big red sideburns, whiskers like General Burnside only they widen out and catch more breeze. They say there isn't a crazier abolitionist in the army. Comes from that abolitionist town of New Era up in northern Illinois. I've heard men say he's a born killer, cool enough when there's no action and then he does like to see blood and hair or at least the piece of an ear on his saber. He risked his neck to get off a horse, under fire, to ease my pain and perhaps save one good leg of mine." The Union Army had lost twenty thousand as against half that many of the enemy. There was muttering, growling, among officers and men about the war running so long with such awful cost. "I am gloomy, the Confederacy may win," wrote Marvel.

Seldom now did Omri ride through Atlas and out to the Wayman farm. When he entered the house there he believed he interrupted no conversation of any kind and that after his leaving the house kept the same heavy silence. Brock, the gay carefree Brock, after the fall crops of '61 were in, had enlisted in the Union Army. Wounded at Shiloh, he died in a Cincinnati hospital and they held burial services in a pine knoll on the Wayman farm. There were tears as the coffin sank into the grave but Omri was struck with a mute grief he saw on faces, Mr. Wayman grown thinner, his cheekbones more bare. Working the farm now he had a Negro man and a Negro boy, slave runaways from southern Missouri, which was not included in the Emancipation Proclamation, wherefore they were still slaves and, under the law, property. In former days they would have been returned to their legal owner or jailed and sold.

In his added cares and duties now Omri had less time for visits and social affairs. He would have gone more often to see Mibs could his wits have devised any thoughts to comfort her. He saw her pressed and torn from many directions. She wanted the Union to win through and perhaps more yet she wanted Rod to live. Omri no longer dared to ask ever so gently, "Any news at all of Rod?" Two years now and no letter from Rod and no word from anyone who had heard of him. Omri saw one grinding twist at her heart, the fear of Rod one of the thousands shoveled into pits and graves marked Unidentified. In Omri's last few talks with her she had been short-spoken, monosyllabic, twice saying, "You talk. Tell me anything. I'll listen. But I can't talk."

In former days he had seen Mrs. Wayman a light and a comfort to Mibs. Now barriers had risen between them. Could Mibs have spoken her Union feeling to her husband's mother? No—Omri was sure. Yet that feeling had somehow betrayed itself or Mrs. Wayman's intuition had read it. This was Barbara's best-beloved son gone South and no word from him in two years, along with the quixotic grief that a younger son had given his life for the Union; these matters preyed on her mind and clawed at her controls. Once on the edge of saying to Mibs, "Her mind isn't what it was, do you think?" Omri knew that wouldn't do.

Mibs had told briefly the news from New Era. Her mother was trying to bear up under the loneliness of Joel Wimbler saying it was his war and then enlisting in the commissary service. Hornsby figured now in all New Era talk, his name there among dispatches reporting front-line valor of Colonel Meadows' cavalry regiment. Danny Hilton, the horse-lover, the boy of wit and daring, the ever friendly man, had died in a cavalry charge at Shiloh. Al Dunnigan, the pleasant Irishman, the blacksmith and horseshoer, the bare-knuckle fighter who feared no man, had proven himself in several battles and come home with an arm gone. Max Mutter's daughter, who wouldn't marry because she had seen her mother's anguish at several childbirths, was a hospital nurse in Virginia. Two Hickory Grove boys back home from service under Frémont in Missouri were saying, "We thought it was a fight for the Union, not to free the nigger."

Omri saw that to Mibs Rod was becoming a phantom, unreal for the present, and Mibs ready to put him in the past as one cherished and adored. He saw Mibs having only one vital consolation—the two children. The second one, born five months after Rod left in March of '61, and named Rodney Wayman Jr., had his father's black hair and jutting chin, and his mother's blue eyes. Omri had seen the gay Mibs of yesterday only when the children were awake and she handling them when Omri called. Then she could laugh, sing, speak follies and make faces. "They'll keep her," he said. "She won't lose her mind. She'll come through for all the black bats I've seen flying far back in her eyes." He wrote to Brooksany Wimbler a letter of affection and respect, telling her he had learned from her daughter how to sing the old revivalist lines:

> We are living, we are dwelling,
> In a grand and awful time,
> In an age on ages telling,
> To be living is sublime.

Omri answered a letter from Annabell Ponder Flack. The second child had come last winter and Annabell reminded him of his promise. She only vaguely hinted at grief that he might help. He wrote her of his cares, duties, chores, quite sure that in late fall or early winter it would do his old bones good to again see her and Henry Flack and the two little ones he had not yet seen. He hesitated and then signed himself "Affectionately yours."

* * * * * * * * * *

Chapter 32

* * * * * * * * * *

Battle Wounds and Prison Hunger

THE soldier Rodney Wayman opened his eyes and turned them in different directions. With little moving of his stiff and sore neck and his head with a ringing pain in it, he kept looking. Now he remembered the place. This triangle of land, covered with gravel, small stones and several boulders, had seen hard fighting the day before. His company with two others had driven the enemy out of it in the morning of that day, had lost it about noon, had with reinforcements retaken it only to lose it again late in the afternoon.

Slowly he loosened kinks in his neck muscles and raised his aching head for a look at his companions. He counted eleven in thirty feet of his eye range. The nearest body, hidden by a boulder except for a shoulder and head, the face with closed eyes turned toward him, not more than five feet away. He had seen the man go down yesterday noon. The orders had been to move back and the man had stayed behind his boulder firing and reloading till enemy crossfire brought him low. The man had on him the only deck left in the company with face cards clean enough to be read. A month ago on a Sunday of preaching in camp this man dealt in a poker game less than twenty feet from the preacher. The next Sunday this man had with six other privates laid his bets on a louse race. Each man had taken off his shirt and picked from the seams nearest the armpits a louse he judged had speed. The racers laid on a line penciled on a piece of canvas, the first grayback to reach a line two feet away took the money for his owner. On a later day the same men staged a louse fight. It ended in a draw and a laughing dispute, one saying, "What's the matter is lice jist don't care for lice blood." And yesterday, this man who could get fun out of cards or lice proved himself worth honorable mention. At his boulder he stayed shouting back to his comrades he would cover for them and then join them. On this still face, two arms' lengths away, had been rippling infectious laughter to cheer other men.

A few feet beyond lay a body with its back toward Rod. He recognized the long head, curly black hair, a boy in another company

914

whose captain had told of the boy wanting a furlough to see his girl in Meridian, Mississippi. The boy had re-enlisted under promise of a furlough. They kept refusing him the furlough and in one skirmish the captain saw the boy lean his rifle against a tree and put out hands and arms for the enemy to shoot at. The boy had laughed to the captain, "I'm feelin for a furlough." Then the boy threatened to go without leave to see his girl in Meridian. The captain warned he would be caught and shot as a deserter. The boy flashed, "I've got a mother in heaven, a father in hell, a girl in Meridian, and I'm going to see one of the three next Saturday night." Then the boy stayed with his company to fight. Now he lay still under a creep of morning mist and the Meridian girl yet to know whether her fingers would again run through the black curls on his long head.

Farther off Rod's eyes caught two bodies clad in butternut. They were barefoot. He had seen them go into action barefoot. Near them lay three bodies in blue jackets, their shoes and socks gone, their wool trousers of a uniform light-blue pulled off. During the night, he guessed, men who wanted better trousers and shoes had taken their chances and crept into the triangle. His eyes moved to his own feet and saw his boots and wool socks gone. He still had his butternut trousers that had replaced his gray wool uniform trousers torn into many shreds in thorn and brier thickets at the last battle. Dropping his eyes he saw that his captain's coat of gray wool and the gray wool shirt underneath were gone. He let his aching head drop back on the gravel and closed his eyes. When again he opened them he knew that he had faded away for a time and before fading away he had wondered about how completely senseless he had been during the night when a coat and shirt could be pulled off him. The burning pain above the elbow of his left arm, as that arm was jerked around to get sleeves of coat and shirt loose from it, should have brought him awake. Then he remembered he had not eaten since yesterday morning. In the close fighting through midday and afternoon there hadn't been time to eat, and near sundown he fell. He could have kept his feet with his bad left arm. It was the sudden scraping grind over the left temple and alongside of the head that brought him down. He had known nothing since then from late afternoon and through the night till this gray light of daybreak. His free right hand went into a trouser pocket and found it empty. He waited for a little strength and moved his hand up over the left side of his head. He could feel the hair wet with blood. His fingers lightly traced the path of the bullet. Had the lead ball struck a quarter- or a half-inch lower he would be lying as still as those nearest him. He had come awake to shiver with cold and each shiver brought fresh pain to the left arm. He was numb, hungry, thirsty. Now that he thought of it he was thirsty more than anything else— and his canteen gone. The thought shouldn't have come to him, his tongue and throat wanted water, two o'clock yesterday afternoon since he tasted water.

He faded away again, possibly slept, opened his eyes to see the morning sun well up, halfway to noon, the warmth of it falling on him and the chill of early daybreak gone. He lay awake with groping thoughts, his mind limp and slack as his body. At high noon the first luxury and warmth of the sun began to change into a heat that pressed down and had him sweating and sweltering. He faded out, came to and lay awake, his wounds burning and aching. Then a moment when he believed he heard stirrings in the underbrush, feet and voices. His mind and senses so vague he wouldn't trust them, his thought he might lie here, too weak to rise, no one ever to come to this little abandoned God-forsaken corner of the world. What forest animals then would have their way with his flesh or buzzards pick his bones clean? The like had happened in this war. He had come a few months ago to a rail-fence corner where a man with leg wounds had so propped himself amid the rails that he sat upright and you could read that he had died with a pipe of tobacco in his left hand and an ambrotype of a woman and two little girls in his right hand and time had passed and rainfalls and changing seasons had wrought their way with him, the flesh faded into dry skin over the bones of the face, the skeleton fingers holding pipe and picture as he wished when he died.

What were those sounds? Were they real or was he imagining? Rod slowly loosened the kinks in his stiff neck. A burning streak ran along the line of his head wound as he raised his head to see two blue-coated men lifting a wounded bluecoat into a litter some forty feet away. He sank back, gave a cry that had the last of his strength in it, "Hi! Hi!" and raised his right arm as high as he could lift it. Then he faded.

In a Union field hospital three days later his wounds had been dressed and he heard a surgeon's judgment that he might be up and around again in three or four weeks. On this third day, too, a litter-bearer told him, "Good thing you raised your arm when you hollered to us. You looked white and dead as any of them." Beef soup and hardtack in plenty were bringing his strength back. For their records they asked his name. He answered, "Captain Rodney Wayman." The nurse who heard this called another to join her in hearing it again. He learned from the two homely and kindly women who had tended him that until they had more evidence he was a commissioned officer they would have to treat him as one of the rank and file.

In a Union Army hospital in Nashville he got better; riding in a railroad boxcar to Louisville two days he got worse. The straw on the boxcar floor had not been changed since the last batch of wounded. The air stank. The soup came lukewarm or cold. Two meals were skipped. Sleep was broken continuously the second night, two men crying for water, a youth out of his mind calling to his mother. The boy of nineteen lying next to Rodney tried to whisper some last message for his home folks in southern Mississippi, gave a final shiver and died with the last words, "It's cold, it's cold." And Rod mumbled more than once in the ten hours on straw next to the boy, "Now no longer cold or if he is he doesn't know it."

At Louisville three dead were taken out of the car and they tasted the first hot soup of quality since leaving Nashville. How many hours passed, whether it was day or night, Rodney didn't know till the last train-stop. A guard called, "Indianapolis and all out!"

Three weeks in Camp Morton Hospital with nourishing food and the care of an able and friendly surgeon. Rod tried to speak deep thanks to that surgeon as he patted his left arm, "Good as new now," and running a hand along the scar on his head, "The hair has grown a cover for it." He pressed both hands to the surgeon's right hand, "You're one of the few Christians in this Christian country—God bless you always."

Then Rodney Wayman was taken by a guard who led him away and dropped him into the swarming slithering human mass of prisoners, walled in and watched, counted and numbered every day, ticketed and tended as animals in a cage. Each cage held three hundred and twenty men. A State Fair grounds, once gay with flags and festoons, brass bands and race horses, blue-ribbon pedigreed swine and cattle led by proud farmers—now Rodney and his companions slept, ate, huddled and shivered through late fall and early winter where cattle had been stalled, with the distinction that the cattle had plenty of fresh straw and captive Confederate soldiers none.

Around Camp Morton ran a twenty-foot wall of smooth thick planks, closely placed sentries at the wall top with only head, shoulders and rifle barrels showing, reflectors at night flooding the walls and near-by ground with a white light. Through the middle of Camp Morton ran a small creek and this open stream carried sewage, contaminations and odors. Eighty feet long, twenty feet wide, ten feet high at the eaves, was the cattle shed where Rod bunked. The lowest tier of bunks ran a foot above bare ground, the second and third tiers each three feet higher, and the fourth level with the eaves. The ten-inch-wide weather boards forming the sides of the shed, Rod noticed, had shrunk, most of the weather strips come loose or warped and fallen away. This was how the wind whistled through and sent its winter cold to the bones of men. Their thin cotton underwear and socks, their butternut trousers, shirts and jackets woven of cotton, with no overcoats and with blankets of cotton, their clothing meant for a climate hundreds of miles to the south—they were men new to the piercing cold of zero weather in the North.

Some had worn and torn their clothes thin and ragged, the bare soiled skin showing. In the spells of colder weather Rod heard unfailing the groans and curses of shivering men. Usually they slept in threes, the blanket of one man under them, two blankets spread over the three, the man between keeping snug and cozy, each taking his turn as the man between. In the colder weather they slept in squads, eight or ten men on their sides, spoon-fashion, and during the night the calls could be heard from squad leaders here and there, the command, "Boys, spoon!" In some squads they had learned to soak the top blankets in water and wring out the blankets so to keep a moisture that helped hold body heat from escaping.

Rod saw pneumonia, consumption of the lungs and other maladies take their toll. What came harder to look at was morning after morning, in zero or near zero weather, the stiff bodies of men pulled from their bunks and taken to the deadhouse, "plain frozen to death," as one phrase had it. And Rod would just as soon it hadn't happened one morning, after a below-zero night, on fuel-squad duty that brought him past the deadhouse, he counted eighteen bodies being carried into that place, "plain frozen to death." Rod heard one body-bearer to another, "Pilin 'em in like cordwood this mornin, eh?" And his own thought ran, "They say plain frozen to death but at least two in our shed I know plain starved to death before they froze."

Food, whether a man could live, stand and walk on the Camp Morton rations, whether by any chance there might be a little more tomorrow or next week, how those with money or watches or jewelry could buy or trade into a little more food—this was the main camp talk. The nearest to a satisfying meal Rod ate in six weeks was when a friend shared with him an ear of hard corn bought for fifteen cents and a small piece of cheese bought for ten cents. He had seen hundreds of men swarm of a morning at the gate opening to let in the bread wagon, rushing around the wagon like hogs at a trough in their shoving and scrambling, and their cry, "Bread! Bread!" To each mess of seven men was rationed daily a loaf of bread seven inches long and about three and a half inches wide and thick, along with a small piece of meat of which each mess member got one-seventh. This with a pint of thin vegetable soup for each man after morning roll call made the day's nourishment.

Rod had seen men slowly go to pieces in mind and behavior, little by little and day by day losing sense and feeling about what was filth. He had seen creatures once brave men in battle feed like hogs and dip their hands over and again and eat what they picked from the swill tubs back of the hospital kitchen. Rod had joined with others to shame, cuff and beat these swill-eaters, making an example of one offender by throwing him head first into a barrel of swill.

Monotony—sunset roll call, all prisoners to bunks—night cold, short sleeps between shivering awake to hear wild groans and curses or again piteous little wails and sharp cries out of delirium—daybreak of gray light creeping into the shed, morning roll call and the dressing for roll call by putting on a hat. Monotony—days of snow and a bitter wind through weather-board cracks—around each of four stoves circles of men, those next the stove too warm, an outer ring still cold. Monotony of vermin—squads in milder weather pulling off shirts and drawers, picking off the graybacks one by one, the labor on other days of carrying water and getting it scalding hot for vermin of infested clothes, lines of men waiting for hours to share their turn at a tub or wash boiler—organized squads seeking the lazy or careless lousy and forcing them to scald their clothes—decisions among prisoners that certain companions indifferent to head lice must have haircuts. Monotony—of rumors around stoves and in bunks, big battles under way, the war to end and all prisoners freed—fresh rumors of thousands of Union prisoners South to be exchanged for Confederates North— no end of the hope deferred that maketh the heart sick.

Brutal punctuations of the monotony: a guard shooting a man to death for too slowly answering "Here" at roll call; a guard drawing revolver and shooting a man leaving after roll call and before the order to break ranks; five prisoners on garbage-wagon detail outside the camp seizing two guards, disarming them and making an escape, these same two guards later that week using sticks of firewood to knock senseless with bloody heads two pale prisoners thin as rails, two prisoner victims of dysentery near daybreak caught going to the sink while wearing both trousers and coat in violation of an order that any prisoner going to the sink must leave either trousers or coat behind, wherefore two patrol guards forced the two men in a deep snow to "mark time," to make march motions without marching, this for more than an hour, one prisoner from frostbite and gangrene later losing both feet—these punctuations of monotony.

The physical corruption of Camp Morton spread its odor. Enforced bodily neglect, degradation and filth gave its stench night and day. Worse yet an incessant rot played in the mind and worked at the invisible fibers of men. Prisoners of tried valor in battle combat slowly became shadows. Some turned mute, refused to talk or listen, in quiet and baffling ways went daft and somehow died, which was their goal.

Somewhere in the upper realms of the authority holding them, believed Rod and some of his intelligent companions, fraud and collusion operated by which food rations meant for them never reached them. Their hate grew ever deeper for the prison guards, men never in front-line service, men lacking a sportsmanship rather common among soldiers in the field, guards known to be shirkers with political pull to keep them safe from campaign marches and firing lines.

Before Chickamauga, Rod had noted among officers and men of his army a feeling that perhaps the Confederacy had seen its high noon and was moving toward sunset and night. The double Union victories of Gettysburg and Vicksburg in July, did they carry the two dark bongs of a big bell? Yet a certain fellowship moved among both officers and men, they could speak no other thought nor feeling to each other: they would fight on till the Confederacy was "gone up." Rod had heard more than one of this fellowship, even in prison, "I think the Confederacy is gone up but we'll fight on hoping it isn't."

Men of this fellowship it was, sixteen of them, who had dug a tunnel for escape. In size the tunnel would accommodate a man crawling on all fours. Over the opening in a shed corner men sat on a blanket and played cards. One held a cord that ran to the digger working with a case knife and his hands; when he had a bag full of dirt he pulled on the cord and the man at the blanket pulled the bag up. Then a circle of men stood around while the dirt taken out of the bag was put into the trousers of men whose trouser ends were held up by socks pulled outside of them. These dirt carriers lazied along to a plank over the sewage creek, looked to see they were not watched, pulled up trousers from the hold of the socks and let the dirt fall into the creek and be washed away.

One day the tunnel was finished and they were figuring what day they would crawl through to freedom. Then the guards came and ordered the diggers of the tunnel to refill it. The informer vanished— to better eating and a warm bed, it was told. Rod heard one of the fellowship, "If Jesus Christ had one Judas among his twelve Apostles I guess maybe we could expect one sonofabitch in our sixteen half-starved half-crazy prisoners."

Week by week Rod saw the eyes of good companions lose their natural luster and take on a queer staring brilliancy, and he knew the same was happening to him. The bones of his hands shone darker and he studied the skinny lengths of his fingers. Two motives kept him going, added strength when the flame-line of the will to live ran low in him and wavered. He had found in this pesthole where humanity festered, rotted, starved and froze to death, a fellowship close, warm, strange yet real. He could count them and name them, men whose decency, honesty, manners, had met final and awful tests.

Always by night and by day the face and shadow of Mibs moved with him. He had caught himself issuing from a daytime stupor when his mind played in vague fantasy at the face and voice of Mibs. A week before leaving hospital he had written her a long letter. On reading it he felt it ran too gay and debonair or again had dark touches that could be misread. He wrote instead a note: "Dear Mibs, my Mibs —am alive and well here at Camp Morton. Night and day my thoughts have been of you as ever the only one, with prayers for you and Clayborn and the little one I hope to see when the war is over and we meet again. My love always and singing ever of thee I'm fondly dreaming—Rod." He added a postscript: "You must not come to see me here. Am alive and well but there are reasons it would do no good. Please write me here. Please write me long long letters."

Weeks had gone by and no letter from Mibs. His daytime reveries of her took on a color of fear. What could have happened to her?

Why not an answer short as his letter to her? Or did his letter fail to reach her? If it did get to her she would have answered. There his faith and certainty were absolute. Could she have gone away from the Wayman farm? Could something have happened to the farm and his father and mother? Could it be sickness? Or near so much of death, could he ask whether death had struck at her too?

In daytime a degree of logic and reason held his mind as to Mibs. Nighttime it took on fantasy. In one dream he saw her in a long white slender coffin, so long it ran out of the front door and far over the porch steps of the Wayman house. He stood twice as tall as when he went away and he wore a tall white silk hat and a long white coat and he bent over the coffin and looked at her long white body in white silk, two white roses fixed in her plaited chestnut hair, five red roses held in her two folded hands, and he thought her eyelids quivered and were about to open—and he turned to the pallbearers, "If she must be buried I am the one to bury her," shouldered the coffin and stalked out into a moonlit mist and with long steps reached a pine knoll where he began digging a grave and came to a coffin and opened it to see his brother Brock in a Union blue uniform; he stepped out to cry over Mibs' face, "It's a lie Brock is dead and a lie you're dead," and Mibs sat up straight in the coffin, brushed sleep from her eyes and spoke with a sleepy drift in her voice, "Rod darling, you here, you here, God is good to us"—then he lifted her from the coffin and they started a slow waltz, in the moonlit mist slowly waltzing, and she was as ever a slim and airy waltzer, featherlight and dreamy, and he heard her murmuring, "It isn't me, Rod, it's a mist woman waltzing, a mist woman, mist is me and me is mist," and his arms empty, he woke in his bunk, his back warm from the body of the man spooned next to him, his empty arms cold and the front of his body cold from the wind whining through the weather boards.

In another dream Rod saw Mibs in a white cape riding a white horse at a slow gallop toward the moon, and alongside her Clayborn on a white pony and on a smaller white pony his two-year-old child he had not yet seen. They rode easy. They waved their hands, smiled to him and rode past him, turned in their saddles to look back toward him still waving and smiling as they went on toward the moon. Suddenly he was on a black horse riding after them, his feet tangled in both stirrups as they rode away from him. He woke to hear his bunkmates tell him to keep his feet quiet. He dropped to sleep again sure the little one on the smaller pony had his own chin and black hair.

Then the weeks of the Plan, days crowded with low-voiced discussion and secret organization, Rod giving little or no thought to Mibs in the daytime though at night always came the float of her face and voice. Rod was one of the first five in on the Plan. Then a second five were brought in. After a time there were seven fives or thirty-five men in all, picked and tested men, they believed, though there would always be the chance of a Judas. Every detail had been worked out beforehand. Each man knew what he was to do and which leader to follow.

The time was evening, just as the bugle sounded for the men to get to their bunks and before the night patrol reached the prison yard. A ditch had been dug next to the Camp Morton twenty-foot wall to keep prisoners from reaching that wall. Here men rushed to overturn a privy shed into that ditch. This made a bridge for the men who swarmed over it with ladders they raised to the top of the wall. Those ladders had been slung together in fast time that very day, from bunk planks spliced with blanket and clothing strips. While the ladders were being set up two guards fired and hit no one while the desperate prisoners below hurled stones, bottles filled with water, hunks of hardwood, that sent the guards running. By their speed, timing and wild abandon, by their cool keen preparations and their seasoned quality as soldiers, every man in the Plan got over the ditch, up the ladders and over the wall. A few were caught the next day. A few made for Canada and reached it. The most of them headed south. They had the names of towns and neighborhoods where over half the people favored any kind of an immediate peace to end the war, these people being known as Peace Democrats or Copperheads, many thousands of them members of one secret society, the Knights of the Golden Circle, or another named the Sons of Liberty. This element in Indiana had sent to the state legislature a controlling majority to block measures and proposals of the Unionist Governor of the state. Part of this element was co-operating with Confederate Army officers in Canada organizing attacks to be launched over the Canadian border on Great Lakes shipping and cities.

Into southern Indiana, sprinkled thick with Southern-blooded Confederate sympathizers, the ragged and desperate prisoners escaped from Camp Morton made their way, found clothes, food, hiding places for rest and going on with new strength.

Nearly half of the escaped men, in their butternut rags and their telltale skinny bodies and staring haunted eyeballs—nearly half were brought back, sullen and worn, to the chills and vermin of Camp Morton where famished human creatures still ransacked daily the swimming particles of the hospital swill barrels.

Among the permanently missing at Camp Morton, no longer answering roll call, was Rodney Wayman. He had followed the ladder men over the privy-shed bridge. Three stones, each about the size of his fist, he had thrown at a sentry up on the wall. Two of the stones missed. The third he spit on and let it go and saw it hit the left elbow of the sentry and he hoped it broke the bone. It gave him a fierce new strength to see the sentry turn and run. Up the flimsy shaking spliced ladder he went and over the wall without time to say good-by or take a farewell look at the most evil house of shame his sight and smell had ever met.

* * * * * * * * * *

Chapter 33

* * * * * * * * * *

God Leaned Down

THE week after the Camp Morton escape, a woman and two small children came to the officer in charge of the prison. She had a note from the Governor of Indiana attesting she was loyal to the Union cause, should be extended every courtesy and an opportunity to interview her husband, who was a prisoner.

"Mrs. Rodney Wayman," read the officer, looked up at her, and curtly, "I think I have heard the name." Then bringing a paper from a desk pigeonhole and scanning it, "Yes, the name is here, Rodney Wayman." He hesitated. This was not the first time his pride or vanity as a keeper of men was touched. Mibs could have said, "The subject seems to be disagreeable to you." He snapped his fingers as though, "Oh, well, let's have this odd little affair over with." Then he told her, brightly he believed, "Your bird has flown, madam. He departed from our hospitality a week ago, without notice or authority. As he is no longer resident here an interview with your Rebel husband is not possible."

She was dismissed. She would have liked to see the prison, perhaps talk with men who had known her husband, who could tell her how he looked and behaved. One fierce satisfaction with shivers of ecstasy ran through her—only bold unbroken men of live wit and unspent strength could have carried through such a dash for freedom.

She walked slowly with her short-stepping children to the hack outside that had brought her. "The Governor's house, please," she told the driver. He gave her of his time, did the Governor. She had come well vouched-for, well attested. Her husband's brother in a Union regiment had died of Shiloh wounds. Her father was an officer in the Union commissary service. She was raised in a northern-Illinois abolitionist community. She loved her husband and wanted him, since it was a matter of *his* personal conscience to fight with the Confederate Army and live through the war and come back to her and their children. Yet, since it was a matter of *her* personal conscience, she wanted the Union cause to win the war.

"We have such a plenty of families in this state who are unanimous against the Union cause," the Governor had remarked when hearing her. "I wish more of those families could be as divided as yours."

An ox of a man, a bulwark, rounded shoulders, a large squarish head with mustache and rather close-trimmed chin beard. Except for his somewhat paunchy girth he reminded Mibs of Hornsby Meadows, both magnificently obstinate. She had read that one of the Governor's ancestors, in direct line on his father's side, came from England with Roger Williams and later in Providence struggled alongside of the great apostle of religious liberty. She told the Governor she had heard about his handling of the state legislature, how the Unionist members walked out and stayed out so there was no quorum and the Copperhead majority was blocked.

"I was reliably advised," the Governor told her, "that they contemplated passing a joint resolution acknowledging the Southern Confederacy, and other mischief. We decided rather to have no legislature at all than a treasonable one."

"This is the first I heard of it," said Mibs.

"We say little of it in public," said the Governor. "It would affect the spirit of men at the fighting fronts if we should be fully candid about it." Then with a searching and pleased look into Mibs' face he added, "Your husband when he returns after the war, as I trust he will, can face you with honor unstained. Had he stayed at home in Pike County, Illinois, and joined his efforts with treasonable political secret organizations I know to be operating there as here in Indiana, your case with him would be quite different."

A secretary entered and laid a paper before the Governor. He glanced over it and said to Mibs, "I sent for a report on Rodney Wayman. He sustained two wounds in the Battle of Chickamauga, made his final recovery from them in the prison hospital here and was dismissed as in excellent condition. There seems to be no record of pernicious activities against him," and here the Governor chuckled, "until this escape of a week ago. That was pernicious," and again he chuckled, then sobered. "I don't like it that some of those escaped men are going to be shooting at our good Union soldiers, but I can say to you in confidence that their strategy and valor in that escape command my admiration. You can have the satisfaction and delight that your husband is a strong and able man or he could not have participated in so furious an affair. They wouldn't have let any spindlings in on it."

Mibs was rising to thank the Governor, and then leave, just as an elderly couple was shown in and the Governor said to Mibs, "You might stay while we visit with these people." The man wore Quaker garb, a black coat to below his hips, a black vest up to near the collar of the white shirt, large farmer hands, and Mibs thought, "What a beautiful head!" A wide meditative mouth, strong cheekbones, wide searching kindly eyes, large ears, with a fall of snow-white hair over them, thinning hair parted in the middle. His stout roly-poly wife too was in Quaker black, a triangle of white linen showing below her neck, a white cap on her head, hair parted in the middle, her hands quietly shifting the ends of a large black kerchief over her shoulders and down below the elbows. "They smell of the good earth." said Mibs to herself, "clover and blue sky and clean barns." .

After greetings the Quaker farmer was telling the Governor: "One day while plowing I heard a voice, whether inside me or outside of me I knew not, but I was awake. It said, 'Go thou and see the President.' I answered, 'Yea, Lord, Thy servant heareth.' And unhitching my plow, I went at once to the house and said to mother, 'Wilt thou go with me to Washington to see the President?' 'Who sends thee?' she asked. 'The Lord,' I answered. 'Where thou goest I will go,' said mother. My friends called me crazed. Some said the trip would be foolish and I could not gain access to the President. We prayed that God would direct our wanderings. It was about early candlelight when we got to Washington. There was so much confusion at the depot and on the street that mother clung to my arm saying, 'Oh, Isaac, we ought not to have come here! It looks like Babylon!' 'But the Lord will help if we have faith that we are doing His will,' I replied, and we walked away from the cars. Under a lamppost there stood a noble-looking man, reading a letter. I stopped before him and said, 'Good friend, wilt thou tell us where to find the President?' He looked us all over before he spoke. We were neat and clean, and soon his face got bright and smiling and he asked us a few plain questions. I told him we were Friends from Indiana who had come all these weary miles to say a few words to the President because the Lord had sent us. He nodded, 'Understand,' took us to a large house called Willard's Hotel and up to a little room. He was gone long and came back with a slip of paper with the writing on it: 'Admit the bearer to the chamber of the President at 9:30 o'clock tomorrow morning.' That night in the hotel was peaceful as those at home in the meadows. The next morning our kind gentleman said, 'You must make your talk with him brief. A big battle has just been fought.'

"The room into which we were first shown was full of people waiting to see the President. Mother whispered, 'Ah, Isaac, we shall not get near him today. See the anxious faces who came before us.' I said to her, 'As God wills.' It was a sad place to be in, truly. There were soldiers' wives and wounded soldiers sitting around the large room, and not a soul but from whom joy and peace seemed to have fled. Some were weeping. Soldiers with clinking spurs and swords walked through the halls. Men with newspapers in their hands were reading the battle news. The house seemed the center of the world."

Mibs sat fascinated at this recital. It was a little like actually going to Washington. She glanced at Clayborn and Rodney sitting together in the big leather chair next to her. They were blinking, listening and blinking at the man, who went on: "When the summons came for us to enter, my knees smote together and for an instant I tottered. Mother whispered, 'Keep heart, Isaac,' and we went forward. Then to be received in that room as if he was our own son made me feel very strange. He shook hands with us and put his chair between us. I said, 'Wilt thou pardon me that I do not remove my hat?' Then his grave face lit up as he said, 'Certainly, I understand it all.' And of that half-hour it does not become me to speak. I will think of it throughout eternity. At last we had to go. The President took a hand of each of us in his, saying, 'I thank you for this visit. May God bless you.' Just then I asked him if he would object to writing a line or two, certifying that I had fulfilled my mission, so that I could show it to the council at home. He sat down to his table and wrote."

From his coat pocket Isaac took out a wallet and unfolded a piece of paper that the Governor read and passed on to Mibs. It read: "I take pleasure in asserting that I have had profitable intercourse with friend Isaac Harvey and his good wife, Sarah Harvey. May the Lord comfort them as they have sustained me.—Abraham Lincoln."

The Governor questioned Isaac, politely and skillfully, and it came out that the Quaker farmer laid before the President a plan for emancipation of the slaves, the Federal Government to pay the slaveowners three hundred dollars "for each man, woman and child held in bondage." The President told Isaac that he agreed it was a just plan, that he must give it every consideration, but he doubted that the Congress would favor it and he doubted further that the leaders or the rank and file of the Confederacy would accept such a proposal. He did agree warmly with Isaac that for the Federal Government to pay the owners of emancipated slaves for their property would make for less of bitterness between North and South when the war should end.

Mibs sat with her head in a whirl. A thousand times perhaps she had heard arguments whether emancipation should be immediate or gradual and if either immediate or gradual whether there should be compensation to the slaveowners. For herself she had always favored gradual compensated emancipation and she could have put her arms around Isaac and hugged him, and likewise the President in Washington.

Their visit over, the Quaker farmer couple left, leaving for Mibs a kind of aura in the room, an attest that humanity was clean rather than foul. Before taking leave, she told the Governor she thought it proper to mention that she had sent two letters containing money to her husband and two more long letters asking why she didn't hear from him. And could it be that the letters were not delivered to him?

For the first time she saw the Governor breathe hard and clench his hands. More than a hundred thousand soldiers from Indiana, young men and boys mostly, had volunteered at his call and he had to care for them and their families besides handling a treasonable legislature. His work never got done and he worked day and night. Camp Morton was named after him. He would like to see it run better and he hoped to find time to straighten it out.

Mibs took his two hands and looked into his stern and weary face. "I understand, sir, I know what you say and what you can't say. I thank you for helping one poor woman hunting her lost husband. You will be in my prayers. I cannot thank you enough." The Governor's hard face softened as he saw her moist eyes and heard her "God bless you" before she walked out holding her two little ones by the hand.

In the dining room of the Bates House that evening Mibs found in one of her supper companions a brigadier general on furlough with disability. Mibs told him of a railroad-coach talk where two men discussed whether the war was a civil war, a sectional war, a war between states, or a war of brothers, as one claimed. The brigadier said you could strictly call it a war of brothers. At the West Point Military Academy he had known John C. Pemberton, a classmate. He remembered Pemberton getting word first of one new baby brother at home and later again news of a second baby brother arriving. And while Pemberton was commanding thirty thousand soldiers defending Vicksburg, the curious fact was that his two grown-up baby brothers were fighting in Pennsylvania regiments of the Union Army. At Vicksburg, said the brigadier, a Confederate regiment from Missouri defended a hill against an attacking Union regiment from Missouri—and in several clashes in Kentucky, Confederate troops from that state fought with Union troops from that same state. He told Mibs of a Kentucky father with one son Union and another son Confederate, both killed in battle and the father burying them in the same grave and on the gravestone: "God knows which was right." He estimated something over three hundred thousand people across lower Illinois, Indiana and Ohio as Southern sympathizers. He had heard estimates of thousands of men from lower Illinois, Indiana and Ohio, gone south for service in the Confederate Army.

Mibs and the little ones slept soundly that night till an hour or two before daybreak. Mibs suddenly sat up in bed, in a sweat, a chill, and a cold fright. Her action and cry woke both the little ones next to her. She had dreamed of morning funeral services at the Wayman farmhouse and a procession to a pine knoll where the grave of Brock Wayman, in his Union blue uniform, had been widened and into the double grave in the white light of a high-noon winter sun, they had let down the body of Rodney Wayman in Confederate gray. And Mibs saw herself as perfectly calm through the services and the burial. It was afterward the endless tears came and the sobs shook her. She had asked Rod's father and mother if on the gravestone over the two sons they should carve the line "God knows which was right." And the mother of Rodney and Brock, even-toned and self-assured, "I might have expected the suggestion from you. We'll put no such nonsense over the grave. God knows one was absolutely right and the other absolutely wrong." Then in the dream the tears came to Mibs and as she sat up in bed awake she could taste salt and later hear Clayborn's gentle voice, "Why are you crying mamma?"

When she arrived at the Wayman farm late the next evening a letter was handed her. She opened it, read it to herself in less than a minute, then read it aloud to Mr. and Mrs. Wayman and saw it heartened them, as good news heartens. She read it over and again to herself during the evening. She slept with it in a pocket of her nightgown. It was from Rod, postmarked Cincinnati. "God leaned down and gave me a lift," he wrote. He was alive and well, would rejoin his regiment, would write her when he could, would see her when the war ended, God willing, his prayers always including her and the two little ones and his father and mother.

Mibs laughed over his being alive and well, caught his song-voice and a personal quirk of his eyes and lips in "God leaned down and gave me a lift." And she cried over how long it might be before his homecoming.

She hunted out verses Rod had copied from some book, many a time reading to her the lines:

> Give me bread and give me wine,
> So my wishes you divine.
> Do not ask me, ask me why—
> If you vex me I shall cry!

> Bread I have, but wine, you gypsy,
> Runs the reddest on your lips—eh?
> Get along, the roses miss you,
> If you vex me I shall kiss you!

And the third verse they had read together sometimes with arms around each other:

> Kiss me? Kiss you! There's the issue!
> Always snatch a juicy cherry!
> Brush the bloom off, the perfume off—
> Take and make a dull heart merry!

Having read these lines one night in a whispered reading, she blew out the lamp, crept between the sheets and pillowed her head with a whispered moan, "Oh God, this bed feels empty!"

PART FIVE

Chapter 34

Blue Smoke and Bird Feathers

THE morning sun of late winter streamed in at a window. Through the glass Omri Winwold could see the span of the Mississippi River and beyond a mist over the thawing mud flats in Illinois. He had finished a plate of buckwheat cakes with butter and sorghum, had begun on a pork chop and two eggs with German-fried potatoes. He had moved his newspaper from where it stood against the caster, turned the caster till the saltcellar came for a sprinkle over his chop and eggs. He had propped the newspaper again at the caster, had sort of luxuriated in the morning sun on his head, shoulders and back, and taken a final glance at the river and the mist creeping over the mud flats beyond.

He wanted to be in the best possible mood for a second reading of the weekly *Salem Exponent,* a Pike County neighbor, Peace Democrat, extremist Copperhead, dead-set against the war and those running it. Omri was reading for a second time the *Exponent* reprint of an editorial from the most widely circulated and most enterprising daily newspaper in the United States, the *New York Herald.* The editorial, dated February 19, 1864, read:

President Lincoln is a joke incarnate. His election was a very sorry joke. The idea that such a man as he should be President of such a country as this is a very ridiculous joke. The manner in which he entered Washington—having fled from Harrisburg in a Scotch cap, a long military cloak and a special night train— was a practical joke. His debut in Washington society was a joke, for he introduced himself and Mrs. Lincoln as "the long and short of the Presidency." His inaugural address was a joke since it was full of promises which he has never performed. His cabinet is and always has been a standing joke. All his state papers are jokes. His letters to our generals, beginning with those to Gen. McClellan, are very cruel jokes. His plan for abolishing slavery in 1900 was a broad joke. His emancipation proclamation was a solemn joke. His recent emancipation proclamation of abolition and amnesty is another joke. His conversation is full of jokes. . . . His title of "Honest" is a satirical joke. The style in which he winks at frauds in the War Department, frauds in the Navy Department . . . and frauds in every department, is a costly joke. His intrigues to secure a renomination and the hopes he appears to entertain of a re-election are, however, the most laughable jokes of all.

Omri ran his eyes over it once more, took a deep quiet laugh that shook his ribs, looked out over the river and murmured, "As the fellow said, it's a delicate situation, there's a hair in the butter." He was thinking of the many times the *Salem Exponent* had howled to the high heavens at the arbitrary and tyrannical Administration in Washington using its power to throttle free speech and to strangle a free press. Across his mind flitted an anecdote he had read, of the President being asked, "Are the newspapers reliable?" and his answer, "Yes, they're reliable. They lie and then they re-lie."

On the sidewalk outside came passers-by. They looked well-fed, well-slept, clothed against the winter chill, most of them. Some looked well-satisfied, prim, chipper, even smug. How many of them, he asked, had the slightest notion of what it was to march twenty miles in either mud or dust, to sleep in rain and snow on the bare ground with only a blanket, to lie wounded and calling for water, to hear nothing for weeks and months from folks at home, to eat cold food and half-rations between spells of action where you couldn't know which of your best friends would not be there to answer roll call? How many heard about these things and yet didn't really hear? How many, and there were such, went along feeling an extra comfort about eating regularly and sleeping clean and warm? How many were there who didn't care one way or another about the war? He had heard a Pike County farmer, after paying two substitutes to go into the Army to fight in place of his two sons, "If it wasn't for the high taxes, I wouldn't know there was a war on, and with corn and pork gone sky-high I'm making money like never before."

Two boys in Union blue, well-fed rosy-cheeked boys, sat at a table next the window in the other corner of the room when he came in. They laughed through their breakfast. He couldn't hear their jokes but he could see their rippling faces. The owner called to them from the cook-stove corner, "When you're through, boys, I want that pay you promised for breakfast." They laughed back to him, "You'll get it, mister, don't worry." Now he saw the boys reaching to the floor next to the wall. Then they stood up and came away from the table on crutches, one with a left leg gone, the other a right leg gone. And in the center of the room they did a crutch dance they had worked out. What could be done with two legs and two crutches was interesting and at times amazing. The owner of the place shook hands with them, laughed and called them by their first names. They stopped at the table where Omri was drinking his breakfast coffee. One of them

930

said, "We buy our shoes together. I get the left," with a nod to his partner, "and he gets the right." Omri gave them a half-dollar apiece and wished them luck.

As he had done a few errands, it was an hour before noon when Omri walked to the house where he had been due for several months. It was four years since he had walked this gravel path between leafless lilac and rose bushes. Both drunk and sober he had walked this path, at midnight and high noon. He rang the bell at the front door and stood waiting. The door opened and there she stood in a plain blue-black gown, her face more narrow, somewhat pinched and worn, but her violet eyes warm and melting and her voice marvelously cool with a hidden warmth.

"Annabell," he said, putting out two hands. "Omri," she said so he could hardly hear her, taking his two hands in hers.

Her hands were not pulling him in. The smile dropped from her face and her grave cool eyes went with her saying, "Don't be surprised at anything, Omri." Her face shaded into something else on his saying, "Whatever you say I'm yours to command."

She led him into the big room where on his last visit he had entered drunk but ambulant to see her for the first time as the wife of Henry Flack. She had had for him that night as she sat in a tall brass-studded black chair nothing less than a quiet majesty and under the spell of it he had mocked and mimicked, then preached and prayed himself sober.

Now he saw Henry Flack in a wheel chair at the fireplace. Henry didn't turn his head. Henry had lost thirty or forty pounds, Omri guessed, the cheeks not puffed out. Where Henry was once round and chunky he was now square with lean shoulders and trunk. He sat with a left hand lying quiet on the right hand, staring into the fireplace.

Omri took a chair next to Henry, Annabell stood with one hand up over her head on the fireplace mantel. Henry turned from staring into the fireplace and looked Omri full in the face. Omri saw Henry as no longer popeyed, the eyeballs set farther back. Henry, after his blank look at Omri, turned his head and resumed his stare into the fireplace. Annabell moved a chair alongside Omri and whispered, "Just wait, he'll come out of it."

Omri looked at his watch—ten minutes past eleven. The two men and the woman sat in quiet looking into the fire. Several times Omri felt the touch of Annabell's hand on his right arm, the hand repeating her whispered, "Just wait, he'll come out of it." Omri was certain she understood he knew well that she had watched Henry through many of these spells. He could hear the feet and voices of children at play in some other room of the house. He was curious to see them— they were wanted children. He looked at his watch again—half-past eleven. He took side glances at Henry and bent toward Annabell's

931

ear and whispered, "You remember I used to call him jug-shaped, now he's more like a box."

Annabell nodded, looked into the fire for a time, leaned close to Omri's ear and whispered, "He never learned to suffer till this came." When Omri looked at his watch again it was a quarter to twelve. Shortly after, Henry turned his head, pivoting it slowly as though it was second nature to him and as though he chose to be deliberate and it was now his way of life. The head swung slowly round and his face looked into that of Omri and Henry spoke. It was not the old bursting and vital speech and it had a faint gleaming delicacy not there in the old days.

Henry was saying, "Omri Winwold, you have been long away from your friends."

Omri rose and stood before Henry, took both Henry's hands, felt the old powerful squeeze gone, Omri saying, "And *you* have been *far* away."

Henry spoke with a laugh, near a titter. "So far I can't tell about it, so much to tell it can't be told, so damned funny I don't know whether to laugh or cry."

"You been in the war, Henry."

"Yes, I been in the war so I won't forget it."

"I'm not asking where you been, Henry. I want to see you take it easy."

"A man goes to war, Omri, up where the shooting is, and he shoots and gets shot and he don't know who he shot nor who shot him and it ain't fixed so the two of 'em that shot each other can write letters back and forth how they're gettin along."

He turned his face and Omri saw what he read as a sweet wistful smile on Henry's mouth. The smile brightened with vitality as he looked beyond Omri and said, "Annabell, ain't it nice to see our old friend Omri here today?"

"Almost too good to be true, Henry," said Annabell. "He stayed away too long."

Henry stared in the fire awhile and then in a sober tone with a touch of anxiety and care, "How's your family in the war, Omri?"

"Marvel, my oldest child, you remember," said Omri, pausing, and hearing Henry's prolonged, "Yes, I remember," this telling Omri that Henry's memory was in good order and he knew that Omri was referring to Bee's child. Omri knew by a featherlight touch on his arm that Annabell, with some kind of delicate instinct, wished him to know that she had seen something pass between them of which she didn't have knowledge. "Marvel, the oldest, twenty-eight now, enlisted in '61 and from battle to battle has gone up to colonel. Milton, the next oldest, twenty-seven, got hit at Shiloh and we have him home now in a wheel chair like yours, he can't walk yet."

"Jesus, Omri."

"Holliday is twenty-four now with Sherman's army deep South. Peter Moore is twenty-three now and in January when he enlisted, and a couple of neighbors were paying for substitutes for their boys, he said if I offered to buy a substitute for him he'd spit in my face. Cedora is twenty-four, a hospital nurse in Virginia, her husband killed at Shiloh. Patrick Henry will be eighteen next fall and says it'll be his turn to go. That leaves our girl Hope, fifteen, and Robert Prindle, fourteen, to help me and two free Negroes work the farm."

"God, Omri, the war hit your family hard. Maybe you don't like to talk about it—like me."

There was a silence. Annabell rose. "Maybe I could get you a drink, Omri. We've got some old Kentucky bourbon, pre-Mexican War."

"Thanks, Annabell, later I might take a glass of beer. I haven't touched hard liquor since I was here last. I took on enough then to last me a lifetime. Let the soldiers do the drinking for the country. The home guards ought to stay sober till the war ends."

Annabell excused herself. Henry stared into the fire. Omri waited, and then, "I had some good times in this house, Henry, I never forget those nights we had." Henry said nothing. Omri wondered if he had lapsed. Then he saw Henry easy and slow take the right hand from under the left and place it on top. Henry turned his head toward Omri and his voice had the stuff of a low distant echo. "Bee died, Omri. It was before I enlisted a man back from San Francisco told me how it was. I'll put it to you short. That Portuguese pimp I told you about—"

"Yes."

"He got all her money and there was a lot of it. He lost it on gambling and other women. Bee got where she was about the lowest and cheapest fat whore in San Francisco, drunk most of the time, kind of crazy between-times. She caught the Portuguese on a steamboat leaving for Buenos Aires—"

Annabell came into the room, her face luminous, hand in hand with two children. She introduced chubby rosy three-year-old Frank Blair Flack. With coaxing, Frank put out a hand for Omri, squirmed, pulled the hand loose and ran out of the room. "Bashful," said Annabell, and then introduced a two-year-old toddler Nathaniel Lyon Flack, who put out a hand without coaxing and laughed and gurgled as he was dandled on Omri's knee. He set Nathaniel down, put the child's hand into his mother's, and called as she walked toward the door, "Beautiful healthy children, Annabell, you can be proud." Annabell was saying before she closed the door, "Dinner soon ready."

Henry in his echo voice that Omri could hear, though it was a little like overhearing, went on, "Like I told you, she caught the Portuguese on a steamboat leaving for Buenos Aires. She pulled a gun, shot him dead, jumped overboard and never came up from salt water." Omri waited. Henry went on. "That's all. You belong to know it, Omri. You will never hear another word from me about Bee except now I

933

can tell you I think it's damn beautiful her boy is a colonel in the army and I'm betting on him."

In his wheel chair at the dinner table Omri noticed Henry's motions correct enough but slow—and Annabell quick to see his every need and meet it, sometimes with a light touch that was a caress. Wheeled back to the big room and the fireplace, Henry dropped to sleep, Omri and Annabell in chairs alongside and Annabell very low-voiced: "First year of the war here Henry made a mistake. It was wild times in St. Louis that summer when the state came near seceding, twenty-eight people killed one day's street fighting here, even two women shot to death. Henry took into our house an old business friend and a kind of sixth cousin from Memphis. They proved this man a spy and they kept Henry in jail for six weeks. Frank Blair, the big politician, heard about Henry's case and came to see him in jail. 'They say you talk against the nigger and you're Secesh,' Blair said, and Henry said, 'I'm ready to fight for the Union but I ain't particular about fightin to free the niggers.'

"Blair got Henry out and Henry got together a company that elected him captain. They saw fighting in different battles in Missouri and Henry went through Vicksburg and then Chickamauga. His company was ordered to charge. One shell exploded that killed two men and laid five others on the ground wounded. Henry wasn't hit by the shell or any piece of it. He just fell to the ground and didn't know anything for hours and he couldn't get up to stand on his feet and they carried him to the hospital and they could stick needles into his legs and he didn't feel it. Since then he has been like you see him, only it was worse at first. For a while he couldn't walk nor talk. Then one day he could talk. It just came to him. Maybe," and Omri heard a catch in her voice and she hesitated and went on, "someday he will walk again. It'll just come like the talking did."

Omri could find no words. He put a hand softly on the back of her hand, which turned toward his, and the two hands spelled out pity and understanding. It was shortly after that Omri was asking, "What is there to Henry's business now, wholesale and retail food?"

"Henry owns control, took in his two best men as partners and they are making money like never before. They have had army food-supply contracts that paid, you might say, too nice, too fat."

"And, Annabell—"

"Yes, I hear you."

"The boy Edward Joshua Ponder."

"You don't forget."

"Some names, some faces, never."

"You can never tell what a growing boy will change into. Josh was a pale spindling, suddenly went in for games and fighting. He got tough and wiry. Last summer he ran away and went into the army as a drummer boy. At Chattanooga two bullets took him, one in the right

934

foot, the other in the left leg. He was unconscious for hours, dragged himself to a tree, sat with his back to it, hollered for help, and no help came. He reached for his drum and sticks and hollered for help while he beat the drum. He fainted away and the next he knew two men were carrying him to a hospital. It was a lonesome timber he was in and the men said the drum saved him, the drum and his quick wits. I go to see him in hospital here three or four days a week. The foot wound is well. The leg will take time. He may lose it. The doctors don't know for sure."

Henry stirred. They saw his eyes open, his hands shifting. He turned his head toward them, looked in their faces, said no word, turned his head and sat in quiet staring in the fire. "He'll come out of it," Annabell murmured.

Omri studied her face. He remembered it once as an image of brief drama: a black-and-gold pansy laughing to the sun after a raindrench. He asked her now, "Did I say that last time you're one of the loveliest blossoms God ever dropped on the earth?"

"Yes." She kept looking straight ahead into the fire. He saw her profile, her lips moving. He heard her and it came a little songlike, "Yes, I remember and it's more than good you remember."

It was still a cherry mouth she had, not bright-red, not gay sunrise-scarlet, but now today rather a sundown-maroon with wisps of violet shadow. He remembered when the hold of her had struck deeper into him. He had brought out antique proverb-poems for her: "Always the impossible happens. For a web begun God sends a thread. The glutted understand little of the hungry. Even a great river's glory ends at the sea. The morning mist goes and life goes." And she sat stone-still, only her lips moving, "Old as the hills. I like 'em. Jawbones drying in the sun. Blue smoke and bird feathers." It was then he felt she was putting knotted thongs around his heart never to come loose. It was then he read to her the poem he had written in the second saloon-stop on the way to Henry's office. He asked her softly now, "The poem I copied for you—has time worn it out for you?" She said "No," a long dreamy No-no-o, threw her head back and with closed eyes recited:

> "Pour from the sea
> one hand of salt.
> Take from a star
> one finger of mist.
> Pick from a heart
> one cry of silver."

Omri heard it through and said, "I'm glad I copied it for you," and heard her with her head still tilted back and eyes closed, "I don't need the copy on paper now, I have copies here," as she made the sign of the cross.

Omri's eyes roved from her head of black hair and white neck down the length of her slim wiry body and said to himself, "Her body calls to me, yes, and she knows it and she knows too it is something else, an added mystic flame-line of likeness we have, that keeps her hold on me." He spoke aloud, "You have chosen from your thorns, and," with a gesture toward Henry, "you have shared with the flamewon."

When she turned with full-open eyes into his, he said, "What I see is blue smoke and bird feathers." Then he added in a dry changed tone, a whiff of laughter in it, "Who would believe it? We have been practical."

A like whiff of laughter was in her saying, "Unless practical we'd have been lost, sunk."

"I'm leaving for home this afternoon because it's practical."

"You could have the same room as before, overnight, if you like."

"No, it's practical to go this afternoon."

"Then I'll be practical and let you go."

"And I shan't stay away so long this time. I shall try to come more often. Time may work for us. Time can be terribly practical." Omri added, "Lord, what full practical days of loving and serving you have here!"

"Henry, the children, keeping house with the help of one good Negro woman, going to hospital to see Josh, going to Henry's office about business."

"Nothing to do till tomorrow."

"And all day to do it in." Then Annabell less gaily, "Don't forget I know you too have your endless round of duty. I know you too share with the flamewon and sometimes cry trying to choose from your thorns."

Annabell now swung a hand toward Henry. "He's my man, now like before. He has a big rich heart. The children love him. Some days they do all sorts of pranks around his chair."

And then she was saying swiftly, her body tensed, "Leaving last time you said, 'When I come again there'll be an awful storm blowing and a million houses will have on the front doorknob a bloody thumbprint.'" Then she queried eagerly, "What prophecies now?"

"Don't set me up for a prophet. There are stuffed prophets and unstuffed. I like to watch them mocking at each other's prophecies. I like to see two prophets contradict the opposite and cancel each other. I have a few small beliefs, if you like, Annabell."

"Like what, please?"

"The war will end in a year or two when the South is down to its last man. The Union will come through. This United States will move into wars with other nations and become a great world power. The cost of it—we can see some of the cost in the room here. Some of it is on your face, in the added dark gravity on your mouth, in smoke shadows that chase each other in your eyes. Yes, and it's there in those little creeps of gray in your black hair."

936

"And I guess it's there in your brown eyes set farther back in the sockets—and there in those sudden white snow-streaks in that chin muffler of whiskers."

Henry stirred, shifted hands, turned toward them with eyes alive. "I hadn't noticed, Annabell. I can see those little streaks in Omri's whiskers. They *are* snow-white."

"I've had a fine visit with Annabell," said Omri. "She's good for you, I can tell that."

"She's a blessing, she's my best hope. I dream of our going to Mass again some Sunday morning, me walking again." He waved a hand toward a corner. "Next time you come, Omri, maybe I will take out the zither and yodel for you and Annabell and the boys." There was more talk. Omri rose to go, took Henry's two hands. "It could have been worse, Henry. You are alive. I'll be praying for you and joining my prayers with all others who pray for you."

On the front porch he hugged the two little ones, held Annabell's two hands, said, "God keep you, Annabell," kissed her swiftly on a plait of black hair above her left ear, and walked down the gravel path between leafless lilac and rose bushes. On the brick sidewalk of the street he turned, threw a kiss with both hands to all three on the porch, saw the children laughing in glee, saw Annabell's two white hands fluttering in the air high over her head almost like a little whirl of snow. Then he walked away without looking back.

* * * * * * * * * *

Chapter 35

* * * * * * * * * *

Cherry Trees in White

A BLOODY month, May of Eighteen Hundred Sixty-Four—the statistics from Virginia and Georgia battlefields a steady drip, a red drip— the open and hidden agony beyond computation or narrative—not told then nor since. Europe looked on, wondering what the end would be. The controlling opinion of men and journals in Britain and on the Continent, as the news reached them from across the Atlantic, held to one viewpoint: If the Union armies won, America would in a long future stand as a world power, incalculable and beyond reckoning or prediction.

Omri Winwold out of his reading and thought tried to interest Mrs. Rodney Wayman in the immensity of the political and military drama of the hour. She had ridden over to his farm one May afternoon for their first visit in many weeks. He could only half interest her in the immense national and international issues. She told him of her trip to Indianapolis and her face had a brightness, her eyes brilliant and her lips swift as he had not seen her in two years or more.

Mibs' old-time voice rippled thrushlike the simple informative sentence, "Rod is alive and well, hard as nails, a regular tiger and a fighting devil," rushing on with details of the escape from Camp Morton. Then the news gushed from her that a short sweet letter had come, postmarked Cincinnati. Rod was alive and heading south to join his regiment, praying for the end of the war so he could join her and the little ones—she had to share this news with Omri. "You're some kind of a sixteenth cousin of mine, if you remember."

Omri's wide mouth twisted in a grin. "As I remember your grandmother on your mother's side telling it to your mother when I was barkeep at the Maple Leaf tavern in Springfield, Massachusetts, she said to your mother: 'Your grandfather's grandfather on your mother's side was a full brother to Omri's grandfather's grandmother on his mother's side.'" And Mibs' even white teeth had flashed with her laugh,. "How you *do* remember! It's a hard fact and the God's truth, of course, yet it sounds a trifle silly."

They had been standing on the front porch, overlooking an orchard and a planted cornfield, trees leafing out, the smell of a fresh green earth in the air, and forty feet away four cherry trees clad in hosannahs of white blossoms. Mibs pointed to the four trees: "A year ago I was saying what do I care about them blossoms, to hell with them blossoms, and today they are a sacred hushed white song telling me believe believe believe." She brought her face close to Omri's in saying this. He read her as wanting a fighting chance, ground to stand on in a little daylight.

"Don't be too gay," said Omri. "Let me show you something." He led Mibs into an end room of the house where in a corner with open windows sat Milton in his wheel chair. For company Milton had the nineteen-year-old son of neighbor William Hoon, one arm gone. Also for company Milton had the twenty-six-year-old son of storekeeper Ed Houseworth, blind in both eyes. Omri introduced Mibs, who shook hands all round. Then Omri led her away. On the front porch, again facing the hushed marvels of the cherry trees in white communion garments, Omri said, "Those three fellows have a language their own. They know, between themselves, whether they are heroes, and if so, what kind. They have wonderful silences together. They beat the Quakers. There is a fellowship of the broken and mutilated and no outsider can get in."

Now, before going, Mibs' face and mood changed. She was traveling the next day up to New Era. Her father, restless through the first year of the war, at fifty-five years of age was commissioned in the commissary service. After Chattanooga and a long siege of malaria and typhoid, he had been furloughed home, taken to bed with a relapse, as Mibs' mother wrote.

With her two children Mibs was to have her first visit in New Era in more than four years. "Our letters got shorter and fewer these four years," said Mibs to Omri. "You know how mixed and tangled things are under the Wayman roof, some things I couldn't even tell you. How could I write them about Rod, gone for years and not a word from him? How could I write them about Rod's mother, her fine friendship with me, a beautiful and lovable woman and her mind slowly failing under the agony and inanity of the war? I couldn't have written them long enough letters, even if there had been time, to make clear to them the miseries that aren't clear to me."

Omri walked with her, saw her mounted and riding away.

* * * * * * * * * *

Chapter 36

* * * * * * * * * *

New Era Homecoming

JOEL WIMBLER was far-gone, a white shrunken face, a wasted body, when one of his pale bony hands lay in the hand of his daughter. Most of his hair had fallen away. She had to search his face for what she had known there. The high moment for all in the house was the wan queer smile at his lips and eyes as his right hand held first one and then the other of the hands of his two grandsons. He died with his mind hazy, too weak for words.

Then came a grinding and terrible week in Mibs' life. Guilt was on her, shame on shame, that she had never begun to realize what loneliness had gnawed at her mother and worn her with her husband away in the war. Mibs looked back at what a couple they had been, her father and mother, the devotion to each other and the understanding between them. Nothing before had ever prepared Brooksany Wimbler for separation from her Joel.

Faintly here and there over the house hovered the smell of leather and oil and beeswax, the harness-maker's odor. It smote Mibs, and her conscience wrangled with her as she saw the white thin war-face of her mother. The old-time still look, inner peace with herself while the world went by, had the pinch of pain on it. Not even the grandchildren could give her ease or comfort, it seemed. "I heard they were born and they were boys and that was all," she said once to Mibs. She saw her mother at times a sort of ghost, bones clothed with a weary and withered flesh. Once when tears came and she had lain down alongside her mother and tried to put an arm under her mother's head, she felt her arm gently pushed away and no words why. From day to day for a week after her father died, Mibs was going to say good-by and leave with the two children. Something told her from day to day not to go.

On the sixth day the mother's only words were, "I don't want to live. I think I began dying when you left us. I did die when Joel died, only you haven't buried me yet." The next day a doctor was there with Mibs and they saw Brooksany Wimbler give her last breath. And there had been one brief moment of wakefulness when her eyes opened in quiet, when Mibs saw again the old still look on the mouth and the little words came that pierced Mibs, melted and shook her, the words along with a soft hand taking Mibs' hand, "I don't blame you, darling, you had to, and I love you all."

As Mibs went about the house, the old home with overwhelming memories, straightening and gathering and discarding, she would pause before the tall mahogany clock from the first home in Arpa, New York, she would look at its face and read the antique script: *Peace Be unto You*, shaking her head and once wagging a finger at it, "Not yet, old clock, not yet—sometime maybe, sometime short or long, sometime maybe." In an upstairs back room she met treasured pieces of furniture stored, her mother's sewing machine, her father's harness-making tools, a box of baby dresses, a little red wagon she had pulled when she was two years old, other articles she could see to later. A box of daguerreotypes, an album of ambrotypes and photographs, her mother's worn black silk dress, lace collars, the plain solid-gold wedding ring, her father's silver watch, a brass one-shot pistol, and two of his awls, these and other keepsakes she was to carry with her. She spent hours with Andrew Biddings, the wagonmaker and McCormick Reaper agent, to whom she was entrusting property affairs.

One afternoon she drove out in a buggy, ran over for a look at Pine Flats Pond, then to the hilltop ridge where once on a winter evening at sunset she stood with skates slung over her shoulder. She could see the town of New Era spread out nearly twice as large as then, new blocks of streets and houses running out over the prairie, nearly four thousand more people, many of them newcomers to America, Swedes, Germans, Irish, English and Scotch. While the war was on, a wave of immigrants had come, two factories, a second brickyard, another sawmill, a sash-door-and-blind mill, a longer Main Street with more stores, double the freight and passenger trains on the railroad, a new big freight shed, an enlarged stockyard for handling cattle and hogs. She knew that hundreds of towns in the North, particularly the Northwest, had grown and prospered like New Era while the war was on. She knew too that hundreds of towns in Southern states had been looted and in part devastated and laid waste. She knew, and had heard the statistics, that the incoming hundreds of thousands of immigrants at the Atlantic ports sought jobs, land and homes in the North, giving their added production strength to the North.

A shiver came to her at one moment when she enfigured the North as vital, hairy, brutal and constantly growing in brute strength, completely beyond the realization of the Southern extremist element that had instigated the war. And a moment of elation came when her mind flashed back to what a little pioneer huddle of cabins New Era was when she grew up as a child, where she had seen unbroken sod and prairie grass to a man's shoulders. Here she had deep roots. Yet she was a stranger. The contradiction troubled her. "I must get away from here," she said.

She was leaving New Era because it would hurt to stay, though she knew very well that in Atlas too it would be hard going. She visited. The widow of Danny Hilton, pleasant and slumberous, had two children for America's future, worth looking at. A fourth-grade schoolteacher, her face once freckled and now a smooth cream-white, her once skimpy body now straight and buxom, her once carroty hair a tall mass of golden braids, her speech sounding almost too Addisonian—Mibs gave a long warm hug to Maureen Whalen, betrothed to the son of Silas Higby, the sawmill man.

"Since you're going to the war," Silas Higby had smiled to his son, "you can have your wife from across the tracks if you come back." Mibs found scandal had been talked about Maureen. For a time, it was said, Herbert Hines, still registered in New Era College, still in flashy clothes and with money aplenty, had been seen often taking Maureen buggy-riding. Then whatever was between them suddenly broke off and Maureen was away two summer months in Peoria, the talk ran. "She was home those two months," said the editor Max Mutter to Mibs. "The goddamnedest lies get going in this town."

Then Max Mutter gave Mibs the cold facts about the gyrations and the sad end of the pale sorry spindling Herbert Hines. The father, always a rugged, daring, take-a-chance man, had come on from California, to straighten out his boy on the war. The boy wanted his father to buy a substitute for him. The father said, "There's been too much of it, too many rich men paying the Irish and the Germans to substitute for their sons. Your three brothers volunteered at the first call in '61. One of them got killed at Gettysburg, another is in Libby Prison, and another fighting with Grant. Now you're going. I won't help you out of it nor let you help yourself out of it. You're going. You might get killed, and you don't know, it might make a real man of you." Then Herbert had packed a bag, sneaked on a train to Chicago. His father followed, after a week located the boy in a luxurious brothel and down to his last silver dollar.

Amos Hines had his son arrested and put in the army. Months later came the published news that Herbert Hines deserted, was captured, tried by court-martial and convicted. And one morning at sunrise in Virginia, his regiment, formed in a hollow square, witnessed Herbert Hines, standing alongside the prepared pine box, take death from a firing squad. Max Mutter had heard Amos Hines say, "I did my duty by the country. It'd be a hell of a country without the Union, a lot of snaggling quarreling sovereign states at war with each other." Max Mutter saw an absent look on Mibs' face and asked what she was thinking. "I'm thinking back to a supper at Silas Higby's when I heard Amos Hines say, 'It can be the country'll have to go through an awful fever that'll burn her bowels and bring her near death, but she'll come through it and be stronger than ever.'" Max Mutter smiled. "He *is* what they call a Union man."

"Have you killed any Know-Nothings since I last saw you?" Mibs asked.

"They're petering out," said Mutter. "They don't like it so many Irish, Germans and Swedes are fighting in the war. A Wisconsin regiment all Norwegians has been marching and fighting since the war began, and about half its men dead or crippled. Some Irish and German outfits have made about the same record. When those who don't get killed come back they'll say it's their country because they fought for it. That makes the Know-Nothings sick. They can't hold their noses up like they used to."

Hornsby Meadows stood out as the New Era hero. Dispatches mentioned the bold attacks, hard riding and endurance under fire, of his cavalry regiment. He seemed to have a high record in the army for the number of enemy troops he had personally sabered to death. "I don't know what to think when I hear of the chances he takes," said his wife Fidelia to Mibs. "Sometimes I wish he wasn't so much of a hero. By his letters I can tell he enjoys the war and he is glad he lived to see the war come." Colonel Meadows had been home a week in late May of '63, furloughed with a light wound. The boy baby that had come in February of '64 he wanted named Theodore Weld. The other two boys he had named Wendell Phillips and Elizur Wright.

"Hornsby wanted the war, don't you think?" asked Mibs.

"Oh yes."

"He told you so?"

"Millicent, he prayed for a war to come. I heard him. I said nothing." Fidelia hesitated, wrung her hands. "I couldn't tell him, you know, I would rather he prayed that it would be God's will and wisdom, rather than his, to bring so terrible a thing as war." Fidelia studied a few moments. Mibs waited. "Hornsby was sure there were men in the South who prayed for war and made ready for it."

"Isn't it queer to think about?" Mibs was asking. "One set of men in the South and another set of men in the North, both reading the same Bible and praying to the same God to send a war?"

"I believe it was just like that, Millicent, and it is queer. North and

South, bold proud uncompromising men like Wendell Phillips and Hornsby here and Rhett and Yancey in the South, they wanted war, all of them, and each had his own reasons and believed his side could win."

The two women talked long. They had mutual travail, griefs, doubts. Each went to bed at night and got up in the morning wondering how and where was the husband. As Mibs was leaving they fell on each other's shoulders in tears.

Mibs turned from the door. "Have you seen these stories printed, Fidelia, about Rebel soldiers hacking off heads of enemy soldiers on the battlefield? It's been printed too that the Rebels carry away the bones of Union soldiers to carve into dice and to shape into rings and bracelets they send home to their women. Another story in many papers says the Rebels when they took prisoners of Union officers commanding Negro regiments, they nailed those officers to trees and crucified them."

"I sent Hornsby some newspaper pieces like those and he said he hadn't heard of them. Furthermore, he wrote, he wouldn't believe such stories without evidence. He writes that the Rebels fight pretty clean and sometimes he feels like coming home to kill certain Copperheads."

"I thought as much, Fidelia." Mibs was in a study for a moment. "It comes back to me now. It didn't come back till the other day when I drove over to Hickory Grove and saw Zadock Wayman, a fifth cousin of my husband's father. He's against the nigger, now as always, says Zadock, but he's still a good Steve Douglas Democrat. Three of his sons went away to the war and one killed. It was years ago, riding back from Hickory Grove and hearing an old Kentuckian sing some songs for me, that something came over me. It wasn't very clear, what came over me. I tried to find words for it and when the words came they were something like this if I remember right:

> "The North and South have secrets from each other.
> Either they must know each other's secrets better,
> Either that or they must somehow love each other more.
> Either they've got to dig deeper in each other's hearts
> For what they'll find there
> Or somehow they've got to love each other more
> In order to get at what they don't understand now.
> Otherwise there'll be a holiday of pride and hate,
> A storm bloody to look at."

"The storm came, Millicent. And it is bloody to look at."

And their arms went about each other and their cheeks pressed in low moan and dry sob.

Mibs' hand was on the doorknob. Again she was about to go. Fidelia was saying, "What you're wearing there, around your neck and down, it's so unusual, what is it?"

"In a leather trunk my father made, at the bottom of the trunk I found it, under letters, papers, keepsakes. Years ago I saw it and it didn't mean anything to me and I clean forgot it." They stepped to a window in the sitting room and Mibs loosened a silver cord at her neck and held in the clear daylight a bronze plaque and they picked out the letters and read together the words, lines, numbers:

The Four Stumbling Blocks to Truth

1. The influence of fragile or unworthy authority.
2. Custom.
3. The imperfection of undisciplined senses.
4. Concealment of ignorance by ostentation of seeming wisdom.

"Only last night I found it," said Mibs. "The wick in the lamp was giving out and the light poor. The bronze was about the color of the leather bottom and if it hadn't been for a loop of silver cord sticking out from under the bronze I probably wouldn't have got my fingers on it."

"It seems old, very old."

"It sounds important, keen like a knife blade of tempered steel," and she hesitated and went on, "like a blade sharpened and worn and sharpened again till it's half its first size."

"Something like that, I do believe, Millicent."

"And shrewd like we say the winter wind is biting and shrewd." Mibs fastened the silver cord at her neck and said to Fidelia, "I'm going to study these four blocks. They may help my ignorance. I do stumble enough and they may help me on my stumbling."

Fidelia smiled. The two of them stood on the front porch and looked at a line of maple trees with a shimmer of the creeping bright-green of oncoming new leaves. The sky shone blue. On the breasts of two robins sitting on a maple branch were slants of copper from a rich afternoon sun. The sounds on the air had quiet, content, sanity—a far-off hen-cackle, hoofs and wagon wheels on a dry dirt road, the chuffing of the engine of the railway local switching stock cars.

The two women stood on the porch and listened.

"Now, Fidelia, who in the hell would believe there is a war on?"

"You are correct, Millicent, but if Hornsby should be here he would say your language is not proper."

Fidelia smiled. So did Mibs. They kissed in parting. Hornsby would not have believed what wishes and prayers went up from those two women that he should return alive and well to a town that now counted his a great name.

Chapter 37

Sanctuary in a Barn

THE annual return, the airy and mystic float of dogwood and shad-blow in blossom, had come to Virginia in 1864 in the old merry month of May—and two armies set for a clutch at each other seeking a strangle-hold. The honeysuckle and huckleberry stood in bloom and the wild rose offered its pink on the air as though here was one more spring like many another spring before.

On red clay and sandy land, amid jack-pine thickets and scrub oak, cedar and ash, in a tanglefoot underbrush, Colonel Marvel Winwold had moved and camped his command, one of a hundred and more regiments. Some of Marvel's men had found where they camped old camp-fires and rusty canteens, rotting artillery axles, skeletons of men and horses. They counted fifty skulls of men on a square of ten rods and found half-open graves thrust out with a rotted trouser leg, a mildewed sleeve or the clean frame of a man's hand. Here the fighting tides of men had swirled in May of last year.

There came ten days of marching, fighting. The battles of the Wilderness and Spotsylvania Courthouse rolled up the most terrible cost in dead, wounded, missing, that any modern war in Europe or America had seen. In smoke, fog and rain sagged the battle lines. No one told then or could tell in later days the whole story, the entire dripping and crimson tale, of the thousands of individual combats, struggles, sacrifices, acts of devotion or fear, that composed the battle drama as a whole. The violence, the chaos, the inexorable incessancy of the changing shambles at the parapets of one salient known as Bloody Angle—any man in it could tell part of it—no man ever gathered the parts into a whole. In mud and blood over ditches filled with dead the living waded and clambered. Muskets went flung like spears over one parapet. Standing on heaped dead and wounded, foeman clutched at foeman, pulled him over the bloody and slippery logs and made him prisoner. Trees nearly two feet thick were gnawed and cut down clean by gunfire. To say that in ten days twenty-six thousand blue-coated men and boys were killed and wounded, and half that many men and boys in butternut and gray, is a smooth numerical statement with no pretense of a debit-and-credit accounting of the passion, hope and will, the agony involved, and saturated in the events.

On a wide clearing between two stretches of woodland on the second afternoon of Spotsylvania, Colonel Marvel Winwold, with his halted infantry in the woods waiting orders, saw the advance of a regiment of dismounted cavalry. Their commander Marvel recognized as Colonel Hornsby Meadows. He saw Hornsby's hat shot off. He saw the gray horse under Hornsby sink and lie writhing. The line was a third of the way across the clearing when Hornsby on a black horse joined them, shouting and flashing his saber. The black horse went down and Marvel saw an officer on a bay horse dismount and give the bay to Hornsby. Marvel questioned his own eyes a little when he believed he saw the bay horse go down after the line had passed more than half the clearing. He was sure his eyes saw Hornsby move on with his troops and then fall. He saw the line of men in Hornsby's command reach the woods beyond, perhaps a third of them scattered and fallen over the clearing they had crossed.

Soon Marvel's own men swept over the clearing and in the woods beyond met fire from rifle and cannon. A bullet went through the cloth of his coat over the left shoulder. Another went through his right trouser leg, scraping the fleshy part of the calf. Later came a ball that stopped him in his tracks, a burning pain along the left forearm, a crackling fiery pounding pain that ran to his head and had him dizzy. His knees gave way and on the ground he sat up, gritting his teeth, and with the help of one of his men cut the sleeve, bared the arm and made a dressing that stanched the blood flow. "Thanks, boy, go on now and join your command, I'm all right," he said as he dragged himself next to a tree trunk, remembering yesterday having seen a soldier's head crushed under a horse hoof.

The next Marvel knew he was in an ambulance, on his aching burning left forearm a clean bandage. He heard after a time a man asking the driver why they had stopped. "About thirty ahead of us unloading."

"How many are we ahead of?"

"About forty, I'd guess."

"Kin the hospital hold us all?"

"Guess so, hope so."

"Where are we?"

"Fredericksburg."

That same afternoon Captain Rodney Wayman had sent four of his best marksmen into trees, veteran sharpshooters. They didn't know it then but two of them talked about it afterward, how they all went to work on the same target in the lines moving across the clearing, a blue-coated officer in a black hat, a tall heavy round-shouldered man on a gray horse. They shot his hat off. They shot a gray horse from under him, then a black horse. They saw him mount a bay and the bay go down. Then as he moved afoot with his men they saw him fall and it was less than ten minutes later that two of Rod's men in the trees were wounded and captured, two shot dead to come toppling from their positions in the trees.

946

To Rod it was like Chickamauga, his men driven back, firing from behind trees, from behind logs and stumps, out of thickets where they hugged the ground. Reinforcements came and orders to charge. They swept over the clearing and into its bordering woods. It was here that Rod lay with six men behind a protective log. He asked for volunteers to run for a thicket forty yards toward the enemy line. One man made it. A second one made it. The third one fell halfway. The other three hesitated. Rod said, "I'll make it, and then you come."

He had made nearly thirty yards, perhaps, when he stopped with a jolt. He spun round, slowly and dizzily spun round and sank into a mass of dwarf juniper. Vaguely, dimly, he knew of a burn and a gash running along the jaw and the right side of his face.

Hours later, before opening his eyes, he caught the smell of hay, of cattle and horses. And sounds came to his ears, voices somewhat hushed, curious confusions of feet, wheels, horses. He opened his eyes on a large barn. He lay with straw between him and bare ground, in a very wide aisle between stalls on both sides, haymows above the stall rows. On both sides of the aisle lay lines of men with their feet toward each other, enough space between the feet for litter-bearers. Perhaps half the men lying down were quiet, the other half moaning feebly, crying sharply and piteously, a few out of their heads and cursing wildly or calling for help. At the end of the barn, with a door through which a load of hay could pass, Rod counted five or six ambulances outside and could see the litter-bearers unloading the wounded and moving them into the barn. As his eyes ranged the two lines of wounded on the floor he guessed about one in four was butternut or gray. The wound along his jaw, he wondered about it. The roaring and splitting ache in his head was from the wound. The rest of his body was whole and intact. He had his arms and legs. He could feel them. He wouldn't have been surprised if any or all of them were gone.

In the line opposite he could see one man in butternut with both legs gone, a cannon ball probably. He could remember a scholarly gentleman, a college professor from Louisiana, who was among those assigned to tip the privy shed into the ditch at Camp Morton and he had heard this pundit several times repeat a rigamarole, "Through God brave men do great things, but in the Providence of God He has not so constituted man that, even though he is brave, he can stop a cannon ball."

Rod gave his head a slow careful sidewise turn that hurt and took a glance at the man next to him. An officer, in blue uniform, a first lieutenant, a smooth face except for a shoebrush chin beard neatly trimmed, the face white and stone-still—the man had died since they bore him in and laid him down.

Rod closed his eyes, made a wish that he could personally thank those who had dressed and bandaged his wound and brought him here. He rested from the aching and throbbing. He opened his eyes, gave a slow sidewise turn of his head toward the right. He forgot the surges of pain in bone, flesh and nerves as his eyes roved the officer in blue next to him. The broad round shoulders and thick arms were familiar. So was the profile of the head. And the sideburns triangular and pointed, the wide positive mouth and the strong nose—there could be no mistake. The moans of the man were a kind of breathing for the relief of pain, they were no call for pity.

"It's come to me at last," he said half to himself, though he had turned his head and was looking at Rod. "I killed in this war eleven men with the saber and four with the revolver. I counted them. I had nine horses shot under me. I counted them. Why shouldn't it come to me now? I've been ready for it and now it's come."

Rod wasn't sure but the man was in a mild delirium. The man looked away from him, stared over the haymow opposite and with half-choked sounds tried to sing the lines, "In the beauty of the lilies Christ was born across the sea. . . . He is trampling out the vintage where the grapes of wrath are stored." The words came blurred. The tongue couldn't shape them and the tune had no song sound. "Shot in the lungs, sir, shot in the stomach," and as his eyes gathered the gray uniform coat of Rod he added, "Compliments of the Southern Confederacy, sir." His eyes opened wider, the brown eyebrows lifting ever so slightly, and now he was saying a little above a whisper and the words clear, "Where have I seen you?"

"Long ago, before the war."

"I remember, I tried to kill you with my bare hands."

"Man, don't think about that now."

"You married Mibs Wimbler?"

"Yes."

"Will you tell her I forgive her?" Rod saw the man's eyes go glassy and his two hands come folded near the hole in his lungs, and then in a dim sigh the words, "Tell her I forgive all."

Rod spoke slowly and thickly the words "I'll tell her, I'll tell her." And he knew the man didn't hear his words and the man lay with earthly hearing gone and he was beyond whispers or thunder.

* * * * * * * * * *

Chapter 38

* * * * * * * * * *

War Is So Damned Impersonal

THE besieged city of Richmond, Virginia, had outlying armies where man had turned mole, beaver, gopher. Entrenchments, tunnels, passageways, bombproofs, underground storehouses and mines, the men of both armies lay close to the earth and wormed their zigzag paths and routes. The shovel had honor equal to the gun. Weeks passed, months passed, and Richmond still held and over the North were murmurs and groans from Union men appalled at the cost in money and blood. Looking toward Georgia gave no comfort, for the army defending Atlanta parried and thrust and faded and the taking of Atlanta seemed far off, maybe never. They could read of the President of the United States, in Philadelphia to dedicate a Sanitary Fair, saying wearily, "It is difficult to say a sensible thing nowadays." Only those inside knew of the secret movement in the President's own National Union party to remove him as head of the ticket and replace him with a man they considered more likely to win in the November election. Then after shell and flame had done their work, Atlanta saw the winning army march in and take over. Shortly after, Union cavalry swept the Shenandoah Valley, its commander saying he had burned two thousand barns and would burn more and a crow flying the valley would have to carry its own rations. The secret movement in his own party, to replace the President with another candidate, collapsed.

When Barbara Billy Wayman that autumn of '64 went broken and mute, lingered pale and voiceless and died because she didn't want to live, she was one of others like her whose world had floated away into nowhere. Only her husband Randolph Rutledge Wayman and her daughter-in-law Millicent Wimbler Wayman knew of the Stars and Bars, the flag of the Confederate States of America, wrapped about her bosom as she lay in her pine-knoll grave next to her son Brock in his uniform of Union Army blue.

"She was a rare and lovely woman," said Mibs to Mr. Wayman, and to Omri Winwold, who called a few days after the burial, "She put on a hard outside front trying to cover an inside that was infinitely sensitive. She was a friend to me, sweet and understanding. Then the war came. The war broke her."

Omri heard a quaver in Mibs' voice. He believed that only her children, those two lively and healthy boys, needing her care and giving her companionship, had kept the war from breaking her. Both he and

949

Mibs had a deepening admiration for Mr. Wayman, his endless patience at first under the many brief sharp rebukes of his wife, his many thoughtful acts and perfect consideration for her in the weeks she had gone mute.

"I had my work every day out under the sky, in weather always changing, with the corn, the livestock and the chores," Mr. Wayman was saying this afternoon. "I tried to get Barbara outdoors more. It might have made a difference." Mibs sensed a flicker of weariness along with an unfathomable patience in Mr. Wayman's voice and manner. The joints of his long bony body seemed almost to creak as he let himself down into a chair or slowly rose and stood up. He was saying, "Working on the land and thinking how eternal the land is and how many generations yet are to work this land, sometimes I clean forget the war."

With one eye closed and the other half-shut and slanted toward Omri, Mr. Wayman went on, "You've been a good enough neighbor, Mr. Winwold, I can tell you I have some consolations. I thought the North was commercial, so devoted to money-making they couldn't fight. They have shown they can fight and sacrifice. I can't mock at my own boy Brock going into the Union Army and ready to die for the flag he chose for himself. I can't mock at your boy Milton in his wheel chair nor that Hoon boy with one arm and that blind boy of Ed Houseworth. They count with me. Naturally I take the most pride in my own boy Rod. It's a consolation to me he led his men in great battles and took wounds and made that wonderful escape from the prison over at Indianapolis. I don't have the shame on me of that man over at Pittsfield whose boy shot himself. They tell me that boy didn't want a substitute. There's an insanity about the war. Somehow men in their right minds, educated men who had time to study and think it over, somehow they could have fixed it if they wanted to. Of course, I'll admit I make my mistakes. The first one was I believed there wouldn't be a war, it couldn't come. The second one was thinking I knew beforehand what the war would be like." And Mr. Wayman looked open-eyed at Mibs.

"They ought to teach it in the schools that you can't tell beforehand what a war or a revolution is going to be. It will always be different from what they figure when it commences. One side and usually both sides find it works out different from what they expected. It has helped my sanity some to dig around in history books I read in Virginia and have been reading again. They seem to teach that no people should brag of being invincible. The road of history is strewn with people who got beat after thinking they were unbeatable.

"I was glad when Rod got thrown out of West Point even though he did turn into a blackface minstrel song-and-dance man. The military men are believers in war. It's their profession, their study. They say they've got armies and tactics that can't be beat. On both sides the generals say that and then comes Bull Run or Shiloh and the generals explain and don't make it clear what happened. When the United States set up as a nation, it was with a tradition new to the rest of the world. They said, No standing armies like the Old World. They said, There is danger in standing armies and a lot of shooting irons ready for war. They were partly afraid of generals using the armies to set up dictatorships and take the government away from the people, as happened so often in Europe and Asia. And they were afraid of the military profession, which thinks in terms of war. There are exceptions in that profession. But the most of them, they like war, they prepare for war and the worst of them want the war they are prepared for. I didn't mention the expense of a standing army and an establishment ready for war. It's been an awful tax-load on the people of Europe and our people didn't like the idea."

Mibs had shuddered at mention of the Pittsfield boy shooting himself. She and others in Pike County were not yet over that affair. He was twenty-two years old, the eldest of six children, and the favorite of his father. He was medium-sized, well-bodied, with a curiously serious face, set with purpose, a mouth and eyes with a touch of melancholy. He had quiet ways, carried mystery about him, and it was said he could have his pick of the girls in Pittsfield. The family lived in a big two-story brick house of twelve rooms and two servants. The father Ezra Winslow had come with the early settlers, owned four farms that he rented, one farm that he managed himself, a brickyard, and a general store. When the son William Bradford Winslow had finished his courses in Illinois College at Jacksonville, his father had taken him in hand, teaching him how to run the father's business. It was clear to Pittsfield people that the father, stern with himself and stern with others, sort of idolized this eldest son.

"He seldom smiles," was said of the father and those who said so wondered whether they saw the boy William Bradford learning to smile less under the guidance and in the company of his father. They believed and it was common talk that when the father paid for a substitute to take the place of his drafted son in the army, it was the father's wish and will, and not the son's. Of this they were certain later when an evening of celebration was punctuated with tragedy.

Two nights after the November day when the North re-elected its President, a Union rally, a ratification meeting, was held in a big hall of the county courthouse. On a platform sat seven sunburned and able-bodied soldiers in Union blue. They had been furloughed home to cast their ballots and were starting back to their armies the next day. In a row in front of the able-bodied sat four camp-fever convalescents hoping soon to return to service, two one-armed men, two with one leg gone, one with no legs, three recovering from intestinal and other wounds, Milton Winwold in his wheel chair, the one-armed Hoon boy, and the blind son of Ed Houseworth. The speakers of the evening paid tribute to these men, one of them naming each soldier and telling how, when and where the sacrifice was enacted. Without such men, said the speakers, men ready to face mutilation and death for their country, the Union would have been lost and there would be no great American nation taking its place in the world.

Earlier some in the audience had turned their heads and seen William Bradford Winslow enter shyly and quietly take a seat in the last row. A few had noticed that he left before the exercises were over and that evening did no mingling with others in the hall. It was the next day that the news ran from mouth to mouth over the town and county that William Bradford Winslow had gone home to his room in the big brick house and put a revolver to his head and sent a bullet through it. They knew then they had not talked an idle gossip when they said it was the father's wish and will the boy should have a substitute.

Mibs and Omri talked it over. The boy could have run away and joined the army, they agreed. But they further agreed they couldn't solve, and no one could, what motives had shaken the boy, his father's idol and the father known to everyone as strong, self-willed, relentless and even cruel in the pressure he could put on those he wanted to dominate. It came to be said of the father, "Before it happened he seldom smiled, and afterward, never."

When they mentioned this to Mr. Wayman, he said, "During a war, you might say, insanity comes natural. One thing the generals like to cover up, so the people back home don't know about it, is the number of men who go to pieces, go mentally broken from camp monotony, from homesickness, from hearing the wounded cry, and from the sight and smell of dead men and dead horses piled and scattered without meaning. I think Barbara began to have a feeling that the war meant agony on both sides and when she saw so many people, newspapers and politicians, sort of satisfied and cheerful about the war, as though they could make sense of it, she put her hands out for supports not there."

Omri took from a pocket a newspaper clipping of the speech of the President last November on the Gettysburg battlefield. Omri read the ten-sentence speech with two fingers fumbling vaguely along the semicircle of his muffler beard. He looked at Mr. Wayman, inquiring, "If he hated the South, that was his chance to say so, a proper place?"

"I suppose so."

"If he meant the Union men were brave and the Union men struggled and the Union men gave their last full share of devotion—if he meant Union men only, he would have said so, don't you think?"

"I remember when reading it that idea came to me and I dismissed it."

"When he says we should here highly resolve that these dead shall not have died in vain, he doesn't say these *Union* dead. Could he possibly mean *both* the Union and Confederate dead should not have died in vain? Doesn't he rather directly imply that?"

"That is possible, Mr. Winwold. I hadn't thought about it. I can see it's possible."

"I think he's trying to get ready for the end of the war, whenever that comes, and he wants as little hate as possible between the North and the South."

Only three or four times in all the years had these neighbors and friends had such a discussion. Their duties and chores had kept them busy. Misgivings had often bade them say nothing, to risk no slightest offense. Mibs felt natural about digging out the old prophecies Hornsby had copied for her, John Luzac in Leyden, Holland, 1780: "If America becomes free, she will someday give the law to Europe," and Barnaby twenty years earlier: "Empire is traveling westward: and everyone is looking forward with eager and impatient expectation to that destined moment when America is to give the law to the rest of the world."

The rough shags of Mibs' eyebrows went up and a sober reserved smile came and went on the oval of her face. "If it could be done, America giving the law to the rest of the world, it would certainly require a united North and South. When I try to see how it might happen that America gives the law to the rest of the world, I can't make the picture. The Atlantic Ocean on one side, the Pacific on the other, they are too big and wide, too far across, for us to send men and guns to give the law to the rest of the world. The picture I get is that when the war ends, if things don't go too bad, the North and the South can get together and work out a peace and prosperity like none ever seen before in any country."

Omri with one eye shut and a sly hint of mischief in the one open, gave his whim. "I can see it in the realm of possibility that New England, having abolished slavery in the South, will be able to give some attention to the wage slavery and the twelve- and fourteen-hour workday in her large, enterprising and ingenious textile mills."

Mibs spoke gravely. "I shall pray for peace and prosperity in the years to come, for my boys, Rod's boys, Mr. Wayman's grandsons." She looked at Mr. Wayman softly, fondly, out of an intimacy grown in a soil of misery and contradictions. His eyes lighted and his right hand with lean fingers ran along a gaunt jawbone as he gave her a quiet look in return. Omri had noticed long ago that Mr. Wayman too had fastened his heart on those boys in a way that his wife hadn't. They had helped bear up their grandfather, who believed he could see them moving into a future having security and affirmation his own life had not known.

Omri was reaching a hand into his coat pocket to bring out a piece of paper. "Four sentences I copied from the last page of *Uncle Tom's Cabin*. We will forget the little lady's omission of sins of commission and omission in New England. The little lady sees America as not alone in the world. She seems to have suspicions that in days to come after this war there may again be hell to pay." And he read her four sentences:

" 'This is an age of the world when nations are trembling and convulsed. A mighty influence is abroad, surging and heaving the world, as with an earthquake. And is America safe? Every nation that carries in its bosom great and unredressed injustice has in it the elements of this last convulsion.' "

They heard the rattle of buggy wheels outside and through the windows saw Rosalind Wayman helped out of the buggy by the Atlas man who had brought her. Three or four times a year she had been making this visit home from Springfield forty miles away.

On the front porch Rosalind put her arms around her father and kissed his lips. In the house she touched a kiss on the cheeks of Mibs, gave her hand to Omri Winwold. Her mass of black curls fell with a kind of wonder over her ears down to her shoulders. She was buxom and robust as ever, it would seem, and her mouth with full underlip drawn far in between her nose and the chin that jutted still indicated she was inclined to be decisive and have her own way. They were not quite prepared for what came from her and abruptly.

They knew she had been engaged to a Major Charles Robert Fellows of Peoria, a recruiting officer she had met and seen often in the two years she had worked in an office clerkship in the state capitol at Springfield. On her visits home three or four times a year she had shown her photographs of the Major, whose full face in two of the camera registers and whose full figure in two others showed a sort of style model of the accepted handsome man. The face and the pose made him out good-looking and meaningless and you would like to know more about him. "He might be a scamp or honest and lazy or maybe a hero," Mibs had said confidentially and very secretly to herself on studying the photographs.

Now Rosalind was telling it. For more than a year Major Fellows had gone with her as "steady company." He had been seen with no other women. In her circle and his it came to be accepted they had "serious intentions." Then suddenly for a month he came no more to see her. In that month the few times Rosalind saw him was on recruiting transactions and he was casual and cool. Then a week ago the word went round that he was to marry the daughter of a well-to-do local merchant. Then day before yesterday came word the wedding was set for yesterday evening. And it was yesterday afternoon Rosalind went to Major Fellows' office and took out a revolver and shot at him and missed him and found herself in the city jail under the charge of attempted homicide. The state's attorney told her Major Fellows didn't care for prosecution of her and she could go on promise to leave the city. So she had packed her things and come home.

She poured out her story mostly in a matter-of-fact tone, her eyes dry though flashing, a faint tremor in her underlip. Her father, Omri, Mibs at moments, were not sure it could be fact she was telling, so cold the words. Then came the downward pinch of her mouth, the underlip spread and flattened. She clutched her hands to her breasts and looked from face to face saying in shaking voice, "I'm so glad I didn't kill him. I would have been so sorry now. It would have been terrible for all of us. And you must have a little pity for me. He was a rat, a treacherous rat, a low slimy rat. He spread it on with me. He told me he loved me and never any other woman. He told me everything except he would marry me. I could never get him to say he would marry me. But he did ask me for everything a woman can give and I gave him everything, the liar, the cheat, the rat. He took liberties with me. He used me. Then without so much as a pleasant good-by he takes up with this other woman he married last night. I must never go near where he is again. I wouldn't trust myself. I might try to kill him."

No one spoke. Her father rose creaking, stepped over and wove his two hands and fingers among her black curls as he stood back of her. "You're my girl, Rosalind. This is your home. Stay with us a while. Stay long as you want to. We're a little lonesome and it will be good to have you."

"I think I could have done just what you did," said Mibs. And in weeks that came Rosalind seemed to shuffle off her old pride, pitched in on the farm and house work, gave cheer to the house, kept saying to Mibs, "He'll come back, I'm betting Rod'll come back." The two of them drove to see Ed Houseworth's blind son, the one-armed Hoon boy, Milton in his wheel chair, and one day Oregon Walker, furloughed home from a bridge-building corps of the Army of Tennessee, shrunken with lung trouble, the eldest son of the free Negro John Walker.

Mibs one night saw a white moon disk move over the sky, then the coming of clouds over the moon, and the beginning of snowfall. She slept and awoke to see out of the window the snow wind-driven and piled in drifts of huddle and curve and under an apple tree a spiral dome with a falling crooked hat. She heard the wind laugh and the snow join in. Then the wind mirth died down and changed to a brawling and roaring, a mockery that too died down, and the land lay quiet under a cold arch of blue sky. A tall hemlock brandished wide arms of snow and stood in a white moonfall that night and, to Mibs, seemed to say, "Can it be I am nothing and you are nothing and the one you wait for is nothing and we are all miserable mimics of nothing? Can it be?"

And she knew she was playing a game with herself in her own mind. The hemlock had a loneliness deep as her own and it shushed her and gave out a dim whisper, "I'll be good for you if you know how to use me."

She spoke of this to Omri, who said, "They go away to leave us lonely and endure a worse loneliness themselves. They go away to starve, to shrink with misery, to groan under wounds, to die, to come home crippled. And you and I have good food and warm corners for sleep and you feel a guilt about it as I do." He had seen the furrows of care deepen on the smooth oval of her face and the first silver in her chestnut hair. She had seen his hair graying and half of his muffler beard turn a snow-white, streaks that ran now in a curious crisscross over the reddish growth of hair under his chin and from ear to ear. "You're beginning to look venerable," said Mibs with her grave smile. "You'll be taken for a prophet."

"Today I'm an anxious father." And he told her of a letter from Marvel, who had broken his engagement to the Missouri girl. It seemed to Omri that Marvel had written the Missouri girl something candid and cruel about himself from the hospital to test the girl. It hurt Omri that the boy didn't write his father and chum the full cold facts about his wound and his condition. He seemed to have written the Missouri girl enough to make her shy away from Marvel for a life companion.

Marvel had written, "It looks, papa, as though I will go through life with a homely little heifer here who has given me everything. I'm tired of beautiful girls. Nine out of ten are cheats and delusions. I've seen enough of women to know what I want." Mibs saw shadows and sorrow in the liquid brown eyes of Omri. Marvel had been his chum. He prayed for all his other children with a special invocation that God watch over Marvel. Now quick as an eyeblink Marvel had put one girl off and taken another on and somehow it had to do with the looks, the face or the body of Marvel and his boy, his chum, doesn't write him about it. Mibs saw pain in Omri's eyes.

"I'm haunted, Mibs," he said. "The war is so damned impersonal. The war don't care who gets killed or crippled. The Hoon boy tells about a wild-eyed wrinkled old woman who came to the hospital and begged for the bones of her boy. 'I've picked up some of his bones,' pointing to a bag she carried, 'and if you can just let me have a few more of his bones I'll thank you to my dying day.' They found some bones for her and she went out and was seen stopping soldiers to ask, 'Can you tell me where I'll find more of the bones of my boy?' The best and bravest struggle on the battle fronts to meet death and mutilation. The laggard, the weak, the dodgers and skedaddlers, stay at home and breed their kind for the future."

Omri had been leaving the Wayman house. Mibs had thrown on a cloak and walked with him to where his horse stood at a hitching post near a corncrib. The sun strayed through a light mist over a melting snow. Omri pointed to the yellow ears of corn shining through the corncrib cracks. "From what I hear, Mibs, there are soldiers in prisons North and South who would leap at the chance to get ears of hard corn like these and to crunch them between their teeth like horses. I'm a haunted man, my sweet girl."

More often, across the years, he had looked straight into her face and eyes to say "my sweet girl" with a deep personal warmth about it. He could hold her two hands, pressing them tight, or he could put his

956

two large hands pressing her shoulders as he said something or gazed into her face in silence—and she had no mistrust of him. She had even held for a moment a thought dismissed on the instant, "If the awful decree should be written that Rod doesn't come back, I wonder what would happen between Omri Winwold and me," and then in a flash, "It's a crazy thought and I'll never let it come again." She could, at times, read him keenly. She was saying, "You're holding something back. You were going to tell it and decided not to bother me. Now I'm asking. Come ahead and bother me. What is it?"

"A dream," said Omri. "The war—the war don't care—the war takes anything it wants—the war don't give a good goddam for anybody." A thin tremor shaded his voice. "The war, my sweet girl, it will take your Rod or my Marvel, if it wants either of them or both." He saw her wince. It was in both her eyes and one mouth corner. His voice softened. "I'm only telling you what I believe led up to the dream." Then he told what had come in his sleep the night before:

"I open a big black box of smooth ebony and find it inlaid with gold pieces. Out of it I take another box and its cover too is inlaid with shining gold disks of coin. Out of this I take another box of smooth ebony, made like the others and fitting perfect. One after another I go on opening boxes, wondering what will be in the last little box. I get furious and work faster from box to box. At last I come to one so small I say it can't hold another box. I loosen the cover of that last little box and what do I find? Nothing. It is empty. While I am saying, 'What kind of a damned swindle is this?' the little box in my hand turns to a gray-white ash, an ash so fine and thin it slips away out of my fingers. I turn to look at the boxes I have piled to the right and left of me and they are gone. Not a side, an end, nor a lid with an inlaid gold piece left. I hear a deep far-off whoosh on some horizon. My clothes slide off me. My hat lifts itself off and away from my head, my coat, vest, trousers, underwear, slide off and slide away. And somehow my shoes get loose and I see them walking away. I am standing bare and naked in a cold wind that keeps getting colder as the flesh shudders on my bones. Then the flesh slides off my bones and I stand there a skeleton. And I begin walking on ice in a deep snow against a cold wind and crying, 'Blow, wind, blow, you can't freeze these bones, blow, wind, blow, these bones shall rise again, these bones shall rise again, rise again, rise again.' And every time I say 'Rise again' a voice riding the wind says, 'Why? Why? Why?' Then suddenly comes a long piercing 'Why-y-y-y' from the wind and it rings and shoots in every bone of me. I stop in my tracks. Slowly all the bone joints of me come apart and fall into a huddle with the skull on top, the skull face grinning at the open sky, grinning while the snow comes down and covers the skull face. Then comes quiet. The howling wind goes down and there is no sound only the snow falling. And under the snow I am saying 'The music of the snow comes very soft, the touch of baby fingers and the

957

print of God's kiss on a baby face and the feel of infinitely delicate yarn is here in the snow falling on me and here under the snow I shall long sleep long sleep long.' And while I am saying this like a solemn lullaby the wind rises and comes howling again and blows away the snow over me. And the wind pushes my bones, mauls them around and knocks them together and then scatters them miles and miles away, leaving only the skull of me on bare ground, face up to the sky."

"It ended there?" asked Mibs, shifting to the plaits of chestnut hair at the side of her head her hands that had been holding her ears to keep them warm.

"The dream ended there. I don't want it again."

"I can make an interpretation," said Mibs, bringing her hands down and taking Omri's two hands.

He leaned over and kissed her on the mouth, then turned and got on his horse. She was looking up at him with a crowded solemn face and saying, "I pray, Omri, I pray and I believe. Both will come home, I believe it."

His horse was walking through the gate she held open and on the road the horse was getting the feel of the slippery snowslush underfoot. Omri turned to see her fastening the gate cleat. That done she called to him with cupped hands at her mouth, "Both will come home, both. I believe, I believe."

* * * * * * * * * *

Chapter 39

* * * * * * * * * *

The Deeper Sorrow That Has Forgotten How to Weep

THE island lay at the harbor mouth. Across the water to the little city of Sandusky, Ohio, was near three miles. A Union Army regiment had a fort and barracks, kept guard over a seventeen-acre tract of ground, walled in, sentry towers at the corners from which men were shot who crossed the well-known deadline. In a few cases men crossing the deadline wanted what came to them, as one of them put it, "a ticket of leave from Johnson's Island."

"Fresh fish!" came the call from more than a thousand men in the prison enclosure. It was a cheer and a jeer, a sardonic welcome to a hundred-odd prisoners arrived in Sandusky that July morning and towed to Johnson's Island. "Fresh fish!" ran the news to the camp and the greeting to the newcomers. They would be salted down. They would lie close to each other as dry mackerel in a barrel. Those passing along the welcome cry had once arrived as fresh fish. And they were not so fresh now. One and all they had a stale odor. And those with scurvy, chronic diarrhea and dysentery, would admit, if pressed about the matter, that they stank and it was not by choice.

Captain Rodney Wayman of the new arrivals had heard the fresh-fish cry at Camp Morton. He was a prison veteran. To be caged, to be held under lock and gun by keepers, for this he was no fresh fish. He was a graduate and had credentials. The other prison was for the Confederate rank and file. This one, Johnson's Island, was for commissioned officers of the Confederate Army.

"They have lanterns along the inside of the twelve-foot wall at night so the guards can see you coming if your aim is to get over the wall," said a prisoner to Rod. "But if he misses you and you do get over the wall, it's easy enough. All you do is swim three miles to Sandusky or walk on the water like Jesus did, if you've got the faith." This interested Rod as fun or irony, that was all. He was in no physical trim to try for an escape. Excellent care they had given him in a northern-Virginia hospital where the bullet wound on the jaw and the right side of the face had slowly healed and left a five-inch scar, a red line that curved over the jaw in a fishhook shape. Then an attack of malaria had set in, a light attack but it left him weak. He had walked up the gangplank of a ship at Norfolk and fainted away as he set foot on the deck. The food, the clean berth, the sea trip to New York, had done him good. Entraining in New York City and looking at crowds on depot platforms along the Erie Railroad, he had glimpsed the war prosperity of the North, what immense resources it yet had to throw at the devastated South that lacked salt and quinine and was scraping the bottom of the flour barrel.

His ragged uniform with six bullet holes in it, a few pocket articles, a blanket—and two or three deep-lying purposes—these were his slim possessions. He would not take the Oath of Amnesty, swear allegiance to the Government of the United States, to get himself better quarters, food, clothes, comfort and a measure of freedom. He would die first, rather than that. For him there were the words Honor and Duty. For those words he had forsaken wife, children, home. For him now to forsake and deny those words would be for him to profane what he had done at Shiloh, Chickamauga, Camp Morton, Spotsylvania Courthouse. After that purpose to hold loyal to a Cause, even a Lost Cause, he would try to be cold, shrewd, calculating toward the purpose of enduring to the end of the war and joining Mibs and the children. It lay in his calculations that Mibs, with others, should they learn where he was, would try to get him out. On this point he had fear. And the fear had an added hold on him because of his weakened body. Sometimes his hands trembled, chills came, then a sweat. This grew worse.

He spent most of October in hospital and came out with that same frequent tremor of the hands. A chronic dysentery weakened and bled him. There were times he averaged day and night hourly visits to the sinks, where because of defective drainage water had risen to cover the floor and to reach almost to the seat. A mild scurvy began to show on his right leg and peculiar mouth sores came. He joined in a petition to the authorities for rations of potatoes and onions with the result that on three days in the following month a potato and an onion came into his hands. He read an announcement, "Potatoes and onions when necessary as antiscorbutics may be purchased from the prison fund on recommendation of a surgeon and approval by the commanding officer."

There came occasional mornings after the cold weather set in when he got out of his bunk and felt grinding twinges of pain in his left hip so he walked slow and limping to go through the routine motions of getting antiscorbutics for his worsening scurvy. He didn't have the reserves of strength and vitality to draw on here that he had at Camp Morton. "Straw is difficult to obtain," he heard from a prison authority in January of '65. His bunk straw had been in use five months and what with his chronic dysentery it needed change, freshening, but the answer was, "Straw is difficult to obtain." He thought about writing to Mibs, just a greeting, a few words to let her know he was among the living. He wrote her one six-line letter, then tore it up, in fear of he knew not what, for he had ended, "I have known the sorrow of endless tears and the deeper sorrow that has forgotten how to weep."

The twenty-five hundred prisoners of last summer and early fall had swollen in January of '65 to more than three thousand. Room space was more crowded. The prisoners drew their food rations for a mess and cooked them in a room allotted to a mess. "Cadavers, that's what they are, cadavers," said Rod one night as he looked at the gaunt men of his mess, each from thirty to sixty pounds underweight, his own onetime hundred and eighty pounds now down to a hundred and fifteen. Some of them ambled and groped rather than walked and they could stare for a long time at nothing.

Yet Rod saw three of these cadaverous fellows, at a given signal, leap at another cadaver who had come through the door. They brought him to the floor and their bones pounded his bones. They choked him, slapped him across the nose, kicked him. Then they threw him out the door. Rod knew what this was. He had seen something like it before only not so cruel. This was the reply of Confederate loyalists to a man, it was known, about to take the Oath of Amnesty. The prison authorities, it was reported, had told such men of materials and carpenters to arrive for the erection of a new building to house those swearing allegiance to the United States Government, but the materials hadn't arrived.

There was a stoop-shouldered major from Virginia who walked with a rheumatic limp and had a sweeping saber scar on his forehead, a

Malvern Hill memento. Rod saw this major face a young lieutenant from Missouri, an open-mouthed fellow who had a habit of smiling too easy and too often to suit other grim ones. "We hear you're taking the Oath," said the major.

"I haven't decided, haven't made up my mind," came the open-mouthed reply with a grin.

"You give us a smile with your big buck teeth and it doesn't say a thing. We can tell if you're for us."

"Uh-uh," said the lieutenant, still wearing his grin.

"Unless they get the new building for you fellows taking the Oath, you'll have to live with us. Has that penetrated your skull?"

"Uh-uh," which could mean anything.

"Go ahead and take the Oath if you want to. But remember when you come back here to sleep and eat with us you'll be knocked flat as the flattest pancake ever was."

He did take the Oath and Rod saw him come back one afternoon and saw them knock him very flat and leave him senseless a long hour. And for days no one of the mess spoke to him and he was peculiarly lonely in a crowded room of men banded in a certain finality of fellowship.

There was a boy from New Orleans, eighteen years old in the spring of '64, whose conduct in battle had won him a commission as a second lieutenant. His service had been in Mississippi and Georgia in the summer and autumn. He had never in his life seen a snowfall till he came to Johnson's Island. The others could see the Northern cold wearing him down. Rod saw him taken to the hospital with pneumonia and heard from a man who lay near that the boy kept murmuring, "I shall never see home again," and turned his face to the wall and died.

Before Christmas of '64 they had seen navigation ice-locked and for weeks the rations and supplies for troop guards and prisoners hauled between the island and Sandusky on ice sleds and small boats with runners. On one night, twenty below zero, it was known the sentries had left their tower lookouts, one of them saying, "Any bird that wants to light out for Sandusky tonight is welcome." The guards knew that no man in the prison could make the trip over the ice to Sandusky and keep warm enough to live. The next day was the first that Rod tried to walk, and his rheumatic hip pain sent him back to his bunk for the day.

He was spending more time in his bunk, half-awake, half-alive in meaningless reverie. His leg scurvy got no better, his mouth sores grew worse. One week a dream came two nights straight. He lay in a four-poster mahogany bed between sheets of fresh white linen. Through a door he had locked and bolted he saw a white shape enter the room through the door without opening it. This white shape began moving toward him gliding rather than walking. As it came nearer it seemed to be a woman seven or eight feet tall, in a glittering white cape from shoulder to heel, the head hooded, the face masked. Her voice came measured, with a slow drop of the words.

She was saying: "Pardon me and pray for me; pray for me, I say. For I am sometimes so fearful that I would creep into a mousehole; sometimes God doth visit me again with His comfort. So He cometh and goeth." At the door, before gliding through, she turned and spoke to him in quavers of low wailing: "Four years thy feet have wandered, Charley Amberson, four pitiless years, Charley Amberson, consider the worth of pity now, Charley Amberson, consider there is such a garment they call love, Charley Amberson; beware of a burnt garment and the bitter ashes of love, Charley Amberson."

He woke from the dream and could sleep no more. Her first speech, "Pardon me and pray for me," Rod knew he was remembering from a scholarly Texas lieutenant who often quoted it as the speech of some famous English martyr. The voice was Mibs', but somehow changed, somehow shadowed and faltering. Yes, it would be four years next month that he had been away from her. He had learned, and it was a hard personal discipline, to brush away thought and memory of her when her face and arms came too close to him. He had seen homesickness and the want of love wither and shrivel men till they were melancholy wordless automatons. He had heard one officer describe another, "He's got one foot in Rappahannock River mud and one on the Other Shore." Had he been merely stubborn? Rod asked himself that. Or had he been truly austere, according to his prayer and desire?

The morning after the second night of his dream, with Mibs' changed voice of unutterable sorrow haunting him, with fresh wonder on him as to his two children and with sharp pangs of curiosity about his father and mother, he took paper and pencil and tried for some kind of a letter to Mibs. The hand tremors that would keep coming, he knew not when beforehand, made the first words into a sprawling scrawl that had twists of terror. He considered having another write for him and decided such a letter would make him look too helpless. So he drifted and let fate work, a little afraid of his more often coming out of long meaningless reveries. He had the wish and desire but knew himself to be completely lacking the strength and vitality to join in lively dramas put on by other fellows who could be gay though gaunt. He went to their blackface-minstrel show and bitterness swept over him that he couldn't be on the stage and be announced for his celebrated soft-shoe dance and his famous rendition of the sad song "In the Bright Mohawk Valley." He admired the workbenches his fellow officers had put up, the charms, rings and breastpins they made out of gutta percha and mussel shells—and the banjo one fellow had cunningly contrived of wood and wire patiently picked up here and there.

He was startled one day passing a nearly finished barracks house where two carpenters were hanging a door. The face of one of them was familiar. He couldn't place it. He came back, went up close to the man, and then walked away. Now he was sure. Now, as he walked away, it came clear that the face was that of a brother of Ed Houseworth, the Atlas storekeeper. Alfred Houseworth, everybody called him Al, and he was a good carpenter when he worked but he was known as easy-going and would lay off work for spells of hard drinking.

The next day Rod's feet strayed again for another look at Al Houseworth. He saw Al lay down a scantling and look up to say, "Was you ever in Atlas, Illinois?" It was a pleasant question. It warmed Rod. He answered, "That's supposed to be my home."

"Ever hear of a fellow named Houseworth there, Ed Houseworth?"

"You're his brother Al, we met in his store a couple of times."

"I heard about your goin South to fight. You've had hard times."

"I'm hoping you don't tell them you saw me here."

"Why not?"

"Because I'd just as soon not have 'em know I'm here."

"If they knowed you was here they'd help you, wouldn't they? Maybe they'd get you out of here."

"I wouldn't want 'em to get me out of here till the war's over."

"Sounds queer, but there's a lot of queer things in a war. Tell you what—"

"Yes."

"If I write any letters back there I won't tell 'em about you."

"I'll thank you to say nothing, I'll appreciate it."

"All right, Mr. Wayman, Captain Wayman. I'll keep mum but it looks foolish to me."

"After the war it might be I'll see you in Atlas and we'll talk about it and have a drink."

"I go for that," and Al put out his hand for a shake, "it's a bargain, after the war we have a talk and a drink in good old Atlas and I can tell you I don't like the rations and the work on this army job and it'll be nice to get back to Pike County and build a few farmhouses." And Al had an afterthought. "If my rheumatism gets worse they can't stop me getting a furlough. Have you had any of this damned rheumatism here?"

"Some days I couldn't walk."

"That bad?"

"Yes."

"Well, I ain't had it that bad yet. If I do it'll be a furlough for me sure as God made little red raspberries."

Al had been in the service three years, rated as an artificer, and being not much of a letter-writer, spending his payday greenbacks for drink, he had little news from Pike County and Atlas. A week later when another carpenter told Rod that Al Houseworth had been furloughed home with disability, Rod could only speculate and guess. He couldn't know that in the decrees of circumstance, so often whimsical and sometimes terrific, Al Houseworth held a long session and spent a pleasant afternoon in the Wayman farmhouse with three persons. He was a short sturdy fellow with a full bushy beard, a mustache that flowed neatly, no growth of hair just below the underlip, and they were fascinated with what came from his testifying lips. They poured for him from a bottle of old Monongahela whisky. Mr. Wayman poured. So did Omri and Mibs. They kept at him and had him repeat more than once every scrap of a word that had come from Rod. There were days Rod couldn't walk, yet there could be thanks he was still alive. The high point of truth and fact stood forth that after the four long years of hazard he was not dead. And Omri saw the pallor of Mibs turn whiter when Al said, "He's thin, what they call *gant*. I couldn't help sayin after a second long look at him, 'Why, it'd take two of you to throw a shadow.'"

* * * * * * * * * *

Chapter 40

* * * * * * * * * *

Charley Amberson Meets a Woman

ROD had awakened at daybreak to say again as a hundred times before, "Consider there is such a garment they call love, Charley Amberson, beware of a burnt garment and the bitter ashes of love, Charley Amberson." It was later that two civilians from Sandusky, one of them a United States Marshal, came to him and said they had orders and he would go with them.

Rod was a little sullen and somewhat suspicious when they put a round black sealskin cap on his head, had him step into overshoes, had him slide into a cowhide overcoat heavy with a hairy warmth. They led him to a small rowboat mounted on runners, had him climb in, and they walked alongside as two soldiers pulled the vehicle over the ice to the Sandusky shore. They walked him the few blocks to a wooden frame building, the New York Central Railroad station. There, in the waiting room, they handed him over to a woman, the Marshal saying to her, "Here's your man and now you take good care of him."

She was in a cloak of blue wool and a blue wool cap. He was encased in the wide loose-hanging stiff cowhide overcoat. Their arms went around each other but it wasn't a real hug. The two long kisses on the mouth had more reality. Yet they were weird kisses. Both knew that in the former days they kissed as equals, as partners strong and matched for kissing. Now it was she alone who had strength and blood. Nor did he notice nor did it occur to him that the scurvy sores inside his mouth were more than hindrance to excellent kissing.

964

In his eyes she saw deep in the sockets a dim lurking flame. Only there in that wavering flame-line in his sunken eyes could she find what she wanted. That was as good to her eyes as any kiss he could now give her. He was still a fighter. Though far-spent he was no beaten man. The old pride, the old flair that had won him to her, she could read it there in blue shadows crossed with a thin sprocket of light. He would mock at himself. She knew that. She would expect it. Mockery at himself would be his resource and weapon.

She had seen, in a flashing instant, the five-inch fishhook scar of red on his right jaw. She wouldn't ask about that for weeks. His hands that trembled so as he held hers and that went on trembling after she let them go, she wouldn't mention that for a long time.

"Mibs, my Mibs," were the only words that came from him after her cry of "Rod!" and their crude silent embrace and the long kisses so unequal. He sank to a bench under the weight of his overcoat and a kind of thunder pulsing in his wrists and forehead temples. A little strength came and she heard his hoarse whisper, "The children—tell me."

"The one you've never seen is named Rodney Wayman Jr., and has your black wavy hair. And Clayborn Joel, he's strong, lusty, all you could ask."

"That's enough. Let me dream about it." And he leaned his head back on the bench and folded his hands that Mibs noticed had become quiet. As her eyes now really caught his hands of skin-and-bone fingers— telling her the whole frame of him was little more than skin and bone— the tears came and she wiped them away and clenched her own hands and set her teeth in a resolve she mustn't cry again.

The cast-iron coal stove near by glowed a rusty red. "Never so warm since last summer," said Rod as he rose, lifting the heavy cowhide over-coat. She helped him out of it and he sank on the bench again, laying aside his sealskin cap. Several bystanders, also waiting for the westbound train, began eying him as Mibs herself for the first time gathered the gray uniform, ragged, patched, stained, grease-spotted, creases from head to toe, a bullet hole at one shoulder, a bullet hole in one sleeve, his only suit of clothes reporting by its surface signs that he had for months worn it every day and slept in it every night.

The black dank beard of him—Mibs shrank from it. It covered a face too fine to hide. His mouth, the subtle corners of it, she didn't want those ugly hairs over it. The hair of his head she noticed as limp and matted, the old waviness gone, and when she saw on the right side of the upper forehead the beginning of a scar and a line, an indentation of the hair over that line, a shudder ran through her. Heavy trouble, deep sorrow, had been her portion. What he had shared was Agony, firsthand, raw, wild, fleeting, credible only to those who were part of the events. In this last he would be to her, in degree, a Stranger, for all time. And it gave her no care. For his wounds, for the limp she had seen as he came into the station, for his tremulous hands, for his

965

shattered skin-and-bone body, she had a sacred regard and a depth of reverence she believed would carry them through. This belief ran strong since she had seen that flickering sprocket of light over blue shadows far back in his eyes.

The smooth clean skin of her face—he had not been close to anything quite like it in a long time. She was pale and there were plain furrows of care at chin and nostril and her black dress he sensed as very sober and proper. A half-inch strip of lace at the top of her collar caught his eyes that moved to her white neck. He had forgotten that any neck anywhere could be so clean. His eyes moved over her face again wondering how skin could be so clean and smooth. Hairy faces, chapped and pitted faces, here and there scurvy faces with running sores —he had been so near them as company night and day that now it was a revelation and a luxury to look at these unspoiled unspotted smooth-flowing cheeks and chin.

She held his right hand, saw his eyes open and heard his husky and throaty "You're good for sore eyes, Mibs, my Mibs."

She waited and heard him, "One thing—tell me—how did you get me out?—I hope it was clean."

"You're an exchanged prisoner. You walked out today because down South somewhere another man as far gone as you walked out to go home to his people."

"But they stopped exchanging prisoners a year ago." And she could see he paused to summon strength to say what was for him hard to say. "Don't you know I wanted no special favor?"

"I knew it well." She pressed his hand. "I sorrowed over it and I revered you for it." Then she too had to pause and summon strength for what was not easy to say to him at this moment. "Do you wish now to go back to Johnson's Island so that a man let out of Andersonville Prison in Georgia today must go back to Andersonville?"

She felt his bony fingers press hers. And she was saying, "We reach Chicago tonight. Tomorrow night you're home with Clayborn Joel, and Rodney Jr. you've never seen, and you'll have every comfort and put meat on your bones in no time." She saw a slight shrug at his spare-boned shoulders. "How do you feel about it?"

His hands trembled again and he stared at the coal stove. "Mibs, I'm just one of God's mistakes. I feel like a rat, since you ask, like a privy rat."

She searched his face. And he didn't look at her and went on. "They were killing them over on the Island—killing them to eat—not a rat left on the Island." He turned to find her anxious eyes searching his. "Mibs," he went on, "do you know I'm so dirty I'll wash and wash and I'll never be clean again, it won't come off?"

She had expected this mockery. It was his way of implying that she and all other outsiders could never know the foul realm of sordid and monotonous routine from which he had this day emerged. And she

966

exulted too, for no one else on earth could have caught as she did a thin edge of trifling in his tone of voice, a vagrant humor that told her he was no hopeless case.

"I'll do the washing, my lord and master. I'll see to the washing myself. I'll get you out of your clothes and put you into that big tin bathtub full of hot water. I'll do the scrubbing and when I'm through you'll laugh and say you're clean all over."

For the first time he now smiled and she saw two teeth gone near one mouth corner. She helped him to the door of the men's closet, heard his patient, "I'm what they call a chronic case."

In the further waiting before the train came in, Mibs noticed Rod indifferent to the curiosity-gazers. A dozen or so of people seemed spellbound in their interest. Here was a piece of the war. Here was a wreck, a guaranteed demolished human ruin, out of the well-known war. At home you ate three squares a day. Off where the war was it could happen you didn't get your three squares. Men and women peered at this specimen, this fish out of the brine of war. And the specimen went along as though he had learned much about what is called privacy and among the least of his personal needs was the right to seclusion. He was immune to witnesses, onlookers, bystanders who didn't give a damn what you were doing.

The train came in. The seats up near the stove at the end of the car were all filled. Rod kept his overcoat on. Mibs had him lay his head on her shoulder a good part of the time and she saw him sleep an hour. She told him of seeing a snowfall begin and how she slept and awoke to see a moonwhite tall hemlock brandishing wide arms of snow and saying to her, "Can it be I am nothing and you are nothing and the one you wait for is nothing and we are all miserable mimics of nothing? Can it be?"

"It was that same week, about that same night," said Rod, "you came to me in a dream." And he told it to her, with its ending words, "Consider there is such a garment they call love, Charley Amberson, beware of a burnt garment and the bitter ashes of love, Charley Amberson."

They stayed overnight in Chicago at the Briggs House. They arrived after dark the next night at the Wayman farmhouse near Atlas.

Chapter 41

Lost Commander

OMRI heard from Annabell writing, "Henry walked to Mass yesterday morning. He gets better. We are pleased and know you will be." Then months later, "The news is not so good about Henry. He has taken a turn for the worse. He still speaks of you and expects a visit from you again." Then in early February of this year of 1865 an abrupt note: "Dear Omri—Henry died last week and it was hard. The doctor has ordered me to a long rest in bed. The children are fine. Come when you can. It will brighten the house for us. And your prayers are needed. Annabell."

She sat up in bed, fixed pillows at her back, held a boy's tin trumpet in one hand, gave Omri the other hand, closed her eyes and leaned back. "It was good you could come, Omri." He saw her white-faced, underweight, a streak of snow-white in a curve of hair over one ear, and very tired. She had been through an ordeal. He would not ask her about it. She would tell it, if the time came.

The boys Nathaniel Lyon and Frank Blair had chalked a diagonal line across the room, curving like the Mississippi twists above St. Louis. They had pulled a small rare antique oak chest out into the river. It was their steamboat. One was captain, the other first mate. They were shouting. The boat couldn't start till mamma blew the trumpet. She blew. It didn't satisfy, not loud enough. They took the trumpet from her hand and handed it to Omri. He blew. And the two boys on their steamboat waved good-by and went upriver. It was later Annabell and Omri heard them at the far corner. They were unloading the wounded at Peoria, chalking a railroad from Peoria to Chicago across the room, and now the oak chest would be a railroad train bringing the wounded from Peoria to Chicago.

"They've heard about the war, it seems," said the mother.

"Only the very deaf haven't," said Omri.

"This was what Henry wanted, children hollering around the house, as he said. They miss him. He had a boy streak in him. In his wheel chair he found ways to play with them." There was a pause. "It was a great day when Henry walked out of the house to a buggy and I drove him to church and he walked in to Mass. Such a day didn't come again. He'd take two or three steps and fall."

She leaned back, with closed eyes again, holding Omri's hand it

968

seemed with a need and with a curiously complete trust in him. The boys finished their steamboat and railroad transport of the wounded. Now they could be heard in the big front hallway and up and down the stairs with a drum and trumpet.

"Playing soldier again," said Annabell softly. "Every day they play soldier. I've had to promise them a sword and a musket. They want to take turns being commander in battle like their father."

The doctor came. He must emphasize as before that she was in excellent health but for exhaustion. She must eat, gain weight and strength, rest in quiet, with no worry. As she again leaned back with closed eyes, Omri held her hand, met its slight quiet occasional pressures, noticed by sleeve ends that she wore some heavy wool garment next her body and over it a light silk jacket of sky-blue with a scrollwork of pink braid at the buttons.

"Becomes you," he said. "Sky-blue is your color, Annabell."

"The deepest and darkest sea-blue was my color one night. If the sea had been outside the door I would have walked into it and let the waves souse me and pound me and let me be forgotten and never found." Her head leaned on the pillows. Only her lips had moved.

"One time I had that feeling. I came to St. Louis and got drunk."

"And I sobered you."

"You did."

"And the next day we were very practical and you went straight home."

"And I say now you were wonderfully practical again when you wanted a deep dark sea to be thrown in."

"The Mississippi is full of ice, mud and sewage. I went and looked at it. It's too dirty to die in."

"Why not deep snow on a prairie in zero cold?"

"And after the snow thaw the body swollen and stinking?"

"You wish to die with embellishment?"

"No, I don't want a fancy death. I merely want to die alone and no fool coroner afterward and no fuss-and-feathers funeral."

"You *do* mean you want to die alone?"

"Either alone—or you holding my hand and hearing my prattle."

Her black eyelashes had lifted. The open eyes looked at him a moment. They swept him with a certain quick flurry he had seen for the first time when he met her in Morissey's five years ago. He could see the lawyer after a Tom and Jerry wiping cream froth from a heavy mustache and studying Annabell in the mirror. "Petite, eh? Quite a bijou." And Omri saying she was doll-faced and he could carve her face on a hazelnut with four quick knife strokes. Then he had shamed himself. "She's sister to a black-and-gold pansy." And the gay sunrise-scarlet of her mouth, brighter than cherry-red, had haunted him. And coming to St. Louis to get drunk and forget the war about to crash, he found her in a tall black chair studded with brass-nail triangles and circles, the wife of his friend Henry Flack, and an image of majesty in flowing, bell-shaped blue with a coif that startled by its white quietude. And he had gone away, she telling him to go and he knowing he must go. Then three years of war and he returned to see the two lusty children that had blossomed from the marriage to Henry—but Henry himself a Chickamauga ruin in a wheel chair. Then he saw her bright mouth rather a sundown-maroon with wisps of violet shadow—and now as he looked at her propped in pillows the mouth was the same with a touch of dusk, heavy dusk and the first evening stars. "A tough wiry body," Henry had said of her, a true heroine of the war in the care, devotion and cheer she gave her paralyzed husband. Now death had come to Henry and with it some ordeal, something brutal and irrational that had near broken this woman who lifted her black eyelashes and swept him a moment with eyes that closed for the rest, the quiet the doctor ordered.

"You go for the sea to die in. Me for the snow." And Omri told of his dream, his clothes sliding off, shoes walking away, the snow over his huddled bones blown away and the skull on the bare ground. "I had that dream out of fear and love and the next week came news of my two oldest boys. A short letter from Holliday, let out of a Georgia prison when Sherman's army opened the gates. 'Of twelve in my company captured, six died, four in hospital I never expect to see again. Two of us are starting home.' Holliday died, with others who died, living skeletons, on the train. Two days after that official army notice arrived, Marvel came home, one forearm a stump cut off above the wrist."

"We are well met. Two days ago they had to take off Josh's foot. They tried their best to save it, I know."

Slowly and sort of rambling, as though he could tell it to a dark music that ran sad and slow, Omri told Annabell of Rod and Mibs, of Mibs' long wait over years of no word from the man she loved, of her bringing Rod home from prison, a living skeleton who might not live on. Omri told of Mrs. Wayman, the mother, going mute and then dying to be buried in a pine knoll on their farm alongside her son who died from wounds at Shiloh. Omri told of his sweetly religious son Milton in his wheel chair fraternizing with the one-armed Hoon boy and the blind Houseworth youth.

"No wonder," said Annabell dreamily. "Not strange at all."

"Is what?"

"Your coming to St. Louis to get drunk, stone-blind drunk. You saw the war coming."

"And I'm not sure but if more people had seen it coming, for what it was when it did come, maybe it wouldn't have come. I don't know. I do know those who wanted the war got a war that wasn't what they expected."

Over a silence of several minutes she held Omri's hand in perfect quiet. He looked at her face. She could be asleep. Then came a long tense pressure on his hand, a tight and fierce hold, and she was saying with eyes still closed, "I'll try to tell you the whole thing. I told it to a coroner's jury and they made a record of every word. I'm telling it to you and then I never want to tell it again."

Then she told it, with eyes now open and then closed. Her eyes seldom strayed to Omri's face and when open they often looked straight into a nowhere beyond the room. Her hand would slip out of Omri's and return after its gesture or pointing.

"Henry's spells that you saw him in, when he wouldn't know anyone, they changed. He'd come out of them gentle, like before, but they wore him, left him spent and weak. We couldn't have the old-time talks. He didn't play with the boys like he used to."

For weeks Henry had Annabell read to him long battle accounts from the newspapers. She had her suspicions that he had excitements he didn't show, more excited than was good for him out of what she read. She tried to stop these readings or to shorten them but he kept her at it for hours every day. One day he said to her with a feverish sly look, new to her, "You know, Annabell, it's strategy wins a battle."

"Strategy?"

"Yeanh, you hit 'em before they expect it when they ain't lookin."

"So that's it."

"Now you wouldn't think I'm a strategist, would you, Annabell?"

"Maybe you are, Henry."

"Why, if I hadn't got this disability I'd have gone up and up in the war as a strategist. Before they could start to flank me I'd flank them. Then having outflanked 'em I'd crush 'em before they could begin to retreat. I been thinkin about it."

He slit his eyes and slid his underlip sidewise and put on a satisfaction with himself that Annabell had never seen before. And it was more mystifying when he struck a posture with his right arm thrust in his coat after the way Napoleon was pictured, his face taking on a noncommittal monkeylike calm as he said, "The great commanders took it cool. No matter what happens they take it cool like I take it cool. I will show them yet how I can command."

There was a week or more of this. "For one who knew Henry it was not easy to look at," said Annabell. "He was never a man for put-on, show-off. When he bought old costly furniture, jewels and books, fancy things, it was for me. Had the best dressmaker in St. Louis fix me out because 'You're a real lady and they don't come often.' Nobody ever saw Henry strut. You loved him for the way he didn't. And now, oh, God, he began to strut. Sitting in his wheel chair he strutted for himself and asked me to watch him strut. For a woman to see her man she knows float away from her and another she don't know at all come in his place—you have to go through it to know it. He would screw his lips into a sly proud mean mouth nobody had ever seen him make. He could lift one eye, look at you from a corner of the other, his lower lip flattened and spreading wide and thick to double what was natural. Henry Flack, the orderly merchant, the friendly neighbor, the playmate of boys, was gone. Someone else had entered his body and brain. For two weeks I lived with that awful Stranger who had taken control of Henry. And a fearful thought flashed sometimes that somewhere away back, it could be, hc was suffering hell, with a glimmer of knowing what he was doing and he couldn't stop it. We can't know. We haven't been in that country."

She was surprised at Henry's energy and ingenuity, coming in one day to see his arrangement of four chairs, ending in the tall brass-studded black one. It seemed he could maneuver in his wheel chair and lift heavy things and put them where he wanted them, a little better than in any other time he had been in the wheel chair. The line of chairs was "the woods," the fireplace beyond was "the ridge," and Henry was saying, "They're in those woods, six brigades of them, my scouts report. They've fortified that ridge runnin up from the woods. My battle plan is to charge the woods, front and flank, drive them from those woods, kill and capture as many as we can, and from the woods we'll shell their fortifications, blast their trenches, then charge up the ridge and take it. It's there, up the ridge, I'll get off my horse and on foot in person I'll lead my men up that ridge. It will end the war. Congress will give a vote of thanks and a medal to General Henry Flack, the Missouri merchant-soldier whose strategy ended the war."

Annabell heard this and saw him again with his hand put inside his coat Napoleon-style, and, "The reports will say that while the battle raged the troops and the corps and brigade commanders took courage from the cool demeanor that characterized their chief, General Henry Flack. They idolized Flack and would go anywhere he ordered. Throughout the contest he exhibited a calm exterior and a grasp of the situation that infected the line officers and the rank and file with his own magnificent resolution."

Annabell confessed to Omri, "I shouldn't have read him so many newspaper columns about the campaigns and battles. It grew on him. He fed on strategy and battle action. Yet I don't know. He was losing his mind, that was plain. But it might have taken a different course if I hadn't followed his wishes from day to day, reading long accounts of how régiments, brigades, corps, were moved here and there for defeat or victory. From reading the battle reports I could never get a clear picture of what happened. But Henry would say, 'That was correct, that's what I would have ordered.' Or, 'That was wrong, he should have moved sooner.' Or, 'He should have waited and made a night attack.' Day after day the idea grew on him that he was the world's greatest war commander.

"The Monday afternoon came he took me by the arm—and his

finger marks were there black-and-blue afterward—and he stretched out his arm pointing, 'Can you see 'em skulkin in the woods there?' Then he moved his arm to the right. 'Can you see where they're finishing the fortifications on the ridge? I think, General Heintzelman, tomorrow we'll show them what strategy can do.' "

This was the first time he had called her General Heintzelman. Till then she had been Annabell or nobody. She had till then been able vaguely and with desperate hope to see it as in part a game of pretensions where he might be still aware who she was. "When he called me General Heintzelman I had a give-out feeling, useless. My head ached, prongs and needles in it. I had run out of ideas for humoring him."

Then came the next day, Tuesday, and she stood beyond his arm reach, and he was saying, "I have delayed the offensive. We attack at daybreak tomorrow, General Schimmelpfennig."

Omri's upward glance found Annabell looking straight ahead, looking into her own nowhere beyond the room. "I was no longer Heintzelman. Now I was Schimmelpfennig." In her black hair, half-hidden and lurking, shone the garnet. It spoke to Omri of the jolly honest sane Henry Flack who adored his Annabell and had lavished jewels on her without her asking. That she, in his mind, could become General Heintzelman and General Schimmelpfennig at a battlefield headquarters where he was a strategist directing an army, this had none of the cool wine-red lucidity of the garnet.

There came the next morning, as foretold, the attack. The commander had made his preparations to conform with his plan. They included armament and munitions others were not aware lay hidden in the house. His light-blue wool trousers, his dark thick wool shirt, they had authority, for he had worn them at Chickamauga and made them his special apparel for this day. The Negro woman Ellie had set his tray on a table alongside the wheel chair. Annabell had brought in her own breakfast tray and set it on the table. Annabell saw Henry pointing with a slow arm and authoritative hand toward the woods, the row of four chairs in place, and again the arm and hand toward the ridge, the fireplace, the commander saying nothing, nodding to himself, first with a grim mouth that was silly, then with a satisfied confident smile likewise silly.

"Orderly," as he looked Annabell in the face, "bring me my field glasses," then as quickly, "No, orderly, stay at your post, I have them here." He took field glasses from a pouch slung by a strap from one shoulder. He studied the woods, the ridge, with the field glasses. He turned to her with a face of no silliness, a smolder in his eyes and a downward pinch to his mouth that she read as both fury and pain.

In a measured voice, curiously hiding a fury definitely there, "General Heintzelman, to your command! Why do you linger here? Obey the orders given you, be instantly ready to attack their left flank in the rear." He was pointing to the door, with hand and eye. She moved to the door and stood there in the open doorway. She saw him throw his tray and land it with crashing glass and victuals in one of the chairs, the first shellfire into the woods. She saw her own tray follow it, artillery fire into the woods, broken chinaware and soft-boiled eggs falling and dripping from the tall brass-studded chair.

He turned with a swift look toward her, pulled a revolver and crying, "General Heintzelman, to your command!" and his shaking hand and fussing trigger finger sent a bullet into the door two feet above her head. She stood outside the door, keeping it open enough to see him reach for a lamp on the table at his left and crash its porcelain and glass into one of the chairs, following with a second lamp, more shells from the cannon firing into the woods.

"Now we're ready to charge them," he was shouting in a tremulous voice near cracking. "Before you fix bayonets give them your musket fire all down the line." He drew out first one musket and then another he had kept hidden and had standing at the left side of his wheel chair. He blazed away, staggered the tall black chair, shattered the glass of a tall window beyond.

Now he was on his horse galloping toward the woods, his arms working the wheel chair, and the woods positions captured he was off his horse, out of his wheel chair, leading his men on foot up the ridge, on toward the fireplace eight feet away. He could move his feet in a weak wobbling shuffle two or three inches forward at a time, leading his men up the ridge, waving two revolvers in his hands, "Come on, men, give 'em hell, they can't stand it, we've got 'em on the run."

One bullet from his loose-handled revolver went up into a chandelier and brought glass pendants shattering down. Another broke the clock face on the mantel. Another bullet put his zither on the mantel out of balance so it fell to the smooth stone flooring in front of the fireplace, toppling toward a burning log and the varnished wood at one end of it catching fire. Three or four more of his shuffling steps and he fell to his knees, calling in a voice that gurgled, "Come on, men, we're near the top." On his knees he sent bullets into a firelog too near his face, the last battery of the enemy on the ridge top.

"I saw from the door," said Annabell, "a splash of embers and a spray of sparks shoot out toward him. He fell to the floor on his back, rolled over with a moan and then lay still and with his fingers picked out a small ember from one eye. I opened the door and ran in and bent over him. His left eye was bleeding and all bloodshot, a dozen embers sizzling on his cheeks and down his neck. I picked two, still smoking, out of his ear.

"He raised himself to look at me and to say very calmly, 'A great commander takes it cool, sir. Others may lose their heads in the face of enemy fire but a great commander—' and there he peered cunning-eyed at me as though suddenly he knew me. While his eyes looked

974

into mine one of his hands found its way to a revolver. He pointed it at my head not two feet away from him and the calm in his voice was cold and awful. 'General Schimmelpfennig, I am not going to wait for a court-martial to order you shot for disobedience and cowardice in the face of the enemy—I will myself execute the sentence of death on you.'

"Then I got one hand on the revolver and another on his wrist. His other hand pushed on my wrist hold and broke it. He wrenched and twisted my own wrist so I thought I would faint. We wrestled for that revolver. I couldn't imagine he would be so strong. I couldn't loosen his hold on the revolver and I was growing weak, I couldn't last. I stood up and with a prayer aimed my right foot at his wrist and sent the revolver spinning away. I ran and picked it up, for he had started to crawl toward it. He lay mumbling but the words came rather clear. 'General Heintzelman, I will have you tried for treason treason sir treason and a firing squad will give you your just deserts sir just deserts.' He was mumbling thick-tongued and repeating those words, 'just deserts just deserts.' Then he went still, his eyes closed, I could put my fingers on his face and hands and feel him going stiff and cold."

Annabell shivered, took her hand from Omri, reached for a knitted white shawl, threw it over her shoulders, tucked it under her chin, and put her hand back to Omri. She again sat looking beyond the room into her own nowhere. At times, in the telling, she had paused long. In these pauses Omri sat quiet as a chair, a bedpost, a chimney in a falling snow. Now she was saying, "That's about all. The doctor said it was a brain hemorrhage and complications. I've told it to you and I never want to tell it again and I make prayers I can forget it."

When Omri left her two days later they had arrived at quiet understandings with very little talk. He consulted with the doctor who agreed, yes, it might be an efficacious cure for her to break away from this house of tragedy and take her three boys and go to a country place with a friendly atmosphere. The doctor added, and in no trifling tone, "I think, Mr. Winwold, you are a good influence for her, a rather tonic effect, I have observed. I have no hesitation in recommending that for the immediate future she be placed under your care."

Where Dark Angels Brushed Light Wings

IN army blue, dark-blue jacket with brass buttons, light-blue trousers, his right-hand trigger finger missing, he had two bullet holes in his crinkled black hat. Thick of body, square-shouldered and short-legged, Asa Ware, nicknamed Ace, seemed less than his five feet eight and all of his hundred and ninety pounds. He had been born with a laughing mouth and after twenty-four years it was still with him. From his ruddy and weather-beaten face came a ten-dollar smile, some said twenty. He was the new husband of Rosalind Wayman.

In the West Wind tavern in Pittsfield, Ace had been drinking for two hours with six other fellows who had stood at the bar with him before the war. One after another had kept saying, "This is on me, bartender," or "I pay for the next one." They were all getting how-come-you-so except Ace. He could hold his liquor. It was a sight, for them, and they kept their eyes on it, how Ace would put his right thumb and middle finger around a glass and hold it as nice as though his trigger finger hadn't been shot off as neat and clean as you like. Except for that missing forefinger and two bullet holes in his hat you wouldn't be sure he had seen fighting. And to look at him, well-fed and hard-muscled, clear-eyed and apple-cheeked, though the apple would be a bronze russet rather than a maiden-blush pippin—you wouldn't guess he enlisted first off in April of '61 and had marched hundreds of miles with the Army of the Potomac and fought in about all of its bloodiest battles and at Sayler's Creek early this April of '65 he lost his trigger finger, and, "They told me they couldn't use me any more and I had done enough for the country."

"Wasn't you ever sick, Ace?"

"Had the shakes a few times, always got shet of 'em. One time I shook like a dog in a wet sack but I came out of it."

"Didn't you get homesick?"

"Wasn't time to be homesick, always something to do."

They asked him about one of the famous battles he was in and what happened.

"We advanced and drove 'em. They came at us and we fell back. Then we advanced and held our positions and won."

Asked about another famous battle, Ace said, "They attacked and we stopped 'em. They attacked again and we stopped 'em. The third time they attacked we didn't stop 'em and we lost."

The question came, "What was the worst time you ever had in the whole war?"

"You mean that?"

"We want to hear you tell it if it don't come too hard."

"Feller from Griggsville, Hoosier folks, a big strappin feller, enlisted when I did. We got to be pardners. Three years we marched together and what was his was mine and what was mine was his. On outpost duty, nothin stirrin for weeks. The cook one day makes a gooseberry pie. My pardner was holdin his piece of pie in his hand and eatin and he was sayin, 'Land of Goshen, that's good pie,' and a bullet takes him in the neck and he's a goner. Only time in the war I was what you call sad."

"What was the funniest thing you saw in the war?"

"I couldn't say. I did take a prisoner last month. A pardner of his deserted the month before,' sayin, 'I've killed as many of them as they have of me and I'm goin home.' Tennessee boy, one time fought under a general that said how to win, 'Get 'em skeered and then keep the skeer on 'em.' "

"And you passed by the purty girls in Virginia to take up with the only Virginia girl left in Pike County."

"Does seem so," he grinned as the men at the bar ordered more rounds of drinks to health and happy days for the newly married couple, Asa Ware and Rosalind Wayman.

"And you're stayin on the Wayman farm?"

"Stayin and I'm goin to raise a power of corn, tall corn. I'm hungry to plow and plant and see the corn come up. You don't know what it is to stay away so long from the corn. Next fall I'll husk against any man of you."

He had met Rosalind at a barn dance three nights after the Appommattox surrender had about ended the war, had taken her to church the next Sunday night and driving her home had said, "I'm a git-up-and-git man, I don't beat about the bush, I'll marry you if you'll have me." And they were married three days later and Rosalind said to Mibs, "His family is respectable and will leave him a big farm someday. He has a good name except for drinking and even there he has a reputation for what he can carry without showing it."

They took a liking to him on the Wayman farm. "The farm will go on," said Mr. Wayman. "He's natural to the land. He'll make crops or know why." Ace had been up at half-past four one morning and coming in at six o'clock after chores, the Negro women asked him from the kitchen if he would like a couple of fried eggs. "I don't dirty my plate for less'n six," he laughed as he wiped his face and threw from the back porch the tin basin of water he had washed his face in. He had come in near dark one evening, after twelve or fourteen hours of plowing and chores, saying to Rosalind, "Hard work never hurt any

977

man. My father brought me up to that. But take your time, he'd say, easy does the trick and just keep at it, keep everlastingly at it."

To Rod he had said once, "I had all the luck there is—and you didn't." And that week Ace had said little more than that, except after pouring about a tablespoon of whisky into a glass, adding water and handing it to Rod, he lifted his own glass with the toast, "You're as good a man, Butternut, as fought in the war." And Rod with a quaver of a smile, lifting his glass, "And you're one of the best there is, Bluebelly." Mibs standing by saw it as a ritual of mutual understanding between two men who had moved in the wildest of front-line fighting, and each having fought fair had for the other an appraisal of respect and affection not quite in the ken of outsiders.

She had seen Rod make slow gains. A sickish yellow tint in his skin took on more of white and pink, at times. On some days his mildewed look was gone. She had burned his clothes with their filth and a smell of filth she believed could never be washed away. She had personally scrubbed his body in hot baths and he had admitted, "Yes, I'm clean now," though later she heard from him, "It may be I won't *feel* clean till the memory is gone."

Slowly by weeks the dysentery had left Rod. But the hand tremors kept coming back. He would knock over the pepper reaching for the salt. The red five-inch fishhook scar on his right jaw, Mibs studied it many a time with infinite thanks the bullet had not plowed into mouth, nose or an eye. She would recall Jeremy Taylor's "What is man?" and the answer, "The dream of a shadow of smoke." Only one heavy anxiety rode her. There would be hours and not a word from him, days with absently spoken greetings. Her fear ran that he might be going mute like his mother. It was a comfort to her to remember back to the months before the war began when he kept these same peculiar silences. There was cheer too in noticing rather strictly that, from week to week, came fewer of these spells of mute quiet.

Rod stood over the sleeping Clayborn Joel one night and murmured to Mibs, "We called him God's kiss, didn't we?" And turning to the crib of Rodney Jr. he asked her whether birth had come hard for her, and hearing it was easier than the first one, he had shifted to a memory. Just before Shiloh he had during the night lain awake an hour listening to the honk and the honk-honk of wild geese flying over the camp toward the north, endless wild geese that he could see crossing Tennessee and Kentucky, some of them the next day perhaps flying over Pike County and the crib of his child he might never see. "And that," said Mibs, "was probably one of the nights I crept between the sheets whispering, 'Oh God, this bed feels empty!' "

One fact stood out. Mibs flung it gaily and daily at Rod. Every week he gained weight. From a hundred and fifteen pounds in February he went to a hundred and thirty-two in the first week of April. "The scales tell it," she warbled at him. "We'll be singing and waltzing again this summer." And it might be, he wasn't sure, that next fall he would start for Texas and bring up the herd of cattle that he was going for when the war started four years ago. On this day in the first week in April came his first try at singing. He didn't quit as she came into the room. He went on:

"Peas, peas, peas, peas,
Eating goober peas.
Goodness, how delicious,
Eating goober peas."

She picked up the guitar and with coaxing had him teach her the song. His voice hadn't come back. It faltered. His lungs and throat couldn't shape singing lines as they once did. "Today is a beginning," said Mibs. He spoke dreamily, "Ever of thee I'm fondly dreaming." She said next summer he would sing it like in the old days and they would run over the old songs and pick up new ones.

Then came from Rod a flow of speech, a little stream of spoken language, an unbroken silver cascade of bright phrases having meaning, a plain historical statement and a quivering love letter sent straight at her with no prediction beforehand that she would get it. She heard it and one glow after another ran over her. One was an adoration of him in a deeper dusk and a brighter splendor than she had ever seen him. In another glow ran her certainty, her first certainty, that he would never go mute. His burst of speech came in a slow measured drawl, as though out of long thoughts and as though the two of them were one and had ahead of them all the time there is: "Sometime I'll tell you about the Union people of East Tennessee, about women who learned how to kill in cold blood, about an ambrotype of a girl in my coat pocket and why I couldn't give it to her, Shiloh and the night march in mud and the wounded in wagons with rain and hail on them, how Doss died and what a man he was—Chickamauga, Camp Morton and the escape, fighting at the Wilderness, Spotsylvania and Hornsby Meadows dying next to me in an old barn with a message he forgives you all—malaria and then the ride to Johnson's Island—how God leaned down and brought you to me—how many times I lost everything but you and one thin sliver of shimmering light and that was my pride in the Lost Cause. My faith in that cause has been hammered on brutal and awful anvils, shot and burnt in the smoke and steel of a thousand battlefields from the Potomac to the Rio Grande. But that pride lives, a bond between men who can never forget what they went through together. I have them and I have you and the two of God's kisses."

She had him lie down, with her alongside, a blanket over them. He closed his eyes and one hand sought hers. She looked from his face out the window to the hemlock tree and its evergreen and five

979

stars fixed over it and beyond that a baby moon, a silver slipper of a moon.

She looked at his forehead and the waviness of his black hair coming back. She ran soft fingers in his hair. It had been matted and stringy with a dank odor of filth. She had washed it twice a week. It was wavy again and smooth and sweet-smelling.

Her fingers parted the hair along the line of the scar curve. She murmured, "This too, when you begin, you'll tell about, a sweet insignia, where a dark angel brushed a light wing tip and went on."

He didn't hear her. In the dim lamplight she saw his mouth and eyes those of a sleeping child. She looked again at the hemlock, the five stars and the baby moon and then his white face so still. She saw his lips purse. He talked in his sleep, loose-lipped words that didn't come clear to her. He repeated and she made out his saying: "Potatoes and onions when necessary as antiscorbutics may be purchased from the prison fund—surgeon—commanding officer—straw difficult obtain —yessir strawsir difficult obtain—potatoes onions difficult obtain—"

She laughed low. She snuggled closer to him. About mid-March it was, what with her attentions, ointment, diet, care, a physician's skill, the scurvy had cleared up, the mouth sores went away. Then he kissed her more freely, more fiercely, nearly as in the old days.

* * * * * * * * * *

Chapter 43

* * * * * * * * * *

Supper at Winwold's

MIBS kept outsiders and newspapers from Rod and told him, "Soaked in the war you've been and the less of newspapers and war talk, the less useless you'll feel."

"Don't baby me too much, honey girl."

"I want you to be slick as a rat, smooth as a fox, bold as a tiger, sudden as chained lightning."

"You pile it on. How could I be all those? And all to wunst, as the man would say."

"You were when you worked out that Camp Morton escape."

He said nothing, a sprocket of blue and white light in his eyes. She went on, "Or if you prefer, sit like Patience on a monument smiling at grief." She saw him almost smile.

She read in April of the surrender at Appomattox, a few days later of the assassination of the President in Washington, and she told him of those dark events and snapped, "Keep your shirt on," then softer than a baby white cloud in an azure sky, "Your old high commander has advice, golden words for you and all your comrades now, *Our duty is to live.*' You've seen enough of death." Rod said nothing. She couldn't read him.

She had seen Omri for the first time since Rod's return. She quoted Omri for him. "Life is a series of punctuations. Being born ends the first period, dying the last. Between periods and strung along are commas, colons, semicolons and dashes, and indeed exclamation points and those endless buttonhook interrogations."

Omri had asked the Waymans to a supper at the Winwold house. He knew her anxiety about Rod. It might upset him, no telling what it might do for him to join in such a gathering. "I would chance it," said Omri. "My idea is it'll do him good, though I can't tell how."

Rod and Mibs arrived early for the supper. Rod wore a black ready-made suit of clothes from a Pittsfield store. It hung loose on him, drooped from his shoulders, bagged and swung as though two of him could have had room in it. His white linen shirt Mibs had refitted for him, the starched collar and the wide green bow tie helping to cut down the lean length of his neck and the spare-bone frame of his face. "I've learned," said Mibs, "how to make myself look less skinny and I can do it with you."

Rod met them and shook hands one by one before they took chairs at the table and supper dishes came on. Omri at his right and Mibs at his left helped him know better the names, faces, people, apparitions at the table. Rod could see Marvel next to his father, in the uniform of a brevetted brigadier general of the United States Army, his left forearm sleeve covering a stump above the wrist; Marvel could handle a fork or spoon for most of his victuals but the roast beef had to be cut for him. Rod noticed that Omri's head of brick-dust hair and his reddish muffler beard had all gone snow-white and there were furrows and clefts around the mouth and nose while the long slash of a mouth was the most sorrow-smitten mouth he had ever seen. Rod studied again those two sides of Omri's face. The peace side was toward him, gentle and beneficent as the purple lilacs swaying in a spring breeze that day. The other side Rod caught in glimpses: a storm path ran over it and Rod thought, "He could have been at Chickamauga." And Rod peered deep into Omri's eyes and saw a faint molten gold in the brown and later said to Mibs, "He didn't pity me but it was like he said 'I've been where you've been, my boy, and we'll get along.'"

Opposite him Rod saw Milton in the wheel chair, patient with a curious sweetness. Omri had asked Milton to say grace over the food and Milton spoke it briefly, sincerely, while all heads bowed. Rod saw Milton's hands tremble before saying grace and once later and the second time heard Mibs' low whisper, "It used to be worse, it's going away like yours will." At Milton's right sat Mr. Wayman, and Rod and Mibs heard part of their conversation to the effect that God made the land for sacred uses and not for desecration. At Mr. Wayman's right was a vacant chair where all understood Brock Wayman of the Union Army would have sat, a turned plate with a crossed knife and fork on the table. Next was a vacant chair for Holliday, who had dreamed to no avail of the food loading the table at which he was a ghost presence. Then around the curve of the table were the two young ones who had stayed home, not quite grown-up, Hope and Robert Prindle.

At Milton's left Rod saw Milton's two special friends he wanted for this evening, the Hoon boy, who had learned to manage one-armed eating with more skill than Marvel, having had longer practice—and next the blind Houseworth youth, who had a knack with his knife and fork and seemed to be the keenest listener at the table. Then further around the table stood three chairs set leaning against the table board. These three were alive, yet to come home, Peter Moore in hospital at Nashville with a wound after the battle there, and Patrick Henry with an army down in North Carolina and soon to come home, and Cedora, Brock's widow, a nurse in Washington and soon to come home.

Next sat two mischievous-looking boys of four and five, fresh-faced and restless, answering to the names of Nathaniel Lyon and Frank Blair. That left two chairs between them and Marvel. Second at Marvel's right was the seventeen-year-old one-legged boy, whose crutch stood handy against the table, a drummer boy, Joshua Ponder. Between him and Marvel sat a woman new to the neighborhood, new to this house, wearing a fadeaway fog-purple gown that became her black hair and violet eyes, Annabell Ponder Flack. Two days ago she was married to Omri Winwold.

Arriving late were Asa and Rosalind Ware, both somewhat tipsy and vague as they took chairs among the younger ones at a table end. Asa wore a suit of black-and-white checks, a light-blue shirt with a flowing red necktie. Rosalind was in a bright-yellow organdie gown with a balloonish effect. To others in the room they seemed to say, "Oh be joyful and sound the glad timbrels." To Omri and to Milton, Ace explained later, "I came near not gettin here at all. I got to thinkin I'd see these other fellows here that got hit in the war and I put in four years fightin and only lost a finger and it wasn't I was bashful, I just couldn't quite figger it out. It ain't right a man should have the luck I had all the way from Bull Run to Sayler's Creek." Rod standing alongside and hearing this couldn't help putting a hand on Ace's shoulder and patting it. Rosalind saw it. She gave Rod a soft kiss on the cheek. She was proud of him and of Ace.

There was talk. They broke into groups and clusters and talked. Of peace and crops and going to church and barn dances and fun, they talked. Of the war being over and the boys and men coming home, they talked. Of the funeral car of the dead President and great crowds, hundreds of thousands in Philadelphia, New York, Albany, and yet to come, Columbus and Indianapolis, Chicago and Springfield, throngs pressing to see his face in the coffin piled with flowers and arched over with blossoms, talking in hushed tones. Somehow the babbling ceased and all listened while Omri read a paragraph from the dead President's Second Inaugural:

" 'Neither party expected for the war the magnitude or the duration which it has already attained. Neither anticipated that the cause of the conflict might cease with, or even before, the conflict itself should cease. Each looked for an easier triumph, and a result less fundamental and astounding. Both read the same Bible, and pray to the same God; and each invokes his aid against the other. It may seem strange that any men should dare to ask a just God's assistance in wringing their bread from the sweat of other men's faces; but let us judge not, that we be not judged. The prayers of both could not be answered—that of neither has been answered fully. The Almighty has his own purposes.' "

Those of the Wayman house drove home. Ace the next morning said, "It was like going to church and hearing good news, I don't know why."

Rod was shut-mouthed for two days. Then Mibs heard him for the first time singing clear-voiced, full-voiced. They took up two guitars and sang together "In the Bright Mohawk Valley." Then he sang for her "Ever of Thee I'm Fondly Dreaming," though his hand tremors came on and she ran along with the accompaniment. Then Rod waltzed a dozen steps with her in old-time style and let go of her. "I'm give-out, honey."

★ ★ ★ ★ ★ ★ ★ ★ ★ ★

Chapter 44

★ ★ ★ ★ ★ ★ ★ ★ ★ ★

A Breakfast Interruption

THE wagons kept going West. During the war they had kept going, by thousands, settlers, homesteaders, homeseekers and silver- and gold-hunters heading for the Great Plains, the Rockies, the West coast. The war ending and a free farm, a quarter-section of land, awaiting any Union soldier who chose to file his claim, there were more wagons West now, more roadside camps.

Mibs came in one morning to see at the eating table a medium-built man with round shoulders, small eyes that seemed to shift often, a grinning mouth that seemed overly satisfied with the pleasure it gave others. He was in Union Army blue. Alongside him sat his girl wife of three weeks, as he told it, perhaps seventeen, could be sixteen, and Mibs couldn't tell whether her rather pretty face was sad, scared, or both. They had put away fried eggs and potatoes and were now working on a stack of buckwheat cakes with molasses. Mibs' eyes swept this in a few seconds as she saw across the table, standing, his hands trembling on the back of a chair, a speaking and hissing Rod, his eyeballs queer and staring, his face at one moment marvelously calm and again the mouth muscles writhing. Mibs stood at the end of the table, certain there was some reason in Rod's acting, certain it couldn't be some new phase of sickness.

Rod was saying as he looked the morning guest in the eye, "You're a yellow dog with a yellow belly, the dirtiest stinkinest yellow God ever made. You're lower than the dirtiest barn rat that ever ate horse-shit and liked it."

Ace Ware had come in and stood by with no word, his ruddy face glowing, for it was a little like being back in the army. He moved over alongside of Mibs, who put her hand in his, as though the two of them would know what to do. Rod hadn't finished. He went on, "If you tried to live with the snakes they wouldn't take you in, for you're lower than they are. When you die and arrive in hell and start burning you'll stink up the place so they'll wonder where to put you." Rod paused. He was trying to think of more compliments and comparisons.

The man eating pushed the last of a buckwheat cake into his mouth, tried for a grin that came a little sickly, and said, "I'm a stranger here, mister, and I don't get your drift."

"You're no stranger here, that's the trouble, yellow-belly," said Rod.

"No?" And what there was of the grin had faded.

"You were on duty at Camp Morton."

"Yes."

"You and another guard caught two fellows going to the sink one winter night with pants and coats on."

"We caught many of them. The rule was they could wear either pants or coat but not both."

"Exactly—and these two fellows in ragged socks and their shoes coming to pieces, you made 'em mark time in the snow for an hour and one of them froze his feet and gangrene set in and he lost the feet and you made him a cripple for life. And you're a sonofabitch and you're what's wrong with the country and your face ought to have had you hung long ago."

"Oh, no."

"Oh, yes. You'll drink your coffee and get out of this house and drive away and you better not look back or a bullet'll burn your ears. Drink your coffee now and get out. I hope you meet the fellow you

984

crippled and he beats the living whey out of you and then tears you to pieces and feeds you to a pack of yellow curs, for hogs couldn't stand the smell of you."

Mr. Wayman and Rosalind had come in. They saw it was an affair between these two men. They waited and saw the man and his girl wife rise from the table. They stood on the front porch and saw Ace and Mibs following Rod, who walked close at the heels of the Camp Morton ex-guard.

Near the corncrib the newcomer wheeled about to face Rod, "I know my rights if I don't live here. No damned Rebel can talk to me like you do. Why don't you go back to Dixie and try to sell your niggers?"

Rod had run out of words. He stood trying to think. When he saw a fist coming toward him, he swung a fist of his own. A blow landed on his jaw, on the fishhook scar, and he reeled and fell on his back. The unexpected morning caller, with one hand pulling his wife along, ran full-speed for his wagon. He had helped his wife up on the seat, had his left foot on a wheel hub to vault up into the seat and drive away. His right foot had just left the ground when it was caught, clutched and given a swift terrific pull by the hands of Ace Ware. His left foot on the hub, his whole weight on that hub, lost its foothold. His face and forehead came down grinding and scraping along the iron wheel rim and the hickory wagon spokes.

He lay on the ground with a deep cut on his forehead, gashes bleeding at one side of the head, one eye closed. Ace stood by, joined by Rod and Mibs, watching him come to. Mr. Wayman and Rosalind came running. A Negro boy brought a pail of water and cloths. Ace washed the cheek gashes and the forehead, tore the man's shirt for a bandage around the forehead, put the man's hat on, helped him up on the seat and told him to drive on. As the horses moved and the wheels turned, Rod called, "I hope it's a scar for life and I hope sometime the fellow you crippled for life meets up with you."

* * * * * * * * * *

Chapter 45

* * * * * * * * * *

Fondly Do We Hope

THE moon had gone down. Some who knew a war song gave the lines, "The stars of heaven are looking kindly down, On the grave of old John Brown."

A great grief had hung in the air over the land since April 14, the night it was said there was blood on the moon. The tolling of bells, the muffled boom of cannon and minute guns, had marked moments of ceremonial. There had been lashing rains and the red gold of rolling prairie sunsets and great bonfires lighting the sky while crowds stood with uncovered heads to see a coffin pass in the night.

Mibs had slept lightly. She saw the moon go down and the sky left in the keep of quiet stars.

She woke Rod. They hitched a span of horses, put a valise and a basket of food in the buggy and took to the roads. Along the roads two and three hours before sunrise they passed or they followed other rigs. There were buggies, wagons, gigs, horsemen—by the hundreds moving in the night toward one point, one center—by the thousands they saw them as they neared Springfield an hour or so after sunrise.

They located Rosalind and Ace, Omri and Annabell, at the barn of a friend of Rosalind where they put up their horses. They stood in line at the state capitol building, ahead of them thousands of city and country folk. It had been so all night long and all of the morning and afternoon of the day before—thousands waiting in line and moving on for a look at the face in the coffin.

That final look itself, the moment or two of gazing at an embalmed body amid heaped fragrance of blossoms, what the eye caught and kept was less in itself than the ritual act of being present and paying silent salutation.

They followed the cortege and procession to a burial vault and stood on a green hillside and heard prayers, hymns, the reading by a Methodist bishop of the Second Inaugural. They heard again the paragraph Omri had read to them at the supper evening and other lines that came rounded and shaped on the spring morning air as though they had life beyond life:

"Fondly do we hope—fervently do we pray—that this mighty scourge of war may speedily pass away. . . . With malice toward none, with charity for all; with firmness in the right, as God gives us to see the right, let us strive on to finish the work we are in . . . to do all which may achieve and cherish a just and lasting peace among ourselves, and with all nations."

They moved among the crowds that packed downtown Springfield. Toward the end of the afternoon Mibs found the wagon of a Pike County farmer and put Rod in the wagon box for a two-hour sleep. They roamed and saw the silk-hatted men in long black shining Prince Albert coats, the day laborers and farmers in their hand-me-downs—women in wide breathless crinoline of silk and the cohorts in gingham and calico. They had taken a bath of multitudes. The papers said seventy-five thousand people had passed through the state capitol building for their last look.

Rod and Mibs took turns driving home, sleeping and driving by turns, saying little, saying almost nothing, brushing shoulders, snuggling close at times, discussing briefly once how inconceivably old the night stars are and yet when you look at them how young and tireless and dependable they seem.

The moon rode white in a silver haze. Past midnight they neared Atlas and home. Rod came out of a short sleep and a long silence to say, "Mibs, do you know—"

"Yes, Rod?"

"I love the old Union, I believe I do truly love the old Union."

"Yes."

"But we won't talk about it. And, Mibs, old girl—"

"Yes, young feller?"

"Been thinking about one letter you never got. You know how it ended?"

"About time you were telling me."

" 'I went out and counted the stars. Every star I counted had your name on it. Does that make sense?' "

"Are you talking or was that the letter?"

"That was the letter."

She had him say it again. She pulled to the side of the road, made him throw back his head and count stars.

"Do they still have my name on 'em, every one?"

"They shore do and I'm askin again if it makes sense."

"You can't ask what's sensible when you're in love." She dropped the reins. She took his head between her hands and gave him long soft kisses on mouth and eyes.

The horses began moving on a slow walk. They knew it was time to go home. Mibs snatched the reins and put them on a slow trot.

★ ★ ★ ★ ★ ★ ★ ★ ★ ★

Chapter 46

★ ★ ★ ★ ★ ★ ★ ★ ★ ★

The Arch Never Sleeps

ONE summer day when apple blossoms were flagrant and luminous in whitening the air the news came. The commander of the Army of Northern Virginia, an idolized figure and a man of few words, had as a paroled soldier applied for a pardon that gave him full restoration of his rights as a citizen of the United States.

Rod made his inquiries and learned of the advice of his old commander: "Our returned soldiers must all set to work, and if they

987

cannot do what they prefer, do what they can. They must put them-selves in a position to take part in government and not to be deterred by obstacles in their way. There is much to be done which they only can do."

Rod and Mibs drove to the courthouse in Pittsfield, had his signed application for pardon made correctly, and sent on to Washington. Driving home they went out of their way to stop at the Winwold house. They sat on the front porch with Omri and Annabell, poured from a big pitcher of cherry punch, and looked out over a mystic float of apple-blossom white. Rod's weight had climbed to a hundred and sixty pounds, Mibs smiled to Omri, who said, "He's getting the old sparkle back," and as Marvel came out, "like this young mustang here —he's bringing his wife home next month and says she's a homely little heifer and just what he wants." Marvel told of his wife's first case in hospital, a lad who was asked how it came he was shot in the face at Bull Run and he laughed, "I run a mile and then looked back."

The talk sobered. Omri ran fingers through his snow-white muffler beard, slanted an eye at Mibs, said he had heard her tell it but now for once he would like to hear from Rod about the San Francisco boy, the young architect.

"He was pure Scotch, as I understand," said Omri, "had a strong face with girlish curves, a tall forehead with straw curls hanging down. A woman had fooled him and failed him and he drank hard. He quoted that ancient line, 'The arch never sleeps.' Then he went far-ther. That's what I'd like to hear from you, Rod."

Rod stood up. It made him restless to remember it. He leaned against a porch post.

"The arch never sleeps. When the arch holds, all else holds. Love stands and hangs by an arch. Hate breaks the arch. The rainbow is an arch. Where you find truth, love, harmony and lasting strength, an arch bends and curves over it as a blessing and an oath. Unity, union, you get it only with an arch. Hate and pride break arches. Love and understanding build unbreakable arches."

They lingered. They drove away, Mibs at the reins. Rod said, "They're a beautiful couple, Omri and his wife."

"Yes, but their waltzing days are over."

"And who wants to waltz life away?"

"I do. I want about a thousand waltzes with you I've missed."

"You can have 'em—since we're good waltzers."

"Good? We're the best in the United States."

"The whole world, you could have said." And he pulled a tassel of her chestnut hair down over an ear. "The whole world—why not?"

Mibs held the reins in one hand, with the other put the tassel of hair back over the ear, turned her head with her eyes slanted at Rod. "Yes, darling, always and ever when you and I see the whole world through the same arch."

★ ★ ★ ★ ★ ★ ★ ★ ★ ★
★   ★
★   *Epilogue*   ★
★   ★
★ ★ ★ ★ ★ ★ ★ ★ ★ ★

STORM AND STARS

Chapter 1

Pete and Ann: Evening of Mist

THE woman in the taxicab watched the raindrops splashing on the skylight glass roof, a September rain, the year 1943. She saw the blowing sheets slow down to a gray drizzle. Her eyes turned toward a man dashing from the front entrance of the Veterans' Hospital. She swung the cab door open and when he had leaped in and closed the door, their arms went around each other. Her lips pressed his tightly. As she drew away it was only vaguely in her mind, and of no importance for the moment, that he had really not met her kiss and had merely brushed his lips to hers with a sidewise shake of the head.

Of the fourteen million American men and boys who had gone into the Second World War, the one in captain's uniform alongside her was the one she preferred to see this day. While waiting in the rain for him her hands had smoothed her Army Nurse uniform and she had murmured in a low tone from some poet, "Life is a kiss and a promise. Death is a kiss and an ashtray."

Now they sat holding hands, once in a while fingers gently pressing, looking at each other with sidelong glances, occasionally turning a head for a full open-eyed gaze, one at the other. He had telephoned to his sister the message for her, "Of course I'd like to see Ann but I couldn't talk. There's little to say." He saw her considerably underweight yet stocky of build, black hair falling in locks and strands of movement around her ears, and a face of natural pallor, eyes that on second look were a deep-brown almost black, a mouth of mournful lips slow in breaking into a smile, and he wondered if this evening he would hear the laugh that used to be utterly Irish and recklessly gay when it came.

She saw him perhaps twenty or thirty pounds under his normal two hundred, and six feet two, bony shoulders, and his uniform coat loose on him, small light-hazel eyes. His chest was still hairy, came one sudden random thought to her, as in days when they had gone swimming together. Her eyes fell on the back of his hairy left hand and one finger with a thickened knuckle joint—she had seen him make the flying tackle which broke that finger.

Now after three years of not seeing him she believed he could be, as before, sudden and casual—like herself. He had been stringing along that last college year with two other girls besides herself when one

991

night he suddenly told her, "You're the one and only for me." He was casual and positive, said it again and took her in a fierce embrace and let her say nothing for the way he put his lips to hers. Then when he heard her soft laugh, partly in a hiss but mostly a whisper, the words came from him, "I was telling you there's nobody else."

Then again her soft laugh, "I won't have to think it over."

They made no plans. There were no pledges or promises. He handed her a thin silver ring saying, "It don't mean a thing but sometime if the cards come up right maybe we'll go in for wedding bells." As she slipped the ring on her finger she gave him her gayest laugh, "You mean nobody's plighting no troths today." That was all. He had been sudden and casual about going into the army without telling her beforehand. And as she looked back now she was hazy about how and why she had drifted into training and become an Army Nurse—and the letters between them had been few and rather factual, more informative than romantic.

Of the large blue goggles he wore, with wide flesh-tinted temple pieces running back to the ears, and the well-made mask rather marvelously simulating his nose and fitted so smoothly on the upper lip and the face contours that your eyes couldn't detect the edges of it, as to this device, this present and temporary arrangement, she had deep curiosity, a few slight misgivings, and nothing at all like fear. She rambled swiftly in memories of him, of how changeable she had seen him, of how there was no telling when next you met him whether he would be high and proud or low and humble. There were the times he was cocksure and swaggering that he would make a great lawyer and again he was afraid he would never be anything but a second-rate pettifogger, saying, "I'm not bright enough to be a shyster." Likewise he would be saying one day, "I can take my pick of the gals," and later the same day, "Any little heifer can take me for a ride." Now for a moment she wondered whether they had so much to tell each other that they didn't dare begin telling it and for the time being it was enough to hold hands and feel snug together over what the evening would bring.

The taxi rolled along spectacular Henry Hudson Parkway and their eyes caught a long bridge in thin evening mist. There was a level horizontal line picked off in parallels of light. There were dangling loops of light, quiet yellow dots on faint blue fog, saying, "Here am I, a bridge, if you wish to cross a river this night."

"Nice, hey, Pete?" with a sweep of her hand toward the bridge.

"I like it, purty."

He had, in the old days, usually said "purty" for "pretty." Now it was more like "kurty," somewhat like an amateur ventriloquist speaking for the dummy on his knees. He couldn't make his lower lip muscles do what he wanted them to do. And of this she had neither misgivings nor fear. She believed she knew her surgeons.

Far down the river they saw two wide brown slabs of light, slanted and leaning. These became, on closer view, two broad squat smokestacks of an ocean liner.

"The *Queen Mary*," said Pete, blurring the "M" in "Mary." "Counting Jake Zinski and me, eighteen thousand of us rode her over the Atlantic." He paused. "No lights. No convoy. Four days and the Q-M had us across, eighteen thousand of us on her, counting Jake Zinski and me."

Ann got nothing from a searching look into the blue goggles. She saw his lips move to say, "Jake Zinski, you never heard of him."

"Who?"

"Jake Zinski."

"I don't remember now," said Ann—and she was telling a white lie, for Pete's sister had told her about Jake Zinski. After a silence she asked, "Why?"

A silence again as the taxi rolled on and his voice came, "Ever hear of Pola Folsom?"

"No."

"That's her name now. Before she married it was Pola Zinski—Jake's sister—we'll see her tonight at the Blue Dipper."

At the brass-studded door of the Blue Dipper entrance, they waited while two privates, first-class, with their girls, argued with the doorman.

"Management's orders—only officers admitted," the doorman kept repeating.

"Tell the management to come out here and we'll bust him in the puss," snarled one of the departing G.I.'s.

Pete brushed by when the doorman bowed to his officer uniform, opening the door with respect. At a table in a dimly lighted corner, they ordered drinks, steaks, and saw a mimic come on into the spotlight, sending his imitations and jokes at men whose faces and half-oval shirt bosoms loomed vague and gray as did the faces and bare shoulders of their women. He did a taxi-driver and a fat lady, two drunks in a conversation with a woman in a second-story window as to which of the two was her husband, a very small husband in bed with his very large wife and resulting complications.

During one prolonged outburst of laughter and hilarity, Ann for a moment saw a red light bobbing on sea water on a dark night. She stood with others at a deck rail watching that red light as the convoy ship sped on. And the red light grew smaller till it vanished. A seaman had fallen overboard, the automatic red light telling his location—and the convoy law absolute: No ship halts in its outlined course unless disabled. The bobbing red signal light grew dim and at last winked out.

Ann in the Blue Dipper drew two fingers across her forehead, swept

993

a wave of hair back of her right ear, saw Pete's face come into sharp focus, and the convoy memory became a blur. "Lordy, lordy," she was saying to herself, "what things we'll be telling if we ever start talking."

Fast music broke across the spotlight cone. They turned their eyes to see a girl tap-dancer in spangled black tights, in stereotyped footwork, a little tired. Four brisk strip-tease dancers, in contrasting silk gowns, one by one went through their acts. "Kinda new?" Pete queried, Ann saying, "About the same—more clothes and trimmings, that's all." In college days they had ventured into burlesque shows and the cheaper night clubs, seeing there the strip tease stark and shameless, also a version of the French cancan, unabashed teasing with no preceding ceremonies of stripping. The old standard designs were changing.

The final act came, an incorrigibly collegiate announcer spieling in marshmallow accents, "You will now have before your eyes the Plastic Lady, in her lithe and lissome body the wiles of the lizard and the cunning of the serpent. While you gaze on her she changes from one tortuous and seductive shape to another, the woman of a thousand fantastic forms. Born forty miles from land and forty miles from sea, she is a sister of mermaids born in sea grottoes and the albatross given birth amid mountain crags. Before her ductile and dazzling mutations men of science acknowledge themselves baffled as to the source and origins of her mysterious bodily gifts. She defies the laws of anatomy and gravity. Prepared to please and mystify you, she is on her way to appear before you, she is here now," and he took her by the hand and proclaimed, "The Princess of the Gargoyles. She turns herself inside out and upside down before you and you'll be saying, 'Is she fish, bird, snake or octopus and where did she come from?' " He bowed toward her. "The one and only Pola Folsom."

She stepped out of sandals and stood barefooted, five feet eight, in the spotlight funnel her white skin a shimmer of silver, her body lean and arrow-smooth, a girdle and tight-fitting trunks of light-bronze silk at her hips and navel, a brassière also light-bronze silk, at her head a snug bob of dark-brown hair. She went into a slow dance with sudden swirls and moved on into five unexpected handsprings, the fifth with one hand, ending with her head between her knees and her upside-down face gazing as though what had happened was a surprise to her. Then she took bows to three rounds of applause and cheers and went into her gargoyles, one piece of fantastic sculpture after another. In the final one she had bent backward and brought her head out between her knees with a writhing face, a slimpsy twist to the head resting loose-hung at the right knee, an illusion of the head perhaps swung off from her neck. She came out of it to cries and handclaps of applause, took several bows keeping her large mournful mouth grave and no smile in her large dark-brown eyes as she bent in a long slow forward sweep of her bob of dark-brown hair.

Pete had folded his hands on the table and shifted fingers in and out throughout Pola Folsom's act. At the final illusion of a head twisted off he put his hands on Ann's wrists, started to say something and let it pass.

In Pola's dressing room Pete shook hands with her and introduced Ann. Tears came to Pola's eyes and she fell into Pete's arms as he was saying, "I saw Jake, Pola, the whole way through. He was a great guy, they all said that, Jake was a great guy. They don't come better." Pete mentioned Jake's showing him photographs of Pola and her husband as a dancing team before her husband went to the South Pacific and another picture of her in shorts with her six-year-old boy and her four-year-old girl, the mother and two children with feet on the floor bent back with hands flat on the floor and Pola once telling Jake, "I want two or three more as limber as these two."

Pola stood at the doorway of the dressing room, her shoulders scrunched forward, the tears rolling down her face, Pete holding her two hands, and the shaken Ann Flaherty noticing Pete's eyes wet and his mouth open and loose. So they stood awhile, Pete leaving with, "It's a promise, Pola, I'll be seeing you."

Walking out of the Blue Dipper Ann clung and hung to Pete's arm and liked it. On the street a drizzle of rain came cool and more than pleasant on her face. They waited a minute or two for a taxi.

"You smell that rain?" she asked.

"It's good, I like it." And she knew the feel of that film-drifting drizzle pleased him more than the floor show, more than the drinks and the float of faces and the gabble and the crowd starting to dance and the jangle of the swing orchestra.

In the taxi on the way to her apartment, Pete said nothing. To the sudden and vehement outburst that came from her he answered with pressure from his large-knuckled right hand in hers. It poured from her in a hoarse fury with some of her syllables in cool black velvet. "Yes," she began. "Yes, I guess so. There are people who can talk and eat and dance far away from a great war—they run their lives so the war won't touch them. They can't forget it because it never came into their minds for them to forget. And it isn't real enough to them for them to be afraid of it. They talk as though they know about the war and the battle fronts and they know where the storm is blowing, lashing, whining, where struggle and death is a clock and the clock goes on night and day and of course they know about it. Those faces, those dancers protecting themselves from the war—a chill kept creeping over me and I was saying to myself, 'Oh, God, this isn't new, it goes with every war.' It's old, so old you wonder how old it can be and whether it goes back to Cain and Abel. These people with satisfied faces taking the war as a thing far away somewhere, never real to them till it shatters their own doorways and blows them into the street with ashes in their hair and mouths, blood streaking their white faces and oozing bellies."

His hand tightened on hers. For a moment it shot pain to her knuckle joints. He knew she was near tears. They rode in silence, each aware of only dry tears, his hand saying, as she believed, "You haven't told the half of it, it can't be told." Then her voice sharply, gutturally, "Nice people, their names get in the papers as nice people. They keep the war far away. They know the war is not nice. The nearer you get to the real thing it stinks with the stink of death and the boys in the dark crying, Medic! Medic! They don't want to smell it or hear it and they guard their minds and imaginations against it. They have worked out a technique of mentally holding their noses and stopping their ears so the war will always be far away."

His hand in hers again brought pain to the knuckles. After another silence she mumbled, "I won't go on, Pete. You get the drift. I had to get that load off my mind."

They rode to the apartment building where Ann was staying. They could see through the revolving door the night elevator man with his eyes on them. Pete pressed her hands in his, leaned close to her face. "Good night, Ann, it was worth the time." He made no move to kiss her, though she believed he at least half wanted to. And she came near reaching her lips toward him.

She held back believing he would rather she didn't. She went through the revolving door with a "Sweet good night and sweet dreams, Pete." She stood inside and watched him, saw him turn and look toward her in his trench coat, his cap visor gleaming over the big blue goggles. She saw him wave to her, she waved back, saw him enter the taxi. As it pulled away he threw her a kiss. She threw him one and blew with her lips out on the opened palm of her right hand toward him.

The elevator man in a dark-blue uniform coat, double-breasted with two rows of brass buttons down the front, spoke easy, not with curiosity, but as one more casual routine matter of the day, as he pulled a lever and the car started, "He was in the war?"

They reached the sixth floor. She was getting out when she answered, casual and routine as he had been, "Yes, he was in the war."

Ann was more than an hour going to sleep. He had wanted the kind of an evening they had had. It ran to his wish. Between white sheets in the smooth sky-blue pajamas of tissue gingham, she reveled at moments in the sheer luxury of a roof and walls about her, a dry corner to sleep in. After the first of this luxuriating, and no sleep coming, she turned on a light, put a second pillow back of her head, reached for newspaper clippings on a table and read about days and nights in cold rain and soggy mud in Italy.

A little man from the State of Indiana, from Hoosierdom, had written these pieces. She had met him, talked with him, seen him several days straight as he shared marching, food, front-line fire. At first he had for her a sharp foxlike face and later nothing foxy at all. His eyes went through and under the tough crusted outside of the G.I. and he could put it into words. Wizened, battered and squeezed by life, he understood others hard-pressed and even misshapen by life. His newspaper pieces, read by millions, brought him nicknames, "The G.I.'s Boswell," "Brother Francis." Ann had met his varied readers, some telling her they felt shame and guilt or inadequacy and help-lessness over comforts at home, good food, sleeping dry and warm, company of kinfolk and friends, a telephone at your elbow to call up friends for a date or a party. Others she knew of his readers only hugged their comforts closer.

She read slowly four of his pieces. She looked at her sky-blue right sleeve. She ran her hand along the soft clean tissue gingham. She wagged her chin back and forth along an immaculate white sheet and its clean smell. And she felt a touch of shame over the perfection of her creature comfort now alongside of K rations eaten in foxholes by men getting "trench feet" with water above their ankles, above their knees, trying to read the enemy by flame flashes cutting across the dark night. The little Hoosier man, it came back how he looked to her, his friendly drawl, his furrowed forehead and his crinkly eyes when he smiled, what a "reg'lar feller" he was, how the boys told him what they couldn't tell their officers. The question came, how would he have written about her and Pete had he seen them in the actions that sent them home? That question floated in her mind.

At Bryn Mawr, Ann and her chum and roommate Maria Enders Windom, Pete's sister, had written for the college paper, played with short-story writing and poems. With two years in the Army as a nurse she had forgotten about writing, many weeks too rushed in duties for letter-writing. Now her mind played with an unwritten dispatch about herself which might have run:

London—Ann Flaherty, 24, daughter of a Chicago paving con-tractor, a Bryn Mawr graduate, will be on a plane for the United States this week on indefinite leave from her duties as a nurse. "It will be sort of homelike on the plane," she said. "I served as a nurse on six flights ferrying wounded to England and carrying medical supplies on return flights. Now I am under orders to keep to my berth and rest and get healed." She was in a plane loaded with hospital supplies that crashed. They lifted her out of a burning plane and after giving her first aid put her on another plane. "I didn't know what happened," she said, "and the first split second when I came to I thought I was still on the plane that crashed. Then several bright and curious pains began reminding me something had happened and I didn't know what it was till they told me."

Her own little story ran smoother as reading than that of Captain Peter Enders, thought Ann. His would be not so good for home-front morale. It might run in part like this, as Ann spoke it in low tones in a voice just above a whisper:

"Captain Peter Enders of the —th Army, —th Regiment, in an operation in Sicily took a hand with men of his company in several vivid exploits. Interviewed in an English hospital he told of his Lieutenant Jacob Zinski leading a platoon up a mountain slope in search for land mines and booby traps. Two explosions lighted the night darkness, followed by enemy fire from machine-gun nests.

"Half the platoon came crawling back on their hands and knees. One reported to Captain Enders, 'Jake is out there!' and the two crept out, zigzagged on their bellies, 'chancing we might help him,' said the Captain. They crawled over slippery bodies of men still warm and the life breath gone. They came to three men in a pile, two of them fallen across Jake's body.

"They bent and crouched low carrying back to their lines Jake's body, a torso with one arm and a head still attached to it.

" 'I went through Jake's pockets,' said Captain Enders, 'for anything the folks back home might like. A pipe, tobacco pouch, pictures of his mother and sister, a black garter with pink rosettes, invasion money, sulfa pills and morphine tablets he hadn't time to use, an address book, two folded maps, his pocketknife, a pocket Testament, four loaded dice, and a letter from his sister Pola Zinski Folsom, the dancer who is winning a name for her wonderful contortion fantasies.

" 'He had no regular sweetheart, but he was sweet on his sister. She wrote him that sometime the war would be over and they would all be together again. She prayed God every night to keep him safe. He would come home and finish his law course and see much of her and mother. He would win medals, wrote the sister, and must save one for her.

" 'We dug a deep hole and a burying detail led a file of men to it, with Jake's torso, right arm and head wrapped in an oilskin for a shroud. I spoke a few words, read verses from his Testament, put one more in a line of white crosses.

" 'The next day I passed a machine-gun post where a German sat as if in the act of firing, his head gone, the bloody neck stump sticking up, his feet and legs sound, his hands on the gun ready to fire, all of him there but his head. I hoped it was him that had blasted Jake Zinski.

" 'The same day, in a house that had served as enemy head-quarters, we saw an officer sit down in a chair and in two seconds every stitch of clothing blown off him and burns all over him with only a fair chance he would live.

" 'Two days later it was I opened the door of a village house, as I had opened the doors of four other houses that day to talk with people living there. In this house the people had gone away. We believed it some kind of a hideout. Two of us jammed our shoulders against the door and broke the lock. The blast that came killed the other man. He was between me and the main force of the explosion. The next I knew I was in the hospital with a face full of shell fragments. Beyond that I don't care to speak.' "

Ann turned off the light, spoke softly to herself. "Yes, beyond that you don't care to speak. You haven't told me a word of it and I still have the ring you gave me and I don't wear it because you say you'd rather I didn't. But you told your story to your sister, my old chum, and she told me."

The light on again, Ann ran over a bunch of cartoons. She had eaten K rations with the little fellow whose drawings of the "dogfaces" were famous. In the code of the dogface, honor and valor might be important but equally so was the question, "When do we eat—or do we?" Being told he had earned a Purple Heart the dogface answered, "Just gimme a coupla aspirin, I already got a Purple Heart." At a door stood a dogface knocking for entrance, as though asking, "May I come in?" the roof and walls of the house fallen away and only this door standing, a dogface on the other side of the door asking, "Who is it?" A world of its own, a world he never made, the dogface world of the overseas foot soldier, a world of which he could never tell the home folks so they would know what he was talking about. The young cartoonist, of rugged service in Africa and Sicily, she had heard him say, "Take sleep now, how the hell you going to tell them about how the dogface sleeps? You do most of your sleeping while you march. It's not a very healthy sleep; you might call it a sort of coma. No matter how much we try we can never give the folks at home any idea of what war really is. I guess you have to go through it to understand its horror. You can't understand it by reading magazines or newspapers or by looking at pictures or by going to newsreels. You have to smell it and feel it all around you."

Cartoons back on the table, she turned off the lights. "A fine lad, gives me a little lift where the heart is heavy."

She wove and shifted in the rich feel of the clean white sheets. A feathersoft outlandish pleasant snow closed around her face and body. She faded into sleep, a blur of slow words in her ears, "Jake was a great guy," and "Good night, Ann, it was worth the time."

She woke during the night clenching her hands, felt of her chin and nose to make sure she was awake. This because she saw a shimmering beautiful human body that seemed cut off with nothing above the navel

—and its head seemed to have come loose to sway and dangle above the right knee, its face with a large mouth and large dark-brown eyes infinitely mournful and alive. Ann at first believed she was asleep and it was a dream. Awake she knew she was remembering Pola Zinski and that Pola couldn't forget her brother Jake any more than Pete Enders could.

She would see Pete again—next week in Washington at Mimah Windom's party at Hopecrest. She hoped he would then say of the evening, "It was worth the time."

* * * * * * * * * *

Chapter 2

* * * * * * * * * *

Justice Windom's Sealed Envelope

AT Hopecrest, where the shadow and voice of the old Justice still lingered in hallways and rooms, the days went by with a strange quality of fury and quiet intermingled for Raymond, the grandson of Justice Orville Brand Windom, and his wife Maria Enders Windom, known to her familiars as Mimah. The wide-fronted, two-story stone house, the large wooded yard with its spread of old oaks and elms and its clump of Scotch pines, the rugged boulder tall as the old Justice himself and wider than it was high, which he had named Remembrance Rock—these led toward quiet. The overhead drone of transport planes and bomber formations, the solemn and implicative newspaper headlines, the broadcasts and announcements pouring from radio sets in relation to mankind's first truly global war—these made the brutal music of the fury of the world storm.

In this mingled quiet and fury Ray and Mimah had read aloud to each other from day to day the long manuscript of Justice Windom, written to them and for them, Books One, Two, Three—the earliest colonists three hundred years ago grappling with a vast naked untamed continent; Lexington, the Declaration of Independence, Valley Forge and the works and self-denials of great men with an utter and complete faith in the American Republic they were founding; the windings of doom, strife and prayer out of which came the amalgamated American Union of States fated to become a world power.

Before and after their daily readings, sometimes as an interruption, came the terrific bulletins, from the colossal and almost incredible Normandy beachheads through the fights and marches across France and the Low Countries into Germany itself, umbrellas of thousands of planes, airborne troops in co-ordination with pronged tank attacks and the ever advancing masses of infantry, this in the west of Europe while on the eastern front day by day and mile by mile the Red Army pressed the invaders of Russia back toward their Faderland. Ray and Mimah looked back toward the people of Bowbong's books and agreed that Miles Standish, Robert Winshore and Hornsby Meadows would all have been perfectly at home in any of the modern fighting, needing only to get acquainted with the new weapons and devices.

Mimah had seen Ray making slow gains mentally and physically from week to week. His spells of black silence still recurred, though less often now did he let go the abruptly cynical remarks, the clipped and cruel comments on life she heard from him at first. Once a week Mimah drove him for consultations at the psychiatric division of a Naval Hospital. The physicians there told her he was making slow but sure gains, that mental readjustment and certain physical rebuildings seemed "satisfactory." Mimah didn't know why she gagged a little at the word "satisfactory." She said to Ray once at breakfast, "You're grand, magnificent and delirious to me and now we'll go to the hospital today and I'll hear again you're plain humdrum satisfactory."

Toward the end of the reading of Book Two, Mimah, holding the manuscript, saw Ray walk around the room slowly and quietly three or four times, and pausing before her, "Whatever he's singing—and I'm not sure what it is—it's good for me. My blood answers to his. I'll get his drift better reading it a second time. I wish he could know he signals me a message, when you look at it, that I haven't been so damned useless after all. That's a help, Mimah. I wish he could know." Again after the reading of Book Three, Ray had said much the same.

At the bottom of the Box they found a sealed envelope with instructions they should open it after reading Book One, Two, Three. Breaking the envelope they read:

My dear children: You have now made with me the long journey of the time of America in the making. You have glimpsed at what America has cost. Each time was its own, with its own actions and secrets, its doubts of the future.

Live with these faces out of the past of America and you find lessons. America as a great world power must confront colossal and staggering problems. Reckoning on ever fresh visions, as in the past, she will come through, she cannot fail. If she forgets where she came from, if the people lose sight of what brought them along, if she listens to the deniers and mockers, then will begin the rot and dissolution.

The hard beginnings, the chaotic obstacles of days when the Republic seemed lost, these must be remembered. To lose them is to lose the Republic.

The day has come for you to know more about Remembrance

Rock. It is, as I often told you, a place to come and remember. I am not sure why I was sensitive about it and held back from telling you what has been placed under the Rock for remembrance sake.

First to go under the Rock was a handful of dust from Plymouth, Massachusetts. Alongside it was placed a Colonial silver snuffbox filled with earth from Valley Forge. Next came a little box of soil from Cemetery Ridge at Gettysburg where my father fought, and side by side with that a handful of dust from the Argonne in France near where my son fell in a La Fayette Escadrille plane.

Now I would request of you that you add to these little sacred deposits some of the rainbow-tinted sand that Ray sent to Mimah from a South Pacific island, adding to it a little black volcanic ash from another island taken at high cost. Perhaps to this last you could add a handful of earth from ground in Italy or France where Mimah's brother Pete shared with his comrades in struggle or sacrifice. I would suggest that this humble and private ceremonial, as between ourselves, be performed on some day shortly after the end of the war. You may use as you please a tiny object, a sacred relic, which I have enclosed in a flat metal-and-leather case at the bottom of the Box which I request you do not open till the day of the ceremonial.

And now please know this is not my final word to you. One further memorandum for you I have given to an old and valued friend. What he brings you at the war's end is my last testament and I pray God keep you.

Ray looking into Mimah's eyes saw them shade from a dark-blue to a flicker of storm-green. Her pale oval face held shifting lights, her wide thin lips parted ever so slightly over her white even teeth. She saw him run a hand through his wavy black hair and the line of his mouth vivid and somber at saying, "What he's telling us, that's the least we could do for old Bowbong."

"And ourselves—pretty the way he put that in, between ourselves."

"Ourselves including the pipsqueak Joe Stilwell Windom and Captain Peter Enders."

Then Ray's face changed. In the mouth above his jutting chin the underlip went out a little, corners pulled down just enough for Mimah to notice. He might be nearing one of his prolonged black silences. He rose, not a word to her, walked out of the room. From a window later she saw him walking around Remembrance Rock, bareheaded, then standing before it a long while, hands in his two back trouser pockets, his elbows triangled back. Not long after, he lay flat on the grass, face down, a late September sunlight falling through yellow afternoon haze.

She smiled to herself, shook her head and smiled. Ray was gaining on himself. He was loosening his thongs. Bowbong had reached into him. So had Remembrance Rock and its dreamdust.

* * * * * * * * * *

Chapter 3

* * * * * * * * * *

Wherein the Lonely Speak

PETE had come to Hopecrest for the week end. He sat in the library with Ray and Mimah in the early afternoon listening to a news broadcast. They began commenting to each other on the news. Next they heard a voice introducing the Librarian of Congress, an artilleryman in the First World War, reading a poem. They liked the color in his voice and a curious monotone quality as he read his lines that had been published in many newspapers with no name signed to them as though propriety lay in printing them anonymously. He read:

The young dead soldiers do not speak.
Nevertheless, they are heard in the still houses: who has not heard them?
They have a silence that speaks for them at night and when the clock counts.
They say: We were young. We have died. Remember us.
They say: We have done what we could but until it is finished it is not done.
They say: We have given our lives but until it is finished no one can know
    what our lives gave.
They say: Our deaths are not ours; they are yours; they will mean what you
    make them.
They say: Whether our lives and our deaths were for peace and a new
    hope or for nothing we cannot say; it is you who must say this.
They say: We leave you our deaths. Give them their meaning. Give them
    an end to the war and a true peace. Give them victory that ends the
    war and a peace afterwards. Give them their meaning.
We were young, they say. We have died. Remember us.

There could have been a pause, perhaps a minute or two of silence. There could have been a stately solemn music. There could have been, with no loss to those listening, a second reading of the awesome and implicative lines. Instead there came instantly after the final line a blaring, excessively cheerful voice, perfectly self-assured, insistent and commanding: "Are you having trouble with your hair? Try Dabbum. Is your hair turning gray? Get Dabbum. Is your hair falling out? Get Dabbum, get Dabbum now. GDN—Gee Dee En—what does GDN mean? Get Dabbum Now. Treat your scalp to a rich fine smooth dose of Dabbum and watch your hair come back to its natural color.

1003

GDN—Get Dabbum now and see your hair grown again. GDN—get Dabbum now."

Pete in his chair at a tall window with sunlight pouring in had been sloped back in lazy comfort. He pursed his lips and spoke, "The sonofabitch!"

"You ain't polite, Pete," laughed Ray. "But I guess I'm with you."

"I vote in the affirmative too," laughed Mimah.

"Whoever was responsible for that program trick," said Pete, "I'd like to see him touch his foot on one of the traps we saw the Germans using in Sicily. It's a long hollow iron tube buried in the ground with the tip exposed. Touch your foot to that tip and the contact sends a bullet through the tube straight up. Usually it shoots you through the foot, but on account of what it did to more than one of them, the G.I.'s named it the 'castrater.' "

"They should have read the poem a second time instead of that vile commercial," said Mimah. "The only line I can remember of the poem now is: 'They say: We were young. We have died. Remember us.' "

"And I remember only one line," said Pete. "It goes: 'They say: Our deaths are not ours; they are yours; they will mean what you make them.' "

Pete had an afterthought. "Think of it, Ray. All we're sure we came back with out of the war is our good hair. And this brass monkey comes into the house and tells us to worry about our hair."

"How did that poem begin?" asked Mimah. " 'The young dead soldiers do not speak,' that was the first line. So I suppose a million people will be saying: The young dead soldiers do not speak—but they are heard in the silent houses—and they say: "Get Dabbum, get Dabbum now."

"Yeah," said Pete. "They died for Dabbum. They died to make men free to sell and buy Dabbum."

Silence for a time while a tall old clock in a rosewood case ticked off a minute or two. Then Pete, "What was the line you remembered, Mimah? Say it."

" 'They say: We were young. We have died. Remember us.' "

"And my line goes: 'They say: Our deaths are not ours; they are yours; they will mean what you make them.' " He paused. The rosewood clock ticked on. Pete ran his hand above the blue goggles, pushed back his thickly grown brown hair, "I'll send for the whole poem. We'll read it and sit quiet and then read it again."

"Right," said Ray. "The poem runs like some of the people talk in Bowbong's books."

"The hair-oil seller and his silly blasphemy," said Mimah, "might have reminded Bowbong of a court clerk he heard in Cincinnati giving an oath in connection with a court paper: 'Hold up your right hand— you do solemnly swear that the contents of this, your affidavit, are true —for which, hand me twenty-five cents—so help you Almighty God.' "

Pete slowly rose out of his chair. He walked with a fine easy deliberation to a window that looked out toward Remembrance Rock. Mimah had read to him Bowbong's memorandum about the memorial dust under the boulder. Pete at the window stood motionless, composed, his hands folded in front of him. Mimah's love of her brother was made of both adoration and reverence and she saw him now as a still image that could be struck into bronze. Years there had been when her love for him included considerable intimate understanding. Now she acknowledged that since his return from the war he was quite beyond her fathoming. She could see certain dark new strengths and she was afraid they might be too stark and ruthless. She was sure he had no slightest vestige of pity for himself of any kind and that anyone by voice or look trying to give him a faint gleam of pity was in turn pitied by him and out of his strengths he was silent and refused to correct or enlighten them. To him there were assumptions beyond his enlightening, ignorance past his correcting. She had seen his composure and peculiar poise, usually having a definite element of warmth rather than cold, act as a tonic and serving health to the mind and will of Ray, who once said, "There are times Pete is good for me like Bowbong was."

As her eyes ranged him there at the window she flashed to old days when he could kick, pass, or run with a pigskin ball down a field and stadium crowds had yelled themselves wild and his helmeted face with a handsome grin had been spread two columns wide in newspapers the country over. That seemed to her now hundreds of years ago. Then he was going to be a lawyer. This morning he told her he would wait a year or two before deciding whether he was for a law career. "A good lawyer certainly must first be a good man." And not until this morning, and not at all at her suggestion and as though the day had come when it could be a proper secret as between an affectionate brother and sister, he had shown her his face before his adjustment of the mask and the goggles. He had put her fingers to his chin where a shell fragment had torn flesh and bone loose, a new chin of metal and plastics replacing the old one. He would be returning to the Valley Forge surgeons for months to come in the slow rebuilding of the lower part of the nose and small sections of cartilage in the upper part.

The sister smiled and laughed when her brother did and she was certain he didn't guess that she went straight to her room and stood at a window and looked toward Remembrance Rock and burst into tears, shook with sobs, then clenched her hands, straightened herself, dried her tears, bowed smiling before two photographs of Orville Brand Windom as a youth and an elder and still smiling, said to herself aloud, "What kind of a fool am I to be weeping? Why should the sister of that kind of a man be crying?" Then she went down to breakfast and neither Pete nor Ray had ever seen her at once so beautifully gay and solemn.

Later alone that morning with Pete she had said to him delicately, tentatively, "Ann phoned me today. She'll be out late this afternoon."

"Yes?" drawled Pete.

"When I think about you and her I can't help a feeling she's got what you need."

And Mimah was amazed at what shook loose from him in a low-toned outburst roused by her few innocent words. "Yes, a dogface like me ought to be living next to her to offer his mouth to her sweet lips. Yes, I should make her life a mess. She's young, years and years ahead of her. She can do better than hook up with me for life. She's got everything. I'm plain nothing wrapped carefully in nothing and the loose ends tucked in. She's keen with a wild streak in her I love down to my toes. I can't do it. She'll get a man that's all there, his face in one piece. Tell her I said so. Maybe you can tell it soft. I can't. Tell it right to her. Tell her I know what I'm doing and she'll thank me all her born days for not putting a hell of a load on her. Suppose we tried it and it was no go. I'd say then it was worse than any misery that ever hit me. I mean a low misery I'd never get over. I'm not her dish. She can do better. I'd rather she hate me for all time than I drag her into a mess. Tell it right to her. Make it easy for her. Let her know it's for the best. She's a grand kid, lovely whether she talks or dances or says nothing and only sweeps me with her eyes. Tell her I said that. And tell her I'm not her dish. I wish I was. She's got everything. Tell her and go soft and easy as you can."

Mimah could read little or nothing of what moved Pete now as he stood at the window, timeless, meditative, motionless. Standing like that in an orchard or an oat field she could see wrens or chickadees lighting on his shoulders or nesting in his thick brown hair. His hands had gone to her two shoulders when she told him of Bowbong's revelation of dust and earth brought from afar and lodged with tender fingers under Remembrance Rock. He could now be in reverie about such a dreamdust so momentously sacred to Bowbong that the old man shied from telling about it while alive. It might even be that Pete could see it proper for Remembrance Rock to hold under it a little of the soil from Sicily where he had found a torso, head and arm of Jake Zinski. Or again he could be studying about the dreaminess of the film of sunlight falling on oak, elm, and pine clump, on the green grass, the scarlet salvia, the elephant ears with spots of saffron, the great outdoor sweep of the bowl of blue sky. Out of such window frames of life, he had told her, he could sometimes hear whispers telling him it was mostly illusion, make-believe, with struggle and cruelty lurking in every part and piece of it, yet until he could penetrate to the last of the series of illusions that lay beyond each first illusion it was his business to enjoy quietly any and all show-pieces of color and form put on by natural forces.

"I could write a book about it," he told his sister. She had answered, "I would understand it better, and you too. Write the book."

"I would like to be," Pete had tossed out for what it was worth, "a tall thick bottle or a big jug so I might know for sure how they make that glug-glug glug-glug when you pour from them."

Mimah let it pass. These came from him every so often and she let them pass. It wasn't quite her line.

Ann came into the room with Ray. She and Mimah put their arms around each other. Mimah laughed a merry greeting. Ann murmured something in low contralto, a little somber, the words not clear. She wore a light gray-blue wool suit, the jacket widely parted showing a white sharkskin blouse, its row of white buttons running high to the top one at her throat, the curves of her full bosom and strong shoulders set off with grace. On her head over the mass of glossy black hair perched a daring and whimsical yellow hat shaped not unlike a crushed bird's nest.

Pete stood looking out the window. Ray and Mimah had fussed around in small talk for several minutes before Pete turned and walked with a slow ease to Ann, took her hand and said, "Good to see you, Ann." She held his hand, "Lovely to be with you, Pete," peering at the blue goggles, trying to fathom what could be lurking in the eyes behind those goggles, for a moment desperately wishing he had a face of shaded expressions she might try to read.

They took chairs and listened to a broadcast from London. Pete had met the news commentator, a North Dakota- and Minnesota-raised boy, of Norwegian parents, a man troubled about humanity and the present global war and the possible next global war. Ever probing, questioning, unblinking, he was relentless as Henrik Ibsen or Roger Williams. Across the Atlantic now came his voice:

The soldier knows the real story of the war; he feels it sharply, but he couldn't tell it to you himself. This war has a thousand faces and a hundred planets. It has a fantastic variety of devilish means for testing a boy's brain, for stretching his nerves, for making him ashamed or making him proud, for exposing his heart or for burying his heart. The war treats no two exactly alike; and so even two soldiers from the same front sometimes don't understand each what the other is talking about.

The soldier's handbook gives little guidance on such matters as how to learn the patience of a saint, how to quench bitterness when his officers make a costly mistake, or how to master the homesickness that comes at sunset.

Who is to relate these things, which make up the real but secret story of the war? Who is to reconstruct, in scenes and acts, the drama of that American on the desolate airfield in the Gulf of Aden? The one who sat three hours, unmindful of the crashing heat, his eyes fixed upon a stone. He had been there eighteen months, and he didn't talk to his comrades any more.

What about the soldier with the child's face who stumbled from the exploding field near Anzio with not a mark on his body but with his eyes too big, his hands senselessly twisting a towel, and his tongue darting in and out between his teeth?

What was it that expanded in the soul of a young man I first knew when he was a press-agent lieutenant three years ago? Then, he was rather silly and talked too much, and his men smiled behind his back. I met him next in a French forest. He had learned control and dignity. He was a major commanding a fighting battalion, and the general was quiet when he spoke.

There was a regimental colonel at Anzio who received notice one night that he could leave next day for Des Moines, where his business was prosperous and his family large. His division had been decimated, but this man's life was now assured. Why, at dawn, at his regular hour, did he risk the mortar shells and crawl on hands and knees from foxhole to foxhole, not missing one, just to speak a confident word to his men?

Who could really explain about that young corporal with the radio post deep in the Burma jungle? The one who rose suddenly from his bunk in the night and walked straight into the woods, walking westward.

This war must be seen to be believed, but it must be lived to be understood. We can tell you only of events, of what men do. We cannot really tell you how or why they do it. We can see, and tell you, that this war is brutalizing some among your sons and yet ennobling others. We can tell you very little more.

War happens inside a man. It happens to one man alone. It can never be communicated. That is the tragedy—and perhaps the blessing.

There was more and the broadcast ended. The words had sunk deep. There was silence, faces seeking faces.

A nursemaid came in holding little Joe Stilwell. "I'm going to push him around in the fresh air a little." Ray stepped over, took the baby from her arms, tossed him high in the air and caught him, chucked him under the chin, slapped him on the legs and buttocks, and handed him back. As the maid was in the doorway Mimah called, "Don't go more than three or four blocks away with him."

Ray took a chair. No one had a word. The broadcast still lingered in the air of the room as an exceedingly fine blue mist.

Ann took off her whimsical yellow bird-nest hat and held it in her lap. She rose, laid it on another chair, and walked to the window where Pete had stood when she came in. Ann too could stand, as Mimah saw her, an image to be struck into bronze. Ann too seemed to be searching the oaks and elms, the green grass and scarlet salvia, the elephant ears with spots of saffron, the great outdoor sweep of the bowl of blue sky and definitely the rugged form of Remembrance Rock. Absently Ann put her two hands above her ears, patted the folds of black hair, and returned her hands folded in front of her.

Mimah was asking Ray, "What is on? Was there something we were going to get about this time?" Ray tuned in and they caught lines being read:

Freedom is a habit
and a coat worn
some born to wear it
some never to know it.
Freedom is cheap
or again as a garment
is so costly
men pay their lives
rather than not have it.
Freedom is baffling:
men having it often
know not they have it
till it is gone and
they no longer have it.
What does this mean?
Is it a riddle?
Yes it is first of all
in the primers of riddles.

Then came the reading of lines, already widely reprinted, from a New York City judge distinguished for his integrity, style and wisdom. A voice gave the lines:

Liberty lies in the hearts of men and women; when it dies there, no constitution, no law, no court can save it; no constitution, no law, no court can even do much to help it. . . . The spirit of liberty is the spirit that is not too sure that it is right; the spirit of liberty is the spirit which seeks to understand the minds of other men and women; the spirit of liberty is the spirit which weighs their interests alongside its own without bias; the spirit of liberty remembers that not even a sparrow falls to earth unheeded; the spirit of liberty is the spirit of Him who, near two thousand years ago, taught mankind that lesson it has never learned but has never quite forgotten: that there may be a kingdom where the least shall be heard and considered side by side with the greatest.

The reading had dignity. The voice came shy with a dim querying touch as though one could be decently shy and hesitant around the word "liberty" and its meaning.

Ann at last moved slowly out of her foot tracks, her face serene as she walked with an easy slouch toward Pete and pulled a chair alongside his. Having seated herself she glanced sidewise toward him. Their eyes met full in a long look. He half-stooped forward, scrunched his shoulders, bent his head and gave her a long upward gaze. She turned her head away as though she didn't care to meet this twist of his or perhaps as though preferring to act as if he were not there. Then she couldn't help herself. She gave her eyes to him. She gave him beseeching black eyes. He began speaking low-voiced, slow. "Did you hear what that fellow was saying from London? Did I get him right, did you?"

"We heard him and you heard him," said Ann lightly with a sober face.

"What was he saying? Did I get him right?"

"He was saying you know what you went through, but we don't."

And Ann knew Pete hadn't been drinking. "No, he said it different and he said it better. You didn't listen. Tell me more he said." There was almost a touch of boozy and overconfident impudence in his tone.

Ann covered her face with her hands. "Let me think."

"You don't have to think. I'll tell you."

Ray looked with curiosity at Pete, Mimah with anxiety. They watched the very deliberate Pete put a faraway gaze toward the window where he and later Ann had stood in contemplation. He gave the impression that what he was to say had its origins beyond this room and far out yonder from the window. He pursed his lips and the words dropped slow with an exceptional clarity for him. " 'War happens inside a man. It happens to one man alone.' " He turned toward Ann, again with scrunched shoulders, the head bent and looking upward into her face. " 'It can never be communicated.' " He waited and gave her that again. " 'It can never be communicated.' "

After a long searching look into Ann's face Pete straightened, turned the line of his goggles toward the window and the far outside world again and very slowly, " 'That is the tragedy—and perhaps the blessing.' " He said it so, just so: *That is the tragedy—and perhaps the blessing.*"

Pete rose casually from his chair, stood before Ann, took her head between his two hands, bent toward her, his palms at her temples, his fingers moving in her hair, saying with tension and in a half-whisper, " 'War happens inside a man. It happens to him alone. It can never be communicated.' "

She was white-faced, with swift blinking eyes. He held her so a moment. Then he let go and sauntered to the door and stood in the doorway perhaps a half-minute while his goggles moved as though his eyes behind them swept the room. Then he stepped away into the hall.

The moment his shoulders faded at the doorway Ann turned to Mimah in a sharp moan, "Did he know me? Do you think he knows me?"

They turned to hear him as he stood in the doorway and there was pain in his cry, "Does he know you? Of course he knows you. He knows you're Ann Flaherty and you've got the face God gave you. He knows Ann Flaherty one time was going to marry him. And he knows and she knows it's off, it's all off, it's gone and clean-gone."

Then days went by and weeks moved into months and the great clock of the war ticked off deaths and dooms by the millions and it was far into the next year before Pete and Ann met again.

★ ★ ★ ★ ★ ★ ★ ★ ★ ★

Chapter 4

★ ★ ★ ★ ★ ★ ★ ★ ★ ★

Floodlights on the Capitol Dome

THE war swept on. Munition dumps ran mile on mile in England, shells and bombs in stacks, pyramids, little mountain ridges. Day by day the propellers whirred and the engines pounded high over the Channel. On medieval Cologne, on modern Munich, on Nuremberg of fame and ill-fame, on the smokestacks of Essen synonymous with the sinister and crafty name of Krupp, fell the cylinders of doom, fell the ash cans of flame. Over the proud capital city of Frederick the Great, the Hohenzollerns and Bismarck, Hindenburg and the Swastika leader Adolf Hitler, over proud Berlin—over the famous world port and once Free City of Hamburg—over the clean well-ordered model municipality of Düsseldorf—the blockbusters dropped and laid swaths of rubble, shambles, roofs fallen in and walls tumbled over the roofs, empty windows framing no living gazers, women and children caught in twisted steel with no service of Extreme Unction. With no letdown the Battle of the Ball Bearings went on, bombers wrecking the plants that made motor bearings, bringing tens of thousands of tanks, planes, trucks and Volkswagen to a standstill before they ever started, for the want of ball bearings. Great power dams sank and fragments floated downriver after bomb blasts, cities, shops and factories going dark. The arrogant and once giant Luftwaffe began shrinking into a timid dwarf needing gas and reinforcements not in sight. The Battle of the Bulge had flared as a final fool gamble of a leadership holding ready its tiny flasks of suicide poison. The Red Army moved on across more than a thousand miles of scorched earth, of destroyed cities and burned villages where fifteen million Russian soldiers and civilians had died—the Red Army marched over the hundreds of miles of ruins and ashes on Russian soil, across Poland, into Czechoslovakia and into East Prussia, and toward Berlin, the Wilhelmstrasse, Potsdam and the old palace grounds of the imperial Hohenzollerns.

On the western front the Eighth Air Force tore the Luftwaffe from the skies, pounded the batteries, machine-gun nests and enemy troop positions in the route of advancing tanks, armored divisions and infantry. The Eighth Air Force, with a hundred-and-twenty-per-cent replacements, its lowest flying formation angle nicknamed the Coffin Corner, vanishing in their crashed planes, tangled in wreckage, burned alive, toppled out of the skies before there was time to reach for a parachute, meeting ack-ack deaths with no time for a split-second prayer —the Eighth Air Force giving back the blood and terror of the Blitz to those who believed they originated lightning war—the Eighth Air Force as it was in the beginning and at the end with its hundred-and-twenty-per-cent replacements, calls for extended narrative and a poem of epic style and length.

The ring of feet and wheels, of steel and flame, day by day pressed deeper into the center of Germany. In the shadows of their commodious and luxurious underground shelters and tunnels dug deep under the heart of Berlin, two little men with their women companions clutched the tiny glass vial and the dependable automatic revolver, and waited for their hour. The shrunken one with a club foot had been Minister of Propaganda and Information of the Third Reich. The other one, with a little mustache under his nose, had been Chancellor of the Third Reich for some twelve years. They had planned and expected to conquer first Europe, then the world, a Greater Germany to rule the world for a thousand years. Yet they had lasted only twelve years. Their calculations were short by nine hundred and eighty-eight years as the great and famous city of Berlin under Red Army fire cried, choked, howled in hoarse fear, burned, crumbled and fell to pieces.

The two little men, the once fearsome and powerful spokesmen of the Greater Germany, they with their women companions made ready with poison and bullet for death and dissolution. Their word to their mighty armies entering Poland and later crossing over into Russia had been "Speed and brutality." Now they bade farewell to the roaring outside world above their tunnels and deeply dug shelters. They could have gone up into daylight and led a resistance and died fighting, as they had taught so many millions of German youth to die. They spoke their farewells to the Greater Germany, it seemed, as though they were sick unto death of the very speed and brutality they had spent their lives teaching the German youth. Did the stench of the millons of deaths they had ordered reach them at all with any faint putrid odor? Who could name the immense variety of fears that told them it was time for them to die? Had they reasoned with calm minds that it was better to die underground from self-taken poison and a self-given bullet than to be strangled with a broken neck in a noosed rope in daylight with the sun pouring down? They left no memoranda, no word. They had for years spoken to a world-wide audience that hung on their words and weighed every sentence. Now they seemed to be hunted and shrunken animals, cornered rats. They had laid their plans and made a timetable with details on how their civilization, the New Order, should spread over the earth. Now they seemed to have had no time, no five or six spare moments, in which to write a final memorandum and a few regrets. They had planned and wrought the deaths of somewhere between twenty to fifty million people. They were busy little men, so busy they couldn't see their own finish till it was on them. One final touch became them, fitted their roles. They ordered their bodies to be gasoline-soaked and burned beyond identification. The evidence was meager as to what they did, hunted and trapped underground, while in the streets over them raged the reversed speed and brutality that had overtaken them.

From the top floor of Hopecrest they could see on the night of May 8, 1945, the figure of a sculptured woman, Armed Freedom, high over the Capitol dome. A matron of wide shoulders and rich bosom, silver-white, impressive and challenging, she stood swathed in the floodlights playing on her. For more than three years she had of nights stood up there in the dark, in the blackout. Now had come V-E Day, Victory in Europe.

Over the night air of the streets came punctuations, vocal fireworks, men howling their glee, sober ones shouting as wildly as the drunk. Others there were who walked in quiet or sat speechless, holding the tongue and the heart still. Who for an hour or two could be still enough at news of the dying down of the awful storm?

Ray and Mimah left the house about dusk. She had lately seen Ray troubled, even tormented, about returning to his flight command in the South Pacific. He seemed to have guilt over not being with fellows whose faces and names were familiar to him; they might have mistaken ideas about him away so long on his leave. He had steadily gained in weight, though not back to old form. He more often overcame his dark moods, which now lasted hours rather than days. Mimah was sure however that he had not built his reserves to carry him through the sort of actions that had worn and broken him. She had followed his anxiety about the war in the Pacific going on another year, perhaps two years or more, and he didn't want a record of staying at home and making his recovery last that long. She had even heard him speak a wish he could have been wounded and mutilated so his disability would be plain to the naked eye and no mistake about it, with none of the queer, intangible and rather unfathomable elements involved in shock, shattered nerves and a mind at times foggy with what was termed "maladjustment."

They were walking a few blocks for dinner and an evening at the house of an old family friend, for years a crony of Ray's grandfather, the widower Nils Rolstadt. On the front porch of his house they saw Rolstadt watching, nodding his head to the singing streaks of light on the Capitol dome. Turning in from the street sidewalk they saw him half-tumble down the front steps, meeting them halfway to take both of Ray's hands in his.

"So this is our little boy, who went away to shoot planes out of the sky in the Pacific, to win medals he leaves at home—I don't see one of them on you, Ray." Rolstadt put a hand with the palm down alongside his right hip. "You came this high when I first saw you." Now Rolstadt smiled with raised eyebrows. "Later you were captain of a winning basketball team and I think you strutted a little. Now you have the finest medals and ribbons there are and you don't wear them. Just like your Grandfather Bowbong you don't wear them. Like Bowbong shy you are."

Ray felt easy before this man, short, stocky, in a loose-hung, rumpled gray suit of clothes, a pink face, blue eyes, a slightly arched nose, light-brown hair, a Danish Jew of international reputation in the field of physics. For two or three minutes they watched together in silence the freshly arrived marvel in the night sky, the shimmering silver-white crosslights half-dancing in exultation around the sculptured and full-bosomed matron Armed Freedom.

They heard a taxi at the curb, saw a figure along the walk. In an easy slouch up the porch steps he came. Mimah kissed him lightly on the mouth. "Mr. Rolstadt, this is my brother Captain Peter Enders." Gravely the blue-eyed physicist tried to peer through the dark goggles. He shook hands with Pete, his lower lip twitched and flattened, then suddenly Rolstadt brought a sunny smile to his entire face. "It is an honor to know you, Captain Enders."

"The sword she carries, and is so proud of, is out of date," said Rolstadt, waving a hand toward the floodlighted Armed Freedom. "But it will do as a symbol. You couldn't expect her to hold a tank in one hand and a plane in the other and a truckload of demolition and incendiary bombs on her head with maybe a machine-gun and a Browning automatic slung over her shoulders." Rolstadt chuckled. "Let her have the sword. Those who made the sword meant it for killing but I doubt whether a dozen soldiers in this war died with a sword run through them. The modern soldier wears a sword for comic effect."

Pete's slow smile came. "In a war now nobody knows who kills who nor how many. A family sits down to supper and before the supper is over there is no family and no house to eat in if there was. And the bombardier streaking home don't know whether he got a hit or a miss."

"We'll go in and eat," said Rolstadt. "We're safe for a while now."

In the house they met Rolstadt's son Hilmer, less thickset than his father, lighter-haired, his face white rather than pink, the skin downy and boyish. He looked ten years younger than his age of thirty-six, had the same blue eyes as his father, his hair a lighter brown, his lips more full. Ray tried to guess why Hilmer held his mouth open a good part of the time. Then Ray decided he would let Hilmer do what

Hilmer wanted to with Hilmer's mouth. Hilmer's wife, Albertina, cut in too often when others were talking, Ray and Mimah noticed. She was taller than her husband, her face moonlike, large darting eyes, a wide mouth and thick lips heavily rouged, black hair slicked down. She was excessively agreeable and seemed to have a constant fear that others might not know she had a cultivated mind. Her husband and his father had adapted themselves to her and took in their stride her interruptions with pointless questions, her abrupt needless additions to what someone else had said. She took pains to give the impression she too was at home in the higher realms of abstract ideas. Her husband and her father-in-law had become accustomed to this habit of hers. They stopped talking when she began, took up again when she quit, and went smoothly on as though nothing had happened.

At dinner Mimah at once and directly led the talk into what she wanted Ray to hear from Nils Rolstadt, as that scientist had given it to her over the telephone. "I can tell you with certainty," said Nils Rolstadt, "that the war with Japan will be over in less than four months, probably three. I cannot tell you how and why I know this to be so, but I can say to you that the prediction is absolutely safe that the war in the Pacific will end before the middle of next September."

Mimah was pleased that in later talk to Ray, Rolstadt spoke as an uncle, spoke as though Ray's grandfather might be present and listening. "You have not made the recovery that you and the men of your command are entitled to," he said. "I am sure your grandfather, if he were here, would join me in the advice that you ought to spend at least three or four months in regaining normal weight and rebuilding lost reserves of strength." He paused. He went on tenderly, lower-voiced, "Bowbong would join me in that." Mimah saw this last was a sort of clincher for Ray. What Ray heard came with a manner of authority as though from old Bowbong himself.

They lingered over the dinner, lingered and talked. Nils Rolstadt drank three cups of black coffee. Ray and Mimah on being pressed by Hilmer and his wife joined them in a second pouring of an old brandy from a bottle that Bowbong had brought to this house six years ago. The elder Rolstadt, after talking about the restlessness of the world of science in its search for new facts and fresh light, told of a well-known professor at a medical college speaking to his class at the end of the year and saying: "Young gentlemen, you are well aware, I believe, I have labored and done my best to give you the latest and most accurate medical facts. Now however the time has come I must warn you that before you have been long in practice one half of what I have told you may be proved untrue. *Unfortunately, gentlemen, I cannot tell you which half.*"

Ray laughed and turned to her with a grin of health, Mimah noticed. Rolstadt went on about people who enjoy belittling a professor, a theorist, abstracted, absent-minded, pathetic as one who bumped into a tree, backing away to apologize, "Excuse me, I thought you were a tree." Or the professor lured by his wife to his first symphony concert, "Very interesting, my dear, but I don't see that it demonstrates anything." And yet, Rolstadt asked with a smile of infinite patience, who is more practical than the professor? Queer they are, yes, queer and quiet and terrific. Take electricity, yes, "the juice," the current of electrodynamic force, the professors found it. Professor Ampère in France, Professor Volta in Italy, Professor Ohm in Germany, theoretical experimental Ben Franklin flying his kite in a thunderstorm in Philadelphia, and the professor at the Royal Institute in London who synthesized the findings of the others, Michael Faraday—theorists, absent-minded, speculative, ready to try anything once, daring men and terribly practical, these professors, they began the modern electrical world. They laid the way for mechanized warfare and transport, projectile velocity, guided missiles, chemical warfare, and it wouldn't come easy to tell what they are doing now in germ warfare and still other ways of making war.

"Man is a changer," Nils Rolstadt was saying as Ann Flaherty entered the room. They arose to say greetings. She put up her hands, "Please don't let me interrupt. I had the day with my father, who came on from Chicago and is at the Wardman, where we had dinner. I am sorry I had to miss dinner with you." She shook hands, took a chair Hilmer Rolstadt drew up to the table for her, put fingers and thumb to a glass of the old brandy Hilmer poured for her, and said, "Now you must go on, Mr. Rolstadt. It will be interesting. You were saying, 'Man is a changer.'"

Rolstadt went on. "God made man a changer. He can change himself into a fish and dive deep and stay under water unafraid of any sea animals. He can change himself into a bird and travel farther with heavier cargo, wider wings, fiercer claws and beaks than any bird. God must have wanted man to be a changer. Else God wouldn't have put that awful unrest in him."

Rolstadt was going farther on this, stopped himself, waited, then abruptly in a snarl, "What we do now, everything in our world of science, is a beginning that leads on into other beginnings. Science never comes to an end. Every ending proves to be a beginning. Each fearful weapon of war we have now can lead to one more fearful—if man lets war go on in the years to come as in the years past." They saw Nils Rolstadt deeply moved, a quaver of the tragic in his voice. He had been casual, warmly pleasant, even a trifle comic. Now they would not be surprised to see tears course down his cheeks. He rose from the table, saying in a subdued tone, "Suppose we go and have a look, just a peep. If Bowbong were here he would want it."

He led them to the large annex, a stone structure, his workroom and experimental laboratory. In the center of the big room hung a replica of the globe of the planet Earth. He pressed a button and it revolved slowly on its axis. He moved about and with a series of motions and releases sent pilotless planes flying at speeds, relative to the actual globe, of six to eight thousand miles an hour. He sent rockets and various guided missiles across oceans with streaks or flares to indicate bombs dropped on targets.

"One of my young assistants keeps working on it, I don't know why," he said. "We could spend all night here, as I have sometimes. I guess I wanted you to see it because of Bowbong." He turned to lead them from the room. "Some night we'll have a real session here."

* * * * * * * * * *

Chapter 5

* * * * * * * * * *

Bright Wonder and a Dark Pride

THE four walked to Hopecrest. They sensed vaguely, though without being particular about it, a change in the air of the city, in the lighting, in whatever went on behind house doors and windows. The end of the war in Europe meant for millions of people less of fear, more of hope, and this was more so in America, the only country at war whose cities stood clean and whole, with never a gash from air raids, its shores and countrysides witness of no invasion scar.

The four walked, Pete alongside of Ray, Mimah up ahead with Ann. Pete on this evening had spoken the most casual kind of greeting to Ann. He gave her the courtesy he might have accorded a stranger woman for whom he picked up a bundle she had dropped on the sidewalk. He walked with Ray, who said little more than, "V-E is your day. V-J will be my day when it comes." Nearing Hopecrest Ray said, "We'll put on some gutbucket blues, shake a couple of drinks, put on Sibelius' *First Symphony* and kiss Ann good night."

"You and Mimah can kiss Ann good night."

"You no like?"

"I like too much and can't figure it."

"Like that?"

"Check."

Up ahead Ann told her old college roommate that Albertina, Hilmer's wife, had asked her to the dinner at Rolstadt's. "She didn't say who were coming. I'm not sure I would have come if she had said Pete was coming."

"You're taking it hard, Ann."

"Is it looking any better? Does he say anything about me?"

"He's the same. Models himself on the Chesapeake Bay clam. Not a word from him, not since long months ago when he said he adores you so completely he can't think of living with you because you're so wonderful."

"I'll wait a little longer. If it doesn't clear up I'll clear out. He's got some disease of conscience, I guess. That's what I say anyhow. And maybe mine is sick too and I ought to tell you and him more than I do."

This last struck Mimah as peculiar. It was the first she knew of Ann being suspicious of herself in keeping back something perhaps both Pete and Mimah ought to know. Yet Mimah sensed both wonder, a bright strange wonder, and pride, a dark mystic pride, a tremulous play of light and shadow, in Ann's voice.

They walked in silence a half-block. Ann said, "The time will come, I think, and then we'll see."

"Maybe the sooner the better."

Another half-block they walked and Ann, "Maybe never at all if it comes too hard." And again the bright wonder and dark pride in Ann's voice.

Ray put on gutbucket blues. Lines came wailing out from a Negro torch singer. "My man's got teeth shine like a lighthouse on the sea." Ann didn't hear it. She was dreamily saying to Pete, "Early summer in the air, you can smell it. You can hear the black-and-gold pansies pushing around, whispering what smooth shades of velvet they pick for this year."

"Don't the pansies ever go snafu?" asked Pete.

"Snafu," said Ann, so definitely out of her dreaminess. "You feeling snafu tonight, Pete?"

They stood at a tall window and looked toward the fresh floodlights blacked out more than three years till this night. "I could wish I was back on one of those planes," said Ann, "bringing water to one basket case, fixing the pus drain of another, getting morphine for a boy crying to his mother he was lonely. If you were on that plane, you'd let me do something for you."

"When we used to talk about getting married I could look you in the face and tell you to look me in the face."

"Why not try and see? Trying won't hurt. You'll never hear a whimper out of me. Can't you see that?"

Pete sipped the last of his Scotch and soda, toyed with the glass in his two hands, looked cool into her face and eyes, pursed his lips, and she would have liked desperately to pierce through the blue goggles and see what could be moving in his eyes. "It's too complicated. Sometimes I think I'm coming out of it. If and when I do I'll tell you."

Her mind wasn't on her drink. She had sipped about a fourth of her glass. She was saying, "So that's the way we stand?"

"As near as I can tell it to you now."

"I'll take it that way. Can you remember I'm a good sport?"

Ann's face and eyes were cool, her voice cool shaded with a light tremolo. Behind his goggles he may have caught her fingers working fierce patterns around the glass of Scotch and soda. He was saying, "All right, we'll leave it lay, just like that." Later, with his third drink, changing to straight bourbon with a chaser of ginger ale, he sang a chorus he had from a sergeant who had been on duty at the headquarters of an Air Force lieutenant general. The song of forty-two verses told what kind of a woman was Aunt Clara, the headquarters staff joining lustily in the chorus:

> We never mention Aunt Clara,
> Her picture is turned to the wall,
> Though she lives on the French Riviera,
> Mother says she is dead to us all.

All kept their chairs, close to each other, in unbroken silence through the Sibelius *First Symphony*. After the final movement they sat in further unbroken silence. Then Pete rose, stood before Ann, took her head between his two hands, gave a gentle slap to one side of her face and then to the other. "Stick around, little girl. We might be chums yet. God only knows. I'm putting it up to God. You better do the same." He walked to the doorway, turned and stood facing them. They all rose. Pete was saying, "It's bedtime for me. Good night, it was worth the time."

Ann fell on Mimah's shoulder, laid her head there. "Help me to stick around like he says." She was sobbing. "Help me. You heard him, didn't you? We might be chums yet. He said it like that. We might be chums yet, God only knows."

Later they called a taxi for her. She would breakfast with her father, a Chicago politician and man of affairs whose fortune of a half-million or so had come in part from street-paving contracts along with selling coal to the city. He never forgot, and he made it a help to him in politics and business, that his father had come from County Kerry, Ireland, and dug gas mains in Chicago for a dollar a day. His heart rich and warm toward his daughter, she barely hinted to him of her main grief and he read her, "It's trouble of the heart y've got, Ann." If it was money she needed for any wish of her heart she could draw on him for any amount, he let her know. He had seen money get results among men and women when nothing else would. Ann had given herself a little sardonic laugh over this side of her father. She had heard Ray tell of two Marines before landing on a Guadalcanal beach. On a ship deck they stood with stacks of silver half-dollars alongside them. Then the two Marines threw their silver half-dollars skimming over the smooth sea waters to see which could send his skimmer the farther.

They were going the next morning, they said, where money was no use and if you had it there was nothing to buy.

Out at Hopecrest Mimah didn't sleep so good, her mind on Ann having said, "Maybe I ought to tell you and Pete more than I do," her mind on the bright wonder and dark pride of Ann's voice.

* * * * * * * * * *

Chapter 6

* * * * * * * * * *

Fellowships of War and Peace

V-J DAY when? A world of onlookers asked and waited there in July of 1945.

Three years since Pearl Harbor's oil slicks and rolling smoke, every battleship of the United States Pacific Fleet blasted or burned, capsized or grounded. Then six desperate months—a makeshift navy, its bases gone and no air cover, hit and faded to return, slowing down the enemy amid open sea, jungle islands and coral sandspits—three thousand miles south of Tokyo. Then help arrived, carriers and "baby" escort carriers enough to slug it out with the enemy and begin rolling him back. Month by month saw flight decks roaring with new fighters and bombers, over welcome horizons new battleships, cruisers, destroyers, landing craft. From one fortified island to another they struck. At enemy battleships, airfields, bombers, thick-walled pillboxes, machine-gun nests in jungle and cave, they struck and took over.

The home front spoke from steel mills on the Utah desert, bomber plants on Texas plains and Midwest cornfields, shipyards on both coasts and endless shops and forges shaping war stuff from guns to gauze, from nylon parachutes to K-ration kits, while tankers, cargo ships and planes made oversea hauls of six to eight thousand miles. Till now who had heard of two fleets fighting and neither in sight of the other? How could the United States planes take off from their flight decks and fly beyond eyesight, beyond the sea and skyline curve, to blast, sink, cripple? Radar had come, youths day and night at an indicator chart plotting ship movements and plane flights fifty and sixty miles away, reading exact enemy locations.

"Rugged" the United States forces called it often on those three thousand miles across three years to Japan's doorstep, rugged and bloody at the Solomons and Guadalcanal, Makin, Midway, New Guinea, Tarawa of the Gilberts, the Marianas with Saipan and Guam,

Kwajalein, Truk, the Philippines, Iwo Jima of the Volcanic Isles, and the longest and deadliest weeks at Okinawa.

Some went down in their ships and planes to vanish in vast waters closing them in a sea-silence as though what had happened was clean-forgotten—some on deck or below, on ships they loved, met death from rocket and bomb and in canvas shrouds and solemn service were given to the sea. Many died wading ashore, more in a running crouch up the beach, still more in shell holes of volcanic ash or in jungle undergrowth from the shots of camouflaged snipers hidden in trees—many dying without time or the benefit of spoken burial like one with a tiny flag pinned on him and assembled comrades hearing the words of Raider Carlson at Guadalcanal: "Father, accept this body of Jack Miller as Thine own. . . . Thou knowest he knew the reasons for which he fought. Give him peace. Amen."

Tankers, troop transports, enemy cargo ships by the hundreds had gone to sea bottom from torpedoes of United States submarines—they were "toys" soon to be wiped out, said the Tokyo radio that later named them "the Black Panthers of the Pacific." Four times the same radio had the carrier *Lexington* sunk and when four times she rose from the sea they named her the *Blue Ghost*.

The kamikazes came, rushing by hundreds as a "divine wind" on United States carriers and destroyers, suicide pilots falling out of the sky by hundreds from counter-divine or diabolical ack-ack and United States fighter planes. A few broke through, one landing a bomb on the loaded flight deck of the carrier *Franklin*, his bomb exploding amid the planes about to take off, killing or wounding a thousand crewmen. Then the attrition began to tell and there were not enough Jap planes for the dedicated suicide pilots to ride as a "divine wind."

Slowly the long-prepared and highly organized armed might of Japan had been crumbling. Her stubby professional generals and admirals with deadpan faces—how were they taking it? Hadn't everything been thought of beforehand? Hadn't they anticipated every contingency? Hadn't they told their people, by an absolutist "thought-control" system, they couldn't lose? Hadn't they told their Emperor, their mild palace captive, the Son of Heaven, that they couldn't lose and that they would take over "Asia for the Asiatics" and include Australia? Yet now came B-29's blasting cities of Japan by the square mile—now what? They, the Nipponese war lords, had won the war, their feet about ready to set foot on the shores of Australia, and then, as had happened before in the history of nations and men arrogantly proud of their might, they began losing the war they had won. Now from across the widest of oceans had come to their shores and home waters a race of mixed breeds they had taught the Japanese people to scorn and despise as inferiors and aliens though nevertheless these same war lords had sent their fleets and troops out armed with weapons, ships and planes copied in admiring imitation of the enemy they were to fight, lacking the later improved models. They had not foreseen a ragged remnant of an American navy fighting with near nothing till something came, nor the naked brawling battle qualities of the United States sea, air and land forces. They had not expected a pilot named Kelly would dive to his own death and sink a Japanese troopship—it was an idea—they would use it and clothe it as a "divine wind." And Guadalcanal, bitter with hunger and heat, death, miasma and madness, dank and dark as Valley Forge—it was not predicted men could thus fight so far from Fresno, Keokuk, Paducah and Brooklyn. Nor had there been forecasts of such scenes as "the Marianas turkey shoot" when Jap planes fell as game birds in season—nor the new tankers hauling alongside United States Fleet ships and refueling on the open sea—and radar, the long-distance detector, the marvelous invisible dependable spy.

Over these matters of violence and science, the once perfectly confident war lords at Tokyo looked now into each other's deadpan faces. Gimleted in their brains lay an unheeded maxim on three June days of '45 when United States planes raided Formosa, Canton, Hong Kong, Balik, Papua and Borneo, Kyushu, the Kuriles and the Marcus Islands and other objectives, half the living area of Tokyo blasted and leveled by flying Superfortresses. Forgotten was a maxim: "The governing condition of War is the Unknown."

"Oh, to be in Okinawa, now that April's there!" Ray Windom threw this paraphrase at Mimah one hot forenoon in July 1945 when the sun-heat waves blistered the sidewalks of Washington. He stood up from his chair at the table. "Win or lose it costs," shaking toward Mimah a scraggly sheet of notebook paper in his right hand. "The wear and tear on the human machine, how can you figure it? At seventeen Mamma's boy, shy about kissing his sixteen-year-old girl next door, can go into the navy four years sooner than he can vote. Mamma's boy can be a navy gunner and learn to sing one of their songs I heard." He looked up at the ceiling, down at the floor, tilted his head low toward his right shoulder, looked at Mimah with a left-eye squint and a crooked mouth. "Wait, chum, wait, and I'll give it to you like I got it from a couple of baby-faces just after Guadalcanal." He raised his head, let go the eye squint and crooked mouth, hummed a few bars of "My Bonnie Lies over the Ocean," then with a queer mock tenderness sang:

> " 'They promised me wings made of silver,
> They promised me wings made of gold,
> Don't worry, my dear darling mother—
> I'll die when I'm eighteen years old.' "

"I don't know—maybe that would break even a heart of glass. Not easy to take, Ray."

"Remember when we heard those Fiske Singers? How did it go,

the song they sang? 'Da ole sheep done know de road, de young lambs must find da way.' " He pushed Mimah into a chair, pulled his own near her and brandishing the scraggly notebook sheet again, "Here's a high-school boy waiting to go to college. Waiting where? Okinawa. When? Last April. How? Here's how. Part of this diary brought home to his father, a Naval surgeon here." He read:

"Standing here with one eye on my throttle man. Getting all kinds of bells—anything can happen. Already had G.Q. [General Quarters] twice tonight. Several times last night. I haven't had over one night's sleep at a time since I can't remember when. Getting to the stage where I just don't give a damn what happens. A hell of a way to feel but a hell of a way to live and a hell of a war too.

"We have settled down to firing about forty rounds an hour now. Every time the gun goes off I jump about three feet. Nerves just about shot. Guess they will go first—the body can stand much more than the mind. We are all getting pretty jumpy. This tin-can life is rotten.

"Just had my messenger put on a pot of 'black joe,' maybe I can hop myself up on that for a while. None of us can think too much of this without a letup.

"Bang! There goes that damn 5 in. 38 again. Hope the bastards are hitting something.

"Getting bells so fast it sounds like a fire engine coming through the engineroom. Guess I'll take the throttle for a while in a little while. It's hard work but one way to stay awake.

"A wagon [battleship] and two cruisers are firing right over our heads. Hope they don't lower their sights too much. I'd hate to get sunk by one of our own ships. After all this can has been through that would be the payoff.

"Noticed a transport with a hole in her bow today. We are paying a price for this lousy Jap island. Hope it's worth it.

"Everything is purring fine down here. Lots of noise but I could sleep right through it. Just let one piece of machinery stop or change speed tho' and I'd wake up in a flash.

"God, but I'll be glad when this war is over. Hope my nerves last that long. One old-timer cracking up last week didn't help any of us. Oh well, maybe he's better off. At least he'll get back to the States. After three years of this damn war, I'm starting to feel the effects."

"What could be sweeter?" Ray was saying with one eye slit and a twist of a grin. Mimah peered into his face, searching. " 'Every time the gun goes off I jump about three feet. This tin-can life is rotten,' " Ray was repeating from the diary, Mimah gathering definitely that at one or more stages Ray himself had done those three-foot jumps when a gun went off. She had never allowed her curiosity to press him for details about what he had been through. He had been flung into terrific actions, she guessed, and he had his own reasons for not picturing to her those actions to him haunting, vivid, perhaps horrible. His slit eye open and his twisted grin vanished, he was saying, "I could put my arm around that boy on the destroyer, crazy for a little sleep, his nerves shot." She saw on Ray's mouth the same tender awareness as when a few weeks ago, after a bitter outbreak about how useless he was, he had suddenly kissed her very softly and said, "Skip it, girl, maybe it's going to work out after all." She was not sure now why he stepped to a table covered with newspapers and magazines and picked up *Information*, a bulletin of the Friends Civilian Public Service.

"You meant for me to see this page where it's open?" he asked.

"Not especially. I let it lay, that's all."

"And a while back you would have hid it from me."

"Definitely."

"You must think I'm coming out of it."

"You are."

He pointed to a paragraph and gave a hoarse laughing grunt, " 'Throttle-pushing bums'—I like that—right on the nose." He folded the paper and slapped her on the cheek with it. "What you slept with last night was a throttle-pushing bum—how do you like it?"

"Like the announcers say, tune in at this same time tomorrow."

Squatted on the edge of a chair, elbows on knees, Ray read aloud from the Quaker journal the letter of an army aviator on active foreign service:

"What are we going to be able to do when this war is over? Flying has pretty well ruined us for indoor desk jobs, and there aren't going to be enough flying jobs. The high nervous pitch of front-line work, with the adrenals pouring adrenalin into the system every time an unidentified plane is sighted, leaves us completely washed-out on the ground. We are so accustomed to being tuned to the topnotch that ordinary work can't keep our attention.

One reason I don't write more often is that I get so nervous when I write or type. In the middle of a letter I have to get up and walk around a while to work it off. For a couple of years we are going to be throttle-pushing bums. Having thousands of horsepower in the palm of your hand is a habit-forming drug that leaves an appetite that few will be able to feed in civilian life. . . .

"You who are left behind had better do something toward providing a better and livable world for us to come back to, for there are a lot of men learning to resolve their troubles with a gun."

"Getting personal," said Ray. "Him and me and who else?" He pressed the button of a Michigan-made chair, sloped its back and lay with his face to the ceiling. "Yes, who else? Only a few million of us bums at the throttles of planes, tanks, armored cars—what will we be doing when the war is over? What do we want? What kind of a world do we want? And if it's the same old world, when does the next world war start? And will it come late enough for bambino Joe Stilwell Windom to grow up and be a throttle-pushing bum like his father?"

Ray's voice growing softer, nearly inaudible, Mimah caught the words, "Who did Bowbong mean by the 'deniers and mockers'? He put them in the three books. They always turn up. Who will they be after this war?" Then Ray faded into sleep. He was learning about sleep, to coax it whenever it came. Mimah felt good about it. He had learned to keep his poise about the deniers and mockers. She had months ago seen his hands flutter and his eyes blaze, his ideas incoherent and his speech vehement, over the careless, the easy-going, the indifferent unbelievers, and those his grandfather might name as "deniers and mockers." Now they still troubled him but he had learned that he must not let them interfere with his return to fighting trim. So it seemed now to Mimah and she was almost afraid of an elation that crept over her.

Mimah mounted a chair, reached to a high shelf for a large envelope she had hidden behind a row of Bowbong's books. In a chair at a corner window she opened the envelope and gave herself to reading its papers, keeping a casual eye on Ray in his sleep. After a time she saw him stir, saw him sit up and press the button that straightened the back of the chair. She walked over to him, drew a chair alongside. Ray was rubbing sleep out of his eyes and saying with a purr to it, "A throttle pushing bum—that's me." He turned his face to hers, fully awake. She put a hand on his fingers on the armrest board. His eyes fell on the papers in her hand. "What goes on here? What's on the pan?"

"I held 'em out on you," said Mimah. "A bunch of letters, type-written copies of letters a man in the Pacific wrote to his wife and two letters to me. He's an assault-transport executive officer, a crew of five hundred under him. Being the censor he could write his wife what he wanted to so long as he didn't endanger security. He's your kind of a man. Bowbong would have had an eye for him.

"I wrote him about you," Mimah went on, "about Bowbong and the Box. He heard Bowbong's broadcast. He knows that your outfit flew cover for his ship, but he never got to meet you, says the war will end sometime and he'll come East and have a look at you."

"What's he got you're so interested?"

"Well, he gets the idea he'll write to you through me. Just now he's in bed in a Naval Hospital at Richmond, California, with orders to rest. He's been many places, seen too much—like you. Now they put him to bed and tell him to forget it."

"I've heard that," said Ray. "Just pull a black curtain over your bright sizzling memory—and forget it—yeah."

Mimah picked a letter. "The day before they put him to bed he wrote this. Can a man love a ship? Listen." She read:

"Today I walked under my ship in dry dock, with the new skipper. The grass was six inches long in spots but her bottom was sound and not a nick in the prop or a dented strake and I patted her old smelly bilge and her grassy streamlined rudder with loving pride. I'd seen her launched and sailed her every mile she'd sailed as we pushed the Japs back from the Gilberts to Okinawa and inside me (not for publication) I know if it hadn't been for me at certain times the old gal would have had worse troubles than a bit of grass along the boot topping. That's just a little thing we have between us, her and me, because no one will ever know what I told the captains one two and three at sudden crossroads or young uncertain officers of the deck on dark raining nights with tactics trouble in the squadron. The things an old sailor does for his ship or from loyalty or in friendship, or just because it's in him to do it, have nothing to do with pay, promotion, or publicity."

Ray was interested. "Go on."

"Age forty now, a licensed master mariner getting his nine hundred dollars a month, he went into the navy as a navigator. He can keep a straight face while laughing—like here." And she read:

"I am one of a new grade in the Navy. 'Lieutenant, super grade.' Neon lights are worn over the stripes in lieu of more gold in purse or braid. The commission reads, 'To rank with but after Majors of the Salvation Army.' . . . These officers, together with ensigns and pelicans of the Chilean coast, are permitted to dip their headgear in salt water in order that their identity may not be confused with that of pollywogs and landlubbers."

In this same letter in June of 1945, before they put him to bed, he wrote somber words that Mimah's voice put to sad music:

" 'Do you think people will be interested in our troubles and struggles when the war is won in Asia? The grass grows so fast.'

"He had come from where the war was," and Mimah stared at the paper and its large script in black ink, moving her fingers to rest on Ray's hand. She quit staring and read:

"I'm supposed to talk at church tomorrow night. I used to talk a lot but since coming back this time it seems hard to do. The dead out there are very silent. Perhaps we should speak for them—but what to say? . . .

"Well, what things are great and what small? To the bulldozer, to the worm, to the frail proud spirit, to the plain common human beings who salt the earth? A green leaf is wonderful to me and a sunset a thing of wonder. Money is just convenient to have, it does not run me or control my thinking. Yet I met a man while I was on leave who evaluated everything in dollars. He had six hundred and sixty acres of magnificent fir. 'Fifty thousand dollars.' He had acres of shore on a lovely bay, 'so much a front foot to the best people.' He had some lovely shrubs in the garden where he liked to work. 'Cost me seventy-five and now worth seven-fifty if a cent.' I guess it is quite a letdown to him to look at rainbows, the pot of gold and all being pure myth. And yet, he was a very nice guy and most kind to us."

"Sounds like good preaching," said Ray.

"Preacher blood in him," said Mimah. "His father a missionary in Africa, where he was born under the American flag over the house and where later he ran away to sea." She turned to the same letter again. "Quite an Easter Sunday he had last spring. The banks of blossoms, the new grass and flowers, his wife and other bright women in their new hats, he missed it for this"—and she read:

"The afternoon we landed at Okinawa (Easter Sunday) I heard a Jap broadcaster from Tokyo say that if Japan lost Okinawa, there was no hope of their winning the war. Then they gave the kamikaze boys a pep talk. Perhaps they were trying to scare us. No full evidence that Easter morning of the fury of their defense. But after the sun set in that yellow battle smoke when we were trying to maneuver in the smoke-obscured waters off Naha town and the suicide planes came diving, crashing, dying down and ships all around throwing up a thunder of fire into a yellow sick sky—darkness falling and still those 'little black bastards' coming in at us between the five-inch bursts and the pepperpot pattern of 40 mm flack. Yes—while the ship next to us flamed from bridge to bow with dead all over her topside and a destroyer close suddenly had no more topsides and a cruiser's stacks hung backwards like old crooked fingers—and while we tried to keep our minds clear and our voices calm, yet heard above all that hellish din, and our eyes keen for dangers to our ship and to see that the orders of reason were carried out in the midst of confusion—we began to see the evidence that Easter Sunday at Okinawa."

A Siamese cat, seal-point-furred with smoky nose and smoky paws, leaped smoothly and silently into Ray's lap. He ran fingers between its smoky ears, then held his hands over its body as it blinked its eyes and settled into a satisfied purring in the quiet room. Mimah was saying, "I'm going to turn the whole batch," lifting the letters, "over to you to read by yourself—only I thought he is so like you and Bowbong that we could share some of the pieces—say like this," and she read:

"I was looking at one of our planes with binoculars when it was hit and burst suddenly into an awful sheet of flame. The plane sideslipped down toward the water, parts of it falling off as it fell toward our boats in the lagoon. One of the men in it fell out. His parachute opened too late just as he hit the water alongside one of our boats. I found myself praying for him even as he fell. Ensign Effner was bringing wounded out to our ship. The body nearly hit his boat on one side, the plane on the other. He got hold of the parachute and pulled the poor broken body in. Every bone was broken, some protruding through the flesh, all of his clothes and hair and skin burnt off. There was no identification. One of the wounded men began to vomit. Effner cut off the parachute and let the poor broken body go. They brought the parachute aboard to the bridge. That night as I was on watch I had the queerest feeling, as if the pilot was very close to me. I went over to the wooden Jap bucket that held the chute and felt the soft silk with my hand and said, 'I'm sorry, fellow.' He may have been a nice clean boy like some we have known."

Mimah's eyes roved to the next page of the letter. "This one to his wife. Lovers, friends and buddies, they are, he says, and writes to her like this:

"It will be some time before I can eat crab again. Off Okinawa one day a dead Jap floated slowly along our ship's side. He was very stocky, dressed in khaki shorts and floating as all dead men do, with the seat of his pants up and legs and head dangling. His back and the sides of his belly were all cut up and then as I looked, a big black crab crawled around his belly. The crab was eating him. If you can think of anything nice about this war except a quick and successful conclusion, I don't know what it would be."

"He's been around and can tell it," said Ray with a grim edge of a smile. His hands gathered the cat and dropped it to the floor with an affectionate command in an undertone, "Now you go chase yourself, Mesopotamia." He stepped to a table, lighted a cigarette and returned to his chair. "He's got the gift of observation, what they call it," said Ray in crypto-classic. "What's his name, this fellow? He signs his letters, I take it."

"Kenneth MacKenzie MacDougall, and here is one of the two letters he has written to me—and to you—and in a way to Bowbong. You'll see before you get through where he's like Bowbong and you. His wife made copies of parts of his letters for two sisters and other relatives. And when they came my way I wrote his wife about us and you, and about her husband, a brave officer and a thinker, a troubled man somewhat like Bowbong's Roger Williams in Book One, and here he is running an assault-transport landing troops on Pacific islands. I asked his wife, in my own polite manner, where did this kind of a man come from and how did he get that way? And along comes this letter to me."

Ray gave a brush-off to Mesopotamia, who had made a smooth swift leap into his lap. He held the letter of three typed pages and read parts that ran:

The letter that came to you was one I happened to write my wife, one of thousands I have written her, for I have spent twenty years at sea. My wife and I are very much in love. We are also very good friends. And I was just expressing to the one person on earth who is closest to me just how I felt. That is all.

Kwajalein is long past now. There have been so many more beaches since. To the men who die, a small engagement is no different from one of the world's famous battles. They contribute their most sacred personal possession. . . . We of the brass and braid get involved in tactics and the precise performance of our duty. But to my way of thinking it is Joe from Brooklyn and Jim from Petaluma who are really doing the job. And when the guns are roaring and I'm trying to go coolly about my work, I always find a few seconds to pray for those boys. . . .

My father came from eastern Maryland. As a little boy he remembered watching grandfather read the paper in the gaslit hall, when Lincoln was shot. My father was a pioneer missionary for thirty years in Angola, Africa, where I was born. The materials for the house came from Germany and an American flag flew from the roof.

My mother is of Scotch ancestry. That's where I get the Kenneth MacKenzie in front of my name. When mother and dad met in Africa, she rode a white ox, with a MacKenzie plaid for a saddle. They were very much in love and had eight children. I'm number six, so I never argue against large families. Father died six years ago at the age of eighty-one. Last time I was home visiting with my wife I caught dad smooching mother behind the kitchen door. They were sweethearts.

We lived one year in Africa, seven in England, and the rest on the West coast or out at sea. I was restless and ornery at seventeen and against my parents' wishes I went to sea in the Merchant Marine, working up in eighteen years from deck boy to captain of my own ship. I was in the Naval Reserve, and two years ago went on active duty in the navy. At present I am navigator on an assault-transport. We have a pretty complicated job here, specializing in enemy real estate with a marine view.

I've been several times around the world and spent thirteen years sailing to the Orient from Seattle. Manchuria, China, Japan, the Philippines, the Indies, the Pacific Islands. Regular Cook's tour.

But if you want me to get enthusiastic, just ask me about my wife and our little boy (when he's good), my son (when he's naughty). They are the ones I live for and sweat for out here in this loveless, eggless portion of the world.

How did I get started on all this? What did you ever do to me? I'm just lonesome, so I just sit here talking with my pen.

It is likely I'd have been much more of a success in life if I hadn't spent so much of it in dreaming and thinking about things that don't concern my job. But I can grow beautiful tulips, and make a sick tomato plant sit up and make a salad. I can tell kids stories, fix my little boy's kites or a broken gate. Old ladies and children love me. I was never much of a hand with the ladies, but for nearly ten years I have been happily married to the lady of my dreams.

There are a lot of fellows just like me and a lot more who have more on the ball or who are nicer fellows to know. We have over five hundred men in our crew, most of them quite young. No two are quite alike. Every one has his points, his faults and his troubles.

We will not all live to see the end of this struggle. But most of us will go back home some day. I like to think that we will be better citizens for this experience. But if you tell that to someone on the street at home it will probably be a letdown. They want to know what it is like to be in a war. General Sherman had a fine answer to that.

Before we got into the war I was running to Japan and China. I came home all fired-up about the Japs and people thought I was crazy. After I'd been out here a while in the war I seemed to lose all perspective—couldn't see the woods for the trees. The hatred, the dying and the possible futility of any lasting peace just about got me. And the loneliness. That's the worst. When you lie awake at night, tired as you are, longing for the arms of your loved one. And you just grit your teeth and slug it out. . . .

We buried a young soldier at sea off Saipan, one of many. The last thing he said was, "I don't want to die. I don't want to die." But he did die. He was still warm when I put my arms around him, lashing iron bars to his canvas shroud. It was the only thing I could do for him. And as I had my arms around his body it seemed as if we had some fellowship together. He had paid the price for freedom I hope I won't be asked to pay. He seemed so lonely there. So much lonelier than I.

But the ageless rain falls and returns to the sky. And new little plants push up through the dead leaf mold. And life goes on.

Please pardon the outburst and please do write again.

Ray looked up from the letter, after sitting silent a while. "Yes, Mimah. He's got streaks of Bowbong, Roger Williams, Oliver Windrow, Ordway Winshore, Omri Winwold."

"You forgot Orton Wingate," said Mimah. "Bowbong never did tell us whether Wingate married Dorothy Temple. He just hinted that her next child would be born in lawful wedlock and Wingate the father."

"He trusted us to guess that much, he had to hurry on with the long story," said Ray.

"The same as he trusted us to guess that surely in due time Remember Spong would get to Providence and look up Resolved Wayfare and ask him how about a little kiss," laughed Mimah. Then she sobered. "MacDougall's wife copied a part of one of his letters for me and said to show it to you sometime because you've got the same kind of stuff. She wrote that the sisters and relatives wouldn't hear of this." And Mimah read:

"I was feeling better some and noting the pressure of things to be done, tailed into the job the best I could. It was an effort to do so. I've worked hard all my life and like to be busy, but this was like dragging uphill. The Captain was always bawling me out for overdoing when I wasn't up to snuff. Our excellent senior surgeon treated me and I noticed that he was keeping an eye on me. When I couldn't take it any more I'd go to bed for a few hours. Two days ago the Doc got me in a corner and gave it to me straight. He said that I haven't got the resistance any more to bounce back and I was heading for serious trouble and that he was going to see the Skipper. He did, and the Old Man laid down the law. I'm still the official Exec, but Smathers has been taken off the watch list and has assumed the entire burden for me until the doctor thinks I can take it again. The Captain told me that I was a passenger and that I must learn to relax. They told me to read light books (not in the mood). The Old Man said that if necessary he'd make me wear a red shirt with *Keep Off* painted on it. So I said that I'd be a good boy. But it is hard to keep out of things. I take my medicine and try to relax. Doc says I need at least two months in pasture, away from it all. As that is impossible now, I'll ride along and try to fight my way back to where I can take over again. The Old Man kept me here principally for my knowledge of seamanship, navigation and piloting, which is no strain. I can always help out that way. However, the main burden of an Exec is the ship's administration, which just takes a lot out of the best of men. It is a twenty-four-hour job.

"I feel ashamed of myself for letting the Captain and the service down, but it's just one of those things. So, you see, I'm not so hot after all.

"I can see him, part of it, I mean, Ray," said Mimah very softly. "He was working and fighting with all he had. Then on top of that he was letting his mind try to bore through and find meanings for now and the days to come."

"Yeah," said Ray. "And you come out of it feeling like a worm that has turned up some curls of dirt and what you do next is turn up more of the same dirt and it comes in the same curls and the monotony wears you down."

Mimah at this briskly sent her fingers to a letter. "This one he wrote to me. I'll read you spots from it, I'll read it for you and for the shadow of Bowbong that keeps bobbing around the doorways and fading." She was about to begin reading, then paused. "I've heard that it is ideas that make civilization. This fellow has ideas, this fellow whose Scottish mother in Africa rode a white ox with a plaid of the MacKenzie clan for a saddle." She now read:

"We have a great cross section of America on this ship. Boys from nearly every state in the Union. Boys from many races and from various home backgrounds. Many are from exceptional homes and the childhood of some has been a mess which is reflected in their actions and attitudes out here. We have Mexicans, Indians, Italians, Spaniards, and boys of varied European descent. As ship's chief censor and as deck-court officer and senior member of the ship's summary court I get an insight into the lives and backgrounds of many of the boys. Of course my assistants read most of the letters, but I spot-check about thirty every day and read most of those which are written in Spanish. In the day-by-day problems which come up and during some of my talks with them, I wonder what they are working and fighting for, what they expect to get from and contribute to life after the war—what kind of a world they expect to go home to when the guns are silent. . . .

"Ninety-five per cent of the letters I censor mention homesickness and talk about going home on leave or after the war. Some express willingness to stay and see it out so 'it won't happen again,' or so it 'won't happen to our son when he grows up.' The last generation thought the same thing and here we are.

"Admiration of the British except as fliers and seamen is practically absent. Yet when they speak of Russia and Germany it is evident that they really aren't worried much about England. It's just a habit. They admire the Russian Army and as *Time* says, realize that Russian lives are saving American lives and bringing us nearer to home. A few who incline strongly to the left admire everything about Russia. Most of them think that the BEAR will be glaring at us across the Atlantic shortly after the defeat of Germany. Some say, 'Let the Russians run Europe. Perhaps they can do it. No one else has yet.' Some think that Russia will not abuse her tremendous power.

"All the boys want Japan and Germany disarmed and kept from any future military power. There seems to be little personal bitterness in their thinking once the temporary hate during action with the enemy has died down. I never heard anyone volunteer for the 'International Police Force.' They want to go home, start life again and let live.

"Well, I've had all these thoughts and more myself.

"I found that when you traveled about the world and even about your own country you saw how the other fellow lived and got his point of view. We seldom quarrel with those we understand. For a long time I have thought that a free radio and air travel would shorten world distances and help the members of world society to understand each other. . . . For years I read Japanese papers and heard their propaganda radio. The average Japanese was cut off entirely from the rest of the world. I knew a few who had influence enough to keep unlawful short-wave radio sets. Not one of them would ever admit to me that there was anything wrong with Japanese aggression in China. Of course I didn't expect them to. They considered themselves as the enlightened and the progressive nation of Asia. They had absorbed what was useful from the West and combined it with the wisdom of the East. We were intruders in Asia. It was up to them to lead all Asia to its 'destiny.' (What destiny? may I ask.)

"I talked to the influential Japanese in Yokohama just a few weeks before Pearl Harbor was attacked. They were eager to know if America intended to fight Japan. Of course we said No, we didn't want to fight. But we didn't like what they were doing in China. They, in turn, were very friendly, and shaking our hands assured us that Japan prized the friendship of the United States and wished to promote 'freedom' in Asia.

"I didn't remind them that I had walked in the rubble of Shanghai and Woosing in 1932 and again in 1937 and that I had seen uncouth Japanese carpetbaggers spending small fortunes in Shanghai shops while the poor starved and raked the bottom of the muddy Hwang Poo for lumps of coal. . . .

"I don't see how I am in a position to say that this or this-and-that will keep the world from war and its people free.

"We see some things all too clearly out here. But in many instances we can't see the woods for the trees. We are tired and underfed and homesick and tired of floating about in a steel prison submitting to military discipline, which is necessary in war but abhorrent to our civilian instincts. For most of us are and remain civilians. We don't believe that gold braid automatically makes a man a gentleman. We don't enjoy power over those who must obey our orders. We want our men to obey us willingly and cheerfully because they have confidence in our ability and integrity. We want to exhibit the same kind of loyalty to our superiors. But that is not military tradition by a long shot.

"This has been a spotty letter. From time to time I've had to go attend to details of the ship's routine and have lost the trend of what I've been trying to say.

"I wanted to get in somewhere that I think the white race has brought both good and bad to Asia. That is another and a long subject.

"Then there is the problem of the Negro and other groups in our own land. I try to treat colored boys as individuals and ignore the color of their skins as much as possible. By that I mean to bear in mind the sensitiveness and background which affect their actions, yet to treat them for what they are. Some are very intelligent and are not getting a fair break. Some are getting the nearest to an education, the best food, pay and treatment they have ever had. Some are lazy and crafty. Their troubles as individuals are not far different from those of the white boys here. But *what* can they expect to go home to?

"We have a few officers from the 'deep South.' It has been interesting to watch how the attitude of the less tolerant ones has improved. Several Southerners aboard, however, are the most kind and understanding of all to the colored boys.

"The interesting point regarding recent action cannot be written about yet. Furthermore it all rolls into a blur after a time. Since Kwajalein the actions seem less clear and fresh in my mind. There have been so many landings, alarms, alerts, attacks like a bad movie without an ending.

"Compared to the foot soldier we live in luxury. But our safety depends on discipline and training. Every man running to his post without delay in the middle of a dark night. Every man must understand his job and do it well and quickly. For every fifteen minutes of action are hours without number standing to the guns, waiting and looking for an enemy who does not come or does not come close enough, or does not come where you can fire at him without endangering your own side. And then at times, out of the quiet comes a sudden increasing roar as an enemy dives out of the sun. Then he either gets you or misses you and you either get him or miss him and in three minutes it is all over. Only your heart is still pounding.

"We do not know what the future holds for us or whether we will live to see it. But we know that we are in God's keeping.

With faith, tho' partly blind, we can travel on toward the lights of home and the hopes of peace to all men of goodwill.

"When we do return again, if we do, it will be our duty to keep peace alive and freedom vital. May we be guided well. Without God's help I do not see how we can succeed.

"Now I have talked a long time and you haven't said a word. Please pardon my rudeness in holding the floor so long.

"It is good to know you."

Mimah waited a few moments and seemed to be pondering, her memory running back to the evening of the broadcast and this room where she and the baby heard Bowbong make his one radio address to the American people. She read now:

"I had a bad cold and a fever (we get 'em in the tropics), my clothes soaking wet from navigating in the rain, when I heard the broadcast of Justice Windom's speech. It rose up and walloped me right between the eyes. He said it, the thing that is so hard to say, the thing you can't blurt out to people even when your soul is brimful of it. To me the speech had the ring of a good ax in a sound oak log. You must send me a copy of the speech, if that can be. About all I remember now goes something like this: 'When we say a patriot is one who loves his country, what kind of love do we mean? A love we can throw on a scale and see how much it weighs? A love we can take apart to see how it ticks? Or is a patriot's love of country a thing invisible, a quality, a human shade and breath, beyond all reckoning and measurement?' Then later, about the time your baby let out the squeal he mentioned, he said we can't unlock the secret that hides in the bosom of a patriot and the dead hold in their clenched hands only that which they have given away. He spoke of a blood-scarlet thread of hardship, toil and combat running through the story of America from the beginning and how it cost to build this nation and in the future there will be cost. As I told you, it rose up and walloped me. He said it. We are safe at anchor this moment but I will be up around 4 A.M. getting the old girl on her way again. But before I get under the shower and into my nice bunk, a luxury lots of fellows lack these days, I wanted to drop you a line.

"Taking up this afternoon from last night—I'll tell you the honest truth about dying—the thing that bothers me most—it is not the pain or trouble of dying, it is not even missing a full life and loved ones—it is the vast silence from which a man cannot speak out to his fellows about the things Justice Windom expressed in his speech. Men paid a cost, in struggle and risk, in self-denial, pain and death, to build this nation. Their dust is sacred in the unfinished dream they died for.

"If there is a hereafter—that is all settled and all right so far as I am concerned. But I love life and I feel that I have so much to live for and I don't want to go down into the silence while some glib-phrased fellow who doesn't know makes a vacuum of what we are trying to do for mankind. And Justice Windom's broadcast made me feel much better about it. So, for the many others out here and in Europe who heard him speak, I thank you, you who were close to him and probably love him for some of his sweet minor blemishes. We are very busy out here. I can't tell you where I am or what's up. I'm awfully tired and have lost a lot of weight, but that is little to lose in a war. Your friendship is close to my heart and I pray that we may meet face to face someday in the Windom house, where my wife and I would like to hold the baby just for the honor."

Mimah looked up from her reading, saw Ray composed and quiet, turned over a sheet of paper. "He says this is a special postscript for you when I think you should get around to it, and he goes on:

"Right now I'm snowed under with work aboard ship. For the last year and more I've had the feeling that life is flying at me so fast I can't handle it. Letters don't get answered. Books don't get read. Bunks don't get slept in enough. Food don't get eaten. Work doesn't get done and no diary kept of the confusion, so many details to remember. I always was a doer and not a detail paperwork man. Oh, well, I guess we'll win the war through 'sheer force of numbers' as the Irishman said. Perhaps you will be able to read my letters. My mind jumps ahead of the pen and it makes an awful mess of nice clean paper. I have to answer a letter tomorrow to a nice lady in Philadelphia whose son we buried off Palau. I just happened to remember him for sure because his name was the same as that of our ship. Private first-class, buried at sea on our ship, and I cried a little when I read his mother's letter—his baby born after he died and that splash as that canvas-covered form went over the side—they always look so lonely as they splash into the sea and I hate military funerals anyway.

"Says it's one of the longest letters he ever wrote," Mimah continued. "Scrawls an apology on another sheet he typed the next day. Says he was haunted at night by Justice Windom and asks me to send him a picture of the grand old man. I think he was beautifully haunted. He typed it narrow-width."

"I believe you may have seen Lincoln's flag-raising speech before the Treasury Building in Philadelphia on his way to inauguration in 1861:

" 'The part assigned to me is to raise the flag, which, if there be no fault in the machinery, I will do, and when up, it will be for the people to keep it up.'

"That was a long time ago. The flag is still flying in spite of faults from time to time in the machinery. And I am sure that notwithstanding our failings and uncertainties we will keep it up. After we are gone, and our children too, the flag will still be flying over the land he gave his life to preserve. And please God, it will be a fairer, freer land than Lincoln dreamed about or we have yet seen.

"We must keep the faith."

Ray said nothing for what seemed to Mimah a long time though had she watched the clock she would have seen it was six minutes. She saw his eyes shift and stare out through a window and keep staring. The boulder, Remembrance Rock, seemed to hold his eyes. Then Ray spoke low-toned, "He does sound like Bowbong, doesn't he, the son-of-a-gun—and Jesus, isn't he just made for hearing Bowbong's idea about the Rock?"

"He'd be soft about it," murmured Mimah.

Ray had a prompting. "That second letter he wrote you. Give me something from that. Then another day I'm going through the whole batch."

"He writes," said Mimah, picking out the letter, "about after the war having a piece of ground overlooking Puget Sound where he can plant and grow things and perhaps write and enjoy his wife without separations and play with his boy. His wife tells him the boy has ordered a sister for him to play with." And Mimah read:

"I would so very much like to write. I have become discouraged with my dream. And yet there still seems to be something bound up inside me, waiting for a form of expression. I have been considered a good seaman and get on well with my shipmates, but somehow have never felt, even after twenty years of it, that I belonged out at sea herding a ship over distant horizons.

"There are so many memories—early days aloft in the rigging— steaming into beautiful Hong Kong at dawn—river life on the muddy Yangtze—a garden in Penang—the jungles of Guadalcanal —the hills of Genoa.

"There was the little Japanese gardener in Yokohama who was my friend for many years. In 1941 sentiment against Americans ran high in Japan. But after selling me some lovely orchid plants, which still grow in my brother's California home, he did not take my money and let me go. Not he. Getting his bicycle he put the plants in the handle-bar basket and walked beside me to the pier. People stared. It was still all right to take an American's money, but to fraternize with him in public? A Japanese cavalry officer swept up on his beautiful horse. Hand arrogantly on his saber hilt he glared at us. With head proudly high the bowlegged little gardener walked silently at my side. We said good-by at the boat landing. I did not shake his hand but paid him the best tribute I knew, bowing sincerely. That was the last I ever saw of him—riding off on his bike past the angry cavalryman.

"It was the kinship of the earth and growing things. I have noticed it all over the world—love me, love my plants. Propaganda blows like a typhoon over that sort of human relationship—wind, noise, confusion and suffering—even war. Still I like to think of that little gardener, hungry now, overtaxed and bombed from the skies, tending the plants he loves—the weak little leaves and stalks and roots which are so much stronger than the angry man on the horse.

"Here I go again. I didn't intend that outburst at all—but my head is full of such thoughts. Somehow they seem more important to me than saying the correct thing to those who command you or to those who may help you. Integrity is so much more important to me than 'correctness.'

"Used as I am to long voyages, I feel so far away. We are in a different world out here. Nothing seems sure and there is little to hang onto but faith."

Mimah handed Ray the large envelope and the letters. "They're out of hiding now. Read 'em all."

"Read 'em and weep?"

"No, like they say in the Victory Gardens, weed 'em and reap."

A letter slid to the floor. Ray picked it up, a typewritten sheet with three lines scrawled lengthwise in ink, the handwriting bold and sweeping. Ray read it and passed it to Mimah with a trick of lifted eyebrows:

Ensign from the *Lexington* tells about Steichen the photographer. A disabled plane didn't take the wave-off and hit the flight deck, killing two men and crippling five others, its whirling propeller blowing off Steichen's cap, hurling him down into the net! So they call him Old Timer on account of his number was up and he's lived past his time.

Mimah looked at Ray, with nothing on her mind worth saying as he looked at her and drew the back of his hand along under his jutted chin, as he was saying, "A big crazy game of craps—the war." He clenched his hand. "The dream will be back tonight, I feel it coming on."

"Dream?"

"It comes when I pick up the whole damned war and try to carry it by my little lonesome."

"The same dream over again?"

"Never changes."

"What's it like?"

"Tell you another time."

The dream came that night to Ray. Blue sky over a blue ocean in the early morning. Peace over the sea waters, quiet over the little hook-shaped island where the hidden enemy waited. Then suddenly smoke over the island, black puffs of smoke over the ships. Planes sweep in; a wing on one plane droops and sags and the plane makes a crash landing. Four men jump out of the plane, precisely in time for two bursting bombs near them, and drop to the ground. One with feet on the face of another one who cries, "Take your damned feet off my face."

And to Ray when he came out of this dream in a sweat soaking his green-striped pajama coat, one oddity was that he had in fact and reality been flung on his back on the ground with his shoes on the forehead and chin of another man—but the other man couldn't talk and Ray couldn't have heard if the other man had talked.

He got into a dry pajama coat, went to Mimah's room and slid quietly into the bed to hear her sleepy, "You had the dream, didn't you?"

"Yes."

"Please, how did it go?"

"I was riding a white horse up and down the Rocky Mountains and it was lonely and I rode the white horse a thousand miles and it got more lonely, for it was desert country and I could hear kiyotes yowling in the night when the moon came up and they made me more lonesome than ever. We were crossing Nevada and we came to a stretch of desert where the moon poured down a drenching white-silver light and the horse seemed galloping along on soft clouds, nice riding. Then up from the clouds and right in our path stood something red, a bright red that stopped us. It was a tall skinny woman in a red silk dress, good to look at for all she was skinny. She was asking for a ride. She was saying, 'Why can't I get on behind and ride?' I asked her why couldn't she walk. She said half-crying, 'My feet hurt, you don't know how my feet hurt.' So I told her to climb on and she was there in a jiffy. I asked her name. She said, 'Maria Enders, Miss Maria Enders.' And the way she came down heavy on the 'Miss' and wanting me to know in particular she was a Miss, I came right out with it and said, 'How about a kiss, how about it?' And there the dream ended and I don't know now whether I ever got the kiss."

They lay looking up at the vague dark blur of the ceiling. From Mimah's lips, after an interval of quiet, came a prolonged, "Whee—ew!" and her voice low and husky, "You're a liar and a fool and you know you got one kiss and you're good for more."

Chapter 7

Home from the Meat-Grinder

RAY woke from his afternoon sleep the next day to see Mimah standing by. "Slicked up you are, Sugarpuss. Can't be my birthday?"

"Good woman coming to see us."

"Good woman might be who? Could be Mary Liebowitz?"

"Bright boy this afternoon," said Mimah, seating herself on the bed. " 'On the distaff side, as they say, we come from the London riffraff rather than the Leyden elect, and the records indicate one of our women was publicly rebuked for the offense termed Unlawful Maternity, the baby arriving three months too soon. Our line seems to favor much love and many babies.' " Bowbong had heard this from Mary Liebowitz and liked quoting it.

After Vassar graduation Mary put in four years moving up from stenographer to confidential secretary to an oil-corporation executive. In those years the sweetheart letters ran long and came often between her and Abel Liebowitz. He was redhaired with a naïve full-mouthed grin, slow-spoken, sober, steady, a short broad-shouldered deep-chested Lithuanian Jew born in New York's swarming East Side. For his meals turning pancakes in the street window of a restaurant having pride in its pancakes, for his room rent tending a coal furnace, he worked his way to a Ph.D. at the University of Michigan, later earning a name in the field of bacteriology, once writing Mary, "I am having fun with fungus." Their three sons and three daughters had pranked with Justice Windom, pulled his hair, rode on his back, and begged him to make faces they liked. Bowbong found the Liebowitz house rocking with fellowship, clean laughter, books, scholarship and a questing for ideas. Mary sometimes quoted a Vassar chum with six little ones doing well in a house in Winnetka, Illinois: "My children are bright as bastards because each one is a love child."

Now two of the Liebowitz daughters had husbands in overseas service. One Liebowitz son in the Normandy beach landings took two light wounds, another was assigned to chemical-warfare research, and a third son, Albert, they buried with military honors in Arlington. Mary had told Ray before the war began, "I'm for the war but more than anything else I don't want any of my boys killed." Ray had answered, "Your kind of honesty, I'm for it."

Mary Liebowitz came in, an elder before Mimah and Ray. What shone from Mary was something like charm yet deeper and more constant. Perhaps it could be that the great love and understanding she had always tried to share with her children now reached out to all others she met. That vaguely was Mimah's feeling. Mary was the Gibson Girl, the Harrison Fisher Girl, of the magazine illustrations of a previous era, not so tall, now more fully rounded, and on the regularly featured loveliness of the face a quaint homeliness super-imposed, some quality of the best gleam of each of her children etched and lined on her face.

Roundabout it had come to Ray and Mimah that Mary Liebowitz had a "heart condition," the doctor saying, "You might go any min-ute, you mustn't walk upstairs or uphill, if you can avoid it, and when walking save your breath and talk as little as possible, for it can affect the heart." Now Ray and Mimah saw her, with her burdens and heavy griefs, a creature of animation and will.

The three in chairs on the back porch, Ray spoke of news soon to come, bloody struggle, the American forces in their landing invasion of Japan itself. "Ten times what Okinawa cost and I hate to think about it," said Ray. Mary had heard an army officer, "Italy all over again, tougher going and longer. The Japs know their home mountain terrains like the Krauts never knew Italy."

Mimah shivered and a slant of pain ran over the pale oval of her face. Ray seemed fairly calm, for him, but she feared the impact on him of the terrific immensity of what was being said. Her thin wide lips set wider. She listened and watched the fine composure of Ray as he put quiet questions to Mary. Mary's eyes of gray-and-blue agate held a mild flash as she had let him know, "With what you have been through you're free to ask me about anything I've been through." Mimah saw in them a kinship of the desperate and her tight anxiety let down a few notches.

Nearly three years now since the Arlington burial of Mary's boy Albert, a graduate of Massachusetts Institute of Technology in aeronautical engineering, killed in a test flight over Boston Harbor. "Nine of his classmates came down to see him buried," said Mary, "nine of the finest American boys you ever saw. They made the night ride from Boston in crowded day coaches, sleeping sitting up, arriving in Wash-ington and straight out to Arlington for the ceremony and the bugler blowing taps and lights out, then the day coaches back to Boston, all nine of them, grand young men, clean serious beautiful young fellows, on a day leave to see their comrade buried with military honors in the National Cemetery. You've heard it, Ray, how they say 'the pick and flower of American youth'—that's what they were. Their training had hardened them, they could carry on with quiet dignity, no cheap fool-ing, no false notes. They had respect and love for each other. You could see it. It is a thing you have seen as Captain Windom, and I'm sure you know it more intimately than I do. Once seen it can never be forgotten. It stays in your deepest memories."

Mimah noticed Ray slowly closing his eyes, his underlip moving out and returning.

Mary went on. "That was near three years ago." Then her voice took on a faintly shaded tremolo. "And now what? Now two of those nine are dead in Italy, two in Germany, one in the Aleutians, one at Iwo Jima."

Mary paused. Her right-hand fingers closed and a thumb moved over two of the fingers. She held the thumb over a first-finger knuckle and went on, tremulous shadows in her voice. Ray saw an almost invisible film of tears over the gray-blue agate of her eyes while her mouth held a brave mocking smile as though she could cry but wouldn't give way. "Of those nine shining boys I saw when the bugle blew taps, lights out, three are alive. Two of those three on combat duty, they will be in the umbrella of planes over the landing invasion of Japan. That leaves one of the nine to be accounted for, alive after a long recovery. Early in the Pacific fighting he lost a leg and an eye."

Ray straightened swiftly, sat up stiff and aware. "That last fellow— I must know him."

"You do?"

"I know a good M.I.T. man who lost a good leg and eye. He was in my squadron."

"Johnny Avolo?"

"That's him, short-looking, hunched shoulders, black eyes and shaggy black eyebrows." And Mary and Ray were both murmuring at the same moment, "Johnny Avolo."

Ray's eyes had a burning quest in them as they peered into the woman's eyes. Tears now ran down her face. Ray turned to see tears coursing down Mimah's cheeks.

"Yes, Johnny Avolo," Ray took up as a cue given him and there was fate in it. Ray's hands shook, a malarial relic Mimah had not seen in months. He looked at his hands, then his face and body at an effort of will or an exercise he had practiced slunk into an easy sag. The hand-trembling ceased. "Yes," Ray went on. "His father came over from Italy at sixteen, ran a garage in a country town in Ohio. The boy worked his way through Antioch College and finished just before he went to M.I.T."

"Ugly at first sight," said Mary, "then less ugly the more you look at him, a crooked mouth with a grin you can't resist."

"That's Johnny," said Ray. "It sticks with me what he told about his father. It happened in 1941, a few months before Pearl Harbor. A farmer, by the name of Jones we'll say, came into the garage for truck repairs. While Johnny's father crawled around on the fixing job Jones kept making remarks about the war in Europe away off, no business of ours, we better keep out of it. And Johnny Avolo's father got tired of these remarks after a while and dropped his tools and stood up facing the farmer and said, 'Mr. Jones, I know Europe, I have lived in Europe and I know what they do to people over there. I don't want to see it in this country. I'm ready to fight Hitler now. I don't want to see his crowd put their feet in this country next. If you knew Europe like I do, Mr. Jones, you would go home and kneel down by the barn and kiss the manure pile!' "

Silence came, broken by six bombers in formation. And in the quiet afterward the quarrels of four wrens in a cedar came clear on the air. Then Ray was saying, "I wish Bowbong could have heard Johnny tell that. He would have liked Johnny's father." And looking into Mary Liebowitz's face, "You've got the rugged stuff of the Avolos. You set me dreaming. I forgot to tell you I get letters from Johnny. His glass eye has been put in. It's the left eye. He says now he won't have to shut it when taking aim. Says he's coming this way for a few days and it might be next week. I'll let you know. That crooked-mouth grin of his, those shaggy black eyebrows and darting black eyes of his— they'll be good for all of us, I know."

They drifted into talk about how the war, the first truly global conflict, had begun, how leaders and supposedly responsible and informed men in nearly every nation at war had said before the shooting started, "There will be no war," and giving their reasons why there would be no war. Yet the war had come. And those men, those leaders and their opinions, now looked not merely silly but idiotic.

The peace after the war, what would it be like? Mimah asked. She had heard about an outer ship in a convoy. "It was camouflaged, painted cleverly, to look as though it was going in the opposite direction. Sailing east it seemed to be headed west."

Mary had heard from a Quaker friend of a legend, a folk tale, passed from mouth to mouth in Europe, printed in the fugitive journals of the Underground. Into a solemn ceremonial service in the Cologne cathedral had walked the high Leader of the Nazis, the author of *Mein Kampf,* with his guards. From the altar steps the minister spoke saying that all who had a Jew for their father must leave the church. Along the aisles to the door moved a score or so. Next came the edict that each having a Jewish grandfather must leave and a half-dozen or more trickled out. Then came the stern pronouncement, "All who have a Jewess for their mother must leave the church." Then from the cross behind the altar where the human form had been nailed with bleeding palms and ankles, with blood-matted hair over the forehead, there stepped down the silent majestic Christ figure, moving in a fantasy almost unbelievable down the wide center aisle and slowly out of the great front door.

"My Quaker friend said the story ends too abruptly," said Mary. "She asked, 'Where did Christ go?' She could see wild winds howling over Europe after the war, more faith and consecration than ever, more ashes and filth and despair than ever before. She could only be sure it wouldn't be the old Europe, never again the old Europe, and the new Europe perhaps worse, perhaps better, than the old."

They phoned for a taxi, saw Mary into it, Ray saying, "We'll tell you when Johnny Avolo comes."

When Ray came down for breakfast the next morning he found Mimah had done the cooking and the maid had phoned she was going to a job at forty-two dollars a week in an airplane plant near Baltimore. "For lunch, if you approve," said Mimah, "I'll fix you some eggs with minced Spam and—"

"You will not," said Ray with a snort.

"Why so? I tried to get ham, but it's scarce these days."

"Listen, honey my sweet, the navy cooks fed us Spam mixed with everything you can think of. O Spam, what crimes have been committed in thy name! They were a long time learning some of us could only eat Spam straight. For the sake of peace in the household don't mince the Spam flavor with the egg taste."

"Okay, boss," said Mimah with a grin and a gay light kiss. "And it'll be all right if I shell some fresh peas and boil them tenderly and scrape some carrots for the pressure cooker?"

"You're stepping on it," grinned Ray. "You're in there pitching with all you've got. I wouldn't trade you for all the oil in Texas."

"Mary Liebowitz was good for you, wasn't she?"

"Her and Johnny Avolo coming soon. They've had their ears knocked down by the war, been through the meat-grinder and it don't get 'em down—that helps."

Ray drove away in their car for two little errands at the Pentagon and hoping for a look-in on Abel Liebowitz in a bacterial-warfare laboratory.

Mimah went into a blue streak. "Have I had my ears knocked down by the war? Have I been through the meat-grinder?" She felt a humiliation over what Mary Liebowitz and Johnny Avolo had with relation to Ray that she didn't have. She had done her best. Circumstance had not allowed her to show her best, hadn't put her on the spots that might have made her completely a war chum of Ray.

She had heard a Negro last winter, "I got the drismals." Now with a little groan, "I got the drismals." And with an added little groan, "I'm shrunk to where I could take a bath in a fountain pen." She nearly smiled at this and realized that the very insignificance she felt about herself was a kind of help and she hadn't reached bottom in "drismals." She carried a kitchen stool and a large pan of carrots and peas-in-the-pod out on a porch that ran sidewise of the kitchen on the east side. Around the corner from where she placed the stool and sat shelling peas ran the rear side of the porch on the south side. She had shelled perhaps a pint of peas when she heard steps in the kitchen, heard the back screen door slam shut, heard chairs drawn on the back porch, then the voices of two men, one of them Ray's and the other one she had never heard.

She heard Ray's voice, "Now you're a hero—so what?" And the laughing answer, "The doctors got me recapped and retreaded. The war make a bum out of me? Not with this plexiglas eye."

"You could always tell 'em where to head in," Ray said.

"I'd like to tell you where to head in once."

Then Ray rather soberly, "Let me have a squint here."

Ray had a long squint. "They both look the same, dandy work, nice work." Ray seemed to be still squinting. He chuckled. "Damned if I can tell which of your two eyes is human."

Mimah, slowly and absently shelling peas, dropped what was in her hands into the pan and said under her breath, "Johnny Avolo—came sooner than expected."

She was about to place pan and peas on the floor and walk around the corner. Then her new humility and "drismals" worked on her. She would let the two chums go on without her, saying, but not out loud, "Have I had my ears knocked down by the war? What do I know about the meat-grinder?" She went on slowly, absently, shelling peas—and listening.

She heard Ray telling Johnny of the visit with Mary yesterday, some of it cold and hard to Johnny, who hadn't met the news of so many of his old M.I.T. bunch having their numbers called and "lights out." For a while Ray had nothing to say nor had Johnny. Then Ray gave Mary's Quaker story of the Christ figure sliding down from the cross and walking out of the cathedral and the Quaker woman wanting to know, "Where did Christ go?" and Johnny abruptly, "Do you know, Ray, my father, me pappy in his Ohio garage, would be asking that? And I'm asking, where did Christ go after He walked out of that big front door?"

The two veterans took up the landing invasion soon expected in Japan, threshed it out from many angles, agreed it would be harder and longer than Italy before they could begin mopping-up operations on that main home island of the Nipponese. They had been reading in the news about a Nazi concentration camp at Manthausen where in one hundred and twenty-three hours two hundred and three persons died one after the other. "The camp register had 'em all dying of the same thing, heart trouble," said Ray. "Kind uh monotonous."

"Yes," said Johnny, "and it was funny, too, they died in alphabetical order."

"The Abrahamsons first, I suppose, and the Zachariahs last," said Ray. He brought a clipping from a hip pocket. "A review of a book by a correspondent we came near meeting in the Pacific, a book about the numbers racket, *Tucker's People*. Bowbong would say it was writ sarcastical and bass ackwards. Bowbong would have liked this, the same as your father:

". . . put your hand out when making a turn. Stop clear of the crosswalk. Honor thy father and mother. Do not talk to the operator while car is in motion. Ask for transfer when paying fare. Spit in your handkerchief. Throw waste in the basket. Love thy neighbor if he's not a Catholic or a Jew or a Seventh Day Adventist or a nigger or a greaser or a ginzo or a hunkie or a bohunk or a frog or a spick or a limey or a heinie or a mick or a chink or a Jap or a Dutchman or a squarehead or a mockie or a slicked-up greaseball from the Argentine, or if he don't scratch himself too loud, or if to love him doesn't cost anything."

"I'll have to send that to my pappy," said Johnny Avolo.

They spoke briefly of Mimah and the baby, Ray as though repeating what he had said in the ride from the Pentagon, "It's great luck, sweet luck, I have them." A hummingbird poised with whirring wings before a trumpet-vine blossom, flashed its long beak into the blossom cup· and again hung poised and watching. "There's the helicopter," said Ray, "the original model." The hummingbird streaked away. They watched buzzing gnats in and out of a blossom cup and it reminded them of Guadalcanal insects, "those mosquitoes, you remember," said Johnny, "and guys saying some of them so particular they lifted up your dogtag to see what blood type you were before they'd try a bite of you." They recalled Marines coming out of weeks of fighting, men and boys who had gone in lean and hard from training and they came out averaging twenty-six pounds of weight loss. One of these Marine outfits had to live for days on rations captured from the Japs. " 'Chocolate like lead for our daily bread and worms in the rice for meat,' " Ray quoted a Marine poet. Johnny remembered only the first line of a song Ray had from Bowbong. Ray with a laugh gave one verse:

> "My Lilla is gentle and fair,
> My Lilla is merry and true—
> Half-dying with love,
> I ate up her glove,
> And drank my champagne from her shoe."

Johnny laughed and there was a pause and Johnny mentioned a case he had seen and they talked about it only in quiet in the hospital. "The poor guy could never again really sleep with a woman. He used to write letters regular to a girl back home. Nobody dared talk about what he would be writing her." Johnny changed the subject suddenly. "We learned the difference between a prostitute and a prosthetist. The fellow who fixes you out with a new leg he's a prosthetist. And what I've got on my stump here is a prosthesis. I'm proud of it. They're smart birds. Give 'em leather and aluminum and what they can do with it! I can dance—would you believe it? Not jive, no boogie-woogie, but a nice slow waltz or a rhumba not played too fast." And

Johnny was saying, "It's good, bejesus, to see you all in one piece, Captain Windom. It's good to be sitting here with you this pretty day shooting the breeze, chewing the fat." And Johnny spoke of how few cases there were of the jerk, the goldbrick, the chicken, "the guy just naturally yellow." Ray was putting in nothing, letting Johnny ramble. Johnny mentioned a Marine he heard, "Anybody who says he wasn't near cracking up on Guadalcanal is a goddamned liar." There was silence a minute or two. Johnny mentioned sodium pentathol. "They told me about it. They use it in bad cases where a man has cracked up. They inject it in your veins and you're hypnotized and you tell anything you ever did and they get a line on you and how to handle your case." There was silence for three or four minutes. Mimah wondered what was passing over their faces—it seemed ominous.

Johnny spoke, rather suddenly, with an ugly twang. "Well, what is it? Spill it."

Ray cut out with a keen low wail. "Goddammit, I want you to know I'm ashamed to be here—ashamed, I say. Night and day I keep saying I belong out there with the boys."

"Yeah," came Johnny's voice with the ugly twang. "I expected it. You damn fool, you need thirty pounds at least before you're fit for combat. You couldn't do right if you went back like you are now. So you pity yourself. So you shame yourself. We heard about it—the doctors. And the boys don't like it. It hurts."

"You got the go-sign," muttered Ray. "Pour it on."

"You went down with malaria. We saw you come back sooner than you should with that tremble in your hands. You should have taken two more weeks or a month. Can't you give 'em credit for having your number? They saw you in one jam down three planes by your lonesome. They saw you get out of your plane and keel over with blood down your face and you had a head wound over your right ear and you come back in five weeks with a grin on your face, your nice wavy black hair covering the scar. Only your wife and us guys know about that scar the hair covers. Then came that crash landing with both wheels gone. Four of us stepped out of that plane alive. All the boys know what happened. It's in the record. Two bombs dropped ten and fifteen yards away, two of the four killed. You went down from the explosion, a shock to your guts and every nerve center of your body. They picked you up for dead and you hadn't been scratched. But you laid flat, paralyzed and half-alive for days—concussion syndrome they called it and some of the best-by-test fighters have had it."

Johnny's voice lost its ugly twang for a moment. "They lifted your feet off my face that time, yes, your dirty shoes right on my bloody face. I would have told you to take them off if I had known about it." And with deliberation Johnny went on in a sharp-edged tone of com-

1047

mand and rebuke. "One day they got anxious about me. Maybe I had a psychoneurosis, what they named it. That's a hummer. I rolled it around my tongue—I said 'psychoneurosis and it's crap, eyewash, scuttlebutt,' I was just worrying, just plain troubled in my mind about how to get along with a leg and eye gone. The Doc saw I didn't have either psycho or neurosis, it was plain old-fashioned anxiety boring in with a heavy auger. The Doc liked me. He liked you. He said you could lick the concussion syndrome but you were a sucker for guilt complex. You hadn't done right by your boys—yeah. You could have done it better—yeah. And I come here and accidentally meet you in the Pentagon and I see you haven't licked it yet. Can't you see the boys know you and they'd bear down heavy on any bastard sayin Ray Windom is, sittin out the war?"

The mean whiplash tone was gone from Johnny's voice. Now it bordered on a subdued cry of pain.

"I suppose you know," Ray put in softly and near a caress, "I wouldn't take this from anybody but you."

"You'd take it from any of the men—it's their idea I should tell you," said Johnny. "You need this information. You better listen. I came East on two counts. One was to see my girl in Boston. She says she'll go through with it and marry me like she promised before the war. But a couple of times we're having fun and what does she do? She breaks down and cries like I never thought a woman could cry. I say to myself three times and she's out. If she pulls that crybaby act again I'll tell her off, she needs a guy all there. Second, I came East to tell you every last man in the old squadron loves you, from the ground up loves you. When some of them say, 'That lousy sonofabitch Windom, why don't he get over it?' it's because they love you and they're worrying. I'll skip it, except to say the old glad hand, the real thing, is there for you. Some of them heard your grandfather's broadcast and you could hear them, 'No wonder Ray is sensitive about the war and his record, growing up with that kind of a grandpappy.' You forget about them needing you, hear me? You get your old weight back. You let the doctors give you the go-sign. For myself, for Johnny Avolo who has had your feet on his face, I'm saying you bitch your own game if you let this guilt complex ride you. You can worry. I hope you worry. I'd like to think of you worrying. But don't let me hear you again you pity yourself and you're ashamed of yourself. You got no right to this pity and shame, with your record. It's the crap."

A long pause and then Ray's voice, "Through, Johnny?"

"If there was more I'd let you have it."

"You're good for me, Johnny. I've made headway, I can tell you. It used to be a lot worse. Could be you've seen the last of it."

It was at this moment of Ray's words that the two veterans heard a peculiar clang and clatter, then a soft thud. Ray sprang in the direction of it. Around the corner, on the side porch, Ray saw an overturned tin pan, scattered carrots, peas, and pods, and on the porch floor lay Mimah crumpled and still, lying partly on one side with an arm flung out, her dress over her knees, her face pale-white and eyes closed. Ray ran into the kitchen, turned a faucet till cold water came, ran to her with a bowl of water he sprinkled with his fingers over her face. Slowly her eyes opened. Ray took her by the shoulders, Johnny the knees, and they carried her to a davenport in the big front room. Ray saw that all the windows were opened, then seated himself at Mimah's side and took one of her hands.

After a few minutes her eyes opened wide and her tongue moved over her lips and a smile came and she said, "I guess for the first time in my life, Ray, I fainted."

"I guess you did, sweetheart."

"I went out there to shell peas and scrape carrots. I did shell and scrape. I went on shelling and scraping and everything was quiet and then came voices. I didn't belong. They had been consecrated as I never have been. They have lived in a fiery furnace I will never know, never can know. I tried to pull myself up to go away. But I couldn't. What they talked about was terrible and marvelous and awful and sacred. It swept over me and I blacked out, like you fellows say." She smiled again. "My first faint, Ray, and I hope my last." She reached a hand toward Johnny Avolo standing near and he took her hand. "I'll call you Johnny and you call me Mimah, like Ray."

Ray gave her a long soft kiss, saying, "I never loved you so much, if you want to know." She stood up, put her arms in those of the two men and walked with them to the back porch. "You walk beautiful, Johnny," she said with a grave mouth and eyes.

"I don't kid myself," he said soberly.

"I'm not kidding. I'll bet you can waltz and like it."

"You'd win your bet," said Johnny. "I'll dance with you any time." Then came over his crooked mouth the grin that Mary Liebowitz had said "you can't resist."

Mimah searched keenly at his two black eyes and only by a faint line of scar tissue around one of them could she make a guess which was the one science had provided.

She walked the two veterans out to Remembrance Rock and had Ray tell Johnny of the dreamdust placed there and how Bowbong alive had been shy about it. While Ray spoke Johnny took off his cap, held it in his two hands, his head bowed. Mimah couldn't take her eyes off his face, his jaw heavy, his nose and mouth crooked, a granitic calm over him, and Mimah saying to herself, "How can a face be so homely and lovely at once?" She knew by Ray's squeeze of her arm that he was reading the same and wanted her to know. "I think he would," Johnny was saying. "My father would be like to cry here."

Seated between them on the back porch, Mimah finished shelling peas and scraping carrots, then fixed lunch with the Spam distinctly separate from the eggs. She helped the nursemaid with Joe Stilwell, watched Ray and Johnny lazying on the grass near Remembrance Rock, later put on the "Missouri Waltz" and went round and round with Johnny Avolo and Ray. And she phoned Mary Liebowitz to come this evening or tomorrow any time, as Johnny Avolo was staying overnight at Hopecrest. "How is Johnny looking?" said Mimah at the phone. "Come and see. That grin of his, you were correct, you can't resist it, it's out of this world."

* * * * * * * * * *

Chapter 8

* * * * * * * * * *

Dream Night at Hopecrest

AUGUST 6, 1945, and four hundred planes swept over southern Kyushu of Japan, their bombs shattering the munition plants of Tarumizu. On the same day of August 6, 1945, a lone Superfortress over the coast of Honshu turned in its course to cross its target, a city of three hundred and forty-three thousand people—and let go one bomb. Down the skyway the bomb started while the Superfortress crew followed instructions, "Scram! Get the hell out of here!" The seconds passed, nearly a minute, eight seconds short of a minute, fifty-two seconds exactly—then the bomb went off. In a quiet flash more dazzling than sunlight it broke over the city of three hundred and forty-three thousand people. A column, a cloud, an umbrella of dust, smoke and chaos, rose, mushroomed and spread. Two-thirds of the city laid level and wiped out in wreck and ruin, the human corpses seventy thousand, the sick, wounded and disabled twice as many as the dead—this foreshadowed what? Hiroshima, the city's name in the news, from then on had only the unknowing, the dumb and comfortable of the round world, saying, "So what?" Weird and creepy with its "nuclear fission," "chain reaction," "radioactivity," the Atomic Bomb struck all men and women of thought and imagination as a foretokening, a dividing line beyond denial, a punctuation absolute in its queries, "Where to? What next?" A legend arose, an anecdote, of the radio operator on the lone Superfortress with orders to report what he saw of the first performance on earth of an atomic bomb. And he could only sit at the transmitter murmuring, "Oh my God, oh my God, oh my God."

The Japanese surrendered. The people's V-J Day came August 14. Nils Rolstadt telephoned Ray and Mimah he was coming over to see them. He arrived to tell them he had from month to month informed Bowbong, his old and trusted friend, of every development coming to his knowledge in the making of the atomic bomb. Rolstadt and his son Hilmer had worked in researches and experiments assigned to them. The intimate relation of their findings to those of other physicists, lifelong friends, had kept them rather close to the achieved results of the project. The Rolstadts knew the approximate time the wanted bomb would be ready for use. The elder Rolstadt handed Ray the memorandum entrusted to him from Bowbong. Ray glanced at the paper and put it in Mimah's hands. She read aloud:

"Dearest Ray and Mimah—You have heard. The news has come. You and Ray share it. You watch its awful impact. Now you see the human family moves out into a fresh adventure. Will it end in a smoking day of doom or a bright dawn of promise?

"You too may consider that for a long time there have been men and women wearing a faith that made them unafraid of a Judgment Day, the Doomsday Book opened, man's life on the earth come to an end. That Last Day, as men visioned it, was to come from the Hand of God. Now, however, do men foresee a new modern up-to-the-minute Day of Doom which, should it arrive, will be from the Hand of Man?

"In the changed world you now enter, my children, armies and navies as we have known them will vanish. The science of mass manslaughter will be statistical and in split seconds, now you see a city and now you don't.

"And in this possible next war, incalculable in speed and finality, the brave man vanishes, the action ending before he has a chance to be brave—valiant and coward, women and babies, sick or idiot, strong heart and faint, go down in one wide kinship of annihilation.

"My friend Rolstadt told me of this event while it was preparing. He can tell you of round-the-earth rockets, of cosmic-ray experiments, of biological warfare, each as ghastly in its potentials as the Atomic Bomb.

"Indeed a changed world you enter, my young dear ones. Now a war can begin before it is declared. When the blights and epidemics commence and the crops fail and the deaths run into millions it will be understood the next war has begun with no certainty who has begun it. To this have we come."

"Would you like a drink, Mr. Rolstadt?" Ray asked. No, Rolstadt was hearing this for the first time. "I brought this paper to you sealed as he gave it to me. I hear Bowbong's voice in it." Rolstadt spoke with a quaver of care and anxiety. Mimah read on:

"The men of science in all nations shared their findings. When at last they shattered the atom and divided the hitherto indivisible, it was a joint international accomplishment. A long exploration began centuries ago and then arrived at its goal. They stood before it saying precisely what free men have on occasion said of their freedom, 'Oh God, now that we have it what shall we do with it?' They were pilgrims who had toiled to a far height to find themselves on a path skirting a precipice and only the strong, only the hairy and hard and strong, could look with calm and ease down into the unfathomable pits of gray mist and rolling black clouds below the steep edge where their feet clung."

Mimah paused, her eyes closed for a moment. "I think he was writing at this the day he asked me if I had heard a voice down the hallway calling 'Telegram, telegram for Mr. Justice Windom.' I guess with what he was seeing ahead for this world he had a right to be hearing strange voices." She read on:

"Long ago Noah saw what was coming and built himself an Ark. But whatever Ark will now save mankind must be built of materials not yet in view. Man must find new materials and shape an Ark never yet seen on this earth.

"Man goes on, my loved ones. Man does not stop. Often I heard Rolstadt, 'Man is a changer. God made him a changer.' It is within possibility that you, my dear ones—and when I say my dear ones I include my important and living grandson, little Joseph Stilwell Windom—you may become the witnesses of the finest and brightest era known to mankind. You shall have music, the nations over the globe shall have music, music instead of murder. It is possible. That is my hope and prayer—for you and for the nations. Now I bid you farewell and say Amen."

Then came his bold sweeping signature in full, Orville Brand Windom, and in tiny printed letters in parenthesis the nickname, Bowbong.

Pete came in. His usual slouch had an added easier roll to it. Mimah said, "You're not jingled, but you *are* feeling pretty good."

"An afternoon with a couple of 82nd Airborne boys a trifle damaged in the well-known war. We thought V-J Day worth two or three toasts and the atomic bomb five or six. We lifted a few to the next war. It'll be a honey, sister. What they say is, the whistle will blow and there won't be time to ring the bell."

"I'll get you black coffee," said Mimah, and gave him Bowbong's memorandum to read. She returned after a time with Scotch and soda for Ray, coffee for Rolstadt and Pete, a bottle of beer for herself, rye bread, Camembert and Cheddar cheese, pickled herring, salted pecans as wanted.

"Kinda wonderful," said Pete, reading the memorandum a second time. "He's really on the beam, the old bird."

"I asked Ann, she'll be in soon and read it when you're through. She's staying overnight. Says she might be heading for a job in Chicago or on the West coast next week."

"It's news. Maybe for the best." And Pete was neither cold nor warm about it, casual as before.

Rolstadt was meditative, sipping his coffee, trailing in the wake of Bowbong's hopes and prayers. "The poor Japs," he said. "We hated them different from the Nazis. They gave us no *Mein Kampf* to understand them better. Now for them and for us, for Germany, Britain and Russia, for Europe and the world, comes a new future."

Mimah heard the doorbell, met Ann Flaherty in the hall, and in their little talk spoke of Pete's face. "Twenty-eight operations in two years, Ann. And now nearly as good as new. He showed me today. A few weeks, he says, and the mask and goggles come off."

"God, that's lovely to hear," came Ann's throaty whisper. "We can see his eyes again." Her finger ends dug into Mimah's arm.

Ann entered the room, nodded to Ray and Rolstadt, took a chair next to Pete, whose goggles seemed to move in slow ranges over Ann from head to hips to knees to toes. Pete mumbled a vague something. Ann was going to ask him to repeat but let it pass. She looked translucent as a blue cloud, her face smooth as a white pebble under clear running water, wearing a light-blue gown that held the snug and even flow of her curves from shoulders to knees.

Mimah poured Rolstadt a second cup of coffee. He drank half of it, put the cup on the table, munched at rye bread and Camembert, and went on as though he had before him one of the University of Chicago classes he used to teach. "Never before such a world storm—and never before any one man or captain of men so insignificant before its sweeping immensity. The First World War was a prelude to the Second and a part of it. The future comes toward us, not creeping, but rushing. Like a breath on a high wind tomorrow will be here before we know it. Epics of the past are dull compared with what our eyes have seen these three years."

Rolstadt's eyes ranged to Ray and then to Pete. Mimah had shown Rolstadt the manuscripts of Books One, Two, and Three, saying he must read them. "Bowbong told me they were about the American Dream and he would try to show people who made that dream have meaning here and the world over. We had long easy talks. I had science for him. He had politics for me. Together we had much that was human. Once I asked him to clarify the American Dream. I think it was about like this." Rolstadt threw back his head, studied the ceiling and recited:

" 'Some sacred seed lurks deep in each human personality, no matter how lowly its arrival on earth. To give any such seed the deepest possible roots and the highest possible flowering is in the vision and hope of those ideas of freedom and discipline that constitute the American Dream.' "

Rolstadt remembered how Bowbong after this dreamy talk stiffened up and spoke sharp, "It's only a whiff, I haven't caught it and no man ever will, it's too chaotic. It takes in all humanity."

Rolstadt rose to go, stood before Pete for a handshake, peering up into the blue-goggled face. When he took Ray by the hand, Mimah saw on the scientist's face a gravity she read as having a reverence for the two young men. To Ray he said, "Bowbong talked about you the last time I saw him. I think you know what he said." Ray said he could pretty well guess. And in the momentary smile on Ray's face Mimah could see a clean bright boyish streak out of earlier days. It gave her a tingle. From day to day Ray was feeling less useless. She spoke of this to Rolstadt, at the door, thanking him as he left.

Through the evening it wasn't easy for the two couples. Pete seemed the least troubled of the four. Ray had begun to join Mimah in her feeling that Pete was making his break with Ann too hard for her. They were afraid they caught a touch of the wanton and cruel in his casual manner toward her.

After dinner and random talk that got nowhere, they put on gutbucket blues, symphonies of Sibelius and César Franck, a Shostakovich concerto. These helped little. At ten o'clock Ann said she would be going to bed.

With a grumbled and half-defiant good night, Pete at the door of his room said to Mimah, "If I ever marry, and no matter who, I will live alone and so will she. I think I'm learning to live alone and like it."

Ray before kissing Mimah good night and going to his room had said, "I feel Bowbong around the place. In every room I feel him. I almost get his voice."

They could hear a light rain falling. Later it came heavy with crashes of thunder. Then followed a quiet aftermath where the ear had to listen twice to catch the little hushed drips of water at roof and eaves, from leaves and branches.

It was dream night at Hopecrest. About an hour before daybreak Ray in his white pajamas striped wide with green came into Mimah's room in the dark and crept into bed to find her wide-awake like himself and in tears. "The awfullest dream I ever had," she sobbed.

"I dreamed too, and not so bad," said Ray, "though it got me awake and I haven't slept for hours."

"Tell me your dream and see if I forget mine." Ray had heard horns blowing a fanfare. In his dream he saw a book tall and wide as Hopecrest house. A voice announced, "We give you the Living Book—out of yesterday—yet alive today!" A big hand reached out and turned pages. A young woman stepped out from one page. She had Mimah's oval face, the skin drawn tight over high cheekbones, thin wide lips parting over marvelously even teeth, coils of chestnut hair with a bright burnish. But it wasn't Mimah. It was Mary Windling, speaking of her archangels and how they never failed her and would keep watch over her daughter Remember and the *Mayflower* Pilgrims in the new unknown world. Out of another page stepped Oliver Windrow pointing at his wood-carved Tower of Babel and his unfinished oaken head of Christ and what it needed and how he didn't have it. Orton Wingate, Resolved Wayfare with Ray Windom's face, Roger Williams, they spoke counsel and hope for the New World. The book shut tight. The big hand and reaching fingers opened it again. There was Ordway Winshore, his face and head the image of Bowbong, saying all was dark and men were slack in faith and yet light would break. Hard-worn as Ray Windom on his return from the Pacific there came Robert Winshore, gaunt with frozen feet at Valley Forge and then his sweetheart Mim, with Mimah's face, crouched on a floor with her hands toward a child toddling to her and Mim saying, "He shall see many dawns!" The book shut tight again. The big hand and reaching fingers opened it and from turning pages stepped out Mibs Wimbler, she too with Mimah's face, saying there must be either more love and understanding or a war of brothers would come crashing. Rodney Wayman, with Raymond Windom's own face, the black wavy hair, the jutting chin, in prison rags, scratching at his armpits and saying unconquered, "Honor is more than a word." Then a page later Omri Winwold, the image of Justice Orville Brand Windom, with the brick-dust hair, the craggy head, the wide slashed mouth, storm on one side of the face and peace on the other, Omri Winwold saying, "It is the divine privilege of any decent man to get drunk as a boiled owl if he sees a war coming and is helpless to stop it."

"I woke up in a sweat," said Ray. "Then when I couldn't sleep I had to come to you if only because Bowbong put your face and heart in all of the books."

Mimah had regained herself, the tears gone, no sobbing. "Your dream makes sense, mine doesn't." She began telling it. In her dream she saw a swaying mocking conventional Mephistopheles, his tail curling and winding, his feet cloven, horns on his head, slick black mustache and goatee, with fire and smoke from his mouth when he talked or didn't. "This is the way I am in the books and on the stage. You can look at me without turning away. I go like this to a party where people expect me to look like this. And then, dear lady, would you believe it, I have working clothes." Then she saw him, the Devil himself, sitting at a large square table in a tight black coat, immense shoulders, short gorilla neck, an enormous head entirely bald, a bland impassive face with a shark mouth shifting in a series of grins that gave off aurora-borealis splinters. The fish-belly white of his eyes changed to a sea-grotto green and a clay-umber. His small glittering eyes watched the table where he nodded and ships at sea went down, where he nodded and planes came toppling from the sky, where he nodded for a beach-head landing and licked his lips at piles of dead men. Then his arms swept the table clean and a great city stood plain with houses, streets, a traffic of people and carts and motorcars. Now he gave a long slow nod of his enormous bald head, wagged his right index finger, and a lone plane made its flight over the heart of the city, dropped a bomb that gave its flash, and under a mushrooming pall of dust and smoke, the city lay leveled in ruin, every wall tumbled, every last inhabitant dead. The enormous bald head on the short gorilla neck flung itself far back and out of the big open shark mouth, its upper and lower black teeth polished and gleaming, came a prolonged piercing howl of laughter. A tongue of yellow flame shot out in a long curve from the mouth roaring triumph. Next in her dream Mimah saw the fearsome huge blob of a figure at the table swiftly move into another change. He stood up from his chair a regular model handsome man, in tails, a wing collar and white tie. He was saying with a smile, "I look like a diplomat and per-haps I am. Why shouldn't the Devil himself look like a diplomat? And am I correct, dear lady, in saying," and his hand made a gesture over the ruined city, "this is the best yet, better than the Tower of Babel, better than Noah's Flood? Could I persuade you that it was I, Satan, the Archdemon, who decoyed man into making this latest, finest, surest device of wholesale death? My time has come. Now I wait to see how God will help man to save himself from this new master device of mine and fresh inventions to surpass it, more secret weapons to come."

Up till then, Mimah told Ray, the dream wasn't so bad and she could take it. Then again came the diplomat's smile, oily rather than gracious, and the figure in tails and white tie went into another change. The body slid down out of the clothes, vanished as another body wrig-gled in, tails and white tie replaced by a loose gray suit, and a short stocky figure and its face that of Nils Rolstadt. Tears rolled down his face and his choked voice and thick tongue shaped only the words, "O my God, O my God, why hast thou forsaken us?"

Ray's right arm was under Mimah's head and he was warm beside her, yet as she spoke, the final "forsaken us" came with a wail and a sob.

Ray was saying, "It is certainly dream night at Hopecrest." They talked of their dreams being creepy and weird and yet also they were close, warm, familiar in the stuff they were made of. Their talk had slowed down and they were going to try for sleep again when they heard a knock at the door. Pete came in, turned a light switch, stood before them in his orange pajamas, his blue goggles faced toward them peering. "I had to come and tell you. I went to sleep with the radio on, listening to a swing band, I don't know how long. I heard the music stop and a clammy goddam announcer telling the world one atomic bomb wiped out Boston, two gave the works to New York, Brooklyn and the Bronx. Said the Philadelphia station he was broadcasting from expected that city to go any minute, Washington to get it next. I dialed and got nothing, all stations dead. Then came over me what happened. I had gone to sleep and had a dream and woke up. I put my hand out and dialed. Here came the swing bands and the night-spot wrens chirping. Business as usual. Then I come and tell you. Why? It's an idea. It burns me. It could happen, some day, it might. Ain't it a cheerful world we got? We fight a war and get a peace mean as the war."

Pete had come to the bed and held Mimah's hand as he told it. "Ray says it's dream night at Hopecrest," said Mimah. "He had a nice one. Mine, Pete, was a pip, terrific as yours. You slide back to bed now. In the morning I'll spoil your breakfast with a cheerful earful, Pete."

Soon they were all lost in sleep, Mimah not mentioning to Ray the last bother of her mind while she was awake, "I wonder what Ann Flaherty drew on this night of dreams."

Mimah knocked softly on the door of Ann's room at seven-thirty in the morning. Hearing Ann's voice, "Come in," she opened the door. She kissed Ann, sat on the bed and told Ray's dream and Pete's, and, "Mine had a dirty flat dark-brown taste—in my mouth yet—wouldn't start your day with it, tell it later. And you—didn't you too ride a dream horse last night?"

"Of course, me too—but I flew with dream birds."

"How did it go?"

"Too good to be true, and then not so good."

Ann in her dream saw herself lying on the grass with Pete in a warm sun before Remembrance Rock. They looked up at blue sky with a single mass of rolling white cloud straight and high over them. "Me for the blue yonder, me with you," said Pete with the first real and sure sweetness she had heard from him since before the war. She answered, "I'm for you and the blue yonder." They watched the cloud mass change to a long horse with short legs, then roll and shift to a thick fat lamb with long legs, then in a slow breeze it spread wide into a flimmering shawl of silver-white. It was here they both fell asleep. She woke at a long deep kiss from Pete. They sat up with twined and caressing fingers, staring at Remembrance Rock, speaking to each other in low tones of the dust brought from far places over the globe and Bowbong's voice once, "I come here to remember."

While they stared, Ann in her dream saw the Rock open at its center, fall apart enough for a bluebird to come out and flutter, trying its wings, dropping to the ground, rising again to try its wings and this time finding them and with a wild wing whirr circling in a spiral, up and on till it was gone in the blue yonder. Pete said only, "Our luck bird?" and Ann, "Through the dark of those goggles I can see in your eyes you know it's our luck bird." They kept staring at the Rock. Two birds, a couple, came loose of whatever had held them in the Rock, two goldfinches, finding their wings right off and sailing in a spiral till they were lost in the blue yonder.

Remembrance Rock stood still a minute or two. Then it seemed the Rock gave birth to a big basket of birds it had held locked and waiting, juncos, wrens, redwings, scarlet tanagers, cardinals, the robin, the grosbeak, the catbird, garrulous bluejays, yellow canaries, unknown uncanny scavenger birds, two large lugubrious crows, kingfishers, teal, herons and cranes, white gulls, homing pigeons, a pair of mockingbirds gushing and trilling, and two lovebirds blue-white-and-red that sat a moment one on Pete's shoulder and one on Ann's before their wings fluttered and took off and away into the freedom of the blue yonder and the thin silver-white flimmer of the cloud shawl.

They sat staring at the Rock. They had seen it tremble as it opened and shook loose one of its many secrets; now again it stood locked, silent, inscrutable. Ann turned to Pete, a shudder running through her, "Is the show over?" And Pete's voice came casual, offhand, baffling again, even cold, "The show's over, it was worth the time."

Ann said to Mimah, "I woke up crying. For weeks I haven't cried, thought I had hold of myself. I head for Chicago tomorrow. Back home with father for a while, then maybe a job on the West coast, far from here."

Mimah sat on the bed, hunting for words to console, to heal. The words wouldn't come. A film of tears blurred her eyes. She lay down and threw her arm around Ann and they held each other. Ann broke away with a little laugh, pushed away sheet and blanket, jumped to the floor, and scampered to the bathroom.

Mimah waited, plucked at vague figures on a spread. Then she saw Ann come out of the bathroom carrying her pajamas, hanging them in a clothes closet and walking to throw on the bed her underthings, stockings, blouse, and skirt for the day.

Mimah leaped off the bed, stood before Ann, startled and wide-eyed, her eyes dropping from Ann's face and then shifting, scared and blinking, over Ann's scrawled body, shoulders to knees.

"Ann, you should have told me." The words seemed to choke and gag in her throat. "Good God, my sweet old friend, you should have told me."

"A hell of a thing to tell," said Ann with a cool smile. "A woman's a woman." And Ann was less cool and her full lips trembled as she took note of a flash of storm-green in the blue eyes of her old chum. By that flash of sea-tint she knew that a whirlwind of mixed anger, love and pity raged in Mimah.

Ann dressed. They went to breakfast. They saw Pete off for a consultation with his favorite Valley Forge surgeon, who was in Washington for the day. "Ann leaves with her father for Chicago tomorrow," Mimah had said to Pete, who was nearly gay in his answer, "We'll make it a farewell party this afternoon."

Morning passed into afternoon. Leading Pete and Ann to a davenport at a window corner overlooking the big rear yard, Ray and Mimah saw them seated and Mimah said, "Pete, if you're saying good-by to this old chum of mine this afternoon, I want you to know she's traveling on her nerve and she's a clean sport. Unless you get closer to her and give in a little she won't spill it to you, what's on her mind. She's lost about all except her face. She's made for you or she isn't. That's between the two of you. You notice I don't come in. But I can tell you, for sheer guts she's got it. For this once try and come off your high horse. Don't be so damned standoffish. Give her a break."

And Pete without a ruffle, "Okay, sure."

Ray and Mimah drove away for an hour, returned to see bottles of bourbon, fizz water and ginger ale on the table before Pete and Ann. Ray went out and brought in Joseph Stilwell Windom and they gave the fourth-generation Hopecrest heir a walking lesson. They put on records, Mimah hovered and flitted about, trying not to seem nosy, yet under her poised exterior anxious and shaken over whether a final farewell afternoon was on between Pete and Ann. She noticed Ann pouring smaller and fewer than Pete with the bourbon and Pete mildly jingled and taking more of his liquor straight. Not being a lip-reader she couldn't make out what Ann was hearing from Pete's mildly lush tongue, "Love is where two people smash into each other with the idea two bare legs and toes to toes makes a marriage, which it don't." With a pathetic boozy animation Pete was saying, "Love is where two people are hungry for something they don't know what it is but they're going to find out and when they do it's something else again." Pete thought this was keen and gave it the approval of such a smile as his not yet fully recovered face muscles would permit. Ann replied with a sad mouth, "Love is where two people lie and lie to each other about how much they mean to each other and when they run out of lies they put their love in a little coffin and bury it." Ann knew, as Mimah would have known, that it was Pete's unfathomable bitterness rather than the straight bourbon that brought Ann's reply.

What-all passed between them Mimah would like to know. She saw Pete sway as he sang a song for Ann. The words didn't come clear to Mimah but Ann heard the lines of a paratroopers' song to the tune of "The Battle Hymn of the Republic":

> "There was blood upon the shroudlines,
> There was blood upon the chutes.
> There was even blood adrippin
> From his paratrooper's boots.

Casey he was dead before he hit the ground,
And he ain't goin to jump no more."

Each guess Mimah made had a hurt in it. Five o'clock had come with
lingering sunslants through the window when she coaxed Pete to go up-
stairs. She put him to bed to sleep it off. At seven she went to call him
for dinner. She shook him awake, saw him refreshed and changed, came
in later when he had washed, dressed and adjusted his mask and gog-
gles. Then she spoke to him, low-toned yet command in her tone: "Lis-
ten, Pete. If you believe I ever loved you so much as a little finger, lis-
ten to me. It's Ann. I saw her this morning in her room. For the first
time since the Bryn Mawr days, I saw her naked, but not as God made
her. Listen, she's scars. All over that curved beautiful body of hers to
her knees, she's scars. Neck to knees long sweeping crisscross scars, crazy
red and white spots, splotches of scars. Shoulders to hips, breasts to
knees—scars and red splotches, I swear. The plane she was on in Africa
crashed. We heard that. We didn't get it clear. It caught fire. She was
lifted out of that plane on fire. For weeks she had hell. Not enough
whole skin left on her for grafting. You know the new skin grafted on
has to come from the person burned."

"You're telling me, where I been, about it."

"Forgive me, Pete, I'm telling it the best I can."

"Go on, don't think I ain't interested."

"You know, of course, they could have taken the skin off her face,
but that wouldn't have been enough to do any good."

"Besides making a difference with her face."

"Listen, I'm telling it the best I can. She's haunted about you. You
lost what she didn't. You both lost, but it's about even—she's a woman.
Can you think at all, Pete, about what I'm telling you?"

"What I think comes easier than it did."

"You know one thing you and Ann have together?"

"Like what?"

"No gripes, both of you game, marvelous what you take in your
stride. I've never seen anything like it. Ray is with me. He says the two
of you do him good, away inside help him. That's all. That's my piece.
I could go on. That's enough."

She could feel her heart slump. Then her heart came back. She
mustn't try to read him. He was beyond reading. She doubted whether
at high moments he could read himself. It could be too that he had
learned certain controls. And she must hold to the idea that what was
going on far inside of him was a secret to which he had a right. She
rebuked herself for what there was of unfair prying in her attempt to
get what was hidden under the icy echoes in his "Thanks, Mimah.
Thanks a million."

"I want to get something for you, I'll be back," and Mimah ran out
of the room and returned with a book she held before Pete's face and

he saw the title, *The Last Days of Sevastopol*, then "Sit," pointing to a chair. Pete sat, sloped. Mimah perched on the bed. "It's short, Pete. You needn't worry. A letter a captain in the Red Army wrote his wife. He was killed. This is what she read from him. I think there were days she wore the letter in her snow-white bosom."

"Read it. Let's have it. Snow-white bosom. Sounds like love love love."

"Here goes." Mimah began reading, her tones barely reaching Pete. She read it matter-of-fact with added subtle accents out of having read the letter a dozen times perhaps, three or four times aloud to herself. A throaty ruffle caught in her voice at some sentences near the end. The letter ran:

". . . I know that when I am dead, for you I will continue to live, and that nobody will edge me away from your careful heart. But if it happens that you meet a man fine enough for your grief whom you will love a little, and as the result of your love you have a new life and it is a son, then let him bear my name. Let him be my continuation, though I am dead and your new friend is alive. This would not punish him, for not everybody must die, and if he cannot understand, then leave him without sorrow and let it be not his but our son. And when a new Sevastopol is built, come here, and somewhere on Chersonese, somewhere near the sea, plant poppies. They grow here very well. And that will be my grave. It may be that you will make a mistake. Maybe it won't be me but another who lies there. It doesn't matter. Someone else will think of her own and plant flowers above me. Nobody will be left out, for we shall lie close, and there will be no space to spare where we lie."

Pete sat puzzled. Then he drawled, in no tone of ice, a shade of flame in his voice. "Say, you're my sister and I'm puttin it to you, did you mean any insinuations the way you read that?"

"Insinuations, hell!" blazed Mimah. "I just wanted you to know it could be there are more kinds of people and more kinds of love in the world than you think."

"Yeah? Well, what is it? He had a load on his mind and he gave it to her. So what?"

An elation that she hid ran over Mimah. She had struck through his barriers for once. He was stubborn. He was putting up a front. But his easy icy controls were gone. She read slow quivers in him, snarling and alive, no more ice. She closed the book, jumped off the bed, ran a hand through Pete's thick hair, walked to the door without a word, and in her room stood whispering lines from an old camp-meeting song that Bowbong's father learned from a Tennessee mountaineer in '64:

"Lord, in the twilight,
Lord, in the deep night,
Lord, in the midnight,
Be thou near."

Dinner saw Pete sober, inscrutable, near wordless, his goggles often pointed toward Ann and held long. He passed his dish to Mimah for a second helping of escalloped oysters with a bland mimicry of Nils Rolstadt, "Man goes on. Man does not stop." As he scooped from an avocado and looked toward Ann alongside him doing the same, he mumbled to her, "Would you say we are playing an avocado duet?"

"Yes," said Ann. "But what, classic or gutbucket?"

Pete sat mute except once when Ann quoted some surgeon, "How tight to tie sutures is a matter of experience, I try to err on the loose side," and Pete kept mumbling, "Err on the loose side, is that so?"

Soon after dinner came Ann's taxi. "I'll put her in," said Pete. When after a few minutes the front door opened and his footsteps were on the hallway rug and he turned into the living room, Mimah asked, "What was the last you said when you put her in the cab?"

"Good night, Ann, it was worth the time—like that."

"Will you write to her?"

"Could be. I might."

Mimah in bed made a slow puzzled drift into sleep. A recurring time-beat ran in her head of an ice echo, "Thanks, Mimah. Thanks a million," and a quizzical meaningless "Good night, Ann, it was worth the time."

* * * * * * * * * *

Chapter 9

* * * * * * * * * *

The Grandson Speaks at Arcadia

NEAR Hopecrest, at the Arcadia School, a girls' junior college, Justice Windom had several times spoken to the students in the opening September week. This year of 1945 they had asked Ray to read to them from writings of Justice Windom and to speak for himself in the same Gothic chapel of time-browned wooden panels and high-backed benches.

Pete was to come from the Valley Forge hospital for the day. He had telephoned from Philadelphia that he might miss being at Arcadia but would surely be on hand for the ceremonial planned at Remembrance Rock the next afternoon.

Ray stood in a pulpit with sheets of paper before him, his finger ends pushing them this way and that. Out in front his eyes ran over a variety of the faces that blended into a mosaic face of the American Girl. Here and there he caught a lovely and thoughtful face and a contrasting few, helpless and fidgety, who tittered at each other about trifles or nothing. In a front-row bench to the right sat Mimah, the gaunt oval of her face shadowed and solemn, her hair in the bright morning light, as Ray saw it, holding a chestnut-bronze haze. Her right arm around little Joseph Stilwell Windom, cuddled asleep against her side, her left hand over a box of animal crackers for an emergency.

"I heard my grandfather say," Ray began, "that it did him good to come here and have a look at you—you being the future." He read from the memorandum:

"Now you see the human family moves out into a fresh adventure. . . . Now do men foresee a new modern up-to-the-minute Day of Doom which, should it arrive, will be from the Hand of Man? In the changed world you now enter, my children, armies and navies as we have known them will vanish. The science of mass manslaughter will be statistical and in split seconds, now you see a city, now you don't . . . the brave man vanishes . . . biological warfare . . . indeed a changed world . . . my young dear ones. . . . When at last they shattered the atom and divided the hitherto indivisible, it was a joint international accomplishment . . . freedom, 'Oh God, now that we have it what shall we do with it?' . . . Long ago Noah saw what was coming and built himself an Ark. But whatever Ark will now save mankind must be built of materials not yet in view. . . . 'Man is a changer. God made him a changer' . . . you may become the witnesses of the finest and brightest era known to mankind. You shall have music, the nations over the globe shall have music, music instead of murder. It is possible. That is my hope and prayer—for you and for the nations. Now I bid you farewell and say Amen."

There had been an interruption at about the middle of the reading and Ray's eyes caught the figure of Pete. The blue goggles gone, the face somehow good to look at, about the same old face Pete used to wear, there he was gliding smoothly and swiftly the few steps from the entrance door to a bench in the last row. There Pete, erect with folded arms, his face one-third hidden by a wooden column, loomed not unlike an apparition. It halted Ray. He could have run down the aisle and put out a hand to Pete, "God, it's good to see you, Pete." Ray repeated a sentence, mumbled it in his reading. Mimah turned her head to see what bothered Ray. Then Mimah bent and stretched till she got a glimpse of the face of her brother, the goggles gone, the face much the same she had always known. She choked down a cry that rose in her throat. She turned her head and by an effort of will sat stiff-necked with a straight gaze at Ray in the pulpit. Ray had flashed an anxious face toward her when, as she twisted for a look at Pete, the child nearly slid down from her knees and arms to the floor. It halted Ray in the middle of a sentence.

Having finished reading the memorandum, Ray's eyes ranged along the rows of faces, the mosaic American Girl face before him, and he believed a few thoughtful ones had moved into a deeper twilight purple of meditation while the fidgety, inclined to tittering at first, had subsided into a mild degree of composure. He told them of Justice Windom having left a further memorandum, an extended one consisting of three books bound with an insistent and repeating scarlet thread of unity.

"He began the writing of those books many years ago," said Ray. "In some of those years he came often to this school. He liked to ramble over these grounds inside. He spoke from this platform several times. If Justice Windom were here today speaking he might try to explain briefly the scarlet thread that gives unity to the three books he wrote, which may be published some day for you to read."

And not until this moment when Ray went into a long pause did Mimah realize how faithfully and completely had Ray absorbed Bowbong's manuscript. She humbled herself in a feeling that swept over her. "The grandson has some of his grandfather's finest stuff," she said to herself as she heard him on the scarlet thread, lost to his audience, abstracted in matters and issues far beyond this little chapel, affairs and events that had knocked his ears down, knocked at his heart and brain till now he spoke and there was a shadow-music in it:

"Always the path of American destiny has been into the Unknown. It was never more true than now. With each new test and each new time it cost and there were those prepared to pay the cost. At Plymouth and Jamestown there was the Unknown of a vast continent of wilderness to be faced. At Philadelphia in the writing of the Declaration and later amid the cold and filth of Valley Forge, there was the Unknown again, no precedents or forerunners to guide. Later in the trials of crossing the Great Plains and pioneering the West coast and in the bloody sectional struggle that hammered national union into a finality, there was ever the Unknown. And never was it more true than now—the path of American destiny leads into the Unknown."

Ray stood silent for a few clockticks, his eyes finding Mimah with Joe Stilwell clutched close and tight to her, on her face the hint of her saying to herself, "He's a new man, he's come through, his grandfather would have cried over him." It came over Ray that he had said his say. He stepped down alongside Mimah, took the little one from her arms. He was looking into the child's face as the applause burst and ran long. The child had never before heard applause and as his ears caught the shattering waves of prolonged handclaps, his face screwed up in a grimace and he began a spell of crying that lasted till Mimah fed animal crackers into his boy mouth.

Chapter 10

Dreamdust and Love

THE evening came in a quiet purple. And Captain Raymond Windom and his wife Maria had little to say to each other because of much said during the day at Arcadia. Pete had shaken hands with them, kissed the baby, and pointing toward a taxi, "See you tomorrow at noon at Remembrance Rock. Anything important, you can get me at the Wardman."

Evening and slow purple lights falling and folding around the pines, the elms, the boulder, seen through the tall windows looking to the back yard. Evening and a silence of health and healing over and around the old stone house. Then a ring at the doorbell and Mimah let in two persons and brought them to Ray, Johnny Avolo and a small shy blonde, plainly born bashful, and Johnny keeping watch that she wouldn't run away, and coaxing her, "You can speak up to them, old friends, nothing to be scared of."

"So she didn't cry for a third time?" said Ray.

"She cried all right," said Johnny. "She put on a terrific act. Then I found it was because she loved me and she was afraid I'd take a runout powder on her."

After a little drink, a toast to the honeymooners, and a long talk in which Mrs. Avolo spoke no word and sat shyly content with Johnny's hand in hers, then Ray, "A long today, a big day tomorrow, we'll hit the sack." Ray showed the honeymooners to their room. At the door Johnny flipped a thumb toward the four-poster bed, "Swell, Ray— thanks a lot."

At Remembrance Rock at high noon they laid in metal-bottomed crevices the little prepared copper boxes—gravel from Sicily, sand from Utah Beach on the Normandy coast, rainbow-tinted sand from a coral atoll in the South Pacific, harsh black volcanic ash from Okinawa. They packed in soil at the base of the boulder, leaving no sign of the sacred receptacle underneath.

They stood by, hands folded in front of them, keeping a silence during one minute of sacramental time. They were Captain Raymond Windom and his wife Maria Enders Windom, Captain Peter Enders, Pola Zinski Folsom, Tail Gunner John Avolo and his wife, Mary Liebowitz, and Nils Rolstadt, the physicist. What the group had done was their private affair, in an intimacy of fellowship that belonged to them alone.

They walked to the house in a quiet sunfall of early autumn, faint streaks of brown and gold, sudden spots of yellow and crimson, in the air the unseen feet of the yearly return of falltime.

Ray, Mimah and Rolstadt in the living room heard Pete in the hallway calling, "Hey, you!" five or six times.

They heard feet on the stairs. They saw entering the room, arm in arm, Pete and Ann Flaherty.

The pair stood before the surprised others. From Pete came the serious words, "How do we look? Would you say we look like a couple, fair enough?" Mimah's heart missed a beat, her eyes falling on Ann's left hand wearing a long-absent and nigh-forgotten silver ring.

"Captain Enders," broke in Ray, "with all due respect, what the hell's been going on here?"

"You request a report, Captain Windom. Then Captain Enders begs to submit the information that early yesterday morning his conscience lay heavy on him and his memory twisted inside of him with a blue and lonesome pain he couldn't stand. He put in a telephone call to Chicago for Miss Ann Flaherty. She caught a plane for Philadelphia. She went off the deep end and got married, hitched and spliced forever to Captain Enders, each of them duly showing their dogtags to the justice of the peace. They began their honeymoon in the Ben Franklin Hotel registered as Captain and Mrs. Pete Enders. From the window of her room here Mrs. Enders saw the ceremony at Remembrance Rock. Now soon the bride and groom are going out to the Rock and watch birds come flying out of it, a thousand birds fluttering and circling in a spiral up to the blue yonder."

"Before you go," said Ray, "join with us in the last thing Bowbong asked us to share with him."

Ray opened the small flat metal-and-leather packet from the bottom of the Box. It held a bronze plaque with a silver neck chain. They read the plaque—the words of Roger Bacon seven centuries ago:

The Four Stumbling Blocks to Truth

1. The influence of fragile or unworthy authority.
2. Custom.
3. The imperfection of undisciplined senses.
4. Concealment of ignorance by ostentation of seeming wisdom.

It passed from hand to hand. Ray read it aloud, then handed it to Mimah.

Mimah fixed the clasps of it around Ann's neck, saying gravely, "You wear it one year and I'll wear it the next." Ann couldn't hold back the tears.

Pete said low-toned to Mimah, "I can't tell her what the chemist said to his wife: 'Go ahead and cry! What are your tears? A moderate percentage of phosphate salts, a touch of sodium chloride and the rest is all water, just plain water.'

"Love love love," said Pete, shaking hands with Johnny Avolo and grinning the best he could. "I've heard about you. You're on the beam here today. You and me can talk."

On seating themselves for lunch and raising their glasses of Burgundy, Ray spoke toasts to Bowbong, to the two newly married couples, to the absent Kenneth MacKenzie MacDougall, to Mary Liebowitz, to Jake Zinski, to the Armed Forces of the U.S.A. And when Ray later said to Mimah, as between them, "You seem to be glad from your shining hair clean down to your fast and wicked feet," Mimah said, "I am," and again went back to Mary Windling in 1608: "My feet may go to hell though my soul will not follow my feet. The good Lord should not have made my feet so glad."

Ann Flaherty Enders at the other side of Ray had heard. She smiled to Mimah. "Say it again, for me, to Pete," which Mimah did.

Then Mimah gave the toast of Mary Windling in 1608: "To the storms to come and the stars coming after the storm."